COMPLETE PROSE WORKS

OF

John Milton

This publication is made possible
through grants of the Bollingen
and Littauer Foundations

Complete Prose Works

OF

John Milton

VOLUME II
1643–1648

NEW HAVEN: YALE UNIVERSITY PRESS

LONDON: OXFORD UNIVERSITY PRESS

MCMLIX

PRINTED IN THE UNITED STATES OF AMERICA BY

H. WOLFF BOOK MANUFACTURING COMPANY, NEW YORK, N. Y.

LIBRARY OF CONGRESS CATALOG CARD NUMBER: 52-5371

EDITORIAL BOARD

EDITOR OF VOLUME II

ERNEST SIRLUCK

PREFACE

The textual principles governing this edition were set out in Volume I, pp. ix and 1040. The present volume adds textual notes (below, pp. 776–92), listing all editorial emendations of the copy texts other than the regular and silent substitution of modern equivalents for archaic printer's symbols (e.g., *w* for *vv*, *J* for appropriate *I*'s, etc.); where emendations affect the meaning, they are also discussed in footnotes. Otherwise, except for such errors as may have defeated our combined vigilances, the text is literal. Variants among different copies of the original editions are listed in the textual notes, and the most important are also discussed in the prefaces. *The Doctrine and Discipline of Divorce* presents a special problem, and the textual arrangement adopted for that tract is described below, p. 218.

In a collaboration of equals it is not always possible to achieve unanimity of view. There are some differences of interpretation within the present volume, and some between this volume and its predecessor; but fewer than had been anticipated, and the materials are provided for the reader to form his own opinions. Such differences seem a small price to pay for the advantages of collaborative scholarship.

The footnotes show some of the editors' debts, but by no means all. The members of the Editorial Board have been anything but perfunctory in the performance of their duties, at all stages of the enterprise working much harder to bring the volume along than could have been expected. R. C. Bald, Gladys Haase, William Haller, William Seaman, James H. Hanford, Ruth Mohl, David C. Searfoss have all in various ways greatly aided the editors, as have the American Council of Learned Societies, the College of Wooster, the Guggenheim Memorial Foundation, the University of Chicago. The library staffs of the British Museum, the Huntington Library, the Newberry Library, the University of Chicago, Union Theological Seminary, and Princeton University have given much patient and sympathetic assistance. All the editors of the *Complete Prose* owe a special debt of thanks to Sue M. Foster, reference librarian at Union Theological Seminary.

CONTENTS

CONTENTS

LIBRARY ABBREVIATIONS

BML	Library of the British Museum
BOD	Bodleian Library, Oxford
CLL	Columbia University Law Library
CUL	Columbia University Library
HCL	Harvard College Library
HHL	Huntington Library
HLH	Houghton Library of Harvard
HDSL	Harvard Divinity School Library
MUL	University of Michigan Library
NEW	Newberry Library, Chicago
NYPL	New York Public Library
PML	Pierpont Morgan Library, New York
PUL	Princeton University Library
SOR	Library of the Sorbonne, University of Paris
UCL	University of Chicago Library
UML	University of Minnesota Library
UTSL	Union Theological Seminary Library

ABBREVIATIONS OF PUBLICATIONS

Bohn	Milton, *Prose Works* (1848–53)
CPB	Milton, *Commonplace Book*
Columbia	Milton, *Works* (1931–38)
Complete Prose	*Complete Prose Works of John Milton*
DNB	*Dictionary of National Biography*
ELH	*Journal of English Literary History*
ERE	*Encyclopaedia of Religion and Ethics*
HLQ	*Huntington Library Quarterly*
JEGP	*Journal of English and Germanic Philology*
McAlpin	*McAlpin Catalogue*
MLN	*Modern Language Notes*
NED, OED	*New English Dictionary*
N&Q	*Notes and Queries*
PMLA	*Publications of the Modern Language Association*
RES	*Review of English Studies*
SP	*Studies in Philology*
TLS	*London Times Literary Supplement*
Thomason	*Catalogue of the Thomason Tracts*

COMPLETE PROSE WORKS

OF

John Milton

PART ONE: THE BACKGROUND

CHAPTER I

1642–1643: SUPREMACY IN THE STATE

LOOKING back in 1654 to the pamphlets reproduced in the present volume and to their relation with those contained in Volume I of the *Complete Prose,* Milton wrote:

> When the bishops could no longer resist the multitude of their assailants, I had leisure to turn my thoughts to other subjects; to the promotion of real and substantial liberty; which is rather to be sought from within than from without. . . . When, therefore, I perceived that there were three species of liberty which are essential to the happiness of social life—religious, domestic, and civil; and as I had already written concerning the first, and the magistrates were strenuously active in obtaining the third, I determined to turn my attention to the second, or the domestic species. As this seemed to involve three material questions, the conditions of the conjugal tie, the education of the children, and the free publication of the thoughts, I made them objects of distinct consideration.[1]

This passage has greatly influenced Milton studies. It bespeaks for the two groups of pamphlets a unity of conception and a singleness of purpose which make them but variant aspects of a single continuous struggle for liberty; and this in fact is how they are usually treated. Nor is such treatment without some justification. There can be no doubt that Milton conceived of his anti-Episcopal pamphlets as in part an effort to liberate the church from an oppressive tyranny, and in this sense they do belong with his subsequent labors on behalf of various kinds of liberty. But Milton's exclusive emphasis on this element of continuity has obscured a radical discontinuity. There is nothing in his account to suggest the enormous difference between the ideas and alignments of the present group of pamphlets and those of the anti-Episcopal pamphlets. From it no one could guess that the men with whom Milton had identified himself in the earlier group had become the enemies of

[1] *The Second Defence,* tr. Robert Fellowes, *The Prose Works of John Milton,* edited by J. A. St. John. Bohn Library (5 vols., London, 1848–1853), I, 258–59.

the later, or that the sects which, in the earlier group, had been seen as an evil suffered by God in order that the sound-hearted might thereby be tried and manifested [2] had, in the later group, become builders of the Temple stirred by God to pursue greater knowledge and understanding.[3] No one could guess, that is, that in the anti-Episcopal tracts Milton was a Presbyterian demanding the immediate institution of the "one right *discipline*," [4] and that the present pamphlets represent the break from Presbyterianism toward the left; but this is, perhaps, the most significant fact about the works of 1643–1645.

In all the thousands of words Milton devoted to his spiritual autobiography he never referred directly to his break from Presbyterianism. Perhaps it was too painful a subject; perhaps he thought it impolitic to draw attention to it; but he is in this break as representative of the Puritan Revolution as in any other respect. In these years the Revolution was itself moving inexorably leftward from Presbyterianism. When Milton was writing the last of his anti-Episcopal pamphlets Presbyterianism was the dominant, almost unchallenged, party in English Puritanism; by the time he published the last of his divorce tracts, it had permanently lost control of the Parliamentary army, was sometimes unable to manage Parliament, and had been displaced or was being challenged in many other strongholds of Puritanism.

Not only in his general tendency but in his particular ideas too Milton in 1643–1645 reflected the revolutionary context. This is not at first obvious, for these were the only years between the summoning of the Long Parliament and the Restoration when the bulk of Milton's publication was on a subject other than the Revolution's main concern of the moment. But even where his object has little connection with the Revolution (as in the divorce tracts), the arguments by which he seeks to achieve it are largely drawn from the rationale of the Revolution, and cannot be fully understood apart therefrom; and at least in the *Areopagitica* both object and argument are products of the Revolution.

1. HISTORICAL SUMMARY

Milton completed his series of anti-Episcopal tracts in March or April, 1642; [1] he published the first of his divorce tracts at the beginning of August, 1643. The introduction to Volume I of *Complete Prose* described the widening and deepening of the differences that were di-

[2] *The Reason of Church-Government* (1642), *Complete Prose*, I, 794–95.
[3] *Areopagitica* (1644); below, pp. 553–55.
[4] *Of Reformation* (1641), *Complete Prose*, I, 605.
[1] See *Complete Prose*, I, 862.

viding England into two opposed camps when *An Apology* was being written; we must now trace the course of events and arguments during the sixteen months that preceded *The Doctrine and Discipline of Divorce*.

When on January 4, 1642, Charles withdrew from Westminster, baffled in his attempt to intimidate Parliament by seizing the persons of its leaders,[2] his intention was to raise a force with which to destroy it. His first hurried efforts came to nothing,[3] and in his messages to Parliament he temporarily adopted a tone which was meant to seem conciliatory; but the chief author of these messages has explained that "though he was resolved in no degree to consent" to Parliament's demand that it share in the control of the militia, "yet he was willing, till all things could be ready for the Queen's journey and so for his own remove, [rather] to delay it than deny it."[4] On February 23 Charles saw Henrietta Maria and the crown jewels sail for Holland; a few days later, having secured the presence of the Prince of Wales, he turned north "to undertake another enterprise, . . . which in truth was the sole motive of his journey into those parts": the seizure of the great magazine of arms at Hull.[5]

Pym and the other parliamentary leaders were in no doubt about Charles' intentions. Having in January frustrated his initial attempts to gain control of Portsmouth, Hull, and Kingston, they looked to preparatory measures of their own. The unprecedented violation of its privileges and the obvious continuing menace restored to Parliament something of its old unity, and in successive steps it placed itself under a guard of its own choosing, ordered the trained bands throughout the country to stand to, secured Hull and the Tower, and submitted to Charles an ordinance which was to place control of the militia in persons nominated by Parliament.[6] Charles refused his assent and started for the north. On March 5 Parliament took the momentous step of voting to effect the Militia Ordinance "by authority of both Houses" alone.[7]

---

[2] *Ibid.*, introduction, pp. 183–86.

[3] Samuel R. Gardiner, *History of England from the Accession of James I to the Outbreak of the Civil War, 1603–1642* (10 vols., London, 1883–84), X, 152–59.

[4] Clarendon, Edward, Earl of, *History of the Rebellion and Civil Wars in England*, IV, 282 (hereafter cited as Clarendon); ed. William D. Macray (6 vols., Oxford, 1888), I, 557. Hereafter cited as Macray. Word supplied by Macray.

[5] Clarendon, V, 88 (Macray, II, 45).

[6] Gardiner, *History of England 1603–1642*, X, 152–67.

[7] *Lords Journals*, IV, 620; Gardiner, *History of England 1603–1642*, X, 171. The first "ordinance," in the sense of an action of Parliament which purported not to require the concurrence of the king, had been made August 20, 1641, and

The five months which were to pass before the first blood was drawn were spent in preparing for war. While Henrietta Maria moved about the Netherlands trying to arrange for foreign aid,[8] Charles moved about northern England trying to raise an army. He was at first scarcely more successful than the queen, being rebuffed in his attempt on Hull and disappointed in his reception at York;[9] but as the Houses at Westminster took their own measures, and in the process assumed one unprecedented power after another, as the individual members were forced to choose sides for the civil war which daily seemed more inevitable, there began that flight to Charles which continued until more than two-fifths of the House of Commons[10] and all but a handful of the peers had abandoned Parliament and formed the nucleus of the new "constitutional" royalism. Thus reinforced, Charles raised his standard at Nottingham on August 22.[11]

Charles knew himself to be militarily weak, and was willing, while his few troops made some sporadic forays, to permit his more pacific counsellors to try what negotiation would do. But Parliament too knew him to be weak, and played a high hand; it threatened not merely to punish Charles' evil counsellors but, more foolishly, to recover all its costs from those whom it had voted, or should yet vote, "delinquents" or "malignants." This reply (September 6) sent thousands of recruits pouring into Charles' headquarters.[12] It is to be hoped that none of them were influenced by Parliament's order of August 24 commanding the better observance of public fasts and prayer,[13] but one wonders what thoughts they entertained of the more famous companion order of September 2; perhaps even such a supporter of Parliament as Milton had mixed feelings about it:

> whereas public Sports do not well agree with public Calamities; nor public Plays with the Seasons of Humiliation; this being an Exercise of sad and pious Solemnity, and the other being Spectacles of Pleasure,

was soon followed by others; see Gardiner, X, 3–5 and 9–10. Since this was done in the days of Parliament's virtual unanimity, there is something unconvincing about the professions of righteous indignation hurled at the unconstitutionality of the Militia Ordinance by many who voted for the earlier ordinances.

[8] Gardiner, *History of England 1603–1642*, X, 187–88, 201, 203–204.

[9] *Ibid.*, pp. 189–95.

[10] D. Brunton and D. H. Pennington, *Members of the Long Parliament* (London: George Allen and Unwin, 1954), p. 187; Mary F. Keeler, *The Long Parliament, 1640–1641: A Biographical Study of its Members* (Philadelphia: American Philosophical Society, 1954), p. 12.

[11] Gardiner, *History of England 1603–1642*, X, 184–85, 196–205, 218–20.

[12] Gardiner, *History of the Great Civil War 1642–1649* (3 vols., London, 1886–91), I, 15–22.

[13] *Lords Journals*, V, 320.

too commonly expressing lascivious Mirth and Leachery: It is, therefore, thought fit and ordained by the Lords and Commons, &c. That
while those sad Courses and set Times of Humiliations do continue,
public Stage-Plays shall cease and be forborne.[14]

Full of confidence and numbers, the Parliamentary army in September set out to find Charles at Nottingham. Charles, however, moved
westward, gaining strength as he went. After some skirmishing, the
main armies met at Edgehill on October 23. The battle was militarily
indecisive, but it effectually ended Parliament's false sense of security.
Essex, the Parliamentary general, while claiming victory, disengaged
toward Warwick, leaving the road to London open. Charles took that
road. When he reached Reading on November 3 he was met by a proposal for negotiation from an uneasy Parliament; he evaded it and
pressed on. At Colnbrook on the 11th he received a renewed appeal;
for answer he attacked Brentford, which he took after hard fighting,
and moved upon London itself. There was great agitation. Milton
posted *"On his dore when the Citty expected an assault"* his appeal to
"Captain or Colonel, or Knight in Arms" for immunity for "the Muses
Bowre," but many preferred to confide in their arms. When Charles
reached Turnham Green, just west of London, he found it occupied in
great strength by an aroused and determined citizenry, and was forced
to draw off. There was some attempt at negotiation, but it came to
nothing and Charles withdrew to Oxford, which he now made his permanent headquarters.[15]

The failure to take London by immediate assault seemed only a
temporary setback to Charles. His new strategy was for himself to pin
Essex down in the centre from Oxford, while Newcastle worked down
from the north and Hopton in from the west to take both banks of the
Thames below London, which would then be starved into submission.
During November and December this strategy enjoyed enough success
to stimulate in London and Westminster a strong growth of sentiment
favoring peace negotiations. After meetings, petitions, and demonstra-
tions in the City, and resolutions in the Houses, the "Treaty" (*i.e.*,
negotiation) of Oxford began on February 1, 1643. It dragged on until
April 14, but Charles' demands, laid down at the outset, were so uncompromising that there never was a real chance of accommodation,
and military operations were pursued even while the discussions pro-

[14] *The Parliamentary or Constitutional History of England, From the Earliest
Times to the Restoration of Charles II* (2 ed., 24 vols., London, 1762–1763),
XI, 411. Usually known as the *Old Parliamentary History*, and hereafter thus
cited.

[15] Gardiner, *Civil War*, I, 27–73.

ceeded.[16] Charles was in fact making quite different arrangements at the same time. In January he had sent to Ormond a secret "Memorial for the Irish Treaty"; [17] by April the business was sufficiently advanced for him to write, "I have sent you herewith a command and power to make a cessation with the rebels; which, though it be not so formally legal as I could wish, yet I desire you earnestly to put those my commands in execution; and as soon as that is done, Ormonde must bring over the Irish Army to Chester." [18] In Scotland plans were made for a royalist rising under Montrose, to be supported by Irish Catholics released for this service by the same cessation which would permit the English troops in Ireland to embark for Chester.[19] For London itself, Charles issued the secret commission of array which was to legalize the projected uprising that is associated with the name of the poet Edmund Waller.[20]

The discovery of these plots during May and June created on the Parliamentary side a mood of fervent indignation which led to the impeachment of the Queen, the Parliamentary Covenant, the acceptance at last by the Lords of the ordinance for an Assembly of Divines, and the dispatch of a Parliamentary committee to Scotland to confer with the Estates on joint action.[21] (The Licensing Order, too, was passed at this time, but it must be doubted whether it had as much connection with the discovery of these plots as Gardiner suggests.[22]) This resolute temper, however, was not proof against a series of grave military reverses. The prospect of utter defeat soon revived and carried to new heights the agitation for peace negotiations, and the first week in August saw the culmination of a bitter struggle between the leaders of this group and those who were determined to continue the war.[23] On August

[16] *Ibid.*, pp. 78–126.

[17] *The Letters, Speeches, and Proclamations of King Charles I,* ed. Sir Charles Petrie (London: Cassell, 1935), pp. 132–34. For the Irish revolt which broke out in 1641 see introduction, *Complete Prose*, I, 168–70.

[18] *Letters,* p. 136; *cf.* Gardiner, *Civil War*, I, 127–48.

[19] Gardiner, *Civil War*, I, 145–48 and 205–207.

[20] *Ibid.*, pp. 128 and 168–73.

[21] *Ibid.*, pp. 170, 174, 208–209.

[22] *Ibid.*, p. 174; see introduction, below, pp. 158–61.

[23] It is unnecessary for our purposes to choose between the traditional view, most fully documented in Gardiner, that Parliament was during 1643 divided into two parties, a peace party and a war party, and the proposal of J. H. Hexter that there were really three groups—a peace party, an extreme war party, and a middle group. Hexter's own analysis finds his extreme war party reduced at the moment of crisis to sullen support of the leadership of the middle group, having lost their bid to control the forces of resistance. See *The Reign of King Pym* (Cambridge: Harvard University Press, 1941), pp. 142–47. Since the "middle

3 the House of Lords prepared propositions to Charles which were, in effect, a capitulation, and besought Essex's concurrence. Pym persuaded Essex not to support the propositions; nevertheless they were formally adopted by the Lords on the 4th, and sent to the Commons, where, on the 6th, an unusually full House voted (by a majority of twenty-nine) to take them into consideration. At this point the anti-royalists of the City, led by Lord Mayor Pennington, intervened. On Sunday the 6th the preachers raised the temperatures of congregations throughout the city, and on the 7th a great and threatening crowd bore into Palace Yard a petition against the propositions. When the Commons divided that day the propositions failed—by seven votes. The following day the peace party, in its turn, tried mob intimidation, but without success.[24]

It was just at this crisis of the civil war that Milton published *The Doctrine and Discipline of Divorce*. We may therefore suspend our narrative of events and turn to the war of ideas.

2. THE ISSUE

The nature of the issue during this year and a half from Charles' withdrawal to the crisis of early August is not easy to state. It has for some years been fashionable to interpret it as a class struggle,[1] and certainly the royalist propaganda, as occasion served, attempted to promulgate something like this view. At the outset the royalists warned

group" was bent upon continuing the war, the clash described in the text above is substantially the same, whether we use Gardiner's bipartite or Hexter's tripartite analysis. Of the latter it may be said that although the argument is far from conclusive, and is in some places demonstrably exaggerated, the notion of three groups shading into each other fits some of the facts—not all—better than the older view.

[24] Gardiner, *Civil War*, I, 175–220.

[1] Perhaps the most forthright statement of this view is in Christopher Hill, *The English Revolution, 1640* (London: Lawrence & Wishart, 1940). R. H. Tawney, whose *Religion and the Rise of Capitalism* (London, 1926) did more than any other work in English to advance among professional historians the interpretation of the Puritan Revolution as essentially bourgeois, seems now to have abandoned this view (see below, pp. 9–10).

A recent variation on the theme of a class struggle, put forward by Hugh Trevor-Roper in *Economic History Review*, Supplement of April, 1953, is that the Revolution resulted not from the rise but from the decline of the lesser gentry. This novel suggestion has attracted more attention than support. For an entertaining but nonetheless searching analysis of the respective statistical and methodological fallacies on which Professors Tawney and Trevor-Roper built, see J. H. Hexter, "Storm Over the Gentry," *Encounter*, X, 5 (May, 1958), 22–34, and subsequent correspondence in the July, August, and September numbers.

Parliament that its doctrines would teach "some *Wat. Tylers* Chaplaine, to preach againe upon that text:

> *When* Adam *dolve and* Eve *span,*
> Who was then a Gentleman." [2]

Here the implication is clear that the parliamentarians would be just as disturbed as the royalists by such a threat to class and property. Later, however, the royalists denounced Parliament for transferring wealth and power to "poor men," [3] and often declared that its leaders were men of no fortune, "beggerly Lords and Gentlemen." [4] But before these later assertions are taken too seriously as evidence that the division was one of class, their context should be understood. As we shall see, a damaging royalist charge was that Parliament's arbitrary procedures subverted the constitution and threatened all personal and property rights. One Parliamentary answer to this was that it was unthinkable that Parliament, consisting of the solidest men of property in England, could intend any threat to property or change of government. Besides making routine accusations of corruption, the royalist assertions about "poor men" were meant to undermine this defense. Actually, the propaganda of both sides held it to be an unquestionable indication of the acceptability of their respective social and political purposes that their leading protagonists were men of large fortune and influence.

A good deal of light is thrown upon this matter by two recent analyses of the personnel of the House of Commons. Using slightly different statistical bases, they report approximately the same findings; we may here use the more detailed. Mary F. Keeler shows that, including replacements to the end of 1641, the House consisted of 547 members, grouped as follows: landed gentry, 334; lawyers, 79; "merchants," 55;

---

[2] *Animadversions Upon Those Notes Which the Late Observator Hath Published* (1642), p. 8. The title page gives the place of publication as London, but Thomason wrote on his copy "Oxon." and entered July 9 as the date that it reached him in London; British Museum shelfmark E107(22). Hereafter, when the month and day are added to the year of publication, this is to be understood to mean (unless otherwise specified) the date on which Thomason received the pamphlet; for matter published in London this date will, during the period of the present volume, usually be soon after the pamphlet's first appearance, but with Oxford, Cambridge, and Scottish publications there is considerable variation. Unless otherwise specified, the shelfmarks given in the notes will be those of the British Museum.

[3] *A Complaint to the House of Commons* (Oxford, January 2, 1643), E244(31), p. 15.

[4] *The Complaint of the Kingdome Against the Evill Members of Both Houses* (1643), 1482.bb.6, p. 23.

administration and church officials and courtiers, 52 ; secretaries or business agents of great men, 13; soldiers, 9; others, 5.[5] In this House
Charles could find virtually no support except from his dependents for
the policy of personal government: there were only 59 votes to spare
Strafford.[6] But the new "constitutional" royalism drew off 226 members,[7] or 41%. It is of the utmost interest that this split is mirrored in
each recognizable social or economic category. Of course personal
careers, as distinct from class, affected choice: the courtiers, church
officials, soldiers, and to a lesser extent administrative officials were
predominantly royalist, and the agents tended to follow the politics of
their patrons. But class is almost no guide to the members' politics:
the dominant landed interest split just in the proportions of the whole
House (39% royalist), the lawyers were a little more than proportionally favorable to Charles (they were about evenly divided), and the
merchants rather less (about a quarter were royalists).[8] Messrs. Brunton and Pennington, analyzing their own essentially similar figures,
observe:

> We found that Royalist and Parliamentarian, so far as can be judged
> from the members of the Long Parliament, were very much the same;
> that the greater and lesser gentry were not on different sides; that it
> made no difference whether a member belonged to an 'old' or to a 'new'
> family; that merchants and lawyers were to be found on both sides, and
> in such proportions as to make it doubtful whether there was any
> general hostility to the King amongst provincial merchants and certain
> that there was none amongst the lawyers.[9]

The failure of the political division to reflect social divisions may
in part be due to coincidence of economic interest in much of what
Namier calls the "political nation," in place of the great economic
clash we have been taught to see. For a century there had been a very
active land market, which strongly emphasized marriage as a source
of new money; there were now few estates which had no connections
with commerce; most prosperous lawyers and tradesmen had direct
or indirect interests in landed property, and many landowners had
commercial investments. In such circumstances a sharp distinction
between a landholding and commercial interest is unrealistic.[10] Professor Tawney, in his introduction to Brunton and Pennington's study,
somewhat surprisingly declares it to have made untenable "the

[5] *The Long Parliament*, p. 21.
[6] Gardiner, *History of England 1603–1642*, IX, 338.
[7] Keeler, *The Long Parliament*, p. 12.   [8] *Ibid.*, p. 22.
[9] *Members of the Long Parliament*, pp. 19–20.
[10] *Ibid.*, pp. 3–6 and 176–82.

venerable legend of a conflict between, on the one side, a monarchy supported by a feudal aristocracy and, on the other, an aspiring *bourgeoisie*." [11]

As the Revolution proceeded it enlarged the political nation, and some of the new groups, Levellers and others, injected into it an element of class conflict; but it never became essentially, and in 1642–1643 was scarcely at all, a class struggle—a fact dramatized for us in the choice of opposite sides by those sons of a City scrivener, John and Christopher Milton.

If the great issue was not economic, what was it? The traditional view, for which Gardiner is the foremost spokesman, is that it was religious. Gardiner believes that there is a clear historical demonstration that the constitutional issue was not in itself seriously divisive. On August 10, 1641, the Scots Treaty was completed and Charles, against the pleas of Parliament, left Westminster for Edinburgh. There was a general belief that his purpose was to return with a Scottish army to reimpose by force the personal government he had so reluctantly signed away in the preceding months. The debates during this emergency show, says Gardiner, that "the men of one party were as ready as the men of the other to put pressure upon the Sovereign, to make preparations for securing the fortresses of the kingdom and for placing the military forces of the country in readiness for action at the bidding of the Houses." Until the constitutional problem merged with the religious, the royal prerogative had no friends but the courtiers. "The rock of offence [upon which Parliamentary unity split] lay in the proposed ecclesiastical legislation of Parliament." [12]

The chief rival to this view (aside from the demonstrably inapplicable economic theory) is the political or constitutional interpretation. J. W. Allen may be taken to represent the extreme form of this viewpoint. Where Gardiner saw the constitutional issue as important only when it became involved in the religious issue, Allen sees religion as divisive only as it became a means to political ends. He believes that when Parliament-men of differing religious opinions attacked Laudianism in 1641 "the House of Commons was thinking politically and not religiously." [13] Even the division on the Root-and-Branch Bill was superficial: the House "was united, still, in desiring to establish complete secular and parliamentary control of the Church." [14] The fundamental issue was whether to trust Charles to keep his word or, in view of his hostility, to seize the means of compelling him to keep it: "The

[11] *Ibid.*, p. xix.   [12] *History of England 1603–1642*, X, 11–12.
[13] *English Political Thought 1603–1644* (London: Methuen, 1938), p. 351.
[14] *Ibid.*, p. 373.

question ultimately involved, the question that lay behind all particular disputes, concerned the power to direct public policy." [15] A modification of this position concedes that religion played a leading part in the great split of 1641, and that it would again divide Parliament in 1645, but denies it any active role in the interim. This view is proposed by J. H. Hexter,[16] who, untroubled by the inconsistency (not present in Allen's view) of a hypothesis that has the same men first precipitating civil war in order to achieve religious reformation, and then not caring about religious reformation, denies to Pym and the leaders of Parliament any "grandiose ideal," [17] and defines their purpose as Allen had: "Parliament had to grow so that the Stuart could be tied." [18]

In either form, this purely constitutional analysis is a grave exaggeration. For a discussion of the dominant role of religion in the great split in the latter part of 1641 (which Allen denies) the reader is referred to the introduction of Volume I; its role during the second year of the civil war (which both Allen and Hexter deny) will be discussed below.[19] But our concern at the moment is with the first year of the civil war and the months just prior to its outbreak, and the exaggeration of the purely constitutional analysis ought not to blind us to the lesser exaggeration of the older, purely religious analysis. The constitutional issue always counted for something; [20] in the year and a half now under scrutiny, as the documents to be discussed in the remainder of this chapter will show, it counted for a very great deal. The fact is that reformation of the church did not dominate public debate in this period, as it had in 1641 and would again in the summer of 1643. Religion, of course, figured prominently in the debate, but for the most part as a source of supporting arguments for constitutional doctrines, rather than as an end. Perhaps it is not safe to assert what the issue during these months really was: intellectual history is an instrument of limited penetration; but it can certainly be said that the issue constantly being debated was supremacy in the state. That for some, perhaps most, this issue mattered chiefly as a means to further ends cannot be doubted (and was to be demonstrated in the later phases of the Revolution, as well in Milton as in others); it was nonetheless the issue upon which the national mind was concentrated during most of the interval between Milton's last anti-Episcopal tract and his first divorce tract.

[15] *Ibid.*, pp. 375–76.   [16] *The Reign of King Pym,* pp. 96–99.
[17] *Ibid.*, p. 199.   [18] *Ibid.*, p. 207.   [19] Pp. 53–136.
[20] See introduction, *Complete Prose,* I, 167–92.

3. THE DEBATE-AT-LAW: PARLIAMENT'S NEW DOCTRINE

The debate was extremely complicated, and it may be well to mark at the outset the most fertile source of confusion for the reader, as it was the most rewarding area of maneuver for the debaters. The English word "law" is in itself radically ambiguous, embracing as it does the distinct if related ideas of *lex, jus,* and *nomos.* In an age in which the concept of sovereignty as containing a nomothetical power was only being worked out,[1] and when, therefore, a constitutional position was seriously jeopardized by the charge of "newness," every party attempted to justify its position in terms of "law," always implying law already essentially in being. Confronted with a situation in which almost unavoidable ambiguity was combined with intentional obscuration, one is tempted to borrow some comprehensive system by which to classify the varying arguments from "law," and one thinks longingly of Hooker, with his distinctions of divine and human, natural and positive, mutable and immutable, higher and lower, etc. But in such matters definition is itself an argument, and Hooker's analysis, magnificent though it is, would mislead us here. There were some on both sides of the Puritan Revolution who employed his system (not always to the same conclusions); some neglected it, either through ignorance or choice; some disingenuously used parts of it, concealing the significance of the rest; some used his terms but changed his values. In these circumstances it seems best to proceed cautiously, which unfortunately means without employing any hierarchical classification. It may, however, be useful simply to list the chief meanings which the term "law" was made to carry in the controversy over supremacy (which is not quite the same thing as the kinds of law involved).

First there was law in the full sense of *lex.* This had been reduced from three branches to two: English common law and English statute law. The historic third branch, canon law, had gone through a series of exigencies that had left it in a bafflingly fluid condition, but one thing may be said of it categorically: canon law was not, in these years, enforceable; it was not *lex.* It figured in the debate as part of the second main idea which may be brought out of our portfolio-concept: "divine" law. It is here that the danger of misunderstanding is greatest, because the term, difficult enough in itself, was made worse by being sometimes used for one or another of its component sections (*e.g.,* the law of Moses), or appropriated to one of its component kinds to distinguish it from another (*e.g.,* to positive divine law as against natural law),

[1] C. H. McIlwain, *The High Court of Parliament* (New Haven, 1910), *passim,* especially pp. 42–256.

or otherwise particularized as a special sanctity was desired for whatever "law" seemed favorable to the author's position. But with the caveat that the term was not always used so broadly, we may say that divine law meant every rule of human conduct that could be attributed to God's authorship, regardless of provenience. Thus everything in Scripture, example as well as precept, might be called divine law; so might such inferences therefrom as the author happened to approve, and therefore the canon law, the fathers, the reformers, or even the schoolmen might be cited as to divine law. The third major component idea of "law" was natural law. We shall speak of this at greater length below; for the present we may content ourselves with observing that while natural law was often treated as part of the divine law, it was sometimes conceived as antithetical to it. Several further meanings of law occupy a lower level of significance. The civil law was, as a code, merely Roman, and could bind Englishmen neither legally nor morally; but it might embody binding law, particularly the law of nature, and hence might be used to show this forth. The law of nations was frequently mentioned and will be discussed below in connection with the law of nature; but it needs to be recognized that while its use is occasionally meaningful, it is more often a fossil, instructive as showing that the civil law has influenced the author, but confusing in the extreme if taken literally. There are also a number of other ideas for which the term "law" was employed, but they are for the most part self-explanatory (*e.g.*, the law of conquest).

The story is familiar of how the political resistance to the first two Stuarts, under the leadership of Coke, Eliot, Hampden, Pym, etc., became identified with the defense of the common and statute laws, while the court position was that kingship was a divine trust which placed the king above the laws of men and answerable only to God.[2] The nature of this divine trust was susceptible of varying definition; to get the debate with which we are now concerned into perspective, nothing is more enlightening than Strafford's conception of this trust, and Parliament's response thereto. Strafford was accused, *inter alia*, of having advised the dissolution of the Short Parliament because it was debating grievances instead of voting subsidies for a war against Scotland, and when that Parliament was dissolved, of having counselled the seizure of supply by illegal means. His words in the Privy Council, according to the elder Vane, were, "Your Majesty having tryed all wayes, and [being] refused; in this case of extream necessity, and for the Safety

[2] From a large bibliography of the subject we may select two studies which are especially illuminating: McIlwain's, cited above, and J. N. Figgis, *The Divine Right of Kings* (Cambridge, 1914).

of Your Kingdom and People, You are loose and absolved from all Rules of Government; You are acquitted before God and Men; You have an Army in Ireland; You may imploy it to reduce this Kingdom." [3] The earl of Bristol, testifying that Strafford had advanced the same doctrine on another occasion, added that he "did use the sentence, *Salus Reipublicae Suprema Lex.*" [4] Commenting upon this and other testimony to the same effect, Strafford, although insisting that if he did use the words which Vane claimed to have noted down at the time he would have been referring to Scotland, not to England, in saying "this Kingdom," made no attempt to deny the doctrine itself. On the contrary: "I say this brings it to that, which is principally for my Defence that must qualify, if not absolutely free me from any blame" for having broken English laws. Matters of fact, such as whether the war against Scotland was defensive or offensive, or whether Parliament had actually refused the subsidy, were arguable, but he could not understand how the doctrine could be brought in question. Kings were "not only accountable for themselves to God Almighty, but also for their Subjects;" [5] from this it followed for him "what a King may do, in case of absolute necessity; certainly in these cases, the ordinary Rules do not take place." [6]

It was Pym who answered on behalf of the House of Commons (in a speech that was immediately published by order of the House) that there could be no appeal from the known laws of England to any "higher" trust or more "fundamental" law. Not that he denied that the safety of the people was fundamental; but because human nature was depraved the people could be safe only under the known laws. It had, he began, already been proved that Strafford had subverted the known laws:

> That which is given me in *charge,* is, to shew the *quality* of the *offence,* how *hainous* it is in the *nature,* how *mischievous* in the *effect* of it; which will best appeare if it be examined by that *Law,* to which he himselfe appealed, that *universall,* that *supreme Law, Salus populi:* This is the *Element* of all Laws, out of which they are derived; the *End* of all Laws, to which they are designed, and in which they are perfected. . . . There is in this *Crime,* a *Seminarie* of all *evils* hurtfull to a *State;* and if you consider the *reasons* of it, it must needs be so: The *Law* is that which puts a *difference* betwixt *good* and *evill,* betwixt *just* and *unjust;* If you take away the *Law,* all things will fall into a *confusion, every man* will become a *Law* to *himselfe,* which in the *depraved condition* of *humane nature,* must needs *produce* many great *enormities: Lust* will become a *Law,* and *Envie* will become a *Law, Covetous-*

[3] John Rushworth, *The Tryal of Thomas Earl of Strafford* (London, 1786), p. 545. [4] *Ibid.,* p. 542. [5] *Ibid.,* p. 643. [6] *Ibid.,* p. 646.

nesse and *Ambition* will become *Lawes*. . . . The *Law* is the *Boundarie*, the *Measure* betwixt the *Kings Prerogative*, and the *Peoples Liberty*. . . . The *Law* is the *safeguard*, the *custody* of all *private interest:* Your *Honours*, your *Lives*, your *Liberties* and *Estates* are all in the *keeping* of the *Law;* without this, every man hath a like *right* to any thing.[7]

It was a memorable speech; all too memorable, as Pym was to find. He was never to hear the end of it.

The following year the struggle over the militia led to a startling reversal of positions. First, the court party was enabled to seize the ground upon which its enemies had hitherto maneuvered so effectively. When the Commons, on January 26, petitioned that the fortresses and militia be placed in hands trusted by Parliament, Charles could reply that the laws of England placed the power of command solely in the crown, and that the petition was therefore one "the Granting whereof would alter the Fundamental Laws, [and] endanger the very Foundation upon which the public Happiness and Welfare of his People is founded and constituted." [8] When Parliament passed the Militia Ordinance (without as yet putting it into effect), it issued (March 7) a "Declaration of both Houses, setting forth the Causes of their Jealousies and Fears" for the safety of the king's person and realm, which had caused them to "apply ourselves to the Use of that Power, for the Security and Defence of both, which, by the Fundamental Laws and Constitutions of this Kingdom, resides in us." [9] Charles' reply (from Huntingdon, March 15) was to insist

> That his *Subjects* cannot be obliged to obey any *Act, Order, or Injunction,* to which his *Majesty* hath not given his *Consent: And therefore he thinks it necessary to publish, That he expects, and hereby requires, Obedience, from all his loving Subjects, to the Laws established; and that they presume not, upon any Pretence of Order or Ordinance to which his Majesty is no Party, concerning the Militia, or any other Thing, to do or execute what is not warranted by those Laws; his Majesty being resolved to observe all the Laws Himself, and to require Obedience to them from all his Subjects.*[10]

Parliament attempted to disguise its action (which, as Charles had correctly said, was legislative in nature, and therefore constitutionally required the royal assent before it could become law) under the aspect

[7] *The Speech or Declaration of John Pym* . . . *12. April, 1641*, E208(8), pp. 2–5; also in Rushworth, *Tryal*, pp. 661–70.

[8] *Old Parliamentary History*, X, 264; *Lords Journals*, IV, 557–58.

[9] *Old Parliamentary History*, X, 338–39.

[10] *Ibid.*, p. 363; *Lords Journals*, IV, 647.

of a judicial declaration.[11] It passed a resolution declaring "That when the Lords and Commons in Parliament, which is the Supreme Court of Judicature in the Kingdom, shall declare what the Law of the Land is, to have This not only questioned and controverted, but contradicted, and a Command that it should not be obeyed, is a high Breach of the Privilege of Parliament," and another that "those Persons that advised his Majesty to this Message are Enemies to the Peace of this Kingdom."[12] Charles (or rather Falkland or Hyde, but we cannot here attempt to establish the authorship of papers bearing Charles' signature) instantly restored the distinction which Parliament was attempting to blur: "We are not satisfied . . . that, under Pretence of declaring what the Law of the Land is, you shall, without us, make a new Law; which is plainly the Case of the Militia; And what is this but to introduce an Arbitrary way of Government?"[13]

It is almost too neat that on the day this was read in the Lords (April 1), Pym, representing the Commons in conference with the Lords about a document which was ultimately to become the Nineteen Propositions of June 2, should have used words which could not fail to recall Strafford's: "We must respect the higher, and not the lower; no Contract can oblige against the Law of God."[14] It is unlikely that Charles needed any reminder of Pym's speech just a year earlier, but he took care to recall it to the nation. "Be sure," he said in a message of April 16, "you have an early speedy Care of the Public; that is, of the only Rule which preserves the Public, the Law of the Land. . . . It was well said in a Speech made by a private Person, but published by Order of the House of Commons this Parliament, *The Law is that which puts a Difference betwixt Good and Evil*"—and he quoted another ten or a dozen lines of the speech, as given above (pp. 14–15). "So said that Gentleman, and much more very well, in Defence of the Law and against arbitrary Power: It is worth looking over and considering."[15]

This was strong ground for an English party to occupy, and from it the royalist propaganda was for some time able to block every move Parliament made to take the initiative in controversy. When Parliament finally put the militia ordinance into execution (May 5) it issued a declaration explaining that, being "intrusted with the Safety of the

[11] See McIlwain for the best account of the transition from the idea of Parliament as a "High Court" which found out and declared how the fundamental and independently existing law applied in a particular situation, to the modern idea that it makes law.

[12] *Old Parliamentary History*, X, 365–66; *Lords Journals*, IV, 650.

[13] March 26; *Old Parliamentary History*, X, 395; *Lords Journals*, IV, 686.

[14] *Old Parliamentary History*, X, 412.

[15] *Ibid.*, p. 437; *Lords Journals*, IV, 722–23.

Kingdom and Peace of the People," it was obligated to "encounter the imminent and approaching Danger" and knew no other way to do so "but by putting the People into a fit Posture of Defence" and requiring all persons to obey it "according to the Fundamental Laws of the Kingdom." [16] In a message of May 12 Charles pointed out that the responsibility for the safety of the kingdom was, by the law, vested in him, and issued a debater's challenge: "By what Law, or Authority, they possess themselves of his Majesty's proper Right and Inheritance, he is confident, that as they have not, so they cannot shew." [17] He triumphantly pursued this tack in *An Answer, by Way of Declaration* (to Parliament's *Declaration* of May 5), dated May 20. If Parliament had not been unable to do so, its *Declaration* "would have told our good Subjects what those Fundamental Laws of the Land are, and where to be found; and would at least have mention'd one Ordinance, from the first Beginning of Parliaments to this present Parliament, which endeavoured to impose any Thing upon the Subject without the King's Consent." [18] Parliament's claim to make new law unilaterally, if allowed, would put all rights of king and people at its mercy.[19]

Parliament's response was very lame. In its *Declaration* of May 19 it stood on its dignity in declining the challenge, and merely repeated its earlier assertions: the Houses had acted, "not by any new Law of their own making, as hath been untruly suggested to his Majesty; but by the most antient Law of this Kingdom, even that which is Fundamental and Essential to the Constitution and Subsistence of it." [20] But what this fundamental law was they did not specify, as Charles, pressing his advantage home, did not fail to point out. No fair man would be deceived, said his *Answer*,[21] "by the meer averring it to be *according to the Fundamental Laws of this Kingdom*, without giving any Direction, that the most cunning and learned Men in the Laws may be able to find those Foundations." [22]

The superiority of the royalist propaganda here was indubitably having its effect. These were the months in which the "constitutional" royalist party was being formed and gaining many recruits, not only from those who had hitherto been neutral but even from those who had been prominent on Parliament's side. One example—a dramatic one—may stand here for many. In June, Lord Paget, one of the few peers

---

[16] *Ibid.*, p. 486; *Lords Journals*, V, 46.

[17] *Ibid.*, p. 509; incomplete in *Lords Journals*, V, 61.

[18] *Ibid.*, XI, 7.   [19] *Ibid.*, p. 8.   [20] *Ibid.*, p. 17.

[21] The Thomason *Catalogue* (I, 111) dates this May 21. The editors of *Old Parliamentary History*, without supplying their evidence, say it was printed some time after May 26 (XI, 63, n.).   [22] *Old Parliamentary History*, XI, 68.

who had chosen to remain in Westminster, changed his mind and fled to York. In *The Copy of a Letter Sent from the Right Honourable, The Lord Paget, unto the Honourable House of Parliament,* he said:

> It may seeme strange, that I, who with all zeale and earnestnesse have prosecuted in the beginning of this Parliament, the Reformation of all disorders in Church, and Common-wealth, should now in a time of such great distractions, desert the cause. . . . But when I found a Preparation of Armes against the KING, under the shadow of Loyaltie, I rather resolved, to obey a good Conscience, then particular ends, and am now on my way to His Majesty.[23]

But the preparation of arms, to be used against Charles if necessary, had not at first alienated Paget. As a matter of fact, he had accepted appointment as Lord Lieutenant to administer the Militia Ordinance in Buckingham, and as late as May 23 had published (with whatever mental reservations) a report "Shewing the great readinesse of that County, to obey the Ordinance of the Parliament, touching the *Militia.*" [24] Clarendon explains Paget's change as due to his having become "convinced in his conscience" [25] (he does not explain or even report Paget's subsequent reconversion to Parliament's side in October, 1644 [26]), and he does in fact seem to exemplify the growing response to the new persuasiveness of the royalist argument.

But already the way had been indicated for the Parliamentary propaganda to outflank the royalist position and reach ground from which a new offensive could be launched. Shortly before April 22 [27] there appeared an anonymous broadside for which no author has been suggested but which one is tempted to call a prior abstract, by the same hand, of John Marsh's *An Argument or, Debate in Law,* published six months later (see below, p. 38). *A Question Answered: How Laws Are To Be Understood, and Obedience Yeelded* [28] boldly concedes the principal fact: "His Majesty (let it be granted) is intrusted by Law with the *Militia.*" But against the consequences which the royalists drew from this fact the broadside opposes an argument from the nature of law. It begins by laying down a distinction: "There is in Laws an equitable,

[23] 669.f.6(35), dated June by the Thomason *Catalogue;* also in *Old Parliamentary History*, XI, 232.

[24] 669.f.6(22).   [25] Clarendon, V, 339 (Macray, II, 182).

[26] *Old Parliamentary History*, XIII, 302–303.

[27] The Thomason *Catalogue* (I, 101) tentatively dates it April 21, but Thomason entered no date on it, and the proposed date leaves insufficient time for notice by Charles's *Message* of the 22nd.

[28] 669.f.6(7). Reprinted in Edward Husbands, *An Exact Collection of All Remonstrances, Declarations* (1643), pp. 150–51, and John Rushworth, *Historical Collections of the Great Civil War* (8 vols., London, 1721), IV, 542–43.

and a litterall sence." When the "Letter of the Law shall be improved against the *equity* of it," the subject is at liberty "to refuse *obedience* to the Letter: for the Law taken abstract from its originall reason and end, is made a shell without a kernell." Now the reason and end of the king's legal command over the militia is "the good and preservation of the Republique." The author appears to anticipate the objection that he is begging the question: "Nor need this *equity* be expressed in the Law, being so naturally implyed and supposed in all Laws that are not meerely Imperiall, from that analogie which all bodies Politicke hold with the Naturall; whence all government and Governours borrow a proportionable respect." He enforces his argument with an illustration which was to become a staple of Parliamentary polemic[29]:

> When the *Militia* of an Army is committed to the Generall, it is not with any expresse condition, that he shall not turn the mouths of his Cannons against his own Souldiers, for that is so naturally and necessarily implyed, that its needlesse to be expressed, insomuch as if he did attempt or command such a thing against the nature of his trust and place, it did *ipso facto* estate the Army, in a right of disobedience, except we thinke that obedience binds Men to cut their owne throats, or at least their companions.

The new Parliamentary doctrine had not quite arrived. Its main foundation, natural law, entered the present argument only as an analogy to supply an "equity" otherwise unexpressed; it had yet to be brought into a more central position, whence it could support consequences for which the notion of equity was too narrow a base. But the ingredients were present, if not in their final arrangement; and if the distinction between the letter and the equity of the law had theoretical inadequacies, it had the enormous tactical advantage of being a distinction "known" and implemented by English law. Charles tacitly acknowledged the broadside's power by immediately dispatching a message to the House of Lords demanding that they find out and punish the author and printer of "such Seditious and Treasonable distinctions," and without waiting for a reply, printed his message in the format (although not with the wording) of a royal proclamation.[30]

About a month later Henry Parker, Parliament's most original lawyer-propagandist, published a pamphlet entitled *Some Few Obser-*

[29] See, *e.g.,* Henry Parker, *Observations upon Some of His Majesties Late Answers* (July 2, 1642), E153(26), p. 4, and *The Contra-Replicant* (January 31, 1643), E87(5), p. 8; John Brinsley, *The Healing of Israels Breaches* (September 30, 1642), E119(14), p. 38; Stephen Marshall, *A Copy of a Letter* (May 18, 1643), E102(10), p. 8.

[30] *His Majesties Message to the House of Peers . . . April 22. 1642,* 669.f.5(6).

*vations upon His Majesties Late Answer to the Declaration . . . of
the 19. of May, 1642.*[31] This develops the position of *A Question
Answered* in the direction of Parliament's fuller theory, but we need
not analyze it here, since Parker's better known and much more important next pamphlet pushed it into the background before it could
occasion much discussion.[32] We may content ourselves with noting
that it introduced the notions that the king's argument was "unnatural," [33] that his rights are conditional and must give way to the
common necessity (which is to be declared by Parliament),[34] and,
more obscurely, that Parliament, without the royal assent, can make
law as well as declare it.[35]

For one more month the debate was conducted largely by the princi-
pals. In its *Remonstrance* of May 26 Parliament asserted that it was
not bound by precedents,[36] that kings were "only intrusted with their
Kingdoms . . . for the Good and Safety and best Advantage thereof"
and their trust was "to be manag'd by the Advice of the Houses of
Parliament, whom the Kingdom hath trusted for that Purpose," [37]
that Parliament could do anything for the public safety, even though
the king chose to absent himself,[38] and that kings had no right to
withhold assent from anything passed by the Houses.[39] A practical
gloss on this document is furnished by the Nineteen Propositions
which Parliament sent to Charles on June 2. Charles was, in effect, to
abdicate supremacy to Parliament, whereupon it would reinstate him
in full command of the military establishment (exercised through
persons nominated by Parliament), and then turn to the settlement of
a happy revenue for him.[40]

Charles, of course, referred everything to the law. On May 27 he
issued a *Proclamation* which, after citing the relevant statute to show
that all armed forces were at the disposal of the crown, prohibited
obedience to the militia ordinance.[41] In his *Answer to the Remonstrance of May 26* he showed that Parliament's claims in that document (each of which he refuted on the basis of cited laws) amounted
to absolute sovereignty, and declared that "the Framers and Contriv-

[31] Thomason, who wrote on the pamphlet, "by Mr Hen: Parker" (E151[23]),
did not date it; the *Catalogue* dates it May 21, but it is in answer to a pamphlet
of that date or later; see above, p. 17, n. 21.

[32] Apparently it drew only one reply, *An Answer or Necessary Animadversions, upon Some Late Impostumate Observations* (August 3, 1642), E108(39).

[33] *Some Few Observations*, E151(23), pp. 2–3.   [34] *Ibid.*, pp. 5–9.

[35] *Ibid.*, p. 12.   [36] *Old Parliamentary History*, XI, 92.   [37] *Ibid.*, p. 94.

[38] *Ibid.*, pp. 94–95.   [39] *Ibid.*, pp. 96–99.   [40] *Ibid.*, pp. 130–35.

[41] Gardiner, *Constitutional Documents of the Puritan Revolution 1625–1660*
(3 ed., Oxford: Clarendon Press, 1947), pp. 248–49.

ers of that Declaration" could no longer be regarded as a Parliament but as a subversive and ambitious faction, and those who continue to support them as "actual Raisers of Sedition." [42] On June 3, at Heyworth Moor, he issued a *Declaration* explaining why he was forming a new "guard." "For the Law," he was careful to explain, "it being the common Inheritance of our People, we shall never inforce any Prerogative of ours beyond it, but submit ourself to it." [43] Similarly, his *Declaration* ten days later to the peers and the Privy Council began, "We do declare, That we will not require, nor exact, any Obedience from you, but what shall be warranted by the known Law of the Land." [44] In a message to Parliament of June 25 he renewed yet again his unaccepted challenge: "Let the Law be Judge by whom it is violated." [45]

Parliament was being goaded into taking the final step that would carry it from the old concept that it "declared" law to the modern concept that it makes law. Bringing up an impeachment of certain peers on June 15, Denzil Holles, on behalf of the Commons, told the Lords that "the Parliament is the Foundation and Basis of Government . . . it creates the Law." [46] For the argument to support this revolutionary assertion we must turn to the most influential pamphlet published on the Parliamentary side in 1642, Parker's *Observations upon Some of His Majesties Late Answers and Expresses* (July 2).[47]

To judge the rival claims of regal and parliamentary power one must, said Parker, consider their respective causes, both in the sense of what created them and to what ends; and these in turn must be sought in the origin of the state. This he finds in a social contract: "Power is originally inherent in the people," and is transferred to their governors by "the Pactions and agreements of such and such politique corporations." [48] The reason men put governors over themselves is that they are by nature social, but since the Fall society is impossible without government:

> Man being depraved by the fall of *Adam* grew so untame and uncivill a creature, that the Law of God written in his brest was not sufficient to restrayne him from mischiefe, or to make him sociable, and therefore

[42] *Old Parliamentary History*, XI, 138–63; especially pp. 139 and 162.

[43] *Ibid.*, p. 166.   [44] *Ibid.*, p. 208.   [45] *Ibid.*, p. 249.   [46] *Ibid.*, p. 200.

[47] I am at a loss to account for J. W. Allen's assertion that "Relatively few of the apologists for Parliament accepted or reproduced the theories of Parker" (*English Political Thought*, p. 424). A bibliography of those who did would be many pages long; the items discussed below are only a selection.

[48] *Observations*, p. 1; quotations are from the corrected second edition, also 1642, reproduced in William Haller, *Tracts on Liberty in the Puritan Revolution 1638–1647* (3 vols., New York: Columbia University Press, 1934), II, 167–213.

without some magistracy to provide new orders, and to judge of old,
and to execute according to justice, no society could be upheld. Without society men could not live, and without lawes men could not be
sociable, and without authority somewhere invested, to judge according
to Law, and execute according to judgement, Law was a vaine and void
thing. It was soon therefore provided that lawes agreeable to the dictates of reason should be ratified by common consent, and that the
execution and interpretation of those Lawes should be intrusted to
some magistrate, for the preventing of common injuries betwixt Subject
and Subject.[49]

From all this "we see that power is but secondary and derivative in
Princes, the fountaine and efficient cause is the people, and from hence
the inference is just, the King, though he be *singulis Major,* yet he is
universis minor, for . . . it is a rule in nature, *quicquid efficit tale, est
magis tale.*" [50]

The people are the final as well as the efficient cause of the king's
power; "indeed it were strange if the people in subjecting it selfe to
command, should ayme at any thing but its owne good in the first and
last place." [51] Now, "that which is the end is farre more honorable and
valuable in nature and policy, then that which is the meanes. This directs us then to the transcendent ἀχμή of all Politiques, to the Paramount Law that shall give Law to all humane Lawes whatsoever, and
that is *Salus Populi.*" [52]

The people then being both efficient and final cause of regal power,
on what terms do they convey that power to a king? As a trust, with a
double condition: "that the subject shall live both safe and free." The
former of these is natural and absolute: "The Charter of nature intitles all Subjects of all Countries whatsoever to safetie by its supreame
Law." The latter is to some extent voluntary and therefore relative:
"Freedome indeed has divers degrees of latitude, and all Countries
therein doe not participate alike, but positive Lawes must every
where assigne those degrees." [53]

Parliament has exactly the same efficient and final causes as have
kings ("if not higher" [54]). After creating the state and its laws, the
people found that it was very difficult to prevent their kings from
ignoring the law and ruling tyrannically. For some time they knew no
recourse but revolution, but at length they "found out an Art and
peaceable Order" by which to give or withhold their consent to particular acts of the king: "by vertue of election and representation, a
few shall act for many." Parliament's power, therefore, resides in the

[49] *Ibid.,* p. 13.   [50] *Ibid.,* p. 2.   [51] *Ibid.*   [52] *Ibid.,* p.3.
[53] *Ibid.,* p. 4.   [54] *Ibid.,* p. 5.

fact that it is the embodiment of "publike consent"; or rather, Parliament is itself "the whole community in its underived Majesty." [55]

With this analysis of the source, nature, and end of regal and Parliamentary powers, Parker turns to their present conflict. In England the "legislative power" is so divided between them that "in ordinary cases, when it concernes not the saving of the people from some great danger or inconvenience," neither can make laws without the other. But where public safety is involved, "if the king will not joyne with the people, the people may without disloyalty save themselves." The king "cites Statutes" to the contrary, statutes "to prove, that the power of levying armes and forces is solely in him;" but "See if this be not contrary to the originall, end, and trust of all power and Lawe." [56] "Since it is unnaturall for any Nation to give away its owne proprietie in it selfe absolutely, . . . wee must not think that it can stand with the intent of any trust, that necessarie defence should be barred, and naturall preservation denyed to any people." [57] The king objects that this is to make "the Law it self subject to your Votes" [58] and to give Parliament "an arbitrary unlimitable power." [59] The people must not be startled by this argument (Parker's is the modern concept of sovereignty). "That there is an Arbitrary power in every State somewhere tis true, tis necessary, and no inconvenience follows upon it. . . . If the State intrusts this to one man, or few, there may be danger in it; but the Parliament is neither one nor few, it is indeed the State it self." [60] The real question in debate is not whether there is such a sovereignty but where it resides; to settle this controversy, "We must retire to the principles of Nature, and there search, whether the King or Kingdom be to be lookt upon as the efficient, and finall cause, and as the proper Subject of all power." [61]

There were difficulties in Parker's argument (the royalists will soon bring them to our attention), but its impact was enormous. Parliament, not long erewhile the great champion of the laws of England, had become vulnerable to accusation by those laws. Confronted by the particular laws it was breaking, it could only refer to some more "fundamental" but embarrassingly undefined law by which it claimed to act for the public safety. Now here was a theory which defined that more fundamental law. It was something called the "law of nature" which, having brought the state into being, remained the criterion of its operations. Men might organize the state according to what rules they pleased ("positive laws"), provided that these rules did not conflict with the fundamental law of nature. But certain positive laws of

[55] Ibid., pp. 13–15.   [56] Ibid., pp. 16–17.   [57] Ibid., p. 20.
[58] Ibid., p. 35.   [59] Ibid., p. 34.   [60] Ibid.   [61] Ibid., p. 44.

England did conflict with the fundamental law of nature: they were therefore invalid.

Of course there was nothing original in the component ideas comprising Parker's theory (they would have had little influence if they had been new). The law of nature is one of those concepts whose origin is obscure because mankind seems never to have been without some form of it. Certainly before the end of the fourth century B.C. it had emerged as the central idea of one of the world's great philosophical systems, Stoicism. The primitive and divine substance which, for the Stoics, unified all being, expressing itself as "hold" and "vital force" at the lower inanimate levels, and as irrational and rational "soul" in animate creatures, was a sublimated "fire" or "seminal reason." Man's reason was a ray of this celestial fire, and hence his "ruling faculty." To live "agreeably to nature"—that is, to conform to the divine order of the universe—therefore meant to obey "right reason," freeing the will from thraldom to pleasure and pain and choosing only what was right and good ("virtue"); this was the sole source of "happiness," every man's object. This "law of nature" was everywhere the same, and the wise man obeyed it regardless of the "laws" of his particular city: he was a "citizen of the city of the world."

Later, during the Middle Stoa, this opposition between the universal law of nature, which the wise man obeyed, and the positive law of individual states, which was the rule for the ignorant, was modified into the demand that positive laws conform to the natural law which bound, or ought to bind, all men. In this form the doctrine was highly suitable for adoption by Rome, which it reached through the Scipionic circle. Rome's empire encompassed many subject peoples, and what validity, if any, to allow their several legal systems was a real administrative and philosophical problem. But if the law of nature or right reason was the law of the universal human community, it could furnish the key to the problem; and Roman law became organized under three rubrics, *jus naturale* (law of nature), *jus gentium* (law of nations), and *jus civile* (civil law, the law of a particular city).

The church fathers and the schoolmen (with some help already available in Pauline theology) adopted the idea of natural law and gave it a Christian sanction by defining the law of fallen nature ("the secondary law of nature") as that remnant of the authoritative pattern written in man's heart at creation ("the law of prime nature," or "the primary law of nature") which is available to the reason of fallen man, variously aided by the enlightenment of grace. Largely, but not wholly, by means of the canon law, the idea of natural law influenced almost every aspect of Christian life throughout the middle ages and the renaissance.[62] English law gave it an ambiguous status. It was a concept fundamental to the canon law, but that was now in a state of flux; it was also fundamental to the civil law, but that had no *legal* status in England; it was not "known" to the common law or to statute law, but all English lawyers had been trained to think of it as identified, or at least closely associated, with a term of great authority, especially in the common law: the "law of reason." [63] It did not, as we shall see, mean the same thing for everyone, but it had for almost everyone what was essential to successful contemporary propaganda— an aura of authority.

The idea of a social contract did not have such status, but neither did it suffer the stigma of newness. It was not unknown in fourth-century Athens, and it enjoyed a kind of intermittent half-life in the first Christian millennium; under the impetus of Aquinas its use grew, and it may be thought the dominant political concept of the seventeenth and eighteenth centuries.[64] It was hardly ever employed without the law of nature, although of course the latter was used by many people who had no sympathy for the social contract.

If these ideas were so central to the main stream of western civilization, it may be thought strange that no Englishman had used them to claim Parliamentary sovereignty before Parker did. In fact, it is not really strange. Parliament had not pursued sovereignty until it became obvious that Charles' constitutional concessions were tactical and were about to be destroyed by force. Thereafter some time was necessary for the champions of Parliament to realize that the historic Parliamentary theory would no longer serve, and to find a new one. Parker's achievement is that he was the first to do this.

4. ROYALIST REPLIES

The royalist propaganda, reacting instantly to what it recognized as a major Parliamentary initiative, developed a counter-offensive along four main lines. The first may be described as a holding operation: it is the continuation of the argument that had done such yeoman service in the preceding months, but a shift in emphasis from royal

[62] The bibliography of the subject is enormous, and no attempt can be made to give it here.

[63] See Christopher St. German, *Dialogue in English, betweene a Doctor of Divinitie, and a Student in the Lawes of England* (especially Dialogue I, chapter 5), which, with its Latin predecessor (first published in 1523), had been a standard textbook for more than a century.

[64] See J. W. Gough, *The Social Contract: A Critical Study of Its Development* (Oxford: Clarendon Press, 1936).

messages and declarations to private (sometimes only apparently private) publications made possible an interesting variation. Early in July a pamphlet purporting to be *A Declaration, or Resolution, of the County of Hereford* began by admitting that "the Kingdom, for many Years past . . . groaned under . . . the . . . dismal Effects of an arbitrary Government, and a high-stretch'd Prerogative," and looked to Parliament for a cure.[1] But Parliament has only produced the same sickness on the other side, violating the laws of the land and the people's rights; and because Hereford does not propose to "cast off the Yoak of one Tyranny to endure many worse," it will support the king.[2] In this brusque form the argument suited the period when Charles' unpopularity was still too great for the royalists to confront it head-on; as it became a staple it was modified. *A Vindication of the King, With Some Observations upon the Two Houses* (September 17) bewailed Charles' "unspeakable misfortune, never to know the misery of the People, till their discontents were grown to that head," and blamed his lack of information on "some ill affected agents." But all that, it continued, was over. "Are not our Rights and Properties already establisht this Parliament, by such acts of Grace, as could never finde Presidents from His Ancestors?" Now that Parliament has divested Charles of the "suspected arbitrary power" which, misinformed of the true meaning of our laws, he had attempted to exercise, what is the meaning of its own claim to be above the law, "unlesse there be that intend the alteration of our Government"?[3] Of course the royalists from time to time repeated Charles' taunt about Parliament's inability to cite the laws it purported to defend: "and yet (having set up as strict an *inquisition* for *presidents* as for *Delinquents*) now after so many monthes elucubrations, not one fragment of law produced to that purpose."[4]

A second line taken by the counter-offensive was for the royalists never more than a clever and effective debating point, but later the Levellers, and after them the New Model, would adopt it in all earnestness, and implement it too. The day before Parker's *Observations* appeared, the king's printer at York published *A Letter from the Sheriff and Gentry of* Nottinghamshire *to their Members* [of the House of Commons]. In rejecting Parliament's claim to make a law without the king, it said, "We never conceived . . . we had such a Power to confer

[1] *Old Parliamentary History*, XI, 273.
[2] *Ibid.*, p. 276.   [3] E118(3), pp. 1–3.
[4] *The Complaint of the Kingdome against the evill Members of both Houses;* 1482.bb.6, p. 5. Not in the Thomason collection. Probably February, 1643, since it refers to several pamphlets of January, one of them dated January 31.

upon you." [5] This was the true royalist view. But it could, if rhetoric required, be temporarily set aside. The first of the many replies to Parker's pamphlet, *Animadversions Upon Those Notes Which The Late Observator hath published* (July 9), showed the way. It repudiates Parker's whole natural-law social-contract theory (this is the pamphlet which warned Parliament that it was reviving the ghost of Wat Tyler),[6] but it adds that the same theory can be turned against Parliament.

> Well, But good Sir, may not the people withdraw the power of representation, which they granted to the Parliament; was their grant so absolute, and so irrevocable, that they dispossest themselves wholly of taking or exercising that power, their owne proper persons? Remember your principles about the conveying of Soveraigne power into the hands of Kings; and if you can shew no better Cards for their power of representation, then the Peoples revocable consent, (and I would faine know why it should be more revocable from Kings then men) you will finde their tenure in it very tickle.[7]

Knowing the future influence of this line, we may think it surprising how slow the other royalists were to take it up; perhaps they found it too distasteful even as a debating point. Aside from an incidental sentence in a pamphlet of November,[8] no use seems to have been made of it until mid-December, when Henry Ferne repeated the warning: "The People being discontented, and having gotten power shall say, The Members of the two Houses do not discharge the trust committed to them, they do not that for which they were chosen and sent for, then may the multitude by this rule and principle now taught them take the Power to themselves, . . . overthrow King and Parliament, fill all with rapine and confusion, draw all to a Folkmoot, and make every Shire a severall Government." [9]

The device really came into its own at the beginning of the new year, with the publication of *A Complaint to the House of Commons, and Resolution taken up by the free Protestant Subjects of the Cities of* London *and* Westminster, *and the Counties Adjacent,* a brilliant piece which gave the Parliamentary side much discomfort (partly be-

[5] *Old Parliamentary History,* XI, 258.

[6] See above, p. 8.   [7] E107(22), p. 12.

[8] *An Answer to a Printed Book, Intituled Observations* (Oxford, November 20, 1642), E242(16), p. 12; for a discussion of this pamphlet see below, pp. 34–36.

[9] *The Resolving of Conscience* (Cambridge, 1642), 701.g.4(4), pp. 29–30; not in the Thomason collection; the imprint reads 1642, and the closer dating is provided by Charles Herle, *A Fuller Answer* (December 29, 1642), E244(27), sig. A2. For a discussion of Ferne's pamphlet see below, pp. 30–31.

cause it enforced each of its accusations of misdemeanor with the names of the doers). After reviewing the history of the struggle along the now familiar royalist line (the conciliar government, for which Laud and Strafford were chiefly responsible, had been arbitrary, but Parliament was now attempting to impose a worse), it ended with the following declaration:

> our Resolution is to re-assume the power we put into you (for . . . wee must work upon your own principles) for you having mainly broken the trust we reposed in you, in subverting all our Laws, (which you should have preserved) we may take back what we gave you, (and we are certain, your elections are more conditionall upon that point then our Kings Crown, which comes by inheritance and succession;) . . . And in case of urgent necessity (which is our case directly) . . . we may defend our selves by Arms, and make use of what is next, and we have a president shown by your selves for the manner of that defence.[10]

Even more disconcerting to Parliament (and, it may be guessed, wonderfully instructive to the future Levellers) was another application of this device. Sir John Spelman, in *A View of a Printed Book Intituled Observations Upon His Majesties Late Answers* (January 26, 1643), after making the point about the sovereign people having the right to revoke Parliament's entrusted powers,[11] shows how Parker's theory lays Parliament open to demands of democratic reform:

> the Commons Vote in right of their electors whom they represent; at least nine parts of the Kingdome, neither doe nor may Vote in their election, . . . all that have not 40. s. per annum free-hold Land, which

[10] E244(31), p. 23. The pamphlet was received by Thomason on January 2, 1643, but since it was published at Oxford it may have appeared some days earlier. Something of the disturbance it caused may be seen in the efforts to answer it. The first is a feeble pamphlet by Peter Bland, of Gray's Inn: *An Answer to the Late Scandalous and Libellous Pamphlet, Entituled, A Complaint* (January 5, 1643), E244(36). Next is a bitter attack inserted into the second edition of Herle's *A Fuller Answer to . . . Doctor Ferne* (January 10, 1643), E245(3), pp. 20–21. The third is very interesting indeed: it is E245(5), January 12, and it imitates the title page of *A Complaint* in all details. It begins the text with the same words, and throughout it employs phrases taken from *A Complaint* and used in opposite contexts. Its general argument is that the earlier pamphlet is a device of crypto-Papists. The reason for the imitated title page can only be guessed, but it is probably that *A Complaint* was enjoying much success and being widely but (because it was contraband) hurriedly bought; the imitated title page might put E245(5) into many hands seeking E244(31), and the aaapted text might confuse and frustrate these readers. The fourth answer was *A Just Complaint, Or Loud Crie, Of All the Well-Affected Subjects* (January 31), E245(27), which is evasive throughout.

[11] E245(22), pp. 13–14.

I imagine, cannot be above a tenth part of the Kingdome. Tell me good Sir, you that list to unsettle principles, power being (you say) nothing else but that might and vigour which a society of men containes in it selfe, why should the might and vigour of these being farre the major part, be over mastred, and concluded by the Votes of those that are deputed by a miner number of the people? or why should halfe the Kingdome in which there are but few Burroughes, be equalled and over-borne in Voting by two Counties, out of which many Burgesses are chosen? *Old Sarum* shal have as many Votes in Parliament, as the Citty of *London,* or County of *Wiltes.*[12]

The idea of recalling entrusted powers did in fact prove a taking doctrine, as Parliament discovered when, in December 1642 and January 1643, under the temporary dominance of the Peace Party, it found that some who supported it most vigorously against Charles had learned how the doctrine could be used to coerce Parliament.[13] They never found it necessary to go beyond the threat, but it is no wonder if an anonymous royalist exulted in the ironical justice that "you should be whipt with a rod of your own making." [14]

A third line along which the royalists conducted their propaganda counter-offensive was a reactivation of the doctrine of the divine right of kings, which had not been much heard since the execution of Strafford. In *Rules to Know a Royall King, From a Disloyall Subject* (July 28, 1642), Thomas Jordan may have been a little simple-minded in formulating the doctrine, but he provides (inadvertently, one sup-poses) an admirable clue to the reasons for its revival just now: "Grace must take precedencie of Nature." [15] That is the essence of the tactic: if Parliament appealed from positive law to a higher law, the royalists would counter with a yet higher. But at its most characteristic the divine-right argument would not oppose divine and natural law, as Parker had opposed natural and English positive; the clergymen who chiefly used this form of the divine-right theory, unlike the pro-ponents of the fourth line discussed below, thought of natural law as a part of divine law,[16] and based their reply on a discrimination of areas of jurisdiction between divine positive law and divine natural law.

---

[12] *Ibid.,* sig. D2.   [13] See below, pp. 45–47.

[14] *An Answer to a Seditious Pamphlet, Intituled, Plain English* (Oxford, 1643), E89(33), p. 18; dated February 12 by Falconer Madan, *Oxford Books* (3 vols., Oxford, 1895–1931), II, 222–23.

[15] E108(14), p. 1.

[16] *E.g.,* while *The Resolving of Conscience* does not deal with natural law, one of the proofs it offers that power is a divine ordinance is that "men are not onely naturally bent to society, but also are bound as they are reasonable crea-tures, to set up and live under government as under an order of that providence by which the world is governed" (701.g.4[4]), p. 16.

Henry Ferne was not the first to answer Parker in these terms,[17] but his was the most influential statement, and we may use it to recover the argument.

The Resolving of Conscience [18] is on the question "Whether upon such a Supposition or Case, as is now usually made (The King will not discharge his trust, but is bent or seduced to subvert Religion, Laws, and Liberties) Subjects may take Arms and resist? and Whether that Case be now?" [19] Ferne begins by limiting the resistance under discussion to the "forcible," for he is ready to agree that "we may and ought to deny obedience to such commands of the Prince, as are unlawfull by the Law of God, yea, by the established Laws of the Land." [20] He deals first, and rather briefly, with the contention of many Puritan preachers that a king must be resisted if he threatens true religion; the example of primitive Christians, together with the teaching of Scripture (particularly Romans 13) is against resistance on behalf of religion. "Conscience . . . heares the Apostle expressely say, *Whosoever resist shall receive to themselves damnation.*" [21]

Then he turns to Parker's argument, and here he distinguishes "*the Power* it self . . . from the *designing of the Person* to bear that power, and the *qualification* of that power according to the divers wayes of executing it in severall forms of government." [22] In the latter functions the people may play a role, and hence no form of government is of divine right; [23] "but the power it self is of God originally and chiefly" [24] and "is still governed under God." [25] The people have no right to "reassume" power which they never had, but must obey the divine ordinance of government. Their good is certainly an end of government (though not the sole end), and the governor (in monarchies the king) is certainly bound by his office to seek it; but if he will not perform his office faithfully he cannot be enforced thereto.[26]

> No, Conscience will look at that Power as the Ordinance of God, and the abuse of that Power as a judgement and scourge of God upon the people, and will not use Arms to resist the Ordinance under pretence of resisting the abuse, but cryes and prayers to God, petitions to the Prince, denials of obedience to his unjust commands, denials of subsidies, aids, and all fair means that are fit for Subjects to use, and when done all, if not succeed, will rather suffer then resist.[27]

---

[17] *E.g., An Answer* (November 20, 1642), E242(16), which will be discussed as representing a different kind of attack (see below, pp. 34–36), is not consistent in its attitude toward natural law, being written by several hands, and at times speaks in a way that might be appropriate to Ferne; *e.g.,* p. 20.

[18] Mid-December, 1642; see above, p. 27, n. 9.   [19] 701.g.4(4), title page.

[20] *Ibid.,* pp. 2–3.   [21] *Ibid.,* p. 5.   [22] *Ibid.,* p. 15.   [23] *Ibid.,* p. 17.

[24] *Ibid.,* p. 15.   [25] *Ibid.,* p. 17.   [26] *Ibid.,* pp. 17–23.   [27] *Ibid.,* p. 31.

This is what the Christian would do were Charles a tyrant. But in fact, so far from governing oppressively, Charles has made great concessions from those prerogative rights which he could fairly claim by precedent; those Parliamentary requests which he has refused to grant were such as he was in duty bound to refuse.[28] The action of Parliament is plain damnable rebellion, and Charles is quite justified in using all means, including foreign troops and Roman Catholic recusants, to suppress it.[29]

This is the dominant form of the divine-right theory in the period under study. Of course there were minor variations. Some of his fellows thought Ferne too liberal with respect to forms of government; thus Griffith Williams, bishop of Ossory, declared that monarchy was the immediate ordinance of God, while other forms were only permitted by him.[30] Sometimes a point would be filled in which Ferne had neglected. He had denied that the good of the people was the sole end of government, but (perhaps intentionally) had not mentioned other ends. Thomas Morton, bishop of Durham, preferred to be explicit. The primary end of all creation is God's praise and glory. But man cannot attain his end, the glorification of God, except in society; "therefore this is the primary, spirituall, supernaturall, and divine finall cause of all Republikes, to which every other end must be secondary, subordinate, and subservient." [31] Morton had no hesitation in including public safety among the secondary ends which must give way to the glory of God.[32] Otherwise, differences were largely a matter of temper; where Ferne was cool, some of his associates insisted on very provocative language. Thus, in another pamphlet, Morton wrote: "We must performe passive obedience and absolute subjection, suffering without resistance, being subject without rebellion, even if they should command the most unjust superstitious, idolatrous, prophane, or irreligious things which can be imagined; yet I say we must not rebell, unless we will renounce Christianity." [23] But allowing for such secondary differences, we may say that Ferne's is the position of those who deny the natural-law social-contract theory on the basis of divine right but who display no animus against natural law.

There is, however, a fourth line of attack against Parker which rises out of a hostility to the idea of natural law itself. With this is associated

[28] *Ibid.*, pp. 40–51.   [29] *Ibid.*, pp. 43–44.

[30] *Vindiciae Regum; or The Grand Rebellion* (Oxford, received by Thomason February 1, 1643), E88(1), p. 48.

[31] *Christus Dei, The Lords Annoynted* (Oxford, received March 7, 1643, by Thomason), E92(4), p. 3.   [32] *Ibid.*, p. 4.

[33] *The Necessity of Christian Subjection* (Oxford, received March 15, 1643, by Thomason), E93(11), p. 13.

another form of the divine-right theory, although somewhat fortuitously; the really integral version of the attack, which was only cautiously employed, is the secular. In either version, this argument constitutes the frontal assault against Parliament's new position.

We spoke above of the aura of authority which the idea of natural law had for almost everyone. It is a mistake to neglect the "almost," although when we find the concept mobilized on both sides of the papal-conciliar controversy, and the papal-imperial, the papal-national, the regal-Parliamentary, and many others, we may be tempted to assume that, if everyone interpreted the idea to suit himself, no one but Machiavelli and Hobbes opposed it. The fact is that although it is hard to find anyone bold enough to deny the existence of a natural law while heresy trials were a present danger, there was always a minority to whom it was simply evil. Nor must it be supposed that these were necessarily obscurantists hating every work of human reason. The great Colet is, together with his friends Erasmus and More, justly credited with the revival of humanistic studies in England; it was to the school he founded, the best in England, that Milton owed his introduction to those liberal arts upon which he proposed to erect his own ideal academy. Let Colet's "Exposition of St. Paul's Epistle to the Romans" exemplify for us this minority tradition of hostility to natural law.

The source of all law is the divine will, "ordaining a beautiful order" and commanding right conduct.[34] The first transgressor was Satan, and Adam soon followed. God drew some few individuals to himself, but if the rest of mankind, sunk in iniquity, "in their wilful perverseness established . . . laws," what could these enjoin but "injustice, folly, and death"?[35] Men "lived without grace, in their fallen nature, and by the corrupt law called the *law of nature:*—not the law of simple, holy, and inviolate nature (for that state of innocence was in paradise alone), but of a defiled and corrupted nature. . . . Under this term, namely, the law of man's nature, I include alike the Law of Nations, Civil Law, Common Custom, human Statutes and Decrees, and the like."[36] God, in his merciful grace, redeemed man from these invalid "laws" by ordaining just ones, first through Moses, then through Christ; and these have been elaborated and made applicable to diverse circumstances by pontifical canons.[37] "We may conclude then . . . that all systems of law may be reduced to two only: the *divine,* or perfect, law; and the *human,* or corrupt. . . . Human reason is the enemy and opponent of grace. If men establish a law of their own, they are not subject to the

[34] John Colet, *Letters to Radulphus . . . Together with Other Treatises,* tr. J. H. Lupton (London, 1876), p. 129.

[35] *Ibid.,* p. 132.　　[36] *Ibid.,* pp. 134–35.　　[37] *Ibid.,* pp. 135–39.

law of God. So also the Municipal Law of this kingdom, a law made up of the absurd decisions of wrangling men, is scouted and exploded by the law of faith and charity." [38] It is really quite remarkable what risks the great Dean took under cover of hunting down Pelagius.

We must not expect to find any royalist champions in 1642 (whatever they may have said a year or two earlier) scouting and exploding English law, but there were some for whom the law of nature was as unredeemed as for Colet. *An Answer or Necessary Animadversions, upon Some Late Impostumate Observations* (August 3, 1642) appears to have been the sole reply to Parker's half-digested pamphlet of May, *Some Few Observations,* and it is even less organized than its target. So far as it can be said to have a position, it is that by constitutional precedent Parliament has no powers without the king's consent, and that the partly-formed natural law argument by which Parker was in May looking for an alternative to constitutional precedent is somehow anti-Christian. "But 'tis Adams pure naturalls, impure nature that makes a Subject covet to be a King; to cry downe the Kings Prerogative, is it to deface nothing of Caesars superscription? . . . Tis better to obey God then man." [39]

William Ball, in *A Caveat For Subjects, Moderating the Observator* (September 19) was more explicit in repudiating natural law politics:

> Though in Nature there is a parity of mankind, and therefore dominion may not seeme to be intended by nature, yet God the authour of Nature, foreseeing the fall of man, and the depravation in nature, which did ensue thereof, intended power and dominion, and that some should bee masters and others servants; some command, and others obey; some should become slaves to tyrants, others subjects to free Monarks; others members of popular Estates: and these things God hath ordained by his divine wisedome, according to his will, and disposes and alters them at his pleasure: *But as for the pot, it ought not to say to the Potter, Why hast thou made mee thus?* It is enough for it to know, that there is no power but of God, and so to be appliable to the use it was made for; if for honour, to honour; if for servility, to servility, being subject *for conscience sake, Rom* 13.5.[40]

Of special interest to us is the fact that Ball is here adapting and modifying a passage in Justinian's *Institutes* which had always been a favorite of the commentators, which Milton was about this time noting in his *Commonplace Book*,[41] and which he too would soon adapt to Christian needs, but in a revealingly different way.[42] Justinian is distin-

---

[38] *Ibid.,* p. 139.   [39] E108(39), p. 23.   [40] E118(7), p. 12.
[41] See *Complete Prose,* I, 426.
[42] *Tetrachordon,* see below, p. 661.

guishing between *jus naturale* and *jus gentium*, which, although both are common to all mankind, may conflict with each other. By the *jus gentium* "nations have settled certain things for themselves as occasion and the necessities of human life required. For instance, wars arose, and then followed captivity and slavery, which are contrary to the law of nature; for by the law of nature all men from the beginning were born free. The law of nations again is the source of almost all contracts; for instance, sale, hire, partnership, deposit, loan for consumption, and very many others." [43] Here the freedom of the law of nature is abrogated by subjection imposed by the law of nations; this is stated as a fact and no attempt is made to justify it. For Ball, the freedom of the law of nature is abrogated by subjection imposed by God's ordinance; the fall of man may be given as the general reason for this, but its justice is not open to human question.

The secular or "rational" version of the attack on natural law at first reading seems an anticipation of Hobbes's method of using the law of nature to neutralize itself; the probability is rather that it already reflects his influence. It is contained in a pamphlet called *An Answer to a Printed Book, Intituled, Observations upon Some of His Majesties Late Answers and Expresses*, printed at Oxford and received by Thomason on November 20, 1642. The Thomason *Catalogue* attributes this to Dudley Digges, and the attribution is generally accepted; [44] but what Thomason actually wrote on the title page was "ffalk. Chiling[w]: Diggs. & y[e] rest of y[e] University." [45] Both the form and the content of the pamphlet are consistent with collaborative authorship: it comprises a series of quotations from Parker and answers to them, and these answers differ considerably in style and idea.

Falkland's participation seems confirmed by a pamphlet signed J. M. (sometimes unconvincingly understood as John Milton [46]) and entitled *A Reply To The Answer (Printed by His Majesties Command at Oxford) to a Printed Booke Intituled Observations* (February 3, 1643). This does not name the author of the pamphlet it attacks, but, after reproducing (somewhat corruptedly) a passage therefrom, it says "I believe the Author preached a quite contrary Doctrine before the Par-

[43] Tr. J. B. Moyle (5 ed., Oxford, 1913), p. 4.

[44] Thus S. Halkett and J. Laing, *A Dictionary of the Anonymous and Pseudonymous Literature of Great Britain* (rev. ed., 7 vols., Edinburgh, 1926–1934); so too *DNB*.

[45] E242(16).

[46] See J. Milton French, *Life Records of John Milton* (5 vols., New Brunswick: Rutgers University Press, 1949–58), II, 84, for an account of the attribution and its rejection; there are, however, no "royalist leanings" in this pamphlet (see below, pp. 34–35).

liament." [47] Digges * was never a member of Parliament. The subject of the excerpt is ship-money; Falkland had a leading role in the Commons' action on this, and brought Finch's impeachment to the Lords. His position was not in fact inconsistent with the reproduced extract; [48] the change is presumably that Falkland was then a Parliamentary champion against arbitrary rule by Charles, and now was on Charles' side. Chillingworth's participation is partly confirmed by what Thomason wrote on the cover of *The Petition of The Most Substantiall Inhabitants of the Citie of London . . . Together with the Answer to the same. And the Reply of the Petitioners* (January 6, 1643): "written by Chilingworth. Vide January ye 31 per parker." [49] This displays many similarities with our *Answer* of November 20.

Now Falkland and Chillingworth were friends of Hobbes. Nor need they have depended exclusively on conversations for some insight into his views on natural law. His *Elements of Law, Natural and Politique* was not published until 1650–1651, but the manuscript circulated among his friends in 1640. Furthermore, his *De Cive* had been published in a very small edition in Paris early in 1642, and it seems very likely that his friends at Oxford would have received it. Of course it is not at all impossible that Hobbes' ideas owed something to the authors of *An Answer:* Falkland and Chillingworth were very brilliant men. In any event, this anonymous pamphlet of November 20, 1642, contains the essential elements of Hobbes' political thought (along with much that is foreign and even contradictory to it, but which we need not notice here).

It is quite true that *salus populi* is the prime end of government, but "How many nations hath this abused principle brought to ruine and confusion!" [50] The abuse of the principle is to make it father the doctrine of popular sovereignty. What is the supremacy of *salus populi* grounded on? As Parker correctly says, on the fact "that the Law of Nature doth allow a man to defend himselfe, and provide for his own preservation." [51] But he need not—and indeed experience teaches that he really cannot—defend himself by his own efforts; his realization of this is the true basis of the social contract (perhaps we ought to say

[47] E245(35), p. 30. The Thomason *Catalogue* mistakenly calls this pamphlet a reply to Spelman's *A View*, discussed above, p. 28.   * *I.e.*, the younger.

[48] See *The Speech or Declaration of the Lord Faulkland . . . Against the Lord Finch* (January 14, 1641), E196(26).

[49] E244(39); misdated December 5, 1642, by the Thomason *Catalogue*. This is a sequel to the "Frivolous Petition" of December 13, 1642 (see below, pp. 41–42). Parker's answer of January 31, 1643, noted by Thomason, was *The Contra-Replicant*.

[50] E242(16), p. 9.   [51] *Ibid.*, p. 20.

"governmental contract," for *An Answer* certainly implies, if it fails explicitly to state, that the contract is unconditional and the sovereignty it confers permanently alienated [52]).

> But the Observer takes no notice, that it is in our power to part with this right, and yet doe nothing contrary to nature, if reason tell us, we shall thereby obtaine a more excellent good, the benefit of Peace and Society; nay, that this restraining our selves by compact of that naturall libertie to defend our selves, will conduce more to that end, for which it was given us, our preservation and safety. Because in probability, we shall be in lesse danger, living amongst men who have agreed to be governed by certaine Lawes, then if every one followed his owne inclination: where one suffers hereby wrongfully, thousands enjoy the benefit of being protected from wrong. And therefore though it should happen to me in particular, to be condemned by the Magistrate without cause, I am bound to suffer patiently, because having made such a bargaine, which might have been profitable, I have no right to recall it, when it appeares disadvantagious. I owe, that I have beene safe thus long, to the benefit of this Covenant, and therefore am bound in justice to share the inconveniences.[53]

Hence Parker's contention that the king is bound to grant what the people think necessary for their preservation is absurd, amounting really to the contention that "a King should bee bound by Law to destroy his people, and kill them out of duty." His true duty is not to "suffer them to be miserable, though they intreat him." [54] "Indeed this is the end of all government; for the people finding they were not fit to governe themselves, resolved to be ruled by those that were wiser, and so committed their safety to the trust of others. Now this were to reduce themselves to that first state, which their sufferings made them weary of, to place a Governour over them, and to governe that Governour." [55] As for Parker's other contention, that the sovereignty of the people is safely vested in Parliament because Parliament is the whole community and can have no private interests to corrupt it, *An Answer* replies in a way which we can hardly help associating with Hobbes: the members "must evidently have more private ends then the King, . . . there being an emptinesse in them, whereas he is full." [56]

In addition to these set royalist positions there were, of course, occasional arguments, fitted to changing situations. Some of these were studiedly moderate in tone and could be very worrisome to Parliament. For example, during the flight of members from Westminster, John

[52] For the distinction between the ideas of a "contract of government" and a "contract of society," see Sir Ernest Barker's admirable introductory essay in *Social Contract: Essays by Locke, Hume and Rousseau* (London: Oxford University Press, World's Classics ed., 1947), pp. 12–13 and *passim*.

[53] E242(16), p. 20.   [54] *Ibid.*, p. 31.   [55] *Ibid.*   [56] *Ibid.*, p. 28.

Price published *Some Few and Short Considerations on the Present Distempers* (July 30, 1642). Instead of taking a clearly partisan stand, he argued that the Houses' claim to legislate without the royal assent would be dubious at best, and must be much more so just now: "If the Votes of whatsoever they passe, though in a compleat body, without His Majesties ratification, be doubted whether efficacious and obligatory, how much rather then, when that body (as at present) is so mutilate and defective, as not to want the head [only], but so many Members too."[57]

Again, during the "Treaty" of Oxford, Thomas Povey published *The Moderator Expecting Sudden Peace, or Certaine Ruine* (February 16, 1643), an urbane argument whose tone anticipated *The Character of a Trimmer* (to which it may have given a hint or two). Povey professes to be not quite committed; he gives some present advantage to the royalist position, while saying that at first that was the worse side. His argument is for an accommodation, not for Charles; the propagandist value of his pamphlet lies in the fact that a peace at this time would have been tantamount to a Parliamentary surrender. It is worth taking space to quote the climax of his argument, a neglected but notable example of the polemical "character":

> *The true Character of a Moderate man, I conceive to be this: He is one that loves his Countrey so well, that he grieves to see it destroyed out of a saving policy, one that is not a friend to this War, not because he is afraid to dy, but because he would hereafter live in an even and well poyzed Temper. One, that could never be so well satisfied of the necessity why this War began, as he is now, why it should see an end; which though he longs for, yet knowes not how to pray for a Victory. One that in earnest loves the King, and thinks him Essentiall to the Being of a Parliament, and the life of this, to the well-being of all hereafter. One that honours, not adores the Parliament because he sees they also are but men: & rather wishes them safe, and what they should be, then Omnipotent. One that would have his Religion nor gawdy nor stripped stark-naked. One that loves both Law and Gospell, and would gladly have those that meddle with either, to hold themselves closer to their Text. One that is equally as much afraid of the medling severe Clergy of New-England, as of the Ambitious pragmatick Clergy of old England. One that is sorry to see it more seasonable then safe, to speake truth. One that would have Peace, not as an effect of War, but of an Accommodation. To conclude he is one that is yet an admirer of Peace, and is earnest to see a farther Tryall who avoids it most, & so hinders him of it: you shall then perhaps have him leave his Center, and betake himselfe to one side, as if by that he had found out his enemy.[58]*

[57] E108(28), pp. 2–3.   [58] E89(21), p. 19.

5. PARLIAMENTARY DEFENSES

The supporters of Parliament, of course, prepared answers against all these forms of attack [1] upon the new doctrine of Parliamentary supremacy, for, as Charles Herle was to say, "The cause would otherwise be sure to suffer as deserted; what in this kind men doe not, 'tis presently concluded they dare not, or they cannot doe." [2] Some of these diverse answers were consistent with and supported each other, but we must not be surprised if, on so broad a front, this is not always so.

To the continuation of the argument from positive laws two kinds of answer were given. By far the most frequent and important was that originally worked out by Parker for just this purpose. His *Animadversions Animadverted, or The Observator Defended* (August 26, 1642) put the position succinctly: "No knowne act of particular Justice or right . . . can clash" with the fundamental law of nature, "but must in equitie vail to it, as to its superintendent." [3] Parker's use of the term "equity" may serve to remind us of the role played by *A Question Answered*,[4] and the argument of that broadside reappeared in more elaborate form in John Marsh's *An Argument or, Debate in Law: Of the Great Question concerning the Militia* (September 30).[5] The Parliamentary supremacy over positive law which Parker's theory entailed could sometimes be expressed with startling candor. Jeremiah Burroughes, in *The Glorious Name of God . . . With a Post Script* (December 1642),[6] wrote: "That is to be accounted Law, which they interpret to be so. I do not say that we are bound to beleeve, that whatsoever interpretation they make was the scope and intention of that Law when it was first made: But this I say, that their interpretation must be accounted as much binding to us for obedience, as the scope and intention of that Parliament that first made that Law." [7] The author of *A New Plea for the Parliament: and the Reserved Man Resolved* (January 5, 1643) took a similar view, but the frankness of both was exceeded by Parker himself in *The Contra-Replicant, His Complaint To His Majestie* (January 31). He ruefully acknowledges that the royalist propaganda based on positive law has had some success.[8] But laws by themselves are not enough: they have not defended the rights of Englishmen "for these 17. yeares last past" (*i.e.*, since

[1] Except that the fourth was not answered until 1644; see below, pp. 132–33.
[2] *An Answer to Doctor Fernes Reply, Entituled Conscience Satisfied* (May 17, 1643), E102(3), p. 3.   [3] E114(19), p. 3.   [4] See above, pp. 18–19.

[5] This pamphlet was signed "J.M. C.L." and has been attributed to Milton (see French, II, 79), but Thomason wrote "J. Marsh Canc [Chancellor] Lincolns Inne" (E119[13]).

[6] See below, p. 46, n. 43.   [7] 693.f.5(4), p. 139.   [8] E87(5), pp. 1–3.

the accession of Charles), nor of the majority in Scotland, nor of the Protestants in Ireland; [9] "they may be imployed either to the benefit or prejudice of any Nation, and . . . they themselves do require to be regulated by further Lawes" [10] or they may be turned (like cannon) against the very objects they were designed to defend.[11] "Laws ayme at *Justice,* Reason of state aimes at *safety.* . . . Reason of State is something more sublime and imperiall then Law. . . . Nothing has done us more harme of late, then this opinion of adhering to Law only for our preservation." [12] With respect to Hull, which involved "both matter of Law and State": "Let our Adversaries . . . upbraid us for declining of Law: I shall like that best which they dislike most in us: I wish we had not observed Law too farre, for they would never so farre recommend it to us, did they not know it might be sometimes unseasonable." [13]

But if English positive laws do not direct the government of England, what is the difference between the English constitution and others? An anonymous black-letter pamphlet entitled *Touching the Fundamentall Lawes, Or Politique Constitution of this Kingdome* (February 24), having presented the natural-law retort to the royalist argument from law, anticipated the objection: "That common rule of *Salus populi* . . . is alike common to all Nations, as well as any; and so what difference?" [14] It replies: "The Fundamentall laws of England are nothing but the Common laws of Equity and Nature reduced into a particular way of policy," and the only difference between the English constitution and others is in the manner of this particularization.[15] Should English "written Laws" run counter to universal fundamentals, they cannot be valid, "for, for a particular branch to ruine the whole foundation by a seeming sense contrary to it, or differing from it, is very absurd." [16]

It may seem surprising that this form of the argument, in which English positive law is professedly stripped of all authority, should have been adopted by the historic champion of English positive law, the "High Court of Parliament"; but such is the case. On June 8 the House of Commons ordered to be printed *A Few Propositions Shewing The Lawfulnesse of Defence Against the Injurious Attempts of Outragious Violence,* which argues the issue of supremacy wholly apart from the particular constitution of England. Throughout the pamphlet runs the unquestioned assumption that positive human laws can have no power to contravene natural law. Indeed, the very form of the argument is based upon that assumption, for it consists of twenty "propositions" derived from the law of nature, each followed by the

[9] *Ibid.,* pp. 5–6.   [10] *Ibid.,* p. 6.   [11] *Ibid.,* pp. 8–9.   [12] *Ibid.,* pp. 18–19.
[13] *Ibid.,* pp. 19–20.   [14] E90(21), p. 5.   [15] *Ibid.*   [16] *Ibid.,* p. 6.

assertion that no human law can deny this right. The pamphlet ends: "Thus far to shew what the law of nature allows to all, and the law of Nations doth not deny to any, nor can be supposed rationally to forbid it. And this under what government soever." Those who want to know how all this "agrees with the particular constitution of Government in this Nation" are referred to "the *Politicall Catechisme* and the *Kingdomes Case.*" [17]

The Commons seemed unaware of the troubles they were preparing for themselves; yet they might have been warned. During the critical fortnight in which the *Doctrine and Discipline of Divorce* was published, the war party in the City thought fit to bring pressure upon a Parliament in which the peace party seemed to be gaining the ascendant; one instrument was *Remonstrans Redivivus* (July 25), which, in ten propositions, gave an extreme and lucid statement of the natural law theory. Parliament was unambiguously vested with supremacy on the basis of being the people's representatives; nothing was argued from "constituted" authority or precedent. Further, every statement was supported with a reference to Parliament's *Book of Declarations*. In short, this would be adaptable, with scarcely a word changed, to the needs of the Levellers and the New Model when they marched to teach the people's representatives the will of the people.

The other answer to the royalist argument from positive law was almost incredibly brazen: it consists of the assertion that the positive laws of England warranted all Parliament's actions. This is the doctrine set forth at numbing length by William Prynne in 1643. Prynne, who had already subscribed to Parliamentary sovereignty both on the basis of Parker's theory and of his own reading of Scripture,[18] published on March 16, 1643 (it had been ordered printed by the House of Commons two months earlier) *The Treachery and Disloyalty of Papists,* the first instalment of what was to become the quadripartite *Soveraigne Power of Parliaments and Kingdomes* (the remaining parts appeared April 15, June 23, and August 28). This, as the general title suggests, proclaimed absolute Parliamentary sovereignty; and while it made use of natural law and scriptural arguments as occasion served, its main effort was to derive the doctrine from common laws, statutes, and precedents.

Since common laws, statutes, and precedents had in fact vested the sovereignty of England in the crown, limited it by the law, and given to Parliament the functions of advice and consent, Prynne's argument was necessarily a feat of legerdemain (if so light a word may be ap-

[17] E106(7), sig. B2v; for a discussion of *A Political Catechism,* see below, pp. 50–51.   [18] *A Soveraign Antidote* (August 18, 1642).

plied to a performance of such wearying heaviness). It has been treated with too much respect by historians, who deprecate his manner but, impressed by his voluntary sufferings, concede his sincerity and occasionally even something of his claim. The sincerity of his religious beliefs is surely beyond question; we do not even question his faith in Parliaments; but his argument in *The Soveraigne Power* is palpably disingenuous and cannot be excused, as is usual, in terms of fanaticism. His method is to cite endless statutes and decisions for those portions of his contention which no one would deny (*e.g.*, that the king cannot lawfully empower his agents to seize the goods of his subjects without due process of law); then, without showing the relevance to the dispute of these abundantly proved propositions at law, to turn to reason and history (foreign, domestic, even natural) [19] for further proof; and then to repeat the whole procedure with another, and then another, such indubitable and uncontested proposition. After the mind has been so bludgeoned that it is reckoned incapable of realizing that neither separately nor together do these demonstrated propositions come near the matter at issue (or of distinguishing between King-in-Parliament and the Houses of Parliament without the King's assent, or between Parliament's function as a court and its function as a council, etc.), Prynne will emerge flaunting his triumphant non-sequitur: "From all which pregnant punctuall domesticke Authorities . . . I presume I may infallibly conclude; That the Parliaments present taking up necessary Defensive Armes, is . . . a just and lawfull Act." [20]

To the royalist debating point that by Parliament's own principles the sovereign people may withdraw the entrusted powers of Parliament as well as those of the king, the Parliamentary defense again returned two kinds of answer. Much the more frequent was the denial that the parallel held, but some Parliamentary supporters conceded the point.

The House of Commons itself seems to have maintained an intentional ambiguity in the matter. It did not take formal cognizance of the argument, but it nevertheless found an opportunity to discuss it. At the height of the peace agitation in December, 1642, the peace party in the City (apparently under crypto-royalist leadership) petitioned Parliament to procure a speedy peace by tendering Charles "such Propositions for Accommodation as he may, with Honour and

---

[19] "Not to trouble you with Histories of Stagges and other beasts which have killed men that chased them, . . . of which there are infinite examples . . . I shall onely recite some few examples even of Kings themselves, who have beene slaine and devoured by such beasts as they have chased." Part III, June 23, 1643, E248(3), p. 18.   [20] E248(3), p. 47.

Safety to the whole Kingdom, accept." [21] The House of Commons published its reply as *An Answer to the London Petition* (December 14).[22] This began by rebuking the petitioners for asking Parliament to offer terms which amounted to submission, not accommodation. It explained that if Charles were not engaged to a party Parliament might think of trusting the terms of a settlement to him, but in fact he was at the disposal of an evil faction of malignants whom it was the Parliament's duty to root out. "Wee are intrusted in this by the whole Kingdome, and that trust wee must not breake upon the solicitation of any part of the kingdome." [23] If any such part attempts to contravene the will of the whole, "wee are bound to withstand it, as much as wee can." [24] What if the will of the whole changes? On this central point, the House chooses not to answer; instead, it makes its displeasure felt, and perhaps hints something of menace:

> We will speak now to you, as we would to the whole bodie of England; if you prefer their cause and beeing before ours, speak it out more plainlie. . . . Yet to deale plainlie with you, and all other Petitioners: We love not to be sollicited at all by the People in any case whatsoever, except when wee doe manifestly faile of our dutie, either out of too much feare, or too much presumption. Howsoever for the present goe peaceablie home.[25]

But Charles Herle, in *A Fuller Answer to a Treatise Written by Doctor Ferne* (December 29),[26] showed how to deny that the people could withdraw their trust from Parliament. To do this meant in some measure repudiating Parker, which Herle does only indirectly. Ferne, he says, spent the fourth section of his book "upon a confutation of any power in the people to *reassume* the power they first betrusted to the *King*, the which no man (for ought I know) maintaines, what need the people *reassume* that which in the first *Coalition* of the Governement they reserved?" [27] Of course Herle knew that Parker had maintained the reassumption of power from the king,[28] but it suited him to substitute reservation, since this permitted a simple answer to Ferne's

---

[21] *Old Parliamentary History*, XII, 102; *Lords Journals*, V, 501.

[22] We may infer a general recognition of the propaganda nature of the petition from Thomason's MS note on the House of Commons *Answer*. Between the words "the" and "London" he inserted "frivolous petition of," and after "Petition" he wrote "presented the 13 Decemb: 1642." Below he wrote the date of the *Answer*, December 14. E130(18); the *Catalogue's* date (December 12) is too early. [23] E130(18), p. 2. [24] *Ibid.*, p. 4. [25] *Ibid.*, pp. 5–6.

[26] This is the date Thomason wrote on the first edition, E244(27).

[27] Quoted from the second edition, January 10, 1643; E245(3), p. 19.

[28] He defended him on positions which were part of this argument; see, *e.g.*, pp. 3 and 9.

great poser: "A second question begg'd is, that *in case the King* and *Parliaments should neither discharge their trust, the people might rise and make resistance against both,* a position which no man (I know) maintaines, the Parliaments is the peoples *owne consent,* which once passed they cannot revoke; hee still pursues his owne dreame of the peoples *reassuming* power, whereas wee acknowledge no power can be imployed but what is *reserved,* and the people have reserved no power in themselves from themselves in Parliament." [29]

This "reservation" of regal power is in England's original "frame" or constitution of government:

> *Englands* is not a simply *subordinative,* and *absolute,* but a *Coordinative,* and *mixt Monarchy;* This *mixture,* or *Coordination* is in the very *Supremacy* of power it selfe, otherwise the *Monarchy* were not *mixt:* all *Monarchies* have a *mixture,* or composition of *subordinate,* and under-officers in them, but here the *Monarchy,* or *highest* power is it selfe *compounded* of 3 *Coordinate* Estates, a *King,* and two *Houses* of Parliament; unto this *mixt* power no *subordinate* authority may in any case make *resistance.* The rule holds still, *Subordinata non pugnant, subordinates* may not strive; but in this our *mixt* highest power, there is no *subordination,* but a *Coordination:* and here the other rule holds as true, *Coordinata invicem supplent, Coordinates* supply each other.[30]

But the difficulty rises that this "constitution" of England can be found nowhere in the historical record. This is where Herle has need of Parker, and he uses him to solve his problem. Of course the fundamental law is not written; "if it be *written* it is *superstructive* and not *fundamentall*"; the fundamental law "is that originall *frame . . . consented* to, and *contrived* by the people in its first *constitution.*" [31]

Thus supplied with an *a priori* constitution which cancels the historical one, Herle's argument becomes wholly "constitutional"; and he states a doctrine of obedience fully as absolute as Ferne's, only to a different "constituted" authority:

> We hold not what ever *cruelty* can be suffered *cause* enough to make *resistance,* 'tis not the *cause,* 'tis the *constitution* of the governement, *reserving* in its *coordination* a power of *resistance,* in order to its *preservation:* otherwise were this an *absolute Monarchy,* should the King alone, or (as it is) should King and Parliament enjoyn us all to deny Christ and worship the *Sun,* we were (though never so able) not to make any *resistance* but by suffering; the *cause* cannot alter the case here, 'tis the *constitution* must doe it.[32]

With all its difficulties, this theory was for almost half a year the best available to those who used the social contract against Charles but would deny that it could be used against Parliament too. Their em-

[29] E245(3), p. 20.   [30] *Ibid.,* p. 2.   [31] *Ibid.,* p. 6.   [32] *Ibid.,* p. 21.

barrassment as they used it to confront the multiplying royalist thrusts is very instructive. "Did ever the Parliament maintain the re-assumption of power more than the knowne Lawes of the Land doe justifie?" asked *A Just Complaint, or Loud Crie, of All the Well-Affected Subjects in England Against that False and Scandalous Pamphlet, Intituled, A Complaint* (January 31, 1643); but it took care not to stay for an answer, having come to this main point only on the last page of a 31-page pamphlet.[33] J. M., in that *Reply to the Answer* (February 3) which has sometimes been attributed to Milton,[34] falls back on phrases: "When hee can make the people to represent the House of Commons, not the House of Commons the people, then shall the peoples judgement for majority carry it."[35] William Bridge, in *The Wounded Conscience Cured* (February 11), which was printed by order of the Commons, vaguely invoked "the authority that they are clothed with" to distinguish Parliament's resistance to Charles from any resistance by the people to Parliament.[36] One pamphlet, *A Disclaimer and Answer of the Commons of* England, *of and unto a Scandalous Libell . . . Intituled* The Remonstrance of the Commons of *England* to the House of Commons (May 4), was driven to something like an echo of the old theory of "interests": "The House of Commons is a part of us, and the choice most excellent and principall part too, and not only our Representative, and are interested and sharing in the publike good and evill as much as any, and more then most of us . . . and to be limitted to be only Proctors to speak for us is senselesse and ridiculous."[37]

The first real improvement on Herle was made by Philip Hunton in *A Treatise of Monarchie* (May 24). By a greatly refined procedure, he reaches exactly Herle's position: that the fundamental English constitution is a limited, mixed monarchy, with the sovereign power in all three co-ordinate estates; unlike Herle, however, who then inconsistently made Parliament supreme, Hunton adheres to this.[38] Now when the sovereign power, or, within its area, the executive branch, commands anything according to the constitution, the subject must obey. But should one of the estates invade the powers of the other two, it tends to "the dissolving of the constituted frame," and private subjects ought "to deny obedience and submission" to these "illegall proceedings." But the co-ordinate estates must do more. It is "the very end and fundamentall aime in constituting all mixed Policies . . . that, if one exorbitate, the power of restraint and providing for the publike safety should be in the rest." Hence "it is their duty, and by the

[33] E245(27).   [34] See above, p. 34.   [35] E245(35), p. 25.
[36] E89(8), p. 37.   [37] E100(23), p. 2.   [38] UCL JC153H9, pp. 40–41.

foundations of the Government they are bound to prevent the dissolution of the established Frame." [39] This does not mean that they possess a sovereign power to command the people to resist the invading estate, but that they must set before the people the threat to the constitution, which the people are obliged to defend. "The Accusing side must make it evident to every mans Conscience. In this case which is beyond the Government, the Appeale must be to the Community, as if there were no Government; and as by Evidence mens Consciences are convinced, they are bound to give their utmost assistance." [40] In the present crisis, therefore, the problem for each man's individual conscience must be one of fact, not of preference: "The resolving enquiry (I thinke) must be, *Whether at the Parliaments taking up of Armes, the Common-wealth, Frame of established Government, or* (which is all one) *the Being and radicall Powers of Parliament were in apparent danger of subversion?* For if so, then the Armes and Force used against the Counsellours or Agents thereof is proved lawfull." [41]

Considered as political theory, the superiority of Hunton's position is that it recognized that the ultimate appeal must be to the community. Considered merely as a defense against the royalist debating point that the people may resist Parliament on the same ground that it resists the king, its superiority lies in his foregoing the temptation, to which his predecessors succumbed, of raising Parliament to supremacy. Consequently, he was able to place the maximum emphasis consistent with Parliament's predicament upon its "constituted," rather than its representative, nature. He was therefore in a better position to say, "I deny the parity of reason: for the two Houses are bodies constituted and endowed with legislative authority, and trust of preservation of the frame, by the Fundamentalls of the Kingdome: which the people out of those Houses are not." [42]

But this rhetorical superiority was not, after all, very great. Hunton was more cautious than Herle: having followed him in attempting to escape the dilemma by retreating from natural law to "constitution," he did not return again unnecessarily to natural law. But he had not been able to escape it, for it was the only possible provenience for his unhistorical "constitution." Some Parliamentary champions thought it better to accept the consequences of the revocable-trust theory. It is very instructive to note that at this time they seem all to be clergymen, although the time would soon come when lawyers, soldiers, professional politicians, and those newly admitted to the "political nation" would join them.

Apparently the first to concede the royalist point was Jeremiah

[39] *Ibid.,* p. 28.   [40] *Ibid.,* p. 29.   [41] *Ibid.,* p. 75.   [42] *Ibid.,* p. 61.

Burroughes, in what appears to have been the first of all the replies to Ferne, *The Glorious Name of God . . . With a Post-Script, Briefly Answering a Late Treatise by Henry Ferne, D.D.* (December, 1642).[43] It is a very hard case that is posed, "but if you can suppose a Parliament so far to degenerate . . . whether a Law of Nature would not allow of standing up to defend our selves, yea to re-assume the power given to them, to discharge them of that power they had, and set up some other, I leave to the light of nature to judge. . . . I know this will be cryed out of as of dangerous consequence, wherefore God deliver us (as I hope he will) for ever making use of such a principle." [44]

Edward Bowles, however, was ready to use it, at least as a threat. In *Plaine English: or, A Discourse Concerning the Accommodation, the Armie, the Association* (January 12, 1643), he said that the issue was between liberty and tyranny, true religion and popery, and such matters could be settled only by conquest, not by negotiation; if Charles entered into an accommodation with the Parliament, it would be with the intention of betraying it. Hitherto, Parliament has on the whole behaved as if it understood this.

> But suppose (if it be lawfull to be supposed) that the Parliament, through the absence of many resolved men, now imployed in particular services for their owne Countries, out of an intolerable wearinesse of this present condition, and feare of the event, agree to the making up of an unsafe unsatisfying Accommodation. This would beget a question, which I hope I shall never have occasion to dispute, whether in case the representative body cannot, or will not, discharge their trust to the satisfaction, not of fancy, but of reason in the people; they may resume (if ever yet they parted with a power to their manifest undoing) and use their power so farre as conduces to their safety; And if this doubt

[43] 693.f.5(4). Since this is not in the Thomason collection, we must recover the date otherwise. The main body of the book, originally two sermons, was ordered printed by the House of Commons December 1, some two weeks before the publication of Ferne's book. Burroughes' volume appeared some time before January 5, 1643, since the *Post-Script* is mentioned by a pamphlet of that date (*A New Plea for the Parliament*, E244[38], pp. 10–11). The outside limits are therefore mid-December to very early January. The *Post-Script* was separately reissued as *A Briefe Answer to Doctor Fernes Booke, Tending to Resolve Conscience* (4175.b.103[21], undated); in this or the original form, Burroughes' is almost certainly the prior answer taken cognizance of by the title of Herle's *A Fuller Answer* (see above, p. 42), since there seems no other candidate (the usual assumption that the reference is to *An Answer to Mis-led Doctor Fearne* of January 10, 1643, must be surrendered, since the first edition of Herle's pamphlet preceded it by almost two weeks; see above, p. 42, nn. 26–27). Hence 693.f.5(4) probably appeared about December 26 or 27, in time for Herle to take cognizance of it in his title but too late to allow him to refer to it in his text. [44] 693.f.5(4), p. 134.

cannot be resolved to the advantage of the people but be found either unlawfull or otherwise impossible, I know but two waies more betwixt which the choise is very hard, hang or flye. As for hanging I should not much like it, though it were in a blue ribband, but for flying . . . it will be full of dishonour and danger.[45]

He therefore proposes an "Association" sworn to the purposes of a true reformation and settlement. This will not only be a good way to support a Parliament true to its trust, but also "It would be a good second string in case the Parliament should unhappily miscarry, whereas otherwise we should be found as sheepe scattered, a fit pray for the *Wolves* of these times." [46] It is little wonder that the peace party in Parliament had to hear that they were being whipped with a rod of their own making.[47]

It is of special interest to students of Milton, and indirectly drawn to their attention by Milton himself,[48] that Herbert Palmer and the other authors of *Scripture and Reason Pleaded for Defensive Armes,* which was printed by order of the House of Commons (April 14), conceded the natural-law principle of revoking a trust with respect to Parliament as well as with respect to the king: "It is lawfull for the people to resist even the Tyranny of a *Parliament,* when altogether outrageous, (as in our Question) not else." [49] Again, if Parliament fails to resist a tyrant, or acquiesces in tyranny, "yet might any one Shire, or part of a Shire, begin to take up Armes to defend themselves by resisting Outragious Attempts of Tyranny against their Religion, Laws, and Liberties, and that from the Naturall Liberty, that all have to be no further Subject then God hath commanded, or themselves consented with Gods consent. . . . Without I say, and even against any Votes or Commands (if any should be) to the contrary." [50]

The royalist argument for immediate divine right and passive obedience caused, as we may well suppose, some particularly active brandishings of chapter and verse by Puritan divines; but before we take our brief notice of these we might observe an epitome of them, by a secular hand, which brings us into the heart of Milton's divorce argument. In *Animadversions Animadverted,* mentioned above,[51] Parker briefly discusses the main divine-right text, Romans 13, to the effect that when its true meaning is recovered it is seen not to aid Charles' cause. The particulars of what he says here are less interesting than his criterion for testing whether a given interpretation can be correct: "S. *Paul* hath not, nor could any where repeale the lawes of nature." [52] That, by and

---

[45] E84(42), p. 20.   [46] *Ibid.,* p. 28.   [47] See above, p. 29.
[48] See below, p. 145.   [49] E247(22), sig. I1v (misnumbered p. 50).
[50] *Ibid.,* pp. 60–61.   [51] See p. 38.   [52] E114(19), p. 8.

large, is how the Puritan divines, at greater length, meet the challenge: they interpret the scriptural texts to show that they do not contain the injunctions the royalists say they do, and then find the positive guidance for political affairs in the natural-law social-contract theory.

John Goodwin, in *Anti-Cavalierisme, or, Truth Pleading as Well the Necessity, as the Lawfulness of this Present War* (October 21, 1642), argued that monarchy is indeed God's ordinance, but only in the sense that all valid forms of government are; that the supreme magistrate is to be obeyed, but so are the subordinate, Parliaments as well as kings; that all political obedience must be within the limits of obedience to God; and that when obedience to God requires disobedience to men, it may in some circumstances not be limitable to passive disobedience. "In such a case, disobedience to Kings by a strong hand, and with forcible resistance, is not only lawfull, but even matter of duty and obedience unto God." [53] As for the royalist inference from the primitive martyrs who, refusing to obey the idolatrous commands of heathen kings, submitted themselves unresistingly to punishment, the cases are simply not parallel. The primitive Christians did not have the strength to resist, did not understand their rights, were mystically inspired to fulfill a special historical role of which they were unaware (the necessary ascension of Anti-christ), and anyway were not, as we are, "invited, countenanced, encouraged, and some waies commanded by as great and as lawfull an Authority as this state hath any" [54] to defend our religion and our civil rights.

Burroughes, in his *Post-Script* answering Ferne, concentrates upon a distinction between the power of government and the governor. Ferne's main reliance had been upon Romans 13, but he had misunderstood it. St. Paul

> doth not say expresly, Whosoever resists the highest men shall receive damnation, but whosoever shall resist the power: *Let every one be subject,* not to the wils of the highest men, but *to the higher power*: there is a great deale of difference betweene these two: . . . We professe against resisting power, authority, though abused: If those who have power to make Laws, shall make sinfull Laws, and so give authority to any to force obedience; we say here there must be either flying or passive obedience; but if one that is in authority command out of his own will, and not by Law, I resist no power, no authority at all, if I neither actively nor passively obey, no I do not so much as resist abused authority.[55]

Agreeing that God is the source of power, Burroughes seizes upon, and exaggerates, Ferne's admission that the designation of the person who

[53] P. 10; in Haller, *Tracts,* II, 228.   [54] *Ibid.,* p. 26.   [55] 693.f.5(4), p. 113.

holds power, and the qualification of its exercise, may involve the people. "If so, mark what follows, then no man can have any of this ruling power, but according as he is designed to it, qualified for it, limited in it by men." [56] Hereafter, all is easy; Burroughes has arrived at the safe haven of "the originall agreement between people and King," [57] where the law of nature rules.

We must not pursue this debate too far, but before leaving it we may notice, because of the pamphlet's special importance for Milton, that *Scripture and Reason Pleaded* belongs to this line. Government is an ordinance of God only in the sense that God requires some institution to effect the laws of nature. The power of government *qua* divine ordinance does not "extend, to the making of any Humane Lawes, but onely to see to the Observation of the Lawes of Nature, and of God by His . . . first, and second Table; and to no other power of coercion, then what the Light of Nature will Argue Necessarie, for the Observation of those Lawes of Nature. And . . . all further power . . . depends upon mans Consent." [58] What is particularly interesting is that the pamphlet Palmer wrote speaks of the relation between Christian, Jew, and natural man in exactly the way the divorce pamphlet he attacked would. Ferne had taunted the Puritan divines with having drawn all their examples of divinely approved resistance to kings from the Old Testament. "Why should he insinuate this to be insufficient? Is not the old Testament Gods word, and a direction for our lives, as well as the new? . . . And if it were lawfull . . . to resist then; how comes it to be unlawfull now? Did Christ come to make Tyrants secure from resistance, who were not before?" [59] Ferne has conceded that, by the law of nature, heathens might resist tyranny; to argue that the Gospel abrogates this natural right is to say that "the Apostles laid a yoake upon the necks of Christians, worse then all the *Jewish* ceremonies, which the Gentiles were ever freed from: For whereas before the *Romans* might resist their tyrannous Emperours, now by becoming Christians their hands must be tyed to have all their throats cut." [60] There is another even more immediate analogy with *The Doctrine and Discipline*, but we shall reserve it for later discussion.[61]

There remains the fourth, and rather special, royalist line, that the law of nature is a law of evil nature and no fit guide for Christians, or indeed for rational men. In time, the parliamentarians presented an answer to this, but not until 1644 (it will help us to understand the

---

[56] *Ibid.*, p. 127.   [57] *Ibid.*, p. 130.   [58] E247(22), p. 31.
[59] *Ibid.*, p. 20.   [60] *Ibid.*, p. 24.

[61] See below, pp. 152–53, for a discussion of the analogy drawn in this and other pamphlets between the institutions of government and marriage.

Tetrachordon, but comes too late for *The Doctrine and Discipline).* In 1642 and 1643 they let it go by default. Possibly they did not think it necessary to meet this argument; they may have felt that the authority of natural law was too great to be shaken, and all they need do was establish that political affairs fell within its jurisdiction. But such unconcern seems unlikely: we may recall what Herle said about the public assuming that what was not answered was unanswerable. Besides, we may infer from a rather panicky anonymous pamphlet entitled *An Answer to Mis-led Doctor Fearne* (January 10, 1643) that some, at least, of the Parliamentary apologists were made uneasy by this attack. The author uses Parker's natural-law social-contract theory as his occasions require, but when Ferne confronts him with its essential postulate he hurriedly repudiates it: "You will suppose that the Parliament holds the power to be in the people, and for this you quote ὁδεῖνα, one mans opinion, the *Observator,* whether he holds so or no I know not, but the Parliament holds the power from God onely." [62] Of course, this inconsistency may have been due to other causes; in any case, whether from inability or negligence, the Parliamentary propaganda did not reply to this fourth royalist line until 1644.

We ought not to end this account of how Parliament defended its natural-law initiative without giving at least one example of its diversionary tactics. We have seen how the royalists embarrassed Parliament by pushing its principles farther than Parliament wished to carry them. But the royalist propaganda was vulnerable to the same maneuver. About March, 1643,[63] the royalists thought it a good time to publish a second, abbreviated version of the answer Charles had made to Parliament's Nineteen Propositions almost a year earlier. Perhaps it would have been as well not to bring it back to attention: it stimulated Henry Parker to write one of his most successful pamphlets, *A Political Catechism, or, Certain Questions Concerning the Government of this Land, Answered in His Majesties Own Words, Taken Out of His Answer to the 19 Propositions* (May 20).[64] Charles' *Answer* had, among other things, argued that Parliament already possessed all the powers

[62] E245(1), p. 7; *cf.* also pp. 8–9. The pamphlet is generally attributed to Herle, but that cannot be correct; see my "Shakespeare and Jonson among the Pamphleteers of the First Civil War," *MP,* LIII (1955), p. 90. What gives this pamphlet a special importance is that it seems to have been the first to hint at regicide (p. 11): "the person of a Tyrant ought to bee inferiour to the Law."

[63] See Madan, *Oxford Books,* II, 246, No. 1299, and Donald Wing, *Short Title Catalogue,* I, 280, No. 2142.

[64] Three days earlier Charles Herle had, in a limited way, included a similar use of Charles' *Answer* in his *An Answer to Doctor Fernes Reply, Entituled Conscience Satisified* (May 17).

it could justly wish, so that its demand for new powers was the preparation for tyranny.[65] Parker's method is to frame questions which are answered by excerpting passages from Charles' argument, and then making "observations" upon these. Here is an example:

> Qu. 22. *But if there be an Attempt or Danger, that the Kings Favorites and Followers go about to change this Regulated Monarchy into an Arbitrary Government, and so into a Tyranny; is there Authority in the Houses sufficient, according to what was fore-mentioned to remedy this?*
> A. Power Legally Placed in both Houses is more then sufficient to prevent and restrain the power of Tyranny. *page 20.*
> *Observ.* 1. Then at least what ever Power is necessary to prevent or restrain the Power of Tyranny is confessed to be Legally placed in both Houses; for else there is not Power sufficient, much less, more then sufficient.
> 2. Then it is Lawful for the two Houses to Raise Arms to defend themselves in case an Army be raised against them, for else they have not power sufficient to restrain the power of Tyranny.[66]

And so on for another half-dozen observations, each of which justifies another of Parliament's contested actions.

It is the same tactic as the royalists used with the doctrine of withdrawing entrusted powers. Charles quite clearly did not wish Parliament to possess adequate powers to restrain arbitrary government; on the contrary, he had always governed arbitrarily. His assertions that England was a mixed monarchy, limited by law, etc., were part of the propaganda battle to win the support of those Englishmen who were not yet committed in the struggle for supremacy, just as was Parliament's social contract theory. What limited the effectiveness of the brilliant court propaganda was the distance between Charles' professions and the record of his government.

6. SIGNIFICANCE FOR MILTON

It would be easy enough to represent the whole complex debate-at-law which we have been examining as a kind of comic ballet, a series of formalized movements, each purporting to be full of meaning, but when the sequence is completed seen to be only a dance. Thus, before the Militia Ordinance, the posture of Parliament is that of the great champion of English common and statute law against invasion by royal prerogative, while the court's position is that where the safety of the realm is involved a higher and more fundamental law warrants the setting aside of positive human laws. After the Militia Ordinance it is Charles' turn to assume the posture of champion of English com-

[65] See Rushworth, *Collections,* IV, 725–35.   [66] E104(7*), p. 11.

mon and statute law, while Parliament's position is that where the safety of the realm is involved a higher and more fundamental law warrants the setting aside of positive human laws. Can this be anything but camouflage for a mere struggle for power?

The answer to the sardonic question is that while it is true that the debate is partially camouflage, it is much more than that. A genuine revolution in political theory was taking place, which the intellectual habits of the time demanded be expressed in terms of law. The positions of the antagonists are not really interchangeable; the terms remain constant, but the connotations change—and so do the relations between the terms. Especially changed are the connotations of the venerable term "law of nature," and its relation to human laws, on the one hand, and divine laws, on the other.

What matters in all this to the student of Milton is that a revolution was also taking place in his thinking, that it too involved obligations and rights and had to be expressed in terms of law, and that in fact it was worked out largely on the basis of Parliament's interpretation of the law of nature and its relation to divine and human laws. So much is this the case that when we come to examine his divorce tracts we will find, not only that he uses the concept in the same way and repeatedly draws attention to the analogy, but also that he struggles unavailingly with a difficulty in his argument until the Parliamentary apologists develop a new refinement to meet an analogous difficulty in their theory, whereupon Milton triumphantly solves his problem with the same refinement.

CHAPTER II

1643–1645: REFORMATION OF THE CHURCH AND RELIGIOUS TOLERATION

1. HISTORICAL SUMMARY

W^E SAW above (p. 7) that, on August 7, 1643, the House of Commons, despite the precarious situation of the Parliamentary forces, rejected, by the barest of majorities, propositions for a peace which would not have been very different from a capitulation. It followed this vote by commissioning Waller to command the western army and Manchester the northeastern, while Essex, as commander-in-chief, kept the main army in the centre.[1] It was this army of the centre which, on September 20, fought the first battle of Newbury against Charles' main army. Although neither side really won this battle, circumstances gave the Parliamentary side most of the advantage; the sharp decline of its fortunes was arrested, and the panic atmosphere of August was relieved.[2] A series of successes in the north (under the Fairfaxes) and east (under Manchester and Cromwell) during September and October contributed to the recovery of morale on the Parliamentary side.[3]

So did an injection of hope from across the Tweed, and of indignation from across the Irish Sea. Parliamentary commissioners had reached Edinburgh on August 7, and on the 17th the Scottish Estates adopted the Solemn League and Covenant, that alliance under which Charles' Scottish Parliament sent an army to assist his English Parliament in making war against him. On September 25 both houses at Westminster, after some amendment, adopted the Solemn League and Covenant.[4] Meanwhile, on September 15, Ormond had, on Charles' behalf, signed the Articles of Cessation with the Catholic Confederation,[5] and late in October the first royalist regiments thus released from Ireland landed at English ports to reinforce Charles' army.[6] It is hard to exaggerate the violence with which Protestant opinion, both in England and Scotland, reacted; one symptom was the revival of the proceedings against Laud, which had been dormant for two years.

During the winter of 1643–1644 the inherent disunity within each

[1] Gardiner, *Civil War*, I, 225–27. [2] *Ibid.*, pp. 244–57.
[3] *Ibid.*, pp. 278–84. [4] *Ibid.*, pp. 268–76. [5] *Ibid.*, pp. 258–64.
[6] *Ibid.*, pp. 287–92.

camp became increasingly apparent. On the Parliamentary side there were many whom the prospect of a Scottish army in England filled with mixed emotions, and Charles attempted a secret negotiation with some of the Independents who feared a church settlement made under such an influence. The Independents proved wary of these advances, and, having received some encouragement from the Presbyterians, continued to rest their hopes for an accommodation—very gingerly, we must suppose—upon the Westminster Assembly of Divines, and, somewhat more confidently, upon Parliament and the army.[7] On the royalist side differences were necessarily less open, but they existed. The true court party encouraged the multifarious intrigues of Charles and Henrietta Maria, while those who had joined Charles only after Parliament's violation of precedent were increasingly anxious about his involvement with Roman Catholics, openly with the English, secretly with the Irish and Continental. Charles' alternate "Parliament," which met at Oxford on January 22, 1644—eleven days before Milton published the revised version of *The Doctrine and Discipline*—soon began to melt away, some members returning to Westminster, others attempting to slip out of all commitment by going quietly home.[8]

In March and April the Parliamentary forces achieved important victories in the west and north (including a juncture with the Scottish army near York), and Charles' centre army seemed entrapped; but partly because of the growing estrangement between Essex and Waller, and partly because of inertia in the peace party and disorganization of the war party (Pym had died on December 8, 1643), the chance to win the war quickly was allowed to slip by.[9] In May and June Rupert moved north, relieving several important royalist strongholds; and at the end of June his forces, having joined those of Newcastle, confronted three Parliamentary armies near York—those of Manchester and Fairfax, and the Scots under Leven. On July 2 they fought the battle of Marston Moor, in which Newcastle's army was destroyed, Rupert's horse broken, the whole north laid open to the Parliamentary forces, and Cromwell's cavalry (he had been promoted to Lieutenant-General of Manchester's army at the beginning of February) replaced Rupert's as the supreme mobile striking force in England.[10] Thereupon the three victorious generals wrote to the Committee of Both Kingdoms (the executive arm of the Solemn League and Covenant) urging it to speed the Presbyterian settlement of the Church, and then separated to pursue various tasks, letting Cromwell's predominantly Independent and sec-

[7] *Ibid.*, pp. 309–15.   [8] *Ibid.*, pp. 347–54.   [9] *Ibid.*, pp. 371–426.
[10] *Ibid.*, pp. 427–48.

tarian sub-command make what it would of the implicit threat.[11] It was about two weeks after this letter that Milton published *Bucer* (he had published *Of Education* early in June).

In August and September Parliament suffered a loss in the west comparable to Charles' at Marston Moor. Essex, notwithstanding the exposure of his rear, attempted to move into Cornwall and was maneuvered into a corner and cut off by Charles. On September 1, having sent his cavalry to safety, Essex slipped away by sea, leaving his second-in-command to surrender the infantry, without fighting, at Lostwithiel.[12] The Presbyterians were made momentarily conciliatory by this humiliation, and Cromwell, temporarily in the Commons because of the inactivity of Manchester's army, exploited the opportunity to get the Accommodation Order of September 13, which was to determine "how far tender Consciences, who cannot in all Things submit to the common Rule which shall be established, may be borne with according to the Word." [13]

In October Parliament gathered all its main forces other than those in the north for an attempt against Charles' army of the centre, but disunity among the Parliamentary generals was so great that the command of the joint armies was vested in a commission. The second battle of Newbury was fought under this arrangement on October 27, and the handicap proved too great: Manchester's refusal to carry out his part in the agreed plan of action allowed Charles to withdraw in good order, and the subsequent inability of the Parliament's command council to adopt any clear course of action exposed their great army, virtually unsupplied, to such rigors of winter that much of it was frittered away or rendered inoperative.[14]

Two separate maneuvers now began at Westminster. The peace party, still hoping for a negotiated settlement, took up an initiative of the Scots, and got Parliament, on November 20, to send peace propositions to Charles. The war party, convinced of the impossibility of a settlement except through a military decision, and of the impossibility of achieving such a decision with forces responsible to local associations and commanded by virtually independent rivals, aimed at a reorganization of the army; their opening move was Cromwell's attack on Manchester in his report to the Commons, November 25, on the failure at Newbury. The first of the rival maneuvers led to the abortive "Treaty" of Uxbridge in January and February; when this negotiation collapsed the success of the second maneuver was assured; even the peace party

[11] *Ibid.*, pp. 450–52.   [12] *Ibid.*, pp. 456–70.
[13] *Commons Journals*, III, 626; Gardiner, *Civil War*, I, 482–83.
[14] Gardiner, *Civil War*, I, 496–518.

supported the creation of a New Model—a standing army, centrally raised and paid, with a unified command.[15] Milton's *Areopagitica* was published during the few days which elapsed between the initial moves of the two sets of maneuvers.

Ever since it had met on July 1, 1643, the Westminster Assembly of Divines, which was overwhelmingly Presbyterian in constitution, had been working to formulate the basis for settling the church, from time to time reporting its progress to Parliament. The first legislation to be completed was the ordinance of January 4, 1645, abolishing the Book of Common Prayer and establishing the new Directory of Worship. (Laud must have felt that there was a macabre propriety in the timing of his execution for six days thereafter.) Having struck this blow at the right, the House of Commons then hit at the left; in a preliminary resolution, passed on January 13, it declared that the Presbyterianism to be established in England would be parochial, without provision for "gathered churches." [16]

But even as Parliament struck at the Independents and the sects beyond them, it was acknowledging its continued and increasing dependence upon them. The wastage and disorganization of its forces, together with arrears of pay, were ruining morale, and overt mutiny broke out in several places. Thus goaded, it pushed the organization of the New Model. Under the terms of the second Self-Denying Ordinance (the Lords had never accepted the more sweeping first), all officers who were members of either House resigned their commissions; there was now nothing to prevent any of them from receiving new appointments, but in fact Essex, Manchester, and Waller were retired, whereas Cromwell was made Lieutenant-General under the younger Fairfax. In these circumstances it is not surprising that the names presented by the general officers to Parliament for commissioning should have included many who, both in religion and in social position, were distasteful to the majority. But the Commons, impressed by the military exigencies, approved the list and sent it up to the Lords on March 3, the day before Milton published *Colasterion* and *Tetrachordon*. The Lords attempted to strike out some of the more notorious Independents, but they had in the end to bow to the Commons.[17] The instrument which, in June, would shatter Charles' power at Naseby, was therefore of such a composition that when the Presbyterian majority in the victorious Parliament attempted to impose a compulsory church unity on the country they would find themselves unable to enforce it. But that story lies beyond the limits of this volume.

[15] *Ibid.*, II, 13–31 and 60–77.   [16] *Ibid.*, pp. 51–52.   [17] *Ibid.*, pp. 141–52.

2. THE SCOTTISH ALLIANCE AND RENEWED PRESSURE FOR REFORMATION

During this period a marked change took place in public controversy. From being a debate between Court and Parliament, it became largely a debate between the various elements within the Parliamentary coalition, with the Oxford press reduced for the most part to the role of the hostile outside observer.[1] Of course the argument over supremacy in the state continued, but it receded from the forefront of controversy until early 1645, when the Levellers brought it back in a greatly altered form. In the latter part of 1643 and throughout 1644 it was supplanted by two other issues: first the issue of reformation of the church, to which, a little later, was added the issue of religious toleration.

Not that the Puritan demand for reformation of the church, which had dominated the Parliamentary scene in the second half of 1641, had lapsed after war broke out. Particularly at moments when the peace party on the Parliamentary side gained influence, true Puritans denounced "Peace without Truth" (*i.e.*, a settlement not including a Puritan church reformation) strenuously enough to incur from many royalists the charge of un-Christian bloodthirstiness. Lionel Gatford, for example, later Hyde's chaplain, thus characterized a number of Puritan sermons in *An Exhortation to Peace: With an Intimation of the Prime Enemies thereof;*[2] more entertaining is Hyde's own similar portrayal of the secular leaders of the war party in his brilliant forgery, *Two Speeches Made in the House of Peers* (January 10, 1643; E84[35]):

> They who think that humane Laws can binde the conscience, and will examine the Oathes they have taken, according to the interpretations of men, will in time fall from us: But such who religiouslie consider that such morall Precepts are fitter for Heathens then for Christians, and

[1] A trickle of something resembling true debate between individual supporters of Court and Parliament continued, some of it on the subject which dominated the debate between the component parts of the parliamentary coalition. One example may be cited. On the fast day, July 27, 1643, Thomas Fuller preached at the Savoy, and published, with John Downam's imprimatur, *A Sermon of Reformation* (August 2; E63[3]). Instantly John Saltmarsh attacked Fuller in *Examinations, Or, A Discovery of some Dangerous Positions* (August 12; E65[5]). Into the imprimatur page (licensed by Herle), Downam inserted a note saying he had been "wronged" by Fuller, who had promised to "amend" certain passages before printing but "did not performe." The following winter Fuller, now in Oxford, continued the controversy with *Truth Maintained* (Oxford; received by Thomason March 8, 1644; E36[9]), to which Saltmarsh replied in *Dawnings of Light* (January 4, 1645; E1168[3]).

[2] 1643; received by Thomason March 24. Gatford's list of such sermons reappears in Clarendon, VI, 40–41 (Macray, II, 320–21).

that we ought to lead our lives according to the Rule of Gods Word; and that the Laws of the Land (being but mans invention) must not check Gods children in doing the work of their heavenlie Father, will not faint in their dutie . . . let us proceed to shed the blood of the ungodlie.[3]

But despite a continuing concern with the needs of reformation, until the summer of 1643 the main emphasis in Parliamentary polemic was, as has been shown, on the issue of supremacy in the state.

It was Parliament's dangerous military situation that returned its major emphasis to reformation of the church. The one promising source for the help Parliament desperately needed was Scotland, and the Scots were not fundamentally interested in the English constitutional issue. To them the great end was a Presbyterian settlement of the Church of England, without which they felt their own Presbyterianism to be in constant danger. In March, 1643, an anonymous pamphlet called *Plaine Scottish, or, Newes from Scotland* had argued that Parliament's wavering position in the Treaty of Oxford showed how right the Scots were not to send an army until Parliament clearly committed itself on the religious issue. "But judge with your selves if this had beene reasonable . . . that an Armie should have been raised by us, to be so suddenly disbanded ere the end pretended had beene effected; your inconstancie and uncertaintie amazeth us, but let your premisses, and principles onely be established, & thence you shal see answerable conclusions . . . according . . . to your desires. . . . For the *quarrel* is whether Jesus shal be *King* or no." [4] In May an even more downright message arrived from the General Assembly of the Kirk of Scotland itself. *The Scots Declaration to the Lords and Commons in Parliament* suggested that Parliament's lowering fortunes were a divine chastisement: "The Lord hath now some Controversie with *England,* which will not bee removed, till first, and before all, the Worship of his Name,

---

[3] Pp. 6–7. The purported speaker was Lord Brooke. The Thomason *Catalogue* calls the pamphlet a satire, but it is in fact a forgery: it was intended to deceive readers into thinking the "speeches" were actually delivered. Brooke was annoyed because it was widely thought to be genuine and he "heard that He was much reproached for so Unchristian a Speech against Peace" (*The Life of Edward Earl of Clarendon,* Oxford, 1759, octavo ed., p. 137; in the folio ed. the reference is p. 161). The other speech, this one favoring accommodation, was attributed to Pembroke, who was pleased because he "heard He was very well spoken of, for having spoken so honestly for Peace" (*ibid.,* p. 138). Charles had often boasted that he could always detect Hyde's hand in anything he wrote, however carefully the latter disguised his manner, and had backed his claim by a wager with Falkland; unknown to Hyde, Falkland tested Charles' boast by placing this pamphlet before him. Charles was completely taken in (*ibid.,* p. 136).

[4] March 21; E247(5), sigs. A3v–A4.

and the Government of his House be setled according to his owne will." [5] Scotland's interest in such a settlement is as strong as England's own, for "what hope can the Kingdome and the Kirk of *Scotland* have of a firm and durable peace" unless "in all His Majesties Dominions there . . . be one Confession of Faith, one Directory of Worship, one publike Catechisme, and one Forme of Kirk-Government." [6] Practical experience indicates that the best place to begin the work of reformation is with church government; nor is there any question what this government must be: "the reformed Kirks do hold without doubting their Kirk Officers, and Kirk-Government by Assemblies higher and lower, in their strong and beautiful subordination to be *jure divino,* and perpetual." [7] To further such a reformation the Kirk is prepared to do "what may be required" of it; [8] and since the Kirk's declaration was approved by the "Lords of the Secret Council" of Scotland, the implication was clear that these were the terms upon which a Scottish army could be secured for Parliament.

This pressure from Scotland coincided with the discovery of Waller's plot and of Charles' communication with the Irish rebels, and together these precipitated a great outburst of renewed demands for church reformation. Representative of scores of sermons delivered during these weeks were the four preached before Parliament on the day of special thanksgiving for the discovery of Waller's plot, June 15. In the morning Stephen Marshall preached to the Commons in St. Margaret's church and Edmund Calamy to the Lords in Westminster Abbey; in the afternoon Obadiah Sedgwick preached to the Commons and Charles Herle to the Lords. The sermons were, as was customary, ordered printed by their respective auditories, and Thomason received all four within the next two weeks. They are much alike: the discovery of the plot is an example of God's special favor, but has the Parliament been really and unreservedly committed to God's service? Each gives the same reply: no. "All this while," said Marshall, "(let me speak freely) how *little* have you done for his honour, and glory? I know your distractions have unavoidably hindered much of what might (and I hope else would) have been done. But say (in this day of your thanksgiving) if you be not infinitely behinde hand with this Lord God Almighty?" [9] Are your wills really engaged in the struggle between Christ and Antichrist, or do some of you intend "to have a stock going on both sides, that you may save your own stake, which side soever win or lose, to save your own skin, whatever become

[5] May 20; E103(4), sig. A2v.   [6] *Ibid.,* sigs. A4 and A2v.
[7] *Ibid.,* sig. A4.   [8] *Ibid.*
[9] *The Song of Moses the Servant of God* (June 29, 1643), E56(5), p. 36.

of the Kingdom?" [10] Let those Parliament men who are really of God's party "beware of *neuters,* and secret *false friends,* who though they take sweet counsell together with you, *and speak you fair, beleeve them not, for there are seven abominations in their hearts."* [11] Let them at last "cast out of this Nation and Church all those reliques, which are the oyl and fuel that feed the flame which burnes amongst us; God calls you *now* to *this* work, and will be with you while you set your hearts and hands to doe it; and doe it *speedily,* it may be it is one Cause, why so many breaches are made upon you, because you have no more vigorously attempted it in the *first place."* [12]

At the same hour, Calamy was similarly exhorting the Lords "to appeare more and more *publikely* in this Cause" rather than to attempt "to be wary and circumspect." [13] Then his tone turned almost threatening.

> It is with us as it was with *Nehemiah* when he undertooke the great worke of rebuilding the Temple, he was opposed by great men especially. The *Nobles of* Tekoah *refused to put their necks to the yoake of the Lord.* This is an eternall brand upon them, *Nehem.* 3.5. Many of the *Nobles of Judah,* did seeme to helpe *Nehemiah,* but they kept secret *correspondency with Tobiah,* and tarried with *Nehemiah* only to give private intelligence to the enemy, and to weaken his hands from going on in the worke, *Neh.* 6.17. Thus it was in *Nehemiah's* dayes. And this is one of the miseries of Civill Warre above all other kinds of Warre: For there are alwayes some false brethren, some *Judasses* in civill Warre. But I beleeve better things of you. The Lord make you more and more faithfull to his Cause! Remember what became of *Judas* for his treachery.[14]

Nor was the threat of retribution confined to individual treacherous peers. In the sermon he was at some pains to reassure the Lords that "It is not the designe of the well-affected party to take away *Temporall Lordships* . . . and to bring all to a popular equality. This is an *Anabaptisticall fury."* [15] But the epistle of the printed version gives a strong hint of what is required to keep the well-affected party of this mind: "the best way for the House of Lords to prosper, is to endeavour earnestly and faithfully to reforme the Lords House." [16]

The afternoon sermons were not less outspoken. Sedgwick too raised the question of treachery indoors: "If any *plotter,* or *intended acter* for this late designe be here present, my earnest councell unto him is only this, *Repent."* [17] Again, "Treachery (I feare) is more at

---

[10] *Ibid.,* p. 42. [11] *Ibid.,* p. 20. [12] *Ibid.,* p. 8.
[13] *The Noble-Mans Patterne of True and Reall Thankfulnesse* (ordered printed June 16, 1643), E56(3), p. 47. [14] *Ibid.,* p. 50. [15] *Ibid.,* p. 46.
[16] *Ibid.,* sig. A4. [17] *Haman's Vanity* (June 26, 1643), E56(6), p. 28.

work this day then open hostility . . . *watch your selves . . . watch your enemies*, and most of all . . . *watch your friends.*" [18] Herle boldly challenged the military backwardness of the upper house: "I make no question but your pieties and wisdomes prompt you with higher considerations; for my part I must confesse I cannot but wonder, that any English Protestant can be contented to fill his hands onely with *Orders* and *Declarations*, while a Papist in the Land hath a *sword* in his." [19]

As a matter of fact, a few days before receiving these stern admonishments, the upper house had at last yielded to the Commons' insistence upon an Assembly of Divines to advise Parliament upon the reformation of the church.[20] There must, however, have been very mixed feelings among the members of both houses when, on July 7, they gathered in the Abbey for their first joint function with the new Assembly, and heard Oliver Bowles, the oldest of the divines, interpret the relation of the two bodies. He thanked Parliament for having "embodied many worthies from among your selves with us," for they "both help to order us who are ignorant of the nature of such meetings, and withall by a seasonable interposall may stay divisions among us." [21] Then, going beyond the Parliamentary committee which sat with the divines, he presented "a double suit" to Parliament as a whole: "1. That you would not suffer the work to be either spun out beyond what is meet, or yet hastily slubber'd over . . . 2. . . . that when the Lawes of Christ, for the due administration of his ordinances, shall be discovered, you would be pleased to account it your greatest honour to submit to them. . . . Be not jealous, as if Christs Government would eclipse your greatnesse." [22] The inferences were pretty clear. In the Assembly, the lay members were not really expected to help find the truth about religion and the church; they were to be helpful as guides to Parliamentary procedure and as referees, while the work was done by the divines. And the function of Parliament itself was to be a super-referee (particularly well equipped to deal with factious Independent ministers) while the work was in progress, and an authorizing or validating agency when the findings were reported—the authority in the sense of having the right and power to establish religion and make the nation conform, but a rubber-stamp with respect to the definition of religion.

[18] *Ibid.*, pp. 30–31.
[19] *Davids Song of Three Parts* (June 29, 1643), E56(4), p. 22.
[20] Rushworth, *Collections*, V, 325; Gardiner, *Civil War*, I, 174.
[21] *Zeale For Gods House Quickned* (August 3, 1643), E63(6), p. 30.
[22] *Ibid.*, pp. 30–31.

Some indications could be found that this view would meet heavy weather in Parliament. The royalist *Mercurius Aulicus* for July 23 furnished one:

> It was also signified, that the new assembly had done little all this while in the explaining of the ten first Articles, (which was the worke they had in hand) most of their time being spent in debating the great question of our Saviour Christ's *descent into Hell*. Concerning which, when they could not agree amongst themselves, (as we expected that they should) Master *Selden* (who is one of the *Lay part* of the *Assembly*) told them he could not choose but wonder, that an Article which had been generally received in the Christian Church 1500 yeares, should now be doubted of: and that if they desired to be better informed in that particular, they might doe well to make a speciall *Committee,* put Dr *Burges* in the Chaire, and send them thither to learne the truth of the matter, and from thence to certifie the same to their brethren here.[23]

But, such individualistic heckling aside, for the moment Parliament chose not to take notice of the Assembly's high line. The only terms on which a Scottish army was to be had were the expectation of a Presbyterian church settlement; and day by day the need for a Scottish army grew more pressing. On July 21 William Spurstowe preached before both Houses. The occasion was an extraordinary fast, the regular monthly fast day not having arrived yet. "Did you not," asked Spurstowe, "take this day to afflict your soules before God, as not knowing whether you might see any more the returne of your monthly Fasts, so exceedingly did the wrath of God hasten it's progresse against you?"[24] The panic was not imaginary. When the English negotiators arrived in Edinburgh on August 8, they carried with them, in addition to more formal documents, "a letter, subscryved by above seventie of their Divines, supplicating, in a most deplorable style, help from us in their present most desperate condition. . . . The letter . . . was so lamentable, that it drew tears from manie."[25] Baillie's description of the letter is not too strong. "God," wrote the seventy divines,

> should we Judge Providences, seems to be angry with our Prayers. . . . Oh give us . . . your Advises, What remains for us further to do, for the making of our own, and the Kingdoms Peace with God? We have lyen in the Dust before him; we have powred out our Hearts in Humiliations to him; we have in sinceritie endeavoured to reforme our Selves; and no lesse sincerely desired, studyed, laboured the publike

[23] August, 1643; E64(11), p. 394.

[24] *Englands Patterne And Duty* (August 4, 1643), E64(2), p. 14.

[25] *The Letters and Journals of Robert Baillie,* ed. David Laing (3 vols., Edinburgh, 1841–1842), II, 89. Hereafter cited as Baillie.

Reformation; nevertthelesse, *The Lord hath not yet turned himself from the fiercenesse of his anger*.[26]

The formal documents opening the negotiation, while more measured, are equally revealing. Parliament's declaration to the Scottish secular authority is relatively perfunctory; its declaration to the Kirk shows that it understood very well where the power in Scotland lay. Interpreting the whole struggle in England as one of religion, it recommends the delegates of the Westminster Assembly to the Scots Kirk, whom it urges "to stirre up that Nation to send some Competent forces in aide of this Parliament and Kingdome, against the many Armies of the Popish and Prelaticall party," [27] not neglecting to add the warning that the Kirk cannot hope to continue in peace unless the Puritans control the Church of England. The Kirk's answer makes no question that, if the church covenant is agreed, Scottish forces will be forthcoming. It leaves the English Parliament in no doubt that the condition for military aid is "the settling of the so much desired union of this whole Island in one forme of Church-government, one confession of Faith, one common Catechisme, and one directory for the worship of God." [28]

The Scots were in a position to dictate terms, and they exploited it. "Above all, diligence was urged," writes Baillie;

> for the report was going alreadie of the losse of Bristoll, from which they feared his Majestie might march to London, and carrie it. For all this, we were not willing to precipitat a businesse of such consequence. . . . The English were for a civill League, we for a religious Covenant. When they were brought to us in this, and Mr. Hendersone had given them a draught of a Covenant, we were not like to agree on the frame; they were, more nor we could assent to, for keeping of a doore open in England to Independencie. Against this we were peremptor.[29]

The Scots had their way—or thought they did. The Solemn League and Covenant bound both countries to

> the preservation of the reformed religion in the Church of Scotland, in doctrine, worship, discipline and government . . .; the reformation of religion in . . . England and Ireland, in doctrine, worship, discipline and government, according to the Word of God, and the example of the best reformed Churches; and . . . [the] endeavour to bring . . . the

[26] *The True Copy of the Letter, Which Was Sent from Divers Ministers, By Mr* Marshall, *and Mr* Nye, *to the Generall Assembly of* Scotland (September 8, 1643), E67(1), p. 5.

[27] *Two Declarations of . . . Parliament . . . The first, to the Convention of the Estates of* Scotland; *The second, to the Generall Assembly of the Kirke of* Scotland. *Together with the Severall Answers* (September 16, 1643), E67(18), p. 9. [28] *Ibid.*, p. 12. [29] Baillie, II, 89–90.

three kingdoms to the nearest conjunction and uniformity in religion, confession of faith, form of Church government. directory for worship and catechising.[30]

The Scots, who had a wrong idea of Vane,[31] cannot have grasped the significance of his amendment to Henderson's draft, the insertion of the words "the Word of God, and"; [32] they would otherwise never have agreed to it.

Had they followed the English Parliamentary debates with greater care they might have been warned. When Pym, the representative of the House of Commons, told the Lords on April 1, 1642, that "the House of Commons considered that the Law of God . . . was only fit for the Representatives of the Body of the Kingdom the House of Commons, and the Lords the hereditary Judges of this Realm, to judge of," [33] he was only voicing, albeit in somewhat more challenging language than usual, the permanently Erastian sentiment of Parliament. By September 25, when the House of Commons subscribed the Solemn League and Covenant, Parliament's military position had improved sufficiently to permit this sentiment to express itself again; it was surely to assert its supremacy, not because of any sudden, temporary conversion to Congregationalism, that the House chose the Independent Philip Nye to "exhort" its joint meeting with the Assembly and the Commissioners for Scotland on the true meaning of a Covenant which the latter, at any rate, had assumed meant making the Church of England conform to the Kirk of Scotland. Nye understood it far otherwise, and the Scots now began their long course of practical instruction in the significance of Vane's phrase, "according to the Word of God."

> What doe we covenant [asked Nye]? . . . Is it not the preservation of Religion, where it is reformed, and the Reformation of Religion, where it needs? . . . And all this to be done according to Gods word, the best Rule, and according to the best reformed Churches, the best interpreters of this Rule. If *England* hath obtained to any greater perfection in so handling the word of righteousnesse, and truths, that are according to godlinesse, as to make men more godly, more righteous: And if in the Churches of *Scotland* any more light and beauty in matters of Order and Discipline, by which their Assemblies are more orderly: Or if to any other Church or person it hath beene given better to have learned Christ in any of his wayes then any of us; wee shall humbly bow, and kisse their lips that can speak right words unto us in this

[30] Gardiner, *Constitutional Documents*, p. 268.
[31] See Baillie's subsequent disillusionment, especially in his letters of September 16 and October 25, 1644 (II, 229–31 and 235–37).
[32] Gardiner, *Civil War*, I, 270–71.
[33] *Old Parliamentary History*, X, 411.

matter, and help us into the nearest uniformity with the word and minde of Christ in this great work of Reformation.[34]

3. CONGREGATIONALISTS AND THE ARGUMENT FOR ACCOMMODATION

Nye's "exhortation" may, for convenience, be taken as an indication of the re-emergence of the Congregationalist drive for recognized status. During the crisis of the summer, when the whole Puritan and Parliamentary cause appeared to depend upon immediate help from Scotland, the leading Congregationalist divines seem to have taken care not to prejudice the prospect of this aid by too much emphasis on their characteristic doctrine of the "gathered" church. They participated energetically in the call for reformation, and refrained from demanding that it be reformation in their sense. Indeed, it is not always easy to distinguish their sermons of this period from those of the Presbyterians. We may take as an example the sermon preached before the House of Commons on April 26 by William Greenhill. England, said Greenhill, despite many warnings of God's judgment impending, has refused truly to reform. Now the judgment has arrived: "God hath given a Commission to the Sword to eate English flesh, and drinke English blood." [1] Only if we "meet God the right way" can we be saved.[2] First, Parliament must exercise justice upon "delinquents"; "when your justice fell upon that great Cedar [3] above a yeare and a halfe agoe did not *England* tremble?" [4] Having thus put the country into a receptive mood, Parliament is to reform religion. Counsels of worldly prudence, which warn against rooting out too abruptly images, ceremonies, and other survivals of popish superstition, are mistaken: "Mens thoughts are, that removall of them will breed disturbance, its their standing not their taking away doth it." [5] Everything is "adulterate" which lacks "Christs superscription," and must be extirpated from the church; no suspected, man-made things, "no worldly rudiments," can be allowed to "prejudice the liberty of tender consciences." [6] Only with this do we arrive at a distinguishable difference from the Presbyterian sermons of this period, and even this is passed over rather rapidly. One is able to sense a difference in emphasis: Greenhill stresses that aspect of reform which lies in the removal of abuses and corruptions, and is somewhat evasive about positive

[34] *The Covenant: With a Narrative of the Proceedings* (October 13, 1643), E70(22), p. 14.

[1] Ἀξίνη πρὸς τὴν Ῥίζαν. *The Axe at the Root*, E103(2), p. 15.

[2] *Ibid.*   [3] Strafford.   [4] *The Axe*, p. 34.   [5] *Ibid.*, p. 42.   [6] *Ibid.*, p. 44.

reformation in the sense of reconstruction according to a fixed pattern, and about Parliament's rights and duties therein.[7]

Even in the Westminster Assembly, the Congregationalist members were, for about three months, virtually indistinguishable in debate from their Presbyterian colleagues (until the end of August the subject under discussion was the first nineteen of the thirty-nine Articles of Religion; in September it was the Solemn League and Covenant).[8] But in the autumn, when the Scottish alliance was secure, when Parliament's own military successes relieved the fear of immediate defeat and so reduced the sense of a desperate unity among the Puritan divines, and particularly when, in response to a Parliamentary ordinance of October 12, the Assembly turned to the subject of church government,[9] the time had come for the Congregationalists to make their move. It was not, to begin with, aimed toward what we should call religious toleration, although after a considerable period of agitation it took a turn in that direction. Its initial object was rather to secure an "accommodation" or permission for orthodox (Calvinist) non-separating Congregationalists to form "gathered churches" outside the jurisdiction of the Presbyterian system of church organization which they expected Parliament to establish.

Late in October Sidrach Simpson published a sermon which he had preached in Westminster "before sundry of the House of Commons" about a year earlier, but which was not at that time printed.[10] In it he presented both a minimal and an optimal objective. If the right ordering of the church could not be obtained, the Congregationalists would accept some arrangement which permitted them their own autonomous gathered churches: "If you cannot indure the Children at the Table

[7] *Ibid.*, p. 49.

[8] W. A. Shaw, *A History of the English Church during the Civil Wars and under the Commonwealth* (2 vols., London, 1900), I, 145–47.

[9] John Lightfoot, "The Journal of the Assembly of Divines," in *The Whole Works of the Rev. John Lightfoot*, ed. J. R. Pitman (13 vols., London, 1825–42), XIII, 17; *Lords Journals*, VI, 254.

[10] *A Sermon Preached at Westminster before Sundry of the House of Commons* (1643). Thomason wrote on the title page "This Sermone was preached about a twelve moneth before. Octob. 28" (E74[3]). The word "Sundry" in the title should be noted; otherwise the absence of the vote of thanks and order to print which ordinarily followed official sermons before one of the Houses will seem due to Simpson's challenging remarks. In fact this sermon does not appear in any of the catalogues of official Parliamentary sermons known to me, and the probability is that it was arranged by some members of the Commons acting privately. There is nothing remarkable in the fact that, at the time, Simpson did not publish his sermon; the significant thing is that a year later circumstances made him decide to bring it out.

. . . amongst you . . . : If the complaints and differences of tender Consciences, who cannot doe as you, cannot be borne . . . allow them yet to be together in some Nurcerie." [11] But in truth church and state ought to be separate; and here Simpson skilfully linked the characteristic Independent demand for separation of church and state to Parliament's own natural-law theory of the state:

> There is a Civill State or Commonwealth . . . and the subjects are men as men, and not as Saints or Christians. The efficient cause, the sociablenes of mans nature. The forme, consociation: The end, theire common good. Their Governour, such as they submit to; The extent of his Power is according to their common good, and the worke he is be-trusted with. As the Lawes of this Kingdome are not in themselves Religious, and therefore bind not conscience in themselves; so it depends not in it selfe upon Religion. Religion is none of the proper Causes of it. An unregenerate man hath right to, and must have Priveledge in this state as well as others, for it is founded in, and upon the Acts of Nature. . . . On the Church of the *Jewes,* the Commonwealth had great dependance. As the Church was civill . . . so the Common-wealth was Ecclesiasticall. . . . In the new Testament, the Common-wealth hath not such dependance . . . the Churches now consist not of Nations, but pickt persons.[12]

Simpson must have been aware that the natural-law view of the state could be, and was, held by many to whom the idea of separating church and state was anathema; nevertheless, he here treats the two ideas as joint and interdependent consequences of a further idea—the idea that there are two orders of being, the order of nature and the order of grace, separate and in some degree opposed, each with its distinct good and its own institution for achieving that good—what A. S. P. Woodhouse, who first in modern times recovered the idea, called "the principle of segregation." [13]

But while Simpson based his argument on the principle of segregation, he was not consistent in applying it. "Falsnesse as well as *Atheisme,* corrupt as well as no Religion brings ruine." [14] "Plucke downe that which hinders [the establishment of true religion], roote and branch," he told his Parliamentary hearers; "you are set over Kingdomes to roote out, pull downe, destroy and throw downe. Do it quickly, doe it thoroughly." [15] The non-separating Congregationalists, as we shall see, never freed themselves from this inconsistency with respect to the relation of the state to religion.

A month after Simpson finally published his year-old sermon, Wil-

[11] *Ibid.,* p. 33.   [12] *Ibid.,* pp. 15–16.
[13] *Puritanism and Liberty, Being the Army Debates (1647–49) . . . with Supplementary Documents* (London: Dent, 1938), introduction, pp. 57–60.
[14] *A Sermon,* p. 11.   [15] *Ibid.,* p. 24.

liam Bridge preached to the House of Commons on their regular monthly fast day. Calling for "exactness" of reformation, he explained how this was to be achieved in a passage interesting enough to quote at some length:

> Be sure of this that you take the right *line* into your hands. Gods word it is our *line*, able to reach unto all particular affaires of the Churches.
> Mistake me not, I pray. A Church is considered two wayes; As a meeting of people, men and women; Or as a Church meeting, a meeting of Saints, apparent Beleevers, *coetus fidelium.* I doe not say that the Word is to be the onely line and rule to the Church in the first respect, so reason may be a rule to men as men; but in the second respect it is, the Word is able to reach unto all things belonging unto a Church as a Church. Our Commission is not larger now then the Apostles Commission was, and their Commission ran thus, *Goe teach and baptize, &c. teaching men to observe what ever I command you, Mat.* 28. If not commanded by Christ, then not to be preached by them nor by us. Jesus Christ was and is as fully Christ in his Propheticall as Priestly office, and his Priestly satisfaction reached unto all our sinnes, though they were never so small, therefore his Propheticall direction reacheth to all our duties, though they be never so little. That which commeth not from heaven, can never bring you into heaven. If you say, There are some things indifferent; It is true, but Christs command is to keep them so then, and not to alter them.[16]

Bridge, dealing with ideas very familiar to his audience, could afford to compress a great deal into little space; it may be well for us to draw out some of the implications of what he said. All dogmatic Christians would agree that ultimately the church is ordered by God, but Bridge is saying that essentially (*i.e.,* as "a meeting of Saints") the church belongs wholly to the order of grace, and that therefore it must be ordered by God *alone,* with nothing added from the realm of nature; that this could be done only by Christ in his own person; that accordingly the whole of this divine regimen was set forth once for all in the gospel, with no intermediary agent empowered to change or add to it in any way. It is true that the church has an incidental aspect as a mere "meeting of people"; in this aspect it belongs to the order of nature, has natural needs not provided for by divine authority, and may meet them by the use of natural reason. But the determinations of some men's reason must not be imposed upon others in the name of religion. Such determinations can have no validity except in "things indifferent," and then only for the individual Christian making them, for what Christ left indifferent he left so designedly, and it must not be made matter of prescription.

[16] *A Sermon Preached before the Honourable House of Commons . . . Novemb. 29, 1643,* E79(11), pp. 25–26.

With this we arrive at the doctrine of Christian liberty in things in-different and the long dispute about its implications. The doctrine may, for practical purposes, be said to derive from St. Paul, and it brings together two ideas which, while related, are nevertheless distinct. On the first of these ideas Paul is everywhere forthright and consistent: the Gospel abrogates the Law of the Old Testament, setting Christians free of the bondage of the Law to obey the spirit of the Gospel. On the second idea Paul is less unambiguous. Granted that Christians are no longer bound by the Law, in what relation do they stand to the things of the Law? It is evident that Paul feared even a voluntary and selective observance of the symbols and ordinances of the Law; he often warned against it, he quarreled with Peter about it, and he came close to forbidding it to the Galatians. Elsewhere, however, and par-ticularly in writing to the Romans, he took another line. He may have been influenced by the Stoic idea that since certain things are beyond our power to influence they are morally irrelevant—"things indiffer-ent"; in any event, he propounded the doctrine that the external things of the Law are in themselves indifferent, and Christians are free to use them or not according to their own judgments, provided that judgment is determined by the spirit of the Gospel.

This ambivalence at the source ensured from the outset that the doctrine's interpretation would be controversial; and as its scope was widened (particularly under the impact of Protestantism) to include ecclesiastical and political affairs, the controversy grew correspond-ingly complex and bitter. Luther, Calvin, and many of the other Re-formers placed great emphasis upon the doctrine, and in England it played an important part in the religious struggles of Elizabeth's reign, especially in the Vestiarian, the Admonition, and the Marprelate con-troversies. The best introduction to its operation in the Puritan Revolu-tion of the seventeenth century is in the discussions of Woodhouse [17] and A. E. Barker.[18] As we attempt, in the pages that follow, to make clear the toleration controversy that began in 1643, we shall have much to say of Christian liberty and indifferency.

To return to Bridge's sermon: he demanded "exactness" of reforma-tion according to the Word of God alone. There is more than a passing glance at the Solemn League and Covenant here. Not that the Congre-gationalists repudiate the example of other reformed churches: rather, they would use the achievement of others to go farther. "You know what other Reformed Churches have done, the Reformation of all

[17] *Puritanism and Liberty*, introduction, pp. *65–68* and *passim.*
[18] *Milton and the Puritan Dilemma* (Toronto: University of Toronto Press, 1942), pp. 52–59 and *passim.*

other Churches are round about you, you have their writings before you, their books, their practices, their examples, and this for many yeeres; can you think that God hath set us now for an hundred yeeres upon their shoulders, to see no farther into Reformation then they have done?"[19] But there are always some who would stop reformation before it is complete: "Oh what a sad thing is this that the spirit of Papists should live in Protestants! . . . that the spirit of Prelats should live in those that are risen up to *fray them away* and *cast them out!*"[20]

During the months immediately following the taking of the Solemn League and Covenant, then, the Assembly Congregationalists were thus making pretty clear to Parliament and public the basis of their demands. But the more explicit they became, the less important their differences from the Separatists seemed; and at this stage the non-separating Congregationalists were interested in emphasizing what they had in common, not with the sects, but with the Presbyterians. Like the latter, they were strictly Calvinist in faith and Puritan in worship,[21]

---

[19] E79(11), p. 24.   [20] *Ibid.*, pp. 20–21.

[21] This unity in worship is obscured, however, in Wilbur K. Jordan's work, *The Development of Religious Toleration in England* (4 vols., Cambridge: Harvard University Press, 1932–1940), III, 58: "When the sturdy Genevan Directory [of Worship] was laid before Parliament it was accompanied by a weighty and eloquent dissent from the Independent leaders which gave eloquent testimony to the losing battle which they had waged on the floor of the Assembly." Here Jordan simply refers to two contemporary news journals, and one is at first at a loss to imagine what "dissent" he has in mind, but the next sentence furnishes a clue: "Parliament sought to restrict the printing of the Independent memorial to three hundred copies for the exclusive use of its members." Again the reference is only to a news journal, but the action of Parliament here reported was taken with respect to only one Independent pamphlet, whose opening leaf carries the following order of the House of Commons, dated December 23, 1644: "That three hundred and no more" be printed, "And the Printer is injoyned (at his perill) not to Print more. . . . It is further Ordered, That no man presume to Re-print, Divulge or Publish the said *Reasons* and *Answers,* or any part of them, till further order." But this pamphlet has nothing to do with worship, as may be seen from the full title: *The Reasons Of The Dissenting Brethren against the Third Proposition, Concerning Presbyterial Government* (Thomason received his copy "about Feb: 5th", 1645; E27[14]). The whole argument is directed against the proposition that (p. 3) *"The Scripture holds forth, that many particular Congregations may be under one Presbyteriall Governement."* In fact the Congregationalists were so far from opposing the Directory of Worship that Baillie records the Presbyterian tactic of using them to help (II, 117) "abolish the great Idol of England, the Service-Book" before breaking with them; and he reports (II, 242) that when the Assembly finally took up the question of transmitting the Directory to Parliament the vote was unanimous and Thomas Goodwin, the leading Congregationalist member, was one

and it was on this solidarity that they were basing their tactics for securing accommodation in the matter of church government. Accordingly, they concurred in and signed a document, drawn up by Stephen Marshall and signed on December 23 by the Prolocutor and many leading members of the Assembly,[22] entitled *Certaine Considerations to Dis-swade Men From Further Gathering of Churches in this Present Juncture of Time*. Although all men have a duty toward reformation, magistrates and ministers have a special responsibility therein (what it is is left carefully unspecified); and since Parliament and Westminster Assembly are now engaged in the work, and since the party of Antichrist is so industrious to promote divisions among "the friends of the cause of Religion," the signatories, to prevent the growth of such divisions, entreat all the godly "to forbeare for a convenient time the joyning of themselves into Church-societies of any kind whatsoever, untill they see whether the right Rule will not bee commended to them" by the Assembly and Parliament.[23] The inducement to the Congregationalists to join in what would otherwise be a self-destructive move was in the following paragraph:

> That it is not to bee doubted, but the councells of the Assembly of Divines, and the care of the Parliament will be, not onely to reforme and set up Religion throughout the Nation, but will concurre to preserve whatever shall appeare to be the rights of particular Congregations, according to the Word; and to beare with such whose Consciences cannot in all things conforme to the publicke Rule, so farre as the word of God would have them borne withall.[24]

There is much that is obscure about this episode. At first Baillie thought quite well of Marshall's idea,[25] but when he next wrote he wished "it had never been moved."[26] These second thoughts of the Scots became official when Henderson preached to the Commons on December 27. The Moderator of the Scottish Kirk did not quite denounce in set form the action which had four days earlier "past with the Assemblie's allowance, but without voyceing,"[27] but he left no

of the "carryers." There was a similar unanimity with respect to the Confession of Faith, and the Congregationalist propaganda continued to stress this area of agreement for a long time (see below, pp. 114–18). We may observe in passing that Jordan is not the only historian who was unhappy in his discussion of *The Reasons of the Dissenting Brethren;* Gardiner allowed himself to say (*Civil War*, II, 51), "On December 23 their [the Dissenting Brethren's] arguments against the establishment of Presbyterianism were produced before the House of Commons; but they proved to be so voluminous that the House sarcastically ordered that no more than three hundred of their reasons should be printed."

[22] Baillie, II, 118.   [23] E79(16), pp. 3–4.   [24] *Ibid.*, p. 3.
[25] See II, 118.   [26] *Ibid.*, p. 121.   [27] *I.e.*, voting; *ibid.*

doubt of what he thought of this English trifling. The work of positive reformation in the English church had scarcely been begun, despite Scotland's good example, and one of the chief impediments was the hopeless attempt to secure the agreement of dissenters: "Nor must yee in this work linger or delay upon any consent or concurrence whatsoever. . . . There be some things wherein we are subject to God alone, and in things of this kind, we are not to wait for counsell or consent from others." [28] Whether the opposition of the Scots killed a genuine move toward accommodation on the part of the English Presbyterians, or whether the latter were never sincere in their implied promise (a year later the Dissenting Brethren called it a "bait" [29]), the whole undertaking died almost as soon as it was born, and by January 3, 1644, five of the Congregationalists in the Assembly had published *An Apologeticall Narration, Humbly Submitted To The Honourable Houses of Parliament.*

The *Apologeticall Narration* is not, as it is sometimes thought to be, a demand for religious toleration; it is still a demand for the "accommodation" we have been noticing. What distinguishes it from its predecessors is that the demand is addressed to Parliament alone, with scarcely the barest pretence that there is any further hope of the Assembly majority helping or favoring the accommodation. The Apologists begin with the narrative of their having gone into voluntary exile from Laudianism "long before some others of our brethren," [30] and having been received very generously by the Reformed Churches in Holland. They then give an account of their church practices abroad and their behavior and circumstances since returning to England. In all this the emphasis is heavily upon their orthodoxy. They have agreed with the Presbyterian majority of the Assembly "in all *points of doctrine.*" [31] Their practice in worship is the same as that "of all other reformed Churches." [32] They have always held all the reformed churches to be *"the true Churches and Body of Christ,"* and gladly hold communion with them.[33] It is true that they differ from the Presbyterians in some points of church government (holding in this "the *Calvinian* Reformed Churches of the first reformation from out of Popery, to stand in need of a further reformation themselves" [34]), but even here their position has been misunderstood; and the Apolo-

[28] *A Sermon Preached to the Honourable House of Commons . . . December 27, 1643* (Thomason's date is January 12, 1644), E81(24), pp. 35–36.

[29] *A Paraenetick, or Humble Addresse to Parliament* (November 30, 1644), E19(10), p. 7; see below, p. 118.

[30] E80(7), p. 2; reproduced in Haller, *Tracts*, II, 306 ff.

[31] *Ibid.,* p. 29.   [32] *Ibid.,* p. 8.   [33] *Ibid.,* p. 6.   [34] *Ibid.,* p. 22.

gists devote a third of their pamphlet to showing how much they differ from Separating Congregationalists.[35] But whereas the churches abroad accorded them "the very same characters and testimonies of difference which are proper to their own Orthodoxe Churches, and whereby they use to distinguish them from all those sects (which they tollerate, but not own)," [36] their English brethren misinterpret and distort their views: "Besides other calumnies, as of *schisme*, &c. . . . *That* proud and insolent title of *Independencie* was affixed unto us, as our claime; . . . which we doe abhor and detest: Or else the odious name of *Brownisme*." [37] The Apologists have hitherto refrained from defending themselves because it is the *"second blow that makes the quarrell,"* [38] and they have been anxious not to exacerbate differences; besides, Parliament had declared its "endeavour and desire to unite the Protestant partie in this Kingdome, that agree in Fundamentall Truths against Popery and other Heresies, and to have that respect to tender consciences as might prevent oppressions and inconveniences," [39] and the Apologists have rested upon "the hopefull expectation we have been entertained with of an happy *latitude* and agreement by means of this *Assembly*, and the wisdom of this Parliament" [40] within "that constitution and government" of the church which is to be "established and declared." [41] But they are now being attacked by "good men"—they do not mention names—"even to the threatning of another banishment," [42] and they are forced to defend themselves. For a moment there is a hint of menace: The Apologists are making their plea to Parliament, but reserve "a more exact and *Scholastique* relation of our judgements in the points of difference . . . as necessity shall after require, to a more publique way of stating and asserting of them" [43] (they had earlier expressed their conviction that they were in a very favorable position to "make and encrease a partie").[44] But immediately the Apologists return to their dominant tone, and end with an appeal to Parliament for "the enjoyment of the ordinances of Christ . . . with the allowance of a latitude to some lesser differences with peaceablenesse." [45]

4. SEPARATISTS, SECULARISTS, AND THE THEORY OF TOLERATION

The Apologetical Narrators very soon heard from the "odious" separation; and as their hopes for an accommodation with Presbyterianism

---

[35] *Ibid.*, pp. 12–22.   [36] *Ibid.*, p. 7.   [37] *Ibid.*, p. 23.   [38] *Ibid.*, p. 25.
[39] *Ibid.*, p. 26.   [40] *Ibid.*   [41] *Ibid.*, p. 23.   [42] *Ibid.*, p. 31.
[43] *Ibid.*, p. 30.   [44] *Ibid.*, p. 24.   [45] *Ibid.*, p. 31.

faded (and as it became obvious that even should such an accommodation be agreed it would be impossible to maintain it against the rising strength of the sects), the non-separating Congregationalists made common cause with the Separatists—in effect, accepted "that proud and insolent title of Independencie"—and worked with the sects for a policy of genuine, if limited, toleration. We must now turn to the Separatists and the sects beyond them, and examine their contribution to tolerationist theory.

In doing so, however, we must try to distinguish the authentic from the merely tactical, although this is not always easy to do. For example, on September 20, 1643, there appeared a broadside entitled *To the . . . House of Commons, . . . The Humble Petition of Many Godly True-Hearted Protestants*.[1] In the usage of the moment, "true-hearted Protestant" implied a contrast with Separatists, and the petition emphasizes this: it purports to be by and on behalf of those who, so far from separating, are much disturbed by the separation of increasing numbers of good men. Such Separatists believe they have been given new truth, which they must follow; at the same time, they strongly insist on their willingness to renounce any of their doctrines shown to be false. The petitioners have therefore urged the Presbyterian ministers to reason with them; and the Separatists are very willing to meet in a public disputation; but the Presbyterians refuse, and this leaves the people confused, uneasy, and suspicious. Let Parliament bring the Westminster Assembly and the Separatists before it for a debate which will make the truth manifest, and quiet the people. Meanwhile, until this debate can be held, let Parliament withdraw any powers it has deputed to anyone to enforce the unenforceable faiths of "conscious" (*i.e.*, conscientious) men, or to silence them from preaching, suppress their writings, or otherwise deprive them of their "liberty of conscience."

Now this appears, on the surface, to be a plea for toleration—that is, for permission to good and sincere men to practise their religion despite certain errors therein. But Thomason wrote on his copy, "Thom: Nutt Late Carier of Norwich," and bound it immediately after another broadside petition, published on the same day and apparently printed by the same press, this one acknowledging Nutt's authorship and bearing the title, *The Humble Request of Certain Christians Reproachfully Called Anabaptists*.[2] In this broadside the well-known Baptist zealot again makes the favorite demand of his sect, a debate with the Westminster Assembly; but this time it is in order to show the falseness of the Presbyterians' pretended "Ministery, Baptisme or Sabboth," by means

[1] 669.f.8(28).   [2] 669.f.8(27).

of a new divine revelation—"a light but very new sprung forth" which must be received and obeyed despite all adverse views.

Nutt's purposes in the two broadsides are clearly different. *The Humble Request* is part of his Baptist proselytizing, part of the demand that falsehood be pulled down and the truth set up. *The Humble Petition* is a device to make this proselytizing possible under the plausible screen of liberty of conscience; hence the false attribution and insincere argument. Whether, if Nutt had been successful in setting up his new truth, he would have adopted the tolerationist advice of *The Humble Petition* is most questionable. Jordan believes that the doctrine of toleration was so intimately connected with the essentials of their faith that the Baptists, much more than other dissidents in the Puritan Revolution, "were able to plead persistently and consistently the cause of toleration," that the use of the idea of toleration as a defensive measure was "almost entirely absent" among them, and that it is likely that if they had achieved political power they would have put the theory of toleration into practice.[3] It may be that they would, but they were not as consistently tolerationist as Jordan thinks. Nutt's equally well-known associate, Mrs. Chidley, leaves no doubt what she meant when she demanded "liberty of conscience." In *A New-Yeares-Gift, Or a Brief Exhortation To Mr. Thomas Edwards,* her method is simply to accept the principles of the arch-antitolerationist but reverse the identities: to agree that error and schism ought not to be tolerated, but to identify Presbyterianism as the schism and the Separation as the true church. "You have brought no argument in your *Antipologia* against *Separation* from a *false Church* and *false Ministry,* but you have challenged all . . . *to bring a ground from Scripture for the lawfulnesse of seperating from a true Church,* which thing wee never strived for, for we know it is utterly unlawfull."[4] "I doe not (neither doe any that are truly religious) plead for such a *Toleration,* as you would father upon us, even a *Toleration to sinne.* . . . But the thing wee plead for, is a peaceable enjoyment of our liberty to worship *God,* publikely, according to his *revealed word.*"[5] "*A toleration of heresie and Scisme* . . . we know is *against the Magistrates duty.*"[6] "It is not wee, that pleade for *different formes of Church Governement.* . . . We pleade but for one intire *governement* established upon *sound principles,* unalterable."[7] She ends by asking, as Nutt had in the broadside he chose to acknowledge, for a debate before Parliament between the Westminster Assembly and the Separatists; and what Nutt did not discuss she makes quite clear: Parliament is to

---

[3] *Religious Toleration,* II, 452 ff., especially pp. 459–60.
[4] January 2, 1645; E23(13), p. 2.
[5] *Ibid.,* pp. 16–17. [6] *Ibid.,* p. 17. [7] *Ibid.,* p. 20.

decide which has made good its claim to be God's one true church, "and as things are cleared, so let them allow, or disallow." [8]

But there was in Separatism a basis for genuine tolerationism. It had received what was perhaps its clearest expression before the Puritan Revolution in John Smith, the Se-Baptist:

> The magistrate is not by virtue of his office to meddle with religion, or matters of conscience, to force or compel men to this or that form of religion or doctrine; but to leave Christian religion free, to every man's conscience, and to handle only civil transgressions.[9]

Now it was brought forward again, and clarified and applied in a more complex situation, by Roger Williams.

Williams' banishment from Massachusetts had made him quick to see the difference between a real and an illusory separation of church and state, and had proved to him "that the frame or constitution" of the Congregational churches of New England "is but implicitly National (which yet they professe against . . .)." [10] In the *Apologeticall Narration* of the Congregational Brethren he saw the same fault, and he adopted a striking way of pointing it out. On January 24, the Scottish Commissioners published a very inflexible reply to the *Apologeticall Narration*,[11] and on February 9 Williams anonymously published *Queries of Highest Consideration, Proposed to the five Holland Ministers and the Scotch Commissioners (So Called)*. He explains that although it would be easy to use the rival arguments against each other, he intends to query only those things in which they agree, "like *Ephraim* and *Manasseh* (though fighting each against other, yet) both against Christ." [12] Apologists and Scots agree, "though with some difference," that the magistrate is to reform and establish religion; but does this not mean that the church will be governed by the World? [13] Both agree that there is more light to come in the church, and profess to desire it;

---

[8] *Ibid.*, p. 22. Mrs. Chidley's reputation as a leading tolerationist is in part due to Masson, who, misled by her attack on the arch-antitolerationist Edwards, assumed that she opposed him in principle as well as in particulars, and credited her (III, 110–11) with fighting for "absolute or universal Toleration."

[9] "The Confession of Fayth," date unknown but probably 1612; reproduced in Walter H. Burgess, *John Smith the Se-Baptist, Thomas Helwys, and the First Baptist Church in England* (London: 1911), pp. 239 ff.; quotation is at p. 255.

[10] *Mr. Cottons Letter Lately Printed, Examined and Answered* (February 5, 1644), E31(16), p. 5.

[11] *Reformation of Church-Government in Scotland, Cleered from Some Mistakes and Prejudices*, by *The Commissioners of the Generall Assembly of the Church of Scotland now at London;* E30(5).

[12] *Publications of the Narragansett Club* (6 vols., Providence: 1866–74), II, 254.   [13] *Ibid.*, pp. 259–60.

then how can they denounce and persecute those who believe they see a further light and therefore dare not join Presbyterian or Independent churches? Is it not the mark of a false church to persecute? Is not Holland's legal toleration of religious diversity closer to Christ's command (as well as being the ground of her great peace and prosperity)? [14] Then, abandoning his queries, Williams asserts that religious compulsion is opposite to everything good, whether in religion or nature. [15] And although Parliament is constantly being told that its first and greatest duty is the reformation of religion, the truth is that it has no responsibility or right therein at all; only "the *Bodies* and *Goods* of the Subject is your charge." [16]

Five months later Williams published his famous *Bloody Tenent, of Persecution, for Cause of Conscience Discussed,* which gave a full and categorical statement of the position suggested by *Queries of the Highest Consideration.* Everything flows from a rigorous application of the principle of segregation and an unflinching acceptance of its furthest consequences. To subject the church, the institution of the order of grace, in any way to establishment, regulation, or supervision by the state, the institution of the order of nature, is fearful sin; it is "to pull *God* and *Christ,* and *Spirit* out of *Heaven,* and subject them unto *naturall,* sinfull, inconstant men, and so consequently to *Sathan* himselfe, by whom all *peoples* naturally are guided." [17] And for the state it is a calamity to become involved in the things of the church, causing "the greatest *breach* of *peace,* and the greatest *distractions* in the world." [18] The function of the magistrate, and hence his rights and duties, are entirely natural, and cannot be augmented from other than natural sources: "This *civill* Nature of the *Magistrate* we have proved to receive no *addition* of *power* from the Magistrates being a *Christian,* no more then it receives *diminution* from his not being a *Christian:* even as the *Common-weale* is a true *Common-weale,* although it have not heard of *Christianitie*; and *Christianitie* professed in it . . . makes it ne're no more a Commonweale, and *Christianitie* taken away, and the *candlestick* removed, makes it ne're the lesse a Commonweale." [19]

The magistrate, then, may not properly pursue other than natural ends. But the principal natural ends, peace and safety in person and goods, are utterly unattainable as long as there is any attempt to enforce religious uniformity; all experience has demonstrated this. Hence it is an inevitable consequence that "a *permission* of the most *Paganish, Jewish, Turkish,* or *Antichristian consciences* and *worships,* bee granted to *all* men in all *Nations* and *Countries*: and they are onely to bee

<hr>

[14] *Ibid.*, pp. 273–74.   [15] *Ibid.*, p. 275.   [16] *Ibid.*, p. 254.
[17] July 15, 1644; E1(2), p. 137.   [18] *Ibid.*, p. 129.   [19] *Ibid.*, p. 202.

fought against with that *Sword* which is only (in *Soule matters*) *able* to *conquer,* to wit, the *Sword of Gods Spirit,* the *Word* of *God.*" [20] (Williams makes a special point of including Roman Catholics in this liberty, "upon good assurance given of *civill obedience* to the *civill State.*" [21]) This "State policy and State necessity," absolute liberty of religion, "will bee found to agree most punctually with the *Rules* of the best *Politician* that ever the *World* saw, the *King of Kings.*" [22] Lest this impunity for sinners distress the reader's sense of justice, Williams frequently reminded him of the fearful and eternal punishments prepared for the damned in hell.

Williams' demand, then, goes beyond liberty for the saint to obey God's commands as revealed to his enlightened conscience (although it includes this); it goes beyond Christian liberty in things indifferent (although it includes this too): it is a demand for natural liberty for all forms of belief or unbelief, and for all religious practices that pose no threat to the safety of the merely natural state. Its primary motive is to safeguard the true church (which is wholly spiritual, consists only of the regenerate, and is governed immediately by Christ) from interference by and subjection to the world, the flesh, and the devil. Its secondary motive is to enable the state to achieve its ends—peace, order, and safety—by removing the worst source of discord, the attempt to achieve religious uniformity.

Radical as Williams' tolerationist demands were, they had already been presented by another group in the Revolution. This group's difference from the Separatists is hard to define, although it can be readily enough felt. When compared with the strict Separatist theory of Williams, it may best be distinguished by its reversal of Williams' emphasis. Williams was motivated by a concern for both the church (conceived as wholly spiritual), and the state (conceived as wholly natural), but the former concern was unquestionably the prior. The group we are now to examine also displayed both concerns, but its emphasis fell on the latter. This is not to say that religion for these men was less important than politics; for some it may have been, for others it was not. But they began from the misery of civil war, and it was for this that they sought a remedy; they found it in religious toleration; they often buttressed this argument with one drawn from the spiritual nature of the true church, and to some of them this was a matter as much of faith as of

[20] *Ibid.,* sig. a2v.   [21] *Ibid.,* p. 107.

[22] *Ibid.,* p. 91. Woodhouse, in *Puritanism and Liberty,* introduction, esp. pp. 66–67 and 84–85, was the first firmly to assert the primacy of Williams' religious concern and its separation from his political concern; theretofore the tendency had been either to regard Williams's primary interest as the peace of the civil state or to confuse his religious and political ends.

tactics; but the primacy lies in the peace and order of the state. It is in this sense, and not with any implication of unconcern with religion, that we may call this group secular. We must add, however, that some —not all—of this group displayed a relativistic attitude towards differences of faith which hints of skepticism.

What seems to be the earliest serious [23] demand, in the Puritan Revo-

[23] This judgment implies some dissent from the view taken in *Complete Prose*, Vol. I, of an anonymous pamphlet of 1641, extant in two states: *A New Petition of the Papists*, E169(7), published in September, and a re-issue in November with no change other than a new title page, *The Humble Petition of the Brownists*, E178(10). My colleague, the editor of Volume I, suggests (introduction, pp. 143–45) that this pamphlet anticipated the full theory of religious liberty, nor is he alone in his opinion; the pamphlet has attracted a good deal of attention, with much variation of judgment. Its ostensible argument is that compulsive religious uniformity produces strife, while toleration brings peace, and that in an atmosphere of free discussion error will wither and truth flourish. Thus, if it is a serious proposal, it does indeed anticipate the full theory of religious liberty. But is it serious? Gardiner, who knew only the second state, found the largeness of its charity suspicious and thought it a hostile caricature of Separatism (*History of England*, X, 35). Theodore C. Pease thought that as satire it would have been too delicate for the age, and therefore took it seriously, conjecturing that it might be by Walwyn (*Leveller Movement*, pp. 256–57). Haller, who was the first to call the bibliographical peculiarity to attention, doubts this attribution and "suspects some Catholic hand" (*Tracts on Liberty*, I, 126). Wolfe thinks it "probable that a Protestant sent out both pamphlets, using ironical titles" (*Complete Prose*, I, 143). Joseph Frank, in *The Levellers* (Cambridge: Harvard University Press, 1955, pp. 32–33), discusses the second form of the pamphlet without seeming to be aware of the earlier, adopts Pease's conjecture that Walwyn was the author, and declares the pamphlet to be "one of the first and one of the most effective . . . pleas for unrestricted religious liberty." I believe it to be a satirical attack upon the idea of religious toleration, employing the method of reduction to absurdity by extension. To begin with, why would a true tolerationist attribute his argument to Roman Catholics? He would know that this was the surest way to prejudice its reception. The predictable Protestant response would be, "We know it is an article of faith with them to extirpate what they call 'heresy'; this universal toleration they now demand is a mere trick to permit the reorganization of the pope's party in England; when they are ready, they will tolerate as much religious diversity here as in Spain." Again, can the following "proof" that religious diversity produces peace have been meant seriously, with twenty-three of the Thirty Years War already fought (p. 3): "This in divers well governed Countries is permitted, as *Holland, Germanie, France,* and *Polonia, &c.* where though their Religion be as opposite as Heaven to Hell, yet their concord is so great, that they say with the Prophet *David, behold how good and pleasant a thing it is for Brethren to dwell together*"? Finally, if the following passage were meant satirically, would it really be too subtle to be effective? Pp. 3–4: "If therefore the Brownists . . . will separate themselves, . . . let them alone. . . . If the *Arminians* will have Bishops, Altars, Lights, Organs, hold Free-will, merit of good workes, and

lution, for a general toleration was of this secular type. It was made
in a remarkable (and hitherto unnoticed) anonymous pamphlet entitled
*A Short Discourse, Touching the Cause of the Present Unhappy Dis-
tractions*, which Thomason acquired on February 8, 1643. *A Short Discourse* begins by isolating religion as the cause of the country's inability
to achieve a settlement. Since "all the Subjects of this KINGDOME"
concur in their "temporall interests" ("the Liberty of mens persons, the
propriety of their goods, and their being governed by the Lawes of the
Kingdome"), a temporal settlement which satisfies any man will satisfy
all men.[24] But in religion the reverse is true, for "there are many
severall perswasions," each convinced of its truth, and this "discrepance
of opinions" means that to satisfy any one group is to displease all the
rest. Hence, so long as men anticipate a settlement which will enforce
religious uniformity, they will strive to control it. There is no possibility of quieting the strife by achieving unity of faith, "mens apprehensions being so various."[25] The only remedy is to ensure that "every
party" knows its religious opinions to be secure against pressure; then
all can unite to achieve a temporal settlement.[26] This "freedome in
matters of Religion" need not necessitate utter disestablishment of the
church, but it strips any surviving establishment of all coercive
powers: "though a certaine tenor of Faith and forme of Divine Worship be agreed of, and established in generall for those that have their
consciences moulded that way; yet others, that cannot yeild their assent thereunto, may to themselves enjoy the freedome of their consciences as long as they do nothing to interrupt the civill society."[27]

Reason thus demonstrates that religious toleration is the only means
to civil peace. But piety itself also demands religious toleration. Persecution to enforce conformity makes men sin by professing what their
consciences reject (their reason not being amenable to force).[28] God,
who has all power at his command, sets us an example by rejecting the
worship of compulsion and requiring men to believe freely.[29] We sin if
we intrude upon that which God reserves to himself.[30] The magistrate
has no jurisdiction in spiritual matters, and his weapons must not be
used in spiritual warfare.[31] Some may fear that under such a toleration

divers others points with the Papists, though as yet no sacrifice with them, upon
their Altars, let them alone. . . . If the *Papists* will have Altars, Priests, Sacrifice and ceremonies, and the Pope for their supreame head in Spirituall affaires
. . . let them alone. . . . Let the *Adamits* Preach in vaults & caves as naked
as their nailes. . . . Let the *Family of Love* meete together in their sweet per-
fum'd Chambers, giving each other the sweet kisse of peace; great pitty it were
to hinder their mutuall charity; let them alone."

[24] E88(28), pp. 1–2.   [25] *Ibid.*, p. 2.   [26] *Ibid.*   [27] *Ibid.*, p. 6.
[28] *Ibid.*, p. 3.   [29] *Ibid.*, pp. 3–4.   [30] *Ibid.*, p. 4.   [31] *Ibid.*, p. 5.

a false doctrine may grow predominant, and thereafter suppress the side now in power; but it is most unlikely—rather, impossible—that falsehood should overcome truth when it has none of the advantages of power. If the party now dominant fears the encounter, it argues "some secret consciousnesse of inward deficiency and weaknesse." Let them "conclude with *Gamaliel*" that if the doctrine they fear is of God nothing can stop it, but if it is false it will fail of itself.[32]

The next secular demand for general toleration seems to have been by William Walwyn. He had already, in November, 1642, made a recommendation which seemed to be for Christian liberty in things indifferent, but whose ambiguity may well have been deliberate. *Some Considerations Tending to the Undeceiving Those, Whose Judgements Are Misinformed* [33] warned that the royalists' best hope lay in fomenting religious divisions among the supporters of Parliament, and that their strategy was already so far successful that "it is almost come to that passe, that the Puritan and Sectaries, as they are called, are more odious to the Protestant, then the Cavalier, Malignant, or Papist." [34] In fact, however, "Protestant" and "Puritan" were at one about the substance of religion, and their "differences concerning formes and circumstances" were unimportant; the author, a "Protestant," could testify that "the Puritan intends no mischiefe to any," and urged that "we" beare with him in circumstantials, "especially when substantiall things lie at the stake." [35]

It is hard to think that this is really a plea for liberty in things indifferent. The general context makes it clear that the inclusiveness of the omnibus phrase, "Puritan and Sectaries," is deliberate, for Walwyn's expressed object was the solidarity of the Parliamentary coalition; but the things dividing many of the sects from more conservative Protestants (and from each other) were not, in any of their theologies, "indifferent"; all were agreed that they were matters of divine prescription, differing from each other only in interpreting these commands. To the somewhat skeptical and fideist Walwyn,[36] indeed, these differences were probably unimportant (he called them "shadows" [37]), but he cannot have been unaware that for the most part they lay outside the scope of the theological principle of Christian liberty in things indifferent. Even this early, then, he may have been trying to insinuate a policy of religious toleration under the camouflage of the familiar doctrine of Christian liberty.

[32] *Ibid.*, p. 7.
[33] November 10, 1642; E126(45); attribution by Haller, *Tracts*, I, 121–27.
[34] *Ibid.*, p. 5.   [35] *Ibid.*, pp. 5–6.
[36] See Haller, *Liberty and Reformation in the Puritan Revolution* (New York: Columbia University Press, 1955), pp. 162–75.   [37] E126(45), p. 5.

By September of 1643, at any rate, he had dispensed with even the appearance of discussing indifferency. *The Power of Love* [38] purports to be a Familist sermon published by one who is not himself a Familist but who has learnt to value and admire that sect. The author of the preface anticipates the reader's hostile reaction to Familism, and for that matter to other sects—Anabaptists, Brownists, Antinomians; for the reader is very likely to have formed his notions of these people from the attacks made against them by "learned" men. But if he will follow the Apostle's bidding and try all things himself, he will find out how falsely the sects have been misrepresented. He will probably find many things to disagree with, but will learn much he had not known, and will be able to "perfect" his own judgment. The Familist preacher would have no man "troubled for any opinion, except such, as make the bloud of Christ ineffectuall, or such as would destroy all that will not submit to their opinions;" [39] and the author of the preface agrees with this policy on the ground that then "truth may come to light, that otherwise may be obscured for particular ends." There is no danger in such toleration because "plaine truth will prove all, sufficient for vanquishing of the most artificiall, sophisticall errour that ever was in the world." [40] Walwyn's theory of toleration was not yet very explicit (and when it became so it proved rather wavering), but his policy already comprehended all Christians who would accept religious diversity.

In November there appeared an anonymous pamphlet entitled *A Discoverie, What God, the Supreame Judge, Through his Servant Hath Caused to Bee Manifested*. Thomason received it on November 21, and wrote on the cover, "by a high German"; and indeed the background of a Germany torn by the Thirty Years War is very evident. The theme of the main body of the pamphlet (somewhat obscured by the furious and rhapsodical style) is that God has forbidden men to take the judgment of religion into their hands. "The whore of Babylon must indeed be destroyed before the end of the world, but it must not be done otherwise, then by, and according to the . . . counsell of the Lord." [41] God has reserved the worst of punishments for those who usurp his role in this. So far, the pamphlet might as easily have been written by a strict Separatist as by a secularist, and perhaps it was; but there is a final summary paragraph which is in so different and so much more lucid a style as to suggest another hand, perhaps the translator's; and here the secular note emerges. Those who persecute religion, even false religion, "doe first and foremost, burden themselves

---

[38] September 19, 1643; E1206(2); attribution by Haller, *Tracts*, I, 121–27. Reproduced in Haller, II, 203 ff.

[39] E1206(2), sig. A7.   [40] *Ibid.*, sig. A7v.   [41] E76(17), sig. A4v.

with great unquietnesse, trouble and labour in vaine to no purpose.
Secondly they bring their country, people and subjects with their rev-
enus, sweate and blood into utter ruine: and then thirdly and consequently . . . they presume to alter or pervert the eternall counsel of
God." [42]

Henry Robinson's *Liberty of Conscience: or the Sole Means to
Obtaine Peace and Truth,* published March 24, 1644, contains every
variety of argument favorable to the policy of toleration, but, as the
title indicates, it is the secular interest which is primary. War, it begins, is the worst scourge of God, and the one which men have the
greatest part in bringing down upon themselves; it is always a threat
everywhere, but the attempt throughout most of Christendom to impose religious uniformity makes it worse there than anywhere else:
"Christendome a spot of ground only, hath continually been the Cock-
pit, & all the world besides but as a breathing place." [43] The policy of
religious uniformity also leads to catastrophic economic losses; for
example, when the Moors of Spain and the Jews of Portugal refused to
conform to Roman Catholicism and were banished, "they conveyed
themselves into *Barbaria* and *Turkey,* with such a stocke of Christian
crafts and pollicie, as not only the Pirates, but those whole Nations are
much advantaged and improved, to the no lesse shame than detriment
of Christianity: Oh let not the like befall *England.*" [44] If it were not
so tragic in its effects, the effort to compel uniformity would be ridiculous, since the whole history of Protestants in Roman Catholic countries, Roman Catholics in Protestant countries, Jews and Moslems in
Christian countries, attests the futility of forcible (and hence only
pretended) conversion.[45]

Coupled to this secular argument is a theological one, and Robinson
uses, but with variable rigor, many of the scriptural texts upon which
the strict Separatists rested: ye are bought with a price,[46] try all
things,[47] Christ's kingdom is not of this world,[48] he that doubteth is
damned if he eateth because he eateth not of faith,[49] to fight against
what is from God is sin,[50] the separation of the tares from the wheat
belongs to the angels' ministry.[51]

In *Liberty of Conscience* Robinson leaves some ambiguity about the
extent of the toleration he desires. For one thing, he nowhere specifies
whether disestablishment is necessary or whether religious liberty
alongside a noncompulsive established church would satisfy him. More
important, he is evasive about Roman Catholicism. He is unwilling

[42] *Ibid.,* sig. B1v.   [43] P. 1; reproduced in Haller, *Tracts,* III, 107 ff.
[44] *Ibid.,* pp. 6–7.   [45] *Ibid.,* pp. 4, 6–7, 31.   [46] *Ibid.,* p. 3.   [47] *Ibid.,* p. 4.
[48] *Ibid.,* p. 7.   [49] *Ibid.,* p. 24.   [50] *Ibid.,* p. 34.   [51] *Ibid.,* p. 51.

to prejudice his cause by frightening off those who might sympathize with a limited toleration but who actively fear Roman Catholicism, while at the same time what he would really like is a general toleration.[52] But we need not examine this matter too particularly, because his later writings leave no doubt that for him the imposition of limits upon toleration was no more than a temporary tactical device.[53]

One aspect of Robinson's argument of special interest to students of Milton is his demand for a free press. The combat between diverse religious views "must be fought out upon eaven ground, on equall termes, neither side must expect to have greater liberty of speech, writing, Printing, or whatsoever else, then the other." [54] Among Robinson's grounds for this necessary freedom, as among Milton's, are the progressive recovery of truth [55] and the constant necessity of re-examining the truth already known:

> [Suppression] would as much as in us lyes, still withhold such saving truth and knowledge as [is] yet undiscovered, and unto which we are to attaine by degrees only, for not any of them but at first sight and hearing, is accounted heresie to most men, and much adoe there is before we will imbrace it: And secondly, in that persecution for Religion, would render us altogether incapable of ever purging and reforming our selves from such erronious doctrines and superstitions, as are amongst us for the present.[56]

What makes freedom for diversity of opinion safe is the invincibility of truth: "doe we suspect that errour should vanquish truth? this is so vaine that no man will confesse so much." [57]

In June or July, Walwyn published his third tolerationist plea, *The Compassionate Samaritane*.[58] Like the two earlier pamphlets discussed above (pp. 81 and 82), this too leaves undefined the extent of the toleration Walwyn desired, but the more circumstantial discussion permits a fuller inference. It complains of the *Apologeticall Narration* that instead of giving "such generall reasons for justification of themselves to the world, as would have justified all the Separation," the plea of the Apologetical Narrators "was grounded rather upon a Remonstrance of the nearenesse betweene them and the Presbyterian," together with great emphasis upon their own difference from the sects, thus "confirming . . . the peoples disesteem of the Separatist." [59] Now

---

[52] See especially sig. A4v and p. 48.   [53] See below, p. 88.

[54] *Liberty of Conscience*, p. 17.

[55] *Cf.* p. 49: "God is pleased only to discover the Gospel to us peecemeals, as we become worthy and capable."

[56] *Ibid.*, p. 50.   [57] *Ibid.*, p. 59.   [58] See Haller, *Tracts*, I, 124–25.

[59] Pp. 7–8 (YUL copy); pp. 1–2 in the more familiar second edition, dated January 5, 1645, by Thomason, and reproduced in Haller, *Tracts*, III, 59 ff.

the anonymous author is no Separatist, but he feels bound to come to the help of persecuted people of such manifest innocence, honesty, and harmlessness [60] (in this again *The Compassionate Samaritane* resembles its predecessors).

> Now because little can bee done in their behalfe, unlesse liberty of Conscience be allowed for every man, or sort of men to worship God in that way, and performe Christs Ordinances in that manner as shall appeare to them most agreeable to Gods Word, and no man be punished or discountenanced by authority for his opinion, unlesse it bee dangerous to the State: I have endeavoured in this discourse to make appeare by the best reason I have, that every man ought to have liberty of Conscience of what opinion soever, with the caution above named.[61]

The references to "Christs Ordinances" and "Gods Word" may seem to limit the toleration to various forms of Christianity, and it is possible that Walwyn thought Roman Catholicism "dangerous to the State," but these limitations seem improbable, both because of his assertion that in order to secure liberty of conscience for the sects it was necessary to adopt a larger liberty, and because of the declaration which follows immediately: "It is the principall interest of the Common wealth, That authority should have [equall] [62] respect, and afford protection to all peaceable good men alike, notwithstanding their difference of opinion, That all men may bee encouraged to be alike serviceable thereunto." [63]

This emphasis on the secular nature of the state makes it probable that Walwyn meant his toleration to be as comprehensive as could be secured. It also helps to explain the most startling aspect of *The Compassionate Samaritane's* theory, its Erastianism. When Roger Williams emphasizes the secular nature of the state, he does so in virtue of the principle of segregation, and primarily in order to preserve the church from secular interference. *The Compassionate Samaritane* does not employ the principle of segregation, and although it gives what by then had become the staple arguments from scrupled conscience [64] it is not motivated primarily by religious concerns. Walwyn's primary interest lay in a just and peaceful community, and this secular orientation, combined with a strong anticlerical bias—one-third of his tract is

---

[60] *Ibid.*, pp. 8–10; pp. 3–4 in 2 ed.

[61] *Ibid.*, pp. 10–11; p. 5 in 2 ed.   [62] Word supplied from 2 ed.

[63] *Compassionate Samaritane*, p. 11; p. 6 in 2 ed.

[64] The judgment cannot be determined by the will but follows reason (pp. 11–12; pp. 6–7 in 2 ed.); human fallibility makes it possible that a compulsive church will enforce error (pp. 15–16; pp. 10–11 in 2 ed.); whatsoever is not of faith is sin (p. 42; p. 43 in 2 ed.); etc.

taken up by a scathing attack on ambitious, greedy, tyrannizing divines, Presbyterian as well as Episcopal—made him willing to put the
church under the governance of the state, apparently in the belief that
there was more chance that Parliament would be tolerant than that
ordained ministers would:

> [The divines'] first interest is to preserve amongst the people the dis-
> tinction concerning government of Ecclesiasticall and Civell, though
> upon consideration it will be found that two Governments in one
> Common wealth hath ever beene, and will ever prove inconsistant with
> the peoples safety: The end of government being to promote vertue,
> restraine vice, and to maintaine to each particular his owne, one sort
> of government which we call the Civell, either is sufficient, or by the
> wisedome of the Parliament may be made sufficient for these ends.[65]

The future Leveller would later find a different solution for the problem of the church.

Of special interest to students of Milton is Walwyn's attack on the
Licensing Order of 1643. He points out in the prefatory address to the
House of Commons that "as it is mine & every mans duty to furnish
You with what wee conceive will advance the common good . . . so
likewise it is Your duty to heare and put in execution whatsoever to
Your owne judgments shall appeare conducing to those good ends and
purposes." [66] He absolves the House of ill intentions in passing the
Licensing Order, which he attributes to the influence of the Westminster Assembly: "It is [67] not to be supposed that You who have so
long spent Your time in recovering the common liberties of *England*,
should in conclusion turne the common into particular; Let the in-
sinuations and suggestions of some in the Synod be what they will, I
make no question but You see both through and beyond them." [68] The
Order itself he attacks vigorously:

> In the beginning of Your Session, when our Divines (as they would
> have us call them) wrote freely against the Bishops, and the Bishops
> made complaint to You for redresse; some of You made answer that
> there was no remedy, for as much as the Presse was to be open and free
> for all in time of Parliament, I shall make bold as a Common of
> *England*, to lay claime to that priviledge, being assured that I write
> nothing scandalous or dangerous to the State (which is justly and upon
> good grounds prohebited by Your Ordinance to that effect) only I
> humbly desire You to consider whether more was not gained by that
> Ordinance than You intended, and that though it was purposed by You
> to restraine the venting and dispersings of the Kings writings and his
> Agents, yet it hath by reason of the qualifications of the Licensers

[65] *Compassionate Samaritane*, p. 24; pp. 20–21 in 2 ed.
[66] *Ibid.*, p. 3; sig. A3 in 2 ed.   [67] 1 ed.: "Is it"; corrected in 2 ed.
[68] *Ibid.*, p. 4; sigs. A3v–A4 in 2 ed.

wrought [69] a wrong way, and stopt the mouthes of good men, who must either not write at all, or no more then is sutable to the judgements and interests of the Licensers.[70]

To suppress this "just *Liberty* in time of *Parliament*" is the greatest argument that the motives of the divines are treacherous.[71] They cannot fear for the truth:

> Truth was not used to feare colours,[72] or to seeke shifts or stratagems for its advancement! I should rather thinke that they who are assured of her should desire that all mens mouthes should be open, that so errour may discover its foulnesse, and truth become more glorious by a victorious conquest after a fight in open field: they shun the battell that doubt their strength.[73]

The tract ends by recommending that parliament stop all repressive proceedings toward the Separation, ensure "that as well particular or private Congregations, as publike, may have publike protection," and provide that "the Presse may bee free for any man, that writes nothing scandalous or dangerous to the State." [74]

The close similarity of all this to the *Areopagitica's* exordium, proposition, and peroration, together with the particular parallels indicated below, leave no doubt that Milton had read and been influenced by *The Compassionate Samaritane*.[75] Most interestingly, the revised edition of the *Samaritane* (January 5, 1645) appears in turn to have been influenced by *Areopagitica*.[76]

In September, Robinson published *John the Baptist, Forerunner of Christ Jesus*.[77] The position is approximately that of *Liberty of Conscience* (the arguments are even more miscellaneous than in that tract), supplemented by a protest against tithes,[78] but the relativistic attitude

[69] Spelt "wrote"; corrected in 2 ed.

[70] *Compassionate Samaritane*, pp. 4–5; sig. A4 in 2 ed.

[71] *Ibid.*, p. 5; sigs. A4v–A5 in 2 ed.   [72] "Colours" dropped in 2 ed.

[73] *Compassionate Samaritane*, pp. 55–56; p. 60 in 2 ed.

[74] *Ibid.*, pp. 70–71; pp. 78–79 in 2 ed.

[75] See below, p. 490, n. 15; p. 542, n. 192; p. 543, n. 197; p. 556, n. 247; p. 563, nn. 270, 277; and pp. 566–67, n. 294.

Masson's assertion (III, 275) that the *Areopagitica* was the first plea for unlicensed printing can no longer be accepted, but it is not being suggested here that Milton's *interest* in the subject was due to the influence of Williams, Robinson, and Walwyn: it had already been displayed in *Bucer* (see below, pp. 140–41), where it grew naturally out of his own experiences.

[76] See below, p. 551, n. 228.

[77] September 23, 1644; E9(13). For the attribution, see Haller, *Tracts*, I, 67–68.

[78] Apparently an afterthought; the two quarto signatures containing the attack on tithes were inserted between the pages numbered 12 and 13 after the original pagination was complete.

towards religion emerges more clearly. Developing the theme that in attempting to enforce religious uniformity the Presbyterians are doing exactly what they so violently denounced the bishops for doing, Robinson asks: "Tell me, Good Reader, what difference dost thou make betwixt being persecuted by an Episcopall or Presbyteriall Clergie? whether hadst thou rather enjoy the Liberty of Conscience in some measure, under a Popish French King, than be persecuted by any Protestant government or discipline whatsoever? nay, deale freely with me, 'tis no time to mince it or dissemble: hadst thou not rather the Great Turke should rule over thee than either?" [79]

Robinson continues to be evasive about whether Roman Catholics ought to be tolerated, but in his *Answer to Prynne,* which Thomason received on November 1, he parenthetically remarks that "the Papists till they renounce some certaine tenets, can be true" to no settlement, thus implying that if Roman Catholicism ceases to be a danger to the state it should be given religious toleration.[80]

In January, 1645, John Lilburne joined the debate with *A Copie of A Letter . . . to Mr. William Prinne Esq.* Some years later, with a truly remarkable impudence, he claimed that he had written Prynne "a sharp Epistle, now in print, dated 7 Jan. 1644 . . . which was the first avowed publick Cannon I know of in England, discharged against the then insulting Presbyter, for the liberty of the consciences of my present bloudy and malicious persecutors . . . they themselves . . . durst then do nothing manlike for themselves; but sate in silence like a company of sneaks without souls or hearts." [81] Perhaps he thought that by reverting to the old style of dating (he had originally signed the *Copie of a Letter* "London, this 7. Jan. 1645.") he could confuse his readers into imagining that the many "avowed publick Cannons" that had in fact preceded his own had really followed it; and, shrewd propagandist that he was, he was doubtless right.

There is nothing novel about Lilburne's argument: Christ has given to his church a perfect and unchangeable model of government, over which the civil magistrate has no jurisdiction and with which he is not to interfere. This government is wholly spiritual, and uses no worldly power. To persecute for conscience' sake is of the devil.[82] What is new is the attitude toward constitutional powers. Prynne had argued that

[79] E9(13), sig. A4.

[80] *An Answer to Mr. William Prynn's Twelve Questions,* E15(5), p. 19. For a further discussion of this pamphlet, see below, pp. 121 and 142.

[81] *The Legall Fundamentall Liberties of the People of England* (1649; UCL), p. 24.

[82] *Letter to Prinne* (January 15, 1645), pp. 3–4; reproduced in Haller, *Tracts,* III, 179 ff.

historically the magistrate has always regulated the religion of his subjects. Lilburne's retort is curt: "I grant you they have; but I demaund of you, by what Right, or by what Authority out of the Word of God they have so done?" [83] This attitude marks the emergence of a new force in the Puritan Revolution. Here the dismissal of precedent, of the custom of the constitution, in order to reconstitute according to abstract right, has a religious context; when it has expanded into a political context Levellerism will have arrived.

Lilburne is not very clear about how comprehensive toleration ought to be, since he does not mention Roman Catholicism, always the most searching test for the Puritan tolerationist. He is willing to accept a noncompulsive state church with what, in the absence of specified limits, must be thought a general toleration:

> *I am not against the Parliaments setting up a State-Government for such a Church as they shall thinke fit, to make the generality of the Land members of, for I for my part leave them to themselves, to doe what they shall thinke good, so that they leave my Conscience free to the Law and Will of My Lord and King.*[84]

Attacks on the Licensing Order had by this time become pretty frequent, but Lilburne's has a special interest for us because it may have been influenced by the *Areopagitica*. Some things in the quotation that follows may remind us of Williams, Robinson, or Walwyn as much as of Milton, but Lilburne's genealogy of the Licensing Order, tracing it backward from Parliament through the Assembly and the bishops to the *imprimatur* of the Inquisition, strongly suggests the influence of the *Areopagitica*:

> You, and the *Blacke-Coates* in the Synod . . . have not dealt fairly with your Antagonists in stopping the Presse against us, while things are in debate, yea robbing us of our Liberty (as we are Subjects) in time of freedome, when the *Parliament* is sitting, who are sufficiently able to punish that man (whatsoever he be) that shall abuse his penne. . . . And truly it argues no manhood nor valour in you nor the *Blacke-Coates*, by force to throw us downe and ty our hands, & then to fall upon us to beat and buffet us, for if you had not beene men that had been affraid of your cause, you would have been willing to have fought and contended with us upon even ground and equall termes, namely that the Presse might be as open for us as for you, and as it was at the beginning of this *Parliament*, which I conceive the *Parliament* did of purpose, that so the freeborne *English* Subjects might enjoy their Liberty and Priviledge, which the Bishops had learned of the *Spanish Inquisition* to rob them of, by locking it up under the Key of an *Imprimatur*, in whose tyrannicall steps the Synod treades.[85]

[83] *Ibid.*, p. 4.   [84] *Ibid.*, p. 7.   [85] *Ibid.*, pp. 2–3.

Three weeks later Walwyn published a pamphlet (also directed against Prynne, and containing a rounder and more downright personal attack against him than was yet usual) which clearly reflects Lilburne's influence. Most important, the Erastianism of *The Compassionate Samaritane* is gone, replaced by an elaboration of Lilburne's attitude into what was to become a permanent Leveller dogma:

> *That the people of a Nation in chusing of a Parliament cannot confer more then that power which was justly in themselves. . . . But all things concerning the worship and service of God, are* [86] *of that nature; that a man cannot without wilfull sin, either binde himselfe to doe any thing therein contrary to his understanding and conscience: nor to forbeare to doe that which his understanding and conscience bindes him to performe: therefore no man can refer matters of Religion to any others regulation.* [87]

More succinctly "what the people cannot entrust that they [*i.e.*, Parliament] cannot have." [88] Another idea apparently adopted from Lilburne is a noncompulsive state church with a toleration of unspecified limits.

When Richard Overton entered the controversy in April the emergent Leveller party became more explicit about the extent of the toleration it would advocate. *The Araignement of Mr. Persecution* is less an argument than a tangle of disparate arguments, both secular and sectarian, held together by satire and passion; Mr. Sovereignty-of-Christ indicts the prisoner as a traitor to the "Prerogative Royall" of Christ, who has "constituted himselfe sole *Head* and *King* for ever over the *Consciences* of men," [89] Mr. Power-of-Parliaments on the ground "that *Persecution* for Conscience is Inconsistant with the *Soveraignty* of *Kingdomes*," [90] and Mr. Public-Good because "that which is destructive to the publique good is *Treasonable,* and not to be suffered in a *Common-wealth,* because it striketh at the *Root* and *Foundation* of *Magistracy,* whose proper end is, that all may lead a *Quiet* and *Peaceable* life under the publique *Protection*." [91] But about the conclusion there is no ambiguity. The basis of Roman Catholic-Protestant fear of each other is the widespread but quite unnecessary assumption of mutual enmity: "If the Papist knew the Protestant, the Protestant the papist to love [one] another: & would not molest or in the least injure one another for their *Conscience,* but live peaceably & quietly one by

---

[86] Text: "and."

[87] *A Helpe to the Right Understanding of a Discourse Concerning Independency. Lately Published by William Pryn* (February 6, 1645), E259(2), p. 4.

[88] *Ibid.,* p. 7.

[89] April 8, 1645, p. 4; reproduced in Haller, *Tracts,* III, 203 ff.

[90] *Ibid.*   [91] *Ibid.,* p. 5.

another; bearing one with another, and so of all Religions: What man would lift up his hand against his Neighbour?"[92] He is equally explicit concerning the Jews. Persecution deprives them of the protection promised them by Christ; "this Incendiary hath caused our Kings, and our Rulers, our Bishops and our preists not to suffer a Jew by authority to live amongst them; how then can we complaine of the vengeance that is at this time upon us & our children, that have been so cruel, so hatefull, so bloody minded to them and their children?"[93] His conclusion is that "all by compulsion are to be forced to the Civill peace and publike unity, and all are to be defended and preserved under the publike freedome, one as well as an other; therefore to this end the Majestrate ought to bind all Religions, that no Religion have power over other, that all in the Generall have Toleration, and none in particular be offensive."[94] From this nothing is to be feared in terms of behavior: "Such publike Transgressions that are uncivill, unnaturall, and unbecoming humaine society, as *open prophanenesse* and *loosenesse* fall under the restraint, and correction of the Magestrate, whose power is over the things of Nature, those being offences of that kind."[95]

Overton too attacks the Licensing Order, and here, like Lilburne, he seems to reflect the influence of the *Areopagitica,* using its genealogy of licensing as his primary weapon (the adoption of this genealogy, indeed, is the only good evidence I have been able to find that the *Areopagitica* had an immediate impact upon the toleration controversy).[96] Officers bearing a warrant for the apprehension of Mr. Persecution,

> making strict search and inquiry after him from Religion to Religion, found him at length amongst the Papists, under the name of Mr. *Spanish-Inquisition;* but the subtile Fox no sooner perceived their *Authority,* but shrunke out of his Roman Papall Robe, and presently turned *Protestant,* clad with an English Episcopall habit, under the name of Mr. *High-Commission,* but [they] . . . being acquainted with his trikes, made after him, whereat he cast of his *Laune sleeves, Hoode, Typpit,* &c. and forthwith, least all Trades should faile, became a zealous *Covenanter,* in the godly shape of a *Presbyter,* changing his name into *Classicall Presbytrie* . . . and then Scholer like . . . jumpt out of *Scotland* into *England,* and turn'd a reverend *Synodian.* . . . And a thousand other trickes, that I cannot reckon, he had; but one above all the rest I must not forget, which was the *master peece* of

[92] *Ibid.,* p. 11.　　[93] *Ibid.,* p. 23.　　[94] *Ibid.,* p. 30.　　[95] *Ibid.,* pp. 32–33.

[96] Perhaps the first adoption of Milton's genealogy of licensing was in December, 1644, by Hezekiah Woodward, so often associated with Milton in these years (see below, pp. 144 and 210–11); the quotation is given below, p. 506, n. 72. For *Areopagitica's* influence upon another contemporary writer (not manifested until 1649), see below, p. 209, n. 7.

all the rest; for to bloke up all passages, stop all mouthes, and fortifie
himselfe round, he turn'd *reverend Imprimatur:* and here the *pursuers*
were at a stand, for all was as fast as the *Divel* and the *Presbyters* could
make it, they sought to Authority to open the *Presse,* and still the *Presbyters* (as their custome is) were in the way, that nothing could be
done.[97]

Overton also adopted Milton's method of ridiculing the formula of
the *imprimatur* (here blended with some reminiscences of the Martin-
Marprelate tracts). The inner cover [98] is a parody of the kind of Parliamentary order, then increasingly common, which began by thanking
the author for his serviceable pains, then desired him to print and
publish, and finally prohibited the printing or publishing by any except
the author's appointee, and which was followed by the author's designation of the publisher. The title page ends with this legend:

> This is Licenced, and printed according to Holy Order, but not Entered
> into the Stationers Monopole. *Angliae Martinis disce favere tuis.*
> Europe. Printed by Martin Claw-Clergie, Printer to the *Reverend
> Assembly of Divines,* and are to be sould at his Shop in *Toleration
> Street,* at the *Signe* of the *Subjects Liberty,* right opposite to *Perse-
> cuting Court.*

5. PRESBYTERIANS: DIVERGENT RATIONALES OF
COMPULSIVE UNIFORMITY

We have seen the Apologists, after revealing some glimpse of ideas
bearing more far-reaching implications, work for an accommodation
with the anticipated Presbyterian settlement, at first through the Westminster Assembly and Parliament, then through Parliament and the
public. We have seen growing up beyond them, and in large measure
based upon ideas which the Apologists shared, a demand by Separatists
and secularists for toleration, variously defined. We shall see the Apologists coming to join in this demand, but first we must go back some
months to see how the Presbyterians contested these several demands,
and how the clash both clarified and extended the principles involved.
   At once we are struck, even more forcefully than in the argument
over supremacy in the state, with the repetitiveness of history (or perhaps it would be better to say the continuity of the substance of the
arguments despite the reversal of roles). In the sixteenth century the
Puritans (led by Presbyterians) had attacked Episcopacy as the creature of man in the temple of the Lord, a usurpation which must be
cast out to make room for God's own prescribed form of church government. The Episcopalian reply had been that part of the law of God was

[97] *Araignement,* pp. 1–2.   [98] Thus in E276(23). In Haller it is sig. A4.

the law of nature, and hence what was done by it was done according to God's will; in man the law of nature expressed itself as right reason; God had left some things to be determined by this right reason, among them the form of church government; in such things the community had the right to establish what it saw fit, and every member of the community was bound to obey. Not so, replied the Puritans; in matters of religion that which is neither prescribed nor prohibited is left to the conscience of the individual: that is the meaning of Christian liberty. Caught by this crossfire, some Episcopalians (particularly the Laudians) took up new ground: Episcopacy was, after all, *jure divino,*[1a] and if it was unable to furnish Biblical prescript, it had scriptural and apostolical example to argue from.

Now it was the turn of the Presbyterians. As they proceeded to establish their own compulsive uniformity, they were met by their own former challenge to the bishops: where was the Biblical prescript for their form of church government? The sequence will be different, but otherwise almost nothing of what has just been said of the Episcopalian response to the Puritan challenge need be changed to apply to the Presbyterian response to the challenge from farther left in Puritanism.

John Brinsley provides the most convenient example of the early stages of the Presbyterian adaptation to their changed circumstances.[1]

[1a] The implications of this change of ground—indeed, even the fact of the change—continue to be rather widely disregarded. *E.g.*, the most recent large-scale history of the period is offended that what it takes to be a moderate and innocuous statement of the case for Episcopacy, written by a bishop who had been rather indulgent to the Puritans in his diocese, should have been answered with unnecessary and unmannerly vehemence; it shows no awareness that the pamphlet in question, so far from being innocuous, marked out more clearly than any publication preceding it that reversal of the rationale of English Episcopacy which attempted to appropriate for itself the main weapon of Puritanism. See C. V. Wedgwood, *The King's War 1641–1647* (London: Collins, 1958), p. 40: "The unfortunate Joseph Hall, in spite of his mildness to the oppressed Puritan clergy, was also the object of pamphlet controversy. He had, at the King's command, published a defence of Episcopacy, a well-mannered and temperate book which had been savaged a few months previously by a pack of Puritan clergy under the collective pseudonym of Smectymnuus. The paper warfare round and about the views of Smectymnuus is remembered today because John Milton was drawn into it. What chiefly mattered, in this December of 1641, was that it had caused the moderation of bishop Hall and his good offices towards the Puritan clergy to be quite forgotten." Incidentally, it may be doubted that Miss Wedgwood has identified the leader of the savage "pack" as the same Stephen Marshall whom she elsewhere (pp. 70–71) describes as "No harsh fanatic, but a warm and lively preacher."

[1] His own circumstances at Yarmouth may well have stimulated his concern; something of their nature in 1642–1643 may be inferred from the account in *DNB* of the arrangement reached in 1650: "[Brinsley] occupied the chancel of the church with the presbyterians, while [William] Bridge with the congrega-

In September, 1642, he published *The Healing of Israels Breaches.* Breaches in the church were made by two kinds of men, strangers (Roman Catholics) and Israelites (Protestants). The divisive Israelites, in turn, were also of two kinds, those who followed error (these might be schismatics and sectaries like Brownists and Anabaptists, or they might be superstitious innovators who burden the conscience with a yoke of carnal ordinances) and those who followed truth, but did so either without wisdom or without love (the non-separating Congregationalists). We must forcibly subdue the "strangers," but the seduced Israelites ought to be "reduced" in "as gentle and tender a way as possibly may be." [2] The magistrate (to whom Brinsley assigns an apparently unlimited power in church affairs) is first to *"take stumbling blockes out of the way"* [3]—those remnants of idolatry and superstition which still serve to cause brethren to take offence and stray. "This being done, then . . . *Let them set up a Standard.* . . . Set up Christ, by the preaching of Christ." [4] Secure in the distinction between the matters involved in these two operations, and confident of the direction in which each tended, Brinsley emphasizes the need for both to be permanently maintained in order to prevent "relapses":

> 1. Having cleared the Churches way by taking the *stumbling-blocks* out of it, *Let them keep it cleare,* and that by vindicating, and asserting (as much as may bee) that which wee call *Christian libertie,* the *libertie of Conscience in the use of things indifferent;* providing that that may not bee pressed and burdened with unnecessary burdens. . . .
> 2. (In the second place) having set up a *standard* for the people, let them *make it a Standard;* by their authority enjoyning, and requiring all in the publicke exercise of Religion to observe the same *rule* and *order,* the same *forme of Publicke worship,* regulated (as neere as may bee) by the lawes of Christ in his Word, and so made conformable to that patterne, that *standard.*[5]

But by June of 1643, when Brinsley published his next discussion of the subject, the situation had greatly altered. We may get a quick view of the tactical situation on the Presbyterian side from *Intelligence from the Armie . . . June 5.* This pleads for unity among "the pretenders to Reformation" lest all be lost in an immediate Royalist victory, but the unity it seeks is of "the more sober part (for as I have forgotten the *Bishops,* so I shall scarce trouble my self with thoughts of the *rigid*

tionalists was in possession of the north aisle, and the south aisle, with the nave, was left to the regular minister. Service in all these was performed simultaneously, the corporation having divided the building for the purpose on the death of the king [actually in 1650], at an expense of 900 *l.*

[2] September 30; E119(14), p. 88.
[3] *Ibid.,* p. 89.　　[4] *Ibid.,* pp. 90–91.　　[5] *Ibid.,* pp. 105–106.

Separatists)." [6] (Since it is a Presbyterian pamphlet, the method it recommends for achieving unity is, of course, that the Independents "for a time" go along with the Presbyterians.) [7] In *Church Reformation Tenderly Handled* Brinsley too has in effect "forgotten the *Bishops*"; the struggle against them was now entrusted wholly to the sword. When theological disputation had still been a significant part of that struggle, Christian liberty had been a very serviceable weapon; but now, not only was the need for it gone, but it was being turned against the Presbyterians themselves by new opponents. Brinsley accordingly revised his interpretation of Christian liberty.

Like *Intelligence From The Armie*, Brinsley scarce troubles himself with thoughts of bringing the rigid Separatist into agreement on church establishment; rather, he denounces and assails "our adversaries of the Seperation" [8] through most of the book, and clearly anticipates their suppression. With "those our brethren, who doe hold communion with us" [8a]—the non-separating Congregationalists—he would proceed more gently. He will not handle the various points of difference between them publicly, for fear of aggravating them; these differences (which are not of doctrine but only of order, and not fundamentals but "Circumstantiall" [9]) should be settled by "that *Authority* to which a *Church-Reforming* power is committed." [10] When church reformation has in this way been authoritatively determined, men must *"humbly submit to it. I, though it should not be every way according to our own minds."* [11] The first church council, we read in the gospel,[12] put certain restraints upon liberty in respect of "things in themselves of an indifferent nature, and so lawfull for them to doe," but which the council thought necessary to enjoin temporarily, for the sake of peace and unity; and the churches submitted "both *humbly* and *joyfully*." [13]

> Surely even such a submission ought Christians to yeald to the *determinations of lawfull Authority* in things not contrariant, but agreeable to the *Rules* of the word, either to the *particular* and expresse rules and directions therein conteyned, or else to those *generall* Rules of *Decencie, Order, Edification,* the three maine *points* of the Churches *compasse,* according to which she is to *steare* her *course,* in the ordering of all such *Church-affaires,* as are not expresly and distinctly stated and regulated in the word; of which nature no question some will be found.[14]

The lecturer at Yarmouth made his shift quickly; in Westminster the Presbyterians showed more embarrassment and took longer. Just

[6] E105(16), p. 2. [7] *Ibid.*, p. 3. [8] June 19; E55(7), p. 18.
[8a] *Ibid.*, p. 34. [9] *Ibid.*, p. 46. [10] *Ibid.*, pp. 34–35. [11] *Ibid.*, p. 69.
[12] Acts 15. [13] E55(7), pp. 69–70. [14] *Ibid.*, p. 70.

before the Assembly convened, Thomas Carter, one of its members, preached before the House of Commons a sermon whose general purpose was exhortation to prayer. Into it he inserted a remarkably oblique defense of the church's right to determine in matters of indifferency. He does not repudiate the arguments which, in common with other Puritans, the Presbyterians had used against Episcopacy.

> Now indeed a thing indifferent both in its nature and use, though not intrinsecally evill; yet because it lookes like a sinne, and carries the face of evill, it ought to be declined, *Abstaine from all appearance of evill*. It is also true, that things in their nature indifferent, yet carrying an appearance of evill, in respect of scandall, should not by authority be imposed, and so be made necessary in their use.[15]

But things which appear evil to some may not be so. They must be judged in their true nature, not by appearances. The criterion is the Word of God; but there are subordinate criteria which may be used when the Word is silent: *"The Lawes and legall Commandements of authority"*; *"The example of Gods people and custome of the Church"*; and "A third rule is each mans *conscience*," but great care is needed to distinguish private fancies from the voice of conscience, and even the true voice of conscience may easily err.[16]

The inferences are not clearly drawn, but the tendency would have been discernible to the audience: while the church ought not to impose evil things, or things which looked evil, under the guise of indifferency, she could impose things truly indifferent despite some people's fancy that they were evil or looked evil; and although in the absence of explicit scriptural instructions the private conscience was a guide, it was an unreliable one and inferior to the guidance of the state, the Old Testament, and select portions of the church's experience.

The summer of 1643, as we have already observed, was a period of co-operation between the Presbyterians and the Congregationalists of the Assembly, and three months passed before another Presbyterian of the Assembly repeated Carter's point (and then with equal caution). On September 27 Anthony Burgess preached to the House of Commons on *The Difficulty of, and the Encouragements to a Reformation.* Like Carter, he reasserted the common Puritan argument against Episcopacy: Scripture is the only rule in matters of religion, and the other "rules" set up by men, such as antiquity, custom, the fathers, etc., are misleading.[17] But, like Carter in this too, he qualified the doctrine to show that "Though it be a rule, yet it does not exclude other minis-

---

[15] *Prayers Prevalencie For Israels Safety*, preached June 28, 1643, received by Thomason July 12; E60(2), p. 8.   [16] *Ibid.*, pp. 8–9.
[17] Thomason received his copy November 3; E71(2), pp. 11–14.

teriall helpes"; [18] and here his argument might have come straight out of Hooker (indeed, it probably did):

> When we say its a rule, it must be extended to that end for which it is a rule; for as the Scripture is not a rule to Physicians or Mathematicians in their proper arts, so neither doth it particularly tend to this, or that individuall action; for all essentials it is a rule, and a generall rule for circumstantials. Nor doth this detract from the perfection of the Scripture, that it doth not command every circumstance, because then a thing is imperfect, when it wants some perfection that is due to it: It is not an imperfection in the body, that its not every where, because this is not requisite to the body, so neither is it to be expected from the Scripture, that all circumstantials must be by name commanded.[19]

The embarrassed and hesitant maneuvers of the English Presbyterians, as they sought to resist the Congregationalist claim to Christian liberty without repudiating their own employment of the doctrine against the bishops, seem to have overtried the patience of the Scottish Commissioners. In what must have been a concerted effort—one which involved them all and which they maintained for four months before their English co-religionists joined them—the Scots hardened the Presbyterian tone.

Henderson took the lead. In the same sermon in which we have already seen him shut the Assembly's door to an accommodation with the non-separating Congregationalists,[20] the Moderator of the Kirk of Scotland summoned the English Parliament to do its duty in the church:

> Civill powers have great authoritie, not onely in things civill, but in matters of Religion; and they sin against God, if they use not the authority which God hath put in their hands, for the good of Religion. . . . The faithfull custody and preservation of Religion, is a part of their office: for they are not onely keepers of the second, but of the first Table of the Law. To them appertaineth the vindication and defence of Religion, against contempt, corruption, and abuses. Religion also expecteth from them the Civill sanction, that the worship of God, and the wholsome constitutions of the Church about Religion, be confirmed and setled by their Laws. Coaction also is theirs, for they by their power are to constrain their Subjects to the duties of Religion, and to coerce and stop them that they do nothing to the contrary.[21]

Having thus utterly rejected any notion of separation of church and state, and having emphasized the magistrates' coercive and punitive role in religion (governed, of course, by God's commandment [22]), Henderson went on to reject any claim to individual liberty in things in-

---

[18] *Ibid.*, p. 8.　　[19] *Ibid.*　　[20] See above, pp. 71–72.
[21] *Sermon* (December 27, 1643), E81(24), pp. 20–21.　　[22] *Ibid.*, p. 22.

different. "The extent of this Reformation is, *whatsoever God hath commanded:* for what God hath commanded must be done; what he hath forbidden must not be done, but abolished; and what is in the nature thereof indifferent must be regulated according to the Commandment of God, which is, no lesse plain and peremptory in our practise of things indifferent, then in any other matters." [23] It is possible, but not very likely, that Henderson saw no difficulty about the assertion that the commandment of God was as "plain and peremptory" in matters of indifferency as in matters of prescription or prohibition; it seems more probable that in this sermon he was concerned to mark out the Scottish position, leaving it to his fellow-countrymen to argue the particulars later; and we must wait for Steuart and Gillespie to explain this point. Meanwhile, Henderson made the application unmistakable. Rabbi Gamaliel was a special favorite of the Independents, but, Henderson told the House, "No Man must be of *Gamaliels* temper; . . . he laid this ground, that the work was either of God or of man; and what was of man would come to nought, and what was of God could not be overthrowne: . . . He would have us . . . do nothing for the advancement of a good cause, but leave it to the providence of God." [24]

When Henderson insisted on the integration of church and state and emphasized the magistrates' powers in religion, it was the Scottish theocracy he had in mind, not the predominantly Erastian English tradition. Some suggestion that Presbyterians subjected the church of God to the inventions of men was made in the *Apologeticall Narration,* of which Henderson's sermon may be called the precipitating cause; and the Scots hurried to make clear that, however wavering the English Presbyterians had lately become on this point, Scottish Presbyterianism stood on the full *jure divino* doctrine. *Reformation of Church-Government in Scotland, Cleered from some mistakes and Prejudices, by the Commissioners of the Generall Assembly of the Church of Scotland, now at London* (which reached Thomason on January 24, 1644) does not name the *Apologeticall Narration,* but is clearly an answer to it. "Nothing," it says of the reformers of the Scottish Kirk, "was farrer from their thoughts & intentions, then to frame in their own forge a Lesbian rule answerable to any particular form of civill polity or complyable with state ends." [25] On the contrary, the Scottish reformers had demonstrated that "the true policy of the Church" is "in it self unalterable, because divine." [26]

The sermon preached to the House of Commons on January 31 by Samuel Rutherford differs from those of his fellow commissioners during this period in being directed more against Episcopacy than against

[23] *Ibid.*   [24] *Ibid.,* p. 35.   [25] E30(5), p. 10.   [26] *Ibid.*

Independency, and is therefore less to our present purpose than the others. He does, however, remind Parliament of its function in the church: "The Lord hath intrusted Christian rulers with the most precious thing he hath on earth, he hath given his bride and spouse to their tutory and faith." [27]

When Robert Baillie's turn came, on February 28, he wasted little of his precious opportunity on the enemies to the right. He attacked popery and Episcopacy of course, but they were remote enemies now, while his letters of this time are full of a growing exasperation with the Congregationalists of the Westminster Assembly. The long epistle in the printed version of his sermon is devoted almost entirely to a complaint about "these extraordinary and unexpected delays of setting up the Government of God in his House," [28] while open vice on the one hand, and deadly heresy and schism on the other, flourish and spread. No other Protestant church has taken so long about the work of reformation; none of them would have achieved reformation at all if they "had taken our present course," if they "had suspended over all their Kingdoms the exercise of any Reformation, till every *puntillo* thereof had been Scholastically debated, in the face of an Assembly; till every Dissenter, over and over, had made to the full, against every part of every Proposition, all the contradiction, his wit, his learning, his eloquence, was able to furnish him." [29]

The sermon itself emphasizes again and again that the motives of those who oppose the building of Zion (*i.e.*, the establishment of Presbyterianism of the Scottish type) are ultimately irrelevant; not only royalists and open malignants, "but also all they, who . . . remaining among us in person, by their means or counsels do oppose the building of the Temple . . . are in the actuall service of Satan, against God." "Yea, for a time, the very regenerate, and these who otherwise walk with God, by the violence or subtilty of a tentation, may be driven to a very evil way." [30] So much, presumably, for those who seek an accommodation for "gathered" but orthodox congregations; as for those who demand more, they prove that this is "an houre of darknesse, wherein all sorts of devils are crept out of their dens, and walk so familiarly with men, that they become bold now to speak of petitioning authority for a toleration, that so this poor kingdome, not onely in these times of

[27] E34(2), p. 4.
[28] *Satan the Leader in Chief to All Who Resist the Reparation of Sion*, E35(17), sig. A2v. For another Scottish sermon before Parliament on this day, not by a Commissioner but possibly of special interest to Milton, see Haller, *Liberty and Reformation*, pp. 122–24.
[29] E35(17), sig. A4.   [30] *Ibid.*, p. 37.

confusion, but for ever should be to them all a place of quiet habitation." [31]

Adam Steuart, who while not a commissioner of the Kirk was one of the Scottish ministers then in London, was the next to be heard, not indeed in a sermon to Parliament but in a pamphlet entitled *Some Observations and Annotations upon the Apologeticall Narration,* which Thomason received on February 29. This supplied the theoretical justification, lacking in the sermons of Henderson and Baillie, for denying individual liberty in things indifferent. It is the Apologists' "subtle way of disputing" to emphasize that what they hold in common with the Presbyterians is directly derived from Scripture, while the Presbyterian positions they reject (which really amount to the synodical structure of authority) are "Additaments" to Scripture.[32] "Ye say . . . *that this challenge of all spirituall power from Christ, had need have a cleer pattent from Christ.*" But the church does not need "any *Pattent* expresly, and formally from Christ: It sufficeth that it have one from Nature, for that sufficeth to binde us all unto obedience. . . . The Author of grace poseth not, but presupposeth the Law of Nature." [33] Not only the synodical structure of the church is of this divine if indirect ordination; so too is the scope of the church's authority, which extends beyond what is expressly prescribed by Scripture and includes among other things the "making of Ecclesiasticall Laws, concerning things indifferent." [34]

Steuart also clarifies the Scottish idea of the magistrate's power in religion. The Apologists are to blame in appealing to Parliament at all, for Parliament

> pretends no *directive powers in matters of religion,* . . . nor any *executive power, that is intrinsecall unto the Church,* . . . but onely an *executive, coercitive, and externall power; which is not in, but about the Church, and for the Church,* whereby it compelleth refractory men to obey the Church. . . . Wherefore if your meaning here be, That the Parliament should judge of the questions in debate, betwixt you and your Brethren; ye go against the Parliaments intention, which esteeming it self, to have no calling of God thereunto, very wisely did convocate an Assembly of Divines to that effect.[35]

The Apologists here and elsewhere hint that they recognize the magistrate's authority more fully than the Presbyterians do, and in fact they seem to "acknowledge the Civill Magistrate to be above them" in "Ecclesiasticall Judgement, that is intrinsecall to the Church": "Here ye symbolize with *Erastus* in many things." [36]

[31] *Ibid.,* p. 26.   [32] E34(23), p. 23.   [33] *Ibid.,* p. 36.   [34] *Ibid.,* p. 42.
[35] *Ibid.,* p. 6.   [36] *Ibid.,* p. 52.

As for the Apologists' distinction between accommodation for them and toleration for heresy, Steuart denies that in the end there can be any real difference. "If it be granted to our Brethren, I cannot see how it can well be denyed to other Sects. If it be said, That other Sects differ more from us, then they do; it is all one, *Magis & minus non mutant Speciem,* in matter of Toleration; for then all must be tolerated, howsoever some more, some lesse: And some of our Brethren grant all the Argument." [37]

George Gillespie, the last of the clerical Commissioners, preached to the House of Commons on March 27. He too took the position that "the Church must observe rules of order and conveniency . . . directed by the . . . light of nature" [38] where Scripture is silent; but he had been made aware (we shall subsequently see how) that this argument sounded very like that once used by the bishops and at that time opposed by the Presbyterians. He therefore drew a distinction between "Common circumstances" and "sacred Ceremonies." [39] The latter are declared to be matters of worship, and Gillespie can reassert the cry against Episcopalian tyranny: "Neither Kings, nor Parliaments, nor Synods, nor any power on earth, may impose or continue the least Ceremony upon the consciences of Gods people, which Christ hath not imposed." [40] But "circumstances of Times, Places, and Persons . . . are none of our holy things: they are only prudentiall accommodations, which are alike common to all humane Societies, both Civill and Ecclesiasticall"; and here the church has the same right to legislate by the "light of nature," and to enforce its laws, as has the state, "providing alwayes, that the generall rules of the Word bee observed." [41]

It was not till late April that any of the English Presbyterians of the Assembly publicly took up the fighting positions prepared for them by their Scottish colleagues. (It may be of some significance that this was done in the City, at the services held on April 23 and 24 by the mayor and aldermen in thanksgiving for certain military successes; in Westminster, at the same time, the House of Commons was listening to a Congregationalist preach a thanksgiving sermon recommending toleration.[42]) Richard Vines was first, and the nature of his sermon may be read in the published title, *The Impostures of Seducing Teachers Discovered.* The chief device by which these seducers trap their victims is to *"promise them liberty,* there is not a more catching bait then *liberty."* [43] Some who mislead are mistaken men, rather than evil: "those

[37] *Ibid.,* pp. 61–62.

[38] *A Sermon Preached before the Honourable House of Commons* (April 16), E43(1), p. 29.   [39] *Ibid.,* p. 29, margin.   [40] *Ibid.,* p. 30.

[41] *Ibid.,* p. 29.   [42] See below, pp. 107–108.   [43] E48(2), p. 30.

that are commonly called Independents" do not intend gospel liberty to be made a cloak for libertinism and heresy; but this must nevertheless be the consequence of taking "the Keyes out of the Churches hand." [44] Thomas Hill, who followed Vines the next day, said it was too early to talk of banishment for the dissenting brethren; more effort should be made to persuade them, and then some thought should be taken of what "indulgence" might be granted them before one came to enforcement. But when he explains the nature of the liberty that may be granted to dissenters, it turns out to be for the strictly private "enjoyment" of very limited variations of opinion in indifferent things; of course "if men will vent their own conceits . . . whereby they puzzle and distract others, it much alters the case, and makes them more *uncapable of connivence*." [45] It is easy to be misled by "the pretence of Christian liberty";[46] but when the apostles left some things indifferent they did so "without the least *violation* of the *Churches Liberty*" [47] —*i.e.*, of the church's right to legislate in things indifferent.

From the Scottish point of view this was not yet satisfactory; the English were still distinguishing between Independents and sectaries. In June Alexander Forbes, another Scottish minister in London, devoted *An Anatomy of Independency* to obliterating the distinction. However loudly the Apologists may emphasize their recognition of the Church of England to be a true church, Forbes repeatedly insisted, their position comes to Separatism in the end.[48] The following month an English Presbyterian minister made as violent an attack upon the Apologists as the Scots could wish; but however satisfactory the notorious *Antapologia* was in itself, it left something more to be desired in that its author, Thomas Edwards, was not a member of the Assembly. At length, on August 13, at a special service of humiliation because of the declining fortunes of Essex's army in Cornwall, the Scots heard what they wanted. Two of the leading members of the Assembly, Hill and Herbert Palmer, preached before a joint audience of Parliament and Assembly what Baillie exultantly described as "two of the most Scottish and free sermons that ever I heard any where." [49] In the morning Hill cited the Solemn League and Covenant to urge his audience to greater efforts against popery and prelacy; [50] in the afternoon Palmer invoked it against heresy and schism: "We have Covenanted with GOD and

[44] *Ibid.*, p. 31.

[45] *The Good Old Way, Gods Way, to Soule-Refreshing Rest* (preached April 24, 1644), E48(4), p. 40.

[46] *Ibid.*, p. 8.   [47] *Ibid.*, p. 42.   [48] June 14, 1644, C59g20(36).

[49] Baillie, II, 220.   [50] *The Season for Englands Selfe-Reflection*, E6(7).

Men, to *extirpate* these *without respect of Persons.*" [51] Not all who err are to be treated alike; those who are truly scrupled in conscience ought to be led to the truth "with all *compassionate tendernesse*"; but those who prove obstinate "must be *saved with Feare.*" [52]

Palmer then adjures his hearers not to "hearken . . . to those, that offer to plead for *Tolerations,*" for this is "*diametrically opposite* and *contradictory*" to both Covenant and Scripture.[53] It can be made to seem plausible, for "the name of *Conscience* hath an *awfull sound* unto a *Conscientious Eare*"; [54] but a glance at what it really involves is enough to show its absurdity. He then gives seven instances of opinions so preposterous and harmful that no one can imagine that Parliament can tolerate them; and it is here that the famous reference to Milton occurs: "If any plead Conscience . . . for divorce for other causes then Christ and His Apostles mention; Of which a *wicked booke* is abroad and *uncensured,* though *deserving to be burnt,* whose *Author* hath been so *impudent* as to *set his Name* to it, and *dedicate it to your selves* . . . will you grant a *Toleration* for all *this?*" [55] Palmer then considers, and dismisses as meaningless, the argument that while toleration cannot be granted in the Second Table, it may in the First: "Are *mens* matters worthy more regard then GODS?" [56] As for the argument that "*no punishment or Restraint can work upon men to convert them. Ans.* It is true, No more can *Exhortation* or *Preaching . . . convert* men, without out Gods *Blessing.* But yet *they must be used, as meanes appointed by God,*" and when God sees fit he blesses these means to their end.[57]

But the denial of toleration was only part of Palmer's object. He was irritated with Parliament, and he showed it. In part his irritation was moral: Parliament made a great show of its special days of humiliation, but how much humility was there in the hearts of Parliament-men? During the service they were to be seen "sitting and leaning at their ease" as if "*they would invite sleepe,*" [58] and their womenfolk came with "*bare breasts,* and *spotted faces,* and *garish apparell* . . . as it were to outface GOD." [59] His fundamental quarrel with Parliament, however, was theological. He knew that the majority would vote to establish Presbyterianism, but he anticipated that they would do so on prudential, rather than *jure divino,* grounds. He could not see how those who say "*That there is no Discipline or Government of the Church to be found in the Word . . .* and yet have Covenanted" could

[51] *The Glasse of Gods Providence Towards His Faithfull Ones;* E6(8), p. 54. Although preached August 13, this was not published until November (it was entered in the *Stationers' Register* November 7).

[52] *Ibid.,* p. 55.   [53] *Ibid.,* pp. 55–56.   [54] *Ibid.,* p. 56.   [55] *Ibid.,* p. 57.
[56] *Ibid.*   [57] *Ibid.,* p. 58.   [58] *Ibid.,* p. 25.   [59] *Ibid.,* p. 24.

be exonerated of a false oath.[60] He insisted "that it concerns us *as well to own what we find in the Word of God, to be from God, as to receive it and set it up.* . . . God will not be satisfied (nor men neither) that the thing be done, or established, if His Authority be overlooked, and mans only pretended for it. . . . Let therefore no man say, *that if we once acknowledge it as from God, then it is unalterable, and we would not have it so.* . . . If God saith, *It shall continue,* it shall continue, that is the *Obligatory* to us, and all posterities." [61]

As a matter of fact, a struggle had begun between the increasingly theocratic Presbyterianism of the Assembly and the fundamentally Erastian Presbyterianism of Parliament. In June Baillie had written, in great indignation, that a Parliamentary Committee was making changes at will in the Assembly's report on ordination, having "scraped out whatever might displease the Independents, or patrons, or Selden and others, who will have no Discipline at all in any Church *Jure Divino,* but settled only upon the free-will and pleasure of the Parliament. . . . We, in private, resolved we would, by all means, stick to our paper; else, this being the first, if we yielded to these most prejudiciall alterations, which the Independents and Civilians underhand had wrought, the Assemblie's reputation was clean overthrowne, and Erastus way would triumph." [62] In July he reported that when the Assembly's committee debated the matter with the Parliamentary Committee, "we were in the midest, over head and ears, of that greatest of our questions, the power of the Parliament in ecclesiastick affairs." [63]

There was, of course, no necessary connection between Erastianism and toleration. When, before the outbreak of the toleration controversy, the royalist propaganda had exploited the general public's fear of religious anarchy, Parliament had replied by declaring "that it is from their purposes to let loose the Reines of golden discipline and Government in Church, to leave private persons in particuler Congregations to take up what forme of divine service they please, for they hold it requisite, that there should be throughout the whole Realme conformity of that order which the Lawes enjoyne, according to the word of God." [64] And now, at the height of the controversy, when for other reasons the *jure divino* Presbyterian divines were making ready to bring to heel the Erastian Presbyterian politicians (particularly the lawyers), Prynne came forward to deny "*that Christ hath peremptorily prescribed one and the selfe same forme of Ecclesiasticall Government . . . to all*

[60] *Ibid.,* p. 51.   [61] *Ibid.,* pp. 52–53.   [62] *Baillie,* II, 198–99.
[63] *Ibid.,* p. 205.
[64] *A Royall Protestation . . . July 23, 1642 . . . Whereunto is Annexed Likewise the Parliaments Protestation* (July 28, 1642), E108(16), sigs. A3v.–A4.

Nations"; [65] but he had no idea of compromising the policy of compulsive uniformity. Christ had authorized each national church to establish the form of government most suitable to its circumstances, and when such a government was established (*"alwayes provided, it be consonant, and no wayes repugnant to the Word of God"*), "all particular Churches Members of that Kingdome & Nation, [are] . . . thereby *actually oblieged in point of Conscience & Christianity, readily to submit thereto,* and no wayes to seeke an exemption from it, under paine of being guiltie of Arrogancie, Scisme, Contumacie, and lyable to such penalties as are due to these offences." [66] Religious toleration is a "detestable" notion,[67] and he urges Parliament "speedily and carefully" to suppress those effects of slack enforcement of uniformity which are already discernible, such as Milton's *"divorce at pleasure."* [68]

But if Erastianism was not necessarily tolerationist, it was usually sensitive to considerations of state, and these might sometimes make it more indulgent than *jure divino* Presbyterianism. The Accommodation Order of September 13 is an example of a relatively indulgent religious temper whose roots are political. We may get an interesting glimpse of this kind of Erastian Presbyterianism in action, as well as of the less accommodating kind, and of *jure divino* Presbyterianism, in three separate news reports of January 23, 1645. *The Parliament Scout* wrote:

> This day the house of Commons debated the businesse of Church Government, as that severall congregations be under one Classis, severall Classis under one Province, and so upward, but the great debate was whether this Church Government is *Jure Divino,* and whether subject to the Civill power; the first was resolved in the negative, the latter in the affirmative, and indeed it were sad if Discipline should once be stretcht to *Jure Divino;* its true, we had dayes in which sometimes this, then that was *Jure Divino,* but now we are grown wiser, and set up as a forme of Church Government that is alterable; yet as neer as can be gathered, according to the practise of the Apostles, and Primative times, which there's no question, but it is above any whatsoever.[69]

Then this Erastian reports a petition, received on the same day, for the suppression of the sects, and comments: "Theres a great difference between universall tolleration, then which, nothing seems more dangerous to a State, and clubbing men out of one opinion into another; for it cannot be instanced, that two in the world, since the world began, have

---

[65] *Twelve Considerable Serious Questions* (September 16, 1644), E257(1), p. 2.
[66] *Ibid.,* p. 2.   [67] *Ibid.,* p. 7.   [68] *Ibid.*   [69] No. 84; E26(12), p. 670.

been of one minde in all things: Why should not then a quiet latitude be allowed, but yet the Magistracy are judge of that." [70]

Mercurius Civicus' Erastianism is more truculent; he approves of Parliament's decision to establish Presbyterianism on its own authority, "for wee see what hold the Bishops tooke of that Statute for their Function to bee by Divine right; . . . but they are (blessed be God) cast out as unsavoury salt we are now going to try another if they prove as burdensome (for men are subject to errors) there is a liberty left to the Parliament to alter." [71] But this denial that there is one right discipline did not lead to sympathy with variations from the discipline chosen by the state. Parliament was deciding whether to permit gathered churches alongside the parochial organization, and *Mercurius Civicus* prints with approval an extract from "the Acts of the Nationall Synod of the Reformed Churches of France" of the previous month instructing the provincial synods *"to take heed that the evill* [of Independent congregations] *take no foot in the Churches of this Kingdom."* [72]

The Scotish Dove was embarrassed. It would fain report the progress made in establishing the Presbyterian church government, but it seems to have been unwilling to report that it was to be on an Erastian basis. Its discussion of this day's Parliamentary business is, in consequence, most confusing. It says nothing of the actual votes of this day, but discusses them obliquely, taking its point of departure from quite another action, the ordinance for the Directory of Worship, passed three weeks earlier.

> The Directory . . . past both Houses . . . and I doubt not will give satisfaction to all, except to such as resolve not to be satisfied but with the fulfilling their owne wills (or rather lusts.) It is my prayer to God, and my request to all that professe to be Disciples of Christ, to forbeare trifles and circumstances, and to cleave to fundamentall and substantiall truths: . . . there is but one way to heaven, why then should not all by-wayes be barred up in a Christian Church and Commonweale? . . . If *Presbytery* government be most agreeable to the Apostles rule and practice (as indeed it is) why seek we after other governments not congruous thereunto? and why doe we mock God? [73]

But whether the Erastian Presbyterians were more sympathetic to the idea of toleration than were the *jure divino* Presbyterians, or as committed as the latter to compulsive uniformity, the fact that they differed in their rationale of Presbyterianism was of great significance in the strategy of the tolerationists. It is now time for us to return to

[70] *Ibid.,* p. 671.   [71] No. 88; E26(13), pp. 803–804.
[72] *Ibid.,* pp. 802–803.   [73] No. 67; E26(16), pp. 526–27.

the further development of the tolerationist argument from the point
at which we left it.

6. "INDEPENDENCY" AND THE REPUDIATION OF ACCOMMODATION IN FAVOR OF TOLERATION

As we have seen, it was among the various sects of the Separation
(and among the secularists) that the idea of toleration was developed;
the non-separating Congregationalists of the Assembly aimed, to begin
with, at quite another end—an accommodation for themselves within
the official Church which they expected Parliament to establish. In
line with this object, they held themselves aloof from the sects and
emphasized their similarity to the Presbyterians. We have now to see
how the Assembly Congregationalists drew nearer to the sects, forming
what was in some respects a coalition with them, and how this coalition
adapted the theory of toleration to the changing situations of 1644–
1645.

A few steps toward the tolerationist position were taken by the Assembly Congregationalists during the heat of the Scottish attack upon
them. Thus, on February 20 and 21, Nye made a demonstration in the
Assembly:

> When it came to his turne in the Assemblie to oppugne the Presbytrie,
> he had, from the 18th of Matthew, drawn in a crooked unformall way,
> which he could never gett in a sillogisme, the inconsistence of a Pres-
> bytrie with a civill State. In this he was cryed doun as impertinent.
> The day following, when he saw the Assemblie full of the prime nobles
> and chiefe members of both Houses, he did fall on that argument
> againe, and very boldlie offered to demonstrate, that our way of draw-
> ing a whole kingdome under one Nationall Assemblie, as formidable,
> yea, pernicious and thrice over pernicious, to civill states and kingdoms.
> All cryed him doune, and some would have had him expelled the
> Assemblie as seditious.[1]

April 23 was a day of thanksgiving for certain Parliamentary victories;
on that day, when Vines was warning the lord mayor and aldermen in
the City against seducers whose bait was liberty,[2] Joseph Caryl, in a
sermon to the House of Commons, became the first of the Assembly
Congregationalists publicly to espouse a policy of toleration:

> Christ himselfe needs no favour from you, but some who are neare to
> him may; He will take it very kindly, if some of your debts to him,
> may be paid over into their bosomes. . . . Yea in their enjoyment of
> their due priviledges, *Christ raignes*. . . . Then a Kingdom is Christs,

[1] Baillie, II, 145–146; the date of the incident is given by Lightfoot, XIII, 169.
[2] See above pp. 101–102.

when all who approve themselves members of Christ may have free
and in-offensive communion with him in all the Ordinances of his
worship.[3]

"All who approve themselves members of Christ"—it is not very explicit, but it clearly looks toward some form of toleration rather than
an institutional accommodation.

But such direct moves were few; frequently repeated, they would
have entailed the necessity of repudiating the policy of accommodation,
and the Accommodation Order of September 13 is evidence that the
Assembly Congregationalists managed to avoid this necessity for a
considerable time. Apparently they decided to close the gap between
themselves and the sects in such a way as would prepare for partial
coalescence should events require it, yet not force a premature relin-
quishment of the advantages which orthodoxy might still hold; at any
rate, that is what happened. New "gathered churches" were constantly
being formed; most of these were somewhat to the left of the Apologists
and cheerfully accepted the name the latter had found so distasteful,
"Independents." Some of these separating Congregationalists now came
to the defense of the *Apologeticall Narration* against the attacks first
of the Scottish and then of the English Presbyterians. While the non-
separating Congregationalists of the Assembly, throughout the spring
and summer, resisted the claims of exclusive Presbyterianism, their
separating co-religionists, in pulpit and press, committed themselves
more and more fully to tolerationism (albeit not an unlimited toleration) ; then, in November, when the Accommodation Order and the
policy it represented had proved abortive, the Assembly Congregationalists came out unequivocally for a toleration which would comprehend
most of the sects, and the coalition known as Independency was, in
effect, acknowledged.

The first Independent defense of the *Apologeticall Narration* was *A
Coole Conference Between the Scottish Commissioners* Cleared Reformation, *and the Holland Ministers* Apologeticall Narration, which
Thomason received on March 4. It was published anonymously, but
Baillie, sending a copy to a friend, said it was by "little Dr. Homes"; [4]
this is consistent with Nathaniel Homes' current position, for although
he subsequently became a Millenarian he had, a few months before
the publication of *A Coole Conference,* collaborated with the famous
Henry Burton in founding St. Matthew's, the Independent congregation
in Friday Street.[5] Homes, after enlarging on the peaceable and modest
character of the *Apologeticall Narration,* which has "not deserved to be

[3] *The Saints Thankfull Acclamation at Christs Resumption of His Great
Power,* E48(1), pp. 48–49.   [4] Baillie, II, 180.   [5] *DNB.*

whipt with a reply," [6] especially one of such bitterness as the Scots put forth, adopts a less defensive tone than the Apologists had used. The Presbyterians, unable to find a warrant in Scripture for imposing synodical authority upon congregations, attempt to justify it in terms of reason, or general consent, or similar notions. But these constitute no basis for church government; and Homes puts forth the *jure divino* position. Then, four separate times, he draws the deadly parallel: "Observe that the same argument that is urged to prove a Presbytery, was formerly urged by the Bishops to prove an Episcopacy." [7]

Two months later, after Adam Steuart had published a reply to this pamphlet, Homes sent forth another and angrier. It heavily attacks the compatriot of the Scottish Commissioners as "this *Incendiary A. S.* . . . who lives out of his Country proudly crowing here over another Nation," [8] and it enlarges the analogy between Presbyterianism and Episcopacy from mere argument to substance, giving it a form which Milton, among others, was to adopt: "A Bishop is but a contracted Presbyterie, and a Presbyterie a diffused Bishop." [9]

The next day Thomason received another pamphlet attacking Steuart, this time for his original reply to the *Apologeticall Narration*. *M. S. To A. S. With a Plea for Libertie of Conscience* came from another new Independent congregation, this one in Coleman Street.[10] The pamphlet's primary tactic is to rouse fears about the theocratic preten-

---

[6] E35(15), p. 2.   [7] *Ibid.*, p. 9, margin; *cf.* pp. 13, 16, 17.

[8] C.C. *The Covenanter Vindicated From Perjurie . . . Injuriously Charged upon Him in a LY-TELL'd by* Adam Steuert (May 2, 1644), E44(20), p. 3.

[9] *Ibid.*, p. 61. *A Coole Conference* (E35[15]), p. 13, had already reported that the "common people" were making this charge "instead of better arguments"; *C. C.* adopts the charge as its own (p. 61), "seeing he puts it so tightly upon us, who before did but say it was *vox populi.*"

[10] Thomason (E45[3]) and Baillie (II, 180) attributed it to John Goodwin, and this attribution has been widely accepted. Haller (*Tracts,* I, 52), pointing out that Goodwin himself later said the pamphlet was written by another pen "ingaged in the same warfare," attributes it to some of his followers. The revised edition, entitled *A Reply of Two of the Brethren to A.S. . . . Formerly called* M.S. *to* A.S. (July 11, 1644; E54[18]), says (sig. A2v.), "two brethren . . . joyned in this Reply." While agreeing with Haller that the tract as a whole is "more loosely argued than is customary" with Goodwin, I think that one section (pp. 61–71) is, both in style and tactics, very much like Goodwin. If this section is by him and the rest by one of his followers, it would account for the contemporary opinion that Goodwin was the author, while at the same time explaining how he could refuse to accept responsibility. Haller argues that Goodwin "did not generally conceal his authorship, and no reason appears for his having done so in this case" since the work expresses views which he elsewhere acknowledged; but there is one important respect in which *M.S. to A.S.* goes beyond limits later accepted by Goodwin (see below, p. 113).

sions reflected by Steuart, and particularly to stimulate a jealous resentment in Parliament. "*A. S.* pag. 5 hath this left-handed expression concerning the Civill Magistrate, *that he arrogates not to himself any Directive power in matters of Religion.*" [11] If what is meant by "Directive power" is the power to command what must be done in religion, then certainly Parliament cannot have it—and neither can the Assembly or any subject; it belongs to God alone. But the Assembly and every well-constituted presbytery may claim the power to advise what ought to be done; so may a member of a private congregation; and Parliament has obviously made such a claim in the very act of constituting and directing the Assembly. Specifically, although Steuart attacks the Apologists for appealing to it in this matter, Parliament unquestionably intends to judge the issue between the opposed groups in the Assembly; otherwise, "to what purpose should they injoyne the Assembly . . . *in case of difference of opinions between them, to present the same, together with the reasons thereof, unto both Houses of Parliament,* if they had no intention to umpire or judge between them?" [12] Steuart's "insinuating unto them a non-vocation from God, to doe any thing with their judgements and understandings *in matters of Religion,* but all things (without exception) with their hand and power, that the Assembly . . . shall propose *or dictate* unto them" [13] is mere theocratic arrogance.

But despite this emphasis on the role of Parliament, *M. S. to A. S.* is not Erastian. The magistrate may advise and aid in religion; he cannot compel. He does not possess that supposed "executive, coercitive, and externall power, which is not in, but about the Church" allotted him by Steuart; no one does. It is only a trick to get Parliament to compel men to obey the Presbytery, and can claim no scriptural warrant other than the example of the kings of Judah. But the Jewish theocracy had no relevance beyond itself; in a Christian country the power of religious compulsion cannot exist; and here *M. S. to A. S.* apparently becomes the first Independent pamphlet avowedly to commit itself to a policy of toleration. "But the Grand Pillar and supporter of this *Coercive power* in Magistrates, is this angry and discontented argument. What? would you have all Religions, sects, and schismes tolerated in Christian Churches? Should Jews, Turks, (and Papists, especially,) be suffered in their Religions? what a confusion must this needs breed both in Church and State?" [14] *M. S.* answers with a distinction: "I. If by *a toleration,* the argument means, either an approbation, or such a connivence which either takes no knowledge of, or however no wayes opposeth such Religions, Sects, or

[11] May 3, 1644, E45(3), p. 32.   [12] *Ibid.,* p. 36.   [13] *Ibid.*   [14] *Ibid.,* p. 53.

Schismes, as are unwarrantable, they are not to be tolerated."[15] Rather, ministers, magistrates, and private Christians have all a duty to preach, argue, and advise against all false ways. If any members of a congregation are obdurate in heresy, the rest of the congregation has an obligation to cast them out. If a whole congregation lapses, and refuses to respond to the admonitions of its neighbor churches, they ought to renounce communion with it. "But Secondly, if by a toleration, the argument means, a non-suppression of such Religions, Sects, and Schismes by a strong hand, as by fineing, imprisoning, disfranchising, banishment, death, or the like, my Answer is, that they ought to be tolerated."[16] This categorical assertion of the principle of toleration is followed by ten reasons against forcible suppression of opinions; the list includes most of the staples, such as spiritual weapons alone being lawful in spiritual war, the nature of magistracy being independent of Christianity, the dangers of compelling men to sin, of fighting against God, of suppressing the growth of new light, and so forth.[17]

M. S. to A. S. is not only the first explicitly tolerationist Independent pamphlet: it is also the most extreme. The toleration it demands is as comprehensive as any demanded by the sectaries and secularists whom we have seen working the policy out; in the months following its publication the Independents, while supporting its commitment to the idea of toleration, retreated significantly from its comprehensiveness. While it was becoming ever clearer that all Congregationalists, whether non-separating or separating, must adopt toleration as a policy, it was not necessary that they should enable the anti-tolerationists to identify them with unlimited toleration. Thus when Prynne, among many others,[18] asked whether Independency were not "a floud-Gate to let in an inundation of all manner of Heresies . . . ? Whether the finall result of it (as Master *Williams* in his late dangerous *Licentious Booke* determines) will not really resolve it selfe into this detestable conclusion, *That every man, whether he be Jew, Turk, Pagan, Papist, Arminian, Anabaptist, &c., ought to be left to his owne free liberty of conscience, without any coertion or restraint, to embrace & publikely to professe what Religion . . . he pleaseth?*"[19] he could be answered by *Certain Briefe Observations and Antiquaeries*, whose authorship was not very different from that of *M. S. to A. S.* five months earlier,[20] that "hee quotes a saying in a Booke called *The bloudy Tenent*, which was

[15] *Ibid.*   [16] *Ibid.*   [17] *Ibid.*, pp. 53–61.
[18] See above, section 5, especially pp. 99–104.
[19] *Twelve Considerable Serious Questions* (September 16, 1644), E257(1), p. 7.
[20] The Thomason *Catalogue* attributes it to John Goodwin; Haller (*Tracts,* I, 53) thinks it came from Goodwin's circle.

written by one as contrary to this [of] the Independents, as he is to the Presbyterians, and they utterly disavow the Booke." [21]

John Goodwin's own most important contribution to the tolerationist controversy was Θεομαχία; or *The Grand Imprudence of Men Running the Hazard of Fighting Against God, in Suppressing any Way, Doctrine, or Practice, Concerning Which They Know not Certainly Whether It Be from God or No. Being the Substance of Two Sermons, Preached in Colemanstreet, upon Occasion of the Late Disaster Sustain'd in the West.* The disaster sustained in the west was the surrender of Lostwithiel on September 2, and Goodwin explains this as God's judgment against the dominant party in Parliament and Assembly for attempting to suppress Independency, the government prescribed by God for his church. But the main thrust of his rhetoric is necessarily directed to the unenlightened, to those who, while agreeing that it is heinous sin to fight against what is from God, do not believe that Independency is from God. Addressing them, Goodwin takes as his text that counsel of Gamaliel which had so angered Henderson:

> And now I say unto you, Refrain from these men, and let them alone: for if this counsel or this work be of men, it will come to nought: But if it be of God, ye cannot overthrow it; lest haply ye be found even to fight against God.[22]

Even

> put the case that that Way or Doctrine, which men shall prosecute with so much violence and fiercenesse of spirit, shall in conclusion be found to have been mistaken, erroneous, and not from God: yet . . . It is extreme madnesse in men, to run the hazard we speak of, I mean, of *fighting against God* . . . because . . . he himself will give testimony from Heaven against them in due time, hee will suppresse and scatter them, and bring them to nought . . . *Vengeance is mine: I will repay, saith the Lord.*[23]

Goodwin's theory of toleration may be elicited from his defense of Independency against the charge that it opens the floodgates to error and heresy. But

> it being certain that error cannot be healed or suppressed but by the manifestation of the truth, as darknesse cannot be destroyed or removed but by the shining of the light; that way which affords the greatest advantages and the best incouragements unto men, both for the searching out, and bringing forth into light the truth being found,

[21] October 4, 1644, E10(33), p. 5, margin.

[22] Acts 5:38–39. Haller (*Tracts,* I, 54 and *Liberty and Reformation,* p. 148) is mistaken in attributing to Goodwin the introduction of this text into the toleration controversy; see above, pp. 81 and 98.

[23] October 7, 1644, pp. 18–20; reproduced in Haller, *Tracts,* III, 3 ff.

must needs be so farre from opening doores unto *errors, heresies, unsound opinions*, &c. that it steers the most advantagious and hopefull course that lightly can be taken, for the evicting, and consequently for the suppression of them.[24]

Independency is perfect in its hatred of heresy, diligent in its pursuit, and relentless in its excommunication when persuasion fails.[25] Goodwin knows what retort to expect: heresy, excommunicated from the Congregational church, remains free to make head in the world; the only sure way is that "error and errant be further restrained by a secular hand, and heresie and heretique put to silence together in the grave."[26] He has a prudential reply, furnished by Tacitus: "To punish men of parts and wit, is to cast a spirit of Authoritie upon them, and to make their reputation glowe."[27] But he does not rely upon this; his authoritative reply is that *"Prisons* and *Swords* are no *Church-officers"*: Christ furnished his church perfectly "without any concurrence of any heterogeneall or externall power."[28]

The same conclusion follows from the nature of magistracy; and here Goodwin gives the usual argument for the secular view of the state and its separation from the church.[29]

Goodwin would appear by this argument to be committed to a policy of toleration as unlimited as that of *M. S. to A. S.*; but there is a reservation to be noted. We saw above that it is madness to attempt to suppress by force what purports to be from God, even though in fact it is not from God—madness, that is, "untill they have proof upon proof, demonstration upon demonstration, evidence upon evidence; yea, all the security that men in an ordinary way (at least) are capable of, that such Wayes or Doctrines only pretend unto God as the author [of] them, and that in truth, they are not at all from him, but either from men, or of a baser parentage."[30] It is an odd reservation, unexpected in the context and inconsistent with the argument, but it is not a heedless one (its substance is repeated on the last page of the pamphlet). Whether or not Goodwin wished to extend toleration to Roman Catholics and Jews, as was done by *M. S. to A. S.* (with whose authorship he very likely had something to do), and as seems to be demanded by the theoretical structure of *Theomachia,* he strove to protect himself against the charge of espousing an unlimited toleration (and this may in part be why he denied the authorship of *M. S. to A. S.*).[31]

This kind of toleration, which, while going far beyond both the right of the saints to carry out God's will and Christian liberty in

---

[24] *Ibid.,* p. 33.   [25] *Ibid.,* p. 34.   [26] *Ibid.*   [27] *Ibid.,* p. 37.
[28] *Ibid.,* pp. 34–35.   [29] *Ibid.,* pp. 48–51.   [30] *Ibid.,* p. 18.
[31] See above, p. 109, n. 10.

things indifferent, yet stops short of a general toleration, now becomes
so regularly espoused by the Independents as to be predictable. In
November Henry Burton, the Congregationalist among the famous
three who in 1637 traded their ears to Laud for the glory and influence
of martyrdom,[32] answered the charges of his Presbyterian fellow-suf-
ferer, Prynne, that Independency must lead to universal toleration, by
laying down two distinctions, "between orthodox Churches, and heterodox" [33] and "between mens consciences and their practices." [34] The
magistrate, as *"The keeper of both Tables,"* [35] must control men's actions, but neither he "nor any man in the world" [36] may use force
against the conscience itself. Burton poses the critical question, and
answers it more directly than was yet usual with Independents:

> But shall we tolerate Popery, and so Idolatry in our land?
> I answer; It is one thing to tolerate Popery and Idolatry publickly
> in a land, and another to tolerate a man in his *Conscience*. Magistrates
> may not tolerate open Popery and Idolatry to be set up in the land:
> but the conscience of a Papist, they are no masters, or judges of.[37]

The distinction between orthodox and heterodox is not fully elaborated,
but Burton's position apparently is that all "orthodox" churches
(which these are is left conveniently unspecified) are to enjoy full
legal rights of "practice" (*i.e.*, public worship), while "heterodox" are
not; and that "heterodox" individuals are to be restrained from acts
which violate the Tables of the Law (*e.g.*, "idolatry"), but must not be
disturbed in their private faith nor compelled to conform to orthodoxy.

In November there appeared an anonymous pamphlet entitled *A
Paraenetick or Humble Addresse to the Parliament and Assembly
For (Not Loose, But) Christian Libertie*. Although it has not in mod-
ern times been attributed to them, it was the work of the Assembly
Congregationalists and was recognized as such at the time.[38] It is in

---

[32] See *Complete Prose*, I, 42–45.

[33] *A Vindication of Churches, Commonly Called Independent* (November 14,
1644), E17(5), p. 39.

[34] *Ibid.*, p. 70.   [35] *Ibid.*   [36] *Ibid.*, p. 39.   [37] *Ibid.*

[38] W. T. Whitely (*A Baptist Bibliography*, 2 vols., London, 1916, I, 33)
ascribed *A Paraenetick* to Roger Williams, and Wing follows this attribution, but
it is not generally accepted. Woodhouse (*Puritanism and Liberty*, introduction,
p. [35]) classes it among "the great Separatist and Baptist pleas for liberty of
conscience" without attempting to identify its author. Jordan (*Religious Toleration*, III, 448) takes it to be by an Independent. Barker quotes from it but does
not attempt to determine its authorship. I became convinced by internal evidence that it was an official, if unsigned, statement by the Assembly Congregationalists (see the discussion below, pp. 117–18), and sought for contemporary
confirmation; this I found in George Gillespie, *Wholsome Severity Reconciled*

fact the document which marks the end of the Assembly Congregationalists' effort to remain uncommitted to either of the alternative
policies of accommodation or toleration. The circumstances of the
pamphlet's publication can be reconstructed with the help of Baillie's
letters and a publication entitled *Papers Given in to the Honorable
Committee of Lords and Commons and Assembly of Divines with the
Commissioners of Scotland. For Accommodation* (1648). The latter contains the official record of the sporadic negotiations which began with
the Accommodation Order of September, 1644, and ended inconclu-
sively in March of 1646. On September 20, 1644, a sub-committee of
the Assembly (called the Sub-Committee of Agreements and consisting
of four Presbyterians and two Congregationalists) was instructed to
report on how to implement the Accommodation Order. On October 15
it reported inability to reach agreement, the Congregationalist minority
making their original demand for an accommodation for gathered
churches and the Presbyterian majority saying, "We having weighed
our Brethrens Principles, do find no probability of accommodation for

*with Christian Liberty . . . And . . . a Paraenetick to the Five Apologists for
Choosing Accommodation rather then Toleration* (January 8, 1645). In the concluding "Paraenetick" (E24[5], p. 38) Gillespie warns the Apologists of the
dangers of their new policy: "Doe not, O doe not involve your selves in the
plea of Toleration with the Separatists and Anabaptists. Do not partake in their
Separation, lest you partake in their *suppression.* Let us heare no more Paraene-
ticks for Toleration, or liberty of Conscience: but as many as you will for a
just and mercifull Accommodation: a thing mentioned by that Author, *pa.* 3, but
not sought after." The quotation from the original *A Paraenetick* and the page
reference are literally accurate, if rather misleadingly used; the passage is given
in full below, p. 117.

   Perhaps the wild fluctuations in assessing the Assembly Congregationalists' relation to toleration are ultimately due to the failure to recognize their authorship
of *A Paraenetick,* for it is not otherwise possible to recover the real history of
their position. Thus Shaw, taking as the whole story their effort to win an accommodation, writes (*The English Church 1640–1660,* II, 35–36): "It was a clerical
conciliation which was then attempted—a mere seeking for some *via media*
whereby Independency could be brought into the fold of presbytery and both together prevail," and assesses it as "rotten at the core." Jordan, on the other hand,
seems not to have understood the meaning of accommodation at all; he writes
(*Religious Toleration,* III, 348): "Not only the more radical sects, but the Erastians and numerous groups of moderates as well, attracted by the tolerant implications of Congregational theory and by the gallant leadership of the Dissenting
Brethren in the Assembly, united to form a party unalterably opposed to the
establishment of another exclusive religious system in England." The recovery of
the Assembly Congregationalists' authorship of *A Paraenetick* allows us, with the
help of the other documents cited in the text, to see precisely how long they clung
to the policy of an accommodation, when and why they abandoned it, and the
circumstances in which they joined the tolerationist coalition.

them." [39] The Committee of Both Kingdoms agreed to take the report into consideration, but before the end of the month the House of Commons put a "cessation" on further proceedings in this matter.

On November 6, 1645, the proceedings were revived and a larger Committee for Accommodation appointed which included all the original Apologetical Narrators. Again it failed to reach agreement, but this time the Presbyterians were willing enough to offer the accommodation they had formerly refused. They deplored their brethren's assertion "that an Accommodation was now impossible, and that the nature and present state of the businesse doth lead them to desire a forbearance [*i.e.,* toleration]." [40] And in fact the Congregationalists refused to "take on us, to call upon the Parliament, to exclude *other tender consciences* from this forbearance and to impose on them." [41] Toleration may *"accidentally* be *an irritation to sin,"* but we must not therefore *"deny* to men, who give undeniable testimony of their Godlinesse, that use of the *ordinances of Christ,* that they may with the peace of their consciences enjoy." [42]

It is clear enough that the key to the position taken in the winter of 1645–1646 is the growing power of the sects; the Presbyterians, following the precept of divide and conquer, were tempting the Congregationalists with what they had before refused to grant, and the Congregationalists were rejecting the bait and maintaining the tolerationist coalition. What happened in the fall of 1644 is less immediately apparent, but we may find the clue in Baillie. Writing just after the passage of the Accommodation Order, he is full of alarm and indignation, speaking of the Order as if it were aimed against the Scots: "Our greatest friends, Sir Henry Vane and the Solicitor, are the main procurers of all this; and that without any regard to us, who have saved their nation, and brought these two persons to the height of the power they now enjoy, and use to our prejudice. . . . Marshall miskens us altogether; he is for a middle way of his own, and draws a faction in the synod to give ordination and excommunication to congregations, albeit dependentlie, in case of mal-administration. God help us! If God be pleased to settle Scotland, and give us Newcastle, all will go well." [43] Some five weeks later he began a letter in continued gloom: "I had not a mind or a hand to write any thing to any while I saw what would be the pleasure of God to doe with us; and howsoever we be yet under the cloud, yet least you should wait so long, I force myselfe to write this to yow." [43a] He reports on military affairs, and then turns to the proceedings on the Accommodation Order. What worries him most is that since

[39] Library of Congress BX9053.A4/1648, p. 6.   [40] *Ibid.,* p. 18.
[41] *Ibid.,* p. 27.   [42] *Ibid.,* p. 37.   [43] Baillie, II, 230–31.   [43a] *Ibid.,* p. 232.

Marshall had arranged the membership of the Assembly's sub-committee "according to his mind," and the Parliamentary sub-committee was dominated by tolerationists, there was great danger that the Assembly would be by-passed.

> At our first meeting, my Lords Say and Wharton, Vane and the Solicitor, pressed vehementlie to debate the propositions of the sub-committee. They knew, when we had debated, and come to voicing, they could carrie all by pluralitie in the committee; and though they should not, yet they were confident, when the report came to the House of Commons, to gett all they desired there past. So, without the Assemblie, they purposed immediatelie from this committee to gett a toleration of Independency concluded in the House of Commons, long before any thing should be gotten so much as reported from the Assemblie anent Presbytries.[44]

Suddenly the tone of the letter changes radically. "While I am wryting, we gett the long expected news of the taking of Newcastle, and that by storme. Blessed be the name of the Lord, who will not for ever contemn the prayer of his people." [45] And a few days later he writes triumphantly,

> Our Committee at Newcastle wrote up to the Houses, to haste the settling of the Church. This motion was well received by all but Say, Vane, and some few Independents. To comfort them, six or eight of the chief Lords came this day in message from the House of Peers, with that letter, entreated the Assemblie to haste; also in that letter the Commons voted, over the Independents bellie, the dissolving of that dangerous committee, which these five weeks has vexed us.[46]

Once again the Scots had tipped the scales against accommodation; and in so doing they also brought to an end the period of ambiguity in the Assembly Congregationalists' policy. They had bankrupted one of the mutually contradictory policies which the Congregationalists had been juggling for most of the year. Accordingly, the Congregationalists now committed themselves fully to the alternative policy. "God," says *A Paraenetick*, "had lately put it into the heart of the Parliament, to consider the just and mercifull accommodation of tender Consciences. Which makes us the more amazed and astonished at the sudden prejudice wee seeme to have received in their affections, and the varied, yea, contrary aspect both of Parliament and Assembly upon us." [47] Do not cheat us of what we have dearly bought with blood and treasure. If you did not intend us to enjoy liberty of conscience, why did the Assembly lead us to believe that you did? And here *A Paraenet-*

---

[44] *Ibid.*, pp. 236–37.   [45] *Ibid.*, p. 237.   [46] *Ibid.*, p. 240.
[47] November 30, 1644, E19(10), p. 3.

ick quotes from *Certain Considerations to Dis-Swade,* the document which marked the high point of that earlier effort at accommodation stopped by the Scots,[48] and contrasts its promises with "some present conclusions, and more menacing agitations" of "Fines, Prisons, Exile." [49] Nor can the Assembly pretend that *Certain Considerations* was an unauthoritative, private thing; its circumstances and signatories show that it was in effect an official document "holding forth to us a bait of timely and seasonable liberty." [50] The ghosts of the hundreds slain fighting for liberty of conscience will ask whether it was a calculated trick from the beginning. "Did you send us out to be cut off, and to make a hand of us? Did you slay part of us in the field with the sword of the Enemy, that you might the easier suppresse the residue at home?" [51]

Then the tone, already pretty warm, hardens. "Doe you stand in no more need of us?" [52] The most diverse groups on the other side are combining "to make their party stronger." [53] "Take heed of walking contrary unto God, of casting shame on those, on whom he hath reflected such eminent honour, both in the Army and otherwise: For I aske you, By whom hath God more deliver'd us hitherto? Who have shewed themselves more valiant in fight? who have oftner put to flight the *Armies of the Aliens* in the North, and els-where, but those men that in the end shall be put to flight themselves, if some may have their will? *The sword of the Lord,* and despised *Gideon,* hath saved this Nation: *Saul hath slaine his thousands, and David his ten thousands.* Let no man envy. God will be acknowledged in his Instruments, as well as in his Attributes." [54]

Balked of their first effort to obtain accommodation through the Assembly, the Congregationalists had turned to Parliament; now balked of their second, they were turning to the army. But this necessarily meant collaborating with the sects constituting a good portion of the strength of Cromwell's command, and accordingly *A Paraenetick* is an "indifferent and generall" discourse, not meant to "beget a good opinion of the *Congregationall way* in speciall" but to "induce liberty . . . for every way not scandalous." [55] With this decisive step the Assembly Congregationalists formally entered the tolerationist coalition.[56]

[48] See above, pp. 71–72.   [49] E19(10), p. 6.   [50] *Ibid.,* p. 7.
[51] *Ibid.,* p. 9.   [52] *Ibid.,* p. 10.   [53] *Ibid.,* p. 11.   [54] *Ibid.,* pp. 11–12.
[55] *Ibid.,* pp. 12–13.

[56] In doing so, however, they took care to reassert, and more challengingly than ever before, their conviction that Congregationalism was *jure divino.* If it is premised that that way is of God which absolutely will not institute anything except from the Word, and that way is of man which denies that God has pre-

The most illuminating statement of the Independent limits to toleration was made in June of the following year by Joshua Sprigge in *The Ancient Bounds, or Liberty of Conscience*. His theory is based on the principle of segregation (indeed, on so full and explicit an account of it that Woodhouse used it as a primary illustrative document [57]), and the resultant separation of church and state makes "the immunity and impunity of differing opinions in Religion, as in relation to the Civill Magistrate . . . a Principle in Nature." [58] Neverthless, "the duty of a Christian Magistrate is somewhat more then of another Magistrate. . . . For it is the duty of *every Christian,* to improve every talent and advantage entrusted with him, for the honour of Christ." [59] In addition to the duties of magistracy *per se,* the Christian magistrate has committed to him the "material" charge of the Second Table of Commandments—"that is, he is not to see God dishonoured by the manifest breach thereof." [60] He is also to be concerned with the First Table "so far as *Nature* carries the candle before him," and it carries the candle far enough to require his suppression of polytheism, atheism, idolatry, and blasphemy.[61] Furthermore, the Christian magistrate is not to restrict himself to "the Principles and light of Nature where they run *lowest,* as among *Heathen,*" but is to enforce them "as they are *improved* and raised by the Gospel, through the common irradiation thereof: For *Consuetudo est altera natura,* Custome or Education is another nature." [62] What is warrantable by the common light of this second nature must be required from the Christian magistrate, for "as he hath his authority from God, so he is to take the *Rise* of exercising it from him *who hath not committed to him the sword in vaine.*" [63] The duties beyond the point to which ordinary nature had already carried the candle are specified. He must suppress all doctrine denying "the article of the *Trinity,* or the *person* and *Office* of Jesus Christ . . . or . . . the Resurrection, or a Judgement Day, *&c.*" [64] He is bound to supervise and rectify the "outward manner and order" of the church, and "to punish disorder." [65]

scribed a perfect pattern of church-government and seeks to eke out what God has provided with the precepts of men, then the inevitable consequence is that all the godly will come to Congregationalism in the end (p. 14): "the *Presbyterian way* is but a step thereto, and will rest here as its center, and end in this as its perfection. For our parts . . . we cannot yeeld to you therein."

[57] *Puritanism and Liberty,* introduction, pp. *39–40.*

[58] June 10, 1645; E287(3), p. 18; attribution by Barbara Kiefer, "The Authorship of *Ancient Bounds,*" in *Church History,* XXII (1953), 3–7; confirmed by the entry in the *Stationers' Registers,* ed. G. E. Briscoe Eyre (3 vols., London, 1913), I, 167, which gives the author as "J:S:M:A:"

[59] E287(3), p. 5.   [60] *Ibid.,* p. 7.   [61] *Ibid.*   [62] *Ibid.,* p. 8.

[63] *Ibid.,* p. 9.   [64] *Ibid.,* p. 8.   [65] *Ibid.,* p. 10.

Sprigge's toleration, then, is for that part of the Christian spectrum lying between Roman Catholicism on the right ("idolatry") and such "errors of manifest scandall and danger . . . as *Arrianisme, Socinianisme, Familisme, &c*" [66] on the left. Freed of attack from the right, some Independents like Burton and Goodwin might have preferred a more comprehensive policy, but this is approximately what the Assembly Congregationalists had in mind when they committed themselves to "liberty . . . for every way not scandalous," and we may recall that they were brought even so far by tactical necessity.

7. THE REPETITIVENESS OF HISTORY AND THE TACTICS OF THE TOLERATIONIST COALITION

As a coalition the tolerationists enjoyed a tactical freedom which would have been impossible for any single group. We have already seen [1] how an Independent might disencumber himself of the resistance aroused by, say, Roger Williams' extremism, while both were in fact, whatever their ultimate differences, pursuing the same immediate end, the disintegration of support for the Presbyterian goal of compulsory religious uniformity; or how John Goodwin might disclaim responsibility for an advanced position assumed somewhat hastily by two of his immediate circle (he may very well have been one of them himself).[2] Or, to illustrate another way in which the flexibility available to a coalition could express itself, two of its members might advance the same proposition, but give it opposite evaluations and employ it to bring opposing groups to what in the circumstances amounted to the same conclusion. Thus in February, 1644, two tolerationists asserted that Presbyterianism and Independency were essentially the same. When Roger Williams made this assertion, as we have seen,[3] the connotations were pejorative, he was addressing himself primarily to the center and left of Puritanism, and his ultimate object was to confirm and strengthen the tendency toward separatism. When Hezekiah Woodward made it (in *A Dialogue, Arguing That . . . The* Presbyteriall *and* Independent . . . *Wayes Are But in Shew Two, and Will Assuredly Meet in One*) the connotations were favorable, he was addressing himself to the center and right of Puritanism, and his ultimate object was to strengthen the movement's sense of unity and common purpose. But the immediate object of both men was toleration (albeit in different degrees).

Many further examples could be given, but their very number and

[66] *Ibid.,* p. 4.   [1] See above, pp. 111–12.   [2] See above, pp. 109 and 113.
[3] See above, pp. 76–77.

variety prevent most of them from having much significance in themselves—past a certain point it is not how flexibility of argument expresses itself that counts, but the fact of flexibility. To this, however, there is one exception, a complex tactical operation so embarrassing to the Presbyterians, so instructive about the nature of debate in the Puritan Revolution, and so influential upon Milton that we must devote some attention to it. This is the exploitation of the division among Presbyterians over whether or not church government is *jure divino*. At one level it is no more than the standard, even predictable, gambit of parading the enemy's inconsistencies; thus Henry Robinson collects a number of statements by the proponents of compulsory Presbyterianism, some of them theocratic and others Erastian, in order to exhibit to the "Presbyterian party . . . the fierce clashings and diametricall contradictions, in which their most eminent champions would inconsiderately involve them," [4] and there are many others who make this debater's point. More troublesome were the straightforward attacks, simultaneous but not necessarily concerted, from opposite points of view, upon each of the contradictory Presbyterian theories of compulsive uniformity.

Prynne's *Twelve Considerable Serious Questions*, published September 16, 1644, may be taken as a convenient starting point for an analysis of these attacks. As we saw above (pp. 104–105), this denied that Christ had prescribed any single form of church government, but insisted on the right of every state to establish church government as it saw fit (*"alwayes provided, it be consonant, and no wayes repugnant to the Word of God"* [5]), and to enforce obedience and conformity. In *An Answer to Mr. William Prynne's Twelve Questions* (November 1), Henry Robinson agrees with the premise that there is no *jure divino* form of church government, but disallows the conclusion that therefore the state is free to impose one; on the contrary, it follows from the premise that therefore "every particular Christian *ought to have under the Gospel a liberty and latitude, to choose such a forme of Church government*, as he himselfe, for his particular use, in his owne reason and understanding apprehendeth to be according to Gods Word." [6]

At the same moment, the true Independents attacked Prynne's pamphlet from the opposite side. *Certain Briefe Observations and Antiquaeries* wanted to know "if no prescript forme in the Word, why not Episcopacy as well as Presbytery? . . . Episcopacy regulated and moderated (if all were knowne) is more consonant and agreeable to a

---

[4] *The Falsehood of Mr. William Pryn's Truth Triumphing* (May 8, 1645), E282(11), sig. A3; attribution by Haller, *Tracts*, I, 67.

[5] E257(1), p. 2. [6] E15(5), p. 2.

Monarchicall government then Presbytery." [7] Again, "if Church government must be suited to States . . . why is an Assembly of Divines called to search the Word about it?" [8] Besides, if it is really the duty of every subject to submit to the government of the national church established by the state, would it not follow that Prynne was "justly stigmatised and censured for speaking against the Bishops and Ceremonies?" [9]

Prynne stood his ground against these Independent questions (he seems to have taken no notice of Robinson's pamphlet until the following July [10]). To the first, *A Full Reply to Certaine Briefe Observations* answered, "If you meane it of Lordly Episcopacy, there are abundant pregnant Texts against it, to prove it opposite to Gods Word. If of moderated or regulated Episcopacy, the same with Presbytery: if the Parliament by the Synods advice unanimously establish it, as most consonant to the Scriptures, and most agreeable to the civill Government, I shall readily submit unto it without opposition." [11] To go with this, he offered an interpretation of the famous martyrdom of 1637 very different from the one current at the time of the event, and rather strange for a leading proponent of the Root-and-Branch bill: "None of us suffered for opposing . . . the Bishops legall authority, or any ceremonies established in our Church by Act of Parliament; *but onely against their pretended divine right to their Episcopall Lordly power, diametrally contrary to Scripture . . . and against their Innovations in doctrine, discipline, ceremonies, canons, &c.* contrary to the Lawes of the land." [12]

Of all men, Henry Burton was in the best position to criticize this interpretation. In *A Vindication of Churches* he cited his indictment in the Court of High Commission to show that it was "my opposing of Bishops themselves, not only their extravagancies" and "all manner of *Ceremonies of humane ordinance,* imposed upon the conscience in the worship of God" that "put the Hang-mans knife . . . so close to the very root of mine ears, that it opened the wider sluces for the blood to stream out (with yours my dear Fellow-sufferers) to fill the Whores cup, and make her drunk and spue, and fall, and rise up no more." [13] To Prynne's Erastianism he opposes the classic *jure divino* argument as used by both Presbyterians and Congregationalists alike against Episcopacy: "To shape Religion . . . *to every Nation . . . and to Civill*

---

[7] October 4, 1644; E10(33), p. 3; for authorship see above, p. 111, n. 20.
[8] *Ibid.,* p. 3.   [9] *Ibid.,* p. 4.
[10] *A Fresh Discovery of Some Prodigious New Wandring-Blazing-Stars, & Firebrands* (July 24, 1645), E261(5).   [11] October 19, 1644; E257(7), p. 6.
[12] *Ibid.,* p. 7.   [13] November 14, 1644; E17(5), p. 72.

Government . . . and so to humane Prudence, (as you say) what is it but to *shape a coat for the Moone?* Whereas the Scripture holds forth unto us, but onely one forme of *Church-government, and Discipline,* which ought not to be altered according to the diversitie of *humane Lawes and Customes . . .* as you affirme," [14] and Prynne's "very question is hereticall." [15] Instructed by God's immediate voice, "we dare not subjugate our conscience to humane lawes, customes, and manners." [16] This is the *jure divino* principle of resistance; since Burton also propounds the principle of toleration which we noticed above (p. 114), he is in an excellent position to make the dread comment: "And whereas you quote in the Margine, 1*Cor.* 14. 40. & 11. 34. on which you ground your liberty to form your Church-government and Discipline sutably to each particular Civill go[vern]ment: Alas, brother, these very Scriptures our Prelats abused to maintain their unlimited liberty of setting up their rites and ceremonies, as suteable to the Civill government." [17]

From this direction the charge that new Presbyter was but old priest writ large troubled particularly the clerical Presbyterians (so much so that in time they felt obliged to quarrel with their Erastian fellow-Presbyterians, and the redoubtable Prynne himself came in for the novel experience of being denounced in the pulpit of St. Margaret's and in pamphlets by such erstwhile allies as Herbert Palmer and George Walker).[18] They naturally attempted to meet the charge by insisting upon Presbyterian claims to a *jus divinum.* Of many examples we may choose one whose circumstances of publication make it particularly illuminating. The day after receiving Burton's pamphlet, Thomason received a tract which was a reissue, with an added title page, of one which Calibut Downing had originally published in 1641 under the title *An Appeale To Every Impartiall . . . Reader: Whether the Presbyterie or Prelacie Be the Better Church Government.* But in 1644 Episcopacy had been overthrown; what point was there in reissuing the pamphlet? The new title page (the only difference from 1641) gives the clue; it reads: *The Cleere Antithesis or Diametrall Opposition Betweene Presbytery and Prelacy.*[19] No one in 1641 was denying that

---

[14] *Ibid.,* p. 4.   [15] *Ibid.,* p. 8.   [16] *Ibid.,* p. 38.   [17] *Ibid.,* p. 6.

[18] See *An Antidote against Foure Dangerous Quaeries* (September 2, 1645), E265(3); George Walker, *A Brotherly Censure of the Errour of a Dear Friend* (September 10), E265(4); and Herbert Palmer, *A Full Answer to a Printed Paper by William Prynne* (September 18), E302(1). In *A Vindication of Foure Serious Questions* (October 3), E265(5), title page, Prynne mentions having been preached against before the House of Commons on September 5 by "a Reverend Brother of Scotland."

[19] November 15, 1644; E17(7). Attribution is by Thomason.

there was a difference between Presbyterianism and Episcopacy: the fact of difference seemed self-evident, and the question was which had the better claim. Downing had addressed himself to this question by setting forth, in parallel columns, the positions of the two systems on thirty points, the Presbyterian position of course representing the truth. But now the *jure divino* critics of Presbyterianism were saying that it was a human invention, a system based on politic considerations—that new Presbyter was but old priest writ large. Hence the original point-by-point contrast could be made to serve again in the new situation; and the first seven articles asserted that Presbyterianism was, and Episcopacy was not, *jure divino*.[20]

But the *jure divino* claim for compulsory Presbyterianism, while more consistent than the Erastian with the Presbyterians' role in the earlier part of the Puritan Revolution, was not without its own difficulties. It, too, was attacked from both sides. On the one hand were those who agreed that there was a *jure divino* form of church government but denied that it was Presbyterian. The most conservative of these, the Assembly Congregationalists, were progressively hardening their tone. In the *Apologeticall Narration* they had said that the synodical structure of the church "was to us a question, and judged to be an *additament*" to Scripture, "which therefore rested on those . . . to make evident and demonstrate," [21] until which time they could not subscribe to it, and ought to be given an accommodation by the side of the Presbyterianism which they expected Parliament to establish. But a year later, in submitting to Parliament *The Reasons of the Dissenting Brethren*, the original five Apologists plus William Greenhill and William Carter declared that the synodical structure of the church *"carries with it so great and manifold incongruities, and inconsistencies, with what the Scripture speaks"* that *"such a Government may not be."* [22] This is what the Separatists and sects had been saying for a long time, inferring therefrom, according to their various tempers, that the Presbyterian ministry was only "pretended," or its church "anti-Christian," and so forth. There was, of course, much emphasis on the parallel between the Presbyterian failure to find explicit scriptural warrant for synods and the Episcopal failure to find such warrant for bishops.

On the other hand, the claim to a Presbyterian *jus divinum* was at-

[20] The remaining twenty-three declared the results of Presbyterianism good, those of Episcopacy bad.

[21] P. 15; Haller, *Tracts*, II, 323.

[22] E27(14), p. 3. The House of Commons on December 23, 1644, ordered the *Reasons* printed, and "about Feb: 5th," 1645, Thomason received the present pamphlet, which consists of the *Reasons* and *The Answer of the Assembly of Divines*. See above, p. 70, n. 21.

tacked by those who denied the premise altogether, particularly the Erastians. We may see this attack at its most telling in several measures taken by Parliament. We saw above (pp. 104–105) that in the summer of 1644 the growing theocratic pretensions of the Assembly had begun to conflict with the permanent Erastian sentiment of Parliament. The Assembly might well have been warned by the Commons' vote of January 23, 1645, declaring that church government was not *jure divino* but subject to the civil power (above, pp. 105–106); instead, it sought means to get Parliament to reverse itself. The story takes us somewhat beyond the period of this volume, but it is so helpful to an appreciation of *Areopagitica* that it will be worthwhile to report it briefly.

"The most of the House of Commons are downright Erastians: they are lyke to create us much more woe than all the sectaries of England," Baillie wrote in April to his friend Spang in the Netherlands. "If yow would sett Apollonius, or Voetius, or Rivett, or Spanheim, when he has done with Ameraud, or all of them, to wryte against Erastus, it will be a great service to us and the [Reformed] churches also . . . L'Emperour promised to write against Selden, for the Jewish ecclesiastick Sanhedrim, and their excommunication. This man is the head of the Erastians: his glory is most in the Jewish learning; he avows every where, that the Jewish State and Church was all one, and that so in England it must be, that the Parliament is the Church." [23] At the same time Baillie was explaining in his public letter home the tactic by which the Assembly hoped to nullify a new Commons' resolution providing for appeals from the national synod to Parliament.[24] A little later he repeats his appeal to Spang for continental support against the Erastianism of Parliament.[25]

The first crisis came in August. Baillie, explaining in his public letter that most of the House of Commons believed "no Church-government to be of divine right, bot all to be a humane constitution," reports: "About this matter we have had, at diverse tymes, much bickering with them: now it is come to a shock." [26] The precipitating issue was the Assembly's demand that the presbyteries be given discretionary power to exclude from the sacrament others besides those falling into categories established by Parliament. This Parliament refused to grant. The Assembly, "after diverse fair papers, at last . . . framed a most zealous, clear, and peremptor one, wherein they held out plainly the Church's divyne right. . . . The House is highly inflamed with this petition, and seems resolute to refuse it." [27] In effect the House did,

[23] Baillie, II, 265–266.   [24] *Ibid.*, p. 267.   [25] *Ibid.*, p. 277.
[26] *Ibid.*, p. 307.   [27] *Ibid.*

but by appointing a committee to meet with a committee of the Assembly,[28] so that an explosion was for the time being averted.

The Assembly learned nothing from this experience. In October Baillie writes that Parliament has at last ordered the erection of presbyteries and synods throughout the country, "yet they give to the ecclesiastick courts so little power, that the Assemblie finding their petitions not granted, are in great doubt whether to sett up any thing, till, by some powerfull petition of many thousand hands, they obtain some more of their just desyres. The only meane to obtain this, and all else we desyre, is our recruited army about Newark." [29] During the winter the relations between Parliament and Assembly continued to deteriorate, and the showdown came in the spring of 1646. In March Parliament passed an ordinance which, among other things, provided for Parliamentary commissioners to decide whether someone accused by a presbytery of scandalous behavior of a kind not enumerated by Parliament should be excluded from the sacrament,[30] and the Assembly promptly petitioned against the ordinance as violating the jurisdiction of the presbyteries, "which we must, as formerly in our petition we have done, say it expressly belongeth to them by Divine right." [31]

The House had had enough. It voted the Assembly's "petition" a breach of privilege, and in its "Narrative of the Matter of Fact" reminded the Assembly that it was created by an ordinance of Parliament for the sole purpose of advising Parliament on such matters as Parliament referred to it. It had given in its advice on the matter covered by the ordinance, after which "Both Houses, after mature Deliberation had thereupon, did, notwithstanding, *ordain*" in a contrary manner:

> The Assembly are not authorised, as an Assembly, by any *Ordinance* or *Order* of Parliament, to interpret the *Covenant*, especially in relation to any Law made or to be made; nor, since the Law passed both Houses concerning the Commissioners, have been required by both or either of the Houses of Parliament, or had any Authority before by Parliament, to deliver their Opinions to the Houses, in Matters already judged and determined by them: Neither have they Power, either to debate or vote, whether what is passed as a Law by both Houses, be agreeing or disagreeing to the Word of God, until they be thereunto required.[32]

Nor was this all. The House sent the Assembly a list of nine questions on the matter of a *jus divinum*. It not only demanded that every feature of the professed *jure divino* church government be individually proved from Scripture, with "the several Texts thereof in the express

---

[28] Shaw, *English Church*, I, 303.   [29] Baillie, II, 318.
[30] *Old Parliamentary History*, XIV, 280–89.   [31] Shaw, I, 304.
[32] *Old Parliamentary History*, XIV, 362.

Words of the same" (in itself an implicit denial of the contention that the church has a divine right to legislate in things indifferent), but it *"Ordered,* That every Minister, present at the Debate of any of these Questions, do, upon every Resolution which shall be presented to the House concerning the same, subscribe his Name, either with the Affirmative or Negative, as he gives his Vote." [33] Since the questions included such dangerous matters as that raised by No. 8 ("Is there any Thing contained in the Word of God, that the Supreme Magistracy, in a Christian State, may not judge and determine what are the aforesaid notorious and scandalous Offences, and the Manner of Suspension for the same, and in what Particulars, concerning the Premises, is the said Supreme Magistracy by the Word of God excluded?" [34]), it is clear that Parliament intended them as a deterrent.

Not surprisingly, the Assembly never finished answering any of the questions. However, it busied itself about the task long enough [35] to incur Selden's mockery:

> When the Queries were sent to the Assembly concerning the *Jus Divinum* of Presbytery, their asking time to answer them, was a Satire upon themselves; for if it were to be seen in the Text, they might quickly turn to the place, and show us it. Their delaying to answer makes us think there's no such thing there. They do just as you have seen a fellow do at a Tavern Reckoning, when he should come to pay his Reckoning; he puts his Hands into his Pockets, and keeps a grabbling and a fumbling, and shaking, at last tells you he has left his Money at home; when all the Company knew at first he had no Money there; for every Man can quickly find his own Money.[36]

The crushing blow to the Assembly's theocratic pretensions delivered by the House cannot be considered simply tolerationist; many who supported it doubtless intended that the church which Parliament was establishing should enforce conformity; but tolerationists took a leading role in the action,[37] and to that extent it may be classified as part of the tactics of the tolerationist coalition. We may conclude our examination of these tactics with a striking illustration of the embarrassment and confusion created among anti-tolerationist Presbyterians by the multiple, various, and encircling attacks against every principle by which they attempted to justify compulsory conformity.

In June of 1645 Sir Simonds D'Ewes published *The Primitive Prac-*

---

[33] *Ibid.,* p. 365.   [34] *Ibid.,* pp. 364–65.   [35] See Shaw, I, 311–13.

[36] *Table Talk,* CXVI, 4; in James C. Thornton, ed., *Table Talk by Various Writers* (London: Dent, 1934), pp. 88–89.

[37] *Old Parliamentary History* remarks (XIV, 360) that the action "confirms . . . the great Increase of Strength the *Independent* Party had, lately, acquired by the new Elections."

tise For Preserving Truth. The "Epistle" explains that the work was written "about eight yeeres since," in part as "a Preparative . . . to fit my self, either for a voluntary exilement, or a necessary suffering," since he lived under the "tyrannie of Bishop *Wren*." D'Ewes was not precipitate in bringing martyrdom on himself, and did not publish the book; as he explains, he knew that "the Presse was then only open to matters of a contrary subject. But now upon the perusall thereof, conceiving that it might be of some use in respect of the many distractions amongst us at this present, when a blessed Reformation is so neere the birth, and yet the Church seemes to want strength to bring it forth, I was content to yeeld to the publishing thereof." [38]

But the lesson it holds forth to "this present" is hard to decipher. The tract's main object, as suited the needs of a convinced Puritan under the Laudian rigor, is to "discover the true madnesse of all persecutors," [39] since persecution for religion is both evil in itself and ineffective as a means of suppression. But D'Ewes was no tolerationist; on the contrary, as Gardiner says, he "held the sects in utter abomination." [40] In speaking in the House in favor of committing the Root-and-Branch bill, he took into consideration the alleged danger of uprooting the existing church government before a new one could be formulated, and dismissed it, saying that an interim discipline "may fully be provided for by a bill or act of twenty lines"; then he added a single particular of this interim government: "in which I would have a clause inserted for the severe punishing of tradesmen and other ignorant persons who shall presume to preach." [41] Nor had his zeal abated when he published *The Primitive Practise;* some four months thereafter, when the classical presbyteries were set up in Suffolk, he was appointed to the tenth division. [42]

If D'Ewes was not in favor of tolerating religious diversity, what contribution did he think he was making in publishing, at a time when toleration was the most agitated issue within Puritanism, a tract which was part of the earlier Presbyterian resistance to compulsive uniformity? The clue would appear to lie in Section XIII of the tract. Here D'Ewes lays down the limits of his position in the odd assertion that while heresy standing alone may be opposed only by instruction and rebuke, when it is joined to a second evil forcible suppression is justified. The argument is an uneasy one and quickly got over: God com-

[38] June 28, 1645, E290(9), sig. A3.   [39] *Ibid.,* p. 11.

[40] *Great Civil War,* I, 482.

[41] Quoted by Shaw (I, 83), who gives the reference as D'Ewes' Manuscripts, III, 1015; when the second volume in chronological sequence of D'Ewes' *Journal* now in process of publication by Yale University Press appears, this entry will presumably be found under June 11, 1641.   [42] Shaw, II, 428.

manded the Jews to put idolaters and blasphemers to death; this was only a judicial law and no evangelical precept, "yet doubtlesse it may thence by the rule of Analogie be concluded, that where Idolatry and Heresie are mixed together, as among *Papists* and *Montanists* or *Altar-adorers*, or where blasphemy and heresie meet in one, as amongst the *Arrians, Pelagians,* or *Anabaptists*, the followers of *Sebastian Castellio*, and *James Arminius*, there a more severe course may be warrantably practised" and "exilement or a greater punishment justly inflicted on them." [43] May we not suppose that D'Ewes thought he was replying to the charge that now that they were in power the Presbyterians had changed their colors and were betraying their earlier role in the Puritan Revolution—were but old priests writ large—by publishing a work which showed that even when the Presbyterians were demanding liberty of conscience from the bishops they were opposed to an unlimited toleration (and specifically to toleration of those sects now become most troublesome)?

In any case, whatever his motive, he furnishes us with an excellent example of the continuity of the argument despite the reversal of the Presbyterian position:

> It is the undoubted mark or brand of the Church *Antichristian* . . . to persecute; of the Church *Christian Orthodox* . . . to be persecuted: For the Truth, if it have but equall countenance and safety, will . . . flourish . . . : But *Falshood* . . . can never be generally & publikely established, without sharp and cruell persecution.[44]
>
> If it be neither warranted by Gods Word, nor consonant to reason, policy, or the property of the true Church to kill an Heretique by a long and noysome imprisonment, or to adjudge him to a violent death: If persecution for conscience sake be accounted, and that justly, a brand of the Antichristian Church . . . how is it possible that Protestant Prelates should persecute any at all with imprisonment and despoiling them of their goods, though convicted of heresie it selfe, but much more such sober and innocent Christians, who by their own confession hold nothing in matter of doctrine contrary to the truth, live inoffensively and vertuously in respect of their conversation, and are ready in all humility to submit to any particulars in matters supposed to be indifferent, which they shall be convinced out of Gods Word to be so? . . . is it possible any *Protestant* Prelate or Divine should stirre up any *Protestant* Prince or State to ruine their *Protestant*-fellow-Ministers, and other Christians, because they cannot submit to such particulars, as in themselves can no way hinder or impeach the unity of faith, nor could breake (if Gods glory were onely aimed at) the bond of love? [45]

[43] E290(9), p. 54.   [44] *Ibid.*, p. 1.

[45] *Ibid.*, pp. 47–48. "To kill an Heretique" is a manuscript correction for an obliterated line of print, and is confirmed by the second edition (3935b15, p. 47).

No word would need to be changed for this to pass as the work of any moderate tolerationist of 1644–1645—as Milton's, but for style—except to substitute "Presbyters" for "Prelates" and "Parliament" for "Prince."

But we must not end with the implication that it was the Presbyterians alone who reversed their position on some principle which they had earlier held forth as fundamental. The Episcopalians, we may recall, had done it before them, conferring the sanction of theology, or withdrawing it, as one or another concept of "law" suited their needs. The Independents would be next, nor would they be the last; but that story belongs to later volumes in this series.

8. THE ISSUE OF SUPREMACY AGAIN: A REFINEMENT OF PARLIAMENTARY THEORY

About the middle of 1643, as we have seen, the issue of supremacy in the state receded from the forefront of public debate, and it did not return to prominence for a year and a half. During this period, although its discussion continued, it was at a much slower pace and was, for the most part, mere repetition of the pattern we analyzed above. There was, however, one significant new development of Parliamentary theory (as it happens, a development of great importance for Milton).

It will be recalled that at the height of the controversy there was one royalist argument which the Parliamentary apologists did not answer, the relatively infrequent one that the law of nature was a law of evil nature and no fit guide for Christians or, indeed, for any rational men. So rarely was this argument advanced that the Parliamentary side seems not to have felt constrained to attempt to meet it. But early in 1644 John Maxwell, then a fugitive from his Scottish diocese of Ross and later archbishop of Tuam, published *Sacro-sancta Regum Majestas: Or, The Sacred and Royall Prerogative of Christian Kings*. He did not professedly adopt the view that the law of nature was opposed to the law of God; for the most part he seemed, like the majority of divine-right royalists, to recognize the law of nature as authoritative while denying that political affairs in a Christian community fell under its jurisdiction. Nevertheless, when he denied the natural-law social-contract theory that kings derived their powers from a sovereign people, he did not limit himself to the assertion that the power of Christian kings derived immediately from God; without troubling about its consistency with his ostensible deference to the law of nature, he introduced something like Hobbes' view of natural law:

There can no other power be conceived to be inherent in the *Community* naturally and properly, but onely *potestas passiva regiminis*, a capacity or susceptibility to be governed. . . . Nature dictates, that government is *necessary*, for the maintenance of the society, for happinesse, for safety and protection, yet every singular and individuall person, by corruption and selfe-love hath . . . a naturall aversenesse and repugnancy to submit to any. . . . It is despaire to attain at government that makes the greatest and most part to submit to government; and that they see and feele, that without government none can enjoy society or safety; this forceth that naturall repugnancy, which is severally and singularly in every one to give way to that universall, naturall, and necessary propension of Nature to Government.[1]

Again, he managed to leave some impression of contrast between what was permissible by the law of nature and what was wished by God. For example, he conceded that aristocracy and democracy were now lawful forms of government;[2] but they would not be were it not for sin:

If *Adam* had not fallen, Divines doubt not but government had beene. . . . [But] Aristocracie, or Democracie, or mixed Government, had never beene existent or apparent in the world. What spece of Government had beene then, I pray you tell me it? . . . . The Argument concludes *a minori ad majus*, from the lesse to the more; if it was necessary in the state of innocency to establish it thus by Gods owne decree, how much more *in statu peccati*, in our decayed and corrupted state by sinne?[3]

Hitherto the English Parliamentarians had avoided this issue, for whatever reasons; but Maxwell was a Scot, and when in October, 1644, his old enemy in the Kirk, Samuel Rutherford, published his answer, *Lex, Rex: The Law and the Prince*, he left nothing out. The distinction in the organization of society before and after the Fall is not between monarchy and other forms of government, but between a society governing itself without rulers and one governed by rulers, whether kings or others.

We are to distinguish betwixt a power of Government, and a power of Government by Magistracy. That we defend our selves from violence by violence, is a consequent of unbroken and sin-lesse nature; but that we defend our selves by devolving our power over in the hands of one, or more Rulers, seemeth rather positively morall, then naturall . . . For which cause I judge that learned Senator *Ferdinandus Vasquius* said well, That Princedom, Empire, Kingdom, or Jurisdiction hath its *rise from a positive and secundary law of Nations* [he expoundeth himself elsewhere to speak of the law of nature secondary], *and not from the law of pure Nature*.[4]

[1] January 30, 1644, E30(22), pp. 90–91. [2] *Ibid.*, p. 85. [3] *Ibid.*, p. 84.
[4] Imprint: October 7, 1644, UCL JN354.R95, pp. 2–3; inserted passage within square brackets is from the repetition of this citation at p. 92.

This does more than deny monarchy the advantage of being the only form of government rooted in unfallen nature. Every form of government possible for fallen man derives from the law of fallen nature; but men must have government or they will perish from the earth;[5] since no one can conceive this to be God's purpose, it follows that the secondary law of nature is the law of God as well as the law of necessity. "It is not in mens free will that they have government or no government, because it is not in their free will to obey, or not to obey the acts of the Court of nature, which is Gods Court, and this Court enacteth that societies suffer not mankind to perish, which must necessarily follow, if they appoint no government."[6]

A few days later Parker advanced the same argument, using slightly different terms. *Jus Populi, Or, A Discourse Wherein Clear Satisfaction Is Given* laid down a difference between "order" and "jurisdiction" or "government," which is the enforcement of order and hence presupposes sin:

> If *Adam* had not sinned in Paradise, order had been sufficient alone without any proper jurisdiction: it may well be supposed, that government, truly so called, had been no more necessary amongst men on earth, then it is now in Heaven amongst Angels. . . . We may then acknowledge that order is of a sublime and celestiall extraction, such as nature in its greatest purity did own; but subjection, or rather servile

[5] Theodore C. Pease's invaluable study, *The Leveller Movement,* is in error on this rather important point. Rutherford, Pease writes (p. 36), "admitted that the law of nature—a divine law—authorized government, and that man's power of ordaining government was, like his social propensities, a gift of God. But, Rutherford added, man was free to accept or reject this gift of God; the union of men in society was purely voluntary." This mistake is the more inexplicable because it attributes to Rutherford a position against which he argues at length. Maxwell had said that if government is derived from the social contract it must be purely voluntary; from which it would follow that it could claim no "majesty," the people as individuals not having sovereignty over each other. Both disputants regard the consequence that government has no "majesty" as manifestly false. For Maxwell its "absurdity" is proof that government does not derive from the social contract. But Rutherford avoids the consequence by qualifying the major premise (p. 44): "For the surrender [of the native right of the individual] is so voluntary, that it is also naturall, and founded on the Law of nature, That men must have Governours, either many, or one supreme Ruler: And it is voluntary . . . Whether the Government be by one supreme Ruler, as in a *Monarchie,* or in many, as in an *Aristocracie*. . . . This Constitution is so voluntary, as it hath below it, the Law of nature for its generall foundation; and above it, the supervenient institution of God, ordaining, That there should be . . . Magistrates . . . because without such, all humane societies should be dissolved."

[6] *Lex, Rex,* p. 8.

subjection, such as attends humane policy amongst us, derives not it self from Nature, unlesse we mean corrupted nature.[7]

Another development of natural-law political theory which influenced Milton (although less evidently in 1644–1645 than later) cannot be called Parliamentary. It is the serious adoption, first by the emergent Leveller party and after them by the "Independent" coalition, of the royalist debating point that if Parliamentary theory sanctioned the sovereign people's withdrawal of trust from the king, it must sanction a similar withdrawal of trust from Parliament should the latter act contrary to the terms of the original compact. The full growth and application of this idea lie beyond the limits of the present volume, but its origins are clearly discernible within them.

The argument is rooted in the fact that while resistance to Charles' political and ecclesiastical policies corresponded to the wishes of the majority of the political nation, the imposition of Parliamentary rule in the state and Presbyterian rule in the church did not. Even during the period when the Puritan leaders were minimizing their differences and presenting something like the appearance of unity there were moments of candor when they admitted that theirs was a minority movement. Anthony Tuckney, for example, the chairman of one of the Assembly's main standing committees, preaching to the House of Commons on August 30, 1643, gave, as a reason for Parliament to enforce reformation with a strong hand, the country's unwillingness to be reformed: "By your faithfulnesse herein (as you are our State-Physicians,) you may keep the disease from proving Epidemicall: for as for the generall body of this people, it hath welnigh overspread all; and therefore the representative bodies integrity (if any thing do) must stand for all, one body for another; you representing us all, as well to God as to man, and so being for the present the only meanes that is left of keeping off a Nationall guilt, and so the wrath of God from this whole Nation." [8] When the precarious unity of Puritanism cracked, the dissidents turned this opposition between the "representative body" and the "generall body" against the dominant group.

It was a religious issue that precipitated this development: in the opening months of 1645, as we saw, some of the characteristic dogmas of Levellerism began to be discernible in the tolerationist pamphlets of

---

[7] October 16, 1644; UCL JC389.P24, p. 3. Thomason's date is so soon after the imprinted date on *Lex, Rex* (October 7) that Parker could hardly have been influenced by Rutherford's published book, and personal influence seems unlikely at a time when the Erastians and the theocrats were at each other's throats.

[8] *The Balme of Gilead, For The Wounds of England;* E69(4), pp. 23–24.

Lilburne, Walwyn, and Overton (see above, pp. 88–92). But from the outset other matters besides religion were involved. For example, on the day of Zouch Tate's report on the charges against Manchester (the day the first Self-Denying Ordinance was introduced) Thomason wrote on a small printed leaflet "Decemb: 9th beinge Monday 1644. Written by some Independant against Ld Gen Essex and Ld gl Manchester, and scatred about yᵉ streets in the night." The term "Independant" is acceptable enough, since at this date it was meant to cover a broad coalition of dissidents, but we may recognize in the leaflet a tone (and perhaps also a technique) soon to be identifiable as Leveller: "Alas pore Parliament, how art thou betrai'd? . . . Wee have brave Generalls that fight for the King, and make pore honest people pay for their owne destructions. . . . Honour without honesty stinkes: away with't: no more Lords and yee love me, they smell o'the Court." [9]

Elsewhere in Thomason's collection there is a manuscript sheet, written by someone other than Thomason, headed "Two Libells." [10] The first, above which Thomason wrote, "This was found in a Church 25. June, 1645," consists of eight couplets such as these:

> Alas the Poore Souldier that Ventures his Life
> Getts nothing to maintain himselfe & his wife
> But asking for money is answered with Noe
> And snibd for his Labor wᵗʰ who bad you go
> We are threatned to ly by'th heeles if we prate
> This makes the Kings Army to hard for the State.
> The Carefull Comitte are shrewdly afraid
> The King would be Conquerd if we should be paid. . . .
> Tis strange that Advantages thus should be lost
> And they be most trusted that hinder us most. . . .

Above the second "Libell" Thomason wrote "June 3, 1645. given in to the parlement"; it reads:

> Wise men labour ⎫   Good Lord from heaven shew
> Good men grieve ⎪   mercy to us
> Knaves plot   ⎬   For Knaves & Fooles will
> Fooles believe ⎭   else undo us.

In fact, the Leveller party was forming. Nothing stimulated its growth more during the summer of 1645 than Lilburne's imprisonment, and this imprisonment at the same time hardened the tone of Lilburne and his associates. In September, after being moved to Newgate, he published *England's Miserie, And Remedie*. The source of the power of the House of Commons is its representative nature; but this makes it

[9] E21(9).   [10] E290(6); not in *Catalogue*.

"but the servant" of the people, and not to be imagined as greater than they. Lilburne quotes approvingly a speech made in the House by Edward Stephens: *"we have not withdrawne our selves from our obedience to the King, to yeild our selves slaves and vassalls to the Tyrannie of our fellow subjects."* [11] It is impossible, Lilburne continues, for men to rule justly by will; Parliament, like kings, must rule by law or degenerate into tyranny. Its imprisonment of Lilburne is tyrannical and cannot be accepted. The House is urged to reverse itself: "This Vote was obtained by *Bastwicke* surreptitiously, when the House was thinne and emptie; and therefore I conceive he may appeale from the House thin and emptie, to the House full and compleat." But if it will not reconsider, that does not end the matter: "if this will not be accepted of, why should he not appeale to the people." [12] Lilburne does not mean an appeal only to the passive sympathy of the people; if Parliament continues to make the multitude feel betrayed, it may expect mass disobedience.[13]

Here, almost fully developed, is the Leveller cry of rebellion. Much had to happen before the threat materialized, but its rationale when it did was what *England's Miserie* predicted; we may, for example, compare Lilburne's warning of 1645 with the title of Overton's pamphlet in July, 1647: *An Appeale From the Degenerate Representative Body the Commons of England Assembled at Westminster: To the Body Represented, the Free People in General.*[14]

9. SIGNIFICANCE FOR MILTON

We have emphasized the repetitiveness of the arguments from indifferency and Christian liberty, or rather the continuity of the argument but with the Presbyterian role reversed. We have seen how this fact created a wonderful tactical opportunity for the tolerationist coalition, and in the next chapter we shall see Milton taking the fullest advantage thereof. Once again, as in the case of civil supremacy, the controversy has something in it of masquerade. But again that is only part of the truth.

Coincident with the revolution in political theory, revolutionary ideas were developing about the role of the church in society and its relation both to the state and to the individual believer. Again these changing ideas had to find expression in traditional terms, and again this altered the meanings of the terms. For some—not all—of the opponents of compulsory Presbyterianism, the scope of indifferency was

[11] September 19; E302(5), p. 2. Attribution by Thomason.
[12] *Ibid.,* p. 3.   [13] *Ibid.,* p. 6.   [14] July 17; E398(28).

so far extended as to change its nature, and with it the nature of Christian liberty. Moreover, this evolution became integrated, for them, with the simultaneous and in some respects parallel evolution in the concept of natural law and its consequence, natural liberty.

One of the opponents of compulsive uniformity of whom this is true, as the next chapter will attempt to show, was Milton.

PART TWO: MILTON'S PAMPHLETS

Chapter III

THE DIVORCE TRACTS AND *AREOPAGITICA*

1. IMMEDIATE OCCASIONS OF THE PAMPHLETS

A MONTH or so after publishing his last anti-Episcopal tract Milton
left London on a mission of which his household knew nothing;
a month later he returned, bringing with him a young wife and
some of her family, royalist gentry from the vicinity of Oxford; in
another month she left him, at first apparently intending no more than
with his permission to spend the remainder of the summer at her family
home, but in the event refusing throughout the first Civil War to return
to him. About a year later Milton published *The Doctrine and Discipline of Divorce: Restor'd to the Good of Both Sexes.*

This chronology has freed Milton studies from a long and distracting
debate. So long as the traditional dating of June, 1643, was accepted
for Milton's marriage, the motivation of *The Doctrine and Discipline*
greatly agitated his admirers. The relevance of the tract to his own
situation could never be questioned, but unwillingness to accept Masson's reluctant picture [1] of Milton, while still on his honeymoon, composing the tract which he expected would release him from Mary, and
issuing it long before he knew she intended not to return from her visit
to her family, led many to insist that the relation was not causal, that
Milton launched his divorce argument out of pure zeal for religious
reformation, and that only later did he find that the case had become
his own. Others, less friendly to Milton, drew very different conclusions.
But with the recovery of the true date of June, 1642, for the marriage [2]
we may return with good confidence to the account of Milton's motives
given by the anonymous "earliest" biographer:

---

[1] *Life*, III, 45–47.

[2] Burns Martin ("The Date of Milton's First Marriage," *SP*, XXV (1928),
457–61, was the first to point to 1642. The argument was put with overwhelming
cogency by B. A. Wright in "Milton's First Marriage," *MLR*, XXVI (1931),
383–400, and XXVII (1932), 6–23.

Hee . . . could ill bear the disappointment hee mett with by her obstinate absenting: And therefore thought upon a Divorce, that hee
might bee free to marry another; concerning which hee also was in
treaty. The lawfulness and expedience of this . . . had upon full consideration & reading good Authors bin formerly his Opinion: And the
necessity of justifying himselfe now concurring with the opportunity,
acceptable to him, of instructing others in a point of so great concern
. . . hee . . . writt *The Doctrine and Discipline of Divorce*.[3]

The reading had not in fact been very full, nor, probably, the consideration; still, there is some reason to believe that, in a not very urgent
way, Milton had had a favorable opinion of divorce before he was
deserted.[4] The rest of the anonymous biographer's account seems wholly
characteristic of Milton: when the blow fell on himself, this favorable
opinion became an urgent conviction which he thought it his duty to
promulgate; and if he contemplated another marriage, he would not
have been satisfied to take advantage of the *de facto* arrangements
which were available (see below, p. 146), but would have felt it necessary to justify such a step publicly.

What and how much Milton expected of marriage, and how bitter
was his disappointment, we need not here recount: it is all passionately
set forth in the divorce tracts (and in *Paradise Lost* and *Samson Agonistes* too). But besides the hurt there was a continuing felt need. In
the poetry of his early manhood there is more than a hint that Milton
for a time contemplated a life of celibacy as a sort of sacrificial dedication of his poetic talents to the service of God. When he changed his
mind and decided to marry, it was presumably because he had decided
that he was not by nature fitted for a celibate life. Now he found himself married but still without a wife, unsuited for celibacy but debarred
a remedy. Already sympathetic on impersonal grounds to the idea of
divorce, he naturally turned to it now, not merely as a deliverance from
a galling and humiliating yoke, but also as a permission to form a better union.

We have little direct information on the reception accorded the first
edition of *The Doctrine and Discipline:* there is no known reference to

[3] "The Life of Mr. John Milton," in *The Early Lives of Milton*, ed. Helen
Darbishire (London: Constable, 1932), p. 23. This has been variously attributed
to Andrew Allan, Dr. Nathan Paget, John Phillips, and, most recently, Cyriack
Skinner; but the present state of the discussion leaves the authorship uncertain.

[4] James H. Hanford, "The Chronology of Milton's Private Studies," *PMLA*,
XXXVI (1921), 251–314, especially pp. 268–78, 286–87, and 294.
Of the many attempts to reconstruct Milton's idea of marriage, the most il-
luminating and convincing is in Haller, *Liberty and Reformation*, pp. 78–99,
based in part on William and Malleville Haller, "The Puritan Art of Love,"
Huntington Library Quarterly, V, 1942, 235–72.

the divorce tracts dating from the half-year during which that pamphlet stood alone. Nevertheless, we can reconstruct the character of the reception well enough. The pamphlet obviously sold fast, since the greatly enlarged second edition appeared within six months. But it was not a success to please Milton. Some of the buyers, he intimates in the epistle of the revised edition, were "the brood of Belial, the draffe of men," who laughed broad to see "so great a strength of Scripture mustering up in favour, as they suppose, of their debausheries." [5] Others, "out of a waterish and queasy conscience," railed at the book as injurious and licentious, if not worse.[6] Still others reacted in a way at which he only hints here: "But this question concerns not us perhaps." [7] They cannot have meant that the problem of divorce was of no concern to a deserted man. Perhaps they were clergymen who declared, among other things, that the reformation of the church was not the concern of the laity. At any rate, although he chose not to be unambiguous about it here, Milton already knew (as he later wrote) that *"some of the Clergie began to inveigh and exclaim on what I was credibly inform'd they had not read."* [8]

However galling this was to Milton, it was not yet enough to alienate him from the Presbyterian clergy. One of the most interesting features of the epistle to the second edition of *The Doctrine and Discipline* is that it was addressed "To the Parlament of England, with the Assembly." [9] It is to this "concourse of so much piety and wisdome" that he appeals from "the clamor of so much envie and impertinence"; [10] and if in fact it was "chiefly to the Parlament" [11] that he looked, nevertheless his inclusion of the Assembly in his address about a month after the Apologetical Narrators had abandoned all hope of it remains a significant indication of where he stood.

By July or August he had given it up. The epistle of *The Judgment of Martin Bucer Concerning Divorce* is addressed to Parliament alone, and in place of the appeal to the Westminster Assembly there is a warning to Parliament not to be guided by *"the scanty and unadequat and inconsistent principles of such as condemn others for adhering to traditions, and are themselves the prostrate worshippers of Custom."* [12]

[5] Below, p. 225.   [6] Below, pp. 225–26.   [7] Below, p. 226.
[8] *Martin Bucer*, below, p. 434.
[9] Below, p. 222.   [10] Below, p. 224.   [11] Below, p. 233.
[12] Below, p. 439. It appears not to have been noticed that the title of Milton's tract derives from a sectional subtitle in *Certain Briefe Treatises* (700.e.32; 1641), the book which occasioned Milton's *Reason of Church-Government* (see *Complete Prose*, I, 738–39 and 768). *Certain Briefe Treatises* contains excerpts and occasional pieces by a number of defenders of Episcopacy (for a full account see *Complete Prose*, I, 193–98). The third section (pp. 43–75) is "The

If Milton had hitherto been unwilling to believe that the Presbyterian clergy would continue to denounce, without deigning to answer, the serious reforming argument of the lay associate of Smectymnuus, he could doubt it no longer. In this half-year, as in the preceding, there are no unmistakeable allusions to the divorce argument (although it may be, as Haller suggests,[13] that such an allusion would have been recognized by Thomas Young's hearers when Milton's old tutor, in a sermon at Westminster on February 28, 1644, warned Parliament against legalizing "digamy"); but *Bucer* leaves us in no doubt that Milton had been woundingly attacked, and by just the people with whom he had been associated against the bishops—men who had previously praised Milton's *"good service to the Church."* [14] They had *"stood now almost this whole year clamouring a farre off, while the book hath bin twice printed, twice bought up, & never once vouchsaft"* [15] to show the author where he was in error; instead, they had *"lavishly traduc't"* him for his opinions and drawn *"odious inferences"* therefrom.[16]

They had also, it would appear, attempted to get *The Doctrine and Discipline* suppressed and perhaps its author punished; at any rate this would seem to be the necessary inference from two passages in *Bucer.* In the epistle, after speaking of the confidence with which he referred the *"judging"* of *The Doctrine and Discipline* to Parliament, Milton continues, *"Nor doth the event hitherto, for some reasons which I shall not heer deliver, faile me of what I conceiv'd so highly."* [17] What was the undisclosed event? The "Postscript," in a passage substantially anticipating the *Areopagitica,* hints at the answer. The works of Bucer and Erasmus on divorce enjoy a free circulation; if Milton's,

> containing but the same thing, shall in a time of reformation, a time of free speaking, free writing, not find a permission to the Presse, I referre me to wisest men, whether truth be suffer'd to be truth, or liberty to be liberty now among us, and be not again in danger of new fetters and captivity after all our hopes and labours lost: and whether learning be not (which our enemies too profetically fear'd) in the way to be trodd'n down again by ignorance. Wherof while time is, out of the faith owing to God and my Country, I bid this Kingdom beware: and doubt not but God who hath dignify'd this Parlament already to so many glorious degrees, will also give them (which is a singular bless-

Originall of Bishops and Metropolitans," of which the first subsection is entitled (p. 45) "The Judgement of Martin Bucer, touching the Originall of Bishops and Metropolitans."

[13] *Liberty and Reformation*, pp. 122–24. [14] Below, p. 437.
[15] Below, p. 436. [16] Below, p. 435. [17] *Ibid.*

ing) to inform themselvs rightly in the midst of an unprincipl'd age; and to prevent this working mystery of ignorance and ecclesiastical thraldom, which under new shapes and disguises begins afresh to grow upon us.[18]

Apparently Milton attempted, and failed, to get *The Doctrine and Discipline* licensed (since *Bucer* was licensed, the reference cannot be to it). He published it anyway. Then something took place which justified Milton's high confidence in referring *The Doctrine and Discipline* to Parliament's judgment. Did someone whom Milton regarded as part of a design to introduce a new ecclesiastical tyranny complain of the unlicensed *Doctrine and Discipline* to Parliament's Committee for Printing? If so, what justified Milton's confidence would be the Committee's decision not to proceed against him.

Milton was now determined that the clergy should not escape dealing with his argument on its merits, and he thought he had found a way to force them to it. When he began to write on divorce, he had not known that some earlier reformers had largely anticipated him. He had made what use he could of a helpful passage in Grotius, but despite this incidental support he had felt alone in taking up this *"rightful cause."* [19] Thinking that the clergy's treatment of the first edition of *The Doctrine and Discipline* might be in part due to its anonymity, he had decided to make it worth their while to answer his argument by showing them a respected name. By now he had learnt that Fagius shared something of his view on divorce, and used this fact in the second edition, assuming it would cause the divines to consider the argument seriously, *"at least to the moderating of their odious inferences."* [20] It had all been to no avail. But about three months later he had found with amazement that the great reformer Bucer had long since set forth virtually his own argument. Here was clearly *"a special Providence of God,"* who during the first reformation had brought Bucer to England to show it how necessary to a general reformation was the restoration of divorce, *"and now in this present renewing of the Church and Common-wealth, which we pray may be more lasting,"* caused *"the same question . . . [to] be again treated and presented to this Parlament, by one enabl'd to use the same reasons without the lest sight or knowledge of what was done before."* [21] Now at last Milton's traducers will be driven to deal with the subject itself; a better reply will be demanded of them than merely to dismiss as *"licentious, new and dangerous"* what Bucer *"so often, and so urgently avoucht to be most lawfull, most necessary, and most Christian."* [22]

[18] Below, p. 479.   [19] Below, p. 434.   [20] Below, p. 435.
[21] Below, p. 437.   [22] Below, p. 436.

Milton underestimated the conviction, on the part of most who are persuaded of their own orthodoxy, that to shout "wickedness, heresy, blasphemy" constitutes a full and satisfactory answer to an argument for reformation. A week after Milton had so hopefully displayed Bucer's support for his own views, Herbert Palmer, in that sermon before Parliament and the Assembly which we have already noticed (see above, pp. 102–104), without discussing Milton's argument, denounced his *"wicked booke"* and its *"impudent"* author and suggested that the former *"be burnt"*; he made no explicit recommendation as to what should be done with the latter.[23] On August 24 the Stationers' Company delivered to the House of Commons a petition whose substance is not known but which that House referred, on the 26th, to its Committee for Printing with instructions to prepare an ordinance and "diligently to inquire out the Authors, Printers, and Publishers of the Pamphlet against the Immortality of the Soul, and concerning Divorce."[24] The *Lords Journals* for September 18 show that the Commons had sent up some ordinance concerning printing, but what it was and what happened to it are not known.[25] In September, as we have seen (above, p. 105), the magisterial Prynne urged Parliament to suppress such dangerous *"Anabaptisticall, Antinomian, Hereticall, Atheisticall opinions, as of the soules mortality, divorce at pleasure, &c."*

Here Milton became the beneficiary of that tactical advantage which we have seen the tolerationist coalition to possess: his right to speak could be defended without its being necessary to espouse his ideas. In varying ways this is, in effect, what Henry Robinson and Henry Burton did in those answers to Prynne which we examined above (pp. 121–23). Since these allusions to Milton have not hitherto been noticed, they are worth giving. Robinson, whose *Answer to Mr. William Prynn's Twelve Questions* appeared on November 1, wrote:

> 'Tis an easie matter to exclaime against *Anabaptisticall, Antinomian, Hereticall, Atheisticall opinions, as of the soules mortality, divorce at pleasure*, &c. but one dram of apposite Scripture, and rectified reason would convince men of their errours, far sooner then the clubs & staves which were and are still imployed against our Saviour and his Saints.[26]

[23] Contemporary allusions to Milton were first systematically collected in William R. Parker, *Milton's Contemporary Reputation* (Columbus: Ohio State University Press, 1940), and amplified in J. Milton French, *The Life Records of John Milton* (5 vols., New Brunswick: Rutgers University Press, 1949–1958), where they may most conveniently be consulted. The only additions to the latter compilation which I have to propose for the years 1642–1646 are the passages from Robinson and Burton which follow immediately in the text, the quotation from Woodward given below, p. 506, n. 72, and the pamphlet discussed in Appendix C below.   [26] E15(5), p. 18.

[25] Masson, III, 274.   [24] French, II, 106–107; Masson, III, 164–65.

Robinson sounds as if he is not too sure that the ideas complained of are heresies; Burton the cleric is surer, and in his *Vindication,* which appeared November 14, he is concerned to free Independency from the blame which Prynne had put upon it for fostering such notions:

> You alledge also *Anabaptisticall, Antinomian, hereticall, Atheisticall opinions,* as of the *Souls mortality, Divorce at pleasure:* will you therefore father all these upon Christs Kingly goverment? In *Luthers* time sundry heresies sprung up; was *Luther* therefore either the cause or occasion of them? Doe wee not know, that Mothes are bred in the purest cloth? [27]

But he too argues against the proposal that Milton's books and the others be suppressed:

> And for means of suppressing errors, what means could suppresse those many errors that sprung up in the successive ages of the Church? Was not the word of God the onely meanes, and not humane power? yea humane power is as well a meanes to maintain heresies, as to suppresse them.[28]

But November was more notable for continued attacks on Milton than for these partial defenses of him. At last he got what he had so vehemently invited, a published reply to his argument. The anonymous *An Answer to a Book, Intituled, The Doctrine and Discipline of Divorce* appeared November 19.[29] To it was prefixed a laudatory statement by the licenser, Joseph Caryl, who spoke of the danger that might be worked "in unstaied mindes and men given to change" by the divorce argument, and commended the "good reason" with which the *Answer* "confuted" it. Also in November, Palmer's sermon of August was published.[30]

It was at this point (November 23, 1644) that the *Areopagitica* appeared. It probably went to the press well before the appearance of the *Answer,* but it is very doubtful that Milton's sense of decorum would have allowed the rhetoric of the *Areopagitica* to be disturbed in order to deal with the *Answer* even if he had seen it (he put in nothing in reply to Palmer or Prynne). He would attend to all these attacks in time. But *Areopagitica's* hit at "the fraud of some old *patentees* and *monopolizers* in the trade of book-selling," [31] its growing anticlericalism, its open threats to the Westminster Assembly, and its thinly veiled warnings to Parliament itself, all show how much that noble argument owes to the attacks upon the author of the divorce tracts.

[27] E17(5), p. 41.   [28] *Ibid.,* pp. 41–42.
[29] Reproduced in Parker, *Milton's Contemporary Reputation,* pp. 170 ff.
[30] See above, p. 103.   [31] Below, p. 570.

These attacks continued unabated. On December 28 the Stationers complained again (this time to the House of Lords) of the "Printing of scandalous Books by divers, as *Hezechia Woodward* and *Jo. Milton.*" [32] The Lords were at the same time receiving complaints about Milton from another source:

> The Assembly of Divines then sitting at Westminster, though formerly obliged by his learned Pen in the defense of Smectymnyus, and other thir controversies with the Bishops, now impatient of having the Clergies Jurisdiction, as they reckon'd it, invaded, instead of answering, or disproving what those books had asserted, caus'd him to be summon'd for them before the Lords.[33]

On receipt of the Stationers' complaint the Lords ordered that Woodward and Milton be examined. Woodward's interrogation appears to have been unpleasant; [34] nothing is known of Milton's save the anonymous biographer's statement that the Lords, "whether approving the Doctrin, or not favoring his Accusers, soon dismiss'd him." [35] On February 7, 1645, there appeared Daniel Featley's Καταβάπτισται κατάπτυστοι. *The Dippers Dipt.* It complains that the sects make "the Presses sweat and groane under the load of their blasphemies." Among the "damnable doctrines" abroad he lists "a Tractate of Divorce, in which the bonds of marriage are let loose to inordinate lust." [36] There were further attacks on Milton, but since they came too late to influence the final divorce tracts they need not be given here.[37]

At the beginning of March Milton published *Colasterion* and *Tetra-*

[32] *Lords Journals*, VII, 116; French, II, 116.

[33] The anonymous "earliest" biography, in Darbishire, p. 24; French, II, 117.

[34] In *Soft Answers, Unto Hard Censures* (February 5, 1645; E268[2]) Woodward defends himself against Thomas Edwards, who charged, among other things, that he had been proceeded against for publishing an unlicensed book. Woodward somewhat ruefully concedes the fact (pp. 1–2): "The *Wardens* have met with, and dealt with it and me as they pleased; or rather, as they said, their Dutie is, and warant in their hands to do. I confesse I took some offence at their Dealing, which they say was not given. I have no disposition, nor were it fitting, to dispute that. But because I took an offence, and, I thought, very justly, therefore will I be the more tender of offending them."

[35] Darbishire, p. 24; French, II, 117. Haller (*Liberty and Reformation*, p. 137) says "There is no record of [Milton] ever having been approached, apprehended, questioned, or further molested [*i.e.*, beyond being named in the documents of August 26 and December 9] by either house or the stationers for anything he had ever printed with or without permission," but he seems to have overlooked the statement in the anonymous biography.

[36] E268(11), sig. B2ᵛ; extract in Parker, p. 74.

[37] Except for the satire discussed in Appendix C below, they are given in Parker and French.

chordon. The former is occasioned entirely by the attacks on him. It devotes some space to Prynne and Caryl,[38] but of course the main "punishment" goes to the "Nameles Answer." *Tetrachordon* is less occasional a piece; it is a genuine enlargement and improvement of theory. However, the epistle thanks Parliament for refraining from giving *"the least interruption or disrepute either to the Author, or to the Book"* despite *"the furious incitements which have been us'd"* to provoke it against *The Doctrine and Discipline,*[39] and goes on to deal with Featley and Palmer. In the latter connection Milton makes a most instructive observation. Having asserted that Palmer was the chief author of *Scripture and Reason Pleaded for Defensive Arms* (see above, pp. 47, 49), he offers *"to make good the same opinion which I there maintain [i.e.,* in *The Doctrine and Discipline], by inevitable consequences drawn parallel from his own principal arguments in that of* Scripture and Reason; *which I shall pardon him, if he can deny, without shaking his own composition to peeces."* [40] It was not an idle boast, as we shall see; and it can teach us much about the source of Milton's ideas at this time.

2. THE ARGUMENT FOR DIVORCE: ORIGINAL FORM

Before the Reformation, the law governing divorce in England was the canon law. Since true marriage was held to be a sacrament, there could be no divorce in the sense of real dissolution of marriage *(a vinculo matrimonii)* with right to remarry. Divorce was only *a mensa et thoro* (separation from bed and board), and even this only by the sentence of an ecclesiastical court. Nullification, however, was possible for any cause which, being in existence before the marriage, interfered with its validity as defined by the canon law (*e.g.,* consanguinity, impotence, precontract, etc.). In England, the grounds of judicial separation were limited, more restrictively than elsewhere, to adultery and cruelty.

The Reformation, denying marriage to be a sacrament, reinstated divorce *a vinculo.* Almost all Protestant states legalized remarriage for the innocent party after divorce for adultery, and many after divorce for desertion. This position was strongly urged in England, was apparently favored by Edward VI, and was incorporated in the *Reformatio Legum Ecclesiasticarum* of 1552. While this code was defeated in the Commons, the provision permitting remarriage for the innocent party after divorce for adultery acquired an independent sanction: in 1548 a commission under Cranmer had approved the remarriage of the divorced Northampton, and in 1552 this was confirmed by Act of Parliament.

---

[38] See below, pp. 722–24 and 727–29.   [39] Below, p. 579.   [40] Below, p. 582.

After the Marian interlude, it became customary to regulate divorce by this provision. Its legality, however, in the uncertain state of the canon law, was very dubious. Furthermore, there was much opposition to it in the Episcopal hierarchy, and in 1597 Convocation declared that there was no legal basis for remarriage after divorce. Elizabeth did not sanction the Canons of 1597, but the limitation of divorce to judicial separation was repeated in those of 1604, which received James's approval. So far as they could, Puritans resisted this reaction. Even while Laud was at the height of his power, many ministers solemnized remarriages of the innocent parties in divorces for adultery or desertion, and when the Westminster Assembly met it approved this practice.[1]

Milton's demand went very much further. It was for the recognition of divorce *a vinculo* with the right of remarriage for both parties; the liberalization of grounds, particularly to include incompatibility; and the removal of divorce from public jurisdiction, whether ecclesiastical or civil, to private.

The framework of his argument was, of course, Scripture, and two of the dominant texts were inevitably the pronouncements of Moses and Christ (Deuteronomy 24:1-2 and Matthew 19:3-9):

> When a man hath taken a wife, and married her, and it come to pass that she find no favour in his eyes, because he hath found some uncleanness in her: then let him write her a bill of divorcement, and give it in her hand, and send her out of his house. And when she is departed out of his house, she may go and be another man's wife.

> The Pharisees also came unto him, tempting him, and saying unto him, Is it lawful for a man to put away his wife for every cause? And he answered and said unto them, Have ye not read, that he which made them at the beginning made them male and female, And said, For this cause shall a man leave father and mother, and shall cleave to his wife: and they twain shall be one flesh? Wherefore they are no more twain, but one flesh. What therefore God hath joined together, let not man put asunder. They say unto him, Why did Moses then command to give a writing of divorcement, and to put her away? He saith unto them, Moses because of the hardness of your hearts suffered you to put away your wives: but from the beginning it was not so. And I say unto you, Whosoever shall put away his wife, except it be for fornication, and shall marry another, committeth adultery: and whoso marrieth her which is put away doth commit adultery.

---

[1] This and the preceding paragraph are based upon *The Late Assembly of Divines Confession of Faith* (1651), p. 263; Gilbert Burnet, *History of the Reformation in the Church of England*, ed. Edward Nares (4 vols., London, 1837), II, 89–93; C. L. Powell, *English Domestic Relations 1487–1653* (New York, 1917), pp. 61–100; M. M. Knappen, *Tudor Puritanism* (Chicago, University of Chicago Press, 1939), pp. 456–61; and Gardiner, *Civil War, passim*.

To these Milton added a third text which was of equal importance in his argument (Genesis 2:18): "And the Lord God said, It is not good that the man should be alone; I will make him an help meet for him."

It is evident that Milton's position must rest upon Deuteronomy. But this involves the problem of the relation between the Old Testament and the New. The view Milton had hitherto taken of this relation would not have permitted him now to exploit the Mosaic permission of divorce:

> For the imperfect and obscure institution of the Law, which the Apostles themselves doubt not oft-times to vilifie, cannot give rules to the compleat and glorious ministration of the Gospell, which lookes on the Law, as on a childe, not as on a tutor. . . . How then the ripe age of the Gospell should be put to schoole againe, and learn to governe her selfe from the infancy of the Law . . . will be a hard undertaking to evince. . . . The whole Judaick law is either politicall, and to take pattern by that, no Christian nation ever thought it selfe oblig'd in conscience; or morall, which containes in it the observation of whatsoever is substantially, and perpetually true and good, either in religion, or course of life. That which is thus morall, besides what we fetch from those unwritten lawes and Ideas which nature hath ingraven in us, the Gospell, as stands with her dignity most, lectures to us from her own authentick hand-writing, and command, not copies out from the borrow'd manuscript of a subservient scrowl, by way of imitating.[2]

But in 1643 he has abandoned this view. For a full statement of the new attitude, for its grounds, and even for some of its most important consequences, we must await the revised edition and the *Tetrachordon*, but already in the first edition of the *Doctrine and Discipline* the "political" content of the Old Testament is subdivided into the *merely* political (that which was made specifically, and is relevant only, for the Jews) and the judicial, which, "being conversant, as it is, about vertue or vice" (below, p. 318), remains, along with the moral law, unabrogated, and is, despite the view previously taken of what behooves the dignity of the gospel, available for the guidance of Christians.

Available; but of course there can be no question of giving it precedence over the commands of Christ. Milton must therefore show that there is no contradiction between what Christ said to the Pharisees and what Moses permitted the Jews, and to do this he must "recover" the "long-lost meaning"[3] of that original institution of marriage to which Christ referred his questioners. To begin with, Milton lays down an axiom (below, p. 245): "All sense and reason and equity reclaimes that any Law or Cov'nant how solemn or strait soever, either between God

---

[2] *Reason of Church-Government* (1642), *Complete Prose*, I, 762–64.
[3] See the subtitle, below, p. 220.

and man, or man and man, though of Gods joyning, should bind against a prime and principall scope of its own institution." What is the prime end of marriage? The words of the institution tell us: "It is not good that the man should be alone; I will make him an help meet for him." From this it is clear that "a meet and happy conversation is the chiefest and the noblest end of mariage." The canon law itself, the chief obstacle to divorce, dissolves marriage on the ground of impotence; and its argument is good, for what frustrates the end of marriage dissolves marriage. But impotence interferes (or, at least, interferes necessarily) only with the subordinate carnal end of marriage; incompatibility, on the other hand, frustrates the primary end, a meet and happy conversation; by the same good argument, therefore, it is a greater cause than impotence for dissolving marriage.

The refusal to recognize incompatibility as a ground for divorce violates Christ's "supreme dictate of charitie," and how essential charity is in this case is soon apparent. Denied the necessary solace of love in lawful wedlock, the victim will be driven to seek it outside, "even against Law." Should he find the strength to resist this temptation, he is likely to succumb to a worse—"to dispair in vertue and mutin against divine providence." [4] In either case his salvation is imperilled; hence incompatibility is analogous with a second cause for dissolving marriage, and a cause more obviously authoritative than impotence, for it is directly expressed in Scripture, not merely inferred therefrom. This cause is idolatry in one partner, imperilling the salvation of the other.

It will be objected that Paul, in writing to the Corinthians, abolished this ground of divorce; but that is to misinterpret the text. There were two reasons for the command to the Jews to divorce idolaters, ceremonial uncleanness and danger to faith. The gospel removes the first reason along with the rest of the ceremonial law, and this is how Paul taught that the unbeliever was sanctified. But Paul does not remove the second reason, nor could he, for it is "morall and perpetuall in the rule of Christian faith," except that under the liberty of the gospel it is not a command but a permission. It is true that Paul advises against breaking a successful marriage for difference of religion, but he takes great care to make it clear that this is only "his counsell in a thing indifferent" *("to the rest speak I, not the Lord")*. We do Paul an injustice, we "outface him," if we take his words as anything more than advisory, for it is only in this sense that "the Apostle may interpose his judgement in a case of Christian libertie without the guilt of adding to Gods word." [5] Hence the Christian remains free to protect himself against

[4] For the passages quoted see below, pp. 246, 250, 253–54.
[5] See below, pp. 262, 266.

temptation by divorcing for idolatry—and, by analogy, for incompatibility.

But what of Christ's apparent prohibition of divorce except for fornication? His words here are commonly taken to mean that one may not divorce except for adultery, and that he who divorces for other reasons, and remarries, commits adultery. But what are the consequences of this interpretation? In the first place, Christ is made to violate his solemn protestation that he would abrogate no jot or tittle of the judicial law. Secondly, he is made to accuse the divine law of being the author of sin, having prescribed for the Jews remarriages which were in fact adulterous. But these consequences are unthinkable, from which it follows that the interpretation of the text is wrong (pp. 250 and 282–86).

What, then, is the true meaning? To recover this, Milton lays down "as a thing not to be deny'd," another principle of Biblical exegesis: the general intention of an obscure text is to be "expounded by considering upon what occasion every thing is set down: and by comparing other Texts." In dealing with the Pharisees it was not Christ's custom "to inform their proud ignorance what *Moses* did in the true intent of the Law"; so now, as they came to tempt him, it was appropriate that he give "a sharp and vehement answer," and as they were licentious men, that he "lay a bridle upon [their] bold abuses" by being as overstrict as they were overlax. Moses made no law on behalf of wicked men: "God forbid"! The permission of divorce was given for the necessary relief of good men. But the law can be no excepter of persons; a general permission must be generally available. Moses knew that wicked men would abuse this permission for evil ends, but such "hardnes of heart" "he held it better to suffer as by accident, where it could not be detected, rather then good men should loose their just and lawfull privilege of remedy." Christ's meaning, then, is that Moses suffered "you"— Pharisees and other licentious men—to put away "your" wives for "your" hardness of heart, not that this was the general intention of the permission; "for it was seasonable that they should hear their own unbounded licence rebuk't, but not seasonable for them to hear a good mans requisit liberty explained." [6]

That Christ was pointing to an unavoidable but accidental consequence of the law of divorce, rather than to its cause, is confirmed (Milton continues) by his reference to the original institution of marriage. "Therefore shall a man cleave to his wife, and they shall be one flesh"; but "therefore" implies a reason, and "this is a solid rule that every command giv'n with a reason, binds our obedience no otherwise then that reason holds." Now what is the reason of inseparability in

[6] Below, pp. 282, 283, 307.

marriage? The remedy of man's loneliness with a "meet help." But if a wife is not a meet help, the reason of inseparability is gone, and with it the inseparability. The law given to original perfection was later, by elaboration of its own grounds ("with due and wise regard had to the premises and reasons of the first command"), divinely adapted to the fallen condition of mankind; and Christ intended neither to rebuke nor to abrogate this Mosaic law.[7]

But to say that Christ gave no such command as is usually attributed to this passage is not to say that he gave no command at all. He did, and it is binding; but when understood it will be seen to clarify and in no way to contradict the law of Moses. The grounds for divorce allowed by Moses were "natural annoyance, defect, or dislike, whether in body or mind, (for so the Hebrew words plainly note)"; the reason for this is that what is natural is permanent. The Pharisees depraved this, and divorced for any cause, however temporary. Christ here declares that "no accidental, temporary, or reconciliable offence" can justify divorce; but to this he makes one exception: fornication. His command therefore leaves divorcive effect in all natural and permanent causes of displeasure, but debars accidental and temporary causes other than fornication.[8]

We have, then, not only the reasons for the Mosaic permission of divorce (with right of remarriage) for incompatibility, but also the evidence that Christ, in accordance with "his fundamental and superior laws of nature and charitie," left that permission intact. It was papal superstition that substituted divorce *a mensa et thoro* for true divorce, and it was papal tyranny that usurped jurisdiction over divorce to its own courts and defined the grounds as it pleased. But God placed the power of divorce in the conscience of the individual, and thither it must be restored. The magistrate ought to protect the property rights of each party, but neither he nor the church may interfere in the divorce itself.[9]

3. THE ARGUMENT FOR DIVORCE: FIRST REFINEMENTS

This is the main argument of the first edition, and its point of greatest weakness is not hard to discern: to accommodate Christ to Moses Milton had to interpret him as speaking, not to mankind, but to a very particular group. In the revised edition, as if to compensate for pleading from the special occasion, Milton greatly enlarges the function in his argument of general ideas: reason, nature, and Christian liberty.

Much of the new matter is brought to reinforce the contention that Christ did not abrogate the Mosaic law of divorce. In the course of

[7] Below, pp. 308–309, 311.   [8] Below, p. 331.   [9] Below, pp. 325, 342–54.

argument Milton formulates a view of the relation between the Old and New Testaments which is virtually a reversal of the view taken in the anti-Episcopal pamphlets: "If we examine over all his [Christ's] sayings, we shall find him not so much interpreting the Law with his words, as referring his owne words to be interpreted by the Law." [1] In the light of this dictum he repeats and amplifies the earlier argument that since to abrogate would involve unthinkable consequences Christ could not have abrogated. It may be objected that nothing is impossible for God, who does what He wills. Milton's reply is a rather militant variety of Christian rationalism:

> God hath not two wills, but one will, much lesse two contrary. If he once will'd adultery should be sinfull . . . all his omnipotence will not allow him to will [its] allowance. . . . The hidden wayes of his providence we adore & search not; but the law is his reveled wil, his complete, his evident, and certain will; herein he appears to us as it were in human shape, enters into cov'nant with us, swears to keep it, binds himself like a just lawgiver to his own prescriptions, gives himself to be understood by men, judges and is judg'd, measures and is commensurat to right reason.[2]

Because his law is commensurate to right reason, God "requires the observance therof not otherwise then to the law of nature and of equity imprinted in us seems correspondent." But the "two prime statutes" of nature are "to joyn it self to that which is good and acceptable and friendly; and to turn aside and depart from what is disagreeable, displeasing and unlike." Divorce for incompatibility is therefore natural, and since "law and nature are not to goe contrary, then to forbid divorce compulsively, is not only against nature, but against law." [3]

In his prefatory address to Parliament and the Westminster Assembly, Milton examines the secret motive of those who pretend that the permission of divorce is abrogated. It is to frustrate the progress of reformation by making the godly life seem too formidable to be attempted. "What greater weakning, what more suttle stratagem against our Christian warfare, when besides the grosse body of real transgressions to encounter; wee shall bee terrify'd by a vain and shadowy menacing of faults that are not: When things indifferent shall be set to overfront us, under the banners of sin, what wonder if we be routed?" (For

[1] Below, p. 301; *contra Church Government*, quoted above, p. 147.

[2] Below, p. 292. Arthur Barker, in "Christian Liberty in Milton's Divorce Pamphlets," *MLR*, XXXV (1940), 153–61, and *Milton and the Puritan Dilemma*, pp. 63–120, demonstrated the stages in the development of Milton's thought within the divorce tracts. The present account, while differing in some respects from Barker's analysis, is heavily indebted to it.

[3] See below, pp. 297, 345–46.

marriage being "a civil, an indifferent" law, it follows that divorce is a thing indifferent.) Those whose task it is to reform a nation must not be deceived by this stratagem, on peril of general failure. "He who wisely would restrain the reasonable Soul of man within due bounds, must first himself know perfectly, how far the territory and dominion extends of just and honest liberty. As little must he offer to bind that which God hath loos'n'd, as to loos'n that which he hath bound." [4]

If this warning is intended primarily for the Assembly, it is explicitly to the Long Parliament that Milton addresses a remarkable and pregnant analogy between divorce and political reformation. That inveterate enemy of truth, Custom (who "rests not . . . untill by secret inclination, shee accorporat her selfe with error"), has distorted the nature of the domestic covenant and denied the "gentle Ordinance" provided against failure, precisely as she has the political covenant and its remedy; therefore,

> Advise yee well, supreme Senat, if charity be thus excluded and expulst, how yee will defend the untainted honour of your own actions and proceedings: He who marries, intends as little to conspire his owne ruine, as he that swears Allegiance: and as a whole people is in proportion to an ill Government, so is one man to an ill mariage. If they against any authority, Covnant, or Statute, may by the soveraign edict of charity, save not only their lives, but honest liberties from unworthy bondage, as well may he against any private Covnant, which hee never enter'd to his mischief, redeem himself from unsupportable disturbances.[5]

It was obviously excellent rhetoric for Milton to relate his own case to that of Parliament in this way. But the analogy was not his invention. When Henry Ferne set out to refute the Parliamentary argument that the social contract justified the people's resumption of power if the king broke his trust, one of his points was that if there was an original covenant, then its terms (as evidenced by the coronation oath) made no provision for the action of Parliament.[6] William Bridge replied that "though there be no such words expressed . . . , in reason that must be implyed," [7] and relied for demonstration upon an analogy between the two institutions ordained by God for man, government and marriage:

> there is a covenant stricken betweene a man and a woman at Marriage; when they marry one another it is not verbally expressed in their agreement, that if one commit Adultery, that party shall be divorced; and

---

[4] Below, pp. 228–29, 227.   [5] Below, pp. 223, 229.
[6] *Resolving of Conscience* (December, 1642), 701g4(4), p. 21.
[7] *The Wounded Conscience Cured* (February 11, 1643), E89(8), p. 31.

yet we know that that covenant of Marriage carries the force of such a condition.[8]

Ferne, of course, repudiated the analogy, but in a way that emphasized its utility to a proponent of divorce who was also a supporter of Parliament:

> That Adultery is the breach of the Mariage Covenant and cause of Divorce, both [9] the institution of Marriage, *They two shall be one flesh*, doth in reason imply, and the Law of God doth expresly declare; and the like implication of reason and declaration of Law must appear, before we can see any warrant for Subjects to resist and provide for their own safety.[10]

All that was needed to bring Bridge's analogy into Milton's service was to extend one of its terms. How this could be done might be learnt from the pamphlet to which Milton directed such particular and challenging attention, claiming his principles in the divorce argument to be only extensions of its principles. *Scripture and Reason Pleaded,* arguing that despite the divine sanction for government the people may resume some of their delegated powers when necessary, uses the analogy between the two ordinances:

> A Wife is tyed to her Husband by the Covenant of God, (so called *Prov. 2.*) by the Ordinance of God more ancient, and no lesse strong then that of Politick Government. She cannot recall wholly her Husbands Authority over her. . . . Yet for her necessity, she may by the Law of God and conscience . . . secure her Person from his violence by absence (though that ordinarily be against the Law of Marriage, and the end of it,) or any other meanes of necessary defence.[11]

Palmer and his associates do not talk of divorce, but they have brought separation of man and wife on grounds other than adultery into relation with Parliament's case for resistance to Charles. Milton had only to push one more step—to advance from separation to divorce—to possess himself of the analogy.

4. THE ARGUMENT FOR DIVORCE: FINAL FORM

The additional ideas introduced by the revision of *The Doctrine and Discipline* are no doubt forceful, and they reveal very clearly the direction in which Milton's thought was developing, but they can hardly be said to overcome the difficulty which vitiated the original argument, that of having to restrict the application of Christ's words to a special

[8] *Ibid.*   [9] Text: "both in."
[10] *Conscience Satisfied* (April 18, 1643), E97(7), p. 70.
[11] April 14, 1643; E247(22), pp. 35–36.

group. It was not until the *Tetrachordon* that Milton found the way to permit Christ's dictum general applicability without having the effect of abrogating the Mosaic permission. This way was through the further elaboration of the concept, already an essential part of his argument, of natural law.

"Hardness of heart," says Milton, has a twofold meaning in Scripture. One of these, "a stubborne resolution to doe evil," we have already noticed, and we have seen that God never makes laws on this behalf—it is only that the nature of the case makes it necessary for the lawmaker to "suffer," as by accident, this hardness of heart to abuse laws made for those who would be good. But the other meaning is general, since it is simply a description of the fallen condition of man. It was on behalf of this hardness of heart, "the imperfection and decay of man from original righteousnesse," that God suffered divorce, and suffered it not only justly but necessarily. "Had men continu'd perfet, it had bin just that all things should have remain'd, as they began to *Adam & Eve*. But after that the sons of men grew violent & injurious, it alter'd the lore of justice, and put the government of things into a new frame." [1] This is the distinction—*i.e.*, between the primary and the secondary laws of nature—which Christ was making when he said "from the beginning it was not so." He meant nothing so absurd as that in the era preceding the promulgation of the Mosaic law marriage was indissoluble: history itself would belie such a meaning, for that was a period when licence went amost unrebuked, or, when, at any rate, there was no manifest and certain rule by which to rebuke it; and the function of Moses was to introduce a stricter discipline. Christ was contrasting the just and necessary permission of the secondary law of nature with the just and necessary prohibition of the primary: "While man and woman were both perfet each to other, there needed no divorce; but when they both degenerated to imperfection, & oft times grew to be an intolerable evil each to other, then law . . . justly did permitt the alienating of that evil." But this contrast implies no abrogation by Christ of the secondary law and restoration of the primary; that would require the restoration of man to his unfallen condition ("the persons . . . must be such as then were").[2]

---

[1] Below, pp. 661–62, 665.

[2] See below, pp. 665–66. Something of the substance of this argument, but not the form or the nomenclature, was briefly anticipated in a digression in the first edition of *The Doctrine and Discipline* (below, p. 326): Christ does not "oblige our performance to that whereto the law never enjoyn'd the fal'n estate of man; for if the first institution must make wedlock, what ever happen, inseparable to us, it must make it also as perfect . . . as God promis'd it should be . . . otherwise it is not equal."

Let us return momentarily to the logical weakness at the centre of the *Doctrine and Discipline*. Why had Milton restricted the application of "hardness of heart" to wicked men? To avoid the received view that Christ explained the permission of divorce as a capitulation by Moses to the uncontrollable licentiousness of his people, and that Christ himself, by bringing new grace into the hearts of believers, first removed the cause and then abrogated the permission.[3] Why (aside from the implausibility of the contention that Christ was veiling the true doctrine) was this restriction damaging to Milton's end? Because there could be no denying that, to whatever effect, Christ had glossed the permission of divorce; and it was, after all, the permissive reason that Milton was restricting even as he went about to effect the indirect rescue of the permission. What was really required was such an interpretation of "hardness of heart" as would embrace—and embrace necessarily—Christians, when the form of the argument could become: the cause continues to exist, hence the permission remains in effect. This interpretation Milton now achieves through the elaboration of his concept of the law of nature.

But it is important to observe that this concept prevents the argument from being limited to Christians, or to Christians plus Jews; if the secondary law of nature is binding at all, it must bind the whole of fallen mankind. Accordingly, the *Tetrachordon* adds to the *Doctrine and Discipline's* demand for Christian liberty a demand for natural liberty. This does not mean that it is an argument for non-Christians to do whatever their individual natures prompt, any more than *Doctrine and Discipline* was an argument for the right of Christians to loosen what God had bound. The secondary law of nature may be a law given to imperfection, but it is nevertheless a law; and it prescribes an objective standard of righteousness (albeit that righteousness is not perfect). Hence, just as the right of Christian liberty depends upon true religion, so the right of "just and naturall privileges" depends upon "inward goodnesse." Because this is pretty well understood, and because both natural virtue and true religion are now somewhat rare, "it may save the wondring why in this age many are so opposite both to human and to Christian liberty." Still, whatever the conditions of natural liberty, it is a liberty available to all men, regardless of their

[3] Thomas Fuller's *Sermon of Reformation*, which reached Thomason the day after he received Milton's first divorce tract, happens to contain a brief statement of this received view. To exemplify his contention that every Christian era was a time of reformation in some degree, Fuller writes (E63[3], p. 5), of, *inter alia*, "the Bill of Divorce cancelled by Christianity, which was permitted to the Jewes, not because that was good, but because they were bad, and by this Toleration were kept from being worse."

faith or lack of faith ("there are left som remains of Gods image in man, as he is meerly man"). Scripture could not justly,[4] and therefore certainly does not, infringe this natural liberty.

When to this is added Milton's axiom that "no ordinance human or from heav'n can binde against the good of man" (as even "Heathens could see"), it is evident that a new test is available for the interpretation of Scripture. The *Doctrine and Discipline* laid it down that any interpretation of the gospel was wrong which contradicted the moral, hence perpetual, content of the Old Testament. It is now added that any interpretation of either Testament is wrong which contradicts the secondary law of nature as that is ascertained by the light of reason; and conversely that this law is the best positive guide of scriptural interpretation: "Nothing sooner might direct them to finde his [Christ's] meaning, then to compare and measure it by the rules of nature and eternall righteousnes, which no writt'n law extinguishes, and the Gospel least of all." (The *Tetrachordon* restates the relation of the Old Testament and the New in terms of three categories of law. The ceremonial law was fulfilled by Christ and is no longer applicable. The judicial is of two kinds: that which was ordained to meet specifically Jewish circumstances—"meerely *judaicall*"—and that which "reaches to human equity in common." The former was abrogated along with the ceremonial law; the latter, with the moral law of which it is an expression, remains in force for Christians.) [5]

The immediate purpose of Milton's new test of interpretations of Scripture is to validate the use of "the lively Sculpture of ancient reason, and humanity" in recovering the permission of divorce, but its ultimate significance is to be vastly greater, for divorce is only a small part of the secondary law of nature. Milton invokes the whole of that law to make clear the force of his argument:

> Partly for this hardnesse of heart, the imperfection and decay of man from original righteousnesse, it was that God suffer'd not divorce onely, but all that which by Civilians is term'd the *secondary law of nature and of nations.* He suffer'd his owne people to wast and spoyle and slay by warre, to lead captives, to be som maisters, som servants, som to be princes, others to be subjects, hee suffer'd propriety to divide all things by severall possession, trade and commerce, not without usury; in his common wealth some to bee undeservedly rich, others to bee undeservingly poore. All which till hardnesse of heart came in, was most unjust; whenas prime Nature made us all equall, made us equall

---

[4] *E.g.*, below, p. 637: "How can this in the vulgar and superficiall sense be a law of Christ, so farre from beeing writt'n in our hearts, that it injures and disallowes . . . nature and morall law." Other quotations in this paragraph: below, pp. 587, 591.   [5] See below, pp. 588, 636, 642.

coheirs by common right and dominion over all creatures. In the same manner, and for the same cause hee suffer'd divorce as well as mariage, our imperfet and degenerat condition of necessity requiring this law among the rest. . . . If therefore we abolish divorce as only suffer'd for hardnes of heart, we may as well abolish the whole law of nations, as only sufferd for the same cause. . . . If nothing now must be suffer'd for hardnes of heart, I say the very prosecution of our right by way of civil justice can no more bee suffer'd among Christians, for the hardnes of heart wherwith most men persue it. And that would next remove all our judiciall lawes, and this restraint of divorce also in the number; which would more then halfe end the controversy.[6]

This is not, of course, a plea for anarchy. It is a demonstration of the validity of the secondary law of nature on the ground that if we reject it anarchy must ensue. But if the secondary law of nature is valid, so is the permission of divorce prescribed by it.

Milton has here gone far beyond his analogy of the preceding year between divorce and Parliament's "own actions and proceedings." He has completely integrated the case for divorce with that for Parliamentary supremacy: they are twin consequences of a single principle, the jurisdiction of the secondary law of nature. Why did he thus merge his argument with the Parliament's? The tactical advantage, of course, is obvious; but there may well be a further reason. Where had Milton learnt to improve his argument by distinguishing, not between Pharisees and other men, but between the primary and secondary laws of nature? He had not known how to use this distinction for his purposes early in 1644.

Surely the answer is that he learnt this where, by his own testimony, and a great deal of independent evidence, he had already learnt so much of his argument: from Parliamentary apologetics. Until October of 1644 the distinction between the primary and secondary laws of nature had not figured in the Parliamentary argument; in that month, as we saw above (pp. 131–33), it entered Parliamentary theory in order to perform the same function as it performs in the *Tetrachordon*: to prevent Christians from being held to a higher moral duty than that imposed by natural law.

This provenience for the distinction would seem to be confirmed by its subsequent role in Milton's thought, for he would next employ it in the direct service of Parliamentary apologetics. When, at the great crisis of the revolution four years later, Milton proclaimed himself a Parliamentary republican, it would be on the basis of the natural-law theory in the form worked out in the *Tetrachordon*. In the *Tetrachordon* the secondary law of nature as determined by the reason of fallen man

[6] Below, pp. 661–62. The earlier quotation is on p. 621.

provides a test of the interpretation of Scripture and of the validity of human laws with reference to marriage; then it will do the same with reference to the state. Now it requires that there be "juridical law and civil power"; then it will prescribe their content.

5. THE HISTORY OF LICENSING

The *Areopagitica* is a document in the history of two distinct if interdependent ideas, freedom of the press and religious liberty. Its background in the latter connection was described in Chapter II; something may now be said of the history of press control.

Milton himself declares that the licensing of books was an invention of "the Councell of Trent, and the Spanish Inquisition engendring together" which "bewitcht of late our Prelats" to imitate it; he denounces the Licensing Order of 1643 as "the immediat image of a Star-chamber decree . . . made in those very times when that Court did the rest of those her pious works, for which she is now fall'n"; and in general he gives the impression that licensing is a thoroughly un-English policy, recently imported by "apishly Romanizing" bishops and perfected only in 1637 (the date of the Star Chamber decree to which he refers).[1] It is remarkable how generally this view has been accepted, for it is widely at variance with the facts. One thing may be said in its defense: the enforcement of licensing in England had been very uneven, and there were considerable periods during which the regulations were largely ignored, so that the rigorous and determined attempt of 1637 to secure universal compliance might well have struck men as something new. But the policy of licensing was far from new, and had been employed not only by Charles and Laud but by kings and churchmen whom Milton thought true Protestant reformers.

One hundred and thirty-seven years before the Council of Trent met (sixty-eight years before printing was introduced in England) archbishop Arundel's Constitutions of 1408 (confirmed by the Parliament of 1414) commanded that "no book . . . be from henceforth read . . . within our province of Canterbury aforesaid, except the same be first examined by the university of Oxford or Cambridge . . . and . . . expressly approved and allowed by us or our successors, and in the name and authority of the university . . . delivered unto the stationers to be copied out." [2] This, it is true, was an emergency measure whose effect was short-lived, but from fifteen years before the first meeting of the

---

[1] See below, pp. 502–504, 569–70. Of course Milton does not suggest that there was no censorship of any kind before 1637; see below, pp. 163–64, 492.

[2] John Foxe, *Acts and Monuments* (8 vols., London, 1844), III, 245.

Council of Trent to twenty years after Milton's death, licensing was a frequently reformulated policy in England. In 1530, before his break with Rome, Henry VIII forbade the printing of "any boke or bokes in englisshe tonge, concernynge holy scripture, not before this tyme printed within this his realme, untyll suche tyme as the same boke or bokes be examyned and approved by the ordinary of the diocese," and required approved books to carry "the name of the examynour" and that of the printer.[3] In 1538, after making religious and political issues almost indistinguishable by assuming the ecclesiastical supremacy, he extended licensing to English books of all kinds, transferred responsibility from the church officers to the Privy Council, and prescribed the form of the imprimatur.[4] The system was reasserted by Edward in a proclamation of 1551, by Mary in proclamations of 1553 and 1558, and by Elizabeth in the royal injunctions of 1559. A Privy Council Order of June 29, 1566, associated the recently incorporated Stationers Company with the administration of the system, and a Star Chamber Decree of June 23, 1586, clarified its procedures. James confirmed the inherited system in the Commissions of 1611 and 1613.[5]

The culmination of this development was Charles' Star Chamber Decree of July 11, 1637. This, the fruit of a century of experience in the control of the press, is the most elaborate instrument in English history for the suppression of undesired publication; nothing was unforeseen except the determination with which it was defied. The decree began by making it a general offence to print, import, or sell "any seditious, scismaticall, or offensive Bookes or Pamphlets."[6] It then forbade anything to be printed which had not first been licensed and entered in the Stationers' Register, or anything to be reprinted, "though formerly printed with licence,"[7] unless relicensed; in all cases the full signed imprimatur was to be printed, along with the names of author and printer. The decree then limited the number of master printers to twenty, specified the number of presses, journeymen, and apprentices each could have, and made it an offence for anyone to own, work, or provide space for an unlicensed press. It empowered the Stationers Company to "search what houses and shops (and at what time they

[3] Proclamation of June, 1530; C18e2(113).

[4] Proclamation of November 16, 1538, reproduced in *Tudor Proclamations* (Oxford, 1897), a facsimile collection made for the British Museum (8 Tab. d3).

[5] F. S. Siebert, *Freedom of the Press in England 1476–1776* (Urbana: University of Illinois Press, 1952), pp. 41–87 and 127–46.

[6] *A Decree of Starre-Chamber, Concerning Printing* (July 11, 1637); 517k3(8), sig. B1. The *Decree*, partially summarized, is printed in Appendix A, below, pp. 793–96.

[7] *Ibid.*, sig. F1. See below, p. 795.

shall think fit)" to discover "printing in Corners without licence,"[8] thus using the Stationers' economic interest in suppressing the competition of unlicensed printers as a means of creating a particularly devoted special police to guard against unlicensed books. Finally, the decree prohibited the import or sale of unlicensed publications.

The abolition of Star Chamber on July 5, 1641, left the press virtually without legal regulation. In essence, if not in detail, Selden was right when, in 1628, he declared that "there is no Law to prevent the printing of any Books in England, only a Decree in Star-Chamber":[9] the whole history of the control of printing had been an exercise of the royal prerogative.

On January 29, 1642, the House of Commons published the following order:

> It is ordered that the Master and Wardens of the Company of Stationers shall be required to take especiall Order, that the Printers doe neither print, nor reprint any thing without the name and consent of the Author: And that if any Printer shall notwithstanding print or reprint any thing without the consent and name of the Author, that he shall then be proceeded against, as both Printer and Author thereof, and their names to be certified to this House.[10]

In his attack on the Licensing Order of seventeen months later, Milton takes this, which we may call the Signature Order, to have been the full implementation of Parliament's original policy for the press, of which the subsequent order was a reversal:

> And as for regulating the Presse, let no man think to have the honour of advising ye better then your selves have done in that Order publisht next before this, that no book be Printed, unlesse the Printers and the Authors name, or at least the Printers be register'd. . . . For this *authentic* Spanish policy of licencing books . . . how it got the upper hand of your precedent Order so well constituted before . . . it may be doubted there was in it the fraud of some.[11]

Had the published order been the whole action of the House on this occasion, had it really been "next before" the Licensing Order, and were there no other evidence to the contrary, it might be possible to support this view. However, the entry in the *Commons Journal* for January 29, 1642 (II, 402) contains the following matter preliminary to the Signature Order as published: "*Ordered,* That the Committee for Printing, and the Bill of Printing, shall be revived; to sit on *Monday* Morning at Eight of Clock, in the Court of Wards; and that the Master and

---

[8] *Ibid.*, sig. G3; see below, p. 796.
[9] Rushworth, *Historical Collections*, I, 665.
[10] E207(2).   [11] Below, pp. 569–70.

Wardens of the Company of Stationers shall be required, etc." This in itself would make it clear that the Signature Order was intended, not as the sole regulation governing the press, but as an interim measure to combat piracy until a bill for the general control of the press could be reported and enacted. Furthermore, two orders intervene between the Signature and Licensing Orders. The first, dated August 26, 1642, begins: "Whereas there hath beene of late great disorders and abuses by Irregular Printing, to the great scandall of Religion and government, and a Bill is in preparation for the redresse of those mischiefes, which by reason of the present distractions cannot be so speedily perfected and passed as is desired"; it then orders "that no person or persons shall Print, publish, or utter, any Booke or Pamphlet, false or scandalous, to the proceedings of the Houses of Parliament, or either of them," and vests in the Stationers and in Black Rod and the Serjeant of the Commons powers of search and seizure.[12] The second intervening order, dated March 9, 1643, broadens the scope to all "scandalous and lying Pamphlets," adds powers of arrest and imprisonment to those earlier enumerated, and adds the Parliamentary printing committees to the administering officials previously named.[13]

The Order of January 29, 1642, then, "revives" a "Bill of Printing," and the Order of August 26, 1642, declares itself to be a temporary measure designed as a stop-gap until a more comprehensive bill which has been in preparation can be completed. This cannot refer to the Order of March 9, 1643, since that merely enlarges some of the provisions of the professedly temporary order. The reference in both cases must be to the bill which finally matured as the Licensing Order. Since this measure had been in process some time before January, 1642, the inference is inescapable that Parliament began to prepare its own licensing system as soon as the Crown's system was abolished, the delay in completing it probably being due as much to resistance by the minority groups in Parliament and Assembly as to the military "distractions" by which the Order of August 26, 1642, sought to explain it.

Impatience at the bill's delays was exhibited from an outside source, as well as by Parliament itself. The regulation of the trade affairs of publishing, along with the censorship of its product, had collapsed with Star Chamber, and the number of presses and printing establishments had steadily increased with the public appetite for news, polemic, and edification. In April, 1643, the Stationers Company petitioned Parliament for the reinstatement of the customary restrictions. Milton,

---

[12] E114(32), sig. A3–4; *Commons Journals*, II, 739.
[13] Husbands, *A Collection*, p. 5; *Commons Journals*, II, 997.

with understandable irritation, described this petition as "the fraud of some old *patentees* and *monopolizers* in the trade of book-selling; who . . . brought divers glosing colours to the House, which were indeed but colours," and attributed to it much influence in procuring the Licensing Order.

The petition begins by arguing that the public interest requires a "well-ordered" press, and that this in turn depends upon the prosperity of the printing trade: "commonly where Printing droops, and Printers grow poor by neglect of Government, there errors and heresies abound" because poverty emboldens printers to "run into enormious disorders." [14] With questionable tact, it proceeds to "give Papists their due; for as well where the Inquisition predominates, as not, regulation is more strict by far, then it is amongst Protestants; we are not so wise in our Generation, nor take so much care to preserve the true Religion as they do the false from alteration." [15] Since Parliament is preparing a bill "for supply of that Government which is faln" [16] with the Star Chamber, the petition, after reminding Parliament that "The main care is to appoint severe Examiners for the licensing of things profitable, and suppressing of things harmfull," urges the inclusion of the Company in enforcing the expected order, since "in matters of the Presse, no man can so effectually prosecute, as Stationers themselves." [17]

With respect to trade affairs, the petition asks for control of the number and condition of printing establishments, presses, and workers, restrictions on foreign competition, and the restoration of the stationers' "ancient Right, Propriety of Copies . . . that in some mens understanding, is the same thing as a Monopoly: Though it be not so much a free priviledge as a necessary right to Stationers." [18]

Finally, on June 14, 1643, Parliament passed the Order against which Milton wrote the *Areopagitica*. Its provisions may well be said to justify Milton's charge that it is "the immediat image" of the decree of 1637 (the Order is reproduced in full in Appendix B, below, pp. 797–99). After repeating the complaints of the earlier orders against "the great late abuses and frequent disorders in Printing" and explaining that the interim measures have been ineffectual "By reason the bill in preparation, for redresse of the said disorders, hath hitherto bin retarded through the present disorders," the Order sets up what is in all essentials the machinery of 1637: licensing, registration, signature,

---

[14] *To the High Court of Parliament: The Humble Remonstrance of the Company of Stationers* (April, 1643); E247(23), sig. A1v. Thomason attributed the drafting of the petition to Henry Parker.

[15] *Ibid.*   [16] *Ibid.*, sig. A2.   [17] *Ibid.*   [18] *Ibid.*, sig. A3.

copyright, import control, search and seizure, arrest, imprisonment by order of Parliamentary committee, and association of the Stationers in administering the Order.

The attack on licensing by Milton and others effected no change in the Long Parliament's policy; on the contrary, it was reasserted in Orders of September 30, 1647,[19] and March 13, 1648.[20] The Commonwealth Parliament followed suit with the Order of September 20, 1649.[21] In substance this was as detailed and stringent as anything that had gone before; what distinguished it from its predecessors was that it was not meant to represent a settled policy, but was an emergency measure carrying a two-year term. (It was under this Order that Milton served as licenser of *Mercurius Politicus* through 1651.) Some fifteen months after it expired, however, the Rump found it necessary to revive it (in the Order of January 7, 1653).[22] Oliver's Order of August 28, 1655, was as severe.[23] There were, of course, important differences in the spirit (and success) with which these orders were applied; but the point to observe in connection with the *Areopagitica* is that, except for the period during which the Long Parliament completed the transfer to itself of the power that had before been exercised by the Crown, and the brief period during which the Commonwealth government experimented with an unlicensed press, the Puritan Revolution preserved unbroken the continuity of licensing in England.

The immediate object of the *Areopagitica* (the first work devoted primarily to freedom of the press) is to achieve "Liberty of Unlicenc'd Printing" by obtaining the repeal of the Licensing Order and a "return" to what Milton saw fit to think the policy underlying the Signature Order. This should not be mistaken for a demand that all forms of control be abolished: "I deny not, but that it is of greatest concernment in the Church and Commonwealth, to have a vigilant eye how Bookes demeane themselves, as well as men; and thereafter to confine, imprison, and do sharpest justice on them as malefactors."[24] Milton distinguishes sharply between such a system of corrective regulation, under which books are freely published on the responsibility of author and printer, who are then answerable to the courts for anything prohibited by law, and the preventive censorship of the Licensing Order, under which nothing was to be published except what had been approved in advance by an official licenser. It was only the censorship

[19] C. H. Firth and R. S. Rait, *Acts and Ordinances of the Interregnum, 1642–1660* (3 vols., London, 1911), I, 1021–1023.   [20] *Commons Journal*, V, 493.

[21] Firth and Rait, *Acts and Ordinances*, II, 245–54; *Commons Journal*, VI, 298.   [22] Firth and Rait, II, 696–99.

[23] *Orders of the Lord Protector for Putting into Execution the Laws made against Printing Unlicensed Books;* E1064(58).   [24] Below, p. 492.

that required that a book "stand before a Jury ere it be borne to the World, and undergo yet in darknesse the judgement of *Radamanth* and his Collegues" that he attacked.[25] At the same time, however, his tolerationist recommendations would greatly liberalize the laws to which he would have the press responsible, especially in the definitions of heresy and schismatic utterance.[26]

6. *AREOPAGITICA:* ARGUMENT

The argument is quadripartite. The first part is historical in method, and is designed to discredit licensing by showing it to be a device invented by the Church of Rome. (As history it is somewhat selective, but, except for its silence about England, not basically inaccurate.) It reviews the practice of the best periods of classical antiquity, and finds them free from any kind of control over publication except punishment after the fact for the authors of atheism, blasphemy, and libel, and suppression of the condemned publications. After Rome became Christian, encroachment upon the liberty of reading and publishing grew proportionally with the power of the papacy, but the final tyranny of licensing had to await those grand efforts to extirpate Protestantism, the Council of Trent and the Inquisition. So unwholesome an origin would of course be no deterrent to the Episcopalian hierarchy which imported the device into England, but it must cause uneasiness to the truly reformed and anti-Episcopal Long Parliament which, after having once abolished it, succumbed to certain pressures for its reinstitution.

The second argument, which proposes to show that the promiscuous reading of bad along with good books is beneficial, seems at first glance, with its citations from prophets, apostles, and fathers, to be an argument from authority. The reverse, however, is true: the primary function of these citations is to free the issue from the influence of miscellaneous Christian authorities (an arbitration not much to Milton's taste, nor, perhaps, to the advantage of his present position). The "authority" of one primitive father is opposed to that of another in such a way as to prevent either from being decisive, and hence the way is cleared for submitting the issue to the test of reason alone. (If, in this matching of opinions, Milton's selection makes the preponderance seem to be in favor of unrestricted reading, that is only a secondary—

---

[25] Below, p. 505.

[26] During the period covered by this volume, Milton issued a total of ten publications (counting all four editions of *Doctrine and Discipline*). Of these, three were licensed: *Of Education, The Judgement of Martin Bucer* (see below, pp. 357 and 416), and *Poems*, 1645 (see *Stationers' Registers* for October 4).

although certainly not accidental—result of the method.) The second argument is really one from principle. It is true that the principle is itself introduced by citations from Scripture, but only in order to prepare a favorable atmosphere for its reception, not as establishing its authority: Scripture had been proved too available an arsenal for the proponents of the contrary principle for a skillful controversialist to resubmit the issue to this kind of arbitration once he had succeeded in freeing it.

The principle is temperance, and its authority is fact. This fact is that the condition of human life is the external inseparability of good and evil. It is impossible to arrange man's life so that he shall confront good and avoid evil circumstances, for good and evil are meaningless terms when applied to circumstances: circumstances are always morally indifferent, equally susceptible of good or evil application ("uncertainly and yet equally working to good, and to evill"). The separation of good from evil cannot in the nature of things be other than a moral act, an act of choice; and therefore God "trusts him [man] with the gift of reason to be his own chooser," to choose from among the things at hand what he will use and what reject, and, of what he uses, whether to good or evil purpose.[1]

Indeed, the very condition of virtue itself is the existence and knowledge of evil and the freedom to choose it. Even if the nature of things were somehow changed, and it became possible to insulate a man from external evil, he could still not aspire to innocence. Innocence is a strictly prelapsarian condition; for our part, impurity is our birthmark; hence our sole alternatives are virtue and vice. To attempt to escape this choice, to try to fence a man from the opportunity of evil, to hope, that is, for innocence, is to fly in the face of fact, to forget that the evil is already there within him. Escape, then, is impossible from evil; but not from vice. "That which purifies us is triall, and triall is by what is contrary."[2] What is necessary is that a man should know evil and all it has to offer, and then reject it and choose the good: this is the only meaning of virtue.

But if the existence of virtue depends on the knowledge of evil, what safer and more convenient way is there to "scout into the regions of sin and falsity then by reading all manner of tractats, and hearing all manner of reason?" Here, then, is the advantage of reading even bad books.[3]

---

[1] Below, pp. 528, 514.   [2] Below, p. 515.

[3] It has not been sufficiently noticed that Milton admits (below, pp. 517–21) that evil books may spread "infection"; he only says that, besides introducing new evils of its own, licensing is unable to prevent this.

The third argument is in a special sense "practical." Its contention is that even if the professed end (to guard faith and manners from infection) were admissible, the licensing of the press would be an ineffective means; and its method is reduction to absurdity by extension. It begins as if it were merely going to deny the wisdom of the most famous of all recommendations that books should be licensed—Plato's; but in fact it uses Plato's own argument to establish its contention that to guard against external infection it cannot be enough "to regulat Printing, . . . we must regulat all recreations and pastimes": had not Plato provided also for the licensing of music and dancing? If evil is transmissible, it is transmissible in numberless ways, and it is absurd to attempt its quarantine by locking one door while leaving open all the many others. It would be necessary to license not only publication, music, and dancing, as Plato recommended; there must also be licensing of diet, of dress, of conversation, of company. And how should all this be possible when every day manifests the unenforceability, in the very seat of Parliamentary power, of the licensing of the press alone? Nor is it only abstract reasoning that demonstrates the inadequacy of the present means to the proposed end; example is not lacking: there have been schisms without book, and what improvement can one detect in the manners of those countries where the Inquisition is unchallenged?

But this whole argument has been artificial. It has proceeded as if it assumed the end to be valid, and it has exposed the insufficiency of the means and the impossibility of adequately extending those means. But the end is not valid: to remind us of this, Milton repeats, in summary, the second argument.

The final argument is much the most complex. It purports to be simple enough: merely an argument from consequences. The preceding argument contended that the Licensing Order could not achieve its end, this one that its operations must have very damaging effects. It must greatly discourage learning, placing as it does all authors under formal suspicion of evil intent, and, in characterizing the whole nation as too stupid and weak to be exposed to unlicensed reading, contemning by implication the worth of the nation's teachers and ministers. (There is a digression here to show that Milton's complaint is not merely personal but genuinely representative of the learned world; we shall presently have to return to this.) Worse, it must weaken the nation's grip on that measure of truth which it already possesses. Most disastrous of all, it must hinder the nation's discovery of further truth beyond that which it now possesses. (There is here a second digression, to show that England is a nation from which real progress in the discovery of truth is to be expected, if only she is granted liberty of enquiry; to this, too, we must return below.)

But why should licensing weaken the nation's hold on what it knows? Because of the nature of truth. Truth has a subjective as well as an objective aspect. Let a doctrine be never so true objectively, it is not truth in its professor if he believes it in the wrong way. The wrong way is to believe because of external authority (a very important qualification of this will be noticed below). "A man may be a heretick in the truth; and if he beleeve things only because his Pastor sayes so, or the Assembly so determins, without knowing other reason, though his belief be true, yet the very truth he holds, becomes his heresie." [4] The right way is to understand the doctrine; where the doctrine is true, this understanding produces a persuasion of its truth. Under licensing, such comprehension must progressively deteriorate. Nothing will be permitted which questions what is generally professed; what is never questioned is never examined; what is not examined is not understood, hence not truly believed, no matter how unanimously it is proclaimed. On the other hand, let an unlicensed press throw up from time to time a book which challenges accepted doctrine: those who rise to the defense of what they profess will have to examine their doctrine, expound its meaning, reveal its grounds—in short, make it understood. Only so can the nation's grip on truth be maintained.

With its final contention, that the Licensing Order is an obstacle to the discovery of unknown truth, the *Areopagitica* moves into the center of the toleration controversy, and it will be worth while to try to determine its relative position in that debate.

England, Milton's argument begins, possesses a "great measure of truth . . . especially in those main points between us and the Pope, with his appertinences the Prelats"; but its reformation has been far from complete. Now God, "decreeing to begin . . . the reforming of Reformation it self," turns "first to his English-men." This is the meaning of the great outburst of religious discussion in London, the "pious forwardnes" with which men have begun "to reassume the ill deputed care of their Religion into their own hands again." [5] At such a time it may well be that "many sectaries and false teachers are . . . busiest in seducing; but yet more true it is, that God then raises to his own work" men who "gain furder and goe on, some new enlightn'd steps in the discovery of truth." Suppose those who "appear to be the leading schismaticks" are in error; then let them be debated with, not forcibly suppressed, for like "dust and cinders . . . they may yet

[4] Below, p. 543.   [5] Below, pp. 549, 553–54.

serve to polish and brighten the armoury of Truth." [6] But if these men denounced as leading schismatics "be of those whom God hath fitted for the speciall use of these times . . . and we in the hast of a precipitant zeal . . . resolve to stop their mouths . . . no lesse then woe to us, while thinking thus to defend the Gospel, we are found the persecutors." [7]

Those who counsel the suppression of "all this flowry crop of knowledge and new light" try to frighten us with "fantastic terrors of sect and schism." But even if "all the windes of doctrin were let loose," we need not fear. Truth is invincible. "Let her and Falshood grapple. . . . Her confuting is the best and surest suppressing." [8]

Nor must we think that every difference, "whether in some point of doctrine or of discipline," every "dividing of one visible congregation from another," involves a challenge to truth. Truth "may have more shapes then one."

> What else is all that rank of things indifferent, wherein Truth may be on this side, or on the other, without being unlike her self. What but a vain shadow else is the abolition of *those ordinances, that hand writing nayl'd to the crosse,* what great purchase is this Christian liberty which *Paul* so often boasts of. His doctrine is, that he who eats or eats not, regards a day, or regards it not, may doe either to the Lord. How many other things might be tolerated in peace, and left to conscience, had we but charity.[9]

Milton does not like men to separate from the church on trivial grounds, nor to withdraw merely because the earthly church cannot meet a standard of purity reserved for the church triumphant. But they must decide these things for themselves: "if all cannot be of one mind, as who looks they should be? this doubtles is more wholsome, more prudent, and more Christian that many be tolerated, rather then all compell'd." [10]

Many are to be tolerated; but not all:

> I mean not tolerated Popery, and open superstition, which as it extirpats all religions and civill supremacies, so it self should be extirpat, provided first that all charitable and compassionat means be us'd to win and regain the weak and the misled: that also which is impious or evil absolutely either against faith or maners no law can possibly permit, that intends not to unlaw it self: but those neighboring differences, or rather indifferences, are what I speak of, whether in some point of doctrine or of discipline, which though they may be many, yet need not interrupt *the unity of Spirit.*[11]

---

[6] Below, pp. 566–67.   [7] Below, pp. 567–68.   [8] Below, pp. 558, 554, 561.
[9] Below, pp. 565, 564, 563.   [10] Below, p. 565.   [11] *Ibid.*

In the context of the toleration controversy, and taking into account Milton's ideas before and after 1644, this argument may well be thought at least as remarkable for what it is not as for what it is. In 1641–1642, Milton had based his argument for church reformation on a principle common to all the Puritan assailants of Episcopacy: the sole authority in matters of religion is the word of God. The Puritan groups who became tolerationists (the coalition of Independents and sects) continued to exploit this principle, now as the basis for their demand that church and state be either wholly separate or at least sufficiently distinguished so that the magistrate would be debarred from prescribing the religion of the subject. This, as we saw (above, pp. 66–130), was a highly effective argument; it embarrassed the *jure divino* Presbyterians, set them and their Erastian co-religionists at odds, and created common ground for the Puritan and the secular tolerationists. Indeed, responsive as it was to so many situations, it became the most widespread and most nearly predictable of all tolerationist arguments. But Milton does not use it; nowhere in the *Areopagitica* is there any suggestion that church and state should be separated.[12]

Milton's failure to use the most nearly universal of tolerationist arguments would be noteworthy even if there were nothing to emphasize it, but there are two considerations which make it even more striking. The first is that time and again in his subsequent tracts Milton urged just the policy which he here evades, the separation of church and state. The second is that, denying himself the support of this argument, he is forced to throw a heavier load upon his remaining principles than they will in logic bear. A brief analysis will make this clear.

Milton demands toleration in behalf of new revelations of divine truth, arguing, not that all the sects have received such revelations, but that some may have. Such toleration is safe because truth itself will always vanquish falsehood. But suppose truth has shown some particular pretender to reformation to be one of the "false teachers" whom Milton admitted to be now "busiest in seducing"; why should not he be silenced? Most tolerationists, knowing that such a distinction between "orthodox" and "heretical" dissenters would be only a device to break up the tolerationist coalition,[13] would have answered that, apart from the difficulty of telling the true from the false, such matters were out-

---

[12] "While things are yet not constituted in Religion," Milton writes (below, p. 541), thereby indicating his awareness of Parliament's intention to revise and settle the faith, worship, and government of the church, and making no attempt to challenge its right to do so.

[13] See, for example, the Presbyterian effort to separate the Assembly Congregationalists from their allies by this method: above, p. 116.

side the jurisdiction of the state. In later years, this is the answer Milton too would give. Now he makes what he can of the difficulty of telling the true from the false, but he has denied himself the rounder part of the answer.

To compensate for this weakness he enormously enlarges the scope of indifferency. Parliament must not violate Christian liberty in things indifferent, and many things which may at first glance seem opposed to truth are in fact indifferent. These include "many other things" beside dietary laws and the observation of the sabbath; they include matters of doctrine and of discipline, things on which congregations divide from each other.

But congregations never divided from each other on matters which both sides thought indifferent, and the external things of the Law do not include points of doctrine and discipline under the Gospel. The object of rhetoric is to persuade. Why should Milton have jeopardized the persuasiveness of the doctrine of Christian liberty (received by all, however variously interpreted) by attempting to extend the scope of indifferency to areas which few would think indifferent?

We are back at the earlier problem. He extended the scope of indifferency because he was trying to compensate for the absence of the argument for separation of church and state. Again we must ask why he evaded this argument.

The object of rhetoric is to persuade, and the most logical case for a policy may not always be the most persuasive. If we examine the *Areopagitica* as a rhetorical structure, we may find the clue for this apparent weakness of argument.

7. *AREOPAGITICA:* RHETORIC AND STRATEGY

The formal articulation is that of regular deliberative rhetoric,[1] as Milton later declared ("I wrote *Areopagitica,* according to the model of a regular speech").[2] The exordium, which occupies the long opening paragraph (pp. 1–3) is followed immediately by the proposition (pp. 3–4, "If ye be thus resolv'd . . . slaies an immortality rather then a

[1] The rules and terminology of classical rhetoric, after being gradually developed over many centuries, were given their fullest and most systematic treatment in Quintilian's *Institutes of Oratory,* which Milton called (below, p. 384) "of classic authoritie," and to which the present analysis conforms.

Wilbur E. Gilman published a formal rhetorical analysis of *Areopagitica* in *Milton's Rhetoric: Studies In His Defense of Liberty* (Columbia: University of Missouri Studies, 1939), pp. 9–44, of which the present study, employing a different method and reaching different findings, has made no use. Similarities of detail are due to our common use of the traditional treatises on rhetoric.

[2] *Second Defence; Works,* ed. Patterson *et al.* VIII, 132–34.

life"),[3] which is so framed as to embrace the fourfold partition. The general confirmation occupies the rest of the speech to the peroration (although within this space occur the remaining formal components); it is, as required by the partition, in four sections (pp. 4–9, "But lest I should be condemn'd . . . the properties it has"; pp. 9–15, "But I have first to finish . . . Inquisition could ever yet contrive"; pp. 15–20, "which is what I promis'd . . . it bears the intention"; pp. 20–35, "I lastly proceed . . . above all liberties"),[4] the last of which is itself subdivided into three (pp. 20–26, "in being first the greatest discouragement . . . a nursing mother to sects"; pp. 26–29, "but I shall easily shew . . . how they will decide it there"; pp. 29–35, "There is yet behind . . . above all liberties").[5] The narration appears as several particular narratives, rather than as a single comprehensive one; *e.g.,* pp. 5–9, "In *Athens* where Books . . . clear yee readily"; pp. 24–25, "I could recount . . . thraldom upon lerning."[6] Similarly, the reprehension occurs piecemeal as required; *e.g.,* pp. 9, 13–15, 15–17, etc.[7] There are two formal digressions, to which passing reference was made above;[8] the first, which we shall call the "personal" digression, rounds out the first subdivision of the last section of the confirmation (pp. 24–26, "And lest som should perswade ye . . . a nursing mother to sects"); the second, which may be called the "national" digression, finishes the final subdivision (pp. 30–35, "Lords and Commons of England . . . above all liberties").[9] The peroration follows immediately.[10]

In rhetoric much depends upon the relation between author and audience, and here the first determining factor is the image of himself which the author establishes in the mind of the audience.[11] Much of

[3] Below, pp. 490–93. The page references cited within the first paragraph of this section are to the original edition.

[4] Below, pp. 493–507, 507–21, 521–30, 530–60.

[5] Below, pp. 530–43, 543–48, 548–60.

[6] Below, pp. 494–507, 537–39.   [7] Below, pp. 507, 517–21, 522–27.

[8] See above, pp. 116–67.   [9] Below, pp. 537–43, 551–60.

[10] This final section may seem to carry too heavy a load of newly introduced ideas and of positive argumentation to be suitably called a "peroration," but this often happens in deliberative rhetoric when the primary intention is critical, for in addition to its ordinary functions the peroration may then be employed to suggest an alternative to the object of criticism. The nomenclature of traditional rhetoric is really better suited to its forensic than to its other forms.

[11] In examining the *Areopagitica* for this we must be clear about our purpose: we are concerned with Milton's rhetoric, which means, in the present application, with the conscious self-portrait here displayed, and not with the more objective picture of the author which we could, perhaps, deduce by combining this with the many incidental and unintentional flashes of self-revelation in the speech.

this picture is, in the *Areopagitica*, furnished by the exordium, whose primary function must always be to secure a favorable atmosphere for the speech's reception.[12] The first trait proclaimed is a passionate love of liberty—a characteristic which is reiterated several times in other parts of the speech. But the moment this is established it is hedged: it is the passion of a practical man with a realistic understanding of the nature and limits of civil liberty. Perfection is not to be expected (a concession subsequently turned to advantage in disposing of Plato's recommendation of licensing) ; [13] only freedom of complaint for the subject, and willingness to redress in the government. Even more reassuringly, the author is one who perceives that true civil liberty has already been in good part achieved, and by the very Parliament he is addressing. He has, indeed, as his earlier publications testify, been a supporter of Parliament since it began its great career. He has, moreover, been wholly sincere in his praise, for he praised Parliament as the restorer and defender of liberty, and that he really believes it to be such is witnessed by the present address of grievance. Next, he is quite without insolence in the present undertaking; the best times of antiquity provide honorable precedent for advice to government by private men of learning. Nor is the comparison immodest; the author is not without natural endowment, and his whole life has been devoted to study.

So far the exordium, establishing the image of one whose principles make it necessary for him to speak, whose ability and preparation make it worth while to listen to him, and whose friendly record makes it not only pleasant but also politically feasible to take his advice. Subsequently (in the personal digression) some rather significant detail is added to this initial sketch. The author is one who has been honored by learned men abroad. He is similarly valued by men of learning at home, among them many supporters of Parliament who are known and respected by the members. He has, in fact, been requested by them to undertake the present address, and is speaking, not really as a private man, but as the representative of learning. In brief, what is here added to the self-portrait (for there is heavy work coming) is influence.

The second, and much more complex, factor in determining the relation of author and audience is the image of the audience that is established in its own mind, first as being the author's view of it, and then as its own recognition of itself. In examining the *Areopagitica* for

[12] Milton calls it an "established axiom" that this is the function of an exordium; see Prolusion I, *Complete Prose*, I, 218–19.

[13] Below, p. 526: "To sequester out of the world into *Atlantick* and *Eutopian* polities, which can never be drawn into use, will not mend our condition."

this, we must recognize that while Milton formally addresses himself to Parliament, his real audience is much broader. As a printed pamphlet the "speech" is addressed also to the general public. In addition, two official organizations were intensely interested in the double issue treated in the *Areopagitica:* the Westminster Assembly and the Parliamentary army; these must be regarded as distinct sections of Milton's audience.

The depiction of Parliament begins in the exordium. Parliament has been faithful, courageous, and wise in recovering the nation from tyranny and superstition. The mildness and justice of its rule will be seen in the magnanimity with which it receives constructive public criticism; in this it is comparable with the great courts of antiquity, except that its superiority to them will be evident in its willingness not merely to entertain such advice, but, when reason warrants, to act on it too—to recognize an error, if it has made one, and remedy it. Subsequently (in the first and third sections of the confirmation) it is added that although licensing is a Tridentine invention, Parliament, in adopting it, cannot be thought to have shown any admiration for its inventors; on the contrary, it surely abhors the logical consequence, a thoroughgoing, home-grown imitation of the Inquisition; it was in error, not in malice, that it yielded to the pressure for licensing.

Nevertheless, the Licensing Order is an action of Parliament, and by it Parliament has insulted the nation—the learned men, the common people, and the ministry (first subsection of section four of the confirmation). Worse, it has threatened the nation, for this is a betrayal of its own principles and achievement; it is an imitation of that Laudian system of enforced uniformity which the nation entrusted Parliament to oppose, and which it did in fact overthrow; it is, in short, giving people cause to think that Parliamentary rule is growing toward a new tyranny (first digression and peroration). Now for Parliament to mount such a threat is for it to endanger its own existence (second digression). Those many free studies and disputes which are complained of represent no danger; on the contrary, they are, in view of the military situation, extraordinary proof of the nation's confidence in Parliament and loyalty to it. Indeed, they are effects of which Parliament has itself been the cause, for they are the actions of liberty, and it is Parliament that has restored liberty. It cannot now suppress liberty without first becoming itself a tyrannical government, and, should it do that, it must expect to be abandoned by the people and left defenseless and helpless against the vengeful armies of Charles. Let it not deceive itself by imagining that to retain the support it has hitherto enjoyed requires only the preservation of just immunities from illegal taxation. Men love peace better than four nobles of Danegelt. The reason the people took up arms against the king on the issue of illegal taxation was that they recognized it as the symptom of the only evil worth breaking the peace to eradicate: tyranny. It may be understood, therefore, what prospect there is of the people "sticking close" to Parliament should it become itself a tyranny.

Now, how is this rough handling of Parliament reconcilable with the opening eulogy (not especially fulsome by contemporary standards, however it may seem to modern taste, but certainly strong praise)? To begin with, it will have been noticed that Parliament was praised outright only for what it had been in the past; the rest was conditional praise for what it might be expected to become once more in the future. But why should Parliament "revert" to a policy so much at odds with that expressed in its current legislation? Because it would be brought to see that it was tricked into an uncharacteristic and dangerous policy by the Westminster Assembly.

To the latter body, and (at least on the present issue) to the mass of the Presbyterian clergy which it represented, the *Areopagitica* takes a uniformly hostile attitude. As the second digression culminates in a thinly veiled threat to Parliament, so does the first in an open one to the Assembly. Its members are upstart tyrants: only lately themselves the victims of suppression, they must now turn to inquisitioning, and are intent to "put it out of controversie that Bishops and Presbyters are the same to us both name and thing." [14] They are teaching the people to understand their strategy, which is aimed not at the destruction but at the capture of the abusive powers of the Episcopacy. They would be safer to take the lesson of their own recent success and the disaster of the bishops: "this obstructing violence meets for the most part with an event utterly opposite to the end which it drives at." [15] All this is repeated and reinforced in the peroration. This compulsive external conformity is but the return of Laudianism: "the ghost of a linnen decency yet haunts us." [16] The nation is not to be deceived by the Assembly's talk of preventing sects and schisms; on the contrary, it recognizes that "this very opinion of theirs, that none must be heard, but whom they like, is the worst and newest opinion of all others; and is the chief cause why sects and schisms do so much abound." [17] The members of the Assembly (their motivation in pride and ignorance was expressed in an earlier passage) are the priests and Pharisees persecuting the Gospel. They were among the beginners of our present reformation; but if it was for evil ends, if the good that they achieved by defying licensing will not move them, and if the fate of the bishops

[14] Below, p. 539.   [15] Below, p. 542.   [16] Below, p. 564.   [17] Below, p. 566.

will not warn them, "but that they will perswade, and execute the most *Dominican* part of the Inquisition over us, and are already with one foot in the stirrup so active at suppressing, it would be no unequall distribution in the first place to suppresse the suppressors themselves." [18]

The distinction that Milton is here insisting on is between Assembly and nation, and to reveal the dimensions of the gap he must portray the character of the nation. It is, to begin with, a liberty-loving nation, whose language is but ill-equipped to furnish the vocabulary of public servitude. Even in those evil days in which it languished under tyranny, it retained enough of freedom to be the envy of foreigners. Now that it has recovered its liberty, it is like a strong man rousing himself from a long sleep, whom to rob will prove some danger. It is, moreover, a learned nation; its very poets are better teachers than famous divines of Scotland and Italy, and for its wisdom it has long been the resort of studious foreigners. It will not readily permit twenty licensers to establish a monopoly over its learning. Above all, this nation, as history shows, is the peculiar favorite of heaven. God has now entrusted to it the reforming of reformation itself, a task which it neither can nor will give over for the complaints of timorous men, or those who love the twilight.

The *Areopagitica* contains no portrait of the Parliamentary army and makes no direct appeal to it; more than four years were to pass before Milton publicly propounded the theory that the army was itself a representative of the nation and entitled to a voice in its government. But there is enough here that would remind the contemporary reader of the form in which God's protection encompassed and surrounded "the mansion house of liberty." [19] Nor was Milton mistaken in the deductions he and everyone else must have made at the time of the Accommodation Order about the importance and nature of the army's influence: the day Milton's unknown friend received his gift copy of *Areopagitica,* the Commons ordered consideration for new-modelling the army; two days later Cromwell launched his attack on Manchester; in another two weeks the Self-Denying Ordinance was moved in the Commons, and ten days later it was passed. [20]

It is clear that the postulate upon which Milton's entire rhetorical structure is raised is that Parliament, whose original and characteristic policy was set out in the Signature Order, was later seduced by the Westminster Assembly into the alien and destructive policy of the Licensing Order. But, as we saw above (pp. 158–61), this postulate is not in accord with the facts: the Signature Order was one of three

[18] Below, pp. 568–69.   [19] Below, p. 554.   [20] See above, pp. 55–56.

interim emergency measures designed to secure some degree of control over the press until Parliament could complete the more comprehensive system which was set out in the Licensing Order. The Westminster Assembly certainly urged Parliament on in the task from which it was so often distracted, but Milton could not have been unaware that Parliament had always intended to devise some replacement for the decree of 1637; the fact is stated in two documents which the *Areopagitica* attacks (the Licensing Order and the Stationers' Petition) and in one which it ignores (the order of August 26, 1642), and was the recorded background for the order it praises. Why then did he attempt to create an image of Parliament so remote from the facts?

If we recall the issues and positions of 1644, it seems obvious that it was because he was aiming his rhetoric primarily at the Erastians. The Independents, the sects, and some of the secular-minded were already committed to toleration and hence opposed to licensing; but they were a minority in Parliament. The only strategy which could offer any hope of getting the Licensing Order repealed was to split the Presbyterian majority. The one issue upon which such a division could be effected was the *jure divino* doctrine of the Westminster Assembly, and the group most likely to respond to this issue, and in the best position to influence the lay Presbyterians in Parliament, were the Erastians, those whom Cromwell was to call the "middle party." [21] The Licensing Order, seen as an expression of the sovereign power of the state, would not worry the Erastians, but if they could be got to see in it a maneuver for furthering the Assembly's pretensions they might well reconsider. Surely this is why Milton represented the Licensing Order as a reversal of Parliament's policy secured, under plausible pretexts, by an Assembly bent upon usurping control of the church.

And here also would appear to be the solution to our other problem, Milton's surprising and (from the point of view of logic) damaging avoidance of the argument for separation of church and state. His best hope lay in enlisting the aid of the Erastians; but to demand the separation of church and state would instantly alienate them. On the other hand, they were precisely the people least likely to be offended by the enlargement of the area of indifferency, Milton's compensation for the absence of the argument for separation. Thus, when the direction of his primary appeal is understood, the logical weaknesses of *Areopagitica's* tolerationist argument turn out to be part of its rhetorical strength.

It should now be possible to discern Milton's tactics. He introduces himself to Parliament as one whom every circumstance makes a compe-

21 In the army debates at Reading, July 16, 1647; see Woodhouse, *Puritanism and Liberty*, p. 419.

tent and trustworthy adviser, speaking, moreover, on behalf of an interest whose continued support is vital to Parliament. He then lays bare the source of Parliament's past strength, and warns it that its present course will alienate it from the nation and leave it at the mercy of the Court party. This course he attributes to the advice of the Westminster Assembly.

Next, he arranges that certain inferences be available to each Parliamentary group in turn. He must not be obtrusive in this, but to quicken perception he finds a patron for his proposals from each of the major groups he wishes to bring together, citing the leading Erastian in the Commons, Selden, as a believer in unrestricted reading, and the late leading Independent in the Lords, Brooke (now a martyr of the Parliamentary cause), as a believer in religious toleration. No Presbyterian is cited.

For the Independents and their allies, the inference amounts to this: our position in this matter is both right and necessary. Nor are we alone: the best among the people and the army are with us. If the rest of Parliament does not conform to our position, the logic of revolution (if only the revolution does not collapse) will make us the inheritors of power.

For the Erastians this is the inference: we have been maneuvered into a false position. What we thought merely a means to make the press responsive to the will of Parliament is in fact a subtle device to impose a theocracy upon England. In this issue we hold or can obtain the balance of power. Our principles require that we join the Independents in this division; so does our interest, as we may see by the temper of the people and the army.

What Milton places before the Presbyterians is something like this. Some of you are more flexible and less committed than others. You have let yourselves be persuaded that the safety of true religion requires this inquisitioning. But it is demonstrable, by rational extension from your own fundamental dogmas, that this is untrue; that, on the contrary, the safety of your religion and the health of your own souls demand its repeal. Is it wise to let your aspiring clergy drive you along the road of your own and Parliament's and the revolution's destruction? Is it not better, on this issue, to join the other parties and restore Parliament to its source of strength in the nation's confidence? As for those of your party who are determined to be the slaves of the Assembly, there is nothing here for them save the warning that they are betraying the Parliament and, so far as it lies with them, destroying all that has been fought for and won.

What he has to say to the Westminster Assembly is simpler: you are revealing yourselves as the imitators of the bishops; be warned in time, or you will share their fate.

Milton's message to the "nation" (*i.e.*, to the part supporting Parliament) is this: Parliament, whose power derives from and is dependent upon you, is beginning to legislate at the dictate of a new priestcraft which regards you with contempt and is animated by limitless ambition. The excuses which are offered to justify the present legislation are intended as a screen for developing tyranny, but they are as transparent as the legislation is harmful. There is in Parliament a firm nucleus of opposition to this policy: support it. There is also a substantial and not really committed group which, on this issue, holds the balance of power and can be persuaded to oppose the Licensing Order: persuade it. Let Parliament understand that if it threatens your liberty you will have no reason to support it against the king.

To the army there is, as has been said, no direct appeal, but the inference available to the increasingly ascendant army Independents and sects was this: we have long understood that the Assembly is not much less our enemy than the bishops and Cavaliers, but it is encouraging to find that the people, too, are coming to understand the clergy's ambitions.

The tactics, then, may be defined fairly clearly. They consist of what may be called a negative and a positive maneuver. The negative maneuver is to define the opposition as restrictively as the most favorable reading of the situation will permit; then to isolate it; and finally to discredit it. The positive maneuver is to construct a coalition from all available elements, each appealed to on grounds of both principle and interest; and then to depict this coalition as being the nation. Milton's faith in these tactics may be judged from the fact that, with astonishingly little modification, they dominated the whole of his subsequent polemic.

8. THE LIMITS OF TOLERATION

The extent of the toleration Milton recommends is consistent with these tactics. He is careful not to jeopardize his appeal to the Erastians and other conservatives by letting them wonder whether he is demanding a general toleration; they are assured that he is only speaking of "those neighboring differences, or rather indifferences . . . which . . . need not interrupt *the unity of Spirit*." At the same time, he has no intention of imperilling the existing tolerationist coalition by menacing specific sects with exclusion. His toleration is limited on the left in a way which few would think directed at themselves: "that . . . which is impious or evil absolutely either against faith or maners no law can possibly permit." (We are reminded of the deliberately coalitionist language, a few days later, of *A Paraenetick,* asking "liberty . . . for every way not scandalous." [1])

Milton is more precise about his limits on the right: "I mean not tolerated Popery, and open superstition, which as it extirpats all religions and civill supremacies, so it self should be extirpat, provided first that all charitable and compassionat means be us'd to win and regain the weak and the misled." [2] Virtually everyone in 1644 who stopped short of general toleration excluded Roman Catholicism. Some Independents who, in the first enthusiasm of the new policy, included Roman Catholicism in their toleration, soon found it a tactical necessity to draw back.[3] But Milton is more severe than was tactically necessary. Some who denied Roman Catholics the public practice of their religion nevertheless forbade the magistrate to inquire into their consciences. Milton's use of the word "open" may seem to raise the possibility that he shared this position, but it would be hard to argue this. Not only does he not make the distinction between belief and practice, but he speaks of "extirpating" Popery—hardly the word one would choose if one meant only to forbid public practice. Rather, Milton's phrase, "Popery, and open superstition," appears to cover the two aspects of Roman Catholicism which, in his opinion, render it intolerable: allegiance to the pope and what he thinks patent or "open" superstition.

If Milton was harsher toward Roman Catholicism than was tactically necessary, what were his reasons?

Partly his view that "it extirpats all . . . civill supremacies." In the seventeenth century the Roman Catholic church's claim to prescriptive authority over the conduct of the believer, even in his capacity of citizen, was very widely considered a standing subversion, or threat of subversion, of national sovereignty. Milton's first two entries under *Subditus* in his Commonplace Book are examples of the voiding by the Vatican of the allegiance of subjects to their kings; [4] and at the end of his life he spells out a final time the argument implied in his quick phrase here: "The Pope . . . pretends right to Kingdoms and States, and especially to this of *England,* Thrones and Unthrones Kings, and absolves the people from their obedience to them." [5] Many of the tolerationists of 1644 excepted Roman Catholics on this ground, nor was the view peculiar to Puritans. Writing three years after the *Areopagitica,* Jeremy Taylor took the same ground:

[1] See above, p. 118.   [2] Below, p. 565.   [3] See above, pp. 111–14.
[4] See *Complete Prose,* I, 444.   [5] *Of True Religion* (1673); C53k18, p. 10.

Such Doctrines as these, The Pope may dispence with all oathes taken to God or man: He may absolve Subjects from their Allegiance to their naturall Prince: Faith is not to be kept with Hereticks, Hereticall Princes may be slaine by their Subjects. These Propositions are so deprest, and doe so immediately communicate with matter, and the interests of men, that they are of the same consideration with matters of fact, and are to be handled accordingly.[6]

Even Locke, nearly half a century later, made the same point. After denouncing as "opposite to the Civil Right of the Community" the doctrines that "Dominion is founded in Grace" and that "Kings excommunicated forfeit their Crowns and Kingdoms," he concludes: "That Church can have no right to be tolerated by the Magistrate, which is constituted upon such a bottom, that all those who enter into it, do thereby, *ipso facto,* deliver themselves up to the Protection and Service of another Prince. For by this means the Magistrate would give way to the settling of a forrein Jurisdiction in his own Country." [7]

But it was first "as it extirpats all religions" that Milton would extirpate Roman Catholicism. He does not mean by this charge merely that Roman Catholicism declares all other creeds false; in some sense this would apply to all churches, and would scarcely form a basis for excluding Roman Catholicism while admitting the rest. To recover Milton's meaning here we must return to the source from which everything in the *Areopagitica* ultimately derives, Milton's conception of truth. Truth is absolute, and susceptible of being absolutely known. Once, by miracle, it was so known. Since then, malice has obscured and distorted much of it. The followers of truth, however, have labored in its recovery.

Truth indeed came once into the world with her divine Master, and was a perfect shape most glorious to look on: but when he ascended, and his Apostles after him were laid asleep, then strait arose a wicked race of deceivers, who . . . took the virgin Truth, hewd her lovely form into a thousand peeces, and scatter'd them to the four winds. From that time ever since, the sad friends of Truth . . . went up and down gathering up limb by limb still as they could find them.[8]

What must be emphasized is that although the truth is now known only in part, this part is absolutely known. But what is this truth? Milton, writing for an audience quick to take—and subscribe—his meaning when he gives thanks for "that great measure of truth which

[6] Θεολογία Ἐκλεκτική. *A Discourse of the Liberty of Prophesying* (1647); E395(2), p. 253.
[7] *A Letter Concerning Toleration* (1689); NEW, pp. 46–47.
[8] Below, p. 549.

we enjoy, especially in those main points between us and the Pope,"
does not trouble to explain; we may, for explication, conveniently turn
a second time to the final summary of his case against Roman Catholicism. "True Religion is the true Worship and Service of God, learnt and
believed from the Word of God only. . . . He hath Reveal'd and taught
it us in the holy Scriptures . . . with strictest command to reject all
other traditions or additions whatsoever." [9] The truth Milton gives
thanks for, then, is that in matters of religion, Scripture is absolutely
and solely authoritative. (This is the qualification referred to above
[p. 167] in noticing Milton's rejection of belief based upon external
authority.) But he thought it the essence of Roman Catholicism to
deny this proposition, and to erect a second, equivalent, and in fact
superior (because interpretative) authority: the traditions of the church
(or, as he would say, of men). This was to subordinate the basis of all
"True Religion" to the inventions of men—"to extirpat all religions."

We may think Milton's proscription of Roman Catholicism unnecessarily severe, but we cannot think it inconsistent with the principles
upon which he based his plea for toleration. He demands toleration of
religious diversity not primarily because truth is relative (although he
enlarged the area in which this was so) but because it is incomplete,
and only toleration will permit the further recovery of its parts. But
this is a rationale which implies a precondition: "To be still searching
what we know not, by what we know, still closing up truth to truth as
we find it (for all her body is *homogeneal,* and proportionall) this is the
golden rule in *Theology.*" [10] "By what we know"—but the fundamental
thing "we know" is, for Milton, precisely what Roman Catholicism
denies. Hence it cannot claim the protection of the tolerationist argument, and self-defense requires its proscription.

9. THE MAJOR INFLUENCE

In 1641–1642 Milton had not been attracted to the doctrine of
indifferency. He had not gone so far as to say, with Lord Brooke,
"Nothing is Indifferent *in Re, in Se;* but to our *Understanding* some
things seeme so, for want of Good light." [1] But the claims of indifferency had not impressed him. Dealing with the objection that the speedy
establishment of Presbyterianism might be politically dangerous, he
had asked: "Who should oppose it? The *Papists?* They dare not. The
Protestants otherwise affected. They were mad. There is nothing will

[9] *Of True Religion* (1673), p. 4.   [10] Below, p. 551.
[1] Robert Greville, Lord Brooke, *A Discourse Opening the Nature of . . .
Episcopacie* (2 ed., 1642), p. 27; reproduced in Haller, *Tracts,* II, 37 ff.

be remoov'd but what to them is profess'dly indifferent." [2] Again, to the Episcopalian argument that the church was empowered to decide in things indifferent, he had not replied that in such things the individual Christian was at liberty to decide for himself; rather, he had insisted that the things at issue were not matters of indifference but of prescription, and had lamented the plight of those who fled to America "because their conscience could not assent to things which the Bishops thought *indifferent*. What more binding then Conscience? what more free then *indifferency*? cruel then must that *indifferency* needs be, that shall violate the strict necessity of Conscience, merciles, and inhumane that free choyse, and liberty that shall break asunder the bonds of Religion." [3]

Nor had he in these years paid much attention to the idea of natural law. He had, of course, from time to time referred to "those unwritten lawes and Ideas which nature hath ingraven in us," [4] but some of these references show that he had not yet considered the great commonplace very carefully. One, for example, seems to anticipate a contradiction between the teachings of nature and grace: "Open your eyes to the light of grace, a better guide then Nature," he replies [5] to that part of Bishop Hall's defense of Episcopacy which had derived from "the light of nature." [6] Another equates natural law with the reason of the regenerate: "they expresse nature best, who in their lives least wander from her safe leading, which may be call'd regenerate reason." [7] These casual utterances are so opposed to what Milton made of the law of nature when he came to use it as a positive factor in his argument that we must infer a relative lack of interest in 1641–1642.

But in 1643–1645 the theory of natural law and the doctrine of indifferency became Milton's principal weapons in defense of liberty. In this

---

[2] *Of Reformation* (1641), *Complete Prose*, I, 602.

[3] *Ibid.*, p. 585. Cf. *An Apology* (1642); *Complete Prose*, I, 925: "a needlesse and jolly persecuter call'd Indifference."

[4] *Reason of Church-Government* (1642), *Complete Prose*, I, 764.

[5] *Animadversions* (1641), *Complete Prose*, I, 702.

[6] *A Defence of the Humble Remonstrance* (1641), 858e10, p. 45. The significance of Milton's remark is emphasized by contrast with what his associates the Smectymnuans said in the same context. Recognizing that Hall's argument from nature (he originally made it in *An Humble Remonstrance to the High Court of Parliament*, 1641, E206[7], pp. 18–19) was subordinate to his main *jure divino* argument, they met it on its own terms: *An Answer to a Booke Entituled, An Humble Remonstrance* (1641, E161[4], pp. 20–21) points out that circumstances alter, "And then the same *light of nature* . . . that did at first command the establishment of [institutions] may and will perswade their abolishment."

[7] *An Apology* (1642), *Complete Prose*, I, 874.

change of attitude the influence of the Parliamentary and the tolerationist coalitions may be seen operating in two ways. It was largely from them that Milton learnt how the traditional formulae could be made to serve his altered needs; and it was chiefly they whom he was trying to persuade.

CHAPTER IV

OF EDUCATION

1. OCCASION

Ｉ N discussing the immediate occasions of the pamphlets (above, pp. 137–45), we passed by *Of Education,* which appeared early in June, 1644,[1] between the second edition of *Doctrine and Discipline* and *Bucer,* for it stands somewhat outside the main series of developments stemming from the unhappy marriage and the first divorce tract. It is, in fact, rather literally an "occasional" piece. It is true that Milton had long reflected upon educational matters (and not wholly "in silence," [2] as the third and seventh prolusions [3] testify); in youth his interest had been stimulated by his rustication, and during our period by the small private school which he had about 1640 begun to keep.[4] Nevertheless, he makes it clear that despite his opinion of the importance and utility of the subject he would not on his own initiative have undertaken its discussion just then, being engrossed "in the persuance of some other assertions." [5] What led him to write the tractate was the "earnest entreaties, and serious conjurements" of Samuel Hartlib, the energetic disciple of the famous educational reformer John Amos Comenius.

2. USUAL ASSOCIATION: COMENIAN

"To tell you," Milton wrote to Hartlib of his plan of education, "what I have benefited herein among old renowned Authors, I shall spare; and to search what many modern *Janua's* and *Didactics* more then ever I shall read, have projected, my inclination leads me not." [1] It is tempting to take this as advice against over-curious examination of the tractate's relations with other educational plans. The temptation must be resisted, but it will be well to acknowledge that it is, in a way, good advice. First with respect to antiquity: Milton borrowed widely and heavily from his old renowned authors, but he did not borrow from them what was essential to his plan. If he had he could not have written that his proposed school was "likest to those ancient and famous schools of *Pythag-*

---

[1] See below, p. 357.　　[2] *Of Education,* below, p. 364.
[3] *Complete Prose,* I, 240–48 and 288–306.　　[4] French, *Life Records,* II, 6–9.
[5] *Of Education,* below, p. 363.　　[1] *Of Education,* below, pp. 364–66.

oras, Plato, Isocrates, Aristotle and such others," [2] for he could not then have remained so blithely unconcerned with—even oblivious to— the fundamental contradictions among his purported exemplars over what constitutes knowledge, and what the end, method, and subject- matter of education ought to be. What Milton took from the great teachers of antiquity was a host of particular suggestions and a large body of readings for his pupils. Of course we must know what his "benefit" therein was (the annotations below include a full account), but however much this knowledge illuminates and clarifies the details of Milton's plan, it will not reveal its main provenience.

With respect to the "modern *Janua's* and *Didactics*" the case is somewhat different. Once again the advice has its merit, this time in the sense that none of Milton's ideas came from Comenius and his followers; nevertheless, here it is the tractate's general relation to Comenianism which, while negative, must be made clear if we are to understand the contemporary significance of Milton's educational thought (and incidentally be prepared to understand the significance of the changes in it by 1659–1660). "Made clear"—for the difficulty is by no means that the tractate has not been seen to be related to Comenian- ism; on the contrary, a relation has been very widely asserted; but, it seems to me, the wrong relation.

Masson, citing Milton's statement above, with its palpable reference to Hartlib's great hero Comenius, comments: "It is as if he had said, 'I know your enthusiasm for your Pansophic friend; but I have not read his books on Education, and do not mean to do so.' This was barely polite." [3] Nevertheless, Masson's method of studying Milton's tractate is to begin with an extended, if somewhat misleading, account of the views of Comenius, his partner John Dury, and Hartlib, and then to compare, and very occasionally contrast, the tractate with them. It is clearly implied throughout that when allowance is made for certain characteristic peculiarities, Milton was, without knowing it, a Comenian reformer.

Foster Watson, whose influence upon historians of education has been comparable to that of Masson upon students of Milton, gives a similar impression by bringing Milton into his discussion always, or almost always, in association with Comenius. For example, he illustrates the English Puritans' interest in the teaching of manners and morals from Milton and a number of other writers on education; then, to give a unified impression of what they advocated, he lists Comenius' rules for moral training. But Comenius was not English, and Watson ex- plains: "Although we are concerned with English education, it is

[2] *Ibid.,* p. 407.   [3] *Life,* III, 235.

remarkable how Comenius' Method seems to be the general view." [4] Again, to document the protest against the study of logic before the acquisition of material knowledge, his sources, among writers on education, are Milton, Comenius, and Dury.[5] On the crucial matter of the study of Latin he writes, "The real Grammar War was . . . [that] fought between the grammar-teachers and the teachers of Latin authors." [6] To represent the latter camp Milton is thrown in with Comenius and "the whole group of Commonwealth educational reformers." [7] Watson makes it quite clear that it is no accident that he thus constantly groups Milton with the Comenians: "Comenius was the leader to whom the Commonwealth writers . . . looked for guidance. It was the organization of 'Reformed' Schools for which they longed." [8]

Masson's view that Milton did not know Comenius' ideas, and somewhat contemptuously declared that he had no intention of finding out about them, has been generally accepted. So, for the most part, has his further view that despite certain particular differences the two programs of reform are so similar in essence that the most profitable way to study Milton's is to report the more "realistic" and "democratic" program of the Comenians, and then show how much of it Milton shared (although more recent students of Milton have placed greater emphasis upon the divergence of the two attitudes as far as the study of literature is concerned). Historians of education, unconcerned with whether Milton had read Comenius, have in general followed Watson in treating the tractate as part of a single great campaign for educational reform whose protagonist was Comenius.[9]

This approach seems to me altogether misleading, and I propose an opposite view: that in 1644—not, perhaps, fifteen years later—Milton's conception of a good educational system was fundamentally opposed to that of Comenius, and that the ideas which Milton and the Comenians admittedly had in common do not at all constitute grounds for associating their general plans—certainly they give no evidence of

---

[4] Foster Watson, *The English Grammar Schools to 1660* (Cambridge, 1908), p. 117.

[5] *Ibid.*, pp. 89–90.   [6] *Ibid.*, p. 276.   [7] *Ibid.*, p. 283.   [8] *Ibid.*, p. 120.

[9] Sometimes, when the interest lies in the history of ideas in general, rather than of educational thought in particular, Milton's tractate is related, through the English Comenians, to Bacon; thus Richard F. Jones, *Ancients and Moderns* (St. Louis: Washington University, 1936), p. 312, note 60; p. 320, note 8; and chapter 5 *passim*. In favor of this variation it may at least be said that Milton does owe something to Bacon (see below, pp. 204–205), while he owes nothing to Comenius. But the debt is a limited one, and Milton's tractate is scarcely more Baconian than Comenian; indeed, as Jones makes clear, Comenianism is for the most part Baconianism in the field of education.

influence. More tentatively, I shall suggest that first Milton and then Hartlib became aware that their educational philosophies were opposed, that this accounts for a curious circumstance of the tractate's publication, and that it is in this light that we should interpret Milton's reference to Januas and Didactics. Finally, I shall indicate what seems to me the true background of the tractate, and therewith its place in contemporary educational thought.

3. FUNDAMENTAL OPPOSITION TO COMENIANISM

In recovering the Comenian educational program it will be safest [1] to limit ourselves to what we may call "official" publications: those of Comenius, John Dury, and Hartlib,[2] and those sponsored by Hartlib. Comenius may be represented by the *Janua* [3] and *A Reformation of Schooles* [4], Hartlib's translation of the most important of Comenius' published essays and of the abstract of *The Great Didactic;* Dury by *Motion Tending to the Publick Good of This Age, The Reformed School,*[5] and *The Reformed Librarie-Keeper, With a Supplement to the Reformed-School;* [6] and Hartlib by *The Parliaments Reformation,* [7] *Considerations Tending to the Happy Accomplishment of Englands Reformation,*[8] and the "Epistle Dedicatory" of *The True and Readie Way to Learne the Latine Tongue.*[9] The rest are Hartlib's translation of Cyprian Kinner's *A Continuation of Mr. John-Amos-Comenius School-Endeavours,*[10] William Petty's *The Advice of W. P. to Mr. Samuel Hartlib. For the Advancement of Some Particular Parts of Learning,*[11] and George Snell's *The Right Teaching of Useful Knowledg.*[12] Except for Comenius' essays, everything on this list which was not written by Hartlib was written at his solicitation.

If a single feature had to be chosen as the most striking in the system of education envisaged by the Comenians, it would be compulsory universal school attendance. The subtitle of Comenius' abstract *Didac-*

---

[1] Because many writers influenced by Comenianism confusingly intermixed bits of it with their own ideas.

[2] Dury set out the terms of their collaboration in *Motion Tending to the Publick Good of this Age, and of Posteritie* (1642), 698.2.e(4), sigs. D3v and E1v; the story is given more fully in G. H. Turnbull, *Hartlib, Dury and Comenius* (London: University Press of Liverpool, 1947).

[3] *Janua Linguarum Reserata* (Leszno, 1631); tr. by John Robotham as *The Gate of Languages Unlocked* (1639). For a description, see below, pp. 201, 206–207.

[4] 1642; 8308.b.17. For publishing history and description, see below, pp. 207–208.   [5] 1649; 1031.a.11(1).   [6] 1650; 1031.a.11(2).

[7] 1646; E349(13).   [8] 1647; E397(25).   [9] 1654; C33.f.18(5).

[10] 1648; E470(26).   [11] 1648; 1031.g.22.   [12] 1649; 1030.a.14.

tic bespeaks *"A certaine and exquisite way for the erecting of such Schooles in all the Cities, Townes, and Villages of any particular Christian Kingdome, as that all young ones, whether males or females, none excepted, may be brought up in learning."* [13] In *The Reformed Librarie-Keeper,* Dury declares that "in a well-Reformed Common wealth . . . all the subjects thereof should in their Youth bee trained up in som Schools fit for their capacities, and that over these Schools, som Overseers should bee appointed to look to the cours of their Education, to see that none should bee left destitute of som benefit of virtuous breeding." [14] (The year before he had, in defining the end of education, been careful to specify "both in the Boyes and Girls.") [15] Petty is equally firm: "That all Children of above seven yeares old may be presented to this kind of Education, none being to be excluded." [16]

Compulsory universal attendance means, of course, a state-operated education. Comenius' abstract, not to leave this to inference from the subtitle, adds, "In the Preface thereof, Magistrates . . . are earnestly exhorted to the diligent education of children." [17] The role of the state is clearly implied in the quotation from Dury given above. Hartlib is more explicit. *Considerations Tending* was addressed to Parliament, which had lately redoubled his zeal for the public good by having provided for "my present maintenance, and future support." [18] Writing with the confidence of one who numbers many friends among his audience, he prescribes the Magistrate's "Duty towards the Young ones"; it is

> to Order the Meanes of their Education aright, to which effect he should see Schools opened, provided with Teachers, endued with Maintenance, regulated with Constitutions, and hee should have Inspectors and Overseers to looke to the observance of good Orders in this businesse. . . . And the right Ordering of these Schooles is to bee lookt upon as the Maine Foundation of a Reformed-Common-wealth, without which no other work of Reformation will ever bee effectuall.[19]

[13] *A Reformation* (1642), p. 92.
[14] Pp. 5–6.
[15] *Reformed School* (1649), p. 18.
[16] *Advice* (1648), p. 4. The sentence continues: "by reason of the poverty and unability of their Parents . . ."; that Petty means that no one is to be excluded, not even on the grounds of poverty, is clear from his frequent insistence on the benefits which will accrue to the children of the wealthy by being required to follow the prescribed studies.
[17] *A Reformation,* p. 93. In *The Great Didactic* itself Comenius was to expatiate largely upon the state's duty to operate a comprehensive educational system; see M. W. Keatinge, *The Great Didactic of John Amos Comenius,* translated into English (London: 1910), pp. 6, 18, 66, 300.
[18] *Considerations* (1647), sig. A1v.   [19] *Ibid.,* pp. 21–22.

Seven years later he made a direct appeal for intervention to Francis
Rous, Speaker of the House of Commons:

> But how to Introduce the Way which is here intimated into the
> Publique Schools of this Common-wealth, will be a matter of further
> deliberation then is fit for me now to enter upon; it may be hoped,
> that the Honourable Committee for the Advancement of Learning, will
> be inclined to reflect upon this matter, and consider the feasablenesse
> thereof: and haply something as a Proposall in this Kinde may be
> offered unto them; wherein Your Grave Recommendation to set their
> thoughts a working may have a special influence in due time.[20]

Snell too proposes a national system of schools established "by authority," staffed and guided by a national "College of Teachers" or "general
college" similarly operated by the state.[21]

We may next consider what was, for the Comenians, the purpose of
education, and here we must exercise some caution, for general statements can be remarkably deceptive. When, for example, Dury lays it
down that it is the object of education "to train them up to know God
in Christ, that they may walke worthy of him in the Gospell; and
become profitable instruments of the Common-wealth in their Generations," [22] he is using language very similar to Milton's; but the education he is defining is, as we shall see, vastly different.

To describe the end of education for the Comenians as utilitarian is
correct enough, but not very meaningful: no one has ever proposed an
education which he did not think, in some sense of the term, useful. The
utility the Comenians sought was so immediate and so predominantly
economic that their educational purpose must be described as vocational. When Comenius complains "that learning is not enough accommodated to the uses of our life" [23] he tells us nothing: it is a complaint
that anyone might have made, and most contemporary writers on education did. It is when he specifies the cause that he reveals himself:
"that inveterate custome, or rather disease of Schooles, whereby all the
time of youth is spent in Grammaticall, Rhetoricall, and Logicall toyes"
to the neglect of "those things which are reall, and fit to enlighten
mens minds, and to prepare them for action." [24] This contempt for the
whole matter of the trivium as "unreal" helps us to interpret the prescription which follows: "The way to remedy this, will be to propound
all things seasonably unto youth, and to make serious exercises the pre-
paratives of serious employments." [25] The language, however, is general

---

[20] *True and Readie Way* (1654), sig. A3v.
[21] *Right Teaching* (1649), pp. 310–27.
[22] *Reformed School* (1649), p. 18.   [23] *A Reformation* (1642), p. 20.
[24] *Ibid.*   [25] *Ibid.*

(it will be remembered that we are dealing with a preliminary essay), and its vocational implications need to be clarified. Dury is a little more specific: "nothing is to bee taught but that which is usefull in it self to the Society of mankind, therin fitting them for employments." [26] Petty is concerned with the "Advancement of Reall Learning." [27] For this he demands "That there be instituted *Ergastula Literaria,* Literary-work-houses, where Children may be taught as well to doe something towards their living, as to Read and Write," wherein "no . . . unnecessary . . . Part of Learning be taught." [28] It is Snell who provides the most unambiguous statement of the vocational end of education. Snell's title is in itself such a declaration: *The Right Teaching of Useful Knowledg, to Fit Scholars for Som Honest Profession; Shewing so much skil as anie man needeth (that is not a Teacher) in all knowledges.* . . . In his "Missive" to Dury and Hartlib he explains that his end is "that our english youths may no longer bee taught to bee emptie Nominalists and verbalists onely . . . but . . . maie henceforth bee *realists* and *materialists;* to know the verie things and matters themselvs, and yet onely such matters as may best further a man for the sufficient doing of all duties and works perteining to his own profession & person." [29] Finally, should anyone have missed the point, he writes, "All learning in the School was but to prepare a Scholar to bee abel to do and execute the duties of a vocation and trade of living." [30]

If this new and heavy educational commitment was to be seriously undertaken, it was necessary that much of the time spent in conventional studies should be saved. Some saving was to be effected through a faster way of teaching Latin, and this object (but not their method for it) the Comenians had in common with Milton (and countless others). But the main economy was to be made by eliminating from the curriculum the whole literature of western civilization, considered as a literature.

> Now these things [wrote Comenius] are to be accounted unnecessary. First, whatsoever is not of the essence of learning, of which sort are the most part of the vanities of the Gentiles, the name of their petty Deities, together with their lying histories, and fables. . . . Lastly, all circumlocutions, and windings, and turnings of expressions, which fetch not out the kernell, but onely make a few assayes upon the shell. Such kind of stuffe is it, wherewith most of our bookes of learning swell.[31]

Kinner's account of his school does not so much as mention the reading of original works other than Scripture; for matter he relies entirely

[26] *Reformed School* (1649), p. 19.   [27] *Advice* (1648), sig. A3.
[28] *Ibid.,* pp. 3–5.   [29] *Right Teaching* (1649), sig. A6.
[30] *Ibid.,* p. 162.   [31] *A Reformation* (1642), pp. 11–12.

upon compilations, always for the Comenians the primary basis of instruction. Dury insists that "the Curious study of Criticismes, and observation of Styles in Authors, and of straines of wit, which speak nothing of Reality in Sciences, are to be left to such as delight in vanityes more then in Truths." [32] It is not until the final portion of their curriculum that his students are to be exposed to any original writings at all, and then only to "choice parcels" and "with directions how to observe the Marrow, and Method of them; and out of them to gather to themselves an Encyclopaedia." [33] Since Snell's Solicitor "abhorreth . . . the teaching of unuseful niceties," [34] the whole literary content of his curriculum is just so much as he thinks necessary to complete the teaching of Latin, and consists of bits of Virgil and "those of *Erasmus*, and other the best Latine Dialogues." [35] He shows the usual unquestioning faith in compilations, which are of course to be the primary basis of instruction. This is worth exemplifying:

> Out of all Histories so much should bee epitomized and collected as may bee esteemed profitabel for an Englishman. In Historie therefore the knowledg of England, Ireland, Scotland, and somwhat of Denmark, Germanie, France and Spain may bee sufficient. The reading of Histories onely for delight, talk, and ostentation, is a prodigal consumption of precious time.[36]

Petty does not even discuss literature; his regard for it may be inferred from the brief statement he devotes to linguistic training: "such as shall have need to learne Forraine Languages (the use whereof would be much lessened, were the Reall and Common Characters brought into practise) may be taught them by incomparably more easie wayes then are now usuall." [37]

Nor must it be imagined that it was especially the lower classes, because of urgent need for economic training, who were to forego literary studies. "As for this School, which at this time I have delineated," wrote Dury, "it is proper to such of the Nobilitie, Gentrie and better sort of Citizens, which are fit to bee made capable to bear Offices in the Common-wealth: the other Schools may bee spoken off in due time, so far as they are distinct from this." [38] It was in fact not reluctantly, nor solely as a spendthrift of time, that the Comenians abolished literature. They disliked it in its own right. It was an enemy of "science."

> The third thing whereby Truth is prejudiced [wrote Comenius], is, as I said, either the carelesnesse, or luxuriance of the stile wherein

[32] *Reformed School* (1649), p. 49.   [33] *Ibid.*, p. 58.
[34] *Right Teaching* (1648), p. 184.   [35] *Ibid.*, p. 206.
[36] *Ibid.*, pp. 256–57.   [37] *Advice* (1648), p. 5.
[38] *Reformed Librarie-Keeper* (1650), A Supplement to the Reformed School, p. 6.

things are expressed. We call that a luxuriating stile, when in the explication of things, improper, tropicall, hyperbolicall, and allusive words or sentences, and expressions are used: especially when Poets, or Oratours (and sometimes Philosophers and Divines acting their parts) falling upon any subject, which they would amplifie, or extenuate according to their manner, use with their figures, and colours so to alter things, that for the most part they appeare not in their native, but in a borrowed, and adventitious forme. Which is nothing else, but a painting, and false glasse, whereas truth ought to be beheld with a pure, and unaltering light.[39]

Worse, it was an enemy of religion. The twenty-fifth chapter heading of the abstract *Didactic* declares that *"if we would have such a reformation of Schooles, as is according to the rules of true Christianity, Profane, and Heathen Authors must be either quite rejected, or used with more choyce and caution."* [40] And *A Reformation* asks, "what wonder can it be that learning doth not enough advance youth towards God? For it is not yet purged, and cleared of the prophanenesse of the Gentiles." [41]

Behind the abolition of literature and the substitution of compilations lay a faith. The Comenians believed that it was possible to achieve final universal knowledge *(Pansophy)* by the investigation of a universal principle of being *(Pan-harmony)*. This is a doctrine not easy to report, for it starts the ghosts of Pythagoras and Plato without indicating when they are to be laid; but it has something to do with an ultimate harmony of "art" (i.e., all conscious human activity), nature, and God. "Art" imitates the forms of things in nature, but nature in turn is a manifestation of the ideas in the mind of God. Hence a knowledge of all things and activities may be built upon a knowledge of these forms, and this, in turn, may be abstracted from things by three instruments: sense, reason, and revelation.[42]

But if this universal knowledge can be attained, it can be recorded; and the great co-operative undertaking which will once and forever fix the mind of man is the compilation of a Universal Christian Encyclopedia. What need then for literature? At its rare best, literature is the record of the preliminary gropings of the human mind toward a truth now to be fully and finally apprehended; more often it is the flight from truth. The editors of the Encyclopedia will, indeed, search all literature; for a moment we seem to be in the free world of the *Areopagitica*:

> that all who have written any thing concerning Piety and good manners, or concerning the Arts and sciences, not respecting whether they be Christians, or Mahumetans, Jewes, or Pagans, and of what sect so ever

[39] *A Reformation* (1642), p. 19.
[40] *Ibid.*, p. 94.   [41] *Ibid.*, p. 21.   [42] *Ibid.*, pp. 34–53.

. . . be admitted, and heard to see what they will bring in for the compiling of this Philosophicall worke. . . . There is no booke so bad, wherein some good thing or other may not be found: and if nothing else, yet it may occasion us to amend some errour.[43]

But it is another country: the *editors* will test all by the universal principle; they will compile what is satisfactory in all authors; "but wherein soever they are convicted to have done, or said any thing unmeet, or contrary to truth, or piety, therein they shall be for ever silenced, lest piety be any more borne down by profanenesse, truth by errour, or light by darknesse." [44]

There are other particular points of difference, but these are the main matters which, taken together, constitute an educational policy to which Milton was fundamentally opposed. By 1659–1660 (and it is perhaps not the least striking indication of the change that the grim experiences of the intervening years wrought in his thinking) Milton had, in modified form, adopted two of the characteristic features of the Comenian educational plan. He called for state-supported schools and libraries (not, certainly, to supplant, but to supplement,[45] private institutions) which should be free of charge to such ministerial students as would undertake to remain in and serve their native locality.[46] These public foundations would combine vocational training with basic education in languages and arts.[47] Here indeed is a change from 1644. Perhaps it ought not to be ascribed wholly to changed ideas; something is no doubt due to the difference of immediate purpose. The object of *Hirelings* is not to formulate an ideal education but to press for the abolition of state maintenance for the clergy, and its free schools, with their component of vocational training, are a means to secure a sufficiently trained ministry capable, where voluntary offerings proved too small, of being economically self-supporting. But even in this the change of thought is apparent; it is not difficult to recognize in a ministry "traind up in the church only, by the scripture and in the original languages therof at schoole; without fetching the compas of other arts and sciences, more then what they can well learn at secondary leasure and at home" [48] the potential practitioners of that "ignorantly zealous Divinity" [49] deprecated in *Of Education*.

The ideal educational scheme of 1644 shows no interest in the inter-

---

[43] *Ibid.*, pp. 30–31.   [44] *Ibid.*, pp. 33–34.

[45] *The Readie & Easie Way to Establish a Free Commonwealth* (March 3, 1660), E1016(11), pp. 16–17.

[46] *Considerations Touching the Likeliest Means to Remove Hirelings Out of the Church* (August, 1659), E2110(2), pp. 95–97 and 140.

[47] *Ibid.*, pp. 97–100.   [48] *Ibid.*, p. 141.   [49] *Of Education*, below, p. 375.

vention of the state, or in the participation of boys of the lower classes, or of girls of any class. It speaks, indeed, of the nation perishing for want of educational reform, and recommends that copies of the ideal academy be established in every city throughout the land; but there can be no doubt that the instrument of this public benefit is to be private initiative. As for the student body, nothing could be simpler than Milton's conception: it is "our noble and our gentle youth"— male, of course.

Nor is there the slightest interest in vocational training. Milton certainly emphasizes the material advantages that may be expected to flow from his plan: the reading of the authors of agriculture should ultimately lead to the improvement of the country's tillage, the study of medicine and of military science to the better condition and use of the armed forces; of political science and rhetoric to the improvement of Parliament, bar, and pulpit. But all these applications to external use, however desirable in themselves, are happy by-products of studies whose primary function is not to make good farmers or soldiers or legislators or lawyers or preachers of the students, but to serve as the materials of a liberal education. Nothing could be more forthright and unambiguous than Milton's statement: "because our understanding cannot in this body found it selfe but on sensible things, nor arrive so cleerly to the knowledge of God and things invisible, as by orderly conning over the visible and inferior creature, the same method is necessarily to be follow'd in all discreet teaching." [50] Indeed, to the extent that schooling has a vocational (which necessarily involves a concentrating and narrowing) effect—to the extent that it produces good farmers who are bad speakers, or good soldiers who are bad legislators—it contravenes Milton's conception of a liberal education, "which fits a man to perform justly, skilfully and magnanimously all the offices both private and publike of peace and war." [51] The fact that a man will presumably never be called upon to perform more than a fraction of these offices is quite irrelevant; it is his fitness (which is integral), not his performance (which must be subject to uncontrollable external influences), that is the criterion of his education.

With respect to the trivium Milton is as far removed as is possible from the Comenians and their contempt for those "Grammaticall, Rhetoricall, and Logicall toyes." The trivium dominates his scheme. It does not, of course, stand alone. The quadrivium is represented, although its weight in the curriculum is inconsiderable (its components usually get picked up "even playing, as the old manner was," or in "the interim

[50] *Ibid.*, below, pp. 368–69.   [51] *Ibid.*, below, pp. 378–79.

of unsweating themselves").[52] Considerable space and an enthusiastic welcome are extended to that study of "things" recommended by Bacon and already approved by Milton while still at Cambridge.[53] Perhaps under the influence of the Civil War—but the "classic authoritie" [54] of Quintilian and the nearer tradition of the renaissance courtier had already pointed the way—military science is included. Because the academy is to be "at once both School and University" [55] (for Oxford and Cambridge were "not yet well recover'd from the Scholastick grosnesse of barbarous ages") it pursues studies beyond the range [56] of the traditional liberal arts: history, political theory, law, ethics, theology, and church history. But at the beginning and end of the whole program stands the trivium, albeit with its sequence (as we shall see) modified and its scope extended. Logic, indeed, Milton approaches with some caution, clearly the result of his aversion from the excesses of scholasticism; he will have "so much as is usefull" [57] of it. But the other arts of the trivium are absolutely fundamental to his scheme. The program is firmly based upon grammar (taken to mean the mastery not of rules but of languages), which is the primary commitment of the first two of what I take to be five phases of study,[58] and enters deeply into the third and fourth; and it culminates in rhetoric (in the explicitly extended sense of including the theory and practice of poetry),

[52] Donald L. Clark, in *John Milton at St. Paul's School* (New York: Columbia University Press, 1948), p. 3, has shown that it was usual in the schools of Renaissance England—and of Imperial Rome too—for the quadrivium to be "honored more than taught." Below, pp. 386–87, 409.

[53] *Of Education*, below, pp. 368–70, 388–94, 411–14.   [54] *Ibid.*, below, p. 384.

[55] *Ibid.*, below, pp. 380, 374.

[56] Of course the traditional liberal arts would have provided an introduction to most (perhaps all) of these further studies; the materials for the study of rhetoric, for example, would be full of information about law, political theory, history, and ethics.

[57] *Of Education*, below, p. 402.

[58] It is not impossible to arrange Milton's program into school forms and college years, but it is hard to feel any confidence that the arrangement is necessarily the one he would have made. It seems to me that the program falls into five phases of varying duration: (1) elementary Latin (including "some delightfull book of Education"), arithmetic, geometry, and religion; (2) natural and physical studies, involving progress in Latin and the beginning of Greek; (3) moral philosophy and some dramatic literature, involving progress in the classical languages and the learning of Italian; (4) political history and philosophy, religious history, theology, and further literary studies, involving, besides the exercise of the languages already mastered, the acquisition of Hebrew and its chief dialects; and (5) the "organic arts": logic, rhetoric, poetics, and the higher composition. Music is separated from the other parts of the quadrivium and placed with "exercise," which also includes military science; the exercises cover the entire period of schooling.

which, having already received considerable preparatory attention in the fourth stage, provides almost the whole substance of the last.

In contrast with the Comenian dislike of literature, it can hardly be necessary to argue that Milton found "the harp of *Orpheus* . . . charming." [59] Nor need we spend much effort elaborating his opposition to the Comenian view that the poets, orators, and philosphers (and especially those of antiquity) distorted science, debased ethics, and profaned religion; it will be enough to recall that they were for him a main source for the study of natural and social science and of ethics, and that he was anxious that Christian students should learn "what Religious, what glorious and magnificent use might be made of Poetry both in divine and humane things." [60] *Of Education* has nothing to say of the digests and compilations that constitute the main matter of Comenian education. This silence may be thought eloquent enough; still, it may not be amiss to notice its active counterpart in the scorn with which he was to point, a few months later, to the minister content "to finish his circuit in an English concordance and a *topic folio,* the gatherings and savings of a sober graduatship, a *Harmony* and a *Catena,* treading the constant round of certain common doctrinall heads, attended with their uses, motives, marks and means, . . . not to reck'n up the infinit helps of interlinearies, breviaries, *synopses,* and other loitering gear." [61] As for the great Comenian end, the compilation of a universal Christian encyclopedia which would forever fix all truth, Milton's short answer would have been that this was not permitted to man: "We have not yet found them [the scattered limbs of Truth] all, Lords and Commons, nor ever shall doe, till her Masters second comming." [62] For his attitude towards the proposed suppression, after the encyclopedia's completion, of writings not therein approved, we may simply refer to the whole thrust of the *Areopagitica.*

4. PARTICULAR SIMILARITIES NOT SIGNIFICANT

What is common to Milton and the Comenians, having been so often discussed, may here be stated summarily. With respect to the end of education, both emphasized the role of religious and moral training. Both complained that prevailing curricula and modes of instruction made studies unnecessarily prolix and difficult and rendered some disciplines almost inutile. They shared two educational maxims: that foreign languages are of value only as instruments, and that

[59] *Of Education,* below, p. 376.   [60] *Ibid.,* below, pp. 405–406.
[61] *Areopagitica,* below, p. 546.   [62] *Ibid.,* below, p. 549.

learning should be a progression from the sensible to the abstract. As consequents of these maxims, both criticized the way languages were generally taught and the position in the usual curriculum of logic, metaphysics, and rhetoric, and they recommended fuller educational use of the natural and applied arts and sciences.

But these are all matters on which rival systems could easily agree. We may begin with the role of religious and moral training. It would be astonishing if this had not been emphasized. "The unity and continuity of Grammar School practice in the 16th and 17th centuries," declares Watson, "are . . . to be sought in the twofold aims of classicism and religious training. In the later part of the period . . . classicism [was] . . . regarded, not as an end in itself, but as subservient and helpful to religion, which was essentially the first motive in the school as in the nation." [1] W. A. L. Vincent reports that before the Civil War "every school, whether public or private, and under whatever patronage, was subject to ecclesiastical control" [2] (this, indeed, was provided for by the Canons of 1603–04 which forebade anyone to keep, or teach in, any school unless he had been licensed by the diocesan authorities [3]), and shows that after the abolition of Episcopacy the Long Parliament, as often as possible, made *ad hoc* arrangements for comparable supervision.[4] In such circumstances at least the profession of a religious and moral end would seem to have been inescapable. "As a matter of course," writes Howard Schultz of the humanistic discussion of education in England, "the educators made their submission to religion." [5]

At St. Paul's School the young Milton had found religion allotted the same centrality in education as he was himself later to prescribe. Colet, in the founding statutes, had declared: "my entent is by thys scole specially to incresse knowledge and worshipping of god and oure lorde Crist Jesu and good Cristen lyff and maners in the Children." [6] William Lily, the school's first High Master, prefixed to his *Grammar* a code for his pupils' conduct; the boys' first daily act therein prescribed was, "Humbly go into the church, and worship God." [7] The

[1] *English Grammar Schools*, p. 539.

[2] *The State and School Education 1640–1660 in England and Wales* (London: Society for the Propagation of Christian Knowledge, 1950), p. 12.

[3] *Constitutions and Canons Ecclesiastical* (1604), Article 77.

[4] *State and School*, pp. 46–55.

[5] *Milton and Forbidden Knowledge* (New York: Oxford University Press, 1955), p. 70.

[6] J. H. Lupton, *A Life of John Colet* (2 ed., London, 1909), p. 279.

[7] "Carmen de Moribus," tr. William Haines, *Lilies Rules Construed* (London, 1770), p. 91.

manuscript "The constant Method of Teaching in St. Pauls Schoole London," preserved in Trinity College, Cambridge, and containing the earliest known curriculum of the school, begins, "A Chapter in the Bible and set prayers in Latine every Morning at 7 of the Clocke." [8] Detailed religious exercises had been laid down by Colet, but these were superseded by the Canons of 1603–04, which may be cited to indicate the importance of religious training in English schools during Milton's boyhood.

> All schoolmasters shall thoroughly instruct their children in the catechism, either in the longer version or in the shorter catechism heretofore published by public authority in Latin, or in English suitable to children's capacity. And so often as a sermon is to be preached upon a holyday or festival within the parish wherein they teach, they shall conduct their pupils to the church wherein the said sermon is to be delivered, they shall take care that they remain there quietly and humbly, and, at some fitting time after their return from church, they shall call up the pupils, one by one, to examine them as to what they have learned from the said sermon. But upon other days, they shall instruct and educate them by means of texts drawn from Holy Scripture, such as seem fitting and especially useful for imbuing their minds with piety. [9]

There is little likelihood that in Milton's time religious instruction would have been scanted at St. Paul's; the interest of his headmaster, the elder Gill, may be inferred from the titles of two of his books: *Treatise concerning the Trinity in Unity of the Deity* (1601), and *The Sacred Philosophie of the Holy Scripture* (1635). [10]

Next, the complaint that studies were made unnecessarily prolix and difficult and some disciplines rendered inutile. While still at Cambridge Milton had levelled these charges, in greater detail and at an even higher temperature, against the scholastic educational tradition. [11] Masson contended that in so doing Milton was proclaiming his sympathy with the Baconian reform movement then struggling to make headway in Cambridge, [12] and his view has been generally accepted. We need not question that Milton was consciously following Bacon's lead; however, we must observe that his own school had already prepared him to take this view. T. W. Baldwin has recently reminded us that

[8] Quoted in Clark, *Milton at St. Paul's*, p. 110.

[9] Article 79, tr. J. W. Adamson, *A Short History of Education* (Cambridge, 1919), pp. 188–89.

[10] The best discussion of Gill's theology is in Arthur E. Barker, "Milton's Schoolmasters," *Modern Language Review*, XXXII (1937), 517–36.

[11] See *Complete Prose*, I, 240–48, 250–51, 300–301.

[12] *Life*, I, 193–232, esp. 202–04 and 211–12.

Colet's friend Erasmus was the basic influence shaping St. Paul's,[13] and Erasmus' antipathy to scholasticism, though so much earlier than Bacon's, was not less vehement.

> My own childhood [he complains bitterly in *De Pueris Instituendis*] was tortured by logical subtleties which had no reference to anything that was true in fact or sound in expression. . . . How much time was spent in sophistries and vain mazes of logic! Further, as to the manner of teaching, what confused methods, what needless toil, characterised instruction! How common it was for a master, for mere display, to cram his lesson with irrelevant matter, wise or foolish, but all equally out of place! All this made for needless difficulty; for there is no virtue in *difficulty*, as such, in instruction. . . . No wonder that learning perishes amongst us. The critical years of a boy's life are allowed to run to waste; he acquires the habit, which cannot be cured, of giving but a fraction of his time and thought to serious pursuits, the rest he squanders on vulgar pleasures.[14]

Hence, in the *De Ratione Studii* which so delighted Colet,[15] he wrote, "If it is claimed that Logic should find a place in the course proposed I do not seriously demur; but I refuse to go beyond Aristotle and I prohibit the verbiage of the schools." [16]

The prohibition continued to be pretty faithfully observed, and we cannot doubt that this partly explains the violence with which Cambridge's scholastic methods shocked and disgusted the unprepared young Milton. Early training as well as taste predisposed him to join in Bacon's strictures.

The maxim that language is only an instrument is yet another view to which Milton would have been exposed as a schoolboy. In *De Ratione Studii* Erasmus wrote:

> All knowledge falls into one of two divisions: the knowledge of "truths" and the knowledge of "words": and if the former is first in importance the latter is acquired first in order of time. They are not to be commended who, in their anxiety to increase their store of truths, neglect the necessary art of expressing them. For ideas are only intelligible to us by means of the words which describe them; wherefore defective knowledge of language reacts upon our apprehension of the truths expressed. . . . Language thus claims the first place in the order of studies and from the outset should include both Greek and Latin

[13] *William Shakspere's Small Latine & Lesse Greeke* (2 vols., Urbana: University of Illinois Press, 1944), I, 75–133. Baldwin goes so far as to say (p. 78), "Paul's was shaped completely by Erasmus."

[14] Tr. W. H. Woodward, *Desiderius Erasmus Concerning the Aim and Method of Education* (Cambridge, 1904), p. 221.

[15] See *The Epistles of Erasmus,* ed. F. M. Nichols (3 vols., London, 1901–1918), II, 24.

[16] Woodward, *Erasmus,* p. 165.

. . . [because] within these two literatures are [*sic*] contained all the knowledge which we recognize as of vital importance to mankind.[17]

The somewhat different emphasis given by Milton to the same proposition (it had been a commonplace for centuries) indicates, not a difference of value from Erasmus, but changed circumstances: in Erasmus' day the study of languages was deficient; in Milton's it had grown to claim a disproportionate—in some places a virtually independent—position.

Their common complaints about the prevailing methods of teaching languages have been taken as the clearest sign that Milton and the Comenians were, whether wittingly or not, allies. Thus, as we have seen, Watson pitches the basic contemporary educational battle "between the grammar-teachers and the teachers of Latin authors." He represents the latter by Eilhard Lubinus, Richard Carew, Comenius, Milton, Thomas Grantham, Hezekiah Woodward, Snell, Petty, Dury, Joseph Webbe, and Hartlib. In fact, however, this concatenation of names represents very diverse views. The only thing common to them all was a protest against a scandalous contemporary condition. We, who sometimes feel that our own exposure to the relatively innocuous pen-of-my-aunt constitutes something of a grievance, can scarcely imagine the dreadful waste of time, effort, and opportunity, and the appalling discouragement, which were the lot of boys in most—happily not quite all—seventeenth-century grammar schools. If there were no other evidence, something of this could be inferred from the ceaseless efforts to revise Lily, the nationally prescribed grammar. But indeed there is no end of evidence; almost all contemporary discussions of education complain of the way languages were taught; in 1622 Webbe had cited over a hundred attackers of the grammar-rule method (and, to show that the evil was as old as the method, had begun his list with Quintilian).[18] In these circumstances the fact that both Milton and the Comenians also complained cannot by itself be taken as ground for grouping them.

When we look to the positive notions of these enemies of the grammar-rules, Watson's indiscriminate catalogue disintegrates. Indeed, if we ask what ends they envisaged and what means they proposed, the names he assembles will serve well enough to indicate the diversity of reformist opinion, and consequently to illuminate, not the solidarity of Milton and the Comenians, but something of the gap between them.

The Comenians are clear on both points. Foreign languages (pri-

[17] *Ibid.*, pp. 162–63.

[18] *An Appeale to Truth, in the Controversie betweene Art, & Use; about the best and most expedient Course in Languages* (1622), C117bb4, p. 3.

marily Latin) are to be acquired so far as is necessary in order to get at information not available in the vernacular.[19] The method is set forth in the *Janua Linguarum Reserata*. This is a compilation, in Latin with vernacular translations, of phrases and sentences drawn from everyday experience; these are to be memorized, constantly re-iterated, and combined with each other in increasingly elaborate patterns. The result is to be a kind of workbench Latin achieved with-out the help of any formal grammar. But it is to be achieved without the help of any Latin authors either: the materials of study are es-pecially created for the purpose of study, and their whole rationale is pedagogic.[20]

Lubinus, Carew, Webbe, Grantham, and Woodward all fail to specify the ultimate object of linguistic training. They assume its necessity, and concern themselves only with the means. The recommendations of the first two reflect the fact that their standpoint is outside the school-room. Lubinus, whose primary concern is with Latin, is sure that by far the best way to teach it is to establish "artificial Roman colonies" where nothing else will be spoken. Conceding grudgingly that this means is unlikely to be widely adopted, he recommends a second-best course: instruction based upon the maximum use of sense-perception. His amplification of this idea constitutes at least an anticipation of Comenius' work in both the *Orbis Sensualium Pictus* and the *Janua,* and quite possibly the suggestion for it. His chief difference from Comenius is that he would follow up the command of the language with a prolonged immersion in its original literature.[21] Carew is more interested in the acquisition of modern languages, but includes Latin in his method, which is that, after a quite minimal preparation in grammar, the student is to go to live where he will hear nothing, and will be unable to make himself understood, except in the language he is studying. Carew, too, would consolidate the new tool by reading.[22]

Webbe, Grantham, and Woodward are professional schoolmasters. Webbe's method is the most radical. He dispenses altogether with the study of grammar, makes the unit of comprehension the clause, and relies entirely upon constant reading.[23] Grantham adopts Webbe's em-phasis on the clause, but, since he combines this with Ascham's fa-

[19] See above, pp. 189–92.

[20] For further evidence that the Comenians were no more "teachers of Latin authors" than they were "grammar teachers," see above, pp. 190–93.

[21] "Epistle" in his edition of the New Testament (1614), tr. by Hartlib in *The True and Readie Way* (1650), pp. 1–44.

[22] "Expressed in Answer to a Quere," *True and Readie Way*, pp. 45–49.

[23] *Appeale to Truth* and *A Petition to the High Court of Parliament, in the Behalfe of Auncient and Authentique Authors* (1623), 12933.b.15.

mous method of double-translation, he must have reintroduced some portion of the formal study of grammar, and his claim to have abolished grammar probably means that he used simplified rules whose memorization he did not require. He too emphasizes authors.[24] Woodward's method is the most eclectic, combining elements from many systems. (Woodward is, of Watson's catalogue, by far the most generous acknowledger of other people's contributions.) He lays a firm base in simplified grammar, by which he means full mastery of "declension and verb." Next the vocabulary is to be developed, with a maximum use of sense-perception after the manner of Comenius. Next, both comprehension and construction are practised by Ascham's method of double-translation. The wide reading of original authors follows, and composition is last.[25]

Milton is like the Comenians in one thing: he is clear as to the end of linguistic training. But it is a very different end from theirs. Languages (including—besides Latin—Greek, Italian, and Hebrew with "the *Chaldey,* and the *Syrian* dialect") are to be mastered (which means to write and speak, as well as to read them), as instruments indeed, but for the acquisition, not merely of factual information, but of the whole cultures incorporated in them. His method begins where all the grammar schools began, with the memorization of the rules of Latin grammar; only it is to be a greatly simplified version of the rules: "some preparatory grounds of speech by their certain forms got into memory," "the chief and necessary rules." (If it is permissible to interpret the 1644 plan in the light of *Accidence Commenc't Grammar* [1669], there was a second easement: the rules would be learnt in English. But this must not be insisted upon; if Milton had it in mind, he neglected to say so.) The great departure from normal theory (for the simplification of the rules is a departure only from practice) is the postponement of composition to a much later stage, and the full immediate concentration upon such reading, "lesson'd throughly to them," as would "bring the whole language quickly into their power." It is only after a very extensive reading, so designed as to perfect the understanding of languages simultaneously with the learning of "the substance of good things, and Arts in due order," that composition, conceived in the most ambitious terms, is to be undertaken.

[24] *The Brainbreakers-Breaker: or the Apologie of Thomas Grantham, for his Method in Teaching* (1644), 1031.g.18, and *A Discourse in Derision of the Teaching in Free-Schooles* (1644), E53(7).

[25] *A Childes Patrimony Laid Out upon the Good Culture or Tilling Over His Whole Man* (1640), 4404.m.19, and *A Light to Grammar, and All Other Arts and Sciences* (1641), Yale Library L674/W63/B641.

This may serve as a rough indication of how great are the differences separating critics of the contemporary teaching of languages. That both Milton and the Comenians were among these critics has no further significance than that both protested against what everyone of intelligence saw to be an intolerable condition. Actually, Milton's complaint, which was that the prevailing method took too long and achieved too little, and even his remedial prescription (except in the important matter of the stage at which composition was to be taught) are quite in the tradition of his own great but rather exceptional school. In *De Ratione Studii*, Erasmus wrote:

> I must make my conviction clear that, whilst a knowledge of the rules of accidence and syntax is most necessary to every student, still they should be as few, as simple, and as carefully framed as possible. I have no patience with the stupidity of the average teacher of grammar who wastes precious years in hammering rules into children's heads. For it is not by learning rules that we acquire the power of speaking a language, but by daily intercourse with those accustomed to express themselves with exactness and refinement, and by copious reading of the best authors. Upon this latter point we do well to choose such works as are not only sound models of style but are instructive by reason of their subject matter.[26]

In this matter, Colet himself is even more emphatic. In the *Aeditio* to which he made the school's statutes refer, he speaks apologetically of preparing a new accidence, saying that it is not because there are not already enough good ones, but so that he may show his love for the school he is founding. But his real motive soon emerges.

> In whiche lytel warke yf ony newe thynges be of me, it is alonely that I have put these partes in a more clere ordre, and have made them a lytel more easy to yonge wyttes than (methynketh) they were before. Judgyng that no thynghe may be to softe nor to famylyer for lytel chyldren, specyally lernynge a tongue unto them al straunge. In whiche lytel boke I have lefte many thynges out of purpose, consyderyng the tendernes and small capacyte of lytel myndes: and that I have spoken, also, I have affyrmed it none otherwyse but as it happeth moost comynly in latyn tongue. For many be the excepcyons, & harde it is ony thynge generally to assure in a speche soo varyous.[27]

After treating the parts of speech, Colet writes:

> Of these viii. partes of speche in ordre well construed be made reasons and sentences and longe oracyons. But how, and in wat maner, and with what construccyon of wordes, & all the varietees and diversitees and chaunges in latyn speche (whiche be innumerable) yf ony man wyl

[26] Woodward, *Erasmus*, pp. 163–64.   [27] Lupton, *Colet*, pp. 290–91.

know, and by that knowlege attayne to understande latyn bokes, and
to speke and to wryte the clene latyn, let hym above al besyly lerne
& rede good latyn authours of chosen poetes and oratours, and note
wysely how they wrote and spake, and studi alway to folowe them:
desyryng none other rules but theyr examples. For in the begynnynge
men spake not latyn bycause suche rules were made, but contrariwyse
bycause men spake suche latyn upon that folowed the rules were made.
That is to saye, latyn speche was before the rules, not the rules before
the latyn speche. Wherfore, welbeloved maysters & techers of grammer,
after the partes of speche sufficiently knowen in your scholes, rede and
expounde playnly unto your scholers good authours, and shewe to them
every worde, and in every sentence what they shal note and observe,
warnynge them besyly to folowe and to do lyke bothe in wrytynge and
in spekynge, & be to them your owne selfe also spekyng with them the
pure latyn veray present, and leve the rules. For redyng of good bokes,
diligent informacyon of taught maysters, studyous advertence &
takynge hede of lerners, heryng eloquent men speke, and fynally besy
imitacyon with tongue and penne, more avayleth shortly to gete the
true eloquent speche than al the tradicions, rules, and preceptes of
maysters.[28]

Milton's final agreement with the Comenians is that learning should
progress from the sensible to the abstract. The maxim itself cannot
be attributed to any single influence, although its application to educational theory apparently received much impetus from Vives.[29] It was,
as Comenius himself says, one of those generally received axioms always honored but rarely applied: "It is indeed the common voyce of
all, that we ought according to the order of nature to proceed from
those things, which are first, to those that follow, from generalls to
those which are more speciall, from things knowne to those which are
more obscure. But who is there, that takes this course?"[30] Milton
implements the maxim by deferring the study of logic, metaphysics,
and rhetoric to the last phase of the curriculum, and importing into the
earlier phases a good deal of natural and applied science. This is
clearly Baconian. It differs from Comenius's prescription (which professes to be Baconian in inspiration) partly in the subordinate, if important, role that Milton gives to natural science, but chiefly in that,
like Bacon, Milton postpones logic, metaphysics, and rhetoric until
the students are mature enough to benefit from their study, whereas
Comenius in effect dispenses altogether with them (see above, pp.
189–90). Bacon complained that

[28] *Ibid.*, pp. 291–92.
[29] See *De Tradendis Disciplinis,* Bk. IV, Chap. 1; tr. by Foster Watson as
Vives: On Education (Cambridge, 1913), pp. 163–71, esp. 168.
[30] *A Reformation* (1642), p. 14.

scholars in universities come too soon and too unripe to logic and rhetoric, arts fitter for graduates than children and novices. For these two, rightly taken, are the gravest of sciences, being the arts of arts; the one for judgment, the other for ornament. And they be the rules and directions how to set forth and dispose matter: and therefore for minds empty and unfraught with matter, and which have not gathered that which Cicero calleth *sylva* and *supellex*, stuff and variety, to begin with those arts (as if one should learn to weigh, or to measure, or to paint the wind) doth work but this effect, that the wisdom of those arts, which is great and universal, is almost made contemptible, and is degenerate into childish sophistry and ridiculous affectation. And further, the untimely learning of them hath drawn on by consequence the superficial and unprofitable teaching and writing of them, as fitteth indeed to the capacity of children.[31]

When this is compared with what Milton wrote (below, pp. 372–75) the correspondence is seen to be so close as to suggest direct borrowing.

Bacon's insistence upon the necessity of what Milton calls "a real tincture of natural knowledge" can scarcely be represented by quotation: it may reasonably be thought to constitute the prime contribution of the *Advancement*. Still, it will be better to illustrate it inadequately than not at all, and a passage may be chosen which Milton appears to have echoed in speaking of unballasted wits being tossed and turmoiled in intellective abstractions:

> Another error hath proceeded from too great a reverence, and a kind of adoration of the mind and understanding of man; by means whereof, men have withdrawn themselves too much from the contemplation of nature, and the observations of experience, and have tumbled up and down in their own reason and conceits. Upon these intellectualists, which are notwithstanding commonly taken for the most sublime and divine philosophers, Heraclitus gave a just censure, saying, 'Men sought truth in their own little worlds, and not in the great and common world'; for they disdain to spell, and so by degrees to read in the volume of God's works: and contrariwise by continual meditation and agitation of wit do urge and as it were invocate their own spirits to divine and give oracles unto them, whereby they are deservedly deluded.[32]

What Milton and the Comenians have in common, then, does not link them. Sometimes it is an inescapable commonplace; sometimes it is a generalization concealing differences more important than the agreement; even where Milton reflects Bacon's influence it is independently of Comenian mediation. On such points people holding the most diverse views about education could, and often did, agree.

[31] *Advancement*, II, Preface, 12; World's Classics ed., pp. 72–73.
[32] *Advancement*, I, v, 6; World's Classics ed., p. 37.

5. HARTLIB'S ROLE

But if the things upon which Milton and the Comenians agreed did not constitute a significant relation between them, and the things about which they differed were fundamental, why should Hartlib, that indefatigable bureau of Comenian propaganda, have solicited Milton's tractate?

I suggest that it was because at first, and with more excuse, he made the same mistake as has plagued the study of the tractate since Masson. He and Milton had had several discussions concerning education. If they talked of how much time was wasted and how little was achieved in English schools and universities, of how cordially and widely these institutions were loathed, what the reasons were for all this, and how it could be remedied—and surely no topics would be more probable—they would have found themselves in what must have seemed very substantial and even detailed agreement. They could have come very close to the chasm which separated them without seeing it: the reason for studying foreign languages, the amount of time that learning them ought to consume—they might have agreed about even such things, without realizing that the agreement concealed quite irreconcilable differences. Hartlib could very easily have concluded that Milton was an appropriate person to solicit for a pamphlet on educational reform.

We shall return to Hartlib in a moment; but first, what are we to make of Milton's reference to "many modern *Janua's* and *Didactics* more then ever I shall read"?

Masson's interpretation, it seems to me, is inherently improbable. If Milton did not know Comenius' ideas, then it follows that he simply went out of his way publicly to perpetrate a motiveless and gratuitous impoliteness against Hartlib's hero, while being, in the same paragraph, elaborately and (we have no reason at all to doubt) sincerely complimentary to Hartlib himself. I cannot think this reasonable, nor indeed any interpretation which leaves Milton without a motive for the allusion to Comenius.

Is it in fact possible that Milton was really ignorant of Comenius' ideas? Let us begin with the *Janua Linguarum Reserata*. Milton tells us that he was aware of its existence, and we hardly need his testimony. The *Janua* had, since its publication in 1631, achieved an enormous success. It had been translated into twelve European and four Asian languages,[1] had reached its sixth English edition before Milton wrote *Of Education,* was widely used by teachers and much discussed by

[1] Keatinge, *Great Didactic,* I, 23.

writers. No contemporary with either a practical or a theoretical interest in education—and Milton had both—could have been unaware of its existence. But it is a book of whose existence one cannot be aware—certainly whose pages one cannot turn over for two minutes—without also being aware of its nature, for, as we have seen, it is simply a compilation, in Latin with vernacular translations, of phrases and sentences drawn from ordinary experience, whose memorization and constant reiteration is meant to teach a kind of reading Latin, without the help of any formal grammar. One might have to spend time with the book to decide whether it was skilfully compiled; one might have to use it in teaching to come to a fair decision about whether it was effective; but one had only to look at it—indeed, only to hear about it—to know its object and method. If, even before he met Hartlib, Milton did not know this much about the *Janua*, he must have been about the only teacher in Europe who didn't.

But the *Janua* is only a way of teaching Latin. Milton may have known its object and method, may even have been skeptical of its value, without in the least knowing whether the general aims of the Comenians were to his taste. Here the crux is *The Great Didactic*, of whose existence he also tells us he was aware; and some consideration of this work will further clarify the problem. The question ought never to have been allowed to rise whether Milton had read the "book": he could not have done so. Comenius had indeed completed the manuscript, in Czech, by 1632,[2] but he had not yet made the Latin translation; that, the first to appear, was not to be published until thirteen years after Milton's tractate. Before 1657, what was meant by Comenius' *Great Didactic* was something much less formidable than the book itself. Hartlib had asked Comenius for some indication of the nature of the work, and Comenius had sent him a descriptive title and the headings of the chapters. This Hartlib had thrice[3] published: first in Latin under the title "Praecipua Capita Didacticae Magnae," occupying the last five and a half pages of the *Conatuum Comenianorum Praeludia*,[4] a volume containing several of Comenius' essays; then again in Latin, in a revised form, as the final pages of a new edition of the *Praeludia* published as *Comenii Pansophiae Prodromus;*[5] and finally in English as the last two and a half pages of *A Reforma-*

[2] *Ibid.*, II, 310.

[3] Keatinge seems to have been unaware of the first two publications; he wrote (*Great Didactic*, I, 41), "The headings of the chapters [Comenius] communicated to Hartlib, who published them in 1642 as an appendix to his *Reforme* [*sic*] *of Schooles.*" George H. Turnbull, *Samuel Hartlib* (London, 1919), pp. 29–30, lists all three publications.

[4] Oxford, 1637; 1012.b.23.7.   [5] 1639; 627.a.1.

tion of Schooles, the body of which was his translation of two of the essays he had already published in Latin. The fame of the *Janua* made people everywhere seize upon this abstract of the more ambitious work, and discuss it widely enough to embarrass the author, whose circumstances prevented him from following it quickly with the work itself; [6] it gave a sufficient indication of the general nature of his educational views; and it is hardly credible that a responsible writer would have referred slightingly to it in print without having taken the bare five minutes necessary to read it.

In Milton's case it is quite impossible to believe this. He tells us that he had at several times discoursed with Hartlib of the best and noblest way of education. Now Hartlib was perhaps the most active of all the proponents of Comenius's ideas, certainly the most active in England. He had already published a good deal of Comenius's work, some of which he translated into English; he had organized a group of influential people to sponsor a new Comenian college in London, and had brought Comenius over to found and direct it; when the collegiate scheme collapsed under the pressure of the Civil War he became the center of a group of teachers and writers who practised and preached Comenian reform; he raised money for the support, during their difficult periods, of Comenius and some of his associates. It is quite beyond question that he would have urged the abstract of the *Didactic* upon Milton; and I think it almost as certain that Milton read it, and probably also the essays with which it was bound.

There is a further fact which we have not yet taken into account; but before we do I want to suggest the hypothesis which I think it confirms. This is that before he met Hartlib Milton's knowledge of Comenianism, if it extended further than the general reputation, did not go beyond the *Janua.* In his conversations with Hartlib he found that if the Comenian method of teaching languages was not his, nevertheless their criticisms of the contemporary educational system, and apparently their ideas for improving it, were very similar. Hartlib then proposed that Milton send him, for publication, a treatise on education, and gave him the abstract *Didactic* so that he would be clear on what the Comenians were doing. Milton agreed to the project. Then he read the *Didactic* (and probably its accompanying essays), and found that for all the apparent harmony of his discussions with Hartlib, the real ends of the Comenians were very different from his own. He therefore thought it wise to dissociate himself from the Comenian program. In doing this, so far from being gratuitously rude, he exercised great courtesy, using, instead of the literal form "I reject," the more urbane

[6] Keatinge, *Great Didactic,* I, 30–31.

form, "I cannot concern myself." It was a not unnecessary precaution. Comenian reform was much in the air; his own prescription for educational reform was addressed to the prime Comenian in England; if he wished to prevent people from assuming, perhaps even without reading his pamphlet, that he too was a Comenian, he had better make the fact plain.

Whether it was plainer to his contemporaries generally [7] than it has been to ours is not clear, but I think it quite clear that Hartlib himself understood perfectly. He did not publish the tractate. Masson recognized this,[8] but its significance seems not to have struck him. It is, however, a fact of great significance. Hartlib solicited writings on education from Comenius, Dury, Milton, Woodward, Kinner, Petty, Snell, John Pell, and Heinrich Scheurl.[9] Except for those of Milton, Woodward, and Snell, he published them all. He offered to publish Snell's book too; in the prefatory "Missive . . . to his verie loving Friends Mr. Durey, and Mr. Hartlib," Snell gratefully acknowledges the proposal, but explains that, because of an unhappy experience with an

[7] John Hall could admire Milton's tract (see Turnbull, *Hartlib, Dury and Comenius,* p. 39) and introduce echoes from it into his own thoroughly Baconian *An Humble Motion to the Parliament of England Concerning the Advancement of Learning and the Reformation of Universities* (1649), as has been pointed out by the editor of that pamphlet, A. K. Croston (Liverpool: Liverpool Un. Press, 1953), introduction, pp. xi–xiv, and notes to pp. 25, 26, and 27 (to which might be added the passages beginning at p. 35, line 11, and p. 44, line 26). But Milton's influence on Hall's pamphlet appears to consist only in matters of expression, particularly in the criticism of current practice and the anticipation of great benefits from reform. For echoes of *Areopagitica,* see Croston's notes to pp. 5–6, 19, 28, and 30 (to which might be added the anecdote at p. 23, lines 24–30, and the phrase at p. 16, 1. 10).

[8] *Life,* III, 233: "The publication had been duly registered, and the publisher was the same Thomas Underhill, of Wood Street, who had published Milton's first three anti-Episcopal pamphlets. The inference is that the thing was printed by Milton himself, and not by Hartlib." (Underhill is not known ever to have done any work for Hartlib.) My colleague Professor Dorian interprets the evidence more cautiously (below, p. 357): "There is no positive evidence to show whether Milton himself or Samuel Hartlib . . . was responsible for publishing the first edition;" *cf.* also p. 362, n. 2. To me the absence of positive evidence is especially significant because—leaving Milton's tract aside for the moment— all the educational writings addressed to Hartlib and published by him have that fact clearly indicated in the title page, publisher's preface, or author's epistle. Strengthening all this negative evidence, moreover, is the striking analogy with Woodward's pamphlet described below, pp. 210–11.

[9] The last two, not mentioned above (p. 187), provided "An Idea of Mathematics" and *"Bibliotheca Augusta,"* published with *The Reformed Librarie-Keeper.* These were not brought into the discussion of the Comenian program because they limit themselves to particular problems.

earlier manuscript which had been printed without his immediate supervision, he thinks it best to arrange publication himself. (He may also have been influenced by the desire to dedicate the book to the kinsman who was supporting him; see "The Epistle Dedicatory.") This leaves only Milton and Woodward, linked yet again [10]—fortuitously, to be sure, but in a way which makes each throw light on the other's relations with Hartlib.

G. H. Turnbull, using Hartlib's newly recovered papers, compiled a bibliography of works which Hartlib "published or intended for publication, or which were dedicated to him." [11] No. 5 is the following manuscript title page in Hartlib's hand: *A Light to Grammar and All Other Arts and Sciences. By Ezek. Woodward. With a Gate to Sciences Opened by a Natural Key. Dedicated to S. H. London. . . . 1641.*[12]

But the title page of the printed volume contains no reference to Hartlib, and the volume is dedicated not to him but to "The High and Mighty Prince Charles."

As the title indicates, the book is in two parts. Each has a preface addressed to Hartlib, and from the first of these we can reconstruct well enough what happened. Hartlib, it is clear, was the initiator: *"My resolution was setled, never in this kind to put Pen to Paper againe, such my discouragement. . . . But see, . . . I am scribling againe. You may thank your selfe, for your intreaty it was, which brake the cords of a very strong resolution to the contrary."* [13] But what Hartlib proposed was quite specific; it was *"but to render a translation touching* precognitions *put into your hand by M.* Brookes 4. *yeares since."* [14] Apparently Woodward, after Hartlib *"came upon* [him] *the second time,"* [15] agreed to this project, for Brookes was his **old friend**, and he was glad to "perfume" his memory and aid in material **assistance** to his destitute children.[16] In the event, however, Woodward **did not** fulfill his promise:

> But Sir, I must tell you, and you will finde it true; I could make his Latine *which was but the contents of two sheets, of no manner of use to the publike, yet of use enough, for it was his, speaking in its owne* Dialect. *You know very well, it was* Technologicall *all along, (he was curious that way) but that would not bee for publike use, for being translated into* English, *it would be* Latine *still. . . . I have followed my owne way, using my owne words, taking the Clue of Nature in my*

[10] See above, pp. 90 and 144 for their other relations during these years.
[11] *Hartlib, Dury and Comenius*, p. 88.   [12] *Ibid.*, p. 90.
[13] *A Light to Grammar* (1641), sig. a4.
[14] *Ibid.*, sig. a6. I have been unable to identify Brookes.
[15] *Ibid.*   [16] *Ibid.*, sig. a6v.

hand all along; what speed I have made, and how neare the White *I
have got, let another judge.*[17]

Not near enough, Hartlib would seem to have judged; at any rate, he
did not publish the result. This need not imply disapproval of Woodward's "way" (Woodward, who was most flattering to Comenius,[18]
adopted some of the latter's devices); it may reflect no more than an
understandable reluctance to pay for the publication of a manuscript
which not only failed to perform what he had bespoken but also was
essentially a repetition of the author's recently published *Childes
Patrimony.*[19]

Woodward, unwilling to lose his labor, published the book himself.
He changed the projected dedication to Hartlib into a preface, and inserted a rather absurd begging dedication to Charles. Why, then, the
prefaces to Hartlib, if the latter had withdrawn his financial support?
We can only speculate, but there are certain advantages to be seen in
Woodward's course: the association with Hartlib would make his book
much more saleable; and the book's origin as a Hartlib project (together with some new matter) might make it seem less a reworking of
the 1640 book.[20]

Hartlib's normal practice, then, was to publish the educational
treatises written at his solicitation (indeed, few busy men would have
undertaken such tasks without this expectation). In one of the two exceptions to this rule,[21] he was disappointed in his expectations and
withdrew his sponsorship. Must we not conclude that the same is true
of the other exception? Milton's manuscript would have disappointed
him even more than Woodward's, and I suggest that, disagreeably surprised to find that it ran counter to his own convictions, he declined to
publish it. Milton, not more willing than Woodward to lose his labor,
thereupon published it himself.

But then why did he retain the original form, that of a letter
to Hartlib? Because, it seems to me, he felt that the little tract required some such setting for its justification. It was by no means the
comprehensive treatise that might well have been addressed to the
problem of education, and Milton went to some lengths to excuse this
on the ground that his mind was "for the present halfe diverted in
the persuance of some other assertions." [22] "But then," he must have

---

[17] *Ibid.*, sigs. a6v–a7.   [18] *Ibid.*, sig. a5v.   [19] See above, p. 202.
[20] *A Childes Patrimony* does not, like *A Light*, purport to be built wholly upon
the single principle of "precognition," but it too insists (p. 160) that "The
Mother-Tongue [must be] . . . a precognition to that tongue he understands
not."   [21] Counting the offer to publish Snell's work as coming within the rule.
[22] Below, p. 363.

anticipated the public reaction, "why publish?" The answer he carefully provided is that he was pressed to do so by a worthy laborer in the public interest.

6. TRUE AFFILIATION

If Milton set himself firmly against those educational reformers whom history seems to have chosen, what relation did his plan have to the contemporary scene? In re-examining those of Milton's ideas which have often been thought to link him with the Comenians, we found our attention directed instead (except for one clear debt to Bacon) always to his own boyhood school. Much has been done, especially by A. F. Leach [1] and T. W. Baldwin,[2] to recover the early curriculum and methods of St. Paul's School, and Masson, R. B. Gardiner,[3] M. J. F. McDonnell,[4] A. E. Barker,[5] and D. L. Clark [6] have given us a good understanding of the personal influence of the masters there during Milton's day (at any rate of the Gills, if Sound and Smythe remain obscure). Clark is the first to have attempted a detailed study on a considerable scale of the Paul's system in relation to Milton's tractate, and he is certainly justified (perhaps more than he shows) in concluding that Milton's "school as he dreamed it was in many respects like St. Paul's School if notably unlike Cambridge." [7] It seems safe to anticipate that further research will confirm the growing impression that the matrix for the views expressed in the tractate (and, perhaps even more important, for the basic assumptions made there) was Milton's own school experience.

There is, however, a caution to be observed. Having shown that Milton approved and was greatly influenced by St. Paul's, Clark writes: "Indeed he approved of the traditional grammar school so emphatically that he would extend and enrich it and abolish the universities altogether save for professional training in law and medicine." [8] Then why, it must be asked, his vehement attack upon the contemporary representatives of "the traditional grammar school"?

It is misleading to take St. Paul's (and especially the St. Paul's of Colet and Erasmus) as representative of the English grammar school of

---

[1] "Milton as Schoolboy and Schoolmaster," *Proceedings of the British Academy*, III (1907–1908), 295–318.

[2] See above, pp. 198–99.

[3] *The Admission Registers of St. Paul's School* (London, 1884).

[4] *A History of St. Paul's School* (London, 1909).

[5] See above, p. 198, n. 10.   [6] *Milton at St. Paul's*, esp. chap. 4.

[7] *Ibid.*, p. 250.   [8] *Ibid.*, pp. 250–51.

the mid-seventeenth century. Baldwin performed a real service in demonstrating that Paul's was the "predominant influence" in the development of the humanistic grammar schools of the early sixteenth century, and that other schools modelled themselves upon it.[9] It is much less clear that the changes which took place during the remainder of the century proceeded as uniformly as he thought.[10] Certainly in the seventeenth century (which falls outside his enquiry) the usual grammar school was very far from the ideas of Erasmus. The reasons for the general decline into the kind of school that Milton and most other thinking men wanted to reform are not clear. The most nearly persuasive explanation so far advanced (by J. W. Adamson) is that the immediate cause lay in the exaggerated Ciceronianism against which Erasmus conducted a losing fight, with its debasement of the venerable doctrine of "imitation" and its domination of the paths to professional advancement.

> The controversy respecting Ciceronianism was in fact a crucial one in the history, not only of classical education, but of all forms of school work. On the defeated side was ranged a sane humanism, desirous of assimilating what was best in the ancient literature in order to reform and fortify contemporary life; the victors included pedants who possessed no notion of an alembic which might transmute ancient into modern by means of a humanism common to both. The failure of Erasmus and his predecessors, Politian and Pico, to secure the adoption of their standpoint in the schools meant the triumph of the study of rhetoric as distinct from pure humanism, of language and modes of expression over literature, of form over content, a victory of grammar-books, phrase-books and similar compilations. The result was a new scholasticism, with Cicero for its Aristotle and St. Thomas Aquinas, and the two classical literatures for its Bible. In consequence the schools of Europe were diverted for generations from paths of knowledge in which humanists like Erasmus and Vives had wished to lead them.[11]

St. Paul's itself, it appears from the reconstruction of its curriculum, had strongly resisted this new scholasticism, and it was in good measure to it (to the living institution he knew, and probably also to the writings of its founder and its philosopher) that Milton looked to pattern his own ideal academy.

Not, of course, to it alone. How freely and richly Milton supplemented the model provided by St. Paul's from his readings among old renowned authors has been studied in detail, but his debt to the educational thought of the Renaissance (except that to Bacon) has been

[9] *Shakspere's Small Latine,* pp. 75–184.
[10] *Ibid.,* pp. 285–428.   [11] *History of Education,* p. 129.

only partly examined.[12] It may not be amiss to suggest that, next to
further study of the St. Paul's of Milton's day, the most promising
field for enlarged research in the provenience of the ideas of Milton's
tractate is in the complex tradition stemming from Castiglione's
Courtier: not only the "courtesy books" themselves, but also the
actual institutions (mostly French) which sought to embody their
doctrine, and the abortive proposals (often English) for further
academies of the same type. By way of reinforcing this guess, we may
adduce one representative of the latter class.

Sir Humphrey Gilbert probably laid his draft of an academy before
Elizabeth about 1570.[13] *The Cambridge Bibliography of English Literature* (I, 379) represents it as published in 1572, but this is erroneous;
there is no evidence of publication before 1827 (in *Archaeologia*),
when it was printed from the manuscript in the British Museum
(Lansdowne 98). We do not know how widely it was known, whether
there were any manuscript copies of the original, whether Milton had
access to it or had even heard of it. We must therefore avoid any suggestion that "Queene Elizabethes Achademy" was a source for *Of Education;* it is introduced here strictly as an analogue.

The proposal, which is as brief as Milton's tractate, is for "The
erection of an Achademy in London for educacion of her Majestes
Wardes, and others the youth of nobility and gentlemen." [14] When
the document's recipient is taken into account, with the restraints that
this imposed, it may be thought that the academy's most striking feature is that it would keep its pupils for the same period as Milton's,
"from xii to his full age"; [15] for Gilbert's reason is the same dislike
that Milton felt for the kind of education available at Oxford and
Cambridge.

> The Comodities which will ensue by erecting this Achademy. At this
> present, the estate of gentlemen cannot well traine up their childeren
> within this Realme but eyther in Oxford or Cambridge, whereof this
> ensueth: ffirst, being theare, they utterly lose their tymes yf they doe
> not follow learning onely. ffor there is no other gentlemanlike qualitie
> to be attained. Also, by the evill example of suche, those which would
> aply their studies are drawn to licentiousnes and Idlenes; and, there-
> fore, yt were every way better that they were in any other place then
> theare. And wheareas in the universities men study onely schole

[12] Howard Schultz, studying Milton's attitude toward curious learning and
vain philosophy, has recently made a fruitful start; see the section entitled
"Curiosity and the Educators" in *Milton and Forbidden Knowledge*, pp. 64–84.

[13] See Henry Ellis, *Archaeologia*, XXI (1827), p. 507.

[14] Ed. F. J. Furnivall, Early English Text Society, Extra Series, VIII (1869), 1.

[15] *Ibid.*, p. 10.

learninges, in this Achademy they shall study matters of accion meet for present practize, both of peace and warre.[16]

The universities would be left to those who sought training for the learned professions; [17] the leaders of society would be educated in Queen Elizabeth's Academy. Almost as striking as this fact (at least for the student of Milton) is the course of study which these prospective men of affairs would follow: "Grammar, both greke and latine," "the Hebrue tounge," French, Italian, Spanish, and "highe duche"; "Logick and Rethorick"; "morall philosophie," but "onely the politique parte thereof" (to be divided into "Civill" and "Martiall pollicy"); "naturall philosophie," "Arithmetick" and "Geometry" (which include "Imbattelinges, fortificacions, and matters of warre, with the practiz of Artillery, and use of all manner of Instrumentes belonging to the same"), "Cosmographie and Astronomy [and] . . . the arte of Navigacion," "phisick," and "Chirurgerie"; "civill law," "common lawes," and "divinitie"; horsemanship, military drill, and weapon training; "Musick" and "dawncing and vawting"; and "Harrowldrie." [18] We do not forget our promise not to treat Gilbert's "Achademy" as a source for Of Education. As an analogue, however, it suggests how much that is usually thought peculiar to Milton's academy is in fact shared by others in the tradition. When reservation is made for the synthetizing and vivifying effects of Milton's own mind, it does not seem too much to say that what in his tractate is not accounted for by St. Paul's (modified by Bacon's criticism and supplemented by particulars borrowed from antiquity) is yet to be found in the Renaissance educational tradition of which St. Paul's was the great institutional exemplar in England.

Have we not here the explanation of Milton's odd notion that his ideal school was simultaneously like the "schools of Pythagoras, Plato, Isocrates, Aristotle and such others"? Milton took from these teachers of antiquity no theory of education, no basic method of instruction, no general curriculum of study, no comprehensive organization: all these, about which Pythagoras and Aristotle, Plato and Isocrates, differed so much, came to him almost unawares while the great school which the boy found so congenial shaped his educational assumptions before he could analyze them. The mature man, who had one large fault to find with the curriculum of St. Paul's, retained its general structure. He had, however, much to add. Some of this was by way of refinement and improvement of detail. More was involved in the extension of his

[16] Ibid.

[17] Not, of course, the law, which would continue to be read at the Inns of Court.   [18] "Achademy," pp. 2–8.

program to embrace education at the university level. In both cases
he sought help among the great teachers of antiquity, and found it in
abundance. Contemplating his plan with that slackened awareness of
the ultimate sources of his thought which accompanies a familiarity so
great as to have become second nature, he might well imagine that this
academy of his, which was to take boys who were already entering
their adolescence and keep them until they reached their majority, and
for which he had taken so many suggestions from the Greeks, was
rather like the famous "academies" of Greece than like St. Paul's,
which took boys fresh from petty school or home tutor and discharged
them in their teens to make their further educational way elsewhere.

But like all these very diverse academies at once? Again the notion
is explicable: he had borrowed from them all, and what he had borrowed was always some particular which he fitted into the underlying,
almost unanalyzed, rationale which he brought from St. Paul's; he did
not become involved in the differences which divided his old renowned
authors because St. Paul's and the tradition which it embodied had
already accommodated them to his eclectic use.

If the present state of information leaves many of the details of the
tractate's relation to the contemporary scene still obscure, the large
outline is clearly discernible. In the schools (but not in the universities) the clerkly education culminating in logic which the sixteenth
century inherited from the Middle Ages succumbed quickly to the
competition of the new "gentlemanly" education culminating in "grammar" and "rhetoric" (or what we should call language and literature).
But, perhaps because the continued domination of the universities by
logic, metaphysics, and theology drove the new humanistic schools in
upon themselves, they deteriorated with extraordinary rapidity, and
in the seventeenth century seemed almost as remote from the needs of
the time as the old scholasticism. They thus created a new rival, vocational education culminating in "real" knowledge immediately applicable to economic use. Although his increasingly desperate concern
with the baffling problem of the relation of church and state was later
to drive Milton into a pretty considerable compromise with this new
education, in 1644 he deliberately rejected it. As aware as the Comenians of the faults of the contemporary grammar schools, he sought
to reform them by a return to their original rationale, corrected
in some particulars with the help of Bacon, refined and enriched from
the experience of antiquity, and vastly extended, in the tradition of
the Renaissance "academy," to achieve independence of the universities with their continuing hostility.

THE DOCTRINE AND
DISCIPLINE OF DIVORCE

August 1, 1643

PREFACE AND NOTES BY LOWELL W. COOLIDGE

HE DOCTRINE AND DISCIPLINE OF DIVORCE was published during Milton's lifetime in four editions.[1] The first of these, bearing neither the author's name nor initials, appeared under the imprint of Thomas Paine and Matthew Simmons about August 1, 1643.[2] One month earlier, the Westminster Assembly, called by Parliament to advise in the reorganization of the Church, had begun its work. That Milton had the Assembly in mind is strongly suggested by his title page; the subject was "Seasonable to be now thought on in the Reformation intended." The second edition, a much amplified revision of the first, came from the press not later than February 2, 1644.[3] Printed probably by Simmons, it carried Milton's initials on the title page and his full name at the end of a prefatory address "To the Parlament of England, with the Assembly." A third and a fourth edition, neither of which shows evidence of Milton's attention, appeared in 1645. The third is a fairly close reproduction of the second, done apparently by the same printer from a new setting-up of type. The fourth, differing noticeably in typography as well as spelling and punctuation, is unchanged from the second and third in content. None of these editions was licensed or registered.

All the main collections of Milton's prose have included *The Doc-*

---

[1] It has been customary to distinguish only two editions and to refer to the third and fourth as "states" of the second. This is not bibliographically justifiable, as William R. Parker has pointed out in *Milton's Contemporary Reputation* (Columbus: Ohio State University Press, 1940), pp. 270–73.

[2] See J. Milton French, *Life Records of John Milton*, II, 87–91. The date is that of the Thomason copy. For details concerning the printing, see William R. Parker, "Milton, Rothwell, and Simmons," *The Library*, Fourth Series, XVIII (1937), pp. 89–103. *The Doctrine and Discipline* was Simmons' first work for Milton; he subsequently printed *The Judgement of Martin Bucer* (see below, p. 416) and several other tracts.

[3] Thomason's dating. See French, II, 96–99.

trine and Discipline. Together with the other three divorce tracts, it has also been once issued in a special collection.[4] Invariably, however, the revised version has been followed, with surprisingly little attention to the initial document. The Columbia edition of *The Works of John Milton* (Vol. III, 1931) provides apparatus for a reconstruction of the 1643 text but prints consecutively only the 1644. There has been no complete commentary. Of explanatory notes dealing with portions of the work, the most extensive are by Merritt Y. Hughes in *John Milton: Prose Selections* (New York: Odyssey Press, 1947) and *John Milton: Complete Poems and Major Prose* (New York: Odyssey Press, 1957). Articles of major importance include Arthur Barker, "Christian Liberty in Milton's Divorce Tracts," *MLR*, XXXV (1940), 153–61, William Haller, " 'Hail, Wedded Love,' " *ELH*, XIII (1946), 79–97, and Kester Svendsen, "Science and Structure in Milton's *Doctrine of Divorce*," *PMLA*, LXVII (1952), 435–45.

The present edition makes available both the original and revised texts, so arranged as to facilitate comparison. The 1643 edition may be read by omitting all matter within arrowheads (◗ ◖), the 1644 edition by omitting all matter within angle brackets (< >) and by consulting the textual notes for spelling and punctuation changes.[5] The 1645 variants have not been supplied since there is no reason to believe that Milton was responsible for them.

The 1643 text is based on the Bridgewater copy in the Henry E. Huntington Library (46429), referred to in the textual notes as "A." It is a quarto measuring 17.5 by 14.1 cm. Collation: 4°, [A¹], B–G⁴, H¹, 26 leaves, pp. [2] 1–48 [2]. Contents: [A1]: title page. (verso blank). B1 [row of ornaments]: heading; text begins. G4: "The end." H₁ [row of ornaments]: text. H1: omitted passages. The "A" copy has been compared with the following copies, either directly or by microfilm: "B," British Museum C.59.g.21(17); "C," Yale Z77.153b; "D," University of Illinois 785829; "E", New York Public *KC 1643; "F," Harvard *EC65.M6427.643d(A); "G," Harvard *EC65.M6427.643d(B); "H," Princeton Ex3859.3257.14.

For the 1644 text Ohio State University Library 744958 has been taken as the "A" copy after collation with the following: "B," Henry E. Huntington 46425; "C," British Museum E.31.(5); "D," University of Illinois 728085; "E," University of Illinois 911141; "F," University of Illinois 953475; "G," University of Illinois (without accession number

---

[4] *The Doctrine and Discipline of Divorce: in Two Books: also The Judgement of Martin Bucer: Tetrachordon: and an Abridgement of Colasterion. With a Preface . . . by a Civilian* (London: Sherwood, Neely, and Jones, 1820).

[5] See below, pp. 781–92.

but marked 2 Apr. 43 Scribner); "H," New York Public *KC 1644
copy 1; "I," New York Public *KC 1644 copy 2; "J," Newberry K.75.-
577; "K," British Museum 117.i.59; "L," British Museum Ashley 1174.
No two of these copies are identical; sheets C, E, F, G, H, I, and K
show variant states of press correction and are bound in different com-
binations. Only the "A" copy appears to contain all the corrected sheets.
It is a quarto measuring 18.6 by 14 cm. Collation: 4°, A–F⁴, G⁴(±G2),
H–L⁴, M¹, 45 leaves, pp. [8] 1–82 (43, 44, 70, 72 misnumbered 45, 46,
76, 70). Contents: [A1]: title page. A2 [row of ornaments]: "To The
Parlament . . ."; A4v: "John Milton." B1 [triple row of ornaments]:
heading; main text begins. M1v: *"The end."* [margin to margin rule]
two lines of errata.

Lowell W. Coolidge

The College of Wooster

John *Milton*

THE
DOCTRINE
AND DISCIPLINE
OF
DIVORCE:
RESTOR'D TO THE GOOD
OF BOTH SEXES,

From the bondage of Canon Law,
and other miſtakes, to Chriſtian freedom,
guided by the Rule of Charity.

Wherein alſo many places of Scripture, have
recover'd their long-loſt meaning.

Seaſonable to be now thought on in the
Reformation intended.

Matth. 13. 52.

*Every Scribe inſtructed to the Kingdome of Heav'n, is like the Maiſter
of a houſe which bringeth out of his treaſurie things old and new.*

LONDON,
Printed by *T. P.* and *M. S.* In Goldſmiths
Alley. 1 6 4 3.

THE
Doctrine & Discipline
OF
DIVORCE

Reſtor'd to the good of both SEXES,
From the bondage of CANON LAW, and
other miſtakes, to the true meaning of Scripture in the Law and Goſpel compar'd.

Wherin alſo are ſet down the bad conſequences of
aboliſhing or condemning of Sin, that which the
Law of God allowes, and Chriſt aboliſht not.

Now the ſecond time revis'd and much augmented,
In TWO BOOKS:
To the Parlament of *England* with the Aſſembly.

The Author *J. M.*

MATTH. 13. 52.
Every Scribe inſtructed to the Kingdome of Heav'n, is like the
Maiſter of a houſe which bringeth out of his treaſury things
new and old.
Prov. 18. 13.
He that anſwereth a matter before he heareth it, it is folly and
ſhame unto him.

LONDON,
Imprinted in the yeare 1 6 4 4.

PARLAMENT OF ENGLAND,

with the ASSEMBLY

I F it were seriously askt, and it would be no untimely question, Renowned Parlament, select Assembly, who of all Teachers and Maisters that have ever taught, hath drawn the most Disciples after him, both in Religion, and in manners, it might bee not untruly answer'd, Custome.[1] Though vertue be commended for the most perswasive in her *Theory;* [2] and Conscience in the plain demonstration of the spirit, finds most evincing,[3] yet whether it be the secret of divine will, or the originall blindnesse we are born in,[4] so it happ'ns for the most part, that Custome still is silently receiv'd for the best instructer. Except it be, because her method is so glib and easie, in some manner like to that vision of *Ezekiel,*[5] rowling up her sudden book of implicit knowledge, for him that will, to take and swallow

---

[1] The power of custom, more particularly its corrupting effect upon religion, was in 1644 hardly a novel theme. *Cf.* Meric Casaubon, *A Treatise of Use and Custome* (1638; HEHL), p. 164: "For in very truth of all things in the World, there is nothing generally that goes by *custome* so much as religion doth, both in point of practice, and in point of opinions. So that there is nothing so horrible of itselfe, or so ridiculous in the judgement of reason and common sense in point of opinions, which long *custome* . . . will not make most plausible and acceptable: *custome having once got the strength of long continuance, insinuates errors and impostures* (bee they never so grosse) *into the minds of most men under the shape and representation of genuine truth:* So *Justin Martyr;* who fetcheth hence especially the origine of Idolatrie."

[2] *Cf. An Apology* (*Complete Prose,* I, 933): "*Theory,* which is often separated from the practick, and judges learnedly without it."

[3] Syntax seems to require that "evincing" be read as a substantive. *NED,* however, records no such usage.

[4] The spiritual blindness (obscuration of right reason) consequent upon the sin of Adam. *Cf. Christian Doctrine,* I, xii.

[5] See Ezekiel 2:8–3:3. In the vision there described the will of God is revealed to the prophet by means of a scroll which he is commanded to eat.

down at pleasure; which proving but of bad nourishment in the concoction,[6] as it was heedlesse in the devouring, puffs up unhealthily, a
certaine big face of pretended learning, mistaken among credulous
men, for the wholsome habit of soundnesse and good constitution;[7]
but is indeed no other, then that swoln visage of counterfeit knowledge and literature, which not onely in private marrs our education,
but also in publick is the common climer into every chaire, where
either Religion is preach't, or Law reported: filling each estate of
life and profession, with abject and servil principles; depressing the
high and Heaven-born spirit of Man, farre beneath the condition
wherein either God created him, or sin hath sunke him.[8] To persue
the Allegory, Custome being but a meer face, as Eccho is a meere
voice, rests not in her unaccomplishment, untill by secret inclination, shee accorporat her selfe with error, who being a blind and
Serpentine body without a head,[9] willingly accepts what he wants,
and supplies what her incompleatnesse went seeking. Hence it is, that
Error supports Custome, Custome count'nances Error.[10] And these
two betweene them would persecute and chase away all truth and
solid wisdome out of humane life, were it not that God, rather then
man, once in many ages, cals together the prudent and Religious
counsels of Men, deputed to represse the encroachments, and to worke

[6] Digestion.

[7] Kester Svendsen points out that the contrasting images of disease and health
establish a rhetorical pattern operative throughout the tract. See "Science and
Structure in Milton's *Doctrine of Divorce,*" *PMLA,* LXVII (1952), 435–45.

[8] *Cf. Christian Doctrine,* I, vii, tr. Sumner: "Man being formed after the
image of God, it followed as a necessary consequence that he should be endued
with natural wisdom, holiness, and righteousness." Although acknowledging the
partial loss of these attributes through original sin (*cf.* above, n. 4), Milton does
not think of man's unregenerate state as wholly depraved.

[9] *Cf.* Spenser's representation of Error in *Faerie Queene,* I, i, 13–24.

[10] An earlier allegorical association of custom and error occurs in the opening
sentences of William Whittingham's preface to Christopher Goodman's *How
Superior Powers Oght to Be Obeyd* (Geneva, 1558; HEHL): "Ignorance the
mother of error and professed ennemie to Gods Trueth, hath two daughters by
whose flatteries and subtile practises she blyndeth mens eyes, obscureth the
Trueth, and withdraweth us from the way of knollage: Custome, and Negligence.
Wherof the first so bewitcheth us, that althogh we wallowe and walter in darcke
blyndenes, yet as it were by dreaming we seme to walke in the bright sunne
shyning: so that Custome and compagnie may farre soner drawe us to perdition,
then Trueth and reason bring us to the understanding of our error." Milton
quotes from this work in the second edition of *Tenure of Kings and Magistrates*
(1650, pp. 52–53).

off the inveterate blots and obscurities wrought upon our mindes by
the suttle insinuating of Error and [A2] Custome: Who with the
numerous and vulgar train of their followers, make it their chiefe
designe to envie and cry-down the industry of free reasoning, under
the terms of humor, and innovation; [11] as if the womb of teeming
Truth were to be clos'd up, if shee presume to bring forth ought, that
sorts not with their unchew'd [12] notions and suppositions. Against
which notorious injury and abuse of mans free soule to testifie and
oppose the utmost that study and true labour can attaine, heretofore
the incitement of men reputed grave hath led me among others; and
now the duty and the right of an instructed Christian cals me through
the chance of good or evill report, to be the sole advocate of a dis-
count'nanc't truth: [13] a high enterprise Lords and Commons, a high
enterprise and a hard, and such as every seventh Son of a seventh
Son [14] does not venture on. Nor have I amidst the clamor of so much
envie and impertinence, whether to appeal, but to the concourse of so
much piety and wisdome heer assembl'd. Bringing in my hands an
ancient and most necessary, most charitable, and yet most injur'd
Statute of *Moses:* [15] not repeald ever by him who only had the
authority, but thrown aside with much inconsiderat neglect, under
the rubbish of Canonicall ignorance: as once the whole law was by
some such like conveyance [16] in *Josiahs* time.[17] And hee who shall
indeavour the amendment of any old neglected grievance in Church
or State, or in the daily course of life, if he be gifted with abilities of
mind that may raise him to so high an undertaking, I grant he hath
already much whereof not to repent him; yet let me arreed him, not
to be the foreman of any mis-judgd opinion, unlesse his resolutions
be firmly seated in a square and constant mind, not conscious to it
self of any deserved blame, and regardles of ungrounded suspicions.
For this let him be sure he shall be boorded presently by the ruder
sort, but not by discreet and well nurtur'd men, with a thousand idle
descants and surmises. Who when they cannot confute the least joynt

[11] Milton's attempt from the outset to forestall charges of innovation is suggested by the phrasing of his title, *The Doctrine and Discipline of Divorce:
Restor'd.* . . .

[12] This figurative use of the word is the earliest listed in *NED.*

[13] *Cf. Martin Bucer,* below, p. 433.

[14] One proverbially destined for great achievements.

[15] Deuteronomy 24:1.   [16] Underhand dealing or contrivance.

[17] See II Kings 22 and 23; also II Chronicles 34.

or sinew of any passage in the book; yet God forbid that truth should be truth, because they have a boistrous conceit of some pretences in the Writer. But were they not more busie and inquisitive then the Apostle commends, they would heare him at least, *rejoycing, so the Truth be preacht, whether of envie or other pretence whatosever:* [18] For Truth is as impossible to be soil'd by any outward touch, as the Sun beam. Though this ill hap wait on her nativity, that shee never comes into the world, but like a Bastard, to the ignominy of him that brought her forth: till Time the Midwife rather then the mother of Truth,[19] have washt and salted the Infant, declar'd her legitimat, and Churcht the father of his young *Minerva*, from the needlesse causes of his purgation.[20] Your selves can best witnesse this, worthy Patriots, and better will, no doubt, hereafter: for who among ye of the formost that have travail'd in her behalfe to the good of Church, or State, hath not been often traduc't to be the agent of his owne by-ends, under pretext of Reformation. So much the more I shall not be unjust to hope, that however Infamy, or Envy may work in other men to doe her fretfull will against this discourse, yet that the experience of your owne uprightnesse mis-interpreted, will put ye in mind to give it free audience and generous construction. What though the brood of Belial,[21] the draffe of men, to whom no liberty is pleasing, but un-bridl'd and vagabond lust without pale or partition, will laugh broad perhaps, to see so great a strength of Scrip- [A2v] ture mustering up in favour, as they suppose, of their debausheries; they will know better, when they shall hence learne, that honest liberty is the greatest foe to dishonest license. And what though others out of a waterish and queasy conscience because ever crazy and never yet sound, will rail

[18] *Cf.* Philippians 1:18.

[19] *Cf. Of Prelatical Episcopacy (Complete Prose,* I, 639), where Truth is referred to as "the daughter not of Time, but of Heaven, only bred up heer below in Christian hearts, between two grave & holy nurses the Doctrine, and Discipline of the Gospel." That Truth is the daughter of Time was a popular maxim.

[20] The image grotesquely mingles classical myth (the coming forth of Minerva from the brain of Jupiter) with the Anglican service of thanksgiving for women after childbirth. This service, commonly known as "churching," was in part derived from Old Testament purification rites; hence the Puritans tended to regard it as an unnecessary piece of ceremonialism.

[21] *Cf. Paradise Lost,* I, 501–502: "the Sons / Of Belial, flown with insolence and wine." The expression "children of Belial" occurs in Deuteronomy 13:13 and elsewhere in the Old Testament.

and fancy to themselves, that injury and licence is the best of this Book? Did not the distemper of their own stomacks affect them with a dizzy megrim, they would soon tie up their tongues, and discern themselves like that *Assyrian* blasphemer [22] all this while reproaching not man but the Almighty, *the holy one of Israel,* whom they doe not deny to have belawgiv'n [23] his owne sacred people with this very allowance, which they now call injury and licence, and dare cry shame on, and will doe yet a while, till they get a little cordiall sobriety to settle their qualming zeale. But this question concerns not us perhaps: Indeed mans disposition though prone to search after vain curiosities, yet when points of difficulty are to be discusst, appertaining to the removall of unreasonable wrong and burden from the perplext life of our brother, it is incredible how cold, how dull, and farre from all fellow feeling we are, without the spurre of self-concernment. Yet if the wisdome, the justice, the purity of God be to be cleer'd from foulest imputations which are not yet avoided, if charity be not to be degraded and trodd'n down under a civil Ordinance, if Matrimony be not to be advanc't like that exalted perdition, writt'n of to the *Thessalonians,*[24] *above all that is called God,* or goodnesse, nay, against them both, then I dare affirm there will be found in the Contents of this Booke, that which may concern us all. You it concerns chiefly, Worthies in Parlament, on whom, as on our deliverers, all our grievances and cares, by the merit of your eminence and fortitude are devolv'd: Me it concerns next, having with much labour and faithfull diligence first found out, or at least with a fearlesse and communicative candor first publisht to the manifest good of Christendome, that which calling to witnesse every thing mortall and immortall, I beleeve unfainedly to be true. Let not other men thinke their conscience bound to search continually after truth, to pray for enlightning from above, to publish what they think they have so obtaind, & debarr me from conceiving my self ty'd by the same duties. Yee have now, doubtlesse by the favour and appointment of God, yee have now in your hands a great and populous Nation to Reform; from what cor-

[22] Sennacherib, king of Assyria, whose threats against Jerusalem during the reign of Hezekiah were denounced as blasphemy "even against the Holy One of Israel." See II Kings 19:22.

[23] "Legislated to." *NED.* The word is probably a Miltonic coinage.

[24] "Son of perdition" may have been the expression which Milton intended. *Cf.* II Thessalonians 2:3–4: "the son of perdition; Who opposeth and exalteth himself above all that is called God, or that is worshipped."

ruption, what blindnes in Religion yee know well; in what a degenerat and fal'n spirit from the apprehension of native liberty, and true manlines, I am sure ye find: with what unbounded licence rushing to whordoms and adulteries needs not long enquiry: insomuch that the fears which men have of too strict a discipline, perhaps exceed the hopes that can bee in others, of ever introducing it with any great successe. What if I should tell yee now of dispensations and indulgences, to give a little the rains, to let them play and nibble with the bait a while; a people as hard of heart as that Egyptian Colony that went to *Canaan*.[25] This is the common doctrine that adulterous and injurious divorces were not conniv'd only, but with eye open allow'd of old for hardnesse of heart. But that opinion, I trust, by then this following argument hath been well read, will be left for one of the mysteries of an indulgent Antichrist, to farm out incest by, and those his other tributary pollutions.[26] What middle way can be tak'n then, may some interrupt, if we must [A3] neither turne to the right nor to the left, and that the people hate to be reform'd: Mark then, Judges and Lawgivers, and yee whose Office is to be our teachers, for I will utter now a doctrine, if ever any other, though neglected or not understood, yet of great and powerfull importance to the governing of mankind. He who wisely would restrain the reasonable Soul of man within due bounds, must first himself know perfectly, how far the territory and dominion extends of just and honest liberty. As little must he offer to bind that which God hath loos'n'd, as to loos'n that which he hath bound.[27] The ignorance and mistake of this high point, hath

[25] The Israelites, whose "hardness of heart" was cited (Matthew 19:8 and Mark 10:5) as the reason for the Mosaic law of divorce.

[26] An allusion to Papal dispensations, specifically to those by which marriages were permitted within the normally forbidden degrees of relationship. That such dispensations were used as a device to obtain revenue was a common Protestant accusation. Thomas Pickering, for example, in the dedication prefixed to William Perkins' *Christian Oeconomie* (1609; HEHL), asserts that "the judgement and determination of causes matrimoniall" were usurped by the church courts. "And among their reasons of policie, this is one of the principall, that they might by this meanes raise a commoditie to the Sea of Rome, by the sale of their dispensations." William Perkins, *The Workes of That Famous and Worthy Minister of Christ in the Universitie of Cambridge* (3 vols., 1609–13; UTSL), III, sig. Rrrr¶¶ (hereafter cited as Perkins, *Works*).

[27] *Cf.* William Whately's earlier statement of the principle in *A Care-Cloth: or A Treatise of the Cumbers and Troubles of Marriage* (1624; HEHL), p. 4: "No man must make more faults then God makes. Our judgement should be alwaies so cleare and sound, that we might esteeme of things as they be, and

heapt up one huge half of all the misery that hath bin since *Adam.* In the Gospel [28] we shall read a supercilious crew of masters, whose holinesse, or rather whose evill eye, grieving that God should be so facil to man, was to set straiter limits to obedience, then God had set; to inslave the dignity of man, to put a garrison upon his neck of empty and overdignifi'd precepts: And we shall read our Saviour never more greev'd and troubl'd, then to meet with such a peevish madnesse among men against their own freedome. How can we expect him to be lesse offended with us, when much of the same folly shall be found yet remaining where it lest ought, to the perishing of thousands. The greatest burden in the world is superstition; not onely of Ceremonies in the Church, but of imaginary and scarcrow sins at home. What greater weakning, what more suttle stratagem against our Christian warfare,[29] when besides the grosse body of real transgressions to encounter; wee shall bee terrify'd by a vain and shadowy menacing of faults that are not: When things indifferent shall be set to over-front us,[30] under the banners of sin, what wonder if wee bee routed, and by this art of our Adversary, fall into the subjection of worst and deadliest offences. The superstition of the Papist is, *touch not, taste not,*[31] when *God* bids both: and ours is, *part not, separat not,* when God and charity both permits and commands. *Let all your things be done with charity,*[32] saith St. *Paul:* and his Master saith, *Shee is the fulfilling of the Law.*[33] Yet now a civil, an indifferent, a somtime diswaded Law of

call that lawfull which is lawfull, as well as that wicked which is wicked: and as in the tribunall of humane Justice, a guiltlesse man must not be sentenced as guiltie: So at the barre of humane reason, a faultlesse action must not bee wrongly burdened with the censure of faultinesse." For the metaphor of binding and loosening, *cf.* Matthew 16:19 and 18:18.

[28] *Cf.* Matthew 12:1–14; 15:1–20; 23:1–33; Mark 2:23–3:6; 7:1–23; Luke 6:1–11; 11:37–54.

[29] John Downame's *Christian Warfare* (1604; HEHL) devotes four chapters of book I to an account "Of Satan's Stratagems."

[30] See introduction above, pp. 68–69.

[31] Colossians 2:21. *Cf.* Whately, *A Care-Cloth* (1624), p. 5: "There is a negative superstition (consisting of *Touch not, taste not, handle not, &c.* that is Do not this and that, for feare of offending God, and hurting your soule, though the Lord have never condemned it) as well as an affirmative superstition, standing in *Doe this,* or *do that,* that you may please God, and benefit your soule."

[32] I Corinthians 16:14.

[33] Romans 13:10. Although Milton is actually quoting St. Paul, he is doubtless thinking of the passage as a restatement of Christ's summary of the Decalogue in Matthew 22:37–40. *Cf.* John Weemse, *An Exposition of the Second Table of*

mariage, must be forc't upon us to fulfill, not onely without charity, but against her. No place in Heav'n or Earth, except Hell, where charity may not enter: yet mariage the Ordinance of our solace and contentment, the remedy of our lonelinesse will not admit now either of charity or mercy to come in and mediate or pacifie the fiercenes of this gentle Ordinance, the unremedied lonelinesse of this remedy. Advise yee well, supreme Senat, if charity be thus excluded and expulst, how yee will defend the untainted honour of your own actions and proceedings: [34] He who marries, intends as little to conspire his own ruine, as he that swears Allegiance: and as a whole people is in proportion to an ill Government, so is one man to an ill mariage. If they against any authority, Covnant, or Statute, may by the soveraign edict of charity, save not only their lives, but honest liberties from unworthy bondage, as well may he against any private Covnant, which hee never enter'd to his mischief, redeem himself from unsupportable disturbances to honest peace, and just contentment: And much the rather, for that to resist the highest Magistrat though tyrannizing, God never gave us expresse allowance, only he gave us reason, charity, nature and good example to bear us out; but in this economical [35] misfortune, thus to demean our selves, besides the warrant of those foure great [A3v] directors, which doth as justly belong hither, we have an expresse law of *God*, and such a law, as wherof our Saviour with a solemn threat forbid the abrogating.[36] For no effect of tyranny can sit more heavy on the Common-wealth, then this household unhappines on the family. And farewell all hope of true Reformation in the state, while such an evill as this lies undiscern'd or

the Morall Law (1636; HEHL), p. 1: "The Lord hath reduced all his Commandements to ten, . . . he reduced them to two, . . . and at last he reduced them to one, *Rom.* 13.10."

[34] That political institutions are subordinate to the ends for which they are established was a principle inevitably invoked by apologists for Parliamentary resistance to the king. Thus Henry Parker had pointed out that the king's "dignitie was erected to preserve the Commonaltie, the Commonaltie was not created for his service: and that which is the end is farre more honorable and valuable in nature and policy then that which is the meanes. This directs us then to the transcendent ἀχμὴ of all Politiques, to the Paramount Law that shall give Law to all humane Lawes whatsoever, and that is *Salus Populi*." *Observations upon Some of His Majesties Late Answers and Expresses* (1642; HEHL), p. 3. See introduction, above, pp. 152–57, for a discussion of the importance for Milton of the analogy he draws between his cause and Parliament's.

[35] Pertaining to a household; domestic.

[36] See Matthew 5:17–19. The "expresse law" is Deuteronomy 24:1.

unregarded in the house. On the redresse wherof depends, not only
the spiritfull and orderly life of our grown men, but the willing, and
carefull education of our children. Let this therefore be new examin'd,
this tenure and free-hold of mankind, this native and domestick Charter giv'n us by a greater Lord then that *Saxon* King the Confessor.[37]
Let the statutes of God be turn'd over, be scann'd a new, and consider'd; not altogether by the narrow intellectuals of quotationists and
common placers, but (as was the ancient right of Counsels) by men
of what liberall profession soever,[38] of eminent spirit and breeding
joyn'd with a diffuse and various knowledge of divine and human
things; able to ballance and define good and evill, right and wrong,
throughout every state of life; able to shew us the waies of the Lord,
strait and faithfull as they are, not full of cranks and contradictions,
and pit falling dispenses, but with divine insight and benignity measur'd out to the proportion of each mind and spirit, each temper and
disposition, created so different each from other, and yet by the skill
of wise conducting, all to become uniform in vertue. To expedite these
knots were worthy a learned and memorable Synod; while our enemies
expect to see the expectation of the Church tir'd out with dependencies and independencies how they will compound, and in what
Calends.[39] Doubt not, worthy Senators, to vindicate the sacred honour
and judgment of *Moses* your predecessor, from the shallow commenting of Scholasticks and Canonists. Doubt not after him to reach out
your steddy hands to the mis-inform'd and wearied life of man; to
restore this his lost heritage into the houshold state; wherwith be
sure that peace and love, the best subsistence of a Christian family
will return home from whence they are now banisht; places of prosti-
tution wil be lesse haunted, the neighbours bed lesse attempted, the
yoke of prudent and manly discipline will be generally submitted to,
sober and well order'd living will soon spring up in the Common-
wealth. Ye have an author great beyond exception, *Moses;* and one

[37] Edward the Confessor (1002–1066), last of the Saxon kings, was remem-
bered with particular affection. *Cf. History of Britain,* Book VI (1670, p. 297):
"His Laws held good and just, and long after desir'd by the English of thir
Norman Kings, are yet extant."

[38] *Cf. Church-Government (Complete Prose,* I, 839), where Milton points out
that laymen were invited to participate in the first Council of Nicaea (325).

[39] Controversy between Presbyterian and Independent elements in the Assembly (*cf.* "dependencies and independencies") became increasingly acute after
publication of *An Apologeticall Narration,* by Thomas Goodwin and others in
January, 1644. How and when ("in what Calends") a compromise could be
effected was a disturbing question. See introduction, above, pp. 65–136.

yet greater, he who hedg'd in from abolishing every smallest jot and tittle of precious equity contain'd in that Law, with a more accurat and lasting Masoreth,[40] then either the Synagogue of *Ezra*,[41] or the *Galilean* School at *Tiberias* [42] hath left us. Whatever els ye can enact, will scarce concern a third part of the Brittish name: but the benefit and good of this your magnanimous example, will easily spread far beyond the banks of *Tweed* and the *Norman* Iles.[43] It would not be the first, or second time, since our ancient *Druides*, by whom this Island was the Cathedrall of Philosophy to *France*, left off their pagan rites, that England hath had this honour vouchsaft from Heav'n, to give out reformation to the World.[44] Who was it but our English *Constantine* that baptiz'd the Roman Empire? [45] who but the *Northumbrian Willibrode*, and *Winifride* of *Devon* with their followers, were the first Apostles of *Germany*? [46] who but *Alcuin* and *Wicklef*

[40] The Masoreth or Masorah (from a Hebrew word commonly understood to mean *tradition*) was a body of marginal notes compiled by rabbinical scholars with the object of preserving the correct form of the Old Testament text. According to *NED*, "Milton (misled by the rendering 'tradition') seems to have supposed the word applicable to the exegetical tradition of the Rabbis, by which the severity of the law was increased." This, however, seems an unnecessary inference. Milton's point is that the words of Christ are the most authoritative commentary on the Mosaic intention.

[41] The reference is probably to the "Great Synagogue," traditionally an assembly of 120 members established in the time of Ezra and Nehemiah (5th century B.C.) and having as one of its objects to "put a fence about the Torah." The biblical basis is Nehemiah 8–10. See *Jewish Encyclopedia*.

[42] The city of Tiberias, on the west shore of the Sea of Galilee, was a famous center of rabbinical scholarship as late as the twelfth century. It was there that the principal system of Hebrew punctuation originated.

[43] The Channel Islands, off the coast of Normandy but belonging to England.

[44] *Cf. History of Britain*, Book II (1670, p. 49), where Milton says of the early inhabitants that "thir Religion was governd by a sort of Priests or Magicians call'd *Druides* from the Greek name of an *Oke*, which Tree they had in great reverence, and the *Missleto* especially growing thereon; *Plinie* writes them skill'd in Magic no less then those of *Persia*: . . . yet Philosophers I cannot call them, reported men factious and ambitious, contending somtimes about the archpriesthood not without civil Warr and slaughter." Julius Caesar, in his account of the Druids (*Commentaries*, VI, 13), observes that their system of doctrine "is thought to have originated in Britain and thence to have been carried over into Gaul." *Cf. Areopagitica*, below, p. 551, nn. 230–32.

[45] Constantine the Great (*ca.* 288–337), the first Roman emperor to accept Christianity, was erroneously supposed of British birth. *Cf. History of Britain*, Book II (1670, p. 89): "There goes a fame, and that seconded by most of our own Historians, though not those the ancientest, that *Constantine* was born in this Iland, his mother *Helena* the Daughter of *Coilus* a *British* Prince."

[46] St. Willibrord or Wilbrord (*ca.* 657–*ca.* 738), "a Priest eminent for learning, past over Sea, having 12 others in Company, with intent to preach the

our Country men open'd the eyes of *Europe*, the one in arts, the other in Religion.[47] Let not England forget her precedence of teaching nations how to live. [A4]

Know, Worthies, know and exercise the privilege of your honour'd Country. A greater title I heer bring ye, then is either in the power or in the policy of *Rome* to give her *Monarchs;* this glorious act will stile ye the defenders of Charity.[48] Nor is this yet the highest inscription that will adorne so religious and so holy a defence as this; behold heer the pure and sacred Law of God, and his yet purer and more sacred name offring themselvs to you first, of all Christian reformers to be acquitted from the long suffer'd ungodly attribute of patronizing Adultery. Deferre not to wipe off instantly these imputative blurrs and stains cast by rude fancies upon the throne and beauty it selfe of inviolable holines: lest some other people more devout and wise then wee, bereav us this offer'd immortal glory, our wonted prerogative, of being the first asserters in every great vindication. For me, as farre as my part leads me, I have already my greatest gain, assurance and inward satisfaction to have don in this nothing unworthy of an honest life, and studies well employ'd. With what event among the wise and right understanding handfull of men, I am secure. But how among the drove of Custom and Prejudice this will be relisht, by such whose capacity, since their youth run ahead into the easie creek of a System or a Medulla,[49] sayls there at will under the blown physiognomy [50] of

Gospel in *Germany*. And coming to *Pepin* Cheif Regent of the *Franks,* who a little before had conquer'd the hither *Frisia,* by his countnance and protection . . . they found the work of conversion much the easier, and *Wilbrod* the first Bishoprick in that Nation." *History of Britain*, Book IV (1670, p. 164). Winfrid (*ca.* 680–755), more commonly known as St. Boniface, was an English Benedictine who suffered martyrdom in Frisia after long and successful missionary activity in Bavaria, Thuringia, and other parts of Germany.

[47] Alcuin (735–804) was born and educated at York. One of the foremost scholars of his age, he figured prominently in the revival of learning at the court of Charlemagne. John Wycliffe (*ca.* 1320–1384) anticipated many of the views of the Continental reformers. *Cf.* Milton's several references to him in the antiprelatical tracts (*Complete Prose*, I, 525, 704, 878), in *Tetrachordon* (below, p. 707), and in *Areopagitica* (below, p. 553).

[48] Milton is thinking of the title "Defender of the Faith" conferred upon Henry VIII in 1521 by Pope Leo X.

[49] The "marrow" of a subject; hence a compendium or abridgment. A popular summation of Calvinistic doctrine was the *Medulla Theologiae* (1623) by William Ames, translated in 1642 (UTSL) as *The Marrow of Sacred Divinity*.

[50] *Cf.* "big face" and "swoln visage" (above, p. 223).

their unlabour'd rudiments, for them, what their tast will be, I have also surety sufficient, from the entire league that hath bin ever between formal ignorance and grave obstinacie. Yet when I remember the little that our Saviour could prevail about this doctrine of Charity against the crabbed textuists of his time, I make no wonder, but rest confident that who so preferrs either Matrimony, or other Ordinance before the good of man and the plain exigence of Charity, let him professe Papist, or Protestant, or what he will, he is no better then a Pharise, and understands not the Gospel: whom as a misinterpreter of Christ I openly protest against; and provoke him to the trial of this truth before all the world: and let him bethink him withall how he will soder up the shifting flaws of his ungirt permissions, his venial and unvenial dispences, wherwith the Law of God pardoning and unpardoning hath bin shamefully branded, for want of heed in gloss-ing, to have eluded and baffl'd out all Faith and chastity from the mariagebed of that holy seed, with politick and judicial adulteries. I seek not to seduce the simple and illiterat; my errand is to find out the choisest and the learnedest, who have this high gift of wisdom to answer solidly, or to be convinc't. I crave it from the piety, the learn-ing and the prudence which is hous'd in this place. It might perhaps more fitly have bin writt'n in another tongue;[51] and I had don so, but that the esteem I have of my Countries judgement, and the love I beare to my native language to serv it first with what I endeavour, made me speak it thus, ere I assay the verdit of outlandish readers. And perhaps also heer I might have ended nameles,[52] but that the addresse of these lines chiefly to the Parlament of *England* might have seem'd ingratefull not to acknowledge by whose Religious care, unwearied watchfulnes, couragious and heroick resolutions, I enjoy the peace and studious leisure to remain,

The Honourer and Attendant of their Noble worth and vertues,
John Milton. [A4v]

[51] *Cf.* Milton's reflection a decade later in *Second Defence* (1654, p. 79), tr. Fellowes: "I regret that I published this work in English; for then it would not have been exposed to the view of those common readers, who are wont to be as ignorant of their own blessings, as they are insensible to others' sufferings."
[52] *Cf. Martin Bucer*, below, p. 434: *"My name I did not publish* [in the first edition], *as not willing it should sway the reader either for me or against me."*

The

Doctrine and Discipline

of Divorce;

Restor'd to the good of both Sexes.

♦ I. BOOKE.

The Preface.

That Man is the occasion of his owne miseries, in most of those evills which hee imputes to Gods inflicting. The absurdity of our canonists in their decrees about divorce. The Christian imperiall Lawes fram'd with more Equity. The opinion of Hugo Grotius, *and* Paulus Fagius: *And the purpose in generall of this Discourse.* ◀

MANY men, whether it be their fate, or fond opinion, easily perswade themselves, if GOD would but be pleas'd a while to withdraw his just punishments from us, and to restraine what power either the devill, or any earthly enemy hath to worke us woe, that then mans nature would find immediate rest and releasement from all evils. But verily they who think so, if they be such as have a minde large anough to take into their thoughts a generall survey of humane things, would soone prove themselves in that opinion farre deceiv'd. For though it were granted us by divine indulgence ♦ [1] ◀ to be exempt from all that can be harmfull to us from without, yet the perversnesse of our folly is so bent, that we should never lin [1] hammering out of our owne hearts, as it were out of a flint, the seeds and sparkles of new <miseries> ♦ misery ◀ to our selves, till all were in a blaze againe. And no marvell if out of our own hearts, for they are evill;[2] but ev'n out of those things which God meant us, either for a principall good, or a pure contentment, we are still hatching and contriving upon our selves matter of continuall

[1] Cease (OE *linnan*).

[2] *Cf.* Genesis 8:21 ("the imagination of man's heart is evil from his youth"); also Matthew 15:19.

234

sorrow and perplexitie. What greater good to man then that revealed rule, whereby God vouchsafes to shew us how he would be worshipt? and yet that not rightly understood, became [1] the cause that once a famous man in *Israel* could not but oblige his conscience to be the sacrificer, or if not, the jayler of his innocent and onely daughter.[3] And was the cause oft-times that Armies of valiant men have given up their throats to a heathenish enemy on the Sabbath day:[4] fondly thinking their defensive resistance to be as then a work unlawfull. What thing more instituted to the solace and delight of man then marriage, and yet the mis-interpreting of some Scripture directed mainly against the abusers of the Law for divorce giv'n <them> by *Moses*,[5] hath chang'd the blessing of matrimony not seldome into a familiar and co-inhabiting mischiefe; at least into a drooping and disconsolate houshold captivitie, without refuge or redemption. So ungovern'd and so wild a race doth superstition run us from one extreme of abused libertie into the other of unmercifull restraint. For although God in the first ordaining of marriage,[6] taught us to what end he did it, in words expresly implying the apt and cheerfull conversation [7] of man with woman, to comfort and refresh him against the evill of solitary life, not mentioning the purpose of generation till afterwards, as being but a secondary end in dignity, though not in necessitie; yet now, if any two be but once handed in the Church, and have tasted in any sort <of> the nuptiall bed, let them finde themselves never so mistak'n in their dispositions through any error, concealment, or misadventure, that through their different tempers, thoughts, and constitutions, they can neither be to one another a

[3] See Judges 11:30–40. Whether Jephthah actually put his daughter to death was "a Question of some moment," according to William Perkins in *Cases of Conscience* (*Works*, 1609–13, II, 98). Perkins adds as his own opinion that Jephthah "onely dedicated her unto God, after the manner of the Nazarites, to the end of her daies, to leade her life apart in a single estate."

[4] Probably the outstanding example of such non-resistance is that recorded in I Maccabees 2:31–38 and in Josephus, *Antiquities of the Jews*, XII, 6. Refusing to defend themselves against a Sabbath attack by Antiochus, the followers of Mattathias were slain "to the number of a thousand people." Josephus also reports that Pompey in his siege of Jerusalem (67 B.C.) took advantage of the Jews' reluctance to fight on the seventh day of the week. See *Antiquities*, XIV, 4, and *Wars of the Jews*, I, 7.

[5] Matthew 5:31–32. For Milton's discussion of the passage, see below, p. 307.

[6] Genesis 2:18.

[7] "The action of consorting or having dealings with others; living together; commerce, intercourse, society, intimacy." *NED.*

remedy against lonelines, nor live in any union or contentment all their dayes, yet they shall, so they be but found suitably weapon'd to the lest possibilitie of sensuall enjoyment, be made, spight of *antipathy* [8] to fadge together, and combine as they may to their unspeakable wearisomnes & despaire of all sociable delight in the ordinance which God establisht to that very end. What a calamitie is this, and as the Wise-man, if he ♦ [2] ◀ were alive, would sigh out in his own phrase, what a *sore evill is this under the Sunne*! [9] All which we can referre justly to no other author then the Canon Law and her adherents,[10] not consulting with charitie, the interpreter and guide of our faith, but resting in the meere element of the Text; doubtles by the policy of the devill to make that gracious ordinance become unsupportable, that what with men not daring to venture upon wedlock, and what with men wearied out of it, all inordinate licence might abound. It was for many ages that mariage lay in disgrace with most of the ancient Doctors, as a [2] work of the flesh, almost a defilement, wholly deny'd to Priests, and the second time disswaded to all, as he that reads *Tertullian* or *Jerom* may see at large.[11] Afterwards it was

[8] Natural contrariety or incompatibility. That Milton is thinking of the word in its original, semi-technical sense is evident from his use of italics.

[9] *Cf.* Ecclesiastes 5:13. The "Wise-man" is King Solomon, to whom Ecclesiastes was commonly attributed.

[10] "The Canon Law consisteth partly of certaine Rules, taken out of the holy Scripture, partly out of the writings of the ancient Fathers of the Church, partly of the ordinances of generall & provinciall Councels, partly of the Decrees of Popes of former ages. Of the Canon Law there are two principall parts, the Decrees & the Decretals. The Decrees are Ecclesiasticall constitutions, made by the Pope and Cardinals, at no mans suit, & are either Rules taken out of the Scripture, or Sentences out of the ancient Fathers, or Decrees of Councels. . . . The Decretals are Canonicall Epistles, written either by the Pope alone, or by the Pope and Cardinals, at the instance or suit of some one or more for the ordering and determining of some matter in controversie." Thomas Ridley, *A View of the Civile and Ecclesiasticall Law* (Oxford, 1634; HEHL), pp. 73–75. Although after 1533 the authority of the *jus canonicum* in England was dependent upon Parliamentary sanction, its principles continued in large measure to determine the practice of the English ecclesiastical courts. See Frederic W. Maitland, *Roman Canon Law in the Church of England* (London, 1898).

[11] Both Tertullian (*ca.* 160–*ca.* 230) and St. Jerome (*ca.* 340–420) reveal strong ascetic leanings. Although their references to marriage are not uniformly disparaging, their emphasis is clearly upon the higher calling of virginity. Among the more severe utterances of Tertullian is the following from his *Exhortation to Chastity*, chapter IX, tr. S. Thelwall, in *The Ante-Nicene Fathers*, ed. Alexander Roberts and James Donaldson (10 vols., Grand Rapids, Michigan: William B. Eerdmans Company, 1951), IV, 55 (hereafter cited as *Fathers A.N.*):

thought so Sacramentall, that no adultery ♦ or desertion ◀ could dissolve it; [12] ♦ and this is the sense of our Canon Courts in *England* to this day, but in no other reformed Church els; [13] ◀ yet there remains ♦ in them also ◀ a burden on it as heavy as the other two were disgracefull or superstitious, and of as much iniquitie, crossing a Law not onely writt'n by *Moses*,[14] but character'd in us by nature, of more antiquitie and deeper ground then mariage it selfe; which Law is to force nothing against the faultles proprieties of nature: [15] yet that this may be colourably done, our Saviours words touching divorce, are as it

"The Lord Himself said, 'Whoever has seen a woman with a view to concupiscence has already violated her in his heart.' But has he who has seen her with a view to marriage done so less or more? . . . It is laws which seem to make the difference between marriage and fornication; through diversity of illicitness, not through the nature of the thing itself. Besides, what is the thing which takes place in all men and women to produce marriage and fornication? Commixture of the flesh, of course; the concupiscence whereof the Lord put on the same footing with fornication. . . . Accordingly, the best thing for a man is not to touch a woman; and, accordingly, the virgin's is the principal sanctity, because it is free from affinity with fornication." Jerome similarly exalts virginity in his treatise *Against Jovinian*.

[12] The sacramental doctrine of marriage, after a long history of development, was explicitly affirmed by the Council of Florence in 1439 and reaffirmed by the Council of Trent. According to this doctrine a consummated marriage validly contracted (*i.e.*, free from all the recognized impediments) is indissoluble. See *Catholic Encyclopedia*.

[13] The Protestant reformers, from Luther on, denied that marriage is a sacrament and generally favored the granting of divorce for adultery, with permission for the innocent party to remarry. The Ordinances of Wittenberg (1553) and of Geneva (1561) recognized as valid grounds for divorce both adultery and desertion. In England a proposed *Reformatio Legum Ecclesiasticarum* in 1552 (see edition of 1571; UTSL) reflected a similarly liberal point of view; and, although this code was never adopted, its principles apparently received considerable acceptance throughout the Elizabethan period. From the beginning of the seventeenth century, however, there was a contrary trend. The *Constitutions and Canons Ecclesiasticall* (1604; UTSL) enjoined closer adherence to pre-Reformation practice, declaring that separations should be granted only with the utmost caution and only upon bond that neither of the parties should remarry during the other's lifetime. The courts having jurisdiction were those (¶ 106, sig. R2) "of the Archbishop within his Province, or of the Bishop within his Diocese, or of the Deane of the Arches, the Judge of the Audience of Canterbury, or of the Vicars general, or other principall Officials." See George E. Howard, *A History of Matrimonial Institutions* (3 vols., Chicago, 1904), II, 60–85, and introduction, above, pp. 145–46.

[14] Deuteronomy 24:1.

[15] That is, the peculiarities of disposition or temperament for which one is not responsible, "that groundwork of nature which God created in him" (*An Apology, Complete Prose*, I, 900).

were congeal'd into a stony rigor, inconsistent both with his doctrine and his office, and that which he preacht onely to the conscience, is by canonicall tyranny snatcht into the compulsive censure of a judiciall Court; where Laws are impos'd even against the venerable & secret power of natures impression, to love what ever cause be found to loath. Which is a hainous barbarisme both against the honour of mariage, the dignitie of man and his soule, the goodnes of Christianitie, and all the humane respects of civilitie. Notwithstanding that some the wisest and gravest among the Christian Emperours, who had about them, to consult with, those of the fathers then living, who for their learning & holines of life are still with us in great renown, have made their statutes & edicts concerning this debate, far more easie and relenting in many necessary cases, wherein the Canon is inflexible.[16] And *Hugo Grotius,* a man of these times, one of the best learned, seems not obscurely to adhere in his perswasion to the equitie of those imperiall decrees, in his notes upon the *Evangelists,*[17] much allaying the outward roughnesse of the Text, which hath for the most part been too immoderately expounded; and excites the diligence of others to enquire further into this question, as contai- ◗ [3] ◖ ning many points <which> ◗ that ◖ have not yet been explain'd. <By which, and by mine owne apprehension of what publick duty each man owes, I conceive my selfe exhorted among the rest > ◗ Which ever likely to re-

---

[16] None of the emperors from Constantine (306–337) to Justinian (527–565) seems to have questioned the validity of earlier Roman practice, which permitted divorce by common consent, without cause being assigned, as well as repudiation in cases of misconduct. Throughout the period of the Empire, marriage was officially regarded as a private and secular matter. Most of the legislation had to do with the grounds of repudiation and the nature of the penalties to be imposed upon the guilty party. Divorce by common consent was not abolished until the time of Leo the Philosopher (886–912). See James Bryce, *Studies in History and Jurisprudence* (2 vols., New York, 1901), II, 799–805.

[17] *Annotationes in Libros Evangeliorum* (Amsterdam, 1641; UTSL). See below, pp. 329 and 335. *Cf.* Milton's statement in *Judgement of Martin Bucer* (below, p. 433): "When I had almost finisht the first edition of *The Doctrine and Discipline* I chanc't to read in the notes of *Hugo Grotius* upon the 5. of Matth. whom I strait understood inclining to reasonable terms in this controversie: and something he whisper'd rather then disputed about the law of charity, and the true end of wedlock. Glad therfore of such an able assistant, how ever at much distance, I resolv'd at length to put off into this wild and calumnious world." Hugo Grotius (1585–1645), Dutch jurist, theologian, poet, and statesman, is now remembered principally for his treatise on international law, *De Jure Belli et Pacis* (1625). During the seventeenth century his Biblical commentaries were highly regarded.

main intricate and hopelesse upon the suppositions commonly stuck
to, the autority of *Paulus Fagius,* one so learned and so eminent in
England once, if it might perswade, would strait acquaint us with a
solution of these differences, no lesse prudent then compendious. He in
his comment on the *Pentateuch* [18] doubted not to maintain that divorces might be as lawfully permitted by the Magistrate to Christians,
as they were to the Jewes. But because he is but briefe, and these
things of great consequence not to be kept obscure, I shall conceave it
nothing above my duty either for the difficulty or the censure that
may passe thereon, ◀ to communicate such thoughts as I ▶ also ◀ have
▶ had ◀, and ▶ do ◀ offer them now in this generall labour of reformation, to the candid view both of Church and Magistrate; especially
because I see it the hope of good men, that those irregular and unspirituall Courts have spun their utmost date in this Land; and some
better course must now be constituted.[19] ▶ This therefore shall be the
task and period [20] of this discourse to prove, first that other reasons
of divorce besides adultery, were by the Law of *Moses,* and are yet to
be allow'd by the Christian Magistrate as a peece of justice, and that
the words of Christ are not hereby contraried. Next, that to prohibit
absolutely any divorce whatsoever except those which *Moses* excepted, is against the reason of Law, as in due place I shall shew out
of *Fagius* with many additions. ◀ He therefore <that> ▶ who ◀
by adventuring shall be so happy as with successe <to ease & set
free the minds of ingenuous and apprehensive men from this needlesse [3] thraldome, he that can prove it lawfull and just to claime
the performance of a fit and matchable conversation, no lesse es-
sentiall to the prime scope of marriage then the gift of bodily con-

[18] *Thargum, Hoc Est, Paraphrasis Onkeli Chaldaica in Sacra Biblia . . .
Additis in Singula Fere Capita Succinctis Annotationibus, autore Paulo Fagio*
(Strassburg, 1546; NYPL). See below, pp. 243 and 344. Paul Fagius (1504–
1549) was a German Protestant divine, an intimate friend of Bucer, and a
Hebraist of high repute. In 1549 he went to England at the invitation of Arch-
bishop Cranmer and was appointed reader in Hebrew at Cambridge. He died
there shortly after his arrival. *Cf. Judgement of Martin Bucer,* below, p. 428.
[19] Termination of the existing ecclesiastical or spiritual courts (*cf.* above, n.
13) was implied by the actions of Parliament which led to the calling of the
Westminster Assembly. Six months after the Assembly had convened, Milton
was apparently less hopeful than at first as to what the "better course" was likely
to be. At least he felt the need for reinforcing his thoughts with a more formally
documented argument.
[20] End or goal. *NED* cites this example.

junction, or els to have an equall plea of divorce as well as for that corporall deficiency; [21] he that can but lend us the clue that windes out this labyrinth of servitude to such a reasonable and expedient liberty as this, deserves> ♦ to light the way of such an expedient liberty and truth as this, shall restore the much wrong'd and over-sorrow'd state of matrimony, not onely to those mercifull and life-giving remedies of *Moses,* but, as much as may be, to that serene and blisfull condition it was in at the beginning; and shall deserv of all aprehensive men (considering the troubles and distempers which for want of this insight have bin so oft in King-domes, in States, and Families) shall deserve ♦ to be reck'n'd among the publick benefactors of civill and humane life; above the inventors of wine and oyle; for this is a far dearer, far nobler, and more desirable cherishing to mans life, unworthily expos'd to sadnes and mistake, which he shall vindicate. Not that licence and levity and unconsented breach of faith should herein be countenanc't, but that some conscionable, and tender pitty might be had of those who have unwarily in a thing they never practiz'd before, made themselves the bondmen of a luckles and helples matrimony. In which Argument he whose courage can serve him to give the first onset, must look ♦ [4] ♦ for two severall oppositions: [22] the one from those who having sworn themselves to long custom and the letter of the Text, will not out of the road: the other from those whose grosse and vulgar apprehensions conceit but low of matrimoniall purposes, and in the work of male and female think they have all. Neverthelesse, it shall be here sought by due wayes to be made appeare, that those words of God in the institution, promising a meet help against lonelines; [23] and those words of Christ, *That his yoke is easie and his burden light,*[24] were not spoken in vaine; for if the knot of marriage may in no case be dissolv'd but for adultery, all the burd'ns and services of the Law [25] are not so intolerable. This onely is desir'd of them who are minded to judge

[21] A marriage contract unconsummated because of the physical incapacity of either party could be nullified on the ground that the matter of the contract was lacking.

[22] In the first of his anti-prelatical tracts Milton had classified "the hinderers of Reformation" as belonging to three groups: "Antiquitarians," "Libertines," and "Polititians." See *Complete Prose,* I, 541.

[23] *Cf.* Genesis 2:18.   [24] Matthew 11:30.

[25] Specifically the ceremonial law of the Old Testament, from the observance of which it was agreed that the Gospel had brought release.

hardly of thus maintaining, that they would be still and heare all out,[26] nor think it equall to answer deliberate reason with sudden heat and noise; remembring this, that many truths now of reverend esteem and credit, had their birth and beginning once from singular and private thoughts; while the most of men were otherwise possest; and had the fate at first to be generally exploded and exclaim'd on by many violent opposers; yet I may erre perhaps in soothing my selfe that this present truth reviv'd, will deserve <to be not ungently receiv'd on all hands; > ◗ on all hands to be not sinisterly receiv'd, ◖ in that it undertakes the cure of an inveterate disease crept into the best part of humane societie: [27] and to doe this with no smarting corrosive, but with a smooth and pleasing lesson, which receiv'd hath the vertue to soften and dispell rooted and knotty sor- [4] rowes; and without enchantment ◗ if that be fear'd, ◖ or spel us'd [28] hath regard at once both to serious pitty, and upright honesty; that tends to the redeeming and restoring of none but such as are the object of compassion; having in an ill houre hamper'd themselves to the utter dispatch of all their most beloved comforts & repose for this lives term. But if wee shall obstinately dislike this new overture of unexpected ease and recovery, what remains but to deplore the frowardnes of our hopeles condition, which neither can endure the estate we are in, nor admit of remedy either sharp or sweet. Sharp we our selves distast; and sweet, under whose hands we are, is scrupl'd and suspected as too lushious. In such a posture Christ found the *Jews*, who were neither won with the austerity of *John the Baptist*, and thought it too much licence to follow freely the charming pipe of him who sounded and proclaim'd liberty and reliefe to all distresses: yet Truth in some age or other will find her witnes, and shall be justify'd at last by her own children.[29] ◗ [5] ◖

[26] *Cf.* the injunction from Proverbs 18:13 placed on the title page of the revised edition.

[27] *Cf.* above, p. 223, n. 7.

[28] Possibly a play is intended on the words "dispell" and "spel." The imagery of the entire passage is subtly compounded.

[29] See Matthew 11:16–19 and Luke 7:31–35. *Cf.* Luke 4:18.

The Position. Prov'd by the Law of Moses. That Law expounded and asserted to a morall and charitable use, first by Paulus Fagius; *next with other additions.* ♦

To remove therefore if it be possible, this great and sad oppression which through the strictnes of a literall interpreting hath invaded and disturb'd the dearest and most peaceable estate of houshold society, to the over-burdning, if not the overwhelming of many Christians better worth then to be so deserted of the Churches considerate care, this position shall be laid down; first proving, then answering what may be objected either from Scripture or light of reason.[1]

That indisposition, unfitnes, or contrariety of mind, arising from a cause in nature unchangable, hindring and ever likely to hinder the main benefits of conjugall society, which are solace and peace, is a greater reason of divorce then naturall frigidity, especially if there be no children, and that there be mutuall consent.[2]

♦ This I gather from the Law in Deut. 24. 1. *When a man hath tak'n a wife and married her, and it come to passe that she find no favour in his eyes, because he hath found some uncleanesse in her, let him write her a bill of divorcement, and give it in her hand, and send her out of his house, &c.* This Law, if the words of Christ may be admitted into our beleef, shall never while the world stands, for him

---

[1] Reference to these as parallel sources of authority is a commonplace in the controversial writing of the time. *Cf.*, for example, *Scripture and Reason Pleaded for Defensive Arms* (1643; UTSL). Actually, it would seem, Milton's problem was to show that scripture, rightly interpreted, is not opposed to a position taken on rational grounds. In the revised edition he attempted to strengthen his constructive case by giving more attention at the outset to scriptural evidence.

[2] *An Answer to a Book, Intituled, The Doctrine and Discipline of Divorce* (1644; HEHL), p. 10, distinguished here four controvertible propositions: "1. That there is in some men and women a disposition, unfitnesse, or contrariety of minde, arising from a cause unchangeable in nature. 2. That such a contrariety of disposition hinders the main benefit of mariage or conjugall society. 3. That solace and peace are the main and chiefe ends of mariage or conjugall society. 4. That such a contrariety of minde or disposition is a greater cause of divorce then naturall frigidity." For Milton's comment on the analysis see *Colasterion,* below, pp. 736–37.

be abrogated.[3] First therfore I here set down what learned *Fagius* hath observ'd on this Law; *The Law of God,* saith he, *permitted divorce for the help of human weaknes. For every one that of necessity separats, cannot live single. That Christ deny'd divorce to his own, hinders not; for what is that to the unregenerate, who hath not attain'd such perfection? Let not the remedy be despis'd which was giv'n to weaknes. And when Christ saith, who marries the divorc't, commits adultery, it is to be understood if he had any plot in the divorce.*[4] The rest I reserve untill it be disputed, how the Magistrate is to doe herein.[5] From hence we may plainly discern a twofold consideration in this Law. First the end of the Lawgiver, and the proper act of the Law to command or to allow somthing just and honest, or indifferent. Secondly, his sufferance from some accidental result of evill by this allowance, which the Law cannot remedy. For if this Law have no other end or act but onely the allowance of a sin, though never to so good intention, that Law is no Law but sin muffl'd in the robe of Law, or Law disguis'd in the loose garment of sin. Both which are ▶ [6] ◀ too foule *Hypotheses* to save the *Phaenomenon* of our Saviours answer to the Pharises about this matter.[6] And I trust anon by the help of an infallible guide to perfet such *Prutenick* tables as shall mend the *Astronomy* of our wide expositors.[7]

[3] *Cf.* Matthew 5:18.

[4] See *Thargum, Hoc Est, Paraphrasis Onkeli Chaldaica in Sacra Biblia* (Strassburg, 1546), sig. Q4. The sentences excerpted by Milton read in the original as follows: "Lex dei in subsidium humanae imbecillitatis divortium permisit. Non enim cuivis datum est celebem agere vitam, Christo attestante. Quod Christus libellum repudii antiquaverit, & negaverit suis, nihil obstat. . . . Quid hoc ad vulgum? qui ad illud perfectionis nondum est eluctatus. . . . Igitur inferioribus proposita medicina non aspernetur. . . . Et quando Christus subiicit in sua responsione, Qui repudiatam duxerit, adulterium committit, id intelligendum est de eo, qui in fraudem prioris matrimonii repudiatam duxerit."

[5] See below, p. 344.

[6] See Matthew 19:3-9. For the phrase "to save the *Phaenomenon*" cf. Bacon, *Essays* (1625), "Of Superstition" *(Works of Francis Bacon,* ed. James Spedding, Robert L. Ellis, and Douglas D. Heath [14 vols., Boston, 1857-74], XII, 136): "It was gravely said by some of the prelates in the council of Trent . . . *that the schoolmen were like astronomers, which did feign eccentrics and epicycles, and such engines of orbs, to save the phenomena; though they knew there were no such things;* and in like manner, that the schoolmen had framed a number of subtle and intricate axioms and theorems, to save the practice of the church."

[7] The Copernican planetary tables of Erasmus Reinhold, which appeared in 1551, were called *Tabulae Prutenicae* in honor of Reinhold's patron, Duke

The cause of divorce mention'd in the Law is translated *some uncleannesse;* but in the Hebrew it sounds *nakednes of ought, or any reall nakednes:* which by all the learned interpreters is refer'd to the mind, as well as to the body.[8] And what greater nakednes or unfitnes of mind then that which hinders ever the solace and peacefull society of the maried couple, and what hinders that more then the unfitnes and defectivenes of an unconjugal mind. The cause therfore of divorce expres't in the position cannot but agree with that describ'd in the best and equalest sense of *Moses* Law. Which being a matter of pure charity, is plainly moral, and more now in force then ever:[9] therfore surely lawfull. For if under the Law such was Gods gracious indulgence, as not to suffer the ordinance of his goodnes and favour, through any error to be ser'd and stigmatiz'd upon his servants to their misery and thraldome, much lesse will he suffer it now under the covenant of grace, by abrogating his former grant of remedy and releef. But the first institution will be objected to have ordain'd mariage inseparable.[10] To that a little patience untill this first part have amply discours't the grave and pious reasons of this divorsive

Albrecht of Prussia. Although more accurate than any of the earlier calculations, they were superseded in 1627 by the *Rudolphine Tables* of Kepler. Theodore H. Banks, in *Milton's Imagery* (New York: Columbia University Press, 1950), pp. 172–73, remarks on the apparent lag in Milton's astronomical information.

[8] *Cf. Tetrachordon,* below, p. 620. Harris Fletcher, in *Milton's Semitic Studies* (Chicago, 1926), p. 68, points out that the expression "occurs several times in the Old Testament with sufficient flexibility of meaning to permit of the interpretation which Milton gives it; in Deuteronomy 23:14 the expression means 'a foul or hateful thing,' while in Isaiah 20:4 and I Samuel 20:30 it more nearly conveys the meaning of 'disgrace' or 'ignominy.' "

[9] *Cf.* William Perkins, *A Discourse of Conscience* (1596) in *Works* (1609–13), I, 519: "Morall law concerns duties of love, partly to God and partly toward our neighbor: . . . and therefore it bindes the consciences of all men at all times. . . ." Perkins, however, in *A Godly and Learned Exposition of Christs Sermon in the Mount* (1608), maintains that the law set forth in Deuteronomy 24:1 (*Works,* 1609–13, III, 68) "was not morall, but civill, or politicke, for the good ordering of the Commonwealth."

[10] Such, in fact, was the objection of Perkins (*Works,* 1609–13, III, 69): "Whereas our Saviour Christ opposeth unto this politicke law of *Moses,* concerning divorce, the law of nature, touching mariage, Gen. 2.24. he giveth us an excellent distinction betweene all politicke lawes, and the law of nature, which is the morall law; for that is a law of eternall equitie, commaunding good, and forbidding evill simply, without respect of man: but politicke lawes are tempered according to the conditions of men, & though they doe not approove, yet sometimes they permit evill, for the avoyding of greater mischiefe: yea, they tolerate that, which before God, and in conscience is condemned."

Law; and then I doubt not but with one gentle stroking to wipe away
ten thousand teares out of the life of man. Yet thus much I shall now
insist on, that what ever the institution were, it could not be so enormous,[11] nor so rebellious against both nature and reason as to exalt
it selfe above the end and person for whom it was instituted.

CHAP. II.

*The first reason of this Law grounded on the prime reason of matrimony.
That no cov'nant whatsoever obliges against the main end both of it self,
and of the parties cov'nanting.* ◀

FOR all sense <and reason> and equity reclaimes [1] that any
Law or Cov'nant how solemn or strait soever, either between
God and man, or man and man, though of Gods joyning, should
bind against a prime and principall scope of its own institution, and
of both or either party ▶ [7] ◀ cov'nanting: [2] neither can it be of force
to ingage a blameles creature to his own perpetuall sorrow, mistak'n
for his expected solace, without suffering charity to step in and doe
a confest good work of parting those whom nothing holds together,
but this of Gods joyning, falsly suppos'd against the expresse end of
his own ordinance. And what his chiefe end was of creating woman to
be [5] joynd with man, his own instituting words declare, and are
infallible to informe us what is mariage, and what is no mariage; unlesse we can think them set there to no purpose: *It is not good*, saith

[11] Unusual, extraordinary.
[1] Cries out in protest, denies.
[2] *Cf.* above, p. 229, n. 34. See also Arthur Barker, *Milton and the Puritan
Dilemma* (Toronto: University of Toronto Press, 1942), pp. 107–12. Milton's
principle is so stated as to make of small consequence the traditional distinction
between civil covenants and those "more than civil." *Cf.* Perkins, *Commentarie
upon the Epistle to the Galatians* (1604), in *Works* (1609–13), II, 242: "Of
covenants some are single, that is, bare promises, not confirmed by oath; and
some againe are with oath. Againe, some covenants are meere civill, being made
of man to man; and some are more then civill, being made of man to God, as
contracts of marriage. Now if covenants bee single covenants, and meerely
civill, then may they bee changed by the makers, or by their successours, if hurts
and losses arise. Yet if covenants bee confirmed by oath, and if they bee made
to God, they may not bee changed, so long as they are lawfull, though great
losses ensue."

he, *that man should be alone; I will make him a help meet for him.*[3] From which words so plain, lesse cannot be concluded, nor is by any learned Interpreter, then that in Gods intention a meet and happy conversation is the chiefest and the noblest end of mariage; for we find here no expression so necessarily implying carnall knowledg, as this prevention of lonelinesse to the mind and spirit of man.♦ To this *Fagius, Calvin, Pareus, Rivetus,* as willingly and largely assent as can be wisht.[4]♦And indeed it is a greater blessing from God, more worthy so excellent a creature as man is, and a higher end to honour and sanctifie the league of mariage, whenas the solace and satisfaction of the minde is regarded and provided for before the sensitive pleasing of the body. And with all generous persons maried thus it is, that where the minde and person pleases aptly, there some unaccomplishment of the bodies delight may be better born with, then when the minde hangs off in an unclosing disproportion, though the body be as it ought; for there all corporall delight will soon become unsavoury and contemptible. And the solitarines of man, which God had namely and principally orderd to prevent by mariage, hath no remedy, but lies under a worse condition then the loneliest single life; for in single life

[3] Genesis 2:18. The King James Version reads "It is not good that *the* man should be alone."

[4] The combined authority of these four names was substantial. For Fagius see above, p. 239, n. 18. Calvin's Biblical commentaries were of course highly regarded. David Paraeus (1548–1622), who taught at Heidelberg from 1584 until his death, was a respected Calvinist theologian and exegete, as was Andrew Rivetus or Rivet (1572–1651). Rivetus, a teacher at Leyden and Breda, had been a leader of the orthodox party at the Synod of Dort. The statements to which Milton refers are presumably the following. (Translations, unless otherwise indicated, are my own.)

"The wife is joined to the husband, to be his partner, not only for procreation but for all the benefits and necessities of life." Fagius, tr. from *Thargum, Hoc Est, Paraphrasis Onkeli Chaldaica in Sacra Biblia* (Strassburg, 1546), sig. a4.

"Howbeit it may be doubted, whether this sentence [Genesis 2:18] ought to be extended to generation. For the wordes simply have this signification. Because it is not good for the man to be alone, we must create for him a wife, that she may be an helpe unto him." Calvin, *A Commentarie upon the First Booke of Moses Called Genesis,* tr. Thomas Tymme (1578; HEHL), p. 72.

"That woman should aid man in the generation of offspring is not the only and principal reason why she is called a helper, for indeed her aid is extended to the intimate companionship of all life." Paraeus, tr. from *In Genesin Mosis Commentarius* (Frankfurt, 1609; NYPL), col. 414.

"This pertains not only to procreation but to all the intercourse of life, and to the uniting of habits, minds, and affections." Rivetus, tr. from *Theologicae & Scholasticae Exercitationes CXC in Genesin* (Leyden, 1633; CUL), p. 120.

the absence and remotenes of a helper might inure him to expect his own comforts out of himselfe, or to seek with hope; but here the continuall sight of his deluded thoughts without cure, must needs be to him, if especially his complexion [5] incline him to melancholy, a daily trouble and paine of losse in some degree like that which Reprobates feel.[6] Lest therefore so noble a creature as man should be shut up incurably under a worse evill by an easie mistake in that ordinance which God gave him to remedy a lesse evill, reaping to himselfe sorrow while he went to rid away solitarines, it cannot avoyd to be concluded, that if the woman be naturally so of disposition, as will not help to remove, but help to encrease that same God-forbidd'n lonelines which will in time draw on with it a ge- ♦ [8] ◀ nerall discomfort and dejection of minde, not beseeming either Christian profession or morall conversation, unprofitable and dangerous to the Common-wealth, when the houshold estate, out of which must flourish forth the vigor and spirit of all publick enterprizes,[7] is so ill contented and procur'd at home, and cannot be supported; such a mariage can be no mariage whereto [6] the most honest end is wanting: and the agrieved person shall doe more manly, to be extraordinary and singular in claiming the due right whereof he is frustrated, then to piece up his lost contentment by visiting the Stews, or stepping to his neighbours bed, which is the common shift in this mis-fortune, or els by suffering his usefull life to wast away and be lost under a secret affliction of an unconscionable size to humane strength. ♦ Against all which evills the mercy of this Mosaick Law was graciously exhibited.

[5] "The combination of the four 'humours' of the body in a certain proportion." *NED*.

[6] *Cf. Christian Doctrine*, I, xxxiii (tr. Sumner, Bohn, IV, 488): "The second death, or the punishment of the damned, seems to consist partly in the loss of the chief good, namely, the favor and protection of God, and the beatific vision of his presence, which is commonly called the punishment of loss."

[7] Perkins, in *Christian Oeconomie* (*Works*, 1609–13, III, 671), states as his final reason for the excellence of marriage the fact that it "was made & appointed by God himselfe, to be the fountaine and seminarie of al other sorts and kinds of life, in the Common-wealth and in the Church."

CHAP. III.

The ignorance & iniquity of Canon law, providing all for the right of the body in mariage, but nothing for the wrongs and greevances of the mind. An objection, that the mind should be better lookt to before contract, answered. ◀

How vain therefore is it, and how preposterous in the Canon Law to have made such carefull provision against the impediment of carnall performance,[1] and to have had no care about the unconversing inability of minde, so defective to the purest and most sacred end of matrimony: and that the vessell of voluptuous enjoyment must be made good to him that has tak'n it upon trust without any caution, when as the minde from whence must flow the acts of peace and love, a far more precious mixture then the quintessence of an excrement,[2] though it be found never so deficient and unable to performe the best duty of mariage in a cheerfull and agreeable conversation, shall be thought good anough, how ever flat & melancholious it be, and must serve though to the eternall disturbance and languishing of him that complains him. Yet wisdom and charity waighing Gods own institution, would think that the pining of a sad spirit wedded to lonelines should deserve to be free'd, aswell as the impatience of a sensuall desire so providently reliev'd. Tis read to us in the Liturgy, that *wee must not marry to satisfie the fleshly appetite, like brute beasts that have no understanding:* [3] but ◗ [9] ◀ the Canon

---

[1] The Gregorian Decretals (Book IV, Title xv) specify sexual incapacity as a cause for annulment, provided that it is antecedent to marriage and is judged after three years to be permanent. See *Corpus Juris Canonici* (2 vols., Leipzig, 1881), II, 720–25.

[2] Human "seed," which was thought to be contained in the menstrual as well as the seminal fluid, is described in Peter de La Primaudaye's *French Academie* (1618; HEHL), p. 540, as "a profitable superfluitie taken from the nourishment of the bloode scattered throughout the whole bodie." The theory of reproductive residues, the *pneuma* or active principle of which was analogous to the heavenly fifth essence, derived from Aristotle's *On the Generation of Animals.*

[3] Cf. *Book of Common Prayer* (1552; HEHL), "Form of Solemnization of Matrimony." The exhortation at the beginning of the service declares that marriage "is not to bee enterprised, nor taken in hande unadvisedly, lightely, or wantonly, to satisfie mennes carnall lustes and appetites, lyke brute beastes that have no understandynge: but reverently, discretely, advisedly, soberly, and in the feare of God."

248

so runs, as if it dreamt of no other matter then such an appetite to be satisfy'd; for if it happen that nature hath stopt or extinguisht the veins of sensuality, that mariage is annull'd. But though all the faculties of the understanding and conversing part after triall appeare to be so ill and so aversly met through natures unalterable working, as that neither peace, nor any sociable contentment can follow, tis as nothing, the contract shall stand as firme as ever, betide what will. What is this but secretly to instruct us, that however many grave reasons are pretended to the maried life, yet that nothing indeed is thought worth regard therein, but the prescrib'd satisfaction of an irrationall heat; which cannot be but ignominious to the state of mariage, dishonourable to the undervalu'd soule of man, and even to Christian doctrine it self. While it seems more mov'd at the disappointing of an impetuous nerve, then at the ingenuous grievance of a minde unreasonably [7] yoakt; and to place more of mariage in the channell of concupiscence, then in the pure influence of peace and love, whereof the souls lawfull contentment is the onely fountain.

But some are ready to object, that the disposition ought seriously to be consider'd before. But let them know again, that for all the warinesse can be us'd, it may yet befall a discreet man to be mistak'n in his choice: ◖ and we have plenty of examples.[4] ◗ the soberest and best govern'd men are lest practiz'd in these affairs; and who knows not that the bashfull mutenes of a virgin may oft-times hide all the unlivelines & naturall sloth which is really unfit for conversation; nor is there that freedom of accesse granted or presum'd, as may suffice to a perfect discerning till too late: and where any indisposition is suspected, what more usuall then the perswasion of friends, that acquaintance, as it encreases, will amend all. And lastly, it is not strange though many who have spent their youth chastly, are in some things not so quick-sighted, while they hast too eagerly to light the nuptiall torch; [5] nor is it therfore that for a modest error a man should forfeit so great a happines, and no charitable means to release him. Since they who have liv'd most loosely by reason of their bold accustoming, prove most succesfull in their matches, because their wild affections unsetling at will, have been as so many divorces to teach them experi-

[4] The insertion of this clause in the revised edition suggests Milton's awareness that the argument might be taken as suspiciously subjective.

[5] The same figure occurs in *Paradise Lost*, XI, 590: "then all in heat / They light the Nuptial Torch."

ence. When as the sober man honouring the appearance of modestie, and hoping well of every sociall vertue under that veile, may easily chance to meet, if not with a body impenetrable, yet often with a minde to all other due conver- ◗ [10] ◖ sation inaccessible, and to all the more estimable and superior purposes of matrimony uselesse and almost liveles: and what a solace, what a fit help such a consort would be through the whole life of a man, is lesse paine to conjecture then to have experience.

◗ CHAP. IIII.

The Second Reason of this Law, because without it, mariage as it happ'ns oft is not a remedy of that which it promises, as any rationall creature would expect. That mariage, if we pattern from the beginning as our Saviour bids, was not properly the remedy of lust, but the fulfilling of conjugall love and helpfulnes. ◖

AND that we may further see what a violent and cruell thing it is to force the continuing of those together, whom God and nature in the gentlest end of mariage never joyn'd, divers evils and extremities that follow upon such a compulsion shall here be set in view. Of evils the first and greatest is that hereby a most absurd and rash imputation is fixt upon God and his holy Laws, of conniving and dispencing with open & common adultery among his chosen people; a thing which the rankest politician [1] would think it shame and dis-worship,[2] that his Laws should countenance; how and in what manner this comes to passe, I shall reserve, till the course of me- [8] thod brings on the unfolding of many Scriptures. Next the Law and Gospel are hereby made liable to more then one contradiction, which I referre also thither. Lastly, the supreme dictate of charitie is hereby many wayes neglected and violated. Which I shall forthwith address to prove. First we know St. *Paul* saith, *It is better to marry then to burne.*[3] Mariage therefore was giv'n as a remedy of that trouble: but

---

[1] *Cf. The Atheisticall Polititian or A Brief Discourse Concerning Ni. Machiavell* (1642; HEHL). The anonymous author observes (p. 7) that "a Common-wealth is like a naturall body, and when it is all together shewes a comely structure, but search into the entrals from whence the true nourishment proceedes, and you shall finde nothing but blood, filth, and stench."

[2] Dishonor, disgrace. *NED* cites this example.   [3] I Corinthians 7:9.

what might this burning mean? Certainly not the meer motion of carnall lust, not the meer goad of a sensitive desire; God does not principally take care for such cattell.[4] What is it then but that desire which God put into *Adam* in Paradise before he knew the sin of incontinence; that desire which God saw it was not good that man should be left alone to burn in; the desire and longing to put off an unkindly solitarines by uniting another body, but not without a fit soule to his in the cheerfull society of wedlock.[5] Which if it were so needfull before the fall, when man was much more perfect in himself, how much more is it needfull now ♦ [11] ◀ against all the sorrows and casualties of this life to have an intimate and speaking help, a ready and reviving associate in marriage: whereof who misses by chancing on a mute and spiritles mate, remains more alone then before, and in a burning lesse to be contain'd then that which is fleshly and more to be consider'd; as being more deeply rooted even in the faultles innocence of nature. As for that other burning, which is but as it were the venom of a lusty and over-abounding concoction, strict life and labour with the abatement of a full diet may keep that low and obedient anough:[6] but this pure and more inbred desire of joyning to it self in conjugall fellowship a fit conversing soul (which desire is properly call'd love) *is stronger then death*, as the Spouse of Christ thought, *many waters cannot quench it, neither can the flouds drown it*.[7] This is that rationall burning that mariage is to remedy, not to be allay'd with fasting, nor with any penance to be subdu'd, which how can he asswage who by mis-hap hath met the unmeetest[8] and most

---

[4] *NED*, citing this passage, defines "cattell" as "rubbish, trash." *Cf.*, however, I Corinthians 9:9 ("Doth God take care for oxen?"), which Milton quotes below, p. 270. *Cf.* also *Paradise Lost*, VIII, 578–85.

[5] For this exegesis Milton could find slight support among either patristic or later commentators. Poole's *Synopsis Criticorum* (5 vols., Frankfurt-am-Main, 1712), V, col. 386, gives only two glosses of "burn": *de igne gehennae* and the much more generally accepted *de libidinis incendio*. Calvin's interpretation is typical: "What Paul here means by the expression 'to burn' is to be inflamed with lust *(libidine aestuare)* so that you cannot resist." See his *In Epistolam Priorem ad Corinthios* (*Opera* [9 vols., Geneva, 1563–1617; UTSL], VIII, 323).

[6] *Cf.* Burton's *Anatomy of Melancholy*, Part 3, Sec. 2, Mem. 5, Subs. 1: "The first rule to be observed in this stubborn and unbridled passion, is exercise and diet. It is an old and well-known sentence, *Sine Cerere et Baccho friget Venus.*" For Milton's account of his own regimen, *cf. An Apology, Complete Prose*, I, 885–86.

[7] *Cf.* Song of Solomon 8:6–7. In their biblical setting the quoted phrases are thought of as applying to the love of Christ and the Church.

[8] Copies of 1644 with sig. C uncorrected read "most unmeetest and unsutable."

unsutable mind? Who hath the power to struggle with an intelligible flame, not in Paradise to be resisted, become now more ardent, by being fail'd of what in reason it lookt for; and even then most unquencht, when the importunity of a provender [9] burning is well anough appeas'd; and yet the soul hath obtain'd nothing of what it justly desires. Certainly such a one forbidd'n to divorce, is in effect forbidd'n to marry, and compell'd to greater difficulties then in a single life; for if there be not a more [9] human burning which mariage must satisfy, or els may be dissolv'd, then that of copulation, mariage cannot be honorable for the meer reducing and terminating of lust between two; seeing many beasts in voluntary and chosen couples live together as unadulterously, and are as truly maried in that respect. But all ingenuous men will see that the dignity & blessing of mariage is plac't rather in the mutual enjoyment of that which the wanting soul needfully seeks, then of that which the plenteous body would jollily [10] give away. Hence it is that *Plato* in his festivall discours brings in *Socrates* relating what he fain'd to have learnt from the Prophetesse *Diotima,* how *Love* was the Sonne of *Penury,* begot of *Plenty* in the garden of *Jupiter.*[11] Which divinely sorts with that which in effect *Moses* tells us; that *Love* was the Son of *Lonelines,* begot in Paradise by that sociable & helpfull aptitude which God implanted between man and woman toward each other.[12] The same also is that burning mention'd by St. *Paul,* whereof marriage ought to be the remedy; the flesh hath other naturall [13] and easie curbes which are in the power of any tempe- ▶ [12] ◀

[9] This adjectival use is noted in *NED* as "perhaps an error of some kind." *Provendered* is a possible emendation. *Cf.* "over provender'd *Episcopants*" (*Of Prelatical Episcopacy, Complete Prose,* I, 650).

[10] Uncorrected copies of 1644 read "joyfully."

[11] *Cf. Symposium,* 203: "On the birthday of Aphrodite there was a feast of the gods, at which the god Poros or Plenty, who is the son of Metis or Discretion, was one of the guests. When the feast was over, Penia or Poverty, as the manner was, came about the doors to beg. Now Plenty, who was the worse for nectar (there was no wine in those days), came into the garden of Zeus and fell into a heavy sleep; and Poverty considering her own straitened circumstances, plotted to have him for a husband, and accordingly she lay down at his side and conceived Love. . . ." *Dialogues of Plato,* tr. Benjamin Jowett (4 vols., Oxford, 1871), I, 519.

[12] *Cf.* Genesis 2:18–24. Farfetched as the parallel may seem, it indicates a pattern of thought which was to enter into the treatment of love in *Paradise Lost,* notably in VIII, 415 ff. See Irene Samuel, *Plato and Milton* (Ithaca: Cornell University Press, 1947), pp. 162–65.

[13] Uncorrected copies of 1644 read "mutuall."

rate man. When therfore this originall and sinles *Penury* or *Lone-lines* of the soul cannot lay it self down by the side of such a meet & acceptable union as God ordain'd in mariage, at least in some propor-tion, it cannot conceive and bring forth *Love,* but remains utterly un-maried under a formall wedlock, and still burnes in the proper meaning of St. *Paul.* Then enters *Hate,* not that Hate that sins, but that which onely is naturall dissatisfaction and the turning aside from a mistaken object:[14] if that mistake have done injury, it fails not to dismisse with recompence, for to retain still, and not be able to love, is to heap ♦ up ◀ more injury. <Thence that wise and pious Law of dis-mission, *Deut.* 24. 1. took beginning; of which anon:> ♦ Thence this wise and pious Law of dismission now defended took beginning: ◀ He therfore who lacking of his due in the most native and humane end of mariage, thinks it better to part then to live sadly and injuriously to that cherfull covnant (for not to be belov'd & yet retain'd, is the greatest injury to a gentle spirit) he I say who therfore seeks to part, is one who highly honours the maried life, and would not stain it: and the reasons which now move him to divorce, are equall to the best of those that could first warrant him to marry; for, as was plainly shewn, both the hate which now diverts him and the lonelines which leads him still powerfully to seek a fit help, hath not the least grain of a sin in it, if he be worthy to understand himself.

♦ CHAP. V.

The Third Reason of this Law, because without it, he who hath happn'd
where he finds nothing but remediles offences and discontents, is in more
and greater temptations then ever before. ◀

THIRDLY, Yet it is next to be feard, if he must be still bound with- [10] out reason by a deafe rigor, that when he per-ceives the just expectance of his mind defeated, he will begin even against Law to cast about where he may find his satisfaction more compleat, unlesse he be a thing heroically vertuous, and that are not the common lump of men for whom chiefly the Laws ought

---

[14] The final elaboration of the myth is of course Milton's own. In his use of Hate to symbolize natural aversion he may have been influenced by the render-ing of Malachi 2:16 which he expounds below, p. 257.

to be made, though not to their sins, yet to their unsinning weaknesses, it being above their strength to endure the lonely estate, which while they shun'd, they are fal'n into. And yet there follows upon this a worse temptation; for if he be such as hath spent his youth unblamably, and layd up his chiefest earthly comforts in the enjoyment of a contented mariage, nor did neglect that furderance which was to be obtain'd herein by constant prayers, when he shall find himselfe bound fast to ▶ [13] ◀ an uncomplying discord of nature, or, as it oft happens, to an image of earth and fleam,[1] with whom he lookt to be the copartner of a sweet and gladsome society, and sees withall that his bondage is now inevitable, though he be almost the strongest Christian, he will be ready to dispair in vertue, and mutin [2] against divine providence: and this doubtles is the reason of those lapses and that melancholy despair which we see in many wedded persons, though they understand it not, or pretend other causes, because they know no remedy, and is of extreme danger; therefore when human frailty surcharg'd, is at such a losse, charity ought to venture much, and use bold physick, lest an over-tost faith endanger to shipwrack.[3]

▶ CHAP. VI.

The Fourth Reason of this Law, that God regards Love and Peace in the family, more then a compulsive performance of mariage, which is more broke by a grievous continuance, then by a needfull divorce. ◀

FOURTHLY, Mariage is a covnant the very beeing whereof consists, not in a forc't cohabitation, and counterfeit performance of duties, but in unfained love and peace. ▶ And of matrimoniall love no doubt but that was chiefly meant, which by the ancient Sages was thus parabl'd, That Love, if he be not twin-born, yet hath a brother wondrous like him, call'd *Anteros:* [1] whom while

---

[1] In the old physiology phlegm was the bodily humour tending to sluggishness and apathy. *Cf. Of Education,* below, p. 392, n. 108.

[2] "To think or say mutinously." *NED.*

[3] Milton's profusion of metaphors results here, as elsewhere, in a combination which is hard to justify. His meaning, however, is unmistakable.

[1] Ancient allusions to Anteros are numerous but often indefinite. The name, signifying love reciprocated, occurs in *Phaedrus,* 255d, without mythical elabora-

he seeks all about, his chance is to meet with many fals and faining
Desires that wander singly up and down in his likenes. By them in
their borrow'd garb, Love, though not wholly blind, as Poets wrong
him,[2] yet having but one eye, as being born an Archer aiming, and
that eye not the quickest in this dark region here below, which is not
Loves proper sphere, partly out of the simplicity, and credulity which
is native to him, often deceiv'd, imbraces and consorts him with these
obvious [3] and suborned [4] striplings, as if they were his Mothers own
Sons, for so he thinks them, while they suttly keep themselves most
on his blind side. But after a while, as his manner is, when soaring up
into the high Towr of his *Apogaeum*,[5] above the shadow of the earth,
he darts out the direct rayes of his then most piercing eyesight upon
the impostures, and trim disguises that were us'd with him, and discerns that this is not his genuin brother, as he imagin'd, he has no
longer the power to hold fellowship with such a personated mate. For
strait his arrows loose their golden heads, and shed their purple
feathers, his silk'n breades [6] untwine, and slip their knots and that
original and firie vertue giv'n him by Fate, all on a sudden goes out
and leaves him [14] undeifi'd, and despoil'd of all his force: [7] till
finding *Anteros* at last, he kindles and repairs the almost faded ammu-
nition of his Deity by the reflection of a coequal & *homogeneal* [8] fire.

tion. In the *Protreptikos* of the fourth century rhetorician Themistius, Anteros
is described as the younger brother of Eros, born to Aphrodite after she had
been told by Themis that Eros would waste away unless he could behold his
own likeness in the person of another. Outstanding among Renaissance treatments is Celio Calcagnini's *Anteros sive de Mutuo Amore* (1544). See Robert V.
Merrill, "Eros and Anteros," *Speculum*, XIX (1944), 265–84.

[2] The conception of Love as blind, although apparently post-classical, had
become established by the end of the fourteenth century. *Cf.* Chaucer, *Knightes
Tale*, l. 1107: "And blind he was, as it is ofte sene." E. K.'s gloss on the March
eclogue of Spenser's *Shepheardes Calender* says "he is described of the Poetes
to be . . . blindfolded because he maketh no difference of Personages."

[3] Frequently met.

[4] Counterfeit.

[5] A term of the Ptolemaic astronomy, denoting the point in the orbit of a
heavenly body at which it is farthest from the earth.

[6] The braids, that is, of his bowstring.

[7] *Cf.* the reverse of this situation in *Paradise Lost*, IV, 763–65:

> Here Love his golden shafts imploies, here lights
> His constant Lamp, and waves his purple wings,
> Reigns here and revels.

[8] Homogeneous. Like *Apogaeum*, the word is drawn from the vocabulary of
traditional science. *Cf. Areopagitica*, below, p. 551.

Thus mine author sung it to me; [9] and by the leave of those who would be counted the only grave ones, this is no meer amatorious novel [10] (though to be wise and skilful in these matters, men heretofore of greatest name in vertue, have esteemd it one of the highest arks that human contemplation circling upward, can make from the glassy Sea [11] wheron she stands)[12] but this is a deep and serious verity, shewing us that Love in mariage cannot live nor subsist, unlesse it be mutual; and where love cannot be, there can be left of wedlock nothing, but the empty husk of an outside matrimony; as undelightfull and unpleasing to God, as any other kind of hypocrisie. So farre is his command from tying men to the observance of duties, which there is no help for, but they must be dissembl'd. ◖ <Thence saith *Salomon* in *Ecclesiastes*,> ◗ If *Salomons* advice be not overfrolick,[13] ◖ *Live joyfully* ◗, saith he, ◖ *with the wife whom thou lovest, all thy dayes, for that is thy portion.* [14] How then, where we find it impossible to rejoyce or to love, can we obay this precept? how miserably doe we defraud our selves of that comfortable portion which God gives us, by striving vainly to glue an error together which God and nature will not joyne, adding but more vexation and violence to that blisfull society by our importunate superstition, that will not heark'n to St. *Paul*, 1 *Cor.* 7. who speaking of mariage and divorce, determines plain anough in generall that God therein *hath call'd us to peace* and not *to bondage*.[15] Yea God himself commands in his Law

[9] By his "author" Milton probably means his own poetic insight. *Cf.* his reference (above, p. 252) to the prophetess Diotima, from whom Socrates "feigned to have learned." St. John (Bohn, I, xvi) calls the passage "a grand dithyrambic digression."

[10] Although *NED* cites this use of "novel" as illustrating the common present meaning, the context points rather to the original sense of Italian *novella. Cf.* Dryden's mention of "the trifling novels which Ariosto, and others, have inserted in their poems." "Dedication of the Aeneis," in *Essays of John Dryden,* ed. W. P. Ker (2 vols., Oxford, 1926), II, 155.

[11] The original reading, "globy sea," is listed as an erratum. Milton evidently intended an allusion to the apocalyptic "sea of glass" (Revelation 4:6 and 15:2).

[12] *Cf.* in *Church-Government (Complete Prose,* I, 812 ff.) Milton's insistence upon the didactic values of imaginative writing. For the view which he there takes of the Apocalypse as "the majestick image of a high and stately Tragedy" he cites "the grave autority of *Pareus.*"

[13] The revision accords with the mock show of deference to "those who would be counted the only grave ones."

[14] Ecclesiastes 9:9.

[15] I Corinthians 7:15: "A brother or a sister is not under bondage in such cases: but God hath called us to peace."

more then once, and by his Prophet *Malachy,* as *Calvin* and the best translations read, that *he who hates let him divorce;* [16] that is, he who cannot love <, or delight.> ♦: hence is it that the Rabbins and *Maimonides* famous among the rest in a Book of his set forth by *Buxtorfius,* tells us that *Divorce was permitted by* Moses *to preserve peace in mariage, and quiet in the family.*[17] Surely the Jewes had their saving peace [18] about them, aswell as we, yet care was tak'n that this wholsom provision for houshold peace should also be allow'd them; and

[16] The reference is to Malachi 2:16, the text of which has suffered in transmission. Calvin (*Praelectiones in Duodecim Prophetas Minores* [Geneva, 1581], p. 753) translates: "*Si odio habeas,* quisquis odio habet, *dimittat,* uxorem, *dicit Iehovah Deus Israel.*" This is also the sense of the Vulgate, and its possible validity is recognized in the marginal reading of the King James translators. However, the preferred reading of the King James Version, in agreement with Tremellius-Junius ("Sibi odio esse dimissionem ait Jehovah Deus Jisraelis"), has a quite contrary import: "For the Lord, the God of Israel, saith that he hateth putting away." Hence the protest in the anonymous *Answer* (1644), p. 35: "And as for *Malachy,* although it be true, that some translations do reade it so, as *Jerome* and some Margents: yet why you should call these the best Interpreters of this Text, I know no reason, but because they agree with your opinion, which you dream to be the best." For Milton's further comment, see *Tetrachordon,* below, p. 615, and *Colasterion,* below, p. 749. See also Harris Fletcher, *The Use of the Bible in Milton's Prose* (Urbana: University of Illinois Press, 1929), pp. 33–36.

It should be noted that Calvin, despite his reading, did not find in the passage a warrant for divorce. See *Praelectiones,* pp. 753–54: "We know indeed that repudiation, properly speaking, had never been divinely sanctioned, for though there was impunity under the Law, there was nevertheless no permission. . . . But by way of comparison, Malachi says that it is a less grave offence to put away a wife than to take many wives." It should perhaps also be noted that the reading has not been sustained by recent textual scholarship. *Cf.* the Revised Standard Version (1952): "For I hate divorce, says the Lord the God of Israel."

[17] *Cf. Rabbi Mosis Maiemonidis Liber Doctor Perplexorum . . . Translatus . . . a Johanne Buxtorfius* (Basle, 1629; UIL), p. 499: "Quando quidem vero nonnunquam accidit, ut nequeant in pace & concordia una vivere, & familiam, sicuti oportet, administrare, idcirco permissum est Marito *Uxorem suam ejicere & repudiare.*" ("Since indeed it sometimes happens that they are unable to live together in peace and quiet, and to manage the family as is fitting, it is permitted the husband to reject and put away his wife.") Maimonides or Moses ben Maimon (1135–1204), born in Cordova, achieved great eminence as a Talmudist, philosopher, and physician. His *Guide to the Perplexed,* written originally in Arabic about 1190, brought together rabbinic Judaism and Aristotelian philosophy. The translator, Johann Buxtorf (1593–1664), was the second of a famous family of scholars who held the chair of Hebrew at the University of Basle.

[18] Peace in the religious sense is a recurrent concept in the Old Testament as well as the New. *Cf.,* for example, Numbers 6:26, Psalms 29:11, Isaiah 26:3.

must this be deny'd to Christians? O perversnes! that the Law should be made more provident of peacemaking then the Gospel! that the Gospel should be put to beg a most necessary help of mercy from the Law, but must not have it: and that to grind in the mill [19] of an undelighted and servil copulation, must be the only forc't work of a Christian mariage, oft times with such a yokefellow, from whom both love and peace, both nature and Religion mourns [20] to be separated.♦ I cannot therefore be so diffident, as not securely to conclude, ♦[15]♦ that he [11] who can receive nothing of the most important helps in mariage, beeing thereby disinabl'd to return that duty which is his, with a clear and hearty countnance; and thus continues to grieve whom he would not, and is no lesse griev'd, that man ought even for loves sake and peace to move divorce upon good and liberall conditions to the divorc't. And it is a lesse breach of wedlock to part with wise and quiet consent betimes, then still to soile and profane that mystery of joy and union [21] with a polluting sadnes and perpetuall distemper; for it is not the outward continuing of marriage that keeps whole that covnant, but whosoever does most according to peace and love, whether in mariage, or in divorce, he it is that breaks mariage lest; it being so often written, that *Love onely is the fulfilling of every Commandment.*[22]

[19] Perhaps a reminiscence of Judges 16:21. *Cf. Samson Agonistes,* 1. 41: "at the mill with slaves."

[20] Has a painful longing.

[21] See Ephesians 5:31–32. *Cf. Paradise Lost,* IV, 750: "Haile wedded Love, mysterious Law."

[22] *Cf.* Romans 13:10: "Love worketh no ill to his neighbour: therefore love is the fulfilling of the law." However, when taken to task by the author of *An Answer* (p. 37) for adding the word "only," Milton replied in *Colasterion* (below, p. 750): "Whereas hee taxes mee of adding to the Scripture in that I said, Love only is the fulfilling of every Commandment, I cited no particular Scripture, but spake a general sense, which might bee collected from many places."

The Fifth Reason, that nothing more hinders and disturbs the whole life of a Christian, then a matrimony found to be uncurably unfit, and doth the same in effect that an Idolatrous match. ♦

FIFTHLY, As those Priests of old were not to be long in sorrow, or if they were, they could not rightly execute their function; [1] so every true Christian in a higher order of Priesthood [2] is a person dedicate to joy and peace, offering himselfe a lively sacrifice of praise and thanksgiving,[3] & there is no Christian duty that is not to be season'd and set off with cherfulnes; [4] which in a thousand outward and intermitting crosses may yet be done well, as in this vale of teares, but in such a bosom affliction as this, <which grindes> ♦ crushing ♦ the very foundations of his inmost nature, when he shall be forc't to love against a possibility, and to use dissimulation against his soul in the perpetuall and ceaseles duties of a husband, doubtles his whole duty of serving God must needs be blurr'd and tainted with a sad unpreparednesse and dejection of spirit, wherein God has no delight. Who sees not therfore how much more Christianly [5] it would be to break by divorce that which is more brok'n by undue and forcible keeping, rather then *to cover the Altar of the Lord with continuall teares, so that he regardeth not the offring any more,*[6] rather then that the whole worship of a Christian mans life should languish and fade away beneath the waight of an immeasurable grief and discouragement. And because some think the childer'n of a second matrimony succeeding a divorce would not be a holy seed, ♦ it hinder'd not the Jews from being so, and ♦ why should we not think them more holy then the offspring ♦ [16] ♦ of a former ill-twisted wedlock, begott'n only out of a bestiall neces-

---

[1] Jewish ceremonial law imposed strict limits upon a priest's participation in acts of mourning. See Leviticus 21:1–6; Ezekiel 44:25–27.

[2] *Cf.* I Peter 2:5. The priesthood of all believers was a cardinal tenet of the Reformation.

[3] *Cf.* Romans 12:1; Hebrews 13:15. *Cf.* also the Order for Holy Communion, *Book of Common Prayer* (1552): "this our Sacrifice of prayse and thanksgiving . . . our selves, our soules, and bodies, to be a reasonable, holy, and lively Sacrifice unto thee."

[4] *Cf.* Romans 12:8; II Corinthians 9:7.

[5] Uncorrected copies of 1644 read "Christianity."   [6] Malachi 2:13.

sitie without any true love or contentment, or joy to their parents, so
that in some sense we may call them the *childern of wrath* [7] and anguish, which will as little conduce to their sanctifying, as if they had
been bastards; for nothing more [12] then disturbance of minde sus-
pends us from approaching to God. Such a disturbance especially as
both assaults our faith and trust in Gods providence, and ends, if
there be not a miracle of vertue on either side, not onely in bitternes
and wrath, the canker of devotion, but in a desperate and vitious
carelesnes; when he sees himself without fault of his train'd by a
deceitfull bait into a snare of misery, betrai'd by an alluring ordinance, and then made the thrall of heavines & discomfort by an undivorcing Law of God, as he erroneously thinks, but of mans iniquitie, as the truth is; for that God preferres the free and cherfull worship of a Christian, before the grievous and exacted observance of an
unhappy mariage, besides that the generall maxims of Religion
assure us, will be more manifest by drawing a paralel argument
from the ground of divorcing an Idolatresse, which was, lest she
should alienate his heart from the true worship of God: [8] and what
difference is there whether she pervert him to superstition by ⟩ her ⟨
enticing sorcery, or disinable him in the whole service of God through
the disturbance of her unhelpful and unfit society, and so drive him
at last through murmuring and despair to thoughts of Atheism:
neither doth it lessen the cause of separating, in that the one willingly allures him from the faith, the other perhaps unwillingly
drives him; for in the account of God it comes all to one that the
wife looses him a servant; and therefore by all the united force of the
Decalogue she ought to be disbanded,[9] unlesse we must set mariage
above God and charitie, which is a doctrine of devils no lesse then
forbidding to marry.[10]

[7] Ephesians 2:3. As there used, the phrase applies to all men in their unregenerate state.

[8] Milton may have taken a hint here from Perkins, *Christian Oeconomie*,
chapter IX (*Works*, 1609–13, III, 687). After citing Ambrose, Lombard, and
Augustine as in favor of divorce for one deserted by an unbelieving partner,
Perkins affirms that "it is farre better that the covenant should be dissolved,
that man and wife have made each with other, then that the Covenant which
man hath made with God. The people of Israel beeing in affliction, were constrained to breake the former made with strange women, that they might keepe
the latter, Ezr. 10.11.19."

[9] Dismissed, sent away. *NED* cites this example.

[10] *Cf.* I Timothy 4:1–3.

♦ CHAP. VIII.

That an idolatrous Heretick ought to be divorc't after a convenient space giv'n to hope of conversion. That place of Corinth. 7. restor'd from a twofold erroneous exposition, and that the common expositers flatly contradict the morall law. ♦

AND here by the way to illustrate the whole question of divorce, ere this treatise end, I shall not be loath to spend a few lines in hope to give a full resolv of that which is yet so much controverted, whether an Idolatrous heretick ought to be divorc't.[1] To the re- ♦ [17] ♦ solving whereof we must first know that the *Jews* were commanded to divorce an unbeleeving Gentile for two causes: first, because all other Nations especially the *Canaanites* were to them unclean. Secondly, to avoid seducement. That other Nations were to the *Jews* impure, even to the separating of mariage, will appear out of *Exod.* 34. 16. *Deut.* 7. 3. 6. compar'd with *Ezra* 9. 2. also chap. 10. 10, 11. *Nehem.* 13. 30. This was the ground of that doubt rais'd among the *Corinthians* by some of the Circumcision; [2] Whether an unbeleever wer not still to be counted an unclean thing, so as that they ought to divorce from such a person. This doubt of theirs St. *Paul* re- [13] moves by an Evangelicall reason, having respect to that vision of St. *Peter*, wherein the distinction of clean and unclean beeing abolisht, all living creatures were sanctify'd to a pure and Christian use, and mankind especially, now invited by a generall call to the covnant of grace.[3] Therefore saith St. *Paul, The unbeleeving wife is sanctify'd*

---

[1] For a phase of the controversy not directly touched by Milton but possibly in the background of his thinking, see Theophilus Philoparnus [Thomas Paget], *A Religious Scrutiny Concerning Unequal Marriage* (1649; HEHL). Paget, who finds support in the private judgment of "some sound and honored English Ministers of the Gospel" relative to the mixed marriage of Charles I, states the issue in the following terms: "Whether the marriages of men, professing the true Religion of God, according to the Faith of Gods elect, and acknowledging the Truth, which is after godliness; contracted and made with the idolatrous daughters of a strange god, and through strong delusion, beleeving a lye, after the working of Satan, in all deceiveableness of unrighteousness; ought not in a due way to be separated, and made voyd, as being a nullity (de jure) from the first? . . . And consequently, whether the marriages of Protestants of the true Christian Religion, made with Papists of the Antichristian, false Religion; ought not to be separated?"

[2] That is, by Christians of Jewish origin.   [3] See Acts 10:9–28.

by the husband; [4] that is, made pure and lawfull to his use; so that he need not put her away for fear lest her unbelief should defile him; but that if he found her love stil towards him, he might rather hope to win her. The second reason of that divorce was to avoid seducement, as is prov'd by comparing those places of the Law, to that which *Ezra* and *Nehemiah* did by divine warrant in compelling the *Jews* to forgoe their wives. And this reason is morall and perpetuall in the rule of Christian faith without evasion. Therefore saith the Apostle 2 *Cor.* 6. *Mis-yoke not together with Infidels,* [5] which is interpreted of mariage in the first place. And although the former legall pollution be now don off, yet there is a spirituall contagion in Idolatry as much to be shunn'd; and though seducement were not to be fear'd, yet where there is no hope of converting, there alwayes ought to be a certain religious aversation and abhorring, which can no way sort with mariage. Therefore saith St. *Paul, What fellowship hath righteousnesse with unrighteousnesse? what communion hath light with darknesse? what concord hath Christ with Beliall? what part hath he that beleeveth with an Infidell?* And in the next verse but one, he moralizes and makes us liable to that command of *Isaiah, Wherfore come out from among them, and be ye separate saith the Lord, touch not the unclean thing, and I will receive ye.* [6] And this command thus Gospelliz'd [7] to us, hath the same force with that whereon *Ezra* grounded the pious necessitie of divorcing. ◆ Neither had he other commission for what he did, then such a generall command in *Deut.* as this, nay not so direct as this; for he is bid there not to marry, [8] but not bid to di- [18] vorce, and yet we see with what a zeal and confidence he was the author of a generall divorce between the faithfull and unfaithfull seed. The Gospell is more plainly on his side according to three of the Evangelists, then the words of the Law; for where the case of divorce is handled with such a severity as was fittest to aggravate the fault of unbounded licence; yet still in the same chapter when it comes into question afterwards whether any civill respect, or natural relation which is dearest, may be our plea to divide, or hinder, or but delay our

---

[4] I Corinthians 7:14.

[5] II Corinthians 6:14: "Be ye not unequally yoked together with unbelievers." Milton gives his own translation of this clause, although in quoting the rest of the passage (see below) he follows the King James Version.

[6] II Corinthians 6:17. The command alluded to is Isaiah 52:11.

[7] Imparted according to the spirit of the gospel. *NED* cites.

[8] Deuteronomy 7:3: "Neither shalt thou make marriages with them."

duty to religion, we heare it determin'd that father and mother, and wife also is not only to be hated, but forsak'n, if we mean to inherit the great reward there promis'd.[9] Nor will it suffice to be put off by saying we must forsake them onely by not consenting or not complying with them, for that were to be don, and roundly too, though being of the same faith they should but seek, out of a fleshly tendernes to weak'n our Christian fortitude with worldly perswasions, or but to unsettle our constancie with timorous and softning suggestions: as we may read with what a vehemence *Job* the patientest of men, rejected the desperat counsels of his wife; [10] and *Moses* the meekest being throughly offended with the prophane speeches of *Zippora*, sent her back to her father.[11] But if they shall perpetually at our elbow seduce us from the true worship of God, or defile and daily scandalize our conscience by their hopeles continuance in misbelief, then ev'n in the due progresse of reason, and that ever-equall proportion which justice proceeds by, it cannot be imagin'd that this cited place, commands lesse then a totall and finall separation from such an adherent; at least that no force should be us'd to keep them together: while we remember that God commanded *Abraham* to send away his irreligious wife and her son for the offences which they gave in a pious family.[12] And it may be guest that *David* for the like cause dispos'd of *Michal* in such a sort, as little differ'd from a dismission.[13] Therefore against reiterated scandals and seducements which never cease, much more can no other remedy or retirement be found but absolute departure. For what kind of matrimony can that remain to be, what one dutie between such can be perform'd as it should be from the heart, when their thoughts and spirits flie asunder as farre as heaven from hell; especially if the time that hope should send forth her expected blossoms be past in vain. It will easily be true that a father or brother may be hated zealously,[14] and lov'd civilly or naturally; for those duties may be perform'd at distance, and doe admit of any long absence: but how the peace and perpetu- [19] all cohabitation of marriage can be kept, how that benevolent and intimate communion of body can be held with one that must be hated with a most operative hatred, must

---

[9] *Cf.* Matthew 19:29; Mark 10:29–30; Luke 18:29–30.
[10] See Job 2:9–10.
[11] See Exodus 18:2; also Numbers 12:3 and Exodus 4:25.
[12] See Genesis 21:9–14.   [13] See II Samuel 6:20–23.
[14] "In the way of religious zeal or devotion." *NED.*

be forsak'n and yet continually dwelt with and accompanied, he who can distinguish, hath the gift of an affection very odly divided and contriv'd: while others both just and wise, and *Salomon* among the rest,[15] if they may not hate and forsake as *Moses* enjoyns, and the Gospell imports, will find it impossible not to love otherwise then will sort with the love of God, whose jealousie brooks no corrivall. And whether is more likely, that Christ bidding to forsake wife for religion, meant it by divorce as *Moses* meant it, whose Law grounded on morall reason, was both his office and his essence to maintain, or that he should bring a new morality into religion, not only new, but contrary to an unchangeable command, and dangerously derogating from our love & worship of God. As if when *Moses* had bid divorce absolutely, and Christ had said, hate & forsake, and his Apostle had said, no communion with Christ & *Belial*, yet that Christ after all this could be understood to say, divorce not, no not for religion, seduce, or seduce not. What mighty and invisible Remora[16] is this in matrimony able to demurre, and to contemne all the divorsive engines in heaven or earth. Both which may now passe away if this be true, for more then many jots or tittles, a whole morall Law is abolisht.[17] But if we dare beleeve it is not, then in the method of religion, and to save the honour and dignity of our faith, we are to retreat, and gather up our selves from the observance of an inferior and civill ordinance, to the strict maintaining of a generall and religious command, which is written, *Thou shalt make no cov'nant with them,* Deut. 7. 2. 3. and that cov'nant which cannot be lawfully made, we have directions and examples lawfully to dissolve. Also 2 Chron. 19. 2.[18] *Shouldst thou love them that hate the Lord?* No doubtlesse: for there is a certain scale of duties, there is a certain Hierarchy of upper and lower commands, which for want of studying in right order, all the world is in confusion.[19] ♦

Upon these principles I answer, that a right beleever ought to

---

[15] See I Kings 11:1–8.

[16] A diminutive fish reputed in antiquity to be capable of holding a ship stationary against oars, winds, and tides. Pliny (*Natural History,* XXXII, i) waxes eloquent on its mysterious powers.

[17] *Cf.* Matthew 5:18: "Till heaven and earth pass, one jot or one tittle shall in no wise pass from the law."

[18] The original edition reads "Chron. 2. 19." Milton's intention, however, is established by the quotation.

[19] *Cf.* Milton's detailed classification of duties in *Christian Doctrine,* Book II.

divorce an idolatrous heretick unlesse upon better hopes: howevei that it is in the beleevers choice to divorce or not.

The former part will be manifest thus; first, an apostate idolater whether husband or wife seducing was to die by the decree of God, *Deut.* 13. 6. 9. that mariage therefore God himself dis-joyns; for others born idolaters the morall reason of their dangerous keeping ▶ [20] ◀ and the incommunicable antagony [20] that is between Christ and *Belial,* will be sufficient to enforce the commandment of those two inspir'd reformers, *Ezra* and *Nehemiah,* to put an Idolater away as well under the Gospel. [14]

The latter part, that although there be no seducement fear'd, yet if there be no hope giv'n, the divorce is lawfull, will appear by this, that idolatrous mariage is still hatefull to God, therefore still it may be divorc't by the pattern of that warrant that *Ezra* had; and by the same everlasting reason: neither can any man give an account wherfore, if those whom God joyns, no man may separate, it should not follow, that, whom he joyns not, but hates to joyn, those man ought to separate: but saith the Lawyer, that which ought not have been don, once don availes. I answer, this is but a crochet of the law,[21] but that brought against it, is plain Scripture. As for what Christ spake concerning divorce, tis confest by all knowing men, he meant onely between them of the same faith.[22] But what shall we say then to St. *Paul,* who seems to bid us not divorce an Infidell willing to stay? We may safely say thus; that wrong collections have been hitherto made out of those words by modern Divines.[23] His drift, as was heard before, is plain: not to command our stay in mariage

[20] Antagonism. *NED* cites as the only instance.

[21] The hostility to legalism is characteristic. *Cf.* the first entry under "Laws" in *CPB* (*Complete Prose,* I, 423), a reference to Savonarola's "fine parable by which he shows 'that one should obey the spirit rather than the letter of the law.' "

[22] *Cf.* Perkins, *Christian Oeconomie* (*Works,* 1609–13, III, 687): "And Christ where he mentioneth the Case of Adulterie, Matt. 19. speaketh of an equall mariage."

[23] The main point of difference between "modern Divines" and the earlier interpreters is stated by John Mayer, *A Commentarie upon the New Testament* (2 vols., 1631; UTSL), II, 199: "*Augustine* and other ancients understood this but as a counsell for the best, so that hee sinneth not which putteth away his unbeleeving wife; but our writers as a precept binding to obey, so that to separate upon this occasion is sinne. And indeed it must needs be so, because otherwise another cause of divorcement besides fornication, should be constituted against that of our Saviour Christ."

with an Infidel, that had been a flat renouncing of the religious and morall Law; but to inform the *Corinthians* that the body of an unbeleever was not defiling, if his desire to live in Christian wedlock shewd any likelihood that his heart was opening to the faith: and therefore advises to forbear departure so long, till nothing have bin neglected to set forward a conversion: this I say he advises, and that with certain cautions; not commands: If we can take up so much credit for him, as to get him beleev'd upon his own word; for what is this els but his counsell in a thing indifferent, *to the rest speak I, not the Lord;* for though it be true that the Lord never spake it, yet from St. *Pauls* mouth wee should have took it as a command, had not himself forewarn'd us, and disclaim'd; which, notwithstanding if we shall still avouch to be a command, he palpably denying it, this is not to expound St. *Paul,* but to out-face him. Neither doth it follow, but that the Apostle may interpose his judgement in a case of Christian libertie without the guilt of adding to Gods word. How doe we know mariage or single life to be of choice, but by such like words as these, *I speak this by permission, not of commandment, I have no command of the Lord, yet I give my judgement.*[24] Why shall not the like words have leave to signifie a freedom in this our present question, ❥ [21] ❧ though *Beza* deny.[25] Neither is the Scripture hereby lesse inspir'd because St. *Paul* confesses to have writt'n therein what he had not of command; for we grant that the Spirit of God led him thus to ex-[15] presse himself to Christian prudence in a matter which God thought best to leave uncommanded. *Beza* therefore must be warily read when he taxes St. *Austin* of Blasphemy, for holding that St. *Paul* spake heer as of a thing indifferent:[26] but if it must be a command, I shall yet the more evince it to be a command that we should heerin be left free:

[24] I Corinthians 7:6, 25.

[25] *Cf.* Theodore Beza's comment on I Corinthians 7:15 (tr. from *Annotationes Majores in Novum Testamentum* [2 vols., 1594; WRUL], II, 189): "Nor does Paul (as some have thought) when he speaks thus, add anything to the precept of Christ, who names adultery as the only cause of divorce."

[26] Commenting on verse 6, Beza says (*Annotationes,* II, 189) that "the word of permission is distorted (*perperam torquetur*) by Augustine in his book *De Bono Conjugali,* Chap. 10." This, however, seems hardly an accusation of blasphemy, nor does his statement on the same point in *Tractatio De Repudiis et Divortiis* (Geneva, 1587; NYPL), p. 108, where he emphatically rejects the interpretation of St. Augustine but does so "with all respect to such a worthy man (*cum tanti viri pace*)."

and that out of the Greek word us'd in the 12. *v.* which instructs us plainly there must be a joynt assent and good liking on both sides; he that will not deprave the Text, must thus render it; *If a brother have an unbeleeving wife, and she joyn in consent to dwell with him* (which cannot utter lesse to us then a mutuall agreement) let him not put her away for the meer surmise of Judaicall uncleannes:[27] and the reason follows, for the body of an Infidell is not polluted, neither to benevolence, nor to procreation. Moreover, this note of mutuall complacency forbids all offer of seducement; which to a person of zeal cannot be attempted without great offence: if therfore seducement be fear'd, this place hinders not divorce. Another caution was put in this supposed command, of not bringing the beleever into *bondage* heerby, which doubtles might prove extreme, if Christian liberty and conscience were left to the humor of a pagan staying at pleasure to play with, or to vexe and wound with a thousand scandals and burdens above strength to bear: if therefore the conceived hope of gaining a soul come to nothing, then charity commands that the beleever be not wearied out with endles waiting under many grievances sore to his spirit; but that respect be had rather to the present suffering of a true Christian, then the uncertain winning of an obdur'd heretick $<$; for this also$>$ ♦. The counsell we have from S. *Paul* to hope, cannot countermand the moral and Evangelick charge we have from God to feare seducement, to separate from the misbeleever, the unclean, the obdurat. The Apostle wisheth us to hope, but does not send us a wooll-gathering after vain hope: he saith, *How knowest thou, O man, whether thou shalt save thy wife,*[28] that is till he try all due means, and set some reasonable time to himselfe after which he may give over washing an Ethiope,[29] if he will heare the advice of the Gospell. *Cast not pearls before swine,* saith Christ himself. *Let him be to thee as a heathen. Shake the dust off thy feet.*[30] If this be not anough, *hate and forsake,*[31]

---

[27] The Greek word to which Milton refers is the compound verb συνευδοκεῖ, the prefix σύν indicating mutuality. In the King James translation the verse reads, "If any brother hath a wife that believeth not, and she be pleased to dwell with him, let him not put her away."

[28] I Corinthians 7:16.

[29] *Cf.* Jeremiah 13:23: "Can the Ethiopian change his skin?"

[30] Matthew 7:6; 18:17; 10:14.

[31] Not a quotation but an inference based apparently on Luke 14:26. See next note.

what relation soever. And this also that follows, ◀ must appertain
to the precept, *Let every man wherein he is call'd therein* ▶ [22] ◀
abide with God, v. 24. that is, so walking in his inferior calling of
mariage, as not by dangerous subjection to that ordinance, to hinder
and disturb the higher calling of his Christianitie.[32] Last, ▶ and never
too oft remembred, ◀ whether this be a command or an advice, we
must look that it be so understood as not to contradict the least
point of morall religion that God hath formerly commanded, otherwise what doe we, but set the morall Law and the Gospel at civill
war together: and who then shall be able to serve those two
masters? [33]

▶ CHAP. IX.

*That adultery is not the greatest breach of matrimony, that there may be
other violations as great.* ◀

Now whether Idolatry or adultery be the greatest violation
of mariage, if any demand, let him thus consider, that
among Christian Writers touching matrimony, there be
three chief ends therof agreed on; Godly society, next civill, and
thirdly, that of the ma-[16] riage-bed.[1] Of these the first in name

[32] *Cf.* Perkins, *Christian Oeconomie* (*Works,* 1609–13, III, 688): "There is a
double calling: The generall, standing in the worship of God: The particular, as
the calling of mariage, or of single life. When these two callings cannot stand
together, the latter must give place to the former: Luk. 14:26. *If any man come
to me, and hate not his father, and mother, and wife, and children, and brethren,
and sisters; yea and his owne life also, he cannot be my disciple.*"
[33] *Cf.* Matthew 6:24: "No man can serve two masters."
[1] *Cf.* "the causes for whiche Matrymonye was ordayned" as stated in the
marriage service of *The Book of Common Prayer.* "One was the procreacion of
children, to be broughte up in the feare and nurtoure of the Lorde, and prayse of
God. Secondlye it was ordeined for a remedye agaynste synne, and to avoide
fornicacion, that suche persons as have not the gyfte of continencie myght
marye, and kepe themselves undefiled members of Christes body. Thirdly, for
the mutuall societie, helpe, and comforte, that the one ought to have of the
other, both in prosperitie and adversitie." Perkins (*Works,* III, 671) names four
ends, distinguishing between procreation *per se* and "procreation of an holy seed,
whereby the Church of God may be kept holy and chaste." Rivetus (*Theologicae
& Scholasticae Exercitationes* [Leyden, 1633], p. 121) adheres to three but
varies the order slightly, naming procreation first, *vitae societas* second, and
avoidance of the evil of incontinence third. Other writers reveal only minor
differences.

to be the highest and most excellent, no baptiz'd man can deny; nor
that Idolatry smites directly against this prime end, nor that such
as the violated end is, such is the violation: but he who affirms
adultery to be the highest breach, affirms the bed to be the highest
of mariage, which is in truth a grosse and borish opinion, how common soever; as farre from the countnance of Scripture, as from the
light of all clean philosophy, or civill nature. And out of question
the cherfull help that may be in mariage toward sanctity of life, is
the purest and so the noblest end of that contract: but if the particular of each person be consider'd, then of those three ends which
God appointed, that to him is greatest which is most necessary: and
mariage is then most brok'n to him, when he utterly wants the
fruition of that which he most sought therin, whether it were religious, civill, or corporall society. Of which wants to do him right
by divorce only for the last and meanest, is a pervers injury, and
the pretended reason of it as frigid as frigidity it self, which the
Code and canon [2] are only sensible of. Thus much of this controversie. I now return to the former argument. [3] And having shewn,
that disproportion, contrariety, or numnesse of minde may justly
be divorc't, by proving already that the prohibition therof opposes
the expresse end of Gods institution, suffers not mariage to satisfie
that intellectuall and innocent desire which God himself kindl'd in
man to be the bond of wedlock, but only to remedy a sublunary [4]
and bestial burning, which frugal diet ◊ [23] ◊ without mariage
would easily chast'n. Next that it drives many to transgresse the
conjugall bed, while the soule wanders after that satisfaction which
it had hope to find at home, but hath mis't. Or els it sits repining
even to Atheism; finding it self hardly dealt with, but misdeeming
the cause to be in Gods Law, which is in mans unrighteous ignorance. I have <shew'd> ◊ shew'n ◊ also how it unties the inward
knot of mariage, which is peace & love (if that can be unti'd
which was never knit) while it aimes to keep fast the outward
formalitie; how it lets perish the Christian man, to compell im-
possibly the maried man.

[2] The term *Code* normally refers to the *Codex* of Justinian, which constitutes
Part III of the *Corpus Juris Civilis* (Geneva, 1591–94). Here, however, there
seems to be an implied reference to the entire body of civil and canon law.

[3] That is, "whether an Idolatrous heretick ought to be divorc't." The 1644
division into chapters somewhat obscures the original rhetorical pattern.

[4] Material, gross. *NED* cites this example.

The Sixth Reason of this Law, that to prohibit divorce sought for natural causes is against nature. ♦

THE sixt place declares this prohibition to be as respectles [1] of human nature ♦ as it is of religion ♦, and therfore is not of God. He teaches that an unlawfull mariage may be lawfully divorc't. And that those who having throughly discern'd each others disposition which ofttimes cannot be till after matrimony, shall then finde a powerfull reluc-[17] tance [2] and recoile of nature on either side blasting all the content of their mutuall society, that such persons are not lawfully maried (to use the Apostles words) *Say I these things as a man, or saith not the Law also the same? for it is writt'n,* Deut. 22. *Thou shalt not sowe thy vineyard with divers seeds, lest thou defile both. Thou shalt not plow with an Oxe and an Asse together,* and the like. I follow the pattern of St. *Pauls* reasoning; *Doth God care for Asses and Oxen,* how ill they yoke together, *or is it not said altogether for our sakes? for our sakes no doubt this is writt'n.*[3] Yea the Apostle himself in the forecited 2 *Cor.* 6. 14. alludes from that place of *Deut.* to forbid mis-yoking mariage; as by the Greek word is evident,[4] though he instance but in one example of mis-matching with an Infidell: yet next to that, what can be a fouler incongruity, a greater violence to the reverend secret of nature, then to force a mixture of minds that cannot unite, & to sowe the furrow of mans nativity with seed of two incoherent and uncombining dispositions. ♦; which act being kindly and voluntarie, as it ought, the Apostle in the language he wrote call'd *Eunoia,* and the Latines *Benevolence,*[5] intimating the original therof to be in the understanding

[1] Regardless, inconsiderate. *NED* cites this example.

[2] Opposition, resistance.

[3] See I Corinthians 9:8–10. St. Paul interprets Deuteronomy 25:4 ("Thou shalt not muzzle the ox when he treadeth out the corn") allegorically. Milton does likewise with Deuteronomy 22:9–10.

[4] The word ἑτεροζυγοῦντες corresponds to the Deuteronomy text in the Septuagint. It does not occur elsewhere in the New Testament.

[5] *Cf.* I Corinthians 7:3: "Let the husband render unto the wife due benevolence: and likewise also the wife unto the husband." Mayer (*Commentarie,* [1631] II, 193) notes that "the word ἐννοιαν, benevolence, doth properly ex-

and the will; if not, surely there is nothing which might more properly be call'd a malevolence rather; and is the most injurious and unnaturall tribute that can be extorted from, a person en-[24] dew'd with reason, to be made pay out the best substance of his body, and of his soul too, as some think,[6] when either for just and powerfull causes he cannot like, or from unequall causes finds not recompence. And that there is a hidden efficacie of love and hatred in man as wel as in other kinds, not morall, but naturall, which though not alwayes in the choyce, yet in the successe of mariage wil ever be most predominant, besides daily experience, the author of *Ecclesiasticus,* whose wisedom hath set him next the Bible,[7] acknowledges, 13. 16. *A man,* saith he, *will cleave to his like.* But what might be the cause, whether each ones alotted *Genius* or proper *Starre,* or whether the supernall influence of Schemes and angular aspects or this elementall *Crasis* [8] here below, whether all these jointly or singly meeting friendly, or unfriendly in either party, I dare not, with the men I am likest to clash, appear so much a Philosopher as to conjecture.[9] The ancient proverb in *Homer* lesse abstruse intitles this worke of leading each like person to his like, peculiarly to God himselfe: [10] which is plain anough also by his naming of a meet or like help in the first espousall in-

presse the affection of the minde, not any act of the body." He acknowledges, however, that "most Expositors understand it of the duty of the marriage bed." Actually the weight of MS evidence inclines to the reading τὴν ὀφειλὴν rather than τὴν ὀφειλημένην εὔνοιαν, upon which the King James translation is based. *Cf.* the Vulgate, *Uxori vir debitum reddat,* and the Revised Standard, "The husband should give to his wife her conjugal rights."

[6] *Cf. Christian Doctrine,* I, vii, tr. Sumner: "If the soul be equally diffused throughout any given whole, and throughout every part of that whole, how can the human seed, the noblest and most intimate part of all the body, be imagined destitute and devoid of the soul of the parents, or at least of the father, when communicated to the son by the laws of generation? It is acknowledged by the common consent of almost all philosophers, that every *form,* to which class the human soul must be considered as belonging, is produced by the power of matter."

[7] Ecclesiasticus and the other books of the Apocrypha, although included in early printings of the King James Version, were not considered by the Reformed churches as belonging to the canon of Scripture.

[8] Combining of elements.

[9] Banks cites this passage, among others, as evidence of an ambiguous but generally skeptical attitude toward astrology; see Banks, *Milton's Imagery,* pp. 173–75.

[10] *Odyssey,* XVII, 218: "God brings like unto like."

stituted; and that every woman is meet for every man, none so absurd as to affirm. Seeing then there is indeed a twofold Seminary or stock in nature, from whence are deriv'd the issues of love and hatred distinctly flowing through the whole masse of created things,[11] and that Gods doing ever is to bring the due likenesses and harmonies of his workes together, except when out of two contraries met to their own destruction, he moulds a third existence, and that it is error, or some evil Angel which either blindly or maliciously hath drawn together in two persons ill imbarkt in wedlock the sleeping discords and enmities of nature lull'd on purpose with some false bait, that they may wake to agony and strife, later then prevention could have wisht, if from the bent of just and honest intentions beginning what was begun, and so continuing, all that is equall, all that is fair and possible hath been tri'd, and no accommodation likely to succeed, what folly is it still to stand combating and battering against invincible causes and effects, with evill upon evill, till either the best of our dayes be linger'd out, or ended with some speeding sorrow. The wise *Ecclesiasticus* advises rather, 37. 27. *My sonne, prove thy soule in thy life, see what is evill for it, and give not that unto it.* Reason he had to say so; for if the noysomnesse or disfigurement of body can soon destroy ◀ <Surely if any noysomnes of body soon destroys> the sympathy of mind to <that work,> ♦ wedlock duties, ◀ much more will the <antipathy> ♦ annoyance and trouble ◀ of minde infuse it self into all the faculties and acts of the body, to render ♦ [25] ◀ them invalid, unkindly, and even unholy against the fundamentall law book of nature; which *Moses* never thwarts, but reverences: therfore he commands us to force nothing against sympathy or naturall order, no not upon the most abject creatures; to shew that such an indignity cannot be offer'd to man without an impious crime. <And when he forbids all unmatchable and unmingling natures to consort, doubtles by all due consequence, if they chance through misadventure to be miscoupl'd, he bids them part asunder, as persons whom God never joyn'd.> ♦ And certainly

---

[11] *Cf.* Pliny's view of "the state of peace or of war which exists between the various departments of Nature." "To these states, known to the Greeks by the respective appellations of 'sympathia' and 'antipathia,' we are indebted," he says, "for the first principles of all things." *Natural History,* XX, i, tr. John Bostock and H. T. Riley (6 vols., London, 1855–57), IV, 206.

those divine meditating words of finding out a meet and like help to man, have in them a consideration of more then the indefinite likenesse of womanhood; nor are they to be made waste paper on, for the dulnesse of Canon divinity: no nor those other allegorick precepts of beneficence fetcht out of the closet of nature to teach us goodnes and compassion in not compelling together unmatchable societies, or if they meet through mischance, by all consequence to dis-joyn them, as God and nature signifies and lectures to us not onely by those recited decrees, but ev'n by the first and last of all his visible works; when by his divorcing command the world first rose out of Chaos,[12] nor can be renew'd again out of confusion but by the separating of unmeet consorts.

CHAP. XI.

The seventh reason, That sometimes continuance in mariage may be evidently the shortning or endangering of life to either party, both Law and divinitie concluding, that life is to be prefer'd before mariage the intended solace of life.

SEVENTHLY, The Canon Law and Divines consent, that if either party be found contriving against the others life, they may be sever'd by divorce;[1] for a sin against the life of mariage is greater then a sin against the bed: the one destroys, the other but defiles: it. The same may be said touching those persons who beeing of a pensive nature and cours of life, have summ'd up all their solace in that free and lightsom conversation which God & man intends in mariage: wherof when they see themselves depriv'd by meeting an unsociable consort, they ofttimes resent one anothers mistake so deeply, that long it is not ere grief end one of them. When therfore this danger is foreseen that the life is in perill by living together, what matter is it whether helples greef, or wilfull practice be the cause? [18] This is certain that the preser-

[12] Genesis 1:4 depicts Creation as initially an act of separation: "and God divided the light from the darkness." Milton repeats the phrase "rose out of Chaos" in *Paradise Lost*, I, 10.

[1] In *Colasterion* Milton cites as authority for this statement the *Decretals of Gregory IX*, book IV, title xix, and Schneidewein's *Commentary on the Institutes of Justinian*, book I, part IV, title x. See below, pp. 753–54.

vation of life is more worth then the compulsory keeping of mariage; and it is no lesse then cruelty to force a man to remain in that state as the solace of his life, which he and his friends know will be either the undoing or the disheartning of his life. And what is life without the vigor and spiritfull exercise ♦ [26] ◀ of life? how can it be usefull either to private or publick employment? shall it <be> therfore ♦ be ◀ quite dejected, though never so valuable, and left to moulder away in heavines for the superstitious and impossible performance of an ill driv'n bargain? nothing more inviolable then vows made to God, yet we read in *Numbers,* that if a wife had made such a vow, the meer will and authority of her husband might break it; [2] how much more may he break the error of his own bonds with an unfit and mistak'n wife, to the saving of his welfare, his life, yea his faith and vertue from the hazard of overstrong temptations; for if man be Lord of the Sabbath, to the curing of a Fevor,[3] can he be lesse then Lord of mariage in such important causes as these?

♦ CHAP. XII.

The eighth reason, It is probable, or rather certain, that every one who happ'ns to marry, hath not the calling, and therefore upon unfitnesse found and consider'd, force ought not to be us'd. ◀

EIGHTHLY, It is most sure that some ev'n of those who are not plainly defective in body, are yet destitute of all other mariagable gifts; and consequently have not the calling to marry; unlesse nothing be requisite therto but a meer instrumentall body; which to affirm, is to that unanimous Covnant a reproach: yet it is as sure that many such not of their own desire, but by ♦ the ◀ perswasion of friends, or not knowing themselves do often enter into wedlock; where finding the difference at length between the duties of a maried life, and the gifts of a single life; what unfitnes of mind, what wearisomnes, what scruples and doubts to an incredible offence and displeasure are like to follow between, may be soon imagin'd: whom thus to shut up and immure together, the

[2] See Numbers 30:6–15.
[3] *Cf.* Matthew 12:8–13; Mark 2:27–28; 3:1–5; Luke 6:5–10.

one with a mischosen mate, the other in a mistak'n calling,[1] is not a course that Christian wisdome and tendernes ought to use. As for the custom that some parents and guardians have of forcing mariages, it will be better to say nothing of such a savage inhumanity, but only this, that the Law which gives not all freedome of divorce to any creature endu'd with reason so assasinated, is next in crueltie.

❧ CHAP. XIII.

The ninth reason, Because mariage is not a meer carnall coition, but a human Society, where that cannot reasonably be had, there can be no true matrimony. Mariage compar'd with all other cov'nants and vowes warrantably bro-[27] ken for the good of man. Mariage the Papists Sacrament, and unfit mariage the Protestants Idoll. ❧

NINTHLY, I suppose it will be allow'd us that mariage is a human society, and that all human society must proceed from the mind rather then the body, els it would be but a kind of animal or beastish meeting; if the mind therfore cannot have that due company by [19] mariage, that it may reasonably and humanly desire, that mariage can be no human society, but a certain formalitie, or gilding over of little better then a brutish congresse, and so in very wisdome and purenes to be dissolv'd.

But mariage is more then human, *the covnant of God,* Pro. 2. 17. therfore man cannot dissolve it.[1] I answer, if it be more then human so much the more it argues the chief society therof to be in the soul

---

[1] As printed in the body of the 1643 text, this clause reads, "whom thus to shut up and immure in an unequall and mischosen match." The expanded form appears on an unnumbered page at the end of the pamphlet (sig. H) under the heading *Omitted pa.* 19. *lin.* 28. On the same page, under the heading *Omitted pa.* 24. *lin.* 22, is a much longer insertion (see below, p. 285). Both passages are probably revisions rather than corrections of printer's omissions. *Cf.* Milton's reference in *Areopagitica* (below, p. 532) to the author "so copious of fancie as to have many things well worth the adding come into his mind . . . while the book is yet under the Presse."

[1] *Cf.* William Ames, *The Marrow of Sacred Divinity* (1638; HEHL), p. 323: "Neither doth this [marriage] perpetually depend upon the will only and covenant of the persons contracting: for then by consent of both parts, a covenant so begun may be unloosed again, as it useth to be between master and servant: but the rule and bond of this covenant is the institution of God, whence also it is in the Scriptures sometimes called the covenant of God. *Prov.* 2. 17."

rather then in the body, and the greatest breach therof to be unfitnes of mind rather then defect of body; for the body can have lest affinity in a covnant more then human, so that the reason of dissolving holds good the rather. Again, I answer, that the Sabbath is a higher institution, a command of the first Table,[2] for the breach wherof God hath far more and oftner testify'd his anger then for divorces, which from *Moses* <till after the captivity> ♦ to *Malachy* ♦ he never took displeasure at, nor then neither, if we mark the Text,[3] and yet as oft as the good of man is concern'd, he not only permits, but commands to break the Sabbath. What covnant more contracted with God, & lesse in mans power then the vow which hath once past his lips? yet if it be found rash, if offensive, if unfruitfull either to Gods glory or the good of man, our doctrin forces not error and unwillingnes irksomly to keep it, but counsels wisdom and better thoughts boldly to break it; [4] therfore to injoyn the indissoluble keeping of a mariage found unfit against the good of man both soul and body, as hath been evidenc't, is to make an Idol of mariage, to advance it above the worship of God and the good of man, to make it a transcendent command, above both the second and the first Table, which is a most prodigious doctrine.

Next, Wheras they cite out of the *Proverbs,* that it is *the covnant of God,* and therfore more then human, that consequence is manifestly false; for so the covnant which *Zedechiah* made with the infidell King of *Babel* is call'd *the covnant of God,* Ezech. 17. 19.[5] which would be strange to hear counted more then a human covnant. So every covnant between man and man, bound by oath, may be call'd the ♦ [28] ♦ covnant of God, because God therin is attested. So of mariage he is the author and the witnes; yet hence will not follow any divine astriction more then what is subordinate to the glory of God and the main good of either party; for as the glory of God & their esteemed fitnes one for the other, was the motive which led them both at first to think without other revelation that God had

[2] *Cf.* Exodus 20:8: "Remember the Sabbath day, to keep it holy." Precepts of the Decalogue concerned directly with man's duty to God constitute the First Table.

[3] *Cf.* Milton's discussion of the Malachi 2:16 text, above, p. 257.

[4] A vow, says Perkins in *Cases of Conscience* (*Works,* 1609–13, II, 97), "must be Lawfull, Possible, & Acceptable to God."

[5] ". . . my covenant that he hath broken, even it will I recompense upon his own head."

joyn'd [20] them together: So when it shall be found by their apparent unfitnes, that their continuing to be man and wife is against the glory of God and their mutuall happines, it may assure them that God never joyn'd them; who hath reveal'd his gratious will not to set the ordinance above the man for whom it was ordain'd: [6] not to canonize mariage either as a tyrannesse or a goddesse over the enfranchiz'd life and soul of man; for wherin can God delight, wherin be worshipt, wherin be glorify'd by the forcible continuing of an improper and ill-yoking couple? He that lov'd not to see the disparity of severall cattell at the plow, cannot be pleas'd with any vast unmeetnes in mariage. Where can be the peace and love which must invite God to such a house, may it not be fear'd that the not divorcing of such a helples disagreement, will be the divorcing of God finally from such a place? But it is a triall of our patience they say: [7] I grant it: but which of *Jobs* afflictions were sent him with that law, that he might not use means to remove any of them if he could? [8] And what if it subvert our patience and our faith too? Who shall answer for the perishing of all those souls perishing by stubborn expositions of particular and inferior precepts, against the general and supreme rule of charitie? They dare not affirm that mariage is either a Sacrament, or a mystery,[9] though all those sacred things give place to man, and yet they invest it with such an awfull sanctity, and give it such adamantine chains [10] to bind with, as if it were to be worshipt like some *Indian* deity,[11] when

[6] Evidently a generalization from Christ's words concerning the Sabbath. *Cf.* above, p. 274.

[7] Milton may have had in mind such advice as that given in *News from Heaven* (1641; HEHL), sig. A3. If a man find himself with a recalcitrant wife, "let him say within himselfe, alas it is the Lords scourge on me, for that I have not beene as I ought to be in obeying *Christ* my spirituall husband."

[8] See the Book of Job, especially chapters 1 and 2.

[9] The sacramental character of marriage had been expressly denied by the Thirty-Nine Articles of the Church of England; see Article XXV. In the language of the Prayer Book it was held to be "an excellent misterie, that in it is signified and represented the spiritual mariage and unitie betwixt Christ and his church." Milton's own reference to it (above, p. 258) as a "mystery of joy and union," although removed from the traditional theological context, is not without an element of ambiguity. *Cf. Colasterion,* below, p. 749, n. 120.

[10] The phrase is repeated in *Paradise Lost,* I, 48: ". . . there to dwell / In Adamantine Chains and penal Fire."

[11] Allan H. Gilbert, in *A Geographical Dictionary of Milton* (New Haven, 1919), cites a passage (p. 155) from the *Pilgrimage* of Samuel Purchas which might have prompted this image.

it can conferre no blessing upon us, but works more and more to our misery. To such teachers the saying of St. *Peter* at the Councell of *Jerusalem* will do well to be apply'd: [12] *Why tempt ye God to put a yoke upon the necks* of Christian men, which neither the *Jews,* Gods ancient people, *nor we are able to bear:* and nothing but unwary expounding hath brought upon us. ◊ [29] ◊

CHAP. XIV.

◊ *Considerations concerning Familisme, Antinomianisme, &c. why it may be thought that such opinions may proceed from the undue restraint of some just liberty, then which no greater cause to contemne discipline.* ◊

To these considerations this also may be added as no improbable conjecture; seeing that sort of men who follow *Anabaptism, Famelism, Antinomianism,* and other *fanatick* dreams,[1] ◊ (if we understand them not amisse) ◊[2] be such most commonly as are by nature addicted to a zeal of Religion, of life also not debausht, and that their opinions having full swinge, do end in satisfaction of the flesh, it may come with reason into the thoughts of a wise man, whether all this proceed not partly, if not cheefly, from the restraint of some lawfull liberty, which ought to be giv'n men, and is deny'd them. As by Physick we learn in men-

---

[12] See Acts 15:6–11.

[1] The Anabaptists were the oldest of the radical Protestant sects. Besides insisting that the only valid baptism was that of adult believers, they generally opposed the Augustinian theology of Luther and advocated complete separation of church and state. Their organization and worship were extremely simple. Although the strongholds of Anabaptism were Germany, Switzerland, and Holland, many members of the group found their way into England by the middle of the sixteenth century. The Familists, or Family of Love, were a much smaller and more esoteric sect, founded by Hendrik Niclaes in Friesland about 1540 and gaining some adherents in England during the late sixteenth and early seventeenth centuries. The basis of Niclaes' teaching was a mystic pantheism. Antinomianism, the belief that Christians had been emancipated from the moral law, was not limited to any specific group; it was, for example, a major tenet of Familism. As terms of abuse, sectarian labels tended to be used loosely.

[2] The addition of this clause is at least suggestive of the direction in which Milton's mind was moving. For an account of some defenses of the sects published between the appearance of the first and second editions of *Doctrine and Discipline,* see introduction, above, pp. 73–76, 80–83. For the completely orthodox attitude see Ephraim Pagitt, *Heresiography* (1645; UTSL).

struous bodies, where natures current hath been stopt, that the suf-[21] focation and upward forcing of some lower part, affects the head and inward sense with dotage and idle fancies.[3] And on the other hand, whether the rest of vulgar men not so religiously professing, doe not give themselves much the more to whordom and adulteries; loving the corrupt and venial discipline of clergy Courts,[4] but hating to hear of perfect reformation: when as they foresee that then fornication shall be austerely censur'd, adultery punisht, and mariage the appointed refuge of nature, though it hap to be never so incongruous & displeasing, must yet of force be worn out, when it can be to no other purpose but of strife and hatred, a thing odious to God. This may be worth the study of skilful men in *Theology*, & the reason of things: and lastly to examin whether some undue and ill grounded strictnes upon the blameles nature of man be not the cause in those places where already reformation is, that the discipline of the Church so often and so unavoidably brok'n, is brought into contempt and derision. And if it be thus, let those who are still bent to hold this obstinate *literality*, so prepare themselves as to share in the account for all these transgressions; when it shall be demanded at the last day by one who will scanne and sift things with more then a literal wisdom of enquiry; [5] for if these reasons be duely ponder'd, and that the Gospel is more jealous of laying on excessive burdens then ever the Law was, lest the soul of a Christian which is inestimable, should be over-tempted and cast away, considering also that many properties of nature, which the power of regeneration it self never alters, may cause dis- ▸ [30] ◂

[3] *Cf. Batman uppon Bartholome, His Booke De Proprietatibus Rerum* (1582; HEHL), f. 31: "Also if ther be superfluous bloud in the body, it breedeth wonderful evills in men, except it be the sooner voyded by kinde or by Physicke: as it fareth in that bloud, that is called, *Sanguis menstrualis,* the which bloud . . . if it be holden beyond due time, is cause and occasion of full great griefes and sickenesse. For sometime it stiffeleth the principall members: sometime it causeth dropsie, and sometime the phrensie."

[4] *Cf.* item XXIII of *The First and Large Petition of the City of London* (1641), which lists as one of the evils of Episcopacy "the great increase and frequencie of whoredomes and Adulteries, occasioned by the *Prelates* Corrupt administration of justice." See *Complete Prose*, I, 982.

[5] *Cf.* Perkins, *Treatise of Christian Equity and Moderation (Works*, 1609–13, II, 437): "As therefore, hee is no way fit to bee a Judge, who hath no knowledge or care to execute the law: so he is but halfe a Judge, who can doe nothing but urge the law, & the plain words of the law, and is not able also to mitigate the rigour of the law, when need so requireth."

like of conversing even between the most sanctify'd, which continually grating in harsh tune together may breed some jarre and discord, and that end in rancor and strife, a thing so opposite both to mariage and to Christianitie, it would perhaps be lesse scandal to divorce a natural disparity, then to link violently together an unchristian dissention, committing two ensnared souls inevitably to kindle one another, not with the fire of love, but with a hatred *inconcileable*,[6] who were they disseverd would be straight friends in any other relation. But if an *alphabetical* servility[7] must be still urg'd, it may so fall out, that the true Church may unwittingly use as much cruelty in forbidding to divorce, as the Church of Antichrist doth wilfully in forbidding to marry.

[6] Irreconcilable. The word is rare, this occurrence being the earliest cited in *NED*.

[7] Servile obedience to the letter of the law. Milton's use here of *alphabetical* in the sense of "literal" is the only instance recorded in *NED*.

♦ THE SECOND BOOK.

CHAP. I.

The Ordinance of Sabbath and mariage compar'd. Hyperbole no unfrequent figure in the Gospel. Excesse cur'd by contrary excesse. Christ neither did, nor could abrogat the Law of divorce, but only reprove the abuse therof.

HITHERTO the Position undertak'n hath bin declar'd, and prov'd by a Law of God; that Law prov'd to be moral, and unabolishable for many reasons equal, honest, charitable, just, annext therto. It follows now that those places of Scripture which have a seeming to revoke the prudence of *Moses,* or rather that mercifull decree of God, be forthwith explain'd and reconcil'd. For ♦ <But> what are all these reasonings worth, will some reply, when as the words of Christ are plainly against all divorce, except in case of fornication; [1] ♦. To whom he whose minde were to answer no more but this, *except also in case of charity,*[2] might safely appeal to the more plain words of Christ in defence of so excepting. *Thou shalt doe no manner of worke* saith the commandment of the Sabbath.[3] Yes saith Christ works of charity. And shall we be more severe in paraphrasing the considerat and tender Gospel, then he was in expounding the rigid and peremptory Law? What was ever in all appearance lesse made for man, and more for God alone then the Sabbath? yet when the good of man comes [31] into the scales, we hear that voice of infinite goodnesse and benignity that *Sabbath was made for man, not man for Sabbath.*[4] What thing ever was more made for man alone and lesse for God then mariage? And shall we load it with a cruel and senceles bondage utterly against both the good of man and the glory of God? Let who so will now listen, I want neither pall nor mitre, I stay neither for ordination nor

---

[1] See Matthew 5:32.
[2] Not a quotation, but Milton's own "paraphrase" based on the analogy which follows.
[3] *Cf.* Exodus 20:10. The version quoted is that of the Prayer Book.
[4] Mark 2:27.

induction, but in the firm faith of a knowing Christian, which is the best and truest endowment of the keyes,[5] I pronounce, the man who shall bind so cruelly a good and gracious ordinance of God, hath not in that the Spirit of Christ. Yet that every text of Scripture seeming opposite may be attended with a due exposition, this other part ensues, and makes account to find no slender arguments for this assertion out of those very Scriptures, which are commonly urg'd against it.

First therfore let us ◀ <let such> remember as a thing not to be deny'd, that all [22] places of Scripture wherin just reason of doubt arises from the letter, are to be expounded by considering upon what occasion every thing is set down: and by comparing other Texts.[6] The occasion which induc't our Saviour to speak of divorce, was either to convince the extravagance of the Pharises in that point, or to give a sharp and vehement answer to a tempting question.[7] And in such cases that we are not to repose all upon the literall terms of so many words, many instances will teach us: [8] Wherin we may plainly discover how Christ meant not to be tak'n word for word, but like a wise Physician, administring one excesse against

---

[5] Cf. Matthew 16:18–19 and Milton's contention in Christian Doctrine, I, xxix, that the passage does not "confer any distinction on Peter beyond what is enjoyed by other professors of the same faith."

[6] Although Milton's independent examination of Scripture was to lead him to unorthodox conclusions, there was nothing unorthodox about his method. Cf. the Westminster Confession of Faith (1647; HEHL), I, ix: "The infallible rule of interpretation of Scripture is the Scripture itself; and therefore, when there is a question about the true and full sense of any Scripture (which is not manifold, but one), it must be searched and known by other places that speak more clearly." For a full discussion see George N. Conklin, Biblical Criticism and Heresy in Milton (New York: King's Crown Press, 1949), pp. 24–40.

[7] Perkins begins his Godly and Learned Exposition of Christs Sermon in the Mount (Works, 1609–13, III, 1) by pointing out that "Christs intent is to cleare the true meaning of Moses and the Prophets, which was corrupted by the false glosse of the Jewish teachers."

[8] Cf. Perkins, Godly and Learned Exposition (Works, 1609–13, III, 53): "First here observe the fraud and cunning of these Pharisies; they would seeme faithful interpreters of the Law, in that they keepe themselves so close to the words, that they will not passe one jot beyond the litterall sense: but yet in the meane time they omit the full meaning and true use of the Law. . . . And the like might be shewed by sundrie examples in all ages; wherby we are taught not to stand upon the proprietie of the words of Scripture onely, but to labour to have the true spirituall sense joyned with them."

another to reduce us to a perfect mean: [9] Where the Pharises were
strict, there Christ seems remisse; where they were too remisse, he
saw it needfull to seem most severe: in one place he censures an
unchast look to be adultery already committed: [10] another time he
passes over actuall adultery with lesse reproof then for an unchast
look; [11] not so heavily condemning secret weaknes, as open malice:
So heer he may be justly thought to have giv'n this rigid sentence
against divorce, not to cut off all remedy from a good man who finds
himself consuming away in a disconsolate and uninjoy'd matrimony,
but to lay a bridle upon the bold abuses of those over-weening
Rabbies; which he could not more effectually doe, then by a coun-
tersway of restraint, curbing their wild exorbitance almost into the
other extreme; as when we bow things the contrary way, to make
them come to thir naturall straitnes.[12] And that this was the only
intention of Christ is most evident; if we attend but to his own
words and protestation made in the same Sermon not many verses
before he treats of divorcing, that he came ◆ [32] ◀ not to abrogate
from the Law *one jot or tittle,* and denounces against them that
shall so teach.[13]

◆ But S. *Luke,* the verse immediatly before going that of divorce
inserts the same caveat,[14] as if the latter could not be understood
without the former; and as a witnesse to produce against this our
wilfull mistake of abrogating, which ◀ <So that the question of
divorce following upon this his open profession,> must needs confirm us, that what ever els in the politicall Law of more speciall
relation to the *Jews,* might cease to us, yet that of those precepts
concerning divorce, not one of them was repeal'd by the doctrine of
Christ; ◆ unlesse we have vow'd not to beleeve his own cautious and
immediat profession; ◀ for if these our Saviours words inveigh

[9] *Cf. Tetrachordon* (below, p. 668): "as the Physician cures him who hath
tak'n down poyson, not by the middling temper of nourishment, but by the other
extreme of *antidote.*"

[10] See Matthew 5:28.   [11] See John 8:3–11.

[12] *Cf.* Aristotle, *Nicomachean Ethics,* II, ix, tr. H. Rackham (New York and
London, 1926), p. 113: "Then we must drag ourselves away in the opposite
direction, for by steering wide of our besetting error we shall make a middle
course. This is the method adopted by carpenters to straighten warped timber."
Milton cites a closely related passage from the *Ethics* in *Colasterion;* see below, p. 745.

[13] See Matthew 5:17–20. The quoted phrase is from verse 18.

[14] Luke 16:17, 18.

against all divorce, and condemn it as adultery, except it be for
adultery, and be not rather understood against the abuse of those
divorces permitted in the Law, then is that Law of *Moses*, Deut. 24.1.
not only repeal'd & wholly anull'd against the promise of Christ &
his known profession, not to meddle in matters judicial, but that
which is more strange, the very substance and purpose of that Law
is contradicted [23] and convinc't both of injustice & impurity, as
having authoriz'd & maintain'd legall adultery by statute. *Moses*
also cannot scape to be guilty of unequall and unwise decrees, punishing one act of secret adultery by death,[15] and permitting a whole
life of open adultery by Law. And albeit Lawyers write that some
politicall Edicts, though not approv'd, are yet allow'd to the scum
of the people and the necessitie of the times;[16] these excuses have
but a weak pulse: for first we read, not that the scoundrel people,
but the choisest, the wisest, the holiest of that nation have frequently us'd these laws, or such as these ◗ in the best and holiest
times ◖. Secondly, Be it yeelded that in matters not very bad or
impure, a human law-giver may slacken somthing of that which is
exactly good, to the disposition of the people and the times: but if
the perfect, the pure, the righteous law of God, for so are all his
statutes and his judgements, be found to have allow'd smoothly
without any certain reprehension, that which Christ afterward declares to be adultery, how can wee free this Law from the horrible
endightment of beeing both impure, unjust, and fallacious.

[15] *Cf.* Leviticus 20:10; Deuteronomy 22:22.
[16] *Cf.* Thomas Aquinas, *Summa Theologica,* part I–II, ques. 96, art. 2, tr. by
the Dominican Fathers (22 vols., London: Burns, Oates & Washburn, 1920–42),
VIII, 66: "Law is framed as a rule or measure of human acts. . . . Wherefore
laws imposed on men should also be in keeping with their condition, for, as
Isidore says (*Etym.* V, 21), law should be *possible both according to nature, and
according to the customs of the country.* . . . In like manner many things are
permissible to men not perfect in virtue, which would be intolerable in a virtuous man."

♦ CHAP. II.

How divorce was permitted for hardnesse of heart, cannot be understood by the common exposition. That the Law cannot permit, much lesse enact a permission of sin. ♦

NEITHER will it serv to say this was permitted for the hardnes of thir hearts, in that sense, as it is usually explain'd,[1] for the Law ♦ [33] ♦ were then but a corrupt and erroneous School-master,[2] teaching us to dash against a vital maxim of religion, by dooing foul evil in hope of some uncertain good.[3] This only text not to be match't again throughout the whole Scripture, wherby God in his perfet Law should seem to have granted to the hard hearts of his holy people under his own hand a civil immunity and free charter to live and die in a long successive adultery, under a covnant of works, till the *Messiah,* and then that indulgent permission to be strictly deny'd by a covnant of grace, besides the incoherence of such a doctrin, cannot, must not be thus interpreted, to the raising of a paradox never known till then, only hanging by the twin'd thred of one doubtfull Scripture, against so many other rules and leading principles of religion, of justice, and purity of life. For what could be granted more either to the fear, or to the lust of any tyrant, or politician,[4] then this autority of *Moses* thus expounded; which opens him a way at will to damme up justice, and not only to

[1] *Cf.* Paraeus, *In S. Matthaei Evangelium Commentarius,* tr. from *Operum Theologicorum* (Frankfurt, 1628; NYPL), I, 644: "Divorce and the bill of repudiation were not of the substance of the moral law, but a concession of the civil law because of the hardness of heart of the Jewish people. . . . Because of this hardness of heart Moses permitted divorces in his state, not that they were not sins, but that it was necessary to tolerate them for the prevention of greater sins." Perkins (*Works,* 1609–13, III, 68) expresses the same view.

[2] *Cf.* Galatians 3:24: "Wherefore the law was our schoolmaster to bring us unto Christ."

[3] In the body of the 1643 text, the next sentence reads: "Wee cannot therfore with safety thus confine the free simplicity of our Saviours meaning to that which meerly amounts from so many letters; whenas it can consist neither with his former, and cautionary words, nor with the scope of charity, commanding by his expresse commission in a higher strain" (*cf.* below, p. 286, l. 16 ff.). The intervening matter, together with the revised form of this sentence, is supplied as the second of two addenda (sig. H). See above, p. 275, n. 1.

[4] Milton almost invariably uses the word in a derogatory sense. *Cf.* above, p. 250.

admit of any *Romish,* or *Austrian* dispences,[5] but to enact a Statute of that which he dares not seem to approve, ev'n to legitimate vice, to make sin it self ◗, the ever alien & vassal sin, ◖ a free Citizen of the Common-wealth, pretending only these or these plausible reasons. And well he might, all the while that *Moses* shall be alleg'd to have don as much without shewing any reason at all. Yet this could not enter into the heart of *David, Psal.* 94. 20. how any such autority as endeavours *to fashion wickednes by* ◗ *a* ◖ *law,* should derive it self from God.[6] And *Isaiah* lays *woe upon them that decree unrighteous decrees,* 10. 1. Now which of these two is the better Lawgiver, and which deservs most a woe, he that gives out an Edict singly unjust, or he that confirms to generations a fixt [H1] and unmolested impunity of that which is not only held to be unjust, but also unclean, and both in a high degree, not only as they themselvs affirm, an injurious expulsion of one wife, but also an unclean freedom by more then a patent to wed another adulterously? How can wee therfore with safety thus dangerously confine the free simplicity of our Saviours meaning to that which meerly amounts from so many letters, whenas it can consist neither with his former and cautionary words, nor with other more pure and holy principles, nor finally with the scope of charity, commanding by his expresse commission in a higher strain. But all rather of necessity must be understood as only against the abuse of that wise and ◗ [34] ◖ ingenuous liberty which *Moses* gave, and to terrify a roaving conscience from sinning under that pretext.

[5] *Cf.* the reference in *Of Reformation* (*Complete Prose,* I, 586) to "many a Popish, and Austrian complotted Treason."

[6] "Shall the throne of iniquity have fellowship with thee, which frameth mischief by a law?"

♦ CHAP. III.

That to allow sin by Law, is against the nature of Law, the end of the law-giver and the good of the people. Impossible therfore in the Law of God. That it makes God the author of sin, more then any thing objected by the Jesuits or Arminians against Predestination.

BUT let us yet further examin upon what consideration a Law of licence could be thus giv'n to a holy people for the hard-nesse of heart. I suppose all wil answer, that for some good end or other. But here the contrary shall be prov'd. First, that many ill effects, but no good end of such a sufferance can be shewn; next, that a thing unlawful can for no good end whatever be either don or allow'd by a positive law. If there were any good end aim'd at, that end was then good, either as to the Law, or to the lawgiver licencing; or as to the person licenc't. That it could not be the end of the Law, whether Moral or Judiciall[1] to licence a sin, I prove easily out of *Rom. 5. 20. The Law enter'd that the offence might abound,* that is, that sin might be made abundantly manifest to be hainous and displeasing to God, that so his offer'd grace might be the more esteem'd. Now if the Law in stead of aggravating and terrifying[2] sin, shall give out licence, it foils it selfe, and turns recreant from its own end: it forestalls the pure grace of Christ which is through righteousnesse, with impure indulgences which are through sin. And instead of discovering sin, for *by the Law is the knowledge therof* saith S. *Paul,*[3] and that by certain and true light for men to walk in safely, it holds out fals and dazling fires to stumble men: or like those miserable flies to run into with delight, and be burnt:[4] for how many soules might easily think that to be

[1] "Morall law concernes duties of love, partly to God and partly towards our neighbour: it is contained in the Decalogue or ten commandments; and it is the very law of nature written in all mens hearts (for substance, though not for the manner of propounding) in the creation of man. . . . Judiciall lawes of Moses are all such as prescribe order for the execution of justice and judgement in the common wealth. They were specially given by God, and directed to the Jewes." Perkins, *A Discourse of Conscience* (*Works,* 1609–13, I, 519–20).

[2] Making terrible. *NED* cites as the only known instance of use in this sense.

[3] Romans 3:20.

[4] The fatal attractiveness of a flame to flies or moths was proverbial. See Morris P. Tilley, *Dictionary of the Proverbs in England in the Sixteenth and Seventeenth Centuries* (Ann Arbor: University of Michigan Press, 1950), p. 224.

lawfull, which the Law and Magistrate allow'd them? Again we read, 1 Tim. 1. 5. *The end of the Commandment is charity, out of a pure heart, and of a good conscience, and of faith unfained.* But never could that be charity to allow a people what they could not use with a pure heart, but with conscience and faith both deceiv'd, or els despis'd. The more particular end of the Judicial Law is set forth to us clearly, *Rom.* 13. that God hath giv'n to that Law *a Sword not in vain, but to be a terror to evil works, a revenge to execute wrath upon him that doth evil.*[5] If this terrible commission should but forbeare to punish wickednes, were it other to be accounted then partial and unjust? but if it [35] begin to write indulgence to vulgar uncleannes can it doe more to corrupt and shame the end of its own being? Lastly, if the Law allow sin, it enters into a kind of covnant with sin, and if it doe, there is not a greater sinner in the world then the Law it selfe. The Law, to use an allegory somthing different from that in *Philo Judaeus* concerning *Amaleck,*[6] though haply more significant, the Law is the *Israelite,* and hath this absolute charge given it Deut. 25. *To blot out the memory of* sin *the Amalekite from under heav'n, not to forget it.* Again, the Law is the *Israelite,* and hath this expresse repeated command *to make no cov'nant with* sin *the Canaanite,*[7] but to expell him, lest he prove a snare. And to say truth it were too rigid and reasonlesse to proclaime such an enmity between man and man, were it not the type of a greater enmity between law and sin. I spake ev'n now, as if sin were condemn'd in a perpetual *villenage* never to be free by law, never to be *manumitted:* but sure sin can have no tenure by law at all, but is rather an eternal outlaw, and in hostility with law past all attonement: both *diagonial*[8] contraries, as much allowing one another, as day and night together in one hemi-

---

[5] *Cf.* Romans 13:3–4. Milton paraphrases freely.

[6] The allusion is to Philo's *Moses,* I, xxxix, tr. F. H. Colson (11 vols., London and New York: Loeb Classical Library, 1950), VI, 387–91. Recounting the first battle of the Israelites with the Amalekites, he interprets allegorically the scriptural statement (Exodus 17:11) that "it came to pass when Moses held up his hand, that Israel prevailed: and when he let down his hand, Amalek prevailed." "Thus, by symbols," says Philo, "God shewed that earth and the lowest region of the universe were the portion assigned as their own to the one party, and the ethereal, the holiest region, to the other; and that, just as heaven holds kingship in the universe and is superior to earth, so this nation should be victorious over its opponents in war."

[7] *Cf.* Deuteronomy 7:1–2.   [8] Diametrically opposed. *NED.*

sphere. Or if it be possible, that sin with his darknes may come to composition, it cannot be without a foul eclipse, and twylight to the law, whose brightnesse ought to surpasse the noon. Thus we see how this unclean permittance defeats the sacred and glorious end both of the Moral and Judicial Law.

As little good can the lawgiver propose to equity by such a lavish remisnes as this: if to remedy hardnes of heart, *Paraeus* and other divines confesse, it more encreases by this liberty, then is lessn'd: [9] and how is it probable that their hearts were more hard in this that it should be yeelded to, then in any other crime? Their hearts were set upon usury, and are to this day, no Nation more; yet that which was the endammaging only of their estates, was narrowly forbid; [10] this which is thought the extreme injury and dishonour of their Wives and daughters with the defilement also of themselves, is bounteously allow'd. Their hearts were as hard under their best Kings to offer in high places, though to the true God; yet that but a small thing is strictly forwarn'd; [11] this accounted a high offence against one of the greatest moral duties, is calmely permitted and establisht. How can it be evaded but that the heavy censure of Christ should fall worse upon this lawgiver of theirs, then upon all the Scribes and Pharises? For they did but omit Judgement and Mercy to trifle in Mint and Cummin, yet all according to Law; [12] but this their Lawgiver altogether as punctuall in such niceties, goes marching on to [36] adulteries, through the violence of divorce by Law against Law. If it were such a cursed act of *Pilat* a subordinate Judge to Caesar, overswayd by those hard hearts with much a doe to suffer one transgression of Law but once,[13] what is it then with lesse a doe to publish a Law of transgression for many ages? Did God for this come down and cover the Mount of *Sinai* with his glory,[14] uttering in thunder those his sacred Ordinances out of the

[9] *Cf.* Paraeus, *In Priorem ad Corinthios Epistolam S. Pauli Commentarius*, tr. from *Operum Theologicorum* (Frankfurt, 1628), II, 488: "For the remedy of divorce did not so much help the hardheartedness of men as the misery of wives; indeed the hardheartedness of the men was not diminished but rather increased."

[10] See Deuteronomy 23:19–20.

[11] Worship of God "in high places" (*i.e.*, at shrines associated with idols) is forbidden in Deuteronomy 12:2. Among the violators of this prohibition was King Solomon; see I Kings 3:2–4.   [12] See Matthew 23:23.

[13] See Matthew 27:11–24, and parallel accounts in the other Gospels.

[14] See Exodus 19:18 ff.

bottomlesse treasures of his wisdome and infinit purenes to patch up an ulcerous and rott'n common-wealth with strict and stern injunctions, to wash the skin and garments for every unclean touch, and such easie permission giv'n to pollute the soule with adulteries by publick authority, without disgrace, or question? No, it had bin better that man had never known Law or matrimony, then that such foul iniquity should be fast'nd upon the holy One of *Israel*, the Judge of all the earth, and such a peece of folly as *Belzebub* [15] would not commit, to divide against himself and pervert his own ends; or if he to compasse more certain mischief, might yeild perhaps to fain some good deed, yet that God should enact a licence of certain evill for uncertain good against His own glory and purenes, is abominable to conceive. And as it is destructive to the end of Law, and blasphemous to the honour of the lawgiver licencing, so is it as pernicious to the person licenc't. If a private friend admonish not, the Scripture saith *he hates his brother, and lets him perish;* [16] but if he sooth him, and allow him in his faults, the Proverbs teach us *he spreads a net for his neighbours feet, and worketh ruin.*[17] If the Magistrate or Prince forget to administer due justice and restrain not sin, *Eli* himself could say *it made the Lords people to transgresse.*[18] But if he count'nance them against law by his own example, what havock it makes both in Religion and vertue among the people, may be guest by the anger it brought upon *Hophni* and *Phineas,* not to be appeas'd *with sacrifice nor offring for ever.*[19] If the Law be silent to declare sin, the people must needs generally goe astray, for the Apostle himselfe saith, *he had not known lust but by the Law:* [20] and surely such a Nation seems not to be under the illuminating guidance of Gods law, but under the horrible doom rather of such as despise the Gospel, *he that is filthy let him be filthy still.*[21] But where the Law it selfe gives a warrant for sin, I know not what condition of misery to imagin miserable anough for such a people, unlesse that portion of the

---

[15] "The prince of the devils" (Matthew 12:24).

[16] *Cf.* Leviticus 19:17.

[17] Proverbs 29:5. The final three words, however, are taken from Proverbs 26:28: "and a flattering mouth worketh ruin."

[18] *Cf.* I Samuel 2:22–24.

[19] I Samuel 3:14. Hophni and Phineas were Eli's sons.

[20] Romans 7:7.

[21] Revelation 22:11.

wicked, or rather of the damned, on whom God threatens in 11. Psalm, *to rain snares:* but that questionlesse cannot be by any Law, which the Apostle saith *is a ministry ordain'd of God unto our good,*[22] and not so many [37]waies and in so high a degree to our destruction, as we have now bin graduating. And this is all the good can come to the person licenc't in his hardnesse of heart.

I am next to mention that which because it is a ground in divinity, Rom. 3. will save the labour of demonstrating,[23] unlesse her giv'n axioms be more doubted then in other Arts (although it be no lesse firm in the precepts of Philosophy) that a thing unlawfull can for no good whatsoever be done, much lesse allow'd by a positive law. And this is the matter [24] why Interpreters upon that passage in *Hosea* will not consent it to be a true story, that the Prophet took a Harlot to wife,[25] because God being a pure Spirit could not command a thing repugnant to his own nature, no not for so good an end as to exhibit more to the life a wholsom and perhaps a converting parable to many an Israelite. Yet that he commanded the allowance of adulterous and injurious divorses for hardnes of heart, a reason obscure and in a wrong sense, they can very savourily perswade themselves; so tenacious is the leven of an old conceit. But they shift it, he permitted only. Yet silence in the Law is consent, and consent is accessory; why then is not the Law being silent, or not active against a crime, accessory to its own conviction, it self judging? For though we should grant, that it approvs not, yet it wills; and the Lawyers maxim is, that *the will compell'd is yet the will.*[26] And though *Aristotle* in his Ethicks call this *a mixt action,* yet he concludes it to be voluntary and inexcusable, if it be

---

[22] Romans 13:4.

[23] See Romans 3:8. The notion that evil may be committed for the sake of good is rejected by St. Paul without argument.

[24] Reason, cause. *NED* cites this example.

[25] See Hosea 1:2–3. Calvin (*Praelectiones in Duodecim Prophetas* [Geneva, 1581], p. 5) likewise observes that here "interpreters labor much because nothing would seem to be more absurd than for the Prophet to take a harlot as a wife." Having summarized the various explanations offered, he states his own view that Hosea was employing a dramatic image to represent the sin of the people.

[26] In his *Maxims of the Law* (1630), Bacon notes exceptions to the rule *Necessitas inducit privilegium.* He concludes that "as *infirmitas culpabilis* excuseth not, no more doth *necessitas culpabilis.*" Spedding, Ellis, and Heath, *Works of Francis Bacon,* XIV, 217.

evill.[27] How justly then might human law and Philosophy rise up against the righteousnesse of *Moses*, if this be true which our vulgar Divinity fathers upon him, yea upon God himselfe; not silently and only negatively to permit, but in his law to divulge a written and generall priviledge to commit and persist in unlawfull divorces with a high hand, with security and no ill fame: for this is more then permitting or conniving, this is maintaining; this is warranting, this is protecting, yea this is doing evill, and such an evil as that reprobat lawgiver did, whose lasting infamy is ingrav'n upon him like a surname *he who made Israel to sin.*[28] This is the lowest pitch contrary to God that publick fraud and injustice can descend.

If it be affirm'd that God as being Lord may doe what he will; yet we must know that God hath not two wills, but one will, much lesse two contrary. If he once will'd adultery should be sinfull, and to be punisht by death, all his omnipotence will not allow him to will the allowance that his holiest people might as it were by his [38] own *Antinomie*, or counter-statute [29] live unreprov'd in the same fact, as he himselfe esteem'd it, according to our common explainers. The hidden wayes of his providence we adore & search not; but the law is his reveled wil, his complete, his evident, and certain will; herein he appears to us as it were in human shape, enters into cov'nant with us, swears to keep it, binds himself like a just lawgiver to his own prescriptions, gives himself to be understood by men, judges and is judg'd, measures and is commensurat to right reason; cannot require lesse of us in one cantle of his Law then in another, his legall justice cannot be so fickle and so variable, sometimes like a devouring fire,[30] and by and by connivent [31] in the embers, or, if I may so say, oscitant and supine. The vigor of his Law could no more remit, then the hallowed fire on his altar could be let goe out.[32] The Lamps that burnt before him might need snuffing, but the light of his Law never. Of this also more beneath, in discussing a solution of *Rivetus*.[33]

---

[27] *Cf. Ethics*, III, 1, tr. Rackham: "Acts of this kind, then, are 'mixed' or composite; but they approximate rather to the voluntary class. For at the actual time when they are done they are chosen or willed."

[28] Manasseh, king of Judah. See II Kings 21:11.

[29] Milton's use of *antinomy* in this sense is the earliest recorded in *NED*.

[30] *Cf.* Exodus 24:17.

[31] Dozing, dormant. *NED*.

[32] *Cf.* Leviticus 6:13.   [33] See below, p. 297.

The Jesuits, and that sect among us which is nam'd of *Arminius*,[34] are wont to charge us [35] of making God the author of sinne in two degrees especially, not to speak of his permissions. 1. Because we hold that he hath decreed some to damnation, and consequently to sinne, say they: Next, because those means which are of saving knowledge to others, he makes to them an occasion of greater sinne. Yet considering the perfection wherin man was created, and might have stood, no decree necessitating his free will, but subsequent though not in time yet in order to causes which were in his owne power, they might, methinks be perswaded to absolve both God and us.[36] Whenas the doctrine of *Plato* and *Chrysippus* with their followers the *Academics* and the *Stoics,* who knew not what a consummat and most adorned *Pandora* was bestow'd upon *Adam* to be the nurse and guide of his arbitrary [37] happinesse and perseverance, I mean his native innocence and perfection, which might have kept him from being our true *Epimetheus*,[38] and though they taught of vertue and vice to be both

[34] Jacobus Arminius (1560–1609), professor of theology at Leyden, was the leader of a movement in the Reformed Church of the Netherlands against the extreme Calvinism prevalent at the beginning of the seventeenth century. His views on Predestination, embodied in the Remonstrance of 1610, were rejected by the Synod of Dort (1618) but became increasingly influential in England as well as on the Continent. Milton's own later position, as defined in *Christian Doctrine,* I, iii and iv, is Arminian.

[35] Here "us" means orthodox Calvinists; in the preceding line it means either members of the Reformed churches generally or members of the Church of England.

[36] *Cf.* Calvin, *Institutio Christianae Religionis,* II, v, 1 (tr. Thomas Norton [1599; UTSL], f. 78): "For if any man will dispute with God, and seeke to escape from his iudgement by this pretence, because he could none otherwise doe: God hath that answere ready which we in another place have spoken of that it is not of creation, but of the corruption of nature that men being made bondslaves to sinne, can will nothing but evill. For whence commeth this want of power which the wicked would gladly pretend, but upon this, that *Adam* of his owne accorde made himselfe subiect to the tyrannie of the Divell? Hereupon therefore grew the corruption, with the bondes whereof we are holden fast tied, for that the first man fell from his Creator. If all men be iustly holden guiltie of his falling away, let them not thinke themselves excused by necessitie, in which it selfe they have a most evident cause of their damnation."

[37] That is, dependent on his own will or choice.

[38] According to classical myth, it was the opening of Pandora's box by Epimetheus which brought man his first experience of evil. See Hesiod, *Theogony,* 570 ff. *Cf.* Milton's application of the story in *Paradise Lost,* IV, 714–19.

the gift of *divine destiny*,[39] they could yet find reasons not invalid, to justifie the counsels of God and Fate from the insulsity of mortall tongues: That mans own freewill self corrupted is the adequat and sufficient cause of his disobedience *besides Fate;* [40] as *Homer* also wanted not to expresse both in his *Iliad* and *Odyssei*.[41] And *Manilius* the Poet, although in his fourth book he tells of some *created both to sinne and punishment;* yet without murmuring and with an industrious cheerfulnes he acquitts the *Deity*.[42] They were not ignorant in their hea-[39] then lore, that it is most God-like to punish those who of his creatures became his enemies with the greatest punishment; and they could attain also to think that the greatest, when God himselfe throws a man furthest from him; which then they held hee did, when he blinded, hard'n'd, and stirr'd up his offendors to finish, and pile up their disperat work since they had undertak'n it. To banish for ever into a locall hell, whether in the aire or in the center, or in that uttermost and bottomlesse gulph of *Chaos*, deeper from holy blisse then the worlds diameter multiply'd,[43] they thought not a punishing so proper and proportionat for God to inflict, as to punish sinne with sinne. Thus were the common sort of Gentiles wont to think, without any

[39] Plato, for example, says that "virtue comes to the virtuous by the gift of God" (*Meno*, 99).

[40] The Stoic Chrysippus (280–207 B.C.) is represented by Cicero (*De Fato*, xvii–xix) as holding a position midway between fatalism and free will but inclining toward the latter. Note especially the following passage, tr. H. Rackham (New York and London: Loeb Classical Library, 1942), p. 237: "But Chrysippus, since he refused on the one hand to accept necessity and held on the other hand that nothing happens without fore-ordained causes, distinguishes different kinds of causation, to enable himself at the same time to escape necessity and to retain fate. 'Some causes,' he says, 'are perfect and principal, others auxiliary and proximate. Hence when we say that everything takes place by fate owing to antecedent causes, what we wish to be understood is not perfect and principal causes but auxiliary and proximate causes.'" In general, Platonic and Stoic ethics emphasized the element of human responsibility.

[41] The theme of the *Iliad* is announced in the opening lines as the wrath of Achilles, "the ruinous wrath that brought on the Achaians woes innumerable." Cf. *Odyssey*, I, 9, and I, 32 ff. Milton quotes the two latter passages at the end of *Christian Doctrine*, I, iv.

[42] See Marcus Manilius, *Astronomicon*, IV, 108–18, in which the poet affirms that fate takes away neither the guilt incurred by evil deeds nor the praise merited by virtue. *In culpam poenasque creatos* (l. 116) is the phrase quoted.

[43] *Cf.* the "locall hell" of *Paradise Lost*, I, 73–74:

As far remov'd from God and light of Heav'n
As from the Center thrice to th' utmost Pole.

wry thoughts cast upon divine governance. And therefore *Cicero* not in his *Tusculan* or *Campanian* retirements among the learned wits of that age; but ev'n in the *Senat* to a mixt auditory (though he were sparing otherwise to broach his Philosophy among Statists and Lawyers) yet as to this point both in his oration against *Piso*, and in that which is about the answers of the Soothsayers against *Clodius*, he declares it publikly as no paradox to common ears, that God cannot punish man more, nor make him more miserable, then still by making him more sinnfull.[44] Thus we see how in this controversie the justice of God stood upright ev'n among heathen disputers. But if any one be truly, and not pretendedly zealous for Gods honour, here I call him forth before men and Angels, to use his best and most advised skill, lest God more unavoidably then ever yet, and in the guiltiest manner be made the author of sin: if he shall not onely deliver over and incite his enemies by rebuks to sin as a punishment, but shall by patent under his own broad seal allow his friends whom he would sanctify and save, whom he would unite to himselfe and not dis-joyne, whom he would correct by wholsome chastning, and not punish as hee doth the damned by lewd sinning, if he shall allow these in his Law the perfect rule of his own purest wil, and our most edify'd conscience, the perpetrating of an odious and manifold sin without the lest contesting. Tis wonder'd how there can be in God a secret, and a reveal'd will; and yet what wonder, if there be in man two answerable causes. But here there must be two revealed wills grappling in a fraternall warre with one another without any reasonable cause apprehended.[45] This cannot be lesse then to ingraft sin into the substance of the law,

[44] *In Pisonem,* 46, tr. N. H. Watts (New York and London, 1931), p. 197: "It is a man's own sin, his own guilt, his own effrontery which unseats his mind from its sanity. These are the Avengers, these the flames, these the brands that hound the wicked." *De Haruspicum Responsis,* 39 (tr. Watts, p. 367): "But what punishment could be visited upon a man by the immortal gods severer than madness and infatuation? . . . Wherefore you are more wretched when your eyes only serve to hurry you into all manner of crime than if you had no eyes at all."

[45] *Cf.* Milton's protest in *Christian Doctrine,* I, iv, against "the scholastic distinction which ascribes a twofold will to God; his revealed will, whereby he prescribes the way in which he desires us to act, and his hidden will, whereby he decrees that we shall never so act; which is much the same as to attribute to the Deity two distinct wills, whereof one is in direct contradiction to the other." Tr. Sumner. See Bohn, IV, 50.

which law is to provoke sin by crossing and forbidding, not by complying with it. Nay this is, which I tremble in uttering, to incarnat sin
into the un-[40] punishing, and well pleas'd will of God. To avoid
these dreadfull consequences that tread upon the heels of those
allowances to sin, will be a task of farre more difficulty then to
appease those minds which perhaps out of a vigilant and wary conscience except against predestination. Thus finally we may conclude,
that a Law wholly giving licence cannot upon any good consideration be giv'n to a holy people for hardnesse of heart in the vulgar
sense.

CHAP. IV.

*That if divorce be no command, no more is mariage. That divorce could be
no dispensation if it were sinfull. The Solution of* Rivetus, *that God dispenc't by some unknown way, ought not to satisfie a Christian mind.* ▶

OTHERS think to evade the matter, by not granting any Law
of divorce, but only a dispensation;[1] which is contrary to
the words of Christ, who himself calls it a Law *Mark* 10. 5.[2]
▶ or if we speak of a command in the strictest definition, then
mariage it selfe is no more a command then divorce, but onely a
free permission to him who cannot contain.[3] But as to dispensation
I affirm, the same as before of the Law, that it can never be giv'n
to the allowance of sin, God cannot give it neither in respect of
himselfe, nor in respect of man: not in respect of himselfe, being a
most pure essence, the just avenger of sin; neither can he make that
cease to be a sinne, which is in it selfe injust and impure, as all
divorces they say were which were not for adultery. Not in respect
of man; for then it must be either to his good or to his evill: Not to
his good; for how can that be imagin'd any good to a sinner whom

---

[1] *Cf.* Calvin, *Mosis Reliqui Libri Quatuor* (Geneva, 1563), p. 364: "That
which pertains to divorce, although conceded to the Jews by indulgence, Christ
nevertheless pronounces not to have been lawful, because directly contrary to
the first institution of God, whence a perpetual and inviolable rule is to be
sought."

[2] In the King James Version the word is "precept." The Greek is ἐντολὴν, command or injunction.

[3] *Cf.* I Corinthians 7:9.

nothing but rebuke and due correction can save, to heare the determinate oracle of divine Law louder then any reproof dispensing and providing for the impunity and convenience of sin; to make that doubtfull, or rather lawfull, which the end of the law was to make most evidently hatefull. Nor to the evill of man can a dispence be given; for if *the Law were ordained unto life,* Ro. 7. 10. how can the same God publish dispences against that Law, which must needs be unto death? Absurd and monstrous would that dispence be, if any Judge or Law should give it a man to cut his own throat, or to damne himselfe. Dispence therefore presupposes full pardon, or els it is not a dispence, but a most baneful & bloody snare. And why should God enter covnant with a people to be holy, as *the Command is holy, and just, and good, Ro.* 7. 12. and yet suffer an impure and treacherous dispence to mislead and betray them under the vizard of Law to a legitimate practice of uncleannesse. God is no covnant breaker, he cannot doe this. [41]

Rivetus, a diligent and learned Writer, having well waigh'd what hath been written by those founders of dispence, and finding the small agreement among them, would fain work himselfe aloof these rocks and quicksands, and thinks it best to conclude that God certainly did dispence, but by some way to us unknown, and so to leave it.[4] But to this I oppose, that a Christian by no meanes ought rest himselfe in such an ignorance; whereby so many absurdities will strait reflect both against the purity, justice, and wisdome of God, the end also both of Law and Gospel, and the comparison of them both together. God indeed in some wayes of his providence, is high and secret past finding out: but in the delivery and execution of his Law, especially in the managing of a duty so daily and so familiar as this is wherof we reason, hath plain anough reveal'd himselfe, and requires the observance therof not otherwise then to the law of nature and of equity imprinted in us seems correspondent. And hee hath taught us to love and to extoll his Lawes, not onely as they are his, but as they are just and good to every wise

---

[4] See *Theologicae & Scholasticae Exercitationes* (Leyden, 1633), pp. 222–30. Rivetus arrives at his conclusion after an extended discussion of Old Testament polygamy. Since polygamy, like divorce, is contrary to the original institution of marriage, the practice of the patriarchs must have been "by God's dispensation, permission, or tolerance" ("sive de dispensatione, sive de permissione, sive de tolerantia Dei"). For Christians the important point is that "Christ has recalled us to the first institution" (p. 228).

and sober understanding. Therefore *Abraham* ev'n to the face of God himselfe, seem'd to doubt of divine justice, if it should swerve from that irradiation wherwith it had enlight'ned the mind of man, and bound it selfe to observe its own rule. *Wilt thou destroy the righteous with the wicked? That be far from thee; shall not the Judge of the earth doe right?* [5] Therby declaring that God hath created a righteousnesse in right it selfe, against which he cannot doe. So *David,* Psal. 119. *The testimonies which thou hast commanded are righteous and very faithfull; thy word is very pure, therfore thy servant loveth it.* [6] Not onely then for the authours sake, but for its owne purity. *He is faithfull,* saith S. *Paul, he cannot deny himselfe,* [7] that is, cannot deny his own promises, cannot but be true to his own rules. He often pleads with men the uprightnesse of his ways by their own principles. How should we imitate him els to *be perfect as he is perfect.* [8] If at pleasure hee can dispence with golden Poetick ages of such pleasing licence, as in the fabl'd reign of old *Saturn.* [9] And this perhaps before the Law might have some covert; [10] but under such an undispencing covenant as *Moses* made with them, and not to tell us why and wherfore indulgence, cannot give quiet to the brest of any intelligent man. We must be resolv'd how the law can be pure and perspicuous, and yet throw a polluted skirt over these *Eleusinian* mysteries, [11] that no man can utter what they mean: worse in this then the worst obscenities of heathen superstition; for their filthines was hid, but the mystick reason therof known to their Sages: But [42] this Jewish imputed filthinesse was daily and open, but the reason of it is not known to our Divines. We know of no designe the Gospel can have to impose new righteousnes upon works, but to remit the old by faith without works, if we mean justifying works: [12] we know no mystery our Saviour could have to lay new bonds upon mariage in the covnant of grace which himselfe had loosn'd to the severity of law. So that *Rivetus* may

[5] Genesis 18:23–25.　　[6] Verses 138, 140.

[7] II Timothy 2:13.　　[8] Matthew 5:48.

[9] *Cf.* "Il Penseroso," 25–26: "in *Saturns* raign, / Such mixture was not held a stain." The Golden Age of Saturn is described in Ovid, *Metamorphoses,* I, 89–112.

[10] Pretext, justification.

[11] Secret rites in honor of Demeter and Persephone, first celebrated at Eleusis in Attica.

[12] *Cf.* Galatians 2:16.

pardon us if we cannot bee contented with his non-solution to remain in such a peck of incertainties and doubts so dangerous and gastly [13] to the fundamentals of our faith.

CHAP. V.

What a Dispensation is.

T HERFORE to get some better satisfaction, we must proceed to enquire as diligently as we can, what a dispensation is, which I find to be either properly so call'd, or improperly. Improperly so call'd, is rather a particular and exceptive law absolving and disobliging from a more general command for some just and reasonable cause. As *Numb.* 9. they who were unclean, or in a journey, had leave to keep the passover, in the second moneth, but otherwise ever in the first. As for that in *Leviticus* of marying the brothers wife, it was a penall statute rather then a dispense; and commands nothing injurious or in it selfe unclean, onely preferres a speciall reason of charitie, before an institutive decencie, and perhaps is meant for life time onely, as is exprest beneath in the prohibition of taking two sisters.[1] What other edict of *Moses,* carrying but the semblance of a Law in any other kind, may beare the name of a dispence, I have not readily to instance. But a dispensation most properly is some particular accident rarely happ'ning and therfore not specify'd in the Law, but left to the decision of charity, ev'n under the bondage of Jewish rites, much more under the liberty of the Gospel. Thus did *David enter into the house of God, and*

---

[13] Frightful, shocking.

[1] This sentence, as it stands, is so obscure as to suggest a hiatus in the text. Unstated but evidently in the background of Milton's thought is the injunction of Deuteronomy 25:5: "If brethren dwell together, and one of them die, and have no child, the wife of the dead shall not marry without unto a stranger: her husband's brother shall go in unto her, and take her to him to wife, and perform the duty of an husband's brother unto her." Seemingly this contradicts the prohibition of marriage with a brother's wife set forth in Leviticus 18:16. Milton offers two explanations: (1) the command in Deuteronomy was a charitable exception to the general rule; (2) the rule itself was perhaps intended to apply only during the life of the first husband. For the latter explanation he finds ground in Leviticus 18:18: "Neither shalt thou take a wife to her sister . . . in her life time."

did eat the Shew bread, he and his followers, which was ceremoni-ally *unlawfull.*[2] Of such dispenses as these it was that *Verdune* the *French* Divine so gravely disputed in the Councell of *Trent* against Friar *Adrian,* who held that the Pope might dispence with any thing. *It is a fond perswasion,* saith *Verdune, that dispencing is a favour, nay it is as good distributive justice, as what is most, and the Priest sins if he give it not: for it is nothing else but a right interpretation of law.*[3] Thus farre that I can learn touching this matter wholsomly decreed. But that God who is the giver of every good and perfect gift, *James* 1.[4] should give out a rule and directory [43] to sin by, should enact a dispensation as long liv'd as a law wherby to live in priviledg'd adultery for hardnes of heart, and yet this obdurat dis-ease cannot bee conceiv'd how it was the more amended by this unclean remedy, is the most deadly and Scorpion like gift[5] that the enemy of mankind could have given to any miserable sinner, and is rather such a dispence as that was which the serpent gave to our first parents. God gave Quails in his wrath,[6] and Kings in his wrath,[7] yet neither of these things evill in themselves, but that hee whose eyes cannot behold impurity, should in the book of his holy covnant, his most unpassionat law, give licence, and statute for uncontroul'd adultery, although it goe for the receiv'd opinion, I shall ever dis-

[2] *Cf.* Matthew 12:3–4; Mark 2:25–26; Luke 6:3–4.

[3] *Cf. CPB,* p. 189 (*Complete Prose,* I, 467), which shows Milton's source to have been Paolo Sarpi's *Historia del Concilio Tridentino* (1619), p. 658. Sarpi reports that in 1563, during the Council's debate on matrimonial impediments, "*Adrian,* a Dominican Friar . . . touching but lightly the matter in question, discoursed at large of dispensations. . . . Hee sayd that authoritie to dispence in humane lawes, was absolute, and unlimited in the Pope, because he was superiour to them all; and therefore when hee did dispence, though without any cause, the dispensation was notwithstanding to bee held for good: that in divine lawes he had power to dispence, but not without a cause." The reply of John Verdun follows. "Hee granted, that in humane lawes a dispensation might lie, in regard of the law-makers imperfection, who could not foresee all cases. . . . But where God is the Law-giver, from whom nothing is concealed, and by whom no accident is not foreseene, the Law can have no exception. . . . [He added] That the world hath conceived a wrong opinion, that to dispence, is to bestow a favour, and that the dispensation is requisite to be given, as any other part of distributive justice to be exercised; that the Prelate doth offend if he give it not to whom it is due. . . . And, in conclusion, he said, that a dispensation was nothing but a declaration or interpretation of the Law." Tr. Nathanael Brent (1620; UTSL), pp. 675–76.

[4] Verse 17: "Every good gift and every perfect gift is from above."

[5] *Cf.* Luke 11:12.   [6] *Cf.* Numbers 11:31–33.   [7] *Cf.* I Samuel 8:1–9.

swade my soul from such a creed, such an indulgence as the shop of Antichrist never forg'd a baser.

CHAP. VI.

That the Jew had no more right to this supposed dispence, then the Christian hath, and rather not so much.

BUT if we must needs dispence, let us for a while so farre dispence with truth, as to grant that sinne may be dispenc't: yet there will be copious reason found to prove that the Jew had no more right to such a suppos'd indulgence, then the Christian, whether we look at the clear knowledge wherin he liv'd, or the strict performance of works wherto he was bound. Besides visions and prophesies they had the Law of God, which in the Psalmes and Proverbs is chiefly prais'd for surenesse and certainty both easie and perfect to the enlightning of the simple.[1] How could it be so obscure then, or they so sottishly blind in this plain morall and houshold duty? They had the same precepts about mariage, Christ added nothing to their clearnesse, for that had argu'd them imperfect; hee opens not the Law, but removes the Pharisaick mists rais'd between the law and the peoples eyes: the onely sentence which he addes, *What God hath joyn'd let no man put asunder,*[2] is as obscure as any clause fetcht out of *Genesis,* and hath encreast a yet undecided controversie of *Clandestine* mariages.[3] If we examine over all his sayings, we shall find him not so much interpreting the Law with his words, as referring his owne words to be interpreted by the Law, and oftner obscures his mind in short, and vehement, and compact sentences, to blind and puzzle them the more who could not understand the Law.[4] The Jewes therfore were as little to be dispenc't with for lack of morall knowledge, as we.

[1] See, for example, Psalms 19:7 and Proverbs 22:20–21.
[2] Matthew 19:6.
[3] *Cf.* CPB, p. 114 (*Complete Prose,* I, 413) for a reference by Milton to Thuanus on the illegality of secret marriages. Such marriages were generally held valid by the Church although strongly condemned. Sarpi comments on the conflicting opinions set forth at the Council of Trent (*History of the Council of Trent,* tr. Brent, 1620, p. 783).
[4] The point is documented in *Tetrachordon,* below, p. 642 ff.

Next, none I think will deny, but that they were as much bound [44] to perform the Law as any Christian. That severe and rigorous knife not sparing the tender fore-skin of any male infant, to carve upon his flesh the mark of that strict and pure covnant wherinto he enter'd, might give us to understand anough against the fancie of dispencing.[5] S. *Paul* testifies that every *circumcis'd man is a debtor to the whole law,* Gal. 5. or els *circumcision is in vain,* Rom. 2. 25.[6] How vain then and how preposterous must it needs be to exact a circumcision of the Flesh from an infant unto an outward signe of purity, and to dispence an uncircumcision in the soul of a grown man to an inward and reall impurity? How vain again was that law to impose tedious expiations for every slight sinne of ignorance and error, and to priviledge without penance or disturbance an odious crime whether of ignorance or obstinacie? How unjust also inflicting death & extirpation for the mark of circumstantial purenes omitted, and proclaiming all honest and liberall indemnity to the act of a substantiall impurenesse committed, making void the covnant that was made against it. Thus if we consider the tenor of the Law, to be circumcis'd and to perform all, not pardoning so much as the scapes[7] of error and ignorance, and compare this with the condition of the Gospel, beleeve and be baptiz'd;[8] I suppose it cannot bee long ere we grant that the Jew was bound as strictly to the performance of every duty as was possible, and therefore could not be dispenc't with more then the Christian, perhaps not so much.

CHAP. VII.

That the Gospel is apter to dispence then the Law: Paraeus *answer'd.* ◗

<But I answer, admitting it to be a dispensation, yet this is a certain rule, that so long as the cause remains, the dispensation ought: Let it be shewn therfore either in the nature of the Gospel, or of man, why this dispensation should be made void. The Gospel indeed exhorts to highest perfection; but bears with weakest infirm-

---

[5] See Genesis 17:10–14.

[6] *Cf.* the King James reading: "But if thou be a breaker of the law, thy circumcision is made uncircumcision."

[7] Omissions.   [8] See Mark 16:16.

ity more then the Law. The nature of man is as weak, and yet as hard: and that weaknes and hardnes as unfit, and as unteachable to be harshly dealt with as [24] ever. I [1] but, say they, there is a greater portion of spirit powr'd upon the Gospel which requires perfecter obedience.[2] But that consequence is deceavable; for it is the Law that is the exacter of our obedience ev'n under the Gospel; [3] how can it then exact concerning divorce, that which it never exacted before? The Gospel is a covnant reveling grace, not commanding a new morality, but assuring justification by faith only, contented if we endeavour to square our moral duty by those wise and equal Mosaick rules, which were as perfect as strict and as unpardonable to the *Jews*, as to us; otherwise the law were unjust, giving grace of pardon without the Gospel, or if it give allowance without pardon, it would be dissolute and deceitfull; saying in general, *do this and live;* [4] and yet deceaving and damning with obscure and hollow permissions. Wee find also by experience that the Spirit of God in the Gospel hath been alwaies more effectual in the illumination of our minds to the gift of faith, then in the moving of our wills to any excellence of vertue, either above the *Jews* or the Heathen.[5] Hence those indulgences in the Gospel; *All cannot receive this saying; Every man hath his proper gift,* with strict charges not to lay on yokes which our Fathers could not bear.[6]

But this that *Moses* suffer'd for the hardnes of thir hearts he suffer'd not by that enacted dispensation, farre be it, but by a meer accidental sufferance of undiscover'd hypocrites, who made ill use of that Law; for that God should enact a dispensation for hard hearts to do that wherby they must live in priviledg'd adultery, however it go for the receav'd opinion, I shall ever disswade my self from so much hardihood as to beleeve: Certainly this is not the

---

[1] Aye.

[2] In the revision (below, p. 304) this contention is ascribed to Paraeus.

[3] *Cf.* Perkins, *A Commentarie or Exposition upon the Five First Chapters of the Epistle to the Galatians (Works,* 1609–13, II, 237): "But I say againe, that the law written in our hearts is still the law of *Moses.*"

[4] Genesis 42:18.

[5] This sentence is not repeated in 1644. For comment on the deletion and the corresponding shift of emphasis in the revision, see Arthur E. Barker, *Milton and the Puritan Dilemma* (Toronto: University of Toronto Press, 1942), pp. 365–66, n. 81; also Barker, "Christian Liberty in Milton's Divorce Pamphlets," *MLR,* XXXV (1940), 157–59.

[6] Matthew 19:11; I Corinthians 7:7; Acts 15:10.

manner of God, whose pure eyes cannot behold, much lesse his perfect Laws dispence with such impurity; [7] and if we consider well, we shall finde that all dispensations are either to avoid wors inconveniences, or to support infirm consciences for a time; but that a dispensation should be as long liv'd as a Law to tolerate adultery for hardnes of heart, both sins perhaps of like degree, and yet this obdurat disease cannot be conceav'd how it is the more amended by this unclean remedy, is a notion of that extravagance [8] from the sage principles of piety, that who considers throughly, cannot but admire, how this hath been digested all this while.>

◗ If then the Law wil afford no reason why the Jew should be more gently dealt with then the Christian, then surely the Gospel can afford as little why the Christian should be lesse gently dealt with then the Jew. The Gospell indeed exhorts to highest perfection but beares with weakest infirmity more then the Law. Hence those indulgencies, *All cannot receive this saying. Every man hath his proper gift,* with expresse charges not to *lay on yokes which our fathers could not beare.* The nature of man still is as weak and yet as hard, and that weaknesse and hardnesse as unfit and as unteachable to bee harshly us'd as ever. I but saith *Paraeus,* there is a greater portion of Spirit powr'd upon the Gospel, which requires from us perfecter obedience.[9] I answer, This does not prove that the law therfore might give allowance to sinne more then the Gospel; and if it were no sin, wee know it the work of the Spirit to *mortifie our corrupt desires and* [45] *evill concupiscence;* [10] but not to root up our naturall affections and disaffections moving to and fro ev'n in wisest men upon just and necessary reasons which were the true ground of that *Mosaick* dispence, and is the utmost extent of our pleading. What is more or lesse perfect we dispute not, but what is sinne or no sinne; and in that I still affirm the Law requir'd as perfect obedience as the Gospell: besides that the prime end of the Gospel is not so much to exact our obedience, as to reveal grace

[7] *Cf.* Habakkuk 1:13.

[8] Deviation. *NED* cites.

[9] *Cf. In Priorem ad Corinthios Epistolam S. Pauli Commentarius (Operum Theologicorum* [Frankfurt, 1628], II, 488): "Now surely among Christians, to whom a more abundant spirit and ampler grace is given, men ought to manifest greater patience and charity towards their wives; likewise from wives there is required fuller obedience and a more modest behavior towards their husbands."

[10] *Cf.* Colossians 3:5.

and the satisfaction of our disobedience.[11] What is now exacted from us, it is the accusing Law that does it ev'n yet under the Gospell; but cannot bee more extreme to us now, then to the Jewes of old: for the Law ever was of works, and the Gospell ever was of grace.

Either then the Law by harmlesse and needfull dispences which the Gospel is now made to deny, must have anticipated and exceeded the grace of the Gospel, or els must be found to have giv'n politick and superficial graces without real pardon, saying in general doe this and live, and yet deceiving and damning under hand, with unsound and hollow permissions, which is utterly abhorring from the end of all Law, as hath bin shewd. But if those indulgences were safe and sinles out of tendernes and compassion, as indeed they were, and yet shall be abrogated by the Gospel, then the Law, whose end is by rigor to magnifie grace, shall it self give grace, and pluck a faire plume from the Gospel, instead of hastning us thither, alluring us from it. And wheras the terror of the Law was as a servant to amplifie and illustrat the mildnesse of grace; now the unmildnesse of Evangelick grace shall turn servant to declare the grace and mildnesse of the rigorous Law. The Law was harsh to extoll the grace of the Gospel, and now the Gospel by a new affected strictnes of her own, shall extenuate the grace, which her self offers. For by exacting a duty which the Law dispenc't, if we perform it, then is grace diminisht, by how much performance advances, unlesse the Apostle argue wrong: [12] if we perform it not, and perish for not performing, then are the conditions of grace harder then those of rigor. If through Faith and Repentance we perish not, yet grace still remains the lesse, by requiring that which rigor did not require, or at least not so strictly. Thus much therfore to *Paraeus*, that if the Gospel require perfecter obedience then the Law as a duty, it exalts the Law and debases it self, which is dishonourable to the work of our Redemption. Seeing therfore that all the causes of any allowance that the Jews might have, remain as well to the Christians, this is a

---

[11] *Cf.* Perkins, *Commentarie or Exposition upon . . . Galatians* (*Works*, 1609–13, II, 236): "The law promiseth life to him that performes perfect obedience, and that for his workes. The Gospell promiseth life to him that doth nothing in the cause of his salvation, but onely beleeves in Christ: and it promiseth salvation to him that beleeveth, yet not for his faith, or for any worke else, but for the merit of Christ. The law then requires doing to salvation, and the Gospell beleeving, and nothing else."

[12] *Cf.* Romans 11:6.

certain rule, that so [46] long as the causes remain the allowance ought. And having thus at length enquir'd the truth concerning Law and dispence, their ends, their uses, their limits, and in what manner both Jew and Christian stands liable to the one, or capable of the other, we may safely conclude, that to affirm the giving of any law, or law-like dispence to sin for hardnesse of heart, is a doctrine of that extravagance from the sage principles of piety, that who so considers throughly, cannot but admire, how this hath been digested all this while.

CHAP. VIII.

The true sence how Moses suffer'd divorce for hardnesse of heart. ◄

W HAT * may we doe then to salve this seeming inconsistence? I must not dissemble that I am confident it can be don no other way then this. [25]

Moses, Deut. 24. 1. establisht a grave and prudent Law, full of moral equity, full of due consideration towards nature, that cannot be resisted; a Law consenting with the Laws of wisest men and civilest nations. That when a man hath maried a wife, if it come to passe he cannot love her by reason of some displeasing natural quality or unfitnes in her, let him write her a bill of divorce. The intent of which Law undoubtedly was this, that if any good and peaceable man should discover some helples disagreement or dislike either of mind or body, wherby he could not cherfully perform the duty of a husband without the perpetual dissembling of offence and disturbance to his spirit, rather then to live uncomfortably and unhappily both to himself and to his wife, rather then to continue undertaking a duty which he could not possibly discharge, he might dismisse her whom he could not tolerably, and so not conscionably retain. And this Law the Spirit of God by the mouth of *Salomon,* Pro. 30. 21. 23. testifies to be a good and a necessary Law; by granting it, that <to *dwell with a hated woman* (for *hated* the hebrew word signifies) *is a thing that nature cannot endure.*> ◄ *a hated woman* (for so the hebrew word signifies, rather then odious though it come all to one)

---

* No paragraph division in 1643.

that a hated woman when she is maried, is a thing that the earth cannot beare.[1] ◀ What follows then but that ♦ the charitable ◀ Law must remedy what nature cannot undergoe. Now that many licentious and hard-hearted men took hold of this Law to cloak thir bad purposes, is nothing strange to beleeve. And these were they, not for whom *Moses* made the Law, God forbid, but whose hardnes of heart taking ill advantage by this Law he held it better to suffer as by accident, where it could not be detected, rather then good men ♦ [47] ◀ should loose their just and lawfull privilege of remedy: Christ therfore having to answer these tempting Pharises, according as his custom was, not meaning to inform their proud ignorance what *Moses* did in the true intent of the Law, which they had ill cited, suppressing the true cause for which *Moses* gave it, and extending it to every slight matter, tells them thir own, what *Moses* was forc't to suffer by their abuse of his Law. Which is yet more plain if wee mark that our Saviour in the fifth of *Matth.* cites not the Law of *Moses,* but the Pharisaical tradition falsly grounded upon that law.[2] And in those other places, *Chap.* 19. & *Mark* 10. the Pharises cite the Law, but conceale the wise and human reason there exprest; which our Saviour corrects not in them whose pride deserv'd not his instruction, only returns them what is proper to them; *Moses for the hardnes of your hearts sufferd you,* that is, such as you *to put away your wives;*[3] and *to you he wrote this precept*[4] for that cause, which [26] (*to you*) must be read with an impression,[5] and understood limitedly of such as cover'd ill purposes under that Law; for it was seasonable that they should hear their own unbounded licence rebuk't, but not seasonable for them to hear a good mans requisit liberty explain'd. ♦ But us he hath taught better, if we have eares to hear. He himselfe acknowledg'd it to be a Law, *Mark* 10. and being a law of God, it must have an undoubted *end of charity, which may be us'd with a pure heart, a good con-*

---

[1] *Cf.* Proverbs 30:21–23 in the King James Version. The Hebrew word there translated "odious" has the literal meaning of "hated," as Milton says, and is so translated in Genesis 29:31 and Deuteronomy 21:15. See Crawford H. Toy, *A Critical and Exegetical Commentary on the Book of Proverbs* (New York, 1903), p. 533. The Revised Standard translates it "unloved."

[2] Verse 31: "It hath been said, Whosoever shall put away his wife, let him give her a writing of divorcement."

[3] Matthew 19:8.   [4] Mark 10:5.

[5] Stress, emphasis. *NED* cites this example.

science, and faith unfained, as was heard: it cannot allow sin, but is purposely to resist sin, as by the same chapter to *Timothy* appears. There we learn also *that the Law is good, if a man use it lawfully.*[6] Out of doubt then there must be a certain good in this Law which *Moses* willingly allow'd; and there might be an unlaw-full use made thereof by hypocrits; and that was it which *Moses* unwillingly suffer'd; fore seeing it in general, but not able to discern it in particulars. Christ therfore mentions not here what *Moses* and the Law intended: for good men might know that by many other rules: and the scornfull Pharises were not fit to be told, untill they could imploy that knowledge they had, lesse abusively. Only he acquaints them with what *Moses* by them was put to suffer.

CHAP. IX.

The words of the Institution how to be understood; and of our Saviours answer to his Disciples. ◀

<And to amaze them the more,> ◆ And to entertain a little their overweening arrogance as best befitted, and to amaze them yet furder, ◀ because <the Pharises> ◆ they ◀ thought it no hard matter to fulfill the Law, he draws them up to that unseparable ◆ [48] ◀ institution which God ordaind in the beginning before the fall when man and woman were both perfect, and could have no cause to separate: just as in the same Chap.[1] he stands not to contend with the arrogant young man who boasted his observance of the whole Law, whether he had indeed kept it or not, but skrues him up higher,[2] to a task of that perfection, which no man is bound to imitate. And in like manner that pattern of the first institution he set before the opinionative Pharises to dazle them and not to bind us. For this is a solid rule that every command giv'n with a reason, binds our obedience no otherwise then that reason holds.[3] Of this sort was that command in *Eden; Therfore shall a man cleave to his wife, and*

---

[6] *Cf.* I Timothy 1:5–8.

[1] Matthew 19:16–22.

[2] That is, tunes him (like a stringed instrument) to a higher pitch.

[3] *Cf.* Milton's entry from Sarpi in *CPB,* p. 179 (*Complete Prose,* I, 424), concerning the effect of reasons added to laws.

they shall be one flesh: [4] which we see is no absolute command, but
with an inference, *Therfore:* the reason then must be first consider'd,
that our obedience be not mis-obedience. The first is, for it is
not single, because the wife is to the husband *flesh of his flesh,* as
in the verse going before. But this reason cannot be sufficient of it
self; for why then should he for his wife leave his father and mother,
with whom he is farre *more flesh of flesh and bone of bone,* as being
made of their substance. And besides it can be but a sorry and
ignoble society of life, whose unseparable injunction depends meerly
upon flesh & bones.[5] Therfore we must look higher, since Christ
himself recalls us to the beginning, and we shall finde that the primitive reason of never divorcing, was that sacred and not vain promise of God to remedy mans lonelines by *making him a <help meet>*
◆ *meet help* ◀ *for him,*[6] though not now in perfection, as at first,
yet still in proportion as things now are. And this is repeated *ver.* 20.
when all other creatures were fitly associated & brought to *Adam,*
as if the divine power had bin in some care and deep thought, because *there was not yet found a help meet for man.* And can wee so
slightly depresse the all-wise purpose of a deliberating God, as if
his consultation had produc't no other good for man, but to joyn
him with an accidentall companion of propagation, which his sudden
word had already made for every beast? nay a farre lesse good to
man it will be found, if she must at all aventures [27] be fasten'd
upon him individually.[7] And therefore even plain sense and equity,
and, which is above them both, the all-interpreting voice of Charity
her self cries loud that this primitive reason, this consulted promise
of God *to make a meet help,* is the onely cause that gives authority
to this command of not divorcing, to be a command. And it might
be further added, that if the true definition of a wife were askt in
good earnest, this clause of beeing *a meet help* would shew it selfe
◆ [49] ◀ so necessary, and so essential in that demonstrative argument, that it might be logically concluded, therfore shee who naturally & perpetually is no meet help, can be no wife; which cleerly
takes away the difficulty of dismissing such a one. ◆ If this be not
thought anough, I answer yet furder, that mariage, unlesse it mean

---

[4] Genesis 2:24.
[5] In *Paradise Lost,* VIII, 499, Milton makes a significant addition to the scriptural figure: "And they shall be one Flesh, one Heart, one Soule."
[6] Genesis 2:18.   [7] Indivisibly, inseparably.

a fit and tolerable mariage, is not inseparable neither by nature nor institution. Not by nature for then those Mosaick divorces had bin against nature, if separable and inseparable be contraries, as who doubts they be: and what is against nature is against Law, if soundest Philosophy abuse us not: [8] by this reckning *Moses* should bee most unmosaick, that is, most illegal, not to say most unnaturall. Nor is it inseparable by the first institution: for then no second institution in the same Law for so many causes could dissolve it: it being most unworthy a human (as *Plato's* judgement is in the fourth book of his Lawes) much more a divine Law-giver to write two several decrees upon the same thing.[9] But what would *Plato* have deem'd if the one of these were good, the other evill to be done? Lastly, suppose it bee inseparable by institution, yet in competition with higher things, as religion and charity in mainest matters, and when the chiefe end is frustrat for which it was ordain'd, as hath been shown, if still it must remain inseparable, it holds a strange and lawlesse propriety from all other works of God under heaven. From these many considerations we may safely gather, ◀ <Hence is manifest,> that so much of the first institution as our Saviour mentions, for he mentions not all, was but to quell and put to nonplus the tempting Pharises; and to lay open their ignorance and shallow understanding of the Scriptures. For, saith he, *have ye not read that he which made them at the beginning, made them male and female, and said, for this cause shall a man cleave to his wife?* [10] which these blind usurpers of *Moses* chair could not gainsay: as if this single respect of male and female were sufficient against a thousand inconveniences and mischiefs to clogge a rational creature to his endles sorrow unrelinquishably ▶, under the guilefull superscription of his intended solace and comfort ◀. What if they had thus answer'd, Master if thou <intend> ▶ mean ◀ to make wedlock as inseparable as it was from the beginning, let it be made also a fit society, as God <intended> ▶ meant ◀ it, which wee shall soon understand it ought to be, if thou recite the whole reason of the Law.

[8] *Cf.*, for example, Cicero, *De Legibus*, I, vi, tr. C. W. Keyes (New York and London: Loeb Classical Library, 1928), p. 317: "Law is the highest reason, implanted in Nature, which commands what ought to be done and forbids the opposite."

[9] See *Laws*, IV, 719, tr. Jowett: "The legislator must give not two rules about the same thing, but one only."

[10] Matthew 19:4–5.

Doubtles our Saviour had applauded their just answer. For then they had expounded this command of Paradise, even as *Moses* himself expounds it by his laws of divorce, that is, with due and wise regard had to the premises and reasons of the first ◗ [50] ◖ command, according to which, without unclean and temporizing permissions he instructs us in this imperfect state what wee may lawfully doe about divorce.

But if it be thought that the Disciples offended at the rigor of Christs answer, could yet obtain no mitigation of the former sentence pronounc't to the Pharises, it may be fully answer'd, that our Saviour continues the same reply to his Disciples, as men leaven'd with the same customary licence, which the Pharises maintain'd; and displeas'd at the removing of a traditional abuse wherto they had so long not unwillingly bin us'd: it was no time then to contend with their slow and prejudicial belief, in a thing wherin an ordinary [28] measure of light in Scripture, with some attention might afterwards inform them well anough. ◗ And yet ere Christ had finisht this argument, they might have pickt out of his own concluding words, an answer more to their minds, and in effect the same with that which hath been all this while entreating audience. *All men,* said he, *cannot receive this saying, save they to whom it is given, he that is able to receive it let him receive it.*[11] What saying is this which is left to a mans choice to receive or not receive? What but the married life. Was our Saviour then so mild and favourable to the weakneſse of a single man, and is he turn'd on the sudden so rigorous and inexorable to the distresses and extremities of an ill wedded man? Did hee so graciously give leave to change the better single life for the worse maried life? Did he open so to us this hazardous and accidentall doore of mariage to shut upon us like the gate of death without retracting or returning, without permitting to change the worst, most insupportable, most unchristian mischance of mariage for all the mischiefes and sorrowes that can ensue, being an ordinance which was especially giv'n as a cordial and exhilarating cup of solace the better to beare our other crosses and afflictions? questionlesse this were a hardheartednesse of undivorcing, worse then that in the Jewes which they say extorted the allowance from *Moses,* and is utterly dissonant from all the doctrine of our Sav-

[11] Matthew 19:11–12.

iour. ◀ After these considerations ◗ therfore ◀ to take a law out of
Paradise giv'n in time of original perfection, and to take it barely
without those just and equal inferences and reasons which mainly
establish it, nor so much as admitting those needfull & safe allowances wherwith *Moses* himself interprets it to the faln condition of
man, argues nothing in us but rashnes and contempt of those means
that God left us in his pure and chast Law, without which it will
not be pos- ◗ [51] ◀ sible for us to perform the strict imposition
of this command: or if we strive beyond our strength, wee shall
strive to obay it otherwise then God commands it. And lamented
experience daily teaches the bitter and vain fruits of this our presumption, forcing men in a thing wherin wee are not able to judge
either of their strength, or ◗ of ◀ their sufferance. Whom neither one
vice nor other by naturall addiction, but only mariage ruins, which
doubtles is not the fault of that ordinance, for God gave it as a
blessing, nor always of mans mis-choosing; it beeing an error above
wisdom to prevent, as examples of wisest men so mistaken manifest:
it is the fault therfore of a pervers opinion that will have it continu'd in despight of nature and reason, when indeed it was never
truly joynd. All those expositers upon the fifth of *Mat.* confesse the
Law of *Moses* to be the Law of the Lord, wherin no addition or
diminution hath place,[12] yet coming to the point of divorce, as if
they fear'd not to be call'd lest in the kingdom of heav'n,[13] any
slight evasion will content them to reconcile those contradictions
which they make between Christ and *Moses,* between Christ and
Christ.

[12] See Matthew Poole, *Synopsis Criticorum* (5 vols., Frankfurt, 1678), IV,
cols. 116–21. Perkins, in his *Godly and Learned Exposition* (*Works,* 1609–13,
III, 1), accuses "the Popish Teachers" of holding "that Christ herein propound-
eth a new Law, farre more perfect then the Law of Moses." "But they erre and
are deceived: for Christs intent is to cleare the true meaning of *Moses* and the
Prophets, which was corrupted by the false glosse of the Jewish teachers; and
not to adde any new Law or counsell thereunto, . . . Againe, there cannot be
given unto man a more perfect rule then *Moses* Law, the summe and scope
whereof is, *To love God with all the heart, with all the soule, and with all the
strength;* then which there cannot be greater perfection in a creature."

[13] *Cf.* Matthew 5:19.

♦ CHAP. X.

The vain shift of those who make the law of divorce to bee onely the premises of a succeeding law. ◀

SOME will have it no Law, but the granted premises of another Law following,[1] contrary to the words of Christ *Mark* 10.5. and all other translations of gravest authority, who render it in form of a Law; agreeable to *Malach.* 2. 16. as it is most anciently and modernly expounded.[2] Besides the bill of divorce ♦, and the particular occasion therein mention'd, ◀ declares it to be orderly & legal. And what avails this to make the matter more righteous, if such an adulterous condition shall be mention'd to build a Law upon without either punishment or so much as forbidding, they pretend it is implicitly reprov'd in these words, *Deut.* 24. 4. *after she is defil'd;* but who sees not that this defilement is only in respect of returning to her former husband after an intermixt mariage; els why was not the *defiling* condition first forbidden, which [29] would have sav'd the labour of this after law; nor is it seemly or piously attributed to the justice of God and his known hatred of sin, that such a hainous fault as this through all the Law should be only wip't with an implicit and oblique touch (which yet is falsly suppos'd) & that his ♦ [52] ◀ peculiar people should be let wallow in adulterous mariages almost two thousand yeares for want of a direct Law to prohibit them; tis rather to be confidently assum'd that this was granted to apparent necessities, as being of unquestionable right and reason in the Law of nature, in that it still passes without inhibition, ev'n when greatest cause is giv'n us to expect it should be directly forbidd'n.

[1] This is the view of Calvin, who insists that the first four verses of Deuteronomy 24 must be read as a unit, the first three constituting the conditions of the fourth. See his *Mosis Reliqui Libri Quatuor* (Geneva, 1563), p. 364. See also *Synopsis Criticorum,* I, cols. 778–79.

[2] See above, p. 257, n. 16.

♦ CHAP. XI.

The other shift of saying divorce was permitted by Law, but not approv'd. More of the Institution. ♦

BUT * it was not approv'd, so much the wors that it was allow'd, as if sin had overmasterd the law of God, to conform her steddy and strait rule to sins crookednes, which is impossible. Besides, what needed a positive grant of that which was not approv'd? it restrain'd no liberty to him that could but use a little fraud, it had bin better silenc't, unlesse it were approv'd in some case or other. ♦ But still it was not approv'd. Miserable excusers! He who doth evil that good may come thereby, approves not what he doth, and yet the grand rule forbids him, and counts *his damnation* just if hee doe it.[1] The Sorceresse *Medea* did not approve her owne evill doings, yet lookt not to be excus'd for that;[2] and it is the constant opinion of *Plato* in *Protagoras* and other of his dialogues agreeing with that proverbiall sentence among the *Greeks,* that no *man is wicked willingly;*[3] which also the *Peripateticks* doe rather distinguish then deny.[4] What great thank then if any man reputed wise and constant, will neither doe nor permit others under his charge to doe that which hee approves not, especially in matter of sinne. But for a Judge, but for a Magistrate the Shepheard of his people to surrender up his approbation against law & his own judgment to the obstinacie of his heard, what more un-Judge-like, more un-Magistrate-like, and in warre

---

* No paragraph division in 1643.

[1] *Cf.* Romans 3:8.

[2] *Cf.* Euripides, *Medea,* ll. 1078–80, tr. Gilbert Murray (New York, 1910), p. 61: "Yea, I know to what bad things I go, but louder than all thought doth cry Anger, which maketh man's worst misery." Murray, in a note on the passage (*ibid.,* p. 94), remarks that "this expression of double consciousness was immensely famous in antiquity. It is quoted by Lucian, Plutarch, Clement, Galen, Synesius, Hierocles, Arrian, Simplicius, besides being imitated, *e.g.,* by Ovid: 'video meliora proboque, Deteriora sequor.' "

[3] *Cf. Protagoras,* 354–58; also *Meno,* 77–78, *Timaeus,* 86.

[4] *Cf. Nicomachean Ethics,* III, 5; also VII, 1–2, and 8–9. The distinction between the Platonic and Aristotelian point of view is somewhat sharper than Milton implies. For a comment on the underlying difference between Milton's ethic and Aristotle's see Ernest Sirluck, "Milton Revises *The Faerie Queene,*" *MP,* XLVIII (1950), 90–96.

more un-commander-like? Twice in a short time it was the un-doing of the Roman State, first when *Pompey,* next when *Marcus Brutus* had not magnanimity anough but to make so poore a resig-nation of what they approv'd, to what the boisterous Tribunes and Souldiers bawl'd for.[5] Twice it was the saving of two the greatest Common-wealths in the world, of *Athens* by *Themistocles* at the Sea fight of *Salamis;* of *Rome* by *Fabius Maximus* in the *Punick* warre, for that these two matchlesse Generalls had the fortitude at home against the rashnes and the clamours of their own Captains and confederates to withstand the doing or permitting of what they [53] could not approve in the duty of their great command.[6] Thus farre of civill prudence. But when we speak of sinne, let us look againe upon the old reverend *Eli;* who in his heavie punishment found no difference between the doing and permitting of what he did not approve.[7] If hardnesse of heart in the people may be any excuse, why then is *Pilat* branded through all memory? Hee ap-prov'd not what he did, he openly protested, he washt his hands and laboured not a little, ere he would yeeld to the hard hearts of a whole people, both Princes and plebeians importuning & tumulting ev'n to the fear of a revolt.[8] Yet is there any will undertake his cause? If therefore Pilat for suffering but one act of cruelty against law, though with much unwillingnesse testify'd, at the violent demand of a whole Nation, shall stand so black upon record to all posterity? Alas for *Moses!* what shall we say for him, while we are taught to beleeve he suffer'd not one act onely both of cruelty and unclean-nesse in one divorce, but made it a plain and lasting law against law whereby ten thousand acts accounted both cruell and unclean,

---

[5] Pompey's decision to offer battle to Caesar at Pharsalia (48 B.C.) was ap-parently contrary to his own judgment. Plutarch says that he "yielded to the diseased passions of his followers." Similarly Brutus was persuaded by Cassius and others to take the lead in the assassination of Caesar. See Plutarch, *Pompey,* LXVII; *Brutus,* VII–X, in *Lives,* tr. Bernadotte Perrin (11 vols., New York and London: Loeb Classical Library, 1914–43), V, 291–93; IV, 139–49.

[6] Themistocles defeated the Persian fleet of Xerxes at Salamis (480 B.C.) by inducing a pitched battle after his associates had determined on withdrawal. In the Second Punic War (218–201 B.C.), Fabius persisted, despite popular dis-approval, in a strategy of delaying action against Hannibal. See Plutarch, *Themistocles,* XI–XV, *Fabius Maximus,* V–XIII, in *Lives,* tr. Perrin, II, 33–45, III, 131–59.

[7] *Cf.* I Samuel 3:12–13.

[8] *Cf.* Matthew 27:22–26.

might be daily committed, and this without the least suit or petition of the people that wee can read of.

And ◀ Can wee conceave without vile thoughts, that the majesty and holines of God could endure so many ages to gratifie a stubborn people in the practice of a foul polluting sin, and could he expect they should abstain, he not signifying his mind in a plain command, at such time especially when he was framing their laws and them to all possible perfection? But they were to look back to the first institution, nay rather why was not that individual institution brought out of Paradise, as was that of the Sabbath, and repeated in the body of the Law,[9] that men might have understood it to be a command? for that any sentence that bears the resemblance of a precept, set there so out of place in another world at such a distance from the whole Law, and not once mention'd there, should be an obliging command to us, is very disputable, and perhaps it might be deny'd to be a command without further dispute: however, it commands not absolutely, as hath bin clear'd, but only with reference to that precedent promise of God, which is the very ground of his institution; if that appeare not in some tolerable sort, how can wee affirm such a matrimony to be the same which God instituted! In such an accident it will best behove our sobernes to follow rather what moral *Sinai* prescribes equal to our strength, then fondly to think within our strength all that lost Paradise [10] relates. ◆ [54] ◀

◆ CHAP. XII.

The third shift of them who esteem it a meer judicial Law. Prov'd again to be a Law of moral equity. ◀

ANOTHER while it shall suffice them, that it was not a moral, but a judicial Law, and so was abrogated. Nay rather <was> not abrogated [30] because judicial; which Law the ministery of Christ came not to deale with. And who put it in mans power to exempt, where Christ speaks in general of not abrogat-

[9] *Cf.* Genesis 2:2–3 and Exodus 20:8–11.

[10] Between this phrase and Milton's epic title there is probably no traceable connection, but its use here is not without significance.

ing *the least jot or tittle,* & in special not that of divorce, because
it follows among those Laws which he promis'd expresly not to
abrogate, but to vindicate from abusive traditions ♦: which is most
evidently to be seen in the 16. of *Luke,*[1] where this caution of not
abrogating is inserted immediatly, and not otherwise then purposely,
when no other point of the Law is toucht, but that of divorce ◀. And
if we mark the 31. *ver.* of *Mat.* the 5. he there cites not the Law
of *Moses,* but the licencious Glosse which traduc't the Law;[2]
that therfore which he cited, that he abrogated, and not only
abrogated but disallow'd and flatly condemn'd, which could not be
the Law of *Moses;* for that had bin fouely to the rebuke of his
great servant. To abrogate a Law made with Gods allowance, had
bin to tell us only that such a Law was now to cease, but to refute
it with an ignominious note of civilizing adultery, casts the reprooff, which was meant only to the Pharises, ev'n upon him who
made the Law. But yet if that be judicial which belongs to a civil
Court, this Law is lesse judicial then nine of the ten Commandements; for antiquaries affirm that divorces proceeded among the
Jews without knowledge of the Magistrate, only with hands and
seales under the testimony of some Rabbies to be then present.[3]
♦ *Perkins* in a *Treatise of Conscience* grants, that what in the judicial Law is of common equity, binds also the Christian. And how
to judge of this, prescribes 2. wayes. If wise Nations have enacted
the like decree. Or if it maintain the good of family, Church or
Common-wealth.[4] This therfore is ◀ <And it was indeed> a pure

---

[1] Verses 17–18.

[2] *Cf.* above, p. 307, "the Pharisaical tradition falsly grounded upon that law."
In *Tetrachordon* (below, p. 639), Milton charges the Pharisees with traducing
the law in two ways. "First, by teaching that to give a bill of divorse was all the
duty which that law requir'd, what ever the cause were. Next by running to
divorse for any triviall, accidentall cause; whenas the law evidently stayes in
the grave causes of naturall and immutable dislike."

[3] The requirements, as set forth in the *Mishnah Gittin,* were the writing of a
bill of divorce at the husband's direction, its attestation by two witnesses, and
its delivery to the wife. For full details, see David W. Amram, *The Jewish Law
of Divorce According to Bible and Talmud* (Philadelphia, 1896), pp. 132–85.

[4] See *A Discourse of Conscience* (*Works,* 1609–13, I, 520–21):
"Judicials of common equitie, are such as are made according to the lawe or
instinct of nature common to all men: & these in respect of their substance,
binde the consciences not only of the Jewes, but also of the Gentiles. . . .
"A judiciall law may be knowne to be a lawe of common equity, if either of
these two things be found in it. First, if wise men not onely among the Jews,

moral *economical* Law, too hastily imputed of tolerating sin; being rather so clear in nature and reason, that it was left to a mans own arbitrement to be determin'd between God and his own conscience ♦ ; not only among the Jews, but in every wise nation; the restraint wherof, who is not too thick sighted, may see how hurtfull and distractive it is to the house, the Church and Common-wealth ♦. And that power which Christ never took from the master of family, but rectify'd only to a right and wary use at home, that power the undiscerning ♦ [55] ♦ Canonist hath improperly usurpt into his Court-leet,[5] and bescribbl'd with a thousand trifling impertinencies, which yet have fil'd the life of man with serious trouble and calamity. Yet grant it were of old a judicial Law, it need not be the lesse moral for that, being conversant, as it is, about vertue or vice.[6] And our Saviour disputes not heer the judicature, for that was not his office, but the morality of divorce, whether it be adultery or no; if therfore he touch the law of *Moses* at all, he touches the moral part therof; which is absurd to imagine that the covnant of grace should reform the exact and perfect law of works, eternal and immutable; or if he touch not the Law at all, then is not the allowance therof disallow'd to us.

but also in other nations, have by naturall reason and conscience judged the same to be equall, just, and necessary, and withall, have justified their judgements by enacting lawes for the common wealths, the same in substance with sundrie of the judiciall lawes given to the Jewes: . . . Secondly, a Judiciall hath common equitie, if it serve directly to explaine and confirme any of the ten precepts of the Decalogue: or, if it serve directly to maintaine and uphold any of the three estates, of the family, the common wealth, the Church."

William Perkins (1558–1602), whom Milton mentions by name at two other points in the *Doctrine and Discipline* (below, pp. 320 and 341), was held in particularly high esteem by the Puritans throughout the seventeenth century. At Cambridge, where he spent most of his active life, he gained a great reputation as a teacher and preacher, a reputation afterwards enlarged by his published writings. Although Milton could hardly claim him as an advocate of divorce, he was able to find in several of his works (especially in the *Christian Oeconomie*) material which he applied to his own purposes.

[5] A district court of minor jurisdiction. Milton uses the term in a transferred sense, obviously disparaging.

[6] *Cf.* Perkins, *Discourse* (*Works,* 1609–13, I, 520): "Againe, judicial lawes, so farre foorth as they have in them the generall or common equitie of the law of nature are morall."

♦ CHAP. XIII.

The ridiculous opinion, that divorce was permitted from the custom in Aegypt. That Moses gave not this Law unwillingly. Perkins *confesses this Law was not abrogated.* ♦

Others are so ridiculous as to allege that this licence of divorcing was giv'n them because they were so accustom'd in Egypt.[1] As if an ill custom were to be kept to all posterity; for the dispensation is [31] both universal and of time unlimited, and so indeed no dispensation at all; for the over-dated dispensation of a thing unlawfull, serves for nothing but to encrease hardnes of heart, and makes men but wax more incorrigible, which were a great reproach to be said of any Law or allowance that God should give us. In these opinions it would be more Religion to advise well, lest wee make our selves juster then God, by censuring rashly that for sin which his unspotted Law without rebuke allows, and his people without being conscious of displeasing him have us'd. And if we can think so of *Moses,* as that the Jewish obstinacy could compell him to write such impure permissions against the rule of God & his own judgement, doubtles it was his part to have protested publickly what straits he was driv'n to, and to have declar'd his conscience when he gave any Law against his minde; for the Law is the touch-stone of sin and of conscience,[2] must not be intermixt with corrupt indulgences; for then it looses the greatest praise it has, of being certain and infallible, not leading into error, as all the *Jews* were led by this connivence of *Moses,* if it were a connivence. But still they fly back to the primitive institution, and would have us re-enter Paradise against the sword that guards it.[3] Whom I again thus reply to, that the place in *Genesis* contains the description of a fit and perfect mariage, with ♦ [56] ♦ an interdict of ever divorcing such a union;

[1] Such is the explanation of Paraeus in his commentary on Matthew 5:32; see *Operum Theologicorum* (Frankfurt, 1628), I, 644.

[2] *Cf.* John Downame, *A Guide to Godlynesse* (1622; HEHL), p. 88: "For the law, as it is the rule of our actions, according to which they ought to be wholy conformed, so also it is the rule of our consciences, whereby they discerne whether they be right or crooked, good or evill."

[3] *Cf.* Genesis 3:24; also *Paradise Lost,* XII, 641–44.

319

but where nature is discover'd to have never joyn'd indeed, but vehemently seeks to part, it cannot be there conceav'd that God forbids it; nay he commands it both in the Law and in the Prophet *Malachy*, which is to be our rule. And *Perkins* upon this chap. of *Mat.* deals plainly that our Saviour heer confutes not *Moses* Law, but the false glosses that deprav'd the Law; [4] which being true, *Perkins* must needs grant, that somthing then is left to that law which Christ found no fault with; and what can that be but the conscionable use of such liberty as the plain words import? So that by his own inference, Christ did not absolutely intend to restrain all divorces to the only cause of adultery. This therfore is the true scope of our Saviours will, that he who looks upon the Law concerning divorce, should look also back upon the first institution, that he may endeavour what is perfectest: and he that looks upon the institution should not refuse as sinfull and unlawfull those allowances which God affords him in his following Law; lest he make himself purer then his maker; and presuming above strength, slip into temptations irrecoverably. For this [32] is wonderfull, that in all those decrees concerning mariage, God should never once mention the prime institution to disswade them from divorcing; and that he should forbid smaller sins as opposite to the hardnes of their hearts, and let this adulterous matter of divorce passe ever unreprov'd. This is also to be marvell'd <at>, that seeing Christ did not condemn whatever it was that *Moses* suffer'd, and that therupon the Christian Magistrate permits usury and open stews, & heer with us adultery to be so slightly punisht, which was punisht by death to these hard-hearted *Jews*,[5] why wee should strain thus at the matter of divorce, which may stand so much with charity to permit, and make no scruple to allow usury, esteem'd to be so much against charity.[6] But this it is to embroile

---

[4] *A Godly and Learned Exposition* (*Works*, 1609–13, III, 69): "Here Christ answereth not to *Moses* law, but to the corrupt interpretation of the Scribes and Pharisies, whereby they depraved that law."

[5] *Cf.* Leviticus 20:10.

[6] Perkins, in the same context (*Works*, 1609–13, III, 69), points out that "the law of this Land in practise tolerates usurie, but usurers must not hereupon think that all is safe and wel with them, and that they sinne not in taking ten in the hundred, because the law of the land permits it; for our law tolerates that, for the preventing of greater usurie, when as the law of God doth utterly condemne the same."

our selves against the righteous and all wise judgements and statutes of God; which are not variable and contrarious, as wee would make them, one while permitting and another while forbidding, but are most constant and most harmonious each to other. For how can the uncorrupt and majestick law of God, bearing in her hand the wages of life and death,[7] harbour such a repugnance within her self, as to require an unexempted and impartial obedience to all her decrees, either from us or from our Mediator, and yet debase her self to faulter so ♦ [57] ◀ many ages with circumcis'd[8] adulteries, by unclean and slubbering permissions.

♦ CHAP. XIV.

That Beza's *opinion of regulating sinne by a politick law,*[1] *cannot be sound.* ◀

YET *Beza's* opinion is that a politick law, but what politick law I know not, unlesse one of *Matchiavel's,* may regulate sin;[2] may bear indeed, I grant, with imperfection for a time, as <those Canons of>[3] the Apostles did in ceremonial things:[4] but as for sin, the essence of it cannot consist with rule; and if the law fall to regulate sin, and not to take it utterly away, it necessarily confirms and establishes sin. To make a regularity of sin by law, either the law must straiten sin into no sin, or sin must crook the law into no law. The judicial law can serve to no other end then to be the protector and champion of Religion and honest

[7] *Cf.* Romans 6:23.

[8] Circumscribed, limited.

[1] All other editions since 1644, following the uncorrected state of sig. I, read *by Apostolick law.*

[2] *Cf.* Beza's comment on Matthew 19:8 (tr. from *Annotationes Majores in Novum Testamentum,* 1594, I, 111): "The moral law, as it is called, enjoins good and prohibits evil without qualification, since it looks to the conscience. Civil laws, if they are well constituted, command nothing which God forbids and forbid nothing which God commands; but because of the wickedness of men they are forced to moderate many things which they cannot completely abolish, and these are the things which are said to be permitted by regulation." Usury is cited as an example.

[3] This deletion, with a consequent resetting of three lines, accompanied the correction in the chapter heading. Uncorrected copies of sig. I retain the 1643 reading.

[4] See Acts 15:22–29.

civility, as is set down plainly *Rom.* 13.[5] and is but the arme of moral law, which can no more be separate from Justice then Justice from vertue: their office also in a different manner steares the same cours; the one teaches what is good by precept, the other unteaches what is bad by punishment. But if we give way to politick dispensations of lewd uncleannesse, the first good consequence of such a relaxe will be the justifying of papal stews,[6] joyn'd with a toleration of epidemick whordom. Justice must revolt from [33] the end of her authority, and become the patron of that wherof she was created the punisher. The example of usury, which is commonly alleg'd makes against the allegation which it brings, as I touch'd before. Besides that usury, so much as is permitted by the Magistrate, and demanded with common equity, is neither against the word of God, nor the rule of charity, as hath been often discus't by men of eminent learning and judgement.[7] There must be therfore some other example found out to shew us wherin civil policy may with warrant from God settle wickednes by law, & make that lawfull which is lawlesse. Although I doubt not but upon deeper consideration, that which is true in Physick, will be found as true in polity: that as of bad pulses those that beat most in order, are much wors then those that keep the most inordinate circuit, so of popular vices those that may be committed legally, will be more pernicious then those which are left to their own cours at peril, not under a stinted priviledge to sin orderly and regularly, which is an implicit contradiction, but under due and fearles execu-

[5] Verse 1: "For there is no power but of God: the powers that be are ordained of God."

[6] *Cf.* Perkins, *Works*, 1609–13, III, 68. The charge that the Papacy not only permitted brothels in Rome but derived revenue from them was repeatedly made by Reformed writers. Thomas Harding, in *A Confutation of a Booke Intituled an Apology of the Church of England* (Antwerp, 1565; HEHL), pp. 155–64, deals with this charge at length. He admits that brothels exist in Rome and that the Pope, by virtue of his civil authority, levies taxes upon them. But these taxes place a restraint upon an evil which cannot be eliminated. "As God suffered the hard necked Jewes to hate their enemies, and to pinche them with usuries, likewise Moses permitted a libell of divorce, not that these thinges were honest, but to the intent by that meanes yet they might the rather love their brethren, and lend them monney freely, and abstaine from murdering their wives."

[7] See *CPB*, p. 160 (*Complete Prose*, I, 418–19). Rivetus, whose belief in the permissibility of usury is there noted, cites Calvin and others in support of his position. *Cf. Christian Doctrine*, II, xiv.

tion of punishment. ♦ [58] ◀ The* political law, since it cannot regulate vice, is to restraine it, by using all means to root it out: but if it suffer the weed to grow up to any pleasurable or contented hight upon what pretext soever, it fastens the root, it prunes and dresses vice, as if it were a good plant. ♦ Let no man doubt therfore to affirm that it is not so hurtfull or dishonourable to a Common wealth, nor so much to the hardning of hearts, when those worse faults pretended to be fear'd, are committed by who so dares under strict and executed penalty, as when those lesse faults tolerated for fear of greater, harden their faces, not their hearts only, under the protection of publick authority. For what lesse indignity were this, then as if Justice her self the Queen of vertues,[8] descending from her scepter'd royalty, instead of conquering, should compound and treat with sin her eternal adversary and rebel, upon ignoble terms. Or as if the judicial Law were like that untrusty steward in the Gospel, and instead of calling in the debts of his moral master, should give out suttle and sly acquittances to keep him self from begging.[9] Or let us person him like some wretched itinerary Judge, who to gratifie his delinquents before him, would let them basely break his head, lest they should pull him from the bench, and throw him over the barre. Unlesse we had rather think both moral and judicial full of malice and deadly purpose conspir'd to let the dettor Israelite the seed of *Abraham* run on upon a banckrout score, flatter'd with insufficient and insnaring discharges, that so he might be hal'd to a more cruel forfeit for all the indulgent arrears which those judicial acquitments had ingaged him in. No no, this cannot be, that the Law whose integrity and faithfulnesse is next to God, should be either the shamelesse broker of our impurities,[10] or the intended instrument of our destruction. The method of holy correction such as became the Common wealth of *Israel,* is not to bribe sin with sin, to capitulate, and hire out one crime with another: but with more noble and gracefull severity then *Popilius* the *Roman legat* us'd with *Antiochus,*[11] to limit and level out the di-

---

* New paragraph in 1644.

[8] The phrase is Cicero's (*De Officiis,* III, vi): "domina et regina virtutum."

[9] See Luke 16:1–8.   [10] Uncorrected copies read "impunities."

[11] Gaius Popilius, halting Antiochus IV in his invasion of Egypt (168 B.C.), drew a circle about him with a stick and ordered him not to step outside it until he had accepted terms imposed by the Roman Senate. See Polybius, *Histories,* XXIX, 27.

rect way from vice to vertu, with straitest and exactest lines on either side, not winding, or indenting so much as to the right hand of fair pretences. Violence indeed and insurrection may force the Law to suffer what it cannot mend: but to write a decree in allowance of sin, as soon can the hand of Justice rot off. Let this be ever concluded as a truth that will outlive the faith of those that seek to bear it down. [59]

CHAP. XV.

That divorce was not giv'n for wives only, as Beza *and* Paraeus *write. More of the Institution.* ♦

LASTLY,* if divorce were granted, <as he sayes,> ♦ as *Beza* and others say, ♦ [1] not for men, but to release afflicted wives, certainly it is not only a dispensation, but a most mercifull Law: and why it should not yet be in force, beeing wholly as needfull, I know not what can be in cause but senselesse cruelty. ♦ But yet to say, divorce was granted for relief of wives, rather then of husbands, is but weakly conjectur'd, and is manifest the extreme shift of a huddl'd exposition. Whenas it could not be found how hardnesse of heart should be lessn'd by liberty of divorce, a fancy was devis'd to hide the flaw by commenting that divorce was permitted only for the help of wives. Palpably uxorious! Who can be ignorant that woman was created for man, and not man for woman; and that a husband may be injur'd as insufferably in mariage as a wife. What an injury is it after wedlock not to be belov'd, what to be slighted, what to be contended with in point of house-rule who shall be the head, not for any parity of wisdome, for that were somthing reasonable, but out of a female pride. *I suffer not* saith S. Paul, *the woman to usurp authority over the man.*[2] If the Apostle could not suffer it, into what mould is he mortify'd that can? *Salomon* saith *that a bad wife is to her husband, as rott'nnesse to his bones, a continual dropping: better dwell in a corner of the*

---

* No paragraph division in 1643.

[1] Beza, in his comment on Matthew 19:8 (*Annotationes Majores*, 1594, I, 111), says that Moses did not approve divorce but that he commanded the giving of a *divortii libellum* to rejected wives for their protection "against the cruelty of husbands." Paraeus (*Operum Theologicorum* [Frankfurt, 1628], I, 784, and II, 488) expresses a similar opinion.   [2] I Timothy 2:12.

house top, or in the wildernes then with such a one.[3] *Who so hideth her hideth the wind, and one of the four mischiefs that the earth cannot bear.*[4] If the Spirit of God wrote such aggravations as these, and as may be guest by these similitudes, counsels the man rather to divorce then to live with such a collegue, and yet on the other side expresses nothing of the wives suffering with a bad husband; is it not most likely that God in his Law had more pitty towards man thus wedlockt, then towards the woman that was created for another. The same Spirit relates to us the cours which the *Medes* and *Persians* took by occasion of *Vashti,* whose meer denial to come at her husbands sending lost her the being Queen any longer, and set up a wholsom Law, *that every man should beare rule in his own house.*[5] And the divine relater shews us not the least signe of disliking what was done; how should he? if *Moses* long before was nothing lesse mindfull of the honour and preeminence due to man. So that to say divorce was granted for woman rather then man, was but fondly invented. ♦ Esteeming therfore to have asserted thus an in- ♦ [60] ♦ jur'd law of *Moses* from the unwarranted and guilty name of a dispensation, to be again a most equall and requisite law, wee have the word of Christ himself, that he came not to alter the least tittle of it; and signifies no small displeasure against him that shall teach to doe so. On which relying, I shall not much waver to affirm that those words which are made to intimate, as if they forbad all divorce but for adultery (though *Moses* have constituted otherwise) those words tak'n circumscriptly, without regard to any precedent law of *Moses* or attestation of Christ himself, or without care to preserve those his fundamental and superior laws of nature and charitie, to which all other ordinances give up their seals, are as much against plain equity, and the mercy of religion, as those words of *Take, eat, this is my body,* elementally understood, are against nature and sense.[6] [34]

[3] Proverbs 12:4, 19:13, 21:9, 21:19.

[4] Proverbs 27:16 and 30:21–23. Milton quotes the first passage directly; the second he summarizes and assimilates to the pattern of the first.

[5] See Esther 1:10–22.

[6] Despite their differing views of the Eucharist, Reformed theologians were unanimous in holding that the Words of Institution (Matthew 26:26, Mark 14:22, I Corinthians 11:24) are not to be understood literally. *Cf.* Article XXVIII of *The Thirty-Nine Articles* (1571; HEHL): "The body of Christe is geven, taken, and eaten in the Supper only after an heavenly and spirituall maner."

And surely the restoring of this degraded law, hath well recompenc't the diligence was us'd, by enlightning us further to finde out wherfore Christ took off the Pharises from alleging the law, and referr'd them to the first institution, not condemning, altering, or abolishing this precept of divorce, which is plainly moral, for that were against his truth, his promise, and his prophetick office; but knowing how fallaciously they had cited, and conceal'd the particular and natural reason of the law, that they might justifie any froward reason of their own, he lets goe that sophistry unconvinc't, for that had bin to teach them els, which his purpose was not. And since they had tak'n a liberty which the law gave not, he amuses [7] & repells their tempting pride with a perfection of paradise, which the law requir'd not; not therby to oblige our performance to that wherto the law never enjoyn'd the fal'n estate of man; for if the first institution must make wedlock, what ever happen, inseparable to us, it must make it also as perfect, as meetly helpfull, and as comfortable as God promis'd it should be, at least in some degree, otherwise it is not equal or proportionable to the strength of man, that he should be reduc't into such indissoluble bonds to his assured misery, if all the other conditions of that covnant be manifestly alter'd.

♦ CHAP. XVI.

How to be understood that they must be one flesh: and how that those whom God hath joyn'd man should not sunder. ♦

NEXT he saith, *they must be one flesh,* which, when all conjecturing is don, wil be found to import no more but <only> to make legitimate ♦ [61] ♦ and good the carnal act, which els might seem to have somthing of pollution in it: And inferrs thus much over, that the fit union of their souls be such as may even incorporate them to love and amity; but that can never be where no correspondence is of the minde; nay instead of beeing one flesh, they will be rather two carkasses chain'd unnaturally together; or as it may happ'n, a living soule bound to a dead corps,

---

[7] Bewilders, confounds.

a punishment too like that inflicted by the tyrant *Mezentius;* [1] so little worthy to be receav'd as that remedy of lonelines which God meant us. Since wee know it is not the joyning of another body will remove lonelines, but the uniting of another compliable mind; and that it is no blessing but a torment, nay a base and brutish condition to be one flesh, unlesse where nature can in some measure fix a unity of disposition. ▶ The meaning therefore of these words, *For this cause shall a man leave his father and his mother and shall cleave to his wife,* [2] was first to shew us the deer affection which naturally & most commonly grows in every not unnatural mariage, ev'n to the leaving of parents, or other familiarity whatsoever: next, it justifies a man in so doing, that nothing is done undutifully to father or mother. But that he should be here sternly commanded to cleave to his error, a disposition which to his he finds will never ciment, a quotidian of sorrow & discontentment in his house, let us be excus'd to pause a little and bethinke us every way round, ere wee lay such a flat solecisme upon the gracious, and certainly not inexorable, not ruthlesse and flinty ordinance of marriage. For if the meaning of these words must be thus blockt up within their owne letters from all equity and fair deduction, they will serve then well indeed their turn, who affirme divorce to have been granted onely for wives; whenas we see no word of this text that bindes women, but men only, what it binds. No marvell then if *Salomith* sister to *Herod,* sent a writ of ease to *Costobarus* her husband; which, as *Josephus* there attests, was lawfull onely to men. [3] No marvell though *Placidia* the sister of *Honorius* threat'n'd the like to Earle *Constantius,* for a triviall cause as *Photius* relates from *Olympiodorus.* [4] No marvell any thing if letters must be turn'd into

---

[1] A mythical Etruscan despot, who, according to Virgil (*Aeneid,* VIII, 485–88), "would even link dead bodies with the living, fitting hand to hand and face to face (grim torture!) and, in the oozy slime and poison of that dread embrace, thus slay them by a lingering death." Tr. H. R. Fairclough (2 vols., New York and London, 1929), II, 93.

[2] Matthew 19:5. *Cf.* Genesis 2:24.

[3] See Josephus, *Antiquities of the Jews,* XV, 7. Josephus remarks that Salome's sending of a bill of divorce was not "according to the Jewish laws: for with us it is lawful for a husband to do so; but a wife, if she depart from her husband, cannot of herself be married to another, unless her former husband put her away." Tr. William Whiston (2 vols., New York, 1821), I, 557.

[4] See Photius, *Bibliotheca,* LXXX (in Migne, *Graeca,* CIII, 255); tr. J. H. Freese, *The Library* (5 vols., London and New York, 1920), I, 145. In his ab-

palisadoes [5] to stake out all requisite sense from entring to their due enlargement. ◀

Lastly, Christ himself tells us who should not be put asunder, namely, those whom God hath joyn'd. A plain solution of this great controversie, if men would but use their eyes; for when is it that God may be said to joyn, when the parties and their friends con-[35] sent? No surely; for that may concurre to leudest ends, or is it ♦ [62] ◀ when Church-rites are finisht? Neither; for the efficacy of those depends upon the presupposed fitnes of either party. Perhaps after carnal knowledge? lest of all: for that may joyn persons whom neither law nor nature dares joyn; tis left, that only then, when the minds are fitly dispos'd, and enabl'd to maintain a cherfull conversation, to the solace and love of each other, according as God intended and promis'd in the very first foundation of matrimony, *I will make him a help meet for him;* for surely what God intended and promis'd, that only can be thought to be of his joyning, and not the contrary. So likewise the Apostle witnesseth 1 *Cor.* 7. 15. that in mariage *God hath call'd us to peace.* And doubtles in what respect he hath call'd us to mariage, in that also he hath joyn'd us. The rest whom either disproportion or deadnes of spirit, or somthing distastfull & avers in the immutable bent of nature renders unconjugal, error may have joyn'd; but God never joyn'd against the meaning of his own ordinance. And if he joynd them not, then is there no power above their own consent to hinder them from unjoyning; when they cannot reap the soberest ends of beeing together in any tolerable sort. Neither can it be said properly that such twain were ever divorc't, but onely parted from each other, as two persons unconjunctive, and unmariable together. But if, whom God hath made a fit help, frowardnes or private injuries have made unfit, that beeing the secret of mariage God can better judge then man, neither is man indeed fit or able to decide this matter; however it be, undoubtedly a peacefull divorce is a lesse evil and lesse in scandal then a hatefull hard-hearted and destructive continuance

stract of the *Histories* of Olympiodorus, which deal with events in the Empire between 407 and 425, Photius tells of a certain magician who appeared at Ravenna during the reign of Honorius and Constantius. This man's presence so offended Placidia that she "threatened to apply for a divorce against Constantius, unless the magician and infidel were removed." He was accordingly put to death, and the divorce was averted.

[5] A fence made of pales or stakes. *NED* cites this example.

of mariage in the judgement of *Moses,* and of Christ, that justifies him in choosing the lesse evil, which if it were an honest & civil prudence in the law, what is there in the Gospel forbidding such a kind of legal wisdom, though wee should admit the common Expositers.[6]

❧ CHAP. XVII.

The sentence of Christ concerning divorce how to be expounded. What Grotius hath observ'd. Other additions. ❧

HAVING thus unfoulded those ambiguous reasons, wherwith Christ, as his wont was, gave to the Pharises that came to sound him, such an answer as they deserv'd, it will not be uneasie [1] to explain the sentence it self that now follows; *Whosoever shall put away his wife, except it be for fornication, and shall marry another, committeth adultery.*[2] First therfore I will set down what is observ'd by *Grotius* upon ❧ [63] ❧ this point, a man of general learning.[3] Next I produce what mine own thoughts gave me,

---

[6] By "the common Expositers" Milton seems to mean primarily such Calvinist exegetes as Perkins, Beza, and Paraeus. The term, however, is open to broader interpretation. For the range and influence of the sixteenth and seventeenth century Biblical commentaries, see Arnold Williams, *The Common Expositor* (Chapel Hill: University of North Carolina Press, 1948).

[1] Difficult.   [2] Matthew 19:9.

[3] See above, p. 238, n. 17. Milton paraphrases closely although with omissions and one change in order. The relevant passages read as follows in the original (*Annotationes in Libros Evangeliorum* [Amsterdam, 1641], pp. 98–99): "Sed contra notat Origenes verba haec poni magis enuntiando quam jubendo. Neque rarum est, ut in tali sermone id quod ex occasione dicitur exempli magis quam adstringendi vim habeat. Non enim in humanis tantum sed & in Dei legibus palam est saepe facti aliquam speciem frequentiorem exprimi, ex qua deinde caetera colligi debeant, ut Exod. xxi, 18, 19, 20, 26. Deut. xix, 5. . . . In omnibus enim legibus, etiam maxime odiosis, quales sunt quae poenam irrogant, receptum est, ut ubi eadem est ratio jus idem valeat: in benignioribus autem legibus etiam a paribus ad paria procedit interpretatio. Quod si diligenter advertamus ad naturam omnium Christi praeceptorum, reperiemus & originem eorum & consummationem in charitate consistere, quae ita nos vult aliis consulere, ut ne in nos ipsos crudeles simus, quemadmodum docet Paulus II Corinth. viii, 13. . . . Et haec causa videri potest, cur Marcus x, 11. & Paulus I Corinth. vii, 10, hoc Christi praeceptum commemorantes, verbis utantur generalibus, nulla exceptione apposita: nimirum quia tales exceptiones ex naturali aequitate venientes tacite insunt legibus quantumvis generaliter pronuntiatis. Videndum ergo est an eadem aequitas non possit etiam in aliis casibus, quanquam

before I had seen his annotations. *Origen,* saith [36] he, notes
that Christ nam'd adultery rather as one example of other like
cases, then as one only exception. And that it is frequent not only
in human but in divine Laws to expresse one kind of fact, wherby
other causes of like nature may have the like plea: as *Exod.* 21. 18,
19, 20, 26. *Deut.* 19. 5. And from the maxims of civil Law he shews
that ev'n in sharpest penal laws, the same reason hath the same
right: and in gentler laws, that from like causes to like the Law
interprets rightly. But it may be objected, saith he, that nothing
destroys the end of wedlock so much as adultery. To which he answers that mariage was not ordain'd only for copulation, but for mutual help and comfort of life; and if we mark diligently the nature of
our Saviours commands, wee shall finde that both their beginning and
their end consists in charity: whose will is that wee should so be good
to others, as that wee be not cruel to our selves. And hence it appears why *Mark* and *Luke* and St. *Paul* to the *Cor.* mentioning
this precept of Christ, adde no exception; because exceptions that
arise from natural equity are included silently under general terms:
it would be consider'd therfore whether the same equity may not
have place in other cases lesse frequent. Thus farre he. From
hence, is what I adde: first, that this saying of Christ, as it is
usually expounded, can be no law at all, that ▶a◀ man for no cause
should separate but for adultery, except it be a supernatural law,
not binding us, as wee now are: [4] had it bin the law of nature, either
the *Jews,* or some other wise and civil Nation would have pres't it:
or let it be so; yet that law *Deut.* 24. 1. wherby a man hath leave
to part, whenas for just and natural cause discover'd he cannot
love, is a law ancienter, and deeper ingrav'n in blameles nature
then the other: therfore the inspired Law-giver *Moses* took care
that this should be specify'd and allow'd: the other he let vanish in
silence, not once repeated in the volume of his law, ev'n as the reason
of it vanisht with Paradise. Secondly, this can be no new command,
for the Gospel enjoyns no new morality, save only the infinit en-

minus frequentibus, ideoque memoratu haud aeque necessariis, locum habere. . . .
Dicat hic forte aliquis adulterium magis quam caetera crimina pugnare cum fine
matrimonii. At enim non prolis solius, sed & mutui auxilii causa conjugium est
institutum: nec quicquam potest contractui tam arctae societatis magis esse
adversum quam quod in vitam committitur."

[4] *Cf.* Milton's discussion "Of the Special Government of Man before the Fall"
in *Christian Doctrine,* I, x.

largement of charity, which in this respect is call'd the *new Commandement* by St. *John;* as being the accomplishment of every command.[5] Thirdly, It is no command of perfection further then it partakes of charity, which is *the bond of perfection.*[6] Those commands therfore which compell us to self-cruelty above our strength, so hardly will help forward to perfection, that they hinder & set backward in all ♦ [64] ♦ the common rudiments of Christianity; as was prov'd. It being thus [37] clear, that the words of Christ can be no kind of command, as they are vulgarly tak'n, wee shall now see in what sense they may be a command, and that an excellent one, the same with that of *Moses,* and no other. *Moses* had granted that only for a natural annoyance, defect, or dislike, whether in body or mind, (for so the Hebrew words plainly note) [7] which a man could not force himself to live with, he might give a bill of divorce; therby forbidding any other cause wherin amendment or reconciliation might have place. This law the Pharises depraving, extended to any slight contentious cause whatsoever. Christ therfore seeing where they halted,[8] urges the negative part of that law, which is necessarily understood (for the determinate permission of *Moses* binds them from further licence) and checking their supercilious drift, declares that no accidental, temporary, or reconciliable offence, except fornication, can justifie a divorce: he touches not heer those natural and perpetual hindrances of society, ♦ whether in body or mind, ♦ which are not to be remov'd: for such, as they are aptest to cause an unchangeable offence, so are they not capable of reconcilement, because not of amendment ♦ ; they do not break indeed, but they annihilate the bands of mariage more then adultery. For that fault committed argues not alwaies a hatred either natural or incidental against whom it is committed; neither does it inferre a disability of all future helpfulnes, or loyalty, or loving agreement, being once past, and pardon'd, where it can be pardon'd: but that which naturally distasts, and *findes no favour in the eyes* of matrimony, can never be conceal'd, never appeas'd, never intermitted, but proves a perpetuall nullity of love and contentment, a solitude, and dead vacation [9] of all acceptable conversing. *Moses* therfore permits divorce, but in cases only that have no hands to joyn, and more need separating then adultery. Christ for-

[5] See John 13:34. [6] Colossians 3:14. [7] *Cf* above, p. 244, n. 8.
[8] Failed, fell short. [9] Absence or cessation.

bids it, but in matters only that may accord, and those lesse then
fornication ♦. Thus is *Moses* Law heer <solidly> ♦ plainly ♦ confirm'd; and those causes which he permitted, not a jot gainsaid.
And that this is the true meaning of this place, I prove also by no
lesse an Author then St. *Paul* himself, 1 *Cor.* 7. 10, 11. upon which
text Interpreters agree, that the Apostle only repeats the precept
of Christ: [10] where while he speaks of *the wives reconcilement to
her husband,* he puts it out of controversie, that our Saviour meant
<only> ♦ chiefly ♦ matters of strife and reconcilement; of which
sort he would not that any difference should be the occasion of divorce, except fornication. ♦ And that we may learn better how to
value [65] a grave and prudent law of *Moses,* and how unadvisedly we smatter with our lips, when we talk of Christs abolishing
any Judiciall law of his great Father, except in some circumstances
which are Judaicall rather than Judicial, and need no abolishing but
cease of themselvs, I say again, that this recited law of *Moses* contains a cause of divorce greater beyond compare then that for adultery; and whoso cannot so conceive it errs and wrongs exceedingly
a law of deep wisdom for want of well fadoming. For let him mark,
no man urges the just divorcing of adultery, as it is a sin, but as it is
an injury to mariage; and though it be but once committed, and
that without malice, whether through importunity or opportunity,[11]
the Gospel does not therfore disswade him who would therfore
divorce; but that natural hatred whenever it arises, is a greater
evil in mariage, then the accident of adultery, a greater de-
frauding, a greater injustice, and yet not blameable, he who understands not after all this representing, I doubt his will like a hard
spleen draws faster then his understanding can well sanguifie.[12]

[10] See, for example, Paraeus, *Operum Theologicorum* (Frankfurt, 1628), II,
487.
[11] The phrase "through importunity or opportunity" (*i.e.,* as a result of solicitation or chance encounter) illustrates Milton's fondness for verbal quibbles. *Cf.*
"Judaicall rather then Judicial" (7 lines above).
[12] According to Renaissance physiology, to "sanguifie" (*i.e.,* to generate
blood) was a function of the liver; impurities in the blood were drawn off by the
spleen. Milton's figure implies an analogous relationship between understanding
and will, the will working upon matter produced by the understanding. The will
of the uncomprehending reader is like an over-active spleen without blood to
draw from. As Kester Svendsen has pointed out, the passage is best explicated
by reference to contemporary encyclopedias of science, such as La Primaudaye's
French Academie (1618 edition [HEHL], pp. 358, 530, 422–25). See Kester
Svendsen, "Milton and Medical Lore," *Bulletin of the History of Medicine,* XIII
(1943), 163–64.

Nor did that man ever know or feel what it is to love truly, nor ever yet comprehend in his thoughts what the true intent of marriage is. And this also will be somwhat above his reach, but yet no lesse a truth for lack of his perspective, that as no man apprehends what vice is, so well as he who is truly vertuous,[13] no man knows hel like him who converses most in heav'n, so there is none that can estimate the evil and the affliction of a naturall hatred in matrimony, unlesse he have a soul gentle anough, and spacious anough to contemplate what is true love.

And the reason why men so disesteem this wise judging Law of God, and count hate, or *the not finding of favour*, as it is there term'd, a humorous,[14] a dishonest, and slight cause of divorce, is because themselves apprehend so little of what true concord means: for if they did, they would be juster in their ballancing between natural hatred and casuall adultery; this being but a transient injury, and soon amended, I mean as to the party against whom the trespasse is: but that other being an unspeakable and unremitting sorrow and offence, wherof no amends can be made, no cure, no ceasing but by divorce, which like a divine touch in one moment heals all; [15] and like the word of God, in one instant hushes outrageous tempests into a sudden stilnesse and peacefull calm.[16] Yet all this so great a good of Gods own enlarging to us, is by the hard rains of them that sit us, wholly diverted and imbezzl'd from us. Maligners of mankind! But who hath taught ye to mangle thus, and make more gashes in [66] the miseries of a blamelesse creature, with the leaden daggers of your literall decrees, to whose ease you cannot adde the tithe of one small atome, but by letting alone your unhelpfull Surgery. As for such as think wandring concupiscence to bee here newly and more precisely forbidd'n, then it was before, if the Apostle can convince them; we know that we are to *know lust by the law*,[17] and not by any new discovery of the Gospel. The Law of *Moses* knew what it permitted, and the Gospel knew what it forbid; hee that under a peevish conceit of debarring concupiscence, shall goe about to make a novice of *Moses*, (not to say a worse thing for reverence sake) and such a one of God himselfe,

[13] *Cf. Areopagitica* (below, p. 514): "He that can apprehend and consider vice," etc.

[14] Fanciful, capricious.

[15] *Cf.* the accounts of Christ's healing: *e.g.*, Matthew 8:3 and 8:15.

[16] *Cf.* Matthew 8:26; Mark 4:39; Luke 8:24.

[17] *Cf.* Romans 7:7.

as is a horror to think, to bind our Saviour in the default of a down-right promise breaking, and to bind the disunions of complaining nature in chains together, and curb them with a canon bit,[18] tis he that commits all the whordom and adultery, which himselfe adjudges, besides the former guilt so manifold that lies upon him. And if none of these considerations with all their wait and gravity, can avail to the dispossessing him of his pretious literalism,[19] let some one or other entreat him but to read on in the same 19. of *Math.* till he come to that place that sayes *Some make themselves Eunuchs for the kingdom of heavns sake.* And if then he please to make use of *Origens* knife, he may doe well to be his own carver.[20]

CHAP. XVIII.

Whether the words of our Saviour be rightly expounded only of actual fornication to be the cause of divorce. The opinion of Grotius *with other reasons.* ◀

BUT because wee know that Christ never gave a judicial law, and that the word *fornication* is variously significant in Scripture, it will be much right don to our Saviours words, to consider diligently, whether it be meant heer, that nothing but actual fornication, prov'd by witnes, can warrant a divorce; for so our Canon Law judges. Neverthelesse, as I find that *Grotius* on this place hath observ'd, the Christian Emperours, *Theodosius* the second, and *Justinian,* men of high wisdom and reputed piety, decree'd it to be a divorsive fornication, if the wife attempted either against the knowledge, or obstinately against the will of her husband, such things as gave open suspicion of adulterizing; as the wilfull haunting of feasts, and invitations with men not of her neer kindred, the lying forth of her hous [38] without probable cause,

[18] A pun on a term drawn from horsemanship. *Cf.* Spenser, *Faerie Queene,* I, vii, 37: ". . . and could manage faire / His stubborne steed with curbed canon bit."

[19] Milton's use here is the earliest recorded in *NED.*

[20] Origen (*ca.* 185–253) is reported to have castrated himself as a result of interpreting Matthew 19:12 too literally. See Eusebius, *Ecclesiastical History,* VI, viii.

the frequenting of Theaters against her husbands mind, her endeavour to prevent, or destroy conception.[1] Hence that of *Jerom, Where fornication is suspected, the wife may lawfully* ▶ [67] ◀ *be divorc't;* not that every motion of a jealous mind should be regarded, but that it should not be exacted to prove all things by the visibility of Law-witnessing, or els to hood-wink the mind: for the Law is not able to judge of these things but by the rule of equity, and by permitting a wise man to walk the middle-way of <a> prudent circumspection, neither wretchedly jealous, nor stupidly and tamely patient. To this purpose hath *Grotius* in his notes.[2] He shews also that fornication is tak'n in Scripture for such a continual headstrong behaviour, as tends to plain contempt of the husband: and proves it out of *Judges* 19. 2. where the Levites wife is said to have playd the whoor against him; which *Josephus* and the *Septuagint,* with the *Chaldaean,* interpret only of stubbornnes and rebellion against her husband: [3] and to this I adde that *Kimchi* and the two other Rabbies who glosse the text, are in the same opinion.[4]

---

[1] *Cf. Annotationes in Libros Evangeliorum* (Amsterdam, 1641), p. 98: "Theodosius junior Imperator Christianus, & pius, & Episcoporum quotidiano usus consilio, in quaestione divortii impudicitiae conjecturas ad sui saeculi mores temperans, sufficere judicavit si mulier viro ignorante vel nolente extraneorum virorum convivia appeteret; si ipso invito, sine justa & probabili causa, foris pernoctaret nisi apud suos parentes; vel si Circensibus theatralibus vel ludis aut arenarum spectaculis ipso prohibente gauderet. Quibus istas addidit Iustinianus: si uxor de industria abortum fecerit; si commune lavacrum cum viris habuerit; si dum est in matrimonio cum alio viro de matrimonio egerit."

[2] "Quo illud Hieronymi pertinet: *ubicunque est fornicatio & fornicationis suspicio, libere uxor dimittitur.* Quod tamen non ita accipiendum est, ut quivis motus animi suspicacis ad pie sancteque faciendum divortium valere debeat: sed ne ad legum subtilitatem res exigatur. In isto autem quaestionum genere nihil certi definiri potest: sed omne hoc ex aequo bonoque aestimandum est, medio itinere inter anxiam credulitatem & crassam supinitatem." This passage immediately precedes the reference to the decrees of Theodosius and Justinian.

[3] Here Milton attributes to Grotius a somewhat more positive tone than the original seems to warrant. Grotius says (*Annotationes,* p. 97) that there are those who give fornication (πορνεία) an extended meaning, and that *they* take their argument (*argumentum sumunt*) from Judges 19:2. Without indicating his own agreement, he then cites the parallel account in Josephus (*Antiquities of the Jews,* V, ii), where the Levite's concubine is said simply to have been *alieno animo a viro,* and notes that this harmonizes with the rendering of the Old Testament text in both the Chaldean paraphrase and the Septuagint.

[4] Harris Fletcher (*Milton's Semitic Studies,* pp. 73–78) argues that Milton for this detail must have used a rabbinical Bible, probably one edited by Johann Buxtorf and published by him at Basle in 1618–19. In Buxtorf's edition the com-

Ben Gersom reasons that had it bin whoordom, a Jew and a Levite would have disdain'd to fetch her again.[5] And this I shall contribute, that had it bin whoordom she would have chosen any other place to run to, then to her fathers house, it being so infamous for an hebrew woman to play the harlot, and so opprobrious to the parents. Fornication then in this place of the *Judges,* is understood for stubborn disobedience against the husband, and not for adultery. A sin of that sudden activity, as to be already committed, when no more is don, but only lookt unchastly: which yet I should be loath to judge worthy a divorce, though in our Saviours language it be call'd adultery.[6] Neverthelesse, when palpable and frequent signes are giv'n, the law of God *Num.* 5. so far gave way to the jealousie of a man, as that the woman set before the Sanctuary with her head uncover'd, was adjur'd by the Priest to swear whether she were fals or no; and constrain'd to drink that *bitter water* with an undoubted *curse of rottennesse, and tympany* to follow, unlesse she were innocent.[7] And the jealous man had not bin guiltles before God, as seems by the last *ver.* if having such a suspicion in his head, he should neglect this trial, which, if to this day it be not to be us'd, or be thought as uncertain of effect, as our antiquated law of *Ordalium,*[8] yet all equity will judge that many adulterous demeanors which are of lewd suspicion and example, may be held sufficient to incurre a divorce; though the act [39] it self hath not bin prov'd. And seeing the generosity of our Nation is so, as to account no reproach more abominable, then to be nick-

mentators are three in number: Kimchi and Ben Gerson, whom Milton names, and Rashi. Fletcher's contention has been challenged by Conklin (*Biblical Criticism and Heresy in Milton,* pp. 64–65), who points out that rabbinical glosses were available at second hand.

[5] The comment of Levi Ben Gerson (otherwise known as Gersonides) is quoted from Buxtorf by Fletcher, pp. 76–77. It reads in part as follows: "And the book adds that in those days, when there was no king in Israel, . . . there was a man, a Levite, a sojourner who dwelt on the outlying slopes of Ephraim. And this man took to himself a wife, a concubine from Beth-Lehem Judah. And she committed adultery against him in that she turned from him and returned to the house of her father to escape from her husband . . . for if she committed adultery against him, it was only in lying apart from him, and it has not been sufficiently emphasized that he went to seek her again in spite of the matter of her so-called 'adultery,' which is thereby explained."

[6] See Matthew 5:28.

[7] See Numbers 5:11–31 (especially verse 27).

[8] Trial by ordeal, abolished in England about 1215. See *NED.*

nam'd the husband of an adultresse, that our law should not be as ample as the law of God to vindicate a man from that ignoble ♦ [68] ❡ sufferance, is our barbarous unskilfulnes, not considering that the law should be exasperated [9] according to our estimation of the injury. And if it must be suffer'd till the act be visibly prov'd, *Salomon* himself whose judgement will be granted to surpasse the acutenes of any Canonist, confesses *Prov.* 30. 19, 20. that for the act of adultery, it is as difficult to be found as the *track of an Eagle in the air, or the way of a ship in the Sea:* so that a man may be put to unmanly indignities, ere it be found out. This therfore may be anough to inform us that divorsive adultery is not limited by our Saviour to the utmost act, and that to be attested always by eye-witnesse: but may be extended also to divers obvious actions, which either plainly lead to adultery, or give such presumtion wherby sensible men may suspect the deed to be already don. And this the rather may be thought, in that our Saviour chose to use the word *fornication,* which word is found to signify other matri-monial transgressions of main breach to that Covnant besides actual adultery. ♦ For that sinne needed not the riddance of divorce, but of death by the Law, which was active ev'n till then by the example of the woman tak'n in adultery; [10] or if the law had been dormant, our Saviour was more likely to have told them of their neglect, then to have let a capitall crime silently scape into a divorce: or if it bee said his businesse was not to tell them what was criminall in the civill Courts, but what was sinfull at the barre of conscience, how dare they then having no other ground then these our Saviours words, draw that into triall of law, which both by *Moses* and our Saviour was left to the jurisdiction of conscience? But wee take from our Saviour, say they, only that it was adultery and our Law of it selfe applies the punishment. But by their leave that so argue, the great Law-giver of all the world who knew best what was adul-tery both to the Jew and to the Gentile appointed no such applying, and never likes when mortall men will be vainly presuming to out-strip his justice.

[9] Rendered more severe. *NED* cites this example.
[10] See John 8:3–11.

CHAP. XIX.

Christs manner of teaching. S. Paul *addes to this matter of divorce without command, to shew the matter to be of equity, not of rigor. That the bondage of a Christian may be as much, and his peace as little in some other mariages besides idolatrous: If those arguments therfore be good in that one case, why not in those other: therfore the Apostle himselfe adds,* ἐν τοῖς τοιούτοις.[1]

THUS at length wee see both by this and by other places, that there is scarse any one saying in the Gospel, but must be read with limitations and distinctions, to be rightly understood; ♦ [69] ♦ for Christ gives no full comments or continu'd discourses, but <scatters> ♦ as *Demetrius* the Rhetorician phrases it, speaks oft in Monosyllables, like a maister,[2] scattering ♦ the heavnly grain of his doctrin like pearle heer and there, which requires a skilfull and laborious gatherer; who must compare the words he finds, with other precepts, with the end of every ordinance, and with the general *analogy* of Evangelick doctrine: [3] otherwise many particular sayings would be but strange repugnant riddles; & the Church would offend in granting divorce for frigidity, which is not heer excepted with adultery, but by them added. And this was it undoubtedly which gave reason to St. *Paul* of his own authority, as he professes, and without command from the Lord, to enlarge the seeming construction of those places in the Gospel, by adding a case wherin a person deserted which is somthing lesse then divorc't, may lawfully marry again. And having declar'd his opinion in one case, he leavs a furder liberty for Christian prudence to determin in cases of like importance; using words so plain as are not to be shifted off, *that a brother or a sister is not under bondage in such cases;* adding also, that [40] *God hath call'd us to peace* in

---

[1] "In such cases" (I Corinthians 7:15).

[2] *Cf.* Demetrius, *On Style*, par. 7, tr. W. Rhys Roberts (Aristotle, *The Poetics. Longinus, On the Sublime. Demetrius, On Style* [Cambridge and London: Loeb Classical Library, 1932], p. 301): "Command is always concise and brief, every master being curt [literally 'monosyllabic'] towards his slave, but supplication and lamentation are lengthy." Although attributed to Demetrius Phalereus (*ca.* 300 B.C.), the work is of uncertain authorship and date. Milton refers to it under the name of Phalereus in *Of Education* (below, p. 402).

[3] *Cf.* above, p. 282, n. 8.

338

mariage.[4] Now if it be plain that a Christian may be brought into unworthy *bondage*, and his religious *peace* not only interrupted now and then, but perpetually and finally hinderd in wedlock by mis-yoking with a diversity of nature as well as of religion, the reasons of St. *Paul* cannot be made special to that one case of infidelity, but are of equal moment to a divorce wherever Christian liberty and peace are without fault equally obstructed. That the ordinance which God gave to our comfort, may not be pinn'd upon us to our undeserved thraldom; to be coop't up as it were in mockery of wedlock, to a perpetual betrothed lonelines and discontent, if nothing wors ensue. There beeing nought els of mariage left between such, but a displeasing and forc't remedy against the sting of a brute desire; which fleshly accustoming [5] without the souls union and commixture of intellectual delight, as it is rather a soiling then a fulfilling of mariage-rites, so is it anough to imbase the mettle of a generous spirit, and sinks him to a low and vulgar pitch of endeavour in all his actions, or, which is wors, leavs him in a dispairing plight of abject and hard'n'd thoughts: which condition, rather then a good man should fall into, a man usefull in the service of God and mankind, Christ himself hath taught us to dispence with the most sacred ordinances of his worship; even for a bodily healing to dispence with that holy & speculative rest ▶ [70] ◀ of Sabbath; [6] much more then with the erroneous observance of an ill-knotted mariage for the sustaining of an overcharg'd faith and perseverance.

▶ CHAP. XX. ◀

The meaning of S. Paul, *that* Charity beleeveth all things. *What is to be said to the licence which is vainly fear'd will grow hereby. What to those who never have don prescribing patience in this case. The Papist most severe against divorce: yet most easie to all licence. Of all the miseries in mariage God is to be clear'd, and the fault to be laid on mans unjust laws.* ◀

AND though bad causes would take licence by this pretext, if that cannot be remedied, upon their conscience be it, who shall so doe. This was that hardnes of heart, & abuse of a good law which *Moses* was content to suffer rather then good men

---

[4] *Cf.* above, p. 256.   [5] Intimacy.   [6] *Cf.* above, p. 281.

should not have it at all to use needfully. And he who to run after
one lost sheep left ninety nine of his own flock at random in the
Wildernes,[1] would little perplex his thought for the obduring[2] of
nine hunder'd and ninety such as will daily take wors liberties
whether they have permission or not. To conclude, as without charity God hath giv'n no commandment to men, so without it, neither
can men rightly beleeve any commandment giv'n. For every act of
true faith, as well that wherby we beleeve the law, as that wherby
wee endeavour[3] the law is wrought in us by charity: according to
that in the divine hymne of St. *Paul*, 1 Cor. 13. *Charity beleeveth
all things:* not as if she were [41] so credulous, which is the exposition hitherto current,[4] for that were a trivial praise, but to teach
us that charity is the high governesse of our belief, and that wee
cannot safely assent to any precept writt'n in the Bible, but as
charity commends it to us. Which agrees with that of the same
Apostle to the *Ephes*. 4. 14, 15. where he tels us that the way to
get a sure undoubted knowledge of things, is to hold that for truth,
which accords most with charity. Whose unerring guidance and
conduct having follow'd as a loadstarre with all diligence and fidelity
in this question, I trust, through the help of that illuminating Spirit
which hath favor'd me, to have done no every daies work: in asserting after many ages the words of Christ with other Scriptures of
great concernment from burdensom & remorsles obscurity, tangl'd
with manifold repugnances, to their native lustre and consent between each other: heerby also dissolving tedious and *Gordian* difficulties, which have hitherto molested the Church of God, and are
now decided not with the sword of *Alexander*, but ♦ [71] ◀ with the
immaculate hands of charity, to the unspeakable good of Christendom.[5] And let the extrem literalist[6] sit down now & revolve[7]
whether this in all necessity be not the due result of our Saviours

---

[1] *Cf.* Matthew 18:12–13; Luke 15:4–6.

[2] Becoming or remaining obdurate. *NED* records no other example of use as a
verbal substantive.

[3] Try to fulfill.

[4] *Cf.* Calvin, *In Epistolam Priorem ad Corinthios* (*Opera*, VIII, 411): "Love
believeth all things. . . . As a consequence the Christian will consider it better
to be imposed upon by his own kindness and easy disposition than to wrong his
brother by an unfriendly suspicion."

[5] Here, as frequently, Milton gives a fresh application to a stock allusion. For
the proverbial aspect of the Gordian knot, see Tilley, *Dictionary*, p. 271.

[6] The earliest use cited in *NED*.   [7] Consider.

words: or if he persist to be otherwise opinion'd, let him well advise, lest thinking to gripe fast the Gospel, he be found in stead with the canon law in his fist: whose boistrous [8] edicts tyrannizing the blessed ordinance of mariage into the quality of a most unnatural and unchristianly yoke, have giv'n the flesh this advantage to hate it, & turn aside, oft-times unwillingly, to all dissolute uncleannesse, even till punishment it self is weary and overcome by the incredible frequency of trading lust, and uncontroull'd adulteries. Yet men whose Creed is custom, I doubt not but will be still endeavouring to hide the sloth of thir own timorous capacities with this pretext, that for all this tis better to endure with patience and silence this affliction which God hath sent. And I agree, tis true; if this be exhorted and not enjoyn'd; but withall, it will be wisely don to be as sure as may be, that what mans iniquity hath laid on, be not imputed to Gods sending; least under the colour of an affected patience wee detain our selves at the gulphs mouth of many hideous temptations, not to be withstood without proper gifts, which as *Perkins* well notes, God gives not ordinarily, no not to most earnest prayers.[9] Therfore wee pray, *Lead us not into temptation,* a vain prayer, if having led our selves thither, wee love to stay in that perilous [42] condition. God sends remedies, as well as evills; under which he who lies and groans, that may lawfully acquitt himself, is accessory to his own ruin: nor will it excuse him, though he suffer, through a sluggish fearfulnes to search throughly what is lawfull, for feare of disquieting the secure falsity of an old opinion. Who doubts not but that it may be piously said to him who would dismiss frigidity, bear your trial, take it as if God would have you live this life of continence: if he exhort this, I hear him as an Angel, though he speak without warrant: but if he would compell me, I know him for Satan. To him who divorces an adulteresse, Piety

[8] Stiff, unyielding.
[9] See *Christian Oeconomie,* chapter III (*Works,* 1609–13, III, 672): "The gifts of God are of two sorts, some are generall, some are Proper. Generall gifts are such as God giveth generally to all, & these may be obtained, if they be asked according to Gods word, lawfully, Jam. 1. 5. . . . Proper gifts, are those which are given onely to some certaine men; of which sort is the gift of continencie, & such like, which though they be often and earnestly asked, yet they are seldome or never granted unto some men." This reference is particularly significant in establishing Milton's familiarity with a work to which at several other points he seems to be indebted. *Cf.* above, p. 247, n. 7; p. 260, n. 8; p. 268, n. 32; below, p. 353, n. 2.

might say; Pardon her; you may shew much mercy, you may win
a soul: yet the law both of God & man leavs it freely to him. For
God loves not to plow out the heart of our endeavours with over-
hard and sad tasks. God delights not to make a drudge of vertue,
whose actions must be all elective and unconstrain'd. Forc't vertu
is as a bolt overshot,[10] it goes neither forward nor backward, &
does no good as it stands. Seeing therfore that neither Scripture nor
reason hath laid this un- ♦ [72] ◀ just austerity upon divorce, we
may resolv that nothing els hath wrought it, but that letter-bound
servility of the Canon Doctors, supposing mariage to be a Sacrament, and out of the art they have to lay unnecessary burdens upon
all men, to make a fair shew in the fleshly observance of matrimony,
though peace & love with all other conjugal respects fare never so
ill. And indeed the Papists who are the strictest forbidders of divorce, are the easiest libertines to admit of grossest uncleannesse;
as if they had a designe by making wedlock a supportles [11] yoke,
to violate it most, under colour of preserving it most inviolable, and
withall delighting, as their mystery [12] is, to make men the day-
labourers of their own <affliction;> ♦afflictions, ◀ as if there were
such a scarcity of miseries from abroad, that wee should be made
to melt our choisest home-blessings, and coin them into crosses,
for want wherby to hold commerce with patience. If any therfore
who shall hap to read this discours, hath bin through misadventure
ill ingag'd in this contracted evill heer complain'd of, and finds the
fits and workings of a high impatience frequently upon him, of all
those wild words which men in misery think to ease themselves by
uttering, let him not op'n his lips against the providence of heav'n,
or tax the waies of God and his divine Truth; for they are equal,
easy, and not burdensome; nor do they ever crosse the just and
reasonable desires of men, nor involve this our portion [43] of mortall life, into a necessity of sadnes and malecontent, by Laws commanding over the unreducible *antipathies* of nature sooner or later
found: but allow us to remedy and shake off those evills into which
human error hath led us through the middest of our best intentions;

[10] Banks (*Milton's Imagery,* p. 84) interprets as referring to a bolt shot from
a crossbow or catapult. But the comparison seems more applicable to the bolt
of a lock, so forced or wedged as to be unworkable.

[11] Insupportable, intolerable.

[12] Secret purpose or policy. There is perhaps an allusion to the Biblical phrase
"mystery of iniquity" (II Thessalonians 2:7).

and to support our incident extremities by that authentick precept of sovran charity; whose grand Commission is to doe and to dispose over all the ordinances of God to man; that love & truth may advance each other to everlasting. While we literally superstitious through customary faintnes of heart, not venturing to peirce with our free thoughts into the full latitude of nature and religion, abandon our selvs to serv under the tyranny of usurpt opinions, suffering those ordinances which were allotted to our solace and reviving, to trample over us and hale us into a multitude of sorrows which God never meant us. And where he set us in a fair allowance of way with honest liberty and prudence to our guard, wee never leave subtilizing and casuisting till wee have straitn'd and par'd that liberal path into a razors edge to walk on between a precipice of unnecessary mischief on either side: [13] and starting at every fals alarum, ⟡ [73] ⟡ wee doe not know which way to set a foot forward with manly confidence and Christian resolution, through the confused ringing in our ears, of *panick* [14] scruples and amazements.

⟡ CHAP. XXI.

That the matter of divorce is not to be try'd by law, but by conscience, as many other sins are. The Magistrate can only see that the condition of divorce be just and equall. The opinion of Fagius, *and the reasons of this assertion.* ⟡

ANOTHER act of papal encroachment it was, to pluck the power & arbitrement of divorce from the master of family, into whose hands God & the law of all Nations had put it, & Christ so left it, preaching only to the conscience, and not authorizing a judiciall Court to tosse about and divulge the unaccountable and secret reasons of disaffection between man & wife, as a thing most improperly answerable to any such kind of trial. But the Popes

[13] Banks suggests a possible origin for this figure in the impression made upon Milton "by his crossing the Alps on his continental tour, an impression to which he refers elsewhere and which may well have been disagreeable to him." See *Milton's Imagery*, p. 76.

[14] "Sounds heard by night on mountains and in valleys were attributed to Pan, and hence he was reputed to be the cause of any sudden or groundless fear." Liddell and Scott as quoted in *NED*.

of *Rome* perceaving the great revenu and high autority it would give them, ev'n over Princes, to have the judging and deciding of such a main consequence in the life of man as was divorce, wrought so upon the superstition of those ages, as to devest them of that right which God from the beginning had entrusted to the husband: by which means they subjected that ancient and naturally domestick prerogative to an external & unbefitting judicature.[1] For although differences in divorce about dowries, jointures, and the like, besides the punishing of adultery, ought not to passe without referring, if need be, to the Magistrate, yet <for him> ♦ that the absolute and final hindring of divorce cannot belong to any civil or earthly power, against the will and consent of both parties, or of the husband alone, some reasons will be here urg'd as shall not need to decline the touch. But first I shall recite what hath bin already yeilded by others in favour of this opinion. *Grotius* and many more agree that notwithstanding what Christ spake therin to the conscience, the Magistrate is not therby enjoyn'd ought against the preservation of civil peace, of equity, and of convenience.[2] Among these *Fagius* is most remarkable, and gives the same liberty of pronouncing divorce to the Christian Magistrate, as the Mosaick had. *For whatever* saith he, *Christ spake to the regenerat, the Judge hath to deal with the vulgar: if therfore any through hardnesse of heart will not be a tolerable wife or husband, it will be lawfull as well now as of old to passe the bill of divorce, not by privat, but by publicke authority. Nor doth man separate* [74] *them then, but God by his law of divorce giv'n by* Moses. *What can hinder the Magistrate from so doing, to whose government all outward things are subject, to separate and remove from perpetual vexation and no small danger, those bodies whose minds are already separate: it being his office to procure peaceable and convenient living in the Common-wealth; and being as certain also, that they so necessarily separated cannot all receive a single life.*[3] And this I observe that our divines doe gen-

---

[1] *Cf. CPB,* p. 112 (*Complete Prose,* I, 406), where Milton notes the expression of a similar idea by Sarpi.

[2] *Cf.* Grotius, *Annotationes in Libros Evangeliorum* (Amsterdam, 1641), p. 98.

[3] *Thargum* (Strassburg, 1546), sig. Q4. The passage is the same as that already quoted in part on p. 243, two sentences being here repeated at the beginning and end in paraphrased form. The additional matter reads as follows in the original: ". . . sed si quis ob duriciam cordis nolit illi commodum exhibere maritum, iam authoritate non propria, sed magistratus licebit hodie ut olim dare libellum

erally condemn separation of bed and board, without the liberty of
second choice: [4] if that therfore in some cases be most purely necessary, as who so blockish to deny, then is this also as needfull. Thus
farre by others is already well stept, to inform us that divorce is
not a matter of Law but of Charity: if there remain a furlong yet
to end the question, these following reasons may serve to gain it
with any apprehension not too unlearned, or too wayward. First
because ofttimes the causes of seeking divorce reside so deeply in
the radical and innocent affections of nature, as is not within the
diocese of Law to tamper with. Other relations may aptly anough
be held together by a civil and vertuous love. But the duties of man
and wife are such as are chiefly conversant in that love, which is
most ancient and meerly [5] naturall; whose two prime statutes are
to joyn it self to that which is good and acceptable and friendly;
and to turn aside and depart from what is disagreeable, displeasing
and unlike: of the two this latter is the strongest, and most equal [6]
to be regarded: for although a man may often be unjust in seeking
that which he loves, yet he can never be unjust or blamable in re-
tiring from his endles trouble and distast, whenas his tarrying can
redound to no true content on either side. Hate is of all things the
mightiest divider, nay, is division it self. To couple hatred therfore
though wedlock try all her golden links, and borrow to her aid all
the iron manacles and fetters of Law, it does but seek to twist a
rope of sand, which was a task, they say, that pos'd the divell. [7]

repudii. Nec iam homo illos ab invicem separat, sed Deus per legem repudii
Mosi datam illos separat. Quid enim prohibere potest, quin magistratus cuius
imperio externa subiecta sunt, tales ab invicem separet, aut periculo eximat,
quorum animi iam sunt separati, & alter vivit in perpetuo cruciatu & gravissimo
periculo? praesertim cum officium magistratus sit, curare ut commode et tranquille in republica vivatur."

[4] Separation *a mensa et thoro,* possible under the Roman canon law in cases
of adultery, found little support among Reformed writers. The general position
of these writers is expressed by Perkins in the following sentence from *Christian
Oeconomie* (*Works,* 1609–13, III, 690): "After the divorcement made, it shall
be lawfull for the harmlesse partie, not having the gift of continencie, upon
leave obtained of the Church, and the Christian Magistrate, to marrie againe."

[5] Absolutely, entirely.

[6] Fit, worthy.

[7] *Cf.* Ben Jonson, *The Devil Is an Ass,* I, i, 118–19: "Get you e'ne backe,
Sir, / To making of your rope of sand againe." "To twist a rope of sand" was a
proverbial expression for an attempt to do the impossible. See Tilley, *Dictionary,*
p. 575.

And that sluggish feind in hell *Ocnus,* whom the Poems tell of, brought his idle cordage to as good effect, which never serv'd to bind with, but to feed the Asse that stood at his elbow.[8] And that the restrictive Law against divorce, attains as little to bind any thing truly in a disjoynted mariage, or to keep it bound, but servs only to feed the ignorance, and definitive impertinence of a doltish Canon, were no absurd allusion.[9] To hinder therfore those deep and serious regresses of nature in a reasonable soul parting from that mistak'n help which he justly seeks in a person created for him, recollecting[10] himself from an unmeet help which was never meant, and to detain [75] him by compulsion in such an unpredestin'd misery as this, is in diameter[11] against both nature and institution: but ◀ to interpose <his> ▶ a ◀ jurisdictive power upon the inward and irremediable disposition of man, to command love and [44] *sympathy,* to forbid dislike against the guiltles instinct of nature, is not within the province of any law to reach, & were indeed an uncommodious rudenes, not a just power <.> ▶ : for that Law may bandy with nature, and traverse her sage motions, was an error in *Callicles* the Rhetorician, whom *Socrates* from high principles confutes in *Plato's Gorgias.*[12] If therfore divorce may be so natural, and that law and nature are not to goe contrary, then to forbid divorce compulsively, is not only against nature, but against law.

Next it must be remember'd that all law is for some good that may be frequently attain'd, without the admixture of a worse inconvenience; and therfore many grosse faults, as ingratitude and the like, which are too farre within the soul, to be cur'd by constraint of law, are left only to be wrought on by conscience and perswasion. Which made *Aristotle* in the 10th of his *Ethicks* to *Nicomachus* aim at a kind of division of law into private or perswasive, and publick or compulsive.[13] Hence it is that the law forbidding divorce,

---

[8] The fate of Ocnus (Indolence), condemned in hell to weave a rope of straw which an ass continually devoured, is described by Propertius (*Elegies,* IV, iii, 21–22). *Cf.* Milton's reference to the story in *Prolusion* III (*Complete Prose,* I, 246).

[9] Application or comparison.

[10] Withdrawing. *NED* cites.

[11] In direct opposition. *NED* cites.

[12] See *Gorgias,* 482–510. Socrates holds that justice is inherent in the nature of things and not, as the Sophist Callicles argues, a mere convention.

[13] See *Ethics,* X, ix. Aristotle affirms the need for public regulation but adds that persuasion privately imparted may at times be more effective.

never attains to any good end of such prohibition, but rather multiplies evil ◀. For if natures resistles sway in love or hate be once compell'd, it grows careles of it self, vitious, useles to friend, unserviceable and spiritles to the Common-wealth. Which *Moses* rightly foresaw, and all wise Lawgivers that ever knew man, what kind of creature he was. The Parliament also and *Clergy* of *England* were not ignorant of this, when they consented that *Harry the 8th* might put away *his Q. Anne of Cleve,* whom he could not like, after he had bin wedded half a year; [14] unles it were that contrary to the Proverb, they made a necessity of that which might have bin a vertu in them to do. For ev'n the freedom and eminence of mans creation gives him to be a Law in this matter to himself, beeing the head of the other sex which was made for him: [15] whom therfore though he ought not to injure, yet neither should he be forc't to retain in society to his own overthrow, nor to hear any judge therin above himself. It being also an unseemly affront to the sequester'd & vail'd modesty of that sex, to have her unpleasingnes and other concealements bandied up and down, and aggravated in open Court by those hir'd maisters of tongue-fence. Such uncomely exigences it befell no lesse a Majesty then *Henry the 8th* to be reduc't to; who finding just reason in his conscience to forgoe his brothers wife, af- ◀ [76] ◀ ter many indignities of beeing deluded, and made a boy of by those his two *cardinal* Judges,[16] was constrain'd at last for want of other prooff, that shee had bin carnally known by Prince *Arthur,* ev'n to uncover the nakednes of that vertuous Lady, & to

[14] Henry's marriage with his fourth wife, Anne of Cleves, was annulled by Convocation, July 10, 1540, approximately six months after the wedding ceremony. The annulment was ratified by both Houses of Parliament on July 12. Deliberations were perfunctory, the King's declaration of "misliking" both before and after the marriage, a "misliking" so great as to deprive him of "the will and power to consummate the same," being considered sufficient to establish the canonical impediment of defective intention. The principal documents are available in Gilbert Burnet, *History of the Reformation of the Church of England* (ed. Nares, 4 vols., London, 1830), IV, 109–13. John Speed, *Historie of Great Britaine* (1632; HEHL), p. 792, briefly states most of the circumstances but is silent about the appeal to canon law.

[15] *Cf.* I Corinthians 11:3: "The head of the woman is the man." *Cf.* also *Paradise Lost,* IV, 440–43.

[16] Cardinals Campeggio and Wolsey, who were delegated by Pope Clement VII to hear Henry's plea for annulment of his marriage with Catherine of Aragon. The legatine court sat during the summer of 1529.

recite openly the obscene evidence of his brothers chamberlain.[17]
Yet it pleas'd God to make him see all the tyranny of *Rome*, by
discovering this which they exercis'd over divorce; and to make
him the beginner of a reformation to this whole Kingdom by first
asserting into his *familiary* [18] power the right of just divorce. Tis
true, an adultres cannot be sham'd anough by any publick proceeding; but that woman whose honour is not appeach't,[19] is lesse injur'd by a silent dismission, being otherwise not illiberally dealt with,
then to endure a clamouring debate of utterles things, in a busines
of that civil secrecy and difficult discerning, as not to be over-much
question'd by neerest friends. Which drew that answer from the
greatest and worthiest *Roman* of his time *Paulus Emilius*, beeing
demanded why he would put away his wife for no visible reason,
This Shoo, <saith> ♦ said ◖ he, and held [45] it out on his foot, *is a
neat shoo, a new shoo, and yet none of* <yee> ♦ *you* ◖ *know where
it wrings me:* [20] much lesse by the unfamiliar cognisance of a fee'd
gamester can such a private difference be examin'd, neither ought it.

<Lastly, All law is for some good that may be frequently attain'd
without the admixture of a wors inconvenience; but the Law forbidding divorce, never attains to any good end of such prohibition,
but rather multiplies evil. If it aim at the establishment of matrimony, wee know that cannot thrive under a loathed and forc't yoke,
but is daily violated: if it seek to prevent the sin of divorcing, that
lies not in the law to prevent; for he that would divorce and marry

---

[17] *Cf.* Speed, *Historie* (1632), pp. 780–81: "Against the lawfulnesse of the
marriage, was alledged the other, formerly solemnized with Prince *Arthur*, the
Kings elder Brother, and the Nuptiall knowledge of Lady *Katherines* body,
which was vehemently prosecuted by the Kings learned Councell, by many
reasons and liklihoods of truth. . . . That she was carnally knowne, was urged
the report of his Chamberlaine, upon certaine words spoken by Prince *Arthur*
the first Morning that he rose from her bed." Speed cites Holinshed and Hall.
Cf. also John Stow, *Annales* (1631), pp. 542–44.

[18] "Pertaining to the control of a family; domestic." *NED*, which cites this as
the only known occurrence.

[19] Impeached, called in question.

[20] See Plutarch, *Aemilius Paulus*, V, 1–2. The remark is not there ascribed to
Aemilius himself but is quoted as applicable to his situation. Plutarch adds that
"it is great and notorious faults that separate many wives from their husbands;
but the slight and frequent frictions arising from some unpleasantness or incongruity of characters, unnoticed as they may be by everybody else, also produce incurable alienations in those whose lives are linked together." Tr. Perrin,
VI, 365.

again, but for the law, hath in the sight of God don it already. Civil or political sin it never was, neither to Jew nor Gentile, nor by any judicial intendment of Christ, only culpable as it transgresses the allowance of *Moses* in the inward man, which not any law but conscience only can evince.> ♦ Again, if Law aim at the firm establishment and preservation of matrimoniall faith, wee know that cannot thrive under violent means, but is the more violated. It is not when two unfortunately met are by the Canon forc't to draw in that yoke an unmercifull dayes work of sorrow till death unharnesse 'em, that then the Law keeps mariage most unviolated and unbrok'n: but when the Law takes order that mariage be accountant and responsible to perform that society, whether it be religious, civill, or corporal, which may be conscionably requir'd and claim'd therein, or else to be dissolv'd if it cannot be undergone: This is to make mariage most indissoluble, by making it a just and equall dealer, a performer of those due helps which instituted the covnant, being otherwise a most unjust contract, and no more to be maintain'd under tuition [21] of law, then the vilest fraud, or cheat, or theft that may be committed. But because this is such a secret kind of fraud or theft, as cannot bee discern'd by law, but only by the plaintife himself, therfore to divorce was never counted a politicall or civil offence neither to *Jew* nor *Gentile*, nor by any judicial intendment of Christ, further then could be discern'd to transgresse the allowance of *Moses*, which was of necessity so large, that it doth all one as if it sent back the matter [77] undeterminable at law, and intractable by rough dealing, to have instructions and admonitions bestow'd about it by them whose spirituall office is to adjure and to denounce, and so left to the conscience. ◀ The law can only ♦ appoint the just and equall conditions of divorce, and is to ◀ look <whether it be> ♦ how it is ◀ an injury to the divorc't, which in truth it can be none, as a meer separation; for if she consent, wherin has the law to right her? or consent not, then is it either just and so deserv'd, or if unjust, such in all likelihood was the divorcer, and to part from an unjust man is a happines, & no injury to be lamented. But suppose it be an injury, the Law is not able to amend it, unlesse she think it other then a miserable redresse to return back from whence she was expell'd, or but entreated to be

[21] Protection.

gon, or els to live apart still maried without mariage, a maried widow. Last, if it be to chast'n the divorcer, what law punishes a deed which is not moral, but natural, a deed which cannot certainly be found to be an injury, or how can it be punisht by prohibiting the divorce, but that the innocent must equally partake ▶ both in the shame and in the smart ◀ ? So that <we see> ▶ which way soever we look ◀ the Law can to no rational purpose forbid divorce, it can only take care that the conditions of divorce be not injurious. ▶ Thus then we see the trial of law how impertinent it is to this question of divorce, how helplesse next, and then how hurtfull.

CHAP. XXII.

The last Reason, why divorce is not to be restrain'd by Law, it being against the Law of nature and of Nations. The larger proof wherof referr'd to Mr. Seldens Book De jure naturali & gentium. *An objection of* Paraeus *answer'd. How it ought to be order'd by the Church. That this will not breed any worse inconvenience nor so bad as is now suffer'd.*

THERFORE the last reason why it should not be, is the example we have, not only from the noblest and wisest Commonwealths, guided by the clearest light of human knowledge, but also from the divine testimonies of God himself, lawgiving in person to a sanctify'd people. That all this is true, who so desires to know at large with least pains, and expects not heer overlong rehersals of that which is by others already so judiciously gather'd, let him hast'n to be acquainted with that noble volume written by our learned *Selden, Of the law of nature & of Nations,*[1] a work more useful and more worthy to be perus'd, whosoever studies to be a great man in wisdom, equity, and justice, then all those *decretals, and sumles sums,*[2] which the *Pontifi-*[78]*cial Clerks* have

---

[1] John Selden (1584–1654), jurist, legal antiquary, and oriental scholar, was a member of the Long Parliament and the Westminster Assembly. His *De Jure Naturali et Gentium, Juxta Disciplinam Ebraeorum* was published in 1640. Book V, chapter vii, to which Milton refers in *CPB*, p. 110 (*Complete Prose*, I, 403), deals with the subject of divorce. For a discussion of Milton's possible indebtedness to this work and to the *Uxor Ebraica* (1646), see Eivion Owen, "Milton and Selden on Divorce," *SP*, XLIII (1946), 233–57. Milton cites and praises Selden's *De Jure Naturali* in *Areopagitica*, below, p. 513.

[2] Endless summas or digests.

doted on, ever since that unfortunat mother famously [3] sinn'd thrice, and dy'd impenitent of her bringing into the world those two misbegott'n infants, & for ever infants *Lombard* & *Gratian*,[4] him the compiler of Canon iniquity, tother the *Tubalcain*[5] of scholastick Sophistry, whose overspreading *barbarism* hath not only infus'd their own bastardy upon the fruitfullest part of human learning; not only dissipated and dejected the clear light of nature in us, & of nations, but hath tainted also the fountains of divine doctrine, & render'd the pure and solid Law of God unbeneficial to us by their calumnious dunceries. Yet this Law which their unskilfulnesse hath made liable to all ignominy, the purity and wisdom of this Law shall be the buckler of our dispute. Liberty of divorce we claim not, we think not but from this Law; the dignity, the faith, the authority therof is now grown among Christians, O astonishment! a labour of no mean difficulty and envy [6] to defend. That it should not be counted a faltring dispence, a flattring permission of sin, the bil of adultery, a snare, is the expence of all this apology. And all that we solicite is, that it may be suffer'd to stand in the place where God set it amidst the firmament of his holy Laws to shine, as it was wont, upon the weaknesses and errors of men perishing els in the sincerity of their honest purposes: for certain there is no memory of whordoms and adulteries left among us now, when this warranted freedom of Gods own giving is made dangerous and discarded for a scrowle of licence. It must be your suffrages and Votes, O English men, that this exploded decree of God and *Moses* may scape, and come off fair without the censure of a shamefull abrogating: which, if yonder Sun ride sure, and mean not to break word with us to morrow, was never yet abrogated by our Saviour. Give sentence, if you please, that the frivolous Canon may reverse the infallible judgement of *Moses* and his great director. Or if it be the

---

[3] Notoriously.

[4] Legend had it that the twelfth-century Italian divines, Johannes Gratian, author of the *Decretum*, and Peter Lombard, author of the *Sententiarum Libri*, were brothers of Peter Comestor, author of the *Historia Scholastica*. "Medieval scholars united in this way, by a fictive kinship, the three great contemporaries who seemed as the fathers of canon law, theology, and Biblical scholarship." *Catholic Encyclopedia*, VI, 730.

[5] Tubal-Cain, according to Genesis 4:22, was "an instructor of every artificer in brass and iron."

[6] Opprobrium.

reformed writers, whose doctrine perswades this rather, their reasons I dare affirm are all silenc't, unlesse it be only this. *Paraeus* on the Corinthians would prove that hardnes of heart in divorce is no more now to be permitted, but to be amerc't with fine and imprisonment.[7] I am not willing to discover the forgettings of reverend men, yet here I must. What article or clause of the whole new Cov'nant can Paraeus bring to exasperat the judicial Law, upon any infirmity under the Gospel? (I say infirmity, for if it were the high hand of sin, the Law as little would have endur'd it as the Gospel) it would not stretch to the dividing of an inheritance; [8] it refus'd to condemn adultery,[9] not that these things should not be [79] don at Law, but to shew that the Gospel hath not the least influence upon judicial Courts, much lesse to make them sharper, and more heavy; lest of all to arraine before a temporal Judge that which the Law without summons acquitted. But saith he, the law was the time of youth, under violent affections, the Gospel in us is mature age, and ought to subdue affections.[10] True, and so ought the Law too, if they be found inordinat, and not meerly natural and blameles. Next I distinguish that the time of the Law is compar'd to youth, and pupillage in respect of the ceremonial part, which led the Jewes as children through corporal and garish rudiments, untill the fulnes of time should reveal to them the higher lessons of faith and redemption. This is not meant of the moral part, therin it soberly concern'd them not to be babies, but to be men in good earnest: the sad and awfull majesty of that Law was not to be jested with; to bring a bearded nonage with lascivious dispensations before that throne, had bin a leud affront, as it is now a grosse mistake. But what discipline is this Paraeus to nourish violent affections in youth, by cockring and wanton indulgences, and

---

[7] *Cf.* the following comment on I Corinthians 7:10–11 (tr. from *Operum Theologicorum*, II, 488): "Those who retain or imitate the hardheartedness of the Jews reveal themselves strangers to the spirit of Christ. . . . The Church is to correct such a one by excluding him from the company of the faithful, the Christian magistrate by subjecting him to imprisonment or fine, in accordance with the precept of the Lord, 'If he neglect to hear the Church, let him be unto thee as an heathen,' and of the Apostle, 'Put away from among yourselves that wicked person.'"

[8] *Cf.* Luke 12:13–14.   [9] *Cf.* John 8:3–11.

[10] *Operum Theologicorum*, II, 488: "In Iudaica gente fuit quasi inventus, quae affectibus violentius rapitur. In nobis est aetas adulta Christi, quae affectibus magis imperare debet."

to chastise them in mature age with a boyish rod of correction. How much more coherent is it to Scripture, that the Law as a strict Schoolmaster should have punisht every trespasse without indulgence so banefull to youth, and that the Gospel should now correct that by admonition and reproof only, in free and mature age, which was punisht with stripes in the childhood and bondage of the Law.[11] What therfore it allow'd then so fairly, much lesse is to be whipt now, especially in penal Courts: and if it ought now to trouble the conscience, why did that angry accuser and condemner Law repreev it? So then, neither from *Moses* nor from Christ hath the Magistrate any authority to proceed against it. ◀ But what? Shall then the disposal of that power return again to the maister of family? Wherfore not? Since God there put it, and the presumptuous Canon thence bereft it.[12] This only must be provided, that the ancient manner be observ'd in presence of the Minister, and other grave selected Elders; who after they shall have admonisht and prest upon him the words of our Saviour, & he shall have protested in the faith of the eternal Gospel, and the hope he has of happy resurrection, that otherwise then thus he cannot doe, and thinks himself, & this his case not contain'd in that prohibition of divorce [46] which Christ pronounc't, the matter not beeing of malice, but of nature, and so not capable of reconciling, to constrain him furder were to unchristen him, to unman him, to throw the moun- ▶ [80] ◀ tain of *Sinai* upon him, with the waight of the whole Law to boot, flat against the liberty and essence of the Gospel, and yet nothing available either to the sanctity of mariage, the good of husband, wife, or childern, nothing profitable either to Church or Common wealth ▶ ; but hurtfull and pernicious to all these respects ◀ . But this <would> ▶ will ◀ bring in confusion. ▶ Yet these cautious mis-

[11] *Cf.* Galatians 3:24–25.

[12] *Cf.* Perkins, *Christian Oeconomie* (*Works,* 1609–13, III, 698): "The *good man* or *master of the familie,* is a person, in whome resteth the private and proper government of the whole houshold, and he comes not unto it by election, as it falleth out in other states, but by the ordinance of God, setled even in the order of nature. The husband indeed naturally beares rule over the wife; parents over their children, masters over their servants: but that person who by the providence of God, hath the place of an husband, a father, a master in his house, the same also by the light of nature, hath the principalitie and soveraigntie therein, and he is *Paterfamilias,* the father and chiefe head of the familie: to him therefore the true right and power over all matters domesticall, of right appertaineth."

trusters might consider, that what they thus object, lights not upon this book, but upon that which I engage against them, the book of God, and of *Moses,* with all the wisdome and providence which had forecast the worst of confusion that could succeed, and yet thought fit of such a permission. But let them be of good cheer, ♦ <Be of good cheer, it would not:> it wrought so little disorder among the *Jews,* that from *Moses* till after the captivity not one of the Profets thought it worth rebuking; for that of *Malachy* well lookt into, will appeare to be, not against divorcing, but rather against keeping strange Concubines, to the vexation of their *Hebrew* wives.[13] If therfore wee Christians may be thought as good and tractable as the *Jews* were, and certainly the prohibiters of divorce presume us to be better, then lesse confusion is to be fear'd for this among us then was among them. If wee bee wors, or but as bad, which lamentable examples confirm wee are, then have wee more, or at least as much need of this permitted law, as they to whom God <expresly> ♦ therfore ♦ gave it ♦ (as they say) ♦ under a harsher covnant. Let not therfore the frailty of man goe on thus inventing needlesse troubles to it self to groan under the fals imagination of a strictnes never impos'd from above, enjoyning that for duty which is an impossible and vain supererogating. *Bee not righteous overmuch,* is the counsel of *Ecclesiastes; why shouldst thou destroy thy self?* [14] Let us not be thus over-curious to strain at *atoms,*[15] and yet to stop every vent and cranny of permissive liberty: lest nature wanting those needful pores, and breathing places which God hath not debarr'd our weaknes, either suddenly break out into some wide rupture of open vice, and frantick heresy, or els inwardly fester with repining and blasphemous thoughts, under an unreasonable and fruitles rigor of unwarranted law. Against which evils nothing can more beseem the religion of the Church or the wisdom of the State, then to consider timely and provide. And in so doing, let them not doubt but they shall vindicate the misreputed honour of God and his great Lawgiver, by suffering him to give his own laws according to the condition of mans nature best known to him, without the unsufferable imputation of dispencing legally with many

---

[13] Malachi 2:14–16. *Cf.* above, p. 257, n. 16.

[14] Ecclesiastes 7:16.

[15] *Cf.* the Biblical "strain at a gnat" (Matthew 23:24). *Atoms,* in popular use, often meant motes or particles of dust. *NED.*

ages of ratify'd adul- ◗ [81] ◖ tery. They shall recover the mis-
attended words of Christ to the sincerity of their true sense from
manifold contradictions, and shall [47] open them with the key of
charity. Many helples Christians they shall raise from the depth of
sadnes and distresse, utterly unfitted, as they are, to serv God or
man: many they shall reclaime from obscure and giddy sects, many
regain from dissolute and brutish licence, many from desperate
hardnes, if ever that were justly pleaded. They shall set free many
daughters of *Israel*, not wanting much of her sad plight *whom
Satan had bound eighteen years.*[16] Man they shall restore to his
just dignity, and prerogative in nature, preferring the souls free
peace before the promiscuous draining of a carnal rage. Mariage
from a perilous hazard and snare, they shall reduce to be a more certain hav'n and retirement of happy society; when they shall judge
according to God and *Moses,* and how not then according to Christ?
when they shall judge it more wisdom and goodnes to break that
covnant seemingly & keep it really, then by compulsion of law to
keep it seemingly, and by compulsion of blameles nature to break it
really, at least if it were ever truly joyn'd. The vigor of discipline
they may then turn with better successe upon the prostitute loose-
nes of the times, when men finding in themselvs the infirmities of
former ages, shall not be constrain'd above the gift of God in them
to unprofitable and impossible observances never requir'd from the
civilest, the wisest, the holiest Nations, whose other excellencies in
moral vertu they never yet could equal. Last of all, to those whose
mind still is to maintain textual restrictions, wherof the bare sound
cannot consist somtimes with humanity, much lesse with charity, I
would ever answer by putting them in remembrance of a command
above all commands, which they seem to have forgot, and who spake
it; in comparison wherof this which they so exalt, is but a petty and
subordinate precept. *Let them goe* therfore with whom I am loath
to couple them, yet they will needs run into the same blindnes with
the Pharises, *let them goe therfore* and consider well what this lesson means, *I will have mercy and not sacrifice;* [17] for on that *saying*

16 *Cf.* Luke 13:16.
17 *Cf.* Matthew 9:13: "But go ye and learn what that meaneth, I will have
mercy and not sacrifice." The words, which refer to Hosea 6:6, were spoken by
Christ to the Pharisees.

all the Law and Profets depend,[18] much more the Gospel whose end and excellence is mercy and peace: Or if they cannot learn that, how will they hear this, which yet I shall not doubt to leave with them as a conclusion: That God the Son hath put all other things under his own feet; but his Commandments he hath left all under the feet of charity.[19]

The end. [48] [20]

▶ Page 15. line 8. *read* it the glassy Sea. p. 32. l. 6. *for* or, *read* nor. p. 39. l. 32. *for* give, *read* find. lin. 34. *for* will, freewill. lin. 38. *read* he acquitts. p. 51. l. 26. for without a comma. [82] ◀

[18] *Cf.* Matthew 22:40, where the law and prophets are said to depend on the love of God and neighbor.

[19] *Cf.* I Corinthians 15:27 and I Timothy 1:5.

[20] The two unnumbered pages of addenda have been incorporated in the text (above, pp. 275 and 285–86).

OF EDUCATION

June, 1644

PREFACE AND NOTES BY DONALD C. DORIAN

THE tractate *Of Education* was first published about June 4 or 5, 1644, as an anonymous pamphlet of eight pages with no title page. It was registered for publication on June 4, 1644, by Thomas Underhill,[1] the registration reading "Entred for his copie under the hands of Master Cranford and Master Man warden, a litle tract touching *Education of Youth,* &c." Thus this slight pamphlet was the first of Milton's works to be registered and licensed (for James Cranford was the licenser) ; and its authorship must have been known to the licenser and to the warden of the Company of Stationers, as it was to George Thomason, who inscribed his copy "By m^r John Milton 5 June 1644."[2] There is no positive evidence to show whether Milton himself or Samuel Hartlib, to whom it was addressed, was responsible for publishing the first edition, except Milton's statement in the text: "I here give you ["these few observations"] to dispose of."[3] Perhaps the publication was intended, as William R. Parker has suggested,[4] for "a limited, almost private circulation," though Milton may have hoped for more than that.

Milton's tractate was one of the many English writings on educational reform that appeared between 1530 and 1660, largely as an attempt to apply the principles of Christian humanism to the practical problems of contemporary life. Yet Milton was not making a deliberate contribution to a series of related works, as in the anti-Episcopal tracts ; on the contrary, his essay is not directly related to any one of the current discussions of education, as is implied by his statement that he was not inclined "to search what many modern *Janua's* and *Didactics* more then ever I shall read, have projected."

---

[1] *A Transcript of the Registers of the Worshipful Company of Stationers,* ed. G. E. Briscoe Eyre (3 vols., London, 1913–14), I, 117.

[2] C59.g.20(12); quoted in French, *Life Records,* II, 101.

[3] Note, however, the view taken in the introduction to this volume, pp. 206–12.

[4] William R. Parker, *Milton's Contemporary Reputation* (Columbus: The Ohio State University Press, 1940), p. 24.

On the other hand, the tractate was written, at Samuel Hartlib's request, as an independent addition to the sequence of proposals for educational reform in England advanced by Hartlib between 1637 and 1654, which are discussed in the introductions to Volume I (pp. 151–66) and the present volume. Some of these proposals, including Milton's, discuss ideas also treated by two important Continental writers: the Spanish humanist Juan Luis Vives (1492–1540) in *De Tradendis Disciplinis;* and John Amos Comenius (1592–1670) in several works, particularly those published in English by Hartlib as *A Reformation of Schooles* (1642). Among English writings on education, Milton's tractate, while broader in purpose and scope than most contemporary ones, does of course treat aspects of the subject that are discussed in detail by other authors before 1644. Some, for example, like Sir Thomas Elyot in *The Governour* (1531), James Cleland in ‘ΗΡΩ-ΠΑΙΔΕΙΑ, *or The Institution of a Young Noble Man* (1607), and Henry Peacham in *The Compleat Gentleman* (1622), share with Milton the purpose of establishing the principles upon which boys should be educated for leadership in the state. Others, like Sir Humphrey Gilbert in *Queene Elizabethes Achademy* (written about 1562),[5] are especially concerned with the more practical question of the right content or curriculum to teach young gentlemen "matters of accion meet for present practize, both of peace and warre"; or, like John Brinsley in *A Consolation for Our Grammar Schooles* (1622), with education for the duties of Christian citizenship; or, like Richard Mulcaster in his *Positions* (1581), and Brinsley in his *Ludus Literarius* (1612), with questions of the best pattern of organization for the schools in regard to age, subjects taught, and exercise. Especially numerous were the writers who urged improvement in the methods of teaching, including Roger Ascham in *The Scholemaster* (1570), John Dury in *A Motion Tending to the Publick Good of This Age, and of Posteritie* (1642, published by Hartlib), Hartlib himself in his collection *The True and Readie Way to Learn the Latin Tongue* (1654; but comprising the earlier methods of Eilhardus Lubinus, Richard Carew, and Montaigne), and (specifically in regard to the improvement of teaching Latin grammar) John Clarke in *Dux Grammaticus Tyronem Scholasticum ad Rectam Orthographiam[,] Syntaxin, & Prosodiam Dirigens* (1633) and Christofer Syms in *An Introduction to, or, The Art of Teaching, the Latine Speach* (1634). At least one writer, too, advocated the establishment of schools throughout England that would make education general if not universal: Samuel Harmar in *Vox Populi, Or Glostersheres Desire* (1642).

As many of these writers range beyond the topics mentioned, so

[5] Ed. F. J. Furnivall, E.E.T.S., Extra Series, No. VIII, 1869, p. 10.

Milton has something in common with each. The distinction of his tractate, aside from its intellectual breadth and its frequent eloquence, consists not in Milton's solution to any specific educational problem of his time, but in the philosophical coherence of his educational principles both throughout the tractate and in relation to his more general views of virtue, liberty, and man's part in the divine scheme of being. These relationships are suggested in the notes that follow; so also are relationships to the contemporary works on education mentioned above. Each of these works and of the books which Milton refers to or recommends in the tractate is described in the notes in an edition available in 1644.

There is little evidence that Milton's writing on education exerted any influence on contemporary writers or practices within his own lifetime.[6] After the first edition of 1644, the tractate was not reprinted until the appearance in 1673 of *POEMS, &c. upon Several Occasions. By Mr. John Milton. Both English and Latin, &c. Composed at several times. With a small Tractate of Education To Mr. Hartlib.* In this volume the second edition of the work appears on pp. 95–117 of the second pagination (sigs. R3–S6), following the Latin poems.

Among the many subsequent editions, the following ones offer especially helpful annotations or other editorial equipment. *Milton's Tractate on Education:* A Facsimile Reprint from the Edition of 1673, edited with an introduction and notes by Oscar Browning (Cambridge, 1890) includes as an introduction the editor's earlier discussion of the tractate in his *Introduction to the History of Educational Theories,* as well as some useful explanatory notes. Brief but valuable notes are also provided in *Selected Essays: Of Education, Areopagitica, The Commonwealth,* by John Milton, edited by Laura E. Lockwood (Boston, 1911). *Milton on Education:* The Tractate *Of Education* with Supplementary Extracts from Other Writings of Milton, edited with an introduction and notes by Oliver Morley Ainsworth (New Haven, 1928), offers some historical discussion of the place of the tractate in relation

---

[6] John Hall of Durham, in *An Humble Motion to the Parliament of England Concerning the Advancement of Learning* (1649; reprinted as *The Advancement of Learning* by Liverpool University Press, 1953), echoes (pp. 26–27), Milton's thoughts about the premature teaching of logic and ethics (Milton's "Proairesis"), with the consequent debasement of the professions of medicine, law, and divinity. Hall indicated in a letter to Hartlib (p. xi, n. 2) that he had read Milton's "excellent discourse of education" (see below, p. 362, n. 2). In addition, Parker in "A Tentative List of Printed Allusions to John Milton, 1641–1674" (*Milton's Contemporary Reputation,* p. 110) quotes one scornful reference in 1670 to "those occasional Writers, that missing preferment in the University, can presently write you their new ways of Education."

to other humanistic writings on education, and a considerable number of passages from Milton's other works bearing on his educational interests, but somewhat limited annotation of the text for a monograph of its scope (355 pages). Ampler assistance, particularly in the treatment of authors mentioned and in the suggestion of significant parallels, may be found in *John Milton: Prose Selections*, edited by Merritt Y. Hughes (New York: The Odyssey Press, 1947).

The present text is based on a copy of the first edition of *Of Education* in the New York Public Library, *KC 1644. It is referred to in the textual notes (below, p. 777) as "A." It is a quarto measuring 18.1 by 13.8 cm. Collation: 4⁰, A⁴, signatures and pagination normal. No title page. A1: line of printer's ornaments; title; text begins. A3v: *"Their Exercise."* A4v: margin-to-margin rule. /*"The end."*/ Margin-to-margin rule. Only two variations in spelling (both on p. 6: "Parliament" in "A" and "B," "Parlament" in all other copies; and "perfected" in "A" and "B," "perfeted" [7] in all others have been found as a result of collation with photostats of the following: "B," Huntington Library 105613; "C," William Andrews Clark Library, University of California at Los Angeles, *PR3570.031; "D," Yale University Library Ij/M642/C641/v.3; "E," Union Theological Seminary 1644/M65; "F," Houghton Library 14496.44.50*.

DONALD C. DORIAN

Douglass College, Rutgers University

---

[7] The Thomason copy, however (British Museum C59.g.20[12]), has "perfited," and shows two other peculiarities: p.. 6, "play writes" for "play-writes," and p. 7, "supper;they" for "supper, they."

Of Education. To Master *Samuel Hartlib.*

Master Hartlib,

Am long since perswaded, that to say, or doe ought worth memory, and imitation, no purpose or respect should sooner move us, then simply the love of God, and of mankinde. Neverthelesse to write now the reforming of Education, though it be one of the greatest and noblest designes, that can be thought on, and for the want whereof this nation perishes, I had not yet at this time been induc't, but by your earnest entreaties, and serious conjurements; as having my minde for the present halfe diverted in the persuance of some other assertions, the knowledge and the use of which, cannot but be a great furtherance both to the enlargement of truth, and honest living, with much more peace. Nor should the lawes of any private friendship have prevail'd with me to divide thus, or transpose my former thoughts, but that I see those aims, those actions which have won you with me the esteem of a person sent hither by some good providence from a farre country to be the occasion and the incitement of great good to this Iland. And, as I heare, you have obtain'd the same repute with men of most approved wisdom, and some of highest authority among us. Not to mention the learned correspondence which you hold in forreigne parts, and the extraordinary pains and diligence which you have us'd in this matter both heer, and beyond the Seas; either by the definite will of God so ruling, or the peculiar sway of nature, which also is Gods working. Neither can I thinke that so reputed, and so valu'd as you are, you would to the forfeit of your own discerning ability, impose upon me an unfit and over ponderous argument, but that the satisfaction which you professe to have receiv'd from those incidentall discourses which we have wander'd into, hath prest & almost constrain'd you into a perswasion, that what you require from me in this point, I neither ought, nor can in conscience deferre beyond this time both of so much need at once, and so much opportunity to trie what God hath determin'd. I will not resist therefore, what ever it is either of divine, or humane obligement that you lay upon me; but will forthwith set down in writing, as you request me, that voluntary *Idea*, which hath long in silence presented it self to me, of a better Education, in extent and comprehension farre more large, and yet of time farre shorter, and of attainment farre more certain, then hath been yet in practice. Briefe I shall endeavour to be; for that which I have to say, assuredly this nation hath extreame need should be done sooner then spok'n. To tell you therefore what I have benefited herein among old renowned Authors, I shall spare; and to search what many modern *Ianua's* and *Didactics* more then ever I shall read, have projected, my inclination leads me not. But if you can accept of these few observations which have flower'd off, and are as it were the burnishing of many studious and contemplative yeers altogether spent in the search of religious and civil knowledge, and such as pleas'd you so well in the relating, I here give you them to dispose of.

A   The

Of Education. To Master *Samuel Hartlib.*[1]

Master Hartlib,[2]

I AM LONG since perswaded, that to say, or doe ought worth
memory, and imitation, no purpose or respect should sooner
move us, then simply the love of God, and of mankinde.[3]
Neverthelesse to write now the reforming of Education, though

[1] The 1673 edition adds, on a separate line: "Written above twenty Years
since."

[2] For an account of Hartlib, particularly in connection with his interest in
educational and other reforms in England and his relationship with John Dury
and John Amos Comenius, see *Complete Prose,* I, 151–66, and Masson, III, 193–
233. Hartlib, of Prussian birth but of Polish and English parentage, studied at
Cambridge in 1625 and 1626 if not earlier (G. H. Turnbull, *Hartlib, Dury and
Comenius* [London: Hodder & Stoughton, 1947], pp. 13–15), and returned to
England to live by 1628. In 1630 he established in Chichester (Turnbull, pp.
16–18) a school "for the education of the gentry of this nation, to advance
piety, learning, morality, and other exercises of industry, not usual then in common schools," though he did not teach in it himself; but as the promised pupils
and boarders did not come in sufficient numbers, he returned to London, in debt,
late in the same year. Still he persevered in his zeal for the improvement of
education; as Dury wrote in a letter of 1635 (Turnbull, p. 116), "he was not
attentive to his owne proffit, but trusting to a blessing from God, continued to
lay out his meanes to begin a reformation of the education of children." He was
particularly interested in the reforms proposed by Comenius, and by 1643 had
published, among eight or more works on various causes he supported (Turnbull, pp. 88–91), at least two by Comenius (for details see below, n. 9). Also by
1643, perhaps through Milton's tutor, Thomas Young, he made Milton's acquaintance, recording in the diary which he entitled *Ephemerides* (Turnbull, p.
40; J. Milton French, *Life Records* [New Brunswick: Rutgers University Press,
II [1950], 82) that "Mr Milton in Aldersgate Street hase written many good
books a great traveller and full of projects and inventions." In keeping with his
efforts to interest Englishmen in the views of Comenius on education, Hartlib
discussed the subject with Milton. Which of them published the brief tractate
which resulted from their discussion is unknown; but there is evidence (Turnbull, p. 39; French, II, 104–105, 115–16) that Hartlib sent copies in 1644 to
Dury and to John Hall of Durham.

[3] *Cf. Church-Government* (*Complete Prose,* I, 810), where Milton, after revealing his hope to "leave something so written to aftertimes, as they should
not willingly let it die," adds his conviction that for this end "there ought no
regard be sooner had, then to Gods glory by the honour and instruction of my
country."

it be one of the greatest and noblest designes, that can be thought on, and for the want whereof this nation perishes,[4] I had not yet at this time been induc't, but by your earnest entreaties, and serious conjurements; as having my minde for the present halfe diverted in the persuance of some other assertions, the knowledge and the use of which, cannot but be a great furtherance both to the enlargement of truth, and honest living, with much more peace. Nor should the lawes of any private friendship have prevail'd with me to divide thus, or transpose my former thoughts, but that I see those aims, those actions which have won you with me the esteem of a person sent hither by some good providence from a farre country to be the occasion and the incitement of great good to this Iland. And, as I hear, you have obtain'd the same repute with men of most approved wisdom, and some of highest authority among us. Not to mention the learned correspondence which you hold in forreigne parts, and the extraordinary pains and diligence which you have us'd in this matter both heer, and beyond the Seas; either by the definite will of God so ruling, or the peculiar sway of nature, which also is Gods working. Neither can I thinke that so reputed, and so valu'd as you are, you would to the forfeit of your own discerning ability, impose upon me an unfit and over ponderous argument, but that the satisfaction which you professe to have receiv'd from those incidentall discourses which we have wander'd into, hath prest & almost constrain'd you into a perswasion, that what you require from me in this point, I neither ought, nor can in conscience deferre beyond this time both of so much need at once, and so much opportunity[5] to trie what God hath determin'd.[6] I will not resist

---

[4] *Cf.* Milton's retrospective description of this tractate in the *Second Defence* (1654, p. 91) as brief but sufficiently long for those who recognize the supreme importance of its subject in inculcating virtue, which is the source of true and inward liberty, and in providing for the sound government and lasting preservation of a commonwealth.

[5] Following the report of June 15, 1641, from the Grand Committee on the Bill for the abolition of "Deans, Deans and Chapters, Archdeacons, Prebendaries, Chanters, Canons and Petty Canons, and their Officers," the House of Commons resolved "That all the Lands, taken by this Bill from the Deans and Chapters, shall be employed to the Advancement of Learning and Piety" (*Commons Journals*, II, 176). Milton probably alluded to this resolution when he wrote in *Animadversions* (published in July, 1641) that "there cannot bee a better way then to take the misbestowed wealth which they ["our misguided Ancestors"] were cheated of, from these our *Prelates*, . . . and to bestow their beneficent

therefore, what ever it is either of divine, or humane obligement that you lay upon me; but will forthwith set down in writing, as you request me, that voluntary *Idea*,[7] which hath long in silence presented it self to me, of a better Education, in extent and comprehension farre more large, and yet of time farre shorter, and of attainment farre more certain, then hath been yet in practice. Briefe I shall endeavour to be; for that which I have to say, assuredly this nation hath extreame need should be done sooner then spok'n.[8] To tell you therefore what I have benefited herein among old renowned Authors, I shall spare; and to search what many modern *Janua's* and *Didactics* [9] more then ever I shall read, have projected,

gifts upon places and meanes of Christian education" (*Complete Prose*, I, 702–703). In later votes the House reaffirmed their intention "to vindicate themselves from the Imputation laid upon them, of Discouraging of Learning" (*Commons Journals*, II, 317), and provided that the revenues of sequestered estates which had formerly supported schools and colleges should continue to be used for this purpose. See William A. L. Vincent, *The State and School Education 1640–1660 in England and Wales* (London: S.P.C.K. for the Church Historical Society, 1950), pp. 29, 46–48, and 77.

[6] See Acts 17:26.

[7] Probably used in the Platonic sense, as suggested by Herbert Agar in *Milton and Plato* (Princeton, 1928), p. 66. On the aspects of Platonism reflected throughout this tractate, see Irene Samuel, *Plato and Milton* (Ithaca: Cornell University Press, 1947), chapter 5, especially pp. 107–109 and 115.

[8] In *Of Reformation* (1641; *Complete Prose*, I, 590) Milton had rebuked the prelates because, instead of the "expences . . . profusely throwne away" in their ceremonies, courts, and ornate decorations, "*Churches* and *Schools* might be built, where they cry out for want, and more added where too few are." As late as 1654, near the conclusion of the *Second Defence* (1654, p. 161), he similarly urged upon Cromwell the need to provide better for the education and morals of youth.

[9] An allusion to *Janua Linguarum Reserata* and *Didactica Magna*, two works of John Amos Comenius (Komenský), Moravian theologian and educator (1592–1670). For an account of the life and principal writings of Comenius, his proposals for a complete educational reformation, and his recent visit to England (September 21, 1641, to June 20, 1642), see *Complete Prose*, I, introduction, pp. 159–65, and above, pp. 184–86.

Hartlib was profoundly interested in Comenius' projects, seeking funds in England to support his work and making every effort to arrange for him to visit England (Turnbull, *Hartlib, Dury and Comenius*, pp. 342–54). When the visit did take place, Comenius stayed with Hartlib throughout (*ibid.*, pp. 357 and 369). There is no evidence that Milton met Comenius at that time; more likely, he learned about him later from Hartlib's reports, and from the reputation and possibly some perusal of his works published up to 1644. The *Didactica Magna*, though probably written between 1628 and 1632, was not published until 1657; but the plan of the work was already known by the inclusion of its chapter titles in some of the publications mentioned below. Various other of Comenius' works had been published in England before 1644, several of them through Hartlib's efforts. The *Janua Linguarum Reserata, sive Seminarium Linguarum et Scientiarum Omnium*, first published at Leszno (Lissa), Poland, in 1631, promptly and repeatedly appeared in English editions. Five of these, with Latin, English, and French in parallel columns, were published under the title *Porta Linguarum Trilinguis Reserata et Aperta* (London, 1631, 1633, 1637, 1639, and 1640; a copy of the last, called *"Quint. Editio"* on the title page, but not listed in *STC*, is in CUL). There followed two further editions, described as the fifth and sixth, containing only Latin and English, under the title *Janua Linguarum Reserata* (London, 1641 and 1643). The plan of all is the same: to teach languages and important facts simultaneously through a series of sentences (1058 in the *Porta* and 1000 in the *Janua*), grouped in 100 chapters or "titles" ranging from external nature through man (his physical being, faculties, and occupations) and useful knowledge of many kinds, on to moral virtues and death, God's providence, and the angels. In 1637 Hartlib published at Oxford the *Conatuum Comenianorum Praeludia*, from a manuscript sent him by Comenius to describe his great Pansophic project, the production of an encyclopedic textbook that would make all knowledge available to all men (see *Complete Prose*, I, 162–63). In the same year, and also at Oxford, a similar publication appeared under the title *Porta Sapientiae Reserata: Sive Pansophiae Christianae Seminarium*, with no indication of Hartlib's connection with it; the fifty-two pages of the text of this edition are followed by six unnumbered pages headed "Praecipua Capita *Didacticae Magnae*" and presenting thirty chapter topics of this unpublished work (UTSL). In 1639 Hartlib brought out at London the *Pansophiae Prodromus*, including the *Praeludia*, the *Dilucidatio* (*Conatuum Pansophicorum Dilucidatio*, published by Comenius at Leszno in 1638 to defend his plan against any suspicion of impiety), and the chapter titles of the *Didactica Magna*. Then in 1642 Hartlib published at London *A Reformation of Schooles*, comprising English translations of the *Praeludia* and the *Dilucidatio*, a table of "The Severall Titles of the Seven Parts of the Temple of Christian Pansophie," and finally thirty-two chapter titles of the *Great Didactic*. These publications, then, are the educational writings of Comenius readily accessible to Milton in England before 1644 if he cared to read them. They express some views on education with which Milton would agree, and some which he probably would not accept. He would agree with Comenius, for example, that too long a time was usually spent in learning the Latin language (*Janua*, 1641, sig. A2) and that it was wasteful to spend several years in learning grammar (*ibid.; A Reformation*, pp. 12 and 20). He probably would not accept Comenius' method of teaching languages through sentences designed to develop the pupils' vocabulary (*Janua*) without leading directly to the reading of "good authors," or Comenius' ardent desire *"that all young ones, whether males or females, none excepted, may be brought up in learning"* (part of the full title of *The Great Didactic* in *A Reformation*, p. 92) and that "all should be taught in everything" (title of chapter X, *ibid.*, p. 94). For further discussion of the relationship between their educational views, see below, nn. 12, 17, 22, and 84.

my inclination leads me not.[10] But if you can accept of these few observations which have flowr'd off, and are as it were the burnishing of many studious and contemplative yeers altogether spent in the search of religious and civil knowledge,[11] and such as pleas'd you so well in the relating, I here give you them to dispose of. [1]

The end then of learning [12] is to repair the ruins [13] of our first

[10] It is not necessary to interpret Milton's allusion to Comenius as more or less contemptuous, as practically all editors of the tractate have done. Milton disclaims intending to survey the writings of such contemporary educational theorists as Comenius, which would be unnecessary to give Hartlib "a generall view in writing . . . of that which at severall times I had discourst with you concerning the best and Noblest way of Education" (below, p. 414). If he had been prejudiced against all such reformers, whose works he appears from this sentence not to have read, it may be questioned why he had spoken above in such high praise of Hartlib, one of their leaders and a principal sponsor of Comenius in England. He based this tractate rather on what he had "benefited herein among old renowned Authors," such as Plato, Isocrates, and Aristotle (below, p. 407); on his own interest for some years past in "the Education of Children" (Commonplace Book, Complete Prose, I, 405–406; first entry about 1635–38); and on his immediate concern with the practical problem of teaching pupils of his own, from 1639 or 1640 until some years after writing the tractate (Masson, III, 253 and 656; French, Life Records, II, 6–8 and passim).

On the relation of Milton to Hartlib, compare, however, the introduction to this volume, above, pp. 206–12.

[11] The years "altogether" so spent were probably, in Milton's opinion, the twelve years since his leaving Cambridge.

[12] The essentially religious purpose of all education affirmed here is the foundation of Milton's whole plan, and underlies the more practical definition in the following paragraph ("I call therefore a compleate and generous Education . . .") as well as the detailed sequence of studies in his program. While this religious end was generally accepted by English educators of the Renaissance, no matter how prominent a place they gave to the pagan classics in their curricula, few if any other writers on education up to this time had given evidence of seeing as clearly as Milton did exactly how secular classical studies and practical knowledge might subserve the religious purpose. Contrast the view of Comenius, in the translation of Conatuum Comenianorum Praeludia published by Hartlib in 1642 as part of A Reformation of Schooles (UTSL), that among "unnecessary" studies are (p. 12) "the most part of the vanities of the Gentiles, the name of their petty Deities, together with their lying histories, and fables"; or (ibid., p. 94, chapter title XXV for the Didactica Magna) "It is plainly demonstrated, that (if we would have such a reformation of Schooles, as is according to the rules of true Christianity) Profane, and Heathen Authors must be either quite rejected, or used with more choice and caution." The Spanish humanist Juan Luis Vives (1492–1540) similarly warns (De Tradendis Disciplinis, in his Joannis Lodovici Vivis Valentini de Disciplinis [Antwerp, 1531; UTSL], f. 103v; there is an accurate translation by Foster Watson published as Vives: On Education [Cambridge, 1913]) that the schoolboy should come to the reading of heathen authors as if entering poisonous fields. Ainsworth (Milton on

parents by regaining to know God aright, and out of that knowledge
to love him, to imitate him, to be like him,[14] as we may the neerest
by possessing our souls of true vertue, which being united to the
heavenly grace of faith [15] makes up the highest perfection. But be-

Education, pp. 42–45) distinguished in Milton's tractate "two objects or ends of
education which do not at once seem to harmonize": the Hebraic one set forth
here (reflecting the traditional assumption of human corruption as stated in
Psalm 14:1–3 and Romans 3:23) and the Greek view of "education as a preparation for service to the State" given in the following paragraph of the text; and
he suggested that the harmonious union of the two is attained when Milton
complements "the systematic study of Nature, including man and his achievements," with theology as "the consummation of the religious teaching." Probably, however, there was not the slightest conflict in Milton's consciousness
between his consistently religious purpose and the carefully planned humanistic
studies he proposed to use in fulfilling it; biblical and Platonic echoes harmonize
even in this sentence of the text (see below, n. 14). Thus Basil Willey (*The
Seventeenth Century Background* [London: Chatto & Windus, 1934], pp. 241–
45) pertinently cites this passage in discussing Milton's attempt "to reconstruct
protestant doctrine in terms of a humanistic ethic."

[13] Hughes (*Prose Selections,* p. 31, n. 6) cites Francis Bacon and Sir Thomas
Browne as examples of other seventeenth-century writers reflecting this traditional belief that the loss of intellectual perfection was incurred in the fall of
man. See Bacon, *De Dignitate et Augmentis Scientiarum,* in *Works,* edited by
James Spedding, Robert Leslie Ellis, and Douglas Denon Heath (15 vols.,
Boston, 1861–64), II, 101; and Browne, *Pseudodoxia Epidemica,* I, v, in *Works,*
edited by Geoffrey Keynes (6 vols., London: Faber & Gwyer, Ltd., 1928–31), II,
40. Milton later elaborated his own view in *Christian Doctrine,* I, xii.

[14] The biblical source of this phrase refers to the life to come (I John 3:2:
"when he shall appear, we shall be like him"), and Milton therefore qualifies it
("as we may the neerest"). Already, in writing *Of Reformation,* Milton had
criticized (*Complete Prose,* I, 571) those who wrote of governing a Christian
commonwealth without teaching "that to govern well is to train up a Nation in
true wisdom and vertue, and that which springs from thence magnanimity,
(take heed of that) and that which is our beginning, regeneration, and happiest
end, likenes to *God,* which in one word we call *godlines.*" *Cf.* also *Church-Government (Complete Prose,* I, 837): "nothing fitter for us to think on, then to
be like him, united to him." At the same time this passage in the text has been
called by J. C. Maxwell ("Plato and Milton," *MLR,* XLIII [1948], 409–10)
"One of the clearest echoes in Milton of a specific passage in Plato." The source
he gives is *Theaetetus,* 176 a–c, where the following phrases are most closely
parallel: "to escape from earth to the dwelling of the gods . . . is to become
like God, so far as this is possible; and to become like God is to become righteous and holy and wise. . . . God is . . . utterly and perfectly righteous, and
there is nothing so like him as that one of us who in turn becomes most nearly
perfect in righteousness" (tr. Harold N. Fowler [London and New York, 1921]).

[15] See II Peter 1:5–8 (Ainsworth, *Milton on Education,* p. 326). Ruth Mohl's
Essay, "Milton and the Idea of Perfection" (*Studies in Spenser, Milton, and the
Theory of Monarchy* [New York: King's Crown Press, 1949]), provides a help-
ful commentary on this sentence.

cause our understanding cannot in this body [16] found it selfe but on
sensible things,[17] nor arrive so cleerly to the knowledge of God and

[16] In the preface to Book II of *Church-Government* (*Complete Prose*, I, 801)
Milton had distinguished between two kinds of knowledge: "that knowledge that
rests in the contemplation of naturall causes and dimensions, which must needs
be a lower wisdom, as the object is low," and the knowledge "of God, and of his
true worship, and what is infallibly good and happy in the state of mans life, . . .
the only high valuable wisdom indeed." Here he is affirming that man cannot
advance from the lower wisdom to the higher except as his education proceeds
from "sensible things" to "the knowledge of God and things invisible." Milton
may have recalled Plato, *Phaedo,* 69, and *Symposium,* 209–12; in the latter
passage Diotima instructs Socrates in the steps by which one may progress from
the love of the individual and concrete beauty to that of the universal and
abstract, from the earthly to the divine. In specific reference to contemporary
schooling, *cf.* Dury, *A Motion* (1642), p. 21: "If wee . . . know that a man is
first naturall, and then spirituall; I thinke it fit to move that assistance may be
given . . . unto those that labour for the rectifying of mens naturall parts, by
reforming and facilitating all the meanes of humane learning for the schooles
aswell of old as young Schollers."

[17] Several writers had anticipated Milton in urging that education should proceed from the "sensible" to the intellectual, from the visible to the invisible,
either in the whole progress Milton has just described or in specific application
to the teaching of languages. (Since he says "the same method is necessarily to
be followed in all discreet teaching," he would presumably endorse both general
and particular instances.) Vives, in *De Tradendis Disciplinis* (*Valentini de
Disciplinis,* 1531), mentions both, though with significant differences from
Milton. In connection with the teaching of Latin he remarks (f. 99; Watson,
p. 103) that pupils learning the first rudiments must learn to name things "quae
sub sensus veniunt," though more advanced students should learn to express
abstract thoughts. Later, after introducing logic as a means of distinguishing
the true from the false, he proposes (ff. 112–112v; Watson, pp. 166–68) that
some qualified students should acquire a knowledge of nature ("rerum naturae
cognitio"), beginning with things accessible to the senses ("sensibus ipsis
pervia"), for these are the entrance to all knowledge ("ad cognitionem omnem
aditus"). Comenius, in the first treatise (*Praeludia*) translated in *A Reformation
of Schooles,* was closer to Milton's view when he argued (pp. 17–18) for "one
and the same symmetry of all things, both sensuall, intellectuall, & revealed.
Now this we cannot behold without a perfect squaring, and unseparable consoli-
dation of the principles of knowledge (Sense, Reason, and Divine Revelation).
. . . And wheresoever sense is deficient, there reason with its certaine rules must
also act its part; but when Reason is [at] a stand, we must then have recourse
unto Divine Revelation." On a more elementary plane, Eilhardus Lubinus (in
Hartlib, *The True and Readie Way,* 1654, p. 34) proposed teaching Latin words
by showing pictures of objects with their Latin names, beginning with most
familiar things in the home; and Dury urges (*A Motion,* 1642, p. 23) that "the
Systeme of things obvious to the sences of children, is to be insinuated unto
their imaginations, with the proper names thereof; that they may have a true
conceipt of the simplest and outward things of the world, as a rude matter of
that whereof afterward they are to receive instructions."

things invisible, as by orderly conning over the visible and inferior creature, the same method is necessarily to be follow'd in all discreet teaching. And seeing every nation [18] affords not experience and tradition anough [19] for all kinde of learning, therefore we are chiefly taught the languages of those people who have at any time been most industrious after wisdom; So that language is but the instrument [20] convaying to us things usefull to be known. And though a linguist should pride himselfe to have all the tongues that *Babel* cleft the world into, yet, if he have not studied the solid things in them as well as the words and lexicons,[21] he were nothing

---

[18] Andrew Bongiorno points out ("Tendencies in Milton's 'Of Education,' " *JGE*, IV [1950], 106–107) that in the tractate Milton exemplifies the "new nationalism" of the Renaissance. He had already shown, in *Church-Government*, his belief that this nationalism harmonized with his duty to God by announcing his decision (*Complete Prose*, I, 810) that in his writing "there ought no regard be sooner had, then to Gods glory by the honour and instruction of my country." Yet, as Bongiorno comments, in Milton's plan of education for the betterment of his own nation, "all the books he prescribes had been produced in Greece, Rome, and Palestine and in the Italy of the Renaissance," with "not a single work written by an Englishman."

[19] The way to Milton's objective in education, James Holly Hanford has observed (*A Milton Handbook* [New York: Crofts, 1946], p. 95), "is through an understanding of the civilization of antiquity, not as a dead or remote thing, but as an experience applicable at every point to modern life."

[20] Read as a whole and in its context, this sentence affirms that utility is the primary value, but not necessarily the exclusive value, of language study. In education as here defined, "we are chiefly taught . . . languages" for the "experience and tradition" of other nations which they make accessible, "So that language is but the instrument convaying to us things usefull to be known." Linguistic study unduly prolonged, as if it were an end in itself, may make the whole learning process "unpleasing" and "unsuccessfull"; but languages studied "chiefly" as an instrument giving prompt access to "the solid things in them" may be learned "easily and delightfully" and open the way to "the substance of good things, and Arts in due order." In "Ad Patrem," ll. 78–89, Milton testified to the rewarding pleasures he had himself found through languages thus studied primarily for the knowledge they made available.

[21] Among those who had anticipated this criticism of studying words rather than the "things" they represent, in addition to Vives, were Erasmus and Francis Bacon. Erasmus opens his essay *De Ratione Studii* with the assertions that all knowledge is either of truths (*rerum*) or of words; and that, though knowledge of words must be earlier, the knowledge of truths is more important. (*De Ratione Studii* [Strasbourg, 1523; CUL], f. 2v: "PRINCIPIO *duplex omnino videtur cognitio, rerum, ac verborum. Verborum prior, rerum potior.*") For discussion of the sources and implications of Erasmus' distinction see Thomas W. Baldwin, *William Shakspere's Small Latine & Lesse Greeke* (2 vols., Urbana: University of Illinois Press, 1944), I, 79; and William H. Woodward, *Desiderius*

so much to be esteem'd a learned man, as any yeoman or tradesman competently wise in his mother dialect only. Hence appear the many mistakes which have made learning generally so unpleasing and so unsuccessfull; first we do amisse to spend seven or eight yeers meerly in scraping together so much miserable Latin, and Greek,[22] as might be learnt otherwise easily and delightfully in one

Erasmus concerning the Aim and Method of Education (Cambridge, 1904), pp. 138–39, with his English version of De Ratione Studii at pp. 162–78. Bacon, in the Advancement of Learning (Works, VI, 120), calls it "the first distemper of learning, when men study words and not matter," adding that "words are but the images of matter."

[22] The protest against delaying the study of authors for their content through unnecessarily prolonged study of grammar alone had become fairly widespread by this time.

Erasmus had condemned (De Ratione Studii, f. 3) the multitude of grammarians who held back the boys for many years in such cramming (inculcandis), maintaining himself that the ability to speak well was best learned from conversation with those who did speak well and from the constant reading of good authors. And, as Milton probably knew, John Colet, who either founded or reorganized and endowed St. Paul's School, had endorsed and expounded this view. In "A lytell proheme to the booke called Grammatices Rudimenta" (No. XIII of A Collection of Miscellanies appended by Samuel Knight to The Life of Dr. John Colet, Dean of S. Paul's [London, 1724; PUL], pp. 451–53) Colet wrote: "For in the begynning men spake not latyn bycause suche rules were made; but contrary wyse, bycause men spake suche latyn, upon that folowed the rules were made. . . . Wherfore well beloved maysters and techers of grammer, after the partes of speche suffyciently knowen in your scholes, rede and expounde playnly unto your scholers good authours, and shewe to them every word and in every sentence what they shall note and observe. . . . For redyng of good bokes, dylygent informacion of taught maysters, studyous advertence, and takyng hede of lerners, heryng eloquent men speke, and finally besy imytacyon with tonge and penne, more avayleth shortly to get the trewe eloquent speche, than all the tradycions, rules, and preceptes of maysters." In 1531 Sir Thomas Elyot had published similar reasons in The Governour, book I, chapter X (Everyman's Library edition, p. 35): "Grammer beinge but an introduction to the understanding of autors, if it be made to longe or exquisite to the lerner, hit in a maner mortifieth his corage: And by that time he cometh to the most swete and pleasant redinge of olde autours, the sparkes of fervent desire of lernynge is extincte with the burdone of grammer, lyke as a lyttel fyre is sone quenched with a great heape of small stickes: so that it can never come to the principall logges where it shuld longe bourne in a great pleasaunt fire." Early in the seventeenth century, James Cleland had deplored ('Ηρωπαιδεία, or The Institution of a Young Noble Man [Oxford, 1607; YUL], pp. 24–25) that "so many hopful young Nobles, borne and ordained for more generous designes," should "trouble their heads seaven or eight yeares with the Heteroclits of Despauter, throw the little Judgment of their Tutors, who often have even as much wit, as a Gnat hath bloud. Such ignorant guides dragging young Noble spirits through so many bryars and brambles, cause them to forsake al good

yeer.[23] And that which casts our proficiency therein so much behinde, is our time lost partly in too oft idle vacancies [24] given both

letters and to despise the verie name of learning and the professors therof."
Comenius, in the first treatise (*Conatuum Comenianorum Praeludia*) translated
in *A Reformation of Schooles,* proposes (pp. 11–12) to correct the "Prolixity of
studies" by omitting such "unnecessary things . . . as weary out mens braines
to little benefit, of which sort are most of the rules of Grammar, which over-
burden children's minds, and consume their yeares." Hartlib's awareness of the
problem is shown by his inclusion in *The True and Readie Way* (1654) of what
had been written by Eilhardus Lubinus in 1614 and by the late Sir Richard
Carew (d. *ca.* 1643) at an undisclosed date. Lubinus criticized too much memorizing of rules without understanding how to put them into practice, and asked (p.
34): "if the Latine Tongue can be learned in two, or surely, three years space,
to what end shall we sweat and toil ten, twelve or more years?" Carew, who
was taught Latin "by the Rules of *Lillies* Grammar," narrated (p. 46) how, "by
reading and talking" on an embassy to France, he "learn'd more French in three
quarters of a year then I had done Latine in above thirteen," and concluded
that "usuall Talking, and much Writing and Reading open a surer and readier
Way to attain any Tongue, then the tedious course which is used in the Latine
by construing and pearsing according to the Rules of Grammar." Thanks to
Colet's influence, Milton himself at St. Paul's School probably studied Latin
grammar for only four years, then Greek grammar for three, and Hebrew
grammar for the last one, the introduction to each language being followed before long by "solid" reading (see Donald L. Clark's "Conjectured Curriculum"
in his *John Milton at St. Paul's School* [New York: Columbia University Press,
1948], p. 121). But Milton would have grammatical study still further "abbreviated," and later proposed to accomplish this for Latin partly by teaching accidence and grammar together in English; hence his *Accedence Commenc't Grammar* (1669, "To the Reader").

[23] Edward Phillips wrote that "in a years time" Milton made him and his
brother John (respectively ten and nine years old when they began) "capable of
interpreting a Latin authour at sight" (Helen Darbishire, ed., *The Early Lives
of Milton* [London, 1932], p. 12; cited hereafter as *Early Lives*). This was
written by Phillips in Aubrey's minutes for Milton's life; Aubrey added that
"Cato, Varro, & Columella de Re rusticâ were the very first Authors they
learn't." In Edward Phillips' own *Life of Milton* are listed the Latin and Greek
authors he and his brother read under Milton (*Early Lives,* p. 60) "through his
excellent judgment and way of Teaching, far above the Pedantry of common
publick Schools (where such Authors are scarce ever heard of) . . . within no
greater compass of time, then from Ten to Fifteen or Sixteen Years of Age."
Of the twenty-one writers Phillips lists, fourteen are also among the forty-eight
authors named in this tractate.

[24] Milton's objection is probably not to regular vacations (*cf.* Prolusion VI
[*Complete Prose,* I, 266]: "The alternation of toil and pleasure usually has the
effect of annihilating the boredom brought about by satiety and of making us
the more eager to resume our interrupted tasks"), but rather to the frequent
holydays, on which secular studies were suspended. Such days were not, however, completely "idle," for Article 79 of the *Constitutiones sive Canones
Ecclesiastici* of 1604 (UTSL) required that schoolmasters take their pupils to

to schools and Universities, partly in a preposterous [25] exaction,
forcing the empty wits of children to compose Theams, verses, and
Orations,[26] which are the acts of ripest judgement and the finall
work of a head fill'd by long reading, and observing, with elegant
maxims,[27] and copious invention.[28] These are not matters to be

church in the parish in which they taught on every sacred and holy day ("sacro
quolibet & Festivo die"), and, on their return, examine them upon what they
had learned there. Later in the tractate Milton recommends the teaching of
theology and church history to advanced students on "Sundayes . . . and every
evening"; his omission of Saints' days suggests that he would have these spent
like any other days in the school week.

[25] In the original sense of *praeposterus*, the last part foremost, or in reversed
order.

[26] In proposing thus to postpone formal training in writing and speaking the
classical tongues until after wide reading in them, Milton is radically opposing
the established practice of the Renaissance grammar schools. While schoolmasters of that era taught the classical authors, the attention of their younger
pupils was in general directed toward observing the eloquent phrases in which
ideas were expressed, rather than toward a full comprehension of those ideas.
Hence the boys collected neat and felicitous examples of classical style in their
notebooks, and with the aid of these, and of printed phrase-books and compilations of models, were taught in their own childish compositions to imitate what
they had read. For a clear exposition of this prevailing system, see Foster
Watson, *The English Grammar Schools to 1660: Their Curriculum and Practice*
(Cambridge, 1908), pp. 5–8, 422–39 (on themes), 454–67 (on orations), and
468–86 (on verse writing, sometimes prescribed as early as the second or fourth
form). For the practices in the school Milton attended, see Clark, *Milton at
St. Paul's*, pp. 198–208 (on verse writing) and 208–13 (on themes). Clark doubts
(p. 213) that in this passage of the text Milton has St. Paul's in mind, since
there the influence of Erasmus and Colet had made "conversing among pure
Authors digested" the basis of the school's educational philosophy. One surviving
theme of Milton's own, an advanced school exercise probably composed during
his final years at St. Paul's, is translated and discussed in *Complete Prose*, I,
1034–39.

[27] The context makes clear Milton's intention: that the boys should select
their own *sententiae* for inclusion in their commonplace books, as their judgment
and taste develop through "long reading," instead of drawing on the ready-made
textbook collections then in use. Prominent among the latter were Erasmus,
Apophthegmatum . . . *Libri Sex* (many editions, including Paris, 1531 [RUL]);
Lycosthenes (Conrad Wolffhart), *Apophthegmata* (many editions, including
London, 1635 [PUL], which contains also the *Parabolae sive Similitudines* of
Erasmus, revised by Lycosthenes); and Thomas Draxe, *Bibliotheca Scholastica
Instructissima* (London, 1616; FSL).

[28] *Inventio* as a part of rhetoric was the discovery of material to use in writing
or speaking, and included a knowledge of where to seek arguments and of how
to recognize material suitable to one's purpose. See Milton's own definition of
the term in his *Art of Logic* (1672, chapter II). Milton's phrase "copious invention" suggests that the goal of *copia verborum* (copiousness as attained

wrung from poor striplings, like blood out of the nose, or the plucking of untimely fruit: besides the ill habit which they get of wretched barbarizing [29] against the Latin and Greek *idiom*, with their untutor'd *Anglicisms*, odious to be read, yet not to be avoided without a well continu'd and judicious conversing [30] among pure Authors [31] digested, which they scarce taste, wheras, if after some preparatory grounds of speech by their certain forms [32] got into memory, they were led to the praxis thereof in some chosen short book lesson'd throughly to them, they might then forthwith proceed

through practice in "varying" phrases by synonymy, tropes, etc.) might be reached according to the plan of Erasmus' *De Copia*, which treats *elocutio* (varying through schemes and tropes) and *inventio* (varying through "topics," or discovery of arguments) as preparation for reading the classical authors and collecting one's own materials from them. See Baldwin, *Shakspere's Small Latine*, II, 176–81, on this aspect of *De Copia*.

[29] In Letter 9 (to Benedetto Buonmattei, September 10, 1638; *Complete Prose*, I, 329–30) Milton affirmed the importance of maintaining pure and correct speech, arguing that a decadent language indicates a decadent people. *Cf. Ad Patrem*, ll. 83–84.

[30] In the sense of "associating," from Latin *conversari*, to live or associate with. *Cf. An Apology* (*Complete Prose*, I, 883): "among whom my conversation hath been."

[31] In teaching the subjects of the medieval trivium (grammar, logic, and rhetoric), the general trend in Renaissance schools was to elevate grammar to the position of first importance which had been given to logic in the Middle Ages, and to introduce literature largely to illustrate grammatical rules. In opposing this tendency, which was widely followed in English schools of the early seventeenth century, Milton is reverting to the more genuinely humanistic position of such sixteenth-century writers as Elyot (*The Governour*, 1531), Ascham (*The Scholemaster*, 1570), Erasmus, and Colet. (See Watson, *English Grammar Schools*, pp. 3–4 and 364–66.) See above, n. 22, for the views of Erasmus and Colet on the importance of proceeding promptly from the study of the rules of grammar to the reading of "good authors." Colet insists more specifically, in his statutes for St. Paul's School, on the study of both Christian and pagan authors who wrote pure Latin (*Statutes of Dean Colet, Founder of St. Paul's School, in 1512 . . . now Re-printed in the Year 1816* [London; NYPL], pp. 12–13): "I would they were taught always in good literature bothe Laten and Greke, and good autors such as have the verrye Romayne eloquence joyned with wisdom, specially Cristen autors that wrote theire wisdome with clean and chaste Laten, other in verse or in prose. . . . I will the Children learne . . . other authors Christian . . . and suche other as shall be thought convenient and most to purpose unto the true laten speeche, all Barbary, all corruption, all Laten adulterate . . . fylthines and all such abusion whiche the later blynde worlde brought in whiche more rather may be called blotterature then Litterature, I utterly abannyshe and exclude out of this Scole."

[32] Probably paradigms, as suggested by Browning (*Milton's Tractate on Education*, p. 28).

to learn the substance of good things, and Arts [33] in due order, which would bring the whole language quickly into their power. This I take to be the most rationall and most profitable way of learning languages, and whereby we may best hope to give account to God of our youth spent herein: And for the usuall method of teaching Arts, I deem it to be an old errour of universities not yet well recover'd from the Scholastick grosnesse [34] of barbarous ages, that in stead of beginning with Arts most easie, and those be such as are most obvious to the sence,[35] they present their young unmatriculated novices at first comming [36] with the most intellective abstractions of Logick [37] & metaphysicks: [38] So that they having but newly

[33] Probably not, as most editors have taken it, a specific reference to the seven "liberal arts"; rather, fields of knowledge in general, as later in this paragraph, where "Arts" includes those studies "most obvious to the sence." Milton customarily uses the full term "liberal arts" when that is clearly his meaning: see the numerous citations in Columbia, *Index, s.v.* "Arts," and "Liberal."

[34] Milton's resentful scorn for the backward curricula and methods of the universities in his day, particularly in their retention of controversies reminiscent of scholasticism at its worst, broke out in his writings again and again. See especially the whole of Prolusion III, "Contra Philosophiam Scholasticam"; also the references to controversies over trifles in Prolusions IV and VII. Similar outbursts after his own student days are no less vehement: see the ridicule of "scragged and thorny lectures of monkish and miserable sophistry" in *Church-Government;* and the censure of scholasticism in *Christian Doctrine,* I, v and xxx. Hanford's *Handbook* (1946, pp. 355–64) contains a useful appendix on "Milton and the Universities." [35] *Cf.* "sensible things," above, p. 368.

[36] The pleonasm, unusual in Milton's writing, emphasizes his strong conviction that such unreadiness and immaturity are insuperable barriers to mastery of these studies.

[37] In advocating postponement of logic, Milton is endorsing the contemporary proposals for the reform of university studies credited largely to the influence of Bacon. Nearly forty years earlier, in the *Advancement of Learning (Works,* VI, 178), Bacon had stated that "scholars in universities come too soon and too unripe to logic and rhetoric; arts fitter for graduates than children and novices: . . . and . . . for minds empty and unfraught with matter, . . . to begin with those arts . . . doth work but this effect, that the wisdom of those arts, which is great and universal, is almost made contemptible, and is degenerate into childish sophistry and ridiculous affectation."

[38] Milton's infrequent uses of the words *metaphysical* and *metaphysics* are all pejorative: see Columbia, *Index,* for instances. *Cf.,* for example, Prolusion VII (*Complete Prose* I, 301): "Metaphysics . . . is not, as the authority of great men would have me believe, an exceedingly rich Art; it is, I say, not an Art at all, but a sinister rock, a Lernian bog of fallacies, devised to cause shipwreck and pestilence." Bongiorno points out ("Tendencies," *JGE,* IV [1950], 109–11) that while logic is postponed in Milton's curriculum, "metaphysics is banished once and for all and is never so much as named again."

left those Grammatick flats & shallows where they stuck unreasonably to learn a few words with lamentable construction, and now
on the sudden transported under another climat [39] to be tost and
turmoild with their unballasted wits in fadomles and unquiet deeps
of controversie,[40] do for the most part grow into hatred and contempt of learning, mockt and deluded all this while with ragged
notions and babblements, while they expected worthy and delightfull
knowledge; till poverty or youthfull yeers call them importunately
their severall wayes, and hasten them with the sway [2] of friends
either to an ambitious and mercenary, or ignorantly zealous Divinity; [41] Some allur'd to the trade of Law,[42] grounding their purposes
not on the prudent, and heavenly contemplation of justice and
equity [43] which was never taught them, but on the promising and
pleasing thoughts of litigious terms,[44] fat contentions, and flowing
fees; others betake them to State affairs, with souls so unprincipl'd in vertue, and true generous breeding, that flattery, and court
shifts [45] and tyrannous aphorismes appear to them the highest

[39] The Greek word κλίμα developed various special meanings, including
the "slope or inclination of the earth and sky from the equator to the poles."
Hence the English derivative was sometimes applied to one of the twenty-four
"climates," each representing the space between the equator and either of the
polar circles "corresponding to an increase of half-an-hour in the length of the
longest day." NED.

[40] Clark points out (Milton at St. Paul's, p. 247) that Prolusions IV and V
are "characteristic examples of the scholastic disputation, . . . which the third
prolusion is at pains to attack."

[41] Among Milton's many criticisms of the English clergy for these two defects
(mercenary ambition and faulty preparation), the most specific may be found
in his Letter 2, to Alexander Gill in 1628 (Complete Prose, I, 314); Lycidas, ll.
112–131; Animadversions (Complete Prose, I, 719–20); and The Likeliest Means
(1659, passim, but especially pp. 131–38).

[42] Though the word trade in itself would not necessarily be derogatory here,
as it was formerly applied to the professions as well as to mercantile and
mechanical occupations (NED), Milton had already expressed his low estimation
of the law as a profession in Ad Patrem, ll. 71–72. Cf. Commonplace Book
(Complete Prose, I, 468), where he notes from Boccalini that the study of laws
is "considered not as a liberal art but as a 'trade and a really mechanical art.' "

[43] Cf. his own provision, p. 398 below, for study of "the grounds of law, and
Legall Justice."

[44] In the legal meaning, as Edward E. Morris pointed out (Milton's Tractate
on Education [1895], p. 36), of the periods during which courts are in session.

[45] Ainsworth (Milton on Education, p. 330) calls attention to Milton's comment on Charles I and his court in Eikonoklastes, Chapter VI: "Certainly Court-
breeding and his perpetual conversation with Flatterers, was but a bad Schoole."

points of wisdom; instilling their barren hearts with a conscientious slavery, if, as I rather think, it be not fain'd. Others lastly of a more delicious [46] and airie [47] spirit, retire themselves knowing no better, to the enjoyments of ease and luxury, living out their daies in feast and jollity; which indeed is the wisest and the safest course of all these, unlesse they were with more integrity undertak'n. And these are the errours, and these are the fruits of mispending our prime youth [48] at the Schools and Universities as we do, either in learning meere words or such things chiefly, as were better unlearnt.

I shall detain you now no longer in the demonstration of what we should not doe, but strait conduct ye to a hill side, where I will point ye out the right path of a vertuous and noble Education; laborious indeed at the first ascent, but else so smooth, so green, so full of goodly prospect, and melodious sounds on every side,[49] that the harp of *Orpheus* [50] was not more charming.[51] I doubt not but ye shall have more adoe to drive our dullest and laziest youth, our

[46] In an obsolete sense: "Addicted to sensuous indulgence; voluptuous, luxurious, dainty." *NED*.

[47] Probably an allusion to the predominance of the element air, which in early physiology was believed to result, through the spirits generated from the humour blood, in a sanguine temperament.

[48] *Cf.* Milton's usage in Sonnet IX: "Lady that in the prime of earliest youth."

[49] *Cf.* the description of the tractate in the anonymous early life (*Early Lives*, p. 24) as "an easy and delightful method for training up Gentry."

[50] *Cf.* "Il Penseroso," ll. 105–108. Orpheus was traditionally regarded not only as a singer who could charm all creatures, including even trees and stones, but also as a symbol of culture. Hughes (*Prose Selections*, p. 34, n. 23) cites Horace's *Art of Poetry*, ll. 391–96, as an early interpretation of the latter conception. Diodorus Siculus, IV, 25; tr. C. H. Oldfather (10 vols., Cambridge and London: Loeb Classical Library, 1935), II, 425, more specifically records that "In culture and song-music and poesy he far surpassed all men of whom we have a record." According to Diodorus, after Orpheus "had devoted his entire time to his education and had learned whatever the myths had to say about the gods, he journeyed to Egypt, where he further increased his knowledge and so became the greatest man among the Greeks both for his knowledge of the gods and for their rites, as well as for his poems and songs." Quintilian said (*Institutio Oratoria*, I, x, 9; tr. H. E. Butler [4 vols., London and New York, 1920], I, 165) that Orpheus united "the roles of musician, poet and philosopher."

[51] *Cf. Comus*, l. 476: "How charming is divine Philosophy!" Milton's use of the words *charm* and *charming* in connection with music is based partly on his deriving them directly from Latin *carmen* and partly on his giving them the connotation of some mysterious influence. See Sigmund G. Spaeth, *Milton's Knowledge of Music* (Princeton, 1913), pp. 88–89.

stocks and stubbs [52] from the infinite desire of such a happy nurture,[53] then we have now to hale and drag our choisest and hopefullest wits to that asinine feast of sowthistles and brambles [54] which is commonly set before them, as all the food and entertainment of their tenderest and most docible age. I call therefore [55] a

[52] Both words originally meant the stumps of trees, and hence were applied to dull or senseless persons. *NED. Cf.* Sonnet XVIII, l. 4: "When all our Fathers worship't Stocks and Stones."

[53] Milton's belief that children can and should enjoy a right education, without at all being indulged, may derive from Plato's doctrine that the early education of freemen should be a kind of amusement, which will best bring out their natural proclivities, whereas learning under compulsion is a kind of slavery and does not impart lasting knowledge. See *Republic,* VII, 536e; *cf. Republic,* IV, 425a, and *Laws,* I, 643c, and VII, 793e. Compare "playing, as the old manner was," pp. 386–87 below.

[54] *Cf.* Prolusion III (*Complete Prose,* I, 243), where Milton would assign to scholastic philosophy only "some waste corner at the very foot of the mountain [Parnassus], . . . tangled and matted with thorns and brambles, overgrown with thistles and nettles"; and Prolusion VII (*Complete Prose,* I, 301), where he compares teachers of logic to "finches which live on thorns and thistles."

[55] The recognized source of the conception of education for both citizenship and leadership affirmed in this sentence is the Greek view as formulated and idealized by Plato; see *Laws,* I, 643c–644b, especially the definition of education at 643e as "training from childhood in goodness, which makes a man eagerly desirous of becoming a perfect citizen, understanding how both to rule and be ruled righteously" (tr. R. G. Bury [2 vols., London and Cambridge: Loeb Classical Library, 1942], I, 65). Quintilian similarly specifies (*Institutio* I, Prooemium 9–10; tr. H. E. Butler, I, 9–11) that for the perfect orator as for the philosopher the "first essential . . . is that he should be a good man . . . who can really play his part as a citizen and is capable of meeting the demands both of public and private business, . . . who can guide a state by his counsels, give it a firm basis by his legislation and purge its vices by his decisions as a judge." Other writers, classical and recent, had advocated education for citizenship and service to the state, though with less specific emphasis than Milton places, here and later in the tractate, on training for the responsibilities of leadership. Aristotle (*Politics,* VIII, i) proposed a public system of education under which all citizens would receive the same training, since all, as parts of the state, belong to it, whether the constitution be that of a democracy or of an oligarchy. Cicero's phrase (*De Officiis,* I, vi), "Virtutis enim laus omnis in actione consistit," though sometimes quoted alone to this effect, has more bearing in its context: *i.e.* (tr. by Walter Miller [London and New York, 1921], p. 21), "to be drawn by study away from active life is contrary to moral duty. For the whole glory of virtue is in activity." Petrus Paulus Vergerius (b. 1349), in writing *De Ingenuis Moribus* (English version by William H. Woodward, *Vittorino da Feltre and Other Humanist Educators* [Cambridge, 1921], p. 102) gives the definition: "We call those studies *liberal* which are worthy of a free man; those studies by which we attain and practise virtue and wisdom; that education which calls forth, trains and develops those highest gifts of body and of mind which ennoble men, and

compleate and generous [56] Education that which fits a man to per-

which are rightly judged to rank next in dignity to virtue only." Vittorino da Feltre (d. 1446) himself wished to educate men (Woodward, p. 37) to "serve God in church and state," regardless of the positions they might later occupy. And Erasmus, in *De Civilitate Morum Puerilium* (*Omnia Opera* [10 vols., Basle, 1540; PUL], I, 862), includes preparation for all the duties of life among the four functions of educating boys. In England this view of education for national service had been most clearly stated by Richard Mulcaster and John Brinsley. Mulcaster, in his *Positions* (1581; reprinted with an appendix by Robert H. Quick [London, 1888]) favors "publike education" of "yong gentlemen" rather than private on the basis of a definition in some respects like Milton's own (pp. 184–85): "*Education* is the bringing up of one, not to live alone, but amongest others, (bycause companie is our naturall cognisaunce) whereby he shall be best able to execute those doings in life, which the state of his calling shall employ him unto, whether *publike* abrode, or *private* at home, according unto the direction of his countrie, whereunto he is borne, and oweth his whole service." And Brinsley, in *A Consolation for Our Grammar Schooles* (1622 [New York: Scholars' Facsimiles & Reprints, 1943], p. 16) speaks of sound education as the means by which "every one shall be the better enabled to pay that debt, which by his very birth he oweth unto the Lord, and to his native countrey. . . . And to this end ought each of us to seeke, as [God] offereth opportunity, to be alwayes paying this debt of ours; which none are likely to discharge, so well as they, who have bene best instructed in their youth."

[56] Literally, appropriate to one of noble birth or spirit; from Latin *generosus*, of good or noble birth. *NED*. That in this tractate Milton's deliberate intention is to provide a plan of education for those boys suited by birth or character to become leaders is shown not only by the selection of this word, as of "magnanimously" later in the same sentence, "liberall" at p. 385 below, and "our noble and our gentle youth" at p. 406; but also by phrases throughout that forecast the pupils' later responsibilities. They may "save an Army" as commanders who have some knowledge of Physick; they may be stronger "pillars of the State" than many recent "great counsellers"; they may "speak in Parliament or counsell" with "honour and attention . . . waiting on their lips"; they may "out of a long warre come forth renowned and perfect Commanders in the service of their country"; and if they travel abroad at the age of twenty-three or twenty-four, "they will by that time be such as shall deserve the regard and honour of all men where they passe, and the society and friendship of those in all places who are best and most eminent." At present Milton is writing of education for leadership; in two tracts published shortly before the Restoration he proposed educational programs with quite different purposes. In *The Likeliest Means*, while discussing other methods than university education for the preparation of ministers for the church, he suggested (1659, pp. 96–98) that the church revenues now in the hands of the civil magistrate might be used "to erect . . . all over the land schooles and competent libraries to those schooles, where languages and arts may be taught free together, . . . and they who are taught freely at the publick cost, might have thir education given them on this condition, that therewith content, they should not gadd for preferment out of thir own countrey. . . ." In these "publick foundations," he stated further, they "may be at once brought up to a competence of learning and to an honest trade; and the hours of teaching so

form justly, skilfully and magnanimously [57] all the offices both private and publike of peace and war.[58] And how all this may be done between twelve, and one and twenty,[59] lesse time then is now bestow'd in pure trifling at Grammar and *Sophistry*, is to be thus order'd.

First to finde out a spatious house and ground about it fit for an *Academy*, and big enough to lodge a hundred and fifty persons,

ordered, as thir studie may be no hindrance to thir labor or other calling." And in *The Readie & Easie Way*, having proposed to secure "the civil rights and advancements of every person according to his merit" by making "every county in the land a little commonwealth," he added (1660, p. 16) that "the nobilitie and chief gentry . . . should have heer also schools and academies at thir own choice, wherin thir children may be bred up in thir own sight to all learning and noble education, not in grammar only, but in all liberal arts and exercises."

[57] Derived from Latin *magnus animus* (soul), originally representing the Aristotelian μεγαλοψυχία. "In Aristotle the word (by modern translators rendered 'greatsouledness,' 'highmindedness') expresses the attitude of one who, rightly conscious of his own great merits, is indifferent to praise except from those whose approval is valuable, regards the chances of fortune with equanimity, and, while ready to confer benefits, will seldom condescend to accept them." *NED*. See *Nicomachean Ethics*, II, vii, 7–8, and IV, iii, 1–34. For Milton's uses of *magnanimity*, *magnanimous*, and *magnanimously* with such connotations, see Columbia, *Index;* and note his own definition of *magnanimitas* in *Christian Doctrine*, II, ix. *Cf.* the passage on fame in *Lycidas*, ll. 70–84. See also *Paradise Lost*, VII, 509–11, on Man as a creature who might

> upright with Front serene
> Govern the rest, self-knowing, and from thence
> Magnanimous to correspond with Heav'n

and the reference in *An Apology* (*Complete Prose* I, 928) to the "just and magnanimous actions" of the Long Parliament.

[58] *Cf.* Aristotle, *Politics*, VII, viii (tr. H. Rackham [London and New York, 1926], pp. 607 and 609): "A man should be capable of engaging in business and war, but still more capable of living in peace and leisure; and he should do what is necessary and useful, but still more should he do what is noble. These then are the aims that ought to be kept in view in the education of the citizens both while still children and at the later ages that require education."

[59] This phrase and the following paragraph best indicate how radically Milton would condense formal schooling. In nine years the boys in his academy would accomplish what normally required fourteen: seven for grammar school, four for the bachelor's degree, and three for the master's. Since seven was the usual age for entering the grammar school, his pupils would begin this stage of their schooling five years later and yet complete their formal education at the customary age of about twenty-one. While it is clear that he expects the entering students to be able to read and write in English, as in that day they would have learned to do in the elementary or petty school before beginning grammar school, it is not within the compass of the present tractate to provide specific uses for the five pre-school years his plan would gain: see below, p. 414.

whereof twenty or thereabout may be attendants, all under the government of one, who shall be thought of desert sufficient, and ability either to doe all, or wisely to direct, and oversee it done. This
place should be at once both School and University, not needing a
remove to any other house of Schollership, except it be some peculiar Colledge of Law, or Physick,[60] where they mean to be practitioners; but as for those generall studies which take up all our time
from Lilly[61] to the commencing, as they term it, Master of Art, it
should be absolute. After this pattern, as many edifices may be con-

[60] The striking omission of one of the three learned professions suggests that
Milton's hostility to university divinity was already approaching the extreme he
stated bluntly in *The Likeliest Means* (1659, pp. 136–37 and 141): "that what
learning either human or divine can be necessary to a minister, may as easily
and less chargeably be had in any private house," and that "it were much better,
there were not one divine in the universitie.

[61] The Latin grammar prepared primarily for use in St. Paul's School by William Lily (*ca.* 1468–*ca.* 1523), first high master of the school, with the collaboration of Colet and Erasmus. From the earliest published form of any part of it in
1513, the work evolved through successive revisions and additions into the
Institutio Compendiaria Totius Grammaticae, dated 1540; and *An Introduction of the Eyght Partes of Speche, and the Construction of the Same,* dated
1542. (Though the Latin *Institutio* is dated earlier, it is extant only bound
with the English *Introduction.*) A preface to the 1542 edition contained an order
of Henry VIII that "this englysshe introduction here ensuing, and the latyne
grammer annexed to the same, and none other," should be used in all English
schools; and through later injunctions and canons ecclesiastical Lily's grammar continued to be exclusively used in Milton's time. By 1548 the two earlier
sections were published together under the title *A Shorte Introduction of Grammer, Generally to be Used in the Kynges Maiesties Dominions, for the Bryngynge
up of all Those that Entende to Atteyne the Knowledge of the Latin Tongue.*
(For the history of the development and authorization of this grammar, see
the facsimile reprint of the 1567 edition with introduction by Vincent J. Flynn
[New York: Scholars' Facsimiles and Reprints, 1945]; also Flynn's "The Grammatical Writings of William Lily," *The Papers of the Bibliographical Society of
America,* XXXVII [1943], 85–113.) Milton himself used the revision first issued
in 1574 (Clark, *Milton at St. Paul's,* p. 133); for a "theme" almost certainly
written by Milton as a schoolboy and evidencing his use of Lily, see *Complete
Prose,* I, 1036–39. This general form of the book used by Milton appeared in
at least fifteen editions between 1574 and 1640. In these editions, *e.g.,* Oxford,
1636 (HHL) the two parts are bound together with separate title pages: *A
Short Introduction of Grammar Generally to be Used,* and *Brevissima Institutio
seu Ratio Grammatices Cognoscendae, ad Omnium Puerorum Utilitatem Prae-
scripta.* The former section includes, in English, "An Introduction of the Eight
Parts of Latine Speech" and "The Concords of Latine Speech," followed by
Lily's Latin "Carmen de Moribus." The latter section, in Latin, deals with orthography, etymology (including accidence: "De Octo Partibus Orationis"),
syntax, and prosody.

verted to this use, as shall be needfull in every City throughout this land,[62] which would tend much to the encrease of learning and civility [63] every where. This number, lesse or more thus collected, to the convenience of a foot company,[64] or interchangeably two troops of cavalry, should divide their daies work [65] into three parts, as it lies orderly. Their studies, their exercise, and their diet.

[62] Milton does not make clear whether he has yet thought out the political and financial basis of what appears to be a proposal for a national educational system, except for the allusion to the present "opportunity" to use funds controlled by the government in the first paragraph of the tractate above (see above, n. 5). The present suggestion, however, perhaps foreshadows the proposal in *The Readie & Easie Way* to provide "schools and academies" for the children of "the nobilitie and chief gentry" in every county (see above, n. 56). This later plan (*The Readie & Easie Way*, 2nd ed., 1660, Columbia, VI, 144–45) is based on a federation of counties, each to contain "one chief town or more, according as the shire is in circuit, made cities, if they be not so call'd alreadie"; the "schools and academies" are apparently to be established in each such city. The implication is that they are to conform to a national pattern or standard, if not to be under national control or supervision. There is no indication, however, whether he advocated government financing of these schools for gentlemen's sons, as he clearly did for the trade schools "at the publick cost" proposed in *The Likeliest Means* (see above, n. 56). Any suggestion of a national educational system was a novelty in England in 1644, whether for the sons of the aristocracy or of the lower classes. In regard to the former Milton seems not to have been anticipated; in regard to the latter, Samuel Harmar had asked, in *Vox Populi, Or Glostersheres Desire: With, The Way and Means to make a Kingdome Happy (by Gods help.) By setting up of Schoole-masters in every Parish throughout the Land generally* (1642 [UCL], sig. A3v): "If the Law of the Land do enjoyne and rate mens estates, toward the relieving of the poore in their Parishes . . . . whether the same Law may not aswell enjoyne a rate upon Mens estates for the maintaining of so charitable a work, which . . . will be a speciall means to prevent Idlenesse among Children, with beggery and theevery."

[63] Probably in the sense, now obsolete, of good citizenship, as in *Church-Government* (*Complete Prose*, I, 816), where the poetic gift is said to be "of power beside the office of a pulpit, to imbreed and cherish in a great people the seeds of vertu, and publick civility."

[64] The usual formation of infantry was a square of ten files each containing ten (or sometimes more) ranks. See J. W. Fortescue, "The Army: Military Service and Equipment," chapter IV in *Shakespeare's England* (2 vols., Oxford, 1916), I, 114–15.

[65] The approximate daily schedule can be constructed by relating Milton's innovations to the practice of his time. In grammar schools of the sixteenth and seventeenth centuries, the boys began their school day at 6 A.M. (Baldwin, *Shakspere's Small Latine*, I, 165, 297, 353–54, 359), though at St. Paul's, which was not a boarding school, the opening hour was 7 (Clark, *Milton at St. Paul's*, p. 44). Studies continued until 11 and were resumed from 1 to 5 P.M. Among the minor modifications proposed, John Brinsley, in *Ludus Literarius* (ed. E. T. Cam-

For their studies, First they should begin with the chief and necessary rules [66] of some good Grammar, either that now us'd, or any better: [67] and while this is doing, their speech is to be fashion'd

pagnac, Liverpool, 1917 [reproduced from the edition of 1627], pp. 296–97), recommended that the boys should have intermissions of "a quarter of an houre at least" at 9 A.M. and 3 P.M. "for the necessity of every one, or their honest recreation"; but he would "countervaile" this time by keeping them at work that much longer after 11 A.M. and 5 P.M. Richard Mulcaster, in his *Positions*, pp. 224–25, goes further, and asks whether the customary hours are not "a great deale more, then a sufficient time for the maister to teach, and the scholer to learne," and suggests (p. 231) that from 7 to 10 A.M. and from 2 to 5 P.M. "be the best and fittest houres, and enough for children wherin to learne . . . . The other times before meat be for exercises." Since Milton does not mention starting the day later than was customary, the pupils in his academy would presumably start their days at 6 A.M.; but they would probably (as Mulcaster suggested) have a longer recess from study at midday than the usual two hours, for Milton reserves at least one and a half hours before their meal for "exercise and due rest afterwards," and would have music both during this rest period and after meals. Before supper, about two hours would be given to military drill. After supper, "till bed-time," there would be religious teaching—Scripture for the younger boys, theology and church history for the older ones. But in the spring all except the two or three lowest forms would give less time to formal studies, traveling instead to learn by observation.

[66] *Cf.* "To the Reader" in Milton's *Accedence Commenc't Grammar* (1669): *"What will not come under Rule, by reason of too much variety in Declension, Gender, or Construction, is also here omitted, least the course and clearness of method be clog'd with Catalogues instead of Rules, or too much interruption between Rule and Rule."*

[67] Though Lily's was the only authorized grammar, others were occasionally published in England, with little or no hope of their general adoption in the schools. Watson (*English Grammar Schools*, pp. 273–74) lists eight printed between 1585 and 1665. The authors of two recent attempts to improve the teaching of grammar had taken pains to relate their new ventures to Lily's standard work: John Clarke, in *Dux Grammaticus Tyronem Scholasticum ad Rectam Orthographiam[,] Syntaxin, & Prosodiam Dirigens* (1633; UCL) gives references to "Regulas Lilianas" in his margins; and Christofer Syms, in *An Introduction to, or, The Art of Teaching, the Latine Speach* (Dublin, 1634; FSL), reiterates in his "Preface to the Reader, proper onely for the Teacher" (sig. B3v), that the work was "begotten in mee by that . . . memorable master *William Lily*," and that "*M. Lily*" would have endorsed his method of "teaching by tipe & figure" and his presentation of the syntax in English. Thomas Farnaby, in his *Systema Grammaticum* (London, 1641; the copy believed to be Milton's, with a marginal correction of a Greek letter by him at p. 102, is in HCL), while referring less deferentially to Lily in his dedication, follows the same general pattern of giving first the accidence in English and then the complete grammar ("etymologia" and "syntaxis") in Latin. There is no evidence to show whether Milton had planned or written his own *Accedence Commenc't Grammar* (1669) as early as 1644.

to a distinct and cleer pronuntiation,[68] as neer as may be to the *Italian,* especially in the vowels. For we Englishmen being farre northerly, doe not open our mouthes in the cold air, wide enough to grace a Southern [3] tongue; but are observ'd by all other nations to speak exceeding close and inward: So that to smatter Latin with an english mouth, is as ill a hearing as law French.[69] Next to make them expert in the usefullest points of grammar, and withall to season them, and win them early to the love of vertue and true labour,[70] ere any flattering seducement, or vain principle seise them wandering, some easie and delightfull book of Education would be

[68] Milton seems to have aroused neither support nor opposition by expressing his disapproval of the Anglicized pronunciation of Latin, though in the sixteenth century the efforts of Sir John Cheke and Sir Thomas Smith to introduce a more accurate pronunciation of Greek at Cambridge had called forth objections from John Caius and others (see *DNB,* articles on Caius and Cheke). The Quaker Thomas Ellwood tells in his autobiography (*The History of Thomas Ellwood,* London, 1714 [UTSL], p. 134) how Milton in 1662 corrected his pronunciation of Latin, with particular attention to the vowels and to the sounding of *c* before *e* or *i* and of *sc* before *i* as in Italian. But pronunciation was omitted from Milton's *Accedence Commenc't Grammar* ("To the Reader") "*since few will be perswaded to pronounce* Latin *otherwise then thir own English.*"

[69] Though the use of either Latin or French in legal proceedings was by this time forbidden, the legal Reports were still written in a degenerate form of Norman French. See Arthur Underhill, "Law," chapter XIII in *Shakespeare's England,* I, 389, and, for a sample concerning a prisoner "que puis son condemnation ject un brickbat a le dit justice que narrowly mist," p. 400. *Cf.* Milton's comment in Prolusion VII (*Complete Prose,* I, 301) that jurisprudence suffers from "a jargon which one might well take for some Red Indian dialect"; and his entry in the *Commonplace Book* (*Complete Prose,* I, 424) on King Alfred's turning the old laws into English: "I would he liv'd now to rid us of this norman gibbrish."

[70] It was a usual practice to teach manners and morals along with elementary Latin grammar in Renaissance England. See, *e.g.,* the *Carmen de Moribus* at the beginning of Lily's *Short Introduction of Grammar* (Oxford, 1636, sig. E4); the dialogue on schoolboys' manners introduced to illustrate the uses of impersonal verbs in John Clarke's *Dux Grammaticus* (1633; UCL), pp. 64–81; and Cato's *Disticha Moralia,* widely used for elementary reading of Latin (1553, with Richard Taverner's English exposition following each Latin passage [CUL]; Leyden, 1626, the Latin text supplemented by Joseph Scaliger's Greek rendering and a Latin exposition by Erasmus [PUL]; and many other editions). But in contrast to these and other contemporary instances (for which see Watson, *English Grammar Schools,* pp. 106–11), Milton is proposing that the boys should develop their "love of vertue" not through epitomes of modern grammarians but through having read to them books "of classic authoritie."

read to them; whereof the Greeks have store as *Cebes*,[71] *Plutarch*,[72] and other Socratic discourses.[73] But in Latin we have none of classic authoritie extant, except the two or three first books of *Quintilian*,[74] and some select peeces elsewhere. But here the main skill and groundwork will be, to temper them [75] such lectures and explanations upon every opportunity, as may lead and draw them in willing

[71] The πίναξ or *Table* of Cebes, erroneously attributed to the Cebes who was a pupil and friend of Socrates. It is described by Richard Parsons (ed., *Cebes' Tablet* [Boston, 1887], introduction, p. 8) as "a dialogue describing and explaining an allegorical picture represented . . . as a votive offering." The chief lesson of the allegory, in the nomenclature of John Healey (see below) is that Beatitude can be reached only through the guidance of Knowledge and her sisters Fortitude, Justice, Integrity of life, Temperance, Modesty, Liberality, Continency, and Clemency. Though the *Pinax* was read in Greek in some English schools before the end of the sixteenth century (Baldwin, *Shakspere's Small Latine*, I, 348 and 417), and had been published in an English translation by John Healey (*Epictetus His Manuall, The Table of Cebes, Theophrastus His Morall Characters*, 1636; FSL), Milton probably desired the use here of a Latin translation; for his proposal is both "to make them expert in the usefullest points of grammar" and to "win them early to the love of vertue" by such reading. There was, for example, an edition with Greek and Latin on opposite pages, issued with Hesiod's *Works and Days* and Cato's *Disticha Moralia* (Strassburg, *ca.* 1515; UTSL). Harris F. Fletcher (*The Intellectual Development of John Milton* [Urbana: University of Illinois Press, 1956—], I, 110–11) gives additional details about the *Pinax*.

[72] Probably a Latin translation of the essay Περὶ παιδῶν ἀγωγῆς (*On the Education of Children*), which Edward Phillips lists among the books Milton had his nephews read in Greek (*Early Lives*, p. 60). The Paris edition of 1572 (*Plutarchi Chaeronensis Moralia*, 2 vols.; PUL) includes this "De Liberis Educandis" (alternatively known as "De Educatione Puerorum") in Vol. I. Fletcher (*Intellectual Development*, I, 112) summarizes the essay.

[73] Probably some of the *Moralia* (see edition in preceding note) which are in the form of dialogues, and perhaps parts of the *Republic* and *Laws* of Plato. Latin texts of Plato suitable for this use in a school might have been difficult to find; the master might use his own copy of Plato to give the boys such "lectures and explanations" as are mentioned in the second following sentence of the text.

[74] In such an edition as *M. Fabii Quintiliani Institutionum Oratoriarum Libri duodecim*, Lyons, 1575 (PUL), pp. 6–205. The first two books lay down Quintilian's theories of education in general and of the teaching of rhetoric in particular, with observations on the capacities and proper treatment of pupils, the values to be sought in reading, the proper relationship between teacher and pupil, etc. Book III, which is chiefly concerned with introducing the technical study of rhetoric, contains little or no material that Milton would find useful for his present purpose.

[75] Adapt to their needs, perhaps also connoting the contemporary meaning of tuning or harmonizing, as in *Lycidas*, l. 33: "Temper'd to th' Oaten Flute."

obedience,[76] enflam'd with the study [77] of learning, and the admiration of vertue; stirr'd up with high hopes of living to be brave men, and worthy patriots, dear to God, and famous to all ages. That they may despise and scorn all their childish, and ill taught qualities, to delight in manly, and liberall [78] exercises: which he who hath the Art, and proper eloquence to catch them with, what with mild and effectuall perswasions, and what with the intimation of some fear,[79] if need be, but chiefly by his own example,[80] might in a short space gain them to an incredible diligence and courage: infusing into their young brests such an ingenuous and noble ardor, as would not fail to make many of them renowned and matchlesse men.[81] At the same

[76] Cf. the entry in the Commonplace Book, under "De Liberis Educandis" (Complete Prose, I, 406): "not to labour, as most men doe to make them bold and pert while they are young which ripens them too soon, and true boldnes and spirit is not bred but of vertuous causes which are wrought in them by sober discipline to this purpose." And see also the insistence in Church-Government (Complete Prose, I, 751) on the importance of discipline "throughout the whole life of man."

[77] In the primary sense, as suggested by Ainsworth (Milton on Education, p. 334), of zeal or eagerness, from Latin studium. Compare "study of revenge," Paradise Lost, I, 107.

[78] Originally "worthy of a free man," as opposed to "servile" or "mechanical"; by Milton's time applied to pursuits or occupations becoming to a gentleman. NED.

[79] In the Preface to Church-Government (Complete Prose, I, 746-47), Milton ascribes to the writings of Plato (see Laws, IV, 718b; cf. VII, 793e) and to the example of Moses the doctrine that persuasion is superior to fear in teaching obedience.

[80] Milton himself was an exacting master but, as Miss Darbishire points out (Early Lives, pp. liv-lv), won the admiration and friendship of a number of his pupils. Aubrey writes (Early Lives, p. 12): "As he was severe on one hand, so he was most familiar and free in his conversation to those to whome most severe in his way of education." The anonymous early biographer mentions (Early Lives, p. 25) "the strictness of his Discipline"; Edward Phillips testifies (Early Lives, p. 60) to "his excellent judgment and way of Teaching, far above the Pedantry of common publick Schools," and adds (pp. 67-68) that "neither his Converse, nor his Writings, nor his manner of Teaching ever savour'd in the least any thing of Pedantry; and probably he might have some prospect of putting into Practice his Academical Institution, according to the Model laid down in his Sheet of Education."

[81] Milton apparently intended the moral readings and explanations in the four preceding sentences—the reading from "some easie and delightful book of Education," the "lectures and explanations," and the "perswasions" and "example" of the master—to replace the usual sequence of elementary Latin readings following the introduction to grammar. Among the commonest readings of the Renaissance school thus omitted (with available editions of each for illustration)

time, some other hour of the day, might be taught them the rules of Arithmetick, and soon after the elements of Geometry [82] even play-

were *Sententiae Pueriles* of Leonhard Culman (1639; FSL), comprising groups of Latin sentences first of two words, then three, then four, and lastly of more, followed by *sententiae sacrae* for holydays and *morum puerilium praecepta;* Cato's *Disticha Moralia* (see editions mentioned in notes 70 and 71; also *STC* for several published in England); and Aesop's *Fabulae* (Lyons, 1579; CUL). For discussion of these and other traditional elementary schoolbooks, see Baldwin, *Shakspere's Small Latine,* I, chapters XXVI–XXVIII; Clark, *Milton at St. Paul's,* pp. 114–25; and Watson, *English Grammar Schools,* pp. 363 and 370–72.

[82] The prominence given to mathematics in Milton's educational plan, here and later, is progressive if not indeed unique for his time. Mulcaster, for example, in his *Positions* (1581), makes no mention of arithmetic in presenting the five subjects of elementary education; Brinsley, in *Ludus Literarius* (1627; ed. E. T. Campagnac, Liverpool, 1917, pp. 25–26) recommends that scholars in the grammar schools learn to read Roman and Arabic numerals "backwards and forwards" so as to be able to find chapters and verses: "If you do require more for any, you must seeke *Records* Arithmetique, . . . and set them to the Cyphering schoole." William Kempe, in *The Education of Children in Learning* (1588 [CUL], sig. H1), would go farther and have scholars about fifteen years old, after mastering logic and rhetoric, "ascend to . . . Arithmetike and Geometrie," and "easely passe through these Artes in halfe a yeere." The Spaniard Vives, in *De Tradendis Disciplinis* (1531 [UTSL], ff. 119–119v.) similarly would make these advanced studies for boys over sixteen, beyond logic and "first philosophy," and relates them to the other subjects of the quadrivium: geometry raised to the heavens becomes astronomy, and arithmetic applied to sounds gives music. He scorns those "crass noblemen" who think it "pulchrum *si deo placet* ac generosum . . . nescire omnino computare," and would have young men learn numbers, addition and subtraction, and algorism.

These authors are among the leading educational thinkers known in England in Milton's time; in general, any knowledge beyond the mere rudiments of arithmetic or geometry was thought distinctly less relevant to school and university education than to the practical training of merchants, soldiers, or architects. Thus Cuthbert Tonstall, author of the first separate mathematical work published in England (*De Arte Supputandi Libri Quattuor* [1522; CUL], sig. A2), relates that he returned to the study of reckoning only after his early training in this skill (probably abroad) had enabled him to save himself from the intended fraud of some money-changers. Sir Humphrey Gilbert, in his practical project for *Queene Elizabethes Achademy* (written about 1562; ed. Frederick J. Furnivall, E.E.T.S., Extra Series, VIII, 1869), where (p. 10) "men . . . shall study matters of accion meet for present practize, both of peace and warre," provides (pp. 4–5) for "two Mathematicians, And the one of them shall one day reade Arithmetick, and the other day Geometry, which shalbe onely employed to Imbattelinges, fortificacions, and matters of warre, . . . The other Mathematician shall reade one day Cosmographie and Astronomy, and the other day tend the practizes thereof, onely to the arte of Navigacion." Similarly when the *Via Regia ad Geometriam* of Ramus (a work Milton seems to have known: see *Art of Logic,* preface) appeared in an English translation by William Bedwell in 1636 (CUL), the title page described it as "necessary and usefull, For / Astronomers. / Geog-

ing, as the old manner was.[83] After evening repast, till bed time their thoughts will be best taken up in the easie grounds of Religion, and the story of Scripture. The next step would be to the Authors

raphers. / Land-meaters. / Sea-men / Engineres. / Architecks. / Carpenters. / Paynters. / Carvers, &c." Hence it is that Samuel Pepys, a university graduate, records (*Diary*, July 1–19, 1662) the lessons he conscientiously took to master the multiplication tables at the age of twenty-nine; and Aubrey comments that Thomas Hobbes, also a university graduate, knew nothing of geometry until he was forty years old. The educational writers closest to agreement with Milton in his plan to include mathematics in the education of future leaders in "all the offices both private and publike of peace and war" were James Cleland and Henry Peacham. Cleland ('Ηρωπαιδεία, *or The Institution of a Young Noble Man* [Oxford, 1607; YUL], pp. 90–92) proposes that after the study of logic and rhetoric the tutor should read to his noble pupil several books on arithmetic and geometry which teach principles applicable to military map-making and architecture. And Peacham (*The Compleat Gentleman*, 1634 [Oxford, 1906], pp. 72–78), also recommending several specific books on the subject, maintains not only that a gentleman may profitably apply geometry in the management of his lands, but more particularly that as a commander in war he will need it for fortification and tactics. Milton, however, seems to be unique in proposing both to introduce mathematics so early into his curriculum (following only Latin grammar and speech) and to carry out this study so thoroughly, as becomes evident later in this paragraph of the text. The thoroughness at least he put into practice in his own teaching, for Edward Phillips mentions (*Early Lives*, p. 61) "reading *Urstisius* his Arithmetick, *Riffs* Geometry, *Petiscus* his Trigonometry, *Joannes de Sacro Bosco de Sphaera*." (See Christianus Urstisius, *Elementa Arithmeticae, Logicis Legibus Deducta*, Basle, 1579 [CUL]; Petrus Ryff, *Quaestiones Geometricae, in Euclidis et P. Rami Στοιχείωσιν*, Frankfurt, 1621 [CUL]; for Petiscus and Sacro Bosco, see notes 103 and 88 respectively.)

[83] In the *Laws* (VII, 819b–20d) Plato endorses the use of games to teach elementary arithmetic and geometry to children, a device he says was invented by the Egyptians; in the *Republic* (VII, 536de) he extends this principle of teaching boys through their amusements from arithmetic and geometry to all that they learn before they begin to reason. (*Cf.* above, n. 53.) Quintilian (*Institutio Oratoria*, I, i, 20 and 26; and iii, 11–12) repeatedly advocates this broader use of amusements and games in education. The use of the name *ludus literarius* for a school furnished Brinsley (*Ludus Literarius*, p. 50; *A Consolation for Our Grammar Schooles*, p. 13) and Peacham (*Compleat Gentleman*, p. 24) with a text for pleading that learning in school should be a pleasant pastime or delight. It is possible that Milton's suggestion that Italian be "easily learnt at any odde hour" represents another application of this principle. The method of learning arithmetic and geometry in this manner is referred to by Montaigne (*Essayes*, book I, chapter XXV; tr. John Florio [3 vols., Everyman's Library edition], I, 186) in telling how he learned Greek "by way of recreation and exercise": "We did tosse our declinations, and conjugations to and fro, as they doe, who by way of a certaine game at tables learne both Arithmetike and Geometrie." Edward Phillips, however, says nothing about "playing" when he mentions Milton's teaching of mathematics.

of *Agriculture*,[84] *Cato*, *Varro*, and *Columella*,[85] for the matter is
most easie,[86] and if the language be difficult, so much the better, it

[84] It is here that the "orderly conning over the visible and inferior creature"
begins, the sequence of studies being carefully planned to lead "to the knowledge
of God and things invisible." First the boys lay a foundation of general knowledge about their world, and gain exercise in the practical use of languages,
through such studies as agriculture, geography, "any compendious method of
naturall Philosophy," and the applications of mathematics. Then, as Balachandra
Rajan has demonstrated in an important exposition of Milton's curriculum
(" 'Simple, Sensuous and Passionate,' " *RES*, XXI [1945], 291–93), the following studies are planned in a sequence closely analogous to progress up the Great
Chain of Being. From matter and plants the ascent proceeds to the highest levels
of human knowledge and understanding, from "sensible things" to "regaining to
know God aright." *Cf.* Raphael's instruction of Adam, *Paradise Lost*, V, 469–
505, and Adam's acknowledgment (ll. 508–12):

> Well hast thou taught the way that might direct
> Our knowledge, and the scale of Nature set
> From centre to circumference, wheron
> In contemplation of created things
> By steps we may ascend to God.

Milton does not make the mistake, however, of suggesting that education by
way of ascending the Great Chain is alone sufficient for the salvation of fallen
man: knowledge (p. 367 above) may lead to virtue, "which being united to the
heavenly grace of faith makes up the highest perfection."

Comenius uses expressions suggesting an analogy to the Great Chain in his
Praeludia (translated in *A Reformation of Schooles*), but with no such continuous sequence in mind: first (pp. 14–15) he urges that in teaching the arts and
sciences there should always be progress from the known to the unknown, "even
as in a chaine, every linke receives and drawes its fellow after it"; and later
(pp. 21–22), in proposing that learning be "purged, and cleared of the prophanenesse of the Gentiles" so that the knowledge of God may be taught everywhere,
he concludes that by this means learning "may be as a sacred ladder for our
minds to clime up by all visible things, unto the invisible top of all things, the
Majesty of the highest God." But these are processes that should go on at every
stage in education, not a progression from one link in the chain of creation to
another, as in Milton.

[85] The *De Re Rustica* of Cato the Censor (234–149 B.C.), the three books *De
Re Rustica* of Marcus Terentius Varro (116–27 B.C.), and the twelve books *De
Re Rustica* of L. Junius Moderatus Columella (first century A.D.). These standard Latin works on agriculture were available in many editions, often combined with each other and sometimes with the thirteen books of Palladius, as
in the following examples: Cato, Varro, Columella, and Palladius (Basle, 1535;
RUL); Cato and Varro (Paris, 1543; RUL); Columella alone (Paris, 1543,
and Lyons, 1548; RUL); Cato, Varro, and Palladius (Lyons, 1549; RUL); and
Cato alone (Leyden, 1598; RUL). Aubrey reports of Milton's teaching his
nephews (*Early Lives*, p. 12): "Cato, Varro, & Columella de Re rusticâ were the
very first Authors they learn't."

[86] Ainsworth (*Milton on Education*, p. 336) called attention to the parallel
with "beginning with Arts most easie" (p. 374 above).

is not a difficultie above their yeers. And here will be an occasion
of inciting and inabling them hereafter to improve the tillage of
their country, to recover the bad soil, and to remedy the wast that
is made of good: for this was one of Hercules praises.[87] Ere halfe
these Authors be read, which will soon be with plying hard, and
dayly, they cannot choose but be masters of any ordinary prose.
So that it will be then seasonable for them to learn in any modern
Author, the use of the Globes, and all the maps [88] first with the old
names; and then with the new: [89] or they might be then capable to

[87] The tradition that the cleansing of the Augean stables led to the introduction of manuring the soil in Italy has been traced to Pliny, *Natural History*,
XVII, 50 (Ainsworth, p. 336).

[88] Probably celestial as well as terrestial globes are intended, since the study
mentioned here is apparently referred to as *"Astronomy,* and *Geography"* later in
the same paragraph. In accordance with the principle stated in this sentence of
using "modern" authors, as distinguished from classical authorities, for these
practical subjects, Milton had his nephews read (*Early Lives,* p. 61) *"Joannes de
Sacro Bosco de Sphaera"* and "in French a great part of Pierre Davity, the
famous Geographer of *France* in his time." The *Sphaera* of Sacro Bosco (John
Halifax of Holywood, thirteenth century) was an interesting little book available
in various editions; for example, the 1574 Venice edition (CUL), of 168 pages,
has several printed circular disks, attached to the page by light string knotted at
each end, so that any of these may be rotated within the larger circular diagram
on the page. The basic system is of course Ptolemaic. The work of Pierre d'Avity
or Davity (1573–1635), first published in 1614, was reprinted, under various
titles, at least ten times in French before 1644, and also three times in Latin.
(See Allan H. Gilbert, "Pierre Davity: His 'Geography' and Its Use by Milton,"
The Geographical Review, VII, 322–38.) Though Milton has not previously
mentioned the study of French in the tractate, Edward Phillips specifically
speaks of "reading . . . in French a great part of Pierre Davity." Presumably,
then, the boys would read one of the many French editions (*e.g., Les Estats,
Empires, et Principautez du monde, Representez par la description des Pays,
Moeurs des habitans, Richesses des Provinces, les Forces, le Gouvernement, la
Religion, & les Princes qui ont gouverné chacun Estat,* [Geneva,] 1619; NYPL).
For Milton's own comment on what geographers should include in their works,
see *A Brief History of Moscovia,* Preface.

[89] Probably in recognition of the need to know both classical and vernacular
place names in order to use the maps of that age. While only one language was
used on many maps, others (*e.g.,* Abraham Ortelius, *Epitome du Théâtre du
Monde,* 1588; PUL) show major place names in Latin and local ones in the
vernacular, or even (Ortelius, *Theatrum Orbis Terrarum,* Antwerp, 1595; PML)
use, in a map of the world, Spanish for the North Atlantic ("Mar del Nort")
and Latin for the South Atlantic ("Oceanus Aethiopicus"). Sometimes (as in
Gerhard Mercator, *Galliae Tabulae Geographicae* [1585; PUL], sigs. b and m)
important names are given in two or more forms, as "MARE BRITANNICUM
vulgo het Caniel à Belgicis nautis dicitur" and "BURGUNDIA SUPERIOR, SIVE
LIBER COMITATUS, vulgò LA FRANCHE COMTE." In Ortelius' *Theatrum Orbis*

read any compendious method of naturall Philosophy. And at the same time might be entring into the Greek tongue,[90] after the same manner as was before prescrib'd in the Latin; whereby the difficulties of Grammar being soon overcome, all the Historicall[91] Physiology of *Aristotle*[92] and *Theophrastus*[93] are open before them, and as I may say, under contribution. The like accesse will be to Vitruvius,[94] to *Senecas* naturall questions,[95] to *Mela*,[96] *Celsus*,[97] *Pliny*,[98]

Terrarum (Antwerp, 1612; PUL) most of the maps, which are by various cartographers, have legends in only Latin or the vernacular or both; but for a few places a choice of three or four ancient and modern names is offered, as, in Map No. 4, "Hæc insula ab incolis Madagascar ab Hispanis S. Laurentij, olim Memithias Ptol. Cerne fortè Plin. dicitur" or, in Map No. 22, "OCEANUS BRITANNICUS. *vulgo Gallico* Manche; *Anglico vulgo* Sleyfe: *Teutonico* Kaniel. *quasi dicas Canal. est enim canalis instar, inter Galliam et Angliam.*" Milton's care to teach both the ancient and the modern names follows the recommendation of Erasmus (*De Ratione Studii*, 1523, f. 5v) in regard to "Cosmographia": "Hic praecipua pars est observasse quæ montium, fluminum, regionum, urbium, vulgo recepta vocabula, quibus antiquis respondeant."

[90] In grammar schools of the time the study of Greek (in grammars written in Latin) was undertaken, like the study of Hebrew, for the primary if not exclusive purpose of reading the Scripture in the original tongue (Baldwin, *Shakspere's Small Latine*, II, 617–19). Milton postpones this Biblical study until the boys are more nearly mature (p. 397 below) and advocates immediate application of Greek to secular authors.

[91] In the rare sense of providing a systematic presentation of certain natural phenomena, not necessarily in chronological arrangement, as in the phrase "natural history." *NED*. Note the similar use in Greek and Latin titles in the two following notes.

[92] Particularly the *Historia Animalium, De Partibus Animalium*, and *De Generatione Animalium*. Various editions of Aristotle's works were available (*Complete Prose*, I, 263 and 443, n. 19), but there is no evidence to show which one Milton used.

[93] Aristotle's pupil and his successor in the leadership of the Peripatetic school; author of two works on plants, the *Enquiry* (Περὶ φυτῶν ἱστορίας) and the *Aetiology* (Περὶ φυτῶν αἰτιῶν). Both would have been available to Milton for example, in the combined Greek and Latin edition of the works of Theophrastus published at Leyden, 1613 (Θεοφράστου τοῦ Ἐρεσίου Ἅπαντα; PUL).

[94] Marcus Vitruvius Pollio (time of Augustus), Roman authority on architecture and engineering. His influential work *De Architectura*, in ten books, treats not only civic and domestic buildings, materials, and methods of construction, but also the rules of proportion in classical temples and in the Greek "Orders." Among the editions available to Milton was that published at Lyons in 1552 (PUL), with diagrams and illustrations of architectural details among the extensive annotations of Gulielmus Philander. Milton used Vitruvius in teaching his nephews (*Early Lives*, p. 60).

[95] The *Quaestiones Naturales* of Lucius Annaeus Seneca (*ca.* 5 B.C.–65 A.D.), a collection of data from earlier Greek and Roman writers on such subjects as air,

or *Solinus*.[99] And having thus past the principles of *Arithmetic,*
Geometry, Astronomy,[100] and *Geography* with a generall compact

fire, water, and the nature of earthquakes and comets. Long regarded as highly
authoritative, the *Naturalium Quaestionum Libri VII* were available not only in
the complete works of Seneca (*e.g., L. Annaei Senecae . . . Opera Quae Extant*
Omnia, Basle, 1557 [CUL], pp. 445–524), but also in separate editions (*e.g.,*
Venice, 1522; NYPL) and in an English translation by Thomas Lodge (*The*
Workes of Lucius Annaeus Seneca, 1620 [CUL], pp. 759–905).

[96] Pomponius Mela (first century A.D.), author of the geographical work *De*
Situ Orbis, a survey of the three known continents and of the countries situated
on the shores of Ocean and its four seas (Caspian, Mediterranean, Red Sea, and
Persian Gulf). Milton cites Mela three times in his *History of Britain* (1670,
pp. 5, 48, and 49), twice merely in marginal references but once as indirectly supporting the historicity of "*Albion* a Giant"; he does not indicate the edition he
used. There were separate Latin editions of this brief work (*e.g., Pomponii Melae*
De Situ Orbis Libri Tres, Antwerp, 1582, with extensive annotations and commentaries; CUL) and also joint editions with works of other authors, such as
Dionysius Periegetes and Solinus (*Dionysii Alex et Pomp. Melae Situs Orbis*
Descriptio. AEthici Cosmographia. C. I. Solini Polyistor, Geneva, 1577; RUL);
see also below, n. 99.

[97] Aulus Cornelius Celsus (first century A.D.), author of an encyclopedic work
of which only the eight books on medicine have survived entire. These books
De Medicina or *De Re Medica* were considered important during the Renaissance
both for their content and for the style of the "Cicero medicorum." Milton
taught Celsus to his nephews (*Early Lives,* p. 60). Contemporary editions (now
rare) include *Aurelii Corn. Celsi de Re Medica Libri Octo,* Geneva, 1625 (YML).

[98] Gaius Plinius Secundus (Pliny the Elder, *ca.* A.D. 23–79), author of the
Historiae Naturalis Libri XXXVII (*e.g.,* 3 vols., Leyden, 1635; PUL). The work
included material on geography, physiology, botany, zoology, mineralogy, and
other topics. Under Milton's tutelage, his nephews read "a great part" of it
(*Early Lives,* p. 60). An English translation by Philemon Holland was published
under the title *The Historie of the World* (2 vols., 1601; CUL).

[99] Gaius Julius Solinus (third century A.D.), whose *Collectanea Rerum Memo-*
rabilium presents a brief description of the known world geographically arranged,
with some information about the inhabitants of the various regions. Although
almost entirely taken from Pliny and Mela, the work adds a few facts about the
British Isles. When revised in the sixth century it was given the title *Polyhistor,*
which was subsequently taken for a name of Solinus. Among available editions
were *C. Iulii Solini Polyhistor, Rerum Toto Orbe Memorabilium Thesaurus*
Locupletissimus. Huic ob Argumenti Similitudinem Pomponii Melae De Situ
Orbis Libros Tres, Basle, 1538 (NYPL), and the Geneva edition of 1577 mentioned above in n. 96. In regard to the authors named in this sentence of the text,
Browning pointed out (*Milton's Tractate on Education,* p. 35) that "the concrete
knowledge contained in these books is to precede the abstract study of the
sciences to which they refer."

[100] Milton used "*Geminus's* Astronomy" in teaching his nephews (*Early Lives,*
p. 60). The work so known was available, for example, in the Leyden edition of
1603 (Γεμίνου Εἰσαγωγὴ εἰς τὰ φαινόμενα; NYPL), which presented the text in
Greek and Latin on opposite pages. The book is an elementary presentation of

of Physicks,[101] they may descend [102] in *Mathematicks* to the instrumentall science of *Trigonometry*,[103] and from thence to Fortification, *Architecture,* Enginry,[104] or navigation. And in naturall Philosophy they may proceed leisurly from the History [105] of *Meteors*,[106] minerals, plants and living creatures as farre as Anatomy. Then also in course might be read to them out of some not tedious writer the institution [107] of Physick; that they may know the tempers,[108] the humors,[109] the seasons,[110] and how to manage a

classical astronomy, suitable for teaching the motions of the sun, moon, and planets, and other important beliefs. Whether Geminus of Rhodes (last century B.C.) or a later editor compiled it is now questioned. It is noteworthy that *Of Education* contains no reference to a book on Copernican astronomy, since both Sacro Bosco (above, n. 88) and Geminus teach the geocentric theory of the universe. Yet in *Areopagitica* (below, p. 538) Milton speaks of "the famous Galileo . . . , a prisner to the Inquisition, for thinking in Astronomy otherwise then the Franciscan and Dominican licencers thought."

[101] A treatise on natural science in general. *NED.*

[102] Proceed from general principles to specific applications. *NED.*

[103] Although two Englishmen wrote or lectured on trigonometry as early as the fourteenth century (David E. Smith, *History of Mathematics* [2 vols., Boston, 1923], II, 235–36), and some slight treatment of the subject was included in Thomas Blundeville's *Exercises, Containing Sixe Treatises,* printed in England in 1594 (Smith, *History,* II, 324), the name itself was first coined when the German mathematician Bartholomäus Pitiscus fused the Greek τρίγωνον and μετρία into the title of his *Trigonometria* (Frankfurt, 1595). Milton was evidently soon familiar with this newly recognized branch of mathematics, for he had his nephews read *"Petiscus* his Trigonometry" (*Early Lives,* p. 61) in addition to specifying the subject here. Pitiscus was by now available in later editions (*e.g., Trigonometriae sive De Dimensione Triangulorum Libri Quinque,* Frankfurt, 1612; CUL), and had been published in an English translation in 1614 (*STC,* 19967).

[104] Here in the obsolete sense, the art of the military engineer.

[105] *Cf.* above, p. 390, n. 91.

[106] Atmospheric phenomena in general; these "were formerly often classed as *aerial* or *airy meteors* (winds), *aqueous* or *watery meteors* (rain, snow, hail, dew, etc.), *luminous meteors* (the aurora, rainbow, halo, etc.), and *igneous* or *fiery meteors* (lightning, shooting stars, etc.)." *NED.* Milton may have taught the elements of meteorology from Seneca's *Quaestiones Naturales* (see above, n. 95), or perhaps from Aristotle's *Meteorologicorum Libri IV.*

[107] In the obsolete sense of an introduction to the subject, an elementary book or treatise. *NED.*

[108] The temperaments of ancient medicine, considered to be the several constitutions of the body resulting from the proportions of the four humours or of the physical qualities (hot or cold, moist or dry). Here, as with the "humors" and "seasons" following, Milton's "Physick" is based upon the traditional associations of the four elements of Empedocles with corresponding qualities, humours, seasons, and temperaments: fire with hot, blood, spring, choleric; earth with

crudity: [111] which he who can wisely and timely doe, is not onely
a great Physician to himselfe, and to his friends, but also may at
some [4] time or other, save an Army by this frugall, and expence-
lesse meanes only; and not let the healthy and stout bodies of young
men rot away under him for want of this discipline; which is a great
pitty, and no lesse a shame to the commander. To set forward all
these proceedings in nature & mathematicks, what hinders, but that
they may procure, as oft as shall be needfull, the helpfull experi-

moist, yellow bile, summer, sanguine; air with dry, black bile, autumn, melan-
cholic; and water with cold, phlegm, winter, phlegmatic.

[109] In the "Hippocratic" work *On the Nature of Man* (attributed by Aristotle
to Polybus, son-in-law of Hippocrates) is stated the doctrine of the four humours
or fluids of the body: blood, phlegm, choler (yellow bile), and melancholy (black
bile). Health was supposed to result from a harmonious blending of the humours,
and sickness from disharmony among them. The Renaissance continued to accept
this doctrine without question; *e.g.*, Sir Thomas Elyot in *The Castel of Helthe*
(1539 ed., New York: Scholars' Facsimiles & Reprints, 1937), a work which was
printed fifteen times between 1539 and 1610, states (f. 8): "In the body of Man
be foure principall humours, whiche contynuinge in the proportion, that nature
hath lymytted, the body is free from all syckenesse. Contrary wise, by the
increase or diminution of any of them in quantitie or qualytie, over or under
their natural assignement, inequall temperature commeth in to the body, whiche
syckenesse, foloweth more or lasse, accordynge to the lapse or decaye of the
temperatures of the sayd humours."

[110] In the works attributed to Hippocrates are many references to the effects of
the seasons on health. For example, in the *Nature of Man,* chapter VII (*Hippocrates,* tr. W. H. S. Jones [4 vols., New York and London, 1931], IV, 19–23) are
set forth the changes in the humours due to the seasons ("Phlegm increases in a
man in winter; for phlegm, being the coldest constituent of the body, is closest
akin to winter," etc.); and in chapter IX (IV, 27) the rule is given: "one
should . . . carry out treatment only after examination of the patient's constitution, age, physique, the season of the year and the fashion of the disease,
sometimes taking away and sometimes adding, . . . and so making changes in
drugging or in regimen to suit the several conditions of age, season, physique
and disease." Celsus (*De Medicina,* book I, 3, 34–39) gives the regimen of diet,
clothing, and sexual gratification appropriate to each season, and also (book II, 1,
6–9) the diseases likeliest to occur in each. Elyot, in *The Castel of Helthe,* similarly presents (1539, ff. 36v–38) seasonal diets with details drawn from Hippocrates, Galen, Diocles of Carystus, and Damascenus, as well as (ff. 86v–83v
[correctly 84v–85v]) discussing the sicknesses "moste commune to particular
tymes of the yere" (*i.e.*, the seasons).

[111] Elyot, *The Castel of Helthe* (1539, f. 74v), explains *crudity* thus: "Fyrste
it shall be necessarye, to consyder, that concoction is an alteration in the stomacke
of meates and drynkes, accordynge to their qualities, wherby they are made lyke
to the substance of the body. Cruditie is a vycious concoction of thynges re-
ceyved, they not beinge holly or perfitely altered."

ences [112] of Hunters, fowlers, Fishermen, Shepherds, Gardeners, *Apothecaries;* and in the other sciences, Architects [,] Engineers, Mariners, *Anatomists;* who doubtlesse would be ready some for reward, and some to favour such a hopefull Seminary. And this will give them such a reall tincture of naturall knowledge,[113] as they shall never forget, but dayly augment with delight. Then also those Poets [114] which are now counted most hard, will be both facil and pleasant, *Orpheus,*[115] *Hesiod,*[116] *Theocritus,*[117] *Aratus,*[118] *Nican-*

[112] The first group of visiting experts would contribute practical knowledge of plants, fishes, birds, and animals—the lower levels in the Great Chain (the apothecaries of that day dealing almost exclusively in botanical remedies); the second group would deal with applications of the technical subjects so far studied. Milton thus proposes to offer both knowledge of classical authorities and acquaintance with modern practitioners in almost all the subjects so far studied: agriculture, "historical physiology," mathematics, *"Architecture, Enginry,* or navigation," and "the History of . . . plants and living creatures as farre as Anatomy."

[113] In this context, not only a knowledge of natural science but also of its uses.

[114] The recommendation of these pagan poets, without warning of the dangers of reading them, is contrary to the principles of both Vives and Comenius. See Vives, *De Tradendis Disciplinis* (1531, f. 104; tr. Watson, p. 128): "There are so many things in the poets, which are charming, beautiful, great and worthy of admiration, that poets ought not to be excluded from boys' study, but should be expurgated"), and the title of chapter XXV of Comenius' *The Great Didactic* (*A Reformation,* p. 94): "It is plainly demonstrated, that (if we would have such a reformation of Schooles, as is according to the Rules of true Christianity) Profane, and Heathen Authors must be either quite rejected, or used with more choyce and caution."

[115] Among the poems attributed to the mythical poet Orpheus, the only one relevant so early in Milton's plan is the *Lithica,* dealing with the properties of precious and other stones, and their uses in divination. The epic *Argonautica* and perhaps the *Hymns* also ascribed to Orpheus might be read when the pupils are prepared for "choice Histories, *heroic poems,* and *Attic* tragedies." All three of these works were available either in Greek ('Ορφέως 'Αργοναυτικά, Venice, 1517; NYPL) or in Latin verse translations (*Opera,* Basle [*ca.* 1552]; CUL).

[116] The *Works and Days* of Hesiod treated farm life and work throughout the year, with advice on the right time for certain operations, on clothing, on lucky and unlucky days, etc. Edward Phillips (*Early Lives,* pp. 12 and 60) listed Hesiod among the poets read under his uncle's direction, but did not specify either the *Works and Days* or the *Theogony;* presumably the former would be studied thus early. It was available, for example, with Greek and Latin on opposite pages (*Hesiodi Ascraei Duo Libri,* Strassburg, *ca.* 1515, bound with Cato's *Moralia* and Cebes' *Tabula;* UTSL).

[117] Theocritus, born in Syracuse, wrote his *Idyls* in Sicily, Cos, and Egypt in the third century B.C. They became the fountain-head of Renaissance pastoral poetry, as Milton's allusions in *Lycidas* reflect (l. 85, "fountain *Arethuse,*" and

der,[119] *Oppian,*[120] *Dionysius* [121] and in Latin *Lucretius,*[122] *Manil-*

l. 133, *"Sicilian* Muse"). These *Idyls,* with those of Bion and Moschus, were available in the Heidelberg edition of 1596 (Θεοκρίτου τοῦ Συρακοσίου εἰδύλλια; NYPL).

[118] Author (third century B.C.) of the Greek *Phaenomena,* a poem on astronomy, and the *Diosemeia,* one on meteorology (now considered a part of the same poem). Milton's nephews read both (*Early Lives,* p. 60). Milton's own copy ('Αράτου Σολέως φαινόμενα, Guillaume Morel edition, Paris, 1559; BML). See Maurice Kelley and Samuel D. Atkins, "Milton's Annotations of Aratus," *PMLA,* LXX (1955), 1090–1106, for a full discussion of his numerous annotations in this copy and the evidence that he also consulted several other editions, with this relevant conclusion: "The Period II entries [1639–52, probably *ca.* 1641–42] suggest . . . that Milton was a conscientious schoolmaster. When he taught Aratus, he did not instruct merely from his general knowledge of Greek and his notes of a decade earlier, but again gave close attention to his Morel text, compared it with Estienne [*Poetae Graeci Principes,* 1566], and in two instances . . . caught errors he had previously overlooked."

[119] Both of the extant Greek poems of Nicander (second century B.C.) would be relevant to the study of medicine: the *Theriaca,* on venomous animals and the treatment of their bites; and the *Alexipharmaca,* on poisons and antidotes. Both are based on the prose work of Apollodorus of Alexandria, early third-century physician. Separate editions of Nicander were rare in the Renaissance, but the Cologne edition of 1530 gives the complete Greek text (Νικάνδρου Θηριακά; PML [Pierre de Ronsard's copy]).

[120] Edward Phillips mentions (*Early Lives,* p. 60) reading *"Oppian's Cynegeticks* & *Halieuticks"* with his uncle. The *Cynegetica,* about hunting, and the *Halieutica,* about fishing, were attributed to Oppian of Cilicia (second century A.D.), though the latter may have been written by Oppian of Syria (third century A.D.). In the Paris edition of 1555 ('Οππιανοῦ 'Αναζαρβέως 'Αλιευτικά; NYPL) a Latin translation is bound with the Greek text of both poems.

[121] Dionysius "Periegetes" (about 300 A.D.), author of the Περιήγησις, a geographical survey of the known world; listed by Edward Phillips (*Early Lives,* pp. 12 and 60) among authors read. In addition to the Geneva edition of 1577 (see above, n. 96), which offered the text of the *Periegesis* in Greek, there would be available in Greek the Paris ("Lutetiae") edition of 1547 (Διονυσίου 'Αλεξανδρέως τῆς οἰκουμένης περιήγησις; NYPL).

[122] Titus Lucretius Carus (about 94–55 B.C.), author of the didactic poem *De Rerum Natura.* Certainly the teaching of this work, which expounds Epicurus' materialistic view of the universe and denies divine participation in it, would not have been approved by Vives or Comenius. Yet Edward Phillips (*Early Lives,* pp. 12 and 60), when he speaks of studying this and the following work, refers to Lucretius and Manilius as examples of "the best of Latin . . . Poetts" and as "the two Egregious Poets." But see *Areopagitica,* below, p. 495, n. 31. Various editions of Lucretius were available; but Maurice Kelley and Samuel Atkins point out ("Milton's Annotations of Aratus," p. 1102), and Harris Fletcher agrees (in a letter to the editor), that Milton's reference to Lucretius in his copy of Aratus (see above, n. 118) fits the page numbering of the Frankfurt edition of 1583 (*T. Lucretii Cari de Rerum Natura Libri VI;* PUL).

ius,[123] and the rurall part of Virgil.[124]

By this time,[125] yeers and good generall precepts will have fur-nisht them more distinctly with that act of reason which in *Ethics* is call'd *Proairesis:* [126] that they may with some judgement contem-plat upon morall good and evill. Then will be requir'd a speciall reinforcement of constant and sound endoctrinating to set them right and firm, instructing them more amply in the knowledge of vertue and the hatred of vice: while their young and pliant affections are led through all the morall works of *Plato*,[127] *Xenophon*,[128] *Cicero*,[129] *Plutarch*,[130] *Laertius*,[131] and those *Locrian* remnants;[132] but still to

[123] Marcus Manilius (contemporary with Augustus and Tiberius), author of the *Astronomica*, a poem largely astrological in its treatment. What edition Milton used to teach his nephews (*Early Lives*, pp. 12 and 60) is unknown, but editions containing the admired commentary of Joseph Scaliger were available (*e.g.*, *M. Manili AstrominicΩn* Paris, 1579; CUL).

[124] Both the *Eclogues* (*Bucolics*) and the *Georgics*. The Paris edition of 1572, entitled *Bucolica* (PUL), contains extensive annotations by Peter Ramus.

[125] Probably three years, or at most four, would have been spent in the pre-ceding elementary studies. Compare Edwards Phillips' statement (*Early Lives*, p. 12) that "within 3 years they went through the best of Latin & Greec Poetts." The boys would now be fifteen to sixteen years old.

[126] The term προαίρεσις (choice) is used by Aristotle (*Nicomachean Ethics*, II, vi, 15) in defining moral virtue. After examining its nature, he describes it (III, ii, 17; see also III, iii, 19) as voluntary action based on reasoning. Milton's use of the term here is the only instance in English recorded in the *NED*.

[127] The "moral works" might include the *Apology* and the dialogues *Crito*, *Menexenus*, *Symposium*, *Phaedo*, *Phaedrus*, and *Philebus* (see Samuel, *Plato and Milton*, pp. 16–17). For Milton's tribute to the virtuous influence of "the divine volumes of Plato, and his equal Xenophon," in his own studies, see *An Apology* (*Complete Prose*, I, 891, and references there).

[128] Probably selections from the *Apology for Socrates*, *Memorabilia*, and *Banquet* (*Symposium*), which Hughes names (*Prose Selections*, p. 41, n. 64), and also the *Cyropaedia*, which Edward Phillips lists (*Early Lives*, p. 60: "*Cyri Institutio*") as being read along with the *Anabasis*. All of these writings were available, with the Greek text and Latin translation in parallel columns, in the one-volume edition of Xenophon's *Opera* published at Basle, 1545 (NYPL).

[129] Primarily the *De Officiis*, a standard ethical work in the Renaissance, endorsed by Erasmus and frequently taught in the schools (see Baldwin, *Shakspere's Small Latine*, II, 585–90). The Paris edition of 1562 (*M. T. Ciceronis ad Filium de Officiis Libri Tres;* PUL) included Latin arguments by Erasmus and copious notes by him and others. Hughes suggests (*Prose Selections*, p. 41, n. 64) *De Amicitia* and *De Finibus* as other "moral works" of Cicero.

[130] The *Moralia*, parts of which the boys might have heard earlier in Latin or English (compare above, nn. 72 and 73), could now be thoroughly studied in Greek in such an edition as that published at Basle in 1574 (Πλουτάρχου τοῦ Χαιρωνέως . . . μικτὰ συγγράμματα; HCL). The so-called *Moralia* were by no means limited to ethical writings; Milton may have had in mind principally

be reduc't [133] in their nightward studies wherewith they close the dayes work, under the determinat sentence of *David,* or *Salomon,* or the Evangels and *Apostolic* scriptures. Being perfit in the knowledge of personall duty, they may then begin the study of Economics.[134] And either now, or before this, they may have easily learnt at any odde hour [135] the *Italian* tongue.[136] And soon after, but with warinesse, and good antidote, it would be wholsome anough to let them tast some choise comedies Greek, Latin,[137] or *Italian:* Those

those known as *De Virtute Morali, De Fraterno Amore, De Amore Prolis,* and *Praecepta Coniugalia.*

[131] The *Lives and Opinions of Eminent Philosophers* attributed to Diogenes Laertius (second or third century A.D.). The Geneva edition of 1594 (Περὶ βίων, δογμάτων καὶ ἀποφθεγμάτων τῶν ἐν φιλοσοφίᾳ εὐδοκιμησάντων; CUL) gave the Greek text and Latin rendering in parallel columns, with the notes of Isaac Casaubon.

[132] The treatise *On the Soul of the World and Nature* (Περὶ ψυχᾶς κόσμου καὶ φύσιος), formerly attributed to Timaeus of Locri, principal speaker in Plato's *Timaeus.* The work is now regarded as a poor paraphrase of that dialogue made about the first century A.D. The Greek text was available in the Paris edition of 1555 (PUL).

[133] In the literal sense, led back (to the "determinat" scriptural authorities). *Cf. Church-Government (Complete Prose,* I, 853 and n. 18): "these be the two fair supporters between which the strength of Prelaty is born up, either of inducing tyranny, or of reducing popery."

[134] "Economics" replaced in 1673 the meaningless "Economies." Milton conceived the scope of "Economics" or management of a household broadly: under "Index Œconomicus" in his *Commonplace Book (Complete Prose,* I, 392–419) he included entries concerning food, dress, marriage, concubinage, the education of children, divorce, slaves, adultery, riches, poverty, alms, and usury. Compare his discussion of the self-discipline needed "to governe a house well" in *Church-Government,* Book I, Chapter I *(Complete Prose,* I, 754); and the treatment of domestic duties in *Christian Doctrine,* Book II, Chapter XV.

[135] Milton applied in his own teaching the principle implied here, that thoroughness in learning Latin and Greek would make the addition of other languages less difficult. Edward Phillips testifies *(Early Lives,* pp. 60–61): "Nor did the time thus Studiously imployed in conquering the *Greek* and *Latin* Tongues, hinder the attaining to the chief Oriental Languages, *viz.* The *Hebrew, Caldee* and *Syriac,* . . . besides an Introduction into several Arts and Sciences . . . and into the *Italian* and *French* Tongues."

[136] Compare Milton's references to his own study of Italian in the poem *Ad Patrem* (ll. 78–85) and in Letter 9, to Benedetto Buonmattei *(Complete Prose,* I, 330).

[137] Classical comedies (both the Greek "New Comedy" and most Roman comedy) dealt with private affairs and family relationships, and classical tragedies rather with characters of great eminence involved in the most profound problems of mankind. Various critics of the Italian Renaissance emphasized this contrast: *e.g.,* Giraldi Cinthio *(Literary Criticism, Plato to Dryden,* ed. Allan

tragedies also that treate of houshold matters, as *Trachiniae, Alcestis* and the like.[138] The next remove must be to the study of *Politics;* [139] to know the beginning, end, and reasons of politicall societies; that they may not in a dangerous fit of the commonwealth be such poor, shaken, uncertain reeds, of such a tottering conscience, as many of our great counsellers have lately shewn themselves, but stedfast pillars of the State. After this they are to dive into the grounds of law, and legall justice; deliver'd first, and with best warrant by *Moses;* [140] and as farre as humane prudence can be trusted, in those extoll'd remains [141] of Grecian Law-givers, *Lycurgus,*[142] *Solon,*[143] *Zaleucus,*[144] *Charondas,*[145] and thence to all

H. Gilbert [New York: American Book Co., 1940], pp. 252–53) and Lodovico Castelvetro (pp. 319–20). Accordingly Milton introduces comedies "soon after" the study of household management, but the reading of tragedies is postponed until after the boys have studied politics, "the grounds of law," and "the highest matters of *Theology.*"

[138] Both these tragedies present devoted wives: in the *Trachiniae* of Sophocles, Deianira, having innocently caused the death of her husband Heracles, remorsefully kills herself; in the *Alcestis* of Euripides, the wife of Admetus gives up her own life to save his. Note Milton's reference in *Church-Government (Complete Prose,* I, 814–15) to Sophocles and Euripides as models he might use in his own writing. Available texts of the *Trachiniae* include the Antwerp edition of 1579 (Σοφοκλέους τραγῳδίαι ζ'; NYPL) of seven plays of Sophocles in Greek, with no annotation. Milton's own copy of the tragedies of Euripides (Εὐριπίδου τραγῳδιῶν ὅσα σῴζονται) is preserved in the Bodleian Library, Oxford (film copy in PUL): it is the Geneva edition of 1602 with Greek text and Latin translation. (See Columbia, XVIII, 566–68, for further description, and XVIII, 304–20.)

[139] In the broad sense of Greek πολιτικός, pertaining to citizens.

[140] Compare Preface to *Church-Government (Complete Prose,* I, 747 and n. 3) on "*Moses . . .* the only Lawgiver that we can believe to have been visibly taught of God."

[141] None of the ancient Greek legal codes referred to here was extant for study in Milton's time; the "remains" are the accounts of the early lawgivers given by later classical writers.

[142] Lycurgus, traditionally described as founder of the Spartan constitution, may have lived at any time from 1100 to 600 B.C. The principal ancient authorities on him are Herodotus, Aristotle, Xenophon, and Plutarch. The last of these specifically states that Lycurgus put none of his laws into writing. He was most highly "extolled" by Xenophon, who in the *Constitution of the Lacedaemonians* repeatedly holds him up for high admiration. Milton later praised Lycurgus for subordinating to the laws his own power as king: see *Eikonoklastes,* Chapter XXVIII, and *A Defence,* Chapter IV.

[143] Athenian legislator (about 640–561 B.C.), whose reforms included remodeling the constitution of his city. Aristotle and Plutarch give considerable infor-

the Romane *Edicts*[146] and tables[147] with their *Justinian;*[148] and so down to the *Saxon* and common laws of England, and the Statutes. Sundayes[149] also and every evening may be now understandingly spent in the highest matters of *Theology,* and Church His-

mation about him. Milton praised him in *Tetrachordon* (see below, p. 588), for setting the good of mankind above strict observance of the letter of the law, and in *Eikonoklastes,* Chapter XXVIII, for making the tyrants of Athens subject to the laws.

[144] Lawgiver of the Greek settlers of Locri Epizephyrii, near the southern tip of Italy. His code, considered the earliest written code of laws in Europe, was composed by the middle of the seventh century B.C. A brief selection attributed to Zaleucus has been preserved in the *Sententiae* of Joannes Stobaeus (for example, the Basle edition, 1549 [RUL], with the Greek of Stobaeus and the Latin of Conrad Gesner in parallel columns, contains two long paragraphs attributed to Zaleucus at p. 279).

[145] Lawgiver of Catana in Sicily, whose written laws, probably composed about 500 B.C., were adopted also by other Greek colonies in Sicily and Italy. Aristotle and Diodorus Siculus give information about him, and Stobaeus (see preceding note) preserved (p. 289) twenty paragraphs attributed to him.

[146] The praetors and other high Roman magistrates could announce publicly, on taking office, the rules and procedures they would observe in administering justice. These annual edicts, customarily accepted by succeeding praetors, developed into a body of legal precedents. About 130 A.D. the jurist Salvius Julianus, by order of the Emperor Hadrian, arranged the praetorian edicts into a codification known as *Edictum Perpetuum.*

[147] The Twelve Tables were the first Roman code of laws, drawn up in 450 B.C. The actual Tables were tablets of bronze or wood, which were lost when Rome fell. About a third of the complete code is thought to survive in the many fragments quoted by Cicero and other authors. *Cf.* Prolusion VII (*Complete Prose,* I, 298), and *Areopagitica,* below, p. 497.

[148] Under the direction of Justinian, Emperor of the East 527–565, were prepared the four legal works which codified the Roman civil law for all Europe: the *Institutiones,* an introductory or elementary book; the *Digesta* or *Pandectae,* a compilation of legal excerpts already three to five centuries old, divided into fifty books; the *Codex Repetitae Praelectionis,* giving the legislative "constitutions" of the emperors from Hadrian to Justinian himself; and the *Novellae Constitutiones,* adding the later enactments of Justinian. Milton was apparently most familiar with the *Institutes,* which he cites in the *Commonplace Book* (*Complete Prose,* I, 410–11) and elsewhere. Editions of one or more of these four works were fairly numerous, because of their great historical authority. Two convenient editions containing all four are *Corpus Juris Civilis* (Geneva, 1594–95; UTSL) and *Corpus Juris Civilis Justinianei Universum* (2 vols., Geneva, 1620; PUL).

[149] Compare Edward Phillips' account (*Early Lives,* p. 61): "The *Sunday's* work was for the most part the Reading each day a Chapter of the *Greek* Testament, and hearing his Learned Exposition upon the same."

tory ancient and modern: [150] and ere this time the Hebrew tongue [151] at a set hour [152] might have been gain'd, that the Scriptures may be now read in their own originall; [153] whereto it would be no impossibility to adde the *Chaldey*,[154] and the *Syrian* [155] dialect. When all these employments are well conquer'd, then will the choise Histories,[156] *heroic poems*,[157] and *Attic* tragedies of statliest, and most

[150] The ecclesiastical historians mentioned in the *Commonplace Book* include Eusebius, Socrates Scholasticus, Sulpicius Severus, Evagrius, Sozomen, Savonarola, Bede, Sarpi, Theodoretus. Entries referring to all of these are dated (in notes to *Commonplace Book, Complete Prose,* I) before 1644.

[151] The elements of Hebrew were taught in a few schools of the time, but more often reserved for the university. Clark believes (*Milton at St. Paul's,* pp. 119 and 121) that Milton began to study Hebrew grammar in the eighth form at St. Paul's. In a letter written in either 1625 or 1627 (*Complete Prose,* I, 311–12), Milton thanks Thomas Young for the gift of a Hebrew Bible, which presumably he could read by then.

[152] In contrast, as several editors have remarked, to learning Italian "at any odde hour."

[153] Compare Milton's statement, in the preface to *Christian Doctrine,* that in his own youth he had assiduously studied both Testaments in the original languages. His nephews, according to Edward Phillips (*Early Lives,* p. 61), acquired a knowledge of "the chief Oriental Languages, *viz.* The *Hebrew, Chaldee* and *Syriac,* so far as to go through the *Pentateuch,* or Five Books of *Moses* in *Hebrew,* to make a good entrance into the *Targum,* or *Chaldee* Paraphrase, and to understand several Chapters of St. *Matthew* in the *Syriac* Testament."

[154] Aramaic, the Semitic dialect in which portions of the books of Ezra and Daniel were preserved, called in Daniel 1:4 "the tongue of the Chaldeans"; also the language of the Targums, or paraphrases of books of the Old Testament.

[155] Syriac, originally the local dialect of Edessa in Mesopotamia, an early Christian center where various versions of the Bible were made. Among the chief of these is the Peshitta version, containing the Old Testament translated from the Hebrew, and the Gospels and much else of the New.

[156] Certainly Herodotus and Thucydides among the Greeks; Sallust among the Romans, and possibly Livy. In writing to Henry de Brass in 1657 (Letter 23), Milton ranked Sallust first among Roman historians, and expressed the view that he who would write worthily of worthy deeds must have as great a mind and experience as he who does such deeds. For texts, Herodotus was available in a Geneva edition, 1570 ('Ηροδότον τοῦ 'Αλικαρνασσέως ἱστορία; CUL), and Thucydides in a Paris edition, 1588 (Θουκυδίδου περὶ τοῦ Πελοποννησιακοῦ πολέμου; PUL). Though some minor historical works of Sallust (*Bellum Catilinae* and *Bellum Iugurthinum*) are extant, his more important *Historiae* has survived only in fragments (some not discovered until 1886); all of these known in Milton's time, as well as some lesser works, were included in the Venice edition, 1584 (C. *Crispi Sallustii De L. Sergij Catilinae Coniuratione, & Bello Iugurthino Historiae;* PUL).

[157] Milton's deliberate intention to postpone the study of the great epics to this comparatively late stage in the curriculum is borne out by the fact that Edward Phillips mentions (*Early Lives,* p. 60) only two minor epics read while studying

regal argument,[158] with all the famous Politicall orations offer themselves; which if they were not only read; but some of them got by memory,[159] and solemnly pronounc't with right accent, and grace, as might be taught, would endue them even with the spirit, and vigor of *Demosthenes* or *Cicero, Euripides,* or *Sophocles.* And now lastly [160] will be the time to read with them those organic arts [161] which inable men to discourse and write perspicuously, elegantly, and according to the fitted stile [162] of lofty, [5] mean, or lowly.[163]

under his uncle between the ages of ten and sixteen: *"Quintus Calaber* his Poem of the *Trojan* War continued from *Homer; Apollonius Rhodius* his *Argonauticks."* At this late point, however, the boys would be thoroughly prepared to understand the heroic characters and actions in the great epics of Homer and Virgil.

[158] Compare the preface to *Samson Agonistes,* where Milton speaks of tragedy as "the gravest, moralest, and most profitable of all other Poems," and refers to Aeschylus, Sophocles, and Euripides as "the three Tragic Poets unequall'd yet by any." See also the entry under "Spectacula" in the *Commonplace Book (Complete Prose,* I, 489–91), where he questions whether in all philosophy there is anything "more important or more sacred or more exalted than a tragedy rightly produced."

[159] Clark points out (*Milton at St. Paul's,* p. 128) that in Milton's day "the traditions of the grammar school required the boy to memorize his Latin grammar, his Greek grammar, and his textbook of rhetoric"; and (pp. 169–70) that Milton, whose "academic exercises, his Prolusions, were delivered not read," is here advocating "the exercise of memorizing fine prose and poetry as a preparation for the pupil's own writing."

[160] Not until now, in the closing years of their schooling, are the pupils to study logic, rhetoric, and poetry—"to compose Theams, verses, and Orations, which are the acts of ripest judgment and the finall work of a head fill'd by long reading, and observing."

[161] Compare Vives, *De Tradendis Disciplinis,* f. 81v: "Certain arts, such as grammar and dialectic, are only instruments of others, and for that reason are called by the Greeks ὄργανα." See *Tetrachordon* (below, pp. 607–608: "Wee shall now . . . summ up the strength wee have, into one argumentative head, with that *organic* force that logic proffers us."

[162] Appropriate to speaker, subject, and audience. Aristotle deals with all three of these kinds of appropriateness or propriety of style in the *Rhetoric:* to the speaker at III, vii, 6; to the subject at III, vii, 2–4; and to the audience at III, xii, 1–2 and 5. The most thorough examination of Milton's theory of style as implied here, in relation to the ancient authors he had studied, is that of Donald L. Clark, "John Milton and 'the fitted stile of lofty, mean, or lowly,'" *Seventeenth-Century News,* XI, no. 4 (winter, 1953), pp. 5–9.

[163] The traditional threefold division of style is found earliest in the *Rhetorica ad Herennium* (IV, 11; tr. Harry Caplan [Cambridge, Mass., and London: Loeb Classical Library, 1954], p. 253): "There are, then, three kinds of style . . . to which discourse, if faultless, confines itself: the first we call the Grand; the second, the Middle; the third, the Simple." The classification into three kinds

Logic therefore so much as is usefull,[164] is to be referr'd to this due place withall her well coucht heads and Topics,[165] untill it be time [166] to open her contracted palm [167] into a gracefull and ornate Rhetorick taught out of the rule of *Plato*,[168] *Aristotle*,[169] *Phalereus*,[170]

was widely accepted, appearing subsequently in Cicero's *De Oratore* (III, xlv, 177; lii, 199; and lv, 212) and *Orator* (v. 20–vi, 21; vii, 23; and xxiii, 75–xxviii, 99), Dionysius of Halicarnassus' *De Demosthene*, and Quintilian's *Institutio Oratoria* (XII, x, 58–59). The Latin names for the three styles, which Milton renders as "lofty, mean, or lowly," varied somewhat: *Rhetorica ad Herennium* gives *gravis, mediocris*, and *extenuata* (literally, thinned or weakened); Cicero (*De Oratore*, III, xlv, 177) first uses *graves, medium*, and *subtiles*, and later, in specific reference to the functions of the orator (*Orator*, xxi, 69), calls them *vehemens, modicum*, and *subtile;* and Quintilian (*Institutio Oratoria*, XII, x, 58–59) names them *floridum, medium*, and *subtile.*

[164] Even while at Cambridge Milton had similarly suggested in Prolusion VII (*Complete Prose*, I, 300–301) a limitation on the study of logic. Compare also the doubts expressed in *The Likeliest Means* (1659, pp. 137–38) whether a knowledge of logic is indispensable to ministers of the Gospel.

[165] See Milton's definition of *Topica* in the *Art of Logic*, Chapter II, as "the invention of arguments"; *invention*, as explained in note 28, meant the discovery or recognition of suitable materials. Clark points out (*Milton at St. Paul's*, pp. 11–12) that *inventio* had been a part of classical rhetoric, but was treated under dialectic by Petrus Ramus (Pierre de la Ramée), whose system of logic Milton studied and later used as the basis of his *Art of Logic.*

[166] Even as early as Prolusion VII (*Complete Prose*, I, 288–89) Milton had said that "he who would be an orator in reality as well as by repute must first acquire a thorough knowledge of all the arts and sciences"; and in *An Apology* (*Complete Prose*, I, 874) had affirmed that "doubtless that indeed according to art is most eloquent, which returns and approaches neerest to nature from whence it came; and they express nature best, who in their lives least wander from her safe leading, which may be call'd regenerate reason. So that how he should be truly eloquent who is not withall a good man, I see not." The last agrees with Quintilian's doctrine (*Institutio Oratoria*, I, Prooemium, 9–11) that the perfect orator must be a good man. John S. Diekhoff (*Milton's "Paradise Lost"* [New York: Columbia University Press, 1946], pp. 15–16) has discussed the significant relationship between this high standard for the orator and the standard at least equally high which Milton set for the poet in *An Apology* (*Complete Prose*, I, 890): That he "ought him selfe to bee a true Poem, that is, a composition, and pattern, of the best and honourablest things." The orator, the poet, and the historian (see above, p. 400, n. 156) must alike be men of exceptional virtue as well as of learning.

[167] The comparison of dialectic to the closed fist, already used by Milton in Prolusion II (*Complete Prose*, I, 234), and of rhetoric to the open hand is attributed to Zeno by Cicero (*De Finibus*, II, 6) and Quintilian (*Institutio Oratoria*, II, xx, 7).

[168] As Clark points out ("Milton and 'the fitted style,' " p. 5), what Milton learned from Plato's *Gorgias* and *Phaedrus* was "the doctrine of the noble rhetoric which makes the teaching of truth and virtue its object." Compare *An*

Cicero,[171] *Hermogenes,*[172] *Longinus.*[173] To which Poetry would be made subsequent, or indeed rather precedent,[174] as being lesse suttle and fine,[175] but more simple, sensuous and passionate.[176] I mean

Apology (*Complete Prose,* I, 948–49): "Although I cannot say that I am utterly untrain'd in those rules which best Rhetoricians have giv'n, . . . yet true eloquence I find to be none, but the serious and hearty love of truth."

[169] Aristotle's *Rhetoric* would have provided especially the doctrine of propriety of style (see above, n. 162).

[170] Milton's reference to the Athenian orator Demetrius Phalereus (born *ca.* 350 B.C.) is actually to the later Greek treatise *On Style* by another Demetrius who probably lived in the first century A.D. but is still almost unknown. This work adds a fourth (the "forcible") to the usual three kinds of style.

[171] The *De Oratore* and the *Orator.* In the latter, an attempt to portray the perfect orator, Cicero deals principally with style. His final summary here of the three styles is (xxix, 100; tr. H. M. Hubbell [Cambridge and London: Loeb Classical Library, 1939]), p. 379: "He in fact is eloquent who can discuss commonplace matters simply, lofty subjects impressively, and topics ranging between in a tempered style" (*"subtiliter . . . graviter et . . . temperate"*). According to a note in his copy of Euripides (Columbia, XVIII, 307), Milton seems also to have accepted the common attribution of the *Rhetorica ad Herennium* to Cicero.

[172] Hermogenes of Tarsus (born *ca.* 150 A.D.), author of a series of writings on school rhetoric. The best known, περὶ ἰδεῶν, was an attempt to arrive at the laws of style by analyzing the work of ancient authors. Clark points out ("Milton and 'the fitted style,'" p. 7) that Milton's use of *"ideas"* in two passages of *An Apology* (*Complete Prose,* I, 899 and 934) shows his familiarity with Hermogenes. The second of these is especially relevant here: "How few among them that know how to write, or speak in a pure stile, much lesse to distinguish the *idea's,* and various kinds of stile."

[173] περὶ ὕψους, a distinguished classical work on the "lofty" style, by an unknown author, but long attributed to Cassius Longinus. The title is usually translated *On the Sublime.*

[174] As Balachandra Rajan explains (" 'Simple, Sensuous and Passionate,'" *RES,* XXI [1945], 294): "Poetry is subsequent to rhetoric in the educational scheme. It is precedent in its value, its intrinsic dignity." His whole article (pp. 289–301) expounds "the part played by the Tractate on Education in the formulation of Milton's theory of poetry," and particularly why we "find the educational process . . . terminating in the study of poetics."

[175] Subtile, literally *fine* or *thin,* is the word used by Cicero and Quintilian (see above, page 401, n. 163) for the plain style of rhetoric, to which Milton's "lowly" corresponds. As applied to rhetorical style, this use of *subtile* is explained (R. G. Austin, ed., *Quintiliani Institutionis Oratoriae Liber XII* [Oxford: Clarendon Press, 1948], p. 198) as "a metaphor from textiles," referring "primarily to its dialectical quality rather than to its simplicity." Milton's distinction is that in rhetoric, even in the "lowly" style, more thin-spun dialectic may be permitted than is proper to poetry.

[176] Poetry is "more simple, sensuous and passionate" than classical rhetoric in being more straightforward, in more directly affecting the senses (*Cf. Para-*

not here the prosody of a verse, which they could not but have hit on before among the rudiments of grammar; [177] but that sublime art which in *Aristotles poetics*,[178] in *Horace*,[179] and the *Italian* commentaries of *Castelvetro*,[180] *Tasso*,[181] *Mazzoni*,[182] and others, teaches

dise Lost, II, 556: "For Eloquence the Soul, Song charms the Sense"), and in more immediately stirring the emotions. See the discussion of these three terms by William P. Ker, *Form and Style in Poetry* (London, 1928), pp. 175–84. His treatment is based on the following explanations (pp. 175–77): " 'Simple' in Milton's description means 'comprehensible,' such as may be taken in at one view, if not at one glance [amplified at p. 180 as seeming "to require . . . immediate unity coming at once to the mind without a long process of explanation"]. . . . 'Sensuous' for Milton meant something like sense perception, immediate knowledge . . . striking direct on the mind in the same way as objects of sight or hearing. 'Passionate' . . . depends on its etymological meaning, ... 'Passio' is a translation of the Greek πάθος, meaning 'suffering'; 'affection' is another term, something by which the mind is affected, to which the being is subject. . . . 'Passionate' includes our common meaning of passion, but it is more general, including everything of feeling, whether strong or weak."

[177] In Lily's *Grammar* (see above, n. 61), prosody is the last topic presented (in the Oxford edition of 1636, pp. 115–30). Clark (*Milton at St. Paul's*, p. 199) suggests that Milton himself probably had to memorize the rules in these pages and may have studied prosody again in connection with Greek grammar.

[178] The *Poetics*, after a preliminary discussion of poetry as a form of imitation, is principally concerned with tragedy and, more briefly, epic poetry. It is in connection with the last that Milton questions, in *Church-Government* (*Complete Prose*, I, 813), "whether the rules of *Aristotle* herein are strictly to be kept, or nature to be follow'd."

[179] The *Ars Poetica*, or Epistle to the Pisos, of which about one-third is concerned with the drama.

[180] Ludovico Castelvetro (1505–1571), translator of Aristotle's *Poetics* into Italian, is credited particularly with formulating the doctrine of the three "unities" in drama, whereas Aristotle had only insisted on the necessity of unity of action and described the practice of writers of tragedy in regard to time. Milton himself followed the doctrine of Castelvetro by observing all three in *Samson Agonistes*, calling particular attention in his foreword to the "circumscription of time" as "according to antient rule, and best example." Ida Langdon has pointed out (*Milton's Theory of Poetry and Fine Art* [New Haven, 1924], p. 150) that Milton also accepted the license granted by the Italian commentators but not by Aristotle in speaking *in propria persona* as an epic poet: "Minturno, Mazzoni, Castelvetro, and Tasso, each in his own way, allow the epic writer to break the course of the story with utterances in his own person. According to Tasso, the poet may blame, praise, comment, and, in doubtful cases, point out the virtuous way. According to Castelvetro, likewise, he may admonish or warn, and, in the role of narrator, may tell of past or future events. But Milton assumed a still larger privilege; he granted the poet leave to speak not only as himself but of himself."

what the laws are of a true *Epic* poem, what of a *Dramatic*, what of a *Lyric*,[183] what decorum [184] is, which is the grand master peece to observe. This would make them soon perceive what despicable creatures our common rimers and play-writes be,[185] and shew them, what Religious, what glorious and magnificent use might be made of

[181] The *Discorsi dell'Arte Poetica, ed in particolare sopra il Poema Eroico,* and *Discorsi del Poema Eroica* of Torquato Tasso (1544–1595). While greatly respecting the ancient poets and critics, Tasso eclectically concluded that the epic poet should add to the classical model the best qualities of the modern romance. See Langdon, *Milton's Theory of Poetry,* pp. 126–28. Milton's high regard for Tasso as himself an exemplary epic poet had already been evidenced in *Church-Government (Complete Prose,* I, 814), where he is the only modern poet named with Homer and Virgil as authors of "diffuse" epics and where his consideration of suitable subjects is cited as a precedent. See also F. T. Prince, *The Italian Element in Milton's Verse* (Oxford: Oxford University Press, 1954), chapters 3 and 7.

[182] The *Discorso Composto in Difesa della Comedia di Dante,* and the longer work that followed, *Della Difesa della Comedia di Dante,* in which Giacomo Mazzoni (1548–1598) defended Dante's poetic practices, partly against judgment by Aristotelian principles. On the bearing which the theories of all the critics named here had on Milton's own poetic planning, see *Church-Government (Complete Prose,* I, 810–17, and notes).

[183] Compare Milton's reflections in *Church-Government (Complete Prose,* I, 813–15) on "that Epick form . . . those Dramatick constitutions . . . those magnifick Odes and Hymns." The preface to *Samson Agonistes* amplifies his view of the "laws" of tragedy. Ida Langdon discusses at some length (*Milton's Theory of Poetry,* pp. 83–153) his theories of drama and of epic, relating these to the precepts of the classical and Renaissance critics.

[184] Compare *Church-Government (Complete Prose,* I, 818): "That which is the main consistence of a true poem, the choys of such persons as they ought to introduce, and what is morall and decent to each one." Milton's clearest specific statement of this principle, however, is in *A Defence,* Chapter V. See also Langdon, pp. 109–15, on his use of the term "with a full sense of its critical value"; and Kester Svendsen, "Epic Address and Reference and the Principle of Decorum in *Paradise Lost,*" *PQ,* XXVIII (1949), 185–87.

[185] Compare *Church-Government (Complete Prose,* I, 818): "the writings and interludes of libidinous and ignorant Poetasters, who having scars ever heard of [decorum], doe for the most part lap up vitious principles in sweet pils to be swallow'd down, and make the tast of vertuous documents harsh and sowr." Note also the comment, in the preface to *Samson Agonistes,* on "the small esteem, or rather infamy, which in the account of many [Tragedy] undergoes at this day with other common Interludes; hap'ning through the Poets error of intermixing Comic stuff with Tragic sadness and gravity; or introducing trivial and vulgar persons, which by all judicious hath bin counted absurd; and brought in without discretion, corruptly to gratifie the people."

Poetry [186] both in divine and humane [187] things. From hence and not till now will be the right season of forming them to be able writers and composers in every excellent matter, when they shall be thus fraught with an universall insight into things.[188] Or whether they be to speak in Parliament or counsell, honour and attention would be waiting on their lips. There would then also appear in Pulpits other visages, other gestures, and stuffe otherwise wrought [189] then what we now sit under, oft times to as great a triall of our patience as any other that they preach to us. These are the studies wherein our noble and our gentle youth [190] ought to bestow their time in a disciplinary way from twelve to one and twenty; unlesse they rely more upon their ancestors dead,[191] then upon themselves living. In which methodicall course it is so suppos'd they must proceed by the steddy pace of learning onward, as at convenient times for memories sake to retire back into the middle ward, and some-

---

[186] Compare the tribute in *Church-Government* (*Complete Prose*, I, 816–17) to poetic abilities as "of power beside the office of a pulpit, to imbreed and cherish in a great people the seeds of vertu, and publick civility, . . . to celebrate in glorious and lofty Hymns the throne and equipage of Gods Almightinesse, . . . to sing . . . the deeds and triumphs of just and pious Nations . . . , to deplore the general relapses of Kingdoms and States from justice and Gods true worship." The whole passage is an expanded statement of the brief suggestion here.

[187] Human: as often spelled until 1700. *NED.*

[188] Compare *An Apology* (*Complete Prose*, I, 890): "he who would not be frustrate of his hope to write well hereafter in laudable things, ought him selfe to bee a true Poem, that is, a composition, and patterne of the best and honourablest things; not presuming to sing high praises of heroick men, or famous Cities, unlesse he have in himselfe the experience and the practice of all that which is praise-worthy." In *Church-Government* (*Complete Prose*, I, 821) Milton spoke of his own need of "insight into all seemly and generous arts and affaires" before he could fulfill his poetic plans.

[189] Hughes points out (*Prose Selections*, p. 45, n. 91) that in *An Apology* (see *Complete Prose*, I, 934) Milton's complaint of the linguistic ignorance of the clergy follows an allusion to their inadequate knowledge of decorum: "How few among them that know to write, or speak in a pure stile, much lesse to distinguish the *idea's,* and various kinds of stile." (On *"idea's,"* see above, n. 172 on Hermogenes.)

[190] See above, p. 378, n. 56.

[191] Compare Milton's description of the Parliament in 1642, in *An Apology* (*Complete Prose*, I, 923): "The most of them being either of ancient and high Nobility, or at least of knowne and well reputed ancestry, which is a great advantage towards vertue one way, but in respect of welth, ease, and flattery, which accompanies a nice and tender education, is as much a hindrance another way."

times into the rear [192] of what they have been taught, untill they have confirm'd, and solidly united the whole body of their perfected knowledge, like the last embattelling of a Romane legion. Now will be worth the seeing what exercises, and what recreations may best agree, and become these studies.

Their Exercise.

The course of study hitherto briefly describ'd, is, what I can guesse by reading, likest to those ancient and famous schools of *Pythagoras*,[1] *Plato*,[2] *Isocrates*,[3] *Aristotle* [4] and such others, out of which were bred up such a number of renowned Philosophers, orators, Historians, Poets and Princes all over *Greece*, *Italy*, and *Asia*, be-

[192] By the sixteenth century *foreward* was the accepted English term for the "first line of embattled troops," *mid-ward* for the second line, and *rear-ward* for the third. See J. W. Fortescue, "The Army: Military Service and Equipment," chapter IV in *Shakespeare's England*, I, 120. As Hughes suggests (*Prose Selections*, p. 45, n. 92), the point of the military metaphor is that a final review will consolidate the "pupils' knowledge of their subjects so as to make it resemble a regiment," all of whose parts are "alike prepared for action." In correspondence with the editor, William B. Hunter, Jr. and Merritt Hughes have suggested that there may also be an echo here of the old faculty psychology, in which memory was seated in the rear ward or ventricle of the brain. *Cf.* Spenser, *Faerie Queene*, II, ix, 47–58.

[1] The "school" of Pythagoras (sixth century B.C.) was a considerable brotherhood to whom he taught his religious and philosophical theories at Croton (modern Crotona) in Italy. Milton again referred to "the school of *Pythagoras*" with high respect in *Areopagitica* (below, p. 551).

[2] The Academy outside Athens, where Plato taught for forty years, took its name originally from a grove dedicated to the hero Academus.

[3] The Athenian orator (426–338 B.C.) taught rhetoric first briefly in Chios and later for about forty years at Athens, achieving a great reputation as teacher at the latter place. Clark comments (*Milton at St. Paul's*, p. 252): "As near as I can guess by reading, Milton's school would be more like that of Isocrates than like the others, for only Isocrates oriented his school toward preparing his pupils 'to speak in Parliament or Counsel,' by making all liberal knowledge function through rhetoric, or more accurately, through that 'philosophy of the logos' which included all the arts of communication in language: grammar, rhetoric, and logic." For further references to Isocrates, see *Areopagitica*, below, pp. 486 and 489) and Sonnet X.

[4] The Lyceum at Athens, where Aristotle, himself a student at Plato's school for nearly twenty years, taught from about 335 to 323 B.C. It came to be known as the Peripatetic school from the covered court ($\pi\epsilon\rho\iota\pi\alpha\tau\sigma\varsigma$) among the buildings there.

sides the flourishing studies [5] of *Cyrene* [6] and *Alexandria.* [7] But herein it shall exceed them, and supply a defect as great as that which *Plato* noted in the common-wealth of *Sparta;* [8] whereas that City train'd up their youth most for warre, and these in their Academies and *Lycaeum,* [9] all for the gown, [10] this institution of breeding which I here delineate, shall be equally good both for Peace and warre. [11] Therefore about an hour and a halfe ere they eat at noon should be allow'd them for exercise and due rest afterwards: But

[5] Milton translates the Latin *studia,* in the sense of endeavors, applications to learning.

[6] Cyrene was known in the fourth century B.C. as a center of mathematical study; it was also the birthplace of Callimachus (*ca.* 305–*ca.* 240 B.C.), who catalogued the library at Alexandria and was author of the so-called "Hymns" which Milton alludes to in *Church-Government* (*Complete Prose,* I, 815), and of Eratosthenes (*ca.* 274–194 B.C.), head librarian at Alexandria and a writer of almost encyclopedic learning. In *Areopagitica* (below, p. 495) Milton refers to "that libertine school of Cyrene," alluding to the hedonistic teachings of Aristippus (fl. *ca.* 400–365 B.C.); note also his reference in *Church-Government* (*Complete Prose,* I, 856) to "*Aristippus* with all his Cyrenaick rout."

[7] At Alexandria the first and second Ptolemies (Soter and Philadelphus) developed the great library and museum that constituted a main center of scientific and literary activity in the last three centuries B.C. Among the scholars and writers at Alexandria, in addition to Callimachus and Eratosthenes (see preceding note), were Apollonius Rhodius, Euclid, Demetrius of Phalerum, Philetas of Cos, and Zenodotus of Ephesus.

[8] Throughout book I of Plato's *Laws,* the Athenian demonstrates this deficiency in the governments of both Crete and Sparta; see especially 626–30, 634–36, and 641b-c.

[9] The schools named above, especially the Academy of Plato and the Lyceum of Aristotle.

[10] In general, the toga as a symbol of peace, as the garment worn in public by Roman citizens in time of peace; more specifically, the "gown" symbolized the magistracy collectively, or the legal and clerical professions. *NED.*

[11] Compare p. 379 above: "to perform justly, skilfully and magnanimously all the offices both private and publike of peace and war." While the tractate was published during the Civil War, less than a month before the Battle of Marston Moor (see Masson, III, 83–96, for the situation in the early months of 1644), Milton would have considered preparation for war an important part of his educational plan at any time. See his entries under the heading "Of Military Discipline" in the *Commonplace Book* (*Complete Prose,* I, 491–96); and note his suggestion in *Church-Government* (*Complete Prose,* I, 818–19) that "because the spirit of man cannot demean it selfe lively in this body without some recreating intermission of labour, and serious things, it were happy for the Common wealth, if our Magistrates . . . would take into their care . . . the managing of our publick sports, and festival pastimes, that they might be . . . such as may inure and harden our bodies by martial exercises to all warlike skil and performance."

the time for this may be enlarg'd at pleasure, according as their rising in the morning shall be early. The exercise which I commend first, is the exact use of their weapon; [12] to guard and to strike safely with edge, or point; this will keep them healthy, nimble, strong, and well in breath, is also the likeliest meanes to make them grow large, and tall, and to inspire them with a gallant and fearlesse courage, which being temper'd with seasonable lectures and precepts [6] to them of true fortitude, and patience,[13] will turn into a native and heroick valour, and make them hate the cowardise of doing wrong.[14] They must be also practiz'd in all the locks and gripes of wrastling,[15] wherein English men were wont to excell, as need may often be in fight to tugge, to grapple, and to close. And this perhaps will be anough, wherein to prove and heat their single strength. The interim of unsweating themselves regularly, and convenient rest before meat may both with profit and delight be taken up in recreating and composing their travail'd spirits with the solemn and divine harmonies of musick heard, or learnt; [16] either

[12] The sword. In the *Second Defence* (1654, pp. 41–42) Milton records that he had formerly kept himself skillful in the use of the sword by daily practice and felt well able to defend himself with it; and the anonymous early biographer testifies (*Early Lives*, p. 32) that "he wore a Sword while hee had his Sight, and was skill'd in using it."

[13] Milton repeatedly affirmed in his later writings that patience was the highest fortitude: *Paradise Lost*, IX, 31–32, and XII, 569–70; and *Samson Agonistes*, ll. 654 and 1288–91.

[14] This forceful phrase is Milton's own, but compare Plato's view (*Laws*, I, 626e) that self-defeat is the most shameful of all defeats.

[15] As Milton implies, wrestling had long been a prominent sport among the English, and several recent writers on education had discussed its values. Mulcaster devotes a chapter of his *Positions* to it, without referring to its worth for military training; Cleland praises it in his Ἡρωπαιδεία (pp. 217–20), asserting that "undoubtedly it shalbe found profitable in warres"; Peacham, on the other hand, considers it (*The Compleat Gentleman*, 1906, p. 215) "not so well beseeming Nobility, but rather soldiers in a Campe." Milton himself had written in Prolusion VI (*Complete Prose*, I, 272) that "those who exercise themselves in wrestling and other sports grow much stronger than others and more ready for all emergencies"; but here he limits the purpose of it in education to its military utility, as Plato does in the *Laws* (VII, 796 and 814d; *cf.* VIII, 832e).

[16] Aubrey reports of Milton's own teaching (*Early Lives*, p. 12): "He made his Nephews Songsters, and sing from the time they were with him." Few educational writers of the time find a place for music, though Sir Humphrey Gilbert (*Queene Elizabethes Achademy*, p. 7) provides for instrumental music, and Mulcaster (*Elementarie*, p. 5; *Positions*, chapter 5) recommends both vocal and instrumental music.

while the skilfull *Organist* plies his grave and fancied [17] descant,[18] in lofty fugues,[19] or the whole Symphony [20] with artfull and unimaginable touches adorn and grace the well studied cords of some choise composer; some times the Lute, or soft organ stop waiting on elegant voices either to Religious, martiall, or civill ditties; [21] which if wise men [22] & prophets be not extreamly out, have a great power

[17] Sigmund G. Spaeth comments (*Milton's Knowledge of Music: Its Sources and its Significance in His Works* [Princeton, 1913], pp. 111–12, n. 1): "Cf. this actual organist with the visionary Jubal [*Paradise Lost*, XI, 556–59] pursuing his themes through all proportions low and high [which Spaeth explains, p. 121, n. 1, as representing the "mathematical relations of the music, . . . not as differing in pitch but in complexity. Simple intervals or rhythms are naturally termed *low*. Conversely, the more complex proportions are *high*."]. When *grave*, the descant or improvisation may be said to be in low proportions, but when *fancied* (*i.e.*, fanciful) the proportions would become complex or high."

[18] Spaeth explains (p. 116, n. 1): "*Descant* implies improvisation on a set theme."

[19] According to Spaeth (pp. 47–48), "Milton's allusion to the fugue . . . denotes a definite style of composition. The fugue of the sixteenth and seventeenth centuries was really a movement in canon form. . . . There were at that time two kinds of fugue—limited fugue, which was in strict canon, and unlimited fugue, which began in canon, but soon broke off into free passages. . . . Fugue, as we now know it, did not exist until the eighteenth century. . . . Milton evidently had a taste for musical embellishment in its proper place. A bewildering series of passages pleased him because of the mathematical order which lay at the bottom of their confusion, and because of the demands made by it upon the analytic powers of the listener. The involved structure of the fugue-form must therefore have appealed to him very strongly."

[20] Milton carefully distinguished between *symphony* and *harmony* as technical terms (see Spaeth, pp. 62–64), but here a less exact meaning is intended. Spaeth explains (p. 112, n.): "The improvisation of the organist is compared with the performance of the well-studied chords of some choice composer *by the entire company* [italics added]. Milton's intention, obviously, is to show how the boys themselves may take part in the music. He speaks above of the 'divine harmonies of music heard or learned.' Here, then, the pupils are represented as playing together, or singing, at times *a cappella,* at times with the accompaniment of lute or organ. The 'artful and unimaginable touches' are in contrast with the natural descant of the organist. Formal set music is here compared with spontaneous improvisation."

[21] Spaeth (p. 159) glosses *ditty* as "a simple but often solemn song."

[22] In spite of the inclusion of "martial . . . ditties" here, Milton is advocating not music that will inflame the boys to desire vigorous military action, but songs that will inculcate virtue, and discipline or calm the emotions. *Cf. Paradise Lost*, I, 549–59, where this distinction is clearly stated of music in "the Dorian mood" which inspired "instead of rage / Deliberate valour." Spaeth comments (p. 66) that of the three ancient "modes" Milton "obviously prefers

over dispositions and manners, to smooth and make them gentle from rustick harshnesse and distemper'd [23] passions. The like also would not be unexpedient after meat to assist and cherish nature in her first concoction,[24] and send their mindes backe to study in good tune and satisfaction. Where having follow'd it close under vigilant eyes till about two hours before supper,[25] they are by a sudden alarum or watch word, to be call'd out to their military motions,[26] under skie or covert, according to the season, as was the Romane wont; first on foot, then as their age permits, on horse back, to all the art of cavalry; That having in sport, but with much exactnesse, and dayly muster, serv'd out the rudiments of their Souldiership in all the skill of embattailing, marching, encamping, fortifying, beseiging and battering, with all the helps of ancient and

the Dorian, and in this he adheres closely to the sentiments of Plato"; but Aristotle also (*Politics,* VIII, 7 [1342b]) considered this mode more sedate than the Phrygian, especially manly, and best suited to the education of younger pupils. Milton's "wise men," therefore, would not include such authorities as Plutarch, who in his *Life of Lycurgus* describes the use of songs to educate boys to look forward eagerly to battle, but would refer rather to Plato (*Republic,* III, 398e–99c and 401b–402a), Aristotle (*Politics,* VIII, 5 [1340a-b]), and Quintilian (*Institutio Oratoria,* I, x, 9–33). The treatment of music in this section of the tractate, under "Exercise," also has its precedent in Plato, who joins music and gymnastic as educative influences (see *Republic,* III, 410b–12a and 441e–42a).

[23] In an obsolete sense, disordered because of the excess or deficiency of one of the bodily humors. *NED.*

[24] Elyot defines concoction (*The Castel of Helthe,* 1539, f. 74v) as "an alteration in the stomacke of meates and drynkes, accordynge to their qualities, wherby they are made lyke to the substance of the body." Sometimes this digestive process was known as "first concoction," the changing of the chyme into blood as "second concoction," and secretion as "third concoction." *NED.*

[25] Miss Lockwood suggests (*Selected Essays,* p. 26, n. 5) that "supper was usually between seven and eight o'clock."

[26] On this military training as "an essential part of Milton's attempt to carry out consistently in a definite educational program the humanistic ideal . . . of a trained leadership, in which practical skill is integrated with and based on liberal culture," and on his own knowledge of ancient and modern military strategy and tactics, see James Holly Hanford, "Milton and the Art of War," *SP,* XVIII (1921), 232–66. The only other English educational treatise of the Renaissance that advocates comparably thorough military training is Gilbert's *Queene Elizabethes Achademy,* pp. 4–5 (see n. 82 above), and this suggests such training as a possible alternative to liberal studies (p. 10): "And yf they will not dispose themselves to letters, yet they may learne languages, or martiall activities for the service of their Cowntrey."

modern stratagems, *Tactiks* and warlike maxims,[27] they may as
it were out of a long warre come forth renowned and perfect Commanders in the service of their country. They would not then, if
they were trusted with fair and hopefull armies, suffer them for
want of just and wise discipline to shed away from about them like
sick feathers, though they be never so oft suppli'd: [28] they would
not suffer their empty & unrecrutible [29] Colonells of twenty men in
a company, to quaffe out, or convay into secret hoards, the wages of
a delusive list, and a miserable remnant: yet in the mean while to
be overmaster'd with a score or two of drunkards, the only souldiery
left about them, or else to comply with all rapines and violences.[30]
No certainly, if they knew ought of that knowledge that belongs to
good men or good governours, they would not suffer these things.
But to return to our own institute, besides these constant exercises
at home, there is another opportunity of gaining experience to be
won from pleasure it selfe abroad; In those vernal seasons of the
yeer, when the air is calm and pleasant, it were an injury and sul-
lennesse against nature not to go out, and see her riches, and par-

[27] Milton's interest in questions of military tactics and policies is demonstrated
by the numerous entries, chiefly historical, in his *Commonplace Book* (*Complete
Prose*, I, 491–506) under the headings "Of Military Discipline," "Of War," "Of
Civil War," "Of Allies," and "Of Besieging a City and of a City Besieged." Edward Phillips records (*Early Lives*, p. 60) reading under Milton's tutelage *"Frontinus* his Stratagems; . . . *Aelian's Tacticks;* and *Polyaenus* his Warlike Stratagems." A Latin edition of Frontinus' *Strategemata* and *Aelian's De Instru-
endis Aciebus,* together with the *De Re Militari* of Flavius Vegetius Renatus,
was published at Antwerp, 1585 (PUL); and the complete works of *Aelian,* in
Greek and Latin, at Zurich (Tiguri), 1556 (Αἰλιανοῦ τὰ εὑρισκόμενα ἅπαντα;
CUL). The *Strategemata* of Polyaenus, in Greek and Latin, was available in the
Lyons edition of 1589 (Πολυαίνου στρατηγμάτων βίβλοι 'οκτώ; PML). See Hanford, "Milton and the Art of War," pp. 233–40 *passim,* on the authority of these
works "as text books and not as classics" at that time.

[28] Samuel R. Gardiner, whom Oscar Browning consulted about this passage
(Browning, *Milton's Tractate on Education,* p. 41), interpreted it as a reference
to Essex: "The constant diminution of his army through 1643 from sickness and
desertion was a constant subject of complaint, and there was information given
to Parliament in the end of that year of companies with only twenty men in
them near London amongst those serving under Essex."

[29] "Incapable of getting recruits." *NED,* quoting this passage.

[30] Later, in the *Second Defence* (1654, p. 145), Milton praised Cromwell as a
commander exhibiting characteristics exactly the opposite of these: an officer
prepared by self-knowledge and self-control to attract and hold good soldiers by
sound discipline and regular pay.

take in her rejoycing with heaven and earth.[31] I should not therefore be a perswader to them of studying much then, after two or
three yeer [32] that they have well laid their grounds, but to ride out
in companies with prudent and staid guides, to all the quarters of
the land: learning and observing all places of strength, all com-
modities of building and of soil, for towns and tillage, harbours
and Ports for trade. Somtimes taking sea as farre as to our Navy,
to learn there also what they can in the practicall knowledge of
sailing and of sea fight. These wayes would trie all their peculiar
gifts of nature,[33] and if there were any secret excellence among
them, would fetch it out, and give it fair opportunities to advance
it selfe by, which could not but mightily re- [7] dound to the good
of this nation, and bring into fashion again those old admired ver-

[31] Compare *Tetrachordon* (below, pp. 596–97): "No mortall nature can endure
either in the actions of Religion, or study of wisdome, without somtime slackning the cords of intense thought and labour: which lest we should think faulty,
God himself conceals us not his own recreations before the world was built:
. . . We cannot therefore alwayes be contemplative, or pragmaticall abroad, but
have need of some delightfull intermissions, wherin the enlarg'd soul may leav
off a while her severe schooling; and like a glad youth in wandring vacancy, may
keep her hollidaies to joy and harmles pastime." Note also Sonnet XXI, "To
Cyriack Skinner," especially ll. 9–14.

[32] The uninflected plural (regular in Old English neuters like *gear*) appears
occasionally in the seventeenth century (*e.g., Hamlet*, V, i, 183) and even now
in some dialects.

[33] While Milton's educational program is the same for all the potential
leaders included (to fit them "to perform . . . all the offices both private and
publike of peace and war"), he recognizes here the individual differences that
would today be called aptitudes, and the rôle these would play in adult life.
Compare *Commonplace Book* (*Complete Prose*, I, 405): "The nature of each
person should be especially observed and not bent in another direction; for God
does not intend all people for one thing, but for each one his own work." Surprisingly enough (especially in view of Castiglione's extensive discussion of the
qualifications of a courtier in *Il Cortegiano*), very few Renaissance writers on
education had previously given consideration to aptitudes. Vives is an exception,
but on a more elementary level of schooling: in *De Tradendis Disciplinis*
(1531, f. 94; tr. Watson, p. 82) he proposes that "Every two or three months
. . . the masters meet together, and deliberate and judge with paternal affection
and grave discretion concerning the minds of their pupils, and send each boy to
that work for which he seems most fit [ad quod aptus videbitur]"; indeed, much
of the advanced study in this work is based on the principle of guidance. In
England, Sir Henry Wotton (1568–1639), in *A Philosophical Survey of Education* (*Reliquiae Wottonianae*, 4th ed., London, 1685, pp. 76–85) entitled the first,
and only published, of his six projected chapters "Touching the Search of
Natural Capacities and Inclinations."

tues and excellencies, with farre more advantage now in this puritie
of Christian knowledge. Nor shall we then need the *Mounsieurs* of
Paris[34] to take our hopefull youth into thir slight and prodigall
custodies and send them over back again transform'd into mimics,
apes & Kicshoes.[35] But if they desire to see other countries at three
or four and twenty yeers of age,[36] not to learn principles, but to enlarge experience, and make wise observation, they will by that time
be such as shall deserve the regard and honour of all men where they
passe, and the society and friendship of those in all places who are
best and most eminent. And perhaps then [37] other Nations will be
glad to visit us for their breeding, or else to imitate us in their
own Country.

Now lastly for their diet there cannot be much to say, save only
that it would be best in the same house; for much time else would
be lost abroad, and many ill habits got; and that it should be plain,
healthfull, and moderat I suppose is out of controversie. Thus Master *Hartlib*, you have a generall view in writing, as your desire was,
of that which at severall times I had discourst with you concerning
the best and Noblest way of Education; not beginning, as some have
done from the cradle,[38] which yet might be worth many considera-

[34] Compare *Commonplace Book* (*Complete Prose*, I, 429–30), under the heading "Customs of Foreign Nations": "a dangerous thing, and an ominous thing,
to imitate with earnestness the fashions of neighbour nations. so the english
ran madding after the french in Edward confessors time. . . . god turn the omen
from these days." The anonymous early biographer says, of Milton's own journey
through France in 1638 (*Early Lives*, p. 19): "In this Kingdom, the manners &
Genius of which hee had in no admiration, hee made small stay."

[35] Here, fantastic persons. *NED*. Compare *Animadversions* (*Complete Prose*,
I, 682): "Is a man therefore bound in the morning to potcht eggs, and vinnegar,
or at noon to Brawn, or Beefe, or at night to fresh Sammon, and French Kick-
shoes?"

[36] This would be two or three years after attaining, in the proposed academy,
the equivalent of a Master's degree. Milton himself had gone abroad for similar
purposes at the age of twenty-nine, nearly six years after his M.A. degree was
conferred.

[37] Milton here affirms his faith that by adopting his plan for providing "a compleat and generous Education," as by following his current proposals for religious
reformation and for freedom of the press, England might regain the clear leadership among nations of which she was capable. Compare the introduction to the
Doctrine and Discipline of Divorce (above, pp. 224–25), and compare *Areopagitica*, below, pp. 551–53.

[38] Milton knew that among the classical authorities he had cited, Plato (*Laws*,
I, 643bc, and VII, 793e) and Quintilian (*Institutio Oratoria*, I, i, 3–5) had

tions, if brevity had not been my scope, many other circumstances also I could have mention'd, but this to such as have the worth in them to make triall, for light and direction may be anough. Only I believe that this is not a bow for every man to shoot in [39] that counts himselfe a teacher; but will require sinews almost equall to those which Homer gave Ulysses,[40] yet I am withall perswaded that it may prove much more easie in the assay, then it now seems at distance, and much more illustrious: howbeit not more difficult then I imagine, and that imagination presents me with nothing but very happy and very possible according to best wishes; if God have so decreed, and this age have spirit and capacity anough to apprehend.

The end. [8]

provided even for early childhood in their programs. He may not have known how many English writers in recent decades had discussed education in early childhood, among them Richard Mulcaster, *Positions* (1581) and *The First Part of the Elementarie* (1582); William Kempe, *The Education of Children in Learning* (1587); James Cleland, Ἡρωπαιδεία (1607); John Brinsley, *Ludus Literarius* (1612); Samuel Harmar, *Vox Populi* (1642); and John Dury (associate of Hartlib and Comenius), *A Motion Tending to the Publick Good of this Age, and of Posteritie* (1642). Most of these works include some treatment of learning to read and write; and Milton assumes that the pupils entering his academy would have learned that much before beginning to study the rules of Latin grammar.

[39] Obsolete idiom for "shoot with." *NED*.

[40] See *Odyssey*, book XXI.

THE JUDGEMENT OF
MARTIN BUCER

July 15, 1644

PREFACE AND NOTES BY ARNOLD WILLIAMS

MILTON's second pamphlet in his campaign for divorce (or third if one counts the two editions of *Doctrine and Discipline of Divorce* as separate publications) was *The Judgement of Martin Bucer*. It was the second of Milton's works to be entered in the *Stationers' Register;* the entry is "15⁰ Julii 1644 . . . Math. Symmons. Entred . . . under the hand of Master Downeham and Master Parker warden, *The Judgment of Martin Bucer concerning* divorse . . . englished by Mʳ Milton . . . vjᵈ" (ed. Eyre and Rivington, I, 122). The date of entry is taken as the date of publication by Masson (III, 255) and Hanford (*Handbook,* p. 88), but it is probably three weeks early. Thomason received his copy August 6, and this date corresponds exactly to Milton's statement that, "by a good providence," he had published *Martin Bucer* "about a week before" Herbert Palmer's sermon of August 13th (see *Tetrachordon,* sig. A2v; below, p. 579). The title page of *Martin Bucer* carries the printer's name (Matthew Simmons), as required by the Licensing Order, but not the author's, which, however, is signed at the end of the address to the Parliament, with which Milton prefaced the work. There was therefore no anonymity. *Martin Bucer* was licensed by John Downham, and the title page carries the official imprimatur. When Milton wrote the pamphlet, however, he apparently feared that permission would be denied, for the "Post Script" contains the germ of the protest against the new strictness of licensing which was to be fully voiced in *Areopagitica,* published in November, 1644.[1] There was only one edition of *Martin Bucer* during Milton's lifetime. It was reprinted in the 1820 collection of divorce tracts (see above, p. 218); otherwise it has been published only as part of editions of Milton's prose works. None of these has contained anything in the way of editorial aids.

[1] See *Areopagitica,* below, p. 480.

Milton himself gives us the approximate time of composition of
Martin Bucer. In the address to Parliament he says it was "wel-nigh
three months, as I best remember" after the publication of the second
edition of *Doctrine and Discipline* when he first learned of Bucer's
opinions about divorce. That would date the discovery late April or
early May. The preparation of the work must therefore fall somewhere between early May and late July. Many features of *Martin
Bucer*, such as the omission of sentences, paragraphs, even whole chapters, incline me to believe that it was rather hastily prepared and got
off to the printer.

The attack which greeted the advocacy of divorce in two editions of
Doctrine and Discipline of Divorce apparently forced Milton to look
about for support. This he found, in considerable abundance, in three
places: in the first generation of the reformers, in some of the fathers,
and in Roman civil law. The support of the first generation of reformers was particularly useful, because of the high reputation they
enjoyed among all Protestants, whether or not Episcopalian. In their
general objection to papacy and all its works the early reformers frequently included the Canon Law on marriage, especially the prohibition of divorce with permission to remarry. Political factors entered,
too. Some early reformers had been involved in the cases of various
princes who wished to divorce their wives. In particular, the ex-Do-
minican Martin Bucer had defended Philip of Hesse in his "bigamy." [2]
Later, Bucer elaborated his theological reasons for divorce in a work
written to the young king of England, Edward VI. Moreover, he had
written this work about 1550, while occupying the chair of divinity at
Cambridge. His substantial agreement with the position advocated in
Doctrine and Discipline of Divorce was therefore very useful to
Milton.

Leaving the other supporting authorities he had found—Erasmus,
Luther, Melancthon, and the rest—for fuller treatment in *Tetrachordon*, Milton concentrated on Bucer; and his second pamphlet in the
divorce controversy is a translation of the appropriate sections of
Bucer's *De Regno Christi* (published posthumously in 1557).

Milton's mood in thus appealing to authority is interesting. He repeatedly insists, both in *Martin Bucer* and in *Tetrachordon*, that he
had come to his own conclusions about divorce quite independently,
with no guide except "infallible Scripture" and, he hints, inspiration
from God. Then, when he had almost finished the first edition of

[2] See Hastings Eels, *The Attitude of Martin Bucer towards the Bigamy of
Philip of Hesse* (New Haven, 1924). The vernacular name of Martin Bucerus
(1491–1551) was probably Kuhhorn, though some authorities insist on Butzer.

Doctrine and Discipline of Divorce, he discovered that Hugo Grotius, perhaps the most learned man in Europe in the second quarter of the seventeenth century and still living when Milton wrote his divorce pamphlets (see below, p. 434, n. 11), agreed with him. Later, he found another ally in Paulus Fagius, one of the first generation of reformers, and, finally, three months after the publication of the second edition of *Doctrine and Discipline of Divorce,* in Martin Bucer. There is no serious reason to doubt this chronology. It does not permit much time for the preparation of *Martin Bucer,* but the pamphlet is probably a rush job.

Milton does not rest his case on authority, either Martin Bucer's or that of anyone else. *Martin Bucer* does not prove something that was in doubt; rather it is presented as a sort of character witness against Milton's traducers. In slandering John Milton they have also slandered one of the holiest and most respected leaders of the reformation, a man especially called from Germany to lead the English out of Papal darkness. Let them explain that away! Moreover, Milton does not add Bucer's reasons to his own, but translates only the parts of *De Regno Christi* which parallel the *Doctrine and Discipline of Divorce.*

Lest any should miss the significance of this agreement, Milton prefixes to *Martin Bucer* a series of encomiums on Bucer. Most of these come from the edition of *De Regno Christi* from which Milton is translating, the second, published in *Scripta Anglicana* (Basle, 1577). (The first edition does not contain some of the material which Milton reproduces from the second, *e.g.,* the passage from Sturmius [p. 3 of text], which is dated 1561 in the *Scripta*—four years after the first edition of *De Regno.*) To the laudatory addresses there contained Milton added a little material from Foxe's *Acts and Monuments* (better known as the *Book of Martyrs*) and some from standard histories and biographical treatments of the reformed divines.

To the translation Milton also added an address to the Parliament and a "Post-Script." The former gives the occasion and purpose of the work, as summarized above, and attempts to convict Milton's defamers of ignorance and prejudice. The latter anticipates both *Tetrachordon* in mentioning other authorities Milton might have appealed to, and *Areopagitica* in protesting against licensing.

In the portion of *De Regno Christi* which Milton translated, Bucer presents mainly three arguments: that the control of marriage is properly the function of the state, not of the Church, which had usurped it in times of ignorance and ecclesiastical delay; that the apparent prohibition of divorce except for adultery in the New Testament (especially Matthew 5:31–32 and 19:3–11) is not to be taken narrowly, but in the light of context and historical situation as a protest against facile and licentious divorce; and that the early church did not interpret these texts as completely forbidding all divorce except for adultery. The scriptural interpretation is not far from what Milton had already worked out for himself in the *Doctrine and Discipline of Divorce*; the contention that marriage is dominantly the affair of the state is implicit, often explicit, in Protestantism; but the evidence of the practice of the early church from some of the fathers and from Roman law probably came as a very useful discovery to Milton, and he made much of it in *Tetrachordon*.

Apart from its position in the divorce controversy, and consequently its interest to both the biographer of Milton and the social historian, *Martin Bucer* is significant to the critic of Milton the artist. It is the longest of his translations, and in it the critic can study many of the elements of compression and emphasis for which the author of *Lycidas* and *Paradise Lost* is noted. Milton's principles and habits of translation are therefore worth study.* In the "Post-Script" he tells us, rather defensively, that he "never could delight in long citations, much lesse in whole traductions." Certainly he made no literal translation. One feels that the haste with which *Martin Bucer* was probably got off to the printer has something to do with the skipping of whole chapters and the drastic reduction of passages. But there is another, and probably more powerful reason: Bucer's prolixity must have offended Milton, useful as were his arguments. Hence we see Milton cutting through the verbosity, making one word do the work of two or three, substituting a hard-hitting English phrase for a more abstract and savorless Latin one. Thus, in the testimonials Calvin writes that Bucer is too copious to be read "ab hominibus alijs occupationibus distractis." Milton hits on the phrase "by over-busied men." He corrects Bucer's love of paraphrase and locution by substituting *Jerom* for "hic vir Dei." "Divortium verum" he makes more specific by changing it to "finall divorce." The notes give ample instances of this sort of stylistic improvement.

At the more drastic alterations, in which Milton ruthlessly prunes away Bucer's verbiage, skipping whole clauses, sentences, and even paragraphs, and recasting the whole, the notes can only hint. A complete analysis of these passages is impossible, if the notes are not to overwhelm the text. For the complete details, I am forced, like Milton, to refer the curious to Bucer's Latin original.

In a very few places Milton has added to the original, where he

* For an extended analysis, see Appendix D below, "Milton As Translator," pp. 808–18.

thought the "meer Englishman" might miss Bucer's point. Where these additions are as extensive as a whole sentence, Milton indicates them by italics. Elsewhere, they are pointed out in the notes. The general effect is either to tighten the original or to point it up by more suggestive phrasing, as when "the whole breed of men" replaces the rather flat "cives."

What is the total effect of these changes? *Martin Bucer* furnishes no clear instance of dishonest or even questionable alteration. The only sample of unscrupulous (by our standards) stretching of evidence in the work is the attempt to make Jerome sanction remarriage after divorce. Here Milton has faithfully followed Bucer through the whole passage; and the fault must be charged to the original. The dropping of some references to Ambrose in Chapter XXXV of the original perhaps results in making Ambrose appear more favorable to divorce in Milton's version than in Bucer's, but the difference is not major. Likewise qualifications and specifications present in the original are absent in Milton's version, but the effect is rather stylistic than argumentative.

The notes are chiefly occupied with pointing out the details of these changes which have just been summarized. I have in such cases put Bucer's Latin original in the note, followed by my own translation in parentheses. In addition, I have indicated Bucer's sources, where citations or references occur in the text. I have made no exhaustive effort to find Bucer's unadmitted sources. Where the reference is patristic the notes indicate the location of the passage in Migne's *Patrologia,* abbreviated Migne, *Latina,* for the Latin fathers, and Migne, *Graeca,* for the Greek.

I have found no textual problems in *Martin Bucer.* The following text was made from a microfilm of a copy in the British Museum (press mark: G19594) and checked against the original and three other copies in the British Museum; no variants were found. Since G19594 has been very badly trimmed, the measurements here given are those of E4(19), Thomason's copy (the collation of all four copies is identical). The title page is also reproduced from Thomason. It is a quarto of 42 pages measuring 18.9 by 14.7 cm. Collation: 4^0, A–E^4 F^1. Contents: A1: title; A2 [row of ornaments]: "Testimonies . . . ". B1 [row of ornaments]: "To the PARLAMENT."; B4v: "JOHN MILTON." C1 [row of ornaments]: Main text begins. E4v: *"The end".* F1 [row of ornaments]: "A POST-SCRIPT."; F1v: *"The end."* Pagination: C1 is p. 1; continuous to E4v, which is p. 24. Signatures normal.

ARNOLD WILLIAMS

Michigan State University

THE
IVDGEMENT
OF
MARTIN BUCER,
CONCERNING
DIVORCE,

Writt'n to *Edward* the fixt, in his fe-
cond Book of the Kingdom of Chrift.
And now Englifht.

Wherin a late Book reftoring the
Doctrine and Difcipline of Divorce,
is heer confirm'd and juftify'd by the
authoritie of MARTIN BUCER.

To the Parlament of England. By

John Milton JOHN 3. 10.

Art thou a teacher of Ifrael, and know'ft not thefe things?

Aug: 6th Publifht by Authoritie.

LONDON,
Printed by *Matthew Simmons,* 1644.

Testimonies of the high approbation

Which learned men have given of *Martin Bucer*.

Simon Grynaeus, 1533.

AMONG all the *Germans*, I give the palm to *Bucer* for excellence in the Scriptures. *Melanchton* in human learning is wondrous fluent; but greater knowledge in the Scripture I attribute to *Bucer*, and speak it unfainedly.[1]

John Calvin, 1539.

Martin Bucer a most faithfull Doctor of the Church of Christ, besides his rare learning, & copious knowledge of many things, besides his cleernes of wit, much reading, and other many and various vertues, wherein he is almost by none now living excell'd, hath few equalls, and excells most, hath this praise peculiar to himself, that none in this age hath us'd exacter diligence in the exposition of Scripture.

And a little beneath.

Bucer is more large then to be read by over-busied men, and too high to be easily understood by unattentive men, and of a low capacitie.[2] [A2[3]]

---

[1] Bucer, *Scripta Anglicana*, ed. Conradus Hubertus (Basle, 1577; UTSL), sig. β1 (hereafter cited as *Scripta*, 1577). This testimony is part of a letter from Grynaeus to Bucer. Milton has used only about a fourth of the letter and has changed *tibi* (to you) to "to Bucer." Simon Grynaeus (Grynäus), 1493–1541, was a German theologian and teacher at Basle (see *New Schaff Hertzog Encyclopedia*). Hubertus (Konrad Hubert), 1507–1577, was a protégé of Oecolampadius and secretary to Bucer at Strassburg.

[2] *Ibid*. Milton has condensed Calvin's *ab hominibus aliis occupationibus distractis* (by men distracted by other occupations) to "by over-busied men."

[3] The prefatory material is unpaginated in the original; hence signatures are given here for cross-reference.

Sir John Cheek,[4] *Tutor to K. Edw. the sixth.* 1551.

Wee have lost our Master, then whom the world scarce held a greater, whether we consider his knowledge of true Religion, or his integrity and innocence of life, or his incessant study of holy things, or his matchless labour of promoting piety, or his authority and amplitude of teaching, or whatever els was praise-worthy and glorious in him. *Script. Anglicana, pag.* 864.[5]

John Sturmius[6] *of Strasborrow.*

No man can be ignorant what a great and constant opinion and estimation of *Bucer* there is in *Italy, France,* and *England.* Whence the saying of *Quintilian* hath oft come to my minde, that he hath well profited in Eloquence whom *Cicero* pleases. The same say I of *Bucer,* that he hath made no small progress in Divinitie, whom *Bucer* pleases; for in his Volumes, which he wrote very many, there is the plain impression to be discern'd of many great vertues, of diligence, of charitie, of truth, of acutenes, of judgment, of learning. Wherin he hath a certain proper kind of writing, wherby he doth not only teach the Reader, but affects him with the sweetness of his sentences, and with the manner of his arguing, which is so teaching, and so logical, that it may be perceiv'd how learnedly he separates probable reasons from necessary, how forcibly he confirms what he has to prove, how suttly he refutes, not with sharpnes, but with truth.[7] [A2v]

---

[4] Sir John Cheke (1514–1557) was a classical scholar, lecturer on Latin and Greek at Cambridge, and tutor to Edward VI. In the sonnet, "A Book was writ of late call'd *Tetrachordon*," Milton uses him as a sort of symbol of true learning. In *Tetrachordon* Milton refers to his assistance in framing the ecclesiastical laws of England, after canon law was abolished by Edward VI. See below, p. 716.

[5] Milton translates Cheke's statement concerning Bucer from *Scripta* (1577), sig. β1; his reference to "pag. 864" is to a three-page account by Cheke of Bucer's death and burial.

[6] John Sturmius (Johann Sturm), 1507–1589, humanist and reformer, taught at Strassburg (see *La Grande Encyclopédie*) and is most noted for his pedagogical works, which earned him the title of "the German Cicero."

[7] *Scripta* (1577), sig. β1v. Milton changes *Fabiani* to "of *Quintilian*"; and omits the last clause, "nor is there any precept of dialectics, according to Aristotle, of which this writer has not many and plain examples."

Theodore Beza on the portraiture of M. Bucer.

This is that countnance of *Bucer,* the mirror of mildnes, temper'd with gravitie; to whom the Citie of *Strasburgh* owes the reformation of her Church. Whose singular learning, and eminent zeal, joyn'd with excellent wisdom, both his learned books, and public disputations in the general diets of the Empire, shall witness to all ages. Him the *German* persecution drove into *England;* where honourably entertain'd by *Edward* the sixt, he was for two years chief professor of Divinity in *Cambridge,* with greatest frequency and applause of all learned and pious men untill his death. 1551. *Bezae Icones.*[8]

M[r] *Fox book of Martyrs, Vol. 3. p.* 763.

Bucer what by writing, but chiefly by reading and preaching openly, wherin being painfull in the Word of GOD, he never spar'd himself, nor regarded his health, brought all men into such an admiration of him, that neither his friends could sufficiently praise him, nor his enemies in any point find fault with his singular life, & sincere doctrine. A most certain tok'n wherof may be his sumptuous burial at *Cambridge,* solemniz'd with so great an assistance of all the Universitie, that it was not possible to devise more to the setting out and amplifying of the same.[9]

---

[8] Theodore Beza, *Icones, Id Est Verae Imagines Virorum Doctrina Simul et Pietate Illustrium* (Geneva, 1580; UTSL). Milton omits Beza's account (sig. G1) of the conversion of Bucer "from the cesspool of the Dominicans" by Luther's defense at Worms and condenses the expression somewhat: *illa tempestas quae Germanicas Ecclesias penè pessundedit* (that storm which had almost destroyed the German churches) becomes "the German persecution." Theodore Beza (de Bèze), 1519–1605, French theologian and author, was Calvin's successor at Geneva. He is named with other great reformers in *Tetrachordon,* below, p. 713.

[9] Milton's page reference fits several editions of Foxe's *Acts and Monuments,* better known as the *Book of Martyrs.* I used the seventh (3 vols., 1631–32; NYPL). See *Complete Prose,* I, 524, 604. As usual, Milton has condensed somewhat. Foxe's beginning reads, "Bucer lived but a little after. During which time, somewhat by writing, but chiefly by reading and preaching openly (wherein the old man, being painfull in the word of God, never spared himself, nor regarded his health)." The rest of Foxe's statement Milton quotes exactly. It is part of his account of the exhuming and burning of the bodies of Bucer and Fagius.

Dr *Pern*¹⁰ *the Popish Vicechancelour of Cambridge his adversary.*

Cardinal *Pool* about the fourth year of Queen *Ma-*[A3]*ry,* intending to reduce the Universitie of *Cambridge* to Popery again, thought no way so effectuall, as to cause the bones of *Martin Bucer* and *Paulus Fagius,* which had been foure years in the grave, to be tak'n up and burnt openly with thir Books, as knowing that those two worthy men had bin of greatest moment to the reformation of that place from Popery, and had left such powerfull seeds of thir doctrine behind them, as would never die, unless the men themselvs were diggd up, and openly condemn'd for heretics by the Universitie it self. This was put in execution, and Doctor *Pern* Vicechancelor appointed to preach against *Bucer.* Who among other things laid to his charge the opinions which he held of the marriage of Priests, of divorcement, and of usury. But immediatly after his Sermon, or somwhat before, as the Book of Martyrs for a truth relates, *Vol. 3. p.* 770. the said Doctor *Pern* smiting himself on the breast, and in manner weeping, wisht with all his heart, that God would grant his soul might then presently depart, and remain with *Bucers*; for he knew his life was such, that if any mans soul were worthy of heaven, he thought *Bucers* in special, to be most worthy, *Histor. de Combust. Buceri, & Fagii.*¹¹

10 Andrew Perne (*ca.* 1519–1589) was Master of Peterhouse, Cambridge, and five times vice-chancellor of the University. Famed as a turncoat, he both preached the sermon when Bucer and Fagius were exhumed and condemned as heretics and presided over the University Senate which, in 1560, restored them to their earlier honors. Cardinal Reginald Pole (spelled *Poole* in Foxe's *Acts and Monuments*), 1500–1558, was a learned kinsman of Henry VIII, whose efforts to reconcile Catholics and Protestants came to nought. As chancellor of Cambridge in Queen Mary's reign, he ordered the restoration of Catholic rites and instigated the burning of the bodies of Bucer and Fagius. Paulus Fagius (Büchlein), 1504–1549, renowned Hebrew scholar and reformer of Strassburg, aided the reform party at Heidelberg, but, like Bucer, at Cranmer's invitation left for England when the triumph of the Emperor over Frederick in 1548 made the position of reformers dangerous in Germany. Fagius' numerous works are listed in *Historia Vera* (see below, n. 11), ed. Konrad Hubert (Conradus Hubertus) (Strassburg, 1562), ff. 114–16v. Milton cites Fagius again in *Tetrachordon,* below, p. 710.

11 This testimonial is a blend of statements by Conradus Hubertus, *Historia Vera: De Vita, Obitu, Sepultura, Accusatione . . . Combustione . . . D. Martini Buceri & Pauli Fagii* (Strassburg, 1562; UTSL), pp. 139–40, partly reprinted in *Scripta Anglicana,* pp. 915–16, and by Foxe, *Acts and Monuments*

Acworth the Universitie Orator.

Soon after that Queen *Elizabeth* came to the crown, this condemnation of *Bucer* and *Fagius* by the Cardinal and his Doctors, was solemnly repeal'd by the [A3v] Universitie; and the memory of those two famous men celebrated in an Oration by *Acworth* the Universitie Orator, which is yet extant in the Book of Martyrs, *Vol.* 3. *p.* 773. and in Latin. *Scripta Anglic. p.* 936.[12]

Nicolas Carre, a learned man, *Walter Haddon* Maister of the Requests to Queen *Elizabeth, Matthew Parker,* afterwards Primate of *England,* with other eminent men, in their funeral Orations and Sermons expresse abundantly how great a man *Martin Bucer* was, what an incredible losse *England* sustain'd in his death; and that with him dy'd the hope of a perfet reformation for that age. *Ibid.*[13]

(1631–32), III, 770. Foxe's account (III, 770) tells of Dr. Perne's charges against Bucer as follows: "Manie other things he patched together of like purpose and effect, as of the supremacie of the Bishop of Rome, of the marriage of Priests, of divorcements, and of shamefull usurie also, as though hee had deemed the same lawfull to be used among Christian people, with divers other of the like sort." Then, in the third paragraph following, appears the account of Dr. Perne's remorse as Milton gives it: "It was reported for a truth, and that by his owne familiar friends testified, that the sayd Doctor Perne himselfe, eyther immediately after his Sermon, or else somewhat before hee went to it, striking himselfe on the breast, and in a manner weeping, wished at home at his house with all his heart, that GOD would grant his soule might even then presently depart & remaine with Bucers. For he knew well enough that his life was such, that if any mans soule were worthy of heaven, he thought his in especiall to be most worthy."

12 George Acworth (d. *ca.* 1578), divine and doctor of civil law, was elected public orator at the University of Cambridge in 1559. Acworth gave the oration restoring to honor Bucer and Fagius, preserved in Foxe, *Acts and Monuments* (1631–32, III, 773) and in *Scripta* (1577), p. 936. His eulogy includes an account of the great changes that have occurred in the religious life of England and closes with the hope that the true faith will henceforth flourish.

13 *Scripta* (1577) gives a letter from Nicholas Carr to Cheke (pp. 867–82) with a report of Haddon's oration; Haddon's oration itself (pp. 882–92); and Parker's sermon (pp. 892–99). Nicholas Carr (1524–1568) was Regius Professor of Greek at Cambridge. Walter Haddon (1516–1572) was Regius Professor of Civil Law at Cambridge and friend of Cheke, Bucer, and Peter Martyr. He held various civil and ecclesiastical offices under Elizabeth. *Cf.* also *Tetrachordon* (below, p. 716), which alludes to the code of ecclesiastical law for which Haddon was partly responsible. Matthew Parker (1504–1575) was, as Archbishop of Canterbury (1559–1575), one of the chief architects of the Elizabethan religious settlement.

Jacobus Verheiden of Grave, in his Elogies
of famous Divines.[14]

Though the name of *Martin Luther* be famous, yet thou *Martin Bucer,* for piety, learning, labour, care, vigilance, and writing, art not to be held inferior to *Luther. Bucer* was a singular instrument of God, so was *Luther.* By the death of this most learned and most faithfull man, the Church of Christ sustaind a heavy losse; as *Calvin* witnesseth; and they who are studious of *Calvin,* are not ignorant how much he ascribes to *Bucer*; for thus he writes in a letter to *Viretus:* [15] What a manifold losse befell the Church of God in the death of *Bucer,* as oft as I call to minde, I feel my heart almost rent asunder. [A4]

Peter Martyr Epist. to Conradus Hubertus.[16]

He is dead, who hath overcome in many battells of the Lord. God lent us for a time this our Father, and our Teacher, never enough prais'd. Death hath divided me from a most unanimous [17] friend, one truly according to mine own heart. My minde is overprest with grief, in so much that I have not power to write more. I bid thee in Christ farewell, and wish thou maist be able to beare the losse of *Bucer,* better then I can beare it.[18]

[14] Jacobus Verheiden, *Praestantium Aliquot Theologorum Qui Rom. Antichristum Praecipue Oppugnarunt Effigies* (The Hague, 1602; UTSL), pp. 74–75. Milton has taken only the first and last sentences, omitting the account of Bucer's life. Jacob Verheiden (fl. 1590) of The Hague was a Dutch biographer.

[15] Petrus Viretus (Pierre Viret), 1511–1571, was a Swiss reformer and one of Calvin's chief aids at Geneva. See *La Grande Encyclopédie.*

[16] Petrus Martyrus Vermilius (Pietro Martire Vermigli), 1500–1562, was an Italian Augustinian friar who became a leading reformer and was Regius Professor of Divinity at Oxford, 1548–1553. This letter is addressed to Conradus Hubertus, secretary to Bucer and editor of *Scripta Anglicana.* See above, p. 422, n. 1.

[17] Unanimous: of one soul.

[18] Hubertus, *Historia* (Strassburg, 1562), ff. 68–70; reprinted in *Scripta* (1577), pp. 900–901. Milton has taken a clause here and there so as to get the essential meaning and achieve a connected style.

Testimonies giv'n by learned men to Paulus Fagius,[19]
who held the same opinion with Martin Bucer
concerning Divorce.

Paulus Fagius born in the *Palatinate,* became most skilfull in the
Hebrew tongue.[20] Beeing call'd to the Ministery at *Isna,* he publisht
many ancient and profitable Hebrew Books, being aided in the ex-
penses by a Senator of that Citie, as *Origen* somtime was by a certain rich man call'd *Ambrosius.* At length invited to *Strasburgh,* he
there famously discharg'd the office of a Teacher; until the same
persecution drove him and *Bucer* into *England,* where he was preferr'd to a Professors place in *Cambridge,* and soon after died.[21]

Melchior Adamus writes his life among the famous *German* Divines.[22]

Sleidan [23] and *Thuanus* [24] mention him with honour in their His-

[19] See above, p. 239.

[20] (M) *Bezae Icones.*

[21] Beza, *Icones* (Geneva, 1580), sig. G3. Milton has considerably condensed
Beza's eulogy. A part of it he follows more closely: "Isnam enim ad pastoris
munus accito, ut olim Origeni Ambrosius, quidam sic Fagio divinitus contigit
Petrus Buflerus, ex ordine illius civitatis senatorio, cuius promptissima sanctis-
simáque liberalitate fretus, illus Judaeorum à multis seculis doctissumum Heliam
ad se accivit, & typographiam instituit hebraeis excudendis libris, non illis
fabulosis, impiis & ineptis, sed utilibus & ad veram religionem accommodatis
destinatam." (To Fagius, called to the office of pastor at Isne, a certain Peter
Bufler, of the senatorial order of that city, providentially gave aid, just as once
Ambrose did to Origen; assisted by whose very prompt and holy liberality,
Fagius summoned that most learned of Jews in many centuries, Elias [Levita],
and set up a press for publishing Hebrew books, not those fabulous, impious,
and useless ones, but those useful and fitted to the purpose of true religion.)

[22] Melchior Adamus, *Vitae Germanorum Theologorum* (Heidelberg, 1620;
UTSL), pp. 204–11 for Fagius; pp. 211–23 for Bucer. Melchior Adamus
(Adam), d. 1622, wrote several volumes of biographies of German theologians,
philosophers, jurists, and physicians.

[23] Johannes Sleidan, *De Statu Religionis et Reipublicae, Carolo Quinto, Caesare,
Commentarii* (Strassburg, 1555; NYPL), book XXI, f. 364. *Cf.* English transla-
tion: *A Famouse Cronicle of Oure Time, Called Sleidanes Commentaries,* tr.
Ihon Daus (1560; BML), f. 331 (sig. NN1v). Johannes Sleidanus (Johann
Philipsohn), *ca.* 1506–1556, was a German jurist, diplomat, and historian. He
was professor of law at Strassburg. See *Complete Prose,* I, 373.

Of Fagius, Sleidan writes: "The Archbishop of Canterbury, Thomas Cranmer, Primate of England, a man of excellent doctrine, was wholly resolved
on furthering studies of letters and piety. When, therefore, he saw the state of
Germany and the danger of learned men there, in numerous letters he urged

tory. And *Verheiden* in his *Elogies*.[25] [A4v]

Bucer first and then Paul Fagius, most expert in the Hebrew tongue, to come
to England, promising them all love and trust."

[24] Jacobus Thuanus, *Historia Sui Temporis* (Geneva, 1626; HCL), book II,
anno 1546 (I, 46); book VI, anno 1549 (I, 173). Jacobus Thuanus (Jacques
Auguste de Thou), 1553–1617, was a French historian. See *Complete Prose*, I,
370.

Thuanus' first reference to Fagius (I, 46) tells of Frederick II's calling Fagius
to Heidelberg to help him abolish papal authority and establish the doctrine of
Luther. "This man," says Thuanus, "had attained a perfect knowledge of the
Holy Tongue [Hebrew] under Wolfgang Capito."

[25] Verheiden, *Effigies* (The Hague, 1602), pp. 79–82.

To the PARLAMENT.[1]

THE *Book which among other great and high points of refor-mation, contains as a principall part thereof, this treatise here presented, Supreme Court of Parlament, was by the famous Author* Martin Bucer, *dedicated to* Edward *the sixt: whose incomparable youth doubtless had brought forth to the Church of England such a glorious manhood, had his life reacht it, as would have left in the affairs of religion, nothing without an excellent pat-tern for us now to follow. But since the secret purpose of divine appointment hath reserv'd no lesse perhaps then the just half of such a sacred work to be accomplisht in this age, and principally, as we trust, by your succesful wisdom and authority, religious Lords and Commons, what wonder if I seek no other, to whose exactest judge-ment, and revieu I may commend these last and worthiest labours of this renowned teacher: whom living, all the pious nobility of those reforming times, your truest and best imitated ancestors, reverenc't and admir'd. Nor was he wanting to a recompence as great as was himself; when both at many times before, and espe-cially among his last sighs and prayers testifying his dear and fatherly affection to the Church and Realm of England, he sin-cerely wisht in the hearing of many devout men,* that what he had in this his last book written to King *Edward* concerning discipline, might have place in this Kingdom.[2] His hope was then that no calamity, no confusion, or deformity would happen to the Com-mon-wealth; but otherwise he fear'd, lest in the midst of all this ardency to know God, yet by the neglect of discipline, our good endeavours would not succeed. *These remarkable words of so godly and so eminent a man at his death, as they are related by a suffi-cient and well known witnes, who heard them; and inserted by* Thuanus[3] *into his grave and serious history, so ought they to be*

---

[1] See introduction, above, pp. 139–41; and Masson, III, 255 ff.

[2] (M) Nicol. Car. de obit Buceri. [(Nicholas Carr concerning the death of Bucer). See above, p. 426, n. 13, for reference.]

[3] Thuanus, *Historia* (Geneva, 1626), book VI, anno 1549 (I, 264). Thuanus, however, does not indicate who the "sufficient and well known witnes" was.

chiefly consider'd by that nation for whose sake they were utter'd,
and more especially by that general Counsel which represents the
body of that nation. If therfore the book, or this part therof, for
necessary causes, be now reviv'd and recommended to the use of
this undisciplin'd age, it hence appears that these reasons [B1]
have not err'd in the choyce of a fit patronage, for a discourse of
such importance. But why the whole tractat is not heer brought
entire, but this matter of divorcement selected in particular, to pre-
vent the full speed of some mis-interpreter, I hasten to disclose.
First, it will be soon manifest to them who know what wise men
should know, that the constitution and reformation of a common-
wealth, if Ezra *and* Nehemiah [4] *did not mis-reform, is, like a build-*
ing, to begin orderly from the foundation therof, which is mariage
and the family, to set right first what ever is amisse therein. How
can there els grow up a race of warrantable men, while the house
and home that breeds them, is troubl'd and disquieted under a
bondage not of Gods constraining with a natureles constraint (if
his most righteous judgements may be our rule) but laid upon us
imperiously in the worst and weakest ages of knowledge, by a
canonicall tyranny of stupid and malicious Monks: who having
rashly vow'd themselves to a single life, which they could not un-
dergoe, invented new fetters to throw on matrimony, that the world
thereby waxing more dissolute, they also in a general loosnes might
sin with more favor. Next, there being yet among many, such a
strange iniquity and perversnes against all necessary divorce, while
they will needs expound the words of our Saviour not duly by com-
paring other places, as they must doe in the resolving of a hunder'd
other Scriptures, but by persisting deafely in the abrupt and Papis-
tical way of a literal apprehension against the direct analogy of
sense, reason, law and Gospel, it therfore may well seem more then
time to apply the sound and holy persuasions of this Apostolic man,
to that part in us, which is not yet fully dispossest of an error as
absurd, as most that we deplore in our blindest adversaries; and to
let his autority and unanswerable reasons be vulgarly known, that
either his name, or the force of his doctrine may work a wholsom

---

[4] The Jews returning from the Captivity pledge themselves to Ezra to put
away their foreign wives, Ezra 10:1–44. Nehemiah later forces certain re-
calcitrants to divorce their foreign wives, Nehemiah 13:23–30. They are cited
again in *Tetrachordon*, below, p. 681, as "two infallible authors."

effect. Lastly, I find it cleer to be the authors intention that this point of divorcement should be held and receav'd as a most necessary and prime part of discipline in every Christian government. And therfore having reduc't his model of reformation to 14. heads, he bestows almost as much time about this one point of divorce, as about all the rest; [5] *which also was the judgement of his heirs and learned friends in Germany, best acquainted with his meaning; who first publishing this his book by* Oporinus *at* Basil *(a Citie for learning and constancie in the true faith, honorable among the first) added a special note in the title,* that there the reader should finde the doctrine of Divorce handl'd so solidly, and so fully, as scars the like in any Writer of that age: [6] *and with this particular commendation they doubted not to dedicate the book, as a most profitable & exquisit discours, to* Christian *the* 3^d, *a worthy & pious King of* Denmark, *as the author himself had done before to our* Edward *the sixt. Yet did not* Bucer *in that volume only declare what his constant opinion was herein, but also in his commentary up-*[B1v]*on* Matthew,[7] *written at* Strasburgh *divers years before, he treats distinctly and copiously the same argument in three severall places; touches it also upon the 7. to the* Romans, *& promises the same solution more largely upon the 1. to the* Corinthians, *omitting no occasion to weed out this last and deepest mischief of the Canon law sown into the opinions of modern men against the lawes and practice both of Gods chosen people, and the best primitive times. Wherin his faithfulnes and powerful evidence prevail'd so farre with all the* Church of Strasburgh, *that they publisht this doctrine of divorce,*

[5] In the edition of *De Regno Christi* which Milton translates, in *Scripta* (1577), sixty-six pages (56–86, 134–70) are devoted to non-matrimonial topics, as against forty-eight pages (86–134) to marriage and divorce. Not all of the section on marriage concerns divorce, as appears from Milton's omissions below. Forty-one pages (93–134) deal with divorce, seven pages (86–93) with the nature of marriage. To fix the cause for Bucer's seeming preoccupation with marriage would be pure speculation; it may be, of course, that Bucer did not complete the treatment of civil polity in a Christian state which he undertook in *De Regno,* but such incompleteness does not appear in the work as published.

[6] Milton refers here to the first edition of *De Regno Christi Jesu Servatoris Nostri* (Basle, 1551; UTSL), from the press of Johann Oporinus (Swiss printer, 1507–1568).

[7] *In Sacra Quatuor Evangelica, Enarrationes* (Basle, 1536; BOD). See below, p. 444, n. 3.

as an article of their confession,[8] *after they had taught so eight and twenty years, through all those times, when that Citie flourisht, and excell'd most, both in religion, lerning, and good goverment, under those first restorers of the Gospel there,* Zellius, Hedio, Capito,[9] Fagius, *and those who incomparably then govern'd the Common-wealth,* Farrerus *and* Sturmius.[10] *If therefore God in the former age found out a servant, and by whom he had converted and reform'd many a citie, by him thought good to restore the most needfull doctrine of divorce from rigorous and harmfull mistakes on the right hand, it can be no strange thing if in this age he stirre up by whatsoever means whom it pleases him, to take in hand & maintain the same assertion. Certainly if it be in mans discerning to sever providence from chance, I could allege many instances, wherein there would appear cause to esteem of me no other then a passive instrument under some power and counsel higher and better then can be human, working to a general good in the whole cours of this matter. For that I ow no light, or leading receav'd from any man in the discovery of this truth, what time I first undertook it in* the doctrine and discipline of divorce, *and had only the infallible grounds of Scripture to be my guide, he who tries the inmost heart, and saw with what severe industry and examination of my self, I set down every period, will be my witnes. When I had almost finisht the first edition, I chanc't to read in the notes of* Hugo Grotius *upon the* 5.

---

[8] "Epitome . . . Doctrinae . . . Quae Argentorati . . . Publicè Sonuit," in *Scripta* (1577), p. 181. In at least one complete text of the Strassburg confessions, *Confessio oder Bekantnüs . . . Strassburg, Costentz, Memmingen, und Lindaw* (Strassburg, 1580; UTSL), the reference to divorce Milton cites from Bucer does not appear.

[9] Zellius (Matthäus Zell), 1477–1548, was a leader in the Reformation in Strassburg. Hedio (Kaspar Heid), 1494–1552, was Zellius' co-worker, as was also Capito (Wolfgang Fabricius Koepfel), 1472–1541. Capito, a famous Hebrew scholar, was teacher of Fagius and co-author with Bucer of the *Confessio oder Bekantnüs,* the articles of faith of Strassburg, Constance, Lindau, and Memmingen. Milton names these three "great divines" again in *Tetrachordon,* below, p. 710.

[10] Farrerus (Mathis Pfarrer), *ca.* 1485–1568, was so revered as a magistrate that he was elected Mayor of Strassburg seven times between 1527 and 1563. He represented Strassburg at the diet of Augsburg in 1530, and was sent as ambassador to the Emperor in Strassburg's behalf. Sturmius (Jakob Sturm), 1489–1553, was Strassburg's greatest statesman and one of the most eminent leaders in the German reformation. These two "renowned magistrates" are named again in *Tetrachordon,* below, p. 710.

of Matth. whom I strait understood inclining to reasonable terms in this controversie: and somthing he whisper'd rather then disputed about the law of charity, and the true end of wedlock.[11] *Glad therfore of such an able assistant, how ever at much distance, I resolv'd at length to put off into this wild and calumnious world. For God, it seems, intended to prove me, whether I durst alone take up a rightful cause against a world of disesteem, & found I durst. My name I did not publish, as not willing it should sway the reader either for me or against me.*[12] *But when I was told, that the stile, which what it ailes to be so soon distinguishable, I cannot tell, was known by most men, and that some of the Clergie began to inveigh and exclaim on what I was credibly inform'd they had not read, I took it then for my proper season both to shew them a name that could easily contemn such an indiscreet kind of censure, and to reinforce the question with a more* [B2] *accurat diligence: that if any of them would be so good as to leav rayling, and to let us hear so much of his lerning and Christian wisdom, as will be strictly demanded of him in his answering to this probleme, care was had he should not spend his preparations against a nameles pamphlet. By this time I had lernt that* Paulus Fagius, *one of the chief Divines in Germany, sent for by* Frederic *the* Palatine,[13] *to reforme his dominion; and after that invited hither in King Edwards dayes to be Professor of Divinity in Cambridge, was of the same opinion touch-*

---

[11] Hugo Grotius, *Annotationes in Libros Evangeliorum* (Amsterdam, 1641; UTSL), pp. 98–99, on Matthew 5. Hugo Grotius (de Groot), 1583–1645, is almost equally famed for his work in theology, belles lettres, and law. According to *Second Defence* (1654, p. 61), John Scudamore, English ambassador in Paris, gave Milton a letter to Hugo Grotius in 1638, when Milton was making his grand tour. Grotius was at that time Swedish ambassador in Paris. *Cf.* Masson, I, 696–703. Milton mentions Grotius among the great reformers in *Tetrachordon*, below, p. 715, and cites there his commentary on Matthew 5.

Grotius' "whisper" concerning charity says (pp. 98–99): "In all laws . . . it is understood that where there is reason the law is strong . . . we find the origin and consummation of all Christ's teachings begin in charity. . . . To put away a wife for whatever cause is cruel, is inhuman."

[12] See *Doctrine and Discipline*, above, p. 217.

[13] Frederick II (1482–1556), Elector and Count Palatine, surnamed "the Wise." He first tried to serve as mediator in the religious strife in Germany, but in 1545 joined the Schmalkald League and in 1546 became a Protestant. In calling Fagius to the Palatinate, he sought help in establishing Protestantism as the official faith.

ing divorce, which these men so lavishly traduc't in me.[14] *What I found, I inserted where fittest place was, thinking sure they would respect so grave an author, at lest to the moderating of their odious inferences. And having now perfected a second edition, I referr'd the judging therof to your high and impartial sentence, honour'd Lords and Commons. For I was confident, if any thing generous, any thing noble, and above the multitude, were left yet in the spirit of England, it could be no where sooner found, and no where sooner understood, then in that house of justice and true liberty where ye sit in counsel. Nor doth the event hitherto, for some reasons which I shall not heer deliver, faile me of what I conceiv'd so highly. Nevertheless being farre otherwise dealt with by some, of whose profession and supposed knowledge I had better hope, and esteem'd the deviser of a new and pernicious paradox,*[15] *I felt no difference within me from that peace & firmnes of minde, which is of neerest kin to patience and contentment: both for that I knew I had divulg'd a truth linkt inseparably with the most fundamental rules of Christianity, to stand or fall together, and was not un-inform'd that divers lerned and judicious men testify'd their daily approbation of the book. Yet at length it hath pleas'd God, who had already giv'n me satisfaction in my self, to afford me now a means wherby I may be fully justify'd also in the eyes of men. When the book had bin now the second time set forth wel-nigh three months, as I best remember, I then first came to hear that* Martin Bucer *had writt'n much concerning divorce: whom earnestly turning over, I soon perceav'd, but not without amazement, in the same opinion, confirm'd with the same reasons which in that publisht book without the help or imitation of any precedent Writer, I had labour'd out, and laid together. Not but that there is some difference in the handling, in the order, and the number of arguments, but still agreeing in the same conclusion. So as I may justly gratulat mine own mind, with*

[14] See Fagius' comment on Deuteronomy 24 in his edition of the "Chaldee" (*i.e.*, Aramaic) Paraphrase, in *Critici Sacri*, ed. John Pearson (Frankfort-am-Main, 1696; UTSL), cols. 1306–1307. Fagius cites ten conditions under which the ancient Jews could divorce a wife, such as hardness of heart, imbecility, adultery, uncleanness, sickness, etc. The Pharisees tempted Christ, who cited Genesis (let no man put asunder) and said no man should divorce for slight cause (Matthew 19). The form of the Jewish bill of divorcement is cited in Hebrew. This material is used again in *Tetrachordon*, below, p. 710.

[15] See introduction, above, pp. 139–41, and *Doctrine and Discipline*, above, pp. 238–39.

*due acknowledgement of assistance from above, which led me, not
as a lerner, but as a collateral teacher, to a sympathy of judgment
with no lesse a man then* Martin Bucer. *And he, if our things heer
below arrive him where he is, does not repent him to see that point
of knowledge which he first, and with an uncheckt freedom preacht
to those more knowing times of England, now found so necessary,
though what he admonisht were lost out of* [B2v] *our memory, yet
that God doth now again create the same doctrin in another unwritt'n table, and raises it up immediatly out of his pure oracle to
the convincement of a pervers age, eager in the reformation of names
and ceremonies, but in realities as traditional and as ignorant as
their forefathers. I would ask now the foremost of my profound
accusers, whether they dare affirm that to be licentious, new and
dangerous, which* Martin Bucer *so often, and so urgently avoucht
to be most lawfull, most necessary, and most Christian, without
the lest blemish to his good name, among all the worthy men of
that age, and since, who testifie so highly of him? If they dare, they
must then set up an arrogance of their own against all those
Churches and Saints who honour'd him without this exception: If
they dare not, how can they now make that licentious doctrin in
another, which was never blam'd, or confuted in* Bucer, *or in*
Fagius? *The truth is, there will be due to them for this their un-
advised rashnes, the best donative that can be giv'n them, I mean,
a round reproof; now that where they thought to be most Magisterial, they have display'd their own want, both of reading, and of
judgement. First, to be so unacquainted in the writings of* Bucer,
which are so obvious [16] *and so usefull in their own faculty; next, to
be so caught in a prejudicating weaknes, as to condemn that for
lewd, which (whether they knew or not) these elect servants of
Christ commended for lawfull; and for new, that which was taught
by these almost the first and greatest authors of reformation, who
were never taxt for so teaching; and dedicated without scruple to
a royall pair of the first reforming Kings in Christendom, and confest in the public confession of a most* orthodoxall *Church & state
in Germany. This is also another fault which I must tell them; that
they have stood now almost this whole year clamouring a farre off,
while the book hath bin twice printed, twice bought up, & never*

---

[16] Frequently met. *OED.*

once vouchsaft a friendly conference with the author, who would be glad and thankfull to be shewn an error, either by privat dispute, or public answer, and could retract, as well as wise men before him; might also be worth the gaining, as one who heertofore, hath done good service to the Church by their own confession. Or if he be obstinat, their confutation would have render'd him without excuse, and reclam'd others of no mean parts who incline to his opinion. But now their work is more then doubl'd; and how they will hold up their heads against the sudden aspect of these two great and reverend Saints whom they have defam'd, how they will make good the censuring of that for a novelty of licence, which Bucer *constantly taught to be a pure and holy law of Christs kingdom, let them advise. For against these my adversaries, who before the examining of a propounded truth in a fit time of reformation, have had the conscience to oppose naught els but their blind reproaches and surmises, that a single innocence might not be opprest and overborn by a crew of mouths for the restoring of a law and doctrin* [B3] *falsely and unlernedly reputed new and scandalous, God, that I may ever magnifie and record this his goodnes, hath unexpectedly rais'd up as it were from the dead, more then one famous light of the first reformation to bear witnes with me, and to doe me honour in that very thing, wherin these men thought to have blotted me: And hath giv'n them the proof of a capacity which they despis'd, running equal, and authentic* [17] *with some of thir chiefest masters unthought of, and in a point of sagest moment. However, if we know at all, when to ascribe the occurrences of this life to the work of a special providence, as nothing is more usual in the talk of good men, what can be more like to a special providence of God, then in the first reformation of England, that this question of divorce, as a main thing to be restor'd to just freedom, was writt'n, and seriously commended to* Edward *the sixt, by a man call'd from another Countrey to be the instructer of our nation, and now in this present renewing of the Church and Common-wealth, which we pray may be more lasting, that the same question should be again treated and presented to this Parlament, by one enabl'd to use the same reasons without the lest sight or knowledge of what was done before. It were no trespas, Lords and Commons, though something of lesse*

---

[17] "Original, first-hand, proto-typical; as opposed to *copied.*" *OED.*

note were attributed to the ordering of a heavnly power; this question therfore of such prime concernment both to Christian and civil welfare, in such an extraordinary manner, not recover'd, but plainly twise born to these latter ages, as from a divine hand I tender to your acceptance, and most considerate thoughts. Think not that God rais'd up in vain a man of greatest autority in the Church to tell a trivial and licentious tale in the eares of that good Prince, and to bequeath it as his last will and testament, nay rather as the testament and royall law of Christ to this Nation, or that it should of it self after so many yeares, as it were in a new feild where it was never sow'n, grow up again as a vitious plant in the minde of another, who had spoke honestest things to the Nation; though he knew not that what his youth [18] *then reason'd without a pattern, had bin heard already, and well allow'd from the gravity and worth of* Martin Bucer: *till meeting with the envy of men ignorant in thir own undertak'n calling, God directed him to the forgott'n Writings of this faithfull Evangelist, to be his defence and warrant against the gross imputation of broaching licence. Ye are now in the glorious way to high vertu, and matchless deeds, trusted with a most inestimable trust, the asserting of our just liberties. Ye have a nation that expects now, and from mighty sufferings aspires to be the example of all Christendom to a perfetest reforming.* [19] *Dare to be as great, as ample, and as eminent in the fair progress of your noble designes, as the full and goodly stature of truth and excellence it self: as unlimited by petty presidents* [20] *and copies, as your unquestionable calling from heaven givs ye power to be. What are all our public immuni-*[B3v]*ties and privileges worth, and how shall it be judg'd that we fight for them with minds worthy to enjoy them, if wee suffer our selvs in the mean while not to understand the most important freedom that God and Nature hath givn us in the family; which no wise Nation ever wanted, till the Popery and superstition of some former ages attempted to remove and alter divine and most prudent Laws for human and most imprudent Canons; wherby good men in the best portion of thir lives, and in that ordinance of God which entitles them from the beginning to most just and requi-*

---

[18] The expression is unexpected: Milton was in his thirty-fifth year when he first published *Doctrine and Discipline.*

[19] *Cf. Areopagitica,* below, pp. 552–53.

[20] Presidents: precedents.

site contentments, are compell'd to civil indignities, which by the law of Moses bad men were not compell'd to. Be not bound about, and straitn'd in the spatious wisdom of your free Spirits, by the scanty and unadequat and inconsistent principles of such as condemn others for adhering to traditions, and are themselvs the prostrate worshippers of Custom; and of such a tradition as they can deduce from no antiquitie, but from the rudest, and thickest barbarism of Antichristian times. But why doe I anticipate the more acceptable, and prevailing voice of lerned Bucer *himself, the pastor of Nations? And O that I could set him living before ye in that doctoral chair, where once the lernedest of* England *thought it no disparagement to sit at his feet! He would be such a pilot, and such a father to ye, as ye would soon find the difference of his hand and skill upon the helm of reformation. Nor doe I forget that faithfull associate of his labours,* Paulus Fagius; *for these thir great names and merits, how pretious so ever, God hath now joyn'd with me necessarily, in the good or evil report of this doctrin which I leav with you. It was writt'n to a religious King of this land; writt'n earnestly, as a main matter wherin this kingdom needed a reform, if it purpos'd to be the kingdom of Christ: Writt'n by him who if any since the daies of* Luther, *merits to be counted the Apostle of our Church; whose unwearied pains and watching for our sakes, as they spent him quickly heer among us, so did they, during the shortnes of his life, incredibly promote the Gospel throughout this Realm.*[21] *The autority, the lerning, the godlines of this man consulted with, is able to out-ballance all that the lightnes of a vulgar opposition can bring to counterpoise. I leav him also as my complete suretie and testimonial, if Truth be not the best witnes to it self, that what I formerly presented to your reading on this subject, was good, and just, and honest, not licentious. Not that I have now more confidence by the addition of these great Authors to my party; for what I wrote was not my opinion, but my knowledge; evn then when I could trace no footstep in the way I went: nor that I think to win upon your apprehensions with numbers and with names, rather then with reasons, yet certainly the worst of my detracters will not except against so good a baile of my integritie and judge-*

---

[21] For an account of Bucer's work in England and a judgment of it, see Constantin Hopf, *Martin Bucer and the English Reformation* (Oxford: Blackwell, 1946).

ment, as now appeares for me. They must els put in the fame of Bucer *and of* Fagius, *as my accom-*[B4]*plices and confederats into the same endightment; they must dig up the good name of these prime worthies (if thir names could be ever buried), they must dig them up and brand them as the Papists did thir bodies; and those thir pure unblamable spirits, which live not only in heaven, but in thir writings, they must attaint with new attaintures which no Protestant ever before aspers't them with. Or if perhaps wee may obtain to get our appeachment new drawn a Writ of Error,[22] not of Libertinism, that those two principal leaders of reformation may not come now to be su'd in a bill of licence, to the scandal of our Church, the brief result will be, that for the error, if thir own works be not thought sufficient to defend them, there livs yet who will be ready, in a fair and christianly discussive way, to debate and sift this matter to the utmost ounce of lerning and religion, in him that shall lay it as an error, either upon* Martin Bucer, *or any other of his opinion. If this be not anough to qualifie[23] my traducers, and that they think it more for the wisdom of thir virulence, not to recant the injuries they have bespoke me, I shall not for much more disturbance then they can bring me, intermitt the prosecution of those thoughts which may render me best serviceable, either to this age, or if it so happ'n, to posteritie; following the fair path which your illustrious exploits, Honourd Lords and Commons, against the brest of tyrany have open'd; and depending so on your happy successes in the hopes that I have conceiv'd either of my self, or of the Nation, as must needs conclude me one who most affectionately wishes and awaits the prosperous issue of your noble and valorous counsels.*

JOHN MILTON. [B4v]

---

[22] Appeachment: criminal charge. Writ of error: a writ to procure reversal of a judgment on grounds of error.

[23] Qualify: moderate or appease.

THE

JUDGEMENT OF
MARTIN BUCER
TOUCHING *DIVORCE*.
Taken out of the second Book
entitl'd

Of the kingdom of Christ writt'n by
Martin Bucer to *Edward* the 6th K. of *England*.

CHAPTER XV.

The 7th Law of the sanctifying and ordering of mariage.

BESIDES these things, Christ our King, and his Churches require from your sacred Majesty, that you would take upon you the just care of mariages.[1] For it is unspeakable, how many good consciences are heerby entangl'd, afflicted, and in danger, because there are no just laws, no speedy way constituted, according to Gods Word, touching this holy society and fountain of mankind. For seeing matrimony is a civil thing, men, that they may rightly [2] contract, inviolably keep, and not without extreme necessitie dissolv mariage, are not only to be taught by the doctrine and discipline of the Church, but also are to be acquitted, aided, and compell'd by laws and judicature of the Common-wealth. Which thing pious Emperours acknowledging, and therin framing themselvs to the law of Nations, gave laws both of contracting and preserving, and also where an unhappy need requir'd, of divorcing mariages. As may be seen in the Code of *Justinian* the 5 Book,

[1] (M) That the ordering of mariage belongs to the civil power.
[2] Rightly: *rité* (with due religious observance).

441

from the beginning through 24 titles.[3] And in the Authentic [4] of *Justinian* the 22, and some others. [1]

But the Antichrists of *Rome*, to get the imperial power into thir own hands, first by fraudulent persuasion, afterwards by force drew to themselvs the whole autority of determining and judging as well in matrimonial causes, as in most other matters.[5] Therfore it hath bin long beleiv'd, that the care and government therof doth not belong to the civil Magistrate. Yet where the Gospel of Christ is receav'd, the laws of Antichrist should be rejected. If therfore Kings and Governours take not this care, by the power of law and justice to provide that mariages be piously contracted, religiously kept, and lawfully dissolv'd, if need require, who sees not what confusion and trouble is brought upon this holy society; and what a rack is prepar'd, evn for many of the best consciences, while they have no certain laws to follow, no justice to implore, if any intolerable thing happen. And how much it concerns the honour and safety of the Commonwealth, that mariages, according to the will of Christ, be made, maintain'd, and not without just cause dissolv'd, who understands not? for unlesse that first and holiest society of man and woman be purely constituted, that houshold discipline may be upheld by them according to Gods law, how can wee expect a race of good men. Let your Majesty therfore know that this is your duty, and in the first place, to reassume to your self the just ordering of matrimony, and by firm laws to establish and defend the religion of this first and divine societie among men, as all wise law-givers of old, and Christian Emperours have carefully don.

The two next Chapters because they cheifly treat about the de-

---

[3] Justinian I, *Corpus Juris Civilis*, ed. Dionysius Gothofredus (Geneva, 1594–95; UTSL), cols. 358–414; *Code*, book V, titles i–xxiv (Scott, XIII, 137–213). Hereafter the *Corpus Juris Civilis* will be cited in this edition as *Juris Civilis* according to its four parts: *Institutes*, *Pandects* (also called *Digest*), *Code*, and *Novellae* (also called *Authentics*), and the subdivisions of these parts: book, title, and, where necessary, paragraph for the first three divisions, and chapter for the *Novellae*. In addition the parentheses contain references to the English translation of the *Corpus Juris: The Civil Law*, tr. S. P. Scott (17 vols., Cincinnati, 1932).

[4] Authentic: the authentics, novellae (the latter is the more usual title and the one used in footnote references in this edition). The novellae, or "novels," are the new laws added by Justinian and later Emperors and constituting one of the parts of the Civil Law. See *Juris Civilis, Novellae*, XXII (Geneva, 1594–95, cols. 72–93; Scott, XVI, 116–42).

[5] (M) The Popes have invaded by fraud and force the ordering of mariage.

grees of Consanguinity and affinity I omit; only setting down a
passage or two concerning the judicial laws of Moses, how fit they
be for Christians to imitate rather then any other.[6]

CHAP. XVII. toward the end.

I CONFESSE that wee beeing free in Christ are not bound to the
civil Laws of *Moses* in every circumstance, yet seeing no laws
can be more honest, just, and wholsom, then those which God
himself gave, who is eternal wisdom & goodnes, I see not why Christians, in things which no lesse appertain to them, ought not to follow the laws of God, rather then of any men. Wee are not to use
circumcision, sacrifice, and those bodily washings prescrib'd to the
Jews; [1] yet by these things wee may rightly learn, with what purity
and devotion both Baptism and the Lords Supper should be administerd and receav'd. How much more is it our duty to observ diligently what the Lord [2] hath commanded, and taught by the examples of his people concerning mariage; wherof wee have the use
no lesse then they.[2]

And because the same worthy Author hath another passage to
this purpose in his Comment upon Matthew, Chap 5. 19. I heer
insert it from p. 46.

Since wee have need of civil laws and the power of punishing, it
will be wisest not to contemn those giv'n by *Moses;* but seriously
rather to consider what the meaning of God was in them, what he
cheifly requir'd, and how much it might be to the good of every
Nation, if they would borrow thence thir manner of governing the
Common-wealth; yet freely all things and with the Spirit of Christ.
For what *Solon,* or *Plato,* or *Aristotle,* what Lawyers or *Caesars*

---

[6] For Milton's use of italics to show his additions to Bucer, see above, p. 420.

[1] *Cf. Scripta* (1577), p. 88: "quae Dominus Judaeis peculiariter per Mosen
praecepit" (which the Lord particularly prescribed to the Jews by Moses).

[2] *Cf. Scripta* (1577), p. 88: "quod nos non minus quam veteres ex Dei constitutione usurpamus? Ista dicta sint de personis, inter quas conveniat copulari
matrimonio" (which things out of God's law, may we not use them no less than
did the ancients? These sayings ought to concern persons who may fittingly be
joined in matrimony).

could make better laws then God? [3] And it is no light argument, that many Magistrates at this day doe not anough acknowledge the kingdom of Christ, though they would seem most Christian, in that they govern thir States by laws so divers from those of *Moses*.

The 18 *Chap. I only mention as determining a thing not heer in question, that mariage without consent of parents ought not to be held good; yet with this qualification fit to be known.*

That if parents admit not the honest desires of thir children, but shall persist to abuse the power they have over them, they are to be mollifi'd by admonitions, entreaties, and persuasions, first of thir freinds and kindred, next of the Church-Elders. Whom if still the hard parents refuse to hear, then ought the Magistrate to interpose his power: lest any by the evil minde of thir parents be detain'd from mariage longer then is meet, or forc't to an unworthy match: in which case the *Roman* laws also provided. *C. de nupt. l.* 11. 13. 26.[4]

[3] Martin Bucer, *In Sacra Quatuor Evangelica, Enarrationes* (Basle, 1536; BOD), p. 122: "Et quia ad tranquille uiuendum omnino legibus ciuilibus, usu gladij & animaduersione nocentium, & hodie opus est, ut sunt renatorum qui spiritu aguntur paucissimi, leges datas per Moschen, minime contemnent, sed religiose potius considerabunt, quo Dominus in illis spectarit, quae potissimum exegerit, & quantum cuique genti & populo commodo esse poterit, ex illis rationem R. pub. instituendae ac moderandae mutuare studebunt, sed libere omnia & ex spiritu Christi. Quis enim Solon, quis Plato, quis Aristoteles, qui denique iureconsulti aut Caesares, potuissent dare leges meliores Deo? Et qui liberet opera manuum Domini & oues pascuae eius, per ipsius leges moderari?" (And since to live altogether peacefully civil laws, the use of the sword, and the punishment of evil doers are today necessary, as there are so few of the reborn whom the spirit moves, they should condemn the laws of Moses very little, but rather will consider religiously what God may have intended in them, what he most strongly required, and how much it might profit each nation and people to study borrowing from the manner of instituting and governing the commonwealth. For what Solon, what Plato, what Aristotle, finally what lawyers or Caesars could give better laws than God? And who shall refuse the handiwork of God and the sheep of his pastures to be governed by his own laws?)

[4] *Juris Civilis, Code,* book V, title iv, paragraphs 11, 12 (not 13), and 25 (not 26) (Geneva, 1594–95, cols. 367–69; Scott, XIII, 148, 153–54). Paragraph 11 provides that the rector of the province will interpose to restore to a husband a wife wrongly detained by her parents; paragraph 12 states that the law does not permit a father to compel his son to take a wife against his will; paragraph 25 protects a daughter from being forced to marry a madman.

CHAP. XIX.

Whether it may be permitted to revoke the promise of mariage.

HEER ariseth another question concerning Contracts, when they ought to be unchangeable; for religious Emperours decree'd that the contract was not indissoluble, until the spouse were brought home, and the solemnities perform'd. They thought it a thing unworthy of divine and human equitie, and the due consideration of mans infirmitie in deliberating and determining, when space is giv'n to renounce other contracts of much lesse moment, which are not yet confirm'd before the Magistrate, to deny that to the most waighty contract of marriage, which requires the greatest care and consultation. Yet lest such a covenant should be brok'n for no just cause, and to the [3] injury of that person to whom mariage was promis'd, they decreed a fine, that he who deni'd mariage to whom he had promis'd, and for some cause not approv'd by the Judges, should pay the double of that pledge which was giv'n at making sure, or as much as the Judge should pronounce might satisfie the dammage or the hinderance of either partie. It beeing most certain that ofttimes after contract, just and honest causes of departing from promise, come to be known and found out, it cannot be other then the duty of pious Princes, to give men the same liberty of unpromising in these cases, as pious Emperours granted: especially where there is only a promise, and not carnal knowledge. And as there is no true mariage between them, who agree not in true consent of mind, so it will be the part of godly Magistrates to procure that no matrimony be among thir Subjects, but what is knit with love and consent.[1] And though your Majesty be not bound to the imperial laws, yet it is the duty of a Christian King to embrace and follow what ever he knows to be any where piously and justly constituted, and to be honest, just and well-pleasing to his people. But why in Gods law and the examples of his Saints nothing heerof is read, no marvell, seeing his ancient people

[1] Milton omits (*Scripta*, 1577, p. 91) "celebrata enim nuptiarum festivitate, atque ita copia facta commixtionis carnalis, tum satis tempestiuum fuerit, nuptialem pactionem suam plenam accipere firmitatem" (after the nuptial festivities have been celebrated and thus plenty of carnal intercourse enjoyed, then it were seasonable enough for their nuptial pact to take full firmness).

445

had power, yea a precept, that who so could not bend his mind to the true love of his wife, should give her a bill of divorce, and send her from him, though after carnal knowledge and long dwelling together. This is anough to authorize a godly Prince in that indulgence [2] which he gives to the changing of a Contract; both because it is certainly the invention of Antichrist, that the promise of mariage *de praesenti* as they call it,[3] should be indissoluble, and because it should be a Princes care that matrimony be so joyn'd, as God ordain'd; which is, that every one should love his wife with such a love as *Adam* exprest to *Eve:* So as wee may hope that they who marry may become one flesh, and one also in the Lord.

CHAP. XX.

Concerns only the celebration of mariage.

CHAP. XXI.

The means of preserving mariage holy and pure.[1]

Now since there ought not to be lesse care that mariage be religiously kept, then that it be piously and deliberately contracted, it will be meet that to every Church be ordan'd certain grave and godly men, who may have this care upon them, to observ whether the [4] husband bear himself wisely toward the wife, loving, & inciting her to all piety and the other duties of this life; and whether the wife be subject to her husband, and study to be truly a meet help to him, as first to all godlines, so to every other use of life. And if they [2] shal find each to other failing of their duty, or the one long absent from the other without just and urgent cause, or giving suspicion of irreligious and impure life, or of living

---

[2] *Cf. Scripta* (1577), p. 91: "ad hujusmodi, de qua dixi, indulgentiam" (that sort of indulgence of which I spoke).

[3] Milton adds "as they call it."

[1] The means . . . pure: *"De conservandis sacris conjugiis"* (concerning the preservation of holy marriage).

[2] They: *illi matrimoniorum custodes* (those guardians of marriages).

in manifest wickednes, let it be admonisht them in time. And if thir autority be contemn'd, let the names of such contemners be brought to the Magistrate, who may use punishment to compell such violaters of mariage, to thir duty, that they may abstain from all probable suspicion of transgressing; and if they admit of suspected company, the Magistrate is to forbid them; whom they not therin obeying, are to be punisht as adulterers, according to the law of *Justinian, Authent.* 117.[3] For if holy wedlock the Fountain and Seminary of good subjects, be not vigilantly preserv'd from all blots and disturbances, what can be hop'd, as I said before, of the springing up of good men, and a right reformation [4] of the Common-wealth. We know it is not anough for Christians to abstain from foul deeds, but from the appearance and suspicion therof.

CHAP. XXII.

Of lawfull divorce, what the ancient Churches have thought.

Now we shall speak about that dissolving of matrimony which may be approv'd in the sight of God, if any greevous necessity require. In which thing the Roman Antichrists have knit many a pernicious entanglement to distressed consciences: for that they might heer also exalt themselvs above God, as if they would be wiser and chaster then God himself is, for no cause, honest, or necessary, will they permit a finall divorce,[1] in the mean while whordoms and adulteries, and worse things then these, not only tolerating in themselvs and others, but cherishing, and throwing men headlong into these evils. For although they also dis-joyn married persons from board and bed, that is, from all conjugall society and communion, and this not only for adultery, but for ill usage, and matrimoniall duties deni'd, yet they forbid those thus parted, to joyn in wedlock with others, but, as I said before, any dishonest associating they permit. And they pronounce the bond of mariage to remain between those whom they have thus

---

[3] *Juris Civilis, Novellae*, CXVII, chapter 15 (Geneva, 1594–95, cols. 278–79; Scott, XVII, 59–60).

[4] Reformation: *constitutione* (constitution).

[1] Finall divorce: *divortium verum* (true divorce).

separat. As if the bond of mariage, God so teaching and pronouncing, were not such a league as bindes the maried couple to all so-[5] ciety of life, and communion in divine & humane things; and so associated keeps them.[2] Somthing indeed out of the latter Fathers they may pretend for this thir tyranny, especially out of *Austine* and some others, who were much tak'n wth a preposterous admiration of single life; yet though these Fathers, from the words of Christ not rightly understood, taught that it was unlawfull to marry again, while the former wife liv'd, whatever cause ther had bin either of desertion or divorce,[3] yet if we mark the custom of the Church, and the common judgement which both in their times and afterward prevail'd, we shall perceave that neither these Fathers did ever cast out of the Church any one for marying after a divorce, approv'd by the Imperiall laws.

Nor only the first Christian Emperours, but the later also, ev'n to *Justinian*, and after him, did grant for certain causes approv'd by Judges, to make a true divorse; which made and confirm'd by law, it might be lawfull to marry again: which if it could not have bin done without displeasing Christ and his Church, surely it would not have been granted by Christian Emperours, nor had the Fathers then winkt at those doings in the Emperours. Hence ye may see that *Jerom* also, though zealous of single life more then anough, and such a condemner of second mariage though after the death of either party, yet forc't by plain equity, defended *Fabiola*, a noble Matron of Rome, who having refus'd [4] her husband for just causes, was married to another.[5] For that the sending of a divorce to her husband was not blame-worthy, he affirms, because the man was hainously vitious, and that if an adulterous wife may be discarded, an adulterous husband is not to be kept. But that she maried again,

---

[2] A paraphrase of *Juris Civilis, Pandects,* XXIII, title ii, paragraph 1 (Geneva, 1594–95, col. 709; Scott, V, 244). See *Tetrachordon,* below, p. 611.

[3] *Cf. Scripta* (1577), p. 93: "vel vir uxorem suam, vel uxor virum suum deseruisset, aut repudiasset" (if a man should either desert or put away his wife, or a wife her husband).

[4] Refus'd: *repudiato* (repudiated, put away).

[5] Jerome, *Epistola,* LXXVII. See *Patrologiae Cursus Completus, Series Latina,* ed. J. P. Migne (217 vols, Paris 1844–65), XXII, 691–92 (hereafter cited as Migne, *Latina*). Bucer, however, misrepresents the whole tone of Jerome's defense, which is that Fabiola's later life of penance and charitable work outweighs the sin of her marriage after divorce. It is very apparent that Jerome is defending not the act, but the person.

while yet her husband was alive, he defends in that the Apostle hath said, *It is better to mary then to burn,* and that yong widows should mary, for such was *Fabiola,* and could not remain in widowhood.

But some one will object that *Jerom* there addes, *Neither did she know the vigor of the Gospel, wherin all cause of marying is debarr'd from women, while thir husbands live,* and again, *while she avoided many wounds of Satan, she receav'd one ere she was aware.* But let the equall Reader minde also what went before; [6] *Because,* saith he soon after the beginning, *there is a rock and storm of slanderers oppos'd against her,*[7] *I will not praise her converted, unlesse I first absolve her guilty.* For why does he call them slanderers who accus'd *Fabiola* of marying again, if he did not judge it a matter of Christian equity and charity, to passe by and pardon that fact, though in his own opinion he held it a fault. And what can this mean? *I will not praise her, unlesse I first absolv her.* For [6] how could he absolv her but by proving that *Fabiola* neither in rejecting her vitious husband, nor in marying another, had committed such a sin, as could be justly condem'd. Nay, he proves both by evident reason, and cleer testimonies of Scripture, that she avoided sin.[8]

This also is hence understood, that *Jerom* [9] by the vigor of the Gospel, meant that height and perfection of our Saviours precept, which might be remitted to those that burn; for he addes, *But if she be accus'd in that she remain'd not unmarried, I shall confesse the fault, so I may relate the necessity.* If then he acknowledg'd a necessity, as he did, because she was young, and could not live in Widowhood, certainly he could not impute her second mariage to her much blame: but when he excuses her out of the word of God,[10] does he not openly declare his thoughts, that the second mariage of *Fabiola* was permitted her by the holy Ghost himself for the necessity which

[6] *Cf. Scripta* (1577), p. 94: "quae hic vir Dei praemisit" (what this man of God put before). Equall: fair minded.

[7] Milton omits (*Scripta,* 1577, p. 94) "quòd secundum sortita matrimonium, prius reliquerit" (that she should leave a first marriage to make a second).

[8] Milton omits a paragraph concerning the "vigor of the Gospel" (*Scripta,* 1577, p. 94), the substance of which appears in the next sentence of Milton's text.

[9] *Cf. Scripta* (1577), p. 94: *hunc virum Dei* (this man of God).

[10] Milton omits (*Scripta,* 1577, p. 94) "quo pronunciatur, melius esse nubere quàm uri, & quo iuniores viduae iubentur nubere" (in which it is said, it is better to marry than to burn, and younger widows are commanded to marry).

she suffer'd, and to shun the danger of fornication, though she went [11] somwhat aside from the vigor of the Gospel.[12] But if any urge that *Fabiola* did public penance for her second mariage, which was not impos'd but for great faults. 'Tis answer'd, she was not enjoyn'd to this pennance, but did it of her own accord, *and not till after her second husbands death*. As in the time of *Cyprian* we read that many [13] were wont to doe voluntary penance for small faults, which were not liable to excommunication.[14]

[11] Milton omits (*Scripta*, 1577, p. 94) *his nuptiis* (in these nuptials).

[12] Milton omits a paragraph (*Scripta*, 1577, p. 94) to the effect that Jerome, like many other fathers, thought that any marriage after a divorce was a decline from the vigor of the Gospel, but to be tolerated because of the weakness of the flesh and to avoid worse sins.

[13] Many: *plerosque ex populo* (and many of the people). Caecilius Cyprianus (d. 258) was an early Latin apologist for Christianity. See *Complete Prose*, I, 392–93.

[14] Bucer's reference is Cyprian's "Sermone de Lapsis." It is difficult to know what passage Bucer has in mind; but it is probably the following (*Liber de Lapsis*, XXVIII, in Migne, *Latina*, IV, 488): "Denique quanto et fide majores et timore meliores sunt qui quivis nullo sacrificii aut libelli facinore constricti, quoniam tamen de hoc vel cogitaverunt hoc ipsum apud sacerdotes Dei dolenter et simpliciter confitentes, exomologesin conscientiae faciunt, animi sui pondus exponunt, salutarem medelam parvis licet et modicis vulneribus exquirunt. . . . Minus plane peccaverit non videndo idola, nec sub oculis circumstantis atque insultantis populi sanctitatem fidei profanando, non polluendo manus suas funestis sacrificiis, nec sceleratis cibis ora maculando. Hoc eo proficit ut sit minor culpa, non ut innocens conscientia. Facilius potest ad veniam criminis pervenire. Non est tamen immunis a crimine. Nec cesset in agenda poenitentia atque in Domini misericordia deprecanda, ne quod minus esse in qualitate delicti videtur, in neglecta satisfactione cumuletur." (Finally, according as they are greater in faith and fear, those are better who, though not forced to sacrifice, or sign a bill repudiating Christianity, nevertheless, since they considered such action, confessing themselves sadly and simply to the priests of God, make a complete confession of their conscience, bare the weight on their soul, and search out a wholesome cure for perhaps small and insignificant wounds. . . . Obviously he will have sinned less in not beholding idols, nor profaning the faith in the eyes of the watching and insulting people, nor polluting his hands by pernicious sacrifice, nor soiling his mouth with infamous food. This counts as a smaller sin, not as an innocent conscience. He can more easily attain to indulgence for his sin. But he is not therefore guiltless of sin. Nor should he cease from doing penance and beseeching the mercy of God, lest, though his sin seems less in gravity, it should grow in neglected satisfaction.) If this is the passage Bucer refers to, he has somewhat stretched its meaning. Cyprian is exhorting the faithful to penance for small sins, not saying that such penance is customary.

That Mariage was granted by the ancient Fathers, e'vn after the vow of single life.
I omit his testimonies out of Cyprian, Gelasius, Epiphanius,[1] contented only to relate what he thence collects to the present purpose.

SOME will say perhaps, wherfore all this concerning mariage after vow of single life, when as the question was of mariage after divorse? For this reason, that they whom it so much moves, because some of the Fathers thought mariage after any kind of divorse, to be condemn'd of our Saviour, may see that this conclusion follows not. The Fathers thought all mariage after divorce to be forbidd'n of our Saviour, therfore they thought such mariage was not to be tolerated in a Christian. For the same Fathers judg'd it forbidd'n to marry after vow; yet such mariages they neither dissolv'd nor excommunicated. For these words of our Saviour, and of the holy Ghost, stood in their way; *All cannot receav this saying, but they to whom it is giv'n. Every one* [7] *hath his proper gift from God, one after this manner, another after that. It is better to marry then to burn. I will that younger Widows marry,*[2] and the like.

So there are many Canons, and Laws extant, wherby Priests, if they maried, were remov'd from their office, yet is it not read that their mariage was dissolv'd, as the Papists now-a-dayes doe, or that they were excommunicated, nay expressly they might communicate as Lay men. If the consideration of human infirmitie, and those testimonies of divine Scripture which grant mariage to every one that wants it, persuaded those Fathers to bear themselvs so humanly toward them who had maried with breach of vow to God, as they beleev'd, and with divorce of that mariage wherin they were in a

---

[1] Gelasius was pope (492–496) during the time of Theodoric. Epiphanius (d. 403), was bishop of Constantia in the isle of Cyprus (310–320). He fought heresy zealously and wrote against all forms of it. Jerome called him the father of all the episcopacy and the last representative of ancient piety. Epiphanius' views on divorce, though omitted here, are given in *Tetrachordon*, below, p. 697.

[2] Milton here is apparently literally translating Bucer's Latin, though the citations are close to the Authorized Version: All *men* cannot receive this saying, *save* they to whom it is given (Matthew 19:11); Everyone hath his proper gift *of* God (I Corinthians 7:7); it is better to marry than to burn (I Corinthians 7:9); I will *therefore* that *the* younger *women* marry (I Timothy 5:14).

manner joyn'd to God, who doubts, but that the same Fathers held
the like humanitie was to be afforded to those who after divorce &
faith broken with men, as they thought, enter'd into second mariage:
for among such are also found no lesse weak, and no lesse burning.

CHAP. XXIV.

Who of the ancient Fathers have granted marriage after divorce.

THIS is cleer both by what hath bin said, and by that which
Origen relates of certain Bishops in his time, *Homil*. 7. in
Matth. *I know some,* saith he, *which are over Churches,
who without Scripture have permitted the wife to mary while her
former husband liv'd. And did this against Scripture which saith,
The wife is bound to her husband so long as he lives, and she shall
be call'd an adulteresse, if, her husband living, she take another man,
yet did they not permit this without cause, perhaps for the infirmitie
of such as had not continence, they permitted evill to avoid worse.*[1]
Ye see *Origen* and the Doctors of his age, not without all cause,
permitted women after divorce to marry, though their former husbands were living: yet writes that they permitted against Scripture.
But what cause could they have to doe so, unlesse they thought our
Saviour in his precepts of divorce, had so forbid'n, as willing to remit
such perfection to his weaker ones, cast into danger of worse faults.

The same thought *Leo,* Bishop of *Rome, Ep.* 85. to the African
Bishops of *Mauritania Caesariensis,* wherin complaining of a certain Priest, who divorcing his wife, or being divorc't by her, as
other copies have it, had maried another, neither dissolvs the matrimony, nor ex-[8]communicates him, only unpreists him.[2] The
fathers therfore as wee see, did not simply and wholly condemn
mariage after divorce.[3]

[1] Origen, *Commentaria in Evangelium Secundum Matthaeum,* XIV, 23, in
Patrologiae Cursus Completus, Series Graeca, ed. J. P. Migne (161 vols., Paris,
1857–66), XIII, 1245 (hereafter cited as Migne, *Graeca*).

[2] Leo Magnus, *Epistola* XII, 3 (Migne, *Latina,* LIV, 648–59). Leo the Great,
Pope (440–446), asserted the universal jurisdiction of the Roman episcopate.

[3] Milton omits a long passage (*Scripta,* 1577, pp. 97–98) to the effect that
though the fathers regarded marriage after divorce as unscriptural, they permitted it because of human weakness. Hence, Bucer reasons, one cannot say
simply that they condemned it in every case and allowed it to no Christian.

But as for me, this remitting of our Saviours precepts, which these ancients allow to the infirm in marrying after vow and divorce, I can in no ways admit; for what so ever plainly consents not with the commandment, cannot, I am certain, be permitted, or suffer'd in any Christian: for heav'n and earth shall passe away, but not a tittle from the commands of God among them who expect life eternal. Let us therfore consider, and waigh the words of our Lord concerning mariage, and divorce, which he pronounc't both by himself, and by his Apostle, and let us compare them with other Oracles of God; for whatsoever is contrary to these, I shall not persuade the least tolerating therof. But if it can be taught to agree with the Word of God, yea to be commanded that most men may have permission giv'n them to divorce and marry again, I must preferre the autority of Gods Word before the opinion of Fathers and Doctors, as they themselvs teach.[4]

CHAP. XXV.

The words of our Lord, and of the holy Ghost by the Apostle Paul concerning Divorce are explain'd.

Bᴜᴛ the words of our Lord and of the holy Ghost, out of which *Austin,* and some others of the Fathers think it concluded that our Saviour forbids mariage after any divorce are these, *Mat.* 5. 31, 32. *It hath bin said &c.* And *Mat.* 19. 7. *They say unto him, why did Moses then command, &c.* And *Mark* the 10ᵗʰ, and *Luke* the 16. *Rom.* 7. 1, 2, 3. I *Cor.* 7. 10, 11.[1] Hence therfore they conclude that all mariage after divorce is call'd adultery; which to commit beeing no ways to be tolerated in any Christian, they think it follows that second mariage is in no case to be permitted either to the divorcer or to the divorsed.[2]

[4] Milton omits a paragraph (*Scripta,* 1577, p. 98) in which Bucer, though admitting his admiration and reverence for the fathers, prefers Scripture even to their opinions.

[1] Bucer gives all the scriptural citations in full. Milton omits a passage (*Scripta,* 1577, p. 99) in which Bucer traces the opinions of Augustine and others that all remarriage after divorce was prohibited to the texts in Mark and Luke, where the exception of fornication is lacking.

[2] Milton condenses this passage (*Scripta,* 1577, p. 99), but without loss of essential sense, *e.g.,* "qui uxorem suam repudiat, & alteram ducit: & repudiatam

But that it may be more fully and plainly perceav'd, what force is in this kind of reasoning, it will be the best cours to lay down certain grounds wherof no Christian can doubt the truth.[3] First it is a wickednes to suspect that our Saviour branded that for adultery, which himself in his own Law, which he came to fulfill, and not to dissolv, did not only permit, but also command; for by him the only Mediator [4] was the whole law of God giv'n. But that by this law of God mariage was permitted after any divorce is certain by *Deut.* 24.1.[5] [9]

CHAP. XXVI.

That God in his law did not only grant, but also command divorce to certain men.

Deut. 24.1. *When a man hath taken a wife, &c.*[1] But in *Mala.* 2. 15, 16. is read the Lords command to put her away whom a man hates, in these words. *Take heed to your spirit, and let none deal injuriously against the wife of his youth. If he hate, let him put away, saith the Lord God of Israel. And he shall hide thy violence with his garment, that maries her divorc't by* thee, *saith the Lord of hosts;* But *take heed to your spirit, and doe no injury.*[2] By these testimonies of the divine law, wee see that the Lord did not only permit, but also expresly and earnestly commanded his people, by whom he would that all holiness and faith of mariage covnant should be observ'd, that he who could not induce

---

ipsam, si vivente priore viro copuletur alteri" (who puts away his wife and takes another, & the wife who, put away, is joined with another while her former husband lives) becomes "to the divorcer or to the divorsed."

[3] (M) The I. axiom that Christ could not condemn of adultery that which he once commanded.

[4] *Cf. Scripta* (1577), p. 99: "unum inter patrem & nos mediatorem, de cuius plenitudine Moses & Prophetae omnes, quaecunque tradiderunt, acceperunt" (the only mediator between the Father and us, of whose fullness Moses and the Prophets, whatever they taught, partook).

[5] Milton omits "ubi lex Dei ita habet" (where the law of God has it thus).

[1] Bucer gives the whole passage (*Scripta*, 1577, p. 99).

[2] Concerning this corrupt passage, see *Tetrachordon*, below, pp. 615–16; also *Doctrine and Discipline*, above, p. 257.

his minde to love his wife with a true conjugal love,[3] might dismisse her that shee might marry to another.

CHAP. XXVII.

That what the Lord permitted and commanded to his ancient people concerning divorce, belongs also to Christians.

Now what the Lord permitted to his first-borne people, that certainly he could not forbid to his own among the Gentils, whom he made coheires and into one body with his people, nor could he ever permit, much lesse command ought that was not good for them, at least so us'd, as he commanded. For beeing God, he is not chang'd as man. Which thing who seriously [1] considers, how can he imagine that God would make that wicked to them that beleeve, and serv him under grace, which he granted and commanded to them that serv'd him under the Law. When as the same causes require the same permission. And who that knows but humane matters, and loves the truth, will deny that many mariages hang as ill together now, as ever they did among the Jews? So that such mariages are liker to torments then true mariages.[2] As therfore the Lord doth always succour and help the oppressed, so he would ever have it provided for injur'd husbands and wives, that under pretence of the mariage-bond, they be not sold to perpetual vexations, instead of the loving and comfortable mariage-duties. And lastly, as God doth always detest hypocrisie, and fraud, so neither doth he approve, that among his people, that should be counted mariage, wherin none of those duties remain, wherby the league of wedlock is chiefly preserv'd. What inconsiderat ne-[10] glect then of Gods law is this, that I may not call it worse, to hold that Christ our Lord would not grant the same remedies both of divorce and second mariage to the weak, or to the evil, if they will needs have it so, but especially to the innocent and wronged, when

[3] *Cf. Scripta* (1577), p. 100: "ut uxorem suam amet, foveatque charitate conjugali" (that he love and cherish his wife with conjugal love).

[1] Seriously: *religiosè* (religiously).

[2] Milton omits a passage (*Scripta*, 1577, p. 100) developing the notion that such husbands and wives are made by their hate murderers and liars.

as the same urgent causes remain, as before; when the discipline of the church and Magistrate hath tri'd what may be tri'd.[3]

CHAP. XXVIII.

That our Lord Christ intended not to make new Laws of mariage and divorce, or of any civil matters.

IT IS agreed by all who determine of the Kingdom, and offices of Christ by the holy Scriptures,[1] as all godly men ought to doe, that our Saviour upon earth took not on him either to give new laws in civil affairs, or to change the old.[2] But it is certain that matrimony and divorce are civil things. Which the Christian Emperours knowing, gave conjugal laws; and reserv'd the administration of them to thir own Courts; which no true ancient Bishop [3] ever condemn'd.

Our Saviour came to preach repentance, and remission; [4] seeing therfore those who put away thir wives without any just cause, were not toucht with conscience of the sin, through misunderstanding of the law, he recall'd them to a right interpretation, and taught that the woman in the beginning was so joyn'd to the man, that there should be a perpetual union both in body and spirit: where this is not, the matrimony is already broke, before there be yet any divorce made or second mariage.

[3] Milton omits (*Scripta*, 1577, p. 101) "ab utraque administratione juxta Dei verbum possit, ut dura illa corda ad conjugalem benevolentiam rursus emolliantur" (what may be done by either power [civil or ecclesiastical] according to the word of God to soften again those hard hearts to conjugal benevolence).

[1] (M) The second Axiom.

[2] Milton omits (*Scripta*, 1577, p. 101) "sed suos, quod ad civilem vitam attinet, subjecisse legibus cuiusque reipublicae, in qua quisque viveret" (but [commanded] his own, in respect to civil life, to subject themselves to the laws of the commonwealth in which they might live).

[3] "nemo sanctorum & verorum Episcoporum" (no holy and true bishop).

[4] Milton omits the rest of the paragraph (*Scripta*, 1577, p. 101) with the next. The omitted material develops the idea that the Jews who put away their wives without cause sinned against the sacredness of marriage.

CHAP. XXIX.

That it is wicked to strain the words of Christ beyond thir purpose.
This is his third Axiom, wherof there needs no explication heer.[1]

CHAP. XXX.

That all places of Scripture about the same thing are to be
joyn'd, and compar'd, to avoid Contradictions.[1]

This he demonstrates at large out of sundry places in the Gospel; and
principally by that precept against swearing,[2] *which compar'd with many*
places of the Law and Prophets, is a flat contradiction of them all, if we
follow superstitiously the letter. Then having repeated briefly his foure
Axioms, he thus proceeds. [11]

T HESE things thus preadmonisht, let us enquire what the undoubted meaning is of our Saviours words; and enquire
according to the rule which is observ'd by all learned and
good men in their expositions; that praying first to God, who is the
only opener of our hearts, wee may first with fear and reverence
consider well the words of our Saviour touching this question. Next,
that wee may compare them with all other places of Scripture,
treating of this matter, to see how they consent with our Saviours
words, and those of his Apostle.

CHAP. XXXI.

This Chapter disputes against Austin and the Papists, who deny
second mariage, ev'n to them who divorce in case of adultery, which
because it is not controverted among true Protestants, but that the
innocent person is easily allow'd to marry, I spare the translating.

---

[1] A very short chapter, comprising the third axiom and consisting of little
beyond the repetition of the title.
[1] (M) Axiom 4.
[2] (M) Mat. 5. 34.

CHAP. XXXII.

That a manifest adulteresse ought to be divorc't, and cannot lawfully be retain'd in mariage by any true Christian.

This though he prove sufficiently, yet I let passe, because this question was not handl'd in the Doctrine and discipline of divorce; to which book I bring so much of this Treatise as runs parallel.

CHAPTER XXXIII.

That adultery is to be punisht by death.

This Chapter also I omitt for the reason last alleg'd.

CHAP. XXXIV.

That it is lawfull for a wife to leav an adulterer, and to marry another husband.

This is generally granted, and therfore excuses me the writing out.

CHAP. XXXV.

Places in the Writings of the Apostle Paul touching divorce explain'd.[1]

LET us consider the answers of the Lord giv'n by the Apostle severally. Concerning the first which is *Rom.* 7. 1. *Know yee not brethren, for I speak to them that know the law, &c.* Ver. 2. *The woman is bound* [12] *by the law to her husband*

---

[1] Milton omits the first paragraph (*Scripta,* 1577, p. 111), which summarizes the places dealing with divorce in the New Testament and cites Ambrose to the effect that divorce is not lawful except for fornication.

so long as he liveth.[2] Heer it is certain that the holy Ghost had no purpose to determine ought of mariage, or divorce, but only to bring an example from the common and ordinary law of wedlock, to shew that as no covnant holds either party beeing dead, so now that wee are not bound to the law, but to Christ our Lord, seeing that through him wee are dead to sin, and to the law; and so joyn'd to Christ that wee may bring forth fruit in him from a willing godlines, and not by the compulsion of law, wherby our sins are more excited, and become more violent.[3] What therfore the holy Spirit heer speaks of matrimony, cannot be extended beyond the general rule.[4]

Besides it is manifest, that the Apostle did allege the law of wedlock, as it was deliver'd to the *Jews;*[5] for, saith he, I speak to them that know the law. They knew no law of God but that by *Moses,* which plainly grants divorce for several reasons. It cannot therfore be said that the Apostle cited this generall example out of the law, to abolish the several exceptions of that law, which God himself granted by giving autority to divorce.

Next when the Apostle brings an example out of Gods law concerning man and wife, it must be necessary that wee understand such for man and wife, as are so indeed according to the same law of God; that is, who are so dispos'd as that they are both willing and able to perform the necessary duties of mariage; not those who under a false title of mariage, keep themselves mutually bound to injuries and disgraces; for such twain are nothing lesse then lawfull man and wife.[6]

The like answer is to be giv'n to all the other places both of the

[2] Milton supplies these texts, to which Bucer has only references (*Scripta,* 1577, p. 111). *Cf.* Milton with the Authorized Version: The woman *which hath an husband.*

[3] Milton omits a passage (*Scripta,* 1577, p. 111) to the effect that the Holy Spirit here institutes nothing concerning the nature and duration of marriage.

[4] Milton omits (*Scripta,* 1577, p. 111) "& eò extrahi, ut causae adulterii exceptionem, quae est duobus locis relata à Matthaeo, faciat inanem & frustraneam" (and to take it thence makes the exception of the cause of adultery, referred to in two places by Matthew, useless and vain).

[5] Jews: *veteri suo populo* (to his ancient people).

[6] Nothing lesse then lawfull man and wife: *cf. Scripta* (1577), p. 112: "qui nihil minus quàm legitimi mariti, & uxores legitimae possunt numerari" (who can be called nothing less than lawful husbands and lawful wives). Milton omits a paragraph dealing with desertion allowed as a cause in I Corinthians 7, and the larger part of another paragraph respecting the point already made about Romans.

Gospel and the Apostle, that what ever exception may be prov'd out of Gods law, be not excluded from those places. For the Spirit of God doth not condemn things formerly granted, and allow'd, where there is like cause and reason.[7] Hence *Ambrose* upon that place, I *Cor.* 7. 15. *A brother or a sister is not under bondage in such cases;* [8] thus expounds; *The reverence of mariage is not due to him who abhors the author of mariage; nor is that mariage ratify'd which is without devotion to God: he sins not therfore who is put away for Gods cause, though he joyn himself to another. For the dishonor of the Creator dissolves the right of matrimony to him who is deserted, that he be not accus'd, though marrying to another. The faith of wedlock is not to be kept with him who departs, that he might not hear the God of Christians to be the author of wedlock. For if* Ezra *caus'd the mis-beleeving wives and husbands to be divorc't, that God might be appeas'd, and not offended, though they took others of thir own faith, how much more shall it be free, if the mis-beleever depart, to marry one of our own Religion. For this is not to be counted matrimony which is against the law of God.*[9] [13]

Two things are heer to be observ'd toward the following discourse, which truth it self, and the force of Gods word hath drawn from this holy man. For those words are very large, *Matrimony is not ratify'd without devotion to God.* And *the dishonour of the Creator dissolvs the right of matrimony.* For devotion is farre off, and dishonor is done to God by all who persist in any wickednes and hainous crime.[10]

---

[7] Milton omits a passage (*Scripta*, 1577, p. 112) citing Ambrose to the effect that a man putting away his wife for adultery should remain unmarried, but is not compelled to.

[8] Text supplied by Milton.

[9] *Commentarium in Epistolam I ad Corinthios*, VII (Migne, *Latina*, XVII, 230).

[10] Milton omits the last paragraph (*Scripta*, 1577, p. 113) of chapter XXXV.

CHAP. XXXVI.

That although it seem in the Gospel, as if our Saviour granted divorce only for adultery, yet in very deed he granted it for other causes also.

Now is to be dealt with this question, Whether it be lawful to divorce and marry again for other causes besides adultery, since our Saviour exprest that only. To this question, if we retain our principles already laid, and must acknowledge it to be a cursed blasphemy, if we say that the words of God doe contradict one another, of necessity we must confesse that our Lord did grant divorce, and mariage after that for other causes besides adultery,[1] notwithstanding what he said in *Matthew*.[2] For first, they who consider but only that place, I *Cor*. 7.[3] which treats of beleevers and misbeleevers matcht together, must of force confesse, that our Lord granted just divorce, and second mariage in the cause of desertion, which is other then the cause of fornication.[4] And if there be one other cause found lawfull, then is it most true that divorce was granted not only for fornication.

Next, it cannot be doubted, as I shew'd before, by them to whom it is giv'n to know God and his judgements out of his own word, but that, what means of peace and safety God ever granted and ordain'd to his elected people, the same he grants and ordains to men of all ages who have equally need of the same remedies. And who, that is but a knowing man, dares say there be not husbands and wives now to be found in such a hardnesse of heart, that they will not perform either conjugal affection, or any requisit duty therof, though it be most deserv'd at thir hands.[5]

Neither can any one deferre to confesse, but that God whose property it is to judge the cause of them that suffer injury, hath provided for innocent and honest persons wedded, how they might free themselvs by lawfull means of divorce, from the bondage and

---

[1] Milton omits "cum viris, tum mulieribus" (as well to men as to women).

[2] Bucer gives the beginning of the text in Matthew 19:9.

[3] Milton adds the citation.

[4] Milton omits a passage of several lines (*Scripta*, 1577, p. 114), keeping only the summary in the next sentence.

[5] Milton omits a section (*Scripta*, 1577, p. 114) substantially repeated in the following paragraph.

iniquity of those who are falsly term'd thir husbands or thir wives. This is cleer out of Deut. 24. 1. Malach. 2. Matth. 19. I Cor. 7. and out of those [14] principles which the Scripture every where teaches, That God changes not his minde, dissents not from himself, is no accepter of persons; but allows the same remedies to all men opprest with the same necessities and infirmities; yea, requires that wee should use them. This he will easily perceave, who considers [6] these things in the Spirit of the Lord.

Lastly, it is most certain, that the Lord hath commanded us to obey the civil laws every one of his own Common-wealth, if they be not against the laws of God.

CHAP. XXXVII.

For what causes divorce is permitted by the civil Law ex 1. consensu Codic. de repudiis.

I T IS also manifest that the law of *Theodosius* and *Valentinian*, which begins *Consensu, &c.*[1] touching divorce, and many other decrees of pious Emperours agreeing heerwith, are not contrary to the word of God. And therfore may be recall'd into use by any Christian Prince or Common-wealth, nay ought to be with due respect had to every nation. For whatsoever is equall and just, that in every thing is to be sought and us'd by Christians. Hence it is plain that divorce is granted by divine approbation, both to husbands and to wives, if either party can convict the other of these following offences before the Magistrate.

If the husband can prove the wife to be an adulteresse, a witch, a murdresse, to have bought or sold to slavery any one free born, to have violated sepulchers, committed sacrilege, favor'd theevs and robbers, desirous of feasting with strangers, the husband not knowing, or not willing, if she lodge forth without a just and probable

---

[6] Considers: *consideraverit & ponderaverit* (will have considered and weighed).

[1] *Juris Civilis, Code,* book V, title xvii, paragraph 8 (Geneva, 1594–95, col. 406; Scott, V, 203–205). The list of causes of divorce is, of course, a summary of this law. See also *Tetrachordon,* below, pp. 700–701, n. 24. Theodosius I was Emperor of the East (378–395), and Valentinian II, Emperor of the West (375–392).

cause, or frequent theaters and sights, he forbidding, if she be privie with those that plot against the State, or if she deale falsly, or offer blows. And if the wife can prove her husband guilty of any those fore-named crimes, and frequent the company of lewd women in her sight; or if he beat her, she had the like liberty to quit herselfe; with this difference, that the man after divorce might forthwith marry again; the woman not till a year after, lest she might chance to have conceav'd.[2] [15]

CHAP. XXXVIII.

An exposition of those places wherein God declares the nature of holy wedlock.

Now to the end it may be seen that this agrees with the divine law, the first institution of mariage is to be consider'd, and those texts in which God establisht the joyning of male and female, and describ'd the duties of them both. When God had determin'd to make woman, and give her as a wife to man, he spake thus, *Gen.* 2. 18. *It is not good for man to be alone, I will make him a help meet for him. And Adam said,* but in the Spirit of God, v. 23. 24. *This is now bone of my bone, and flesh of my flesh. Therfore shall a man leav his father and mother, and shall cleav to his wife, and they shall be one flesh.*[1]

To this first institution did Christ recall his own; when answering the Pharises, he condemn'd the licence of unlawfull divorce. He taught therfore by his example, that we, according to this first institution, and what God hath spok'n therof, ought to determin

---

[2] This whole paragraph is considerably condensed from Bucer (*Scripta*, 1577, p. 115), who, for instance, repeats the list of crimes for which the woman may divorce the man, where Milton has "fore-named crimes," and reduces "si se verberibus (quae ingenuis aliena sunt) adficientem" (if he give her blows, which are repugnant to the free) to "if he beat her."

[1] The scriptural passages are neither a translation of Bucer's Latin (*Scripta*, 1577, p. 116) nor quotations from the Authorized Version, but a blend. *Cf.* the Authorized Version: "It is not good that the man should be alone; I will make him an help meet for him. . . . And Adam said, This is now bone of my bones, and flesh of my flesh. . . . Therefore shall a man leave his father and his mother and cleave unto his wife, and they shall be one flesh."

what kind of covnant mariage is, how to be kept, and how farre; and lastly, for what causes to be dissolv'd. To which decrees of God these also are to be joyn'd, which the holy Ghost hath taught by his Apostle, that neither the husband nor the wife *hath power of their own body, but mutually each of eithers.* That *the husband shall love the wife as his own body, yea as Christ loves his Church, and that the wife ought to be subject to her husband, as the Church is to Christ.*[2]

By these things the nature of holy wedlock is certainly known; whereof if only one be wanting in both or either party, and that either by obstinate malevolence, or too deep inbred weaknes of minde, or lastly, through incurable impotence of body, it cannot then be said that the covnant of matrimony holds good between such; if we mean that covnant which God instituted and call'd Mariage, and that wherof only it must be understood that our Saviour[3] said, *Those whom God hath joyn'd, let no man separate.*[4]

And hence is concluded, that matrimony requires continuall co-habitation and living together, unlesse the calling of God be otherwise evident; which union if the parties themselves dis-joyn either by mutuall consent, or one against the others will depart, the marriage is then brok'n. Wherein the Papists, as in other things oppose themselvs against God; while they separate for many causes from bed and board, & yet will have the bond of matrimony remain, as if this covnant could be other then the conjunction and communion not only of bed & board, but of all other loving and helpfull duties. This we may see in these [16] words;[5] *I will make him a help meet for him;*[6] *bone of his bones, and flesh of his flesh; for this cause shall he leav father and mother, and cleav to his wife, and*

---

[2] Milton translates Bucer's paraphrase of I Corinthians 7:4 and Ephesians 5:23–24.

[3] Saviour: *Dominus* (Lord).

[4] Milton translates Bucer's Latin. Following, Milton omits three paragraphs (*Scripta*, 1577, p. 116) in which Bucer makes the point that marriage consists essentially in continuous cohabitation, except for special cause and for short periods. Without this cohabitation marriage is no remedy for temptation.

[5] This . . . words: cf. *Scripta* (1577), p. 117: "Sed videamus nunc, qualem etiam vitae communicationem atque consuetudinem Deus inter conjuges postulet" (But let us now see what communication and agreement of life God indeed supposes between spouses).

[6] Milton omits "et Adam, suggerente Domino" (and Adam at the Lord's inspiration).

they twain shall be one flesh.[7] By which words who discerns not, that God requires of them both so to live together, and to be united not only in body but in mind also, with such an affection as none may be dearer and more ardent among all the relations of mankind, nor of more efficacy to the mutuall offices of love, and loyalty.[8] They must communicate and consent in all things both divine and human, which have any moment to well and happy living.[9] The wife must honour and obey her husband, as the Church honours and obeys Christ her head. The husband must love and cherish his wife, as Christ his Church. Thus they must be to each other, if they will be true man and wife in the sight of God, whom certainly the Churches ought to follow in thir judgement. Now the proper and ultimate end of mariage is not copulation, or children, for then there was not true matrimony between *Joseph* and *Mary* the mother of Christ, nor between many holy persons more; but the full and proper and main end of mariage, is the communicating of all duties, both divine and humane, each to other, with utmost benevolence and affection.[10]

CHAP. XXXIX.

The properties of a true and Christian mariage, more distinctly repeated.

BY which definition wee may know that God esteems and reckons upon these foure [1] necessary properties to be in every true mariage. 1. That they should live together, unlesse the calling of God require otherwise for a time. 2. That they should

---

[7] *They twain* is apparently Milton's own translation. After the Scripture Milton omits (*Scripta*, 1577, p. 117) "Ex quo conclusit Dominus in Evangelio, oportere conjuges, quos Dominus matrimonio junxit, esse non duo, sed unam carnem" (from which the Lord concluded in the Gospel that it behooves spouses whom the Lord has joined in marriage to be not two, but one flesh).

[8] Milton omits a paragraph (*Scripta*, 1577, p. 117) on the love that ought to be between parents and children.

[9] The rest of the chapter is a condensation of Bucer, with many verbal omissions.

[10] This definition of marriage is repeated and developed in the first paragraph of chapter XXXIX in Bucer.

[1] Milton here puts the "foure" properties named in Bucer's margin (*Scripta*, 1577, p. 118) into the text itself.

love one another to the height of dearnes, and that in the Lord,
and in the communion of true Religion. 3. That the husband beare
himself as the head and preserver of his wife,[2] instructing her to
all godlines and intigritie of life; [3] that the wife also be to her
husband a help, according to her place, especially furdering him
in the true worship of God, and next in all the occasions of civil life.
And 4. That they defraud not each other of conjugal benevolence,
as the Apostle commands, I *Cor.* 7. Hence it follows according to
the sentence of God, which all Christians ought to be rul'd by, that
between those who either through obstinacy, or helples inabilitie,
cannot or will not perform these repeated duties, between those
there can be no true matrimony, nor ought they to be counted man
and wife. [17]

CHAP. XL.

*Whether those crimes recited Chap. 37. out of the civil law dissolv
matrimony in Gods account.*

Now if a husband or wife be found guilty of any those crimes,
which by the law *consensu* are made causes of divorce, 'tis
manifest that such a man cannot be the head, and preserver of his wife, nor such a woman be a meet help to her husband,
as the divine law in true wedlock requires; for these faults are punisht either by death, or deportation, or extream infamy, which are
directly opposite to the covnant of mariage. If they deserve death,
as adultery and the like,[1] doubtles God would not that any should
live in wedlock with them whom he would not have to live at all.
Or if it be not death, but the incurring of notorious infamy, certain
it is neither just, nor expedient, nor meet, that an honest man should
be coupl'd with an infamous woman, nor an honest matron with an

---

[2] Milton omits "sicut CHRISTUS se praestat Ecclesiae, hoc est" (As Christ is
to the church, that is).

[3] Milton omits (*Scripta,* 1577, p. 118) "avocet & abarceat ab omni peccato,
& Dei offensione: tùm externè etiam nutriat, foveatque, sicut carnem propriam"
(that he distract and withdraw her from all sin and offense to God, as well as
nourish and cherish her outwardly, as his own flesh).

[1] Bucer lists the other crimes: murder, witchcraft, plotting against the state,
robbery, and sacrilege.

infamous man. The wise Roman Princes had so great regard to the
equal honour of either wedded person, that they counted those
mariages of no force which were made between the one of good
repute, and the other of evill note.[2] How much more will all honest
regard of Christian expedience and comlines beseem & concern those
who are set free and dignify'd in Christ, then it could the Roman
Senate, or thir sons for whom that law was provided.

And this all godly men will soon apprehend, that he who ought
to be the head and preserver not only of his wife, but also of his
children and family, as Christ is of his Church, had need be one
of honest name: so likewise the wife which is to be the meet help of
an honest and good man, the mother of an honest off-spring and
family, the glory of the man, ev'n as the man is the glory of Christ,
should not be tainted with ignominy; as neither of them can avoid
to be, having bin justly appeacht of those forenamed crimes; and
therfore cannot be worthy to hold thir place in a Christian family:
yea they themselvs turn out themselvs and dissolv that holy covnant. And they who are true brethren and sisters in the Lord, are
no more in bondage to such violaters of mariage.

But heer the Patrons of wickednes and dissolvers of Christian
discipline will object, that it is the part of man and wife to bear one
anothers crosse, whether in calamitie, or infamy, that they might
gain each other, if not to a good name, yet to repentance and amendment. But they who thus object, seek the impunity of wickednes,
and the favour of wicked men, not the duties of true charity; which
preferrs [18] public honesty before private interest; and had rather
the remedies of wholsom punishment appointed by God should be
in use, then that by remisness the licence of evil doing should
encrease. For if they who by committing such offences, have made
void the holy knott of mariage, be capable of repentance, they will

---

[2] Milton omits (*Scripta*, 1577, p. 119) "Ut si quis Senator, Senatorisve filius,
nepos aut pronepos, duxisset uxorem quae artem ludicram exercuisset, aut
corpus suum prostituisset, aut lenocinium fecisset, aut publico judicio fuisset
condemnata: vel, si filia Senatoris, neptis, aut proneptis nupsisset viro talibus
notis commaculato" (if a senator, or a senator's son, grandson, or great grandson
should take a wife who had performed in the theatre, or prostituted her body,
or pandered, or been condemned in a public judgment: or, if a senator's daughter,
granddaughter, or great granddaughter should marry a man tainted with such
offenses).

be sooner mov'd when due punishment is executed on them, then when it is remitted.[3]

Wee must ever beware, lest, in contriving what will be best for the souls health of delinquents, wee make our selvs wiser and discreeter then God. He that religiously waighs his oracles concerning mariage, cannot doubt that they who have committed the foresaid transgressions, have lost the right of matrimony, and are unworthy to hold thir dignity in an honest and Christian family.

But if any husband or wife see such signes of repentance in thir transgressor,[4] as that they doubt not to regain them by continuing with them, and partaking of thir miseries and attaintures, they may be left to thir own hopes, and thir own mind, saving ever the right of Church and Common-wealth, that it receav no scandal by the neglect of due severity, and thir children no harm by this invitation to licence, and want of good education.[5]

From all these considerations, if they be thought on, as in the presence of God, and out of his Word, any one may perceav, who desires to determine of these things by the Scripture, that those causes of lawfull divorce, which the most religious Emperours *Theodosius* and *Valentinian* set forth in the forecited place,[6] are according to the law of God, and the prime institution of mariage. *And were still more and more straitn'd, as the Church and State of the Empire still more and more corrupted and degenerated.*[7] Therfore pious Princes & Common-wealths both may and ought establish them again, if they have a mind to restore the honour, sanctitie, and religion of holy wedlock to thir people, and dis-intangle many

---

[3] Milton omits (*Scripta,* 1577, p. 120) "Quo enim hi Dei severitatem contra sua flagitia pleniùs sentiunt, eo facilius, siquidem ex Deo nati sint, & à Deo respiciantur, flagitiorum suorum agnoscunt atrocitatem" (by which indeed they feel the severity of God against their wickedness more fully and easily, especially if they are born of God, and may heed God, than if they do not know the atrocity of their sins).

[4] Transgressor: *cf. Scripta* (1577), p. 120: "vir aliquis uxorem suam lapsam, vel si qua mulier virum suum depraehensum in flagitio" (any husband his fallen wife, or a woman her husband caught in sin).

[5] Milton omits a paragraph (*Scripta,* 1577, p. 120), already summarized above, pp. 462–63, giving causes for which a woman may divorce her husband, or a man his wife.

[6] See above, p. 462. Bucer gives the reference.

[7] This sentence is added by Milton; hence the italics.

consciences from a miserable and perilous condition, to a chaste and honest life.

To those recited causes wherfore a wife might send a divorce to her husband, *Justinian* added foure more, *Constit*. 117. And foure more, for which a man might put away his wife. Three other causes were added in the *Code de repudiis l. Jubemus*. All which causes are so cleerly contrary to the first intent of mariage, that they plainly dissolv it. *I set them not down beeing easie to be found in the body of the civil Law.*[8]

It was permitted also by Christian Emperours, that they who would divorce by mutuall consent, might without impediment.[9] *Or if there were any difficulty at all in it, the law expresses the reason, that it was only* [19] *in favour of the children, so that if there were none, the law of those godly Emperours made no other difficulty of a divorce by consent.*[10] Or if any were minded without consent of the other to divorce, and without those causes which have bin nam'd, the Christian Emperours laid no other punishment upon them, then that the husband wrongfully divorcing his wife should give back her dowry, and the use of that which was call'd *Donatio propter nuptias;* or if there were no dowry nor no donation, that he should then give her the fourth part of his goods. The like penalty was inflicted on the wife departing without just cause. But that they who were once maried should be compell'd to remain so

[8] Bucer details the causes (*Scripta*, 1577, p. 121): For a woman to divorce a man he lists four: (1) failure to defend the wife against malicious gossip, (2) failure to defend her reputation for chastity, (3) charging her with adultery without proof, (4) consorting with another woman and refusing to desist on the pleas of his wife's parent or of other honest people. Bucer likewise gives four causes for the husband's divorcing his wife: (1) adultery, (2) procuring abortion, (3) frequenting the baths with other men for lascivious purposes, (4) bigamy. Milton has apparently misread Bucer, who gives only four causes in all for the husband's divorcing his wife, not seven, as Milton states. The first of Bucer's causes is from Novella CXVII, the other three from Jubemus, not four from the novella and three more from Jubemus. Moreover, it should be observed that the three from Jubemus cannot be an addition to those in the novella, since the novella comes after the Code, in which Jubemus occurs. See *Juris Civilis, Code*, book V, title 17, paragraph 11; and *Novellae*, CXVII, chapter 8 (Geneva, 1594–95, cols. 408–409, 273–74; Scott, XIII, 206–207; XVII, 54–56).

[9] Milton omits (*Scripta*, 1577, p. 121) "sed eam concessionem Justinianus rursum sustulit" (but this concession Justinian recalled). See *Tetrachordon*, below, p. 701, for Milton's discussion of Justinian's recall of divorce *de consensu*.

[10] Added by Milton from the Civil Law. See *Tetrachordon*, below, p. 700.

ever against thir wills, was not exacted. Wherin those pious Princes follow'd the law of God in *Deut.* 24. 1.[11] and his expresse charge by the Profet *Malachy* to dismisse from him the wife whom he hates. For God never meant in mariage to give to man a perpetuall torment, instead of a meet help. Neither can God approve that to the violation of this holy league (which is violated as soon as true affection ceases and is lost,) should be added murder, which is already committed by either of them who resolvedly hates the other, as I shew'd out of I *John* 15.[12] *Who so hateth his brother is a murderer.*[13]

CHAP. XLI.

Whether the husband or wife deserted may marry to another.

THE wives desertion of her husband the Christian Emperours plainly decreed to be a just cause of divorce, when as they granted him the right therof, if she had but lain out one night against his will without probable cause. But of the man deserting his wife they did not so determine: [1] Yet if we look into the Word of God, wee shall find, that he who though but for a year without just cause forsakes his wife,[2] and neither provides for her maintenance,[3] nor signifies his purpose of returning, and good will towards her, when as he may, hath forfeited his right in her so forsak'n. For the Spirit of God speaks plainly, that both man and wife hath such power over one anothers person, as that they cannot

[11] Reference added by Milton.
[12] Verse added by Milton. The reference should be I John 3:15.
[13] *Who so:* Authorized Version, *whosoever.*
[1] Milton omits a passage (*Scripta,* 1577, p. 122) giving the information that Constantine allowed divorce to a wife whose husband was on military duty and for four years did not communicate with her, and that Justinian abrogated that law and required a wife to wait for her husband, whether he was absent in the military, or in school, or in business. Milton uses this information in *Tetrachordon.* See below, p. 700.
[2] Without just cause forsakes: *cf. Scripta* (1577), p. 122: "non propter necessariam militiam, aut alia justa de causa" (not because of military necessity or other just cause).
[3] For her maintenance: *cf. Scripta* (1577), p. 122: "nec uxori interim & liberis de alimentis prospiciat" (nor meanwhile provides for the maintenance of the wife and children).

deprive each other of living together, but by consent and for a time.[4]

Hither may be added that the holy Spirit grants desertion to be a cause of divorce, in those answers giv'n to the *Corinthians* concerning a brother or sister deserted by a mis-beleever. *If he depart, let him depart, a brother or a sister is not under bondage in such cases.* In which words, who sees not that the holy Ghost openly pronounc't, that the party without cause deserted, is not bound for anothers wilfull desertion, to abstain from mariage, if he have need therof. [20]

But some will say, that this is spok'n of a mis-beleever [5] departing. But I beseech yee, doth not he reject the faith of Christ in his deeds, who rashly [6] breaks the holy covnant of wedlock instituted by God? [7] And besides this, the holy Spirit does not make the misbeleeving of him who departs, but the departing of him who misbeleevs to be the just cause of freedom to the brother or sister.

Since therfore it will be agreed among Christians, that they who depart from wedlock without just cause, doe not only deny the faith of matrimony, but of Christ also, what ever they professe with thir mouths, it is but reason to conclude, that the party deserted is not bound in case of causlesse desertion, but that he may lawfully seek another consort, if it be needfull to him toward a pure and blameles conversation.[8]

[4] For a time: *cf. Scripta* (1577), p. 122: *& religionis causa* (and because of religion).

[5] Mis-beleever: *cf. Scripta* (1577), p. 122: "ὁ ἄπιστος id est a fide CHRISTI alienus" (unbeliever, that is, stranger from the faith of Christ).

[6] Rashly: *cf. Scripta* (1577), p. 122: "non minus impiè quàm temerè" (not less impiously than rashly).

[7] Milton omits (*Scripta*, 1577, p. 122) "& uxorem deserit suam, quam debet, ut carnem propriam, imò ut CHRISTUS Ecclesiam, diligere atque fovere" (and deserts his wife, whom he ought to watch over and cherish, even as Christ does the Church).

[8] Blameles conversation: *cf. Scripta* (1577), p. 122: *sancte piéque vivendum* (holy and pious living).

CHAP. XLII.

That impotence of body, leprosie, madnes, &c. are just causes of divorce.[1]

OF THIS, because it was not disputed in the doctrine and discipline of divorce, him that would know furder I commend to the Latin original.

CHAP. XLIII.

That to grant divorce for all the causes which have bin hitherto brought, disagrees not from the words of Christ naming only the cause of adultery.

Now wee must see how these things can stand with the words of our Saviour, who seems directly to forbid all divorce [1] except it be for adultery. To the understanding wherof, wee must ever remember this: That in the words of our Saviour there can be no contrarietie. That his words and answers are not to be stretcht beyond the question propos'd. That our Saviour did not there purpose to treat of all the causes for which it might be lawfull to divorce and marry again; *for then that in the Corinthians of marrying again without guilt of adultery could not be added.*[2] That it is not good for that man to be alone who hath not the special gift from above.[3] That it is good for every such one to be married, that he may shun fornication.

With regard to these principles let us see what our Lord answered to the tempting Pharises about divorce, and second mariage, and how farre his answer doth extend.

[1] Bucer in this chapter (*Scripta*, 1577, p. 123) mentions that in Germany princes permitted divorce and remarriage to husbands whose wives had incurable maladies rendering intercourse impossible. See *Tetrachordon*, below, p. 711.

[1] Divorce: *cf. Scripta* (1577), p. 125: "uxorem . . . dimittere, & alteram ducere" (to dismiss a wife and take another).

[2] Matter in italics added by Milton.

[3] Who . . . above: *cf. Scripta* (1577), p. 125: "qui castrationem propter regnum coelorum non capiunt, ac ideo in periculo versantur fornicationis" (who do not receive the castration for the kingdom of heaven, and are therefore put in danger of fornication).

First, No man who is not very contentious, will deny that the Pha-[21]rises askt our Lord whether it were lawfull to put away such a wife, as was truly, and according to Gods law, to be counted a wife; that is, such a one as would dwell with her husband, and both would & could perform the necessary duties of wedlock tolerably. But shee who will not dwell with her husband, is not put away by him, but goes of her self: and shee who denies to be a meet help, or to be so, hath made her self unfit by open misdemeanours, or through incurable impotencies cannot be able, is not by the law of God to be esteem'd a wife; as hath bin shewn both from the first institution, and other places of Scripture. Neither certainly would the Pharises propound a question concerning such an unconjugall wife; *for thir depravation of the law had brought them to that passe, as to think a man had right to put away his wife for any cause, though never so slight.*[4] Since therfore it is manifest that Christ answer'd the Pharises concerning a fit and meet wife according to the law of God, whom he forbid to divorce for any cause but fornication. Who sees not that it is a wickednes so to wrest and extend that answer of his, as if it forbad to divorce her who hath already forsak'n, or hath lost the place and dignitie of a wife by deserved infamy,[5] *or hath undertak'n to be that which she hath not naturall ability to be.*[6]

This truth is so powerfull that it hath mov'd the Papists to grant their kind of divorce for other causes besides adultery, as for ill usage, and the not performing of conjugal dutie; and to separate from bed and board for these causes, which is as much divorce, as they grant for adultery.

But some perhaps will object, that though it be yeilded, that our Lord granted divorce not only for adultery, yet it is not certain that he permitted mariage after divorce, unlesse for that only cause. I answer, first, that the sentence of divorce, and second mariage, is one and the same. So that when the right of divorce is evinc't to belong not only to the cause of fornication, the power of second

---

[4] Matter in italics added by Milton.

[5] Here Milton has considerably condensed Bucer, omitting a passage (*Scripta*, 1577, p. 125) in which Bucer tries to prove that Christ was speaking only of a "fit and meet wife," and preserving the summary.

[6] Material in italics added by Milton, who omits a paragraph (*Scripta*, 1577, pp. 125–26) in which Bucer argues that I Corinthians 7 proves that the causes of divorce are not restricted to adultery.

mariage is also prov'd to be not limited to that cause only; and that most evidently, when as the holy Ghost, I *Cor.* 7.[7] so frees the deserted party from bondage, as that he may not only send a just divorce in case of desertion, but may seek another marriage.

Lastly, Seeing God will not that any should live in danger of fornication and utter ruine for the default of another, and hath commanded the husband to send away with a bill of divorce her whom he could not love, it is impossible that the charge of adultery should belong to him who for lawfull causes divorces and marries, or to her who marries after she hath bin unjustly rejected, or to him who re-[22]ceavs her without all fraud to the former wedlock.[8] For this were a horrid blasphemy against God, so to interpret his words, as to make him dissent from himself; [9] for who sees not a flat contradiction in this, to enthrall blameles men and women to miseries and injuries, under a false and soothing title of mariage, and yet to declare by his Apostle that a brother or sister is not under bondage in such cases. No lesse doe these two things conflict with themselvs, to enforce the innocent and faultles to endure the pain and misery of anothers perversnes, or els to live in unavoidable temptation; and to affirm elswhere that he lays on no man the burden of another mans sin, nor doth constrain any man to the endangering of his soul.[10]

CHAP. XLIV.

That to those also who are justly divorc't, second mariage ought to be permitted.

This although it be well prov'd, yet because it concerns only the offendor, I leav him to search out his own charter himself in the Author.

[7] Reference added by Milton.

[8] Milton omits a passage (*Scripta,* 1577, p. 126) developing the danger of fornication to a man compelled to live with an intolerable wife.

[9] Milton has considerably compressed the expression here, omitting several clauses that substantially summarize the preceding argument.

[10] Milton omits two paragraphs (*Scripta,* 1577, p. 127) consisting of repetition and summary of the foregoing arguments against restricting divorce to adultery.

CHAP. XLV.

*That some persons are so ordain'd to mariage, as that they cannot obtain
the gift of continence, no not by earnest prayer, and that therin every
one is to be left to his own judgement, and conscience, and not to have
a burden laid upon him by any other.*

CHAP. XLVI.

The words of the Apostle concerning the praise of single life unfolded.

THESE two Chapters not so immediatly debating the right
of divorce, I chose rather not to insert.

CHAP. XLVII.

The Conclusion of this Treatise.

THESE things, most renowned King, I have brought together,
both to explain for what causes the unhappy, but sometimes
most necessary help of divorce ought to be granted, according to Gods Word, by Princes and Rulers: as also to explain
how the words of Christ doe consent with such a grant. I have bin
large indeed both in handling [23] those Oracles of God, and in
laying down those certain principles, which he who will know what
the mind of God is in this matter, must ever think on, and remember. But if wee consider what mist and obscuritie hath been powrd
out by Antichrist upon this question, and how deep this pernicious
contempt of wedlock, and admiration of single life, ev'n in those
who are not call'd therto, hath sunk into many mens persuasions, I
fear lest all that hath bin said, be hardly anough to persuade such
that they would cease at length to make themselvs wiser & holier
then God himself, in beeing so severe to grant lawfull mariage, and
so easie to connive at all, not only whordoms, but deflowrings, and

adulteries. When as among the people of God, no whordom [1] was to be tolerated.

Our Lord Jesus Christ, who came to destroy the works of Satan, send down his Spirit upon all Christians, and principally upon Christian Governours both in Church and Common-wealth (for of the cleer judgement of your royall Majesty I nothing doubt, revolving the Scripture so often as yee doe) that they may acknowledge how much they provoke the anger of God against us, when as all kind of unchastity is tolerated, fornications and adulteries winkt at: But holy and honourable wedlock is oft withheld by the meer persuasion of Antichrist, from such as without this remedy, cannot preserve themselves from damnation! For none who hath but a spark of honesty will deny that Princes and States ought to use diligence toward the maintaining of pure and honest life among all men, without which [2] all justice, all fear of God, and true religion decayes.

And who knows not that chastity and purenes of life, can never be restor'd, or continu'd in the Common-wealth, unlesse it be first establisht in private houses, from whence the whole breed of men [3] is to come forth. To effect this, no wise man [4] can doubt that it is necessary for Princes and Magistrates first with severity to punish whordom and adultery; [5] next to see that mariages be lawfully contracted, and in the Lord, then that they be faithfully kept; and lastly, when that unhappines urges, that they be lawfully dissolv'd, [6] and other mariage granted, according as the law of God, and of nature, and the Constitutions of pious Princes have decreed; as I have shewn both by evident autorities of Scripture, together with the writings of the ancient Fathers, and other testimonies. Only the

---

[1] No whordom: cf. Scripta (1577), p. 133: "Nullus omnino scortator, nullumque scortum debeat tolerari" (No whoremonger at all and no whoredom ought to be tolerated).

[2] Without which: qua neglecta (by the neglect of which).

[3] Whole breed of men: cives (citizens).

[4] No wise man: cf. Scripta (1577), p. 133: "nemo unquam sapientum, & honestae vitae amantium" (no wise man and lover of honest life).

[5] Whordom and adultery: cf. Scripta (1577), p. 133: "non stupra tantùm, & adulteria, sed etiam omnes vagas libidines, omnes illegitimas marium & foeminarum conjunctiones" (not only whoredoms and adulteries, but also all loose passions, all lawless conjunctions of men and women).

[6] Lawfully dissolv'd; cf. Scripta (1577), p. 133: "sed non nisi legitimè, dissolvantur" (dissolved, but not otherwise than lawfully).

Lord grant that we may learn to preferre his ever just and saving Word, before the Comments of Antichrist, too deeply rooted in many, and the false and blasphemous exposition of our Saviours words. *Amen.*

The end [24]

A Post-Script.[1]

THUS farre *Martin Bucer*; Whom where I might without injury to either part of the cause, I deny not to have *epitomiz'd:* in the rest observing a well-warranted rule, not to give an Inventory of so many words, but to weigh thir force. I could have added that eloquent and right Christian discours, writt'n by *Erasmus*[2] on this Argument, not disagreeing in effect from *Bucer.* But this, I hope, will be anough to excuse me with the meer *Englishman,*[3] to be no forger of new and loose opinions. Others may read him in his own phrase on the first to the *Corinthians,* and ease me who never could delight in long citations, much lesse in whole traductions; Whether it be natural disposition or education in me, or that my mother bore me a speaker of what God made mine own, and not a translator. There be others also whom I could reck'n up, of no mean account in the Church (and *Peter Martyr*[4] among the first) who are more then half our own in this controversie. But this is a providence not to be slighted, that as *Bucer* wrote this tractat of divorce in *England* and for *England,* so *Erasmus* professes he begun heer among us the same subject, especially out of compassion, for the need he saw this Nation had of some charitable redresse heerin; and seriously exhorts others to use thir best industry in the cleering of this point, wherin custom hath a greater sway then verity.[5] That therfore which came into the minde of these two admired strangers to doe for *England,* and in a touch of highest prudence which they took to be not yet recover'd from monastic superstition, if I a native am found to have don for [F1] mine own Country, altogether sutably and conformly to their so large and

---

[1] The "Post-Script" is unpaginated.

[2] The arguments of Erasmus are epitomized in *Tetrachordon,* below, pp. 620, 709.

[3] Meer Englishman: a person who can read only English.

[4] Peter Martyr's opinions are dealt with in *Tetrachordon,* below, p. 681.

[5] On I Corinthians 7 Erasmus writes, "Miserabat me illorum, quos videbam hujusmodi vinculis inextricabilibus implicatos, quos sciebam esse plurimos, praesertim apud Britannos, apud quos hoc opus primum deformabam" (I pitied those, whom I saw thus caught in inextricable bonds, whom I knew to be many, especially among the English, among whom I first designed this work). *Omnia Opera* (9 vols., Basle, 1540–41; UTSL), VI, 480.

cleer understanding, yet without the lest help of theirs, I suppose that hence-forward among conscionable and judicious persons, it will no more be thought to my discredit, or at all to this Nations dishonor. And if these thir books, the one shall be printed often, with best allowance in most religious Cities, the other with express autority of *Leo* the tenth a Pope, shall for the propagating of truth be publisht and republisht, though against the receav'd opinion of that Church,[6] and mine containing but the same thing, shall in a time of reformation, a time of free speaking, free writing, not find a permission to the Presse,[7] I referre me to wisest men, whether truth be suffer'd to be truth, or liberty to be liberty now among us, and be not again in danger of new fetters and captivity after all our hopes and labours lost: and whether learning be not (which our enemies too profetically fear'd) in the way to be trodd'n down again by ignorance. Wherof while time is, out of the faith owing to God and my Country, I bid this Kingdom beware: and doubt not but God who hath dignify'd this Parlament already to so many glorious degrees, will also give them (which is a singular blessing) to inform themselvs rightly in the midst of an unprincipl'd age; and to prevent this working mystery of ignorance and ecclesiastical thraldom, which under new shapes and disguises begins afresh to grow upon us.

The end. [F1v]

[6] It is hard to know how far Milton's statement that the *De Regno Christi* was "printed often, with best allowance in most religious Cities" is accurate. I have been able to find record of only one edition besides the two published at Basle: *Deux Livres du Royaume de Jesus Christ Nostre Sauveur . . .* , tr. J. Rivery (?), (Lausanne [?], 1558; BML). There were in addition at least two separately published extracts from the *De Regno Christi* (see British Museum *Catalogue of Printed Books*); neither is relevant to the divorce argument, but they open the possibility that Milton was more justified than at first appears in referring to Bucer's "book" as "printed often."

The implication in Milton's statement concerning Erasmus needs some correction. Though Erasmus' commentaries were published with ecclesiastical sanction in the early part of the sixteenth century, all his works were put on the Index by Pope Paul IV in 1559. A commission of the Council of Trent somewhat relaxed the prohibition by making it apply only to the *Institution of Christian Marriage* and all the works on religion until they were expurgated by the Sorbonne. See Preserved Smith, *Erasmus* (New York, 1923), p. 422.

[7] A direct anticipation of *Areopagitica;* see preface, above, p. 418, and introduction, pp. 140–43.

AREOPAGITICA

November, 1644

PREFACE AND NOTES BY ERNEST SIRLUCK

THE *Areopagitica*, although it bears Milton's name on the title page, was unlicensed, unregistered, and issued without imprint of publisher or printer (who remain unknown). The unknown recipient of the presentation copy now in the Yale Library, the title page of which is here reproduced, added "nov: 23" to the imprint "*LONDON*, Printed in the Yeare, 1644." Thomason dated his presentation copy a day later. Two other presentation copies are known, one to John Rous for the Bodleian, where it remains, and one to Patrick Young, now in the library of Trinity College, Dublin; but each formed part of a presentation collection and neither is separately dated. A. Geffroy (*Étude sur les Pamphlets Politiques et Religieux de Milton* [Paris, 1848], p. 232) asserted that the original manuscript was in the British Museum; no one has been able to find it.

There was no further edition during Milton's lifetime, nor (except in the collected editions of Milton's prose in 1697 and 1698 [1]) during the remainder of the seventeenth century, although several more or less extensive, if unacknowledged, adaptations were published during the latter part of the century at moments when censorship was in agitation.[2] The first separate republication (with a preface by the poet James Thomson) was in 1738, when it was widely feared that the renewal of stage licensing would soon be followed by renewed licensing of the press. *Areopagitica* has since become the most frequently republished of Milton's prose works. The most important annotated editions are those of:

T. Holt White (London, 1819). Gives bibliographical history prior to 1819. First systematically annotated edition, containing many useful explications adopted by subsequent editors. Reprints the adaptation by Mirabeau (see below).

[1] See *Complete Prose*, I, vii.

[2] See T. Holt White, *Areopagitica* (London, 1819), introduction, pp. lvii and cxxi; Macaulay, *History of England*, Book III, chapter 19 (Everyman ed., London, 1906, III, 186–88); and George F. Sensabaugh, *That Grand Whig Milton* (Stanford: Stanford University Press, 1952), pp. 55–61 and 155–62.

J. A. St. John, in the Bohn *Prose Works* (London, 1848). Inaccurate text, sporadic and uneven annotations. Has had a serious corrupting influence upon the text (many popular editions still repeat the errors it introduced).

Edward Arber, in *English Reprints* (London, 1868). Few notes, but almost completely accurate literal text, and contains *A Decree of Starre-Chamber, Concerning Printing* (1637), the House of Commons Orders of January 29, 1642, and March 9, 1643, and *An Order of the Lords and Commons . . . for the Regulating of Printing . . . 14 June 1643* (see above, introduction, pp. 158–61, for an account of these documents).

Sir Richard Jebb, whose *Commentary*, privately printed in 1872, was reprinted with the text and supplementary material by A. W. Verity (Cambridge, 1918); several reprints (to 1940).

John W. Hales (Oxford, 1874). Reissued several times, with minor revisions, to 1939. Very full and informative notes on classical and biblical background; with respect to the seventeenth century it has been in part outmoded by more recent scholarship.

Laura E. Lockwood, in *Of Education, Areopagitica, The Commonwealth* (New York, 1911).

Merritt Y. Hughes, in *John Milton: Prose Selections* (New York: Odyssey Press, 1947); notes revised and amplified in *John Milton: Complete Poems and Major Prose* (New York: Odyssey Press, 1957).

A facsimile reproduction of the first edition was published simultaneously in *The Noel Douglas Replicas* (London, 1927) and *The English Replicas* (New York, 1927). The Columbia *Works* presents a critical text, but finds no variants.

Areopagitica has been several times translated into French and German; there are complete translations in Russian, Italian, and Spanish, and partial ones in Dutch and classical Greek. The most dramatic foreign rendering is less a translation than an adaptation: Mirabeau's *Tract sur la Liberté de la Presse, imité de l'Anglois de Milton* ("Londres" [*i.e.*, Paris?], 1788 and 1789; second edition, Paris, 1792). The most scholarly foreign edition is the translation, with introduction and notes, by Olivier Lutaud (Paris: Aubier, 1956). A paraphrase into nineteenth-century English, with explanatory annotations, was published by Samuel Lobb (Calcutta, 1872).

The context in which Milton wrote *Areopagitica*, together with its organization, method, and success, has been discussed at some length in the introduction (see above, pp. 53–136 and 158–81).

The present text is based upon the Thomason copy, British Museum C55c22(9), referred to in the textual notes (below, p. 778) as "A."

It is a quarto measuring 18.6 x 14.6 cm.[3] Collation: A-E⁴F². Contents: A1, title-page; A2-F1v text; F2 blank. A2 [row of 16 ornaments, an Irish harp surmounted by a crown] head-title: "For the Liberty of unlicenc'd Printing." F1v, *"The End."*/[margin-to-margin rule]. The blank leaf F2 is often missing. Signatures are normal; pagination 1–40. A2 is page 1, and pagination is continuous without error. "A" has been collated with these other copies of the first edition: "B" (the Rous presentation copy), Bodleian Arch. G.e.44; "C" (the Yale presentation copy), Yale University Library Ij.M642.C641.v.3; "D," British Museum C120. b12(1); "E," British Museum G608; "F," Bodleian Wood. B.29; "G," Bodleian C.14.5.Linc.; "H," Union Theological Seminary, McAlpin Cat., II, 301; "I," New York Public *KC 1644 Milton. In addition, the Librarian of Trinity College, Dublin, has generously examined the Young presentation copy for the manuscript corrections described in the textual notes.

Gathering A exists in two states. The earlier is represented by copy "A," which contains a superfluous and reversed oblique at p. 1, l. 5 (below, p. 468, l. 7), and has "unboekish" at p. 5, l. 29 (below, p. 496, l. 8). The second state, which includes all other copies examined, deletes the obtruding mark and corrects to "unbookish." Since p. 1 is A2r and p. 5 is A4r, it will be seen that only the inner forme underwent correction; the outer forme contains an uncorrected repeated word at p. 4, l. 34 (below, p. 493, l. 12).

Gathering B probably has only one state, the difference between copies at p. 8, l. 21 (below, p. 503, l. 18) being almost certainly due to the gradual deterioration of a faulty character.

Gathering C shows two variations, but it is doubtful whether either involved resetting. That at p. 17, l. 5 (below, p. 526, l. 5) is probably due to deterioration, and that at p. 19, l. 4 (below, p. 778, l. 1) to a turned colon printing like a period after some impressions had been taken.

Gathering D has only one state.

Gathering E exists in two states. The earlier is represented by copies "A," "C," and "D," which have *"treasuves"* at p. 36, l. 4 (below, p. 562, l. 7). The second state, represented by "B," "E," "F," "G," "H," and "I," corrects to *"treasures."* P. 36 is E3v, thus belonging to the inner forme. The outer forme has three uncorrected errors: at p. 34, l. 15 (below, p. 559, l. 3), p. 38, ll. 16–17 (below, p. 567, l. 3), and p. 38, l. 27 (below, p. 567, l. 14). Gathering F exists in two states. The earlier is represented by copy "A," which has "fore judge" at p. 39, ll. 1–2 (below,

[3] Copies have been variously trimmed; the largest encountered ("D"), which may be fairly close to the original size, is 19.2 x 14.6 cm.

p. 567, l. 26). The second state, which includes all other copies examined, corrects to "fore-judge" (line-end hyphen). An error four lines down (below, p. 568, l. 4) remains uncorrected.

None of these press corrections suggests the intervention of the author; rather, the unsystematic nature of the corrections suggests his absence from the press, and so makes it more probable that the correction noted below, p. 515, n. 102, represents his belated intervention.

ERNEST SIRLUCK

University of Chicago

AREOPAGITICA;

A

SPEECH

OF

Mr. JOHN MILTON

For the Liberty of VNLICENC'D PRINTING,

To the PARLAMENT of ENGLAND.

Τυλδ'θερρι δ' ἐκῆνε, εἴ τις θέλχ πόλι
Χρηςὸν τι βέλλμ' εἰς μέσον φέρειν, ἔχω.
Καὶ ταῦθ' ὁ χρῄζων, λαμπρὸς ἔσθ', ὁ μὴ θέλων,
Σιγᾷ, τί τέτων ἐστὶν ἰσαίτερον πόλι;

Euripid. Hicetid.

This is true Liberty when free born men
Having to advise the public may speak free,
Which he who can, and will, deserv's high praise,
Who neither can nor will, may hold his peace;
What can be juster in a State then this?

Euripid. Hicetid.

LONDON,
Printed in the Yeare, 1644.

For the Liberty of unlicenc'd Printing.

THEY who to States [3] and Governours of the Commonwealth direct their Speech, High Court of Parlament, or wanting such accesse in a private condition, write that which they foresee may advance the publick good; I suppose them as at the beginning of no meane endeavour, not a little alter'd and mov'd inwardly in their mindes: Some with doubt of what will be the successe, others with feare of what will be the censure; some with hope, others with confidence of what they have to speake. And me perhaps each of these dispositions, as the subject was whereon I enter'd, may have at other times [4] variously affected; and likely might in these

[1] Title page, first line, *Areopagitica*. The Seventh Oration of Isocrates, usually called the *Areopagitic Discourse* or *Areopagiticus,* was written *ca.* 355 B.C. (R. C. Jebb, *The Attic Orators* [2 vols., London, 1893], II, 203–206). Isocrates (436–338 B.C.) conducted a famous school of rhetoric at Athens. Physical and nervous weakness prevented him from speaking in public; hence he composed his "orations" to be read. His greatest interest was political, but his only real influence was stylistic. The parallel of the *Areopagitic Discourse* with the *Areopagitica* lies chiefly in the form (a "speech" designed to be read, not spoken) and situation (a private citizen urging a change of policy in a discourse to what Milton calls "the Parlament of Athens"; below, p. 489, n. 12). In purpose, Isocrates differs so strikingly from Milton that the latter's choice of title is rather curious. In the fourth century B.C. the Court of the Areopagus retained only such of its former powers as served to make it a criminal court of very limited jurisdiction; Isocrates urges the restoration to it of those functions which had once made it a dominant political power, especially the control of education and the general censorship of manners (Jebb, II, 206–14). It is just possible that Milton intended that his title call to the reader's mind another "Areopagitic discource" (to which he refers elsewhere in the *Areopagitica;* see below, nn. 75 and 76): that of Paul, reported in Acts 17:18–34. Some connection may be seen between Milton's idea of the nature of truth and his attack on compulsory religious conformity, and the words of Paul: "Ye men of Athens, I perceive that in all things ye are too superstitious. . . . Whom therefore ye ignorantly worship, him declare I unto you."

[2] Title page, 1. 19, *Euripid. Hicetid.:* Euripides, *The Suppliants.*

[3] Heads of state.

[4] Of the seven prose works that had preceded the *Areopagitica*, only the revised edition of *Doctrine and Discipline of Divorce* (1644) and *The Judgment of Martin Bucer* (1644) had been formally addressed to Parliament; all of them, of course, had been written with Parliament in mind.

formost expressions now also disclose which of them sway'd most, but that the very attempt of this addresse thus made, and the thought of whom it hath recourse to, hath got the power within me to a passion, farre more welcome then incidentall to a Preface. Which though I stay not to confesse ere any aske, I shall be blamelesse, if it be no other, then the joy and gratulation which it [5] brings to all who wish and promote their Countries liberty; whereof this whole Discourse propos'd will be a certaine testimony, if not a Trophey. For this is not the liberty which wee can hope, that no grievance ever should arise in the Commonwealth, that let no man in this World expect; but when complaints are freely heard, deeply consider'd, and speedily reform'd, then is the utmost bound of civill liberty attain'd, that wise men looke for. To which if I now manifest by the very sound of this which I shall utter, that wee are already in good part arriv'd, and yet from such a steepe disadvantage of tyranny and superstition grounded into our principles as was beyond the manhood of a *Roman* recovery, it will bee attributed first, as is most due, to the strong assistance of God our deliverer, next to your faithfull guidance and undaunted Wisdome, Lords and Commons of *England*. Neither is it in Gods esteeme the diminution of his glory, when honourable things are spoken of good men and worthy Magistrates; which if I now first should begin to [1] doe,[6] after so fair a progresse of your laudable deeds, and such a long obligement [7] upon the whole Realme to your indefatigable vertues, I might be justly reckn'd among the tardiest, and the unwillingest of them that praise yee. Neverthelesse there being three principall things, without which all praising is but Courtship and flattery, First, when that only is prais'd which is solidly worth praise: next when greatest likelihoods are brought that such things are truly and really in those persons to whom they are ascrib'd, the other, when he who praises, by shewing that such his actuall perswasion is of whom he writes, can demonstrate that he flatters not; the former two of these I have heretofore endeavour'd, rescuing the employ-

---

[5] it: The antecedent is "the very attempt of this addresse thus made."

[6] The most striking instance of Milton's earlier praise of the Long Parliament is in *An Apology* (*Complete Prose*, I, 922–28). In comparison with this panegyric, the praise contained in the address to Parliament prefixed to the second edition of *Doctrine and Discipline* (above, pp. 224–26) is relatively cautious.

[7] The Long Parliament met November 3, 1640, four years before *Areopagitica*. See *Complete Prose*, I, 56–59.

ment from him who went about to impaire your merits with a triviall
and malignant *Encomium;* [8] the latter as belonging chiefly to mine
owne acquittall, that whom I so extoll'd I did not flatter, hath been
reserv'd opportunely to this occasion. For he who freely magnifies
what hath been nobly done, and fears not to declare as freely what
might be done better, gives ye the best cov'nant of his fidelity;
and that his loyalest affection and his hope waits on your proceedings. His highest praising is not flattery, and his plainest advice is
a kinde of praising; for though I should affirme and hold by argument, that it would fare better with truth, with learning, and the
Commonwealth, if one of your publisht Orders which I should
name, were call'd in, yet at the same time it could not but much
redound to the lustre of your milde and equall Government, when
as private persons are hereby animated to thinke ye better pleas'd
with publick advice, then other statists have been delighted heretofore with publicke flattery.[9] And men will then see what difference
there is between the magnanimity of a trienniall Parlament,[10] and

[8] Joseph Hall, bishop of Norwich, 1574–1656; see *Complete Prose*, I, 28–33.
Hall's *Humble Remonstrance to the High Court of Parliament* (1641) precipitated the Smectymnuan controversy, to which Milton contributed *Animadversions* (1641) and *Apology against a Pamphlet* (1642). In the latter Milton
attacks a passage in Hall's *Modest Confutation of a Slanderous and Scurrilous
Libel* (1642) as revealing royalist sympathy even while pretending to praise
the Parliament (*Complete Prose*, I, 919–20). After this analysis he writes (p.
922), "to testifie the gratitude which I owe to those publick benefactors of their
country . . . I shall be so troublesome to this declamer for once, as to shew
him what he might have better said in their praise," and then fills several pages
with the better praise. "Malignant" was a stock term by which the Parliamentary
party designated its opponents.

[9] *Cf.* Herbert Palmer, who, in urging speedier reformation in a sermon to the
House of Commons (*The Necessity and Encouragement of Utmost Venturing*,
June 21, 1643; E60[3], p. 49), said: "We have long, and too justly complained
of *Princes being flattered,* by them that least should, and how much we and
they have been *undone* by it. Let it, I beseech you, be *your glory* (and God will
make it so) that *you had rather be twice admonisht,* even without cause, then
to want it once, when there is just cause." An important difference from Milton,
however, was that a clergyman was thought to have a duty to admonish his
hearers.

[10] The Triennial Parliaments Act (February 16, 1641) provided for the auto-
matic issue of writs for a new Parliament if the king failed to summon one
within three years of the dissolution of the last. Milton seems to suggest that
Parliament, thus secured against a long intermission, has become more magnanimous than when it could meet only at the king's pleasure. He does not mention an Act of vastly greater consequence to the power of the Long Parliament:
that of May 10, 1641, providing against its dissolution except by its own consent.

that jealous hautinesse of Prelates and cabin Counsellours that usurpt of late, when as they shall observe yee in the midd'st of your Victories and successes [11] more gently brooking writt'n exceptions against a voted Order, then other Courts, which had produc't nothing worth memory but the weake ostentation of wealth, would have endur'd the least signifi'd dislike at any sudden Proclamation. If I should thus farre presume upon the meek demeanour of your civill and gentle greatnesse, Lords and Commons, as what your publisht Order hath directly said, that to gainsay, I might defend my selfe with ease, if any should accuse me of being new or insolent, did they but know how much better I find ye esteem it to imitate the old and elegant humanity of Greece, [2] then the barbarick pride of a *Hunnish* and *Norwegian* statelines. And out of those ages, to whose polite wisdom and letters we ow that we are not yet *Gothes* and *Jutlanders,* I could name him who from his private house wrote that discourse to the Parlament of *Athens,*[12] that perswades them to change the forme of *Democraty* which was then establisht. Such honour was done in those dayes to men who profest the study of wisdome and eloquence, not only in their own Country, but in other Lands, that Cities and Siniories heard them gladly, and with great respect, if they had ought in publick to admonish the State. Thus did *Dion Prusaeus* [13] a stranger and a privat Orator counsell the *Rhodians* against a former Edict: and I abound with other like examples, which to set heer would be superfluous. But if from the industry of a life wholly dedicated to studi-

[11] Milton is being tactful; "in the midd'st of your Victories and successes" would have been a much more accurate description of Parliament's situation in July than in the autumn and early winter. See above, introduction, pp. 54–55.

[12] him: Isocrates; see above, p. 486, n. 1. "The Parlament of Athens" is not a reference to the Court of the Areopagus, as is sometimes supposed (see, *e.g.,* Lockwood, p. 31, and James H. Hanford, *A Milton Handbook* [New York: F. S. Crofts, 1946], p. 101). Isocrates addressed the *ecclesia,* or popular assembly, on the *subject* of the powers of the Areopagus (Jebb, *Attic Orators,* II, 203); for Milton to term the *ecclesia* the "Parlament of Athens" seems a permissible licence.

[13] Dion Prusaeus died *ca.* A.D. 117. A Greek rhetorician of Prusa in Bithynia, he went to Egypt and then to Rome, whence he was expelled for political reasons by Domitian. On the accession of his friend Nerva he returned to Rome, and was honored by both Nerva and Trajan. His speeches are largely philosophical (advocating a modified Stoicism) and political. His "Rhodian Discourse" advises repeal of the law permitting the removal of the original names from public monuments and the substitution of new ones.

ous labours, and those naturall endowments haply not the worst for two and fifty degrees of northern latitude,[14] so much must be derogated, as to count me not equall to any of those who had this priviledge, I would obtain to be thought not so inferior, as your selves are superior to the most of them who receiv'd their counsell: and how farre you excell them, be assur'd, Lords and Commons, there can no greater testimony appear, then when your prudent spirit acknowledges and obeyes the voice of reason from what quarter soever it be heard speaking; and renders ye as willing to repeal any Act of your own setting forth, as any set forth by your Predecessors.[15]

If ye be thus resolv'd, as it were injury to thinke ye were not, I know not what should withhold me from presenting ye with a fit instance wherein to shew both that love of truth which ye eminently professe, and that uprightnesse of your judgement which is not wont to be partiall to your selves; by judging over again that Order

[14] In the suppressed digression in *History of Britain,* Book III, Milton cites the northern climate as a cause of the intellectual shortcomings of his countrymen (Columbia, X, 325; not in 1670 ed.): "For the sunn, which wee want, ripens witts as well as fruits." See also *Reason of Church-Government, Complete Prose,* I, 814; "Manso," 1.28; *Paradise Lost,* IX, 44–45. The idea is discussed in Zera S. Fink, "Milton and the Theory of Climatic Influence," *MLQ,* II (1941), 67–80.

[15] With this *exordium* and the *propositio* that follows immediately (see introduction, above, pp. 170–71), *cf.* William Walwyn's *The Compassionate Samaritane* (1644), which opens with an address "To The Commons of England" (pp. 3–5): "To you whom the People have chosen for the managing of their affaires, I present this necessary Treatise without boldnesse and without feare: For I am well assured that as it is mine & every mans duty to furnish You with what wee conceive will advance the common good, . . . so likewise it is Your duty to heare and put in execution whatsoever to your owne judgements shall appeare conducing to those good ends. . . . In the beginning of Your Session, when our Divines (as they would have us call them) wrote freely against the Bishops, and the Bishops made complaint to You for redresse; some of You made answer that there was no remedy, for as much as the Presse was to be open and free for all in time of Parliament, I shall make bold as a Common of *England* to lay claime to that priviledge, being assured that I write nothing scandalous or dangerous to the State (which is justly and upon good grounds prohebited by Your Ordinance to that effect) only I humbly desire You to consider whether more was not gained by that Ordinance then You intended, and that though it was purposed by You to restraine the venting and dispersings of the Kings writings and his Agents, yet it hath by reason of the qualifications of the *Licensers* wrot a wrong way, and stopt the mouthes of good men, who must either not write at all, or no more then is sutable to the judgements and interests of the *Licensers.*" For evidence that Milton knew this pamphlet, see introduction, above, pp. 84–87.

which ye have ordain'd [16] *to regulate Printing. That no Book, pamphlet, or paper shall be henceforth Printed, unlesse the same be first approv'd and licenc't by such,* or at least one of such as shall be thereto appointed. For that part [17] which preserves justly every mans Copy to himselfe, or provides for the poor, I touch not, only wish they be not made pretenses to abuse and persecute honest and painfull Men, who offend not in either of these particulars. But that other clause of Licencing Books,[18] which we thought had dy'd with his brother *quadragesimal* and *matrimonial* [19] when the Prelats expir'd,[20] I shall now attend with such a Homily, as shall lay before ye, first the inventors of it to bee those whom ye will be loath to own; next what is to be thought in [3] generall of reading, what ever sort the Books be; and that this Order avails nothing to the suppressing of scandalous, seditious, and libellous Books, which were mainly intended to be supprest. Last, that it will be primely to the discouragement of all learning, and the stop of Truth, not only by disexercising and blunting our abilities in what we know

---

[16] See introduction, above, pp. 162–63.

[17] See Appendix B, below, p. 798.

[18] See Appendix B, below, p. 797.

[19] "Quadragesimal" means Lenten, and the reference is to dispensations from dietary restrictions given by the bishops to individual applicants. Matrimonial licences were dispensations by the bishops from the required publication of the banns. Milton's opposition is not, of course, really to the power of exemption, but to the original power of restriction, which he thinks a tyrannical usurpation. A misleading ambiguity rises from the dominant modern meaning of "marriage licence" as a civil registration; it should therefore be recalled that Milton had, in the divorce tracts, urged such a development, and was later to welcome its first appearance enthusiastically (*Likeliest Means*, [1659], pp. 74–76): "As for marriages, that ministers should meddle with them, as not sanctifi'd or legitimat without their celebration, I finde no ground in scripture either of precept or example . . . being of it self a civil ordinance, a houshold contract, a thing indifferent and free to the whole race of mankinde, not as religious, but as men. . . . Our divines denie it to be a sacrament; yet retain the celebration, till prudently a late parlament recoverd the civil liberty of marriage from thir incroachment; and transferrd the ratifying and registring thereof from the canonical shop to the proper cognisance of civil magistrates." (The Act of 1656 here praised was repealed at the Restoration, and civil licensing was not reintroduced in England until the Marriage Act of 1753.)

[20] Presbyterianism was not established by law until January 28, 1645, and Episcopacy was not formally abolished until October 9, 1646, but the bishops may be said in effect to have "expired" on February 13, 1642, when Charles gave his consent to the Bishops Exclusion Bill. See Gardiner, *History of England*, X, 165–66.

already, but by hindring and cropping the discovery that might bee yet further made both in religious and civill Wisdome.[21]

I deny not, but that it is of greatest concernment in the Church and Commonwealth, to have a vigilant eye how Bookes demeane themselves, as well as men; and thereafter to confine, imprison, and do sharpest justice on them as malefactors: For Books are not absolutely dead things, but doe contain a potencie of life in them to be as active as that soule was whose progeny they are; nay they do preserve as in a violl the purest efficacie and extraction of that living intellect that bred them.[22] I know they are as lively, and as vigorously productive, as those fabulous Dragons teeth; and being sown up and down, may chance to spring up armed men.[23] And yet on the other hand unlesse warinesse be us'd, as good almost kill a Man as kill a good Book; who kills a Man kills a reasonable creature, Gods Image; but hee who destroyes a good Booke, kills reason it selfe, kills the Image of God, as it were in the eye. Many

[21] Cf. Henry Robinson, Liberty of Conscience (1644), p. 50: "An inquisition or persecution for matters of Religion may not be tollerated: First, because it would as much as in us lyes, still withold such saving truth and knowledge as [is] yet undiscovered, and unto which we are to attaine by degrees only, for not any of them but at first sight and hearing, is accounted heresie to most men, and much adoe there is before we will imbrace it: And secondly, in that persecution for Religion would render us altogether incapable of ever purging and reforming our selves from such erronious doctrines and superstitions, as are amongst us for the present." For evidence that Milton knew this pamphlet, see introduction, above, p. 84, and below, nn. 195, 206, 240, 265, 292, 302.

[22] Cf. Bacon's Advancement of Learning, I, viii, 6 (World's Classics, Oxford, 1929), p. 65: "The images of men's wits and knowledges remain in books. . . . Neither are they fitly to be called images, because they generate still, and cast their seeds in the minds of others, provoking and causing infinite actions and opinions in succeeding ages."

[23] See Ovid's stories of Cadmus (Metamorphoses, III, 101–30) and Jason (VII, 121–42). Milton's familiarity with Ovid contributed the image, but the association was probably suggested by the following passage in Pietro Sarpi's History of the Inquisition, tr. Robert Gentilis (1639), p. 69: "The matter of Bookes seemes to be a thing of small moment, because it treats of words, but through these words comes opinions into the world, which cause partialities, seditions, and finally warres. They are words, it is true, but such as in consequence draw after them Hosts of armed men." Milton, who refers to and copiously borrows from Sarpi's Historie of the Councel of Trent (see below, p. 500 and note 54), does not mention his Inquisition, but see below, notes 62 and 156, for further evidence that he knew it. (The English translation had been published in 1639 by Humphrey Moseley, who was to publish Milton's Poems the year after the publication of the Areopagitica.)

a man lives a burden to the Earth; but a good Booke is the pretious
life-blood of a master spirit, imbalm'd and treasur'd up on purpose
to a life beyond life. 'Tis true, no age can restore a life, whereof
perhaps there is no great losse; and revolutions of ages doe not oft
recover the losse of a rejected truth, for the want of which whole
Nations fare the worse. We should be wary therefore what persecution we raise against the living labours of publick men, how we
spill [24] that season'd life of man preserv'd and stor'd up in Books;
since we see a kinde of homicide may be thus committed, sometimes a martyrdome, and if it extend to the whole impression, a
kinde of massacre, whereof the execution ends not in the slaying
of an elementall life, but strikes at that ethereall and fift essence,[25]
the breath of reason it selfe, slaies an immortality rather then a life.
But lest I should be condemn'd of introducing licence, while I
oppose Licencing, I refuse not the paines to be so much Historicall,
as will serve to shew what hath been done by ancient and famous
Commonwealths, against this disorder, till the very time that this
project of licencing crept out of the *Inquisition*,[26] was catcht up [4]
by our Prelates, and hath caught some of our Presbyters.

[24] spill: O.E. *spillan*, to destroy. *Cf. Faerie Queene*, III, vii, 54, where the
Squire of Dames bids his lady to "commaund my life to save or spill."

[25] The first four—earth, water, air, and fire—are "elemental," *i.e.*, they are
the elements of the material world. The fifth is "ethereal"; from it are formed
the stars (*Paradise Lost*, III, 714–18):

> Swift to their several Quarters hasted then
> The cumbrous Elements, Earth, Flood, Aire, Fire,
> And this Ethereal quintessence of Heav'n
> Flew upward . . .
>   and turned to Starrs.

Hence the modern *quintessence*, the most essential part or feature of a substance or of a non-material thing.

[26] The inquiry after and the suppression of heresy by ecclesiastical and civil
authority is as old as the Christian church, but the Inquisition as a distinct ecclesiastical tribunal did not come into being until 1231, when the rescripts of the
Emperor Frederick II were adopted into ecclesiastical criminal law by Pope
Honorius III. For the next two and a half centuries its operations were much
more extensive in Germany, France, and Italy than in Spain, but Ferdinand and
Isabella encouraged its reorganization in that country, and, in 1478, Torquemada
was appointed first Grand Inquisitor. Thereafter the operations of the "Holy
Office" in Spain were sufficiently formidable—so much so, indeed, that today the
term Inquisition is more often than not used to mean the Spanish Inquisition;
Milton appears to have used it in the same way: *cf.* pp. 502 ("Spanish Inquisition"), [529] ("the model of . . . *Sevil*"), and [569] ("this *authentic* Spanish

In *Athens* where Books and Wits were ever busier then in any other part of *Greece,* I finde but only two sorts of writings which the Magistrate car'd to take notice of; those either blasphemous and Atheisticall, or Libellous. Thus the Books of *Protagoras* [27] were by the Judges of *Areopagus* [28] commanded to be burnt, and himselfe banisht the territory for a discourse begun with his confessing not to know *whether there were gods, or whether not:* And against defaming, it was decreed that none should be traduc'd by name, as was the manner of *Vetus Comœdia,*[29] whereby we may guesse how they censur'd libelling: And this course was quick enough, as *Cicero* writes,[30] to quell both the desperate wits of other Atheists, and the open way of defaming, as the event shew'd. Of other sects and opinions though tending to voluptuousnesse, and the denying of divine providence they tooke no heed. Therefore we do not read that either

policy"). The Office was suppressed by Napoleon, but revived in 1814. In Spain it was finally suppressed by the Revolution of 1868. In Rome its coercive powers ended with the entry of the Italian army in 1870, but the Office still exists and functions.

[27] *Cf.* Cicero's *On the Nature of the Gods,* I, 23; tr. C. D. Yonge (New York, 1888), p. 231: "Protagoras . . . was banished by order of the Athenians from their city and territories, and his books were publicly burned, because these words were in the beginning of his treatise concerning the Gods: 'I am unable to arrive at any knowledge whether there are, or are not, any Gods.' This treatment of him, I imagine, restrained many from professing their disbelief in a Deity." Protagoras (*ca.* 480–*ca.* 410 B.C.), the famous Sophist, was born in Abdera; a pupil of Democritus, he was influenced by Heraclitus' doctrine of the eternal flux of matter, which he adapted to knowledge. Hence his most celebrated proposition: "Man is the measure of all things: of those which are, that they are; of those which are not, that they are not." As Hales points out (p. 70), Milton "does not aim at being exhaustive, or he might have mentioned the indictments of Anaxagoras and of Aspasia for 'impiety.' "

[28] See above, p. 486, n. 1.

[29] The virulent personal lampooning which characterized the "Old Comedy" was absent from the Middle and New Comedy. Largely on the authority of Horace (*Ars Poetica,* 282 ff., esp. 306–10), it has been traditional to suppose, as Milton does, that this was due to legislation; but Gilbert Norwood (*History of Greek Comedy* [Boston, 1932], pp. 26–29), in re-examining the evidence, finds that there was only one Athenian decree restraining lampooning, that it endured only from 440 to 437 B.C. (*i.e.,* during the middle, not the final, years of the Old Comedy), that it "was an experiment that was felt to have failed," and that the changed tone of comedy after 404 B.C. was due to the change of mood that accompanied the defeat of Athens.

[30] Quoted in note 27 above. Cicero says nothing with respect to "defaming," and Milton's sentence should be interpreted: "this method restrained both atheistical writings (as Cicero said) and libellous (as the event showed)."

Epicurus,[31] or that libertine school of *Cyrene*,[32] or what the *Cynick* [33] impudence utter'd, was ever question'd by the Laws. Neither is it recorded that the writings of those old Comedians were supprest, though the acting of them were forbid; and that *Plato* commended the reading of *Aristophanes* the loosest of them all, to his royall scholler *Dionysius*,[34] is commonly known, and may be excus'd, if holy *Chrysostome*,[35] as is reported, nightly studied so much the same

[31] The disrepute into which the teaching of Epicurus fell was due partly to the slanders of his professional rivals, partly to misunderstanding of his doctrine that pleasure is the chief good. Milton shared the widespread prejudice against him, despite the spirited defense (now generally accepted) of Diogenes Laertius, who, after recording all the usual calumnies, writes (*Lives and Opinions of Eminent Philosophers*, X, 9–10 [2 vols., London: Loeb Classical Library, 1925] II, 537–39): "But these people are stark mad. For our philosopher has abundance of witnesses to attest his unsurpassed good will to all men . . . [and] the siren-charms of his doctrine. . . . His piety towards the gods and his affection for his country no words can describe." All Milton's references to Epicurus (*cf.* below, p. [517]; *Reason of Church-Government, Complete Prose*, I, 856; *Defence of Himself* (1655), p. 118; *Paradise Regained*, IV, 299) are uniformly hostile, notwithstanding the inclusion of Lucretius in the readings prescribed by *Of Education* (see above, p. 395), where the natural science of the poem, not its Epicurean philosophy, is the basis of recommendation.

[32] The followers of Aristippus (*ca.* 435–356 B.C.). Born in Cyrene, he studied in Athens under Socrates, and subsequently returned to Cyrene, where he established his school. His was a hedonism which made no distinction in kind among pleasures, only in degree and duration; virtue is a good only insofar as it is productive of pleasure. There would appear to be better ground for impeaching the Cyrenaic manners and doctrine than the Epicurean; see the life of Aristippus in Diogenes Laertius, II. *Cf. Reason of Church-Government, Complete Prose*, I, 856.

[33] The school founded by Antisthenes (*ca.* 440–*ca.* 370 B.C.) in the gymnasium Cynosarges, whence the name Cynics. Antisthenes taught the complete sufficiency of virtue and wisdom, and contempt for pleasure and ostentation. He gained fame as much for the sharpness of his rebukes as for his positive teaching. The school's reputation for "impudence" really comes from his most famous pupil, Diogenes of Sinope, *ca.* 412–323 B.C. (to be distinguished from Diogenes of Babylonia, the Stoic, to whom note 43 refers), who exaggerated both the doctrine and the bitterness of Antisthenes, and erected studied insolence into a principle of conduct. He is best known today for his tub and lamp. See Diogenes Laertius, VI, for the lives of both men.

[34] The source of this tradition appears to be the anonymous ancient *Life* of Aristophanes: "They say that when Dionysius the tyrant wished to learn about the constitution of the Athenians, Plato sent him to the poetry of Aristophanes" (sec. ix; given in the Teubner edition of Aristophanes, ed. Theodorus Bergk, Leipzig, 1852, p. 37).

[35] Chrysostom (St. John, *ca.* 347–407), bishop of Constantinople and archbishop of Antioch, one of the most influential of the Greek church Fathers, was

Author and had the art to cleanse a scurrilous vehemence into the stile of a rousing Sermon. That other leading City of *Greece, Lacedaemon,* considering that *Lycurgus* their Law-giver was so addicted to elegant learning, as to have been the first that brought out of *Ionia* the scatter'd workes of *Homer,* and sent the Poet *Thales* from *Creet* to prepare and mollifie the *Spartan* surlinesse with his smooth songs and odes, the better to plant among them law and civility,[36] it is to be wonder'd how muselesse and unbookish they were, minding nought but the feats of Warre. There needed no licencing of Books among them for they dislik'd all, but their owne *Laconick Apothegms,* and took a slight occasion to chase *Archilochus*[37] out of their City, perhaps for composing in a higher straine then their owne souldierly ballats and roundels could reach to: Or if it were for his broad verses, they were not therein so cautious, but they were as dissolute in their promiscuous conversing; whence *Euripides* affirmes in *Andromache,*[38] that their women were all unchaste. Thus much may give us light after what sort Bookes were prohibited

deprived and banished for opposing the moral "corruption," and more especially the semi-idolatry, of the Court. His use of Aristophanes was reported by Aemilius Portus in an epistle to Bisetus (quoted in *Encyclopaedia Metropolitana, History of Greek Literature*).

[36] "Thales" or Thaletas (to be distinguished from Thales of Miletus, the philosopher), probably seventh century B.C., was a poet and musician; assisted in perfecting Terpander's musical system at Sparta. Lycurgus, probably ninth century B.C., was the semi-legendary founder of the Spartan constitution. Both anecdotes are in Plutarch's *Lives* ("Lycurgus," IV; Bohn ed. [4 vols., London, 1906] I, 70); the one concerning the relation between Lycurgus and Thales is manifestly impossible because of the disparity in their dates. Milton had already used the story of Lycurgus collecting the Homeric fragments; see Prolusion VII, *Complete Prose,* I, 298.

[37] Archilochus of Paros, seventh century B.C., was a lyric and satiric poet, inventor of the iambic trimeter and trochaic tetrameter. Valerius Maximus (VI, 3) says that his poems were suppressed in Sparta because of their licentiousness; Plutarch (*Instituta Laconica,* 239B) says that the poet himself was expelled from the city because of his contention that it was better to throw away one's shield than one's life. Milton appears to have telescoped the literary and personal anecdotes into one. For an earlier reference to Archilochus, see "On the Bishop of Ely," ll. 20–22.

[38] Ll. 590–93: "No! a Spartan maid could not be chaste, e'en if she would, who leaves her home and bares her limbs and lets her robe float free, to share with youths their races and their sports,—customs I cannot away with" (tr. E. P. Coleridge). Spartan men and women publicly performed gymnastic exercises together in the nude. The practice and its real or imagined moral effects were widely discussed; Plato (*Laws,* 806ª) and Aristotle (*Politics,* II, 9) share Euripides' view; Plutarch (*Lives,* "Lycurgus," XIII–XIV) defends the practice.

among the Greeks. The Romans also for many ages train'd up
on-[5]ly to a military roughnes, resembling most the *Lacedae-
monian* guise, knew of learning little but what their twelve Tables,[39]
and the *Pontifick* College [40] with their *Augurs* [41] and *Flamins* [42]
taught them in Religion and Law, so unacquainted with other learning, that when *Carneades* and *Critolaus*, with the *Stoick Diogenes*
comming Embassadors to *Rome*, tooke thereby occasion to give the
City a tast of their Philosophy, they were suspected for seducers by
no lesse a man then *Cato* the Censor, who mov'd it in the Senat to
dismisse them speedily, and to banish all such *Attick* bablers out of
Italy.[43] But *Scipio* [44] and others of the noblest Senators withstood
him and his old *Sabin* austerity; honour'd and admir'd the men;

[39] The importance in education attributed to the twelve "tables" by Milton is
confirmed by the fact that to the end of the Republic they were memorized by
Roman schoolboys. In 451 B.C. decemvirs were commissioned to reduce the unwritten customary laws of Rome into a regular legal code. They formulated ten
"tables," which, in the following year, were supplemented by two more. These
Twelve Tables, engraved in bronze, became the basis of the whole sytem of
Roman jurisprudence.

[40] Besides ordering all matters connected with religious ceremonial, the pontific
college, which was the supreme ecclesiastical authority of ancient Rome, possessed (or at least could legally claim) a monopoly of certain kinds of knowledge,
especially those concerned with number and measure; hence it was entrusted
with the management of the intricate Roman calendar, and dominated all public
engineering projects. Its institution is attributed to Numa. The tempting etymology of the name, from the office of erecting or demolishing the sacred and
politically important bridge (*pons*) over the Tiber, has long been in dispute.

[41] The Roman priestly college whose function it was to take and declare the
auspices, *i.e.*, to determine from the actions of birds (and later by supplementary
means) whether any given public project had the approval of the gods; *cf.* below,
p. 558, n. 256.

[42] Pre-eminently the priests of the sacrificial fires. There were fifteen of them,
each in the service of a particular god, and each performing sacrifice daily. *Cf.*
"Nativity Ode," l. 94.

[43] The incident took place in 155 B.C. Athens, having sacked Oropus, was
sentenced by the Roman senate to pay a heavy fine; this embassy was to ask its
remission. The action of Cato, here ridiculed by Milton, has often been defended.
Carneades was at least injudicious in his illustration of Sceptic dialectics: he
delivered two public lectures on justice, the first of which upheld its reality,
while the second demolished all the former arguments (Cicero, *De Re Publica*,
III, 6). Carneades (*ca.* 213–129 B.C.) was born at Cyrene, came to Athens,
studied especially the Stoics. He established the Third, or New (Sceptic),
Academy. Critolaus (*ca.* 192–*ca.* 110 B.C.) was head of the Peripatetic School
about the middle of the century. Diogenes of Babylonia, the Stoic (to be distinguished from Diogenes of Sinope, the Cynic, to whom note 33 refers), fl. in
the second century B.C. He was head of the Stoic School about the middle of the

and the Censor himself at last in his old age fell to the study of that whereof before hee was so scrupulous.[45] And yet at the same time *Naevius* and *Plautus* the first Latine comedians had fill'd the City with all the borrow'd Scenes of *Menander* and *Philemon*.[46] Then began to be consider'd there also what was to be don to libellous books and Authors; for *Naevius* was quickly cast into prison for his unbridl'd pen, and releas'd by the *Tribunes* upon his recantation: We read also that libels were burnt, and the makers punisht by *Augustus*.[47] The like severity no doubt was us'd if ought were impiously writt'n against their esteemed gods. Except in these two points, how the world went in Books, the Magistrat kept no reckning. And therefore *Lucretius* [48] without impeachment versifies his Epicurism to *Memmius*, and had the honour to be set forth the second time by *Cicero* so great a father of the Commonwealth; although himselfe disputes against that opinion in his own writings.[49] Nor was the Satyricall sharpnesse, or naked plainnes of *Lucilius*,

century. Cato the Censor (Marcus Porcius, 234–149 B.C.), after a distinguished military career, became censor of Rome in 184, administering his office with great rigor in opposition to all innovation, especially Greek influence. "Sabin austerity": although born in Tusculum, Cato was brought up on his father's farm in the Sabine territory, and thither he periodically returned throughout his life.

[44] Cicero consistently represents Scipio the Younger (185–129 B.C.) as a friend of Cato, but Diogenes Laertius (*Lives*, "Cato," *passim*) makes it clear that they were at least unfriendly rivals, if not outright enemies. Scipio was a leading Roman patron of Greek culture.

[45] The anecdote, reported in Cicero's *De Senectute*, VIII, 26, and Cornelius Nepos' *Life of Cato*, III, was often repeated.

[46] Naevius (*ca.* 264–*ca.* 202 B.C.), a Roman epic and dramatic poet, was imprisoned for satirizing Scipio and the Metelli in several of his comedies. Released by the Tribunes after recanting, he soon offended again, and was exiled. Plautus (*ca.* 254–184 B.C.) was the most popular comic dramatist of Rome. Menander (342–291 B.C.) was the chief dramatist of the Athenian "New Comedy." Philemon (*ca.* 361–263 B.C.) was another very popular dramatist of the New Comedy. Milton's "at the same time" needs to be taken in conjunction with the pluperfect "had filled"; at the time of this embassy (see note 43) some eighty years had passed since the performance of Naevius' first comedy, seventy since Plautus' first.

[47] See Tacitus, *Annals*, I, 72. In fact there had been a law of libel since 450 B.C. (in the Eighth Table), reinforced by a statute of 302 B.C.; see Horace, *Epistles*, II, i, 152–54.

[48] The *De Rerum Natura* of Lucretius (*ca.* 98–55 B.C.) expounds the doctrine of Epicurus (see above, p. 495, n. 31). Memmius was praetor in 58 B.C.

[49] The story that Cicero edited the *De Rerum Natura* is in Jerome's additions to the chronicle of Eusebius, although he appears to mean that this was the poem's first appearance, rather than, as Milton says, "the second time." Cicero

or *Catullus,* or *Flaccus,*[50] by any order prohibited. And for matters of State, the story of *Titus Livius,*[51] though it extoll'd that part which *Pompey* held, was not therefore supprest by *Octavius Caesar* of the other Faction. But that *Naso* [52] was by him banisht in his old age, for the wanton Poems of his youth, was but a meer covert of State over some secret cause: and besides, the Books were neither banisht nor call'd in. From hence we shall meet with little else but

attacks Epicureanism in *De Natura Deorum,* I and II, *De Finibus,* I and II, and *Tusculan Disputations,* II and III; the weight of these attacks, when measured against the slightness of Jerome's authority in this matter, has caused many scholars to doubt that Cicero edited Lucretius' poem, but Lucretius' editor, H. A. J. Munro, argues in favor of the tradition, largely on the ground that "Jerome's additions to the chronicle are servilely copied from the lost work of Suetonius de viris illustribus," to which high authority attaches (*Lucretius,* Cambridge, 1873, pp. 297–301).

[50] Lucilius (*ca.* 148–103 B.C.) was the founder of a very strong tradition of poetical satire; Horace's *Satires,* I, iv, is partly, and I, x, wholly, devoted to a discussion of his work. Catullus (87–*ca.* 54 B.C.) lampooned, among others, Julius Caesar. Quintius Horatius Flaccus is the full name of Horace (65–8 B.C.).

[51] The portion of Livy's *History* treating the war between Augustus and Pompey (books 109–16) has not survived, except in very brief summary. Milton's source is Tacitus' account of the defense of Cremutius Cordus, a chronicler living in the reign of Tiberius, against the charge of *lèse-majesté* in that he published praises of Brutus and Cassius. Cordus cited Livy as one of the examples of historians who reported with impunity truths unpalatable to rulers. The passage in Tacitus is of considerable interest. Ben Jonson had already translated it into English verse to form a scene in his *Sejanus* (III, i, 375–470), and Tacitus' own comment is germane enough to the *Areopagitica* to warrant quoting (*Annals,* IV, 35, tr. Arthur Murphy; *The Historical Works* [2 vols., Everyman, London: 1943], I, 207): "The fathers ordered his book to be burned by the aediles; but to destroy it was not in their power. It was preserved in secret, and copies have been multiplied: so vain and senseless is the attempt, by an arbitrary act, to extinguish the light of truth, and defraud posterity of due information. Genius thrives under oppression: persecute the author, and you enhance the value of his work." Milton quotes part of this below; see p. 542, n. 193.

[52] Publius Ovidius Naso is the full name of Ovid (43 B.C. to A.D. 18). No more is known now than in Milton's day of the real cause of Ovid's exile; most scholars share Milton's view that the alleged immorality of the *Ars Amatoria* was only a pretext to cover a court scandal, and point out that Augustus' granddaughter Julia was banished about the same time. To speak of the poems as belonging to Ovid's youth, and the banishment as taking place in his old age, is an exaggeration: Ovid was forty-three when he was banished; the *Ars Amatoria* was published a decade earlier. Milton is right in saying that his books were not suppressed, but the *Ars Amatoria* was ordered withdrawn from the public libraries. Recently, however, there has been some disposition to think the poem "the true as well as the official cause," as L. P. Wilkinson argues; see *Ovid Recalled* (Cambridge: Cambridge University Press, 1955), p. 298.

tyranny in the Roman Empire, that we may not marvell, if not so often bad, as good Books were silenc't. I shall therefore deem to have bin large anough in producing what among the ancients was punishable to write, save only which, all other arguments were free to treat on.

By this time [53] the Emperors were become Christians, whose discipline in this point I doe not finde to have bin more severe then what [6] was formerly in practice.[54] The Books of those whom they

[53] Constantine, the first emperor publicly professing Christianity, reigned A.D. 306–337.

[54] From this point to note 63 Milton draws so heavily upon Sarpi's *Historie of the Councel of Trent* (see notes 58, 59, 81, 88, and 109) that, despite its length, the relevant passage must be quoted (tr. Nathaniel Brent, 1620, pp. 472–73): "In the Church of Martyrs there was no Ecclesiasticall prohibition, though some godly men made conscience of reading bad bookes. . . . [For parts of the deleted passages, see notes 81, 88, and 109.] About the yeere 400. a Councell in *Carthage* did forbid to reade the bookes of the Gentiles, but allowed them to reade the bookes of the heretiques; the Decree whereof is amongst the Canons, collected by *Gratian*. And this was the first prohibition by way of Canon. . . . The bookes of heretiques, containing doctrine condemned by Councels, were often forbid by the Emperours for good governement. . . . It suffised the Councels and Bishops to shew what bookes did containe damned or apocryphall doctrine. So did *Gelasius* in the yeere 494. and went no further, leaving it to the conscience of every one to avoide them, or reade them to a good end. After the yeere 800. the Popes of *Rome*, as they assumed a great part of the politique governement, so they caused the bookes, whose authors they did condemne, to bee burned, and forbad the reading of them. Notwithstanding one shall finde but few bookes forbid in that sort, untill this age. A generall prohibition of reading bookes containing doctrine of heretiques, or suspected of heresies, upon paine of excommunication, without any further sentence, was not used. *Martinus* 5. doth in a Bull excommunicate all the Sects of heretiques, especially *Wiglefists*, and *Hussites*, not mentioning those who read their bookes, though many of them went about. *Leo* the tenth condemning *Luther*, did withall forbid all his bookes, upon paine of excommunication. The Popes following, in the Bull called *In Coena*, having condemned and excommunicated all heretiques, did excommunicate those also who reade their bookes. . . . The *Inquisitors*, being more diligent, made Catalogues of those which they knew. . . . *Philip*, King of *Spaine*, who was the first that gave a more convenient forme, in the yeere 1558, making a Law that the Catalogue of bookes prohibited by *Inquisition* should be printed. According to this example *Paul* 4. also ordayned, that an *Index* should be composed by that office, and printed; and so it was in the yeere 1559. in which they did proceed many steps further then formerly they had done. . . . Untill that time they contayned themselves within the tearmes of the bookes of the heretiques" [but, Sarpi continues, after 1559 the Index was extended to include books which were entirely irrelevant to doctrine]. Milton noted Sarpi's account in *CPB* (*Complete Prose*, I, 451), and made twelve other entries from *The Historie of Trent*; see *Complete Prose*, I, 396.

took to be grand Hereticks were examin'd, refuted, and condemn'd in the generall Councels; [55] and not till then were prohibited, or burnt by autority of the Emperor. As for the writings of Heathen authors, unlesse they were plaine invectives against Christianity, as those of *Porphyrius* and *Proclus*,[56] they met with no interdict that can be cited, till about the year 400. in a *Carthaginian* Councel,[57] wherein Bishops themselves were forbid to read the Books of Gentiles, but Heresies they might read: while others long before them on the contrary scrupl'd more the Books of Hereticks, then of Gentiles. And that the primitive Councels and Bishops were wont only to declare what Books were not commendable, passing no furder, but leaving it to each ones conscience to read or to lay by, till after the yeare 800. is observ'd already by *Padre Paolo* [58] the great unmasker of the *Trentine* Councel. After which time the Popes of *Rome* engrossing what they pleas'd of Politicall rule into their owne hands, extended their dominion over mens eyes, as they

[55] As distinguished from local or regional synods. The first general or oecumenical council was convoked by Constantine in Nicaea, Bithynia, in 325, to consider the problem of Arianism; it formulated the Nicene Creed.

[56] Porphyrius, 233–305. Originally a pupil of Origen, he turned against Christianity after coming under the influence of Plotinus and wrote a treatise entitled *Against the Christians*. His works were burned by Constantine; the date is not clear, but Constantine refers to it in the past tense in a letter of 325 (Socrates, *Ecclesiastical History*, I, ix; Bohn ed., London, 1853, p. 31). Proclus, 412–85. A Neoplatonist, he was a declared and persistent enemy of Christianity. I have been unable to find any record of his writings being suppressed, except as they were covered by the edict, forty-four years after his death, in which Justinian suppressed the Athenian philosophical schools (Gibbon, *Decline and Fall*, chapter 40; Bohn variorum ed. [7 vols., London: 1867], IV, 354–55).

[57] Without citing his source, Jebb (p. 74) gives 412 as the date of this council. Hales (p. 81), citing Hallam's *Middle Ages*, calls this the "fourth Council of Carthage" and dates it 398; Hughes (1947, p. 213) gives the same title and date. Carthaginian councils were at this period so frequent (they had become almost annual affairs), and the records have suffered so severely, that many conciliar enactments cannot be accurately dated. There does not appear to have been a general council at Carthage during either 398 or 412. The regulation may belong to one of the two councils of 397, to that of 401, or possibly to 403 (*Catholic Encyclopedia*), but the effort to determine which council Milton had in mind is a fallacious approach: he was merely quoting Sarpi (see above, p. 500, n. 54).

[58] Paolo Servita was the religious name of Pietro Sarpi (1552–1623), one of the leaders of Venice in its fight to abolish papal secular supremacy. His most important works were the *Historie of the Councel of Trent* (see above, note 54) and the *History of the Inquisition* (see above, note 23). See *Complete Prose*. I, 396.

had before over their judgements, burning and prohibiting to be read, what they fansied not; yet sparing in their censures, and the Books not many which they so dealt with: till *Martin* the 5.[59] by his Bull not only prohibited, but was the first that excommunicated the reading of hereticall Books; for about that time *Wicklef* and *Husse* growing terrible, were they who first drove the Papall Court to a stricter policy of prohibiting. Which cours *Leo* the 10,[60] and his successors follow'd, untill the Councell of Trent,[61] and the Spanish

[59] Martin V (Otto Colonna, 1368–1431) was pope from 1417. John Wyclif (*ca*. 1324–1384) and John Huss (*ca*. 1373–1415) were the great English and Bohemian precursors of the Protestant Reformation. Milton's silent contradiction of Sarpi here (see above, note 54) is very suggestive. The matter is somewhat involved. Martin's bull of 1418 (*Inter cunctas*) was apparently published in two forms: section 16 instructs archbishops, bishops, etc., to publish it "omitting the articles and interrogatories herein contained" (*Magnum Bullarium Romanorum*, Taurinensio ed. [25 vols., 1859], IV, 675). If Sarpi saw the bull only in the abridged form, it was very natural that he should have reported that it took no action against those who merely read, without approving, Wyclifite and Hussite books. John Foxe, however, had seen the complete bull in "a certain old monument remaining in the hands of Master Hackluyt, Student in the Temple" (*Acts and Monuments*, 3 vols., 1641, I, 857). Having in an earlier context already reported the "Articles of John Wickliff to be enquired upon," he omitted these; otherwise he published the bull entire. The "interrogatories" are twenty-eight questions to be put to such as are suspected of sympathy with the ideas of Wyclif and Huss. The ninth and tenth are as follows: "9. Item, whether he have in his custodie any treatises, smal workes, epistles, or other writings in what language or tongue soever, set forth and translated by any of these heretikes, John Wickliffe, John Hus, and Jerome, or any other of their false disciples and followers, that he may deliver them to the ordinaries of that place, or his commissary, or to the inquisitors upon his oath. . . . 10. Item, whether he knoweth any that hath [such] treatises, [etc.] . . . and that he detect and manifest the same, for the purgation of their faith and execution of justice" (p. 855). The general tone of the bull (not only those who are, but even those who are only "suspected to be beleevers, followers, fautors, defenders, or receivers" of Wyclifite or Hussite ideas are "to be excommunicate every Sunday and festivall day, in the presence of the people" [p. 856]) leaves little doubt that, whether any may have escaped who readily confessed under question nine, Martin intended that those who waited to be accused under question ten should be excommunicated. For a discussion of the light thrown on Milton's critical methods by this and other changes from Sarpi's account, see Ernest Sirluck, "Milton's Critical Use of Historical Sources," *Modern Philology*, L (1953), 226–31.

[60] Leo X (Giovanni dei Medici, 1475–1521) was pope from 1513. His bull of May 3, 1515, extended censorship to all writings.

[61] The nineteenth oecumenical council, which, with several intermissions, met at Trent from December 13, 1545, to December 4, 1563, was one of the most important in history. Its primary object was a determination of doctrine to meet the challenge of Protestantism; a secondary object was reformation of ecclesi-

Inquisition engendring together brought forth, or perfeted those Catalogues, and expurging Indexes that rake through the entralls of many an old good Author, with a violation wors then any could be offer'd to his tomb.[62] Nor did they stay in matters Hereticall, but any subject that was not to their palat, they either condemn'd in a prohibition, or had it strait into the new Purgatory of an Index. To fill up the measure of encroachment, their last invention was to ordain that no Book, pamphlet, or paper should be Printed (as if S. *Peter* had bequeath'd them the keys of the Presse also out of Paradise) unlesse it were approv'd and licenc't under the hands of 2 or 3 glutton Friers.[63] For example:

> Let the Chancellor *Cini* be pleas'd to see if in this present work
> be contain'd ought that may withstand the Printing,
>
> $\qquad\qquad$ *Vincent Rabatta* Vicar of *Florence.* [7]

> I have seen this present work, and finde nothing athwart the
> Catholick faith and good manners: In witnesse whereof I have
> given, &c.
>
> $\qquad\qquad$ *Nicolò Cini* Chancellor of *Florence.*

astical organization and practices. Its basic decree was that in matters of faith and morals the tradition of the church is, together with the Bible, the standard of supernatural revelation; immensely important derivative decrees fixed the dogmas of justification and of the sacraments. Among the decrees of practice were two (February 25, 1562, and December 3, 1563) concerning the cataloguing of prohibited books. The Inquisition (see above, p. 493, n. 26) was reorganized by Paul III in a bull of July 21, 1542, and was charged with the supervision of books; all publication was forbidden without prior licence from the Inquisition. In 1559, during the sittings and with the advice of the Council of Trent, Paul IV issued the first *Index of Prohibited Books,* together with the *Index of Expurgations* from books otherwise permitted to be read. There had been many catalogues of forbidden books since that issued in 405 by Innocent I; what was new in the *Index* (aside from the name and form) was that, in consequence of the bull of 1515 (see above, note 60), it was universally applicable. The Index has since been frequently revised and constantly enforced.

[62] The anatomical image may have been suggested by a passage in Sarpi's *Inquisition* (tr. Gentilis, 1639, p. 71), in which he returned to the subject already discussed in his *Trent:* "They have gelded the bookes of ancient Authors by new printing of them, and taken out all which might serve for Temporall authority." *Cf.* above, p. 492, n. 23.

[63] With this point Milton diverges from Sarpi. Sarpi altogether approves of licensing; his point is that the licensing power ought to belong to the church only in matters of religion, and that in secular affairs it properly belongs to the state, from which the church has usurped it. Milton's point is that licensing is in itself wrong. (Of course this does not mean that he would do away with all control over the press; see introduction, above, pp. 163–64.)

Attending the precedent relation, it is allow'd that this present
work of *Davanzati* [64] may be Printed,

Vincent Rabatta, &c.

It may be Printed, *July* 15.
Friar *Simon Mompei* d'*Amelia* Chancellor of the holy office
in *Florence.*

Sure they have a conceit, if he of the bottomlesse pit had not long
since broke prison, that this quadruple exorcism would barre him
down. I feare their next designe will be to get into their custody the
licencing of that which they say * *Claudius* intended, but went not
through with. Voutsafe to see another of their forms the Roman
stamp:

Imprimatur, If it seem good to the reverend Master of the holy
Palace,

Belcastro Vicegerent.

Imprimatur

Friar *Nicolò Rodolphi* Master of the holy Palace.

Sometimes 5 *Imprimaturs* are seen together dialogue-wise in the
Piatza of one Title page, complementing and ducking each to other
with their shav'n reverences,[65] whether the Author, who stands by
in perplexity at the foot of his Epistle, shall to the Presse or to the
spunge. These are the prety responsories, these are the deare An-
tiphonies that so bewitcht of late our Prelats, and their Chaplaines
with the goodly Eccho they made; and besotted us to the gay imitation of a lordly *Imprimatur,* one from Lambeth house, another
from the West end of *Pauls;* [66] so apishly Romanizing, that the word

---

* *Quo veniam daret flatum crepitumque ventris in convivio emittendi. Sueton.
in Claudio.* (M)

[64] Bernardo Davanzati Bostichi (1529–1606), Florentine scholar and historian; the passages in the text are Milton's translations of the permissions on
the flyleaf of his *Scisma d'Inghilterra,* posthumously published in Florence, 1638.
Hales (p. 84) points out the possibility that the book appeared while Milton was
in Florence. For Milton's further use of this book, see below, p. 518, n. 118.

[65] An allusion to the tonsure; the licensers appointed by the Inquisition were
usually Dominicans.

[66] Lambeth House (now called Lambeth Palace) is the London residence of
the Archbishop of Canterbury. The palace of the Bishop of London used to be
in the precincts of St. Paul's Cathedral. *A Decree of Starre-Chamber, Concerning Printing* (1637), after reserving certain classes of books to the licensing of
the senior legal authorities, the universities, the secretaries of state, and the Earl

of command still was set downe in Latine; as if the learned Grammaticall pen that wrote it, would cast no ink without Latine: or perhaps, as they thought, because no vulgar tongue was worthy to expresse the pure conceit of an *Imprimatur;* but rather, as I hope, for that our English, the language of men ever famous, and formost in the atchievements of liberty, will not easily finde servile letters anow to spell such a dictatorie presumption English. And thus ye have the Inventors and the originall of Book-licencing ript up, and drawn as lineally as any pedigree. We have it not, that can be heard of, from any [8] ancient State, or politie, or Church, nor by any Statute [67] left us by our Ancestors elder or later; nor from the moderne custom of any reformed Citty, or Church abroad; but from the most Antichristian Councel, and the most tyrannous Inquisition that ever inquir'd. Till then Books were ever as freely admitted into the World as any other birth; the issue of the brain was no more stifl'd then the issue of the womb: no envious *Juno* sate cros-leg'd [68] over the nativity of any mans intellectuall off spring; but if it prov'd a Monster, who denies, but that it was justly burnt, or sunk into the Sea. But that a Book in wors condition then a peccant soul, should be to stand before a Jury ere it be borne to the World, and undergo yet in darknesse the judgement of *Radamanth* and his Collegues,

Marshal, provided (517 k 3, sig. B3v) that "All other Books, whether of Divinitie, Phisicke, Philosophie, Poetry, or whatsoever, shall be allowed by the Lord Arch-Bishop of *Canterbury,* or Bishop of *London* for the time being, or by their appointment." (See introduction, above, pp. 159–60.)

[67] Milton is distinguishing between "statute" and "decree." Selden, during the Parliament of 1628, said (Rushworth, *Collections,* 1721, I, 655), "There is no Law to prevent the printing of any Books in England, only a Decree in Star-Chamber."

[68] Milton does not mean that Juno performed in person this traditional charm to prevent or retard childbirth, but that she caused Ilythia, the goddess of delivery, to do so. On the day that Juno's current rival for Jove's attentions, Alcmena, was due to be delivered of Hercules, Ilythia, according to Ovid (*Metamorphoses,* IX, especially 281–323; tr. F. J. Miller [2 vols., London: Loeb Classical Library, 1928], II, 23–25), "sat upon the altar before the door, listening to my groans, with her right knee crossed over her left, and with her fingers interlocked; and so she stayed the birth" for seven days. Clement Walker had, in the previous year, made a curiously similar application of the story in *An Answer to Col: Nathaniel Fiennes* (September 23, 1643; E67[36], sig. A2): "when this Pamphlet was ready for the Presse, I found the Presse obstructed, whereby I was inforced to keep it in a moneth before I could be delivered of this Birth, some malicious *Juno* sitting crosse legged at the labour." There is nothing to indicate whether Milton knew this pamphlet.

ere it can passe the ferry backward into light,[69] was never heard before, till that mysterious iniquity [70] provokt and troubl'd at the first
entrance of Reformation, sought out new limbo's [71] and new hells
wherein they might include our Books also within the number of
their damned.[72] And this was the rare morsell so officiously snatcht

[69] Rhadamanthus, Minos, and Aeacus were the judges of Hades. Antique literature contains many accounts of the souls of the dead pressing to get into
Charon's boat, to be ferried across the Acheron into Hades proper. Virgil's account (*Aeneid,* VI, 295–330) contains an image that is echoed in *Paradise Lost,*
I, 301–302: the spirits are "Countless as forest leaves that fluttering fall / In
the first chill of autumn" (*Poems,* tr. James Rhoades, World's Classics ed. [Ox-
ford, 1929] p. 134). "Backward into light" is a reversal emphasizing the absurdity of being judged before birth. For the ordinary progression, *cf. Richard
III,* I, iv, 45–47: "I pass'd (methought) the melancholy flood, / With that sour
ferryman which poets write of, / Unto the kingdom of perpetual night."

[70] *Cf.* Revelation 17:1–5: "The great whore that sitteth upon many waters:
With whom the kings of the earth have committed fornication. . . . And upon
her forehead was a name written, Mystery, Babylon the Great, the mother of
harlots and abominations of the earth." The Reformation treated Babylon as the
"type" of Rome; Milton's phrase is a reference to the papacy.

[71] "Limbo" does not here possess the slightly comic quality which it acquires
when used for Fool's Paradise (*cf. Paradise Lost,* III, 440–97); it means a
genuinely infernal region (Hales [p. 87] cites *Faerie Queene,* I, ii, 32: "What
voice of *damned* ghost from limbo lake?"). The meaning of the passage has been
perplexed by unnecessarily ingenious interpretation; it would appear to be, quite
simply, that since hell proper was made for the accommodation of damned *souls,*
the papacy was, as it were, obliged to extend the borders (*limbus:* a border) of
hell to accommodate the *books* it proposed to damn. Five months before
Areopagitica, a royalist verse satire entitled *Sampsons Foxes Agreed to Fire a
Kingdom,* arguing that Puritans were really just like Jesuits, said (Oxford, June
22, 1644; E52[6], p. 5):

> *Limbus* and Purgatorie they believe,
> For lesser sinners, that is, I conceive,
> Malignants onelie; you this trick does please,
> For the same cause y' have made new *Limbus's,*
> Where we may lie imprison'd long, ere we
> A day of judgment in your Court shall see.

[72] Hezekiah Woodward, whose name was bracketed with Milton's in a complaint about unlicensed books which the Stationers made to the House of Lords,
and in the order the Lords issued thereupon (see introduction, above, p. 114),
published, about a month after *Areopagitica,* a pamphlet entitled *Inquiries into
the Causes of our Miseries* (December 23, 1644). Among other indications that
it was influenced by *Areopagitica* is the following (E22[1], p. 1): "Touching my
licence here, I have no *Imprimatur,* no licence to speak. To which I could answer,
Yes, that I have, for by the grace of God, *Truth,* and *Reason,* the old Licensers
of old, have licenced my words all along. And truly my spirit could never go forth
with any other way of licensing, or *midwifring* such births as are books into the
world . . . And if he be *Libellous,* as too many are, let his own place the pillory
instruct him to better manners. But if he has blasphemed *God,* or the *King of*

up, and so ilfavourdly imitated by our inquisiturient Bishops, and
the attendant minorites their Chaplains.[73] That ye like not now
these most certain Authors of this licencing order, and that all
sinister intention was farre distant from your thoughts, when ye
were importun'd the passing it, all men who know the integrity of
your actions, and how ye honour Truth, will clear yee readily.

But some will say, What though the Inventors were bad, the
thing for all that may be good? It may so; yet if that thing be no
such deep invention, but obvious, and easie for any man to light on,
and yet best and wisest Commonwealths through all ages, and occasions have forborne to use it, and falsest seducers, and oppressors
of men were the first who tooke it up, and to no other purpose but
to obstruct and hinder the first approach of Reformation; I am of
those who beleeve, it will be a harder alchymy then *Lullius* [74] ever
knew, to sublimat any good use out of such an invention. Yet this
only is what I request to gain from this reason, that it may be held
a dangerous and suspicious fruit, as certainly it deserves, for the
tree that bore it, untill I can dissect one by one the properties it
has. But I have first to finish, as was propounded, what is to be
thought in generall of reading Books, what ever sort they be, and
whether be more the benefit, or the harm that thence proceeds?

Not to insist upon the examples of *Moses, Daniel & Paul,* who
were [9] skilfull in all the learning of the Ægyptians, Caldeans,

Saints, let him find neither friend nor enemy, but let him dye, if he has
blasphemed his God. Gods Law this, and mans Law that, carried all along
through a series of time, and never interrupted, nor reversed, or made null till
it came thorough the Inquisition Court at Rome, whence we have our *Imprimatur,* Let this be printed. And then sure enough it served to promote the
Doctrines, and practices of the Church there, which my soul abominates." Woodward appears to have been the first of several tolerationists to adopt Milton's
genealogy of licensing (see introduction, above, pp. 87, 89, 91).

[73] The name Friars Minor was adopted to represent the humility enjoined
upon his order by Francis ("Let no one be called prior, but let all be called
lesser brethren"). It was an especial reproach of the Reformation that the order
proclaimed humility and practised arrogance; the Puritans thought that the
office and conduct of the chaplains of English bishops opened them to the same
charge.

[74] Raymond Lully (*ca.* 1234–1315) was an Italian born at Majorca. The
memory of his death (he was stoned by the Moslems of Mauretania, whom he
was attempting to convert to Christianity) was soon overwhelmed by the fame
of his writings on chemistry, medicine, and logic, and he became a kind of patron
saint of alchemists.

and Greeks,[75] which could not probably be without reading their
Books of all sorts, in *Paul* especially, who thought it no defilement
to insert into holy Scripture the sentences of three Greek Poets,[76]
and one of them a Tragedian, the question was, notwithstanding,
sometimes controverted among the Primitive Doctors, but with
great odds on that side which affirm'd it both lawfull and profitable,
as was then evidently perceiv'd, when *Julian* the Apostat, and sut-
tlest enemy to our faith, made a decree forbidding Christians the
study of heathen learning: for, said he, they wound us with our
own weapons, and with our owne arts and sciences they overcome
us.[77] And indeed the Christians were put so to their shifts by this

<hr/>

[75] Acts 7:22: "And Moses was learned in all the widom of the Egyptians, and
was mighty in words and in deeds." Daniel 1:17: "As for these four children,
God gave them knowledge and skill in all learning and wisdom: and Daniel had
understanding in all visions and dreams." Basil uses the examples of Moses and
Daniel to the same purpose, and in approximately this language, in "The Right
Use of Greek Literature" (F. M. Padelford, tr., *Essays by Plutarch and Basil*,
New York, 1902, p. 104); since Milton refers to this essay elsewhere in the
Areopagitica (see below, p. 510, n. 84), it is probable that it was his source
here. Paul's education was predominantly Hebrew (Acts 22:3: "I am verily a
man which am a Jew, born in Tarsus, a city in Cilicia, yet brought up in this
city [Jerusalem] at the feet of Gamaliel, and taught according to the perfect
manner of the law of the fathers"), but he made effective use of what knowledge
he had of Greek literature; for example, when preaching to the Athenians he
sought to make them more receptive to his doctrine by representing it as in part
their own (Acts 17:28): "For in him we live, and move, and have our being; as
certain also of your own poets have said, For we are also his offspring."

[76] The sentences (*sententiae*) are the one which closes the preceding note,
from Aratus; Titus 1:12, from Epimenedes; and I Corinthians 15:33, from
Euripides ("one of them a tragedian"; *cf.* Milton's preface to *Samson Agonistes*).
Milton's source was Socrates' *Ecclesiastical History*, III, 16, where he shows that
Paul was quoting from the Greek poets, and uses this as evidence that it is
proper for Christians to read pagan books. Milton had noted this passage in
CPB, probably 1635–1637; see *Complete Prose*, I, 376–77; for evidence that
Milton had Socrates before him as he wrote this paragraph, see below, note 79.

[77] Julian the Apostate (Flavius Claudius Julianus, 331–63), emperor of Rome
from 361. The nephew of Constantine, he was originally a Christian; subsequently he became a convert to the old Roman gods, and, as Emperor, made
some efforts to return Rome to its earlier religion. The story of the decree is in
Socrates (III, 12), but with a different version of Julian's comment; Milton's
source just here was a passage (noted in *CPB* probably 1635–1637; see *Complete
Prose*, I, 377), in Theodoret, *History of the Church*, III, 8 (Bohn, London,
1854, p. 135): Julian "prohibited the . . . Christians from being instructed in
poetry, rhetoric, or philosophy. 'For we,' said he, 'are, according to the old
proverb, smitten by our own wings; for our authors furnish weapons to carry

crafty means, and so much in danger to decline into all ignorance, that the two *Apollinarii* were fain as a man may say, to coin all the seven liberall Sciences [78] out of the Bible, reducing it into divers forms of Orations, Poems, Dialogues, ev'n to the calculating of a new Christian Grammar. But saith the Historian *Socrates*,[79] The providence of God provided better then the industry of *Apollinarius* and his son, by taking away that illiterat law with the life of him who devis'd it. So great an injury they then held it to be depriv'd of *Hellenick* learning; and thought it a persecution more undermining, and secretly decaying the Church, then the open cruelty of *Decius* or *Dioclesian*.[80] And perhaps it was the same politick drift that the

on war against us.' " There is some confusion here. Julian's decree forbade the election of Christians as teachers, but it was constantly represented by Christians as forbidding their children to be taught the arts. Gibbon, in a footnote, explains this disparity convincingly (*Decline and Fall,* chap. 23; Bohn, II, 541–42): "The Christians were *directly* forbidden to teach; they were indirectly forbidden to learn, since they would not frequent the schools of the Pagans."

[78] The seven liberal "sciences" were the *trivium* (grammar, logic, and rhetoric) and the *quadrivium* (arithmetic, geometry, astronomy, and music).

[79] Socrates Scholasticus (*ca.* 385–*ca.* 440), the great church historian, whose *Ecclesiastical History,* together with that of Eusebius (of which it is a continuation; see below, p. 511, n. 87) is still the primary source of information on the primitive church; see *Complete Prose,* I, 376–77, note 1. Milton is paraphrasing a passage in Book III, Chapter 16 (Bohn, London, 1853, pp. 191–92): "The imperial law which forbade Christians to study Grecian literature, rendered the two Appolinares . . . much more distinguished than before. For both being skilled in polite learning, the father as a grammarian, and the son as a rhetorician, they each became exceedingly serviceable to the Christians at this crisis. For the former, according to his art, composed a grammar consistent with the Christian faith: he also translated the books of Moses into heroic verse; and paraphrased all the historical books of the Old Testament, putting them partly into dactylic measure, and partly reducing them to the form of dramatic tragedy. He purposely employed all kinds of verse, that no form of expression peculiar to the Greek language might be unknown or unheard of amongst Christians. The younger Appolinaris, who was well trained in eloquence, expounded the Gospels and apostolic doctrines in the way of dialogue, following Plato among the Greeks as his model. By this joint service to the Christian cause, they baffled the emperor's subtlety. But Divine Providence was more potent than either of their labours, or the craft they had to contend with: for death in carrying off its framer . . . rendered the law wholly inoperative." Julian's successor, Jovian, who was a Christian, emancipated the Christians from all legal disabilities.

[80] Decius Trajanus (201–251), emperor of Rome from 249. In his effort to restore the ancient religion of Rome, he instituted a systematic persecution of Christianity. Diocletian (245–313), emperor from 284 to his abdication in 305. He returned to the anti-Christian policy of Decius.

Divell whipt St. *Jerom* [81] in a lenten dream, for reading *Cicero;*
or else it was a fantasm bred by the feaver which had then seis'd
him. For had an Angel bin his discipliner, unlesse it were for dwelling too much upon Ciceronianisms,[82] & had chastiz'd the reading,
not the vanity, it had bin plainly partiall; first to correct him for
grave *Cicero,* and not for scurrill *Plautus* [83] whom he confesses to
have bin reading not long before; next to correct him only, and let
so many more ancient Fathers wax old in those pleasant and florid
studies without the lash of such a tutoring apparition; insomuch
that *Basil* [84] teaches how some good use may be made of *Margites* [85]

[81] Jerome (*ca.* 340–420) was a scholar, controversialist, and the author of the
revised translation of the Bible which goes by his name and which became (with
some revision) the Vulgate. His love of Roman literature interfered, for some
time, with his devotion to Christian doctrine, and his renunciation of secular
studies cost him much pain. His eighteenth *Epistle,* "To Eustochium on Virginity," tells of falling into a severe fever during Lent, of being caught up in
spirit and brought before God, and of being questioned with regard to the state
of his soul. He answered that he was a Christian, but the answer was not accepted, for his heart was possessed by the writings of Cicero, and an angel
promoted his reformation with the lash. Jerome strove to prevent the affair
from being dismissed as only a dream (always thought a less certain form of
divine illumination than a vision); he insisted that he had not been asleep, and
that when he issued from the vision he found the marks of the whipping on his
body. He neglected to provide against Milton's alternative deprecation, that it
was a real enough whipping, but administered by the devil impersonating an
angel. Milton found the suggestion in Sarpi; one of the deletions mentioned in
note 54 is: "Yet they thought there was greater danger in the bookes of the
Gentiles, then of the heretiques, the reading whereof was more abhorred and
reprehended, because it was more used by Christian Doctors for a vanitie of
learned eloquence. For this cause S. *Hierom,* either in a vision, or in a sleepe,
was beaten by the Devill" (*Trent,* p. 472).

[82] The exaggerated devotion to the style of Cicero of many Renaissance pur-
ists was frequently remarked and ridiculed; see, *e.g.,* the *Ciceronianus* of
Erasmus.

[83] See Jerome, Epistle XVIII. For Plautus, see above, p. 498, n. 46.

[84] Basil the Great (*ca.* 330–379), bishop of Caesarea from 370, was the author
of the "Rules" followed by Basilian monks. The general sense of *The Right Use*
(see note 75) is that good Christian use may be made of pagan writings (*e.g.,*
"Now this is my counsel, that you should not unqualifiedly give over your minds
to these men, as a ship is surrendered to the rudder, to follow whither they list,
but that, while receiving whatever of value they have to offer, you yet recognize
what it is wise to ignore" [Padelford, p. 102]). Basil illustrates the method
copiously from, among others, Homer, but not from the *Margites,* which he mentions only once and in a different connection. Milton may however mean that
Basil "teaches" how to make good use of the *Margites,* not directly, but by ex-

a sportfull Poem, not now extant, writ by *Homer;* and why not then of *Morgante* [86] an Italian Romanze much to the same purpose. But if it be agreed we shall be try'd by visions, there is a vision recorded by *Eusebius* [87] far ancienter then this tale of *Jerom* to the Nun *Eustochium,* and besides has nothing of a feavor in it. *Dionysius Alexandrinus* [88] was about the year 240, a person of great name in the Church for piety and learning, who had wont to avail himself much against hereticks by [10] being conversant in their Books; untill a certain Presbyter laid it scrupulously to his conscience, how he durst venture himselfe among those defiling volumes. The worthy man loath to give offence fell into a new debate with himselfe what was to be thought; when suddenly a vision sent from God, it is his own Epistle [89] that so averrs it, confirm'd him in these words: Read any books what ever come to thy hands, for thou art sufficient both to judge aright, and to examine each matter. To this revelation he assented the sooner, as he confesses, because it was answerable to that of the Apostle to the Thessalonians, Prove

ample, since he uses it in another context to help make the point that idleness is unworthy (p. 113).

[85] A mock-heroic poem (of which only four lines are extant) ascribed to Homer by, among others, Plato (*Second Alcibiades,* 147ᶜ) and Aristotle (*Poetics,* IV, 10); its true authorship is not known.

[86] Luigi Pulci published his mock-heroic romance *Il Morgante Maggiore* at Venice in 1481.

[87] Eusebius Pamphilius (*ca.* 264–*ca.* 340), bishop of Caesarea, is called "Father of ecclesiastical history"; his is the first organized account of the church, and (together with the continuation by Socrates; see above, note 79) it remains the primary source of information on the primitive church. See *Complete Prose,* I, 376–77.

[88] Dionysius Alexandrinus (*ca.* 190–265) was bishop of Alexandria from 247. The story derives from his "Third Epistle, Concerning Baptism, to Philemon," and is reported in Eusebius, VII, 7, where Milton appears first to have seen it (he entered it in *CPB* from Eusebius; see *Complete Prose,* I, 377); but neither of these sources assigns a date to the incident. Milton apparently took the date from Sarpi's *Trent.* The second deletion mentioned in note 54 is: "But . . . the example of *Dionysius,* Bishop of *Alexandria,* a famous Doctor, did happen, who about the yeere of our Lord 240. being reprehended by his Priests for these causes, and troubled with these respects, had a vision that hee should reade all bookes, because hee was able to judge of them" (p. 472).

[89] It is unlikely that Milton means that he went from Eusebius, to whom he has already attributed the story, to Dionysius' own epistle for verification; rather, he seems to be emphasizing the fact that Eusebius states (VII, 7) that he is quoting the epistle directly.

all things, hold fast that which is good.[90] And he might have added another remarkable saying of the same Author; To the pure all things are pure,[91] not only meats and drinks, but all kinde of knowledge whether of good or evill; the knowledge cannot defile, nor consequently the books, if the will and conscience be not defil'd. For books are as meats and viands are; some of good, some of evill substance; and yet God in that unapocryphall vision,[92] said without exception, Rise *Peter*, kill and eat, leaving the choice to each mans discretion. Wholesome meats to a vitiated stomach differ little or nothing from unwholesome; and best books to a naughty mind are not unappliable to occasions of evill.[93] Bad meats will scarce breed good nourishment in the healthiest concoction; [94] but herein the difference is of bad books, that they to a discreet and judicious Reader serve in many respects to discover, to confute, to forewarn, and to

[90] I Thessalonians 5:21. Milton's quotation of this verse is a remarkable substitution for what he found. Dionysius' epistle actually says (*St. Dionysius of Alexandria, Letters and Treatises*, tr. C. L. Feltoe, London, 1918, p. 57), "I acknowledged the vision as in agreement with the apostolic voice which says to the more able: 'Approve yourselves bankers of repute,' " and is so reported in Eusebius. This "apostolic" injunction, although attested by Origen and Jerome, had long before Milton's day been rejected as apocryphal, and no longer appeared in Scripture. But in the digression of Socrates which Milton used for the story of the Appolinarii (see above, p. 509, n. 79) there occurs the following (III, 16; Bohn, p. 193): "Both Christ and his apostle enjoin us 'to become discriminating money-changers, so that we might "prove all things, and hold fast that which is good." ' " Milton apparently remembered this linkage of the apocryphal to a canonical verse, and regarded it as justifying the substitution.

[91] Titus 1:15.

[92] Acts 10:9-16. Peter, who had hitherto observed the Jewish ceremonial law, was hungry, and had a vision of a vessel let down from heaven, full of animals prohibited by the dietary law. He was bidden to eat, and further events caused him to interpret this to mean that it was no longer unlawful for a Jew to associate with Gentiles. However, the passage can be made to bear Milton's interpretation. Cf. *Doctrine and Discipline*, above, p. 261. "Unapocryphall," in contrast to Jerome's "fantasm."

[93] This observation could be made with an intent opposite to Milton's; thus the Presbyterian Richard Vines, in a sermon exhorting the City against toleration, urged that a claim to the warrant of Scripture was no assurance that a doctrine was sound, and continued: "The Spider sucks poyson out of the Rose, not that I would imply that there is any such thing in the Word it selfe (for *ex veris nil nisi verum*) but that a corrupt stomacke concocts wholesome food into disease." See *The Impostures of Seducing Teachers* (April 23, 1644), E48(2), p. 13.

[94] Digestion. Cf. *Of Education*, above, p. 411: "The like also would not be unexpedient after Meat to assist and cherish Nature in her first concoction."

illustrate. Wherof what better witnes can ye expect I should produce, then one of your own now sitting in Parlament, the chief of learned men reputed in this Land, Mr. *Selden,* whose volume of naturall & national laws proves, not only by great autorities brought together, but by exquisite reasons and theorems almost mathematically demonstrative, that all opinions, yea errors, known, read, and collated, are of main service & assistance toward the speedy attainment of what is truest.[95] I conceive therefore, that when God did enlarge the universall diet of mans body, saving ever the rules of temperance, he then also, as before, left arbitrary the dyeting and repasting of our minds; as wherein every mature man might have to exercise his owne leading capacity. How great a vertue is temperance, how much of moment through the whole life of man? yet God committs the managing so great a trust, without particular Law or prescription, wholly to the demeanour of every grown man. And therefore when he himself tabl'd the Jews from heaven,[96] that Omer which was every mans daily portion of [11] Manna, is computed to have bin more then might have well suffic'd the heartiest feeder thrice as many meals. For those actions which enter into a man, rather then issue out of him, and therefore defile not,[97] God

[95] John Selden (1584–1654) was a lawyer, legal historian, orientalist, and parliamentarian. He was several times imprisoned by Charles for his opposition to the extreme interpretation of the royal prerogative, and became one of the leaders of the Erastian group in the Long Parliament. His *De Jure Naturali et Gentium juxta Disciplinam Ebraeorum* (1640; UCL, p. 2) opens with a prefatory statement containing the following passage: "Among these men it is a firmly established usage not only to make known what they have come upon among others, in exact or approximate agreement with their own convictions or those of the groups and sects with which they are associated, but also on many occasions similarly to publish opposed and disagreeing views and ordinances of other sects. They have very weighty reasons for this, for in this way they not only confirm their own doctrines to no small degree by the approval of others, but they further acquire the means of detecting and delimiting with nicety the subtle lines of demarcation which distinguish their tenets from dissenting ones, of removing the mask from the falsehood which often approximates and counterfeits truth, and of accomplishing more readily whatever else of this nature a scrupulous search for the truth is likely to entail." (This translation was made for me by my colleague Richard T. Bruère, Professor of Latin at the University of Chicago.) Milton had already praised the *De Jure Naturali* for its demonstration that positive law must not contravene natural law; see *Doctrine and Discipline,* above, p. 350.

[96] Exodus 16.

[97] Matthew 15:17–20; Mark 7:14–23.

uses not to captivat under a perpetuall childhood of prescription, but trusts him with the gift of reason to be his own chooser; there were but little work left for preaching, if law and compulsion should grow so fast upon those things which hertofore were govern'd only by exhortation. *Salomon* informs us that much reading is a wearines to the flesh; [98] but neither he, nor other inspir'd author tells us that such, or such reading is unlawfull: yet certainly had God thought good to limit us herein, it had bin much more expedient to have told us what was unlawfull, then what was wearisome. As for the burning of those Ephesian books by St. *Pauls* converts, tis reply'd the books were magick, the Syriack so renders them.[99] It was a privat act, a voluntary act, and leaves us to a voluntary imitation: the men in remorse burnt those books which were their own; the Magistrat by this example is not appointed: these men practiz'd the books, another might perhaps have read them in some sort usefully. Good and evill we know in the field of this World grow up together almost inseparably; and the knowledge of good is so involv'd and interwoven with the knowledge of evill, and in so many cunning resemblances hardly to be discern'd, that those confused seeds which were impos'd on *Psyche* as an incessant labour to cull out, and sort asunder, were not more intermixt.[100] It was from out the rinde of one apple tasted, that the knowledge of good and evill as two twins cleaving together leapt forth into the World.[101] And perhaps this is that doom which *Adam* fell into of knowing good and evill, that is to say of knowing good by evill. As therefore the state of man now is; what wisdome can there be to choose, what continence to forbeare without the knowledge of evill? He that can apprehend and consider vice with all her baits and seeming pleasures, and yet abstain, and yet distinguish, and yet prefer that which

[98] Ecclesiastes 12:12.

[99] Acts 19:19.

[100] The story of Cupid and Psyche is in Apuleius, *The Golden Ass*, IV–VI. Venus, as part of the abuse she visited upon her daughter-in-law, "tooke a great quantity of wheat, of barly, poppy seede, peason, lintles, and beanes, and mingled them altogether on a heape saying . . . see that thou separate all these graines one from another, disposing them orderly in their quantity, and let it be done before night" (tr. William Adlington, 1566 [London, John Lehman, 1946], p. 125). The seeds were sorted out by helpful ants.

[101] Genesis 3:5 and 22.

is truly better, he is the true warfaring [102] Christian. I cannot praise a fugitive and cloister'd vertue, unexercis'd & unbreath'd, that never sallies out and sees her adversary, but slinks out of the race, where that immortall garland [103] is to be run for, not without dust and heat. Assuredly we bring not innocence into the world, we bring impurity much rather: [104] that which purifies us is triall, and triall is by what is contrary. That vertue therefore which is but a young-ling in the contemplation of evill, and knows not the utmost [12] that vice promises to her followers, and rejects it, is but a blank

[102] The printed text has *wayfaring*. All four presentation copies and "F" have the y crossed through in ink and an r written above it. (Three more copies, which I have not examined and which have no known connection with Milton, are reported to have the same correction: one is in the University Library of Lausanne, the other two in the University Library at Cambridge; see G. A. Bonnard, *R.E.S.*, IV [1928], 434–38, and Helen Darbishire, *R.E.S.*, VII [1931], 72–73.) In the presentation copies (but not in "F") the inserted r's all have a similar form, resembling Milton's r's. It has been contended that the changes were made by Milton himself, but this cannot be proved (Miss Darbishire argues against it). The changes were probably not made out of the same inkwell: in the Young copy the ink is, like that of all four inscriptions, faded brown; in the Yale copy it is dark gray; in the Thomason and Rous copies it is still shiny black. Furthermore, in the Thomason copy the change was not made in the same ink as the correction on p. [34] (see below, p. 778, textual notes), since that is faded brown (in *Rous, Yale,* and "F" the ink at p. [34] is similar to that at p. [12] in each copy; *Young* does not contain the later correction). It can scarcely be doubted, however, that the change has Milton's authority, and was made, if not by himself, by the printer or bookseller after the error was discovered. (1) All known presentation copies, and some others, have it. (2) Milton's manuscript r's are easily confusable with y's. (3) There is no other instance in Milton of either "wayfaring" or "warfaring," but "Christian warfare" occurs several times, while the image of the Christian pilgrimage, frequently found elsewhere, never occurs in Milton. (4) The argument from literary propriety is not decisive, but its weight is on the side of "warfaring." "Wayfaring" has been thought to have some relation to the image of a race, but is it the pilgrim or the warrior who participates in such games? And the main image is that of struggle; *e.g.,* "adversary," and "triall is by what is contrary." Earlier in 1644 Milton had used the phrase "Christian warfare" in a context very similar to this one (*Doctrine and Discipline,* above, p. 228).

[103] "that immortal garland": Reference uncertain, but the image of the race suggests 1 Corinthians 9:24–25 ("Know ye not that they which run in a race run all, but one receiveth the prize? . . . Now they do it to obtain a corruptible crown; but we an incorruptible."), while the idea of resisting temptation suggests James 1:12 ("Blessed is the man that endureth temptation: for when he is tried he shall receive the crown of life.").

[104] *Christian Doctrine,* I, 11: "The sin which is common to all men is that which our first parents, and in them all their posterity committed."

vertue, not a pure; her whitenesse is but an excrementall [105] whitenesse; Which was the reason why our sage and serious Poet *Spencer,*
whom I dare be known to think a better teacher [106] then *Scotus* or
Aquinas,[107] describing true temperance under the person of *Guion,*
brings him in with his palmer through the cave of Mammon,[108] and
the bowr of earthly blisse that he might see and know, and yet
abstain. Since therefore the knowledge and survay of vice is in this
world so necessary to the constituting of human vertue, and the
scanning of error to the confirmation of truth, how can we more

[105] excrementall: *OED* cites this passage (Def.a.²), deriving the word from
ex, out, and *crescere,* to grow, and defining it as "of the nature of an outgrowth
or excrescence." Milton seems to have in mind that "excrements" in this sense
(*e.g.,* hair, nails, etc.) are on the surface, for the phrase clearly means "superficial whiteness." It also seems to be one of the series of echoes of Laudianism
(*cf.* below, notes 140, 141, 155, 167, etc.) which grow increasingly frequent
until they have prepared for the charge that "Bishops and Presbyters are the
same to us both name and thing" (see below, p. [539]). I have been unable to
locate it, but Laud appears to have issued a regulation governing "excrementals";
this, at least, seems a necessary inference from a passage in *The Spie, Communicating Intelligence from Oxford* (February 20, 1644), which describes the
disguise (cloak, cassock, band, etc.) by means of which the journalistic spy
entered Oxford, and continues (E33[27], p. 26): "And afterwards I to the
Barbers, where I most happily met with a fellow which had served an appren-
tiship to the Cardinals Cut, who most officiously innovated my beard according to *Canterbury* his Canon for the regulating of *Excrementals.*"

[106] *Cf.* "Il Penseroso," ll. 116–20; *Comus,* ll. 512–19 and l. 821; *Animadversions, Complete Prose,* I, 722–23. Dryden ("Preface" to the *Fables*) says,
"Milton has acknowledged to me that Spenser was his original."

[107] Duns Scotus and Aquinas are presumably named as representatives of
medieval theology and philosophy at its most influential.

[108] This is one of Milton's most interesting errors (the Palmer did not accompany Guyon to the Cave of Mammon; see *Faerie Queene,* II, vii, 2, and
viii, 3). It is evidence not merely that Milton thought he knew the poem too
well to need to check the incident, but also that he missed the exact point of
Spenser's psychology in a rather important matter. Guyon does indeed require
the active intervention of reason (the Palmer) in order to resist the temptations
of Acrasia's Bower of Bliss (Canto xii); but before confronting him with
Mammon Spenser separates him from the Palmer, partly to show that the mere
habit of temperance is sufficient to withstand the solicitations of that god. De-
posited in the memory of the more strenuous and (it may be suspected) more
realistic Milton, this incident gets worked over; when it re-emerges, there has
been no separation of Guyon and the Palmer. Milton is in this matter less
Aristotelian than Spenser; he is less disposed to rely on the security of habit;
in all significant situations, choosing (to adapt the famous phrase on p. [527]) is,
for him, active reasoning. For a fuller discussion of the significance of this error,
see Ernest Sirluck, "Milton Revises *The Faerie Queene,*" *Modern Philology,*
XLVIII (1950), pp. 90–96.

safely, and with lesse danger scout into the regions of sin and falsity
then by reading all manner of tractats, and hearing all manner of
reason? And this is the benefit which may be had of books promis-
cuously read. But of the harm that may result hence three kinds
are usually reckn'd. First, is fear'd the infection that may spread;[109]
but then all human learning and controversie in religious points must
remove out of the world, yea the Bible it selfe; for that oftimes relates blasphemy not nicely, it describes the carnall sense of wicked
men not unelegantly, it brings in holiest men passionately murmuring against providence through all the arguments of *Epicurus:* in
other great disputes it answers dubiously and darkly to the common
reader: And ask a Talmudist [110] what ails the modesty of his marginall Keri, that *Moses* and all the Prophets cannot perswade him
to pronounce the textuall Chetiv.[111] For these causes we all know
the Bible it selfe put by the Papist into the first rank of prohibited
books. The ancientest Fathers must be next remov'd, as *Clement
of Alexandria,*[112] and that *Eusebian* book of Evangelick preparation,[113] transmitting our ears through a hoard of heathenish obscen-

[109] The third deletion mentioned in note 54 is: "some godly men made conscience of reading bad bookes, for feare of offending against one of the three
points of the Law of God, to avoid the contagion of evill; not to expose ones
selfe to temptation, without necessitie or profite; and not to spend time vainely"
(*Trent,* p. 472). *Cf.* below, p. 521, and note 129.

[110] The *Talmud* (noun related to the verb *limmed,* to teach) embraces both
the primary (*Mishnah*) and secondary (*Gemara*) Hebraic commentaries upon
Scripture. It is thus the codification of an oral tradition of Biblical exegesis laying claim to an authority second only to Scripture itself. It exists in two redac-
tions, the *Talmud* of the West (usually called the Jerusalem *Talmud*) and the
more comprehensive and systematic Babylonian *Talmud*. Milton evidently means
by Talmudist not a compiler but a student of the *Talmud*.

[111] *Keri* and *Chetiv* are technical terms of *Masorah*, the textual criticism of
Hebrew Scripture. When a textual reading (*Chetiv*) is suspected of corruption,
or when it is thought unseemly (*e.g.,* the use of the names of pagan deities to
indicate Jehovah), or when, in the frequently recurrent case of the tetragram-
maton *YHWH*, it is forbidden to pronounce it, the margin provides an emendation or a euphemism to be read (*Keri*); an alteration of the received text itself
is not considered permissible. *Cf. An Apology, Complete Prose*, I, 902.

[112] Clement of Alexandria (*fl.* second century) was the first church father to
bring an intimate knowledge of Greek religion, philosophy, and art into the
service of Christianity. Milton is thinking of Clement's *Hortatory Address to
the Greeks*, in which, to dissuade his hearers from participation in certain pagan
rites, he describes these with much emphasis on their lewdness and obscenity.

[113] See above, p. 511, n. 87. What was said of Clement's *Hortatory Address*
in note 112 is applicable to Eusebius' *Evangelical Preparation*.

ities to receive the Gospel. Who finds not that *Irenaeus, Epiphanius, Jerom*,[114] and others discover more heresies then they well confute, and that oft for heresie which is the truer opinion. Nor boots it to say for these, and all the heathen Writers of greatest infection, if it must be thought so, with whom is bound up the life of human learning, that they writ in an unknown tongue, so long as we are sure those languages are known as well to the worst of men, who are both most able, and most diligent to instill the poison they suck, first into the Courts of Princes, acquainting them with the choisest delights, and criticisms [115] of sin. As perhaps did that *Petronius* [116] whom *Nero* call'd his *Arbiter*, the Master of his revels; and that notorious ribald of *Arezzo*,[117] dreaded, and yet dear to the Italian Courtiers. I name not him for posterities sake, whom [13] *Harry* the 8. nam'd in merriment his Vicar of hell.[118] By which compendious way all the contagion that foreine books can infuse, will finde a passage to the people farre easier and shorter then an Indian voyage, though it could be sail'd either by the North of *Cataio*

[114] Irenaeus (*ca.* 140–*ca.* 202) was bishop of Lyons from 177. His only surviving work is *Against Heresies*. Epiphanius (315–403) was bishop of Constantia from 367. His chief work, *Panarion*, describes and attacks eighty heresies. For Jerome, see above, p. 510, n. 81.

[115] Criticisms: critical refinements, *elegantiae*.

[116] Gaius Petronius (d. A.D. 66), author of the famous *Satyricon*, was the favorite of Nero. The title *arbiter elegantiarum* is reported in Tacitus, *Annals*, XVI, 18.

[117] Pietro Aretino (1492–1557) was born in Arezzo. He was an accomplished poet of lewdness and the most famous of all literary blackmailers.

[118] Until recently there was lively speculation on the identity concealed beneath this phrase; among the many suggested identifications were Skelton, Wolsey, Thomas Cromwell, Andrew Borde, and a ballad-maker named Gray. Hughes (1947, p. 227) was the first to suggest Anne Boleyn's cousin, "the very minor poet Sir Francis Brian, to whom Thomas Cromwell repeatedly referred as 'the Vicar of Hell.'" Harris Fletcher has since put this identification out of controversy by finding the following passage in Davanzati's *English Schism*, a book we know Milton to have used in writing the *Areopagitica* (see above, p. 504, n. 64): "[Sir] Thomas [Boleyn] had by this his wife a daughter, half-grown, whom the King saw when he went to visit her mother, and whom he took to court and to his bedroom, and once he asked Francis Bryan, born of the Boleyn family, the finest of all the very wicked courtiers of which the court was full, 'What sin would he have committed who lay first with the mother, and then with the daughter?' He [Bryan] answered, 'The same as he who eats first the hen and then the pullet.' The King died of laughing and said, 'You are indeed my Vicar of Hell' (he was already called the King's Vicar of Hell because of his ungodliness) whence everyone afterward so called him." See *Journal of English and Germanic Philology*, XLVII (1948), 387–89.

Eastward, or of *Canada* Westward,[119] while our Spanish licencing gags the English Presse never so severely. But on the other side that infection which is from books of controversie in Religion, is more doubtfull and dangerous to the learned, then to the ignorant; and yet those books must be permitted untoucht by the licencer.[120] It will be hard to instance where any ignorant man hath bin ever seduc't by Papisticall book in English, unlesse it were commended and expounded to him by some of that Clergy: and indeed all such tractats whether false or true are as the Prophesie of *Isaiah* was to the *Eunuch,* not to be *understood without a guide*.[121] But of our Priests and Doctors how many have bin corrupted by studying the comments of Jesuits and *Sorbonists,*[122] and how fast they could transfuse that corruption into the people, our experience is both late and sad.[123] It is not forgot, since the acute and distinct *Arminius*

[119] The principal goal of marine exploration was still the discovery of Northeast or Northwest passages to the "Indies." *Cataio* is a variant of Cathay, or China.

[120] Milton is here strangely forgetful or somewhat naively sophistical. The Licensing Order does not contain the slightest suggestion that "books of controversie in Religion" were to be exempted; on the contrary, the licensing of such books was specifically provided for (see Appendix B, below, p. 797). Indeed, it may well be supposed that such books were, next to royalist publications, the chief object of the Order—a supposition shared by Milton himself, if the over-all emphasis of the argument in *Areopagitica* is any evidence (and see below, note 218). The meaning of "must be permitted untouched by the licenser" has therefore to be sought elsewhere than in the Order. It is to be found in the fourth sentence below: such books "cannot be suppressed without the fall of learning." The inference is that since Parliament will be unwilling to bring about the fall of learning, it will be obliged to exempt books of religious controversy, thus leaving open a gate of infection so important that it will render the whole scheme of licensing nugatory. How such an argument could be advanced against the evidence of the already existent Order is difficult to understand.

[121] Acts 8:27–35.

[122] The Sorbonne was originally the theological school founded in 1252 by Robert de Sorbon, but its distinction was such that the whole faculty of theology in the University of Paris came to be known by that name (ultimately the name was extended to embrace the faculties of letters and science). It was one of the most influential centres of Roman Catholic polemic. *Cf. A Defence,* Chapter III.

[123] "Our Priests" and "our experience" suggest that Milton is thinking, in this sentence, of English churchmen, separately from his reference to Arminius in the next sentence. It was a standard Puritan complaint that the Episcopalian clergy were very susceptible to, and even promoted, Roman Catholic proselytization; *e.g.,* Harbottle Grimston's speech in the Commons seconding the motion to impeach Laud (John Nalson, *An Impartial Collection of the Great Affairs of State* [2 vols., 1682; UCL] I, 690): "Who is it Mr. *Speaker* but he only that

was perverted meerly by the perusing of a namelesse discours
writt'n at *Delf,* which at first he took in hand to confute.[124] Seeing
therefore that those books, & those in great abundance which are
likeliest to taint both life and doctrine, cannot be supprest without
the fall of learning, and of all ability in disputation, and that these
books of either sort are most and soonest catching to the learned,
from whom to the common people what ever is hereticall or dissolute may quickly be convey'd, and that evill manners are as perfectly learnt without books a thousand other ways which cannot be
stopt, and evill doctrine not with books can propagate, except a
teacher guide, which he might also doe without writing, and so beyond prohibiting, I am not able to unfold, how this cautelous [125]
enterprise of licencing can be exempted from the number of vain
and impossible attempts. And he who were pleasantly dispos'd,
could not well avoid to lik'n it to the exploit of that gallant man
who thought to pound up the crows by shutting his Parkgate. Besides another inconvenience, if learned men be the first receivers
out of books, & dispredders both of vice and error, how shall the
licencers themselves be confided in, unlesse we can conferr upon

hath advanced all our Popish Bishops. I shall name but some of them, Bishop
Manering, the Bishop of *Bath and Wells,* the Bishop of *Oxford,* and Bishop
Wren, the least of all these birds, but one of the most unclean ones. These are
the men that should have fed Christ's Flock, but they are the Wolves that have
devoured them." *Cf.* "Lycidas," ll. 128–29.

[124] Milton's own subsequent conversion to Arminianism (see especially *Christian Doctrine,* I, iv, "On Predestination") lends both force and irony here.
Arminius (Jacob Hermanns, 1560–1609) became so famous as professor of
theology at the University of Leyden that a movement which was already strong
before he joined it was given his name. It began in 1554 when Calvin's erstwhile
colleague, Castellion, attacked (from the relative safety of Basle) the forcible
imposition of religious uniformity in Geneva (recently exemplified by the burning of Servetus). The main features of his position were general predestination,
as opposed to particular; conditional, as opposed to unconditional, election; free
will; and toleration of religious diversity. "Bellianism," as Beza called it, flour-
ished in the Netherlands under the leadership of Dirck Coornhert; and Arminius,
then an orthodox Calvinist minister at Amsterdam, was, in 1589, called upon to
answer some tracts (anonymous, but possibly written by Coornhert) circulating
in Delft. His change of view followed, as described by Milton; the movement
gained increasing momentum, securing, by 1630, official permission. Its influence
in England was not confined to any religious party: Calvinists denounced as
Arminian such diverse people as Archbishop Laud and the Independent preacher
John Goodwin. (This note is in part based upon J. W. Allen, *History of Political
Thought in the Sixteenth Century,* pp. 73–102.)

[125] deceitful, crafty.

them, or they assume to themselves above all others in the Land, the grace of infallibility, and uncorruptednesse? And again if it be true, that a wise man like a good refiner can gather gold out of the drossiest volume, and that a fool will be a fool with [14] the best book, yea or without book, there is no reason that we should deprive a wise man of any advantage to his wisdome, while we seek to restrain from a fool, that which being restrain'd will be no hindrance to his folly. For if there should be so much exactnesse always us'd to keep that from him which is unfit for his reading, we should in the judgement of *Aristotle* [126] not only, but of *Salomon*,[127] and of our Saviour,[128] not voutsafe him good precepts, and by consequence not willingly admit him to good books; as being certain that a wise man will make better use of an idle pamphlet, then a fool will do of sacred Scripture. 'Tis next alleg'd we must not expose our selves to temptations without necessity, and next to that, not imploy our time in vain things.[129] To both these objections one answer will serve, out of the grounds already laid, that to all men such books are not temptations, nor vanities; but usefull drugs and materialls wherewith to temper and compose effective and strong med'cins, which mans life cannot want.[130] The rest, as children and childish men, who have not the art to qualifie and prepare these working mineralls, well may be exhorted to forbear, but hinder'd forcibly they cannot be by all the licencing that Sainted [131] Inquisition could ever yet contrive; which is what I promis'd to deliver next, That this order of licencing conduces nothing to the end for which it was fram'd; and hath almost prevented me by being clear already while thus much hath bin explaining. See the ingenuity of Truth, who when she gets a free and willing hand, opens her self faster, then the pace of method and discours can overtake her. It was the task which I began with, To shew that no Nation, or well

[126] *Ethics*, I, iii; 1095^a (tr. W. D. Ross, in *Introduction to Aristotle*, ed. Richard McKeon, New York; Modern Library, 1947, p. 310): "Since he tends to follow his passions, his study will be vain and unprofitable."

[127] Proverbs 23:9: "Speak not in the ears of a fool: for he will despise the wisdom of thy words."

[128] Matthew 7:6: "Give not that which is holy unto the dogs, neither cast ye your pearls before swine."

[129] See above, p. 517, n. 109.

[130] *I.e.*, with which men cannot dispense.

[131] A jibe at the official name adopted by the Inquisition in 1542: "The Sacred Congregation of the Holy Office."

instituted State, if they valu'd books at all, did ever use this way of licencing; and it might be answer'd, that this is a piece of prudence lately discover'd. To which I return, that as it was a thing slight and obvious to think on, so if it had bin difficult to finde out, there wanted not among them long since, who suggested such a cours; which they not following, leave us a pattern of their judgement, that it was not the not knowing, but the not approving, which was the cause of their not using it. *Plato,* a man of high autority indeed, but least of all for his Commonwealth, in the book of his laws,[132] which no City ever yet receiv'd, fed his fancie with making many edicts to his ayrie Burgomasters, which they who otherwise admire him, wish had bin rather buried and excus'd in the *genial* cups of an *Academick* night-sitting.[133] By which laws he seems to tolerat no kind of learning, but by unalterable decree, con-[15] sisting most of practicall traditions, to the attainment whereof a Library of smaller bulk then his own dialogues would be abundant. And there also enacts that no Poet should so much as read to any privat man, what he had writt'n, untill the Judges and Law-keepers had seen it, and allow'd it: But that *Plato* meant this Law peculiarly to that Commonwealth which he had imagin'd, and to no

[132] The presence in this passage of "Commonwealth," "ayrie Burgomasters," and "his fancied republic, which in this world could have no place" may seem to suggest the *Republic,* which formulates a frankly ideal state, rather than the *Laws,* which aims at the best possible actual state; and "to tolerat no kind of learning, but by unalterable decree" is as readily applicable to the *Republic* (books II and III) as to the *Laws* (book VII). But the rest of the passage makes it clear that the reference is to the *Laws.* The description of tolerated learning as "consisting most of practicall traditions" is accurate only if applied to the *Laws;* "there . . . enacts that no Poet should so much as read to any privat man, what he had writt'n, untill the Judges . . . had . . . allow'd it" is a paraphrase of a passage in *Laws,* VII, 801; finally the statement that the dialogue under examination contributed least to Plato's "autority," and was deprecated by his admirers, can, in view of the respective reputations of the two books, refer only to the *Laws.* The meaning, therefore, of Plato's "Commonwealth, in the book of his laws" is "the state which he depicted in the book entitled the *Laws,*" and the utopian nature of the state must be taken as indicating, not Plato's intention, but Milton's opinion of the result.

[133] Plato's *Symposium* does not discuss the tenet against which Milton is here arguing. The function of the allusion (the original meaning of "symposium" was an intellectual drinking party, and *"Academick"* is formed from Plato's "Academy") is indirect deprecation, for the reminder of the circumstances of some of Plato's dialogues serves momentarily to give to them all an air of vinous irresponsibility.

other, is evident. Why was he not else a Law-giver to himself, but a transgressor, and to be expell'd by his own Magistrats; both for the wanton epigrams and dialogues which he made,[134] and his perpetuall reading of *Sophron Mimus*,[135] and *Aristophanes*, books of grossest infamy, and also for commending the latter of them though he were the malicious libeller of his chief friends, to be read by the Tyrant *Dionysius*,[136] who had little need of such trash to spend his time on? But that he knew this licencing of Poems had reference and dependence to many other proviso's there set down in his fancied republic, which in this world could have no place: and so neither he himself, nor any Magistrat, or City ever imitated that cours, which tak'n apart from those other collaterall injunctions must needs be vain and fruitlesse. For if they fell upon one kind of strictnesse, unlesse their care were equall to regulat all other things of like aptnes to corrupt the mind, that single endeavour they knew would be but a fond labour; to shut and fortifie one gate against corruption, and be necessitated to leave others round about wide open. If we think to regulat Printing, thereby to rectifie manners, we must regulat all recreations and pastimes, all that is delightfull to man. No musick must be heard, no song be set or sung, but what is grave and *Dorick*.[137] There must be licencing dancers, that no gesture, motion, or deportment be taught our youth but what by their allowance shall be thought honest; for such *Plato*

[134] For the epigrams, see Diogenes Laertius, III, 23; the dialogues are probably the *Symposium* and the *Phaedrus*. Hales (p. 104) and Lockwood (p. 78) feel that "the epithet [wanton] is certainly too violent and unsparing." They have, presumably, the language in mind, which is not wanton; but Milton is thinking of the matter represented: homosexual love. *E.g.*, Shelley's well-known translation of one of the epigrams is entitled "Kissing Helena," and seems unobjectionable if ardent; but in the original epigram the name of the person embraced was Agathon.

[135] Sophron "Mimus" (fl. fifth century B.C.) was a popular writer of mimes, or realistic dramatic sketches. Milton's authority for Plato's addiction to Sophron is Diogenes Laertius (III, 13), to whom he attributes the story in *An Apology, Complete Prose*, I, 879.

[136] See above, p. 495, n. 34. Aristophanes satirizes Socrates in the *Clouds*, Nicias in the *Knights*.

[137] *Laws*, VII, contains an extensive discussion of the kinds of music to be permitted and those to be proscribed, but does not give them geographical or national names. Milton draws the term *"Dorick"* from the earlier discussion in *Republic*, III, 398–99, which divides music into four styles, the "relaxed" Lydian and Ionian (to be suppressed), and the more "manly" Dorian and Phrygian (to be permitted). *Cf. Lycidas*, l. 189: "warbling his Doric lay."

was provided of; [138] It will ask more then the work of twenty licencers to examin all the lutes, the violins, and the ghittarrs in every house; they must not be suffer'd to prattle as they doe, but must be licenc'd what they may say. And who shall silence all the airs and madrigalls, that whisper softnes in chambers? The Windows also, and the *Balcone's* must be thought on, there are shrewd books, with dangerous Frontispices [139] set to sale; who shall prohibit them, shall twenty licencers? The villages also must have their visitors [140]

[138] *Laws,* VII, 802. This part of Milton's *reductio ad absurdum* had been demanded in all seriousness by George Wither, who, in dedicating to Parliament his *Haleluiah or, Britans Second Remembrancer* (1641; C70a13, sigs. A6–7) complained that many "Scurrilous and obscaene *Songs* are impudently . . . *Sung, and Acted,* with . . . abominable gesticulations. . . . For Prevention whereof, I am an humble Petitioner, that some order may be provided, by the Wisdome and Pietie, of your *Assemblies;* Seeing upon due examination of this Abuse, it may soone be discovered, that, as well *Censores Canticorum,* as *Librorum* will be necessary in these Times."

[139] Frontispices: This orthography is usually treated as a printer's vagary; in fact it is more strictly accurate than that now standard, which derives from a false popular etymology connecting the final syllable with "piece," whereas it actually is from *specio,* to behold, and comes to English by way of medieval *frontispicium,* the front-look or facade of a building (*cf. Paradise Lost,* III, 506); hence the pun consists in achieving the analogy with books not by bestowing a new meaning, but by applying the original. There appears to be an allusion here to the display methods of brothel-keepers; *cf.* Middleton, *A Chaste Maid in Cheapside,* V, i, 160–61, where Allwit, proposing to return to brothel-keeping, speaks of being "stock'd with cloth-of-tissue cushions / To furnish out bay-windows."

[140] An allusion to one of the most hated features of Laud's administration of the church. After 1634, every bishop was required to send ecclesiastical censors ("visitors") to examine and report upon the state of every parish; in 1636 these visitations were extended to include the universities (Gardiner, *History of England,* VIII, 108 and 147). Daniel Neal, in *The History of the Puritans* (2 vols., London, 1754), I, 590–91, says that individual bishops framed *"new articles of visitation in their own names, without the king's seal and authority. . . .* This was an outrage upon the laws . . . but the bishops presumed upon . . . the indulgence of the crown. . . . The most remarkable and curious were Dr. *Wren's* bishop of *Norwich. . . .* The book contains one hundred and thirty-nine articles, in which are eight hundred and ninety-seven questions, some very insignificant, others highly superstitious, and several impossible to be answered." An anonymous pamphlet entitled *The Bishop of Canterbury His Confession* (February 3, 1644) has Laud saying (E31[9], p. 4): "I had my Pantacousts or my Church Scouts, that went abroad to hear Sermons, and if they could bring me any accusation against the Puritan Preachers, I would interpret it to be a point of *Lesa Majestatis vel Religionis,* either Treason against Majestie, or against Piety." Milton's point is that this Laudian system must, in consistency, now be imposed by the enemies of Laud upon the very music of the village.

to enquire what lectures [141] the bagpipe and the rebbeck [142] reads ev'n to the ballatry, and the gammuth of every *municipal* fidler, for these are the Countrymans *Arcadia's* [143] and his *Monte May-ors.* [144] Next, what more Nationall corruption, for which England hears ill abroad, then houshold gluttony; [145] [16] who shall be the

[141] This amplifies the rhetorical effect of "visitors" discussed in note 140. "Lecturers" were ordained ministers, but not members of the parish clergy; they were employed by corporations or individuals to preach and to do nothing more. As they did not have to read the service, they were in an especially favorable position for avoiding conformity, and in fact the Sunday afternoon lecture became the great opportunity of English puritanism. At Laud's instigation Charles placed severe restrictions upon lecturers in 1629, and again in 1633; these were set aside by the House of Commons in 1641 (Gardiner, *History of England,* VII, 130–32 and 303–306, and X, 16). Neal (*History of the Puritans,* I, 593) gives a number of examples of how various bishops dealt with the lecturers; *e.g.,* "Dr. *Pierse* bishop of *Bath* and *Wells,* suppressed all lectures in market-towns, and elsewhere throughout his diocese, alledging *that he saw no such need of preaching now, as was in the apostles days. . . .* All the new bishops went in the same tract; and some of them upon this sad principle, *That afternoon sermons on Sundays, were an impediment to the revels in the evening.*"

[142] A rudimentary two-stringed violin; *cf.* "L'Allegro," l. 94.

[143] Sir Philip Sidney's prose romance, *The Countesse of Pembrokes Arcadia* (published 1590, revised edition, 1593) was immensely popular. There is no hostility in this reference; Milton's famous description, five years later, of the *Arcadia* as a "vain amatorious poem" (*Eikonoklastes,* Chapter I) must be taken in context: "a book in that kind full of worth and wit, but among religious thoughts and duties not worthy to be named." See *Complete Prose,* III, for a discussion of this point.

[144] Jorge de Montemayor's *Diana* (published *ca.* 1559), was the first Spanish prose romance; it started a major literary fashion, and achieved an almost unprecedented European popularity.

[145] For corroboration of this charge, see Mary Bateson in H. D. Traill and J. S. Mann, *Social England* (6 vols., London, 1894–97), IV, 214–36, especially p. 220. Hears ill: Hales (p. 108) cites several parallels for this Englishing of a Greek idiom; *e.g.,* Ben Jonson, in the dedication of *Volpone,* writes that his is "an age wherein poetry and the professors of it hear so ill on all sides."

On the question of drunkenness there would seem to be at first glance a contradiction between *Areopagitica* and *Tetrachordon* (see below, p. 634). *Areopagitica* says that drunkenness (among other things) "will be, and must be," and that wisdom consists not in attempting to eradicate the ineradicable, but in making it "lest hurtful." *Tetrachordon* seems not to agree that drunkenness is ineradicable: "what more foul and common sin among us then drunkennes, and who can bee ignorant, that if the importation of Wine, and the use of all strong drink were forbid, it would both clean ridde the possibility of committing that odious vice, and men might afterwards live happily and healthfully, without the use of those intoxicating licors." But *Tetrachordon* is not advocating prohibition; it goes on to say that drunkenness will not be eradicated because not even the severest and holiest of reformers would think of surrendering his own (per-

rectors of our daily rioting? and what shall be done to inhibit the multitudes that frequent those houses where drunk'nes is sold and harbour'd? Our garments also should be referr'd to the licencing of some more sober work-masters to see them cut into a lesse wanton garb.[146] Who shall regulat all the mixt conversation of our youth, male and female together, as is the fashion of this Country, who shall still appoint what shall be discours'd, what presum'd, and no furder? Lastly, who shall forbid and separat all idle resort, all evill company? These things will be, and must be; but how they shall be lest hurtfull, how lest enticing, herein consists the grave and governing wisdom of a State. To sequester out of the world into *Atlantick* and *Eutopian* polities,[147] which never can be drawn into use, will not mend our condition; but to ordain wisely as in this world of evill, in the midd'st whereof God hath plac't us unavoidably. Nor is it *Plato's* licencing of books will doe this, which necessarily pulls along with it so many other kinds of licencing, as will make us all both ridiculous and weary, and yet frustrat; but those unwritt'n, or at least unconstraining laws of vertuous education, religious and civill nurture, which *Plato* there mentions,[148] as the bonds and ligaments of the Commonwealth, the pillars and the sustainers of every writt'n Statute; these they be which will bear chief sway

fectly legitimate) use of drink in order to make impossible its abuse by others. Milton's point is that by common consent and the example of daily life the abuse of a permission does not make the permission invalid, and that the right use of divorce should no more than the right use of wine be abolished because of abuse.

[146] Between 1363 and 1597 there had in fact been a number of sumptuary laws, but of increasingly negligible effect.

[147] Plato's *Critias* purports to give an account of the "Kingdom of Atlantis," an island beyond the Pillars of Hercules that was later sunk into the ocean. Ideal, and hence unattainable, commonwealths are depicted in More's *Utopia* (1516) and Bacon's *New Atlantis* (1627). On other occasions Milton could be friendlier to utopian speculation; cf. *An Apology* (*Complete Prose*, I, 881), where he praises "That grave and noble invention which the greatest and sublimest wits in sundry ages, *Plato* in *Critias*, and our two famous countreymen, the one in his *Utopia*, the other in his *new Atlantis* chose . . . to display the largenesse of their spirits by teaching this our world better and exacter things, then were yet known." Ironically, Milton's own polity would one day be jeered at as utopian; see *The Censure of the Rota Upon Mr. Miltons Book* (1660), E 1019(5*), pp. 13–14.

[148] This is usually taken as an allusion to *Republic*, IV, 424–33, a passage which fits Milton's description; but "there mentions" would suggest that the reference is to *Laws*, I, 643–44; see note 132.

in such matters as these, when all licencing will be easily eluded. Impunity and remissenes, for certain are the bane of a Commonwealth, but here the great art lyes to discern in what the law is to bid restraint and punishment, and in what things perswasion only is to work. If every action which is good, or evill in man at ripe years, were to be under pittance,[149] and prescription, and compulsion, what were vertue but a name, what praise could be then due to well-doing, what grammercy to be sober, just or continent? many there be that complain of divin Providence for suffering *Adam* to transgresse, foolish tongues! when God gave him reason, he gave him freedom to choose, for reason is but choosing; [150] he had bin else a meer artificiall *Adam,* such an *Adam* as he is in the motions.[151] We our selves esteem not of that obedience, or love, or gift, which is of force: God therefore left him free, set before him a provoking object, ever almost in his eyes; herein consisted his merit, herein the right of his reward, the praise of his abstinence. Wherefore did he creat passions within us, pleasures round about us, but that these rightly temper'd are the very ingredients of vertu? They are not skilfull considerers of human things, who [17] imagin to remove sin by removing the matter of sin; for, besides that it is a huge heap increasing under the very act of diminishing, though some part of it may for a time be withdrawn from some persons, it cannot from all, in such a universall thing as books are; and when this is done, yet the sin remains entire. Though ye take from a covetous man all his treasure, he has yet one jewell left, ye cannot bereave him of his covetousnesse. Banish all objects of lust, shut up all youth into the severest discipline that can be exercis'd in any hermitage, ye cannot make them chaste, that came not thither so: such great care and wisdom is requir'd to the right managing of this point. Suppose we could expell sin by this means; look how much we thus expell of sin, so much we expell of vertue: [152] for the matter of them both is the same; remove that, and ye remove them both alike. This justifies the high providence of God, who

---

[149] Hales (p. 110) suggests this means "not so much an 'allowance,' as 'allowancing,' i.e., a system of allowance."

[150] *Cf.* Aristotle, *Ethics,* III, 2; *Paradise Lost,* III, 95–128.

[151] Puppet-shows.

[152] *Cf.* Sir Thomas Browne, *Religio Medici* (London, Everyman Library: 1934), p. 71: "They that endeavour to abolish Vice, destroy also Virtue."

though he command us temperance, justice, continence, yet powrs out before us ev'n to a profusenes all desirable things, and gives us minds that can wander beyond all limit and satiety. Why should we then affect a rigor contrary to the manner of God and of nature, by abridging or scanting those means, which books freely permitted are, both to the triall of vertue, and the exercise of truth. It would be better done to learn that the law must needs be frivolous which goes to restrain things, uncertainly and yet equally working to good, and to evill. And were I the chooser, a dram of well-doing should be preferr'd before many times as much the forcible hindrance of evill-doing. For God sure esteems the growth and compleating of one vertuous person, more then the restraint of ten vitious. And albeit what ever thing we hear or see, sitting, walking, travelling, or conversing may be fitly call'd our book, and is of the same effect that writings are, yet grant the thing to be prohibited were only books, it appears that this order hitherto is far insufficient to the end which it intends. Do we not see, not once or oftner, but weekly that continu'd Court-libell [153] against the Parlament and City, Printed, as the wet sheets can witnes, and dispers't among us, for all that licencing can doe? yet this is the prime service a man would think, wherein this order should give proof of it self. If it were executed, you'l say. But certain, if execution be remisse or blindfold now, and in this particular, what will it be hereafter, and in other books. If then the order shall not be vain and frustrat, behold a new labour, Lords and Commons, ye must repeal and proscribe all scandalous and unlicenc't books already printed and divulg'd; after ye have [18] drawn them up into a list, that all may know which are

---

[153] *Mercurius Aulicus*, a newspaper published weekly from early 1642 to late 1645, and sporadically for some time thereafter. Established largely to counter the effects of *Mercurius Britanicus* [*sic*], the Parliamentary newspaper, it was written by Sir John Birkenhead and published at Oxford by the appointment of Charles. Even in areas controlled by Parliament it managed to achieve a wide underground circulation, and, as Milton says, it was reprinted by secret presses within London itself. *The Parliament Scout . . . Numb. 73*, reporting for the period a fortnight before *Areopagitica's* publication, says (November 14, 1644; E17 [4], p. 585): "*Aulicus* may come through all the Watches, Courts of Guards, and call the Parliament-men Rebells, Traitours, jeer and scoff city, countrey, Clergy, and what not? and he may be suffered within the walls of London, yea, to be reprinted, and disperst in the face of Westminister Hall; and may not a true friend to the Parliament tell his friends and the Parliament the truth . . . ?"

condemn'd, and which not; and ordain that no forrein books be deliver'd out of custody, till they have bin read over.[154] This office will require the whole time of not a few overseers, and those no vulgar men. There be also books which are partly usefull and excellent, partly culpable and pernicious; this work will ask as many more officials,[155] to make expurgations, and expunctions, that the Commonwealth of learning be not damnify'd.[156] In fine, when the multitude of books encrease upon their hands, ye must be fain to catalogue all those Printers who are found frequently offending, and forbidd the importation of their whole suspected *typography*. In a word, that this your order may be exact, and not deficient, ye must reform it perfectly according to the model of *Trent* and *Sevil*,[157] which I know ye abhorre to doe. Yet though ye should condiscend to this, which God forbid, the order still would be but fruitlesse and defective to that end whereto ye meant it. If to prevent sects and schisms, who is so unread or so uncatechis'd in story, that hath not heard of many sects refusing books as a hindrance, and preserving their doctrine unmixt for many ages, only by unwritt'n traditions.[158] The Christian faith, for that was once a schism, is not unknown to have spread all over *Asia*, ere any Gospel or Epistle was seen in writing. If the amendment of manners be aym'd

[154] This provision against foreign books was in fact made in section VI of the Star-Chamber Decree of 1637; see Appendix A, below, p. 794.

[155] White (pp. 92–93) has shown how hateful this word was at the time of the *Areopagitica:* "An *official* was the name of the officer in the Ecclesiastical Courts to whom the Bishops deputed the cognizance of spiritual offences. Laud had let them loose over the country." He quotes from *Of Reformation* (*Complete Prose*, I, 543: "to goe about circl'd with a band of rooking Officials") and cites the title of the Root-and-Branch Bill of 1641 ("a bill for the utter eradication of Bishops, Deans, and Chapters; with all Chancellors, *Officials*, and all officers and other Persons belonging to either of them").

[156] *Cf.* Sarpi, *Inquisition*, p. 81: "It is a folly to thinke that the Commonwealth may be damnified by the printing of an evill booke, and not if it be printed in another place, and so scattered abroad"; *cf.* note 154.

[157] See above, p. 493, note 26, and p. 502, n. 61.

[158] One reason this was so widely known was that historians constantly used it to explain inadequacy of documentary evidence. *E.g.*, Drayton's *Poly-Olbion* with Selden's "Illustrations" (1612; Milton appears to have known this: *cf.* below, p. 551, n. 230) declares (Song X) that the Druids "To letters never would their mysteries commit, / For which the breasts of men they deem'd to be more fit"; and Selden's note compares the Jewish Cabalists, who "until of late time wrote not, but taught and learnt by mouth and diligent hearing of their rabbins."

at, look into Italy and Spain, whether those places be one scruple the better, the honester, the wiser, the chaster, since all the inquisitionall rigor that hath bin executed upon books.

Another reason, whereby to make it plain that this order will misse the end it seeks, consider by the quality which ought to be in every licencer. It cannot be deny'd but that he who is made judge to sit upon the birth, or death of books whether they may be wafted [159] into this world, or not, had need to be a man above the common measure, both studious, learned, and judicious; there may be else no mean mistakes in the censure of what is passable or not; which is also no mean injury. If he be of such worth as behoovs him, there cannot be a more tedious and unpleasing journey-work, a greater losse of time levied upon his head, then to be made the perpetuall reader of unchosen books and pamphlets, oftimes huge volumes. There is no book that is acceptable unlesse at certain seasons; but to be enjoyn'd the reading of that at all times, and in a hand scars legible, whereof three pages would not down at any time in the fairest Print, is an imposition which I cannot beleeve how he that values time, and his own [19] studies, or is but of a sensible nostrill should be able to endure. In this one thing I crave leave of the present licencers to be pardon'd for so thinking: who doubtlesse took this office up, looking on it through their obedience to the Parlament, whose command perhaps made all things seem easie and unlaborious to them; but that this short triall hath wearied them out already, their own expressions and excuses to them who make so many journeys to sollicit their licence, are testimony anough. Seeing therefore those who now possesse the imployment, by all evident signs wish themselves well ridd of it, and that no man of worth, none that is not a plain unthrift of his own hours is ever likely to succeed them, except he mean to put himself to the salary of a Presse-corrector, we may easily foresee what kind of licencers we are to expect hereafter, either ignorant, imperious, and remisse, or basely pecuniary. This is what I had to shew wherein this order cannot conduce to that end, whereof it bears the intention.

I lastly proceed from the no good it can do, to the manifest hurt it causes, in being first the greatest discouragement and affront, that can be offer'd to learning and to learned men. It was the com-

[159] The image assumes the mythical river dividing the unborn souls from the living world; see Plato's *Phaedo*, 113.

plaint and lamentation of Prelats, upon every least breath of a motion to remove pluralities, and distribute more equally Church revennu's, that then all learning would be for ever dasht and discourag'd.[160] But as for that opinion, I never found cause to think that the tenth part of learning stood or fell with the Clergy: nor could I ever but hold it for a sordid and unworthy speech of any Churchman who had a competency left him.[161] If therefore ye be loath to dishearten utterly and discontent, not the mercenary crew of false pretenders to learning, but the free and ingenuous sort of such as evidently were born to study, and love lerning for it self, not for lucre, or any other end, but the service of God and of truth, and perhaps that lasting fame and perpetuity of praise which God and good men have consented shall be the reward of those whose publisht labours advance the good of mankind, then know, that so far to distrust the judgement & the honesty of one who hath but a common repute in learning, and never yet offended, as not to count him fit to print his mind without a tutor and examiner, lest he should drop a scism, or something of corruption, is the greatest displeasure and indignity to a free and knowing spirit that can be put upon him. What advantage is it to be a man over it is to be a boy at school, if we have only scapt the ferular,[162] to come under the fescu [163] of an *Imprimatur*? if serious and elaborat writings, as if they were no [20] more then the theam of a Grammar lad under his Pedagogue must not be utter'd [164] without the cursory eyes of a temporizing and extemporizing licencer. He who is not trusted with his own actions, his drift not being known to be evill, and standing to the hazard of law and penalty, has no great argument to think himself reputed in the Commonwealth wherin he was born,

---

[160] Howard Schultz, *Milton and Forbidden Knowledge*, pp. 288–89, gives a selective bibliography of Episcopalians who advanced this defense of pluralities and Puritans who attacked it.

[161] *Cf., e.g., Animadversions, Complete Prose*, I, 718–23 (which includes the quotation from "our admired *Spencer*" of *Shepheardes Calendar*, May eclogue, ll. 103–31), and *Church-Government, Complete Prose*, I, 855–56. Milton often returned to this point in later years; *cf., e.g., Likeliest Means* (1659), pp. 140–41. The *tenth* part of learning: a glance at tithes.

[162] Ferula is the giant fennel, and, from its use in Roman times, a cane, rod, or other instrument of punishment, especially in school discipline. Ferular is another form of the same word.

[163] Originally a straw or twig, finally a pointer used as an aid to instruction.

[164] Published.

for other then a fool or a foreiner. When a man writes to the world, he summons up all his reason and deliberation to assist him; he searches, meditats, is industrious, and likely consults and conferrs with his judicious friends; after all which done he takes himself to be inform'd in what he writes, as well as any that writ before him; if in this the most consummat act of his fidelity and ripenesse, no years, no industry, no former proof of his abilities can bring him to that state of maturity, as not to be still mistrusted and suspected, unlesse he carry all his considerat diligence, all his midnight watchings, and expence of *Palladian* [165] oyl, to the hasty view of an unleasur'd licencer, perhaps much his younger, perhaps far his inferiour in judgement, perhaps one who never knew the labour of book-writing, and if he be not repulst, or slighted, must appear in Print like a punie [166] with his guardian, and his censors hand on the back of his title to be his bayl and surety, that he is no idiot, or seducer, it cannot be but a dishonor and derogation to the author, to the book, to the priviledge and dignity of Learning. And what if the author shall be one so copious of fancie, as to have many things well worth the adding, come into his mind after licencing, while the book is yet under the Presse, which not seldom happ'ns to the best and diligentest writers; and that perhaps a dozen times in one book. The Printer dares not go beyond his licenc't copy; so often then must the author trudge to his leav-giver, that those his new insertions may be viewd; and many a jaunt will be made, ere that licencer, for it must be the same man, can either be found, or found at leisure; mean while either the Presse must stand still, which is no small damage, or the author loose his accuratest thoughts, & send the book forth wors then he had made it, which to a diligent writer is the greatest melancholy and vexation that can befall. And how can a man teach with autority, which is the life

---

[165] Pertaining to Pallas Athene, goddess of wisdom. The olive was sacred to her, and she taught man to extract its oil; one of its uses was to feed the lamps by which the devotees of wisdom studied and wrote.

[166] Old French *puis-ne*, after-born; hence a minor. In the schools it meant, technically, a freshman (*NED*, B2), but might be applied to one whose status had not advanced with his years, which is Milton's meaning here; *cf.* Thomas Grantham, *A Discourse in Derision of the Teaching in Free-Schooles* (July 1, 1644), E53(7), p. 8: "Very few of our Gentry are Schollers, for at fourteen or fifteen the bloud growes hot, and they scorn a yoak, and then they are but punies, in the Common-Schooles, under the lowest or second Usher."

of teaching, how can he be a Doctor in his book as he ought to be, or else had better be silent, whenas all he teaches, all he delivers, is but under the tuition, under the correction of his patriarchal [167] licencer to blot or alter [168] what precisely accords not with the hidebound humor which he calls his his judgement. When every a-[21] cute reader upon the first sight of a pedantick licence, will be ready with these like words to ding the book a coits distance from him, I hate a pupil teacher, I endure not an instructer that comes to me under the wardship of an overseeing fist. I know nothing of the

[167] There is a pun here, giving yet another implicit comparison of the Licensing Order with Laud's administration of the Church. There was a widespread belief that Laud had labored to return England to the Roman Catholic Church, the price to be the erection of a Patriarchate of the Western Church, with himself first in office. See, e.g., A True Delineation, or other Parallel, between Cardinal Wolsey, Arch-bishop of York, and Wm. Laud, Arch-bishop of Canterbury (1641; in Somers Tracts, IV, 434): "They both favored the See of Rome and respected his holinesse in it: the Cardinal did professe it publickly, the Arch-bishop did professe it privately. The Cardinal's ambition was to be Pope: the Arch-bishop strove to be Patriarch: they both bid fairly for it; yet lost their aime." Cf. Of Reformation, Complete Prose, I, 529: "And doutles, when ever the Pope shall fall, . . . the Bishops . . . will leave him, and fall to scrambling, catch who may, hee a Patriarch-dome, and another what comes next hand; as the French Cardinall of late, and the See of Canterbury hath plainly affected." At Laud's trial some months before Areopagitica, one charge was that he had attempted "to reconcile the church of England with the church of Rome" and "agreeably to this he assumed to himself the title of PATRIARCH, or pope of Great Britain, alterius orbis papa." See Neal, History of the Puritans, II, 154. See following note.

[168] Milton's charge is that the licensers not merely deleted but even changed what they did not approve. Since this was one of the charges the House of Commons had brought against Laud (see Neal, II, 149–151), it strongly reinforces the allusion implicit in "patriarchal"; see preceding note. James Howell tells of an incident that took place sometime between 1643 and 1646. The printer Richard Heron (or Hearne) took a thirty-year-old sermon of the late Thomas Brightman "to him who was appointed by the Synod to license for the Press peeces of that nature, to get an Imprimatur, but the Synodical man having kept the Sermon above three daies by him, the Printer went for his Sermon, and found it formally licenc'd for the Press, but most pittifully falsify'd, interlin'd and adulterated in many places; For whereas the opinion of Brightman throughout the whole Sermon, was, that a National and General Covenant was agreeable to the Word of God, Provided, the King did give his Royall assent thereunto, without which it was both detestable and damnable; The holy Synodical man had expunged the word King every where, and foisted in the room of it, sometimes the word Parlement, sometimes the Trustees of the Common wealth; sometimes the men in Authority. . . . I saw the said Sermon, and the maner how it was so basely sophisticated" (Philanglus, 1655; quoted by W. M. Clyde, "Parliament and the Press," The Library, Fourth Series, XIII [1932], 413–14).

licencer, but that I have his own hand here for his arrogance; who shall warrant me his judgement? The State Sir, replies the Stationer, but has a quick return, The State shall be my governours, but not my criticks; they may be mistak'n in the choice of a licencer, as easily as this licencer may be mistak'n in an author: This is some common stuffe; and he might adde from Sir *Francis Bacon*, That *such authoriz'd books are but the language of the times.*[169] For though a licencer should happ'n to be judicious more then ordnary, which will be a great jeopardy of the next succession, yet his very office, and his commission enjoyns him to let passe nothing but what is vulgarly receiv'd already. Nay, which is more lamentable, if the work of any deceased author, though never so famous in his life time, and even to this day, come to their hands for licence to be Printed, or Reprinted, if there be found in his book one sentence of a ventrous edge, utter'd in the height of zeal, and who knows whether it might not be the dictat of a divine Spirit, yet not suiting with every low decrepit humor of their own, though it were *Knox* himself, the Reformer of a Kingdom that spake it, they will not pardon him their dash: the sense of that great man shall to all posterity be lost, for the fearfulnesse, or the presumptuous rashnesse of a perfunctory licencer. And to what an author [170] this violence hath bin lately done, and in what book of greatest consequence to be faithfully publisht, I could now instance, but shall forbear till a more convenient season. Yet if these things be not resented seriously and timely by them who have the remedy in their power, but that such iron moulds as these shall have autority to knaw out the choisest periods of exquisitest books, and to commit such a treacherous fraud against the orphan remainders of worthiest men after

---

[169] *An Advertisement Touching the Controversies of the Church of England;* James Spedding, *Letters and Life of Francis Bacon* (3 vols., London: 1861), I, 78. The preceding part of this sentence is quoted later; see below, p. 542, n. 193. *Cf.* also *Animadversions, Complete Prose,* I, 668. Bacon wrote this piece for private circulation in 1589, at the height of the Admonition controversy; it was first published as *A Wise and Moderate Discourse Concerning Church-Affaires,* in 1640 (as Spedding thought) or 1641. See introduction, *Complete Prose,* I, 22–28.

[170] Identity uncertain; White (pp. 106–108) suggests Edward Coke, Part II of whose *Institutes,* posthumously published by Parliamentary warrant in 1641, was widely understood to have undergone mutilation; or possibly Knox, from whose *History of the Reformation in Scotland* (pub. 1584) several passages were expunged in the 1644 edition.

death, the more sorrow will belong to that haples race of men, whose misfortune it is to have understanding. Henceforth let no man care to learn, or care to be more then worldly wise; for certainly in higher matters to be ignorant and slothfull, to be a common stedfast dunce will be the only pleasant life, and only in request.

And as it is a particular disesteem of every knowing person alive, and most injurious to the writt'n labours and monuments of the dead, so to me it seems an undervaluing and vilifying of the whole Nation. I [22] cannot set so light by all the invention, the art, the wit, the grave and solid judgement which is in England, as that it can be comprehended in any twenty [171] capacities how good soever, much lesse that it should not passe except their superintendence be over it, except it be sifted and strain'd with their strainers, that it should be uncurrant without their manuall stamp. Truth and understanding are not such wares as to be monopoliz'd [172] and traded in by tickets and statutes, and standards.[173] We must not

[171] This gives the impression that there were twenty licensers (cf. also below, p. 558, n. 257). The list announced by Parliament six days after the Licensing Order totals thirty-four, not including the Parliamentary Committee for Printing (Siebert, *Freedom of the Press in England 1476–1776*, pp. 187–88). It is possible that they had been reduced to twenty by November, 1644, but I can find no record to suggest it.

[172] Another word associating the Licensing Order with a widely detested feature of Charles' reign. Commodity monopolies were abolished (except for new inventions) in 1624, but were prominent among the illegal exactions into which Charles was led by his determination to rule without Parliament. Considerable attention was paid them by Parliament's *Grand Remonstrance* of 1641 (see articles 27 and 115–19; Gardiner, *Constitutional Documents*, pp. 212 and 221–22; see also *Complete Prose*, I, 171–73). Cf. below, notes 205 and 259.

[173] Tickets: Here probably certificates of special trading prerogatives (*NED* quotes Greene's *James IV*, III, ii, "I am the king's purveyor. . . . Here's my ticket") rather than, as usually glossed, acknowledgements for goods obtained on credit. Such a special authorization would automatically entail restrictions on those not so authorized; *e.g.*, goods loaded or unloaded at the London quays could in the seventeenth century be handled only by "Ticket Porters," a body of men licensed by the City Corporation, whose numbers were limited and whose right to do the work was a jealously guarded monopoly. statutes: This may refer to bonds given to creditors (statutes merchant, statutes staple) or possibly, in view of the phrase in the following sentence, "to mark and licence it like our broad cloath," to certain kinds of cloth, of breadth fixed by statute; but more probably it means such statutes of the realm as either impose the special restrictions upon trade involved in monopolies and tickets, or enforce fixed standards of measurement (*NED* quotes Bacon's *Henry VII*, p. 101, "There was also a Statute, for the dispersing of the Standard of the Exchequor, throughout England; thereby to size Weights and Measures").

think to make a staple commodity [174] of all the knowledge in the
Land, to mark and licence it like our broad cloath, and our wooll
packs. What is it but a servitude like that impos'd by the Philistims,
not to be allow'd the sharpning of our own axes and coulters,[175]
but we must repair from all quarters to twenty licencing forges.
Had any one writt'n and divulg'd erroneous things & scandalous
to honest life, misusing and forfeiting the esteem had of his reason
among men, if after conviction this only censure were adjudg'd
him, that he should never henceforth write, but what were first
examin'd by an appointed officer, whose hand should be annext to
passe his credit for him, that now he might be safely read, it could
not be apprehended lesse then a disgracefull punishment. Whence
to include the whole Nation, and those that never yet thus offended,
under such a diffident and suspectfull prohibition, may plainly be
understood what a disparagement it is. So much the more, when
as dettors and delinquents may walk abroad without a keeper,[176]
but unoffensive books must not stirre forth without a visible jaylor
in thir title. Nor is it to the common people lesse then a reproach;
for if we be so jealous over them, as that we dare not trust them
with an English pamphlet, what doe we but censure them for a
giddy, vitious, and ungrounded people; in such a sick and weak
estate of faith and discretion, as to be able to take nothing down

[174] staple commodity: *NED:* "An article of merchandise the trade in which is
subjected to the regulations of the Staple" (the town or place or body of merchants possessing royal authority to control a particular traffic).

[175] I Samuel 13:19–20.

[176] Debtors were, of course, jailed if caught on unprivileged ground; but the
precincts of the dissolved monasteries were sanctuaries where they could live
unmolested, and "Alsatias" like Blackfriars and St. Martin le Grand swarmed
with them (see 8 & 9 William III *cap* XXVII). Even imprisoned debtors might
enjoy considerable liberty, since the "rules" of some debtors' prisons (*e.g.*, the
Marshalsea) included whole streets of ordinary houses where, if the keeper
consented, a prisoner could maintain a pretty ordinary life. Delinquents:
On March 27, 1643, Parliament had declared all who had assisted the king to
be "delinquents," sequestered their property, and made them liable to imprisonment; but on January 30, 1644, it offered pardon to those who submitted before
a certain date, and permitted them to compound for their confiscated estates by
paying an assessment (usually about two years' revenue). See Gardiner, *Civil
War,* I, 116 and 353, and III, 7. Milton's brother Christopher appears to have
experienced both the original and the milder ordinances; see French, *Life
Records,* II, 92, 99, 103, 109. Contemporary records are full of compositions
only partially paid; perhaps this is what Milton means by delinquents walking
abroad.

but through the pipe of a licencer. That this is care or love of them, we cannot pretend, whenas in those Popish places where the Laity are most hated and dispis'd the same strictnes is us'd over them. Wisdom we cannot call it, because it stops but one breach of licence, nor that neither; whenas those corruptions which it seeks to prevent, break in faster at other dores which cannot be shut.

And in conclusion it reflects to the disrepute of our Ministers also, of whose labours we should hope better, and of the proficiencie which thir flock reaps by them, then that after all this light of the Gospel which is, and is to be, and all this continuall preaching, they [23] should be still frequented with such an unprincipl'd, unedify'd, and laick rabble,[177] as that the whiffe of every new pamphlet should stagger them out of thir catechism, and Christian walking. This may have much reason to discourage the Ministers when such a low conceit is had of all their exhortations, and the benefiting of their hearers, as that they are not thought fit to be turn'd loose to three sheets of paper without a licencer, that all the Sermons, all the Lectures preacht, printed, vented in such numbers, and such volumes, as have now wellnigh made all other books unsalable, should not be armor anough against one single *enchiridion*,[178] without the castle St. *Angelo* [179] of an *Imprimatur*.

And lest som should perswade ye, Lords and Commons, that these arguments of lerned mens discouragement at this your order, are meer flourishes, and not reall, I could recount what I have seen and heard in other Countries, where this kind of inquisition tyrannizes; when I have sat among their lerned men, for that honor I had, and bin counted happy to be born in such a place of *Philosophic* freedom, as they suppos'd England was, while themselvs did nothing but bemoan the servil condition into which lerning amongst

---

[177] Another anti-Laudian echo; one of the most emotion-charged complaints against Laud was that he sought to reduce the laity to a wholly passive role in the church. Milton voiced a representative Puritan view when he argued (*Reason of Church-Government, Complete Prose*, I, 838) that the people were "not now any more to be separated in the Church by vails and partitions as laicks and unclean, but admitted to wait upon the tabernacle as the rightfull Clergy of Christ, a chosen generation, a royal Priesthood."

[178] A pun exploiting both meanings of *enchiridion:* hand-knife and hand-book.

[179] Although the castle of St. Angelo was originally an imperial mausoleum and in Milton's time a papal prison, it was an appropriate symbol of a fortress, having been decisive in Belisarius' victorious defense of Rome against the great siege of Vitiges (537–538).

them was brought; that this was it which had dampt the glory of
Italian wits; that nothing had bin there writt'n now these many
years but flattery and fustian. There it was that I found and visited
the famous *Galileo* [180] grown old, a prisner to the Inquisition, for
thinking in Astronomy otherwise then the Franciscan and Dominican licencers thought. And though I knew that England then [181]
was groaning loudest under the Prelaticall yoak, neverthelesse I
took it as a pledge of future happines, that other Nations were so
perswaded of her liberty. Yet was it beyond my hope that those
Worthies were then breathing in her air, who should be her leaders

---

[180] In 1632 the great physicist and astronomer (1564–1642) published his
Dialogue on the Two Chief Systems, which confirmed the Copernican cosmology.
He was forced to recant by the Inquisition, which thereafter kept him imprisoned
in the Villa Martinelli, near Florence. S. B. Liljegren (*Studies in Milton,* Lund,
1918, pp. 3–36) charged that Milton merely invented this visit. His argument is
based on two contentions: that such a visit would have been almost impossible,
and that Milton is not a credible witness. The first has been disposed of by the
work of three scholars: Marjorie Nicolson ("Milton and the Telescope," *ELH,*
II [1935], pp. 1–32, especially 8–10), who showed that, besides the relatives and
known friends allowed by Liljegren, Galileo had other visitors (the records of at
least four during the period 1638–1641 being extant), and that the editor of the
official national edition of his works, writing after Liljegren, continues to believe
the meeting took place; and James H. Hanford (*John Milton, Englishman* [New
York: Crown, 1949], pp. 79–81) and D. C. Dorian (*The English Diodatis* [New
Brunswick: Rutgers U. Press, 1950], pp. 172–73), who showed how suitable
were Milton's connections, and how good his opportunities, for arranging such a
meeting. As for Milton's alleged unreliability as a witness, Liljegren's argument
is as follows. (1) Milton gave an account of his Italian journey in the *Second
Defence* and did not repeat his claim to have met Galileo. Inference: the *Second
Defence,* being in Latin, would be understood by Italians in a position to know
the facts; therefore Milton decided against repeating the Galileo story. (2) Also
in the *Second Defence,* Milton referred to some great men who were blind and
did not include Galileo. Inference: Milton was unaware that Galileo had gone
blind, and (since this occurred before Milton's European tour) had therefore
not met him. (3) Milton planted the famous "Pamela prayer" in the *Eikon
Basilike* (see Vol. III). Inference: Milton was a dishonest man. What is serious
in all this is the charge that Milton forged the Pamela prayer, and it has been
finally disproved by F. F. Madan, *A New Bibliography of the Eikon Basilike*
(London: Bernard Quaritch, 1950), pp. 120–21; *cf.* also M. Y. Hughes, "New
Evidence on the Charge That Milton Forged the Pamela Prayer," *Review of
English Studies,* n.s. III (1952), pp. 130–40. All that is left, then, of Liljegren's
famous attack is just what Bernhardi had observed some forty years earlier:
that it was surprising that Milton did not, in 1654, make the use that might have
been expected of the man he had met in 1638 (Wilhelm Bernhardi, *John Miltons
Politische Hauptschriften* [3 vols., Berlin, 1876], II, 215–16).

[181] Milton's European tour took place in 1638–1639.

to such a deliverance, as shall never be forgott'n by any revolution
of time that this world hath to finish. When that was once begun,
it was as little in my fear, that what words of complaint I heard
among lerned men of other parts utter'd against the Inquisition, the
same I should hear by as lerned men at home utterd in time of
Parlament against an order of licencing; and that so generally,
that when I had disclos'd my self a companion of their discontent, I
might say, if without envy, that he whom an honest *quaestorship*
had indear'd to the *Sicilians*,[182] was not more by them importun'd
against *Verres*, then the favourable opinion which I had among
many who honour ye, and are known and respected by ye, [24]
loaded me with entreaties and perswasions; that I would not despair to lay together that which just reason should bring into my
mind, toward the removal of an undeserved thraldom upon lerning.
That this is not therefore the disburdning of a particular fancie,
but the common grievance of all those who had prepar'd their
minds and studies above the vulgar pitch to advance truth in others,
and from others to entertain it, thus much may satisfie. And in
their name I shall for neither friend nor foe conceal what the generall murmur is; that if it come to inquisitioning again, and licencing, and that we are so timorous of our selvs, and so suspicious of
all men, as to fear each book, and the shaking of every leaf, before
we know what the contents are, if some who but of late were little
better then silenc't from preaching, shall come now to silence us
from reading, except what they please, it cannot be guest what is
intended by som but a second tyranny over learning: and will soon
put it out of controversie that Bishops and Presbyters are the same
to us both name and thing.[183] That those evills of Prelaty which be-

---

[182] Cicero was quaestor in Sicily in 75 B.C. Verres was praetor there, 73–71 B.C.
It was in indictment of the latter's extortions that Cicero composed his Verrine
Orations; only the first two were delivered, after which Verres went into exile.

[183] An ironical history underlies this line of attack. On the one hand, it had
always been a basic Puritan contention that the hierarchical structure of the
Church of England was invalid, since there was nothing to indicate that the
Gospel recognized a third ecclesiastical order besides priest (for which "bishop"
and "presbyter" were synonyms) and deacon; thus, in *Of Prelatical Episcopacy*,
Milton provided an elaborate philological, exegetical, and historical argument to
show (*Complete Prose*, I, 650) that "a Bishop and *Presbyter* is all one both in
name, and office." On the other hand, the defenders of Episcopacy had always
contended that Presbyterianism would vest tyrannical power in each minister.
Thus Bishop Hall warned (*Episcopacie by Divine Right*, 1640; *Works*, ed. Philip

fore from five or six and twenty Sees were distributivly charg'd upon the whole people, will now light wholly upon learning, is not obscure to us: whenas now the Pastor of a small unlearned Parish, on the sudden shall be exalted Archbishop over a large dioces of books, and yet not remove, but keep his other cure too, a mysticall pluralist. He who but of late cry'd down the sole ordination of every novice Batchelor of Art, and deny'd sole jurisdiction over the simplest Parishioner,[184] shall now at home in his privat chair assume both these over worthiest and excellentest books and ablest authors that write them. This is not, Yee Covnants [185] and Protestations [186]

Wynter [10 vols., London, 1863], IX, 270) against setting up "a pope and his conclave of cardinals within his own parish," and Sir Thomas Aston (*A Remonstrance against Presbitery* [1641, E163 (1)], p. 250) pictured the Presbyterian minister as "the little Bishop, absolute Pope of every parish." Milton's bitter jest thus means that the controversy about whether "bishop" and "presbyter" mean the same thing will soon end, since the conduct of the Presbyterian divines confirms simultaneously both the Episcopalian argument from consequences (that they will prove petty tyrants) and the Puritan argument from definition (that they are the same as bishops). Compare the pun in the sonnet *con coda* of a year or two later: "*New Presbyter* is but *Old Priest* writ large" (the etymology of "priest" is a series of elisions from "presbyter"). See introduction, above, pp. 109, 123–24, 129–30.

[184] The bishops' claim to possess the sole right to ordain ministers and to exercise spiritual jurisdiction within their dioceses had, of course, been strongly contested by the Presbyterians. Milton illustrates the Presbyterian position on both points in *Animadversions,* section XIII (*Complete Prose,* I, 710 ff.); his more extensive discussion of jurisdiction in *Reason of Church-Government* (*Complete Prose,* I, 830 ff.) has moved somewhat to the left of Presbyterian orthodoxy.

[185] The Scots' National Covenant (February 28, 1638) formalized the Presbyterian resistance to the effort of Charles and Laud to impose Episcopacy on Scotland. This became the basis of the Solemn League and Covenant between England and Scotland (ratified by Parliament September 25, 1643, and ordered for subscription for all Englishmen February 5, 1644), which was, in effect, a treaty bringing a Scottish army to the assistance of the Long Parliament. It undertook to abolish Episcopacy and reform religion in the Church of England. Whether or not the Licensing Order was consistent with its terms was a matter of interpretation (and interpretation of the Covenant was to became fiercely divisive in the following years); certainly, despite Milton's view, it was consistent with the intent at the time of the treaty of the Scots and of the Presbyterian majority in the Parliament that promulgated it. For a fuller discussion see introduction, above, pp. 53–54, 57–65.

[186] At the beginning of May, 1641, Charles, despairing of other means to protect Strafford, prepared to use force against Parliament. One of Parliament's defensive measures was the Protestation (May 3–4), taken by members of both Houses and subscribed by many citizens, which undertook to defend, besides religion, Crown, and Parliament, "the lawful rights and liberties of the subjects";

that we have made, this is not to put down Prelaty, this is but to chop [187] an Episcopacy, this is but to translate the Palace *Metropolitan* from one kind of dominion into another, this is but an old canonicall slight of *commuting* our penance.[188] To startle thus betimes at a meer unlicenc't pamphlet will after a while be afraid of every conventicle, and a while after will make a conventicle of every Christian meeting. But I am certain that a State govern'd by the rules of justice and fortitude, or a Church built and founded upon the rock of faith and true knowledge, cannot be so pusillanimous. While things are yet not constituted in Religion,[189] that freedom of writing should be restrain'd by a discipline imitated from the Prelats, and learnt by them from the Inquisition to shut us up all again into the brest of a licencer, must needs give cause of doubt and [25] discouragement to all learned and religious men. Who cannot but discern the finenes of this politic drift, and who are the contrivers; that while Bishops were to be baited down, then all Presses might be open; it was the peoples birthright and priviledge in time of Parlament, it was the breaking forth of light. But now the Bishops abrogated and voided out of the Church, as if our Reformation sought no more, but to make room for others into their seats under another name, the Episcopall arts begin to bud again, the cruse of truth must run no more oyle,[190] liberty of Printing must be enthrall'd again under a Prelaticall commission of twenty, the privilege of the people nullify'd, and which is wors, the freedom of learning must

see Gardiner, *History of England*, IX, 354. As in the case of the Covenant, the consistency of the Licensing Order with the Protestation is a matter of interpretation.

[187] *NED* (v.2·7.) cites this passage and defines "chop" as "to change" (*i.e.,* alter), explaining that "the meaning of 'change' [from 'chop and change'] passes over into *chop* alone"; but the context suggests rather the earlier meaning "to exchange" (*i.e.,* barter).

[188] One of the charges against Laud was that he took "several large sums of money by way of composition for fines in the high commission court, making use of the method of *commutation*." Laud replied that the money had gone to repair "the west end of St. *Paul's*," and "he thought it his duty to get as much money for so good a work as he could, even by way of *commutation* for certain crimes." See Neal, *History of the Puritans*, II, 129.

[189] The Assembly of Divines (Westminster Assembly), whose task it was to advise Parliament on a settlement of the Church, was still, at the time of writing, debating the matter; its famous *Confession of Faith* was not in its entirety submitted to Parliament until December 7, 1646. See introduction, above, pp. 61–72, 92–107.

[190] See I Kings 17:9–16.

groan again, and to her old fetters; all this the Parlament yet sitting.[191] Although their own late arguments and defences against the Prelats might remember them that this obstructing violence meets for the most part with an event utterly opposite to the end which it drives at: instead of suppressing sects and schisms, it raises them and invests them with a reputation: [192] *The punishing of wits enhaunces their autority,* saith the Vicount St. *Albans, and a forbidd'n writing is thought to be a certain spark of truth that flies up in the faces of them who seeke to tread it out.*[193] This order therefore may

[191] *Cf.* Henry Robinson, *John the Baptist* (September 23, 1644), E9(13), pp. 23–24: "Had it not been for that blessed liberty of Printing which this Kingdome has enjoyed some two or three yeares together after the first sitting of this Parliament, we had yet remained in ignorance of much saving truth, and amongst other mischiefes beene still as deeply engaged for Episcopacie, as ever; but since God thereby has already given so great a blessing to us, as an earnest of his greater bounty hereafter, why doe we stifle it in the birth? . . . If . . . Presbytery be Gospel proofe, why is it afraid to come to triall? . . . the necessity of suffering erroneous opinions to be published, lest truth thereby should be stifled, is so cleare and necessary to the eye of reason, as it is for him that hath lost any thing, to seek it where it is not, as well as where it is." See introduction, above, pp. 87–88.

[192] *Cf.* Walwyn's *Compassionate Samaritane,* pp. 17–23, for a close parallel to this double argument, simultaneously warning the Presbyterians of their danger and impugning their motives: "A compultion is of all wayes the most unlikely to beget unity of mind, and uniformity in practise, which experience will make evident. For, The Fines, Imprisonments, Pillories, Banishments, &c. used by the Bishops as meanes to unite, rather confirmed men in their judgements, and begot the abomination and *odium* which these times have cast upon the Hierarchy. . . . And therefore in these times men should consider what they doe. For if they who have the publique countenance doe beare themselves after the same manner towards [those] . . . that cannot comply with them in judgement or practise . . . what can we judge of them but that their ends and intentions are the same with the Bishops? . . . Now . . . men doe speake very strangly, some say the tyrannie over conscience that was exercised by the Bishops, is like to be continued by the Presbyter: that the oppressors are only changed, but the oppression not like to be removed. . . . Nay some say further, that they did well indeede in being so zealous against the Bishops, those Drones and Caterpillers of the Common wealth, in making deservedly odious to the people their oppressive Courts, Fines, Censures, and imprisonments. But they beginne to feare that some bad ends of their owne were aimed [at] herein, and not so much the liberty of the people, [as that] they might get up into the chaire and become to them instead of a Lord Bishop, a ruling Presbytery" (bracketed inserts are from the second edition, pp. 12–19; in Haller, *Tracts,* III, 61 ff.). For a discussion of this pamphlet and evidence that Milton knew it, see introduction, above, pp. 84–87.

[193] See above, p. 534, n. 169. Milton knew that Bacon took the first epigram from Tacitus (see above, p. 499, n. 51), but Bacon's contemporary prestige made his the more useful name to invoke.

prove a nursing mother to sects, but I shall easily shew how it will be a step-dame to Truth: and first by disinabling us to the maintenance of what is known already.

Well knows he who uses to consider, that our faith and knowledge thrives by exercise, as well as our limbs and complexion. Truth is compar'd in Scripture to a streaming fountain; [194] if her waters flow not in a perpetuall progression, they sick'n into a muddy pool of conformity and tradition.[195] A man may be a heretick in the truth; and if he beleeve things only because his Pastor sayes so, or the Assembly [196] so determins, without knowing other reason, though his belief be true, yet the very truth he holds, becomes his heresie.[197] There is not any burden that som would gladlier post off to another, then the charge and care of their Religion. There be, who knows not that there be of Protestants and professors [198] who live and dye in as arrant an implicit faith,[199] as any lay Papist of

[194] This is usually taken to be a reference to Psalm 85:11 ("Truth shall spring out of the earth"), but Milton may be thinking of the allegorical interpretation of the Song of Solomon 4:15 ("a fountain of gardens, a well of living waters").

[195] Cf. Robinson's Liberty of Conscience, sig. a1: "there is no medium between an implicite faith, and that which a mans owne judgement and understanding leads him to." See introduction, above, pp. 83–84, for a discussion of this pamphlet and evidence that Milton knew it; also note 21 above.

[196] See above, p. 541, n. 189.

[197] Cf. Walwyn's Compassionate Samaritane, pp. 41–42: "If we must beleeve as the Synod would have us, what is this but to be brought into their miserable condition that must beleeve as the Church beleeves, and so become, (as said an honest man,) not the Disciples of Christ, but of the Synod?" See introduction, above, pp. 84–87.

[198] NED defines this to include anyone who "makes open profession of religion," but by 1644 the word had become restricted to Puritans.

[199] The medieval church distinguished between the "explicit faith" required of the higher clergy (acceptance of the doctrines of the church with a clear understanding of their nature and grounds) and the "implicit faith" which would suffice for the lower clergy and the laity (acceptance of the same doctrines on the authority of the church). In periods of ecclesiastical rigor and inquisition the second category naturally became a general refuge, and so attracted the special hostility of the reformers; e.g., Calvin, Institutes of the Christian Religion, III, ii, 2–3, tr. Henry Beveridge (3 vols.: Edinburgh, 1865), II, 97–98: "They have invented the fiction of implicit faith, with which name decking the grossest ignorance, they delude the wretched populace to their great destruction. . . . Is it faith to understand nothing, and merely submit your convictions implicitly to the Church? . . . Faith consists in the knowledge of God and Christ, . . . not in reverence for the Church. And we see what a labyrinth they have formed out of this implicit faith—every thing, sometimes even the most monstrous errors, being received by the ignorant as oracles without any dis-

Loretto.[200] A wealthy man [201] addicted to his pleasure and to his profits, finds Religion to be a traffick so entangl'd, and of so many piddling accounts, that of all mysteries [202] he cannot skill to keep a stock going upon that trade. What should he doe? fain he would have the name to be religious, fain he would bear up with his neighbours in that. What does he therefore, but resolvs to give over toy-[26]ling, and to find himself out som factor, to whose care and credit he may commit the whole managing of his religious affairs; som Divine of note and estimation that must be. To him he adheres, resigns the whole ware-house of his religion, with all the locks and keyes into his custody; and indeed makes the very person of that man his religion; esteems his associating with him a sufficient evidence and commendatory of his own piety. So that a man may say his religion is now no more within himself, but is becom a dividuall movable, and goes and comes neer him, according as that good man frequents the house. He entertains him, gives him gifts, feasts him, lodges him; his religion comes home at night, praies, is liberally supt, and sumptuously laid to sleep, rises, is saluted, and after the malmsey, or some well spic't bruage, and better breakfasted then he whose morning appetite would have gladly fed on green figs between *Bethany* and *Jerusalem*,[203] his Religion walks abroad at eight,

crimination, provided they are prescribed to them under the name of the Church. This inconsiderate facility, though the surest precipice to destruction, is, however, excused on the ground that it believes nothing definitely, but only with the appended condition, If such is the faith of the Church." In *Animadversions* (*Complete Prose,* I, 728) Milton had accused the English Episcopacy of trying to cheat Protestants "into a blind and implicite obedience," and to the end of his life he argued that censorship and enforced conformity produce "that Papistical implicit faith which we all disclaim," while permission of argument and diversity "must needs conduce much . . . to the general confirmation of unimplicit truth." See *Of True Religion* (1673), p. 16.

[200] The popularity of this shrine was due to the presence within the cathedral of a structure reputed to be the house in which Mary was born and Jesus conceived, conveyed from Nazareth by angels in 1291. The belief was authorized by successive popes, and finally became institutionalized in the Feast of the Translation of the Holy House (see *Catholic Encyclopedia*). It was for long a favorite target for Protestant witticism.

[201] This passage (to the end of the paragraph) has been discussed in relation to the character-writing of the revolutionary period by Benjamin Boyce, *The Polemic Character 1640–1661* (Lincoln: University of Nebraska Press, 1955). pp. 24, 85–86, and 94.

[202] Mysteries: Crafts, trades, and professions.

[203] Matthew 21:17–19; Mark 11:12–14.

and leavs his kind entertainer in the shop trading all day without his religion.

Another sort there be who when they hear that all things shall be order'd, all things regulated and setl'd; nothing writt'n but what passes through the custom-house of certain Publicans [204] that have the tunaging and the poundaging [205] of all free spok'n truth, will strait give themselvs up into your hands, mak'em, & cut'em out what religion ye please; there be delights, there be recreations and jolly pastimes that will fetch the day about from sun to sun, and rock the tedious year as in a delightfull dream. What need they torture their heads with that which others have tak'n so strictly, and so unalterably into their own pourveying.[206] These are the fruits which a dull ease and cessation of our knowledge will bring forth among the people. How goodly, and how to be wisht were such an obedient unanimity as this, what a fine conformity would it starch us all into? doubtles a stanch and solid peece of frame-work, as any January could freeze together.[207]

[204] Here, tax collectors.

[205] Another effort to associate the Licensing Order with an unpopular feature of Charles' administration. The main revenue producer in the customs was a form of tariff known as tunnage and poundage. In the first session of a new reign, Parliament had traditionally granted it for the king's lifetime, but refused to do so on the accession of Charles, whose subsequent attempts to collect it on his own authority became one of the most persistent and irritating of the grievances disturbing the country before the convening of the Long Parliament; the *Grand Remonstrance* said it was "without colour or pretence of law." See Gardiner, *Constitutional Documents,* pp. 210–11; *cf.* above, p. 535, n. 172, and below, p. 559, n. 259. On June 22, 1641, Charles gave his consent to a bill declaring it illegal for the king to levy customs duties without parliamentary consent. The "modernization" of *tunage* to *tonnage* in most editions betrays a misconception of the nature of the tariff: it was a tax of three shillings on each tun (barrel) of wine and one shilling in the pound on the value (not weight) of other goods.

[206] *Cf.* Robinson, *Liberty of Conscience,* sig. a1: "Such will be found carelesse, if not negligent, in the choice of their Religion, as little troubling themselves to *trie the spirits whether they be of God or no,* 1 John 4.1. or examine the opinions and doctrines which are taught, receive them currantly, what ever they be, so they come sealed and delivered by authority of State. . . . To be of a Religion because it is countenanced by the law in that Countrey where thou livest, or because most men are of the same, is no good reason." See introduction, above, pp. 83–84.

[207] Shortly after the publication of *Areopagitica,* John Saltmarsh was to write (*Dawnings of Light,* January 4, 1645, E1168[3], p. 44): "For their [Roman Catholic] *unity,* it hath such cold principles as freeze and congeale *multitudes*

Nor much better will be the consequence ev'n among the Clergy themselvs; it is no new thing never heard of before, for a *parochiall* [208] Minister, who has his reward, and is at his *Hercules* pillars [209] in a warm benefice, to be easily inclinable, if he have nothing else that may rouse up his studies, to finish his circuit in an English concordance and a *topic folio*,[210] the gatherings and savings of a sober graduatship, a *Harmony* and a *Catena*,[211] treading the constant round of certain common doctrinall heads, attended with their uses, motives, marks and [27] means,[212] out of which as out of an alphabet or sol fa [213] by forming and transforming, joyning and dis-joyning variously a little book-craft, and two hours meditation might furnish him unspeakably to the performance of more then a weekly charge of sermoning: not to reck'n up the infinit helps of interlinearies, breviaries, *synopses,* and other loitering gear.[214] But as for the multitude of Sermons ready printed and pil'd up, on every text that is not difficult, our London trading St. *Thomas* in his vestry, and adde to boot St. *Martin,* and St. *Hugh,* have not within their hallow'd limits more vendible ware of all sorts ready

heterrogeneally together in the *worship of God.*" I have been unable to determine whether Saltmarsh knew the *Areopagitica.*

[208] Milton had not heretofore italicized this word (*cf. Complete Prose,* I, 537, 782, 789). Presumably he did so here to enforce the pun (minister of a parish, and parochial-minded minister).

[209] Calpe (Gibraltar) and Abyla (on the African side) were said by the ancients to have been erected by Hercules to mark the limit of his navigation, and thus became a symbol for the ultimate in achievement.

[210] Commonplace-book.

[211] *Harmony:* a handbook whose object is to bring into agreement apparently discordant passages in Scripture, especially the four gospels. *Catena:* a chain of extracts from the fathers, forming a commentary on some portion of Scripture.

[212] "doctrinall heads . . . means": Milton is listing the "parts" into which most contemporary sermons were organized. After expounding the text, the sermon would normally draw from it one or more "doctrines," give their "applications" or "uses," show what "incitements" or "motives" there were for applying the doctrines in the prescribed ways, by what "marks" they could be known, what "means" could be employed in their application, etc.

[213] Musical scale.

[214] *Cf.* Henry Robinson, *John the Baptist* (September 23, 1644), E9(13), sig. B2v (p. 12 of insert), criticizing the method of determining the fitness of a candidate for ordination: "Perhaps they . . . examine such a one upon some few questions, and give him a Text to try whether his Common-place bookes, with such like ready helps can furnish him with a Sermon." For an earlier comment by Milton on dependence upon "loitering gear" see *Doctrine and Discipline,* above, pp. 232–33. "Interlinearies" are line-beneath-line translations.

made: [215] so that penury he never need fear of Pulpit provision, having where so plenteously to refresh his magazin. But if his rear and flanks be not impal'd,[216] if his back dore be not secur'd by the rigid licencer, but that a bold book may now and then issue forth, and give the assault to some of his old collections in their trenches, it will concern him then to keep waking, to stand in watch, to set good guards and sentinells about his receiv'd opinions, to walk the round and counter-round with his fellow inspectors, fearing lest any of his flock be seduc't, who also then would be better instructed, better exercis'd and disciplin'd. And God send that the fear of this diligence which must then be us'd, doe not make us affect the lazines of a licencing Church.

For if we be sure we are in the right, and doe not hold the truth guiltily, which becomes not, if we our selves condemn not our own weak and frivolous teaching, and the people for an untaught and irreligious gadding rout, what can be more fair, then when a man judicious, learned, and of a conscience, for ought we know, as good

[215] The general purport of this passage is clear enough, but the allusions are difficult. If "hallow'd limits" is taken to mean actual "precincts," then the only reference I can identify is to St. Martin le Grand; this liberty was a very busy centre of small (and often shady) commerce. If "hallow'd limits" is understood less technically to mean the area "sanctified" by the presence of a church, "St. Thomas" would appear to be a reference, by its older name, to Mercer's Chapel (originally Church of St. Thomas Acon); then "vestry" would be a pun on the clothes-markets which dominated the area. (Alternatively, if "vestry" is thought to indicate a parish church, the reference may be to the church of St. Thomas Apostle in Knightrider Street, which, being just south of St. Paul's, was in the centre of the bookselling trade.) See C. L. Kingsford's edition of Stow's *London* (2 vols., Oxford, 1908) for all these churches. There is no record of any church in London dedicated to St. Hugh, but a saint of this name became identified with the shoe trade. As members of the Cordwainers' Company the shoemakers had Crispin for patron saint; nevertheless, they seem to have felt the need for a sort of deputy patron reserved for themselves alone. One version of this un-official sanctification is given in Rowley's *A Shoo-maker a Gentleman* (*ca.* 1609), where a Welsh prince named Sir Hugh, who has spent some time as a shoemaker, is martyred for Christianity (IV, ii, 209–20): "He shall no more be call'd Sir Hugh, but St. Hugh, and the Saint for ever of all the Shooemakers in England. . . . All our working tooles, from this time for ever, shall be call'd St. Hugh's bones." In the more familiar *Shoemaker's Holiday* of Dekker, Simon Eyre, wholly ignoring St. Crispin, explains (V, v, 157–60) that his fellows are "All shoemakers, my liege; all gentlemen of the Gentle Craft, true Trojans, coura-geous cordwainers; they all kneel to the shrine of St. Hugh." The sense of the passage: the materials to save a lazy preacher from the need to think for himself are as abundant as the merchandise available in the London areas and trades associated with these saints. [216] Protected by palisading.

as theirs that taught us what we know, shall not privily from house to house, which is more dangerous, but openly by writing publish to the world what his opinion is, what his reasons, and wherefore that which is now thought cannot be sound. Christ urg'd it as wherewith to justifie himself, that he preacht in publick; [217] yet writing is more publick then preaching; and more easie to refutation, if need be, there being so many whose businesse and profession meerly it is, to be the champions of Truth; which if they neglect, what can be imputed but their sloth, or unability?

Thus much we are hinder'd and dis-inur'd by this cours of licencing toward the true knowledge of what we seem to know. For how much it hurts and hinders the licencers themselves in the calling of their Ministery,[218] more then any secular employment, if they will [28] discharge that office as they ought, so that of necessity they must neglect either the one duty or the other, I insist not, because it is a particular, but leave it to their own conscience, how they will decide it there.

There is yet behind of what I purpos'd to lay open, the incredible losse, and detriment that this plot of licencing puts us to, more then if som enemy at sea should stop up all our hav'ns and ports, and creeks, it hinders and retards the importation of our richest Marchandize, Truth: [219] nay it was first establisht and put in practice by Antichristian malice and mystery on set purpose to extinguish, if it were possible, the light of Reformation, and to settle falshood; little differing from that policie wherewith the Turk upholds his *Alcoran*, by the prohibition of Printing.[220] 'Tis not deny'd, but gladly confest,

---

217 John 18:19–20.

218 This is written as if all the licensers were clergymen. Since in fact divinity accounted for only twelve of thirty-four, the other licensers being drawn from the appropriate professions (Siebert, *Freedom of the Press*, pp. 186–87), Milton's emphasis strongly suggests that he thought the main object of the Licensing Order—aside from the suppression of royalist propaganda—to be "books of controversie in Religion"; *cf.* above, p. 519, n. 120.

219 Possibly an echo of Matthew 13:45–46: "The kingdom of heaven is like unto a merchant man, seeking goodly pearls: who, when he had found one pearl of great price, went and sold all that he had, and bought it."

220 Foxe, in a digression on "The Benefit and Invention of Printing," declares (3 vols., 1641; I, 927) that, after Rome had overwhelmed the Wyclif and Huss movements, it was the providence of God that furnished men with the art of printing as an instrument of Reformation; "Wherefore I suppose, that either the Pope must abolish Printing, or he must seeke a new world to raigne over; for else, as this world standeth, Printing doubtlesse will abolish him."

we are to send our thanks and vows to heav'n, louder then most of Nations, for that great measure of truth which we enjoy, especially in those main points between us and the Pope, with his appertinences the Prelats: but he who thinks we are to pitch our tent here, and have attain'd the utmost prospect of reformation, that the mortall glasse wherein we contemplate, can shew us, till we come to *beatific* vision,[221] that man by this very opinion declares, that he is yet farre short of Truth.

Truth indeed came once into the world with her divine Master, and was a perfect shape most glorious to look on: but when he ascended, and his Apostles after him were laid asleep, then strait arose a wicked race of deceivers, who as that story goes of the *AEgyptian Typhon* with his conspirators, how they dealt with the good *Osiris*, took the virgin Truth, hewd her lovely form into a thousand peeces, and scatter'd them to the four winds. From that time ever since, the sad friends of Truth, such as durst appear, imitating the carefull search that *Isis* made for the mangl'd body of *Osiris*, went up and down gathering up limb by limb still as they could find them.[222] We have not yet found them all, Lords and Commons, nor ever shall doe, till her Masters second comming; he shall bring together every joynt and member, and shall mould them into an immortall feature [223] of lovelines and perfection. Suffer not these licencing prohibitions to stand at every place of opportunity forbidding and disturbing them that continue seeking, that continue

[221] I Corinthians 13:12: "For now we see through [by means of] a glass, darkly; but then face to face."

[222] The appropriateness of the Egyptian myth was probably suggested to Milton by Plutarch's "On Isis and Osiris," which, reporting the narrative legend much as Milton summarizes it, repeatedly insists that it must be understood as an allegory, and records the numerous extant interpretations. Plutarch himself (*Moralia*, 351–52; tr. F. C. Babbitt [14 vols., Loeb Classical Library, London: 1927 et seq.], V, 9) likens it to "the effort to arrive at the Truth, and especially the truth about the gods. . . . [Typhon] tears to pieces and scatters to the winds the sacred writings, which the goddess collects and puts together and gives into the keeping of those that are initiated into the holy rites . . . the end and aim of which is the knowledge of Him who is the First, the Lord of All, the Ideal One. Him does the goddess urge us to seek." Milton's friendliness to Isis and Osiris here is in marked contrast with "Nativity Ode," ll. 211–23, and *Paradise Lost*, I, 475–82.

[223] feature: From *factura*: shape, *facere*: to make; *NED* def. 1c: "Something formed or shaped." *Cf. Paradise Lost*, X, 278: "So scented the grim feature."

to do our obsequies to the torn body of our martyr'd Saint.[224] We boast our light; but if we look not wisely on the Sun it self, it smites us into darknes. Who can discern those [29] planets that are oft *Combust*,[225] and those stars of brightest magnitude that rise and set with the Sun, untill the opposite motion of their orbs bring them to such a place in the firmament, where they may be seen evning or morning. The light which we have gain'd, was giv'n us, not to be ever staring on, but by it to discover onward things more remote from our knowledge.[226] It is not the unfrocking of a Priest, the unmitring of a Bishop, and the removing him from off the *Presbyterian* shoulders that will make us a happy Nation, no, if other things as great in the Church, and in the rule of life both economicall and politicall be not lookt into and reform'd, we have lookt so long upon the blaze that *Zuinglius*[227] and *Calvin* hath beacon'd up to us, that we are stark blind. There be who perpetually complain of schisms and sects, and make it such a calamity that any man dissents from their maxims. 'Tis their own pride and ignorance which causes the disturbing, who neither will hear with meeknes, nor can convince, yet all must be supprest which is not found in their *Syntagma*. They are the troublers, they are the dividers of unity, who neglect and permit not others to unite those dissever'd

---

[224] In his anonymous *Queries of Highest Consideration* (February 9, 1644), Roger Williams confessed that he had not even tried to get his pamphlet licensed, knowing it would be useless. Then he added (*Publications of the Narragansett Club*, II, 253): "By such Circumscribing and immuring of your selves by such a *Guard* (their Persons we honour and esteem) it is rarely possible that any other *Light*, but what their Hemispheare affoords, shall ever shine on your *Honours* Souls, though ne're so *sweet*, so *necessary*, and though it come from *God*, from *Heaven.*"

[225] Within 8° 30′ of the sun; in such positions their "influence" was "burnt up." The planets frequently combust are Venus, Mars, and Vulcan.

[226] *Cf.* William Sedgewick, *Scripture A Perfect Rule* (December 28, 1643), E79(21), p. 34: "We may without arrogance thinke the Gospel hath gotten something in these fourescore yeeres, there is some more cleare light. They lived in the dawning of the day, we enjoy more light, that which succeeds us will be greater: and therefore it is no dishonour to them for us to proceed in a further reformation."

[227] Huldrich Zwingli (1484–1531) secured the first legal sanction for the Reformation in Switzerland (in Zurich, 1519). Although his doctrines were later submerged by the more uncompromising ones of Calvin, he was reckoned of equal rank as a founder of the Reformed Church.

peeces which are yet wanting to the body of Truth.[228] To be still searching what we know not, by what we know, still closing up truth to truth as we find it (for all her body is *homogeneal,* and proportionall) this is the golden rule [229] in *Theology* as well as in Arithmetick, and makes up the best harmony in a Church; not the forc't and outward union of cold, and neutrall, and inwardly divided minds.

Lords and Commons of England, consider what Nation it is wherof ye are, and wherof ye are the governours: a Nation not slow and dull, but of a quick, ingenious, and piercing spirit, acute to invent, suttle and sinewy to discours, not beneath the reach of any point the highest that human capacity can soar to. Therefore the studies of learning in her deepest Sciences have bin so ancient, and so eminent among us, that Writers of good antiquity, and ablest judgement have bin perswaded that ev'n the school of *Pythagoras,*[230] and the *Persian* wisdom [231] took beginning from the old

[228] Many Puritans (but in this the Presbyterians had not assumed their usual predominance) had levelled this charge at the bishops; *e.g.,* Lord Brooke, "They cry out of Schisme, Schisme, Sects and Schismes; and well they may: They make them, and it is strange they should not know them. . . . *Schismes* in the *Conscience* are of greatest danger; and to prevent these, if I am forct to that, which they please to call a *Schisme* in the Church, Woe to him that so forceth me." See *A Discourse Opening the Nature of that Episcopacie, which is Exercised in England* (1641), second ed., 1642 (in Haller, *Tracts,* II), p. 92. Hence, when Milton had taken the same line (*e.g.,* in 1642, *Reason of Church-Government, Complete Prose,* I, 779 ff.) he was one of many. He appears, however, to have been the first in print to turn the argument against the Presbyterians. The next occurrence of the charge seems to be in the revised edition of *The Compassionate Samaritane* (January 5, 1645; pp. 49–50), where its insertion appears to be one of the very rare indications discoverable of immediate influence by the *Areopagitica:* "And then for the charge of Separating, for their making a Scisme. . . . May not I say this, Reverend Synod: . . . to be proceeded against by such carnall sandy principles, such humane ordinances, by which the Separatists stand prejudiced, [is] . . . to have made the greatest and most transcendent scisme which England ever knew or heard of, since the Papistrie was discarded." See introduction, above, p. 87. Syntagma: compilation, collection.

[229] The Rule of Proportion is often called the "golden rule of arithmetic" because of its great serviceability in determining unknown quantities.

[230] This is a complex allusion. The primary reference is to the doctrine of metempsychosis. Drayton (*Poly-Olbion,* 1613, UCL, p. 2) attributes the doctrine to the British Druids, and Selden defends his friend's poetic licence by saying (pp. 14–15), "*Lipsius* doubts whether *Pythagoras* received it from the *Druids,* or they from him, because in his travels he converst as well with *Gaulish* as *Indian* Philosophers." Milton's own strong early interest in Pythagoras was

Philosophy of this Iland. And that wise and civill Roman, *Julius Agricola,* who govern'd once here for *Caesar,* preferr'd the naturall wits of Britain, before the labour'd studies of the French.[232] Nor is it for nothing that the grave and frugal *Transilvanian* sends out yearly from as farre as the mountanous borders of *Russia,* and beyond the *Hercynian* wildernes, not their youth, but their stay'd men, to learn our language, and our *theologic* [30] arts.[233] Yet that which is above all this, the favour and the love of heav'n we have great argument to think in a peculiar manner propitious and propending towards us. Why else was this Nation chos'n before any other, that out of her as out of *Sion* should be proclam'd and sounded forth the first tidings and trumpet of Reformation to all *Europ.* And had it not bin the obstinat perversnes of our Prelats

based on the doctrine of harmony; see, *e.g.,* Prolusion II, *Complete Prose,* I, 234 ff. Since Milton has only one of Pythagoras' doctrines in mind (and not the one which really interested him), his phrase is somewhat comprehensive. This is because of a secondary reference to a famous twelfth-century building in Cambridge, originally known as the Stone House, then as Merton Hall, and since the sixteenth century as the "School of Pythagoras." The latter name seems to be due to what is sometimes called the oldest inter-university sport, the "lying match" regarding the relative antiquity of Oxford and Cambridge; see J. M. Gray, *The School of Pythagoras (Merton Hall) Cambridge* (Cambridge, 1932), pp. 37–38.

[231] *I.e.,* the art of magic. Milton is echoing Pliny the Elder, who having said (*Natural History,* XXX, 2; tr. H. Rackham [10 vols., Loeb Classical Library, 1938 ff], V, 222), "There is no doubt that this art originated in Persia, under Zoroaster," emphasizes the extent of its influence by saying (XXX, 4; Rackham, V, 426), "At the present day, struck with fascination, Britannia still cultivates this art, and that, with ceremonials so august, that she might almost seem to have been the first to communicate them to the people of Persia [*ut dedisse Persis videri possit*]." Milton is using everything he can find; this "wisdom," in which he says the ancient Britons may have been "acute" enough to anticipate the Persians, seemed to his source (*ibid.,* Rackham, V, 427) "those monstrous rites, in accordance with which, to murder a man was to do an act of the greatest devoutness, and to eat his flesh was to secure the highest blessings of health." *Cf. History of Britain,* Book II (1670, p. 49) and *Doctrine and Discipline,* above, p. 231.

[232] Tacitus, *Agricola,* 21. Agricola (A.D. 37–93) was proconsul in Britain, 78–85. He therefore actually governed for three Caesars: Vespasian, Titus, and Domitian. *Cf.* Milton's *History of Britain,* Book II (1670, p. 71).

[233] Transylvania (now part of Roumania) was independent from 1535 to 1689, and was strongly Protestant; many of its divines came to study theology at the great Protestant universities of the west. *Hyrcania Silva* was the general name given by Julius Caesar to the mountains and forests of central and southern Germany.

against the divine and admirable spirit of *Wicklef*, to suppresse him as a schismatic and *innovator*, perhaps neither the *Bohemian Husse* and *Jerom*,[234] no nor the name of *Luther*, or of *Calvin* had bin ever known: the glory of reforming all our neighbours had bin compleatly ours. But now, as our obdurat Clergy have with violence demean'd the matter, we are become hitherto the latest and the backwardest Schollers, of whom God offer'd to have made us the teachers. Now once again by all concurrence of signs, and by the generall instinct of holy and devout men, as they daily and solemnly expresse their thoughts, God is decreeing to begin some new and great period in his Church, ev'n to the reforming of Reformation it self: what does he then but reveal Himself to his servants, and as his manner is, first to his English-men; [235] I say as his manner is, first to us, though we mark not the method of his counsels, and are unworthy. Behold now this vast City; a City of refuge,[236] the

---

[234] For Wyclif and Huss, see above, p. 502, n. 59. Jerome of Prague (*ca.* 1365–1416) was a disciple of both Wyclif and Huss. For an earlier expression of the idea that the English were a chosen people whose mission of reforming the church had been frustrated by its clergy, see *Of Reformation, Complete Prose*, I, 525–26; *cf.* also *Doctrine and Discipline*, above, pp. 231–32, and *Tetrachordon*, below, p. 707.

[235] *Cf.* Thomas Goodwin *et al.*, *An Apologeticall Narration* (1644), pp. 22–23: "We do professedly judge the *Calvinian* Reformed Churches of the first reformation from out of Popery, to stand in need of a further reformation themselves; And it may without prejudice to them, or the imputation of Schisme in us from them, be thought, that they comming new out of Popery (as well as *England*) and the founders of that reformation not having *Apostolique infallibility*, might not be fully perfect the first day. Yea and it may hopefully be conceived, that *God* in his secret, yet wise and gratious dispensation, had left *England* more unreformed as touching the outward form, both of worship & Church government, then the neighbour Churches were, . . . as having in his infinite mercy on purpose reserved and *provided some better thing* for this Nation when it should come to be reformed, that the other Churches might not be made *perfect without it*, as the Apostle speaks." See introduction, above, pp. 72–73.

In *Doctrine and Discipline* (above, p. 232) Milton had sounded more confident of England's "wonted prerogative, of being the first asserters in every vindication" of God's glory. *Cf.* also *Martin Bucer* (above, p. 438): "a nation that expects now, and from mighty sufferings aspires to be the example of all Christendom to a perfetest reforming."

[236] Numbers 35 instructs the Jews to establish six "cities of refuge" where those who have committed unpremeditated manslaughter may take sanctuary from "the revenger of blood." The parallel was not as embarrassing as it may seem. Milton's audience was unlikely to think of the followers of Parliament as manslaughterers, and he was not at all reluctant that they should conceive of (and fear) the royalists as revengers of blood (see introduction, above, pp. 55–56).

mansion house of liberty, encompast and surrounded with his protection; the shop of warre hath not there more anvils and hammers
waking, to fashion out the plates and instruments of armed Justice
in defence of beleaguer'd Truth, then there be pens and heads there,
sitting by their studious lamps, musing, searching, revolving new
notions and idea's wherewith to present, as with their homage and
their fealty the approaching Reformation: [237] others as fast reading,
trying all things, assenting to the force of reason and convincement.
What could a man require more from a Nation so pliant and so
prone to seek after knowledge. What wants there to such a towardly
and pregnant soile, but wise and faithfull labourers, to make a
knowing people, a Nation of Prophets,[238] of Sages, and of Worthies.
We reck'n more then five months yet to harvest; there need not be
five weeks, had we but eyes to lift up, the fields are white already.[239]
Where there is much desire to learn, there of necessity will be much
arguing, much writing, many opinions; for opinion in good men is
but knowledge in the making. Under these fantastic terrors of [31]
sect and schism, we wrong the earnest and zealous thirst after
knowledge and understanding which God hath stirr'd up in this
City. What some lament of, we rather should rejoyce at, should
rather praise this pious forwardnes among men, to reassume the ill
deputed care of their Religion into their own hands again.[240] A
little generous prudence, a little forbearance of one another,[241] and
som grain of charity might win all these diligences to joyn, and
unite into one generall and brotherly search after Truth; could we
but forgoe this Prelaticall tradition of crowding free consciences
and Christian liberties [242] into canons and precepts of men. I doubt

237 The flourishing condition of the arms industry was due to the state of the
Civil War; that of the publishing industry in good part to the toleration controversy, to which the *Areopagitica* belonged (see introduction, above, pp. 57–130).

238 *Cf.* below, p. 556, n. 245.

239 This is an adaptation of John 4:35, with five months substituted for four;
Milton's reason for the change is obscure. *Cf. Hirelings* (1659), p. 87, where the
waiting period is omitted altogether.

240 *Cf.* Robinson, *Liberty of Conscience*, sig. a1: "Amongst all those that
professe Christianity, I conceive it may easily be observed, that such as study
the variety of opinions, and trie the spirits out of a zeale to truth, choosing their
Religion by their owne judgements, though erronious, are yet more jealous of
Gods worship, and conscionable towards men." See introduction, above, pp. 83–84.

241 Ephesians 4:2.

242 See below, p. 563, n. 275, and introduction, above, pp. 65–69.

not, if some great and worthy stranger should come among us, wise
to discern the mould and temper of a people, and how to govern it,
observing the high hopes and aims, the diligent alacrity of our extended thoughts and reasonings in the pursuance of truth and freedom, but that he would cry out as *Pirrhus* did, admiring the Roman
docility and courage, if such were my *Epirots,* I would not despair
the greatest design that could be attempted to make a Church or
Kingdom happy.[243] Yet these are the men cry'd out against for
schismaticks and sectaries; as if, while the Temple of the Lord
was building, some cutting, some squaring the marble, others hewing
the cedars, there should be a sort of irrationall men who could not
consider there must be many schisms and many dissections made
in the quarry and in the timber, ere the house of God can be built.[244]
And when every stone is laid artfully together, it cannot be united
into a continuity, it can but be contiguous in this world; neither
can every peece of the building be of one form; nay rather the perfection consists in this, that out of many moderat varieties and
brotherly dissimilitudes that are not vastly disproportionall arises
the goodly and the gracefull symmetry that commends the whole
pile and structure. Let us therefore be more considerat builders,
more wise in spirituall architecture, when great reformation is expected. For now the time seems come, wherein *Moses* the great
Prophet may sit in heav'n rejoycing to see that memorable and
glorious wish of his fulfill'd, when not only our sev'nty Elders, but

[243] Pyrrhus (*ca.* 318–272 B.C.), king of Epirus, defeated the Romans under
Valerius Laevinus at Heraclea, 280 B.C. Florus (*Epitome Rerum Romanorum,* I,
18) says that after the battle he declared that he would think it easy to conquer
the world if either his own soldiers were like the Romans, or if he were king of
Rome.

[244] This is a remarkable example of Milton's technique of reversing a damaging received inference from a scriptural text by enlarging the scope of the reference. In building the Temple, Solomon had the stones cut to size before being
brought to the construction site, so that the quiet of the holy place would be
undisturbed. This became one of the arguments for religious conformity; *e.g.,*
Thomas Hill, *The Good Old Way, Gods Way* (April 24, 1644), E48(4), p. 39:
"It is an observation of a *Learned Divine,* from that passage in 1 *Kin.* 6.7. while
the Temple was in building, there *was neither hammer, nor axe, nor any toole
of iron heard in the house* . . . That no noise *of contentions and schismes* (saith
hee) *might be heard, O that God would grant this mercy, that in his house wee
might all thinke and speake the same thing."* Milton turns attention from this
particular verse to the general account occupying two chapters (I Kings 5–6),
and echoes enough of it to bring the necessary cutting operations to the fore.

all the Lords people are become Prophets.[245] No marvell then though some men, and some good men too perhaps, but young in goodnesse, as *Joshua* then was, envy them. They fret, and out of their own weaknes are in agony, lest these divisions and subdivisions will undoe us. [32] The adversarie again applauds, and waits the hour, when they have brancht themselves out, saith he, small anough into parties and partitions, then will be our time.[246] Fool! he sees not the firm root, out of which we all grow, though into branches: [247] nor will beware untill he see our small divided maniples [248] cutting through at every angle of his ill united and unweildy brigade. And that we are to hope better of all these supposed sects and schisms, and that we shall not need that solicitude honest perhaps though over timorous of them that vex in this behalf, but shall laugh in the end, at those malicious applauders of our differences, I have these reasons to perswade me.

First, when a City shall be as it were besieg'd and blockt about,

[245] Numbers 11:27–29: "And there ran a young man, and told Moses, and said, Eldad and Medad do prophecy in the camp. And Joshua the son of Nun, the servant of Moses, one of his young men, answered and said, My lord Moses, forbid them. And Moses said unto him, Enviest thou for my sake? would God that all the Lord's people were prophets, and that the Lord would put his spirit upon them!"

[246] This was, of course, a recurrent theme of royalist propaganda. *E.g.,* *Mercurius Aulicus* for August 10, 1643 (E65[26], p. 431): "The heates in *London* (according to the season) doe still increase; and . . . the discontents which have late beene growing betweene the remaining partie in the two *Houses,* are at the last improved to a *sedition,* if not unto a *Civill Warre* amongst themselves"; again, on August 18, 1644 (E9[5], p. 1127): "A sharpe difference betwixt the *Conqueror* and the *Wood-monger* (commonly called Sir *William Waller* and Colonell *Browne*) who have broken out into such unbrotherly language, as if one were an *Independent,* and the other a *Presbyterian* . . . the *Conqueror* posted up to *Westminster* . . . and complained that Colonell *Browne* would yeild him no obedience."

[247] Cf. Walwyn, *Compassionate Samaritane,* p. 44, which, anticipating the objection that "nothing is more dangerous to a State, espeacially in these times, than division," answers, "that the diversity of mens judgements are not the occasion of division because the word division hath reference to a falling off from the Common cause. Now, though the provocations and incitements against the Brownists and Anabaptists, and some of the Independents have beene many, yet their affections to the Publike weale are so hearty in them, and grounded upon such sound principalls of reason, that no assay of the Synod can make them cease to love and assist their Country." See introduction, above, pp. 84–87.

[248] Tactical unit in the Roman army, approximately equivalent to the modern infantry company.

her navigable river infested, inrodes and incursions round, defiance and battell oft rumor'd to be marching up ev'n to her walls, and suburb trenches,[249] that then the people, or the greater part, more then at other times, wholly tak'n up with the study of highest and most important matters to be reform'd, should be disputing, reasoning, reading, inventing, discoursing, ev'n to a rarity, and admiration,[250] things not before discourst or writt'n of, argues first a singular good will, contentednesse and confidence in your prudent foresight, and safe government, Lords and Commons; and from thence derives it self to a gallant bravery and well grounded contempt of their enemies, as if there were no small number of as great spirits among us, as his was, who when Rome was nigh besieg'd by *Hanibal*, being in the City, bought that peece of ground at no cheap rate, whereon *Hanibal* himself encampt his own regiment.[251] Next it is a lively and cherfull presage of our happy successe and victory. For as in a body, when the blood is fresh, the spirits pure and vigorous, not only to vital, but to rationall faculties, and those in the acutest, and the pertest operations of wit and suttlety, it argues in what good plight and constitution the body is, so when the cherfulnesse of the people is so sprightly up, as that it has, not only wherewith to guard well its own freedom and safety, but to spare, and to bestow upon the solidest and sublimest points of controversie, and new invention, it betok'ns us not degenerated, nor drooping to a fatall decay, but casting off the old and wrincl'd skin of corruption to outlive these pangs and wax young again, entring the glorious waies of Truth and prosperous vertue destin'd to be-[33]come great and honourable in these latter ages.[252] Methinks I

---

[249] In November, 1642, the royalist army advanced as far as Turnham Green and threatened an attack on London, then unfortified; faced by Essex, it fell back to Reading. The following summer the city erected a fortification based upon a twelve-mile circuit of "suburb trenches." For some time thereafter, with Arundel, Reading, and Newport Pagnell being royalist strongholds, London was under intermittent threat. See introduction, above, p. 5.

[250] admiration: Here, in the sense of astonishment.

[251] The story is in Livy, 26, 11.

[252] For a discussion of the contemporary debate on whether nature had outlived its vigor and was decaying, see Victor Harris, *All Coherence Gone* (Chicago: University of Chicago Press, 1949). In 1628, in "Naturam non Pati Senium," Milton had espoused the negative (perhaps on assignment; see *Complete Prose*, I, 313–14); in 1631–1632, in the seventh prolusion, he had let the affirmative go unchallenged, but this need not indicate agreement (he was prob-

see in my mind a noble and puissant Nation rousing herself like a strong man after sleep, and shaking her invincible locks: [253] Methinks I see her as an Eagle muing [254] her mighty youth, and kindling her undazl'd eyes at the full midday beam; purging and unscaling her long abused sight at the fountain it self of heav'nly radiance; [255] while the whole noise of timorous and flocking birds, with those also that love the twilight, flutter about, amaz'd at what she means, and in their envious gabble would prognosticat [256] a year of sects and schisms.

What should ye doe then, should ye suppresse all this flowry crop of knowledge and new light sprung up and yet springing daily in this City, should ye set an *Oligarchy* of twenty ingrossers [257]

ably setting the stage for his doctrine of true glory; see *Complete Prose*, I, 302). The use of the snake as a symbol of the revitalization of England may seem strange in the author of *Paradise Lost*, but it had been a literary favorite at least since Virgil's description (*Georgics*, III, 437–38) of the serpent in summer "when, slipped his slough, / To glittering youth transformed he winds his spires," *Poems*, tr. James Rhoades (Oxford: World's Classics, 1929), p. 364.

[253] The reference is to Samson frustrating the first three attempts of Delila and the Philistines to subdue him in his sleep (Judges 16:6–14). Milton had already used Samson as a symbol of England; see *Reason of Church-Government*, *Complete Prose*, I, 858–59.

[254] So in the original. *Mew* is a term in falconry meaning to moult; hence it can carry the secondary meeting of renewal, which is apparently Milton's intention here (*cf.* the snake, above, p. 557, n. 252). Some editions treat "muing" as a misprint for "newing" or "renuing"; the argument for the former is in R. S. Loomis, *Modern Language Notes*, XXXII (1917), 437–38, and for the latter in G. M. Yule, *Review of English Studies*, XIX (1943), 61–67. The argument against "muing" fails to take account of the tradition associating the moulting of eagles with renewal (see next note).

[255] The image derives from the bestiaries. We do not know whether Milton was accustomed to using the antique or the medieval form; a thirteenth-century English version (translated from the *Physiologus* of Theobaldus) runs: "*Natura aquile.* / Kiðen i wille ðe ernes kinde, / Also ic it o boke rede, / wu he neweð his guðhede, / hu he cumeð ut of elde . . . . / A welle he sekeð ðat springeð ai / boðe bi nigt *and* bi dai, / ðer-over he flegeð, *and* up he teð, / til ðat he ðe hevene seð, / ðurg skies sexe *and* sevene / til he cumeð to hevene; / So rigt so he cunne / he hoveð in ðe sunne; / ðe sunne swideð al his fligt, / *and* oc it makeð his egen brigt. / Hise feðres fallen for ðe hete, / *and* he dun mide to ðe wete / falleð in ðat welle grund, / ðer he wurdeð heil *and* sund, / *and* cumeð ut al newe." See E.E.T.S., vol. 49, p. 3.

[256] Would prognosticat: *I.e.*, the noises they make, unintelligible to ordinary men ("gabble"), are intended to cause the augurs to prognosticate to this effect; *cf.* above, p. 497, n. 41.

[257] *Cf.* above, p. 535, n. 171.

over it, to bring a famin upon our minds again, when we shall know
nothing but what is measur'd to us by their bushel? Beleeve it,
Lords and Commons, they who counsell ye to such a suppressing,
doe as good as bid ye suppresse your selves; and I will soon shew
how. If it be desir'd to know the immediat cause of all this free
writing and free speaking, there cannot be assign'd a truer then
your own mild, and free, and human government; it is the liberty,
Lords and Commons, which your own valorous and happy counsels
have purchast us, liberty which is the nurse of all great wits; this
is that which hath rarify'd and enlightn'd our spirits like the influence of heav'n; this is that which hath enfranchis'd, enlarg'd and
lifted up our apprehensions degrees above themselves. Ye cannot
make us now lesse capable, lesse knowing, lesse eagarly pursuing of
the truth, unlesse ye first make your selves, that made us so, lesse
the lovers, lesse the founders of our true liberty. We can grow ignorant again, brutish, formall, and slavish, as ye found us; but you
then must first become that which ye cannot be, oppressive, arbitrary, and tyrannous, as they were from whom ye have free'd us.
That our hearts are now more capacious, our thoughts more erected
to the search and expectation of greatest and exactest things, is the
issue of your owne vertu propagated in us; ye cannot suppresse that
unlesse ye reinforce an abrogated and mercilesse law, that fathers
may dispatch at will their own children.[258] And who shall then stick
closest to ye, and excite others? not he who takes up armes for
cote and conduct, and his four nobles of Danegelt.[259] Although I

[258] The absolute legal power of the Roman father over his children (*jus vitae
et necis*) had fallen into desuetude much earlier, but was not formally abolished
until 318 A.D.; it was never revived.

[259] cote and conduct: A form of taxation levied on the counties, to pay for the
clothing and transportation of new troops recruited within their boundaries.
noble: A coin worth 6s. 8d. Danegelt: shipmoney, which was originally levied to
raise money for a fleet to oppose, or a bribe to placate, the Danes. Charles'
effort to levy and collect these taxes without the consent of Parliament was
another violation of "just immunities" contributing greatly to the national discontent; see the *Grand Remonstrance* of 1641 (Gardiner, *Constitutional Documents*, pp. 211 and 221). *Cf.* above, p. 535, n. 172, and p. 545, n. 205. The
passage is variously interpreted, and its sense is not beyond dispute, but it would
seem to be: If you suppress liberty your supporters will abandon you; their
initial adherence may have been given on the issue of illegal taxation, but what
concerned them in that was less the money (which they value below peace) than
the threat to liberty inherent in such a procedure.
Cf. M.S. to A.S. (May 3, 1644), E45 (3), sig. N1v (page misnumbered 82):

dispraise not the defence of just immunities, yet love my [34] peace better, if that were all. Give me the liberty to know, to utter, and to argue freely according to conscience, above all liberties.

What would be best advis'd then, if it be found so hurtfull and so unequall to suppresse opinions for the newnes, or the unsutablenes to a customary acceptance, will not be my task to say; I only shall repeat what I have learnt from one of your own honourable number, a right noble and pious Lord, who had he not sacrific'd his life and fortunes to the Church and Commonwealth, we had not now mist and bewayl'd a worthy and undoubted patron of this argument. Ye know him I am sure; yet I for honours sake, and may it be eternall to him, shall name him, the Lord *Brook*.[260] He writing of Episcopacy, and by the way treating of sects and schisms, left Ye his vote, or rather now the last words of his dying charge,

"For men that are truly conscientious, civill libertie (as it is called) *i*. freedome from illegall taxes, impositions, exactions, imprisonments, without libertie of conscience, is an accommodation of little value; yea without this, such men are not capable of much ease or benefit by the other. They are still in danger of hearing in trouble and molestation from the State, for their conscience sake."

Just immunities: A few months earlier, in the address to Parliament in *Martin Bucer*, Milton had laid down a similar challenge (above, p. 438): "What are all our public immunities and privileges worth, and how shall it be judg'd that we fight for them with minds worthy to enjoy them, if wee suffer our selvs in the mean while not to understand the most important freedom that God and Nature hath givn us in the family."

260 Robert Greville, second Lord Brooke (1608–1643), one of the leaders of the Parliamentary party in the House of Lords and a general of the Parliamentary army, had been killed assaulting Lichfield; *cf*. *Complete Prose*, I, 145–48. The whole final section of his *Discourse of Episcopacie* (already cited in note 228; and see introduction, above, p. 181) is relevant to Milton's argument here, but there appears to be a particular reference to the conclusion (1642 ed., pp. 117–18): "But when God shall so enlarge his Hand, and unveil his face, that the poore creature is brought into communion and acquaintance with his Creator: steered in all his wayes, by his spirit; and by it carried up above shame, feare, pleasure, comfort, losses, grave, and death it selfe; Let us not censure such Tempers, but blesse God for them. . . . God assisting me, my desire, prayer, endeavour shall still be, as much as in me lies, to follow peace and holinesse; and though there may haply be some little dissent betweene my darke judgement, weake conscience, and other Good men, that are much more cleare and strong; yet my prayer still shall be, to *keepe the Unity of the Spirit in the Bond of Peace*. And as many as walke after this Rule, Peace I hope shall still be on them, and the whole Israel of God." George W. Whiting ("Milton and Lord Brooke on the Church," *Modern Language Notes*, LI [1936], pp. 161–66) has shown that Brooke's *Discourse* is in turn indebted to Milton's *Of Prelatical Episcopacie*.

which I know will ever be of dear and honour'd regard with Ye, so full of meeknes and breathing charity, that next to his last testament, who bequeath'd love and peace to his Disciples,[261] I cannot call to mind where I have read or heard words more mild and peacefull. He there exhorts us to hear with patience and humility those, however they be miscall'd, that desire to live purely, in such a use of Gods Ordinances, as the best guidance of their conscience gives them, and to tolerat them, though in some disconformity to our selves. The book it self will tell us more at large being publisht to the world, and dedicated to the Parlament by him who both for his life and for his death deserves, that what advice he left be not laid by without perusall.

And now the time in speciall is,[262] by priviledge to write and speak what may help to the furder discussing of matters in agitation. The Temple of *Janus* with his two *controversal* faces might now not unsignificantly be set open.[263] And though all the windes of doctrin were let loose to play upon the earth,[264] so Truth be in the field, we do injuriously by licencing and prohibiting to misdoubt her strength. Let her and Falshood grapple; who ever knew Truth put to the wors, in a free and open encounter.[265] Her confuting is the best and surest suppressing.[266] He who hears what praying there is

---

[261] John 14:15–31, especially 21 and 27.

[262] Because Parliament was in session, the Westminster Assembly in convention, and the Civil War in progress.

[263] The image of Janus, the Roman god of gateways, had two heads facing in opposite directions (*"controversal"*). His temple in the Forum was open during war, shut in peace.

[264] Ephesians 4:14–15: "That we henceforth be no more children, tossed to and fro, and carried about with every wind of doctrine, by the sleight of men, and cunning craftiness, whereby they lie in wait to deceive; but speaking the truth in love, may grow up into him in all things, which is the head, even Christ."

[265] *Cf.* Robinson, *Liberty of Conscience*, p. 59: "Doe we suspect that errour should vanquish truth? this is so vaine that no man will confesse so much." See introduction, above, pp. 83–84.

[266] *Cf.* John Goodwin, *Theomachia* (1644; E12[1]), p. 33: "It being certain that error cannot be healed or suppressed but by the manifestation of the truth, as darknesse cannot be destroyed or removed but by the shining of the light; that way which affords the greatest advantages and the best incouragements unto men, both for the searching out, and bringing forth into light the truth being found, must needs be so farre from opening doores unto *errors, heresies, unsound opinions*, &c. that it steers the most advantagious and hopefull course that lightly can be taken, for the evicting, and consequently for the suppression of them." See introduction, above, pp. 112–13. There is a pleasant irony in the fact

for light and clearer knowledge to be sent down among us, would think of other matters to be constituted beyond the discipline of *Geneva*, fram'd and fabric't already to our hands.[267] Yet when the [35] new light which we beg for shines in upon us, there be who envy, and oppose, if it come not first in at their casements.[268] What a collusion is this, whenas we are exhorted by the wise man to use diligence, *to seek for wisdom as for hidd'n treasures* [269] early and late, that another order shall enjoyn us to know nothing but by statute. When a man hath bin labouring the hardest labour in the deep mines of knowledge, hath furnisht out his findings in all their equipage, drawn forth his reasons as it were a battell raung'd, scatter'd and defeated all objections in his way, calls out his adversary into the plain, offers him the advantage of wind and sun, if he please; only that he may try the matter by dint of argument, for his opponents then to sculk, to lay ambushments, to keep a narrow bridge of licencing where the challenger should passe, though it be valour anough in shouldiership, is but weaknes and cowardise in the wars of Truth. For who knows not that Truth is strong next to the

that two pamphlets published in the same month as *Areopagitica*, agreeing with the tenet here proclaimed by Milton, declare that it shows the only way to suppress Milton's own doctrine of divorce; see introduction, above, pp. 142–43.

[267] *Cf.* William Bridge, *A Sermon Preached Before the Honourable House of Commons* (November 29, 1643), E79(11), p. 24: "You know what other Reformed Churches have done, the Reformation of all other Churches are round about you, you have their writings before you, their books, their practices, their examples, and this for many yeeres; can you think that God hath set us now for an hundred yeeres upon their shoulders, to see no farther into Reformation then they have done?" The "discipline of *Geneva*" is Presbyterianism.

[268] *Cf.* Roger Williams, *Queries of Highest Consideration* (February 9, 1644; *Publications of the Narragansett Club*, II, 273): "Since you both professe to want more Light, and that a greater Light is yet to be expected; . . . how can you professe and Sweare to Persecute all others as Schismatiques, Hereticks, &c., that beleeve they see a further Light and dare not joyn with either of your Churches?" *Cf.* also Brooke, *Discourse of Episcopacie* (second ed., 1642), p. 116: "The Light, still, will, must, cannot but encrease; why then doe wee shut our eyes? Let it not bee said of us, that Light came in & grew up among us, yet we would not use it (for we cannot but receive it) because we loved darknesse."

[269] Reference is usually made to Matthew 13:44 ("the kingdom of heaven is like unto treasure hidden in a field") or Proverbs 8:11 ("wisdom is better than rubies"). Neither of these is close enough to justify Milton's use of italics (*i.e.*, mark of quotation), and the former is not even "by the wise man," which means Solomon. Milton's allusion is to Proverbs 2:4–5: "If thou seekest her [wisdom] as silver, and searchest for her as for hid treasures; then shalt thou understand the fear of the Lord, and find the knowledge of God."

Almighty; she needs no policies, nor stratagems, nor licencings to make her victorious, those are the shifts and the defences that error uses against her power: [270] give her but room, & do not bind her when she sleeps, for then she speaks not true, as the old *Proteus* did, who spake oracles only when he was caught & bound,[271] but then rather she turns herself into all shapes, except her own, and perhaps tunes her voice according to the time, as *Micaiah* did before *Ahab*,[272] untill she be adjur'd into her own likenes. Yet is it not impossible that she may have more shapes then one. What else is all that rank of things indifferent,[273] wherein Truth may be on this side, or on the other, without being unlike her self. What but a vain shadow else is the abolition of *those ordinances, that hand writing nayl'd to the crosse*,[274] what great purchase is this Christian liberty which *Paul* so often boasts of.[275] His doctrine is, that he who eats or eats not, regards a day, or regards it not, may doe either to the Lord.[276] How many other things might be tolerated in peace, and left to conscience, had we but charity, and were it not the chief strong hold of our hypocrisie to be ever judging one another.[277] I fear yet this iron yoke of outward conformity hath left

[270] *Cf.* Walwyn's *Compassionate Samaritane*, pp. 55–56: "But then for the assurance of the Divines that their conclusions & Articles are certainly true, if it bee built upon certaine foundations, they neede not avoid the cumbat with any sort of men of what opinion soever: Truth was not used to feare colours, or to seeke shifts or stratagems for its advancement! I should rather thinke that they who are assured of her should desire that all mens mouthes should be open, that so errour may discover its foulnesse, and truth become more glorious by a victorious conquest after a fight in open field: they shun the battell that doubt their strength." See introduction, above, pp. 84–87.

[271] *Odyssey*, IV, 384–93; *cf. Georgics*, IV, 387–452.   [272] I Kings 22:1–36.

[273] See introduction, above, pp. 68–69.   [274] Colossians, 2:14.

[275] Especially in Romans and Galatians.   [276] Romans 14:1–13.

[277] *Cf.* Walwyn's "Good Counnsell," originally published as the final section of *The Compassionate Samaritane*, pp. 78–79: "[Christ] allowed them to be fully perswaded in their own minds using no meanes but argument and perswasion to alter or controle their judgements: Hee knew that men might live peaceably and lovingly together, though they differ in judgement one from another. . . . His servant and Apostle *Paul* was of the same mind also . . . : hee desires that those who are strong in faith, should beare with those that are weake, adviseth him that eateth, that hee should not condemne him that eateth not: where one observeth a day to the Lord, and others not, (though a matter of great moment) yet he alloweth every one to be fully perswaded in his own mind. Now . . . what spirit are they of, whose Ministers are they, that would have al men compelled to submit to their probabilities and doubtfull determinations." (Not in second edition.) See introduction, above, pp. 84–87.

a slavish print upon our necks; the ghost of a linnen decency [278]
yet haunts us. We stumble and are impatient at the least dividing
of one visible congregation from another, though it be not in fundamentalls; [279] and through our forwardnes to suppresse, and our
backwardnes to recover any [36] enthrall'd peece of truth out of
the gripe of custom,[280] we care not to keep truth separated from
truth, which is the fiercest rent and disunion of all. We doe not see
that while we still affect by all means a rigid externall formality,
we may as soon fall again into a grosse conforming stupidity, a
stark and dead congealment of *wood and hay and stubble* [281] forc't
and frozen together, which is more to the sudden degenerating of
a Church then many *subdichotomies* of petty schisms.[282] Not that
I can think well of every light separation, or that all in a Church
is to be expected *gold and silver and pretious stones:* [283] it is not
possible for man to sever the wheat from the tares, the good fish
from the other frie; that must be the Angels Ministery at the end

278 It was in the name of "decency" that Laud enforced uniformity in rites and
ceremonies; see, *e.g.,* articles VII–VIII, *Constitutions and Canons Ecclesiasticall*
(1640); *Complete Prose,* I, 992–93. "Linnen" alludes to the vestments long
hated by the Puritans; *cf. Mercurius Britanicus. Numb. 52* (October 7, 1644),
E13(10), p. 413: "The Bishops cheating tricks, whereby they deluded the consciences of men, and under the name of *Decencie,* and *Conformity to reverend
Antiquity,* brought in many *Popish Innovations,* and in their Surplices, Copes,
and Hoods, had well nigh ushered the Pope into *England."*

279 For an example of Presbyterian insistence on excommunication for differences of opinion or practice admittedly not "fundamental," see the Scottish Commissioners' *Reformation of Church-Government in Scotland, Cleered from some
Mistakes and Prejudices* (January 24, 1644), E30(5), pp. 20–21: "To limit the
censure of excommunication, in matter of opinion to the common and uncon-
troverted principles, and in the matter of manners to the common, and universall
practises of Christianitie, and in both to the parties known light, is the dangerous
doctrine of the Arminians, and Socinians, openeth a wide dore, and proclaimeth
libertie to all other practises and errors, which are not fundamentall, and universally abhorred by all Christians, and tendeth to the overthrow of the Reformed Religion."

280 For a fuller statement of the opposition of truth and custom, see the opening of *Doctrine and Discipline of Divorce,* above, pp. 222–26. See also Ernest
Sirluck, "Milton Revises *The Faerie Queene," Modern Philology,* XLVIII
(1950), 90–96.

281 I Corinthians 3:10–13.

282 Cf. Brooke, *Discourse* (second ed., 1642), p. 91: "The Spaniard indeed by
his cruell *Inquisition,* hath inclined his Subjects to a kinde of *Unity;* but an
Unity of Darknesse and Ignorance; so that the Remedy proves worse than the
Disease."

283 I Corinthians 3:10–13.

of mortall things.[284] Yet if all cannot be of one mind, as who looks they should be? this doubtles is more wholsome, more prudent, and more Christian that many be tolerated, rather then all compell'd. I mean not tolerated Popery, and open superstition, which as it extirpats all religions [285] and civill supremacies,[286] so it self should be extirpat, provided first that all charitable and compassionat means be us'd to win and regain the weak and the misled: that also which is impious or evil absolutely either against faith or maners [287] no law can possibly permit, that intends not to unlaw it self: but those neighboring differences, or rather indifferences, are what I speak of, whether in some point of doctrine or of discipline, which though they may be many, yet need not interrupt *the unity of Spirit*, if we could but find among us *the bond of peace*.[288] In the mean while if any one would write, and bring his helpfull hand to the slow-moving Reformation which we labour under, if Truth have spok'n to him before others, or but seem'd at least to speak, who hath so bejesuited us that we should trouble that man with asking licence to doe so worthy a deed? and not consider this, that if it come to prohibiting, there is not ought more likely to be prohibited then truth it self; whose first appearance to our eyes blear'd and dimm'd with prejudice and custom, is more unsightly and unplausible then many errors,[289] ev'n as the person is of many a great

[284] Matthew 13:24–30 and 36–43.

[285] *Cf.* John Pym, *March 17. Master Pyms Speech in Parliament* (1642), E200(37), p. 6: "The Religion of the Papists is a Religion incomputable [*sic*] to any other Religion, destructive to all others, and doth not endure any thing that doth oppose it; and whosoever doth withstand their Religion, (if it lie in their power) they bring them to ruine." See introduction, above, pp. 179–81, for a discussion of the form this standing Protestant charge takes in Milton.

[286] *Cf.* the secular argument of John Locke, who says that such Roman Catholic doctrines as "Dominion is founded in Grace" and "Kings excommunicated forfeit their Crowns and Kingdoms" make it impossible for a non-Catholic state to tolerate the Roman Catholic Church, "for by this means the Magistrate would give way to the settling of a forrein Jurisdiction in his own Country." (First *Letter of Toleration*, 1689, pp. 46–47). See introduction, above, p. 180.

[287] See introduction, above, pp. 180–81.

[288] Ephesians 4:3.

[289] *Cf.* Brooke, *Discourse* (second ed., 1642), p. 115: "These whom they so brand, may maintaine some errors, may not carry on the truth in the glory of it; who is so pe[r]fect? but oft-times in the midst of thickest ore we finde the purest gold: discover their errors and reject them; but doe not refuse what is good, because they hold it forth but darkly: no truth can shine in its perfect lustre at the first: light is darknesse when it first appeareth."

man slight and contemptible to see to.[290] And what doe they tell
us vainly of new opinions, when this very opinion of theirs, that
none must be heard, but whom they like, is the worst and newest
opinion of all others; and is the chief cause why sects and schisms
doe so much abound, and true knowledge is kept at distance from
us; besides yet a greater [37] danger which is in it. For when God
shakes a Kingdome with strong and healthfull commotions to a
generall reforming,[291] 'tis not untrue that many sectaries and false
teachers are then busiest in seducing; but yet more true it is, that
God then raises to his own work men of rare abilities, and more
then common industry not only to look back and revise what hath
bin taught heretofore, but to gain furder and goe on, some new
enlightn'd steps in the discovery of truth.[292] For such is the order
of Gods enlightning his Church, to dispense and deal out by degrees his beam, so as our earthly eyes may best sustain it. Neither
is God appointed and confin'd, where and out of what place these
his chosen shall be first heard to speak; for he sees not as man sees,
chooses not as man chooses,[293] lest we should devote our selves again
to set places, and assemblies, and outward callings of men; [294]

290 An echo of the criticism Paul recorded of himself (II Corinthians 10:10):
"For his letters, say they, are weighty and powerful; but his bodily presence is
weak, and his speech contemptible."

291 Haggai 2:7: "I will shake all nations, and the desire of all nations shall
come, and I will fill this house with glory, saith the Lord of hosts."

292 Cf. Robinson, *Liberty of Conscience*, p. 56: "It is true that if liberty be
given for men to teach what they will, there will appeare more false Teachers
then ever, yet it were better that many false doctrines were published, especially
with a good intention and out of weaknesse only, then that one sound truth
should be forcibly smothered or wilfully concealed; and by the incongruities and
absurdities which accompany erroneous and unsound doctrines, the truth appears
still more glorious, and wins others to the love thereof." See introduction, above,
pp. 83–84.

293 I Corinthians 26:29: "Not many wise men after the flesh, not many
mighty, not many noble, are called: but God hath chosen the foolish things of
the world to confound the wise; and God hath chosen the weak things of the
world to confound the things which are mighty; and base things of the world, and
things which are despised, hath God chosen, yea, and things which are not, to
bring to nought things which are: that no flesh should glory in his presence."

294 Cf. Walwyn, *Compassionate Samaritane*, pp. 26–28: "The . . . interest of
the Divine is to preserve amongst the people the distinction of Clergie & Laity,
though not now in those termes. . . . Because otherwise if the people did not
believe so, they would examine all that was said, and not take things upon trust
from their Ministers . . . : they would then try al things, & what they found

planting our faith one while in the old Convocation house, and another while in the Chappell at Westminster; [295] when all the faith and religion that shall be there canoniz'd,[296] is not sufficient without plain convincement, and the charity of patient instruction to supple the least bruise of conscience, to edifie the meanest Christian, who desires to walk in the Spirit, and not in the letter of human trust, for all the number of voices that can be there made; no though *Harry* the 7. himself there,[297] with all his leige tombs about him, should lend them voices from the dead, to swell their number. And if the men be erroneous who appear to be the leading schismaticks, what witholds us but our sloth, our self-will, and distrust in the right cause, that we doe not give them gentle meetings and gentle dismissions, that we debate not and examin the matter throughly with liberall and frequent audience; if not for their sakes, yet for our own? seeing no man who hath tasted learning, but will confesse the many waies of profiting by those who not contented with stale receits are able to manage, and set forth new positions to the world. And were they but as the dust and cinders of our feet, so long as in that notion they may yet serve to polish and brighten the armoury of Truth, ev'n for that respect they were not utterly to be cast away. But if they be of those whom God hath fitted for the speciall use of these times with eminent and ample gifts, and those perhaps neither among the Priests, nor among the Pharisees, and we in the hast of a precipitant zeal shall make no distinction, but resolve to stop their mouths, because we fear they [38] come with new and dangerous opinions, as we commonly forejudge them ere

to be truth, they would imbrace as from God, for God is the authour of truth; what they found to bee otherwise, they would reject. . . . . He that bade us to try all things, and hold fast that which was good, did suppose that men have faculties and abilities wherewithall to try all things, or else the counsel had bin given in vaine." See introduction, above, pp. 84–87.

[295] Convocation was held in the Chapter-house at Westminster from Wolsey's time through Laud's. The Long Parliament transferred the powers of Convocation (with some augmentation) to the Assembly of Divines, which met in Henry VII's Chapel in Westminster.

[296] The Assembly was then working upon, and was expected shortly to report, a Confession of Faith, a Directory of Worship, a Catechism, and a Frame of Church-government; the intention of the Presbyterians was that these should be established and made obligatory by Parliament ("canoniz'd").

[297] He was buried in the Chapel in which the Assembly met.

we understand them,* no lesse then woe to us, while thinking thus to defend the Gospel, we are found the persecutors.[298]

There have bin not a few since the beginning of this Parlament, both of the Presbytery and others who by their unlicenc't books to the contempt of an *Imprimatur* first broke that triple ice clung about our hearts, and taught the people to see day: I hope that none of those were the perswaders to renew upon us this bondage which they themselves have wrought so much good by contemning. But if neither the check that *Moses* gave to young *Joshua*,[299] nor the countermand which our Saviour gave to young *John,* who was so ready to prohibit those whom he thought unlicenc't,[300] be not anough to admonish our Elders how unacceptable to God their testy mood of prohibiting is, if neither their own remembrance what evill hath abounded in the Church by this lett of licencing, and what good they themselves have begun by transgressing it, be not anough, but that they will perswade, and execute the most *Domini-can* part of the Inquisition[301] over us, and are already with one foot in the stirrup so active at suppressing, it would be no unequall distribution in the first place to suppresse the suppressors them-

* Milton would probably have conceded that, despite the sympathy he had now come to feel for the sects, this stricture applied in some measure to himself. As late as the first edition of *Doctrine and Discipline* he was still writing (above, p. 278) of "*Anabaptism, Famelism, Antinomianism,* and other fanatick dreams"; by the time he revised the pamphlet he was beginning to be less certain that everything taught by the extreme sects was necessarily lunacy, and he added the parenthetic comment, "if we understand them not amisse."

298 *Cf.* John Goodwin's *Theomachia* (1644), which was the substance of two sermons preached after the surrender to the royalists of Essex's army in Cornwall on September 2. The text was Acts 5:38–39, in which Rabbi Gamaliel advises against executing the imprisoned apostles: "Refrain from these men, and let them alone: for if this counsel or this work be of men, it will come to nought: but if it be of God, ye cannot overthrow it; lest haply ye be found even to fight against God." Goodwin's subtitle is "The Grand Imprudence of men, running the hazard of *Fighting against God,* in suppressing any Way, Doctrine, or Practice, concerning which they know not certainly whether it be from God, or no." His application is that the military disaster was God's punishment of the Parliamentary party for persecuting the sects. See introduction, above, pp. 112–13.

299 See above, p. 556, n. 245.

300 Luke 9:49–50: "John . . . said, Master, we saw one casting out devils in thy name; and we forbad him, because he followeth not with us. And Jesus said unto him, Forbid him not: for he that is not against us is for us."

301 See above, notes 65, 26 and 63.

selves; whom the change of their condition hath puft up, more then their late experience of harder times hath made wise.[302]

And as for regulating the Presse, let no man think to have the honour of advising ye better then your selves have done in that Order publisht next before this,[303] that no book be Printed, unlesse the Printers and the Authors name, or at least the Printers be regis-ter'd. Those which otherwise [304] come forth, if they be found mis-chievous and libellous, the fire and the executioner [305] will be the timeliest and the most effectuall remedy, that mans prevention can use. For this *authentic* Spanish [306] policy of licencing books, if I have said ought, will prove the most unlicenc't book it self within a short while; and was the immediat image of a Star-chamber de-cree [307] to that purpose made in those very times when that Court

[302] In March Henry Robinson had written (*Liberty of Conscience*, pp. 31–32): "But what hath been the end of the grand Politicians and Persecuters? may it not be observed, that . . . very many . . . have been taken in their own nets . . . ? *Let such as thinke they stand take heed lest they fall,* and may it be far from any of Gods good servants to imagine that God delivered them out of persecution to the end they might be inabled to persecute their brethren: Perse-cution is a sinne, a signe of the Church malignant, . . . the whole Kingdome did acknowledge it whilest Popery domineered, the greatest part are weary of it in Prelacie; O let Presbytery be forewarned thereby, and know that they have the same temptation which was common to both the other Governments, and wherein they miscarried." A few weeks before *Areopagitica* appeared he had gone further; *An Answer to Mr.* William Prynn's *Twelve Questions* (November 1, 1644), E15(5), p. 21, demanded: "if Episcopacie and Presbytery have set the State on fire through an ambitious desire of Empire, together with a pestilent spirit of persecuting one another, may not the serving both alike reduce us to quietnesse againe?" See introduction, above, p. 121.

[303] Actually, the Order next-but-two before this. Milton is quoting from the Order of January 29, 1642. Between it and the Licensing Order there intervened two orders, one of August 26, 1642, and one of March 9, 1643; see introduction, above, pp. 160–61. It seems unlikely that Milton could have been unaware of these orders.

[304] There is an ambiguity here. It was a legal offence for books to be pub-lished anonymously or without the publisher's imprint, even though they were neither "mischievous" nor libellous; it was another offence to publish "mischief" or libel, even though the publication carried the name of author and publisher.

[305] The normal procedure for condemned books was to confiscate the pub-lisher's stocks and "call in" distributed copies, and have the whole imprint burnt by the executioner, who also carried out any corporal punishment ordered for author or printer (*e.g.*, pillory, ear-cropping, nose-slitting, *etc.*).

[306] See above, p. 493, n. 26.

[307] Decree of July 11, 1637; see introduction, above, pp. 159–60, and above, p. 505, n. 67.

did the rest of those her pious works, for which she is now fall'n [308] from the Starres with *Lucifer*. Whereby ye may guesse what kinde of State prudence, what love of the people, what care of Religion, or good manners there was at the contriving, although with singular hypocrisie it pretended to bind books to their good behaviour. [39] And how it got the upper hand of your precedent Order so well constituted before, if we may beleeve those men whose profession gives them cause to enquire most, it may be doubted there was in it the fraud of some old *patentees* and *monopolizers* in the trade of book-selling; who under pretence of the poor in their Company not to be defrauded, and the just retaining of each man his severall copy, which God forbid should be gainsaid, brought divers glosing colours to the House, which were indeed but colours, and serving to no end except it be to exercise a superiority over their neighbours, men who doe not therefore labour in an honest profession to which learning is indetted, that they should be made other mens vassalls. Another end is thought was aym'd at by some of them in procuring by petition [309] this Order, that having power in their hands, malignant books might the easier scape abroad, as the event shews. But of these *Sophisms* and *Elenchs* [310] of marchandize I skill not: This I know, that errors in a good government and in a bad are equally almost incident; for what Magistrate may not be mis-inform'd, and much the sooner, if liberty of Printing be reduc't into the power of a few; but to redresse willingly and speedily what hath bin err'd, and in highest autority to esteem a plain advertisement more then others have done a sumptuous bribe, is a vertue (honour'd Lords and Commons) answerable to Your highest actions, and whereof none can participat but greatest and wisest men.

The End. [40]

[308] The Court of Star-Chamber was abolished July 5, 1641.

[309] For the Petition, dated April 1643, see introduction, above, pp. 161–62.

[310] *Sophisms* and *Elenchs:* here, apparently, positive and negative logical deceit. The Stationers are being accused of using sophistical arguments to establish false propositions, and elenchical arguments (in the sense of false refutations) to defend themselves against true charges or sound objections.

TETRACHORDON

March 4, 1645

PREFACE AND NOTES BY ARNOLD WILLIAMS

*T*etrachordon was published, according to the date on the Thomason copy in the British Museum, on March 4, 1644, old style, or 1645, new style. It followed *Martin Bucer* by about seven months. The title page of the first edition (the only one published in Milton's lifetime) carries the date 1645, apparently, as was common, an anticipation of the official change of the year on March 25. Thomason has corrected this to 1644 and has written in "March 4th." The title page gives only Milton's initials, but the address "To the Parlament" is signed with his full name, so that there is no question of anonymity. However, the title page does not give the printer's name, as required by the Licensing Order, nor was *Tetrachordon* licensed or registered. William R. Parker suggests that *Tetrachordon* was printed in two parts by Thomas Paine and Matthew Simmons, who were then partners.[1] There was no further edition in Milton's lifetime. It has since been republished only in comprehensive editions and in the 1820 collection of divorce tracts (see above, p. 218) ; there has been no attempt at systematic annotation.

The title *Tetrachordon* means literally "four-stringed." It was the common term for the primitive Greek scale of four tones. According to Sigmund Spaeth, "Milton probably had this primitive four-part 'harmony' in mind" when he named the pamphlet, since it was a harmony of the "foure chief places in Scripture which treat of Mariage or nullities of Mariage."[2] These four chief places are given on the title page, and the main purpose of the work is to prove that divorce has the sanction of Scripture. According to the preface, certain judicious men had been impressed by the reasons offered in the *Doctrine and Discipline of Divorce* but wished, for complete conviction, that "The Scriptures there alleg'd, might be discuss'd more fully."

---

[1] "Milton, Rothwell, and Simmons," *The Library,* Fourth Series, XVIII (1937), 89–103, esp. 99–100.

[2] *Milton's Knowledge of Music* (Princeton, 1913), p. 171.

To the discussion of the four places in Scripture Milton prefixed an address to Parliament and appended a list of authorities who support, more or less, his position. The address to Parliament is largely a vindication of himself from the attacks of two ministers, Herbert Palmer and Dr. Daniel Featley. The former had called for the suppression of *Doctrine and Discipline of Divorce* in a sermon preached before Parliament August 13, 1644. Featley had included the doctrine of divorce among detestable Anabaptist tenets.[3] These two Milton apparently considered minor adversaries; the major ones he reserved for greater wrath in *Colasterion*, published on the same day as *Tetrachordon*.

The list of authorities, patristic, legal, and theological, with which Milton closed *Tetrachordon* is a continuation of the argumentative technique of *Martin Bucer*; in fact, some of them appear in the preface and postscript to that work. As always, Milton presents the argument from authority rather apologetically: it is not a valid type of argument to reasonable men; but so many men are unreasonable that one needs must use it, to silence if not to convince.

Tetrachordon is a product of scholarly research, far more than any pamphlet Milton had hitherto written. Its substance was dug out of books. In form and method it belongs to perhaps the prime genre of Renaissance scholarship, scriptural exegesis. Anyone who has read a sixteenth- or seventeenth-century commentary on the Bible knows whence *Tetrachordon* is hewn. Just like scores of commentators, Milton takes up a passage of Scripture, divides it into phrases, sometimes subdivides the phrase into words, and discusses each detail fully. Milton follows the less formal methods of commentary. He uses linguistic analysis and comparison of texts only in a few places. He does not follow the literal exposition of the text by questions, disputations, or problems in the scholastic manner; nor does he add homiletic material by way of moral or allegorical interpretations. All these deviations from the pattern are to be explained by Milton's special purpose: he is interpreting the texts not from all points of view, but from only one. The result, in spite of differences, closely resembles the type of commentary one finds in David Paraeus' exegetical works, two of which, the commentary on Genesis and that on Matthew, Milton uses extensively.

That *Tetrachordon* is in form and method a commentary needs emphasis, for the reader unacquainted with Renaissance Biblical exegesis may easily be misled by Milton's numerous slighting references to "common expositers" and "vulgar expositions." These do not mean that

---

[3] *The Dippers Dipped* (February 7, 1645). sig. B2v: "Witnesse a Tractate of Divorce, in which the bonds of marriage are let loose to inordinate lust."

Milton rejected the methods of commentary current in his times. He used nearly all of them. He objects only to the abuse of these methods by men of small comprehension.

The evidences of Milton's scholarship are impressive both in the four sections of scriptural interpretation which comprise the bulk of the work and in the roll call of authorities with which it ends. His citations range from the fathers, through Roman and canon law, to the theologians and lawyers of the sixteenth and seventeenth centuries. Classical authors are cited mainly for illustration and prestige. A good sample is the passage from Euripides' *Medea* which appears on the title page. The two authorities on Jewish tradition and practice, Josephus and Philo, though both wrote in Greek, should not be included among classical authors; Milton cites them for evidence of the historical background against which the texts in Matthew must be understood. The church fathers, likewise, are cited for evidence: they tell us what the practice of the primitive church was. So does Roman law, for it was framed or sanctioned by Christian emperors, hence, Milton argues, following Bucer, approved by leaders of the church. Renaissance theologians and lawyers are cited for somewhat different reasons. Some, like Erasmus and Luther, show by their support of Milton's whole position on divorce that he was advocating nothing novel or heretical. Others merely buttress one detail or another of Milton's argument.

One must be careful to distinguish these two kinds of authority. It is obvious that Milton cites Beza only to refute him. When he cites Cameron on the meaning of the Greek preposition κατά, one must not suppose that Cameron supports Milton's general argument on divorce. In fact, he does not; and Milton nowhere says that he does. On the other hand, Erasmus, Bucer, Luther, and Melancthon support Milton's main argument. Careful reading will usually disclose whether Milton is citing because of general agreement, as with Erasmus, or merely agreement on one detail, as with Cameron, Wesenbechius, and several others. I have noted only one place in which Milton seriously misleads the reader. This is one of the references to Cicero, who according to Milton defends Epaminondas for breaking the letter of a law in order to fulfill its intent. Actually, the passage to which Milton refers is pure academic illustration, neatly balanced with another passage in which Cicero prosecutes Epaminondas for the same deed. The point at issue, however, is rather minor; and I am inclined to believe that haste or carelessness is the worst fault of which Milton can be impeached.

It must also be observed that Milton's erudition is not quite so great as might appear without a study of his sources. He did not need to discover for himself each of the authorities he cites. Most of the Roman law and much of the patristic material which he cites are commonplaces in the literature of the period dealing with divorce. For instance, the Theodosian law *consensu* is cited in *Martin Bucer,* in Paraeus, and elsewhere. All Milton had to do, and there are indications that he did this faithfully, was to check the original. Sometimes he found further material there, as when a reference to Ambrose in *Martin Bucer* leads him to other passages in Ambrose, which he uses in *Tetrachordon.* We may suppose that in checking Bucer's references to Roman law in the *Corpus Juris Civilis* he ran on the laws concerning guardianship ("tutelage") and the freeing of slaves to which he alludes. Recondite as they appear to the modern reader, few of the sources cited in *Tetrachordon* were not standard references in theology, law, or history during the period when Milton lived.

Milton's practice in the use of quotations also needs some explaining to the modern reader. Though generally above the standard of honesty of his age, Milton considers that all reasonable requirements have been met when he reproduces the sense of the author he is quoting. The use of italics does not, as the use of quotation marks would with us, promise literal accuracy. Of course, the question of literal quotation does not often arise, for Milton was translating from Latin most of the passages he italicized. But in the process of translating he also rearranges, omits, and recasts. At no time is he a slave to the letter. Even with the Bible, the most important of Milton's sources, this is true. Although he follows the Authorized Version in the main, his departures from the literal text are numerous. Some of these are to be explained as independent translations from the Hebrew or Greek; in at least one instance Milton disagrees with the reading of the Authorized Version; but the bulk of variations can only be taken as manifestations of Milton's literary independence.[4]

The notes are mainly devoted to Milton's sources. Where the quotation or abstract is substantially what appears in the original, without other changes than slight verbal ones, I have given only the citation. Where I have thought that the reader would profit from seeing the passage as it is in the original, I have given it, often at some length. The reader can then judge for himself the extent and effect of Milton's alterations, his stylistic preferences, and the context from which the quotation is taken. This procedure is not always possible. In some instances I could not be entirely sure of Milton's exact source, or of the exact passage he had in mind. In others, his habit of sweeping over several

---

[4] Milton's use of the Bible has been intensively studied by Harris Fletcher, *The Use of the Bible in Milton's Prose* (Urbana, 1929). See also below, Appendix D, pp. 808–18.

pages, taking a phrase here, an idea there, a sentence somewhere else, makes it impossible to give the source in full.

In accordance with the style of this edition, all the sources are given in English translation. Unless otherwise noted, the translation is mine. Variations from the Authorized Version are also noted. For the convenience of the reader the notes give, in parentheses, the location in Migne's *Patrologia,* abbreviated as Migne, *Latina* and Migne, *Graeca,* of all passages from the Fathers.

The present text is based upon the Thomason copy, British Museum E271(12), referred to in the textual notes (below, pp. 779–80) as "A." It is a quarto measuring 18.7 by 13.8 cm. Collation A–O⁴; pagination begins B1, continues without error to F4v, which is p. 40; G1 reverts to 37 and the new series continues without further error (except that copy "C" has the 9 of p. 39 reversed to resemble 36) to O3v, which is p. 98. Contents: A1: title-page. A2–O3v text; O4 blank. A2 [row of ornaments]: "To the PARLAMENT." A4v: "JOHN MILTON." B1: heading. Text begins. G1 [row of ornaments]: heading; text continues. O3v [margin-to-margin rule]: *"The End."*/[rule]/*"Errata."*/[rule]. "A" has been collated with these other copies of the first edition: "B," BM G19594; "C," BM 5175.dd.32; "D," BM Ashley 1177; and "E," BM 108.b.53. Variants other than accidents of inking, etc., are to be found in three signatures. Sig. A exists in two states, one represented by copies "A," "B," and "C," the other by copies "D" and "E." Each state corrects one error found in the other, and there are six words spelt differently. The only variant in sig. G is that "C" has the reversed numeral mentioned in the collation. In sig. I an error found in "B," "C," and "E" is corrected in "A" and "D."

ARNOLD WILLIAMS

Michigan State University

Tetrachordon: _12_

EXPOSITIONS
UPON
The foure chief places in Scripture,
which treat of Mariage, or nullities in Mariage.

On $\left\{\begin{array}{l}\text{Gen.1.27.28. compar'd and explain'd by Gen. 2.}\\ \text{Deut.24. 1. 2.} \qquad\qquad\qquad\qquad (18.23.24.\\ \text{Matth.5.31.32. with Matth.19. from the 3}^d\text{. v. to}\\ \text{1 Cor. 7. from the 10}^{th}\text{ to the 16}^{th}. \qquad \text{(the 11}^{th}.\end{array}\right.$

Wherin the Doctrine and Discipline of Divorce, as was
lately publish'd, is confirm'd by explanation of Scripture, by testimony of ancient Fathers, of civill lawes
in the Primitive Church, of famousest
Reformed Divines,

And lastly, by an intended Act of the Parlament and
Church of England in the last yeare of
E D VV A R D the sixth.

By the former Author J. M.

—— Σκαιοῖσι καινὰ προσφέρων σοφὰ
Δόξεις ἀχρεῖος, κ' ου σοφὸς πεφυχέναι·
Τῶν δ' αὖ δοχύντων εἰδέναι τι ποιχίλον,
Κρείσσων νομισθεὶς ἐν πόλει, λυπρὸς φανῇ. _Euripid. Medea._

Church. 44 · _LONDON:_
Printed in the yeare 1645. _1644_

To the PARLAMENT.[1]

THAT WHICH *I knew to be the part of a good Magistrate, aiming at true liberty through the right information of religious and civil life, and that which I saw, and was partaker, of your Vows and solemne Cov'nants, Parlament of England,*[2] *your actions also manifestly tending to exalt the truth, and to depresse the tyranny of error, and ill custome, with more constancy and prowesse then ever yet any, since that Parlament which put the first Scepter of this Kingdom into his hand whom God and extraordinary vertue made thir Monarch,*[3] *were the causes that mov'd me, one else not placing much in the eminence of a dedication, to present your high notice with a Discourse, conscious to it self of nothing more then of diligence, and firm affection to the publick good. And that ye took it so as wise and impartial men, obtaining so great power and dignitie, are wont to accept, in matters both doubtfull and important, what they think offer'd them well meant, and from a rational ability, I had no lesse then to perswade me. And on that perswasion am return'd, as to a famous and free Port, my self also bound by more then a* maritime *Law, to expose as freely what fraughtage I conceave to bring of no trifles.*[4] *For although it be generally known, how and by whom ye have been instigated to a hard censure of that former book entitl'd,* The Doctrine, and Discipline of Divorce, *an opinion held by some of the*

1 Title page, *Medea*, ll. 298–301: "For if thou bring strange wisdom unto dullards / Useless thou shalt be counted and not wise / And, if thy fame outshine those heretofore / Held wise, thou shalt be odious in men's eyes," tr. Arthur S. Way (London and New York: Loeb Classical Library, 1912–19). Milton's text varies slightly from the Loeb text.

2 The allusion is to the Solemn Covenant taken by the Commons and the Westminster Assembly on September 25, 1643, and by the Lords on October 15. From this passage it is evident that Milton himself signed the Covenant, a partial text of which may be found in Masson, III, 13–15. See introduction, above, pp. 61–65.

3 Possibly the Parliament which passed the Act of Supremacy making Henry VIII head of the English Church in 1534.

4 A "free port" is one open to the ships of all nations, as opposed to a "closed port." Milton proposes to declare what kind of ideas *Tetrachordon* contains, just as he would make a customs declaration when docking at a free port.

*best among reformed Writers without scandal or confutement,
though now thought new and dangerous by some of our severe
Gnostics,*[5] *whose little reading, and lesse meditating holds ever with
hardest obstinacy that which it took up with easiest credulity, I
do not find yet that ought, for the furious incitements which have
been us'd, hath issu'd by your appointment, that might give the least
interruption or disrepute either to the Author, or to the Book.
Which he who will be better advis'd then to call your neglect, or
connivence at a thing imagin'd so perilous, can attribute it to nothing more justly, then to the deep and quiet streame of your direct
and calme deliberations; that gave not way either to the fervent
rashnesse, or the immaterial gravity of those who ceas'd not to
exasperate without cause. For which uprightnesse and incorrupt
refusall of what ye were incens'd to, Lords and Commons, (though
it were don to justice, not to me, and was a peculiar demonstration
how farre your waies are different from the rash vulgar) besides
those allegiances of oath and* [A2] *duty, which are my public debt
to your public labours, I have yet a store of gratitude laid up,
which cannot be exhausted; and such thanks perhaps they may live
to be, as shall more then whisper to the next ages. Yet that the
Author may be known to ground himself upon his own innocence,
and the merit of his cause, not upon the favour of a diversion, or a
delay to any just censure, but wishes rather he might see those his
detracters at any fair meeting, as learned debatements are privi-
leg'd with a due freedome under equall Moderators, I shall here
briefly single one of them*[6] *(because he hath oblig'd me to it) who
I perswade me having scarse read the book, nor knowing him who
writ it, or at least faining the latter, hath not forborn to scandalize
him, unconferr'd with, unadmonisht, undealt with by any Pastorly
or brotherly convincement, in the most open and invective manner,
and at the most bitter opportunity that drift or set designe could
have invented. And this, when as the Canon Law, though commonly
most favouring the boldnesse of their Priests, punishes the naming*

[5] The Gnostics held that the body and all its works were evil; hence the desires of the flesh were to be suppressed, even marriage itself. Milton implies that
those who oppose divorce because of such reasons as incompatibility are as
opposed to the legitimate enjoyment of carnal pleasure as the Gnostics.

[6] Herbert Palmer, a minister who preached before Parliament on the Extraordinary Day of Humiliation, August 13, 1644. See introduction, above, pp.
103, 142, for the details of Palmer's attack and its danger to Milton.

or traducing of any person in the Pulpit,[7] *was by him made no scruple. If I shall therfore take licence by the right of nature, and that liberty wherin I was born, to defend my self publicly against a printed Calumny, and do willingly appeal to those Judges to whom I am accus'd, it can be no immoderate, or unallowable course of seeking so just and needfull reparations. Which I had don long since, had not these employments, which are now visible, deferr'd me. It was preacht before ye, Lords and Commons, in August last upon a special day of humiliation, that* there was a wicked Book abroad, *and ye were taxt of sin that it was yet* uncensur'd, the book deserving to be burnt, *and* impudence *also was charg'd upon the Author, who durst* set his name to it, and dedicate it to your selves.[8] *First, Lords and Commons, I pray to that God, before whom ye then were prostrate, so to forgive ye those omissions and trespasses, which ye desire most should find forgivness, as I shall soon shew to the world how easily ye absolve your selves of that which this man calls your sin, and is indeed your wisdome, and your Noblenesse, whereof to this day ye have don well not to repent. He terms it* a wicked book, *and why but* for allowing other causes of Divorce, then Christ and his Apostles mention; *and with the same censure condemns of wickednesse not onely* Martin Bucer *that elect Instrument of Reformation, highly honour'd and had in reverence by* Edward *the sixth, and his whole Parlament, whom also I had publisht in English by a good providence, about a week before this calumnious digression was preach'd;* [9] *so that if he knew not* Bucer *then, as he ought to have known, he might at least have known him some months after, ere the Sermon came in print,*[10] [A2v] *wherein*

---

[7] The Fifth Lateran Council, session xi (1516), condemned "that scandalous practice of defaming the character of bishops, prelates, and other superiors before the people." H. J. Schoeder, O.P., *Disciplinary Decrees of the General Councils* (St. Louis: Herder, 1937), p. 505. I have not been able to find any decree as broad as Milton indicates.

[8] See introduction, above, p. 103.

[9] *Martin Bucer* appeared, according to Thomason, August 6, 1644. Palmer's sermon was preached on August 13.

[10] The exact date of the publication of Palmer's sermon is unknown. Thomason did not date it, and it is entered in the *Tracts* under August 13, 1644, the date of its delivery. Masson (III, 298) gives "September or October" as the time of publication, but offers no reason for the guess. Milton's phrase "some months" accords better with the date of registration, November 7 (*Stationers' Registers,* I, 136).

notwithstanding he persists in his former sentence, and condemnes again of wickednesse, either ignorantly or wilfully, not onely Martin Bucer, *and all the choisest and holiest of our Reformers, but the whole Parlament and Church of England in those best and purest times of* Edward *the sixth. All which I shall prove with good evidence, at the end of these Explanations. And then let it be judg'd and seriously consider'd with what hope the affairs of our Religion are committed to one among others, who hath now onely left him which of the twain he will choose, whether this shall be his palpable ignorance, or the same wickednesse of his own book, which he so lavishly imputes to the writings of other men: and whether this of his, that thus peremptorily defames and attaints of wickednesse unspotted Churches, unblemisht Parlaments, and the most eminent restorers of Christian Doctrine, deserve not to be burnt first. And if his heat had burst out onely against the opinion, his wonted passion had no doubt bin silently born with wonted patience. But since against the charity of that solemne place and meeting, it serv'd him furder to inveigh opprobriously against the person, branding him with no lesse then impudence, onely for setting his name to what he had writt'n, I must be excus'd not to be so wanting to the defence of an honest name, or to the reputation of those good men who afford me their society, but to be sensible of such a foule endeavour'd disgrace: not knowing ought either in mine own deserts, or the Laws of this Land, why I should be subject, in such a notorious and illegal manner, to the intemperancies of this mans preaching choler. And indeed to be so prompt and ready in the midst of his humblenesse, to tosse reproaches of this bulk and size, argues as if they were the weapons of his exercise, I am sure not of his Ministery, or of that dayes work. Certainly to subscribe my name at what I was to own, was what the State had order'd and requires. And he who lists not to be malicious; would call it ingenuity,*[11] *cleer conscience, willingnesse to avouch what might be question'd, or to be better instructed. And if God were so displeas'd with those,* Isa. 58. who on the solemne fast were wont to smite with the fist of wickednesse,[12] *it could be no signe of his own humiliation accepted, which dispos'd him to smite so keenly with a reviling tongue. But if*

---

[11] Ingenuity: L. *ingenuitas* (frankness).

[12] V. 4: "Behold ye fast for strife and debate, and to smite with the fist of wickedness."

onely to have writ my name must be counted impudence, *how doth this but justifie another, who might affirm with as good warrant, that the late Discourse of* Scripture and Reason,[13] *which is certain to be chiefly his own draught, was publisht without a name, out of base fear, and the sly avoidance of what might follow to his detriment, if the party at Court should hap to reach him. And I, to have set my name, where he accuses me to have set it, am so far from recanting, that I offer my hand also if need be, to make good the same opinion which I there maintain, by inevitable consequences drawn parallel from his own principal arguments* [14] *in that of* Scripture and Rea-[A3]son; *which I shall pardon him, if he can deny, without shaking his own composition to peeces. The* impudence *therfore, since he waigh'd so little what a grosse revile that was to give his equall, I send him back again for a* phylactery *to stitch upon his arrogance, that censures not onely before conviction so bitterly without so much as one reason giv'n, but censures the Congregation of his Governors to their faces, for not being so hasty as himself to censure.*

And whereas my other crime is, that I address'd the Dedication of what I had studied, to the Parlament, how could I better declare the loyalty which I owe to that supreme and majestick Tribunal, and the opinion which I have of the high-entrusted judgement, and personall worth assembl'd in that place. With the same affections therfore, and the same addicted fidelity, Parlament of England, I here again have brought to your perusal on the same argument these following Expositions of Scripture. The former book, as pleas'd some to think, who were thought judicious, had of reason in it to a sufficiencie; what they requir'd, was that the Scriptures there alleg'd, might be discuss'd more fully. To their desires, thus much furder hath been labour'd in the Scriptures. Another sort also who wanted more autorities, and citations, have not been here unthought of. If all this attain not to satisfie them, as I am confident that none of those our great controversies at this day, hath had a more demonstrative explaining, I must confesse to admire what it is, for doubtlesse it is not reason now adayes that satisfies, or suborns the common credence of men, to yeeld so easily, and grow so vehement in matters much more disputable, and farre lesse conducing to the

---

[13] Concerning *Scripture and Reason,* see introduction, above, pp. 47–49.
[14] See introduction, above, pp. 145, 153.

daily good and peace of life. Some whose necessary shifts have long enur'd them to cloak the defects of their unstudied yeers, and hatred now to learn, under the appearance of a grave solidity, which estimation they have gain'd among weak perceivers, find the ease of slighting what they cannot refute, and are determin'd, as I hear, to hold it not worth the answering. In which number I must be forc'd to reck'n that Doctor,[15] *who in a late equivocating Treatise plausibly set afloat against the* Dippers, *diving the while himself with a more deep prelatical malignance against the present state, & Church-government, mentions with ignominy the* Tractate of Divorce; *yet answers nothing, but instead thereof (for which I do not commend his marshalling) sets* Moses *also among the crew of his Anabaptists; as one who to a holy Nation, the Common-wealth of Israel, gave Laws* breaking the bonds of mariage to inordinate lust. *These are no mean surges of blasphemy, not onely dipping Moses the divine Lawgiver, but dashing with a high hand against the justice and purity of God himself; as these ensuing Scriptures plainly and freely handl'd shall verifie to the launcing of that old* apostemated [16] *error. Him therefore I leave now to his repentance.* [A3v]

Others, which is their courtesie, confesse that wit and parts may do much to make that seem true which is not (as was objected to Socrates *by them who could not resist his efficacy, that he ever made the worse cause seem the better)* [17] *and thus thinking themselves discharg'd of the difficulty, love not to wade furder into the fear of a convincement. These will be their excuses to decline the full examining of this serious point. So much the more I presse it and repeat it, Lords and Commons, that ye beware while time is, ere this grand secret, and onely art of ignorance affecting tyrany, grow powerfull and rule among us. For if sound argument and reason shall be thus put off, either by an undervaluing silence, or the maisterly censuring of a rayling word or two in the Pulpit, or by rejecting the force of truth, as the meer cunning of eloquence, and Sophis-*

---

[15] Dr. Daniel Featley, author of *The Dippers Dipt* (1645), an attack on the Anabaptists, which included divorce as one of their tenets. See introduction, above, p. 144, and preface, above, p. 572, n. 3.

[16] Apostemated: abscessed. An "aposteme" is a deep abscess.

[17] Plato, *Apology,* I, 18 (tr. Jowett): "But far more dangerous are the others . . . telling of one Socrates, a wise man, who speculated about the heaven above, and searched into the earth beneath, and made the worse appear the better cause."

try, what can be the end of this, but that all good learning and knowledge will suddenly decay: Ignorance, and illiterate presumption, which is yet but our disease, will turn at length into our very constitution, and prove the hectic *evill of this age: worse to be fear'd, if it get once to reign over us, then any fift Monarchy.*[18] *If this shall be the course, that what was wont to be a chief commendation, and the ground of other mens confidence in an Author, his diligence, his learning, his elocution whether by right, or by ill meaning granted him, shall be turn'd now to a disadvantage and suspicion against him, that he writes though unconfuted, must therefore be mistrusted, therfore not receiv'd for the industry, the exactnesse, the labour in it, confess'd to be more then ordnary; as if wisdome had now forsak'n the thirstie and laborious inquirer to dwell against her nature with the arrogant and shallow babler, to what purpose all those pains and that continual searching requir'd of us by* Solomon *to the attainment of understanding;* [19] *why are men bred up with such care and expence to a life of perpetual studies, why do your selves with such endeavour seek to wipe off the imputation of intending to discourage the progresse and advance of learning? He therfore whose heart can bear him to the high pitch of your noble enterprises, may easily assure himself that the prudence and farre-judging circumspectnesse of so grave a Magistracy sitting in Parlament, who have before them the prepar'd and purpos'd Act*[20] *of their most religious predecessors to imitate in this question, cannot reject the cleernesse of these reasons, and these allegations both here and formerly offer'd them; nor can over-look the necessity of ordaining more wholsomly and more humanly in the casualties of Divorce, then our Laws have yet establisht: if the most urgent and excessive grievances hapning in domestick life, be worth the laying to heart, which, unlesse charity be farre from us, cannot*

---

[18] The Fifth Monarchy is the last of the kingdoms foretold in Daniel 2:44, generally understood as the reign of Christ in the millennium. A sect of Milton's time expected the coming of Christ and the beginning of the fifth monarchy in the immediate future. Adherents of that sect, "Fifth Monarchy Men," proposed to set up the millennial reign of Christ by force. Sometimes the word means only "fanaticism." See *Complete Prose*, I, 149–50.

Hectic: In the Greek sense of habitual or constitutional; *cf. Church-Government, Complete Prose*, I, 836, "that hectick disposition to evill, the sourse of all vice."

[19] Probably Proverbs 2:4.   [20] See below, p. 716.

be neglected. And that these things both in the right constitution, and in the right reformation of a Common-wealth call for speediest redresse, and ought to be the first consider'd, anough was urg'd in what was [A4] prefac'd to that monument of Bucer which I brought to your remembrance, and the other time before. Hence forth, except new cause be giv'n, I shall say lesse and lesse. For if the Law make not timely provision, let the Law, as reason is, bear the censure of those consequences, which her own default now more evidently produces. And if men want manlinesse to expostulate the right of their due ransom, and to second their own occasions, they may sit hereafter and bemoan themselves to have neglected through faintnesse the onely remedy of their sufferings, which a seasonable and well grounded speaking might have purchas'd them. And perhaps in time to come, others will know how to esteem what is not every day put into their hands, when they have markt events, and better weigh'd how hurtfull and unwise it is, to hide a secret and pernicious rupture under the ill counsell of a bashfull silence. But who would distrust ought, or not be ample in his hopes of your wise and Christian determinations? who have the prudence to consider, and should have the goodnesse like gods, as ye are call'd,[21] to find out readily, and by just Law to administer those redresses which have of old, not without God ordaining, bin granted to the adversities of mankind, ere they who needed, were put to ask. Certainly, if any other have enlarg'd his thoughts to expect from this government so justly undertak'n, and by frequent assistances from heaven so apparently upheld, glorious changes and renovations both in Church and State, he among the formost might be nam'd, who prayes that the fate of England may tarry for no other Deliverers.

JOHN MILTON. [A4v]

---

[21] One of the Hebrew words for God, *Elohim*, probably meaning originally "the powers," is also used to mean "rulers," "judges," and the like, *e.g.*, in Exodus 21:6: "Then his master shall bring him before the judges." For a full discussion of the several meanings of *Elohim*, see *Christian Doctrine*, I, v, where several texts are cited. (Note suggested by the late Ralph Marcus, Professor of Jewish Antiquities at the University of Chicago.)

TETRACHORDON,

Expofitions upon the foure chiefe places in Scripture which treat of Mariage, or nullities in Mariage.

Gen. 1. 27.

So God created man in his owne image, in the image of God created he him; male and female created he them.

28. *And God blessed them, and God said unto them be fruitfull, &c.*

Gen. 2. 18.

And the Lord God said, It is not good that man [1] *should be alone, I will make him a helpe meet for him.*

23. *And Adam said, This is now bone of my bones, and flesh of my flesh; she shall be called Woman, because she was taken out of Man.*

24. *Therefore shall a man leave his father and his mother, and shall cleave unto his wife, and they shall be one flesh.*

Gen. 1. 27.

So GOD *created man in his owne image.*] To be inform'd aright in the whole History of Mariage, that we may know for certain, not by a forc't yoke, but by an impartial definition, what Mariage is, and what is not Mariage; it will undoubtedly be safest, fairest, and most with our obedience, to enquire, as our

---

[1] Man: Authorized Version, *the* man. The Authorized Version translates the Hebrew literally; Milton uses *man* generically, without the article. The Authorized Version renders the identical Hebrew construction by the generic noun without an article in Genesis 1:27: "So God created man." See Harris Fletcher, *The Use of the Bible in Milton's Prose* (Urbana, 1929), p. 31.

Saviours direction is, how it was in the beginning. And that we begin so high as man created after Gods owne Image, there want not earnest causes. For nothing now adayes is more degenerately forgott'n, then the true dignity of man, almost in every respect, but especially in this prime institution of Matrimony, wherein his native pre-eminence ought most to shine. Although if we consider that just and naturall privileges man neither can rightly seek, nor dare fully claime, unlesse they be ally'd to inward goodnesse, and stedfast knowledge, and that the want of this quells them to a servile sense of their own [1] conscious unworthinesse, it may save the wondring why in this age many are so opposite both to human and to Christian liberty,[2] either while they understand not, or envy others that do; contenting, or rather priding themselves in a specious humility and strictnesse bred out of low ignorance that never yet conceiv'd the freedome of the Gospel; and is therefore by the Apostle to the Colossians rankt with no better company, then Will-worship and the meer shew of wisdome.[3] And how injurious herein they are, if not to themselves, yet to their neighbours, and not to them only, but to the all-wise and bounteous grace offer'd us in our redemption, will orderly appear.

[*In the Image of God created he him.*] It is anough determin'd, that this Image of God wherin man was created, is meant Wisdom, Purity, Justice, and rule over all creatures.[4] All which being lost in *Adam,* was recover'd with gain by the merits of Christ. For albeit our first parent had lordship over sea, and land, and aire, yet there was a law without him, as a guard set over him. But Christ having cancell'd [5] the hand writing of ordinances which was against us, *Coloss.* 2. 14. and interpreted the fulfilling of all through charity, hath in that respect set us over law, in the free custody of his love,

[2] Concerning the distinction between human and Christian liberty see the full discussion in Barker, *Milton and the Puritan Dilemma,* pp. 98–120; see also introduction, pp. 65–70.

[3] Colossians 2:23: "Which things have indeed a shew of wisdom in will worship."

[4] Milton here summarizes the opinions of the Renaissance commentators on Genesis, particularly that of Paraeus, who understood the image of God to consist in those qualities of man in which he most resembled God. For other opinions and a discussion of the interpretation of the image of God see Arnold Williams, *The Common Expositor* (Chapel Hill: North Carolina University Press, 1948), pp. 72–74.

[5] Having cancell'd: Authorized Version, "blotting out."

and left us victorious under the guidance of his living Spirit, not
under the dead letter; to follow that which most edifies, most
aides and furders a religious life, makes us holiest and likest to his
immortall Image, not that which makes us most conformable and
captive to civill and subordinat precepts; whereof the strictest observance may oftimes prove the destruction not only of many innocent persons and families, but of whole Nations. Although indeed
no ordinance human or from heav'n can binde against the good of
man; so that to keep them strictly against that end, is all one with
to breake them. Men of most renowned vertu have sometimes by
transgressing, most truly kept the law; and wisest Magistrates
have permitted and dispenc't it; while they lookt not peevishly at
the letter, but with a greater spirit at the good of mankinde, if
alwayes not writt'n in the characters of law, yet engrav'n in the
heart of man by a divine impression. This Heathens could see, as
the well-read in story can recount of *Solon* and *Epaminondas*, whom
Cicero in his first booke of *invention* nobly defends. *All law*, saith
he, *we ought referr to the common good, and interpret by that, not
by the scrowl of letters. No man observes law for laws sake, but for
the good of them for whom it was made.*[6] The rest might serv well
to lecture these times, deluded through belly-doctrines [7] into a devout slavery. The Scripture also affords us *David* in the shew-bread,
Hezechiah [2] in the passeover [8] sound and safe transgressors of
the literall command, which also dispenc'd not seldom with it self;
and taught us on what just occasions to doe so: untill our Saviour
for whom that great and God-like work was reserv'd, redeem'd us
to a state above prescriptions by dissolving the whole law into
charity.[9] And have we not the soul to understand this, and must

---

[6] *De Inventione,* I, xxxviii, tr. H. M. Hubbell (Cambridge, 1929), pp. 111–13.
It is not quite accurate to say that Cicero defends Epaminondas. In the passage
to which Milton refers he merely illustrates a type of argument, which he drama-
tizes by supposing it offered as a defense of Epaminondas, who by refusing to
hand over the command of his army to another, as required by law, defeated
the Lacedaemonians. Previously in the same work (I, xxxiii), Cicero has illustrated another type of argument by similarly composing the accusation of
Epaminondas.

[7] Romans 16:18: "For they that are such serve not our Lord Jesus Christ,
but their own belly."

[8] David and the showbread: I Samuel 21:2–6; Hezekiah: II Chronicles
30:18–19.

[9] See *Doctrine and Discipline,* above, pp. 228–29.

we against this glory of Gods transcendent love towards us be still the servants of a literall indightment?

[*Created he him.*] It might be doubted why he saith, *In the Image of God created he him*, not them, as well as *male and female them*; especially since that Image might be common to them both, but *male and female* could not, however the Jewes fable, and please themselvs with the accidentall concurrence of *Plato's* wit, as if man at first had bin created *Hermaphrodite:* [10] but then it must have bin male and female created he him. So had the Image of God bin equally common to them both, it had no doubt bin said, In the image of God created he them. But *St. Paul* ends the controversie by explaining that the woman is not primarily and immediatly the image of God, but in reference to the man. *The head of the woman*, saith he, I *Cor.* 11. *is the man: he the image and glory of God, she the glory of the man:* he not for her, but she for him. Therefore his precept is, *Wives be subject to your husbands* [11] *as is fit in the Lord, Coloss.* 3. 18. *In every thing, Eph.* 5. 24. Neverthelesse man is not to hold her as a servant, but receives her into a part of that empire which God proclaims him to, though not equally, yet largely, as his own image and glory: for it is no small glory to him, that a creature so like him, should be made subject to him. Not but that particular exceptions may have place, if she exceed her husband in prudence and dexterity, and he contentedly yeeld, for then a superior and more naturall law comes in, that the wiser should govern the lesse wise, whether male or female. But that which far more easily and obediently follows from this verse, is that, seeing woman was purposely made for man, and he her head, it cannot stand before the breath of this divine utterance, that man the portraiture of God, joyning to himself for his intended good and solace an inferiour sexe, should so becom her thrall, whose wilfulnes or inability to be a wife frustrates the occasionall end of her creation,[12] but that he may acquitt himself to freedom by his naturall birth-

[10] The commentaries frequently reported the notion that man was originally created a hermaphrodite. Jewish sources and Plato's *Symposium* both appear as sources. See Williams, *The Common Expositor*, p. 92.

[11] Authorized Version: "Wives submit yourselves unto your own husbands." This is probably an example of Milton's independent translation from the Greek.

[12] Occasionall end: the end for which woman was made. See Williams, p. 85, for Augustine's definition of woman as an "occasional animal." However, Milton makes companionship, rather than procreation, the occasion.

right, and that indeleble character of priority which God crown'd him with. If it be urg'd that sin hath lost him this, the answer is not far to seek, that from her the sin first proceeded, which keeps her justly in the same proportion still beneath. She is not to gain by be-[3]ing first in the transgression, that man should furder loose to her, because already he hath lost by her means. Oft it happens that in this matter he is without fault; so that his punishment herein is causeles: and God hath the praise in our speeches of him, to sort his punishment in the same kind with the offence. Suppose he err'd; it is not the intent of God or man, to hunt an error so to the death with a revenge beyond all measure and proportion. But if we argue thus, this affliction is befaln him for his sin, therefore he must bear it, without seeking the only remedy, first it will be false that all affliction comes for sin, as in the case of *Job,* and of the man born blind, *Joh.* 9. 3,[13] was evident: next by that reason, all miseries comming for sin, we must let them all lye upon us like the vermin of an Indian *Catharist,*[14] which his fond religion forbids him to molest. Were it a particular punishment inflicted through the anger of God upon a person, or upon a land, no law hinders us in that regard, no law but bidds us remove it if we can: much more if it be a dangerous temptation withall, much more yet, if it be certainly a temptation, and not certainly a punishment, though a pain. As for what they say we must bear with patience, to bear with patience, and to seek effectuall remedies, implies no contradiction. It may no lesse be for our disobedience, our unfaithfulnes, and other sins against God, that wives becom adulterous to the bed, and questionles we ought to take the affliction as patiently, as christian prudence would wish; yet hereby is not lost the right of divorcing for adultery. No you say, because our Saviour excepted that only. But why, if he were so bent to punish our sins, and try our patience in binding on us a disastrous mariage, why did he except adultery? Certainly to have bin bound from divorce in that case also had bin as plentifull a punishment to our sins, and not too

---

[13] "And his disciples asked him, saying, Master who did sin, this man, or his parents, that he was born blind? Jesus answered, Neither hath this man sinned, nor his parents: but that the works of God should be made manifest in him."

[14] Indian *Catharist:* ascetic. The Catharists were an ascetic sect prominent, under the name of Albigenses and other names, in Europe in the twelfth and thirteenth centuries. Milton transfers the meaning of the word to ascetics in general.

little work for the patientest. Nay perhaps they will say it was too great a sufferance: And with as slight a reason, for no wise man but would sooner pardon the act of adultery once and again committed by a person worthy pitty and forgivnes, then to lead a wearisom life of unloving & unquiet conversation with one who neither affects nor is affected, much lesse with one who exercises all bitternes, and would commit adultery too, but for envy lest the persecuted condition should thereby get the benefit of his freedom. 'Tis plain therefore that God enjoyns not this supposed strictnes of not divorcing either to punish us, or to try our patience.

Moreover, if man be the image of God, which consists in holines, and woman ought in the same respect to be the image and companion of man, in such wise to be lov'd, as the Church is belov'd of Christ, and if, as God [4] is the head of Christ, and Christ the head of man, so man is the head of woman; I cannot see by this golden dependance of headship and subjection, but that Piety and Religion is the main tye of Christian Matrimony: So as if there be found between the pair a notorious disparity either of wickednes or heresie, the husband by all manner of right is disingag'd from a creature, not made and inflicted on him to the vexation of his righteousnes; the wife also, as her subjection is terminated in the Lord, being her self the redeem'd of Christ, is not still bound to be the vassall of him, who is the bondslave of Satan: she being now neither the image nor the glory of such a person, nor made for him, nor left in bondage to him; but hath recours to the wing of charity, and protection of the Church; unless there be a hope on either side; yet such a hope must be meant, as may be a rationall hope, and not an endles servitude. Of which hereafter.[15]

But usually it is objected, that if it be thus, then there can be no true mariage between misbeleevers and irreligious persons? I might answer, let them see to that who are such; the Church hath no commission to judge those without, I *Cor.* 5.[16] But this they will say perhaps, is but penuriously to resolv a doubt. I answer therefore, that where they are both irreligious, the mariage may be yet true anough to them in a civill relation. For there are left som remains of Gods image in man, as he is meerly man; which reason God

15 See below, pp. 682–83.
16 V. 12: "For what have I to do to judge them also that are without?"

gives against the shedding of mans bloud, *Gen.* 9.[17] as being made
in Gods image, without expression whether he were a good man or
a bad, to exempt the slayer from punishment. So that in those
mariages where the parties are alike void of Religion, the wife owes
a civill homage and subjection, the husband owes a civill loyalty.
But where the yoke is mis-yok't, heretick with faithfull, godly with
ungodly, to the grievance and manifest endangering of a brother
or sister, reasons of a higher strain then matrimoniall bear sway;
unlesse the Gospel instead of freeing us, debase it self to make us
bondmen, and suffer evill to controule good.

[*Male and female created he them.*] This contains another end
of matching man and woman, being the right, and lawfulnes of the
mariage bed; though much inferior to the former end of her being
his image and helpe in religious society. And who of weakest insight
may not see that this creating of them male and female, cannot in
any order of reason, or Christianity, be of such moment against the
better and higher purposes of their creation, as to enthrall husband
or wife to duties or to sufferings, unworthy and unbeseeming the
image of God in them? Now when as [5] not only men, but good
men doe stand upon their right, their estimation, their dignity in
all other actions and deportments with warrant anough and good
conscience, as having the image of God in them, it will not be difficult to determin what is unworthy and unseemly for a man to do or
suffer in wedlock; and the like proportionally may be found for
woman: if we love not to stand disputing below the principles of
humanity. He that said, *Male and female created he them,* immediatly before that said also in the same verse, *In the Image of God
created he him,* and redoubl'd it, that our thoughts might not be so
full of dregs as to urge this poor consideration of *male and female,*
without remembring the noblenes of that former repetition; lest
when God sends a wise eye to examin our triviall glosses, they be
found extremly to creep upon the ground: especially since they
confesse that what here concerns mariage is but a brief touch, only
preparative to the institution which follows more expressely in the
next Chapter: and that Christ so took it, as desiring to be briefest
with them who came to tempt him, account shall be given in due
place.

[17] V. 6: "Whoso sheddeth man's blood, by man shall his blood be shed: for in
the image of God made he man."

V. 28. *And God blessed them, and God said unto them, be fruit-full, and multiply, and replenish the earth,* &c.

This declares another end of Matrimony, the propagation of mankind; and is again repeated to *Noah* and his sons.[18] Many things might be noted on this place not ordinary, nor unworth the noting; but I undertook not a generall Comment. Hence therefore we see the desire of children is honest and pious; if we be not lesse zealous in our Christianity, then *Plato* was in his heathenism; who in the sixt *of his laws,* counts off-spring therefore desirable, that we may leav in our stead sons of our sons, continuall servants of God: [19] a religious and prudent desire, if people knew as well what were requir'd to breeding as to begetting; which desire perhaps was a cause why the Jews hardly could endure a barren wedlock: and *Philo* in his book of speciall laws esteems him only worth pardon that sends not barrennes away.[20] *Carvilius* the first recorded in Rome to have sought divorce, had it granted him for the barrennes of his wife, upon his oath that he maried to the end he might have children; as *Dionysius* and *Gellius* are authors.[21] But to dismisse a

[18] Genesis 9:1: "And God blessed Noah and his sons, and said unto them, Be fruitful, and multiply, and replenish the earth."

[19] *Laws,* VI, 774A, in *Plato,* tr. H. N. Fowler and others (10 vols., London and New York, 1914–26), I, 465.

[20] *Special Laws,* III, 35, in *Philo,* tr. F. H. Colson and G. H. Whittaker (7 vols., Cambridge, 1929), VII, 497. The compression of Milton's epitome somewhat obscures Philo's meaning, which more strongly supports Milton's case than is evident here. Philo has been condemning those who marry barren women. Since they cannot hope for offspring, their motive must be mere lust. It is the duty of husbands of childless women to put them away, though certain concessions may be made: "Those who marry maidens in ignorance at the time of their capacity or incapacity for successful motherhood, and later refuse to dismiss them, when prolonged childlessness shews them to be barren, deserve our pardon. Familiarity, that most constraining influence, is too strong for them, and they are unable to rid themselves of the charm of old affection imprinted on their souls by long companionship."

[21] Dionysius of Halicarnassus, *Roman Antiquities,* II, 25, tr. Earnest Cary (6 vols., Cambridge and London: Loeb Classical Library, 1937–47), I, 385; Aulus Gellius, *Noctes Atticae,* IV, 3, tr. John C. Rolfe (2 vols., Cambridge: Loeb Classical Library, 1946–48), I, 323. Milton seems to be following Dionysius rather than Gellius. Like Milton, Dionysius says that Carvilius was obliged by the censors to swear that he married to have children. Gellius, however, says that Carvilius held his wife in high esteem, but held higher the oath which the censors had compelled him to take that he would marry for the purpose of begetting children. Dionysius adds that he was ever afterward hated by the people.

wife only for barrennes, is hard: and yet in som the desire of children is so great, and so just, yea somtime so necessary, that to condemn such a one to a childles age, the fault apparently not being in
him, might seem perhaps more strict then [6] needed. Somtimes
inheritances, crowns, and dignities are so interested and annext in
their common peace and good to such or such lineall descent, that
it may prove a great moment both in the affairs of men and of religion, to consider throughly what might be don heerin, notwithstanding the waywardnes of our School Doctors.

Gen. 2. 18.

*And the Lord said, it is not good that man should be alone; I will
make him a help meet for him.*
V. 23. *And Adam said, &c.* V. 24. *Therefore shall a man leave,
&c.*

T HIS second Chapter is granted to be a commentary on the
first; [22] and these verses granted to be an exposition of
that former verse, *Male and female created he them,* and
yet when this male and female is by the explicit words of God
himselfe heer declar'd to be not meant other then a fit help, and
meet society; som who would ingrosse to themselves the whole
trade of interpreting, will not suffer the cleer text of God to doe
the office of explaining it self.

[*And the Lord God said it is not good.*] A man would think that
the consideration of who spake, should raise up the attention of our
minds to enquire better, and obey the purpos of so great a Speaker:
for as we order the busines of Mariage, that which he heer speaks
is all made vain; and in the decision of matrimony, or not matrimony, nothing at all regarded. Our presumption, hath utterly
chang'd the state and condition of this ordinance: God ordain'd it
in love and helpfulnes to be indissoluble, and we in outward act

---

[22] A common statement in the commentaries on Genesis, *e.g.,* David Paraeus,
In Genesin Mosis Commentarius (Geneva, 1614; UTSL, cols. 251–52: "This
chapter is an epilogue and illuminating commentary on the whole work of the
days." David Paraeus (Wängler), 1548–1622, a Calvinist theologian, taught at
Heidelberg from 1584 until his death. See *Doctrine and Discipline,* above, p. 246.

and formality to be a forc't bondage; so that being subject to a thousand errors in the best men, if it prove a blessing to any, it is of meer accident, as mans law hath handl'd it, and not of institution.

[*It is not good for man to be alone.*] [23] Hitherto all things that have bin nam'd, were approv'd of God to be very good: lonelines is the first thing which Gods eye nam'd not good: whether it be a thing, or the want of somthing, I labour not; let it be their tendance, who have the art to be industriously idle. And heer *alone* is meant alone without woman; otherwise *Adam* had the company of God himself, and Angels to convers with; all creatures to delight him seriously, or to make him sport. God could have created him out of the same mould a thousand friends and brother *Adams* to have bin his consorts, yet for all this till *Eve* was giv'n him, God reckn'd him to be alone. [7]

[*It is not good.*] God heer presents himself like to a man deliberating; both to shew us that the matter is of high consequence, and that he intended to found it according to naturall reason, not impulsive command, but that the duty should arise from the reason of it, not the reason be swallow'd up in a reasonlesse duty. *Not good,* was as much to *Adam* before his fall, as not pleasing, not expedient; but since the comming of sin into the world, to him who hath not receiv'd the continence, it is not only not expedient to be alone, but plainly sinfull. And therefore he who wilfully abstains from mariage, not being supernaturally gifted, and he who by making the yoke of mariage unjust and intolerable, causes men to abhorr it, are both in a diabolicall sin, equall to that of Antichrist who forbids to marry.[24] For what difference at all whether he abstain men from marrying, or restrain them in a mariage hapning totally discommodious, distastfull, dishonest and pernicious to him without the appearance of his fault? For God does not heer precisely say, I make a female to this male, as he did briefly before, but expounding himselfe heer on purpos, he saith, because it is not good for man to be alone, I make him therefore a meet help. God supplies the privation of not good, with the perfect gift of a reall and positive good; it is mans pervers cooking who hath turn'd this bounty of God into a Scorpion, either by weak and shallow constructions, or

---

[23] Authorized Version: "that the man should be alone." *Cf.* above, p. 463.

[24] Apparently an exaggerated interpretation of the Roman Catholic insistence on the vow of chastity for priests.

by proud arrogance and cruelty to them who neither in their purposes nor in their actions have offended against the due honour of
wedlock.

Now whereas the Apostle speaking in the Spirit, I *Cor. 7.* pronounces quite contrary to this word of God, *It is good for a man
not to touch a woman,* and God cannot contradict himself, it instructs us that his commands and words, especially such as bear the
manifest title of som good to man, are not to be so strictly wrung,
as to command without regard to the most naturall and miserable
necessities of mankind. Therefore the Apostle adds a limitation
in the 26 v. of that chap. for the present necessity it is good; which
he gives us doubtlesse as a pattern how to reconcile other places by
the generall rule of charity.[25]

[*For man to be alone.*] Som would have the sense heerof to be
in respect of procreation only: and *Austin* contests that manly
friendship in all other regards had bin a more becomming solace
for *Adam,* then to spend so many secret years in an empty world
with one woman.[26] But our Writers [27] deservedly reject this crabbed
opinion; [28] and defend that there is a peculiar comfort in the
maried state besides the genial [29] bed, which no other society affords. No mortall nature can endure either in the actions [8] of
Religion, or study of wisdome, without somtime slackning the cords
of intense thought and labour: which lest we should think faulty,
God himself conceals us not his own recreations before the world
was built; *I was,* saith the eternall wisdome, *dayly his delight,*

[25] Paraeus, *In Genesin* (Geneva, 1614), col. 413, considers these same texts
in the same connection. His conclusion is that in Genesis, God speaks about the
whole species of man; whereas Paul speaks only about "the present necessity,"
in which single men can better withstand persecution than married men. Milton's
use of the phrase "present necessity," a literal translation of the Latin text
Paraeus cites, instead of the Authorized Version's "present distress," makes it
probable that he was prompted to this passage by Paraeus.

[26] Augustine, *De Genesi ad Litteram,* IX, 5 (Migne, *Latina,* XXXIV, 396):
"How much more fitting therefore for living and conversing together would it
be for two friends to live together equally than a man and a woman." Paraeus,
In Genesin (Geneva, 1614), cols. 410–11, quotes the whole passage, and it is frequently cited or alluded to by other commentators.

[27] *I.e.,* Protestant commentators.

[28] Not only Protestants, but also Catholic commentators of the sixteenth and
seventeenth centuries emphasize the social purposes of marriage. See Williams,
The Common Expositor, pp. 85–86.

[29] Genial: for procreation.

playing always before him.[30] And to him indeed wisdom is as a high towr of pleasure, but to us a steep hill, and we toyling ever about the bottom: he executes with ease the exploits of his omnipotence, as easie as with us it is to will: but no worthy enterprise can be don by us without continuall plodding and wearisomnes to our faint and sensitive abilities. We cannot therefore alwayes be contemplative, or pragmaticall abroad, but have need of som delightfull intermissions, wherin the enlarg'd soul may leav off a while her severe schooling; and like a glad youth in wandring vacancy, may keep her hollidaies to joy and harmles pastime: which as she cannot well doe without company, so in no company so well as where the different sexe in most resembling unlikenes, and most unlike resemblance cannot but please best and be pleas'd in the aptitude of that variety. Wherof lest we should be too timorous, in the aw that our flat sages would form us and dresse us, wisest *Salomon* among his gravest Proverbs [31] countenances a kinde of ravishment and erring fondnes in the entertainment of wedded leisures; and in the Song of Songs, which is generally beleev'd, even in the jolliest expressions to figure the spousals of the Church with Christ, sings of a thousand raptures between those two lovely ones farre on the hither side of carnall enjoyment. By these instances, and more which might be brought, we may imagine how indulgently God provided against mans lonelines; that he approv'd it not, as by himself declar'd not good; that he approv'd the remedy therof, as of his own ordaining, consequently good; and as he ordain'd it, so doubtles proportionably to our fal'n estate he gives it; els were his ordinance at least in vain, and we for all his gift still empty handed. Nay such an unbounteous giver we should make him, as in the fables *Jupiter* was to *Ixion,* giving him *a cloud* instead of *Juno,* giving him a monstrous issue by her, the breed of *Centaures* a neglected and unlov'd race,[32] the fruits of a delusive mariage,

---

[30] Proverbs 8:30. Playing: Authorized Version, "rejoicing." Fletcher, *Use of the Bible,* p. 32, calls this an independent translation from the Hebrew. Milton alludes to the passage again in *Paradise Lost,* VII, 5–12.

[31] Proverbs 5:18–19: "Rejoice with the wife of thy youth. Let her be as the loving hind and pleasant roe; let her breasts satisfy thee at all times; and be thou ravished always with her love."

[32] See Pindar, *Pythian Odes,* II, 20–48. Natale Conti, *Mythologiae* (Frankfurt, 1596), p. 628, interprets the fable of Ixion as an example of ingratitude for divine gifts.

and lastly giving him her with a damnation to that wheele in hell, from a life thrown into the midst of temptations and disorders. But God is no deceitfull giver, to bestow that on us for a remedy of lonelines, which if it bring not a sociable minde as well as a conjunctive body, leavs us no lesse alone then [9] before; and if it bring a minde perpetually avers and disagreeable, betraies us to a wors condition then the most deserted lonelines. God cannot in the justice of his own promise and institution so unexpectedly mock us by forcing that upon us as the remedy of solitude, which wraps us in a misery worse then any wildernes, as the Spirit of God himself judges, Prov. 19.[33] especially knowing that the best and wisest men amidst the sincere and most cordiall designes of their heart doe dayly erre in choosing. We may conclude therfore seeing orthodoxall Expositers confesse to our hands, that by lonelines is not only meant the want of copulation,[34] and that man is not lesse alone by turning in a body to him, unlesse there be within it a minde answerable, that it is a work more worthy the care and consultation of God to provide for the worthiest part of man which is his minde, and not unnaturally to set it beneath the formalities and respects of the body, to make it a servant of its owne vassall, I say we may conclude that such a mariage, wherin the minde is so disgrac't and vilify'd below the bodies interest, and can have no just or tolerable contentment, is not of Gods institution, and therfore no mariage. Nay in concluding this, I say we conclude no more then what the common Expositers themselves give us, both in that which I have recited and much more hereafter. But the truth is, they give us in such a manner, as they who leav their own mature positions like the eggs of an Ostrich in the dust; I do but lay them in the sun; their own pregnancies hatch the truth; and I am taxt of novelties and strange producements, while they, like that inconsiderat bird, know not that these are their own naturall breed.

[*I will make him a help meet for him.*] Heer the heavnly instituter, as if he labour'd, not to be mistak'n by the supercilious hypocrisie of those that love to maister their brethren, and to make us

---

[33] V. 13: "The contentions of a wife are a continual dropping."

[34] *E.g.*, Paraeus, *In Genesin* (Geneva, 1614), cols. 416–17: "In the second place, woman is an aid to man in society and in mutual and true friendship, that is, an undivided and faithful companion in intimate and most sweet conversation and social cohabitation."

sure that he gave us not now a servil yoke, but an amiable knot; contents not himself to say, I will make him a wife, but resolving to give us first the meaning before the name of a wife, saith graciously, *I will make him a help meet for him*. And heer again, as before, I doe not require more full and fair deductions then the whole consent of our Divines usually raise from this text, that in matrimony there must be first a mutuall help to piety, next to civill fellowship of love and amity, then to generation, so to houshold affairs, lastly the remedy of incontinence.[35] And commonly they reck'n them in such order, as leavs generation and incon-[10] tinence to be last consider'd. This I amaze me at, that though all the superior and nobler ends both of mariage and of the maried persons be absolutely frustrat, the matrimony stirs not, looses no hold, remains as rooted as the center: but if the body bring but in a complaint of frigidity, by that cold application only, this adaman-tine *Alpe* of wedlock has leav to dissolve; which els all the machi-nations of religious or civill reason at the suit of a distressed mind, either for divine worship or humane conversation violated, cannot unfasten. What courts of concupiscence are these, wherein fleshly appetite is heard before right reason, lust before love or devotion? They may be pious Christians together, they may be loving and friendly, they may be helpfull to each other in the family, but they cannot couple; that shall divorce them though either party would not.[36] They can neither serv God together, nor one be at peace with the other, nor be good in the family one to other, but live as they were dead, or live as they were deadly enemies in a cage together; tis all one, they can couple, they shall not divorce till death, no though this sentence be their death. What is this, besides tyranny, but to turn nature upside down, to make both religion, and the minde of man wait upon the slavish errands of the body, and not

[35] This is exactly the order in Paraeus, *In Genesin* (Geneva, 1614), cols. 416–18.

[36] The canons on frigidity and impotence as barriers to marriage and causes of divorce, and the comments on these canons, are extremely complicated, abounding in contradictions, exceptions, and distinctions. There is, however, con-siderable opinion that impotence, if unknown to the potent party before the marriage, is cause for divorce. I can find no hint in this discussion that im-potence requires the termination of a marriage, even against the will of the parties, as Milton seems to say. For an exceptionally complete discussion of the problem, see Joseph Freisen, *Geschichte des Canonischen Eherechts* (Paderborn, 1893), pp. 330–64.

the body to follow either the sanctity, or the sovranty of the mind unspeakably wrong'd, and with all equity complaining? what is this but to abuse the sacred and misterious bed of mariage to be the compulsive stie of an ingratefull and malignant lust, stirr'd up only from a carnall acrimony,[37] without either love or peace, or regard to any other thing holy or human. This I admire how possibly it should inhabit thus long in the sense of so many disputing *Theologians,* unlesse it be the lowest lees of a canonicall infection livergrown [38] to their sides; which perhaps will never uncling, without the strong abstersive of som heroick magistrat, whose mind equall to his high office dares lead him both to know and to do without their frivolous case-putting. For certain he shall have God and this institution plainly on his side. And if it be true both in divinity and law, that consent alone,[39] though copulation never follow, makes a mariage, how can they dissolv it for the want of that which made it not, and not dissolv it for that not continuing which made it, and should preserve it in love and reason, and difference it from a brute conjugality.

[*Meet for him.*] The originall heer is more expressive then other [11] languages word for word can render it; but all agree effectuall conformity of disposition and affection to be heerby signify'd; [40] which God as it were not satisfy'd with the naming of a help, goes on describing *another self, a second self, a very self it self.* Yet now there is nothing in the life of man through our misconstruction, made more uncertain, more hazardous and full of chance then this divine blessing with such favorable significance heer conferr'd upon us, which if we do but erre in our choice the most unblamable error that can be, erre but one minute, one moment after those mighty syllables pronounc't which take upon them to joyn heavn and hell together unpardnably till death pardon, this divine blessing that lookt but now with such a human smile upon us, and spoke such gentle reason, strait vanishes like a fair skie and brings on such a scene of cloud and tempest, as turns all to shipwrack without havn

---

[37] Acrimony: sharpness. By "carnal acrimony" Milton means passion or lust.
[38] Liver-grown: adherent as an enlarged liver.
[39] See below, p. 609, n. 55.
[40] Paraeus, *In Genesin* (Geneva, 1614), cols. 407–408, has a textual note giving the Hebrew, the Septuagint Greek, and Luther's German, the meaning of which he summarizes as "not as a servant, but as an undivided companion of life, that is, one who intimately lives together with him."

or shoar but to a ransomles captivity. And then they tell us it is our sin; but let them be told again, that sin through the mercy of God hath not made such wast upon us, as to make utterly void to our use any temporall benefit, much lesse any so much availing to a peacefull and sanctify'd life, meerly for a most incident error which no warines can certainly shun. And wherfore servs our happy redemption, and the liberty we have in Christ, but to deliver us from calamitous yokes not to be liv'd under without the endangerment of our souls, and to restore us in som competent measure to a right in every good thing both of this life, and the other. Thus we see how treatably and distinctly God hath heer taught us what the prime ends of mariage are, mutuall solace and help. That we are now, upon the most irreprehensible mistake in choosing, defeated and defrauded of all this originall benignity, was begun first through the snare of Antichristian canons long since obtruded upon the Church of Rome,[41] and not yet scour'd off by reformation, out of a lingring vain-glory that abides among us to make fair shews in formall ordinances, and to enjoyn continence & bearing of crosses in such a garb as no Scripture binds us, under the thickest arrows of temptation, where we need not stand. Now we shall see with what acknowledgement and assent *Adam* receiv'd this new associat, which God brought him. [12]

V. 23. *And Adam said this is now bone of my bones, and flesh of my flesh, she shall be called Woman, because she was tak'n out of Man.*

That there was a neerer alliance between *Adam* and *Eve*, then could be ever after between man and wife, is visible to any. For no other woman was ever moulded out of her husbands rib, but of meer strangers for the most part they com to have that consanguinity which they have by wedlock. And if we look neerly upon the matter, though mariage be most agreeable to holines, to purity and justice, yet is it not a naturall, but a civill and ordain'd relation. For if it were in nature, no law or crime could disanull it, to make a wife, or husband, otherwise then still a wife or husband, but only death; as nothing but that can make a father no father, or a son no son. But divorce for adultery or desertion, as all our Churches agree

[41] See *Doctrine and Discipline,* above, pp. 236–38, and below, pp. 704–706.

but England,[42] not only separats, but nullifies, and extinguishes the
relation it self of matrimony, so that they are no more man and
wife; otherwise the innocent party could not marry else-where,
without the guilt of adultery; next were it meerly naturall why was
it heer ordain'd more then the rest of morall law to man in his
originall rectitude, in whose brest all that was naturall or morall
was engrav'n without externall constitutions and edicts. *Adam* therfore in these words does not establish an indissoluble bond of mariage
in the carnall ligaments of flesh and bones, for if he did, it would
belong only to himself in the literall sense; every one of us being
neerer in flesh of flesh, and bone of bones to our parents then to a
wife; they therfore were not to be left for her in that respect. But
Adam who had the wisdom giv'n him to know all creatures,[43] and to
name them according to their properties, no doubt but had the gift
to discern perfectly, that which concern'd him much more; and to
apprehend at first sight the true fitnes of that consort which God
provided him. And therfore spake in reference to those words which
God pronounc't before; as if he had said, this is she by whose meet
help and society I shall no more be alone; this is she who was made
my image, ev'n as I the Image of God; not so much in body, as in
unity of mind and heart. And he might as easily know what were the
words of God, as he knew so readily what had bin don with his rib,
while he slept so soundly.[44] He might well know, if God took a rib out
of his inside, to form of it a double good to him, he would far [13]
sooner dis-joyn it from his outside, to prevent a treble mischief to
him: and far sooner cut it quite off from all relation for his undoubted
ease, then nail it into his body again, to stick for ever there a thorn
in his heart. When as nature teaches us to divide any limb from the
body to the saving of his fellows, though it be the maiming and deformity of the whole; how much more is it her doctrin to sever by
incision, not a true limb so much, though that be lawfull, but an adherent, a sore, the gangrene of a limb, to the recovery of a whole man.

---

[42] See *Doctrine and Discipline*, above, p. 237.

[43] Concerning this commonplace, see Williams, *The Common Expositor*, pp.
81–82.

[44] The common explanation was that Adam knew what God had done while
he slept either by some sort of revelation, perhaps in a dream, or by his naturally
perfect knowledge of all things that concerned him. Paraeus, *In Genesin*
(Geneva, 1614), col. 438, prefers the latter explanation, though reporting the
other; in *Paradise Lost*, VIII, 452 ff. Milton chooses the former.

But if in these words we shall make *Adam* to erect a new establishment of mariage in the meer flesh, which God so lately had instituted, and founded in the sweet and mild familiarity of love and solace and mutuall fitnes, what do we but use the mouth of our generall parent, the first time it opens, to an arrogant opposition, and correcting of Gods wiser ordinance. These words therfore cannot import any thing new in mariage, but either that which belongs to *Adam* only, or to us in reference only to the instituting words of God which made a meet help against lonelines. *Adam* spake like *Adam* the words of flesh and bones, the shell and rinde of matrimony; but God spake like God, of love and solace and meet help, the soul both of *Adams* words and of matrimony.

V. 24. *Therefore shall a man leav his father and his mother, and shall cleav unto his wife; and they shall be one flesh.*

This vers, as our common heed expounds it, is the great knot tier, which hath undon by tying, and by tangling, millions of guiltles consciences: this is that greisly Porter, who having drawn men and wisest men by suttle allurement within the train of an unhappy matrimony, claps the dungeon gate upon them, as irrecoverable as the grave. But if we view him well, and hear him with not too hasty and prejudicant ears, we shall finde no such terror in him. For first, it is not heer said absolutely without all reason he shall cleave to his wife, be it to his weal or to his destruction as it happens, but he shall doe this upon the premises and considerations of that meet help and society before mention'd, *Therefore he shall cleave to his wife,* no otherwise a wife, then a fit help. He is not bid to leave the dear cohabitation of his father, mother, brothers and sisters, to link himself inseparably with the meer carcas of a Mariage, perhaps an enemy. [14] This joyning particle *Therefore* is in all equity, nay in all necessity of construction to comprehend first and most principally what God spake concerning the inward essence of Mariage in his institution; that we may learn how far to attend what *Adam* spake of the outward materials therof in his approbation. For if we shall bind these words of *Adam* only to a corporall meaning, and that the force of this injunction upon all us his sons to live individually with any woman which hath befaln us in the most mistak'n wedlock, shall consist not in those morall and relative causes of

Eves creation, but in the meer anatomy of a rib, and that *Adams* insight concerning wedlock reacht no furder, we shall make him as very an idiot as the Socinians [45] make him; which would not be reverently don of us. Let us be content to allow our great forefather so much wisdom, as to take the instituting words of God along with him into this sentence, which if they be well minded, wil assure us that flesh and ribs are but of a weak and dead efficacy to keep Mariage united where there is no other fitnes. The rib of Mariage, to all since *Adam,* is a relation much rather then a bone; the nerves and sinews therof are love and meet help, they knit not every couple that maries, and where they knit they seldom break, but where they break, which for the most part is where they never truly joyn'd, to such at the same instant both flesh and rib cease to be in common; so that heer they argue nothing to the continuance of a false or violated Mariage, but must be led back to receive their meaning from those institutive words of God which give them all the life and vigor they have.

[*Therefore shall a man leav his father, &c.*] What to a mans thinking more plain by this appointment, that the fatherly power should give place to conjugall prerogative? yet it is generally held by reformed writers against the Papist, that though in persons at discretion the Mariage in it self be never so fit, though it be fully accomplisht with benediction, board and bed, yet the father not consenting, his main will without dispute shall dissolv all. And this they affirm only from collective reason, not from any direct law: for that in *Exod.* 22. 17. which is most particular, speaks that a father may refuse to marry his daughter to one who hath deflour'd her, not that he may take her away from one who hath soberly married her. Yet because the generall honor due to parents is great, they hold he may, and perhaps hold not amisse. But again when the question is of harsh and rugged parents who deferr [15] to bestow their childern seasonably, they agree joyntly that the Church or Magistrat may bestow them, though without the Fathers consent: and for this they have no express autority in Scripture. So that they may see by thir own handling of this very place, that it is not the stubborn letter must govern us, but the divine and softning breath of charity which turns and windes the dictat of every posi-

---

[45] The Socinians, according to their adversaries, taught that Adam was created entirely ignorant and acquired knowledge after eating of the tree of knowledge.

tive command, and shapes it to the good of mankind. Shall the outward accessory of a Fathers will wanting, rend the fittest and most affectionat mariage in twain, after all nuptial consummations, and shall not the want of love and the privation of all civil and religious concord, which is the inward essence of wedlock, doe as much to part those who were never truly wedded? shall a Father have this power to vindicate his own wilfull honour and autority to the utter breach of a most dearly-united mariage, and shall not a man in his own power have the permission to free his Soul, his life, and all his comfort of life from the disastre of a no-mariage. Shall fatherhood, which is but man, for his own pleasure dissolve matrimony, and shall not matrimony, which is Gods Ordinance, for its own honour and better conservation, dissolv it self, when it is wrong, and not fitted to any of the cheif ends which it owes us?

[*And they shall bee one flesh.*] These words also inferre that there ought to be an individualty in Mariage; but without all question presuppose the joyning causes. Not a rule yet that we have met with, so universall in this whole institution, but hath admitted limitations and conditions according to human necessity. The very foundation of Matrimony, though God laid it so deliberatly, *that it is not good for man to bee alone* holds not always, if the Apostle can secure us. Soon after wee are bid leav Father and Mother, and cleav to a Wife, but must understand the Fathers consent withall, els not. *Cleav to a Wife,* but let her bee a wife, let her be a meet help, a solace, not a nothing, not an adversary, not a desertrice; [46] can any law or command be so unreasonable as to make men cleav to calamity, to ruin, to perdition? In like manner heer, *They shall be one flesh*; but let the causes hold, and be made really good, which only have the possibility to make them one flesh. Wee know that flesh can neither joyn, nor keep together two bodies of it self; what is it then must make them one flesh, but likenes, but fitnes of mind and disposition, which may breed the Spirit of concord, and union between them? If that be not in the nature [16] of either, and that there has bin a remediles mistake, as vain wee goe about to compell them into one flesh, as if wee undertook to weav a garment of drie sand. It were more easy to compell the vegetable and nutritive power of nature to assimilations and mixtures which are not alter-

[46] Desertrice: female deserter. Milton's use here is the only citation in *NED*.

able each by other; or force the concoctive stomach to turn that into flesh which is so totaliy unlike that substance, as not to be wrought on. For as the unity of minde is neerer and greater then the union of bodies, so doubtles, is the dissimilitude greater, and more dividuall, as that which makes between bodies all difference and distinction. Especially when as besides the singular and substantial differences of every Soul, there is an intimat quality of good or evil, through the whol progeny of *Adam,* which like a radical heat, or mortal chilnes joyns them, or disjoyns them irresistibly. In whom therefore either the will, or the faculty is found to have never joyn'd, or now not to continue so, 'tis not to say, they shall be one flesh, for they cannot be one flesh. God commands not impossibilities; and all the Ecclesiastical glue, that Liturgy, or Laymen can compound, is not able to soder up two such incongruous natures into the one flesh of a true beseeming Mariage. Why did *Moses* then set down thir uniting into one flesh? And I again ask, why the Gospel so oft repeats the eating of our Saviours flesh, the drinking of his blood? *That wee are one body with him, the members of his body, flesh of his flesh and bone of his bone. Ephes.* 5.[47] Yet lest wee should be Capernaitans,[48] as wee are told there that the flesh profiteth nothing, so wee are told heer, if we be not deaf as adders, that this union of the flesh proceeds from the union of a fit help and solace. Wee know that there was never a more spiritual mystery then this Gospel taught us under the terms of body and flesh; yet nothing less intended then that wee should stick there. What a stupidnes then is it, that in Mariage, which is the neerest resemblance of our union with Christ, wee should deject our selvs to such a sluggish and underfoot Philosophy, as to esteem the validity of Mariage meerly by the flesh; though never so brokn and disjoynted from love and peace, which only can give a human qualification to that act of the flesh, and distinguish it from the bestial. The Text therefore uses this phrase, that *they shall bee one flesh,* to justify and make legitimat the rites of the Mariage bed; which was not un-

---

[47] V. 30. Authorized Version: "For we are members of his body, of his flesh, and of his bones." Fletcher, *Use of the Bible,* pp. 38 and 41, gives this text as an example of Milton's alterations to fit quotations into the context of his own argument.

[48] Capernaitans: inhabitants of Capernaum, who are denounced for their want of faith in Matthew 11:23 and Luke 10:15.

needfull, if for all this warrant, they were suspected of pollution by some sects of Philosophy, and Religions of old, and latelier among the [17] Papists, and other heretics elder then they.[49] Som think there is a high mystery in those words, from that which *Paul* saith of them, *Ephes.* 5. *This is a great mystery, but I speak of Christ and the Church:* [50] and thence they would conclude mariage to be inseparable. For me I dispute not now whether matrimony bee a mystery or no; if it bee of Christ and his Church, certainly it is not meant of every ungodly and miswedded mariage, but then only mysterious, when it is a holy, happy, and peacefull match. But when a Saint is joyn'd with a reprobate, or both alike, wicked with wicked, fool with fool, a hee drunkard with a she, when the bed hath bin nothing els for twenty yeares or more, but an old haunt of lust and malice mixt together, no love, no goodnes, no loyalty, but counter-plotting, and secret wishing one anothers dissolution, this is to me the greatest mystery in the world, if such a mariage as this, can be the mystery of ought, unless it bee the mystery of iniquity: [51] According to that which *Paraeus* cites out of *Chrysostom,* that a bad wife is a help for the devill,[52] and the like may be said of a bad husband. Since therfore none but a fit and pious matrimony can signify the union of Christ and his Church, ther cannot hence be any hindrance of divorce to that wedlock wherin ther can be no good mystery. Rather it might to a Christian Conscience bee matter of finding it self so much less satisfy'd then before, in the continuance of an unhappy yoke, wherein there can be no representation either of Christ, or of his Church.

Thus having enquir'd the institution how it was in the beginning, both from the I Chap. of *Gen.* where it was only mention'd in part, and from the second, where it was plainly and evidently instituted, and having attended each clause and word necessary, with a diligence not drousy, wee shall now fix with som advantage; and by a short view backward gather up the ground wee have gon; and summ up the strength wee have, into one argumentative head,

[49] In nearly all periods of the church, copulation, hence marriage, has been held sinful by some sects: Gnostics, Manichees, Cathari. The Pythagoreans were the chief ancient philosophical sect advocating chastity.

[50] V. 32. Authorized Version: "concerning Christ."

[51] II Thessalonians 2:7.

[52] *In Genesin* (Geneva, 1614), col. 420: "Of such Chrysostom, homily 5 on John: a hostile wife is an aid to the devil, not to her husband."

with that *organic* [53] force that *logic* proffers us. All arts acknowledge that then only we know certainly, when we can define; for definition is that which refines the pure essence of things from the circumstance. If therfore we can attain in this our Controversy to define exactly what mariage is, wee shall soon lern, when there is a nullity thereof, and when a divorce.

The part therfore of this Chapter which hath bin heer treated, doth orderly and readily resolv it self into a definition of mariage, and a [18] consectary from thence. To the definition these words cheifly contribute. *It is not good, &c. I will make, &c.* Where the consectary begins this connexion *Therfore* informs us, *Therfore shall a man,* &c. Definition is decreed by Logicians to consist only of causes constituting the essence of a thing. What is not therfore among the causes constituting mariage, must not stay in the definition. Those causes are concluded to be *matter,* and, as the Artist calls it, *Form.*[54] But inasmuch as the same thing may be a cause more waies then one, and that in relations and institutions which have no corporal subsistence, but only a respective beeing, the *Form* by which the thing is what it is, is oft so slender and undistinguishable, that it would soon confuse, were it not sustain'd by the efficient and final causes, which concurre to make up the form invalid otherwise of it self, it will bee needfull to take in all the fowr causes into the definition. First therfore the material cause of matrimony is man and woman; the Author and efficient, God and their consent, the internal *Form* and the soul of this relation, is conjugal love arising from a mutual fitnes to the final causes of wedlock, help and society in Religious, Civil and Domestic conversation, which includes as an inferior end the fulfilling of natural desire, and specifical increase; these are the final causes both moving the *efficient,* and perfeting the *form.* And although copulation be consider'd among the ends of mariage, yet the act therof in a right

[53] Aristotle's chief work on logic is the *Organon* (tool). *Cf. Of Education,* above, p. 401: "those organic arts," logic, rhetoric, and poetry.

[54] The four causes in Aristotelian logic are the material, the matter out of which a thing is made; the formal, the form or pattern according to which it is made; the efficient, the maker; and the final, or purpose for which it is made. Thus, the material cause of a house is wood, the formal is the architect's plans, the efficient is the contractor, the final is its use as a dwelling. The best commentary on Milton's logic, which follows Ramus rather than Aristotle, is Milton's own *Art of Logic.*

esteem can no longer be matrimonial, then it is an effect of conjugal love. When love findes it self utterly unmatcht, and justly vanishes, nay rather cannot but vanish, the fleshly act indeed may continue, but not holy, not pure, not beseeming the sacred bond of mariage; beeing at best but an animal excretion, but more truly wors and more ignoble then that mute kindlyness * among the heards and flocks: in that proceeding as it ought from intellective principles, it participates of nothing rational, but that which the feild and the fould equalls. For in human actions the soule is the agent, the body in a manner passive. If then the body doe out of sensitive force, what the soul complies not with, how can man, and not rather somthing beneath man be thought the doer.

But to proceed in the persute of an accurat definition, it will avail us somthing, and whet our thoughts, to examin what fabric heerof others have already reard. *Paraeus* on *Gen.* defines Mariage to be *an indissoluble conjunction of one man and one woman to an individual and inti-*[19]*mat conversation, and mutual benevolence,*[55] *&c.* Wherin is to be markt his placing of intimat conversation before bodily benevolence; for bodily is meant, though indeed *benevolence* rather sounds will then body.[56] Why then shall divorce be granted for want of bodily performance, and not for want of fitnes to intimat conversation, when as corporal benevolence cannot in any human fashion bee without this? Thus his definition places the ends of Mariage in one order, and esteems them in another. His *Tautology* also of indissoluble and individual[57] is not to be imitated; especially since neither indissoluble, nor individual hath ought to doe in the exact definition, beeing but a consectary flowing from thence, as appears by plain Scripture, *Therfore shall a man*

---

* Kindlyness: following natural instinct.

[55] Paraeus protests (*In Genesin,* Geneva, 1614, col. 416) that those who restrict the manner in which woman aids man to procreation do not sufficiently consider the nature of marriage. Milton omits the last part of the passage: "and divinely established for the procreation of legitimate children, so that an honest society of men may be propagated and served, and the Church may take form, to the end that God may be celebrated in eternity. The particular and only cause why woman is called עֵזֶר [help] to man is not that she aids in the procreation of offspring, but this aid is extended to the intimate habit of all life."

[56] "Benevolence" has the technical meaning of "yielding the rights of the body." Milton is here thinking partly of the etymology (from *bene volens,* "well willing"), partly that yielding is of its nature an act of the will.

[57] "Individual" means "indivisible" or "undivided," hence the tautology.

leav. &c. For Mariage is not true mariage by beeing individual, but therfore individual, if it be true Mariage. No argument but causes enter the definition; a Consectary is but the effect of those causes. Besides, that Mariage is indissoluble, is not *Catholickly* true; wee know it dissoluble for Adultery, and for desertion by the verdit of all Reformed Churches. Dr. *Ames* defines it *an individual conjunction of one man and one woman, to communion of body and mutual society of life;* [58] But this perverts the order of God, who in the institution places meet help and society of life before communion of body. And vulgar estimation undervalues beyond comparison all society of life and communion of minde beneath the communion of body; granting no divorce, but to the want, or miscommunicating of that. *Hemingius,* an approved Author, *Melanchtons* Scholler, and who next to *Bucer* and *Erasmus* writes of divorce most like a Divine, thus comprises, *Mariage is a conjunction of one man and one woman lawfully consenting, into one flesh, for mutual helps sake, ordain'd of God.* [59] And in his explanation stands punctually upon the conditions of consent, that it be not in any main matter deluded, as beeing the life of wedloc, and no true marriage without a true consent. *Into one flesh* he expounds into one minde, as well as one body, and makes it the formal cause: [60] Heerin only missing, while he puts the effect into his definition instead of the cause which the Text affords him. For *one flesh* is not the formal essence of wedloc, but one end, or one effect of *a meet help;* The end oft times beeing the effect and fruit of the form, as Logic teaches: Els many aged and holy matrimonies, and more eminently that of *Joseph* and *Mary,* would bee no true mariage. And that *maxim* generally receiv'd, would be fals, [20] that *consent alone, though*

[58] *The Marrow of Sacred Divinity* (1642; UTSL), II, 19; p. 321: "Marriage is an individuall conjunction of one man and one woman by lawfull consent, for a mutuall communion of their bodies, and society of life among themselves." Milton may have used the Latin original, *Medulla Theologiae* (1630; UTSL), p. 567. William Ames (1576–1633) was a Puritan theologian, whose *Medulla Theologiae* was the only considerable manual of systematic theology by an Englishman of the sixteenth or early seventeenth century.

[59] Nicolaus Hemmingus, "De Conjugio," *Opuscula Theologica* (Geneva, 1586; BML), col. 941. Nicolaus Hemming (Niels Hemmingsen) (1513–1600) was a Danish theologian.

[60] *Ibid.,* col. 993: "Since indeed one flesh is made in matrimony, marriage is the height of being united by the conjunction of souls (or minds) and bodies."

copulation never follow, makes the mariage.[61] Therefore to consent lawfully into one flesh, is not the formal cause of Matrimony, but only one of the effects. The Civil Lawyers, and first *Justinian* or *Tribonian* [62] defines Matrimony a *conjunction of man and woman containing individual accustom of life.*[63] Wherin first, individual is not so bad as indissoluble put in by others: [64] And although much cavil might be made in the distinguishing between indivisible, and individual, yet the one tak'n for possible, the other for actuall, neither the one nor the other can belong to the essence of mariage; especially when a Civilian defines, by which Law mariage is actually divorc't for many causes, and with good leav, by mutual consent. Therfore where *conjunction* is said, they who comment the *Institutes,*[65] agree that conjunction of minde is by the Law meant, not necessarily conjunction of body. That Law then had good reason attending to its own definition, that divorce should be granted for the breaking of that conjunction which it holds necessary, sooner then for the want of that conjunction which it holds not necessary. And wheras *Tuningus* a famous Lawyer excuses individual as the purpos of Mariage, not always the success, it suffices not.[66] Purpos is not able to constitute the essence of a thing. Nature her self the universal Mother intends nothing but her own perfection and preservation; yet is not the more indissoluble for that. The *Pandects* out of *Modestinus,* though not define, yet well describe Mariage, *the conjunction of male and female, the society of all life, the communion of divine and human right:* [67] which *Bucer*

[61] A maxim of *Juris Civilis,* quoted in many places, *e.g.,* Paraeus, *In Genesin* (Geneva, 1614), col. 436.

[62] Tribonianus (d. *ca.* 543–545) was the head of a commission appointed by Justinian to codify the law. The *Institutes* are presumably of his composition, or he at least oversaw the composition. See next note.

[63] *Juris Civilis, Institutes,* book I, title ix (Geneva, 1594–95, col. 28; Scott, II, 13). The definition of marriage cited here by Milton is translated by Scott: "Marriage, or matrimony, is the union of man and wife entailing the obligation to live together."

[64] Note that above, p. 609, Milton has called *individual* and *indissoluble* a "tautology."

[65] Commentators on the civil law, such as Tuningus, mentioned immediately below, and others referred to in the last section, below, pp. 714–15.

[66] Gerardus Tuningus, *In Quatuor Libros Institutionum Juris Civilis Divi Justiniani Commentarius,* title x, "De Nuptiis" (Leyden, 1618; BML), p. 66.

[67] *Juris Civilis, Pandects,* XXIII, title ii, paragraph 1 (Geneva, 1594–95, col. 709; Scott, V, 244). The *Pandects* are a compilation of the opinions of the most

also imitates on the fifth to the *Ephesians*.[68] But it seems rather to comprehend the several ends of Mariage, then to contain the more constituting cause that makes it what it is.

That I therefore among others (for who sings not *Hylas*) [69] may give as well as take matter to be judg'd on, it will be lookt I should produce another definition then these which have not stood the tryal. Thus then I suppose that Mariage by the natural and plain order of Gods institution in the Text may be more demonstratively and essentially defin'd. *Mariage is a divine institution joyning man and woman in a love fitly dispos'd to the helps and comforts of domestic life. A divine institution.* This contains the prime efficient cause of Mariage; as for consent of Parents and Guardians, it seems rather a concurrence then a cause; for as many, that marry are in thir own power as not; and where they are not thir own, yet are they not subjected beyond [21] reason. Now though efficient causes are not requisite in a definition, yet divine institution hath such influence upon the *Form,* and is so a conserving cause of it, that without it the *Form* is not sufficient to distinguish matrimony from other conjunctions of male and female, which are not to be counted mariage. *Joyning man and woman in a love, &c.* This brings in the parties consent; until which be, the mariage hath no true beeing. When I say *consent,* I mean not error, for error is not properly consent: And why should not consent be heer understood with equity and good to either part, as in all other freindly covnants, and not be strain'd and cruelly urg'd to the mischeif and destruction of both? Neither doe I mean that singular act of consent which made the contract, for that may remain, and yet the mariage not true nor lawful; and that may cease, and yet the mariage both true and lawful, to their sin that break it. So that either as no efficient at all, or but a transitory, it comes not into the definition.

eminent Roman legal authorities, one of whom is Herennius Modestinus (*fl.* 222–244). Apparently Milton regards Modestinus' statement as a description rather than a definition because it lacks one of the formal elements of a definition, the differentia. Scott's translation is: "Marriage is the union of a man and a woman, forming an association during their entire lives, and involving the common enjoyment of divine and human privileges."

68 Also in the part of the *De Regno Christi* which Milton translated. See above, p. 448.

69 Hylas was the son of Theodamus, king of the Dryopes, and companion of Hercules. He was drowned (or kidnaped by nymphs) at Cios. See especially Theocritus, *Idyll* XIII.

That consent I mean which is a love fitly dispos'd to mutual help and comfort of life; this is that happy *Form* of mariage naturally arising from the very heart of divine institution in the Text, in all the former definitions either obscurely, and under mistak'n terms exprest, or not at all. This gives mariage all her due, all her benefits, all her beeing, all her distinct and proper beeing. This makes mariage not a bondage, a blessing not a curse, a gift of God not a snare. Unless ther be a love, and that love born of fitnes, how can it last? unless it last how can the best and sweetest purposes of mariage be attain'd, and they not attain'd, which are the cheif ends, and with a lawful love constitute the formal cause it self of mariage, how can the essence thereof subsist, how can it bee indeed what it goes for? Conclude therfore by all the power of reason, that where this essence of mariage is not, there can bee no true mariage; and the parties either one of them, or both are free, and without fault rather by a nullity, then by a divorce may betake them to a second choys; if thir present condition be not tolerable to them. If any shall ask, why *domestic* in the definition? I answer, that because both in the Scriptures, and in the gravest Poets and Philosophers I finde the properties and excellencies of a wife set out only from domestic vertues; if they extend furder, it diffuses them into the notion of som more common duty then matrimonial.

Thus farre of the definition; the *Consectary* which flows from [22] thence, and altogether depends theron, is manifestly brought in by this connexive particle *Therfore;* and branches it self into a double consequence; First individual Society, *therfore shall a man leav father and mother:* Secondly conjugal benevolence, *and they shall bee one flesh.* Which as was shewn, is not without cause heer mention'd, to prevent and to abolish the suspect of pollution in that natural and undefiled act. These consequences therfore cannot either in Religion, Law, or Reason bee bound, and posted upon mankind to his sorrow and misery, but receiv what force they have from the meetnes of help and solace, which is the *formal* cause and end of that definition that sustains them. And although it be not for the Majesty of Scripture to humble her self in artificial *theorems,* and definitions, and *Corollaries,* like a professor in the Schools, but looks to be *analys'd,* and interpreted by the logical industry of her Disciples and followers, and to bee reduc't by them, as oft as need is, into those *Sciential* rules, which are the implements of instruction, yet *Moses,* as if foreseeing the miserable work that mans ignorance and pusillanimity would make in this matrimonious busines, and endevouring his utmost to prevent it, condescends in this place to such a methodical and School-like way of defining, and consequencing, as in no place of the whole Law more.

Thus wee have seen, and if wee be not contentious, may know what was Mariage in the beginning, to which in the Gospel wee are referr'd; and what from hence to judge of nullity, or divorce. Heer I esteem the work don; in this field the controversie decided; but because other places of Scripture seem to look aversly upon this our decision, although indeed they keep all harmony with it, and because it is a better work to reconcile the seeming diversities of Scripture, then the reall dissentions of neerest friends, I shall assay in three following Discourses to perform that Office.

Deut. 24. 1, 2.

1 *When a man hath taken a Wife, and married her, and it come to pass that she find no favour in his eyes, because he hath found som uncleannes in her, then let him write her a bill of divorcement, and give it in her hand, and send her out of his house.* [23]

2 *And when she is departed out of his house, she may goe and be another mans wife.*

THAT which is the only discommodity of speaking in a cleer matter, the abundance of argument that presses to bee utter'd, and the suspense of judgement what to choose, and how in the multitude of reason, to be not tedious, is the greatest difficulty which I expect heer to meet with. Yet much hath bin said formerly concerning this Law in *the Doctrine of divorce:* [1] Wherof I shall repeat no more then what is necessary. Two things are heer doubted: First, and that but of late, whether this bee a Law or no, next what this reason of *uncleannes* might mean for which the Law is granted; That it is a plain Law no man ever question'd, till *Vatablus* [2] within

---

[1] See *Doctrine and Discipline,* above, pp. 306–34.

[2] This is not in Vatablus' notes to Deuteronomy. Franciscus Vatablus (François Vatable or Vatablé), d. 1547, was a French scholar of Hebrew, best known for his notes to the Old Testament, published by Robert Étienne (Stephanus) in his *Biblia* (Paris, 1545; UTSL).

these hunder'd years profess'd *Hebrew* at *Paris*, a man of no Religion, as *Beza* deciphers him.[3] Yet som there be who follow him, not only against the current of all antiquity, both Jewish and Christian, but the evidence of Scripture also, Malach. 2.16. *Let him who hateth put away saith the Lord God of Israel.* Although this place also hath bin tamper'd with, as if it were to be thus render'd, *The Lord God saith, that hee hateth putting away.*[4] But this new interpretation rests only in the autority of *Junius;*[5] for neither *Calvin,*[6] nor *Vatablus*[7] himself, nor any other known Divine so interpreted before.[8] And they of best note who have translated the Scripture since, and *Diodati*[9] for one, follow not his reading. And

---

[3] Beza, *Icones* ([Geneva], 1580), sig. V1: "But you, Vatablus, whose teaching of Hebrew, which indeed astounded the Jews themselves, many Christians heard with great fruit, now how shall we regard you, who interpreting sacred letters imparted to others that which you so far neglected as finally to abandon? Let, therefore, your great erudition and diligence prepare a place for you also in the court of this sacristy to which you have introduced others, but yourself have never been seen to enter." On Beza's biography see *Martin Bucer,* above, p. 424. See also *Doctrine and Discipline,* above, p. 257, n. 16.

[4] Authorized Version: "For the Lord, the God of Israel, saith that he hateth putting away." The text is corrupt, as Milton notes, and the Authorized Version gives as an alternative reading, "if he hate her, put her away." See Fletcher, *Use of the Bible,* pp. 34–36.

[5] Junius' rendering is "Sibi odio esse dimissionem ait Jehova Deus Jisraelis" (Jehovah God of Israel saith that putting away is hateful to him). *Testamenti Veteris Biblia Sacra . . . Immanuele Tremellio, & Francisco Junio* (Geneva, 1630; UTSL), f. 292. Franciscus Junius (Du Jon) the Elder, 1545–1602, was a Dutch or Flemish theologian, most noted for a translation of the Old Testament into Latin. Matthew Poole, *Synopsis Criticorum* (5 vols., Utrecht, 1684–86; UTSL), III, cols. 2163–64, says that Piscator also preferred this reading. Poole's *Synopsis Criticorum* is a compendium of the biblical scholarship in text and exegesis of the sixteenth and seventeenth centuries.

[6] Calvin's reading is, "Si odio habeas (quisquis odio habet) dimittat (uxorem), dicit Jehova Deus Israel" (If you have her in hate—whoever has her in hate—let him dismiss—his wife—says Jehovah the God of Israel). *Praelectiones in Duodecim Prophetas* (Geneva, 1559; UTSL), p. 772.

[7] Vatablus preserves the Vulgate reading: "Si odio habueris, dimitte" (If you have her in hate, put away).

[8] Milton ignores the Authorized Version's "For the Lord, the God of Israel, saith that he hateth putting away," which, however, is not *before* Junius.

[9] Diodati's translation is, "Che se pur l'odia, rimandila" (That if he hate, let him put her away). See also his commentary: "If the husbands love be alienated from his wife, it were more tolerable for him to make use of the permission of divorce, *Deut. 24.* 1, then to keep and afflict her by means of these strange women." *Pious Annotations upon the Holy Bible* (3rd ed., 1651;), sig. Llll3. John (Giovanni or Jean) Diodati was an Italian refugee Protestant who taught

perhaps they might reject it, if for nothing els, for these two reasons: First, it introduces in a new manner the person of God speaking less Majestic then he is ever wont; When God speaks by his Profet, he ever speaks in the first person; thereby signifying his Majesty and omni-presence. Hee would have said, I hate putting away, saith the Lord; and not sent word by *Malachi* in a sudden faln stile, The *Lord God saith that hee hateth putting away:* that were a phrase to shrink the glorious omnipresence of God speaking, into a kind of circumscriptive absence. And were as if a Herald in the *Atcheivment* [10] of a King, should commit the *indecorum* to set his helmet sidewaies and close, not full fac't and open in the posture of direction and command. Wee cannot think therfore that this last Profet would thus in a new fashion absent the person of God from his own words as if he came not along with them. For it would also be wide from the proper scope of this place: hee that reads attentively will soon [24] perceav, that God blames not heer the Jews for putting away thir wives, but for keeping strange Concubines, to the *profaning of Juda's holines,* and the vexation of thir Hebrew wives, v. 11. and 14. *Judah hath maried the daughter of a strange God:* [11] And exhorts them rather to put thir wives away whom they hate, as the Law permitted, then to keep them under such affronts. And it is receiv'd that this Profet livd in those times of *Ezra* and *Nehemiah* (nay by som is thought to bee *Ezra* himself) [12] when the people were forc't by these two Worthies to put thir strange wives away. So that what the story of those times, and the plain context of the 11 verse, from whence this rebuke begins, can give us to

at Geneva. He translated the Bible into Italian. He was the uncle of Charles Diodati, Milton's close friend, and Milton says that he visited John in Geneva, *Second Defence* (1654), p. 64. See also Donald C. Dorian, *The English Diodatis* (New Brunswick: Rutgers University Press, 1950), pp. 98–101.

[10] *Atcheivment:* the heraldic term for the escutcheon or ensign armorial, granted usually in memory of some achievement.

[11] V. 11: "Judah hath profaned the holiness of the Lord which he loved, and hath married the daughter of a strange god."

[12] Poole, *Synopsis Criticorum* (Utrecht, 1684–86), III, col. 1245, lists three opinions about the authorship of Malachi: 1. That it was written not by a man, but by an angel (Hebrew *malachi* means "my messenger"); 2. that Ezra was the real author; and 3. that the real author lived in the time of the building of the second temple, hence of Ezra and Nehemiah. The sources he cites for the second opinion are, besides unidentified Jewish ones, Pagnini, Jerome, and Ribera. The majority of commentators, including Vatablus, Drusius, and Grotius, favor the third interpretation.

conjecture of the obscure and curt *Ebraisms* that follow, this Profet does not forbid putting away, but forbids keeping, and commands putting away according to Gods Law, which is the plainest interpreter both of what God will, and what he can best suffer. Thus much evinces that God there commanded divorce by *Malachi,* and this confirmes that he commands it also heer by *Moses*.

I may the less doubt to mention by the way an Author, though counted Apocryphal, yet of no small account for piety and wisdom, the Author of *Ecclesiasticus*. Which book begun by the Grand-father of that *Jesus* who is call'd the Son of *Sirach,* might have bin writt'n in part, not much after the time when *Malachi* livd; if wee compute by the Reigne of *Ptolemaeus Euergetes*.[13] It professes to explain the Law and the Profets; and yet exhorts us to divorce for incurable causes, and to cut off from the flesh those whom it there describes, *Ecclesiastic*. 25.26.[14] Which doubtles that wise and ancient Writer would never have advis'd, had either *Malachi* so lately forbidd'n it, or the Law by a full precept not left it lawful. But I urge not this for want of better prooff; our Saviour himself allows divorce to be a command, *Mark* 10.3.5. Neither doe they weak'n this assertion, who say it was only a sufferance, as shall be prov'd at large in that place of *Matthew*. But suppose it were not a writt'n Law, they never can deny it was a custom, and so effect nothing. For the same reasons

[13] I have found no source for this dating. Hugo Grotius, one of the few Protestants to comment on Ecclesiasticus, dated the book "not much before the time of Antiochus," meaning probably Antiochus III (223–187 B.C.). *Annotata ad Vetus Testamentum* (3 vols., Paris, 1644; UTSL), III, 81. Milton, however, may have worked out his own chronology on the basis of the two prefaces to Ecclesiasticus and the general opinion on the date of Ezra. Poole, *Synopsis Criticorum* (Utrecht, 1684–86), I, cols. 885–87, dates Ezra as late sixth century, but gives him a very long life, 132 years, to satisfy the allusions in the book of Ezra. The preface to Ecclesiasticus by the unknown author says that the book was started by one Jesus, grandfather to the Jesus of Sirach to whom it is assigned, "in the latter times, after the people had been led away captive." The preface by Jesus of Sirach tells us that he translated the Hebrew original of his grandfather into Greek in the reign of Ptolemy Euergetes (246–21 B.C.). Whether the dating is Milton's or another's, it strikes us as loose, even for Milton's time. The dating of Ezra current in Milton's time would have him die hardly later than 450 B.C. leaving a gap of two hundred years between Ezra and the Greek translation of Ecclesiasticus. Even allowing that the Hebrew original was written by Jesus of Sirach's grandfather a hundred years before the Greek translation, one still has a century to explain away.

[14] "If she go not as thou wouldest have her, cut her off from thy flesh, and give her a bill of divorce, and let her go."

that induce them why it should not bee a law, will strait'n them as hard why it should bee allow'd a custom. All custom is either evil or not evil; if it be evil, this is the very end of Law-giving, to abolish evil customs by wholsom Laws; unless wee imagin *Moses* weaker then every negligent and startling [15] Politician. If [25] it be, as they make this of divorce to be, a custom against nature, against justice, against chastity, how, upon this most impure custom tolerated, could the God of purenes erect a nice and precise Law, that the wife marryed after divorce could not return to her former husband, as beeing defil'd? What was all this following nicenes worth, built upon the leud foundation of a wicked thing allow'd? In few words then, this custom of divorce either was allowable, or not allowable; if not allowable, how could it be allow'd? if it were allowable, all who understand Law will consent, that a tolerated custom hath the force of a Law, and is indeed no other, but an unwritt'n Law, as *Justinian* calls it, and is as prevalent as any writt'n statute.[16] So that thir shift of turning this Law into a custom wheels about, and gives the onset upon thir own flanks; not disproving, but concluding it to be the more firm law, because it was without controversy a granted custom; as cleer in the reason of common life, as those giv'n rules wheron *Euclides* builds his propositions.

Thus beeing every way a Law of God, who can without blasphemy doubt it to be a just and pure Law. *Moses* continually disavows the giving them any statute, or judgement, but what hee learnt of God; of whom also in his Song hee saith, Deut. 32. *Hee is the rock, his work is perfet, all* [17] *his waies are judgement, a God of truth and without iniquity, just and right is hee.* And *David* testifies, the judgements of the Lord *are true and righteous altogether.*[18] Not partly right and partly wrong, much less wrong altogether, as Divines of now adaies dare censure them. *Moses* again of that people to whom hee gave this Law saith, Deut. 14. *Yee are the childern of*

---

[15] Startling: The *OED*, citing this passage, defines the word as "fickle, irresolute." However, "upstart" seems the better gloss.

[16] *Juris Civilis, Pandects*, book I, title 3, especially paragraphs 33, 35 (Geneva, 1594–95, col. 138; Scott, II, 226), which are the opinions of Ulpian and Hermogenian. Ulpian: "It is usual for long established custom to be observed as law in those matters which have not come down in writing." Hermogenian: "Those rules which have been approved by long established custom and have been observed for many years, by, as it were, a tacit agreement of citizens, are no less to be obeyed than laws which have been committed to writing."

[17] Authorized Version: "perfect: for all his ways." [18] Psalms 19:9.

the Lord your God,[19] *the Lord hath chosen thee to bee a peculiar people to himself above all the nations*[20] *upon the earth, that thou shouldst keep all his Commandements; and be high in praise, in name, and in honour, holy to the Lord.* Chap. 26.[21] And in the fourth, *Behold I have taught you statutes and judgements eevn as the Lord my God commanded mee,*[22] *keep therfore and doe them. For this is your wisdom and your understanding in the sight of Nations*[23] *that shall*[24] *hear all these Statutes and say, surely this great Nation is a wise and understanding people. For what Nation is ther so great, who hath God so nigh to*[25] *them?*[26] *and what Nation*[27] *that hath Statutes and Judgements so righteous as all this Law which I set before you this day?* Thus whether wee look at the purity and justice of God himself, the jealousy of his honour among other Nations, the holines and moral perfection which [26] hee intended by his Law to teach this people, wee cannot possibly think how he could indure to let them slugg & grow inveteratly wicked, under base allowances, & whole adulterous lives by dispensation. They might not eat, they might not touch an unclean thing; to what hypocrisy then were they train'd up, if by prescription of the same Law, they might be unjust, they might be adulterous for term of life? forbid to soile thir garments with a coy imaginary pollution,[28] but not forbid, but countnanc't and animated by Law to soile thir soules with deepest defilements. What more unlike to God, what more like that God should hate, then that his Law should bee so curious to wash vessels, and vestures, and so careles to leav unwasht, unregarded, so foul a scab of *Egypt* in thir Soules? what would wee

[19] Vv. 1–2. Milton omits "ye shall not cut yourselves, nor make any baldness between your eyes for the dead. For thou art an holy people unto the Lord thy God."

[20] Milton omits "that are."   [21] Deuteronomy 26:18–19.

[22] Milton omits "that ye should do so in the land whither ye go to possess it."

[23] Authorized Version: "sight of the nations."

[24] Authorized Version: "which shall."   [25] Authorized Version: "unto."

[26] Milton omits "as the Lord our God is in all things that we call upon him for."

[27] Milton omits "is there so great."

[28] *Coy* means "secluded, hidden." Milton probably has in mind some such passage as Deuteronomy 23:10–11: "If there be among you any man, that is not clean by reason of uncleanness that chanceth him by night, then shall he go abroad out of the camp, he shall not come within the camp: but it shall be, when evening cometh on, he shall wash himself with water: and when the sun is down, he shall come into the camp again."

more? the Statutes of the Lord are all pure and just: and if all, then this of Divorce.

[*Because he hath found som uncleannes in her.*] That wee may not esteem this law to bee a meer authorizing of licence, as the Pharises took it, *Moses* adds the reason, for *som uncleannes found.* Som heertofore have bin so ignorant, as to have thought, that this *uncleannes* means adultery. But *Erasmus,* who for having writ an excellent Treatise of Divorce, was wrote against by som burly standard Divine, perhaps of *Cullen,* or of *Lovain,*[29] who calls himself *Phimostomus,* shews learnedly out of the Fathers with other Testimonies and Reasons, that *uncleannes* is not heer so understood; defends his former work, though new to that age, and perhaps counted licentious, and fears not to ingage all his fame on the Argument.[30] Afterward, when Expositers began to understand the Hebrew Text, which they had not done of many ages before, they translated word for word not *uncleannes,* but *the nakednes of any thing;* and considering that nakednes is usually referr'd in Scripture to the minde as well as to the body, they constantly expound it any defect, annoyance, or ill quality in nature, which to bee joyn'd with, makes life tedious, and such company wors then solitude. So that heer will be no cause to vary from the generall consent of exposition, which gives us freely that God permitted divorce, for whatever was unalterably distastful, whether in body or mind. But with this admonishment, that if the *Roman* law especially in contracts and dowries left many things to equity with these cautions, *ex fide bonâ, quod aequius melius erit, ut inter bonos bene agier,*[31]

[29] *Cullen:* Cologne, where there was a famous Catholic school of Divinity, as there was also at Louvain. Milton's guess that "Phimostomus," whom I cannot identify, was from Cologne or Louvain is probably pure surmise. See also below, p. 709.

[30] *Responsio ad Disputationem cujusdam Phimostomi de Divortio,* in *Omnia Opera* (10 vols., Basle, 1540), IX, 775–83. Erasmus renders the word for *uncleanness* as *rem indecoram* (unsuitable thing). It should be noted, however, that he is arguing from the Greek text of Matthew 5:19, not from the Hebrew of Deuteronomy. The fathers whom he cites are Ambrose, Origen, and Tertullian, whom Milton also uses. See below, pp. 697–99. Several commentators understood the word in the sense Milton accepts. Poole, *Synopsis Criticorum* (Utrecht, 1684–86), I, col. 843, gives Drusius and Ainsworth for the interpretation *nuditatem rei* (nakedness of a thing), and Arias Montanus and Malvenda for the interpretation *nuditatem verbi* (nakedness of the word).

[31] In good faith; that the more just will be the better; as it is well to be done between good men. These are oft-repeated qualifications in the *Pandects.*

wee will not grudge to think that God intended not licence heer to every humor, but to such remediles greevan-[27]ces as might move a good, and honest, and faithfull man then to divorce, when it can no more bee peace or comfort to either of them continuing thus joyn'd. And although it could not be avoided, but that men of hard hearts would abuse this liberty, yet doubtles it was intended as all other privileges in Law are, to good men principally, to bad only by accident. So that the sin was not in the permission, nor simply in the action of divorce (for then the permitting also had bin sin) but only in the abuse. But that this Law should, as it were, bee wrung from God and *Moses,* only to serve the hard heartednes, and the lust of injurious men, how remote it is from all sense, and law, and honesty, and therfore surely from the meaning of Christ, shall abundantly be manifest in due order.

Now although *Moses* needed not to adde other reason of this law then that one there exprest, yet to these ages wherin Canons, and *Scotisms,*[32] and *Lumbard*[33] Laws, have dull'd, and almost obliterated the lively Sculpture of ancient reason, and humanity, it will be requisit to heap reason upon reason, and all little enough to vindicat the whitenes and the innocence of this divine Law, from the calumny it findes at this day, of beeing a dore to licence and confusion. When as indeed there is not a judicial point in all *Moses,* consisting of more true equity, high wisdom, and God-like pitty then this Law; not derogating, but preserving the honour and peace of Mariage, and exactly agreeing with the sense and mind of that institution in *Genesis.*

For first, if Mariage be but an ordain'd relation, as it seems not more, it cannot take place above the prime dictats of nature; and if it bee of natural right, yet it must yeeld to that which is more natural, and before it by eldership and precedence in nature. Now it is not natural that *Hugh* marries *Beatrice,* or *Thomas Rebecca,* beeing only a civill contract, and full of many chances, but that these men seek them meet helps, that only is natural; and that they espouse them such, that only is mariage. But if they find them neither fit helps, nor tolerable society, what thing more natural, more original and first in nature then to depart from that which is

[32] The teachings of the medieval philosopher, Duns Scotus (*ca.* 1265–1308).
[33] A reference to the *Sententiae* of Peter Lombard (*ca.* 1100–1160), the standard medieval manual of dogmatic and moral theology.

irksom, greevous, actively hateful, and injurious eevn to hostility,
especially in a conjugal respect, wherin antipathies are invincible,
and wher the forc't abiding of the one, can bee no true good, no real
comfort to the other. For if hee find no contentment from the other,
how can he re-[28]turn it from himself, or no acceptance, how
can hee mutually accept? what more equal, more pious then to untie
a civil knot for a natural enmity held by violence from parting, to
dissolv an accidental conjunction of this or that man & woman, for
the most natural and most necessary disagreement of meet from
unmeet, guilty from guiltles, contrary from contrary? It beeing
certain that the mystical and blessed unity of mariage can bee no
way more unhallow'd and profan'd, then by the forcible uniting of
such disunions and separations. Which if wee see oft times they
cannot joyn or peece up to a common friendship, or to a willing conversation in the same house, how should they possibly agree to the
most familiar and united amity of wedlock? *Abraham* and *Lot,*
though dear friends and brethren in a strange Country, chose
rather to part asunder, then to infect thir friendship with the strife
of thir servants: [34] *Paul* and *Barnabas* joyn'd together by the Holy
Ghost to a Spiritual work, thought it better to separate when once
they grew at variance.[35] If these great Saints joynd by nature,
friendship, religion, high providence, and revelation, could not so
govern a casual difference, a sudden passion, but must in wisdom
divide from the outward duties of a friendship, or a Collegueship in
the same family, or in the same journey, lest it should grow to a
wors division, can any thing bee more absurd and barbarous then
that they whom only error, casualty, art or plot hath joynd, should
be compell'd, not against a sudden passion but against the permanent and radical discords of nature, to the most intimat and incorporating duties of love and imbracement, therin only rational and
human, as they are free and voluntary; beeing els an abject and
servile yoke, scars not brutish. And that there is in man such a peculiar sway of liking, or disliking in the affairs of matrimony is evidently seen before mariage among those who can bee freindly, can
respect each other, yet to marry each other would not for any perswasion. If then this unfitnes and disparity bee not till after
mariage discover'd, through many causes, and colours, and con-

[34] Genesis 13:6–12.   [35] Acts 15:37–40.

cealements, that may overshadow; undoubtedly it will produce the same effects and perhaps with more vehemence, that such a mistakn pair, would give the world to be unmarried again. And thir condition *Solomon* to the plain justification of divorce expresses, *Prov.* 30.21.23. Where hee tells us of his own accord, that a *hated*, or a *hatefull* woman, *when shee is married, is a thing for which the earth is disquieted and cannot* [29] *bear it*; [36] thus giving divine testimony to this divine Law, which bids us nothing more then is the first and most innocent lesson of nature, to turn away peaceably from that which afflicts and hazards our destruction; especially when our staying can doe no good, and is expos'd to all evil.

Secondly, It is unjust that any Ordinance ordain'd to the good and comfort of man, where that end is missing, without his fault, should be forc't upon him to an unsufferable misery and discomfort, if not commonly ruin. All Ordinances are establisht in thir end; the end of Law is the vertu, is the righteousnes of Law. And therfore him wee count an ill Expounder who urges Law against the intention therof. The general end of every Ordinance, of every severest, every divinest, eevn of Sabbath is the good of man, yea his temporal good not excluded. But marriage is one of the benignest ordinances of God to man, wherof both the general and particular end is the peace and contentment of mans mind, as the institution declares. Contentment of body they grant, which if it bee defrauded, the plea of frigidity shall divorce: But heer lies the fadomles absurdity, that granting this for bodily defect, they will not grant it for any defect of the mind, any violation of religious or civil society. When as, if the argument of Christ bee firm against the ruler of the Synagogue, Luk. 13. *Thou hypocrite, doth not each of you on the Sabbath day loos'n his Oxe or his Asse from the stall, and lead him to watering, and should not I unbind a daughter of Abraham from this bond of Satan?* [37] it stands as good heer, yee have regard in mariage to the

---

[36] Authorized Version: "For three things the earth is disquieted, and for four which it cannot bear. . . . For an odious woman when she is married." "Hated or hateful" probably represents Milton's independent translation from the Hebrew. See Fletcher, *Use of the Bible*, p. 33.

[37] V. 15–16. Milton condenses the Authorized Version: "The Lord then answered him, and said, Thou hypocrite, doth not each of you on the sabbath loose his ox or his ass from the stall, and lead him away to watering? And ought not this woman, being a daughter of Abraham, whom Satan hath bound, lo, these eighteen years, be loosed from this bond on the sabbath day?"

greevance of body, should you not regard more the greevances of the mind, seeing the Soul as much excells the body, as the outward man excells the Ass and more; for that *animal* is yet a living creature, perfet in it self; but the body without the Soul is a meer senseles trunck. No Ordinance therfore givn particularly to the good both spiritual and temporal of man, can bee urg'd upon him to his mischeif, and if they yeeld this to the unworthier part, the body, wherabout are they in thir principles, that they yeeld it not to the more worthy, the mind of a good man?

Thirdly, As no Ordinance, so no Covnant, no not between God and man, much less between man and man, beeing as all are, intended to the good of both parties, can hold to the deluding or making miserable of them both. For equity is understood in every Covnant, [30] eevn between enemies, though the terms bee not exprest. If equity therfore made it, extremity may dissolv it. But Mariage, they use to say, is the Covnant of God. Undoubted: and so is any covnant frequently call'd in Scripture, wherin God is call'd to witnes: the covnant of freindship between *David* and *Jonathan*, is call'd *the Covnant of the Lord*, I Sam. 20. The covnant of *Zedechiah* with the King of *Babel*,[38] a Covnant to bee doubted whether lawfull or no, yet in respect of God invok't thereto, is call'd *the Oath, and the Covnant of God*, Ezech. 17. Mariage also is call'd the *Covnant of God*, Prov. 2.17. Why, but as before, because God is the witnes therof, Malach. 2.14. So that this denomination adds nothing to the Covnant of Mariage, above any other civil and solemn contract: nor is it more indissoluble for this reason then any other against the end of its own ordination, nor is any vow or Oath to God exacted with such a rigor, where superstition reignes not. For look how much divine the Covnant is, so much the more equal; So much the more to bee expected that every article therof should bee fairly made good, no fals dealing, or unperforming should be thrust upon men without redress, if the covnant bee so divine. But faith they say must bee kept in Covnant, though to our dammage. I answer, that only holds true, where the other side performs, which failing, hee is no longer bound. Again, this is true, when the keeping of faith can bee of any use, or benefit to the other. But in Mariage a league of love and willingnes, if faith bee not willingly

38 See Ezekiel 17:19.

kept, it scars is worth the keeping; nor can bee any delight to a generous minde, with whom it is forcibly kept: and the question still supposes the one brought to an impossibility of keeping it as hee ought, by the others default, and to keep it formally, not only with a thousand shifts and dissimulations, but with open anguish, perpetual sadnes and disturbance, no willingnes, no cheerfulnes, no contentment, cannot bee any good to a minde not basely poor and shallow, with whom the contract of love is so kept. A Covnant therfore brought to that passe, is on the unfaulty side without injury dissolv'd.

Fourthly, The Law is not to neglect men under greatest sufferances, but to see Covnants of greatest moment faithfullest perform'd. And what injury comparable to that sustain'd in a frustrat and fals dealing Mariage, to loose, for anothers fault against him, the best portion of his temporal comforts, and of his spiritual too, as it may fall out. [31] It was the Law, that for mans good and quiet, reduc't things to propriety, which were at first in common; how much more Law-like were it to assist nature in disappropriating that evil which by continuing proper becomes destructive. But hee might have bewar'd. So hee might in any other covnant, wherin the Law does not constrain error to so dear a forfeit. And yet in these matters wherin the wisest are apt to erre, all the warines that can bee, oft times nothing avails. But the Law can compell the offending party to bee more duteous. Yes, if all these kind of offences were fit in public to bee complain'd on, or beeing compell'd were any satisfaction to a mate not sottish, or malicious. And these injuries work so vehemently, that if the Law remedy them not, by separating the cause when no way els will pacify, the person not releev'd betakes him either to such disorderly courses, or to such a dull dejection, as renders him either infamous, or useles to the service of God and his Country. Which the Law ought to prevent as a thing pernicious to the Common wealth; and what better prevention then this which *Moses* us'd?

Fifthly, The Law is to tender the liberty and human dignity of them that live under the Law, whether it bee the mans right above the woman, or the womans just appeal against wrong, and servitude. But the duties of mariage contain in them a duty of benevolence, which to doe by compulsion against the Soul, where ther can bee neither peace, nor joy, nor love, but an enthrallment to one who

either cannot, or will not bee mutual in the godliest and the civilest
ends of that society, is the ignoblest, and the lowest slavery that a
human shape can bee put to. This Law therfore justly and piously
provides against such an unmanly task of bondage as this. The civil
Law, though it favour'd the setting free of a slave, yet if hee prov'd
ungratefull to his Patron, reduc't him to a servil condition.[39] If that
Law did well to reduce from liberty to bondage for an ingratitude
not the greatest, much more became it the Law of God to enact the
restorement of a free born man from an unpurpos'd, and unworthy
bondage to a rightfull liberty for the most unnatural fraud and ingratitude that can be committed against him. And if that Civilian
Emperour in his title of *Donations,* permit the giver to recall his
guift from him who proves unthankful towards him, yea, though hee
had subscrib'd and sign'd in the deed of his guift, not to recall it
though for this very cause of ingratitude,[40] with much more equity
doth *Moses* [32] permit heer the giver to recall no petty guift, but
the guift of himself from one who most injuriously & deceitfully
uses him against the main ends and conditions of his giving himself, exprest in Gods institution.

Sixthly, Although ther bee nothing in the plain words of this Law,
that seems to regard the afflictions of a wife, how great so ever, yet
Expositers determin, and doubtles determin rightly, that God was
not uncompassionat of them also in the framing of this Law. For
should the rescript of *Antoninus* in the Civil Law give release to serv-

---

[39] *Juris Civilis, Code,* book VII, title vii, paragraph 2 (Geneva, 1594–95, col.
478; Scott, XIII, 305): "If a slave, who has been manumitted, has manifested
ingratitude towards his patron, and has behaved towards him with insolence or
obstinacy, or has been guilty of some slight offence against him, he shall again
be placed under the control and authority of his master, if the latter can prove
that he was ungrateful in a complaint brought before an ordinary judge, or
judges specially appointed."

[40] Probably *Juris Civilis, Code,* book VIII, title lvi, paragraphs 1, 10 (Geneva,
1594–95, cols. 750, 752; Scott, XIV, 347–50). "We decree, in general, that all
donations made in conformity with law shall be valid and irrecoverable, and if
he who receives the donation is not found to be guilty of ingratitude towards the
donor, as, for instance, where he has inflicted atrocious injury on him, or has
been guilty of personal violence towards him, or of having, by treachery, caused
him to suffer great pecuniary losses which sensibly diminished his estate, or has
exposed him to losing his life, or is unwilling to comply with any agreements
inserted in the document evidencing the donation, or even if these were not
committed to writing, and he, as the recipient of the donation, promised to observe them, but failed to do so."

ants flying to refuge to the Emperours statue, by giving leav to change thir cruel Maisters,[41] and should God who in his Law also is good to injur'd servants, by granting them thir freedom in divers cases, not consider the wrongs and miseries of a wife which is no servant.[42] Though heerin the counter sense of our Divines, to me, I must confesse seems admirable; who teach that God gave this as a mercifull Law, not for man whom he heer names, and to whom by name hee gives this power, but for the wife whom hee names not, and to whom by name hee gives no power at all.[43] For certainly if man be liable to injuries in mariage, as well as woman, and man be the worthier person, it were a preposterous law to respect only the less worthy; her whom God made for mariage, and not him at all for whom mariage was made.

Seventhly, The Law of mariage gives place to the power of Parents: for wee hold that consent of Parents not had may break the wedlock, though els accomplisht. It gives place to maisterly power,

[41] *Juris Civilis, Institutes,* book I, title viii, paragraph 2 (Geneva, 1594–95, col. 28; Scott, II, 13): "For by a Constitution of the Divine Pius Antoninus he who kills his slave without a reason shall not be punished with less severity than he who kills the slave of another; and by the Constitution of the same sovereign the excessive severity of masters is still further repressed; for having been consulted by certain governors of provinces with reference to slaves who flee for refuge to a sacred edifice or to the statues of the Emperors, he decreed that if the barbarity of the masters appeared to be intolerable, they could be forced to sell their slaves under favorable conditions and have the price paid to them."

[42] Most of the commentaries I have seen specifically say that divorce was forbidden to women, except at the permission of the husband. Josephus is commonly cited to the effect that Salome was the first woman to attempt divorcing her husband. Poole, *Synopsis Criticorum* (Utrecht, 1684–86), I, 843, says that the question whether a woman could divorce a man was disputed, and lists Jacques Bonfrère and Cornelius à Lapide as contending that she could. À Lapide's comment is, "But if this [statement of Josephus] is true, it was introduced by custom, by which husbands usurped this right. Wives could thus for adultery or for other just causes make a divorce of bed. This indeed the law of nature permits to Christians and to all nations." *Commentaria in Pentateuchum Mosis* (Antwerp, 1630; UTSL), p. 1000. It is noteworthy that both à Lapide and Bonfrerius were Catholics, and Milton does not commonly accept the interpretations of Catholics. Also à Lapide is speaking of "divorce from bed and board," which the Catholics allowed (see below, p. 706), not of final divorce with permission to remarry. I have not been able to find in the better-known commentaries on Deuteronomy or in the sources Milton commonly consulted any authority for this passage.

[43] See below, p. 652, and *Doctrine and Discipline,* above, pp. 324–25 for the view, which Milton rejects, that divorce was permitted to men by the Old Law so that they would not persecute their wives, but would divorce them.

for the Maister might take away from an Hebrew servant the wife which hee gave him, *Exod.* 21.[44] If it be answer'd that the mariage of servants is no matrimony: tis reply'd, that this in the ancient *Roman* Law is true,[45] not in the *Mosaic.* If it bee added, she was a stranger not an Hebrew, therfore easily divorc't, it will be answerd that strangers not beeing *Canaanites,* and they also beeing Converts might bee lawfully maryed, as *Rahab* was.[46] And her conversion is heer suppos'd; for an Hebrew maister could not lawfully give a heathen wife to an Hebrew servant. However, the divorcing of an Israelitish woman was as easy by the Law, as the divorcing of a stranger, and almost in the same words permitted, *Deut.* 24. and *Deut.* 21. Lastly, it gives place to the right of warr, for a captiv woman lawfully maryed, and afterward not belov'd, might bee dismist, only without ransom, *Deut.* 21.[47] If mariage may bee dissolv'd by so [33] many exterior powers, not superior, as wee think, why may not the power of mariage it self for its own peace and honour dissolv it self, wher the persons wedded be free persons, why may not a greater and more natural power complaining dissolv mariage? for the ends why matrimony was ordain'd, are certainly and by all Logic above the Ordinance it self, why may not that dissolv mariage without which that institution hath no force at all? for the prime ends of mariage, are the whole strength and validity therof, without

[44] V. 4: "If his master have given him a wife, and she have borne him sons or daughters; the wife and her children shall be her master's, and he shall go out by himself."

[45] See *Institutes of Gaius,* VII, 56, 57a (Scott, I, 89): "Roman citizens are understood to have contracted marriage according to civil law . . . if they marry Roman citizens, or even Latins or foreigners whom they have a right to marry . . . Marriage, however, cannot take place with persons of a servile condition." Also *Opinions of Paulus,* XXI, 1–18 (Scott, I, 277); and W. W. Buckland, *The Main Institutions of Roman Private Law* (Cambridge, 1931), p. 41: "Though slaves could not marry, they contracted unions similar to marriage in all but legal effect."

[46] The Rahab mentioned in Matthew 1:5 among the ancestors of Jesus is usually understood by the commentators as the Rahab of Joshua 2:1–21, the harlot of Jericho who protected Joshua's spies and smuggled them out of Jericho. In return Joshua spared her after the capture of Jericho. See Bucer on Matthew 1:5 in *In Sacra Quatuor Evangelia Enarrationes* (Basle, 1536), p. 6, and other commentaries on Matthew, some of which also repeat the tradition that Joshua himself married Rahab.

[47] V. 14: "And it shall be, if thou have no delight in her, then thou shalt let her go whither she will; but thou shalt not sell her at all for money, thou shalt not make merchandise of her, because thou hast humbled her."

which matrimony is like an Idol, nothing in the world. But those former allowances were all for hardnes of heart. Be that granted, untill we come where to understand it better: if the Law suffer thus farr the obstinacy of a bad man, is it not more righteous heer, to doe willingly what is but equal, to remove in season the extrimities of a good man?

Eightly, If a man had deflowr'd a Virgin, or brought an ill name on his wife that shee came not a Virgin to him, hee was amerc't in certain shekles of Silver, and bound never to divorce her all his daies, *Deut. 22*, which shews that the Law gave no liberty to divorce, wher the injury was palpable; and that the absolute forbidding to divorce, was in part the punishment of a deflowrer, and a defamer. Yet not so but that the wife questionles might depart when shee pleas'd. Otherwise this cours had not so much righted her, as deliverd her up to more spight and cruel usage. This Law therfore doth justly distinguish the privilege of an honest and blameles man in the matter of divorce from the punishment of a notorious offender.

Ninthly, Suppose it might bee imputed to a man, that hee was too rash in his choyce and why took hee not better heed, let him now smart, and bear his folly as he may; although the Law of God, that terrible law doe not thus upbraid the infirmities and unwilling mistakes of man in his integrity: But suppose these and the like proud aggravations of som stern hypocrite, more merciles in his mercies, then any literall Law in the vigor of severity, must be patiently heard; yet all Law, and Gods Law especially grants every where to error easy remitments, eevn where the utmost penalty exacted were no undoing. With great reason therfore and mercy doth it heer not torment an error, if it be so, with the endurance of a whole life lost to all houshold comfort and society, a punishment of too vast and huge dimensions for an error, and the more unreasonable for that the like objection may be oppos'd against the plea of divorcing for adultery; hee [34] might have lookt better before to her breeding under religious Parents: why did hee not then more diligently inquire into her manners, into what company she kept? every glaunce of her eye, every step of her gate would have propheci'd adultery, if the quick sent of these discerners had bin took along; they had the divination to have foretold you all this; as they have now the divinity to punish an error inhumanly. As good reason to be content, and forc't to be content with your adultress, if these objecters might be the judges of human frailtie. But God more mild and good to man, then man to his brother, in all this liberty givn to divorcement, mentions not a word of our past errors and mistakes, if any were, which these men objecting from their own inventions prosecute with all violence and iniquity. For if the one bee to look so narrowly what hee takes, at the peril of ever keeping, why should not the other bee made as wary what is promis'd, by the peril of loosing? for without those promises the treaty of mariage had not proceeded. Why should his own error bind him, rather then the others fraud acquit him? Let the buyer beware, saith the old Law-beaten termer. Belike then ther is no more honesty, nor ingenuity in the bargain of a wedloc, then in the buying of a colt: Wee must it seems drive it on as craftily with those whose affinity wee seek, as if they were a pack of sale men and complotters. But the deceiver deceivs himself in the unprosperous mariage, and therin is sufficiently punisht. I answer, that the most of those who deceiv, are such as either understand not, or value not the true purposes of mariage; they have the prey they seek, not the punishment: yet say it prove to them som cross, it is not equal that error and fraud should be linkt in the same degree of forfeture, but rather that error should be acquitted, and fraud bereav'd his morsel: if the mistake were not on both sides, for then on both sides the acquitment will be reasonable, if the bondage be intolerable; which this Law graciously determins, not unmindful of the wife, as was granted willingly to the common Expositers, though beyond the letter of this law, yet not beyond the spirit of charity.

Tenthly, Mariage is a solemn thing, som say a holy, the resemblance of Christ and his Church; and so indeed it is where the persons are truly religious; and wee know all Sacred things not perform'd sincerely as they ought, are no way acceptable to God in thir outward formality. And that wherin it differs from personal duties, if they be [35] not truly don, the fault is in our selves; but mariage to be a true and pious mariage is not in the single power of any person; the essence whereof, as of all other Covnants is in relation to another, the making and maintaining causes thereof are all mutual, and must be a communion of spiritual and temporal comforts. If then either of them cannot, or obstinatly will not be answerable in these duties, so as that the other can have no peaceful living, or enduring the want of what he justly seeks, and sees no hope, then strait from that dwelling love, which is the soul of wedloc, takes his flight, leaving only som cold performances of civil and common respects, but the true bond of mariage, if there were ever any there, is already burst like a rott'n thred. Then follows dissimulation, suspicion, fals colours, fals pretences, and wors then these, disturbance, annoyance, vexation, sorrow, temtation eevn in the faultles person, weary of himself, and of all action public or domestic; then comes disorder, neglect, hatred, and perpetual strife, all these the enemies of holines and christianity, and every one of these persisted in, a remediles violation to matrimony. Therfore God who hates all faining and formality, wher there should bee all faith and sincerenes, and abhorrs to see inevitable discord, wher there should be greatest concord, when through anothers default, faith and concord cannot bee, counts it neither just to punish the innocent with the transgressor, nor holy, nor honourable for the sanctity of mariage, that should bee the union of peace and love, to be made the commitment, and close fight of enmity and hate. And therfore doth in this Law, what best agrees with his goodnes, loosning a sacred thing to peace and charity, rather then binding it to hatred and contention; loosning only the outward and formal tie of that which is already inwardly, and really brokn, or els was really never joyn'd.

Eleventhly, One of the cheif matrimonial ends is said to seek a holy seed; [48] but where an unfit mariage administers continual cause of hatred and distemper, there, as was heard before, cannot choose but much unholines abide. Nothing more unhallows a man, more unprepares him to the service of God in any duty, then a habit of wrath and perturbation, arising from the importunity of troublous causes never absent. And wher the houshold stands in this plight, what love can ther bee to the unfortunat issue, what care of thir breeding, which is of main conducement to thir beeing holy. God therfore knowing [36] how unhappy it would bee for children to bee born in such a family, gives this Law either as a prevention, that beeing an unhappy pair, they should not adde to bee unhappy parents, or els as a remedy that if ther be children, while they are fewest, they may follow either parent, as shall bee agreed, or judg'd, from the house of hatred and discord, to a place of more holy and peaceable education.

Twelfthly, All Law is available to som good end, but the final pro-

[48] Malachi 2:15.

hibition of divorce avails to no good end, causing only the endles aggravation of evil, and therfore this permission of divorce was givn to the Jews by the wisdom and fatherly providence of God; who knew that Law cannot command love, without which, matrimony hath no true beeing, no good, no solace, nothing of Gods instituting, nothing but so sordid and so low, as to bee disdain'd of any generous person. Law cannot inable natural inability either of body, or mind, which gives the greevance; it cannot make equal those inequalities, it cannot make fit those unfitnesses; and where there is malice more then defect of nature, it cannot hinder ten thousand injuries, and bitter actions of despight too suttle and too unapparent for Law to deal with. And while it seeks to remedy more outward wrongs, it exposes the injur'd person to other more inward and more cutting. All these evils unavoidably will redound upon the children, if any be, and the whole family. It degenerates and disorders the best spirits, leavs them to unsettl'd imaginations, and degraded hopes, careles of themselvs, their houshold and their freinds, unactive to all public service, dead to the Common-wealth; wherin they are by one mishapp, and no willing trespas of theirs, outlaw'd from all the benefits and comforts of married life and posterity. It conferrs as little to the honour and inviolable keeping of Matrimony, but sooner stirrs up temptations, and occasions to secret adulteries, and unchast roaving. But it maintaines public honesty. Public folly rather, who shall judge of public honesty? the Law of God, and of ancientest Christians, and all Civil Nations, or the illegitimat Law of Monks and Canonists, the most malevolent, most unexperienc't, and incompetent judges of Matrimony?

These reasons, and many more that might bee alleg'd, afford us plainly to perceav, both what good cause this Law had to doe for good men in mischances, and what necessity it had to suffer accidentally the hard heartednes of bad men, which it could not certainly [37] discover, or discovering could not subdue, no nor indeavour to restrain without multiplying sorrow to them, for whom all was indeavour'd. The guiltles therfore were not depriv'd thir needful redresses, and the hard hearts of others unchastisable in those judicial Courts, were so remitted there, as bound over to the higher Session of Conscience.

Nothwithstanding all this, ther is a loud exception against this Law of God, nor can the holy Author save his Law from this exception, that it opens a dore to all licence and confusion. But this is the rudest, I was almost saying the most graceles objection, and with the least reverence to God and *Moses,* that could bee devis'd: This is to cite God before mans Tribunal, to arrogate a wisdom and holines above him. Did not God then foresee what event of licence or confusion could follow? did not hee know how to ponder these abuses with more prevailing respects, in the most eevn ballance of his justice and purenes, till these correctors came up to shew him better? The Law is, if it stirre up sin any way, to stirre it up by forbidding, as one contrary excites another, *Rom.* 7.[49] but if it once come to provoke sin, by granting licence to sin, according to Laws that have no other honest end, but only to permit the fulfilling of obstinat lust, how is God not made the contradicter of himself? No man denies that best things may bee abus'd: but it is a rule resulting from many pregnant experiences, that what doth most harm in the abusing, us'd rightly doth most good. And such a good to take away from honest men, for beeing abus'd by such as abuse all things, is the greatest abuse of all. That the whole Law is no furder usefull, then as man uses it lawfully, St. *Paul* teaches 1. *Tim.* 1.[50] And that Christian liberty may bee us'd for an occasion to the flesh, the same Apostle confesses, *Galat.* 5.[51] yet thinks not of removing it for that, but bidds us rather *Stand fast in the liberty wherwith Christ hath freed us, and not bee held again in the yoke of bondage.*[52] The very permission which Christ gave to divorce for adultery, may bee fouly abus'd, by any whose hardnes of heart can either fain adultery, or dares committ, that hee may divorce. And for this cause the Pope, and hitherto the Church of *England,* forbid all divorce from the bond of mariage, though for openest adultery. If then it bee righteous to hinder for the fear of abuse, that which Gods Law notwithstanding that caution, hath warranted to bee don, doth not our righteousnes come short of Antichrist, or doe we not rather [38] heerin conform our selves to his unrighteousnes in this undue and unwise fear. For God regards more to releev by this Law the just complaints of good

[49] V. 7: "Nay, I had not known sin, but by the law: for I had not known lust, except the law had said, Thou shalt not covet."

[50] V. 8: "But we know that the law is good, if a man use it lawfully."

[51] V. 13: "For, brethren, ye have been called unto liberty; only use not liberty for an occasion to the flesh, but by love serve one another."

[52] V. 1: Authorized Version: "Stand fast therefore in the liberty wherewith Christ hath made us free, and be not entangled again with the yoke of bondage."

men, then to curb the licence of wicked men, to the crushing withall, and the overwhelming of his afflicted servants. He loves more that his Law should look with pitty upon the difficulties of his own, then with rigor upon the boundlesse riots of them who serv another Maister, and hinder'd heer by strictnes, will break another way to wors enormities. If this Law therfore have many good reasons for which God gave it, and no intention of giving scope to leudnes, but as abuse by accident comes in with every good Law, and every good thing, it cannot be wisdom in us, while we can content us with Gods wisdom, nor can be purity, if his purity will suffice us, to except against this Law, as if it foster'd licence. But if they affirm this Law had no other end, but to permitt obdurat lust, because it would bee obdurat, making the Law of God intentionally to proclame and enact sin lawful, as if the will of God were becom sinfull, or sin stronger then his direct and Law-giving will, the men would bee admonisht to look well to it, that while they are so eager to shut the dore against licence, they do not open a wors dore to blasphemy. And yet they shall bee heer furder shewn thir iniquity; what more foul and common sin among us then drunkennes, and who can bee ignorant, that if the importation of Wine, and the use of all strong drink were forbid, it would both clean ridde the possibility of committing that odious vice, and men might afterwards live happily and healthfully, without the use of those intoxicating licors. Yet who is ther the severest of them all, that ever propounded to loos his Sack, his Ale, toward the certain abolishing of so great a sin, who is ther of them, the holiest, that less loves his rich Canary at meals, though it bee fetcht from places that hazard the Religion of them who fetch it, and though it make his neighbour drunk out of the same Tunne? While they forbid not therfore the use of that liquid Marchandise, which forbidd'n would utterly remove a most loathsom sin, and not impair either the health, or the refreshment of mankind, suppli'd many other wayes, why doe they forbid a Law of God, the forbidding wherof brings into an excessive bondage, oft times the best of men, and betters not the wors? Hee to remove a Nationall vice, will not pardon his cupps, nor think it concerns him to forbear the quaffing of that outlandish Grape, in his unnecessary fullnes, though other men [39] abuse it never so much, nor is hee so abstemious as to intercede with the Magistrate that all matter of drunkennes be banisht the Common-wealth, and yet for the fear of a less inconvenience unpardnably requires of his brethren, in thir extreme necessity to debarre themselves the use of Gods permissive Law, though it might bee thir saving, and no mans indangering the more. Thus this peremptory strictnes we may discern of what sort it is, how unequal, and how unjust.

But it will breed confusion. What confusion it would breed, God himself took the care to prevent in the fourth verse of this Chapter, that the divorc't beeing maried to another, might not return to her former Husband. And *Justinians* law counsels the same in his title of *Nuptials*.[53] And what confusion els can ther bee in separation, to separat, upon extrem urgency, the Religious from the irreligious, the fit from the unfit, the willing from the wilfull, the abus'd from the abuser, such a separation is quite contrary to confusion. But to binde and mixe together holy with Atheist, hevnly with hellish, fitnes with unfitnes, light with darknes, antipathy with antipathy, the injur'd with the injurer, and force them into the most inward neernes of a detested union, this doubtles is the most horrid, the most unnatural mixture, the greatest confusion that can be confus'd!

Thus by this plain and Christian *Talmud*[54] vindicating the Law of God from irreverent and unwary expositions, I trust, wher it shall meet with intelligible perusers, som stay at least of mens thoughts will bee obtain'd, to consider these many prudent and righteous ends of this divorcing permission. That it may have, for the great Authors sake, heerafter som competent allowance to bee counted a little purer then the prerogative of a legal and public ribaldry, granted to that holy seed. So that from hence wee shall hope to finde the way still more open to the reconciling of those places which treat this matter in the Gospel. And thether now without interruption the cours of method brings us. [40]

[53] Not in *Institutes*, I, x ("Of Marriage"), nor have I been able to find this "counsel" elsewhere in the *Corpus*.
[54] *Talmud:* study, interpretation.

TETRACHORDON,

MATT. 5. 31, 32.

31 *It hath beene said whosoever shall put away his wife, let him give her a writing of divorcement.*

32 *But I say unto you that whosoever shall put away his wife, &c.*

MATT. 19. 3, 4, &c.

3 *And the Pharises also came unto him tempting him, &c.*

*I*t hath beene said.] What hitherto hath beene spoke upon the law of God touching Matrimony or divorce, hee who will deny to have bin argu'd according to reason, and all equity of Scripture, I cannot edifie how, or by what rule of proportion that mans vertue calculates, what his *elements* [1] are, nor what his *analytics*.[2] Confidently to those who have read good bookes, and to those whose reason is not an illiterate booke to themselves I appeale, whether they would not confesse all this to bee the commentary of truth and justice, were it not for these recited words of our Saviour. And if they take not backe that which they thus grant, nothing sooner might perswade them that Christ heer teaches no new precept, and nothing sooner might direct them to finde his meaning, then to compare and measure it by the rules of nature and eternall righteousnes, which no writt'n law extinguishes, and the Gospel least of all. For what can be more opposite and disparaging to the cov'nant of love, of freedom, & of our manhood in grace, then to bee made the yoaking pedagogue of new severities, the scribe of syllables and rigid letters, not only greevous to the best of men, but different and strange from the light of reason in them, save only as they are fain to stretch & distort their apprehensions, for feare of displeasing the verbal straightnesse of a text, which our owne servil feare gives us not the leisure to understand aright. If the law of Christ shall be

[1] Elements: The first principles of an art or science (*OED*). Edifie: *OED* cites this passage and defines: "to frame a notion; 'make out,' imagine."

[2] Analytics: his system of logic, an allusion to Aristotle's two logical treatises, the *Prior* and the *Posterior Analytics*.

writt'n in our hearts, as was promis'd to the Gospel, *Jer.* [37²] 31,[3] how can this in the vulgar and superficiall sense be a law of Christ, so farre from beeing writt'n in our hearts, that it injures and disallowes not onely the free dictates of nature and morall law, but of charity also and religion in our hearts. Our Saviours doctrine is, that the end, and the fulfilling of every command is charity; [4] no faith without it, no truth without it, no worship, no workes pleasing to God but as they partake of charity. He himselfe sets us an example, breaking the solemnest and the strictest ordinance of religious rest, and justify'd the breaking, not to cure a dying man, but such whose cure might without danger have beene deferr'd.[5] And wherefore needes must the sick mans bed be carried home on that day by his appointment, and why were the Disciples who could not forbeare on that day to pluck the corne,[6] so industriously defended, but to shew us that if he preferr'd the slightest occasions of mans good before the observing of highest and severest ordinances, hee gave us much more easie leave to breake the intolerable yoake of a never well joyn'd wedlocke for the removing of our heaviest afflictions. Therefore it is that the most of evangelick precepts are given us in proverbiall formes, to drive us from the letter, though we love ever to be sticking there. For no other cause did Christ assure us that whatsoever things wee binde, or slacken on earth, are so in heaven, but to signifie that the christian arbitrement of charity is supreme decider of all controversie, and supreme resolver of all Scripture; not as the Pope determines for his owne tyrany, but as the Church ought to determine for its owne true liberty. Hence *Eusebius* not far from beginning his History, compares the state of Christians to that of *Noah* and the Patriarkes before the Law.[7] And this indeede was the

---

[3] V. 33. "I will put my law in their inward parts, and write it in their hearts."
[4] I Timothy 1:5. [5] John 5:1–16.
[6] Matthew 12:1–8; Mark 2:23–28.
[7] Eusebius, *Ecclesiastical Histories*, I, iv (Migne, *Graeca*, XX, 77–78): "And indeed, even before the flood, there were some who were distinguished for virtue; and after this others, both of the sons and posterity of Noah, among whom we would mention Abraham, celebrated by the Hebrews as the founder and progenitor of their nation. Should anyone, beginning from Abraham, and going back to the first man, pronounce those who have had the testimony of righteousness, Christians in fact, though not in name, he would not be far from the truth. For as the name Christians is intended to indicate this very idea, that a man, by the knowledge and doctrine of Christ, is distinguished by modesty and justice, by patience and a virtuous fortitude, and by a profession of piety towards the

reason, why *Apostolick* tradition in the antient Church was counted nigh equall to the writt'n word, though it carried them at length awry, for want of considering that tradition was not left to bee impos'd as law, but to be a patterne of that Christian prudence, and liberty which holy men by right assum'd of old, which truth was so evident, that it found entrance even into the Councell of *Trent,* when the point of tradition came to be discusst. And *Marinaro* [8] a learned *Carmelite* for approaching too neere the true cause that gave esteeme to tradition, that is to say, the difference betweene the Old and New Testament, the one punctually prescribing writt'n Law, the other guiding by the inward spirit, was reprehended by Cardinall *Poole* [9] as one that had spoken more worthy a *German Colloquie,* then a generall councell.[10] I omit many instances, many proofes and arguments of this kind, which alone would compile a just vo-[38²]lume, and shall content me heer to have shew'n breifly, that the great and almost only commandment of the Gospel, is to

one and only true and supreme God; all this was no less studiously cultivated bv them than by us." Tr. Christian F. Crusé, *The Ecclesiastical History* (Philadelphia, 1836), p. 27. Eusebius of Caesarea or Pamphili (*ca.* 275–340) was a Greek father who opposed the Arians and wrote a church history. See *Complete Prose,* I, 630, n. 19.

[8] Antonius Marinarius (probably Antonio Marinario in Italian) entered the Carmelite Order in 1531 and died in 1570. Concerning his works, certain and probable, see Cosmas de Villiers, *Bibliotheca Carmelitana,* ed. Gabriel Wessels (Rome, 1927), I, cols. 176–80. See Sarpi's mention of him, below, n. 10.

[9] Reginald Pole (1500–1558), cardinal and archbishop, opposed Henry VIII and was papal legate to England in the reign of Mary and chief instrument of Mary's religious policies. See above, p. 425.

[10] Paolo Sarpi, *Historie of the Councel of Trent,* tr. Nathaniel Brent (1640; UTSL), pp. 151–52: "But *Anthonius Marinarus,* a Carmelite Friar, thought fit to refraine speaking of traditions, and said, that for decision of the first Article in this matter, it was meet first to determine whether the question were *facti,* or *juris:* that is, if the Christian doctrine have two parts, one which was written by the will of God, and the other which was forbidden to be writ, but onely taught by word of mouth; or if in the whole body of doctrine it hath accidentally happened, that all having beene taught, some part hath not beene committed to writing. He added, that it was a cleere case that the Majestie of God ordaining the law of the Old Testament, appointed it should be necessary to have it in writing. . . . This fell not out in the Gospell, which the Sonne of God wrote in the hearts, for which neither tables, nor chest, nor book is necessary: yea, the Church was most perfect before any of the Apostles wrote; and though they had writ nothing, the Church would have wanted nothing of its perfection. . . . The Friars opinion pleased but few; yea, Cardinall *Poole* reprehended it, and said, it better beseemed a Colloquie in *Germany,* than a Councell of the universall Church."

command nothing against the good of man, and much more no civil command, against his civil good. If we understand not this, we are but crakt cimbals,[11] we do but tinckle, we know nothing, we doe nothing, all the sweat of our toilsomest obedience will but mock us. And what wee suffer superstitiously returnes us no thankes. Thus med'cining our eyes wee neede not doubt to see more into the meaning of these our Saviours words, then many who have gone before us.

[*It hath beene said, whosoever shall put away his wife.*] Our Saviour was by the doctors of his time suspected of intending to dissolve the law. In this chapter he wipes off this aspersion upon his accusers, and shewes how they were the law breakers. In every common wealth when it decayes, corruption makes two maine steps; first when men cease to doe according to the inward and uncompell'd actions of vertue, caring only to live by the outward constraint of law, and turne the Simplicity of reall good, into the craft of seeming so by law. To this hypocritical honesty was Rome declin'd in that age, wherein *Horace* liv'd and discover'd it to *Quintius.*

> *Whom doe we count a good man, whom but he*
> *Who keepes the lawes and statutes of the Senate,*
> *Who judges in great suits and controversies,*
> *Whose witnesse and opinion winnes the cause;*
> *But his owne house, and the whole neighbourhood*
> *Sees his foule inside through his whited skin.*[12]

The next declining is, when law becomes now too straight for the secular manners, and those too loose for the cincture of law. This brings in false and crooked interpretations to eeke out law, and invents the suttle encroachment of obscure traditions hard to be disprov'd. To both these descents the Pharises themselves were fall'n. Our Saviour therefore shews them both where they broke the law in not marking the divine intent thereof, but onely the letter, and where they deprav'd the letter also with sophisticall expositions. This law of divorse they had deprav'd both waies. First, by teaching that to give a bill of divorse was all the duty which that law requir'd, what ever the cause were. Next by running to divorse for any triviall, accidentall cause; whenas the law evidently stayes in the grave causes of naturall and immutable dislike. [*It hath been said*] saith he. Christ doth not put any contempt or disesteeme upon the

[11] I Corinthians 13:1.
[12] *Epistles*, I, xvi, 40–45; Milton's translation.

[39²] law of *Moses,* by citing it so briefly; for in the same manner God himselfe cites a law of greatest caution, *Jer.* 3. *They say if a man put away his wife, shall he returne to her againe, &c.*[13] Nor doth he more abolish it then the law of swearing, cited next with the same brevity, and more appearance of contradicting. For divorce hath an exception left it, but we are charg'd there, as absolutely as words can charge us, *not to sweare at all*: yet who denies the lawfulnesse of an oath,[14] though here it be in no case permitted? And what shall become of his solemne protestation not to abolish one law, or one tittle of any law,[15] especially of those which hee mentions in this chapter. And that hee meant more particularly the not abolishing of *Mosaic* divorse, is beyond all cavill manifest in *Luke* 16. 17, 18. where this clause against abrogating is inserted immediately before the sentence against divorse, as if it were call'd thither on purpose to defend the equity of this particular law against the foreseene rashnesse of common textuaries, who abolish lawes, as the rable demolish images, in the zeale of their hammers oft violating the Sepulchers of good men, like *Pentheus* in the tragedies, they see that for *Thebes* which is not,[16] and take that for superstition, as these men in the heate of their annulling perceive not how they abolish right, and equall, and justice under the appearance of *judicial*. And yet are confessing all the while, that these sayings of Christ stand not in contradiction to the law of *Moses,* but to the false doctrine of the Pharises rais'd from thence; that the law of God is perfect, not liable to additions or diminutions, & *Paraeus* accuses the Jesuite *Maldonatus* [17] of greatest falsity for limiting the perfection of that law only to the rudenes of the Jewes. He adds *that the law promiseth life to the performers thereof; therefore needs not perfecter precepts, then such as bring to life;* that *if the corrections of Christ stand opposite, not to the corruptions of the Pharises, but to the law it selfe of God, the heresie of Manes would*

[13] V. 1. After *wife* Milton omits "and she go from him, and become another man's."

[14] Milton was surely aware that the Anabaptists ("Dippers") and the other sects that were beginning to accept Anabaptist beliefs took this prohibition against oaths literally.

[15] Matthew 5:17–19.

[16] Euripides, *Bacchae,* esp. ll. 918–22. Pentheus, seeking to root out the festival orgies of Dionysius, is hypnotized by the god so that he does not know what he is doing or where he is.

[17] Johannes Maldonatus (Juan Maldonado), 1534–1583, was a Jesuit exegete.

follow, one God of the old Testament, and another of the New. That Christ saith not here except your righteousnesse exceede the righteousnesse of Moses law, but of the Scribes and Pharises.[18] That all this may be true, whether is common sense flown asquint, if we can maintaine that Christ forbid the Mosaic divorce utterly, and yet abolisht not the law that permits it? For if the conscience onely were checkt, and the law not repeal'd, what meanes the *fanatic* boldnesse of this age that dares tutor Christ to be more strict then he thought fit? ye shall have the evasion, it was a judiciall law. What could infancy and slumber have invented more childish? judiciall or not judiciall, it was one of those lawes expresly, which he forewarn'd us with protestation, that his [40²] mind was not to abrogate: and if we marke the stearage of his words, what course they hold, wee may perceive that what he protested not to disolve (that he might faithfully & not deceitfully remove a suspition from himselfe) was principally concerning the judiciall law; for of that sort are all these here which he vindicates; except the last. Of the Ceremonial law he told them true, that nothing of it should passe *untill all were fullfill'd.*[19] Of the morall law he knew the Pharises did not suspect he meant to nullifie that: for so doing would soone have undone his authority, and advanc'd theirs. Of the judiciall law therefore cheifly this Apologie was meant: For how is that fullfill'd longer then the common equity thereof remaines in force? And how is this our Saviours defence of himselfe, not made fallacious, if the Pharises chiefe feare be, least he should abolish the judiciall law, and he to satisfie them, protests his good intention to the Moral law.

[18] *In S. Matthaei Evangelium Commentarius* (Geneva, 1641), pp. 171–72. Paraeus accuses Anabaptists and Jesuits of minimizing the perfection of the Law: "That it was, however, perfect according to the rude fashion of the Jewish people, as Maldonatus limits it, is most false. . . . The Law perfectly promises life to those who obey it, Leviticus 18:5, 'Which if a man do, he shall live in them.' Therefore for the acquisition of life by works there is no need of more perfect precepts. .. The opinion of the Anabaptists and the Jesuits is a heresy, derived from the Manichees. Indeed Faustus Manichaeus contended that Christ added somewhat to the Law of the Peoples and to that of Moses, that He taught somewhat contrary . . . If Christ by saying 'But I say unto you,' opposed himself not to the elders of the Pharisees, but to God the lawgiver, it would indeed follow that there is a god of the Old Testament other than the God of the New Testament. . . . He does not say 'Except your righteousness shall exceed the righteousness of Moses,' that is of the Mosaic Law, but 'shall exceed the righteousness of the scribes and Pharisees.' "
[19] Matthew 5:18.

It is the generall grant of Divines,[20] that what in the Judicial law is not meerely *judicall,* but reaches to human equity in common, was never in the thought of being abrogated. If our Saviour tooke away ought of law, it was the burthensome of it,[21] not the ease of burden, it was the bondage, not the liberty of any divine law that he remov'd: this he often profest to be the end of his comming. But what if the law of divorce be a morall law, as most certainly it is fundamentally, and hath been so prov'd in the reasons thereof. For though the giving of a bill may be judiciall, yet the act of divorce is altogether conversant in good or evill, and so absolutely moral. So farr as it is good it never can be abolisht being morall; so farr as it is simply evil it never could be judiciall, as hath been shewen at large in *the Doctrine of divorce,*[22] and will be reassum'd anon. Whence one of these two necessities follow, that either it was never establisht, or never abolisht. Thus much may be enough to have said on this place. The following verse will be better unfolded in the 19. Chapter, where it meets us againe, after a large debatement on the question, between our Saviour and his adversaries.

MAT. 19. 3, 4. &c.

V. 3. *And the Pharises came unto him tempting him and saying unto him.*

[*Tempting him.*] The manner of these men comming to our Saviour, not to learne, but to tempt him, may give us to expect that their answer will bee such as is fittest for them, not so much a teaching, as an intangling. No man though never so willing or so well enabl'd to in-[41]struct, but if he discerne his willingnesse and candor made use of to intrapp him, will suddainly draw in himselfe, and laying aside the facil vein of perspicuity, will know his time to utter clouds and riddles; If he be not lesse wise then that noted Fish,[23] when as he should bee not unwiser then the Serpent.[24] Our Saviour at no time exprest any great desire to teach

20 See *Doctrine and Discipline,* above, pp. 244, 317–18.
21 Burthensome: supply *part.* Since this passage is the only citation in the *OED* for *burdensome* as a substantive, it seems likely that some such word as *part* has been omitted.
22 See *Doctrine and Discipline,* above, pp. 319–24.
23 The "noted Fish" is probably the squid, which, in the medieval bestiaries, escapes by surrounding itself with a cloud of ink.
24 Matthew 10:16: "Be ye therefore wise as serpents, and harmless as doves."

the obstinate and unteachable Pharises; but when they came to tempt him, then least of all. As now about the liberty of divorce, so another time about the punishment of adultery [25] they came to sound him, and what satisfaction got they from his answer, either to themselves or to us, that might direct a law under the Gospel, new from that of *Moses*, unlesse we draw his absolution of adultery into an edict. So about the tribute, who is there can picke out a full solution, what and when we must give to *Caesar*, by the answer which he gave the Pharises? [26] If we must give to *Caesar* that which is *Caesars*, and all be *Caesars*, which hath his image, wee must either new stamp our Coine, or we may goe new stamp our Foreheads with the superscription of slaves in stead of freemen. Besides it is a generall precept, not only of Christ, but of all other Sages, not to instruct the unworthy and the conceited who love tradition more then truth,[27] but to perplex and stumble them purposely with contriv'd obscurities. No wonder then if they who would determine of divorce by this place, have ever found it difficult, and unsatisfying through all the ages of the Church, as *Austine* himselfe [28] and other great writers confesse. Lastly it is manifest to be the principal scope of our Saviour both here, and in the 5. of *Mat.* to convince the Pharises of what they being evill did licentiously, not to explaine what others being good and blamelesse men might be permitted to doe in case of extremity. Neither was it seasonable to talke of honest and conscientious liberty among them who had abused legall and civil liberty to uncivil licence. We doe not say to a servant what we say to a sonne; nor was it expedient to preach freedome to those who had transgrest in wantonnesse. When we rebuke a Prodigal, we admonish him of thrift, not of magnificence, or bounty. And to school a proud man we labour to make him humble, not magnanimous. So Christ to

[25] John 8:3–11. When the Pharisees brought to Jesus a woman taken in adultery, He said, "He that is without sin among you, let him first cast a stone at her."

[26] Matthew 22:17–21: "Render therefore unto Caesar the things which are Caesar's; and unto God the things that are God's." Also Mark 12:14; and Luke 20:22.

[27] With respect to Christ, Milton may have had in mind some such passage as Matthew 7:6: "Give not that which is holy unto the dogs, neither cast ye your pearls before swine."

[28] Augustine, *De Conjugiis Adulterinis ad Pollentium*, I, 11 (Migne, *Latina*, XL, 458). See below, pp. 698–99.

retort these arrogant inquisitors their own, tooke the course to lay their hautinesse under a severity which they deserv'd; not to acquaint them, or make them judges either of the just mans right and privilege, or of the afflicted mans necessity. And if wee may have leave to conjecture, there is a likelyhood offer'd us by *Tertullian* in his 4. against *Marcion*,[29] whereby it may seeme very probable that the Pharises had a private drift of malice against our Saviours life in proposing this questi-[42]on; and our Saviour had a peculiar aim in the rigor of his answer, both to let them know the freedome of his spirit, and the sharpenesse of his discerning. *This I must now shew, saith Tertullian, Whence our Lord deduc'd this sentence, and which way he directed it, whereby it will more fully appeare that he intended not to dissolve Moses.* And thereupon tells us that the vehemence of this our Saviours speech was cheifly darted against *Herod* and *Herodias.* The story is out of *Josephus:* [30] *Herod* had beene a long time married to the daughter of *Aretas* King of *Petra,* til hapning on his jorney towards *Rome* to be entertain'd at his brother *Philips* house, he cast his eye unlawfully and unguestlike upon *Herodias* there, the wife of *Philip,* but daughter to *Aristobulus* their common brother, and durst make words of marrying her his Neece from his brothers bed. She assented upon agreement he should expell his former wife. All was accomplisht, and by the *Baptist* rebuk't with the losse of his head. Though doubtlesse that staid not the various discourses of men upon the fact, which while the *Herodian* flatterers, and not a few perhaps among the Pharises endevour'd to defend by wresting the law, it might be a meanes to bring the question of divorce into a

[29] *Adversus Marcionem,* IV, 34 (Migne, *Latina,* II, 474). See below, p. 694. Quintus Septimus Florens Tertullianus *(ca.* 150–220) was a Latin father, apologist, and opponent of several heresies. See *Complete Prose,* I, 552–53.

[30] *Antiquities,* XVIII, 5 (7 in old editions): "*Herode* the Tetrarch married *Aretas* daughter, with whome hee had lived maried a verie long time. Afterwardes taking his journey towards Rome, he lodged with *Herode* his halfe brother by the fathers side . . . and there being surprized with the love of *Herodias* his brothers wife, which was the daughter of *Aristobulus,* their brother, and sister to the great *Agrippa,* he was so bold as to offer her some speech of marriage: which when she had accepted, the accords were made betweene them, that at such time as hee should returne from Rome, he should displace her, and lead her away with him." *The Famous and Memorable Workes of Josephus,* tr. Thomas Lodge (1609; BML), p. 470. Elsewhere in the account the half-brother's name is give as Philip. Flavius Josephus *(ca.* 37–95) was a Hellenistic Jewish historian.

hot agitation among the people, how farre *Moses* gave allowance. The Pharises therefore knowing our Saviour to be a friend of *John* the Baptist, and no doubt but having heard much of his Sermon in the Mount, wherein he spake rigidly against the licence of divorce, they put him this question both in hope to find him a contradicter of *Moses,* and a condemner of *Herod*; so to insnare him within compasse of the same accusation which had ended his friend; and our Saviour so orders his answer, as that they might perceive *Herod* and his Adultresse only not nam'd; so lively it concern'd them both what he spake. No wonder then if the sentence of our Saviour sounded stricter then his custome was; which his conscious attempters doubtlesse apprehended sooner then his other auditors. Thus much we gaine from hence to informe us, that what Christ intends to speake here of divorce, will be rather the forbidding of what we may not doe herein passionately and abusively, as *Herod* and *Herodias* did, then the discussing of what herein we may doe reasonably and necessarily.

[*Is it lawfull for a man to put away his wife.*] It might be render'd more exactly from the Greeke, *to loosen or to set free;* which though it seeme to have a milder signification then the two Hebrew words commonly us'd for divorce, yet Interpreters have noted, that the Greeke also is read in the *Septuagint,* for an act which is not without constraint.[31] As when *A-*[43]*chish* drove from his presence *David* counterfeiting madnesse, *Psal.* 34. the Greeke word is the same with this here, to put away. And *Erasmus* quotes *Hilary* rendering it by an expression, not so soft.[32] Whence may be doubted, whether the Pharises did not state this question in the strict right of the man, not tarrying for the wives consent. And if our Saviour answer directly according to what was askt in the tearm of putting away, it may be questionable, whether the rigor of his sentence did not forbid only such putting away as is without mutuall consent, in a violent and harsh manner, or without any reason, but will, as the *Tetrarch* did. Which might be the cause that those Christian Emperours fear'd not in their constitutions to dissolve mariage by

---

[31] A common remark on this place. See Poole, *Synopsis Criticorum* (Utrecht, 1684–86), IV, col. 470, where approximately the same comment is made.

[32] "Enarratio," Psalm XXXIII, *Omnia Opera* (Basle, 1540), V. 317. Erasmus cites Jerome, however, not Hilary. Hilarius was elected Pope in 461 and died in 468.

mutuall consent; In that our Saviour seemes here, as the case is most likely, not to condemne all divorce but all injury and violence in divorce. But no injury can be done to them who seeke it, as the *Ethics* of *Aristotle* sufficiently prove.[33] True it is, that an unjust thing may be done to one though willing, and so may justly be forbid'n: But divorce being in it selfe no unjust or evill thing, but only as it is joyn'd with injury, or lust, injury it cannot be at law, if consent be, and *Aristotle* erre not. And lust it may as frequently not be, while charity hath the judging of so many private greevances in a misfortun'd Wedlock, which may pard'nably seeke a redemption. But whether it be or not, the law cannot discerne, or examine lust, so long as it walkes from one lawfull terme to another, from divorce to marriage both in themselves indifferent. For if the law cannot take hold to punish many actions apparently covetous, ambitious, ingratefull, proud, how can it forbid and punish that for lust, which is but only surmis'd so, and can no more be certainly prov'd in the divorcing now, then before in the marrying. Whence if divorce be no unjust thing, but through lust, a cause not discernable by law, as law is wont to discerne in other cases, and can be no injury where consent is, there can be nothing in the equity of law, why divorce by consent may not be lawfull: leaving secrecies to conscience, the thing which our Saviour here aimes to rectifie, not to revoke the statutes of *Moses*. In the meane while the word *To put away*, being in the Greeke, to loosen or disolve, utterly takes away that vaine papisticall distinction of divorce from bed, and divorce from bond, evincing plainly that both Christ and the Pharises meane here that divorce which finally disolves the bond and frees both parties to a second marriage.

[*For every cause.*] This the Pharises held, that for every cause they might divorce, for every accidentall cause, any quarrell or difference [44] that might happ'n. So both *Josephus*[34] and *Philo*,[35]

[33] *Nicomachean Ethics*, V, ix, 1139b.

[34] *Antiquities*, IV, 253, tr. H. St. J. Thackeray (7 vols., London: Loeb Classical Library, 1926–43), IV, 597: "He who desires to be divorced from the wife who is living with him for whatsoever cause—and with mortals many such may arise—must certify in writing that he will have no further intercourse with her."

[35] *Special Laws*, III, 5: "Another commandment is that if a woman after parting from her husband. . . ." *Philo*, tr. F. H. Colson, VII, 493. The aorist passive participle ἀπαλλαγεῖσα here translated "parting" must be understood in the sense of "divorced," since, according to most authorities, including Philo, a woman may not divorce her husband under Mosaic Law. This quotation does

men who liv'd in the same age, explain; and the *Syriac* translater, whose antiquity is thought parallel to the *Evangelists* themselves, reads it conformably *upon any occasion or pretence.*[36] Divines also generally agree that thus the Pharises meant. *Cameron*[37] a late writer much applauded, commenting this place not undiligently, affirmes that the Greeke preposition κατὰ translated unusually (For)[38] hath a force in it implying the suddennesse of those Pharisaic divorces; and that their question was to this effect, *whether for any cause, whatever it chanc't to be, straight as it rose, the divorse might be lawfull.* This he freely gives what ever mov'd him, and I as freely take, nor can deny his observation to be acute & learned. If therfore we insist upon the word of *putting away,* that it imports a constraint without consent, as might be insisted, and may enjoy what *Cameron* bestowes on us, that for every cause is to be understood, *according as any cause may happen,* with a relation to the speedinesse of those divorces and that *Herodian* act especially, as is already brought us, the sentence of our Saviour wil appeare nothing so strict a prohibition as hath beene long conceiv'd, forbidding only to divorce for casuall & temporary causes, that may be soon ended, or soone remedied; & likewise forbidding to divorce rashly, & on

not seem to fit Milton's purpose very well, but it seems to be the only passage in Philo that has any bearing upon the matter, and it was cited by several authorities to show that Philo believed in divorce for any cause. Philo Judaeus (*ca.* 20 B.C.–50 A.D.) was a Hellenistic Jewish philosopher and theologian.

[36] Martinus Trostius, ed., *Novum Domini Nostri Jesu Christi Testamentum Syriacè, cum Versione Latina* (Anhalt, 1621; UTSL), p. 63, translates the Syriac of this phrase *qualibet occasione.* Milton's rendering seems based on this Latin translation, as are also his remarks on the antiquity of the Syriac version. Martinus writes, in the "Prefatio," sig. (?) 4: "This Syrian version is of all the first and oldest: it is the version, I assert, to be preferred before all others as fuller and more correct: it is the version, I say moreover, either of one of the Evangelists or at least of those who lived in Antioch while those Apostles were there, whom they could consult and hear concerning many obscure places."

[37] Johannes Cameron, *Myrothecium Evangelicum* (Geneva, 1632; UTSL), pp. 92–93: "for κατὰ certainly does not mean properly *because of,* but *according to* (secundum), *in accordance with* (iuxta) . . . We have therefore the intention of the Pharisees; they asked whether for any cause, whatever it might be, just as it is given, it might be lawful to divorce." John Cameron (*ca.* 1579–1625) was a Scots theologian who studied and taught at various Scottish and French universities.

[38] The Greek is κατὰ πᾶσαν αἰτίαν. Tyndale, Geneva, and Douay all agree with the Authorized Version in translating κατά "for." Milton's point is apparently that κατά with the accusative is usually translated "according to" or "concerning." See Cameron's remark in note 37.

the sudden heate, except it be for adultery. If these qualifications may be admitted, as partly we offer them, partly are offer'd them by some of their own opinion, and that where nothing is repugnant why they should not bee admitted, nothing can wrest them from us, the severe sentence of our Saviour will straight unbend the seeming frowne into that gentlenesse and compassion which was so abundant in all his actions, his office and his doctrine, from all which otherwise it stands off at no meane distance.

Vers. 4. *And he answered and said unto them, have ye not read that he which made them at the beginning, made them Male and Female?*

Vers. 5. *And said, for this cause shall a man leave Father and Mother, and shall cleave to his wife, and they twaine shall be one flesh?*

Vers. 6. *Wherefore they are no more twaine but one flesh, what therefore God hath joyned together, let no man* [39] *put asunder.*

[4. and 5. *Made them Male and Female, And said for this cause, &c.*] We see it here undeniably, that the law which our Saviour cites to prove that divorce was forbidd'n, is not an absolute and tyrannicall command without reason, as now adaies wee make it little better, but is grounded [45] upon some rationall cause not difficult to be apprehended, being in a matter which equally concernes the meanest and the plainest sort of persons in a houshold life. Our next way then will be to inquire if there bee not more reasons then one, and if there be, whether this be the best and cheifest. That we shall finde by turning to the first institution, to which Christ referrs our owne reading; He himselfe having to deale with treacherous assailants, useth brevity, and lighting on the first place in *Genesis* that mentions any thing tending to Marriage in the first chapter, joynes it immediately to the 24. verse of the 2 chapter, omitting all the prime words between, which create the institution, and containe the noblest and purest ends of Matrimony, without which attain'd, that conjunction hath nothing in it above what is common to us with beasts. So likewise beneath in this very chapter, to the young man who came not tempting him, but to learne of him,

---

[39] Authorized Version: "let not man."

asking him which commandments hee should keepe, he neither repeates the first table, nor all the second, nor that in order which
he repeates. If heere then being tempted, hee desire to bee the
shorter, and the darker in his conference, and omitt to cite that from
the second of *Genesis,* which all Divines confesse is a commentary
to what he cites out of the first, the *making them Male and Female*;
what are we to doe, but to search the institution our selves; and
we shall finde there his owne authority giving other manner of reasons why such firme union is to bee in matrimony, without which
reasons their being male and female can be no cause of joyning them
unseparably: for if it be, then no Adultery can sever. Therefore the
prohibition of divorce depends not upon this reason heere exprest
to the Pharises, but upon the plainer & more eminent causes omitted
heere and referr'd to the institution; which causes not being found
in a particular and casuall Matrimony, this sensitive and materious
cause alone can no more hinder a divorce against those higher and
more human reasons urging it, then it can alone without them to
warrant a copulation, but leaves it arbitrary to those who in their
chance of marriage finde not why divorce is forbidd them, but why
it is permitted them; and finde both here and in *Genesis,* that the
forbidding is not absolute, but according to the reasons there taught
us, not here. And that our Saviour taught them no better, but uses
the most vulgar, most animal and corporal argument, to convince
them, is first to shew us, that as through their licentious divorces
they made no more of mariage then as if to marry, were no more
then to be male and female, so hee goes no higher in his confutation; deeming them unworthy to be talkt with in a [46] higher
straine, but to bee ty'd in marriage by the meere material cause
thereof, since their owne licence testify'd that nothing matrimonial
was in their thought but to be male and female. Next it might be
don to discover the brute ignorance of these carnall Doctors, who
taking on them to dispute of marriage and divorce, were put to
silence with such a slender opposition as this, and outed from their
hold with scarce one quarter of an argument. That we may beleeve
this, his entertainment of the young man soon after may perswade
us. Whom, though he came to preach eternall life by faith only, he
dismisses with a salvation taught him by workes only. On which
place *Paraeus* notes, *That this man was to be convinc't by a false
perswasion; and that Christ is wont otherwise to answer hypocrites,*

otherwise those that are docible.[40] Much rather then may we thinke that in handling these tempters, he forgot not so to frame his prudent ambiguities and concealements, as was to the troubling of those peremtory disputants most wholsome. When therefore we would know what right there may be, in ill accidents, to divorce, wee must repaire thither where God professes to teach his servants by the prime institution, and not where we see him intending to dazle sophisters: Wee must not reade *hee made them Male and Female,* & not understand he made them more intendedly *a meet helpe* to remove the evill of being *alone.* We must take both these together, and then we may inferre compleatly as from the whole cause why a man shall cleave to his wife, and they twaine shall be one flesh: but if the full and cheife cause why we may not divorce, be wanting heer, this place may skirmish with the rabbies while it will, but to the true christian it prohibits nothing beyond the full reason of its own prohibiting, which is best knowne by the institution.

Vers. 6. [*Wherefore they are no more twaine, but one flesh.*] This is true in the generall right of marriage, but not in the chance medley of every particular match. For if they who were once undoubtedly one flesh, yet become twain by adultery, then sure they who were never one flesh rightly, never helps meete for each other according to the plain prescript of God, may with lesse adoe then a volume be concluded still twaine. And so long as we account a Magistrate no Magistrate, if there be but a flaw in his election, why should we not much rather count a Matrimony no Matrimony, if it cannot be in any reasonable manner according to the words of Gods institution.

[*What therefore God hath joyned, let no man put asunder.*] But heare the christian prudence lies to consider what God hath joyn'd; shall wee say [47] that God hath joyn'd error, fraud, unfitnesse, wrath, contention, perpetuall lonelinesse, perpetuall discord; what ever lust, or wine, or witchery, threate, or inticement, avarice or ambition hath joyn'd together, faithfull with unfaithfull, christian with antichristian, hate with hate, or hate with love, shall we say this is Gods joyning?

[40] *In S. Matthaei Evangelium Commentarius* (Geneva, 1641), p. 749. Paraeus is attacking the use of this passage by Maldonatus, Bellarmine, and other Catholic commentators to support salvation by works and the achievement of a more perfect life by monastic vows.

[*Let not man put asunder.*] That is to say, what God hath joyn'd;
for if it be, as how oft we see it may be, not of Gods joyning, and
his law tells us he joynes not unmachable things but hates to joyne
them, as an abominable confusion, then the divine law of *Moses*
puts them asunder, his owne divine will in the institution puts them
asunder, as oft as the reasons be not extant, for which only God
ordain'd their joyning. Man only puts asunder when his inordinate
desires, his passion, his violence, his injury makes the breach: not
when the utter want of that which lawfully was the end of his joyning, when wrongs and extremities, and unsupportable greevances
compell him to disjoyne: when such as *Herod* & the pharises divorce
beside law, or against law, then only man separates, and to such
only this prohibition belongs. In a word, if it be unlawful for man
to put asunder that which God hath joyn'd, let man take heede it
be not detestable to joyne that by compulsion which God hath put
assunder.

Vers. 7. *They say unto him, why did Moses then command to
give a writing of divorcement, and to put her away?*
Vers. 8. *He saith unto them, Moses because of the hardnesse of
your hearts suffered you to put away your wives, but from the beginning it was not so.*

[*Moses because of the hardnesse of your hearts suffered you.*]
Hence the divinity now current argues that this judiciall *Moses* [41]
is abolisht. But suppose it were so, though it hath bin prov'd otherwise, the firmenesse of such right to divorce as here pleads, is fetcht
from the prime institution, does not stand or fall with the judiciall
Jew, but is as morall as what is moralest. Yet as I have shewn positively that this law cannot bee abrogated, both by the words of our
Saviour pronouncing the contrary, and by that unabolishable equity
which it convaies to us, so I shall now bring to view those appearances of strength which are levied from this text to maintaine the
most grosse and massy paradox that ever did violence to reason
and religion, bred onely under the shadow of these words, to all other

[41] Judiciall *Moses:* the judicial law of Moses, *i.e.*, the secular as opposed to
the moral legislation. It was often held that the ceremonial and judicial laws
of Moses were abrogated in the New Testament, but not the moral. See *Christian Doctrine*, I, xxvii.

piety or philosophy strange and insolent, that God by act of law
[48] drew out a line of adultery almost two thousand yeares long:
although to detect the prodigy of this surmise, the former booke [42]
set forth on this argument hath already beene copious. I shall not
repeate much though I might borrow of mine own, but shall endeavour to adde something either yet untoucht, or not largely anough
explain'd. First it shal be manifest that the common exposition cannot possibly consist with christian doctrine: next a truer meaning
of this our Saviours reply shall be left in the roome. The receiv'd
exposition is, that God though not approving did enact a law to
permit adultery by divorcement simply unlawfull. And this conceit
they feede with fond supposals that have not the least footing in
Scripture. As that the Jews learnt this custome of divorce in *Egypt*,
and therefore God would not unteach it them till Christ came, but let
it stick as a notorious botch of deformity in the midst of his most
perfect and severe law. And yet he saith, *Levit.* the 18th *after the
doings of Egypt ye shall not do.*[43] Another while they invent a
slander (as what thing more bold then teaching Ignorance when he
shifts to hide his nakednes) that the Jews were naturally to their
wives the cruellest men in the world; would poison, braine, and doe
I know not what, if they might not divorce.[44] Certain, if it were a
fault heavily punisht, to bring an evill report upon the land which
God gave, what is it to raise a groundles calumny against the people

---

[42] See *Doctrine and Discipline,* above, pp. 285–326.

[43] Authorized Version: "After the doings of the land of Egypt, wherein ye
dwelt, shall ye not do."

[44] Paraeus, *In S. Matthaei Evangelium Commentarius* (Geneva, 1641), p. 190,
on Matthew 5:32. The Mosaic law of divorce, says Paraeus, is not of the substance of the moral law, which was not changed by Christ, but is rather an indulgence of the civil law according to the hardness of heart of the Jews "who,
become accustomed to gentile manners in Egypt, had used to make divorce. Indeed, as soon as someone began to hate his wife, he dismissed her from his house
and took another into it, in the manner of the Egyptians." On Matthew 19:8,
p. 734, Paraeus gives the cruelty of the Jews to their wives as a reason for the
permission to divorce: "for there was danger lest husbands of a hard heart, that
is, petulant, easily moved, inhuman, and cruel, should treat their hated wives
tyrannically, even kill them, if indeed they were forced to live with them permanently. To prevent which evil and protect the reputations and lives of women
[Moses] permitted divorce to such husbands." Cornelius à Lapide, *Commentaria
in Pentateuchum* (Antwerp, 1630; BML), p. 1000, on Deuteronomy 24, has the
same sort of comment: "I respond that this hardness was the cause why God
conceded putting away, lest certainly the Jews should kill their wives whom they
could not put away."

which God made choise of? But that this bold interpretament, how commonly so ever sided with, cannot stand a minute with any competent reverence to God or his law, or his people, nor with any other maxim of religion, or good manners, might bee prov'd through all the heads and *Topics* of argumentation: but I shall willingly bee as concise as possible. First the law, not onely the moral, but the judicial given by *Moses* is just and pure; for such is God who gave it. *Harken O Israel*, saith *Moses, Deut.* 4. *unto the statutes and* [45] *the judgements which I teach you,* [46] *to doe them, that ye may live, &c. ye shall not adde unto the word which I command you, neither shall ye diminish ought from it, that ye may keepe the commandements of the Lord your God which I command you.* And onward in the chapter, *Behold I have taught you statutes and judgements, even as the Lord my God commanded me. Keepe therefore and doe them, for this is your wisedome and your understanding. For what nation hath God so nigh unto them, and what nation hath statutes and judgements so righteous as all this law which I set before ye this day.* [47] Is it imaginable there should bee among these a law which God allow'd not, a law giving permissions laxative to unmarry a wife and marry a lust, a law to suffer a kind of *tribunall* adultery? Many [49] other scriptures might be brought to assert the purity of this judicial law, and many I have alleg'd before; this law therefore is pure and just. But if it permit, if it teach, if it defend that which is both unjust and impure, as by the common doctrine it doth, what thinke we? The three generall doctrines of *Justinians* law, are *To live in honesty, To hurt no man, To give every one his due.* [48] Shall the *Roman civil* law observe these three things, as the onely end of law, and shall a statute be found in the civil law of God, enacted simply and totally against all these three precepts of nature and morality?

Secondly, the gifts of God are all perfet, and certainly the law is of all his other gifts one of the perfetest. But if it give that outwardly which it takes away really, & give that seemingly, which, if a man take it, wraps him into sinne and damns him, what gift of an enemy can be more dangerous and destroying then this.

---

[45] Milton omits "unto."   [46] Milton omits "for."   [47] *Cf.* above, p. 619.
[48] *Juris Civilis, Institutes,* book I, title i (Geneva, 1594–95, col. 23; Scott, II, 5); also *Pandects,* book I, title i, paragraph 10 (Geneva, 1594–95, col. 130; Scott, II, 211), where the same statement is quoted from Ulpian.

Thirdly, *Moses* every where commends his lawes, preferrs them before all of other nations, and warrants them to be the way of life and safety to all that walke therein, *Levit.* 18.[49] But if they containe statutes which God approves not, and traine men unweeting to committ injustice and adultery, under the shelter of law, if those things bee sin, and death sins wages, what is this law but the snare of death?

Fourthly, the statutes and judgements of the Lord, which without exception are often told us to be such, as doing wee may live by them, are doubtles to be counted the rule of knowledge and of conscience. *For I had not known lust,* saith the Apostle, *but by the law.*[50] But if the law come downe from the state of her incorruptible majesty to grant lust his boon, palpably it darkns and confounds both knowledge and conscience; it goes against the common office of all goodnes and freindlinesse, which is at lest to counsel and admonish; it subverts the rules of all sober education; and is it selfe a most negligent debaushing tutor.

Fiftly, if the law permit a thing unlawfull, it permitts that which else where it hath forbid; so that hereby it contradicts it selfe, and transgresses it selfe. But if the law become a transgressor, it stands guilty to it selfe, and how then shall it save another; it makes a confederacy with sin, how then can it justly condemne a sinner? and thus reducing it selfe to the state of neither saving nor condemning, it will not faile to expire solemnely ridiculous.

Sixtly, the Prophets in Scripture declare severely against the decreeing of that which is unjust, *Psal.* 94. 20. *Isaiah* the 10th. But it was done, they [50] say, for hardnesse of heart; To which objection the Apostles rule, *not to doe evill that good may come thereby,*[51] gives an invincible repuls; and here especially, where it cannot be shewn how any good came by doing this evil, how rather more evil did not hereon abound; for the giving way to hardnesse of heart hard'ns the more, and adds more to the number. God to an evil and adulterous generation would not *grant a signe;* [52] much lesse would he for their hardnesse of heart pollute his law with an adulter-

[49] V. 5: "Ye shall therefore keep my statutes, and my judgments: which if a man do, he shall live in them."
[50] Romans 7:7: "Nay, I had not known sin, but by the law: for I had not known lust, except the law had said, Thou shalt not covet."
[51] Romans 3:8.　　[52] Matthew 12:39; Mark 8:12; Luke 11:29.

ous permission. Yea but to permitt evil is not to doe evil. Yes, it is in a most eminent manner to doe evil: where else are all our grave and faithfull sayings, that he whose office is to forbid and forbids not, bids, exhorts, encourages. Why hath God denounc't his anger against parents, maisters, freinds, magistrates neglectfull of forbidding what they ought, if law the common father, maister, friend, and perpetuall magistrate shall not onely not forbidd, but enact, exhibit, and uphold with countnance and protection a deede every way dishonest, what ever the pretence be. If it were of those inward vices, which the law cannot by outward constraint remedy, but leaves to conscience and perswasion, it had bin guiltlesse in being silent: but to write a decree of that which can be no way lawfull, and might with ease be hinder'd, makes law by the doome of law it selfe accessory in the highest degree.

Seventhly, it makes God the direct author of sin. For although he bee not made the authour of what he silently permitts in his providence, yet in his law, the image of his will, when in plaine expression he constitutes and ordaines a fact utterly unlawfull, what wants hee to authorize it, and what wants that to be the author?

Eightly, to establish by law a thing wholly unlawfull and dishonest, is an affirmation was never heard of before in any law, reason, philosophy, or religion, till it was rais'd by inconsiderat glossists, from the mistake of this text. And though the Civilians have bin contented to chew this opinion, after the canon had subdu'd them, yet they never could bring example or authority either from divine writt, or human learning, or human practice in any nation, or well-form'd republick, but only from the customary abuse of this text. Usually they allege the Epistle of *Cicero* to *Atticus;* wherein *Cato* is blam'd for giving sentence to the scumme of *Romulus,* as if he were in *Plato's* common wealth. *Cato* would have call'd some great one into judgement for bribery, *Cicero* as the time stood, advis'd against it. *Cato,* not to endammage the public treasury, would not grant to the Roman Knights, that the *Asian* taxes might bee farm'd them at a [51] lesse rate. *Cicero* wisht it granted.[53]

---

[53] Cicero, *Letters to Atticus*, II, 1, tr. E. O. Winstedt (3 vols., New York and London, 1912–18), I, 109: "For our friend Cato is not more to you than to me: but still with the best of intentions and unimpeachable honesty at times he does harm to the country: for the opinions that he delivers would be more in place in Plato's *Republic* than among the dregs of humanity collected by Romulus. That

Nothing in all this will bee like the establishing of a law to sinne: here are no lawes made, here onely the execution of law is crav'd might be suspended: between which and our question is a broad difference. And what if human law givers have confest that they could not frame their lawes to that perfection which they desir'd, we heare of no such confession from *Moses* concerning the lawes of God, but rather all praise and high testimony of perfection given them. And although mans nature cannot beare exactest lawes, yet still within the confines of good it may and must; so long as lesse good is far anough from altogether evil. As for what they instance of usury,[54] let them first prove usury to be wholly unlawfull, as the law allowes it; which learned men as numerous on the other side will deny them. Or if it be altogether unlawfull, why is it tolerated more then divorce? he who said divorse not, said also *lend hoping for nothing againe,* Luk. 6. 35. But then they put in, that trade could not stand. And so to serve the commodity of insatiable trading, usury shall be permitted, but divorce, the onely meanes oft times to right the innocent, & outrageously wrong'd, shall be utterly forbid. This is egregious doctrine, and for which one day charity will much thanke them. *Beza* [55] not finding how to salve this perplexity, and *Cameron* since him, would secure us; although the latter confesses that to *permit a wicked thing by law, is a wickednesse from which God abhorrs; yet to limit sin, and prescribe it a certaine measure, is good.*[56] First this evasion wil not helpe heere; for this

a man who accepts a bribe for the verdict he returns at a trial should be put on trial himself is as fair a principle as one could wish. Cato voted for it and won the House's assent. Result, a war of the knights with the Senate, but not with me. I was against it. That the tax-collectors should repudiate their bargain was a most shameless proceeding. But we ought to have put up with the loss in order to keep their good-will. Cato resisted and carried the day. Result, though we've had a consul in prison, and frequent riots, not a breath of encouragement from one of those, who in my own consulship and that of my successors used to rally round us to defend the country."

[54] Milton's point is that some thought usury unlawful but to be permitted. For a discussion of the changing attitude towards usury in the sixteenth century see R. H. Tawney's introduction to his edition of Thomas Wilson, *A Discourse upon Usury* (New York, 1925), esp. pp. 106–108. Wilson uses the argument that usury must be suffered to avoid worse evils, pp. 239–40. William Perkins, *The Golden Chain,* chapter 27, in *Works* (3 vols., 1612; UCL), I, 63–64, allows usury within certain limitations. (References suggested by Jerald C. Brauer, Professor of Church History, University of Chicago.)

[55] *Tractatio de Repudiis et Divortiis* (Geneva, 1596; BML), p. 168.

[56] *Myrothecium Evangelicum* (Geneva, 1632), p. 99.

law bounded no man; he might put away whatever found not favour in his eyes. And how could it forbid to divorce, whom it could not forbidd to dislike, or command to love. If these be the limits of law to restraine sinne, who so lame a sinner but may hoppe over them more easily then over those *Romulean* circumscriptions,[57] not as *Remus* did with hard succes, but with all indemnity. Such a limiting as this were not worth the mischeif that accompanies it. This law therefore not bounding the supposed sinne, by permitting enlarges it, gives it enfranchisement. And never greater confusion, then when law and sin move their land markes, mixe their territories, and correspond, have intercourse and traffic together. When law contracts a kindred and hospitality with transgression, becomes the godfather of sinne and names it Lawfull; when sin revels and gossips within the arcenal of law, plaies, and dandles the artillery of justice that should be bent against her, this is a faire limitation indeede. Besides it is an absurdity to say that law can measure sin, or moderate sin; sin is not a predicament [58] to be measur'd [52] and modify'd, but is alwaies an excesse. The least sinne that is, exceeds the measure of the largest law that can bee good; and is as boundlesse as that vacuity beyond the world. If once it square to the measure of Law, it ceases to be an excesse, and consequently ceases to be a sinne; or else law conforming it selfe to the obliquity of sin, betraies it selfe to be not strait, but crooked, and so immediatly no law. And the improper conceit of moderating sin by law will appeare, if wee can imagin any lawgiver so senselesse as to decree that so farre a man may steale, and thus farre bee drunk, that moderately he may cozen, and moderatly committ adultery. To the same extent it would be as pithily absurd to publish that a man may moderately divorce, if to doe that be intirely naught. But to end this moot, the law of *Moses* is manifest to fixe no limit therein at all, or such at lest as impeaches the fraudulent abuser no more then if it were not set; only requires the dismissive writing without other caution, leaves that to the inner man, and the barre of conscience. But it stopt other sins. This is as vaine as the rest, and dangerously uncertain: the contrary to be fear'd rather, that one sin admitted courteously by law, open'd the gate to another. However

[57] *Romulean* circumscriptions: walls, like those which Romulus built about Rome. Remus jumped over the wall and Romulus killed him.
[58] Predicament: state of being.

evil must not be don for good. And it were a fall to be lamented, an indignity unspeakable, if law should becom tributary to sin her slave, and forc't to yeild up into his hands her awfull minister Punishment, should buy out her peace with sinne for sinne, paying as it were her so many *Philistian* foreskins [59] to the proud demand of Transgression. But suppose it any way possible to limit sinne, to put a girdle about that *Chaos,* suppose it also good; yet if to permitt sin by Law bee an abomination in the eyes of God, as *Cameron* acknowledges, the evil of permitting will eate out the good of limiting.[60] For though sin be not limited, there can but evil come out of evil; but if it be permitted & decreed lawfull by divine law, of force then sin must proceed from the infinit Good, which is a dreadfull thought. But if the restraining of sinne by this permission beeing good, as this author testifies, be more good then the permission of more sin by the restraint of divorce, and that God waighing both these like two ingots in the perfet scales of his justice and providence found them so, and others coming without authority from God, shall change this counterpoise, and judge it better to let sin multiply by setting a judicial restraint upon divorce, which Christ never set, then to limit sin by this permission, as God himselfe thought best to permitt it, it will behoove them to consult betimes whether these their ballances be not fals and abominable; and this their limiting that which God loosen'd, and their loosning the sinnes that he limited, which they [53] confesse was good to doe: and were it possible to doe by law, doubtlesse it would be most morally good; and they so beleeving, as we heare they doe, and yet abolishing a law so good and moral, the limiter of sin, what are they else but contrary to themselves? for they can never bring us to that time wherein it will not be good to limit sinne, and they can never limit it better then so as God prescrib'd in his law.

Others conceave it a more defensible retirement to say this permission to divorce sinfully for hardnesse of heart was a dispensation. But surely they either know not, or attend not what a dispensation meanes. A dispensation is for no long time, is particular to som persons rather then generall to a whole people; alwaies hath charity the end, is granted to necessities and infirmities, not to obstinat lust. This permission is another creature, hath all those evils and absurdities following the name of a dispensation, as when it was

[59] I Samuel 18:25-27.   [60] See above, p. 656.

nam'd a law; and is the very *antarctic pole* against charity, nothing more advers, ensnaring and ruining those that trust in it, or use it; so leud and criminous as never durst enter into the head of any Politician, Jew, or Proselyte, till they became the apt Schollers of this canonistic exposition. Ought in it, that can allude in the lest manner to charity, or goodnes, belongs with more full right to the christian under grace and liberty, then to the Jew under law and bondage. To Jewish ignorance it could not be dispenc't without a horrid imputation laid upon the law, to dispence fouly, in stead of teaching fairly; like that dispensation that first polluted Christendom with Idolatry, permitting to lay men images in stead of bookes and preaching. Sloth or malice in the law would they have this calld? But what ignorance can be pretended for the Jewes, who had all the same precepts about mariage, that we now: for Christ referrs all to the institution. It was as reasonable for them to know then as for us now, and concern'd them alike: for wherein hath the gospel alter'd the nature of matrimony? All these considerations, or many of them have bin furder amplify'd in *the doctrine of divorce.*[61] And what *Rivetus* [62] and *Paraeus* [63] hath objected, or giv'n over as past cure hath bin there discusst. Whereby it may be plain anough to men of eyes, that the vulgar exposition of a permittance by law to an entire sin, what ever the colour may be, is an opinion both ungodly, unpolitic, unvertuous, and void of all honesty & civil sense. It appertaines therefore to every zealous Christian both for the honour of Gods law, & the vindication of our Saviours words, that such an irreligious depravement no longer may be sooth'd and flatter'd through custome, but with all diligence and speed solidly refuted,

[61] *Doctrine and Discipline,* above, pp. 285–326.

[62] Andraeus Rivetus, *Tractatus Tertius,* quaestio xvi, "De divortio ob adulterium," *Operum Theologicorum* (3 vols., Rotterdam, 1651–60; HCL), III, 333–36. Andraeus Rivetus (André Rivet), 1572–1651, was a Huguenot theologian who taught at Leyden and Breda.

[63] *In S. Matthaei Evangelium Commentarius* (Geneva, 1641), pp. 736–38. Asking whether there are any other causes of divorce besides fornication, Paraeus notes that Paul added desertion by the infidel partner and that the civil law allowed other causes. Commenting on the question of the disciples whether, if divorce was allowed only for fornication, it were not better not to marry, Paraeus paraphrases the question: what shall be done by one who has a drunken, wrathful, ill-mannered, lustful, gluttonous, inconstant, abusive wife? Would it not be better to fight concupiscence alone in a celibate life than to sustain such injuries? But he can find no remedy. To refuse to marry would violate divine precept, for if none married there could be no human race, no church.

and in the room a better explanation giv'n; which is now our next endeavour. [54]

[*Moses suffer'd you to put away*, &c.] Not commanded you, saies the common observer, and therefore car'd not how soon it were abolisht, being but suffer'd; heerin declaring his annotation to be slight & nothing law prudent. For in this place *commanded* and *suffer'd* are interchangeably us'd in the same sense both by our Saviour and the Pharises. Our Saviour who heer saith, *Moses suffer'd you*, in the 10th of *Marke* saith, *Moses wrote you this command*.[64] And the Pharisees who heer say, *Moses commanded*, and would mainly have it a command, in that place of *Marke* say *Moses suffer'd*, which had made against them in their owne mouthes, if the word of *suffering* had weakn'd the command. So that *suffer'd* and *commanded* is heer taken for the same thing on both sides of the controversy: as *Cameron*[65] also and others on this place acknowledge. And Lawyers know that all the precepts of law are devided into obligatorie and permissive, containing either what we must doe, or what wee may doe; and of this latter sort are as many precepts, as of the former, and all as lawfull. Tutelage, an ordainment then which nothing more just, being for the defence of Orfanes, the *Institutes* of *Justinian* say, *is given and permitted by the civil law:* and *to parents it is permitted to choose and appoint by will the guardians of their children*.[66] What more equall, and yet the civil law calls this *permission*. So likewise to *manumise*, to adopt, to make a will, and to be made an heire is call'd *permission* by law. Marriage it selfe, and this which is already granted, to divorce for adultery, obliges no man, is but a permission by law, is but suffer'd. By this we may see how weakly it hath bin thought that all divorce is utterly unlawfull, because the law is said to suffer it: whenas to *suffer* is but the legall phrase denoting what by law a man may doe or not doe.

[*Because of the hardnesse of your hearts*.] Hence they argue that

---

[64] V. 5. Authorized Version: "precept."

[65] *Myrothecium Evangelicum* (Geneva, 1632), p. 98: "For the Hebrew word צוה means both *command* and *permit*, since it fits both of them, as we thus may see, by analogy."

[66] *Juris Civilis, Institutes*, book I, title xiii, paragraphs 1, 3 (Geneva, 1594–95, col. 32; Scott, II, 20): "Guardianship, as Servius defines it, is the right and authority over a free person granted and allowed by the Civil Law for the protection of one who, on account of his age, cannot protect himself. . . . Parents, therefore, are allowed to appoint guardians by will for children not arrived at puberty and who are under their control."

therefore he allowd it not; and therefore it must be abolisht. But
the contrary to this will sooner follow, that because he suffer'd it for
a cause, therefore in relation to that cause he allow'd it. Next, if he
in his wisedome, and in the midst of his severity allow'd it for hardnesse of heart, it can be nothing better then arrogance and presumption to take stricter courses against hardnes of heart then God
ever set an example, and that under the Gospel which warrants them
to no judicial act of compulsion in this matter, much lesse to be more
severe against hardnes of extremity, then God thought good to bee
against hardnes of heart. He suffer'd it, rather then worse inconveniences; these men wiser as they make themselves, will suffer the
worst and hainousest inconveniences to follow, rather then [55] they
will suffer what God suffer'd. Although they can know when they
please, that Christ spake only to the conscience, did not judge on
the civil bench, but alwaies disavow'd it. What can be more contrary to the waies of God then these their doings? If they bee such
enemies to hardnes of heart, although this groundlesse rigor proclaims it to be in themselves, they may yet learne, or consider that
hardnesse of heart hath a twofould acception in the Gospel. One,
when it is in a good man taken for infirmity, and imperfection, which
was in all the Apostles, whose weaknesse only, not utter want of
beleef is call'd hardnes of heart, *Marke* 16. partly for this hardnesse
of heart, the imperfection and decay of man from original righteousnesse, it was that God suffer'd not divorce onely, but all that which
by Civilians is term'd the *secondary law of nature and of nations.*[67]
He suffer'd his owne people to wast and spoyle and slay by warre,
to lead captives, to be som maisters, som servants, som to be
princes, others to be subjects, hee suffer'd propriety to divide all
things by severall possession, trade and commerce, not without
usury; in his common wealth some to bee undeservedly rich, others
to bee undeservingly poore. All which till hardnesse of heart came
in, was most unjust; whenas prime Nature made us all equall, made
us equall coheirs by common right and dominion over all creatures.
In the same manner, and for the same cause hee suffer'd divorce
as well as mariage, our imperfet and degenerat condition of necessity requiring this law among the rest, as a remedy against intolerable wrong and servitude above the patience of man to beare. Nor
was it giv'n only because our infirmity, or if it must be so call'd,

[67] See introduction, above, pp. 130–33.

hardnesse of heart could not endure all things, but because the hardnes of anothers heart might not inflict all things upon an innocent person, whom far other ends brought into a league of love and not of bondage and indignity. If therefore we abolish divorce as only suffer'd for hardnes of heart, we may as well abolish the whole law of nations, as only sufferd for the same cause; it being shown us by Saint *Paul* I *Cor.* 6. that the very seeking of a mans right by law, and at the hands of a worldly magistrat, is not without the hardnesse of our hearts. *For why doe ye not rather take wrong,* saith he, *why suffer ye not rather your selves to be defrauded?* [68] If nothing now must be suffer'd for hardnes of heart, I say the very prosecution of our right by way of civil justice can no more bee suffer'd among Christians, for the hardnes of heart wherwith most men persue it. And that would next remove all our judiciall lawes, and this restraint of divorce also in the number; which would more then halfe [56] end the controversy. But if it be plaine that the whole juridical law and civil power is only suffer'd under the Gospel, for the hardnes of our hearts, then wherefore should not that which *Moses* suffer'd, be suffer'd still by the same reason?

In a second signification hardnes of heart is tak'n for a stubborne resolution to doe evil. And that God ever makes any law purposely to such, I deny; for he voutsafes not to enter cov'nant with them, but as they fortune to be mixt with good men, and passe undiscover'd; much lesse that he should decree an unlawfull thing only to serve their licentiousnes. But that God *suffers* this reprobate hardnes of heart I affirm, not only in this law of divorce, but throughout all his best and purest commandements. He commands all to worship in singlenes of heart according to all his Ordinances; and yet suffers the wicked man to performe all the rites of religion hypocritically and in the hardnes of his heart. He gives us generall statutes & privileges in all civil matters, just & good of themselves, yet suffers unworthiest men, to use them & by them to prosecute their own right, or any colour of right, though for the most part maliciously, covetously, rigorously, revengefully. He allow'd by law the discreet father and husband to forbidd, if he thought fit, the religious vows of his wife or daughter: *Num.* 30. and in the same law suffer'd the hard heartednes of impious and covetous fathers or

[68] Authorized Version: "Why do ye not rather suffer yourselves to be defrauded?"

husbands abusing this law to forbidd their wives or daughters in their offrings and devotions of greatest zeal. If then God suffer hardnes of heart equally in the best laws as in this of divorce, there can be no reason that for this cause this law should be abolisht. But other lawes, they object, may be well us'd, this never. How often shall I answer both from the institution of mariage, and from other general rules in Scripture, that this law of divorce hath many wise and charitable ends besides the being suffer'd for hardnes of heart; which is indeed no end, but an accident happning through the whole law; which gives to good men right, and to bad men who abuse right under false pretences, gives only sufferance. Now although Christ express no other reasons here, but only what was suffer'd, it nothing followes that this law had no other reason to be permitted but for hardnes of heart. The Scripture seldome, or never in one place sets down all the reasons of what it grants or commands, especially when it talks to enemies and tempters. St. *Paul* permitting mariage, I *Cor*. 7. seems to permit even that also for hardnes of heart only, lest we should run into fornication; [69] yet no intelligent man thence concludes mariage allow'd in the Gospel [57] only to avoid an evill, because no other end is there exprest. Thus *Moses* of necessity suffer'd many to put away their wives for hardnesse of heart; but enacted the law of divorce doubtles for other good causes, not for this only sufferance. He permitted not divorce by law as an evil, for that was impossible to divine law, but permitted by accident the evil of them who divorc't against the lawes intention undiscoverably. This also may be thought not improbably, that Christ stirr'd up in his spirit against these tempting Pharises, answer'd them in a certain forme of indignation usual among good authors; wherby the question, or the truth is not directly answer'd, but som thing which is fitter for them, who aske, to heare. So in the ecclesiastical stories one demanding how God imploy'd himself before the world was made, had answer; that he was making hel for curious questioners.[70] Another (and *Libanius* the *Sophist* as I remember) asking

[69] V. 2: "Nevertheless, to avoid fornication, let every man have his own wife, and let every woman have her own husband."

[70] Augustine, *Confessions*, XI, 12, tr. William Watts (2 vols., London and New York, 1912), II, 233: "See, I now return answer to the demand; What did God do before he made heaven and earth? But I will not answer so as one was said to have done merrily, to break the violence of the question: God was a preparing hell, saith he, for those that should pry into such profound mysteries."

in derision som Christian, what the Carpenter, meaning our Saviour, was doing, now that *Julian* so prevail'd, had it return'd him, that the Carpenter was making a coffin for the Apostat.[71] So Christ being demanded maliciously why *Moses* made the law of divorce, answers them in a vehement *scheme*,[72] not telling them the cause why he made it, but what was fittest to be told them, that *for the hardnes of their hearts* he suffer'd them to abuse it. And all beit *Mark* say not he suffer'd you, but *to you he wrote this precept; Mark* may be warrantably expounded by *Mathew* the larger. And whether he suffer'd, or gave precept, being all one as was heard, it changes not the *trope* of indignation, fittest account for such askers. Next for the hardnes of *your hearts to you he wrote this precept,* inferrs not therfore for this cause only he wrote it, as was parallell'd by other Scriptures. Lastly, It may be worth the observing, that Christ speaking to the Pharises does not say in general that for hardnes of heart he gave this precept, but *you he suffer'd,* & *to you he gave this precept for your* hardnes of heart. It cannot be easily thought that Christ heer included all the children of Israel under the person of these tempting Pharises but that he conceals wherefore he gave the better sort of them this law, and expresses by saying emphatically *To you* how he gave it to the worser, such as the Pharises best represented, that is to say for the hardnes of your hearts: as indeed to wicked men and hardn'd hearts he gives the whole law and the Gospel also, to hard'n them the more. Thus many waies it may orthodoxally be understood how God or *Moses* suffer'd such as the demanders were, to divorce for hardnes of heart. Whereas the vulgar expositer beset with contradictions and absurdities round, and resolving at any peril to make an exposition of it, as [58] there is nothing more violent and boistrous then a reverend ignorance in fear to be convicted, rushes brutely and impetuously against all the

---

[71] Theodoret, *Ecclesiasticae Historiae,* III, xviii (Migne, *Graeca,* LXXXII, 1115), gives the story as follows: "For there was at Antioch a certain very good man, a teacher of boys, who was familiar with the principal learned man of that age, that is Labanius, a celebrated Sophist. The latter, since he was impious and expected a victory, now that Julian changed his mind, making fun of our teacher asked him what the son of the carpenter would do. But the former, filled with divine grace, predicted what was to come to pass. Sophist, he said, the creator of the best things, whom you in scorn have called the son of a carpenter, even now makes a coffin. Indeed after a few days the death of that furious one (Julian) was announced, and he was laid in a coffin."

[72] Scheme: rhetorical figure.

principles both of nature, piety, and moral goodnes; and in the fury
of his literal expounding overturns them all.

[*But from the beginning it was not so.*] Not how from the beginning doe they suppose, that men might not divorce at all, not
necessarily, not deliberatly except for adultery, but that som law,
like canon law presently attacht them both before and after the
flood, till stricter *Moses* came, and with law brought licence into
the world? that were a fancy indeed to smile at. Undoubtedly as to
point of judiciall law, divorce was more permissive from the beginning before *Moses* then under *Moses*. But from the beginning, that
is to say, by the institution in Paradice it was not intended that
matrimony should dissolve for every trivial cause as you Pharises
accustome. But that it was not thus suffer'd from the beginning ever
since the race of men corrupted, & laws were made, he who will
affirme, must have found out other antiquities then are yet known.
Besides we must consider now, what can be so as from the beginning, not only what should be so. In the beginning, had men continu'd perfet, it had bin just that all things should have remain'd, as
they began to *Adam & Eve*. But after that the sons of men grew
violent & injurious, it alter'd the lore of justice, and put the goverment of things into a new frame. While man and woman were both
perfet each to other, there needed no divorce; but when they both
degenerated to imperfection, & oft times grew to be an intolerable
evil each to other, then law more justly did permitt the alienating of
that evil which mistake made proper, then it did the appropriating
of that good which Nature at first made common. For if the absence
of outward good be not so bad as the presence of a close evil, & that
propriety, whether by cov'nant or possession, be but the attainment
of some outward good, it is more natural & righteous that the law
should sever us from an intimat evil, then appropriate any outward
good to us from the community of nature. The Gospel indeed tending ever to that which is perfetest, aim'd at the restorement of all
things, as they were in the beginning. And therefore all things were
in common to those primitive Christians in the Acts, which *Ananias
& Sapphira* dearly felt.[73] That custome also continu'd more or less
till the time of *Justin Martyr*, as may be read in his 2ᵈ *Apology*,[74]

[73] Acts 5:1–10.
[74] The passage to which Milton refers is probably *Apologia I* (formerly *II*)
Pro Christianis, 15 (Migne, *Graeca*, VI, 347–48): "So that after we have be-

which might be writt after that act of communion perhaps some 40. yeares above a hunder'd.[75] But who will be the man shall introduce this kind of common wealth, as christianity now goes? If then mariage must [59] be as in the beginning, the persons that marry must be such as then were, the institution must make good, in som tolerable sort, what it promises toeeither party. If not, it is but madnes to drag this one ordinance back to the beginning, and draw down all other to the present necessity, and condition farre from the beginning even to the tolerating of extortions and oppressions. Christ only told us that from the beginning it was not so; that is to say, not so as the Pharises manur'd[76] the busines; did not command us that it should be forcibly so again in all points, as at the beginning; or so at least in our intentions and desires, but so in execution, as reason, and present nature can bear. Although we are not to seek, that the institution it selfe from the first beginning was never but conditional, as all cov'nants are: because thus and thus, therefore so and so; if not thus, then not so. Then moreover was perfetest to fulfill each law in it selfe; now is perfetest in this estate of things, to ask of charity how much law may be fulfill'd: els the fulfilling, oft times is the greatest breaking. If any therefore demand, which is now most perfection, to ease an extremity by divorce, or to enrage and fester it by the greevous observance of a miserable wedloc, I am not destitute to say which is most perfection (although som who beleev they thinke favourably of divorce, esteem it only venial to infirmity). Him I hold more in the way to perfection who forgoes an unfit ungodly & discordant wedloc, to live according to peace & love, & Gods institution in a fitter chois, then he who debarrs himself the happy experience of all godly, which is peaceful conversation in his family, to live a contentious, and unchristian life not to be avoided, in temptations not to be liv'd in, only for the fals keeping of a most unreal nullity, a mariage that hath no affinity with

lieved in the Word we abandon those deeds, and follow only the understanding of God by his son . . . and we who formerly sought the ways of wealth and possession now even hold all we have in common and divide it with the needy." Justin Martyr (ca. 100–165) was a Christian apologist. See *Complete Prose*, I, 397.

[75] That act of communion: Pentecost. Milton means that Justin Martyr wrote about 140 years after Pentecost, or ca. 170. Modern chronology would put him a little earlier.

[76] Manur'd: handled (from *manoeuvre*).

Gods intention, a daring phantasm, a meer toy of terror awing weak senses, to the lamentable superstition of ruining themselves; the remedy wherof God in his law voutsafes us. Which not to dare use, he warranting, is not our perfection, is our infirmity, our little faith, our timorous and low conceit of charity: and in them who force us, it is their masking pride and vanity, to seem holier & more circumspect then God. So far is it that we need impute to him infirmity, who thus divorces: since the rule of perfection is not so much that which was don in the beginning, as that which now is nearest to the rule of charity. This is the greatest, the perfetest, the highest commandment.

V. 9. *And I say unto you, who so shall put away his wife, except it be for Fornication, and shall marry another, committeth adultery; and who so marrieth her which is put away, doth commit adultery.* [60]

[*And I say unto you.*] That this restrictive denouncement of Christ contradicts and refutes that permissive precept of *Moses,* common expositers themselves disclaime: and that it does not traverse from the closet of conscience to the courts of civil or canon law, with any Christian rightly commenc't requires not long evincing. If Christ then did not heer check permissive *Moses,* nor did reduce matrimony to the beginning more then all other things, as the reason of mans condition could beare, we would know precisely what it was which he did, and what the end was of his declaring thus austerely against divorce. For this is a confest oracle in law, that he who lookes not at the intention of a precept, the more superstitious he is of the letter,[77] the more he misinterprets. Was it to shame *Moses?* that had beene monstrous: or all those purest ages of Israel, to whom the permission was granted? that were as incredible. Or was it that he who came to abrogate the burden of law, not the equity, should put this yoke upon a blamelesse person, to league himselfe in chaines with a begirting mischeif, not to separat till death? hee who taught us that no man puts a peece of new

---

[77] Although the idea is, as Milton says, very familiar, it has not been possible to find it recorded as a legal maxim. It is easy to illustrate the idea from the writings of non-lawyers; *e.g.,* Luther: "Without love and natural justice you can never be in accord with the will of God, though you have devoured the Jurists and all their works. The more you ponder them, the more you will err" (*Von Weltliger Uberkeyt,* quoted by J. W. Allen, *A History of Political Thought in the Sixteenth Century* [London, 1928], p. 22).

cloth upon an old garment, nor new wine into old bottles, that he should sow this patch of strictnes upon the old apparel of our frailty, to make a rent more incurable, when as in all other amendments his doctrine still charges, that regard be had to the garment, and to the vessel, what it can endure; this were an irregular and single peece of rigor, not onely sounding disproportion to the whole Gospel, but outstretching the most rigorous nervs of law and rigor it selfe. No other end therefore can bee left imaginable of this excessive restraint, but to bridle those erroneous and licentious postillers [78] the Pharises; not by telling them what may bee done in necessity, but what censure they deserve who divorce abusively, which their Tetrarch had done. And as the offence was in one extreme, so the rebuke, to bring more efficaciously to a rectitude and mediocrity, stands not in the middle way of duty, but in the other extreme. Which art of powerfull reclaiming, wisest men have also taught in their ethical precepts and *gnomologies*; [79] resembling it, as when wee bend a crooked wand the contrary way; not that it should stand so bent, but that the overbending might reduce it to a straitnesse by its own reluctance. And as the Physician cures him who hath tak'n down poyson, not by the middling temper of nourishment, but by the other extreme of *antidote,* so Christ administers heer a sharp & corrosive sentence against a foul and putrid licence; not to eate into the flesh, but into the sore. And knowing that our divines through all their comments make [61] no scruple, where they please, to soften the high and vehement speeches of our Saviour, which they call *hyperbolies,* why in this one text should they be such crabbed *masorites* [80] of the Letter, as not to mollifie a transcendence of literal rigidity, which they confess to find often elsewhere in his manner of delivery, but must make their exposition

[78] Postillers: commentators. A "postil" (L. *postilla*) is a note or annotation. One of the most famous of medieval commentaries on the Bible is Nicholas de Lyra's *Postillae.*

[79] Gnomologies: collections of maxims and wise sayings, the most famous of which was the Distichs of Cato, studied in the Middle Ages and into the seventeenth century as a reading text in grammar school. *Mediocrity: OED* cites this passage in illustration of the quasi-technical use of the word with reference to the Aristotelian mean.

[80] *Mazorites:* Jewish scholars who fixed the text of the Hebrew Scriptures especially by the provision of vowel points, the determination of spelling, and the glossing of words of obscure meaning and etymology. Milton here uses the term pejoratively: strict literalists.

heer such an obdurat *Cyclops,* to have but one eye for this text, and that onely open to cruelty and enthralment, such as no divine, or human law before ever heard of. No, let the foppish canonist with his fardel of matrimonial cases goe and be vendible where men bee so unhappy as to cheap'n him; the words of Christ shall be asserted from such elementall notaries, and resolv'd by the now-only lawgiving mouth of charity; which may be done undoubtedly by understanding them as followes.

[*Whosoever shall put away his wife.*] That is to say, shall so put away as the propounders of this question, the Pharisees were wont to doe and covertly defended *Herod* for so doing; whom to rebuke, our Saviour heer mainely intends, and not to determine all the cases of divorce, as appeares by Saint *Paul.*[81] Whosoever shall put away, either violently without mutuall consent for urgent reasons, or conspiringly by plot of lust, or cunning malice, shall put away for any sudden mood, or contingency of disagreement, which is not daily practice, but may blow soone over, and be reconcil'd, except it bee fornication; whosoever shall put away rashly, as his choler prompts him, without due time of deliberating, and thinke his conscience discharg'd only by the bill of divorce giv'n, and the outward law satisfi'd; whosoever lastly shall put away his wife, that is a wife indeede, & not in name only, such a one who both can and is willing to bee a meet helpe toward the cheif ends of mariage both civil, and sanctify'd, except fornication be the cause, that man, or that pair committ adultery. Not he who puts away by mutuall consent, with all the considerations and respects of humanity and gentlenesse without malicious or lustfull drift. Not he who after sober and coole experience, and long debate within himself, puts away whom though he cannot love or suffer as a wife, with that sincere affection that marriage requires, yet loves at lest with that civility and goodnesse, as not to keepe her under a neglected and unwelcom residence, where nothing can be hearty, and not beeing, it must needs bee both unjoyous and injurious to any perceaving person so detain'd, and more injurious, then to be freely, and upon good termes dismist. Nor doth hee put away adulterously who complaines of causes rooted in immutable nature, utter unfitnesse, utter disconformity, not concileable, be-[62]cause not to be amended

---

[81] In I Corinthians 7:10–16, the fourth of the scriptural texts discussed in *Tetrachordon.* See below, p. 680.

without a miracle. Nor hee who puts away an unquenshable vexation
from his bosom, and flies an evil then which a greater cannot befall
human society. Nor hee who puts away with the full sufferage and
applause of his conscience, not relying on the writt'n bill of law, but
claiming by faith and fulnes of perswasion the rights and promises
of Gods institution, of which hee finds himselfe in a mistak'n wedlock defrauded. Doubtlesse this man hath baile anough to bee no
adulterer giving divorce for these causes.

[*His Wife.*] This word is not to be idle here, a meere word without a sense, much lesse a fallacious word signifying contrary to what
it pretends; but faithfully signifies a wife, that is, a comfortable
helpe and society, as God instituted; does not signify deceitfully
under this name, an intolerable adversary, not a helpelesse, unaffec-
tionate and sullen masse whose very company represents the visible
and exactest figure of lonlines it selfe. Such an associate he who
puts away, divorces not a wife, but disjoyns a nullity which God
never joyn'd, if she be neither willing, nor to her proper and requisite duties sufficient, as the words of God institute her. And this also
is *Bucers* explication of this place.[82]

[*Except it bee for fornication, or saving for the cause of fornication, as Matt.* 5th.] This declares what kind of causes our Saviour
meant; fornication being no natural and perpetual cause, but onely
accidental and temporary; therefore shewes that head of causes
from whence it is excepted, to bee meant of the same sort. For exceptions are not logically deduc't from a divers kind, as to say who
so puts away for any naturall cause except fornication, the exception would want salt. And if they understand it, who so for any
cause what ever, they cast [83] themselves; granting divorce for frigidity a naturall cause of their own allowing, though not heer exprest, and for desertion without infidelity when as he who marries,
as they allow him for a desertion, deserts as well as is deserted, and
finally puts away, for another cause besides adultery. It will with
all due reason therefore be thus better understood, who so puts

---

[82] *In Sacra Quatuor Evangelia Enarrationes* (Basle, 1536), p. 197: "For this
saying of the Lord is to be accepted of a wife strictly speaking. Who knows not
what a wife is, that she is one who may be joined to a man and may serve the
purposes of a wife? If therefore for any cause she cannot be a wife, as we have
certainly shown, who does not see that this response of Christ does not fit, so
that she cannot be put away."

[83] Cast: defeat or condemn.

away for any accidental and temporary causes, except one of them, which is fornication. Thus this exception finds out the causes from whence it is excepted, to be of the same kind, that is, casuall, not continuall.

[*Saving for the cause of fornication.*] The New Testament, though it be said originally writt in Greeke, yet hath nothing neer so many *Atticisms* as *Hebraisms*, & *Syriacisms* which was the Majesty of God, not filing the tongue of Scripture to a Gentilish *Idiom*, but in a princely manner off-[63]ring to them as to Gentiles and Foreiners grace and mercy, though not in forein words, yet in a forein stile that might induce them to the fountaines; and though their calling were high and happy, yet still to acknowledge Gods ancient people their betters, and that language the *Metropolitan* language. He therefore who thinks to *Scholiaze* upon the Gospel, though Greek, according to his Greek *Analogies,* and hath not bin Auditor to the oriental dialects, shall want in the heat of his *Analysis* no accomodation to stumble.[84] In this place, as the 5th of *Matth.* reads it, *Saving for the cause of fornication,* the Greek, such as it is, sounds it, except for the *word, report, speech, or proportion* of fornication. In which regard with other inducements, many ancient and learned writers have understood this exception as comprehending any fault equivalent and proportional to fornication. But truth is, the Evangelist heer *Hebraizes*, taking *word* or *speech* for *cause* or *matter* in the common eastern phrase, meaning perhaps no more then if he had said for fornication, as in this 19th chapter. And yet the word is found in the 5th of *Exodus* also signifying *Proportion*; where the Israelites are commanded to doe their tasks, *The matter of each day in his day.* A task we know is a proportion of work, not doing the same thing absolutely every day, but so much.

[84] A fairly frequent remark. See, *e.g.,* Jacobus Martinus, "Prefatio," to Martinus Trostius, ed., *Novum Domini Nostri Jesu Christi Testamentum Syriacè, cum Versione Latina* (Anhalt, 1621), sig. (?)4: "This [Syriac] is indeed that tongue which not merely illustrates the Hebrew books of the Old Testament; but is also outstanding for the understanding and interpretation of the phrase of the New Testament. For though the New Testament was originally Greek, the Greek did not flow so pure; but was mixed with the water of the Hebrew and Syriac languages. Wherefore let the reader of the New Testament in the Greek tongue be dextrously founded and informed; who is ignorant of the Hebrew and Syriac will be unhappily mistaken in the Greek reading of it: certainly a great many obstacles arise, Hebraisms and Syriacisms, even many whole Syriac phrases and idioms."

Whereby it may be doubtfull yet, whether heer be not excepted not
only fornication it self, but other causes equipollent, and proportional to fornication. Which very word also to understand rightly,
wee must of necessity, have recours again to the Ebrew. For in the
Greek and Latin sense by fornication is meant the common prosti-
tution of body for sale. So that they who are so exact for the letter,
shall be dealt with by the *Lexicon,* and the *Etymologicon* too if they
please, and must be bound to forbidd divorce for adultery also, untill it come to open whoredom and trade, like that for which *Claudius* divorc't *Messalina.*[85] Since therfore they take not heer the word
fornication in the common significance for an open exercise in the
stews, but grant divorce for one single act of privatest adultery,
notwithstanding that the word speakes a public and notorious frequency of fact, not without price, we may reason with as good leav,
and as little straining to the text, that our Saviour on set purpose
chose this word *Fornication,* improperly appli'd to the lapse of adultery, that we might not think our selvs bound from all divorce, except when that fault hath bin actually committed. For the language
of Scripture signifies by fornication (and others beside St. *Austin* [86]
so expound it) not only the trespas of body nor perhaps that between maried persons, unlesse in a degree or quality as [64] shame-
les as the *Bordello,* but signifies also any notable disobedience, or
intractable cariage of the wife to the husband, as Judg. the 19. 2.
Whereof at large in *the Doctrin of Divorce, l. 2. c.* 18. Secondly
signifies the apparent alienation of mind not to idolatry, (which may
seeme to answer the act of adultery) but farre on this side, to any
point of will worship, though to the true God; some times it notes
the love of earthly things, or worldly pleasures though in a right
beleever, some times the least suspicion of unwitting idolatry. As

---

[85] For the story of Claudius and Messalina see Suetonius, *Lives of the Caesars,*
"The Deified Claudius," XXVI; Tacitus, *Annals,* XI, i–iii, xxvi–xxxviii; Dio
Cassius, *Roman History,* LX–LXI. All three authors tell of her licentiousness
and cupidity, but none says that Claudius divorced her. Instead, according to
Suetonius and Dio, Claudius had her slain; Tacitus ascribes the slaying to a
tribune, urged on by Narcissus, Claudius' freedman. Perhaps Milton, citing from
memory, has confused Messalina's end with those of her two predecessors as
wife to Claudius, Plautia Urgulanilla and Aelia Paetina, both of whom were
divorced.

[86] *De Sermone Domini in Monte,* I, 16 (Migne, *Latina,* XXXIV, 1251–55).

Num. 15. 39.[87] willfull disobedience to any the least of Gods commandements is call'd fornication. *Psal.* 73. 26, 27. a distrust only in God, and withdrawing from that neernes of zeal and confidence which ought to be, is call'd fornication. We may be sure it could not import thus much less then Idolatry in the borrow'd metaphor between God and man, unless it signifi'd as much less then adultery in the ordinary acception between man and wife. Adde also that there was no need our Saviour should grant divorce for adultery, it being death by law, and law then in force. Which was the cause why *Joseph* sought to put away his betrothed wife privately,[88] least he should make her an example of capitall punishment, as lernedest expounders affirm, *Herod* being a great zelot of the Mosaic law, and the Pharises great maisters of the text, as the woman tak'n in adultery doubtless had cause to fear. Or if they can prove it was neglected, which they cannot doe, why did our Saviour shape his answer to the corruption of that age, and not rather tell them of their neglect? If they say he came not to meddle with their judicatures, much less then was it in his thought to make them new ones, or that divorce should be judicially restrain'd in a stricter manner by these his words, more then adultery judicially acquitted by those his words to the adultres. His sentence doth no more by law forbidd divorce heer, then by law it doth absolve adultery there. To them therefore, who have drawn this yoke upon Christians from his words thus wrested, nothing remaines but the guilt of a presumption and perversnes which will be hard for them to answer. Thus much that the word fornication is to be understood as the language of Christ understands it, for a constant alienation and disaffection of mind, or for the continual practise of disobedience and crossnes from the duties of love and peace, that is in summ, when to be a tolerable wife is either naturally not in their power, or obstinatly not in their will, and this opinion also is St. *Austins,* least it should hap to be suspected

---

[87] Which commands the Israelites to put fringes and blue ribbons on their garments to remind them of the Lord's commandments, "and that ye seek not after your own heart and your own eyes, after which ye use to go a whoring." The Hebrew word here translated *whoring* is elsewhere rendered *fornication.*

[88] Paraeus, *In Matthaei Evangelium Commentarius* (Geneva, 1641), p. 49, describes Joseph's dilemma at learning of Mary's pregnancy thus: "If he said nothing he was beaten for aiding by criminal silence; if at length he announced it, he foresaw that his act would deprive his dearest wife of reputation and life and subject her to the penalty of stoning by the law."

TETRACHORDON

of novelty. Yet grant the thing heer meant were only adultery, the reason of things will afford more to our asserti-[65]on, then did the reason of words. For why is divorce unlawfull but only for adultery? because, say they, that crime only breaks the matrimony. But this, I reply, the institution it selfe gainsaies: for that which is most contrary to the words and meaning of the institution, that most breaks the matrimony; but a perpetuall unmeetnes and unwillingnesse to all the duties of helpe, of love and tranquillity is most contrary to the words and meaning of the institution; that therefore much more breaks matrimony then the act of adultery though repeated. For this, as it is not felt, nor troubles him who perceaves it not, so beeing perceav'd, may soon be repented, soon amended, soon, if it can be pardon'd, may be redeem'd wth the more ardent love and duty in her who hath the pardon. But this naturall unmeetnes both cannot be unknown long, and ever after cannot be amended, if it be natural, and will not, if it be farre gon obstinat. So that wanting ought in the instant to be as great a breach as adultery, it gains it in the perpetuity to be greater. Next adultery does not exclude her other fitnes, her other pleasingnes; she may be otherwise both loving and prevalent, as many adultresses be; but in this general unfitnes or alienation she can be nothing to him that can please. In adultery nothing is given from the husband, which he misses, or enjoyes the less, as it may be suttly giv'n: but this unfitnes defrauds him of the whole contentment which is sought in wedloc. And what benefit to him, though nothing be giv'n by the stealth of adultery to another, if that which there is to give, whether it be solace, or society, be not such as may justly content him? and so not only deprives him of what it should give him, but gives him sorrow and affliction, which it did not ow him. Besides is adultery the greatest breach of matrimony in respect of the offence to God, or of the injury to man? if in the former, then other sins may offend God more, and sooner cause him to disunite his servant from being one flesh with such an offender. If in respect of the latter, other injuries are demonstrated therein more heavy to mans nature then the iterated act of adultery. God therfore in his wisedom would not so dispose his remedies, as to provide them for the less injuries, and not allow them for the greater. Thus is won both from the word fornication, & the reason of adultery, that the exception of divorce is not limitted to that act, but enlarg'd to the causes above specify'd.

[*And who so marieth her which is put away doth committ adultery.*]

By this clause alone, if by nothing els, we may assure us, that Christ intended not to deliver heer the whole doctrin of divorce, but only to condemn abuses. Otherwise to marry after desertion, which the Apostle, [66] and the reformed Churches at this day permitt, is heer forbid, as adultery. Be she never so wrongfully deserted, or put away, as the law then suffer'd, if thus forsak'n and expulst, she accept the refuge and protection of any honester man who would love her better, and give her self in mariage to him, by what the letter guides us, it shall be present adultery to them both. This is either harsh and cruel, or all the Churches teaching as they doe the contrary, are loos and remiss; besides that the Apostle himselfe stands deeply fin'd in a contradiction against our Saviour. What shall we make of this? what rather the common interpreter can make of it, for they be his own markets, let him now trie; let him trie which way he can wind in his *Vertumnian*[89] distinctions and evasions, if his canonical gabardine of text and letter do not now sit too close about him, and pinch his activity; which if I erre not, hath heer hamper'd it selfe in a springe fitt for those who put their confidence in Alphabets. *Spanheim*[90] a writer of *Evangelic doubts* comes now and confesses that our Saviours words *are to be limited beyond the limitation there exprest, and excepted beyond their own exception,* as not speaking of what happn'd rarely, but what most commonly. Is it so rare *Spanheim,* to be deserted, or was it then so rare to put away injuriously, that a person so hatefully expell'd, should to the heaping of more injury be turn'd like an infectious thing out of all maried fruition upon pain of adultery, as not considerable to the brevity of this halfe sentence? Of what then speakes our Saviour? of *that collusion,* saith he, *which was then most frequent among the Jews of changing wives and husbands, through inconstancy and unchast desires.*[91] Colluders your selves, as violent to

---

[89] *Vertumnian:* Vertumnus was the Roman god of seasons; possibly also an allusion to the work of the eccentric Flemish scholar Goropius Becanus, whose *Vertumnus* abounds in fantastic knowledge.

[90] Friedrich Spanheim (1600–1649) was a German Calvinist theologian, professor of divinity at Geneva and Leyden.

[91] Friedrich Spanheim, *Dubiorum Evangelicorum* (3 parts, Geneva, 1639; UTSL). The discussion of divorce is covered in part III, *Dubia* 120–21 (pp. 603–14) and 147–48 (pp. 886–910). Milton uses the second of these passages, in

this law of God by your unmercifull binding, as the Pharises by their unbounded loosning! Have thousands of Christian souls perisht as to this life, and God knows what hath betided their consciences, for want of this healing explanation, and is it now at last obscurely drawn forth, only to cure a scratch, and leave the main wound spouting? *Who so ever putteth away his wife except for fornication committeth adultery*; That shall be spoke of all ages, and all men, though never so justly otherwise mov'd to divorce: in the very next breath, *And who so marieth her which is put away committeth adultery*, the men are new and miraculous, they tell you now *you are to limit it to that age, when it was in fashion to chop matrimonies; and must be meant of him who puts away with his wives consent through the lightnes, and leudnes of them both.* But what rule of Logic, or indeed of reason is our commission to understand the *Antecedent* one way and the *Consequent* another; for in the habitude this whole vers may be [67] consider'd: or at least to take the parts of a *copulat axiom*, both absolutely affirmative, and to say that first is absolutely true, the other not, but must bee limited to a certain time and custome; which is no lesse then to say they are both false. For in this *compound axiom*, be the parts never so many, if one of them doe but falter, & be not equally absolute and generall, the rest are all fals. If therefore, that *he who marries her which is put away committs adultery*, be not generally true, neither is it generally true that *he committs adultery who puts away for other cause then fornication.* And if the marrying her which is put away, must be understood limited, which they cannot but yeild it must, with the same limitation must be understood the putting away. Thus doth the common exposition confound it selfe, and justify this which is heer brought; that our Saviour as well in the first part of this sentence as in the second, prohibited only such divorses

which Spanheim tries to reconcile Matthew 19:9, which allows divorce only for fornication, with I Corinthians 7:12–15, where divorce is allowed for desertion. Spanheim rejects the argument, employed by Milton, that Christ's words referred only to the Jewish practice of easy divorce for light reasons, and contends that it applied to those divorces, then frequent, in which husband and wife by collusion agreed to divorce for some light and frivolous reason. Milton's exasperation is probably to be explained by Spanheim's rejection of several arguments which Milton, following Erasmus and Bucer, thought valid, as that "fornication" is to be interpreted broadly to include other faults. The matter Milton puts in italics is paraphrase rather than direct quotation.

as the Jewes then made through malice or through plotted licence, not those which are for necessary and just causes; where charity and wisedome disjoyns, that which not God, but Error and Disastre joyn'd.

And there is yet to this our exposition, a stronger siding freind, then any can be an adversary, unlesse Saint *Paul* be doubted, who repeating a command concerning divorce, I *Cor.* 7. which is agreed by writers to be the same with this of our Saviour, and appointing that the *wife remaine unmaried, or be reconcil'd to her husband,* leavs it infallible that our Saviour spake cheifly against putting away for casual and choleric disagreements, or any other cause which may with human patience and wisedom be reconcil'd, not hereby meaning to hale and dash together the irreconcilable aversations of nature, nor to tie up a faultlesse person like a parricide, as it were into one sack with an enemy,[92] to be his causelesse tormenter and executioner the length of a long life. Lastly, let this sentence of Christ bee understood how it will, yet that it was never intended for a judicial law, to be inforc'd by the Magistrat, besides that the office of our Saviour had no such purpose in the Gospel, this latter part of the sentence may assure us, *And who so marrieth her which is put away committs adultery.* Shall the exception for adultery belong to this clause or not? if not, it would be strange, that he who marries a woman really divorc't for adultery, as Christ permitted, should becom an adulter by marrying one who is now no other mans wife, himself being also free, who might by this meanes reclaim her from common whordome. And if the exception must belong hither, then it followes that he who marries an adultresse divorc'd, commits no adultry; which would soone discover to us what an absurd and [68] senseles peece of injustice this would be, to make a civil statute of, in penal courts; whereby the adultresse put away may marry another safely, and without a crime to him that marries her: but the innocent and wrongfully divorc'd shall not marry again without the guilt of adultery both to her selfe and to her second husband. This saying of Christ therefore cannot be made a temporal law, were it but for

---

[92] "Together with a snake, a cock, an ape, and a dog (unclean man with unclean beasts), the murderer [of his father] is sewed in a sack, which is pulled to the sea by two black oxen and there sunk, so that neither earth, nor water, nor sun may be defiled by his death." E. Hoffmann-Krayer, *Handwörterbuch des deutschen Aberglaubens* (Berlin and Leipzig, 1936–37, 10 vols.), VIII, 1513, "Vater."

this reason. Nor is it easie to say what coherence there is at all in it from the letter, to any perfet sense not obnoxious to som absurdity, and seems much lesse agreeable to what ever els of the Gospel is left us written; doubtles by our Saviour spok'n in that fiercenes and abstruse intricacy, first to amuse [93] his tempters, and admonish in general the abusers of that Mosaic law; next to let *Herod* know a second knower of his unlawfull act, though the Baptist were beheaded; last that his Disciples and all good men might learne to expound him in this place, as in all other his precepts, not by the written letter, but by that unerring paraphrase of Christian love and Charity, which is the summe of all commands, and the perfection.

Vers. 10. *His Disciples say unto him, if the case of the man be so with his wife, it is not good to marry.*

This verse I adde, to leave no objection behind unanswer'd: for some may thinke, if this our Saviours sentence be so faire, as not commanding ought that patience or nature cannot brook, why then did the Disciples murmur and say, *it is not good to marry.* I answer that the Disciples had bin longer bred up under the Pharisaean doctrin, then under that of Christ, and so no marvel though they yet retain'd the infection of loving old licentious customs; no marvel though they thought it hard they might not for any offence that throughly anger'd them, divorce a wife, as well as put away a servant; since it was but giving her a bill, as they were taught. Secondly, it was no unwonted thing with them not to understand our Saviour in matters farre easier. So that bee it granted their conceit of this text was the same which is now commonly conceiv'd, according to the usuall rate of their capacity then, it will not hurt a better interpretation. But why did not Christ seeing their error informe them? for good cause; it was his profest method not to teach them all things at all times, but each thing in due place and season. Christ said *Luke* 22. that *hee who had no sword should sell* [94] *his garment and buy one:* the Disciples tooke it in a manifest wrong sense, yet our Saviour did not there informe them better. He told [69] them *it was easier for a Camell to go through a needles eye,* [95] then a rich

---

[93] Amuse: bemuse, bewilder.   [94] Authorized Version: "let him sell."
[95] Matthew 19:24.

man in at heav'n gate. They were *amaz'd exceedingly:* he explain'd himselfe to meane of those *who trust in riches, Mark* 10. *They were amaz'd* [96] *then out of measure,* for so *Marke* relates it; as if his explaining had increas'd their amazement, in such a plaine case, and which concern'd so neerely their calling to be inform'd in. Good reason therefore, if Christ at that time did not stand amplifying, to the thick prejudice and tradition wherein they were, this question of more difficulty, and lesse concernment to any perhaps of them in particular. Yet did he not omitt to sow within them the seeds of sufficient determining, agen the time that his promis'd spirit should bring all things to their memory. Hee had declar'd in their hearing not long before, how distant hee was from abolishing the law it selfe of divorce; hee had referr'd them to the institution; and after all this, gives them a set answer, from which they might collect what was cleer anough, that *all men cannot receive all sayings,*[97] verse 11. If such regard bee had to each mans receiving of mariage or single life, what can arise, that the same christian regard should not bee had in most necessary divorce? All which instructed both them and us, that it beseem'd his Disciples to learne the deciding of this question, which hath nothing new in it, first by the institution, then by the generall grounds of religion, not by a particular saying here or there, temper'd and level'd only to an incident occasion, the riddance of a tempting assault. For what can this bee but weake and shallow apprehension, to forsake the standard principles of institution, faith, & charity; then to be blanke & various at every occurrence in Scripture, and in a cold *Spasm* of scruple, to reare peculiar doctrines upon the place; that shall bid the gray autority of most unchangeable and sovran rules to stand by & be contradicted. Thus to this Evangelic precept of famous difficulty, which for these many ages weakly understood, and violently put in practice, hath made a shambles rather then an ordinance of matrimony, I am firme a truer exposition cannot be given. If this or that argument heer us'd, please not every one, there is no scarsity of arguments, any halfe of them will suffice. Or should they all faile, as Truth it selfe can faile as soon, I should content me with the institution alone to wage this controversie, and not distrust to evince. If any need it not, the happier; yet

---

[96] Authorized Version: *astonished.* The parallel account in Matthew 19:25 has *exceedingly amazed.*

[97] Matthew 19:11. Authorized Version: *this saying.*

Christians ought to study earnestly what may be anothers need. But if, as mortall mischances are, som hap to need it, let them be sure they abuse not, and give God his thanks, who hath reviv'd this remedy, not too late for them, and scowr'd off an inveterat misexposition from the [70] Gospel: a work not to perish by the vaine breath or doome of this age. Our next industry shall bee, under the same guidance, to try with what fidelity that remaining passage in the *Epistles* touching this matter, hath bin commented.

I COR. 7. 10, &c.

10. *And unto the maried I command, &c.*

11. *And let not the husband put away his wife.*

THIS intimates but what our Saviour taught before, that divorce is not rashly to be made, but reconcilement to be persuaded and endevor'd, as oft as the cause can have to doe with reconcilement, & is not under the dominion of blameles nature; which may have reason to depart though seldomest and last from charitable love, yet somtimes from friendly, and familiar, and somthing oftner from conjugal love, which requires not only moral, but natural causes to the making and maintayning; and may be warrantably excus'd to retire from the deception of what it justly seeks, and the ill requitals which unjustly it finds. For Nature hath her *Zodiac* also, keepes her great annual circuit over human things as truly as the Sun and Planets in the firmament; hath her *anomalies,* hath her obliquities in ascensions and declinations, accesses and recesses,[1] as blamelessly as they in heaven. And sitting in her planetary Orb with two rains in each hand, one strait, the other loos, tempers the cours of minds as well as bodies to several conjunctions and oppositions, freindly, or unfreindly aspects,[2] consenting oftest with

---

[1] Anomalies: discrepancies between computed and observed positions of planets. Obliquities: inclinations away from the straight line, especially of the sun away from the equator. Accesses and recesses: approaches and departures, as of the sun in spring and autumn.

[2] The imagery here is astrological rather than astronomical. Planets in conjunction are in the same longitude; planets in opposition are in longitudes of 180 degrees difference. Astrology interprets these conjunctions and opposition as friendly or unfriendly.

reason, but never contrary. This in the effect no man of meanest reach but daily sees; and though to every one it appeare not in the cause, yet to a cleare capacity, well nurtur'd with good reading and observation, it cannot but be plaine and visible. Other exposition therefore then hath bin given to former places that give light to these two summary verses, will not be needfull: save onely that these precepts are meant to those maried who differ not in religion.

[*But to the rest speake I, not the Lord; if any brother hath a wife that beleeveth not, and she be pleased to dwell with him, let him not put her away.*]

Now followes what is to be done, if the persons wedded be of a different faith. The common beleef is, that a christian is heer commanded not to divorce, if the infidel please to stay, though it be but to vexe, or to deride, or to seduce the christian. This doctrin will be the easie worke of a refutation. The other opinion is, that a christian is heer conditionally [71] permitted to hold wedloc with a misbeleever only upon hopes limited by christian prudence, which without much difficulty shall be defended. That this heer spoken by *Paul,* not by the Lord cannot be a command, these reasons avouch. First the law of *Moses, Exod.* 34. 16. *Deut.* 7. 3. 6. interpreted by *Ezra,* and *Nehemiah* two infallible authors, commands to divorce an infidel not for the feare onely of a ceremonious defilement, but of an irreligious seducement, fear'd both in respect of the beleever himselfe, and of his children in danger to bee perverted by the misbeleeving parent, *Nehem.* 13. 24. 26. and *Peter Martyr* thought this a convincing reason.[3] If therefore the legal pollution vanishing have abrogated the ceremony of this law, so that a christian may be permitted to retaine an infidel without uncleannes, yet the moral reason of divorcing stands to eternity, which neither Apostle nor Angel from heaven can countermand. All that they reply to this, is their human warrant, that God will preserve us in our obedience to this command against the danger of seducement. And so undoubtedly he will, if we understand his commands aright; if we turn not this evangelic permission into a legal, and yet illegal command: if we turne not hope into bondage, the charitable and free hope of gaining another, into the forc't and servil temptation of loosing our selves;

---

[3] Pietro Martiro Vermigli, *In selectissimam D. Pauli priorem ad Corinthios . . . commentarii doctissimi* (Zurich, 1567), ff. 86v–91v. See also below, p. 711. For Peter Martyr see *Martin Bucer,* above, p. 427.

but more of this beneath. Thus these words of *Paul* by common doctrin made a command, are made a contradiction to the morall law.

Secondly, not the law only, but the Gospel from the law, and from it selfe requires even in the same chapter, where divorce between them of one religion is so narrowly forbidd, rather then our christian love should come into danger of backsliding, to forsake all relations how neer so ever, and the wife expresly, with promise of a high reward, *Mat.* 19.[4] And he who hates not father or mother, wife, or children hindring his christian cours, much more, if they despise or assault it, cannot be a Disciple, *Luke* 14.[5] How can the Apostle then command us, to love and continue in that matrimony, which our Saviour bids us hate, and forsake? They can as soon teach our faculty of respiration to contract and to dilate it selfe at once, to breath and to fetch breath in the same instant, as teach our minds how to doe such contrary acts as these, towards the same object, and as they must be done in the same moment. For either the hatred of her religion, & her hatred to our religion will work powerfully against the love of her society, or the love of that will by degrees flatter out all our zealous hatred and forsaking and soone ensnare us to unchristianly compliances.

Thirdly, In mariage there ought not only to be a civil love, but such a [72] love as Christ loves his Church; but where the religion is contrary without hope of conversion, there can be no love, no faith, no peacefull society, (they of the other opinion confess it) nay there ought not to be, furder then in expectation of gaining a soul; when that ceases, we know God hath put enmity between the seed of the woman, and the seed of the Serpent. Neither should *we love them that hate the Lord,* as the Prophet told *Jehosaphat. 2 Chron.* 19. And this Apostle himselfe in another place, warns us *that we be not unequally yokt with Infidels,* 2 Cor. 6.[6] for that there can be no fellowship, no communion, no concord between such. Outward commerce and civil intercours cannot perhaps be avoided; but true friendship and familiarity there can be none. How vainly therefore,

[4] V. 29: "And every one that hath forsaken houses, or brethren, or sisters, or father, or mother, or wife, or children, or lands, for my name's sake, shall receive an hundredfold, and shall inherit everlasting life."

[5] V. 26: "And if any man come to me, and hate not his father, and mother, and wife, and children, and brethren, and sisters, yea, and his own life also, he cannot be my disciple."

[6] V. 14: "Be ye not unequally yoked together with infidels."

not to say how impiously would the most inward and dear alliance of mariage or continuance in mariage be commanded, where true freindship is confest impossible. For say they, wee are forbidd heer to marry with an infidel, not bid to divorce. But to rob the words thus of their full sense will not be allow'd them: it is not said, enter not into the yoke, but *be not unequally yokt;* which plainly forbids the thing in present act, as well as in purpose; and his manifest conclusion is, not only that *we should not touch,* but that having toucht, *we should come out from among them, and be separat;* with the promise of a blessing thereupon that *God will receave us, will be our father, and we his sons and daughters.* v. 17. 18.[7] Why we should stay with an Infidel after the expence of all our hopes, can be but for a civil relation; but why we should depart from a seducer, setting aside the misconstruction of this place, is from a religious necessity of departing. The wors cause therefore of staying (if it be any cause at all, for civil government forces it not) must not overtop the religious cause of separating, executed with such an urgent zeal, & such a prostrate humiliation by *Ezra* and *Nehemiah.* What God hates to joyn, certainly he cannot love should continue joyn'd: it being all one in matter of ill consequence, to marry, or to continue maried with an Infidel, save only so long as we wait willingly, and with a safe hope. St. *Paul* therefore citing heer a command of *the Lord Almighty,* for so he terms it, that we should *separate,* cannot have bound us with that which he calls his own whether command or counsel that we should not separate.

Which is the fourth reason, for he himselfe takes care least we should mistake him, [*But to the rest speak I, not the Lord.*] If the Lord spake not, then man spake it and man hath no Lordship to command the conscience: yet modern interpreters [8] will have it a command maugre St. [73] *Paul* himselfe, they will make him a Prophet like *Caiaphas* [9] to speak the word of the Lord not thinking, nay denying to think; though he disavow to have receav'd it from the Lord, his word shall not be tak'n, though an Apostle, he shall

[7] "Wherefore come out from among them, and be ye separate, saith the Lord, and touch not the unclean thing, and I will receive you. And will be a Father unto you, and ye shall be my sons and daughters."

[8] *E.g.,* Beza; see note 10 below.

[9] The text Milton probably alludes to is John 18:14: "Now Caiaphas was he, which gave counsel to the Jews, that it was expedient that one man should die for the people." See also John 11:49–51.

be born down in his own Epistle, by a race of expositers who presume to know from whom he spake, better then he himselfe. *Paul* deposes that the Lord speaks not this, they, that the Lord speaks it: can this be less then to brave him with a full fac't contradiction? Certainly to such a violence as this, for I cannot call it an expounding, what a man should answer I know not, unless that if it be their pleasure next to put a gag into the Apostles mouth, they are already furnisht with a commodious audacity toward the attempt. *Beza* would seem to shun the contradictory by telling us that the Lord spake it not in person, as he did the former precept.[10] But how many other doctrines doth St. *Paul* deliver which the Lord spake not in person, and yet never uses this preamble but in things indifferent? So long as we receave him for a messenger of God, for him to stand sorting sentences what the Lord spake in person, and what he, not the Lord in person, would be but a chill trifling, and his readers might catch an ague the while. But if we shall supply the grammatical *Ellipsis* regularly, and as we must in the sam *tense,* all will be then cleer, for we cannot supply it thus, to the rest I speake, the Lord spake not, but I speake, the Lord speaks not. If then the Lord neither spake in person, nor speakes it now, the Apostle testifying both, it follows duely, that this can be no command. Forsooth the fear is, least this not being a command, would prove an evangelic counsel, & so make way for supererogations. As if the Apostle could not speak his mind in things indifferent, as he doth in fowr or five several places of this chapter with the like preface of not commanding, but that the doubted inconvenience of supererogating must needs rush in. And how adds it to the word of the Lord, (for this also they object) when as the Apostle by his christian prudence guids us in the liberty which God hath left us to, without command? could not the spirit of God instruct us by him what was free, as well as what was not? But what need I more, when *Cameron* an ingenuous writer, and in high esteem, solidly confutes the surmise of a command heer,

---

[10] *Tractatio de Repudiis et Divortiis* (Geneva, 1596), pp. 286–87: "Fifthly, since the Apostle prefaces that not the Lord but he himself speaks this, some are heard to say triflingly that humanity makes this sentence, not divinity; whence that following sentence of Paul does not obligate us; nor was the Apostle's mind otherwise when he used that preface. I respond that this objection is not without blasphemy. Unless we firmly hold this, that whatever the Apostles taught in the Churches, was taught by the Holy Spirit, the whole teaching of the Apostles would necessarily fall. I thus say whatever they taught."

and among other words hath these. That *when Paul speaks as an Apostle, he uses this forme,* The Lord saith, not I, v. 10. *but as a privat man he saith,* I speak, not the Lord.[11] And thus also all the prime fathers *Austin,*[12] *Jerom,*[13] and the rest understood this place.

Fiftly, The very stating of the question declares this to be no com-[74]mand; *If any brother hath an unbeleeving wife, and she be pleased to dwell with him, let him not put her away.* For the Greek word συνευδοκεῖ does not imply only her being pleas'd to stay, but his being pleas'd to let her stay; it must be a consent of them both. Nor can the force of this word be render'd less, without either much negligence or iniquity of him that otherwise translates it. And thus the Greek Church also and their Synods understood it, who best knew what their own language meant, as appeares by *Matthaeus Monachus* an author set forth by *Leunclavius* and of antiquity perhaps not inferior to *Balsamon* who writes upon the canons of the Apostles; this Author in his chap. *that mariage is not to be made with heretics,* thus recites the second canon of the 6. Synod, *As to the Corinthians Paul determins, If the beleeving wife choos to live with the unbeleeving husband, or the beleeving husband with the unbeleeving wife. Mark* saith he, *how the Apostle heer condescends, if the beleever please to dwell with the unbeleever; so that if he please not, out of doubt the mariage is dissolv'd. And I am perswaded it was so in the beginning, and thus preach't.*[14] And thereupon gives an example of one, who though not deserted, yet by the decree of *Theodotus* the Patriarch divorc't an unbeleeving wife. What therefore depends in the plain state of this question on the consent and well liking of them both, must not be a command. Lay next the latter end of the 11. v. to the twelf (for wherefore els is Logic taught us) in a *discrete axiom,* as it can be no other by the phrase, *The Lord saith, let not the husband put away*

[11] *Myrothecium Evangelicum* (Geneva, 1632), p. 208.

[12] *De Conjugiis Adulterinis ad Pollentium,* I, 13 (Migne, *Latina,* XL, 459).

[13] On I Corinthians 19 (Migne, *Latina,* XXIX, 790): "It will be more blessed to remain so, according to my counsel. I think also that I may have the Spirit of God."

[14] Johannes Leunclavius, ed., *Juris Graeco-Romani tam Canonici quam Civilis* (Frankfurt, 1596; CULL), book VIII, p. 506. Leunclavius (Johann Löwenklau), 1533–1593, was a historian, orientalist, and classical scholar mentioned by Milton in his *Commonplace Book.* See *Complete Prose,* I, 401. Balsamon (d. *ca.* 1200) was a Byzantine commentator on canon law. I have not been able to get any biographical information on Mattheus.

his wife. But I say let him not put away a misbeleeving wife; this sounds as if by the judgement of *Paul,* a man might put away any wife but the misbeleeving; or els the parts are not *discrete,* or *dissentanie,*[15] for both conclude not putting away, and consequently in such a form the proposition is ridiculous. Of necessity therfore the former part of this sentence must be conceav'd, as understood, and silently granted, that although the Lord command to divorce an infidel, yet I, not the Lord command you? No, but give my judgement, that for som evangelic reasons a christian may be permitted not to divorce her. Thus while we reduce the brevity of St. *Paul* to a plainer sense, by the needfull supply of that which was granted between him and the Corinthians, the very logic of his speech extracts him confessing that the Lords command lay in a seeming contrariety to this his counsel: and that he meant not to thrust out a command of the Lord by a new one of his own, as one nail drives another, but to release us from the rigor of it, by the right of the Gospel, so farre forth as a charitable cause leads us on in the [75] hope of winning another soule without the peril of loosing our own. For this is the glory of the Gospel to teach us that *the end of the commandment is charity,* I *Tim.* 1. not the drudging out a poore and worthlesse duty forc't from us by the taxe, and taile [16] of so many letters. This doctrine therefore can bee no command, but it must contradict the moral law, the Gospel, and the Apostle himselfe both else where, and heere also eevn in the act of speaking.

If then it be no command, it must remain to be a permission, and that not absolute, for so it would be still contrary to the law, but with such a caution as breaks not the law, but as the manner of the Gospel is, fulfills it through charity. The law had two reasons, the one was ceremonial, the pollution that all Gentiles were to the Jewes; this the vision of *Peter* had abolisht, Acts 10. and clens'd all creatures to the use of a Christian. The *Corinthians* understood not this, but fear'd lest dwelling in matrimony with an unbeleever, they were defil'd. The Apostle discusses that scruple with an Evangelic reason, shewing them that although God heretofore under the law, not intending the conversion of the Gentiles, except some special ones, held them as polluted things to the Jew, yet now pur-

---

[15] Dissentanie: contradictory or contrary. Cited in *OED*.

[16] Taxe, and taile: impost. Milton is protesting against the reckoning up of Christian duty as one would reckon a tax.

posing to call them in, he hath purify'd them from that legal un-cleannesse wherein they stood, to use and to be us'd in a pure manner.

For saith he, *The unbeleeving husband is sanctifi'd by the wife, and the unbeleeving wife, is sanctifi'd by the husband, else were your children uncleane; but now they are holy.* That is, they are sanctify'd to you, from that legal impurity which you so feare; and are brought into a neer capacity to be holy, if they beleeve, and to have free accesse to holy things. In the mean time, as being Gods creatures, a christian hath power to use them according to their proper use; in as much as now, *all things to the pure are become pure.* In this legal respect therefore ye need not doubt to continue in mariage with an unbeleever. Thus others also expound this place and *Cameron especially.*[17] This reason warrants us onely what wee may doe without feare of pollution, does not binde us that we must. But the other reason to divorce an infidel was moral, the avoiding of enticement from the true faith. This cannot shrink; but remains in as full force as ever, to save the actuall christian from the snare of a misbeleever. Yet if a Christian full of grace and spirituall gifts finding the misbeleever not frowardly affected, feares not a seduc-ing, but hopes rather a gaining, who sees not that this morall reason is not violated by not divorcing, which the law commanded to doe, but better ful-[76]fill'd by the excellence of the Gospel working through charity. For neither the faithfull is seduc't, and the un-faithfull is either sav'd, or with all discharge of love, and evangelic duty sought to be sav'd. But contrarywise if the infirme Christian shall bee commanded here against his minde, against his hope, and against his strength, to dwell with all the scandals, the houshold persecutions, or alluring temptations of an infidel, how is not the Gospel by this made harsher then the law, and more yoaking? There-fore the Apostle ere he deliver this other reason why wee need not in all hast put away an infidel, his mind misgiving him least he should seem to be the imposer of a new command, staies not for method, but with an abrupt speed inserts the declaration of their liberty in this matter.

[17] *Myrothecium Evangelicum* (Geneva, 1632), p. 208: "That we may know of what holiness and impurity Paul here speaks, it is noteworthy that in the Corinthian Church there were women who fled congress with their infidel hus-bands, and men similarly who would not mix with their infidel wives, because they thought that they were polluted thereby."

But if the unbeleeving depart, let him depart; a brother or a sister is not under bondage in such cases: but God hath called us to peace.

[*But if the unbeleeving depart.*] This cannot be restrain'd to locall departure only; for who knows not that an offencive society is worse then a forsaking. If his purpose of cohabitation be to endanger the life, or the conscience, *Beza* himselfe is halfe perswaded, that this may purchase to the faithfull person the same freedome that a desertion may; [18] and so *Gerard* and others whom he cites.[19] If therefore he depart in affection, if hee depart from giving hope of his conversion, if he disturb, or scoffe at religion, seduce, or tempt, if he rage, doubtlesse not the weake only, but the strong may leave him, if not for feare, yet for the dignities sake of religion, which cannot be liable to all base affronts, meerely for the worshiping of a civil mariage. I take therefore *departing* to bee as large as the negative of being well pleas'd: that is, if he be not pleas'd for the present to live lovingly, quietly, inoffensively, so as may give good hope; which appeares well by that which followes.

[*A brother or a sister is not under bondage in such cases.*] If Saint *Paul* provide seriously against the bondage of a christian, it is not the only bondage to live unmaried for a deserting infidel, but to endure his presence intolerably, to beare indignities against his religion in words or deedes, to be wearied with seducements, to have idolatries and superstitions ever before his eyes, to be tormented with impure and prophane conversation, this must needs be bondage to a christian; is this left all unprovided for, without remedy, or freedom granted? undoubtedly no, for the Apostle leavs it furder to be consider'd with prudence, what bondage a brother or sister is not under, not onely in this case, but as hee speaks himselfe plurally, *in such cases.* [77]

[*But God hath called us to peace.*] To peace, not to bondage, not to brabbles and contentions with him who is not pleas'd to live peaceably, as mariage and christianity requires. And where strife arises from a cause hopelesse to be allayd, what better way to peace

---

[18] *Tractatio de Repudiis et Divortiis* (Geneva, 1596), pp. 167–68.

[19] Johannis Gerhardus, *Locorum Theologicorum* (9 vols., Geneva, 1639; BML), VII, col. 768. The "others" whom Gerhard cites are "Melancthon, Burgenhagius, Brentius, Wigandus, Mentzerus." Johannes Gerhardus (Johann Gerhard), 1582–1637, was a German theologian and exegete.

then by separating that which is ill joyn'd? It is not divorce, that first breaks the peace of family, as som fondly comment on this place, but it is peace already brok'n, which, when other cures fail, can only be restor'd to the faultles person by a necessary divorce. And Saint *Paul* heer warrants us to seeke peace, rather then to remain in bondage. If God hath call'd us to peace, why should we not follow him, why should we miserably stay in perpetual discord under a servitude not requir'd?

[*For what knowest thou O wife, whether thou shalt save thy husband, &c.*] St. *Paul* having thus clear'd himselfe, not to go about the mining of our christian liberty, not *to cast a snare upon us,* which to doe hee so much hated, returnes now to the second reason of that law to put away an infidel, for feare of seducement, which hee does not heer contradict with a command now to venture that; but if neither the infirmity of the Christian, nor the strength of the unbeleever be fear'd, but hopes appearing that he may be won, he judges it no breaking of that law, though the beleever be permitted to forbeare divorce, and can abide, without the peril of seducement, to offer the charity of a salvation to wife or husband, which is the fulfilling, not the transgressing of that law; and well worth the undertaking with much hazard and patience. For what knowest thou whether thou shalt save thy wife, that is, till all meanes convenient and possible with discretion and probability, as human things are, have bin us'd. For Christ himselfe sends not our hope on pilgrimage to the worlds end; [20] but sets it bounds beyond which we need not wait on a brother, much lesse on an infidell. If after such a time we may count a professing Christian no better then a heathen, after less time perhaps wee may cease to hope of a heathen, that hee will turne christian. Otherwise, to binde us harder then the law, and tell us wee are not under bondage, is meere mockery. If till the unbeleever please to part, we may not stirre from the house of our bondage, then certain this our liberty is not grounded in the purchas of Christ, but in the pleasure of a miscreant. What knowes the loyal husband whether he may not save the adulteresse, he is not therfore bound to receive her. What knowes the wife but shee may reclaim her husband who hath deserted her? yet the reformed Churches doe not enjoyn her to wait longer then after the contempt of an Ecclesi-

[20] Matthew 18:15–17.

astical [78] Summons. *Beza* himselfe heer befriends us with a remarkable speech, *what could be firmly constituted in human matters if under pretence of expecting grace from above, it should be never lawfull for us to seeke our right.*[21] And yet in other cases not lesse reasonable to obtain a most just and needfull remedy by divorce, he turnes the innocent party to a taske of prayers beyond the multitude of beads and *rosaries,* to beg the gift of chastity in recompence of an injurious mariage. But the Apostle is evident anough, *we are not under bondage,* trusting that he writes to those who are not ignorant what bondage is, to let supercilious determiners cheat them out of their freedome. God hath call'd us to peace, and so doubtlesse hath left in our hands how to obtaine it seasonably; if it be not our own choise to sit ever like novices wretchedly servile.

Thus much the Apostle on this question between Christian and Pagan, to us now of little use; yet supposing it written for our instruction as it may be rightly apply'd, I doubt not but that the difference between a true beleever and a heretic, or any one truely religious either deserted or seeking divorce from any one grossly erroneous or profane may be referr'd hither. For St. *Paul* leaves us heer the solution not of this case only, which little concernes us, but of *such like cases,* which may occurr to us. For where the reasons directly square, who can forbid why the verdit should not be the same? But this the common writers allow us not. And yet from this text which in plaine words gives liberty to none unlesse deserted by an infidel, they collect the same freedome though the desertion bee not for religion, which, as I conceive, they neede not doe; but may without straining reduce it to the cause of fornication. For first they confesse that desertion is seldome without a just suspition of adultery: next it is a breach of mariage in the same kind, and in some sort worse: for adultery though it give to another, yet it bereaves not al; but the deserter wholly denies all right, and makes one flesh twain, which is counted the absolutest breach of matrimony, and causes the other, as much as in him lies, to commit sin, by being so left. Neverthelesse those reasons which they bring of establishing by this place the like liberty from any desertion, are faire and solid: and if the thing be lawfull, and can be prov'd so,

[21]*Tractatio de Repudiis et Divortiis* (Geneva, 1596), p. 285.

more waies then one, so much the safer. Their arguments I shall heer
recite, and that they may not com idle, shall use them to make good
the like freedome to divorce for other causes; and that we are no
more under bondage to any hainous default against the main ends
of matrimony, then to a desertion: First they allege that to *Tim.*
1. 5. 8. If any provide not for [79] *those of his own house,*[22] *hee*
hath deny'd the faith, and is worse then an Infidel. But a deserter,
say they, *can have no care of them who are most his owne, there-*
fore the deserted party is not lesse to bee righted against such a one
then against an infidel.[23] With the same evidence I argue, that man
or wife who hates in wedloc, is perpetually unsociable, unpeacefull,
or unduteous, either not being able, or not willing to performe what
the maine ends of mariage demand in helpe and solace, cannot bee
said to care for who should bee dearest in the house; therefore is
worse then an infidel in both regards, either in undertaking a duty
which he cannot performe, to the undeserved and unspeakable injury
of the other party so defrauded and betrai'd, or not performing
what he hath undertaken, whenas he may or might have, to the per-
jury of himselfe more irreligious then heathenisme. The blamelesse
person therefore hath as good a plea to sue out his delivery from
this bondage, as from the desertion of an infidel. Since most writers
cannot but grant that desertion is not only a local absence, but an
intolerable society; or if they grant it not, the reasons of Saint *Paul*
grant it, with all as much leave as they grant to enlarge a particular
freedom from paganisme, into a general freedom from any desertion. Secondly, they reason from the likenes of either fact, *the same*
losse redounds to the deserted by a christian, as by an infidel, the
same peril of temptation. And I in like manner affirme that if honest
and free persons may be allow'd to know what is most to their owne
losse, the same losse and discontent, but worse disquiet with continuall misery and temptation resides in the company, or better
call'd the persecution of an unfit, or an unpeaceable consort, then by
his desertion. For then the deserted may enjoy himselfe at least.
And he who deserts is more favourable to the party whom his presence afflicts, then that importunat thing which is and will be ever

---

[22] Authorized Version: "If any provide not for his own, and specially for
those of his own house."

[23] In this and the other italicized passages following Milton does not seem to
be quoting, but summarizing the opinions of Beza, Cameron, and others.

conversant before the eyes a loyal and individual vexation. As for those who still rudely urge it no loss to mariage, no desertion, so long as the flesh is present and offers a benevolence that hates, or is justly hated, I am not of that vulgar and low perswasion, to thinke such forc'd embracements as these worth the honour, or the humanity of mariage, but farre beneath the soul of a rational and freeborne man. Thirdly, they say, *it is not the infidelity of the deserter, but the desertion of the infidel from which the Apostle gives this freedom;* and I joyne that the Apostle could as little require our subjection to an unfit and injurious bondage present, as to an infidel absent. To free us from that which is an evil by being distant, and not from that which is an inmate, and in the bosome [80] evil, argues an improvident and careles deliverer. And thus all occasions, which way so ever they turn, are not unofficious to administer somthing which may conduce to explain, or to defend the assertion of this book touching divorce. I complain of nothing, but that it is indeed too copious to be the matter of a dispute, or a defence, rather to be yeelded, as in the best ages, a thing of common reason, not of controversie. What have I left to say? I fear to be more elaborat in such a perspicuity as this; lest I should seem not to teach, but to upbraid the dulnes of an age; not to commun with reason in men, but to deplore the loss of reason from among men: this only, and not the want of more to say, is the limit of my discours.

Who among the fathers have interpreted the words of Christ concerning divorce, as is heer interpreted; and what the civil law of Christian Emperors in the primitive Church determin'd.

ALTHOUGH testimony be in Logic an argument rightly call'd *inartificial*,[1] & doth not solidly fetch the truth by multiplicity of Authors, nor argue a thing false by the few that hold so, yet seeing most men from their youth so accustom, as not to scanne reason, nor cleerly to apprehend it, but to trust for that the names and numbers of such, as have got, and many times undeservedly, the reputation among them to know much, and because there is a vulgar also of teachers, who are as blindly by whom they fancy led, as they lead the people, it will not be amiss for them who had rather

---

[1] Inartificial: not according to the art of logic.

list themselves under this weaker sort, and follow authorities, to take notice that this opinion which I bring, hath bin favour'd, and by som of those affirm'd, who in their time were able to carry what they taught, had they urg'd it, through all Christendom; or to have left it such a credit with all good men, as they who could not bouldly use the opinion, would have fear'd to censure it. But since by his appointment on whom the times and seasons wait, every point of doctrin is not fatall to be throughly sifted out in every age, it will be anough for me to find, that the thoughts of wisest heads heertofore, and hearts no less reverenc't for devotion have tended this way, and contributed their lot in some good measure towards this which hath bin heer attain'd. Others of them and modern especially, have bin as full in the assertion, though not so full in the reason; so that either in this regard, or in the former, I shall be manifest in a middle fortune to meet the praise or dispraise of beeing [81] somthing first. But I deferr not what I undertooke to shew, that in the Church both primitive and reformed, the words of Christ have bin understood to grant divorce for other causes then adultery; and that the word *fornication* in mariage hath a larger sense then that commonly suppos'd.

Justin Martyr in his first Apology writt'n within 50. yeares after St. *John* dy'd, relates a story which *Eusebius* transcribes,[2] that a

---

[2] Justin Martyr, *Apologia II* [not *I*] *pro Christianis*, ii (Migne, *Graeca*, VI, 443); Eusebius Pamphili, *Historiae Ecclesiasticae*, IV, 17 (Migne, *Graeca*, XX, 569–70): "A certain woman, says he [Justin Martyr] had a husband that was intemperate. She herself, had also previously led a dissolute life; but after she was made acquainted with the doctrines of Christ, she became modest, and endeavoured to persuade her husband also to lead a virtuous life, presenting to his mind the doctrines of Christ, and the punishment of eternal fire awaiting those who would not live virtuously, and according to right reason. But he still continuing in the same lascivious habits, wholly alienated his wife's affections by his practices. Finally, the woman considering it wicked to live with one who, contrary to the law of nature and propriety, was intent upon every course to gratify his lusts, contemplated a divorce. But when she was encouraged by her friends, who advised her still to remain with him, as if he might give hopes of a change in life, she did violence to herself and remained. Afterwards, however, her husband, who had gone to Alexandria, was reported to be acting much worse. Fearing, therefore, lest she should become a sharer in his unrighteousness and impieties, if she continued united to him, and should be his companion, she sent him what is called a bill of divorce, and was separated." *Ecclesiastical History*, tr. C. F. Crusé (London, 1903), pp. 152–53. Milton found this passage cited in Matthaeus Wesenbechius, *In Pandectas Juris Civilis & Codicis Justinanei, lib. iix* [*sic*] *Comentarii* (Lyons, 1583; BML), p. 101.

certain matron of Rome, the wife of a vitious husband, her selfe also formerly vitious, but converted to the faith, and persuading the same to her husband, at lest the amendment of his wicked life, upon his not yeilding to her daily entreaties and persuasions in this behalf, procur'd by law to be divorc't from him. This was neither for adultery, nor desertion, but as the relation saies, *Esteeming it an ungodly thing to be the consort of bed with him, who against the law of nature and of right sought out voluptuous waies.* Suppose he endeavour'd som unnaturall abuse, as the Greek admitts that meaning, it cannot yet be call'd adultery; it therefore could be thought worthy of divorce no otherwise then as equivalent, or wors; and other vices will appear in other respects as much divorsive. Next tis said her freinds advis'd her to stay a while; and what reason gave they? not because they held unlawfull what she purpos'd, but because they thought she might longer yet hope his repentance. She obey'd, till the man going to *Alexandria*, and from thence reported to grow still more impenitent, not for any adultery or desertion, wherof neither can be gather'd, but, saith the *Martyr*, and speaks it like one approving, *lest she should be partaker of his unrighteous and ungodly deeds, remaining in wedloc, the communion of bed and board with such a person, she left him by a lawfull divorce.* This cannot but give us the judgement of the Church in those pure and next to Apostolic times. For how els could the woman have bin permitted, or heer not reprehended; and if a wife might then doe this without reprooff, a husband certainly might no less, if not more.

Tertullian in the same age writing his 4. book against *Marcion* [3] witnesses *that Christ by his answer to the Pharises protected the constitution of Moses as his own, and directed the institution of the creator,* for I alter not his *Carthaginian* phrase; [4] *he excus'd rather then destroi'd the constitution of Moses; I say he forbidd conditionally, if any one therefore put away that he may marry another: so that if he prohibited conditionally, then not wholly; and what he forbadd not wholly, he permitted otherwise, where the cause ceases for which he prohibited*: that is when a man makes it not the cause of [82] his putting away, meerly that he may marry again. *Christ teaches not contrary to Moses, the justice of divorce hath Christ the*

---

[3] *Adversus Marcionem*, IV, 34 (Migne, *Latina*, II, 472–73).

[4] Carthaginian phrase: Tertullian was a native of Carthage. Milton blames the shaky Latin syntax on this fact.

asserter: he would not have mariage separat, nor kept with igno-miny, permitting then a divorce, and guesses that this vehemence of our Saviours sentence was cheifly bent against *Herod,* as was cited before. Which leavs it evident how *Tertullian* interpreted this pro-hibition of our Saviour; for wheras the text is, *Whosoever putteth away and marieth another,* wherfore should *Tertullian* explain it, *Whosoever putteth away that he may marry another,* but to signify his opinion that our Saviour did not forbidd divorce from an un-worthy yoke, but forbidd the malice or the lust of a needles change and cheifly those plotted divorces then in use.

Origen in the next century testifies to have known certain who had the government of Churches in his time, who permitted som to marry, while yet their former husbands liv'd, and excuses the deed, as don *not without cause, though without Scripture,* which confirms that cause not to be adultery; for how then was it against Scripture that they maried again.[5] And a little beneath, for I cite his 7. homily on *Matthew,* saith he, *To endure faults wors then adultery and fornication, seems a thing unreasonable,* and disputes therfore that Christ did not speak by *way of precept, but as it were expounding.* By which and the like speeches *Origen* declares his mind farre from thinking that our Saviour confin'd all the causes of divorce to actual adultery.

Lactantius of the age that succeeded speaking of this matter in the 6. of his *institutions,* hath these words.[6] *But lest any think he may circumscribe divine precepts, let this be added, that all mis-interpreting, and occasion of fraud, or death may be remov'd, he commits adultery who marries the divorc't wife, and, besides the crime of adultery, divorces a wife that he may marry another.* To divorce and marry another, and to divorce that he may marry another, are two different things; and imply that *Lactantius* thought not this place the forbidding of all necessary divorce, but such only as proceeded from the wanton desire of a future chois, not from the burden of a present affliction.

[5] *Commentaria in Evangelium Secundum Matthaeum,* XIV, 24 (Migne, *Graeca,* XIII, 1247). Also cited in *Martin Bucer,* above, p. 452, and by Wesen-bechius, *Pandectas* (Lyons, 1583), p. 101.

[6] *Divinarum Institutionum,* VI, 23 (Migne, *Latina,* VI, 720). Lucius Caelicus Firmianus Lactantius (early fourth century) was a Christian apologist. Milton's debt to him is studied in Kathleen Ellen Hartwell, *Lactantius and Milton* (Cambridge, 1929). See *Complete Prose,* I, 363, 364, 369, 373, 422, etc.

About this time the Councel of *Eliberis* in *Spain*[7] decreed the husband excommunicat, *If he kept his wife being an adultress; but if he left her, he might after ten yeares be receav'd into communion, if he retain'd her any while in his house after the adultery known.* The councel of *Neocaesarea*[8] in the year 314. decreed, that if the wife of any *Laic* were convicted of adultery, that man could not be admitted into the ministery: if after ordination it [83] were committed, he was to divorce her; if not, he could not hold his ministery. The councel of *Nantes*[9] condemn'd in 7. yeares penance the husband that would reconcile with an adultress. But how proves this that other causes may divorce? it proves thus; there can be but two causes why these councels enjoyn'd so strictly the divorsing of an adultress, either as an offender against God, or against the husband; in the latter respect they could not impose on him to divorce; for every man is the maister of his own forgivenes; who shal hinder him to pardon the injuries don against himself? it follows therfore that the divorce of an adultress was commanded by these three councels, as it was a sin against God; and by all consequence they could not but beleeve that other sins as hainous might with equal justice be the ground of a divorce.

[7] *Conciliorum Omnium tam Generalium quam Provincialium . . . Sixti V. Pontificis Maxime* (5 vols., Lyons, 1585), I, 605. This work dates the Council of Eliberis (Elvira, near Granada) *ca.* 313. Karl Joseph Hefele, *Histoire des Conciles,* Benedictine edition (20 vols., Paris, 1907–52), the modern authority on the councils, dates it *ca.* 300 and calls it a provincial synod. There were several collections of councils before Milton wrote *Tetrachordon,* concerning the bibliography of which, see Hefele, I, 97–124.

[8] *Conciliorum Omnium* (Lyons, 1585), I, 470, gives three texts of the canons of the Council of Neocaesarea. Milton has substantially translated the third of these, that of Gentianus Hervetus. *Conciliorum Omnium* gives 316 as the probable date, remarking that authorities differ, some putting it as late as 320. Hefele, *Histoire,* I, 326–27, gives the dates as between 314 and 325.

[9] *Conciliorum Omnium* (Lyons, 1585), IV, 43: "If someone's wife committed adultery, and this was discovered by the husband and published, he may dismiss the wife for fornication: she shall do penance for seven years. Her husband shall in no wise take another wife while she lives. But if he wishes to be reconciled with the adultress, he shall have leave, provided that he does penance equally with her, and strict penance after seven years shall admit them to the communion [of the Church]. The same rule shall apply to the wife, if her husband commits adultery against her." *Conciliorum Omnium* notes that the date of this provincial synod is uncertain; other collections of the sixteenth and seventeenth centuries date it in 895. Hefele, *Histoire,* III, 296–98, gives 658 as the probable date.

Basil in his 73. rule, as *Chamier* numbers it, thus determins, that divorce ought not to be, unlesse for adultery, *or the hindrance to a godly life.*[10] What doth this but proclaime aloud more causes of divorce then adultery, if by other sins besides this, in wife or husband, the godlines of the better person may be certainly hinder'd, and endanger'd.

Epiphanius[11] no less ancient, writing against Heretics, & therefore should himself be orthodoxal above others, acquaints us in his second book *Tom.* 1, not that his private persuasion was, but that the whole Church in his time generally thought other causes of divorce lawful besides adultery, as comprehended under that name;[12] *If,* saith he, *a divorce happ'n for any cause either fornication, or adultery, or any hainous fault, the word of God blames not either the man or wife marrying again, nor cutts them off from the congregation, or from life, but beares with the infirmity; not that he may keep both wives, but that leaving the former he may be lawfully joyn'd to the latter, the holy word, and the holy Church of God commiserates this man, especially, if he be otherwise of good conversation, and live according to Gods law.* This place is cleerer then exposition, and needs no comment.

Ambrose on the 16. of *Luke,* teaches *that all wedloc is not Gods joyning* and to the 19. of *Pro.* That a *wife is prepard of the Lord,* as the old latin translates it, he answers that the septuagint renders it, *a wife is fitted by the Lord, and temper'd to a kind of harmony; and where that harmony is there God joyns; where it is not, there dissention reigns, which is not from God, for God is love.*[13] This he

---

[10] Danielus Chamierus, *Panstratiae Catholicae* (4 vols. in 2, Frankfurt, 1627; UTSL), III, 348: "it is not lawful for a husband to be separated from his wife, or a wife from her husband, except for adultery, or because there is an impediment to piety." Daniel Chamier (d. 1621) was a French Protestant theologian.

[11] Epiphanius (d. 535) was Patriarch of Constantinople and author of several letters to Pope Hormisdas.

[12] *Adversus Haereses,* I, i, Haereses LIX (or XXIX), "Contra Catharos" (Migne, *Graeca,* XLI, 1021).

[13] All three texts are dealt with in *Expositionis in Lucam,* VIII, 2–8 (Migne, *Latina,* XV, 1855–58). On Proverbs 19:14 Ambrose writes: "Who reads this in Greek does not think there is any contrary. The Greek indeed says ἁρμονία; harmony in fact is said conveniently and aptly of all things composing unity. Therefore where there are marriages, there is harmony; where there is harmony, God joins. Where there is no harmony, strife and dissension is, which is not from God, for God is love." Wesenbechius, *Pandectas* (Lyons, 1583), p. 101, also cites Ambrose.

brings to prove the marrying of Christian with Gentile to be no mariage, and consequently divorc't without sin: but he who sees not this argument how plainly it serves to divorce any untunable, or unattonable matrimony, sees little. On the 1 to the *Cor.* 7,[14] he grants a wo-[84]man may leave her husband not only for fornication, *but for Apostacy, and inverting nature, though not marry again; but the man may*: heer are causes of divorce assign'd other then adultery. And going on he affirms, *that the cause of God is greater then the cause of matrimony; that the reverence of wedloc is not due to him who hates the author thereof; that no matrimony is firm without devotion to God; that dishonour don to God acquitts the other being deserted from the bond of matrimony; that the faith of mariage is not to be kept with such.* If these contorted sentences be ought worth, it is not the desertion that breaks what is broken, but the impiety; and who then may not for that cause better divorce, then tarry to be deserted? or these grave sayings of St. *Ambrose* are but knacks.

Jerom on the 19. of *Matthew* explains, that for the cause of fornication, or the *suspicion thereof a man may freely divorce.*[15] What can breed that suspicion, but sundry faults leading that way? by *Jeroms* consent therfore divorce is free not only for actuall adultery, but for any cause that may encline a wise man to the just suspicion therof.

Austin also must be remember'd among those who hold that this instance of fornication gives equal inference to other faults equally hateful, for which to divorce: [16] & therfore in his books to *Pollen-*

---

[14] Ambrose's extended treatment of I Corinthians is in *Commentarium in Epistolam I ad Corinthios,* VII (Migne, *Latina,* XVII, 230). The passage Milton summarizes is: "If therefore the man apostasizes, or seeks to pervert the use of his wife, neither can the woman marry another, nor return to him. 'And the husband shall not dismiss his wife.' But there is added 'except for the cause of fornication.' Wherefore he well subjects her, saying thus concerning the woman: that if she dismisses, she shall remain so, for to the man it is lawful to take another wife, if he dismisses his sinning wife, for the man is not so restricted by the law as the woman: the head of the woman in truth is the man." The rest of the passage is taken from Ambrose's comment *passim.*

[15] *Commentaria in Evangelium Secundum Matthaeum,* XIX (Migne, *Latina,* XXVI, 140): "Wherever therefore there is fornication, and the suspicion of fornication, the wife may freely be dismissed."

[16] *De Conjugiis Adulterinis ad Pollentium,* I, 17 (Migne, *Latina,* XL, 462). Apparently this is the passage Milton has in mind: "For if a man is permitted to be separated from his consort because of fornication of the body, how much more is fornication of the mind to be detested in the consort? that is, infidelity."

tius he disputes that *infidelity, as being a greater sin then adultery, ought so much the rather cause a divorce.* And on the Sermon in the Mount, under the name of fornication will have *idolatry, or any harmfull superstition* contain'd, which are not thought to disturb matrimony so directly as som other obstinacies and dissaffections, more against the daily duties of that cov'nant, & in the eastern tongues not unfrequently call'd fornication, as hath bin shew'n. *Hence is understood,* saith he, *that not only for bodily fornication, but for that which draws the mind from Gods law, and fouly corrupts it, a man may without fault put away his wife, and a wife her husband, because the Lord excepts the cause of fornication, which fornication we are constrain'd to interpret in a general sense.*[17] And in the first book of his *retractions* chap. 16.[18] he retracts not this his opinion, but commends it to serious consideration; and explains that he counted not there all sin to be fornication, but the more detestable sort of sins.[19] The cause of fornication therefore is not in this discours newly interpreted to signify other faults infringing the duties of wedloc, besides adultery.

Lastly the councel of *Agatha* in the year 506. can. 25. decreed, that *if lay men who divorc't without some great fault, or giving no probable cause, therfore divorc't, that they might marry som unlawfull person, or som other* [85] *mans,*[20] *if before the provinciall Bishops were made acquainted, or judgements past, they presum'd this, excommunication was the penalty.*[21] Whence it followes, that if the cause of divorce were som great offence, or that they gave probable causes for what they did, and did not therefore divorce that they might presume with som unlawfull person, or what was another mans, the censure of Church in those daies did not touch them.

---

[17] *De Sermone Domini in Monte,* I, 16 (Migne, *Latina,* XXXIV, 1252–53): "For especially is the idolatry which infidels follow, and any noxious superstition, fornication," and henceforth substantially as Milton renders it. Cited by Wesenbechius, p. 101.

[18] "16" is probably an error (reversed letter?) for "19," the chapter numbering in all editions, modern and older, which I have seen.

[19] *Retractionum,* I, xix (Migne, *Latina,* XXXII, 615–16).

[20] The Latin indicates that some such word as "wife" should be supplied for the sense.

[21] *Conciliorum Omnium* (Lyons, 1585), II, 506; Hefele, *Histoire,* II, 973–80, 991. "Agatha" is Agde in Languedoc. Milton condenses the full formula of excommunication: "shall be excluded from the communion of the church and from the society of holy people, because they defile faith and marriage."

Thus having alleg'd anough to shew after what manner the primitive Church for above 500. yeares understood our Saviours words touching divorce, I shall now with a labour less disperst, and sooner dispatcht, bring under view what the civil law of those times constituted about this matter: I say the civil law, which is the honour of every true Civilian to stand for, rather then to count that for law, which the *pontificall* Canon hath enthrall'd them to, and in stead of interpreting a generous and elegant law, made them the drudges of a blockish *Rubric*.

Theodosius and *Valentinian,* pious Emperors both, ordain'd that *as by consent lawfull mariages were made, so by consent, but not without the bill of divorce, they might be dissolv'd; and to dissolve was the more difficult, onely in favour of the children.*[22] We see the wisedome and piety of that age one of the purest and learnedest since Christ, conceav'd no hindrance in the words of our Saviour, but that a divorce mutually consented, might bee suffer'd by the law, especially if there were no children, or if there were, carefull provision was made. And further saith that law (supposing there wanted the consent of either) *wee designe the causes of divorce by this most wholsom law; for as we forbid the dissolving of mariage without just cause, so we desire that a husband or a wife distrest by som advers necessity, should be freed, though by an unhappy, yet a necessary releefe.* What dramm of wisedome, or religion (for charity is truest religion) could there be in that knowing age, which is not virtually summ'd up in this most just law? As for those other Christian Emperours, from *Constantine* the first of them, finding the Roman law in this point so answerable to the Mosaic, it might bee the likeliest cause why they alter'd nothing to restraint, but if ought, rather to liberty, for the helpe, and consideration of the weaker sexe, according as the Gospel seems to make the wife more equal to her husband in these conjugal respects then the law of *Moses* doth. Therefore *if a man were absent from his wife foure yeares, and in that space not heard of, though gon to warre in the service of the Empire,* she might divorce, and mary another by the edict of *Constantine* to *Dalmatius. Co. l. 5. tit.* 17.[23] And this was

[22] *Juris Civilis, Code,* book V, title 17, paragraph 8 (Geneva, 1591–95, cols. 406–407; Scott, XIII, 203). Cited in *Martin Bucer,* above, p. 462; also by Peter Martyr, below, p. 711, n. 59; and in several other sources used by Milton.

[23] Paragraph 7 (Geneva, 1591–95, col. 406; Scott, XIII, 202).

an age of the Church both antient, and cry'd up still for the most flouri-[86]shing in knowledge and pious government since the Apostles. But to returne to this law of *Theodosius,* with this observation by the way, that still as the Church corrupted, as the Clergie grew more ignorant, and yet more usurping on the Magistrate, who also now declin'd, so still divorce grew more restrain'd; though certainly if better times permitted the thing that worse times restrain'd, it would not weakly argue that the permission was better, and the restraint worse. This law therefore of *Theodosius* wiser in this then the most of his successors, though not wiser then God and *Moses,* reduc't the causes of divorce to a certain number which by the judiciall law of God, and all recorded humanitie were left before to the brest of each husband, provided that the dismisse was not without reasonable conditions to the wife. But this was a restraint not yet come to extreames. For besides adultery and that not only actual, but suspected by many signes there set down, any fault equally punishable with adultery, or equally infamous might bee the cause of a divorce. Which informes us how the wisest of those ages understood that place in the Gospel, whereby, not the pilfering of a benevolence was consider'd as the main and only breach of wedloc, as is now thought, but the breach of love and peace, a more holy union then that of the flesh; and the dignity of an honest person was regarded, not to bee held in bondage with one whose ignominy was infectious. To this purpose was constituted *Cod. l.* 5. *tit.* 17. and *Authent. collat.* 4. *tit.* 1. *Novell.* 22. where *Justinian* added three causes more.[24] In the 117. *Novell.* most of the same causes are allow'd, but the liberty of divorcing by consent is repeal'd: but by whom? by *Justinian,* not a wiser, not a more religious emperor then either of the former, but noted by judicious writers for his fickle head in making and unmaking lawes; and how *Procopius* a good historian, and a counselor of state then living deciphers him in his

---

[24] *Juris Civilis, Code,* book V, title 17, paragraph 11 (Geneva, 1591–95, col. 408; Scott, XIII, 207), allows divorce to the husband whose wife procures an abortion by her own efforts, or who goes to baths with men for lascivious purposes, or who, while still married, tries to get a new husband. *Novella* CXVII, chapter 10 (Geneva, 1591–95, col. 275), abrogates divorce by consent, "because indeed people have, up to now, dissolved marriages one after another by consent, we command that from now on this shall not be done in any manner, unless some should do it out of a desire for chastity [*i.e.,* to enter monastic life]." References to the two *Novellae* are in Henningus Arnisaeus, *De Jure Connubiorum* (Frankfurt, 1613; BML), p. 279.

other actions, I willingly omitt.[25] Nor was the Church then in better case, but had the corruption of a 100. declining yeare swept on it, when the statute of *consent* was call'd in; which as I said, gives us every way more reason to suspect this restraint, more then that liberty: which therfore in the reign of *Justin* the succeeding Emperor was recall'd, *Novel.* 140. & establisht with a preface more wise & christianly then [26] for those times,[27] declaring the necessity to restore that *Theodosian* law, if no other meanes of reconcilement could be found. And by whom this law was abrogated, or how long after, I doe not finde; but that those other causes remain'd in force, as long as the Greek empire subsisted, and were assented by that Church, is to bee read [87] in the Canons and edicts compar'd by *Photius* the Patriarch,[28] with the avertiments of *Balsamon,* and *Matthaeus Monachus* thereon.[29]

[25] Procopius' *Anecdota* (or *Secret History*) abounds in descriptions of Justinian's vices. A sample passage (X, 21), which Milton may have had in mind, runs, "Accordingly, when Justinian took over the Empire he immediately succeeded in bringing confusion upon everything. For things which previously had been forbidden by law he kept introducing into the constitution, and tearing down all existing institutions and those made familiar by custom, as if he had put on the imperial garb on the condition that he should change all things also into another garb." Tr. H. B. Dewing (7 vols., New York and London: Loeb Classical Library, 1914–40), VI, 129. Procopius (*ca.* 490–562) was the chief historian of Justinian's era.

[26] Supply some such word as "usual" for the sense.

[27] *Novella* CXL (Geneva, 1591–95, cols. 348–49; Scott, XVII, 158–60), after a preface concerning the irreconcilable hatred which produces constant strife in some houses and gives rise to a desire by the husband and wife to separate by mutual consent, provides that "in conformity to the ancient rule, it shall be lawful to dissolve marriages by common consent." The Theodosian requirement of a bill of divorce is insisted on and the Justinian laws on divorce for other causes reaffirmed.

[28] Photius (*ca.* 815–897) was Patriarch of Constantinople and chief leader in the schism between Eastern and Western Churches.

[29] Photius, *Nomocanon,* title 13, chapter 4 (Migne, *Graeca,* CIV, 1190–94). The text is the same as that of Photius' *Syntagma Canonum,* title 13, chapter 4 (Migne, *Graeca,* CIV, 903–11), with the addition of scholia, chiefly by Theodore Balsamon. The Renaissance editions of Photius (Basle, 1561, and Paris, 1615) contain these scholia by Balsamon, which refer to the civil law on divorce, without any indication of its abrogation. I have not seen any edition of Photius with scholia by Matthaeus Monachus. Perhaps the "avertiment" of Matthaeus to which Milton refers is his treatment of divorce in Leunclavius, *Juris Graeco-Romani* (Frankfurt, 1596; CULL), I, 507–508, where he lists the causes of divorce "especially enumerated by religious emperors, for which alone it is lawful to dissolve marriage." These include (1) conspiracy of the wife

But long before those dayes [30] *Leo* the son of *Basilius Macedo* [31] reigning about the yeare 886. and for his excellent wisdome sur- nam'd the *Philosopher,* constituted *that in case of madnesse the hus- band might divorce after three yeares, the wife after 5. Constitut. Leon.* 111. 112.[32] This declares how hee expounded our Saviour, and deriv'd his reasons from the institution, which in his preface with great eloquence are set downe; whereof a passage or two may give som proofe, though better not divided from the rest. *There is not,* saith he, *a thing more necessary to preserve mankind, then the helpe giv'n him from his own rib; both God and nature so teaching us: which being so, it was requisite that the providence of law, or if any other care be to the good of man, should teach and ordaine those things which are to the helpe and comfort of maried persons, and confirme the end of mariage purpos'd in the beginning, not those things which afflict and bring perpetuall misery to them.* Then an- swers the objection that they are one flesh; *if Matrimony had held so as God ordain'd it, he were wicked that would dissolve it. But if we respect this in matrimony, that it be contracted to the good of both, how shall he, who for some great evil feard, perswades not to marry though contracted, not perswade to unmarry, if after mar- riage a calamity befall? should we bid beware least any fall into an evil, and leave him helplesse who by humane error is fall'n therein? This were as if we should use remedies to prevent a disease, but let the sick die without remedy.* The rest will be worth reading in the author.

And thus we have the judgement first of primitive fathers; next of the imperial law not disallow'd by the universal Church in ages

against the reigning prince, when this is unknown to the husband; (2) convic- tion of adultery; (3) plotting against the life of the husband; (4) the wife's remaining away from home without the husband's consent, except perhaps with her parents; and (5) the wife's frequenting circuses, spectacles, or the arena, without the husband's knowledge or against his will.

[30] That is, before the days of Balsamon (d. after 1195) and Matthaeus(?), not of Photius (d. 891), who was contemporary with Leo.

[31] Leo VI was Emperor, 886–912.

[32] *Imp. Leonis Augusti Constitutiones Novellae,* ed. Henricus Agylaeus ([Paris?], 1650). Agylaeus' preface, pp. 4–6, supplies Milton with the in- formation about Leo. Constitution CXI, pp. 180–82 (Scott, XVII, 293–94), prescribes that a husband may divorce for madness after three years; Constitu- tion CXII, pp. 182–85 (Scott, XVII, 295–96), allows the wife the same privilege after five years. The passage Milton translates follows, pp. 182–83 (Scott, p. 294).

of her best authority; and lastly of the whole Greeke Church and civil state, incorporating their Canons and edicts together, that divorce was lawfull for other causes equivalent to adultery, contain'd under the word fornication. So that the exposition of our saviours sentence heer alleg'd hath all these ancient and great asserters, is therefore neither new nor licentious, as some now would perswade the commonalty; although it be neerer truth that nothing is more new then those teachers themselves, & nothing more licentious then some known to be, whose hypocrisie yet shames not to take offence at this doctrine for licence; when as indeed they feare it would remove licence, and leave them but few companions. [88]

That the Popes Canon law incroaching upon civil Magistracy abolisht all divorce eevn for adultery. What the reformed Divines have recover'd; and that the famousest of them have taught according to the assertion of this booke.

But in these western parts of the empire it will appeare almost unquestionable that the cited law of *Theodosius* and *Valentinian* stood in force untill the blindest and corruptest times of Popedom displac't it. For that the volumes of *Justinian* never came into *Italy,* or beyond *Illiricum,* is the opinion of good Antiquaries. And that only manuscript thereof found in *Apulia* by *Lotharius* the *Saxon,* and giv'n to the state of *Pisa* for their aid at sea against the *Normans* of *Sicily,* was receav'd as a rarity not to bee matcht. And although the *Gothes,* and after them the *Lombards* and *Franks* who over-run the most of *Europ* except this Island (unlesse wee make our *Saxons* and *Normans* a limm of them) brought in their owne customes, yet that they follow'd the Roman laws in their contracts and mariages, *Agathias* [33] the historian is alleg'd. And other testimonies relate that *Alaricus* [34] & *Theodoric* [35] their Kings writ their statutes out of this *Theodosian Code* which hath the recited law of Divorce.[36] Never-

[33] Agathias (*ca.* 536–582) was a Byzantine historian who continued the work of Procopius.

[34] Alaric was King of the Visigoths *ca.* 370–410.

[35] Theodoric (*ca.* 454–526) was King of the Ostrogoths and conqueror of Italy.

[36] Based on Marquardus Freherus, "Epistola Dedicatoria" to Leunclavius, ed., *Juris Graeco-Romani,* I, ff. iii^v–iv. It does not appear, writes Freherus, that the Justinian Code was "either published or proposed for observation by the same Justinian in the City of Rome, or in any part of Italy, still less in the other Latin provinces, except Illyria. . . . For at the same time when Justinian, in his third consulate, composed and issued those books in Greece, Italy had al-

thelesse while the Monarchs of Christendome were yet barbarous, and but halfe Christian, the Popes tooke this advantage of their weake superstition, to raise a corpulent law out of the canons and *decretals* of audacious preists; and presum'd also to set this in the front; *That the constitutions of princes are not above the constitutions of clergy, but beneath them.* Using this very instance of divorce as the first prop of their tyranny; by a false consequence drawn from a passage of *Ambrose* upon *Luke* where hee saith, though *Mans law grant it, yet Gods prohibits it.* Whence *Gregory* the Pope [37] writing to *Theoctista* inferrs that Ecclesiasticall Courts cannot be dissolv'd by the Magistrate.[38] A faire conclusion from a double error. First in saying that the divine law prohibited divorce, for what will hee make of *Moses;* next supposing that it did, how will it follow, that what ever Christ forbids in his Evangelic pre-

ready been occupied sixty years by the Goths and bound by their barbarian laws: when the domination of the Goths had lasted a little less than eight years, the kingdom of the Lombards followed, and then that of the Franks. . . . And Agathias, no mean author, describing the Franks and the Germans, clearly enough witnesses that they were not entirely deprived of Roman polity and used Roman laws among themselves and Roman customs in their contracts and marriages. Of which indeed remains often appear, got, it seems clear to us, probably from the codes of Theodosius and of Gregorius Hermogenius (all of which, as they have somewhat of the Jurists Gaius, Paulus, and Papinian, whence both Alaric King of the Goths, and Theodoric King of the Franks, took their laws), not from the Justinian Code, whose body of laws does not appear by any sign to have reached any part [of Italy], concerning which indeed there is complete silence in Isadore of Seville and Dagobert, King of the Franks, where they enumerate the origins of law and especially remember the Theodosian Code; nor in the capitularies of Charlemagne and Louis collected by Ansegisus are there any remains of it. . . . Nor can I satisfactorily explain by what fortune Lotharius the Saxon Emperor may have found those books six centuries after their publication, whose fame is certainly first among the learned. . . . These are certainly the most ancient copy of the Pandects, which if not of the age of Justinian (as some think) and the prototype of Trebonian himself, at least were written not long after in Greece itself and kept at one time either in the library of Byzantium or in that of Ravenna, or otherwise at the city of Amalfi. The book may have belonged to Apulia, in whose sack it was discovered about the year 1336 and given by the Emperor Lotharius II and the Pope Innocent II to the Pisans as a reward for a distinguished naval action, which they helped carry out against Roger the Norman. They bore it home with the greatest veneration of antiquity."

[37] Gregory I (*ca.* 540–604), surnamed "the Great," is famous both for his numerous writings and for his organizational ability as Pope.

[38] Gregorius Magnus, *Epistolarum Liber* XI, XLV (Migne, *Latina*, LXXVII, 1160–62).

cepts, should be hal'd into a judicial constraint against the patterne
of a divine law: Certainely the Gospel came not to enact such com-
pulsions. In the meane while wee may note heere that the restraint
of divorce was one of the first faire seeming pleas which the Pope
had, to step into secular authority, and with his Antichristian rigor
to abolish the permissive law of Christian princes conforming to a
sacred lawgiver. Which if we consider, this papal and un-[89]just
restriction of divorce need not be so deere to us, since the plausible
restraining of that, was in a manner the first loosning of Antichrist;
and as it were the substance of his eldest horn. Nor doe we less
remarkably ow the first meanes of his fall heer in *England* to the
contemning of that restraint by *Henry* 8. whose divorce he oppos'd.
Yet was not that rigour executed anciently in spiritual Courts untill
Alexander the third,[39] who trod upon the neck of *Frederic Barbarossa* [40] the Emperor, and summond our Henry 2.[41] into *Normandy* about the death of *Becket.* He it was, that the worthy author
may be known, who first actually repeal'd the imperial law of divorce, and decreed this tyranous decree, that matrimony for no
cause should be dissolv'd, though for many causes it might separate;
as may be seen *decret. Gregor. l.* 4. *tit.* 19. and in other places of the
Canonicall Tomes.[42] The main good of which invention, wherein it
consists who can tell? but that it hath one vertue incomparable, to
fill all christendom with whordomes, and adulteries beyond the art
of *Balaams* [43] or of divells. Yet neither can these, though so per-
verse, but acknowledge that the words of Christ under the name of
fornication allow putting away for other causes then adultery both
from *bed and bord,* but not from the *bond;* their only reason is, because mariage they beleeve to bee a Sacrament. But our Divines
who would seem long since to have renounc't that reason, have so

[39] Pope Alexander III (1159–1181) is most noted for upholding Papal supremacy in the quarrels with Frederic Barbarossa and Henry II.

[40] Frederic Barbarossa, German Emperor (1152–1190), became involved with
Alexander III in a dispute over investiture. His repentance at Canossa is historical, but the story that Alexander placed his foot on Frederic's neck is now
usually regarded as fable.

[41] Henry II (1133–1189) is perhaps most noted for his quarrel with Thomas
À Becket (*ca.* 1118–1170) over church rights.

[42] *Corpus Juris Canonici, Emendatum et Notis Illustratum Gregorii XIII*
(Lyons, 1591), col. 588. Title 19 allows divorces (*i.e.,* separation from bed
and board) for plotting against spouse's life, for witchcraft and corruption of
faith, for adultery, for heresy and infidelity.

[43] See Numbers 23 and 24; and Revelation 2:14.

forgot them selves, as yet to hold the absurdity, which but for that reason, unlesse there be some mystery of Satan in it, perhaps the Papist would not hold. Tis true, we grant divorce for actual & prov'd adultery, and not for lesse then many tedious and unreparable yeares of desertion, wherein a man shall loose all his hope of posterity, which great and holy men have bewail'd, ere he can be righted; and then perhaps on the confines of his old age, when all is not worth the while. But grant this were seasonably don; what are these two causes to many other, which afflict the state of mariage as bad, and yet find no redresse? What hath the soule of man deserv'd, if it be in the way of salvation, that it should be morgag'd thus, and may not redeem it selfe according to conscience out of the hands of such ignorant and slothfull teachers as these, who are neither able nor mindful to give due tendance to that pretious cure which they rashly undertake; nor have in them the noble goodnesse to consider these distresses and accidents of mans life; but are bent rather to fill their mouthes with Tithe and oblation. Yet if they can learne to follow, as well as they can seeke to be follow'd, I shall direct them to a faire number of renowned men, worthy to be their leaders, who will commend to them a doctrin in this point wiser then their own, and if they bee not [90] impatient, it will be the same doctrin which this treatis hath defended.

Wicklef that Englishman honor'd of God to be the first preacher of a general reformation to all *Europe,* was not in this thing better taught of God, then to teach among his cheifest recoveries of truth, that divorce is lawfull to the christian for many other causes equall to adultery. This book indeed through the poverty of our Libraries [44] I am forc't to cite from *Arnisaeus* of *Halberstad on the right of mariage,* who cites it from *Corasius* of *Tolouse, c.* 4. *Cent. Sct.* and he from *Wicklef, l.* 4. *Dial. c.* 21.[45] So much the sorrier, for that I

---

[44] It is remarkable that none of Wycliffe's English works were printed before Milton's time and almost none of the Latin. Manuscripts of the Latin works were and are extremely few in England. Most of the manuscripts used in the Wycliffe Society editions come from Bohemia and are now found in Prague or Vienna libraries. See *Complete Prose,* I, 525.

[45] Hennigus Arnisaeus, *De Jure Connubiorum* (Frankfurt, 1613), p. 325. Arnisaeus cites from Alciatus, who cites from Corasius, and Corasius from Wycliffe. Arnisaeus also has references to Erasmus on I Corinthians and to the Theodosian and Justinian Codes. Arnisaeus (d. 1636?) was a German writer on philosophy and jurisprudence. Johannes Corasius (Jean Coras or de Coras), 1513–1572, was a French jurist.

never lookt into author cited by his adversary upon this occasion, but found him more conducible to the question, then his quotation render'd him.

Next *Luther,* how great a servant of God, in his book of *conjugal life* quoted by *Gerard* out of the Dutch,[46] allowes divorce for the obstinate denial of conjugal duty; and *that a man may send away a proud Vashti, and marry an Esther in her stead.*[47] It seemes, if this example shall not be impertinent, that *Luther* meant not onely the refusall of benevolence, but a stubborn denial of any main conjugal duty; or if he did not, it will be evinc't from what he allowes. For out of question, with men that are not barbarous, love and peace, and fitnesse will be yeelded as essential to mariage, as corporal benevolence. *Though I give my body to be burnt,* saith Saint *Paul, and have not charity, it profits me nothing.*[48] So though the body prostitute it selfe to whom the mind affords no other love or peace, but constant malice and vexation, can this bodily benevolence deserv to be call'd a mariage between Christians and rationall creatures.

Melanchton, the third great luminary of reformation in his book *concerning marriage* grants divorce for cruell usage, and danger of life, urging the authority of that *Theodosian* law, which he esteemes written with the grave deliberation of godly men; *and that they who reject this law, and thinke it disagreeing from the Gospel, understand not the difference of law and Gospel; that the Magistrat ought not only to defend life, but to succour the weake conscience, lest broke with greif and indignation it relinquish praier, and turn to som unlawfull thing.*[49] What if this heavy plight of despaire arise from other discontents in wedloc which may goe to the soule of a

---

[46] Dutch: *i.e.,* German.

[47] *Locum Theologicorum,* VII (Geneva, 1639), col. 774: "But that persistent, *constant,* and long-lasting denial of the conjugal debt is a kind of desertion, and that therefore the husband after private and public admonitions made in vain by the authority of the magistrate, may repudiate that desertress and take another Esther in the place of that proud Vashti in lawful wedlock."

[48] I Corinthians 13:3. Authorized Version: "profiteth."

[49] "De Conjugio," *Loci Communes Theologici* (Basle, 1561), pp. 724–25: "But the Theodosian Code, which I suppose written after grave deliberation by pious men, as divorce is there restricted to certain causes, conceded in fact divorce in these cases [because of cruelty and plotting against life]," and thence forward as Milton translates. Philipp Melanchthon (Schwartzerde), 1497–1560, was a renowned German reformer, chief lieutenant of Luther.

good man more then the danger of his life, or cruel using, which a man cannot bee liable to, suppose it be ingratefull usage, suppose it be perpetuall spight and disobedience, suppose a hatred, shall not the Magistrat free him from this disquiet which interrupts his prayers, and disturbs the cours of his service to God and his Country all as much, and brings him such a mise-[91]ry, as that he more desires to leave his life then feares to loose it: Shall not this equally concerne the office of civil protection, and much more the charity of a true Church to remedy?

Erasmus who for learning was the wonder of his age, both in his *notes* on *Matthew*,[50] and on the first to the *Corinthians*[51] in a large and eloquent discourse, and in his answer to *Phimostomus* a Papist,[52] maintaines (and no protestant then living contradicted him) that the words of Christ comprehend many other causes of divorce under the name of fornication.

Bucer, whom our famous D[r] *Rainolds* was wont to preferr before *Calvin*,[53] in his comment on *Matthew*, and in his second booke *of the Kingdome of Christ*, treats of divorce at large to the same effect, as is written in *the doctrine and discipline of divorce* lately publisht, and the translation is extant: whom lest I should be thought to have wrested to mine own purpose, take somthing more out of his 49. Chap. which I then for brevity omitted. *It will be the duty of pious princes, and all who govern Church, or common*

---

[50] *Annotationes in Matthaeum* in *Omnia Opera* (Basle, 1540), VI, 82–83. The principal point of the passage is that Christ was protesting the lightness of divorce among the Jews.

[51] *Ibid.*, VI, 485. Erasmus protests against restricting the meaning of fornication to bodily intercourse.

[52] See above, p. 620.

[53] This is not in *A Defence of the Judgment of the Reformed Churches* (1610; UTSL), where Bucer is mentioned along with other leading Protestant divines as agreeing that (p. 61) "our Saviour doth allow marriage after divorcement for adulterie"; and Bucer and Luther are cited as (p. 64) "graunting second marriage afer divorcement for moe causes then whordome." The whole treatise is dedicated to proving, against Bellarmine and other Roman apologists, that remarriage after divorce for adultery is scriptural. Milton may have known this treatise, but it was of little use to him, beyond perhaps providing some references, which, however, are commonplaces in the literature dealing with marriage and divorce. John Rainoldes (1549–1607) was an Elizabethan rhetorician and divine. For a sketch of his life see *Oratio in Laudem Artis Poeticae*, ed. and tr. William Ringler and Wreter Allen, Jr. (Princeton: Princeton University Press, 1940), esp. pp. 2–7. For Milton's earlier concern with his writings, see *Complete Prose*, I, 104, 115–18, and 618.

wealth, if any, whether husband or wife, shall affirme their want of such who either will, or can tolerably performe the necessary duties of maried life, to grant that they may seeke them such, and marry them; if they make it appeare that such they have not.[54] This book he wrote heer in *England*, where he liv'd the greatest admir'd man, and this hee dedicated to *Edward* the sixth.

Fagius rankt among the famous divines of *Germany*, whom *Frederic* at that time the *Palatine* sent for to be the reformer of his Dominion, and whom afterwards *England* sought to, and obtain'd of him to come and teach her, differs not in this opinion from *Bucer*, as his notes on the *Chaldey paraphrast* well testify.[55]

The whole Church of *Strasburgh* in her most flourishing time, when *Zellius, Hedio, Capito*,[56] and other great Divines taught there, and those two renouned magistrates *Farrerus* and *Sturmius* [57] govern'd that common wealth and Academy to the admiration of all *Germany*, hath thus on the 21. Article. *We teach that if according to the word of God, yea or against it, divorces happen, to doe according to Gods word, Deut.* 24. 1. *Mat.* 19. 1 *Cor.* 7. *and the observation of the primitive Church, and the Christian constitution of pious Caesars.*[58]

Peter Martyr seems in word our easy adversary, but is in deed for us: toward which though it be somthing when he saith of this opinion, *that it is not wicked, and can hardly be refuted*, this which followes is much more, *I speake not heer* saith he, *of natural impediments which may so happ'n that* [92] *the matrimony can no longer hold*: but adding, *that he often wonder'd, how the antient and most christian Emperors establisht those lawes of divorce, and neither* Ambrose, *who had such influence upon the lawes of* Theodosius, *nor any of those holy fathers found fault, nor any of the Churches, why the Magistrats of this day should be so loth to constitute the same. Perhaps they feare an inundation of divorces,*

---

[54] *Scripta Anglicana* (Basle, 1577), p. 130.

[55] In *Critici Sacri*, ed. John Pearson (Frankfurt, 1696), I, cols. 1306–1307. On Fagius see *Martin Bucer*, above, pp. 428–29.

[56] See *Martin Bucer*, above, p. 433.

[57] See *Martin Bucer*, above, p. 433.

[58] "Epitome . . . doctrinae . . . quae Argentorati . . . publice sonuit," in Bucer, *Scripta Anglicana* (Basle, 1577), p. 181. In addition to the scriptural references Milton preserves, there is one to Ambrose, cited by Milton, above, p. 698. See also *Martin Bucer*, above, p. 460.

which is not likely, whenas we reade not either among the Ebrews, Greeks, *or* Romans *that they were much frequent where they were most permitted. If they judge christian men worse then Jewes or Pagans, they both injure that name, and by this reason will bee constrain'd to grant divorces the rather; because it was permitted as a remedy of evil, for who would remove the medcin, while the disease is yet so rife?* This being read both in his *common places,* & on the first *to the Corinthians,*[59] with what we shall relate more of him yet ere the end,[60] sets him absolutely on this side. Not to insist that in both these, & other places of his commentaries hee grants divorce not onely for desertion, but for the seducement and scandalous demeanour of a heretical consort.

Musculus a divine of no obscure fame distinguishes betweene the religious and civil determination of divorce; and leaving the civil wholly to the lawyers, pronounces a conscionable divorce for impotence not only natural, but accidental, if it be durable.[61] His equity it seems, can enlarge the words of Christ to one cause more then adultery; why may not the reason of another man as wise, enlarge them to another cause.

Gualter of *Zuric* a well known judicious commentator in his Homilies on *Matthew,* allows divorce for *Leprosie, or any other cause which renders unfit for wedloc,* and calls this rather *a nullity of mariage then a divorce,* and who, that is not himselfe a meer body, can restrain all the unfitnes of mariage only to a corporal defect.[62]

Hemingius an Author highly esteem'd, and his works printed at *Geneva,* writing of divorce, confesses that lerned men *vary in this*

---

[59] Comment on I Corinthians 7 in *In Selectissimam D. Pauli Priorem ad Corinthios Epistolam,* f. 87v; also *Loci Communes* (1583), p. 237.

[60] Milton refers to Peter Martyr's participation in the committee to frame ecclesiastical laws for England in the time of Edward VI. See below, p. 716.

[61] Wolfgang Musculus, *In Evangelistam Matthaeum Commentarii* (Basle, 1548), pp. 101–103 (on Matthew 5): "Those who cannot satisfy the laws of marriage because of impotence, either natural or accidental, of a lasting sort, can rightly be separated." Wolfgangus Musculus (Wolfgang Mäuslin, Müslin, or Moesel), 1497–1563, was a Benedictine monk, who later professed Protestantism and taught at Strassburg, Augsburg, and Berne, and visited England in 1548.

[62] Rodolphus Gualtherius, *Archetypi Homiliarum in Quatuor Evangelia* (Zurich, 1601; UTSL), ff. 40v, 133v. Rodolphus Gualtherius (Rudolph Walther), 1519–1586, was a follower of Zwingli and also a classical scholar. There is also a son of the same name (1552–1577), who wrote Latin poetry.

question, some granting three causes thereof, some five, others many more; he himselfe gives us sixe, *adultery, desertion, inability, error, evill usage, and impiety,* using argument *that Christ under one special containes the whole kind, & under the name & example of fornication* he includes *other causes equipollent.*[63] This discours he wrote at the [93] request of many who had the judging of these causes in *Denmark and Norway,* who by all likelyhood follow'd his advice.

Hunnius a Doctor of *Wittenberg,* well known both in Divinity & other arts, on the 19. of *Matt.* affirmes *that the exception of fornication exprest by our Saviour excludes not other causes equalling adultery, or destructive to the substantials of matrimony; but was oppos'd to the custom of the Jewes who made divorce for every light cause.*[64]

Felix Bidenbachius an eminent Divine in the Dutchy of *Wirtemberg* affirmes *that the obstinat refusal of conjugal due is a lawful cause of divorce,* and gives an instance *that the consistory of that state so judg'd.*[65]

Gerard cites *Harbardus* [66] an author not unknown, and *Arnisaeus* [67] cites *Wigandus,*[68] both yeelding divorce *in case of cruel usage;* and another author who testifies *to have seen in a dukedom of Germany mariages disjoynd for some implacable enmities arising.*[69]

---

[63] Nicolaus Hemmingus, "De Devortiis," in *Opuscula Theologica* (Geneva, 1586; BML), cols. 1006–1008. Milton summarizes the passage. Hemmingus cites three causes from Ambrose and twelve from the canonists. I can find no list of five. The six of Hemmingus himself are as Milton gives them.

[64] Aegidius Hunnius, *Commentarius in Evangelium de Jesu Christo Secundum Matthaeum,* in *Operum Latinorum* (5 vols., Wittenberg and Frankfurt, 1606–1609; UTSL), III, 433. Aegidius Hunnius (1550–1603) wrote polemics against Catholics and Calvinists.

[65] *De Causis Matrimonialibus Tractatus* (Frankfurt, 1608), p. 99. Felix Bidenbachius (1564–1612), a German theologian, is especially noted for his two works on marriage.

[66] Harbardus is unknown to modern reference works.

[67] *Locorum Theologicorum* (Geneva, 1639), VII, col. 774.

[68] Johann Wigand (also Vigand, 1523–1587), was a Lutheran divine.

[69] *De Jure Connubiorum* (Frankfurt, 1613), in the course of arguing that hatred is not a legitimate cause of divorce, cites Wigandus, pp. 299–300, that an unjustly deserted partner may, according to the constitution and custom of Saxony, avail himself of the Pauline privilege. Elsewhere, p. 334, Arnisaeus cites "Borch, in tract. de Grace. inducata Megap." who had seen "publicly contracted marriages separated because of implacable enmities arising." I suspect that Milton had no more success than I have had in solving the abbreviation "Borch."

Beza one of the strictest against divorce, denies it not *for danger of life from a Heretic,* or *importunat solicitation to doe ought against religion:* and counts it *all one whether the heretic desert, or would stay upon intolerable conditions.*[70] But this decision well examin'd will be found of no solidity. For *Beza* would be askt why, if God so strictly exact our stay in any kind of wedloc, wee had not better stay and hazard a murdering for Religion at the hand of a wife, or husband, as he and others enjoyn us to stay and venture it for all other causes but that? and why a mans life is not as well and warrantably sav'd by divorcing from an orthodox murderer, as a heretical? Againe, if desertion be confest by him to consist not only in the forsaking, but in the unsufferable conditions of staying, a man may as well deduce the lawfulnesse of divorcing from any intolerable conditions (if his grant bee good that wee may divorce thereupon from a heretic) as he can deduce it lawfull to divorce from any deserter, by finding it lawful to divorce from a deserting infidel. For this is plaine, if Saint *Pauls* permission to divorce an infidel deserter, inferre it lawfull for any malicious desertion, then doth *Beza's* definition of a deserter transferr it selfe with like facility from the cause of religion to the cause of malice, and proves it as good to divorce from him who intolerably stayes as from him who purposely departs; and leaves it as lawfull to depart from him who urgently requires a [94] wicked thing, though professing the same religion, as from him who urges a heathenish or superstitious compliance in a different faith. For if there be such necessity of our abiding, wee ought rather to abide the utmost for religion then for any other cause; seeing both the cause of our stay is pretended our religion to mariage, and the cause of our suffering is suppos'd our constant mariage to religion. *Beza* therfore by his owne definition of a deserter justifies a divorce from any wicked or intolerable conditions rather in the same religion then in a different.

Aretius a famous Divine of *Bern* approves many causes of divorce in his *Problemes,* and adds *that the lawes and consistories of Swizzerland approve them also.* As first, *adultery, and that not ac-*

"Inducata" is doubtless, as Milton read it, an error for "in ducatu" (in the duchy). He may not have recognized "Megap." as "Megalopolis," *i.e.*, Mecklenburg.

[70] *Tractatio de Repudiis et Divortiis* (Geneva, 1596), pp. 176–77, 280, 294–95. I have not found the quotation, though Beza makes the point.

tual only, but intentional, alleging *Matthew* the fifth, *Whosoever looketh to lust, hath committed adultery already in his heart. Wherby* saith he, *our Saviour shewes that the breach of matrimony may be not only by outward act, but by the heart and desire; when that hath once possest, it renders the conversation intolerable, and commonly the fact followes.* Other causes to the number of 9. or 10. consenting in most with the imperial lawes, may bee read in the author himselfe, who averrs them *to be grave and weighty.*[71] All these are men of name in Divinity, and to these if need were, might be added more. Nor have the Civilians bin all so blinded by the Canon, as not to avouch the justice of those old permissions touching divorce.

Alciat of *Millain,* a man of extraordinary wisedome and learning, in the sixt book of his *Parerga* defends those imperial lawes, *not repugnant to the Gospel, as the Church then interpreted.* For saith hee, *the antients understood him separat by man, whom passions and corrupt affections divorc't, not, if the provincial Bishops first heard the matter, and judg'd, as the councel of Agatha declares;* and on some part of the Code hee names *Isidorus Hispalensis* the first computer of Canons, *to be in the same minde.* And in the former place gives his opinion *that divorce might be more lawfully permitted then usury.*[72]

Corasius recorded by *Helvicus*[73] among the famous Lawyers hath been already cited of the same judgement.

[71] Benedictus Aretius, *Problema Theologica* (Mainz, 1583), pp. 579–82). On Swiss practice: "Thirdly, our laws and courts today admit other causes of divorce." "Our" Milton rendered "of Swizzerland," since Aretius lived in Berne. "Other causes" means other than those allowed in Roman law. Aretius considers Matthew 5:28 (p. 580): "In which Christ reasonably shows that the dissipation of marriage is not only an external deed: but by hardness of heart. Where a man has that, he makes conversation with his spouse intolerable; so that in fact the deed commonly follows." "Nine or ten": it is impossible to tell whether "insanity which breaks out into manifest madness" and "disease" are one cause or two in Aretius' numbering, hence Milton's "nine or ten." Benedictus Aretius (1505–1574) was a Swiss theologian who also wrote on botany.

[72] Andraeus Alciatus, Παρέργων *Juris* (Lyons, 1554; BML), p. 48. Andraeus Alciatus (Andrea Alciato, 1492–1550, was an Italian jurist more noted for his *Emblemata* than for his annotations to the *Code* and other legal works.

[73] Christophorus Helvicus, *Theatrum Historicum* (Giessen, 1609), table XXXIX: "I Corasius died 1572." The *Theatrum Historicum* is a series of tables of kings, popes, councils, and the like, with lists of famous men who lived in the epoch covered by each table. For the reference to Corasius, see above, p. 707.

Wesembechius a much nam'd Civilian in his comment on this law defends it, and affirms *that our Saviour excluded not other faults* [95] *equall to adultery; and that the word fornication signifies larger among the Hebrewes then with us, comprehending every fault which alienates from him to whom obedience is due, and that the primitive Church interpreted so.*[74]

Grotius yet living, and one of prime note among learned men retires plainly from the Canon to the antient civility, yea to the Mosaic law, *as being most just and undecevable.* On the fifth of *Matt.* he saith, *that Christ made no civil lawes, but taught us how to use law: that the law sent not a husband to the Judge about this matter of divorce, but left him to his owne conscience; that Christ therfore cannot be thought to send him; that adultery may be judg'd by a vehement suspition; that the exception of adultery seems an example of other like offences;* proves it *from the manner of speech, the maxims of law, the reason of charity, and common equity.*[75]

These authorities without long search I had to produce, all excellent men, som of them such as many ages had brought forth none greater: almost the meanest of them might deserve to obtain credit in a singularity; what might not then all of them joyn'd in an opinion so consonant to reason? For although som speak of this cause, others of that, why divorce may be, yet all agreeing in the necessary enlargement of that textual straitnes, leave the matter to equity, not to literal bondage, and so the opinion closes. Nor could I have wanted more testimonies, had the cause needed a more sollicitous enquiry. But herein the satisfaction of others hath bin studied, not the gaining of more assurance to mine own perswasion:

[74] In *Pandectas Juris Civilis* (Lyons, 1583), p. 212: "But the Lord did not exclude faults heavier or equal to adultery, which in fact destroy the substance of marriage. For the word πορνείας, which is used, has a wider meaning, especially among the Hebrews, who comprehended every crime which alienates us from him to whom obedience is due under the word πορνείας, or fornication. . . . Nor was that saying of Christ accepted in any other fashion in the ancient Church." Matthaeus Wesenbecius (Matthew Wesenbeck), 1531–1596, was a Flemish jurist who taught at Jena and Wittenberg.

[75] Hugo Grotius, *Annotationes in Libros Evangeliorum* (Amsterdam, 1641), pp. 97–98, on Matthew 5: "It is to be noted that in the whole sermon [on the mount] Christ did not institute civil laws, but gave precepts to individual souls," and so on approximately as Milton quotes. Note that by dropping the qualification "in the whole sermon," Milton has generalized Grotius' remarks perhaps beyond Grotius' intention. See also *Doctrine and Discipline*, above, pp. 238, 329 ff., and *Martin Bucer*, above, p. 434.

although authorities contributing reason withall, bee a good confirmation and a welcom. But God, I solemnly attest him, withheld
from my knowledge the consenting judgement of these men so late,
untill they could not bee my instructers, but only my unexpected
witnesses to partial men, that in this work I had not given the worst
experiment of an industry joyn'd with integrity and the free utterance though of an unpopular truth. Which yet to the people of
England may, if God so please, prove a memorable informing;
certainly a benefit which was intended them long since by men of
highest repute for wisedome & piety *Bucer & Erasmus*. Only this
one autority more, whether in place or out of place, I am not to
omitt; which if any can think a small one, I must bee pati-[96]ent:
it is no smaller then the whole assembl'd autority of *England* both
Church and State; and in those times which are on record for the
purest and sincerest that ever shon yet on the reformation of this
Iland, the time of *Edward* the 6th. That worthy Prince having utterly abolisht the Canon Law out of his Dominions, as his Father
did before him,[76] appointed by full vote of Parlament, a Committy
of two and thirty chosen men, Divines and Lawyers, of whom *Cranmer* the Archbishop, *Peter Martyr*, and *Walter Haddon,* (not without the assistance of Sir *John Cheeke* the Kings Tutor, a man at
that time counted the learnedest of Englishmen, & for piety not
inferior) were the cheif, to frame anew som Ecclesiastical Laws,
that might be in stead of what was abrogated. The work with great
diligence was finisht, and with as great approbation of that reforming age was receav'd; and had bin doubtlesse, as the learned Preface
thereof testifies, establisht by Act of Parlament, had not the good

---

[76] The statement that Henry VIII abolished canon law appears to be substantially, though not strictly, true. Such legislation as the forbidding of appeals to
Rome (1533) and the Act of Supremacy (1534) necessarily had the effect of
throwing the actual administration of canon law into chaos, so that Pollard
speaks of the "wreck of Canon law" by 1535 (A. F. Pollard, *Henry VIII* [Lon-
don, 1925], p. 336). Pollard also speaks of an act of 1535 authorizing the appointment of a commission to draft a new ecclesiastical code. The committee to
which Milton alludes immediately below was appointed pursuant to an act
passed in 1544. The committee reported a new code, which according to the
accompanying letter utterly abolished "the corrupt laws, decrees, and statutes,
that proceeded from the Bishops of Rome." Henry did not sign the letter or
approve the new code. They were revised and finished in the reign of Edward VI.
See John Strype, *Memorials of Thomas Cranmer* (2 vols., Oxford, 1812), I,
190–92.

Kings death so soon ensuing, arrested the furder growth of Religion also, from that season to this. Those laws, thus founded on the memorable wisedome and piety of that religious Parlament and Synod, allow divorce and second mariage *not only for adultery or desertion, but for any capital enmity or plot laid against the others life, and likewise for evil and fierce usage;* nay the 12. Chap. of that title by plaine consequence declares, *that lesser contentions, if they be perpetual, may obtaine divorce:* [77] which is all one really with the position by me held in the former treatise publisht on this argument, herein only differing that there the cause of perpetual strife was put for example in the unchangeable discord of som natures; but in these lawes intended us by the best of our ancestors, the effect of continual strife is determin'd no unjust plea of divorce, whether the cause be naturall or wilfull. Wherby the warinesse and deliberation from which that discourse proceeded, will appeare, & that God hath aided us to make no bad conclusion of this point; seeing the opinion which of late hath undergon ill censures among the vulgar, hath now prov'd to have don no violence to Scripture, unlesse all these famous Authors alleg'd have done the like; nor hath affirm'd ought more then what indeed the most nominated Fathers

---

[77] The proposals of the commission appointed by Edward VI to reform ecclesiastical law were printed during the reign of Elizabeth: *Reformatio Legum Ecclesiasticarum*, ed. John Foxe (1571; UTSL). Another edition in two issues (*STC* 6007 and 6008) was published in 1640, and this is the one Milton probably used. The following references are to the 1571 edition. The preface names Cranmer, Walter Haddon, and Sir John Cheke among the members of the commission (sig. A4v), and the letter of Edward VI to Cranmer, here quoted, names Peter Martyr as one of the theologians (sig. B3v). The preface also contains the information (sig. B1) that the work was pushed forward with great diligence and received greatest applause and approbation and that the law would doubtless have been established by act of Parliament, but for the untimely death of Edward VI. The section dealing with divorce covers fols. 24–28v. Chapter 8 (fol. 25v) allows divorce for desertion, chapter 10 (fol. 26) for "capital hatreds." Chapter 12 (fols. 26v–27) is titled "Small contentions unless they are perpetual do not lead to divorce," and provides that in the case of minor contentions Paul's "moderate sentence" ought to be applied, that no pains should be spared to procure a reconciliation of the wife and the husband, or at least that the wife should get along without a new husband. No mention is made of granting divorce for minor contentions if they are "perpetual," and Milton, as he admits, has inferred this interpretation from the title. Chapter 13 (fol. 27) denies divorce for incurable disease. The remainder of the section is devoted to the punishment of adultery and incest, separation from bed and board, and the determination of legitimacy.

of the Church both ancient and modern are unexpectedly found affirming, the lawes of Gods pe-[97]culiar people, & of primitive Christendom found to have practis'd, reformed Churches and states to have imitated, and especially the most pious Church-times of this Kingdom to have fram'd and publisht, and, but for sad hindrances in the sudden change of religion, had enacted by Parlament. Hence forth let them who condemn the assertion of this book for new and licentious, be sorry; lest, while they think to be of the graver sort, and take on them to be teachers, they expose themselves rather to be pledg'd up and down by men who intimatly know them, to the discovery and contempt of their ignorance and presumption.

The End.

Errata.

Pag. 57. *lin.* 16. *and by them to prosecute, no comma between.*
Pag. 88. *lin.* 3. Basilius Macedo, *no comma between.* [98]

COLASTERION

March 4, 1645

PREFACE AND NOTES BY LOWELL W. COOLIDGE

*C*olasterion: A Reply to a Nameles Answer against The Doctrine and Discipline of Divorce was published on or before March 4, 1645, the date recorded on the copy in the Thomason Collection. Like *Tetrachordon,* also dated March 4 by Thomason, it was unlicensed and unregistered. The printer, quite understandably, omitted not only his name and the place of publication but also all ornamental capitals and other devices making for ready identification. There is no reason to doubt that it was published in London, however, and its apparently simultaneous issue with *Tetrachordon,* as well as certain typographical similarities in the two pamphlets, lends weight to the surmise that both came from the same shop—most likely that of Matthew Simmons. See William R. Parker, "Milton, Rothwell, and Simmons," *The Library,* Fourth Series, XVIII (1937), 89–103.

The occasion of *Colasterion* is indicated by its subtitle. *An Answer to a Book, Intituled, The Doctrine and Discipline of Divorce, or, A Plea for Ladies and Gentlewomen, and all other Maried Women against Divorce* had appeared in London during the preceding November, having been licensed on the fourteenth of the month and having reached the hands of Thomason five days later. This pamphlet, a facsimile reproduction of which is accessible in William R. Parker's *Milton's Contemporary Reputation* (Columbus: Ohio State University Press, 1940), pp. 170–216, is a small quarto containing 44 pages of text and designed as a point-by-point refutation of Milton's arguments in the 1643 *Doctrine and Discipline.* It was published by William Lee and bears the imprimatur of Joseph Caryl, but its actual authorship remains unknown.

Milton must have addressed himself to his counter-reply sometime between the latter part of November, 1644, and the middle of the following February. His assertion that the *Answer* had been delayed until the *Doctrine and Discipline* had "a whole year bin publisht the second time" (see p. 726 below) suggests that it did not come immediately to his attention. Even if it did, he was probably still occupied with *Tetra-*

719

chordon, which in part at least was composed prior to *Colasterion* as two references in the latter work make evident (pp. 736 and 749 below). *Colasterion* required little new investigation. That it was written rather rapidly, nearer the late than the early limit, seems a reasonable conjecture.

Colasterion was not reprinted during Milton's lifetime. Although included with the other divorce tracts in the earliest collected editions of his prose (1697 and 1698), as well as in the principal eighteenth and nineteenth century collections,[1] it has received relatively little scholarly attention. Until the Columbia edition (1931) there was no critical treatment of the text, and until now there has been no attempt at a detailed annotation.

The present text is reproduced from a copy of the original edition in the Henry E. Huntington Library (105707). It is a quarto measuring 18.2 by 14.1 cm. Collation: [A^2], B–D^4, E^2. B1 is page 1; pagination is continuous to E2r, which is p. 27. Contents: B1: heading [margin-to-margin rule]; text begins. [E2] [margin-to-margin rule]: *"The End."* Huntington copy 105707 has been collated with another copy in the Huntington Library (46432), formerly in the library of Bridgewater House, with copies in the Clark Library, University of California at Los Angeles (*PR3570/C61), the New York Public Library (*KC1645), and the Newberry Library (K75.5782), and with three copies in the British Museum: Ashley 1178, G.19594(4), and E271(11). No variants have been found. Emendations have been restricted to obvious printer's errors and are recorded in the textual notes (below, p. 780).

LOWELL W. COOLIDGE

The College of Wooster

---

[1] *Colasterion* was abridged for the 1820 collection of the divorce tracts. See preface to *Doctrine and Discipline,* above, p. 218; also pp. 416 and 571.

COLASTERION:
A
REPLY TO
A
NAMELES ANSVVER
AGAINST
The Doctrine and Discipline of Divorce.

WHEREIN
The trivial Author of that Anſwer is diſco-
ver'd, the Licencer conferr'd with, and the
Opinion which they traduce defended.

By the former Author, *J. M.*

Prov. 26. 5.

*Anſwer a Fool according to his folly, leſt bee bee wiſe in his
own conceit.*

Printed in the Year, 1645.

COLASTERION:[1]

A Reply to a nameless Answer against the
Doctrine and Discipline of Divorce.

A FTER MANY rumors of confutations and convictions forth
comming against *The Doctrine and Discipline of Divorce,*
and now and then a by-blow from the Pulpit,[2] featherd with
a censure strict indeed, but how true, more beholding to the autority
of that devout place which it borrow'd to bee utterd in, then to any
sound reason which it could oracle, while I still hop'd as for a blessing
to see som peece of diligence, or lerned discretion come from them,
it was my hap at length lighting on a certain parcel of *Quaeries,*[3] that
seek and finde not, to finde not seeking, at the taile of *Anabaptistical,
Antinomian, Heretical, Atheistical* epithets, a jolly [4] slander, call'd
Divorce at pleasure: [5] I stood a while and wonder'd, what wee might
doe to a mans heart, or what anatomie use, to finde in it sincerity;
for all our wonted marks every day fail us, and where wee thought it

---

[1] A transliteration of the Greek κολαστήριον, which means *a place* (or *an instrument*) *of punishment.* In choosing this word for his title, Milton may have had in mind Lucian's use of it in *Menippus* 14: "Leaving then the place of judgment, we came to the place of punishment."

[2] Except for the comment in Herbert Palmer's sermon of August 13, 1644, with which Milton deals at length in *Tetrachordon* (above, p. 579), no unmistakable pulpit references to the *Doctrine and Discipline* are on record. A possible veiled reproof by Milton's former tutor, Thomas Young, in a sermon before Parliament on February 28, 1644, has been suggested by William Haller. See his *Liberty and Reformation in the Puritan Revolution* (New York: Columbia University Press, 1955), pp. 122–24.

[3] A tract by William Prynne, *Twelve Considerable Serious Questions Touching Church Government* (1644). It was dated by Thomason September 16.

[4] Bold, arrogant.

[5] *Cf.* Prynne, *Twelve Considerable Serious Questions,* p. 7: "And whether such a Government as this [Independency] ought to be embraced, much lesse established among us (the sad effects wherof we have already experimentally felt, by the late dangerous increase of many *Anabaptisticall, Antinomian, Hereticall, Atheisticall opinions, as of the soules mortality, divorce at pleasure, &c.* lately broached, preached, printed in this famous City, which I hope our grand Councell will speedily and carefully suppresse, and by our divisions betweene som of our Commanders refusing to be *dependent* or subordinat one to another;) I referre to the judgment of all such who have any sparkes of love to God, Religion, their bleeding dying distracted native Country flaming in their brests, or any remainder of right reason residing in their braines."

was, wee see it is not, for alter and change residence it cannot sure. And yet I see no good of body or of minde secure to a man for all his past labours without perpetual watchfulnes, and perseverance. When as one above others who hath suffer'd much and long [6] in the defence of Truth, shall after all this, give her cause to leav him so destitute and so vacant of her defence, as to yeild his mouth to bee the common road of Truth and Falshood, and such falshood as is joyn'd with the rash and heedles calumny of his neighbour. For what book hath hee ever met with, as his complaint is, *Printed in the City,* maintaining either in the title, or in the whole persuance, *Divorce at pleasure?* Tis true, that to divorce upon extreme necessity, when through the perversnes, or the apparent unfitnes of either, the continuance can bee to both no good at all, but an into-[1]lerable injury and temptation to the wronged and the defrauded, to divorce then, there is a book that writes it lawfull. And that this Law is a pure and wholsom national [7] Law, not to be with-held from good men, because others likely anough may abuse it to thir pleasure, can not bee charg'd upon that book, but must bee enterd a bold and impious accusation against God himself; who did not for this abuse withhold it from his own people. It will bee just therfore, and best for the reputation of him who in his *Subitanes* [8] hath thus censur'd, to recall his sentence. And if, out of the abundance of his volumes, and the readiness of his quill, and the vastness of his other imploiments, especially in the great audit for accounts,[9] hee can spare us ought to the better understanding of this point, hee shall bee thankt in public, and what hath offended in the book, shall willingly submitt to his correction. Provided he bee sure not to come with those old and stale suppositions, unless hee can take away cleerly what that discours hath urg'd against them, by one who will expect other arguments to bee per-

[6] Prynne's militant Puritanism had resulted in his almost continuous imprisonment from 1633 to 1640. He had also been fined, pilloried, branded, and deprived of his ears. See *Complete Prose,* I, 39–42.

[7] *I.e.,* in accordance with the law of nations. *Cf.* Thomas Ridley, *A View of the Civile and Ecclesiasticall Law* (Oxford, 1634; HEHL), p. 3: "The law of Nations is that which common reason hath established among men, and is observed alike in all Nations."

[8] A sarcastic allusion to what Prynne in the opening paragraph of *Twelve Considerable Serious Questions* called his "subitane [*i.e.,* sudden] apprehensions." The word was not in common use. See *NED.*

[9] Prynne was an active member of the Committee for Accounts, appointed by Parliament in February, 1644, to check on all payments made from public funds.

swaded the good health of a sound answer, then the gout and dropsy of a big margent,[10] litter'd and overlaid with crude and huddl'd quotations. But as I still was waiting, when these light arm'd refuters would have don pelting at thir three lines utterd with a sage delivery of no reason, but an impotent and wors then *Bonner*-like censure [11] to burn that which provokes them to a fair dispute, at length a book was brought to my hands, entitl'd *An Answer to the Doctrine and Discipline of Divorce*. Gladly I receiv'd it, and very attentively compos'd my self to read; hoping that now som good man had voutsaft the pains to instruct mee better, then I could yet learn out of all the volumes which for this purpos I had visited. Only this I marvel'd, and other men have since, when as I, in a Subject so new to this age, and so hazardous to please, conceal'd not my name,[12] why this Author defending that part which is so creeded by the people, would conceal his? But ere I could enter three leaves into the Pamflet, (for I deferr the peasantly rudenes, which by the Licencers leav, I met with afterwards) my satisfaction came in abundantly, that it could bee nothing why hee durst not name himself, but the guilt of his own wretchednes. For first, not to speak of his abrupt and bald beginning,[13] his very first page notoriously bewraies him an illiterat, and arrogant presumer in that which hee understands not; bearing us in hand as if hee knew both Greek and Ebrew, and is not able to [2] spell it;[14] which had hee bin, it had bin either writt'n as it ought, or scor'd upon

---

10 The wide margins of Prynne's tracts were almost always filled with prooftexts, most of them scriptural. *Cf.* the canceled line of Milton's "On the New Forcers of Conscience" as it appears in the Trinity College Ms.: "Cropp yee as close as marginall P—s eares."

11 Edmund Bonner (*ca.* 1500–1569), bishop of London, was popularly regarded as one of the chief agents in the burnings at Smithfield and elsewhere during the reign of Queen Mary. Robert Greville, Lord Brooke, asserts that "oft when the Bishops could not reply, they would start up and sweare by the *Faith of their Body*, that this was a dangerous, grosse, & Hereticall opinion; And all this was but a Prologue to that Tragedy, whose Epilogue was Flame and Fagot." See *A Discourse Opening the Nature of that Episcopacie which is Exercised in England* (1642; HEHL), p. 104.

12 As a matter of fact, Milton's name did not appear in the first edition of *Doctrine and Discipline,* which was the edition used by the Answerer.

13 Milton repeatedly points out his opponent's lack of the rhetorical and stylistic graces which he himself cultivated.

14 See *An Answer to a Book . . . of Divorce* (1644; HEHL), pp. 1–2. The errors consist in the substitution of short vowels for long in two Greek words (ε for η in ἀποπομπή, ο for ω in ἀποπέμπω), and in the general omission of accents. The Hebrew words are transliterated.

the Printer.[15] If it bee excus'd as the carelesnes of his deputy, bee it known, the lerned Author himself is inventoried, and summ'd up, to the utmost value of his Livery cloak. Who ever hee bee, though this to som may seem a slight contest, I shall yet continue to think that man full of other secret injustice, and deceitfull pride, who shall offer in public to assume the skill, though it bee but of a tongue which hee hath not, and would catch his readers to beleeve of his ability, that which is not in him. The Licencer indeed, as his autority now stands, may licence much; but if these Greek *Orthographies* were of his licencing, the boyes at School might reck'n with him at his Grammar. Nor did I finde this his want of the pretended Languages alone, but accompanied with such a low and home-spun expression of his Mother *English* all along, without joynt or frame, as made mee, ere I knew furder of him, often stop, and conclude, that this Author could for certain bee no other then som mechanic. Nor was the stile flat and rude, and the matter grave and solid, for then ther had bin pardon, but so shallow and so unwary was that also, as gave sufficiently the character of a gross and sluggish, yet a contentious and overweening pretender. For first, it behooving him to shew, as hee promises, what divorce is, and what the true doctrine and Discipline therof, and this beeing to doe by such principles and prooffs as are receav'd on both sides, hee performes neither of these; but shews it first from the *Judaical* practice,[16] which hee himself disallows,[17] and next from the practice of Canon Law, which the Book hee would confute, utterly rejects, and all Laws depending theron; which this puny Clark calls *The Laws of England*,[18] and yet pronounces them

[15] *I.e.*, included in the list of errata. Such a list, far from complete, appears in *An Answer* directly below the imprimatur.

[16] *Cf. An Answer* (1644), p. 2: "First, as it hath been practised by the Jewes according as they thought directed by *Moses's* Law, and so Divorce was a free and a voluntary act of the Husband, made known by writing, whereby he did dismisse and for ever put away his Wife, and give her leave to marry to another man."

[17] Milton refers to the following passage in *An Answer*, p. 26: "We answer to your Text *Deut*. 24. 1. . . . then may that be a good positive law made by *Moses*, during the time of the Jewish politie or government, properly called Mosaicall: yet now Christ under the New Testament hath abolished that law to all his followers."

[18] See *An Answer*, p. 2: "In the second place we will consider of it as practised by the lawes of England.

"And so Divorce is a sentence pronounced by an Ecclesiasticall Judge, whereby a man and a woman formerly married, are separated or parted."

by an Ecclesiastical judge: as if that were to bee accounted the Law
of *England,* which depended on the Popery of *England;* or if it were,
this Parlament hee might know hath now damn'd that judicature.[19]
So that whether his meaning were to inform his own party, or to confute his adversary, instead of shewing us the true Doctrin and Discipline of Divorce, hee shews us nothing but his own contemptible
ignorance. For what is the *Mosaic* Law to his opinion, and what is
the Canon utterly now antiquated, either to that or to mine? Yee see
already what a faithfull definer wee have him. From such a wind-
egg [20] of definition as this, they who expect any of his other arguments to bee well hatcht, let them enjoy the [3] vertu of thir worthy
Champion. But one thing more I observ'd, a singular note of his
stupidity, and that his Trade is not to meddle with Books, much less
with Confutations. When as *the Doctrin of Divorce* had now a whole
year [21] bin publisht the second time, with many Arguments added;
and the former ones better'd and confirm'd,[22] this idle pamflet comes
reeling forth against the first Edition only; as may appear to any by
the pages quoted. Which put me in minde of what by chance I had
notice of to this purpos the last Summer, as nothing so serious, but
happns oft times to bee attended with a ridiculous accident, it was
then told mee that *the Doctrin of divorce* was answerd, and the answer half printed against the first Edition; not by one, but by a pack
of heads; of whom the cheif, by circumstance, was intimated to mee,
and since ratifi'd to bee no other, if any can hold laughter,[23] and I
am sure none will guess him lower, then an actual Serving-man. This
creature, for the Story must on, (and what though hee bee the lowest
person of an interlude, hee may deserv a canvasing,) [24] transplanted

---

[19] The ecclesiastical courts had been under attack by the Long Parliament
since November, 1640. On July 5, 1641, Charles I had signed bills abolishing the
courts of Star Chamber and High Commission. See *Complete Prose,* I, 61 ff., 129.
Cf. Milton's statement in *Doctrine and Discipline* (above, p. 239) that he sees
"it the hope of good men, that those irregular and unspirituall Courts have spun
their utmost date in this Land."

[20] An imperfect or unproductive egg. *NED* quotes Milton's figurative use here.

[21] If Thomason's dates are approximately those of publication, the interval
was only about nine and a half months (Feb. 2–Nov. 19). But see p. 719 above.

[22] See introduction, above, pp. 150–53.

[23] A pun on *lofter* (higher) is probably intended. See *NED* for examples of
loft as an adjective.

[24] Shaking or buffeting. The meaning derives from the practice of tossing a
person in a canvas sheet as a sport or punishment.

himself, and to the improvment of his wages, and your better notice of his capacity, turn'd Solliciter. And having convers'd much with a stripling Divine or two of those newly fledge *Probationers,* that usually come scouting from the University, and ly heer no lame *legers* [25] to pop into the *Bethesda* [26] of som Knights Chaplainship, where they bring grace to his good cheer, but no peace or benediction els to his house; these made the *Champarty,*[27] hee contributed the Law, and both joynd in the Divinity. Which made mee intend, following the advice also of freinds, to lay aside the thought of mis-spending a Reply to the buzze of such a Drones nest. But finding that it lay, what ever was the matter, half a year after unfinisht in the press, and hearing for certain that a Divine of note, out of his good will to the opinion, had takn it into his revise, and somthing had put out, somthing put in, and stuck it heer and there with a clove of his own *Calligraphy,* to keep it from tainting, and furder when I saw the stuff, though very cours and thred-bare, garnisht and trimly fac't with the commendations of a Licencer, I resolv'd, so soon, as leisure granted mee the recreation, that my man of Law should not altogether loose his solliciting. Although I impute a share of the making to him whose name [28] I find in the approbation, who may take, as his mind servs him, this Reply. In the mean while it shall bee seen, I refuse no occasion, and avoid no adversary, either to main-[4]tane what I have begun, or to give it up for better reason.

To begin then with the Licencer and his censure.[29] For a Licencer is not contented now to give his single *Imprimatur,* but brings his chair into the Title leaf; there sits and judges up or judges down what book hee pleases; if this bee suffer'd, what worthles Author, or what cunning Printer will not bee ambitious of such a Stale [30] to put off the heaviest gear; which may in time bring in round fees to the

---

[25] Residents.   [26] See John 5:2–4.

[27] "A combination for an evil purpose." *NED.*

[28] Joseph Caryl (1602–1673), a member of the Westminster Assembly and a frequent preacher before the Long Parliament. He was one of twelve ministers named by the House of Commons (June 21, 1643) to license books of divinity.

[29] The full text of Caryl's statement is as follows: "To preserve the strength of the Mariage-bond and the Honour of that estate, against those sad breaches and dangerous abuses of it, which common discontents (on this side Adultery) are likely to make in unstaied mindes and men given to change, by taking in or grounding themselves upon the opinion answered, and with good reason confuted in this Treatise, I have approved the printing and publishing of it."

[30] Decoy.

Licencer, and wretched mis-leading to the People. But to the matter: he approves *the publishing of this Book, to preserv the strength and honour of Mariage against those sad breaches and dangerous abuses of it.* Belike then the wrongfull suffering of all those sad breaches and abuses in Mariage to a remediless thraldom, is *the strength and honour of Mariage;* a boistrous and bestial strength, a dis-honourable honour, an infatuated Doctrine, wors then the *salvo jure* [31] of tyrannizing, which wee all fight against. Next hee saith that *common discontents make these breaches in unstaid mindes, and men givn to change.* His words may be apprehended, as if they disallow'd only to divorce for *common discontents in unstaid mindes,* having no cause, but a *desire of change,* and then wee agree. But if hee take all discontents *on this side adultery,* to bee common, that is to say, not difficult to endure, and to affect only *unstaid mindes,* it might administer just cause to think him the unfittest man that could bee, to offer at a comment upon *Job;* [32] as seeming by this to have no more true sense of a good man in his afflictions, then those *Edomitish* Freinds [33] had, of whom *Job* complains, and against whom God testifies his anger. Shall a man of your own coat, who hath espous'd his flock; and represents Christ more, in beeing the true husband of his Congregation, then an ordnary man doth in beeing the husband of his wife, and yet this representment is thought a cheif cause why Mariage must bee inseparable, shall this spiritual man ordnarily for the increase of his maintenance, or any slight cause forsake that wedded cure of souls, that should bee dearest to him, and marry another, and another, and shall not a person wrongfully afflicted, and persecuted eevn to extremity, forsake an unfit, injurious, and pestilent mate, ty'd only by a civil and fleshly covnant? If you bee a man so much hating change, hate that other change; if your self bee not guilty, counsel your brethren [34] to hate it; and leav to bee the super-

[31] An expression of legal exception, as in *salvo jure coronae,* "without prejudice to the right of the crown."

[32] Caryl's *Exposition with Practicall Observations upon the Three First Chapters of the Booke of Job, Delivered in XXI Lectures, at Magnus neare the Bridge, London* had been published in 1643 and reprinted in 1644.

[33] See Job 2:11 ff. *Edomitish* is probably used with allusion to Psalm 137:7. *Cf. Animadversions, Complete Prose,* I, 725.

[34] This is one of Milton's earliest expressions of suspicion concerning the personal ambitions of the Presbyterian clergy. Caryl, incidentally, remained in the parish of St. Magnus for the rest of his active ministry.

cilious judge of other mens miseries and changes, that your own bee
not judg'd. The reasons of your licenc't pamflet, you say [5] *are good;*
they must bee better then your own then, I shall wonder els how such
a trivial fellow was accepted and commended, to bee the confuter of
so dangerous an opinion as yee give out mine.

Now therfore to your *Atturney,* since no worthier an adversary
makes his appearance, nor this neither his appearance, but lurking
under the safety of his nameles obscurity: such as yee turn him forth
at the Postern, I must accept him; and in a better temper then *Ajax,*
doe mean to scourge this *Ramme* for yee, till I meet with his *Ulysses.*[35]

Hee begins with Law,[36] and wee have it of him as good cheap, as
any hucster at Law, newly set up, can possibly afford, and as impertinent; but for that hee hath receiv'd his hansel.[37] Hee presumes
also to cite the Civil Law,[38] which, I perceav by his citing never came
within his *dormitory,* yet what hee cites makes but against himself.

His second thing [39] therfore is to refute the advers position, and
very methodically, three pages before hee sets it down; and sets his
own in the place, *that disagreement of minde or disposition, though
shewing it self in much sharpnes is not by the Law of God, or man, a
just cause of divorce.*

[35] Enraged because the arms of Achilles had been awarded to Ulysses, Ajax
mistook the Greeks' sheep and cattle for the human objects of his vengeance.
Sophocles (*Ajax,* 1–133) represents him as binding one of these beasts and
scourging it under the delusion that it was Ulysses himself.

[36] See *An Answer,* pp. 2 ff. The author cites cases from two major collections
of common law *Reports,* those of Sir Edward Coke and of Sir James Dyer. Most
of his legal detail, however, seems to have been drawn from Sir Edward's
Commentary upon Littleton (book 3, chapter 5, section 380), otherwise known
as *The First Part of the Institutes of the Laws of England* (1628; HEHL).

[37] A first token or payment upon beginning a new enterprise.

[38] See *An Answer,* pp. 3–4: "So *Cod. lib. 5. tit. 1. leg. 2. const. sponsa post
biennium, &c.* allowed to marry after two years absence, but *tit.* 27. after three
years, *leg.* 27. after four years." *Cf.* Milton's own citations of the civil law in
Tetrachordon (above, pp. 700–703).
Dormitory: *NED* cites this passage to illustrate the figurative use of the word
to mean "a resting place."

[39] *Cf. An Answer,* p. 4: "And so now we leave this first thing what Divorce is,
and the doctrine and discipline thereof, and come to the second thing. And that
is to prove that whatsoever other causes of Divorce may be allowed of, yet that
disagreement of minde or disposition between husband and wife, yea though it
shewes it selfe in much sharpnesse each to other, is not by the law of God
allowed of for a just cause of divorce, neither ought to be allowed of by the
lawes of man."

To this position I answer, that it lays no battery against mine, no, nor so much as faces it, but tacks about, long ere it come neer, like a harmles and respectfull confutement. For I confess that disagreement of minde or disposition, though in much sharpnes, is not alwaies a just cause of divorce; for much may bee endur'd. But what if the sharpnes bee much more then his much? To that point it is our mis-hap wee have not heer his grave decision. Hee that will contradict the positive which I alleg'd, must hold that no disagreement of minde, or disposition, can divorce, though shewn in most sharpnes; otherwise hee leaves a place for equity to appoint limits, and so his following arguments will either not prove his own position, or not disprove mine.

His first Argument,[40] all but what hobbles to no purpos is this. *Wher the Scripture commands a thing to bee don, it appoints when, how, and for what, as in the case of death or excommunication. But the Scripture directs not what measure of disagreement or contrariety may divorce; Therfore, the Scripture allows not any divorce for disagreement.*

Answer, First I deny your *major,* the Scripture appoints many things, [6] and yet leaves the circumstance to mans discretion, particularly, in your own examples; Excommunication is not taught when, and for what to bee, but left to the Church. How could the Licencer let pass this childish ignorance and call it *good?* Next, in matter of death, the Laws of *England,* wherof you have intruded to bee an opiniastrous * *Sub advocate,* and are bound to defend them, conceave it not enjoyn'd in Scripture, when or for what cause they shall put to death, as in adultery, theft, and the like; your *minor* also is fals, for the Scripture plainly sets down for what measure of disagreement a man may divorce, *Deut.* 24. 1. Learn better what that phrase means, *if shee finde no favour in his eyes.*

Your second Argument,[41] without more tedious fumbling is breifly thus. *If diversity in Religion, which breeds a greater dislike then any natural disagreement may not cause a divorce, then may not the lesser disagreement: but diversity of Religion may not; Ergo.*

Answer, First, I deny in the *major,* that diversity of Religion, breeds a greater dislike to mariage duties, then natural disagreement.

---

[40] *Cf. An Answer,* p. 5.
* This is the only example cited by *OED* for this form of the word.
[41] *An Answer,* p. 5.

For between *Israelite,* or Christian and Infidel more often hath bin seen too much love: but between them who perpetually clash in natural contrarieties, it is repugnant that ther should bee ever any maried love or concord. Next, I deny your *minor,* that it is commanded not to divorce in diversity of Religion, if the Infidel will stay: for that place in St. *Paul,*[42] commands nothing, as *that book* [43] at large affirm'd, though you over-skipt it.

Secondly, if it doe command, it is but with condition, that the Infidel bee content, and well pleas'd to stay, which cuts off the supposal of any great hatred or disquiet between them; seeing the Infidel had liberty to depart at pleasure; and so this comparison avails nothing.

Your third Argument [44] is from Deut. 22. *If a man hate his wife, and raise an ill report, that hee found her no virgin,* if this were fals, *he might not put her away,* though hated never so much.

Answer, This was a malicious hatred bent against her life, or to send her out of dores without her portion. Such a hater looses by due punishment that privilege, Deut. 24.1. to divorce for a natural dislike, which though it could not love conjugally, yet sent away civilly, and with just conditions. But doubtles the Wife in that former case had liberty to depart from her fals accuser, lest his hatred [7] should prove mortal; els that Law peculiarly made to right the woman, had turn'd to her greatest mischeif.

Your fourth Argument,[45] *One Christian ought to bear the infirmities of another, but cheifly of his Wife.*

Answer, I grant, infirmities, but not outrages, not perpetual defraudments of truest conjugal society, not injuries and vexations as importunat as fire. Yet to endure very much, might doe well an exhortation, but not a compulsive Law. For the Spirit of God himself by *Solomon* [46] declares that such a consort *the earth cannot bear, and better dwell in a corner on the house top, or in the Wildernes.* Burdens may bee born, but still with consideration to the strength of an honest man complaining. Charity indeed bids us forgive our enemies, yet doth not force us to continue freindship and familiarity with those freinds who have bin fals or unworthy toward us; but is contented in our peace with them, at a fair distance. Charity commands not the husband to receav again into his bosom the adulterous Wife,

---

[42] I Corinthians 7:12.   [43] *Doctrine and Discipline,* above, pp. 261–68.
[44] *An Answer,* pp. 5–6.   [45] *Ibid.,* p. 6.
[46] See Proverbs 30:21–23; 21:9; 21:19.

but thinks it anough, if hee dismiss her with a beneficent and peace-full dismission. No more doth Charity command, nor can her rule compell, to retain in neerest union of wedloc, one whose other gross-est faults, or disabilities to perform what was covnanted, are the just causes of as much greevance and dissention in a Family, as the private act of adultery. Let not therfore under the name of fulfill-ing Charity, such an unmercifull, and more then legal yoke, bee padlockt upon the neck of any Christian.

Your fifth Argument,[47] *If the husband ought love his Wife, as Christ his Church, then ought shee not to bee put away for contrariety of minde.*

Answer, This similitude turnes against him. For if the husband must bee as Christ to the Wife, then must the wife bee as the Church to her husband. If ther bee a perpetual contrariety of minde in the Church toward Christ, Christ himselfe threat'ns to divorce such a Spouse, and hath often don it. If they urge, this was no true Church, I urge again, that was no true Wife.

His sixth Argument [48] is from the 5 of *Matthew* 32. which hee expounds after the old fashion, and never takes notice of what I brought against that exposition; Let him therfore seek his answer there.[49] Yet can hee not leav this Argument, but hee must needs first shew us a curvett of his madnes, holding out an objection, and running him-[8]self upon the point. *For,* saith hee, *if Christ except no cause but adultery, then all other causes as frigidity, incestuous mariage, &c. are no causes of divorce;* and answers *that the speech of Christ holds universally, as hee intended it namely to condemn such divorce, as was groundlesly practiz'd among the Jews, for every cause which they thought sufficient; not checking the law of consanguinities or affinities, or forbidding other cause which makes mariage void, Ipso facto.*

Answ. Look to it now you be not found taking fees on both sides, for if you once bring limitations to the universal words of Christ, another will doe as much with as good autority, and affirm, that neither did hee check the Law Deut. 24.1. nor forbid the causes that make mariage void actually; which if any thing in the world doth, unfitnes doth, and contrariety of minde; yea, more then adul-

---

[47] *An Answer,* p. 6. Ephesians 5:29 is cited as authority.
[48] *An Answer,* pp. 6–7.
[49] See *Doctrine and Discipline,* above, pp. 329–37.

tery, for that makes not the mariage void, nor much more unfit, but for the time, if the offended party forgive; but unfitnes and contrariety frustrates and nullifies for ever, unless it bee a rare chance, all the good and peace of wedded conversation; and leaves nothing between them enjoyable, but a prone and savage necessity, not worth the name of mariage, unaccompanied with love. Thus much his own objection hath don against himself.

Argu. 7.[50] Hee insists, *that man and wife are one flesh, therfore must not separat.* But must bee sent to look again upon the 35. pag. of that book,[51] where hee might have read an answer, which hee stirrs not. Yet can hee not abstain, but hee must doe us another pleasure ere hee goes; Although I call the Common Pleas to witness, I have not hir'd his tongue, whatever men may think by his arguing. For besides adultery, hee excepts *other causes which dissolv the union of beeing one flesh, either directly, or by consequence.* If only adultery bee excepted by our Saviour, and hee voluntarily can adde other exceptions that dissolv that union *both directly and by consequence,* these words of Christ, the main obstacle of divorce, are open to us by his own invitation to include what ever causes dissolv that union of flesh, *either directly or by consequence.* Which, till hee name other causes more likely, I affirm to bee don soonest by unfitness and contrariety of minde. For that induces hatred, which is the greatest dissolver, both of spiritual and corporal union, turning the minde and consequently the body to other objects. Thus our doubty adversary, *either directly, or by consequence* yeilds us the question with his own mouth, [9] and the next thing hee does, recants it again.

His eighth Argument [52] shivers in the uttering, and hee confesses *to bee not over confident of it,* but of the rest it may bee sworn hee is. St. *Paul,* I *Cor.* 7. saith, that *the married have trouble in the flesh,* therfore wee must bear it, though never so intolerable.

I Answer, if this bee a true consequence, why are not all troubles to bee born alike? why are wee suffer'd to divorce adulteries, desertions, or frigidities? Who knows not that trouble and affliction is the decree of God upon every state of life? follows it therfore, that though they grow excessive, and insupportable, wee must not avoid

---

[50] *An Answer,* p. 7.
[51] *Doctrine and Discipline,* above, p. 326.
[52] *An Answer,* p. 8.

them? if wee may in all other conditions, and not in mariage, the doom of our suffering ties us not by the trouble, but by the bond of mariage; and that must bee prov'd inseparable from other reasons, not from this place. And his own confession declares the weaknes of this Argument, yet his ungovern'd arrogance could not bee disswaded from venting it.

His ninth Argument [53] is, *That a husband must love his wife as himself, therfore hee may not divorce for any disagreement, no more then hee may separat his soul from his body.*

I Answer, if hee love his wife as himself, hee must love her so farre as hee may preserv himself to her in a cherfull and comfortable manner, and not so as to ruin himself by anguish and sorrow, without any benefit to her. Next, if the husband must love his wife as himself, shee must bee understood a wife in som reasonable measure, willing, and sufficient to perform the cheif duties of her Covnant, els by the hold of this argument, it would bee his great sin to divorce either for adultery, or desertion. The rest of this will run circuit with the union of one flesh, which was answer'd before. And that to divorce a relative and *Metaphorical* union of two bodies into one flesh, cannot bee likn'd in all things to the dividing of that natural union of soul and body into one person, is apparent of it self.

His last Argument [54] hee fetches *from the inconveniences that would follow upon this freedom of divorce, to the corrupting of mens mindes, and the overturning of all human society.*

But for mee, let God and *Moses* answer this blasphemer, who dares bring in such a foul endightment against the divine Law. Why did God permit this to his people the Jewes, but that the right and good which came directly therby, was more in his esteem, then the wrong [10] and evil which came by accident. And for those weak supposes [55] of Infants that would be left in their mothers belly, (which must needs bee good news for Chamber-maids, to hear a Serving-man grown so provident for great bellies) and portions, and joyntures likely to incurr imbezlement heerby, the ancient civil Law

---

[53] *Ibid.*　　[54] *Ibid.,* pp. 8–9.

[55] *Cf. An Answer,* p. 8: "Who sees not, how many thousands of lustfull and libidinous men would be parting from their Wives every week and marying others: and upon this, who should keep the children of these divorcers which somtimes they would leave in their Wives bellies? how shall they come by their Portions, of whom, or where? and how shall the Wife be endowed of her Husbands estate?"

instructs us plentifully how to award, which our profound opposite knew not, for it was not in his Tenures.[56]

His Arguments are spun, now follows the Chaplain with his Antiquities, wiser if hee had refrain'd, for his very touching ought that is lerned, soiles it, and lays him still more and more open a conspicuous gull. There beeing both Fathers and Councels more ancient, wherwith to have serv'd his purpos better then with what hee cites, how may we doe to know the suttle drift that mov'd him to begin first with the *twelfth Councel of Toledo*? [57] I would not undervalue the depth of his notion, but perhaps he had heard that the men of *Toledo* had store of good blade-mettle, and were excellent at cuttling; who can tell but it might bee the reach of his policy, that these able men of decision, would doe best to have the prime stroke among his testimonies in deciding this cause. But all this craft avails him not; for seeing they allow no cause of divorce but fornication, what doe these keen Doctors heer but cut him over the sinews with thir Toledo's, for holding in the precedent page other causes of divorce besides, *both directly, and by consequence*. As evil doth that *Saxon* Councel, next quoted,[58] bestead him. For if it allow divorce precisely for no cause but fornication, it thwarts his own Exposition: and if it understand fornication largely, it sides with whom hee would confute. However the autority of that Synod can bee but small,[59] beeing under *Theodorus,* the *Canterbury*

[56] The work by Sir Thomas Littleton which furnished the basis for Coke's *Commentary* was entitled *Les Tenures*. See above, p. 729, n. 36.

[57] See *An Answer*, p. 9: "*Concil. Tolet. 12. Can. 8. Preceptum Domini est, ut excepta causa fornicationis, uxor a viro dimitti non debeat. &c.* Its the command of the Lord, the Wife should not be put away but for fornication." As Milton implies, this council was hardly of major importance; the date was 681.

[58] *An Answer*, p. 9: "So *Concil. Anglic.* 670. *Can.* 10. No man may put away his Wife, except as the Gospell teacheth for fornication." The reference is evidently to the first of the English provincial councils, commonly known as the Synod of Hertford, which was convened by Theodore, Archbishop of Canterbury, in 673 rather than 670. Bede's *Historia Ecclesiastica* (book IV, chapter 5) gives a full account, including the text of the canons.

[59] Milton's reasoning here is perhaps open to question. *Cf.* his own reference to Theodore in *History of Britain* (1670, p. 163): "In *Kent, Ercombert* expiring, was succeeded by his Son *Ecbert*. In whose fowrth year, by means of *Theodore,* a learned Greekish Monk of Tarsus whom Pope *Vitalian* had ordain'd Archbishop of *Canterbury*, the Greek and Latin Tongue, with other liberal Arts, Arithmetic, Music, Astronomie, and the like, began first to flourish among the *Saxons;* as did also the whole Land, under potent and religious Kings, more then ever before, as *Bede* affirms, till his own days."

Bishop, a Grecian Monk of *Tarsus,* revolted from his own Church to the Pope. What have wee next? The Civil Law stufft in between two Councels, as if the *Code* had bin som Synod; for that hee understood himself in this quotation is incredible; where the Law, *Cod. l. 3. tit. 38. leg.* 11.[60] speaks not of divorce, but against the dividing of possessions to divers heires, wherby the maried servants of a great family were divided perhaps into distant Countries, and Colonies, Father from Son, Wife from Husband, sore against thir will. Somwhat lower hee confesses, *that the Civill Law allows many reasons of divorce, but the Cannon Law decrees otherwise.*[61] A fair credit to his Cause; and I amaze me, though the fancy of this [11] doult bee as obtuse and sad as any mallet, how the Licencer could sleep out all this, and suffer him to uphold his opinion, by Canons, & *Gregorian decretals,*[62] a Law which not only his adversary, but the whole reformation of this Church and state hath branded and rejected. As ignorantly, and too ignorantly to deceav any Reader but an unlerned, hee talks of *Justin Martyrs* Apology, not telling us which of the twain; for that passage in the beginning of his first, which I have cited els-where,[63] plainly makes against him: So doth *Tertullian,* cited next, and next *Erasmus,* the one against *Marcion,*[64] the other in his Annotations on *Matthew,* and to the *Corinthians.*[65] And thus yee have the List of his choice Antiquities, as pleasantly chosen as yee would wish from a man of his handy Vocation, puft up with no luck at all, above the stint of his capacity.

Now hee comes to the Position, which I sett down whole; and

[60] *Cf. An Answer,* p. 9: "*Quis ferat, &c.* who can endure that Children from Parents, and Wives from Husbands should be separate?"

[61] *Cf. An Answer,* p. 9: "It is true, some of the Imperiall lawes allow Homicide, Sacriledge, Robbery, Manstealing, &c. for causes of divorce. *Cod. lib.* 5. *tit.* 17. *leg.* 8. but the Canon law decrees otherwise."

[62] The Answerer at this point (p. 9) refers not to the *Decretals* but to the *Decretum Gratiani* as is shown by the form of his citations ("*Greg. causa* 29. *quest.* 7. *cap.* 19. . . . *Zach. causa* 29. *quest.* 2. *cap.* 2."). The first citation is inaccurate.

[63] See *Tetrachordon,* above, p. 693. Actually Milton's reference is to what is now known as the *Second Apology.* His opponent probably had in mind chapter XV of the *First Apology,* especially the following sentence (*Fathers, A.N.,* I, 167): "So that all, who by human law, are twice married, are in the eye of our Master sinners, and those who look upon a woman to lust after her."

[64] *Cf. Tetrachordon,* above, p. 694. But the Answerer refers specifically to the tract *On Monogamy* (p. 9): "Tertullian agrees *lib. de Monogamia.*"

[65] *Cf. Martin Bucer,* above, p. 478; also *Tetrachordon,* above, p. 709.

like an able text man slits it into fowr, that hee may the better
come at it with his Barbar Surgery, and his sleevs turn'd up. Wherin
first hee denies *that any disposition, unfitness, or contrariety of
minde is unchangeable in nature, but that by the help of diet and
physic it may be alter'd.*[66]

I mean not to dispute Philosophy with this Pork, who never read
any. But I appeal to all experience, though there bee many drugs
to purge those redundant humors, and circulations that commonly
impair health, and are not natural, whether any man can with the
safety of his life bring a healthy constitution into physic with this
designe, to alter his natural temperament, and disposition of minde.
How much more vain, and ridiculous would it bee, by altering and
rooting up the grounds of nature,[67] which is most likely to produce
death or madnes, to hope the reducing of a minde to this or that
fitnes, or two disagreeing mindes to a mutual sympathy. Suppose
they might, and that with great danger of thir lives and right senses,
alter one temperature,[68] how can they know that the succeeding
disposition will not bee as farre from fitnes and agreement? They
would perhaps change Melancholy into Sanguin, but what if fleam,
and choler in as great a measure come instead, the unfitnes will be
still as difficult and troublesom.[69] But lastly, whether these things
bee changeable, or not, experience teacheth us, and our Position
supposes that they seldom doe change in any time commensurable
to the necessities of man, or convenient to the ends of mariage.
And if the fault bee in the one, shall the other live all his daies in
bondage and misery [12] for anothers perversnes, or immedicable
disaffection? To my freinds, of which may fewest bee so unhappy,

[66] *An Answer*, p. 10. In support of this assertion the author adds, "so teacheth
Philosophy." His authority was perhaps one of the several popular expositions
of theology, ethics, and pseudo-science, such as Pierre de La Primaudaye's *The
French Academie* (earliest complete English edition 1618; HEHL). The fourth
part of La Primaudaye's work was entitled *Christian Philosophie*.

[67] *Cf.* Milton's earlier insistence in *An Apology* (*Complete Prose*, I, 900) that
no man is "forc't wholly to dissolve the groundwork of nature which God created
in him."

[68] Temperature: temperament.

[69] *Cf.* La Primaudaye, *The French Academie* (1618), p. 535: "True it is, . . .
that no body is so framed, or hath such an harmony and equalitie throughout,
but there is some disagreement & inequalitie. . . . and as every humour ruleth
more or lesse in every one, so he is called either sanguine, or flegmatike, or
cholerike, or melancholike."

I have a remedy, as they know, more wise and manly to prescribe: but for his freinds and followers (of which many may deserv justly to feel themselvs the unhappines which they consider not in others) I send them by his advice to sit upon the stool and strain, till their cross dispositions and contrarieties of minde shall change to a better correspondence, and to a quicker apprehension of common sense, and thir own good.

His second Reason [70] is as heedles, *because that grace may change the disposition, therfore no indisposition may cause divorce.*

Answ. First, it will not bee deniable that many persons, gracious both, may yet happn to bee very unfitly marryed, to the great disturbance of either. Secondly, what if one have grace, the other not, and will not alter, as the Scripture testifies ther bee of those, in whom wee may expect a change, when *the Blackamore changes his colour, or the Leopard his spots,* Jer. 13. 23.[71] shall the gracious therfore dwell in torment all his life, for the ungracious? Wee see that holiest precepts, then which ther can no better physic bee administerd to the minde of man, and set on with powerfull preaching, cannot work this cure, no not in the family, not in the wife of him that Preaches day and night to her. What an unreasonable thing it is that men, and Clergy-men especially, should exact such wondrous changes in another mans house, and are seen to work so little in thir own?

To the second point of the position, that this *unfitnes* hinders the main ends, and benefits of mariage, hee answers, *if I mean the unfitnes of choler, or sullen disposition, that soft words according to Solomon, pacify wrath.*[72]

But I reply, that the saying of *Salomon,* is a Proverb frequently true, not universally, as both the event shews, and many other sentences writtn by the same Author particularly of an evill woman, *Prov.* 21. 9. 19. and in other Chapters, that shee is better shun'd then dwelt with, and a desert is preferr'd before her society. What need the Spirit of God put this chois into our heads, if soft words could alwaies take effect with her? How frivolous is, not only this disputer, but hee that taught him thus, and let him come abroad.

[70] *An Answer,* p. 10.

[71] The form of the translation appears to be Milton's own. The Authorized Version reads, "Can the Ethiopian change his skinne? or the leopard his spots?"

[72] *An Answer,* p. 11. The quotation from Solomon is found in Proverbs 15:1.

To his second answer [73] I return this, that although there bee not easily found such an *antipathy, as to hate one another like a toad or poison,* yet [13] that there is oft such a dislike in both, or either, to conjugal love, as hinders all the comfort of Matrimony, scars any can bee so simple, as not to apprehend. And what can be *that favour, found* or not found *in the eyes of the Husband,* but a natural liking or disliking, wherof the Law of God, *Deut.* 24. beares witnes, as of an ordnary accident, and determins wisely, and divinely therafter. And this disaffection happning to bee in the one, not without the unspeakable discomfort of the other, must hee bee left like a thing consecrated to calamity, and despair without redemption?

Against the third branch of the position hee denies *that solace, and peace, which is contrary to discord and variance, is the main end of mariage.* What then? Hee will have it *the solace of male, and female.*[74] Came this doctrin out of som School, or som stie? Who but one forsak'n of all sense and civil nature, and cheifly of Christianity, will deny that peace contrary to discord, is the calling and the general end of every Christian, and of all his actions, and more especially of mariage, which is the dearest league of love, and the dearest resemblance of that love which in Christ is dearest to his Church; how then can peace and comfort, as it is contrary to discord, which God hates to dwell with, not bee the main end of mariage? Discord then wee ought to fly, and to pursue peace, farre above the observance of a civil covnant, already brokn, and the breaking dayly iterated on the other side. And what better testimony then the words of the institution it self, to prove, that a conversing solace, & peacefull society is the prime end of mariage, without which no other help, or office can bee mutual, beseeming the dignity of reasonable creatures, that such as they should be coupl'd in the rites of nature by the meer compulsion of lust, without love, or peace, wors then wild beasts. Nor was it half so wisely spokn, as some deem, though *Austin* spake it, that if God had intended other then copulation in Mariage, he would for *Adam* have created a freind, rather

[73] *Cf. An Answer,* p. 11: "If by contrarietie of minde or disposition he will mean some unheard of thing, which God and Nature hath planted on purpose in such a man and woman who afterwards shall marry, who shall hate one another with that mutuall antypathie as a man doth a Toad or Poyson; . . . if he can finde such an example in the World, let him send his Book to them for to take the benefit of it."

[74] See *An Answer,* p. 12.

then a wife, to convers with;[75] and our own writers blame him for
this opinion; for which and the like passages, concerning mariage,
hee might bee justly taxt of rusticity in these affairs. For this cannot but bee with ease conceav'd, that there is one society of grave
freindship, and another amiable and attractive society of conjugal
love, besides the deed of procreation, which of it self soon cloies,
and is despis'd, unless it bee cherisht and re-incited with a pleasing
conversation. Which if ignoble and [14] swainish mindes cannot
apprehend, shall such merit therfore to be the censurers of more
generous and vertuous Spirits?

Against the last point of the position, to prove that contrariety of
minde is not a greater cause of divorce, then corporal frigidity, hee
enters into such a tedious and drawling tale of *burning, and burning, and lust and burning*,[76] that the dull argument it self burnes to,
for want of stirring; and yet all this burning is not able to expell
the frigidity of his brain. So long therfore, as that cause in the
position shall bee prov'd a sufficient cause of divorce, rather then
spend words with this fleamy [77] clodd of an *Antagonist*, more then
of necessity, and a little merriment, I will not now contend whether
it bee a greater cause then frigidity, or no.

His next attempt is upon the Arguments which I brought to prove
the position. And for the first,[78] not finding it of that structure, as
to bee scal'd with his short ladder, hee retreats with a bravado,
that it deservs no answer. And I as much wonder what the whole

[75] Cf. *Tetrachordon*, above, p. 596. *An Answer* (p. 12) states the idea without mention of St. Augustine: "For then would it have been every wayes as
much, yea more content and solace to *Adam;* and so consequently to every man,
to have had another man made to him of his Rib in stead of *Eve:* this is apparent by experience, which shews, that man ordinarily exceeds woman in
naturall gifts of minde, and in delectablenesse of converse."

[76] *An Answer*, pp. 12–13. Within this space the author uses the phrase "burning in lust" or "to burn in lust" six times. His equally repetitious use of "frigidity" in the same passage gives point to Milton's jibe at "the frigidity of his
brain."

[77] Phlegmatic. Cf. *Batman uppon Bartholome* (1582; HEHL), f. 32: "A very
fleumaticke man is of body unlustie, heavie and slow, dull of wit, and of thought
forgetfull."

[78] *An Answer*, p. 14: "*Your first proofe is the institution of mariage Gen. 2.
to make woman a meet help for man, because it was not good that man should
be alone. . . .*

"Will it follow, think you, that because the end of mariage is, that woman
should bee a meet helpe to man, therfore if shee prove not so meet as is expected, he may then put her away and take another: I hope no: Such kind of
reasoning deserves no answer at all."

book deserv'd to bee thus troubl'd and sollicited by such a paltry
Solliciter. I would hee had not cast the gracious eye of his duncery
upon the small deserts of a pamflet, whose every line meddl'd with,
uncases him to scorn and laughter.

That which hee takes for the second Argument,[79] if hee look
better, is no argument, but an induction to those that follow. Then
hee stumbles that I should say, the gentlest ends of Mariage, confessing that hee understands it not. And I beleev him heartily: for
how should hee, a Servingman both by nature and by function, an
Idiot by breeding, and a Solliciter by presumption, ever come to
know, or feel within himself, what the meaning is of gentle? Hee
blames it for *a neat phrase*,[80] for nothing angers him more then his
own proper contrary. Yet altogether without art sure hee is not;
for who could have devis'd to give us more breifly a better description of his own Servility?

But what will become now of the busines I know not; for the
man is suddenly takn with a lunacy of Law, and speaks revelations
out of the *Atturneys Academy*,[81] only from a lying spirit: for hee
saies that *where a thing is void,* ipso facto, *there needs no legal
proceeding to make it void.*[82] Which is fals, for mariage is void by
adultery, or frigidity, yet not made void without legal proceeding.
Then asks my opinion of *John a Nokes, and John a Stiles;*[83] and I
answer him, that I for my [15] part think *John Dory*,[84] was a better

[79] *An Answer,* p. 14: "His second Argument is, *From the violence and cruelty
which is in forcing the continuance of those maried persons together, whom God
and nature in the gentlest ends of mariage never joyned.*"

[80] *Cf. An Answer,* p. 14: "As for the phrase of the gentlest ends of mariage,
its too abstruse and of no use, except it be as you think to please the Reader with
a neet phrase."

[81] *The Attourneys Academy: or, The Manner and Forme of Proceeding Practically, upon any Suite, Plaint or Action whatsoever, in any Court of Record
whatsoever within this Kingdome* . . . (1623; HEHL) was the title of a professional handbook compiled by Thomas Powell (*ca.* 1572–*ca.* 1635). Actually
An Answer shows no specific indebtedness to it.

[82] *An Answer,* p. 14.

[83] Names commonly used to designate the parties in a legal action. The Answerer states a hypothetical—and irrelevant—case.

[84] The hero of a popular ballad beginning

> As it fell on a holy day,
>   And upon an holy tide a:
> John Dory bought him an ambling Nag,
>   In Paris for to ride a.

Nine stanzas were printed with musical setting in Thomas Ravenscroft's *Deuter-
omelia: or the Second Part of Musicks Melodie* (1609; HEHL).

man then both of them: for certainly, they were the greatest wran-
glers that ever liv'd, and have fill'd all our Law-books with the obtunding [85] story of thir suits and trials.

After this hee tells us a miraculous peece of antiquity,[86] how
two *Romans, Titus, and Sempronius made feoffments,* at *Rome*
sure, and *levied Fines* by the Common Law. But now his fit of Law
past, yet hardly come to himself, hee maintains, that if Mariage
bee void, as beeing neither of God nor nature, *there needs no legal
proceeding to part it,* and I tell him, that offends not mee; *Then,*
quoth hee, *this is no thing to your book, beeing the Doctrin and
Disciplin of Divorce.* But that I deny him; for all Discipline is not
legal, that is to say juridical, but som is personal, som Economical,
and som Ecclesiastical. Lastly, if I prove that contrary dispositions
are joyn'd neither of God nor nature, and so the mariage void,
hee will give mee the controversy.[87] I have prov'd it in that book
to any wise man, and without more a doe the Institution proves
it.

Where I answer an Objection usually made, that the disposition
ought to bee known before mariage, and shew how difficult it is to
choose a fit consort, and how easie to mistake, the Servitor would
know what I mean by conversation, declaring his capacity nothing
refin'd since his Law-puddering, but still the same it was in the
Pantry, and at the Dresser. Shall I argue of conversation [88] with
this hoyd'n [89] to goe and practice at his opportunities in the Larder?
To men of quality I have said anough, and experience confirms by
daily example, that wisest, sobrest, justest men are somtimes miserably mistak'n in thir chois. Whom to leav thus without remedy, tost

---

[85] obtunding: deadening. *NED* quotes.

[86] *An Answer,* p. 15. The author states another hypothetical common law case,
substituting Roman names for the conventional English ones.

[87] *Ibid.* The promise is qualified: "In the mean time it is too great a begging
of the question."

[88] Milton's evident irritation here results from a personal allusion. His opponent writes (p. 16): "It is true, if every man were of your breeding and capacitie,
there were some colour for this plea; for we believe you count no woman to due
conversation accessible, as to you, except she can speak Hebrew, Greek, Latine,
& French, and dispute against the Canon law as well as you, or at least be able
to hold discourse with you. But other Gentlemen of good qualitie are content
with meaner and fewer endowments, as you know well enough."

[89] A rude, ignorant fellow. Now obsolete as applied to males, the word in the
17th century was common to both sexes.

and tempested in a most unquiet sea of afflictions and temptations, I say is most unchristianly.

But hee goes on to untruss my Arguments, imagining them his Maisters points.[90] Only in the passage following, I cannot but admire the ripenes, and the pregnance of his native trechery, endeavouring to bee more a Fox then his wit will suffer him. Wheras I breifly mention'd certain heads of Discours,[91] which I referr'd to a place more proper according to my method, to bee treated there at full with all thir Reasons about them, this Brain-worm against all the Laws of Dispute, will needs deal with them heer. And as a Country Hinde somtimes ambitious to shew his betters that hee is not so simple as you take him, and that hee knows his advantages, will teach us a new [16] trick to confute by. And would you think to what a pride hee swels in the contemplation of his rare stratagem, offring to carp at the language of a book, which yet hee confesses to bee generally commended; [92] while himself will bee acknowledg'd by all that read him, the basest and the hungriest endighter, that could take the boldnes to look abroad. Observ now the arrogance of a groom, how it will mount. I had writt'n, that common adultery is a thing which the rankest Politician would think it shame and disworship that his Law should countenance. First, it offends him that rankest should signify ought, but his own smell; who, that knows *English,* would not understand mee, when I say a rank Serving-man, a rank petti-fogger, to mean a meer Servingman, a meer and arrant petti-fogger, who lately was so hardy, as to lay aside his buckram wallet, and make himself a fool in Print, with confuting books, which are above him. Next the word Politician is not us'd to his maw, and therupon hee plaies the most notorious hobbihors, jesting and frisking in the luxury of his non-sense with such poor fetches to

[90] Tagged laces or cords used for fastening parts of a costume.

[91] See *Doctrine and Discipline,* above, p. 250. Brain-worm: Apparently an allusion to *Brainworm,* the contriving servant in *Every Man in His Humour.* See Ernest Sirluck, "Shakespere and Jonson among the Pamphleteers of the First Civil War," *MP,* LIII (1955), p. 96.

[92] *Cf. An Answer,* p. 17: "Your phrase is, *That such an imputation as would be cast upon the Law of God by this means, the rankest Polititian would think it shame and dis-worship that his lawes should be charged with any such thing.*

"Is this the fine language that your Book is commended for: Good your worship look a little upon your Rhetorick in this one piece, shall I say of nonsense: however I am sure it is contrary to all lawes and customes of speaking. *Rankest Polititian.* Wonderfull!"

cog a laughter from us, that no antic hobnaile at a Morris, but is more hansomly facetious.

Concerning that place Deut. 24.1. which hee saith to bee *the main pillar of my opinion*,[93] though I rely more on the institution [94] then on that. These two pillars I doe indeed confess are to mee as those two in the porch of the Temple, *Jachin* and *Boaz*,[95] which names import establishment, and strength; nor doe I fear, who can shake them. The exposition of *Deut.* which I brought,[96] is the receav'd Exposition both ancient and modern, by all lerned men, unless it bee a Monkish Papist heer and there: and the gloss which hee and his obscure assistant would perswade us to, is meerly new, and absurd, presuming out of his utter ignorance in the Ebrew, to interpret those words of the Text, first in a mistakn sense of *uncleanness*, against all approved Writers. Secondly, in a limited sense, when as the original speaks without limitation, *some uncleannes, or any;* and it had bin a wise Law indeed to mean it self particular, and not to express the case which this acute Rabbie hath all this while bin hooking for. Wherby they who are most partial to him, may guess that somthing is in this doctrin which I allege, that forces the adversary to such a new & strain'd Exposition, wherin hee does nothing for above foure pages,[97] but founder himself to and fro in his own objections, one while denying [17] *that divorce was permitted*, another while affirming, *that it was permitted for the wives sake*, and after all distrusts himself. And for his surest retirement, betakes him to those old suppositions, *that Christ abolisht the Mosaic Law of divorce; that the Jews had not sufficient knowledge in this point, through the darknes of the dispensation of heavnly things; that under the plenteous grace of the Gospel, wee are ty'd by cruellest compulsion, to live in mariage till death, with the wickedest, the worst, the most persecuting mate.*[98] These ignorant and

[93] *Ibid.*, p. 19.   [94] Genesis 2:18. See *Doctrine and Discipline*, above, p. 245.
[95] See I Kings 7:21; also II Chronicles 3:17.
[96] *Doctrine and Discipline*, above, pp. 306 ff.
[97] Milton uses "pages" here in the sense of *leaves*. The exposition to which he refers takes somewhat over eight pages (19–27).
[98] *An Answer*, p. 27: Although ostensibly a quotation or paraphrase, the final clause of this sentence is Milton's own inference from his opponent's assertion that "whosoever will . . . professe himself to have received the plenteous grace of the Gospell . . . must be so farre from turning his Wife out of doores for her ill cariage . . . that he must use all mildnesse, and love, and godly means to reforme her."

doting surmises, he might have read confuted at large, eevn in the first Edition;[99] but found it safer to pass that part over in silence. So that they who see not the sottishnes of this his new and tedious Exposition, are worthy to love it dearly.

His Explanation don, hee charges mee with a *wicked gloss, and almost blasphemy,*[100] for saying that Christ in teaching meant not always to bee tak'n word for word; but like a wise Physician administring one excess against another, to reduce us to a perfet mean. Certainly to teach thus, were no dishonest method: Christ himself hath often us'd *hyperbolies* in his teaching; and gravest Authors, both *Aristotle* in the second of his *Ethics* to *Nichomachus,*[101] and *Seneca* in his seventh *De Beneficiis,*[102] advise us to stretch out the line of precept oft times beyond measure, that while wee tend furder, the mean might bee the easier attain'd. And who-ever comments that fifth of *Matthew,* when hee comes to the *turning of cheek after cheek to blows,* and the *parting both with cloak and coat,*[103] if any please to bee the rifler, will bee forc't to recommend himself to the same Exposition, though this catering Law-monger bee bold to call it *wicked.* Now note another pretious peece of him; *Christ,* saith hee, *doth not say that an unchast look is adultery, but the lusting after her;* as if the looking unchastly, could bee without lusting. This gear is Licenc't for good reason: *Imprimatur.*

Next hee would prove that the speech of Christ is not utter'd in excess against the Pharises,[104] First, *Because hee speaks it to his Disciples, Matth.* 5. which is fals, for hee spake it to the multitude, as by the first *vers.* is evident, among which in all likelihood were many Pharises, but out of doubt, all of them Pharisaean disciples, and bred up in their Doctrin; from which extremes of error and falsity, Christ throughout his whole Sermon labours to reclaim the people. Secondly, saith hee, *Because Christ forbidds not only put-*

[99] *Doctrine and Discipline,* above, pp. 316 ff.

[100] *An Answer,* p. 28.

[101] Chapter 9, concluding sentence (tr. H. Rackham): "Thus much then is clear, that it is the middle disposition in each department of conduct that is to be praised, but that one should lean sometimes to the side of excess and sometimes to that of deficiency, since this is the easiest way of hitting the mean and the right course."

[102] Chapter 22: *Quaedam praecipimus ultra modum, ut ad verum et suum redeant.* "We stretch some precepts beyond measure in order that they may return to what is true and proper."

[103] Verses 39 and 40.   [104] *An Answer,* p. 29.

ting away, but [18] *marrying her who is put away.* Acutely, as if the Pharises might not have offended as much in marrying the divorc'd, as in divorcing the maried. The precept may bind all, rightly understood; and yet the vehement manner of giving it, may bee occasion'd only by the Pharises.

Finally, hee windes up his Text with much doubt and trepidation; for it may bee his trenchers were not scrap't, and that which never yet afforded corn of savour to his noddle, the Salt-seller was not rubb'd: and therfore in this hast *easily granting, that his answers fall foule upon each other,* and praying, you would not think *hee writes as a profet, but as a man,*[105] hee runns to the black jack,[106] fills his flagon, spreds the table, and servs up dinner.

After waiting and voiding,[107] hee thinks to void my second Argument, and the contradictions that will follow, both in the Law and Gospel, if the *Mosaic* Law were abrogated by our Saviour, and a compulsive prohibition fixt instead: and sings his old song, *that the Gospel counts unlawfull that which the Law allow'd,* instancing in *Circumcision, Sacrifices, Washings.*[108] But what are these Ceremonial things to the changing of a morall point in houshold dutie, equally belonging to Jew and Gentile; divorce was then right, now wrong; then permitted in the rigorous time of Law, now forbidd'n by Law eevn to the most extremely afflicted in the favourable time of grace and freedom. But this is not for an unbutton'd fellow to discuss in the Garret, at his tressle, and dimension of candle by the snuffe; which brought forth his cullionly paraphrase on St. *Paul,*[109]

---

[105] *An Answer,* p. 29: "If any shall think these answers to fall foul upon each other, we easily grant it, and say its usuall in this kinde; and besides we write not as Prophets but as men: and if any of the answers be to the point, and overthrow that which we conceived to be an error, its sufficient."

[106] A large leather jug for beer, ale, etc.

[107] Clearing the table.

[108] *An Answer,* p. 30.

[109] *Cf. An Answer,* p. 31: "I *Paul* am a Batchelour, and I never met with any fit and meet conversing soule, to fit my desire, to discourse and converse with me as I had when I was in *Adam;* but I speake to you Virgins and Widowes, although it be thus with me, yet it were good if you could remaine solitary without any fit conversing soule to discourse with you: but if you cannot live altogether alone all the dayes of your life (however I shift for my selfe) yet doe you marrie, *viz.* get some fit conversing soules, such an one as *Adam* thought of when he was alone in the garden, and no bodie created but he. For it is better for you seeing you cannot live alwaies alone, to have some such fit conversing soule, to drive away the time with, then to pine away like a Dove in a Wildernesse, where

whom he brings in, discoursing such idle stuff to the *Maids, and Widdows,* as his own servile inurbanity forbeares not to put into the Apostles mouth, *of the soules conversing:* and this hee presumes to doe beeing a bayard,[110] who never had the soul to know, what conversing means, but as his provender, and the familiarity of the Kitchin school'd his conceptions.

Hee passes to the third Argument, like a Boar in a Vinyard, doing nought els, but still as hee goes, champing and chewing over, what I could mean by this *Chimera* of a fit conversing Soul,[111] notions and words never made for those chopps; but like a generous Wine, only by overworking the settl'd mudd of his fancy, to make him drunk, and disgorge his vileness the more openly. All persons of gentle breeding (I say gentle, though this Barrow grunt at the word) I [19] know will apprehend and bee satisfy'd in what I spake, how unpleasing and discontenting the society of body must needs be between those whose mindes cannot bee sociable. But what should a man say more to a snout in this pickle, what language can be low and degenerat anough?

The fourth Argument which I had, was, that Mariage beeing a Covnant, the very beeing wherof consists in the performance of unfained love and peace, if that were not tolerably perform'd, the Covnant became broke and revocable. Which how can any in whose minde the principles of right reason and justice are not cancell'd, deny; for how can a thing subsist, when the true essence therof is dissolv'd? yet this hee denies, and yet in such a manner as alters my assertion, for hee puts in, *though the main end bee not attain'd in full measure:*[112] but my position is, if it be not tolerably attain'd, as throughout the whole Discours is apparent.

Now for his Reasons; *Heman found not that peace and solace, which is the main end of communion with God, should hee therfore break off that communion?*[113]

there is none to beare her company."

The paraphrase was intended as a reduction to absurdity of Milton's own exposition of I Corinthians 7:9. See *Doctrine and Discipline,* above, pp. 250–51.

[110] A self-confident ignoramus. *NED* quotes Milton's use here.

[111] *Cf. An Answer,* p. 32: "But enough of this: only we desire the next time you write, to tell us the meaning of this fit conversing soule."

[112] See *An Answer,* p. 33.

[113] The reference is to Psalm 88, attributed to Heman the Ezrahite. See *An Answer,* p. 33.

I answer, that if *Heman* found it not, the fault was certainly his own: but in Mariage it happns farre otherwise: Somtimes the fault is plainly not his who seeks Divorce: Somtimes it cannot bee discern'd, whose fault it is: and therfore cannot in reason or equity bee the matter of an absolute prohibition.

His other instance declares, what a right handicrafts man hee is of petty cases, and how unfitt to bee ought els at highest, but a hacney of the Law. *I change houses with a man; it is suppos'd I doe it for mine own ends; I attain them not in this house; I shall not therfore goe from my bargain.*[114] How without fear might the young *Charinus* in *Andria* [115] now cry out, *what likenes can bee heer to a Mariage?* In this bargain was no capitulation, but the yeilding of possession to one another, wherin each of them had his several end apart: in Mariage there is a solemn vow of love and fidelity each to other: this bargain is fully accomplisht in the change; In Mariage the covnant still is in performing. If one of them perform nothing tolerably, but instead of love, abound in disaffection, disobedience, fraud, and hatred, what thing in the nature of a covnant shall bind the other to such a perdurable mischeif? Keep to your Problems of ten groats, these matters are not for pragmatics, and folkmooters to babble in. [20]

[114] *Cf. An Answer*, pp. 33–34: "Or how think you; suppose you should covenant with a man at *Hackney*, that he should dwell in your house at Aldersgate-street, & you in requital would dwel in his house at *Hackney* for a time; I doubt not but your main end in this your Covenant was your own solace, peace, and refreshing. Well, but suppose when you come there, the *Cavaliers* or other Souldiers should trouble you, and should be quartered there; who peradventure if they did not quite put you out, yet would lie in your most pleasant Chamber best scituate for your solace and refreshing; and divers other waies would annoy you; by meanes whereof you could not enjoy that pleasure and delight which you intended in your Covenant, when you changed houses with the other. Think you in this case it would be lawfull or accepted on by the other partie if now you should come to him and say; Sir, I covenanted for your house at *Hackney* for my own refreshing, comfort, and solace, but I am disturbed of it, I do not enjoy the end of my Covenant, give me my own house again, and go you live there. He would tel you, and so he might justly, stay Sir, take your own fortune, a bargain is a bargain, you must even stand to it."

The reference to Milton's house on Aldersgate Street suggests at least a slight knowledge of his personal circumstances.

[115] The plot of Terence's *Andria* turns partly on the fear of Charinus that his beloved Philumena is to be married to his friend, Pamphilus. In *Art of Logic*, II, vi, Milton again alludes to this comedy, quoting directly from Act II, Scene i.

Concerning the place of *Paul*, that *God hath call'd us to peace,*
I Cor. 7. and therfore certainly, if any where in this world, wee
have a right to claim it reasonably in mariage, tis plain anough in
the sense which I gave,[116] and confess'd by *Paraeus*,[117] and other
Orthodox Divines, to bee a good sense, and this Answerer, doth
not weak'n it. The other place, *that hee who hateth, may put away,*
which, if I shew him, he promises to yeeld the whole controversie,[118]
is, besides, *Deut.* 24. 1. *Deut.* 21. 14. and before this, *Exod.* 21. 8.
Of *Malachy* I have spok'n more in another place;[119] and say again
that the best interpreters, all the ancient, and most of the modern
translate it, as I cited, and very few otherwise, wherof perhaps
Junius is the cheif.

Another thing troubles him, that mariage is call'd the mystery
of Joy.[120] Let it still trouble him; for what hath hee to doe either
with joy, or with mystery? He thinks it *frantic divinity* to say, It
is not the outward continuance of mariage, that keeps the covnant
of mariage whole, but whosoever doth most according to peace and
love, whether in mariage or divorce, hee breaks mariage lest. If I
shall spell it to him, *Hee breaks mariage lest,* is to say, hee dis-
honours not mariage; for *least* is tak'n in the Bible, and other good
Authors, for, *not at all.* And a particular mariage a man may break,
if for a lawfull cause, and yet not break, that is, not violate, or dishonour the Ordnance of Mariage. Hence those two questions that

---

[116] *Doctrine and Discipline,* above, p. 256. *Cf.* pp. 328 and 338–39.

[117] See David Paraeus, *In Priorem ad Corinthios Epistolam S. Pauli . . .
Commentarius* in *Operum Theologicorum* (2 vols., Frankfurt, 1628; NYPL), II,
494 (misnumbered 498). The issue is whether the clause "but God hath called
us to peace" is to be understood as completing the thought of verse 15, as Milton
had assumed, or whether it is an introduction to the next verse. Paraeus, although
favoring the latter interpretation, acknowledges that the clause "can be connected with the preceding as a reason why the faithful is not bound." He adds
that "this sense is not bad (*Quae sententia non mala est*)."

[118] *Cf. An Answer,* p. 35: "We desire you to shew out of your new Scripture (if
any such you have) where God in his Law commands, and that more then once,
that he who hateth his Wife, should put her away; shew it but one time and we
will yeild you the whole controversie."

[119] *Tetrachordon,* above, pp. 615–17. *Cf. Doctrine and Discipline,* above, p.
257.

[120] *An Answer,* p. 36: "Mysterie of joy, what language is this? is mariage now
a Sacrament signifying joy? this I never heard of before: the Papists indeed
make it a Sacrament, but not of joy, and yet I doubt they can say more for their
opinion then you for yours."

follow,[121] are left ridiculous; and the *Maids at Algate*,[122] whom hee flouts, are likely to have more witt then the Servingman at Addlegate.

Whereas hee taxes mee of adding to the Scripture in that I said, Love only is the fulfilling of every Commandment,[123] I cited no particular Scripture, but spake a general sense, which might bee collected from many places. For seeing love includes Faith, what is ther that can fulfill every commandment but only love? And I meant, as any intelligent Reader might apprehend, every positive, and civil commandment, wherof Christ hath taught us that *man is the Lord*.[124] It is not the formal duty of worship, or the sitting still, that keeps the holy rest of Sabbath; but whosoever doth most according to charity, whether hee work, or work not; hee breaks the holy rest of Sabbath least. So Mariage beeing a civil Ordinance made for man, not man for it; hee who doth that which most accords with charity, first to himself, next to whom hee next ows it, whether in mariage or divorce, hee breaks the Ordinance of mariage least. And what in Re-[21]ligious prudence, can bee charity to himself, and what to his Wife, either in continuing, or in dissolving the mariage knot, hath bin already oft anough discours'd. So that what St. *Paul* saith of circumcision,[125] the same I stick not to say of a civil ordinance, made to the good, and comfort of man, not to his ruin; mariage is nothing, and divorce is nothing, *but faith, which worketh by love*. And this I trust none can mistake.

[121] *An Answer*, p. 37.

[122] *Cf. An Answer*, p. 36: "We answer: this is a wilde, mad, and frantick divinitie, just like to the opinions of the Maids of Algate: Oh say they, we live in Christ, and Christ doth all for us; we are Christed with Christ and Godded with God, and at the same time we sin here, we joyned to Christ do justice in him, for our life is hid with God in Christ."

The opinions ascribed to "the Maids of Algate" are those popularly identified with Antinomianism. See Ephraim Pagitt, *Heresiography: or, A Description of the Heretickes and Sectaries of These Latter Times* (1645; HEHL), pp. 88–101. According to Pagitt, the first of the English Antinomians was the curate of a church near Aldgate, John Eaton (p. 89): "There is a booke set forth in his name, called the *Honey-comb of free Justification by Christ alone*, . . . the maine subject of which booke is to prove that *God doth not, will not, nor cannot see any sin in any of his justified children*."

[123] Assuming that Milton had reference to Romans 13:10, his opponent objects (p. 37), "You must remember you put in the word only, and so adde to the Scripture."

[124] See Matthew 12:8; Mark 2:27–28; Luke 6:5.   [125] Galatians 5:6.

Against the fifth Argument, That a Christian in a higher order of Preist-hood, then that Levitical, is a person dedicat to joy and peace; and therfore needs not in Subjection to a civil Ordnance, made to no other end but for his good (when without his fault hee findes it impossible to bee decently or tolerably observ'd) to plunge himself into immeasurable distractions and temptations, above his strength; against this hee proves nothing, but gadds into silly conjectures [126] of what abuses would follow, and with as good reason might declaim against the best things that are.

Against the sixt Argument, that to force the continuance of mariage between mindes found utterly unfit, and disproportional, is against nature, and seems forbidd under that *allegorical* precept of *Moses, Not to sow a field with divers seeds, lest both bee defil'd, not to plough with an Oxe and an Ass together*,[127] which I deduc'd by the pattern of St. *Pauls* reasoning what was meant *by not muzzling the Oxe*,[128] hee rambles over a long narration,[129] to tell us that by *the Oxen are meant the Preachers:* which is not doubted. Then hee demands, *if this my reasoning bee like St. Pauls*, and I answer him, yes. Hee replies that *sure St. Paul would bee asham'd to reason thus*. And I tell him, No. Hee grants that place which I alleg'd, 2 *Cor.* 6. of unequal yoking, *may allude to that of Moses,* but saies, *I cannot prove it makes to my purpos,* and shews not first, how hee can disprove it. Waigh, Gentlemen, and consider, whether my affirmations, backt with reason, may hold ballance against the bare denials of this ponderous confuter, elected by his ghostly Patrons to bee my copes-mate.[130]

Proceeding on to speak of mysterious things in nature, I had occasion to fit the language therafter, matters not for the reading of this odious fool, who thus ever when hee meets with ought above the cogitation of his breeding, leavs the noysom stench of his rude *slot* [131] behind him, maligning that any thing should bee spoke or understood, above his own *genuine* [132] basenes; and gives sentence

[126] *An Answer*, pp. 38–39.   [127] Deuteronomy 22:9–10.
[128] I Corinthians 9:8–10.
[129] *An Answer*, pp. 39–40.
[130] Adversary. *NED* quotes Milton's use here.
[131] slot: the track or trail of an animal. *NED* quotes as an example of figurative use.
[132] Innate (Latin *genuinus*).

that his confu-[22]ting hath bin imploy'd about *a frothy, im-meritous and undeserving discours.*[133] Who could have beleevd so much insolence durst vent it self from out the hide of a varlet, as thus to censure that which men of mature judgement have applauded to bee writ with good reason. But this contents him not, hee falls now to rave in his barbarous abusivenes; and why? a reason be-fitting such an Artificer, because he saith *the Book is contrary to all human lerning;* when as the world knows that all, both human and divine lerning, till the Canon Law, allow'd divorce by consent, and for many causes without consent. Next he dooms it, *as contrary to Truth;* when as it hath bin disputable among lerned men, ever since it was prohibited: and is by *Peter Martyr* thought an *opinion not impious, but hard to bee refuted;* [134] and by *Erasmus* deem'd a Doctrin *so charitable and pious, as, if it cannot bee us'd, were to bee wisht it could;* [135] but is by *Martin Bucer,* a man of dearest and

---

[133] *An Answer,* p. 41: "This frothie discourse, were it not sugred over with a little neat language, would appear so immeritous and undeserving, so contrary to all humane learning, yea, truth and common experience it self, that all that reade it must needs count it worthie to be burnt by the Hangman."

[134] *Cf. Loci Communes D. Petri Martyris Vermilii* (1583; HEHL), p. 302: *Quae licet impia non sit, et fortasse non facile refelli possit.* The context, in the Elizabethan translation of Anthonie Marten [*The Common Places . . . Doctor Peter Martyr* (1583; HEHL), part II, pp. 457–58], is as follows: "But as touch-ing the cause of adulterie, which Christ excepted, some doubt whether that be the onlie cause; and they are bold to saie, that Christs meaning was to compre-hend therin all other wickednesse, which is either equall, or more heinous then adulterie: and they saie, that the maner of the holie scriptures is, that in one cause rehearsed, they include others like unto it. . . . This (as I have declared) is the opinion of some, which although it be not wicked, and perhaps it cannot easily be confuted: yet for my part, as I with all my hart imbrase those causes, which be expressed in the scriptures; so can I hardlie indure, that divorsement should stretch beyond these bonds."

[135] *Cf. Desiderii Erasmi Roterodami Opera Omnia* (10 vols., Leyden, 1703, VI, 693-A): *Videmus autem tot hominum millia infelici conjugio sibi cohaerere cum exitio utriusque, qui fortasse disjuncti servari possent. Quod si fieri possit citra injuriam divini praecepti, optandum opinor omnibus piis: sin minus, votum tamen ipsum pium arbitror, praesertim quum charitas optet nonnunquam et quae fieri non possunt.* The passage is from the annotations on I Corinthians 7. Nycolas Lesse translates in *The Censure and Judgement of the Famous Clark Erasmus* (ca. 1550; HEHL), sig. A viii: "For we do se many thousands so unlockelye copeled togyther, wyth as evyl agrement, that bothe partes do peryshe therby, which peradventure might be saved, if they had bin set a sonder one from the other. Whyche thing if it myght be broughte to passe, without doing prejudice and wrong to the holy commandementes of God, it ought to be the desire of al godly men, but if it be so that it can not stand with the law of God,

most religious memory in the Church, taught and maintan'd to bee either most lawfully us'd, or most lawfully permitted.[136] And for this, for I affirm no more then *Bucer,* what censure doe you think, Readers he hath condemn'd the book to? To a death no less infamous then *to be burnt by the hangman.* Mr. Licencer, for I deal not now with this caitif, never worth my earnest, & now not seasonable for my jest, you are reputed a man discreet anough, religious anough, honest anough, that is, to an ordnary competence in all these. But now your turn is, to hear what your own hand hath earn'd ye, that when you suffer'd this nameles hangman to cast into public such a despightfull contumely upon a name and person deserving of the Church and State equally to your self, and one who hath don more to the present advancement of your own Tribe,[137] then you or many of them have don for themselvs, you forgot to bee either honest, Religious, or discreet. What ever the State might doe concerning it, suppos'd a matter to expect evill from, I should not doubt to meet among them with wise, and honourable, and knowing men. But as to this brute Libel, so much the more impudent and lawless for the abus'd autority which it bears, I say again, that I abominat the censure of Rascalls and their Licencers.

With difficulty I return to what remains of this ignoble task, for the disdain I have to change a period more with the filth and venom of this gourmand, swell'd into a confuter. Yet for the satisfaction of others, I endure all this. [23]

Against the seventh Argument, that if the Canon Law and Divines allow divorce for conspiracy of death, they may as well allow it to avoid the same consequence from the likelihood of naturall causes;

First, hee denies that the Canon so decrees.[138]

I Answer, that it decrees for danger of life, as much as for adultery. *Decret. Gregor. l.* 4. *tit.* 19.[139] and in other places: and the

---

yet I do take it to be a good wish and desire, forsomuch as charite often tymes doth desyre those things which can not be."

[136] See *Martin Bucer,* above, pp. 416 ff.

[137] Milton's claim here is of course based upon his tracts against Episcopacy.

[138] *An Answer,* p. 42.

[139] *Decretales Gregorii IX, Liber IV, Titulus XIX.* Chapter I under this title declares that a man whose wife conspires with others against his life may dismiss her and, after her death, may marry again. For the full text of the Gregorian Decretals on divorce, see *Corpus Juris Canonici* (2 vols., Leipzig, 1881), II, 720–25.

best Civilians who cite the Canon Law, so collect, as *Schneidewin in institut. tit.* 10. *p.* 4. *de divort.*[140] and indeed who would have deny'd it, but one of a reprobate ignorance in all hee meddles with.

Secondly, hee saith, the case alters, for there the offender *who seeks the life, doth implicitly at least act a divorce.*[141]

And I answer, that heer nature though no offender, doth the same. But if an offender *by acting a divorce,* shall release the offended, this is an ample grant against himself. Hee saith, *nature teacheth to save life from one who seeks it.* And I say she teaches no less to save it from any other cause that endangers it. Hee saith, *that heer they are both actors.* Admit they were, it would not be uncharitable to part them; yet somtimes they are not both actors, but the one of them most lamentedly passive. So hee concludes, *Wee must not take advantage of our own faults and corruptions to release us from our duties.* But shall wee take no advantage to save our selvs from the faults of another, who hath anull'd his right to our duty? No, saith hee, *Let them die of the sullens, and try who will pitty them.* Barbarian, the shame of all honest Atturneys, why doe they not hoiss him over the barre, and blanket him? [142]

Against the eighth Argument, that they who are destitute of all mariageable guifts, except a body not plainly unfit, have not the calling to marry, and consequently married and so found, may bee divorc'd, this, hee saith, *is nothing to the purpose,* and not fit to bee answer'd.[143] I leav it therfore to the judgement of his Maisters.

Against the ninth Argument, that mariage is a human society, and so cheifly seated in agreement and unity of minde: If therfore the minde cannot have that due society by mariage, that it may reasonably and humanly desire, it can bee no human society, and

[140] Johann Schneidewein (1519–1568), otherwise known as Joannes Oinotomus, was a German Protestant, a professor of legal institutions at Wittenberg. See his *In Quattuor Institutionum Imperialium Justiniani Imp. Libros Commentarii* (Venice, 1612; CUL), book I, part IV, title x. Among "such causes of divorce as are set forth in the canon law and are still observed by us" he notes as the first (p. 41) "when one of the marriage partners deliberately plots the death of the other."

[141] *An Answer,* p. 42.

[142] Toss him in a blanket. *Cf.* "hee may deserv a canvasing" (above, p. 726).

[143] *Cf. An Answer,* pp. 42–43: "Briefly to this simple Argument, quite besides that which ought to be the scope of your Book, for what is here to contrariety of dispositions, now it is a disabilitie to all maried duties: This wavering & shaking in your opinion is not fit to be answered."

so not without reason divorcible, heer hee falsifies, and turnes what the position requir'd of a reasonable agreement in the main matters of society, into *an agreement in all things,* which makes the opinion not mine, and so hee leavs it.[144] [24]

At last, and in good howr we are com to his farewell,[145] which is to bee a concluding taste of his jabberment in Law,[146] the flashiest and the fustiest that ever corrupted in such an unswill'd hogshead.

Against my tenth Argument, as he calls it, but as I intended it, my other position,[147] that Divorce is not a thing determinable by a compulsive Law, for that all Law is for som good that may be frequently attain'd without the admixture of a wors inconvenience; but the Law forbidding divorce, never attains to any good end of such prohibition, but rather multiplies evill; therfore, the prohibition of divorce is no good Law. Now for his Atturneys prise: but first, like a right cunning and sturdy Logician, hee denies my Argument not mattering whether in the *major* or *minor:* and saith, *there are many Laws made for good, and yet that good is not attain'd, through the defaults of the party, but a greater inconvenience follows.*[148]

But I reply that this Answer builds upon a shallow foundation, and most unjustly supposes every one in default, who seeks divorce from the most injurious wedloc. The default therfore will bee found in the Law it self; which is neither able to punish the offender, but the innocent must withall suffer; nor can right the innocent, in what is cheifly sought, the obtainment of love or quietnes. His instances out of the Common Law, are all so quite beside the matter which hee would prove, as may bee a warning to all clients how they venture thir busines with such a cock-braind Solliciter. For beeing to shew som Law of *England,* attaining to no good end, and yet through no

---

[144] *An Answer,* p. 43: "The consent of the minde ought to be had in mariage, or else it will hardly become a humane societie: but that after mariage the mindes of the Husband and Wife must in all things agree, or else the mariage becomes no humane societie, is a new principle unheard of till now, and so I leave it."

[145] *An Answer,* p. 43: "Now a word to your last Argument and so farewell."

[146] The original edition reads "jabberment at in Law," and it is possible that *at* is the preposition which Milton intended. In most copies examined, however, the *at* has been canceled. This is the only occurrence of *jabberment* recorded in *NED.*

[147] See *Doctrine and Discipline,* above, p. 348.

[148] *An Answer,* p. 43.

default of the party, who is therby debarr'd all remedy, hee shews us only how som doe loos the benefit of good Laws through their own default. His first example saith, *It is a just Law that every one shall peaceably enjoy his estate in Lands or otherwise.* Does this Law attain to no good end? the Barr will blush at this most incogitant woodcock. But see if a draft of *Littleton* [149] will recover him to his senses. *If this man having Fee simple in his Lands, yet will take a Leas of his own Lands, from another, this shall bee an Estoppel to him in an Assise from the recovering of his own Land.* Mark now, and register him. How many are there of ten thousand who have such a Fee simple in their sconse, as to take a Leas of their own Lands from another? So that this inconvenience lights upon scars one in an age, and by his own default; and the Law of enjoying each man his own, is good to all others. But on the contrary, this prohibition of divorce is good [25] to none, and brings inconvenience to numbers, who lie under intolerable greevances, without thir own default, through the wickednes or folly of another; and all this iniquity the Law remedies not, but in a manner maintains. His other cases [150] are directly to the same purpos, and might have bin spar'd, but that hee is a tradsman of the Law, and must be born with at his first setting up, to lay forth his best ware, which is only gibbrish.

I have now don that, which for many causes I might have thought, could not likely have bin my fortune, to bee put to this under-work of scowring and unrubbishing the low and sordid ignorance of such a presumptuous lozel. Yet *Hercules* had the labour once impos'd upon him to carry dung out of the *Augean* stable.[151] At any hand I would bee ridd of him: for I had rather, since the life of man is likn'd to a Scene,[152] that all my entrances and *exits* might mixe with such persons only, whose worth erects them and their actions to a grave and *tragic* deportment, and not to have to doe with *Clowns and*

---

[149] *Cf.* above, pp. 729 and 735, nn. 36 and 56. The *Answer* makes no mention of Littleton at this point but twice cites Sir Robert Brooke, whose *La Graunde Abridgement* (1568) was a standard legal reference book of the day. The form of the citations suggests that the immediate source was a small volume of selections from the *Abridgement*, first published under the title *Ascuns Novel Cases* (1578; HEHL) and familiarly known as "Petty Brooke."

[150] *An Answer*, pp. 43–44. There are four other cases, three dealing with questions of tenure. All, as Milton says, are quite unrelated to the argument.

[151] The story is in Apollodorus, *Bibliotheca*, II, v, 5.

[152] *Cf.* Shakespeare, *As You Like It*, II, vii, 147 ff. But the comparison was almost proverbial.

Vices.[153] But if a man cannot peaceably walk into the world, but must bee infested, somtimes at his face, with dorrs and horsflies, somtimes beneath, with bauling whippets, and shin-barkers, and these to bee set on by plot and consultation with a *Junto* of Clergy men and Licencers, commended also and rejoyc't in by those whose partiality cannot yet forgoe old papisticall principles, have I not cause to bee in such a manner defensive, as may procure mee freedom to pass more unmolested heerafter by these incumbrances, not so much regarded for themselvs, as for those who incite them. And what defence can properly bee us'd in such a despicable encounter as this, but either the flap or the spurn? If they can afford mee none but a ridiculous adversary, the blame belongs not to mee, though the whole Dispute bee strew'd and scatter'd with ridiculous. And if hee have such an ambition to know no better who are his mates, but among those needy thoughts, which though his two faculties of Servingman and Solliciter, should compound into one mongrel, would bee but thin and meager, if in this penury of Soul hee can bee possible to have the lustiness to think of fame, let him but send mee how hee calls himself, and I may chance not fail to endorse him on the backside of posterity, not a *golden*, but a brazen Asse.[154] Since my fate extorts from mee a talent of sport, which I had thought to hide in a napkin, hee shall bee my *Batrachomuomachia*,[155] my *Bavius*,[156] my *Ca-*[26]*landrino*,[157] the common adagy of ignorance and overweening. Nay perhaps, as the provocation may bee, I may bee driv'n to curle up this gliding prose into a rough *Sotadic*,[158] that shall rime him into such a condition, as instead of judging good Books to bee burnt by the executioner, hee shall be readier to be his own hangman. Thus much to this *Nuisance*.

But as for the Subject it self which I have writt, and now defend, according as the opposition beares, if any man equal to the matter

---

[153] Buffoons in the morality plays.

[154] The *Metamorphoses* of Lucius Apuleius had been translated into English by William Adlington as *The XI Bookes of the Golden Asse* (1566).

[155] The title of a mock-epic poem (*Battle of the Frogs and Mice*), ascribed in antiquity to Homer but probably of much later date.

[156] A poetaster, lampooned by Virgil. See *Eclogues*, III, 90.

[157] "A simpleton of uncouth manners" (*uom simplice e di nuovi costumi*) in the *Decameron* of Boccaccio. See *Decameron*, day VIII, novel III.

[158] A satire after the manner of Sotades, a Greek poet of the third century B.C., whose writings were notoriously scurrilous.

shall think it appertains him to take in hand this controversy, either excepting against ought writt'n, or perswaded hee can shew better how this question of such moment to bee throughly known may receav a true determination, not leaning on the old and rott'n suggestions wheron it yet leanes, if his intents bee sincere to the public, and shall carry him on without bitternes to the opinion, or to the person dissenting, let him not, I entreate him, guess by the handling, which meritoriously hath bin bestowd on this object of contempt and laughter, that I account it any displeasure don mee to bee contradicted in Print: but as it leads to the attainment of any thing more true, shall esteem it a benefit; and shall know how to return his civility and faire Argument in such a sort, as hee shall confess that to doe so is my choise, and to have don thus was my chance.

The End. [27]

MILTON'S PRIVATE CORRESPON-
DENCE

1647–1648

TRANSLATIONS, PREFACES, AND NOTES BY
W. ARTHUR TURNER AND ALBERTA T. TURNER

MILTON's correspondence for the period through 1639 appeared in Volume I of this edition. General principles for the translation and edition of the correspondence and problems involved in the text are presented in *Complete Prose*, I, 307–10. In accordance with the policy adopted for the edition, Milton's Latin and Dati's Italian texts of letters in Volume II are not given. They may be consulted most readily in the Columbia edition, Volume XII. The present translations have been based on Milton's 1674 edition and on the manuscripts, as indicated in the prefaces to individual letters.

LETTER 11, TO CARLO DATI, 1647

This is Familiar Letter number 10 in the 1674 edition. The holograph manuscript of it is now in the New York Public Library, with a manuscript of Dati's reply to it (Letter V in this volume). How the manuscripts came to be together is not certainly known, but it seems possible that they have been together since Dati penned the reply. Both manuscripts are from a collection of Milton papers owned by John Fitchett Marsh in 1833. They were bought and catalogued by Quaritch in 1882. They were then acquired by the Lenox Library, which became part of the New York Public Library. The last thirteen lines of Milton's letter are written on the reverse of the paper, and ink erosion has now made these and the first fifteen lines very difficult to read. But fortunately Marsh printed some of these lines in his *Papers Connected with the Affairs of Milton and His Family,* and photostats of the manuscript were made while the manuscript was in better condition than it is now. The present editors are indebted to Maurice Kelley for the loan of a good photostat in his possession.

Both Marsh and Masson believed that Milton's letter was the copy received by Dati, and it seems likely that that is so. The manuscript bears the full superscription "Carolo Dato Patricio Florentino Joannes Miltonius Londinensis S.P.D.," as if for the complete formality and full identification of a letter to be sent. It is written carefully and has few alterations. It is dated "Londini Pascatis feriâ tertiâ MDCXLVII," a form which seems appropriate in a letter sent to a Roman Catholic and is certainly a formal dating. The 1674 text is headed simply "Carolo Dato Patricio Florentino" and is dated "*Londino,* Aprilis 21. 1647." Both of these forms are in keeping with the usage in the 1674 edition and are briefer than those in the manuscript.

There is a discrepancy in the dating, between the manuscript and the printed letter, which at first is disconcerting. "Pascatis feriâ tertiâ MDCXLVII" ought to mean "on the third day of Easter week 1647." When Milton published the letter in 1674 this would have been April 21st; but in 1647 it would have been April 20th. It is difficult to believe that in preparing the letter for publication in 1674 Milton converted this Latin phrase to the appropriate date for that year, not remembering that Easter is a moveable holiday. It seems more likely, for the following reasons, that in 1647 he simply dated his own copy a day later than the copy sent. For only two other letters in the 1674 edition do we have manuscripts, and in both cases they appear to be the copies sent to the addressee: the letter to Holstenius (Letter 9 in 1674) and the letter to Mylius (Letter 11 in 1674).

A holograph of the letter to Holstenius was discovered by Professor J. McG. Bottkol and reproduced, with full and able discussion, in *PMLA*, LXVIII (1953), 617–27. The manuscript is almost certainly the copy received by Holstenius: it was found in the Vatican Library, where Holstenius was librarian when Milton wrote to him, and it bears a full and formal superscription like that of the manuscript letter to Dati. It is dated "Mart. 29, 1639." But again, the letter printed in 1674 is dated "*Florentiae,* Martii 30. 1639."—a day later than the manuscript. In both cases one can imagine Milton finishing a fair copy and then on the next day, perhaps when he sent the letter or when he put away his draft, dating the draft. Clearly something very much like this happened in the case of the letter to Mylius; the manuscript is certainly the one received by Mylius, for it was found among his papers. The manuscript is in the hand of an amanuensis. The date was first written "ultimo xbris 1651" (presumably the date of composition) and later changed to "2 Jan:1652." But the printed letter in 1674 bears no date. Since the letter deals with actions which occurred on stated days, and "today" presumably refers to the last day of December, 1651, the later date would actually be an error on the letter sent. Possibly the amanuensis had been instructed to date the draft and had re-dated the letter instead; certainly if he had then dated the draft, it would have borne a date two days later than the accurate date for the letter Mylius received, and that date on the draft would have appeared in the 1674 edition. From these three instances we are certainly not justified in assuming that Milton always gave to the drafts of his letters, or to the copies he kept, later dates than those on the copies sent; but we should apparently be wrong in supposing that he never did. Therefore we need not let the discrepancy in dates on the two states of the letter to Dati keep us from assuming that the surviving manuscript was the copy which Dati received.

Moreover, the manuscript of Dati's reply, which has been with Milton's manuscript at least since they were acquired by Marsh, looks like a draft. It is not carefully written. It contains many errors in quotation and reference. And, most convincing perhaps, it contains many abbreviations, some so brief as to be almost cryptic.

All three manuscript letters contain variants from the 1674 edition. But in no case do the variants indicate which is earlier, the manuscript or the copy from which the 1674 edition was set. This may be accounted for by the assumption that Milton did a certain amount of revision for the 1674 edition.

We are apparently justified in drawing two conclusions from the evidence before us: (1) that the three surviving manuscripts of the letters printed in 1674 are the fair copies received by the addressees, and therefore (2) that no drafts, or revised copies for the 1674 edition, have been recovered. Presumably, then, the manuscripts represent Milton's intention at the time the letters were dispatched and the printed text represents his final intention as authorized for publication. For the sake of consistency with the other letters published by Milton, we have based our translation on the 1674 text.

Carlo Roberto Dati was born in Florence on October 2, 1619, and died there January 11, 1676. He was one of the stimulating young intellectuals whom Milton met on his memorable visits to Florence in 1638 and 1639, whose friendship he mentioned with such pride and gratitude in the *Second Defence*. Milton headed the published letter to "Carolo Dato, Patricio Florentino," the appellation with which Dati had signed an encomium to Milton. He seems not to have been a nobleman, but he was certainly a "gentleman" of some means, very popular as a person, and well known as a scholar in his day. He was a member of many of the academies in Florence; in 1663 he was made secretary of the *Della Crusca*, in which he was known as *Smarrito*, "the bewildered." On the death of Giovanni Battista Doni (December 1, 1647), another of the group, he became Professor of Greek and Latin Literature in the Florentine Academy. Altogether he wrote many tracts on literature, language, science, and painting, and edited a collection of works of the Della Cruscans. Though he wrote some occasional verse (notably some laudatory verses to Louis XIV, who gave him a pension), he was primarily a scholar. Milton may have been especially interested in him because, like Buonmattei (see *Complete Prose* I, 328–32), he was interested in the proper use of language. His admiration for Milton he first expressed in a Latin prose encomium while Milton was still in Florence; this Milton published with his *Poems*, 1645.

SOURCES

Columbia Edition, XII, 383–84, 395–97; J. Milton French, *Life Records of John Milton*, II, 185–91, 201–09; John Fitchett Marsh, *Papers Connected with the Affairs of Milton and His Family* (Chetham Society Publications, XXIV, 1851); Masson, I (rev. ed., 1881), 774–75; III, 455, 650–55; *Nouvelle Biographie Générale*, III, 156–57; J. M. Botthol, "The Holograph of Milton's letter to Holstenius, *PMLA*, LXVIII (1953), 617–27; Milton, *Epistolarum Familiarium Liber Unus*, 1674; the holograph manuscripts of Milton's letter and of Dati's reply, in the New York Public Library, and photostats of these manuscripts.

TO CHARLES DATI, NOBLEMAN OF FLORENCE

How NEW and great a joy fills me, my Charles, at the unexpected arrival of your letter; [1] since I cannot describe it adequately, I want you to form some idea of it, at least from that attendant pain without which men have scarcely ever known delight. For while running through the first part of your letter, in which elegance vies so beautifully with friendship, I should have called my feeling one of unmixed joy, especially since I see that you take pains to make friendship the victor. But as soon as I reach that passage in which you write that you have already sent me three letters,[2] which I know have been lost, then, first, that sincere joy begins to be tainted, and disturbed by a sad longing; soon an even heavier mood creeps over me, a mood in which I am accustomed often to bewail my lot, to lament that those whom perhaps proximity or some unprofitable tie has bound to me, whether by accident or by law, those, commendable in no other way, daily sit beside me, weary me—even exhaust me, in fact—as often as they please; [3] whereas those whom character, temperament, interests

[1] The letter has not survived.

[2] Evidently these were never recovered.

[3] Milton's household had been in turmoil for a year. In the Barbican house, which he took on his wife Mary's return to him in 1645, there were his father, his nephews John and Edward Phillips, and perhaps other boarding students, certainly other day students. Then in June, 1646, on the surrender of Oxford, Mary's father, mother, brothers, and sisters came to live with them. In July Mary's first child was born. Though Milton evidently got along well with Mary after her return, he cannot have been fond of her family. Her father had never paid him her dowry and owed other money besides; her mother had evidently been partially responsible for Mary's desertion, and she never liked Milton. They were all royalists; Milton had supported Parliament in the first civil war and would end the second a republican. But in January, 1647, Mr. Powell died, in March Milton's father died, and soon afterward the Powells were able to move

had so finely united are now nearly all grudged me by death or most.
hostile distance and are for the most part so quickly torn from my
sight that I am forced to live in almost perpetual solitude.[4] I
strongly congratulate myself that ever since I left Florence,[5] you
have, you say, been concerned about my health and have always
kept me in mind; and I congratulate myself that the feeling was
equal and mutual which I, perhaps with reason, had thought was
mine alone. That separation, I may not conceal from you, was also
very painful for me; and it fixed those stings in my heart which
even now rankle whenever I think that, reluctant and actually torn
away, I left so many companions and at the same time such good
friends, and such congenial ones in a single city—a city distant indeed but to me most dear. I call to witness the tomb of Damon [6]
(which shall always be sacred and solemn to me) that when I was
burdened with the task of adorning it with every tribute of grief,
when I wanted to turn to what comforts I could and pause for
breath, I could think of nothing pleasanter than to recall my dearest
memory of you all, of you, Dati, especially. All this you must have
read for yourself long since, if indeed that poem reached you, as
from you I now first hear it did. I had had it sent purposely, so that
it might be, however small a proof of talent, by no means an obscure
proof of my love for you, at least in those few little verses inserted
—as it were inlaid [7]—there. I thought by this means to entice

away. Then Milton gave up most of his students, moved to a smaller house in
Holborn, and turned again to his studies. Here he reveals the strain he felt, but
as usual omits intimate details of his troubles. See W. A. Turner, *The Known
English Acquaintances of John Milton* (Ohio State University Doctoral Disserta-
tion, 1946), articles on the Powells.

[4] We do not know who all these friends were. Diodati was long dead, Mrs.
Katherine Thomason (of Sonnet XIV) had died in 1646, his father more recently, and young Gill had left London and was probably dead. He probably did
not yet know Marvell or Cyriack Skinner. He may have known Lady Ranelagh.
He knew Hartlib, bookseller Thomason, Lawes, and Lady Margaret Ley and her
husband, but may have found it inconvenient to visit them at this time. (See
Turner, cited above, articles on persons named.)

[5] He left Florence for the last time about the first of April, 1639.

[6] Damon is Charles Diodati, whose death Milton had lamented in "Epitaphium
Damonis." (See preface to Letter I, *Complete Prose*, I, 310–11.) Milton had
evidently sent copies to his Italian friends.

[7] "emblematis ad morem." In the manner of little gems set in a mosaic or
ornamented vessel. Throughout the "Epitaphium Damonis" Milton mentions or
alludes to persons and places in Florence and to his visits there. He specifically
names Francini and Dati, who had given him written encomia.

either you or another to write; for if I wrote first, I had either to write to all, or, by preferring one, to offend, I feared, those of the others who came to know it—since I hope there still survive among you [8] many who could surely claim that attention from me. Now you, first, have freed my long-due correspondence from the reproach of the others, both by this letter's most friendly appeal and by your previous triple repetition of the courtesy. Yet I confess that, since I returned home, there has been an additional reason for silence in the extremely turbulent state of our Britain, which quickly compelled me to turn my mind from my studies to protecting life and property in any way I could.[9] Do you think there can be any safe retreat for literary leisure among so many civil battles, so much slaughter, flight, and pillaging of goods? Nevertheless, since you ask about my studies, know that even among these evils we have given to the light not a few things in our native language,[10] which, were they not in English, I should gladly send all of you, whose opinions I value highly. Yet since you wish it, I shall shortly send you that part of the poems which is in Latin; and I should have sent it of my own accord long since, had I not suspected that they would be unpleasing to your ears because of those words spoken rather sharply on some pages against the Roman Pope.[11] Now I beg you to obtain from my other friends (for of you I am certain) that same indulgence to freedom of speech which, as you know, you have been used to granting in the past with singular kindness—I do not mean to your Dante and Petrarch in this case, but to me; I crave it now whenever mention be made of your religion according to our custom. I am reading with pleasure your description of the funeral of King Louis,[12] in which I recognize your Mercury, not that presiding

[8] Most of the people Milton had met in Italy were still alive in 1647. Buonmattei had died January 27, 1647.

[9] We have no knowledge of what Milton did to protect himself. Instead of staying at Horton he took a house in London; instead of staying out of trouble he wrote the anti-Episcopal tracts; and he married a royalist's daughter. But his concern for his safety is perhaps reflected in the sonnet "When the Assault was Intended to the City."

[10] Since his Italian visit, he had published the anti-Episcopal tracts, the divorce tracts, *Of Education, Areopagitica,* and his *Poems* (1645).

[11] Milton perhaps had in mind the "In Proditionem Bombardicam" poems, "In Inventorem Bombardae," and "In Quintum Novembris."

[12] Louis XIII of France had died on May 14, 1643. The Duke of Tuscany honored his memory with public services in Florence. Milton no doubt refers to

over the cross-roads and dedicated to merchandise, which you jest that you have been cultivating recently, but that which is eloquent, welcome to the Muses, and protector of Mercurial men.[13] It remains for us to decide upon some means whereby our letters may come and go by a sure route. This does not seem very difficult, since so many of our merchants have both large and numerous business transactions in your city; their letter carriers run back and forth every week, and their ships sail from both sides not much less often. This business I shall entrust, rightly I hope, to James, the bookseller, or to his master,[14] a most familiar acquaintance of mine. Meanwhile, my Charles, farewell and give my best greeting to Coltellini, Francini, Frescobaldi, Malatesta, Chimentelli the younger, and any other of our group whom you know to be especially fond of me—in short to the whole Gaddian Academy.[15] Again farewell.

London, April 21, 1647.[16]

a little tract entitled *Esequie della Maesta Christianiss: di Luigi XIII. il Giusto, Re di Francia e di Navarra, celebrate in Firenze dall. altezza serenissima di Ferdinando Granduca di Tosc., e discritte da Carlo Dati* (Florence, 1644).

[13] Milton is here playing upon the different functions of Mercury. Mercury was patron of business men and of messengers, but he was also the patron god of literary men. Dati's business might have been only such matters as the affairs of the academies, in which he was very active, or details of the funeral which he described; in his next letter to Milton (Letter V, below, p. 767) we learn that he was busy with details of the funeral of his friend Rovai and was preparing a volume of tributes. But Milton recognizes rather the literary aspect of Dati's work and in his words *Mercurialium Virorum* echoes Horace verbatim (*Carmina,* II, 29–30) in calling literary men Mercurial men.

[14] Booksellers were often agents of communication. This one has not been identified.

[15] For Milton's Florentine friends, see Masson, I, 773–80. Agostino Coltellini was an energetic scholar and founder of the *Apatisti* academy. Antonio Francini was a poet of some renown and had given Milton a verse encomium which Milton had published, with Dati's prose encomium, in his *Poems.* Pietro Frescobaldi, Antonio Malatesta, and Valerio Chimentelli were all members of the circle. All these men, plus Giovanni Battista Doni, Benedetto Buonmattei, and Jacopo Gaddi, were members of about the same academies. They formed the group Milton had known in Florence.

[16] See discussion of date in headnote, above, p. 760.

LETTER V, CARLO DATI TO MILTON, 1647

TRANSLATED BY LAWRENCE A. WILSON

This letter is clearly a reply to Milton's letter of April 21 (Letter 11), and the manuscript is with Milton's in the New York Public Library. Our translation is based on a photostat of that manuscript. For the history and status of the manuscript, see the headnote to Letter 11, above, p. 759.

It is interesting to notice that many of Dati's quotations (in illustration of the usage of *rapidus*) are of a nature which might bring some philosophic comfort to one suffering because of love. If this is more than coincidence, we may suppose that Dati knew more of Milton's domestic troubles than he had learned from Milton's letter. Possibly rumors of Mary's earlier desertion had reached Italy.

Many of Dati's quotations are inaccurate, but only to an extent which suggests that he was working from hastily written notes or at times even from memory, and that perhaps the manuscript is a draft. The letter is in Italian.

TO THE MOST ILLUSTRIOUS SIGNOR JOHN MILTON, LONDON.

W HEN ALL hope was dead within me notwithstanding the liveliest desire to receive your letters, there appears one [1] from you which is more welcome than this pen can express. Oh, how many reasons for boundless joy that little paper brought to my heart! That paper, written by so accomplished and so dear a friend, which after so long a time and from so far a land brought me word of your health, as much desired as feared for, and which assured me that remembrance of me is kept so fresh and affectionate in the most generous soul of John Milton. I learned, moreover, in what esteem you hold my country, which numbers among its excellences having in great England (divided from our world, as that poet [2] said) one who extols its glories, loves its people, celebrates its writers, and writes and discourses so correctly and in so polished a manner in its beautiful language. And it is precisely this which moved me to answer your very Latin letter in the Tuscan,

[1] Letter 11.
[2] Virgil, *Eclogue I*, l. 60. Dati may have been reminded of this by line 59, which contains the word *rapidum*.

gifted as you are for making dead languages live again and for making foreign tongues your own, hoping that the sound of one you possess and speak so well will be pleasing to you. For the same reason I shall be so bold as to beseech you to honor with your verses the glorious memory of Signor Francesco Rovai,[3] worthy Florentine poet dead before his prime and, I believe, well known to you. My friends, those most excellent patrons and men of letters of our age Nicholas Heinsius and Isaac Vossius [4] of Holland, have done as much at my request. Signor Francesco was of noble birth, endowed by Nature with the loftiest genius, enriched by art and indefatigable study of the finest disciplines. He understood Greek very well, spoke French, composed in Latin and Tuscan marvellously well. He wrote tragedies and distinguished himself by his lyric poetry, in which he lauded the Heroes and scourged vice—particularly in those seven Canzoni directed against the Seven Deadly Sins. He was polite, courtly, beloved of princes, of uncorrupted and devout manners. He died young without having published his works. Sumptuous exequies are being prepared by his friends, and all that lacks is the funeral oration, with which I have been charged. If (as I hope) you will deign to send me to this end some fruit of your delightful wit, you will oblige not merely me, but all my country; and when Signor Francesco's poetry and the eulogies of him are published, copies will be sent you. But since I have begun to speak of our language and of our poets, I take pleasure in imparting to you one of my animadversions relative to our writers which I compose now and then in the rare moments of leisure allowed me by my business pursuits.[5]

[3] Rovai's poems, edited by Niccolo Rovai (a brother?), were published at Florence in 1652. There is no evidence, other than Dati's remark, that Milton knew him.

[4] Heinsius and Vossius knew each other and corresponded frequently. Vossius went to Italy and met many of the people Milton knew. He was royal librarian to Christina of Sweden during Milton's controversy with Salmasius, who was also at Christina's court, and so observed the effect of Milton's books on his enemy. Neither Heinsius nor Vossius knew Milton or sympathized with his cause, but both admired his books tremendously and judged him the victor. Their interest in Milton continued through the Morus controversy. Masson, IV, *passim; Nouvelle Biographie Générale*, XXIII, 793–95.

[5] Business pursuits. Nature unknown, but possibly only a kind of writing which he feels is merely utilitarian; Milton's allusion in Letter 11 seems to justify such an interpretation.

The other day, while I was pondering that tercet of Petrarch, *The Triumph of Love,* Canto 3,

> Love's stern law, though unjust,
> Must be obeyed since it extends
> From heaven to earth, universal, primordial,[6]

I saw that the most learned Castelvetro [7] had already noted that this passage had some resemblance to one from Horace, *Odes,* I, 33, 10—

> Such is the decree of Venus, whose delight it is in cruel sport
> to force beneath her brazen yoke bodies and hearts ill-mated.[8]

This is most aptly imitated by Gabriel Chiabrera, resuscitator of Pindaric and Anacreontic verse, in the fifth of his *Canzonetta,*

> Ah, that a lover, suffering, become ashes
> Even though faithful,
> Thus Venus wills it,
> Cruel goddess of Ocean born.[9]

Recognizable in the above verses is not only a bit taken from Horace, but also the remnant taken—not without noteworthy improvement—from Tibullus, in whose *Elegies,* Book I, Elegy 2, one reads this threat against those who betray the secrets of love:

> For, if any man turn prater, he shall find that Venus is the
> child of blood and the whirling [*rapido*] sea.[10]

The adjective *rapido* applied here to the sea to me appearing to have little or no force, I would read *rabido,* by which term—simply by inverting a single letter—the greatest vigor is added to Tibullus' conceit, his desire being to depict Venus as relentless and cruel in punishing such a crime. To this emendation all the printed texts and all the commentaries on the aforesaid poet are opposed, all of them reading *rapido,* an epithet much more befitting the swift flow of rivers than the surge of the sea, but which is nevertheless applied to the sea by many poets, to wit—Catullus, on Berecynthia and Attis,

---

[6] Petrarch: Canto III, 148–50.

[7] Castelvetro: *Le Rime del Petrarca brevemente sposte per Ludovico Castelvetro* (Basle, 1582; private library of Andrew Bongiorno, Oberlin), p. 224.

[8] Horace: *Odes,* I, 33, 10–12. Ms. has 23 for 33.

[9] Chiabrera: *Canzonetta,* 5. Ms. has 18ª.

[10] Tibullus: *Liber I, Elegia 2,* ll. 40–41.

[Ye Gallae . . . who] endured the fast-flowing brine [*rapidum salum*] and the savage seas; [11]

Virgil, or rather, according to Scaliger, Cornelius Severus in the *Aetna,*

Even as when the rapid sea is seen with curving swell; [12]

Seneca, in the *Hercules Oetaeus,* line 552,

And as a bull, with horns quick-sprouting on his brow, clove through the boisterous sea [*rapidum mare*], bearing the Assyrian maid; [13]

Valerius Flaccus, *Argonautica,* Book IV,

The sea that contending winds make boisterous [*rapidum*]; [14]

Claudian,

He [sought] Tyre through so many struggles of the rapid sea.[15]

And others still. But note that all speak of tempests or seek to express the fury of the stormy sea, wherefore they nicely hit upon calling it *rapido.* And Catullus on the Argonauts [16] very aptly called the sea of Hellespont *rapido* because the contrary and changing tides run continuously through these straits. But it spoils Tibullus' conceit to say "Praters shall find that Venus is the child of blood and the whirling sea" rather than "child of blood and the savage sea." All those poets who have called the sea *wild, savage, mad, angry,* or otherwise, with a view of expressing cruelty, favor my opinion; but the passages I have considered make it doubly clear. Seneca, in the *Hippolytus,* line 273,

Goddess born of the pitiless sea; [17]

and Virgil, *Aeneid,* V, 802, who makes Neptune say in addressing Venus,

[11] Catullus: *Carmina,* LXIII, 16.
[12] Virgil . . . Severus: *Aetna,* I, 495. The original text is in such confusion that it is impossible to be certain of the authorship. Editions containing Scaliger's comments appeared in 1575, 1595, 1596.
[13] Seneca: *Hercules Oetaeus,* ll. 552–53.
[14] Flaccus: *Argonautica,* IV, 270.
[15] Claudian: This seems to be Dati's error. We have found no such line in Claudian. Since he omits the exact references given for his other quotations, he may be depending on memory.
[16] Catullus: *Carmina,* LXIV, 358–60.
[17] Seneca: *Hippolytus,* or *Phaedra,* l. 274.

Every right hast thou, Cythera's queen, to trust in my realms
—those realms whence thou drawest birth! And I have merited
so! Often have I quelled the madness and dread fury [*rabiem*]
of sky and sea. . . . [18]

The very same Virgil confirms my interpretation when he says
"*rabies Scyllaea*," [19] Scylla's savagery, as does Valerius Flaccus, IV,
about line 508,

In so fleet [*rapido*] a whirlwind do they pass over peoples and
seas afar, nor are suffered to settle in any land,

and in line 582,

Only when a ship shall have penetrated the sea and cruel
[*rabidi*] mountains have stood fast in the flood; [20]

Silius Italicus, Book 15,

when he saw there the van. Like a great beast of the angry
[*rabidi*] deep.[21]

Precisely the same error has slipped into Horace's *Poetics* according
to which, speaking of Orpheus, one commonly reads

He is said from this to tame tigers and swift [*rapidos*] lions,[22]

where everyone of middling wit perceives how cold and inconsequent
a conceit it is to say that the song of Orpheus had the power of
taming the swiftest lions, and how much better the figure is, reading
with Cruquius [23] and Lambinus [24] in some manuscripts,

He is said from this to tame tigers and raging [*rabidos*] lions,

since taming best suits the "raging," an adjective befitting lions.
Wherefore Cornelius Gallus (or, according to better opinion, Maximian the poet) in his first *Elegy*,

Broken the wrath of the long raging [*diu rabidi*] lion,

[18] Virgil: *Aeneid*, V, 800–802.
[19] Virgil: *Aeneid*, I, 200. Again perhaps quoting from memory. For Virgil's
Scyllaeam rabiem Dati has *rabies Scyllaea*.
[20] Flaccus: *Argonautica*, IV, 510–11; 581–82.
[21] Silius: *Punica*, XV, 784. Ms. has 13 for 15.   [22] Horace: *Ars Poetica*, l.
393.
[23] Cruquius: Jacob de Crusque's edition of Horace, Antwerp, 1578.
[24] Lambinus: Lambin's edition of Horace, 1561 and republished several times
in Paris and elsewhere.

although afterwards in the same poet's fifth Elegy one reads

You cause the fleet [*rapidas*] tigers to know love,[25]

which, by the same reasoning as applies to the passage from Horace, would make better sense as "ravening" [*rabidas*], as Virgil, *Georgics*, II, 151, styles them,

But the cruel [*rabidae*] tigers are not there, nor the lions' fierce speed.[26]

But perhaps I have ventured too far, both in words and zeal. Returning, therefore, to my first intent, which was to emend Tibullus and to clarify Chiabrera, I say that the birth of Venus from the sea is well known, as amply indicated by Natalis Comes' *Mythology;* [27] Giglio Gregorio Giraldi's *On the Gods of the Heathen*, article 13; [28] Martin del Rio on line 273 of Seneca's *Hippolytus*,[29] and Ludovico della Cerda's on Virgil's *Aeneid*, V, 802.[30] According to the poets, it is no less certain that being born of the sea was an infallible sign of cruelty. As Aulus Gellius says, XV, 21, "The sons of Neptune . . . were most haughty and cruel, and strangers to all refinement, as being sprung from the sea." [31] Likewise Tibullus, Elegy 4, Book 3,

For the waves of the vasty sea did not bear you; [32]

Catullus on the Argonauts,

What sea conceived thee and vomited thee forth from its foaming waves? [33]

[25] Cornelius . . . Maximian: *Elegy I*, l. 271; *Elegy V*, l. 145. For the false attribution of the poet Maximian's works to Cornelius Gallus, friend of Virgil and Octavianus, see Richard Webster, ed., *The Elegies of Maximianus* (Princeton, 1900), p. 15.

[26] Virgil: As cited, ll. 151–52.

[27] *Mythology* of . . . Comes: Natale (or Noël) Conti, *Mythologiae* (Venice, 1568, and several later editions elsewhere) was a well-known encyclopedia.

[28] Giraldi: Lilius (or Giglius) Gregorius Geraldus, *De Deis Gentium Libri sive Syntagmata* (Leyden, 1565).

[29] Del Rio: *Syntagma Tragoediae Latinae, seu Fragmenta veterum Tragicorum et L. Ann. Senecae Tragoediae, Cum Commentariis* (Antwerp, 1593).

[30] Joannes Ludovicus de la Cerda, *P. Vergilii Maronis Aeneidos . . . Argumentis Explicationibus, Notis Illustrati* (1612).

[31] Gellius: Aulus Gellius, *Noctium Atticarum*, XV, 21, ll. 3–5.

[32] Tibullus: *Lygdamus*, IV, 85.

[33] Catullus: *Carmina*, LXIV, 155.

Ovid in his epistle from Ariadne to Theseus,

> Neither is Aegeus your father, nor are you the son of Pittheus'
> daughter Aethra; they who begot you were the rocks and the
> deep; [34]

Homer in the sixteenth book, line 34, of the *Iliad*,

> —γλαυκὴ δὲ σ᾽ ἔτικτε θάλασσα
> πέτραι τ᾽ ἠλίβατοι, ὅτι τοι νόος ἐστὶν ἀπηνής.[35]

that is,

> Thou of the blue sea, of the lofty crags, wert born; hence thou
> art cruel of mind;

and our own Torquato Tasso, imitator, nay! rival of the poets cited
above, sang in the sixteenth canto of his *Jerusalem Delivered,*

> Sofia bore thee not, nor wert thou born
> Of the blood of Azzio. Thou the mad waves of sea bore,
> And the frozen Caucasus, the dugs of an Hircanian tigress fed.[36]

Nor let anyone marvel that Venus, so pleasing and so gracious a
goddess, is called by Chiabrera a cruel divinity, since Horace called
her "imperious mother of love," [37] and Seneca in the *Hercules
Oetaeus,* line 543, [describes Cupid as] "youth dreaded by his savage mother." [38] I communicate these reflections of mine to you,
confident of being excused and of being affectionately admonished
by your exquisite learning, a favor I earnestly request, beseeching
you to forgive me if my excessive affection, my having been so long
a time without word of you, and the great distance between us, have
led me to transgress the limits prescribed for letters. It grieves me
much that the disorders [39] of the realm have disturbed your studies,
and I am anxiously awaiting your poems,[40] in which I believe that
I shall be given ample reason for admiring the fineness of your wit,
save in those, however, which are in dispraise of my religion, and

---

[34] Ovid: *Heroides,* X, 131–32.

[35] Homer: *Iliad,* XVI, 34–35. Dati quotes the Greek and then furnishes a
translation in Italian, which Milton must have thought a little unflattering.

[36] Tasso: *Gerusalemme Liberata,* XVI, stanza 57, ll. 1–4.

[37] Horace: *Odes,* I, xix, 1.   [38] Seneca: *Hercules Oetaeus,* l. 543.

[39] Disorders: See Letter 11, above, p. 764.

[40] your poems: See Letter 11. That Milton sent the poems is shown by Dati's
next, Letter VI.

which, although coming from the lips of a friend, can only be excused, not praised. But this will be no obstacle to my welcoming the others, if my zealous freeness be excused. Meanwhile, as I pray that Heaven will make and keep you happy, may you keep a place for me in your thoughts, giving me sign thereof by your ever-welcome commands. All your friends,[41] whom I greeted affectionately in your name, send you their respectful salutations.

Your most devoted servant,[42]

Carlo Dati

Florence, November 1, 1647

LETTER VI, CARLO DATI TO MILTON, 1648

TRANSLATED BY LAWRENCE A. WILSON

The original manuscript of this letter, in Italian, is in BML, MS. Add. 5016*, which also contains the two letters from Diodati, one from Aizema, and one from Heimbach. Perhaps the best reason for supposing that the letters are the copies Milton received and not drafts is that they are thus together, although they are of different dates and their authors were far apart. Toland mentions the Diodati letters in his *Life* (p. 23), and a note by Birch on one of the sheets reads "These 2 Greek Epistles of the famous *Diodati* to *Milton* were given me by Mr. Toland who writ the life of ye said JM." Possibly Toland obtained all the letters from Milton's widow. They were together in the British Museum before the middle of the nineteenth century and were printed in Mitford's *Life* prefixed to Pickering's edition of Milton's *Works*, 1851. The Dati letter appears in Volume I, cxcv-vi. It is not signed; but it is in Dati's hand, and it bears on the cover a full and formal address to Milton (see at the end of our translation). There is no apparent reason for doubting its authenticity.

SOURCES

Columbia Edition, XII, 393–97; photostat of Dati's letter, BML, MS. Add. 5016*, ff. 9–10v; French, *Life Records*, II, 221–24; Masson, II, 690–91.

[41] friends: See names at end of Letter 11.
[42] servant: Literally, "Your most illustrious lordship's most devoted servant," but the English would have a specific social meaning not in the Italian.

[CARLO DATI TO MILTON]

Most illustrious and most honored Sir,

A s LONG ago as the past year I replied to your most courteous and elegant letter, thanking you affectionately for the kind memory you are pleased to entertain of me. I wrote in the Tuscan, as I do now, knowing that my language is so dear and familiar that it does not seem foreign in your mouth. I have received since then two copies of your most learned poems, than which there could not have come to me a dearer gift; for, however small, it contains within itself infinite worth, being a gem from the treasury of John Milton. And, as Theocritus said,

—ἦ μεγάλα χάρις
δώρῳ ξὺν ὀλίγῳ· πάντα δὲ τίματα τὰ πὰρ φίλων.[1]

A small gift has great value,
And what comes from friends demands honor.

I therefore return the fullest thanks I can, and I pray Heaven grant me the good fortune of being able to prove my devotion to your merits. I shall not keep from you some news that I am confident will be pleasing to you. The Most Serene Grand Duke,[2] my master, has been pleased to confer upon me the chair and lectureship of Humane Letters of the Florentine Academy, vacant through the death of the most learned Giovanni Doni,[3] a gentleman of Florence. This is a most honorable post, and it has always been filled by gentlemen and men of letters of this city, as already by Politian,[4] the two Vettori,[5] the two Adriani [6]—literary lights all. Last week on the death of the Most Serene Prince Lorenzo [7] of Tuscany, uncle

[1] Theocritus: *Idylls*, XXVIII, 24–25. Dati quotes the Greek and provides an Italian translation, as he had done for Homer in Letter V.

[2] Grand Duke Ferdinand de Medici II, 1610–1670. Like his predecessors, he liberally patronized science and letters.

[3] Doni: Doni died December 1, 1647.

[4] Politian: Ambroginio Poliziano, 1454–1494, a famous humanist.

[5] Vettori: One of these was certainly Pietro Vettori, 1499–1585, editor of many Greek and Roman authors. The other may well have been Francesco Vettori, 1474–1539, who also spent much time in Florence and was a favorite of the Medici.

[6] Adriani: Marcello Adriani, 1464–1521, and Giovanni-Battista Adriani, 1511–1579.

[7] Lorenzo: Lorenzo de Medici, uncle of Duke Ferdinand II, died 1648.

of the reigning Grand Duke, I gave the funeral oration; when it is published it will be my care to send you [8] a copy [9] of it. I am working on several pieces which, God willing, I shall strive to dispose of as my learned and kind friends think best. Valerio Chimentelli has been chosen by His Highness as Professor of Greek Literature at Pisa, with great expectations of his worth.

Messrs. Frescobaldi, Coltellini, Francini, Galilei,[10] and many others join in sending you their affectionate greetings. And I, as more than any other obliged to you, reminding you of my desire to receive your commands, subscribe myself

Your most devoted servant,[11]

[Carlo Dati]

Florence, December 4, 1648

To the most illustrious and honored Mr. John Milton, London. [on cover.]

[8] You: Literally, "to your most illustrious lordship."

[9] Copy: We do not know that Milton received a copy.

[10] Chimentelli . . . Galilei: All Milton's acquaintances. The Galilei is not the famous Galileo (who died in 1642) but his son Vincenzio, 1600–1649; this is the only evidence that Milton knew the young mathematician. For the other names see note to Letter 11.

[11] Your: For literal translation, see above, Letter V, p. 773, n. 42.

TEXTUAL NOTES

DOCTRINE AND DISCIPLINE OF DIVORCE [1]

In each set of textual notes below, the word following the bracket is Milton's original. The word preceding the bracket is the emendation as it appears in the text in this volume. Errors in punctuation are similarly recorded.

Page	Line	
232	2	England] England,
233	9	and] And
233	11	world:] world.
248	5	How] (No paragraph in 1643)
252	23	burning] burnining
261	21	Christian] christian
266	5	advises] advices
266	25	Christian] christian
267	10	offence:] offence,
267	14	Christian] christian
268	5	Christianitie] christianitie
275	2	Christian] christian
277	4	reveal'd] revel'd
277	9	couple?] couple;
277	17	could?] could.
287	8	prov'd.] prov'd
292	3	fathers] Fathers
292	7	conniving] contriving (Ink corrections in most copies)
292	11	contrary] cantrary
294	1	find] give (Corrected in errata)

Page	Line	
294	3	freewill] will (Corrected in errata)
294	8	he acquitts] acquits (Corrected in errata)
297	14	and] anc
298	13	rules.] rules
298	14	principles.] principles
299	5	satisfaction,] satisfaction.
299	12	first.] first,
301	2	forg'd] fotg'd
302	13	odious] odi-dious (Word divided at end of line)
311	24	Was] was
314	9	But] but
325	10	*Vashti*] *Vasthi*
330	6	20,] 20.
331	29	incidental] indicental (Ink correction in many copies)
332	26	yet] yer
338	26	Christian] christian
342	18	withall] with all
346	11	an] a
352	23	redemption.] redemption,

[1] For spelling and punctuation changes in the 1644 edition of *Doctrine and Discipline,* see below, pp. 781–92.

OF EDUCATION

Page	Line		Page	Line	
362	1	or doe] 1644: ot doe] Corrected from 1673.	397	4–5	Economics.] 1644: Economies.] Corrected from 1673.
364	10	Authors] 1644: Authots] Corrected from 1673.	401	5	*Cicero*] 1644: *Cicere*] Correct in 1673.
369	1	invisible,] 1644: invisible,,] 1673 deletes superfluous comma.		7	which inable men] 1644: which in able men] Corrected from 1673.
376	7	these are the errours, and] 1673 omits.	412	12	No] 1644: no] Corrected from 1673.
394	2	*Architects,*] 1644: *Architects*] Comma supplied from 1673.			

MARTIN BUCER

Page	Line		Page	Line	
423	22	prove, how] prove how	446	1	his mind] hismind
425	16	the said] The said	446	10	such a] sucha
426	2	after that] after, that	447	8	*Authent.*] *Authent*
432	9	the true faith] the the true faith	449	7	and again] *and again*
433	17	any man] anyman	450	4	'Tis] T'is
433	18	in *the doctrine*] *in the doctrine*	456	14	Saviour] Savour
440	4	buried), they] buried) they	463	15	female] famale
			466	18	'tis] tis
			475	11	Treatise] Trearise

AREOPAGITICA

Page	Line	
486	5	endeavour,] *A:* endeavour, \ All other copies: the reversed oblique deleted.
493	12	ethereall and fift] ethereall and and fift
494	5	Judges] Iudges (Except for this and the two further instances noted below, the printer observed the modern usage of *I* and *J,* both in roman and italic.)
496	5	*Ionia] Jonia* (swash *J*)
496	8	unbookish] A: unboekish All other copies: unbookish, with imperfect and smudgy second *o.*
503	17	*Nicolò*] *i* faint but discernible in *C, D, E, G, H,* and *I.* Failed to print in *A, B,* and *F.*
508	4	notwithstanding,] notwithstanding
515	1	warfaring] wayfaring For explanation of the editorial change, see below, p. 515, n. 102.
521	10	judgement] judgemenr
526	5	conversation] *t* faint but discernible in all copies except *A,* where it failed to print.
527	15	eyes;] eyes

Page	Line	
529	4	men.] *H:* men: (colon faint) All other copies: men.
530	22	doubtlesse] doublesse
	28	it, and] it, aud
544	21	*Jerusalem] Jeruslaem*
559	3	Lords] Lord Three of the four presentation copies (not *Young*) and *D* and *F* have a manuscript *s* added. The ink of the *Thomason* correction is faded brown, and was therefore not made simultaneously with that at p. 12 (see above, p. 515, n. 102). In *Rous, Yale,* and *F* the ink is similar to that at p. 12 in each copy (*D* lacks the earlier correction.)
562	7	*treasures*] *A, C,* and *D: treasuves* (but the *v* is not precisely like other italic *v*'s in the pamphlet). *B, E, F, G, H,* and *I: treasures*
567	3	sufficient] suffi-/ent
	14	liberall and] liberall aud
	26	forejudge] *A:* fore·judge All other copies: forejudge (line-end hyphen).
568	4	unlicenc't] unlicen't

TETRACHORDON

Page	Line	
578	4	civil] Thus in A, B, C. D, E have civill
578	18	perswasion] A, B, C: perswaston (corrected in D, E)
579	12	immaterial] Thus in A, B, C. D, E have immateriall
583	8	while] Thus in A, B, C. D, E have whole
583	9	prelatical] Thus in A, B, C. D, E have prelaticall
584	15	continual] Thus in A, B, C. D, E have continuall
584	17	perpetual] Thus in A, B, C. D, E have perpetuall
592	13	mariage] marige
600	5	without] withour
606	33	of the Mariage] of Mariage
608	13	a thing.] a thing,
614	28	in the] in the
617	19	Mark] Mark.
619	4	Chap. 26] Chap. 26
620	3	her.]] both brackets supplied
635	18	confus'd!] confus'd?
637	1	Several pages are misnumbered here; see collation, above, p. 575. Superior numbers are used in this text to distinguish the two pages with the same number.
639	36	said]] bracket supplied
642	13	in the Doctrine] in the Doctrine
645	3	John the Baptist] John the Baptist
645	14–15	forbidding of] forbidding of of
645	18	wife.] period supplied
645	24	madnesse,] madnesse.
645	32	reason, but] bnt
649	19	forbidd] farbidd
649	21	according] accordiug

Page	Line	
649	38	notes,] notes.
652	7	explain'd.] period supplied
653	8	Deut.] Dent.
654	15	which] wich
654	34	hardnes of heart] heatt
655	15	sin. For] sin, For
658	37	creature] creatnre
659	6	christian] chri-an (line break)
660	6	commanded and suffer'd] commanded and suffer'd
660	21	Justinian say,] Justinian, say
661	16	doings?] doings.
661	29	possession, trade] comma supplied
662	32	by them to] A, D: themt, o (corrected from M's errata) B, C, E have been corrected, but errata unchanged.
663	16	St.] period supplied
663	26	undiscoverably.] period supplied
665	3	from the beginning] the the beginning
665	15	yet known] yer
666	25	infirmity).] period supplied
670	21	Matt. 5th.]] bracket supplied
672	20	expound] expounded (A, D, E: last two letters deleted in ink)
672	23	Judg. the 19.] period after 19 supplied
672	24	in the Doctrine] in
673	2	Psal. 72. 26. 27. a] A
675	2	adultery]] bracket supplied
675	5–6	which the] whic hthe
679	34	suffice.] suffice,
680	13	not rashly] no rashly (A, D, E have t inked in)
680	14	endevor'd] endoevor'd

Page	*Line*		*Page*	*Line*	
681	10	away.]] bracket supplied	701	10	successors] successor (*A*,
681	19	reasons.] rea- (line break,			*D, E* have the *s* inked
		last four letters omit-			in)
		ted from following line;	703	1	*Basilius Macedo*]
		A, D, E have them			*Basilius, Macedo* (cor-
		inked in)			rected from M's errata)
681	25	misbeleeving parent,]	703	5	This] this
		parent.	705	9	*prohibits*] *probibits*
682	30	Infidels,] comma supplied	707	21	bee not] not—
683	27	*speak I, not*] *If not* (*A,*	707	29	*Tolouse*] Tolouse
		D, E: corrected in ink)	707	30	*Wicklef,*] *Wicklef.*
685	2	I, v. 10.] I v 10.	709	19	in *the doctrine*] *in the*
687	22	commanded] conmanded			*doctrine*
688	27	no, for the Apostle] no,	711	7	his *common*] *his common*
		for, the	713	17	Saint] Saiut
689	1	ill joyn'd?] question mark	716	12	patient] pati-tient (line
		supplied			break)
692	26	determin'd] determi'nd	716	12	patient:] punctuation
698	4	*Cor.*] *Cor,*			supplied
699	19	*Agatha*] *Agatba*	717	6	usage;] usage?

COLASTERION

Page	*Line*		*Page*	*Line*	
725	10	licencing,] licencing;	745	12	*Beneficiis,*] *Beneficiis.*
726	22	printed] Printed	746	9	hast] *hast*
728	7	Doctrine,] Doctrine.	748	15	in] In
729	2	licenc't] licen't	751	28	occasion] oc-sion (Word
730	19	*Answer,*] *Answer;*			divided at end of line)
730	23	good?] good.	752	8	when] When
730	29	Learn] learn	754	10	it.] it,
731	22	mischeif.] mischeif,	755	6	jabberment in]
737	7	any.] any,			jabberment at in
737	24	mariage.] mariage,	756	18	maintains.] maintains?
744	24	*sake,*] *sake.*			

THE DOCTRINE AND DISCIPLINE OF DIVORCE

SPELLING AND PUNCTUATION CHANGES IN 1644

Page and line references are to the present text. The first reading given is that of the 1643 text; the second, 1644. The 1644 readings are those of the "A" copy.

Page	Line		Page	Line	
234	8	restraine] restrain	251	13	sorrowes;] sorrowes:
	9	worke] work		14	enchantment]
	12	minde] mind			inchantment
	12	anough] enough		14	spel us'd] spell us'd,
	13	humane] human		18	&] and
	14	soone] soon		18	wee] we
235	3	and] And	242	4	therefore] therfore
	5	jayler] jaylor		7	over-burdning]
	5	onely] only			over-burdening
	10	marriage,] marriage?		13	*unchangable*
	14	captivitie] captivity			*unchangeable*
	16	libertie] liberty	245	9	reclaimes] reclaims
	22	necessitie] necessity		10	solemn] solemne
	23	finde] find		20	mariage;] mariage:
236	3	lest possibilitie]	246	4	mariage;] mariage:
		least possibility		5	knowledg] knowledge
	5	&] and		6	lonelinesse] lonelines
	6	calamitie] calamity		10	mariage] marriage
237	4	heavy] heavie		11	minde] mind
	5	iniquitie] iniquity		13	minde] mind
	6	antiquitie] antiquity		14	minde] mind
	7	mariage] marriage		18	orderd] order'd
238	3	canonicall] Canonicall	247	2	himselfe,] himselfe
	4	&] and		5	paine] pain
	7	dignitie] dignity		5	some] som
	10	fathers] Fathers		5	Reprobates] Reprobats
	11	&] and		6	therefore] therfore
	11	renown] renowne		9	avoyd] avoid
	12	&] and		11	encrease] increase
	15	equitie] equity		13	minde] mind
	15	imperiall] Imperiall		22	mis-fortune,]
239	15	better] beter			mis-fortune;
240	16	countenanc't] countnanc't		23	away] away,
	17	conscionable,]	248	5	therefore] therfore
		conscionable		8	minde] mind
	29	vaine] vain		11	minde] mind

Page	Line		Page	Line	
248	12	precious] pretious	253	5	unmaried] unmarried
	14	mariage] marriage		6	St.] S.
	15	&] and		9	recompence,]
	16	serve] serve,			recompence;
	21	*wee*] *we*		13	humane] human
	22	*understanding:*] *under-*		15	cherfull] cheerfull
		standing;		18	which] whch
249	13	self] selfe		20	lonelines] lonelinesse
	15	minde] mind		22	himself] himselfe
	21	choice:] choice		26	feard] fear'd
	21	the soberest] The sobrest	254	1	sins,] sins
	22	lest] least		10	society,] society
	22	knows] knowes		17	therefore] therfore
	24	&] and		23	covnant] cov'nant
	28	encreases] increases		23	whereof] wherof
	31	therfore] therefore		24	counterfeit] counterfet
250	1	modestie] modesty	256	15	find] finde
	4	minde] mind		16	obay] obey
	7	paine] pain		17	doe] do
	16	joyn'd] joynd		19	joyne,] joyn;
	17	compulsion] compulsion,		22	anough] enough
	18	is] is,		22	generall] generall,
	20	dispencing] dispensing	258	8	therefore] therfore
	20	&] and		10	beeing thereby] being
	29	*burne*] *burn*			therby
	29	therefore] therfore		17	marriage] mariage
251	9	himself] himselfe		18	covnant] cov'nant
	17	labour] labour,		20	lest] least
	19	anough] enough		20	*onely*] *only*
	19	self] selfe		20	*fulfilling*] *fullfilling*
	21	Spouse] spouse	259	4	As] as
	22	*flouds*] *floods*		7	himselfe] himself
	24	which] whch		8	&] and
252	2	Paradise] paradice		9	cherfulnes] cheerfulnes
	5	soul] soule		11	teares] tears
	9	satisfy] satisfie		11	bosom] bosome
	11	two;] two:		14	soul] soule
	12	couples] couples,		17	wherein] wherin
	16	festivall] festival		19	brok'n] broken
	18	Sonne] sonne		21	*offring*] *offering*
	20	us;] us,		22	waight] weight
	20	Son] son		23	grief] griefe
	21	&] and		24	childer'n] childr'n
	23	St.] S.		26	offspring] off-spring
	23	marriage] mariage	260	2	*childern*] *children*
	24	flesh] Flesh		4	minde] mind
	25	curbes] curbs		9	himself] himselfe
253	2	self] selfe		9	his] his,
	2	&] and		11	&] and
	3	mariage] marriage		13	cherfull] cheerfull

Page	Line		Page	Line	
260	15	mariage] marriage	265	23	St.] S.
	15	maxims] maximes		23	seems] seemes
	16	paralel] parallell	266	5	therefore] therfore
	21	unhelpful] unhelpfull		5	forbear] forbeare
	21	society,] society;		5	bin] been
	22	Atheism:] Atheisme;		11	St.] S.
	23	separating,] separating		11	wee] we
	26	therefore] therfore		14	St.] S.
	28	charitie] charity		16	libertie] liberty
261	7	resolv] resolve		22	St.] S.
	9	whereof] wherof		24	himself] himselfe
	11	Nations] Nations,		27	St. *Austin*] S. *Austine*
	17	wer] were		27	Blasphemy,] *Blasphemy*
	18	St.] S.		27	St.] S.
	20	St.] S.		28	indifferent: but]
	20	wherein] wherin			indifferent. But
	20	beeing] being		29	heerin] herein
	21	sanctify'd] sanctified	267	1	*v.*] v.
	22	generall] general		2	plainly] plainly,
	22	covnant] cov'nant		4	*joyn*] *joyne*
	23	St.] S.		7	Infidell] infidell
262	8	Therefore] Therfore		9	mutuall complacency]
	9	*Infidels*] *infidels*			mutual complacencie
	12	shunn'd] shun'd		10	therfore] therefore
	15	Therefore] Therfore		15	vexe] vex
	15	St.] S.		16	burdens] burdens,
	16	*darknesse*] *darknes*		16	if therefore] if therfore
	17	*Beliall*] *Belial*		17	soul] soul,
	18	*Infidell*] *infidel*		18	endles] endlesse
	18	one,] one	268	2	*wherein*] *wherin*
	19	*Wherfore*] *Wherefore*		2	*therein*] *therin*
	20	*separate*] *separate,*		3	*God, v.*] *God.* v.
	22	whereon] wheron		5	Christianitie] Christianity
	23	necessitie] necessity		7	look] looke
265	1	heretick] heretick,		7	understood] understood,
	5	*Deut.*] Deut.		9	we,] we
	5	therefore] therfore		9	Gospel] Gospell
	5	himself dis-joyns;]		14	adultery] Adultery
		himselfe dis-joyns:		17	chief] chiefe
	6	keeping] keeping,		17	therof] thereof
	12	appear] appeare	269	8	cherfull] cheerfull
	13	mariage] marriage		15	pervers] perverse
	13	therefore] therfore		16	self] selfe
	14	pattern] patern		17	canon] Canon
	15	neither] Neither		18	shewn,] shewn
	15	wherfore] wherefore		31	&] and
	18	separate: but]		33	compell] compel
		separate. But	270	3	respectles] respectlesse
	19	don availes] don, avails		7	ofttimes] oft-times
	19	law] Law		8	finde] find

Page	Line		Page	Line	
270	8	powerfull] powerful	275	20	*covnant*] Covnant
	19	*Deut.*] Deut.		20	Pro.] Prov.
	21	that,] that		21	human] human.
	23	&] and		22	chief] chiefe
272	24	will] wil		22	therof] thereof
	25	minde] mind		22	soul] soule
	25	self] selfe	276	1	unfitnes] unfitnesse
	27	nature;] nature,		2	body;] body:
	28	therfore] therefore		2	lest] least
273	20	mariage] mariage,		6	far] farre
	20	destroys] destroyes		6	anger] anger,
	22	beeing] being		9	Text,] Text;
	22	summ'd] sum'd		9	only] onely
	23	lightsom] lightsome		11	&] and
	24	&] and		11	power] power,
	24	mariage] marriage		13	doctrin] doctrine
	25	ofttimes] oft-times		14	wisdom] wisedome
	26	grief] griefe		15	injoyn] enjoyn
	27	foreseen] foreseen,		17	been] bin
	28	greef] griefe		21	Wheras] wheras
	29	certain] certain,		21	*the covnant*] the *Covnant*
274	2	cruelty] crueltie		23	false;] false:
	9	ill driv'n] ill-driv'n		23	infidell] Infidell
	9	nothing] Nothing		24	*Babel*] *Babel,*
	10	vows] vowes		24	*the covnant of God,*
	10	God,] God:			Ezech.] the *Covnant*
	10	*Numbers,*] *Numbers*			*of God.* Ezek.
	11	authority] authoritie		25	hear] heare
	12	it;] it:		28	author] authour
	12	break] breake		31	&] and
	23	gifts;] gifts,		31	fitnes] fitnesse
	25	Covnant] Covenant	277	1	joyn'd] joynd
	26	such] such,		2	unfitnes] unfitnesse
	27	themselves do]		3	happines] happinesse
		themselves, doe		4	gratious] gracious
	29	maried] married		7	man;] man:
	30	wearisomnes]		8	wherin] wherein
		wearisomnesse		11	unmeetnes] unmeetnesse
275	2	course] cours		13	helples] helplesse
	2	wisdome] wisedome		18	souls] soules
	2	tendernes] tendernesse		19	precepts,] precepts
	3	custom] custome		20	general] generall
	5	freedome] freedom		20	charitie] charity
	6	crueltie] cruelty		24	*Indian*] Indian
	13	society] Society	278	2	St.] S.
	15	animal] animall		3	do] doe
	18	formalitie,] formality;		12	*Famelism*] *Familism*
	18	gilding] guilding		12	and] &
	19	purenes] purenesse		12	*fanatick*] fanatick

Page	Line		Page	Line	
278	13	dreams,] dreams	284	4	&] and
	14	Religion,] religion;		5	judicial] Judicial
	18	cheefly] chiefly		7	convinc't] covinc't
279	5	doe] do		7	&] and
	5	themselves] themselvs		8	&] and
	5	whordom] whoredom		12	Edicts] edicts
	6	adulteries;] adulteries,		13	necessitie] necessity
	6	clergy] clergie		14	first] first,
	7	hear] heare		15	choisest] choicest
	10	&] and		16	laws] lawes
	12	skilful] skilfull		17	Be] be
	12	*Theology*] Theology		17	yeelded] yeelded,
	13	&] and		18	law-giver] law giver
	13	examin] examine		18	somthing] something
	14	strictnes] strictnesse		23	wee] we
	14	blameles] blamelesse		24	beeing] being
	14	man] man,	285	4	will] wil
	19	transgressions;]		4	serv] serve
		transgressions,		5	thir] their
	20	scanne] scan		5	sense,] sense
	21	literal wisdom] literall		7	vital] vitall
		wisedome		8	dooing] doing
	21	enquiry; for] enquiry.		9	only text] onely Text
		For		10	perfet] perfect
	22	duely] duly		11	own hand] owne hand,
	22	Gospel] Gospell		11	civil] civill
	23	soul] soule		13	covnant] covenant
	26	self] selfe		14	grace,] grace;
280	2	together] together,		15	doctrin] doctrine
	4	Christianitie] Christianity		16	till] til
	4	scandal] schandall		16	only] onely
	5	natural] naturall		20	autority] authority
	6	souls] soules		21	only] onely
	8	disseverd] dissever'd,	286	1	*Romish,*] *Romish*
	9	*alphabetical*] alphabeticall		1	Statute] statute
281	11	when as] whenas		2	seem] seeme
	12	in case of fornication]		3	sin] sinne
		in case of fornication		3	self] selfe
283	12	restraint,] restraint		4	only] onely
	14	straitnes] straitnesse		5	alleg'd] alledg'd
	16	Sermon] Sermon,		6	don] done
	25	us,] us		8	endeavours] endevours
	25	politicall Law] political		8	self] selfe
		law		9	lays] layes
	25	speciall] special		11	deservs] deserves
	26	*Jews,*] Jews		11	Edict] edict
	28	Christ;] Christ,		13	only] onely
284	4	only] onely		14	themselvs] themselves
	4	&] and		16	wee] we
	4	anull'd] annull'd		24	terrify] terrifie

Page	Line		
296	14	matter,]	matter
	15	only]	onely
	15	dispensation;]	dispensation,
	16	himself]	himselfe
	16	Law *Mark*]	*Law, Mark.*
306	14	*Moses, Deut.*]	*Moses Deut.*
	17	nations]	Nations
	20	Law]	law
	22	cherfully]	cheerfully
	28	Law]	law
	29	it,]	it
307	4	hard-hearted]	hard hearted
	4	thir]	their
	9	privilege]	priviledge
	14	thir]	their
	16	wee]	we
	18	*Chap.*]	Chap.
	18	& *Mark*]	and *Mark.*
	20	them]	them,
	22	*hardnes*]	*hardnesse*
	22	*hearts sufferd*]	*heart suffer'd*
	26	Law;]	Law:
	26	rebuk't]	rebukt
308	19	ordaind]	ordain'd
	19	fall]	fall,
	27	rule]	rule,
309	10	&]	and
	15	*ver.*]	vers.
	16	&]	and
	18	wee]	we
	20	man,]	man
	30	beeing]	being
	32	concluded,]	concluded:
	32	shee]	she
	33	&]	and
310	21	nonplus]	non-plus
	27	mischiefs]	mischiefes,
	27	rational]	rationall
	28	endles]	endlesse
	30	Master]	Master,
	31	beginning]	begining
	32	wee]	we
	33	Law]	law
311	1	Doubtles]	Doubtlesse
	3	himself]	himselfe
	3	laws]	lawes
311	6	wee]	we
	8	rigor]	rigour
	12	maintain'd;]	maintain'd,
	13	traditional]	traditionall
	17	inform]	informe
312	2	original]	originall
	3	equal]	equall
	4	&]	and
	5	himself]	himselfe
	6	rashnes]	rashnesse
	6	means]	meanes
	9	wee]	we
	12	wee]	we
	14	naturall]	natural
	14	only mariage]	onely marriage
	15	doubtles]	doubtlesse
	16	always]	alwayes
	16	beeing]	being
	18	pervers]	perverse
	19	despight]	despite
	20	joynd]	joyn'd
	20	*Mat.*]	*Matthew*
	22	place,]	place;
	23	lest]	least
313	4	Christ]	Christ,
	9	be]	bee
	9	& legal]	and legall
	10	shall]	shal
	11	Law]	law
	11	punishment]	punishment,
	12	forbidding,]	forbidding;
	14	only]	onely
	15	*defiling*]	defiling
	16	forbidden]	forbidd'n
	18	sin]	sinne
	19	Law]	Law,
	19	only]	onely
	20	&]	and
	22	tis]	'tis
	25	still]	stil
314	3	wors]	worse
	4	over masterd]	over-masterd
	5	crookednes]	crookednesse
316	3	Can wee conceave]	can we conceive
	20	wee]	we
	27	moral,]	moral
	28	and]	&

Page	Line	
316	29	abrogated] abrogated,
	29	judicial;] judicial:
	30	deale] deal
317	1	&] and
	2	Laws] Laws,
	7	*ver.*] vers.
	13	cease,] cease:
	15	reprooff] reproof
	15	Pharises,] Pharises
	19	*Jews*] Jews
318	8	home,] home;
	11	fil'd] fill'd
	17	covnant] cov'nant
319	13	wee] we
	16	*Moses*] Moses
	18	&] and
	21	minde] mind
	24	*Jews*] Jews
	25	*Moses,*] Moses
	28	*Genesis*] Genesis
320	2	conceav'd] conceiv'd
	5	*Mat.*] *Matth.*
	5	plainly] plainly,
	10	own] owne
	11	only] onely
	11	therfore] therefore
	13	Law] law
	16	Law;] Law,
	17	himself] himselfe
	21	sins] sinnes
	22	hardnes] hardnesse
	23	This] This (new ¶)
	23	be] bee
	26	& heer] and here
	26	be] bee
	27	hard-hearted *Jews*] hard hearted Jewes
	29	usury,] usury
321	1	all wise judgements] all-wise Judgements
	1	statutes] Statutes
	2	wee] we
	5	law] Law
	6	her self] herselfe
	7	impartial] impartiall
	9	self] selfe
	12	law] Law
	13	law] Law
	14	bear] beare
	15	ceremonial] ceremoniall

Page	Line	
321	16–19	sin] sinne (7 times)
	19	judicial] Judiciall
	20	be] bee
322	1	plainly] plainly,
	1	arme] arm
	2	moral] morall
	2	Justice . . . Justice] justice . . . justice
	3	steares] steers
	7	be] bee
	7	papal] Papal
	10	usury,] usury
	11	alleg'd] alleg'd,
	16	therfore] therefore
	16	wherin civil] wherein civill
	17	&] and
	19	will] wil
	20	polity] politie
	21	wors] worse
	21	inordinate] inordinat
	22	be] bee
	22	will] wil
	24	peril] perill
	25	fearles] fearlesse
323	2	restraine] restrain
	3	hight] height
324	11	wives,] wives;
	13	beeing] being
325	20	wee] we
	22	doe] do
	23	affirm] affirm,
	28	charitie] charity
326	2	finde] find
	8	law] Law
	10	els] else
	12	&] and
	12	paradise] Paradise
	17	comfortable] comfortable,
	17	degree,] degree
	20	covnant] cov'nant
	25	wil] will
	30	beeing] being
327	2	receav'd] receiv'd
	2	lonelines] lonelinesse
	3	wee] we
	6	unlesse where] unles wher
328	3	himself] himselfe
	3	be] bee

Page	Line	
328	4	namely,] namely
	6	be] bee
	7	surely;] surely,
	7	leudest ends, or] lewdest ends. Or
	8	Church-rites] Church rites
	8	efficacy] efficacie
	9	fitnes] fitnesse
	9	Perhaps] Perhaps,
	10	carnal] carnall
	10	lest] Least
	10	all:] all;
	11	joyn;] joyn:
	12	cherfull] cheerfull
	15	*him;*] *him:*
	16	only] onely
	17	witnesseth] witnesseth,
	18	doubtles] doubtlesse
	19	he . . . he] hee . . . hee
	20	deadnes] deadnesse
	21	somthing distastfull] something distastful
	21	avers] averse
	22	unconjugal] unconjugall
	22	joyn'd;] joyn'd,
	25	unjoyning;] unjoyning,
	25	soberest] sobrest
	25	beeing] being
	29	frowardnes] frowardnesse
	30	beeing] being
	32	evil] evill,
	33	scandal] scandall
	33	hard-hearted] hardhearted
329	1	mariage] mariage,
	1	*Moses,*] Moses
	2	evil] evill
	2	& civil] and civill
	3	Gospel] Gospell
	4	legal] legall
	8	unfoulded] unfolded
	8	wherwith] wherewith
	11	self] selfe
	15	general] generall
330	3	frequent] frequent,
	4	Laws] Laws,
	8	laws] Lawes

Page	Line	
330	9	he] hee
	10	destroys] destroyes
	11	answers] answers,
	11	ordain'd] ordaind
	11	mutual] mutuall
	15	be] bee
	15	cruel] cruell
	15	appears] appeares
	16	*Mark*] *Marke,*
	16	*Luke*] *Luke,*
	16	St.] S.
	17	exception;] exception:
	18	natural equity] naturall equity,
	18	general] generall
	19	be] bee
	23	be a supernatural] bee a supernaturall
	24	us,] us
	24	wee] we
	25	*Jews*] Jews
	25	civil Nation] civill nation
	27	whenas] when as
	27	natural] naturall
	29	*Moses*] Moses
331	1	*Commandement*] commandement
	2	St.] S.
	5	self-cruelty] self cruelty
	6	&] and
	7	Christianity;] Christianity,
	9	wee] we
	10	sense] sence
	13	mind,] mind
	14	himself] himselfe
	15	divorce;] divorce,
	16	law] Law
	21	reconciliable] reconcileable
	23	heer] here
	26	reconcilement,] reconcilement
332	2	heer] here
	2	confirm'd;] confirm'd,
	5	St.] S.
	6	agree,] agree
	9	reconcilement;] reconcilement:

Page	Line		Page	Line	
334	15	wee] wee	337	2	law] Law
	15	judicial law] Judiciall Law		3	unskilfulnes] unskilfulnesse
	17	will] wil		6	himself] himselfe
	17	don] done		7	acutenes] acutenesse
	19	actual] actuall		7	confesses *Prov.* 30.19,20.]
	19	divorce;] divorce,			confesses, *Pro.* 30.19.-20.
	20	Canon Law] canon law		9	*air] aire*
	20	Neverthelesse,] Neverthelesse		11	be] bee
	22	decree'd] decreed		11	us] us,
	23	be] bee		12	always] alwayes
	24	obstinately] obstinatly		13	eye-witnesse:] eye witnesse,
	25	suspicion] suspition		13	be] bee
	25	adulterizing;] adulterizing:		14	presumtion] presumption,
	27	hous] house		15	be] bee
335	2	prevent,] prevent		16	be] bee
	6	Law-witnessing] Law witnessing		17	*fornication,] Fornication,*
	7	Law] law		17	signify] signifie
	8	middle-way] middle way		17	matrimonial] matrimoniall
	14	playd] plaid		17	Covnant] covnant
	15	*Chaldaean] Chaldean*		18	actual] actuall
	15	only] onely	338	8	scarse] scarce
	15	stubbornes] stubbornesse		8	be] bee
336	1	reasons] reasons,		9	be] bee
	1	Levite] Levit		10	continu'd] continued
	3	bin whoordom] been whoordom,		12	heavnly] heavenly
	5	hebrew] Hebrew		13	doctrin] doctrine
	6	*Judges,] Judges*		13	pearle] pearl
	8	activity,] activity		14	gatherer;] gatherer,
	9	don] done		15	finds] findes
	9	only] onely		16	general *analogy*] generall *analogie*
	10	be] bee		17	be] bee
	11	be] bee		17	&] and
	11	Neverthelesse,] Neverthelesse		19	heer] here
	12	God *Num.*] God, *Numb.*		20	St.] S.
	13	a man,] a man		21	he] hee
	15	fals] false		22	Gospel,] Gospell;
	16	*rottennesse,] rottennesse*		23	deserted] deserted,
	18	*ver.*] verse,		25	leavs] leaves
	18	suspicion] suspition		25	determin] determine
	19	trial, which,] triall; which		28	*cases;] cases,*
	23	divorce;] divorce,	339	2	only] onely
	24	self] selfe		3	hinderd] hinder'd
	24	bin] been		5	St.] S.
	25	be] bee		5	special] speciall
				6	divorce] divorce,

Page	Line		Page	Line	
343	25	& . . . &] and . . . and	347	17	&] and
	25	only] onely		17	unpleasingnes] unpleasingnesse
	28	&] and		18	concealements] concealments
	29	trial] triall		19	maisters] masters
344	1	perceaving] perceiving		20	*the 8th*] the eighth
	1	revenu] revenue		22	beeing] being
	1	autority] authority		23	*cardinal*] Cardinall
	2	them,] them		24	prooff] proof
	4	devest] divest		24	shee] she
	6	means] meanes		24	bin:] been
	7	external &] externall and		25	nakednes] nakednesse
	7	judicature] Judicature		25	&] and
	8	dowries, jointures] Dowries, Jointures	348	1	chamberlain] Chamberlain
346	15	*sympathy*] sympathy		4	Kingdom] Kingdome
	16	province] Province		6	adultres] adultresse
	16	law] Law		6	proceeding;] proceeding:
	16	&] and		9	utterles] utterlesse
	17	rudnes] rudenesse		10	civil] civill
347	2	resistles] resistlesse		10	be] bee
	2	be] bee		12	beeing] being
	3	careles] carelesse		13	he] hee
	3	self] selfe	349	28	law] Law
	3	useles] uselesse		29	only] onely
	4	spiritles] spiritlesse		32	law] Law
	4	*Moses*] Moses		32	not,] not;
	5	Lawgivers] Law-givers		33	just] just,
	6	Parliament] Parlament		33	deserv'd,] deserv'd;
	6	*Clergy* of *England*] Clergy of England		34	happines, &] happinesse, and
	7	*the*] the		35	be] bee
	8	*8th*] eighth		35	Law] law
	8	*his Q. Anne of Cleve*] his Queen *Anne* of *Cleve*		36	unlesse] unles
	8	like,] like		36	redresse] redress
	9	bin] been		37	entreated] intreated
	9	half a year] halfe a yeare	350	1	gon] gone
	9	unles] unlesse		1	els] else
	10	Proverb] proverb		2	law] Law
	10	bin] been		3	moral] morall
	11	vertu] vertue		6	smart?] smart.
	11	do] doe		7	rational] rationall
	11	ev'n] even		8	injurious] injurous
	11	freedom] freedome	353	15	Minister,] Minister
	12	himself, beeing] himselfe, being		17	&] and
	13	sex] Sex		20	&] and
	13	therfore] therefore		21	beeing] being
	15	hear] heare		24	waight] weight
	16	sequester'd] sequestr'd		27	children] children

Page	Line		Page	Line	
353	27	Common wealth.]	354	25	debarr'd] debar'd
		Common-wealth;		26	weaknes] weaknesse
354	7	*Jews*] Jews		27	heresy] heresie
	7	captivity] captivity,		27	els] else
	7	Profets] Prophets		29	fruitles] fruitlesse
	11	therfore wee] therefore		29	evils] evills
		we		30	Church] Church,
	12	*Jews*] Jews		30	wisdom] wisedom
	13	be] bee	355	5	serv] serve
	13	us] us,		12	carnal] carnall
	14	wors] worse		13	be] bee
	15	wee . . . wee]		17	&] and
		we . . . we		21	themselvs] themselves
	19	self] self,		22	them] them,
	20	above,] above;		25	moral vertu] morall
	21	and] &			vertue
	21	*Bee*] *Be*		25	equal] equall
	22	counsel] counsell		26	textual] textuall
	22	*Ecclesiastes;*]	356	1	*Profets*] *Prophets*
		Ecclesiastes,		5	he] hee
	22	*self*] *selfe*		6	charity] Charity
	24	liberty:] liberty;		7	The end.] *The end.*
	25	needful] needfull			

APPENDIX A

THE STAR CHAMBER DECREE OF 1637

A Decree of Starre-Chamber, Concerning Printing, Made the eleventh day of July last past. 1637.[1] *. . . Whereas the three and twentieth day of June in the eight and twentieth yere of the reigne of the late Queene Elizabeth, and before, divers Decrees and Ordinances have beene made for the better government and regulating of Printers and Printing, which Orders and Decrees have beene found by experience to be defective in some particulars; And divers abuses have sithence arisen, and beene practised by the craft and malice of wicked and evill disposed persons, to the prejudice of the publike; And divers libellous, seditious, and mutinous bookes have beene unduly printed, and other bookes and papers without licence, to the disturbance of the peace of the Church and State: For prevention whereof in time to come, It is now Ordered and Decreed, That the said former Decrees and Ordinances shall stand in force with these Additions, Explanations, and Alterations following, viz. . . . Imprimis,* That no person or persons whatsoever shall presume to print, or cause to bee printed, either in the parts beyond the Seas, or in this Realme, or other his Majesties Dominions, any seditious, scismaticall, or offensive Bookes or Pamphlets, to the scandall of Religion, or the Church, or the Government, or Governours of the Church or State, or Commonwealth, or of any Corporation, or particular person or persons whatsoever, nor shall import any such Booke or Bookes, nor sell or dispose of them, or any of them, nor cause any such to be bound, stitched, or sowed, upon paine that he or they so offending, shall lose all such Bookes & Pamphlets, and also have, and suffer such correction, and severe punishment, either by Fine, imprisonment, or other corporall punishment, or otherwise, as by this Court, or by His Majesties Commissioners for causes Ecclesiasticall in the high Commission Court, respectively, as the several causes shall require, shall be thought fit to be inflicted upon him, or them, for such their offence and contempt.

II. *Item,* That no person or persons whatsoever, shall at any time print or cause to be imprinted, any Booke or Pamphlet whatsoever, unlesse the same Booke or Pamphlet, and also all and every the Titles, Epistles, Prefaces, Proems, Preambles, Introductions, Tables, Dedications, and other matters and things whatsoever thereunto annexed, or therewith imprinted, shall be first lawfully licenced and authorized onely by such person and persons as are hereafter expressed, and by no other, and shall be also first

[1] 517.k.3.8.

entred into the Registers Booke of the Company of Stationers; upon paine that every Printer offending therein, shall be for ever hereafter disabled to use or exercise the Art or Mysterie of Printing, and receive such further punishment, as by this Court or the high Commission Court respectively, as the severall causes shall require, shall be thought fitting.

III. *Item,* That all Bookes concerning the common Lawes of this Realme shall be printed by the especiall allowance of the Lords chiefe Justices, and the Lord chiefe Baron for the time being, or one or more of them, or by their appointment; And that all Books of History, belonging to this State, and present times, or any other Booke of State affaires, shall be licenced by the principall Secretaries of State, or one of them, or by their appointment; And that all Bookes concerning Heraldry, Titles of Honour and Armes, or otherwise concerning the Office of Earle Marshall, shall be licenced by the Earle Marshall, or by his appointment; And further, that all other Books, whether of Divinitie, Phisicke, Philosophie, Poetry, or whatsoever, shall be allowed by the Lord Arch-Bishop of *Canterbury,* or Bishop of *London* for the time being, or by their appointment, or the Chancellours, or Vice-Chancellors of either of the Universities of this Realme for the time being.

Always provided, that the Chancellour or Vice-Chancellour, of either of the Universities, shall Licence onely such Booke or Bookes that are to be Printed within the limits of the Universities respectively, but not in *London,* or elsewhere, not medling either with Bookes of the common Law, or matters of State.

IV. [Provides that the licensing authority is to certify two copies of all manuscripts, keeping one (against which the printed book may be checked); and that the] license or approbation shall be imprinted in the beginning of the same Booke, with the name, or names of him or them that shall authorize or license the same, for a testimonie of the allowance thereof.

V and VI. [Provide that the licensing authority be furnished with catalogues of all printed matter to be imported, and that a representative of the authority be present at the opening of all such shipments, with power to confiscate any "seditious, schismaticall or offensive" books, and to initiate action against the offender.]

VII. [Provides against the printing or importing of privileged or registered matter except by the holder of the patent, order, or registration.]

VIII. *Item,* Every person and persons that shall hereafter Print, or cause to be Printed, any Bookes, Ballads, Charts, Portraiture, or any other thing or things whatsoever, shall thereunto or theron Print and set his and their owne name or names, as also the name or names of the Author or Authors, Maker or Makers of the same, and by, or for whom any such booke, or other thing is, or shall be printed. . . .

IX. [Provides against the use of any printer's name or imprint without his permission.]

X, XI, and XII. [Provide against the retailing of books by anyone who has not served the seven-year apprenticeship to one of the publishing trades, the importation of books all or most of which are in the English language, and the importation or retailing of books by foreigners other than those made free of the Stationers Company.]

XIII and XIV. [Provide against erecting a press, or furnishing space or equipment for it, without prior notice to the Stationers Company.]

XV. *Item,* The Court doth declare, that as formerly, so now, there shall be but Twentie Master Printers allowed to have the use of one Presse or more, as is after specified, and doth hereby nominate, allow, and admit these persons whose names hereafter follow, to the number of Twentie, to have the use of a Presse, or Presses and Printing-house, for the time being, *viz. Felix Kingstone, Adam Islip, Thomas Purfoot, Miles Flesher, Thomas Harper, John Beale, John Legat, Robert Young, John Haviland, George Miller, Richard Badger, Thomas Cotes, Bernard Alsop, Richard Bishop, Edward Griffin, Thomas Purslow, Richard Hodgkinsonne, John Dawson, John Raworth, Marmaduke Parsons.* And further, the Court doth order and decree, That it shall be lawfull for the Lord Arch-Bishop of *Canterbury,* or the Lord Bishop of *London,* for the time being, taking to him or them six other high Commissioners, to supply the place or places of those, which are now already Printers by this Court, as they shall fall void by death, or Censure, or otherwise: Provided that they exceed not the number of Twentie, besides His Majesties Printers, and the Printers allowed for the Universities.

XVI. [Requires from each printer a three hundred pound bond that his press will not be used for unlicensed matter.]

XVII. [Limits printers who have been Masters or upper Wardens of the Company to three presses each, and all others to two.]

XVIII. *Item,* That no person or persons, do hereafter reprint, or cause to bee reprinted, any booke or bookes whatsoever (though formerly printed with licence) without being reviewed, and a new Licence obtained for the reprinting thereof. . . .

XIX. [Limits printers who have been Masters or upper Wardens to three apprentices each, those who are of the Livery to two, and those of the Yeomanry to one.]

XX and XXI. . . . Because a great part of the secret printing in corners hath been caused for want of orderly imployment for Journeyman printers, [provide that every master printer must employ at least one journeyman, whether or not he needs him, and that unemployed journeymen must accept employment when it is offered.]

XXII. [Exempts the printers of the universities from sections XIX, XX, and XXI, but requires them to furnish employment to all their own journeymen.]

XXIII. [Provides against the employment on case or press of any but Freemen of the Company and their apprentices.]

XXIV. *Item*, The Court doth hereby declare their firme resolution, that if any person or persons, that is not allowed Printer, shall hereafter presume to set up any Presse for printing, or shall worke at any such Presse, or Set, or Compose any Letters to bee wrought by any such Presse; hee, or they so offending, shall from time to time, by the Order of this Court, bee set in the Pillorie, and Whipt through the Citie of *London*, and suffer such other punishment, as this Court shall Order or thinke fit to inflict upon them, upon Complaint or proofe of such offence or offences, or shalbe otherwise punished, as the Court of High Commission shall thinke fit, and is agreeable to their Commission.

XXV. *Item*, That for the better discovery of printing in Corners without licence; The Master and Wardens of the Company of Stationers for the time being, or any two licensed Master-Printers, which shall be appointed by the Lord Arch-Bishop of *Canterbury*, or Lord Bishop of *London* for the time being, shall have power and authority, to take unto themselves such assistance as they shall think needfull, and to search what houses and shops (and at what time they shall think fit) especially Printing-houses, and to view what is in printing, and to call for the license to see whether it be licenced or no, and if not, to seize upon so much as is printed, together with the severall offenders, and to bring them before the Lord Arch-Bishop of *Canterbury*, or the Lord Bishop of *London* for the time being, that they or either of them may take such further order therein as shall appertaine to Justice.

XXVI. *Item*, The Court doth declare, that it shall be lawfull also for the said Searchers, if upon search they find any book or bookes, or part of booke or books which they suspect to containe matter in it or them, contrary to the doctrine and discipline of the Church of *England*, or against the State and Government, upon such suspition to seize upon such book or books, or part of booke or books, and to bring it, or them, to the Lord Arch-Bishop of *Canterbury*, or the Lord Bishop of *London* for the time being, who shall take such further course therein, as to their Lordships, or either of them shall seeme fit.

XXVII, XXVIII, XXIX, and XXX. [Limit to four the number of type-founders (appointing John Grismand, Thomas Wright, Arthur Nichols, and Alexander Fifeild, and empowering the Archbishop of Canterbury or the Bishop of London to fill vacancies), and to two the number of apprentices each may keep; require the employment of journeymen founders after the pattern established for printers in sections XX and XXI; and prohibit the employment of all other persons in the making of type.]

XXXI. [Provides that in addition to being punished, anyone who violates any of these regulations must post surety for future obedience.]

XXXII. [Prohibits merchants and mariners from landing printed matter anywhere but the Port of London.]

XXXIII. [Sanctions the agreement of the Company to deposit one copy of every new or reprinted book in the Bodleian Library.]

THE LICENSING ORDER OF 1643

An Order of the Lords and Commons Assembled in Parliament.[1] . . .
Printed . . . June 16, 1643
  Die Mercurii, 14 Junii. 1643.
Whereas divers good Orders have bin lately made by both Houses
of Parliament, for suppressing the great late abuses and frequent
disorders in Printing many false forged, scandalous, seditious, libellous, and unlicensed Papers, Pamphlets, and Books to the great defa-
mation of Religion and government. Which orders (notwithstanding
the diligence of the Company of *Stationers,* to put them in full execution) have taken little or no effect: By reason the bill in preparation, for
redresse of the said disorders, hath hitherto bin retarded through the
present distractions, and very many, as well *Stationers* and *Printers,* as
others of sundry other professions not free of the *Stationers* Company,
have taken upon them to set up sundry private Printing Presses in corners,
and to print, vend, publish and disperse Books, pamphlets and papers, in
such multitudes, that no industry could be suficient to discover or bring
to punishment, all the severall abounding delinquents; And by reason that
divers of the *Stationers* Company and others being Delinquents (contrary
to former orders and the constant custome used among the said Company) have taken liberty to Print, Vend and publish, the most profitable
vendible Copies of Books, belonging to the Company and other *Stationers,*
especially of such Agents as are imployed in putting the said Orders in
Execution, and that by way of revenge for giveing information against
them to the Houses for their Delinquences in Printing, to the great
prejudice of the said Company of *Stationers* and Agents, & to their discouragement in this publik service.

It is therefore Ordered by the Lords and Commons in *Parliament,* That
no Order or Declaration of both, or either House of *Parliament* shall be
printed by any, but by order of one or both the said Houses: Nor other
Book, Pamphlet, paper, nor part of any such Book, Pamphlet, or paper,
shall from henceforth be printed, bound, stitched or put to sale by any
person or persons whatsoever, unlesse the same be first approved of and
licensed under the hands of such person or persons as both, or either of
the said Houses shall appoint for the licensing of the same, and entred in

[1] E106 (15). The text is in black letter.

the Register Book of the Company of *Stationers*, according to Ancient custom, and the Printer therof to put his name thereto. And that no person or persons shall hereafter print, or cause to be reprinted any Book or Books, or part of Book, or Books heretofore allowed of and granted to the said Company of *Stationers* for their relief and maintenance of their poore, without the licence or consent of the Master, Wardens and Assistants of the said Company; Nor any Book or Books lawfully licensed and entred in the Register of the said Company for any particular member thereof, without the license and consent of the Owner or Owners therof. Nor yet import any such Book or Books, or part of Book or Books formerly Printed here, from beyond the Seas, upon paine of forfeiting the same to the Owner, or Owners of the Copies of the said Books, and such further punishment as shall be thought fit.

And the Master and Wardens of the said Company, the Gentleman Usher of the House of *Peers*, the Sergeant of the Commons House and their deputies, together with the persons formerly appointed by the Committee of the House of Commons for Examinations, are hereby Authorized and required, from time to time, to make diligent search in all places, where they shall think meete, for all unlicensed Printing Presses, and all Presses any way imployed in the printing of scandalous or unlicensed Papers, Pamphlets, Books, or any Copies of Books belonging to the said Company, or any member thereof, without their approbation and consents, and to seize and carry away such printing Presses Letters, together with the Nut, Spindle, and other materialls of every such irregular Printer, which they find so misimployed, unto the Common Hall of the said Company, there to be defaced and made unserviceable according to Ancient Custom; And likewise to make diligent search in all suspected Printing-houses, Ware-houses, Shops and other places for such scandalous and unlicensed Books, papers, Pamphlets and all other Books, not entred, nor signed with the Printers name as aforesaid, being printed, or reprinted by such as have no lawfull interest in them, or any way contrary to this Order, and the same to seize and carry away to the said common hall, there to remain till both or either House of *Parliament* shall dispose thereof, And likewise to apprehend all Authors, Printers, and other persons whatsoever imployed in compiling, printing, stitching, binding, publishing and dispersing of the said scandalous, unlicensed, and unwarrantable papers, books and pamphlets as aforesaid, and all those who shall resist the said Parties in searching after them, and to bring them afore either of the Houses or the Committee of Examinations, that so they may receive such further punishments, as their Offences shall demerit, and not to be released untill they have given satisfaction to the Parties imployed in their apprehension for their paines and charges, and given sufficient caution not to offend in like sort for the future. And all Justices of the Peace, Captaines, Constables and other officers, are hereby ordered and required to be aiding, and assisting to the foresaid persons in the due execution of all, and singular the premisses and in the apprehension of all Offenders against the same. And in case of opposition to break open Doores and Locks.

And it is further ordered, that this Order be forthwith Printed and Published, to the end that notice may be taken thereof, and all Contemners of it left inexcusable.

FINIS.

LITTLE NON-SUCH: A SATIRE ON MILTON'S DIVORCE
ARGUMENT?

BY ERNEST SIRLUCK

On September 3, 1646, Thomason received a quarto pamphlet of sixteen pages entitled *Little Non-Such: or, Certaine New Questions
Moved out of Ancient Truths,* which I believe to be a satire on promul-
gators of novel ideas subversive of established doctrines and institutions, with Milton's divorce argument supplying the main basis for the
reductio ad absurdum.

The pamphlet seems always to have been noticed—so far as it has
been noticed—in connection with Milton's divorce argument, as a
parallel demand for lifting a legal prohibition concerning marriage
(this time the interdiction of marriage with the next of kin). The famous Sion College pamphlet of 1648, *A Testimony to the Truth of
Jesus Christ, and to Our Solemn League and Covenant; as Also
Against the Errours, Heresies and Blasphemies of these Times, and the
Toleration of them,* contains "A Catalogue of divers of the said
Errours," organized under nineteen rubrics. One of these is "Errours
touching Marriage and Divorce,"[1] consisting of four entries, three being quotations from *Little Non-Such* and the fourth from *Doctrine and
Discipline.*[2] Later in 1648 there appeared *A Glasse for the Times . . .
by T. C. a Friend to Truth,* which contained "A briefe Collection of the
Errors of our Times," stated to be based upon the catalogue in the Sion
College *Testimony.*[3] A classification headed "These following are so
grosse, they need no further Confutation" ends as follows: "In the
booke called, *Little Nonsuch,* concerning Marriage. The very next of
kin may joyne in Marriage by custome and command, for *Sarah* was
Abrahams sister whom he took to wife. In the doctrine of divorce by
John Milton. That unfitnesse or contrariety of minde betwixt man and

[1] January 18; Newberry C65.51, p. 19.
[2] *Little Non-Such* also appears under "Errours against the Nature and Essence of God," p. 6, where Milton does not figure.
[3] July 29; E455(10), p. 2.

wife, from a naturall cause which hindereth solace and peace are a great reason of divorce." [4]

Masson described *A Testimony,* noted its citation of *Little Non-Such,* and observed, "Milton comes in company with this *Little Nonsuch,* as hardly less worthy of execration on account of his Divorce Doctrine." [5] Parker quotes the allusions to Milton in both pamphlets,[6] and notes the association with *Little Non-Such,*[7] which he emphasizes in his introduction: "The doctrine of 'divorce at pleasure' soon became a half-remembered, half-legendary heresy of the age. It was recalled when *Little Nonsuch* created a momentary stir in 1646." [8]

The interpretation of *Little Non-Such* as a serious demand for the permission of incestuous marriages, it should be noted, stems wholly from the Sion College "Catalogue." T. C., as we saw, stated that his "Collection" was based on the earlier "Catalogue," and makes no claim to have read *Little Non-Such;* neither does Masson (who repeats part of the "Catalogue's" citation from *Little Non-Such*) or Parker.

I think that the fifty-eight Presbyterian ministers in London who subscribed *A Testimony,* or the committee whom they probably delegated to compile their "Catalogue of . . . Errours," unwilling to omit any monstrosities but having other things to do, took as a serious and heretical novelty what was intended as a parody, probably by an Episcopalian, of the method by which novel doctrines were being advanced on all sides. It has not been fully recognized how prominent a feature such parodies were of the polemic of this period; for one of the most brilliant, written by Hyde, see above, pp. 57–58, and others are discussed above, pp. 28, 79–80, and 92. That *Little Non-Such* belongs to this genre is, I think, manifest from the utter incongruity of its framework with its ostensible argument; indeed the framework scarcely comes short of declaring that the ostensible argument is a parody.

The pamphlet begins with an "Advertisement" of a page and a half, continues with three "Questions," and ends with a "Postscript" of about a page. The tone of the "Advertisement," one would have said,

---

[4] *Ibid.,* pp. 5–6.

[5] *Life,* III, 678. H. J. Todd, *The Poetical Works of John Milton* (7 vols., London: 1809), I,55, and Dora N. Raymond, *Oliver's Secretary* (New York, 1932), pp. 84 and 101, noticed the attack on Milton in *A Glasse,* but did not mention *Little Non-Such.*

[6] As does French, *Life Records,* II, 211–12 and 218, who does not, however, mention *Little Non-Such.*

[7] *Milton's Contemporary Reputation,* pp. 77–78.

[8] *Ibid.,* p. 21. The comment is rather odd in view of the fact that all but one of the 1646 allusions to the divorce tracts printed by Parker *preceded* the publication of *Little Non-Such.*

was unmistakable: the removal of tried and necessary controls had led to doctrinal chaos, with every heresy pleading scriptural warrant.

> Since these late eruptions in Church and State the minds of men are become much distracted; and no marvell, seeing . . . that all the heresies fomented at severall times, in former ages, and condemned by severall Councels, are now extant, attended with as many more; and how shall it be otherwaies? when both Fathers and Councels are derided and contemn'd (without controle) by the very off-scouring of the people; yea, even such as setled and confirmed our Christian faith (by refuting errors and heresies the first 400 yeeres) which till now the Christian world hath received for Orthodox: yet is it no wonder to see the Scripture abused and mis-interpreted by every *Mechanicke*, mis-applying the sence to their fantasticke humors; seeing there was never heresie broached, but came with *verbum Dei* Scripture in the mouth.[9]

Then, with a sudden change of tone, but professing that *"herein we detest to be curiously inquisitive in things not necessary, but onely covet the health of our soules,"* [10] the pamphlet plunges into its Questions. The first two, treated very briefly (two pages cover both), are precisely of the type of "curious" and unnecessary speculation whose condemnation by almost everyone Howard Schultz has recently demonstrated: [11] whether God has a bodily shape, and whether that was a material apple which Adam ate.[12] The third Question, to which we will return, occupies the bulk of the pamphlet (pp. 5–15), and purports to recommend marriage to the next of kin. With the "Postscript" the tone returns to that of the "Advertisement." The author lists some of the novelties he has seen genuinely maintained in print:

> 1. *We have lately seen a little Booke which saith, the sinne against the holy Ghost hath hitherto been mistaken.*
> 2. *We have seen another maintaine that* Independency *is no Schism.*
> 3. *We have seen another maintaine (out of Scripture) that our Saviour Christ shall live 1000 yeers with his Saints upon earth.*
> 4. *We have seen books writ against baptizing of Infants, though the custome hath been so for 1400 yeeres.*[13]

(It is here that the author's Episcopalian sympathies become evident [pp. 15–16]: *"We see the Office of Bishops of no repute, though their Function hath continued since the time of the Apostles; and what Heresies were by them refuted in the first four generall Counsels?"* [14]) Then he ends by echoing the complaint of the "Advertisement": "Salo. *Nothing remaines certain under the Sunne."* [15]

On the hypothesis of a satirical parody the title of the pamphlet,

---

[9] E353(8), p. 2.   [10] *Ibid.*, p. 3.   [11] See above, p. 214.
[12] E353(8), pp. 3–5.   [13] *Ibid.*, p. 15.   [14] *Ibid.*, pp. 15–16.
[15] *Ibid.*, p. 16.

which is ludicrously inappropriate to a serious reforming intent, becomes wholly fitting: it is a sarcastic jeer, and shares with the rest of the framework the function of making clear the real intention of the pamphlet.

If *Little Non-Such* is parody, the third and main "Question" is almost certainly directed at Milton's divorce argument. The force of parody depends upon the reader's recognition of the original behind the caricature, and there was no other widely known contemporary thesis to which the argument of the third Question corresponds. It corresponds very closely to Milton's argument, then still at or near the height of its notoriety; as the following outline and extracts should show, it is a cruel but not unskillful caricature. Its ground for the permission of incest is the same as Milton's for the permission of divorce, the institution of marriage in Genesis; it assigns the same reason as Milton does for the distorted received interpretation of the institution, papal greed; and it exemplifies the newly recovered true meaning from the Old Testament, making the examples applicable by comparative exegesis. Then it examines a Scriptural text which seems to contradict its interpretation of the institution. First it denies that this prohibition can mean what it seems to mean because that would involve giving man the power to dispense with God's laws. Then it deals with the reinterpreted prohibition on the basis of the abrogation of laws made to suit the special needs of the Jews. It finds historical evidence that the true intent of the text conforms to general practice prior to its enactment, and philological evidence that apparent Gospel prohibitions refer only to a special aspect without affecting the original permission. It then defines the limits of its thesis and argues that any popish denial of human rights within those limits is against the law of nature and reason, as any statute prohibition is against Christian liberty.

All this is argued with the wildest kind of nonsequitur and most flagrant misrepresentation of universally known Scriptural texts, sometimes with the comedy forcing its way to the surface but more often preserving the classic seeming unawareness of the tradition of parody. The language, like the organization and method, is often reminiscent of Milton, and the Question ends with a passage, emphasized by the word "Note." in the margin, which may echo Bramhall's attack on Milton as a "young novice" [16] defaming the martyrs of the Church of England. The passages reproduced below should suffice to convey the pamphlet's character and relation to Milton's argument:

[16] John Bramhall, *The Serpent Salve, or, A Remedie For the Biting of an Aspe* (? Dublin, 1643), pp. 211–12; quoted by Parker, *Milton's Contemporary Reputation*, p. 73.

The next question is of marriage, *Genesis. And the Lord God said it is not good for man to be alone, I wil make him a help meet for him. vers.21,22.* God tooke one of *Adams* ribs, made a woman, and brought her unto him, *v* 23. *Adam* said, *this is bone of my bone, and flesh of my flesh,* which is one flesh, *v.*24. How comes it then that there are forbidden degrees in marriage? or is it not so in truth, but a *Popish injunction for their profit?* for in that respect they have given their dispensations *ad infinitum* to the neerest kindred. To recite particulars in a matter so well known (as the houses of *Austria, Burbon,* and many others, where profit or State policy is at stake) were onely to spend Inke and Paper. Then if it may be done by dispensation, and for money, which is but an Ordinance of man; why may it not much more be done without, seeing it is the Ordinance of God himselfe? . . . And here we see the woman is not of the man derivatively, and by descent, but of his own *proper substance;* then in regard there can be no more matches of this nature, the very next of kin were to joyn in marriage, and that both by custome and command. For example, we finde that *Sara* was *Abrahams* sister, whom he took to wife; a better president we can not have, for he was the father of the faithfull; his seed should be multiplied as the Stars in Heaven; all the Nations of the earth be blessed therein, &c. If it be said, that when *Abraham* went down to sojourne in *Ægypt* because of the famine, he wish'd his wife to say she was his sister, lest the *Ægyptians* should kill him and take her to themselves, for she was a faire woman to looke upon. And from thence you will argue, that to be but simulation betwixt them to save his life; then it will appeare in the same book of *Genesis* that in his returne to the South Countrey, they used the like practice, in saying she was his sister. . . .[17] And so naturally confident were the servants of God in propagating by the next of kin, that *Lots daughters* (when they fled out of *Sodome* with their father, where the rest of their kindred perished) did not doubt to raise up seed to their father, saying, *There is not a man alive to come in unto us after the manner of the earth, therefore let us lie with him, &c.* Now there were thousands (not to be numbered) left alive, but there was none of their *Tribe and kindred,* for so the Text seems to infer. We know also that many things are writ for our instruction not for our imitation; and so *Lot* might justly be blamed for drinking so liberally, that he perceived not what he did (which we ought not to imitate) yet we finde no reproofe upon the daughters, because (it seems) what they did was onely for propagation, according to the institution, and not to satisfie appetite.[18]

There follow several other examples of comparable cogency, and then a difficulty is anticipated:

Well, yet let us object *Levit.* 18. the prohibition there, with the glosse upon the Text, entituled unlawfull marriages; but we suppose it is a Popish glosse, and of purpose mis-interpreted to increase his coffers: for it will appeare hereafter that the uncovering of nakednesse there mentioned, is meant of *fornication onely, and not of marriage:*

[17] E353(8), pp. 5–6.   [18] *Ibid.,* p. 6.

yet the *Popes purse* upon that pretence hath pickt up many large fees,
especially where the joyning of *Kingdomes* or *Dukedomes* together
hath been sought more for politick ends, (and chiefly if his owne
cause hath been interested) then the parties owne particular liking.
But now who is so ignorant to believe that any *sinfull man* can dispense with what God hath commanded or forbidden. . . . But to
returne, the Answer to the foresaid prohibition in *Leviticus* 18. is, that
the many Lawes given in that booke were not perpetuall, but onely
given to busie the minds of the children of *Israel* for that present, and
to divert their inclination from *Idolatry*. . . . They were also peculiar to that people, and therefore not binding elsewhere, especially to
Christians under the Gospel. But to make the matter more cleare, let
us see how we can prove the prohibition in these degrees, to be meant
of Fornication, as is formerly mentioned, and not of the holy institution of marriage, for instance in the foresaid, 18 *ch. &* 16. *ver.* it
is said, *Thou shalt not uncover the nakednesse of thy brothers wife,
it is thy brothers nakednesse:* uncover the nakednesse, marke that;
though the *Pope and ambitious men* would delude us, the holy Ghost
is very wary; the Text here speaks not of marriage, but uncovering
nakednesse: and now repaire to *Deut.* 25. vers. 5. There you shall
finde that if a brother die the wife of the dead shall not marry unto a
stranger, *her husbands brother shall goe in unto her, take her to wife,
and performe the duty of a husbands brother unto her.* The rest of
the verses following shewes how disgracefully, and with what reproach
he was to be used that refused to perform this duty. So you see there
is a vast difference betwixt uncovering of nakednesse, and taking to
wife; for else did not these two Texts controvert each other *point-
blanke,* if they were meant of one and the selfesame matter? what is
then the right exposition? no other then this, by uncovering of nakednesse is meant fornication, as is formerly said, which in kindred is
utterly forbidden; but the other Text in *Deutronomy* speakes expresly
of marriage, and taking to wife, which is like-wise in kindred as directly commanded. . . . And that this practice of marriage with
kindred was in use, not onely before the prohibition in *Leviticus,*
already answered, but eversithence, and never forbid, in the *Law or
Gospell,* for ought we can finde, is the next thing we shall endeavour
to prove.[19]

Among the "examples" here given is this:

the passage betwixt *Ammon* and *Tamar,* where it is said, that *Ammon*
loved *Tamar* in an unlawfull manner, which the mayd as discreetly
reproved, desiring him not to force her, but to aske her of the King
for a wife, in that sence she knew the King would not withhold her,
but *Ammon* after his lust was satisfied, despised her, which act turned
to his confusion, and was the occasion of his slaughter. Still we see the
sister did not doubt to be her brothers wife, but did detest the act of
fornication, (which certainly is the thing meant in the forbidden degrees formerly mentioned). And assuredly also that act proceeding
from lust in kindred, is the highest degree of *fornication,* and of some

[19] *Ibid.,* pp. 7–9.

perhaps not improperly termed *incest,* if there be such a distinction: But for the holy institution of marriage with the next of Kindred, we see (by all examples *before and after*), it hath not onely been permitted but commanded.[20]

Now *Little Non-Such* reaches the New Testament:

Neither doe we finde any thing to the contrary in the whole progresse of the Gospell, but still reproofe of fornication, and especially amongst kindred, which seems to confirme what is formerly said; for so St. *Paul, It is reported commonly that there is fornication amongst you, and such as is not used among the Gentiles, but one should have his fathers wife.* But the same Saint *Paul* hath these following words in the same booke, *Ch.* 7, *v.* 3. touching marriage. *To avoyd fornication, let every man* (excepting no degree or profession) *have his own wife, and let every woman have her own husband.* And in verse 4. *the wife hath not power of her own body, but the husband; nor the husband power of his own body, but the wife,* in the singular number. From hence may be inferred, that men since the Gospell ought not to have *plurality of wives,* but neither there, nor in any other place where the like precept is given, is there any exception to the next of kin, but in case of *fornication* aforesaid. Then let *every man have his own wife* . . . in the singular number aforesaid; but then (seeing there is not one word in the Gospell to the contrary) that any Popish Ordinance or other should bar a man to choose that single woman he liketh best to be his wife (if she be also consenting, and of ripe judgement) seems to be both against the law of nature and reason. Wherefore we conclude this point with the Apostles words, that the forbidding of marriage is the *doctrine of devils.* . . . And if the prohibition in the law formerly mentioned, were meant of marriage, as it is fully and amply proved to intend *fornication onely,* because of the practice in marrying with their next of kin, as well after as before, formerly proved also; yet were it not binding now, for we understand the Law contained in Ordinances to be abolished. And againe, blotting out the hand-writing of Ordinances that was against us, nayling it to the Crosse, *Colos.* 2. 14. . . . But how, what liberty? to doe the works of the flesh, formerly touched; no, God forbid, The holy Ghost will witnesse with those that the Lord hath made his Covenant with, he will put lawes into their hearts, and in their minds will he write them. . . . So then we perceive by this *Tract* and all the rest, it is fornication, uncleannesse, and these forenamed works of the flesh, which is forbidden; but for that excellent and sacred institution of marriage, from which Ordinance the blessed elect of Gods children doe proceed; that holy Order, we see, is honorable amongst all without exception, as is formerly proved. Now then without all dispute that marriage is most just, which is made without any ambitious or covetous end; and if this liking and mutuall correspondency happen betwixt the neerest of kindred, then is it also the most naturall, the most lawfull, and according to the *primitive purity* and practice: nor is there now any *Popish Canons* to restraine it, which perhaps some consciences might boggle at in regard

[20] *Ibid.,* p. 10.

of the precept, *you are to obey the Magistrate for conscience sake.*
And indeed we would not argue any thing here against higher powers
that are in true orthodox authority; but onely desire that no Law or
prohibition should bind the conscience in matters that the *Gospell of
Christ* hath left free unto Christian people.[21]

What he is recommending is, after all, no more than liberty in a
thing indifferent:

> Now we know the vulgar sort (that lookes no further then the times
> they live in) will bogle at this doctrine, and thinke it a *Novell.* Then
> here we will put you in mind of what some of you do yet remember;
> namely, a quality of two eminent men esteemed very wise (especially
> in the lawes) the one would not abide a *sholder of Veale,* the other did
> not love a *Duck:* what? would you have thought these men wise to
> proclaime it unlawfull for any other to eate these kind of meats, be-
> cause they did not love them? surely no, you would have held them
> rediculous: So our question is not how any mans appetite likes, or dis-
> likes; we onely desire to know yea, or no, whether the matter in it
> selfe be unlawfull, or where it is repugnant to Scripture, when all
> places of *this subject* are compared together.[22]

Finally, there is the apparently insignificant passage which is nevertheless important enough to warrant the pamphlet's only marginal
"Note" (p. 15): "And if it be controverted (not with Heathen fables,
or mens bare opinions, but by Scripture proofe) by one that is learned,
and of a refin'd wit, it may satisfie; but [not] if it come from a young
head not halfe codled." [23]

Bishop Hall reported his unbelieving first reaction to the "licentious
pamphlet" of a "wild Novelist," Milton's *Doctrine and Discipline of
Divorce:* "I must seriously professe when I first did cast my eye upon
the front of the booke, I supposed some great wit meant to try his
skill in the maintenance of this so wild, and improbable a paradoxe." [24]
The author of *Little Non-Such,* it seems to me, must also have believed
that divorce argued on Scriptural grounds was a wild paradox, and
thought that reducing it to manifest absurdity by extension from
divorce to incest would serve to throw ridicule upon the whole species
of new doctrines which he believed it to typify.

[21] *Ibid.,* pp. 10–13.   [22] *Ibid.,* pp. 14–15.   [23] *Ibid.,* p. 15.
[24] Joseph Hall, *Resolutions and Decisions of Divers Practicall Cases of
Conscience* (1649), p. 392; quoted by Parker, *Milton's Contemporary Reputation,* pp. 78–79.

Appendix D

MILTON AS TRANSLATOR: NOTES ON MILTON'S METHOD OF TRANSLATION IN *THE JUDGEMENT OF MARTIN BUCER*

BY ARNOLD WILLIAMS

The Judgement of Martin Bucer is unique among Milton's prose works. In other works Milton translates a few lines of Greek or Latin verse or paraphrases a passage from one of the Latin authorities he is using.[1] But virtually all of *Martin Bucer* is a translation, even the "testimonies" preceding the piece. Only the address to the Parliament at the beginning and the "Post-Script" at the end, plus a few sentences here and there (always put in italics) are Milton's own composition. Commentary on *Martin Bucer* would therefore be incomplete without some attention to Milton's methods and habits of translation and adaptation.

It would not, however, be accurate to generalize Milton's practice in this work into a theory of translation, for two reasons. The first is that Martin Bucer's *De Regno Christi* is written in the Latin style common to most of the divines of the sixteenth century, whether Protestant or Catholic, which is substantially that of the great scholastics of the thirteenth century, and quite different from the compressed periods of a Cicero or a Tacitus. The scholastics (and Bucer originally belonged to the order of the greatest of them, Thomas Aquinas) passed on to the sixteenth century an admirable vehicle for the discussion of abstract questions, simple, easy, and generally unambiguous. It inherits much of the colloquialism of the oral disputations required in the medieval university curriculum. Above all, it is self-effacing; the emphasis is always on the matter, never on the manner.

For these very reasons, this sort of Latin style came under severe criticism from the humanists. Milton, who was more humanist than theologian, must have found the style of Bucer often prolix, loose, and graceless, no matter how useful his arguments. It certainly lacks

[1] *E.g.*, from Horace in *Tetrachordon*, above, p. 639.

the compression and hard-hitting emphasis which Milton constantly strove for, in prose as well as in verse.

Moreover, Milton is not making a translation in the usual sense of the word. A translator's task calls for self-effacement; he must be a mere medium through which the original author expresses himself in a different tongue. In the "Post-Script" Milton distinctly disclaims this office: "Whether it be natural disposition or education in me, or that my mother bore me a speaker of what God made mine own, and not a translator." Certainly, Milton's purpose in the work is to make available to the "meer Englishman," who cannot read the Latin original, only so much of Bucer's argument as parallels and supports what he himself, without benefit of authorities, has already written in *The Doctrine and Discipline of Divorce*.

Thus, Milton's natural inclination, his purpose, and the nature of the language he is translating combine to produce a practice almost diametrically opposite that of the great Elizabethan translators, as analyzed by the late Professor Matthiessen.[2] Philemon Holland, the "translator general" of the age, whose works embraced Livy and Suetonius, accomplished his most striking effects by elaboration and amplification, in which a bare statement such as "Consules in sedem processere suam" is expanded into *"Then came the consuls forth, took their places and set them down on the tribunall seat."* [3]

Martin Bucer furnishes few examples of this sort of amplification. One is the translation of *ciues* by "the whole breed of men," [4] which enlarges the scope of the statement and gives it an oratorical roundness: the chaste and pure home is necessary not merely to produce virtuous burgesses and citizens, but virtuous men, whatever their station. An interesting example of such enlargement instantly compensated for by a compression is "the promise of mariage *de praesenti* as they call it, should be indissoluble," which translates "promissionem matrimonii verbis de praesenti factam, esse insolubilem." [5] Milton has added "as they call it," doubtless because he could find no satisfactory translation of the canonical term *de praesenti,* but he balanced the account by dropping "verbis" and "factam."

For the rest, Milton's additions are of specific texts, references, or details which he thought the reader needed for comprehension. An

[2] F. O. Matthiessen, *Translation: an Elizabethan Art* (Cambridge, Massachusetts, 1931), esp. pp. 129–227.

[3] *Ibid.*, p. 189. Italics are used here, as elsewhere, to denote words found in one version, but lacking in the other.

[4] *Scripta*, p. 133; above, p. 476.

[5] *Scripta*, p. 91; above, p. 446.

interesting case is one in which Bucer is making the point that the Christian emperors of Rome in allowing divorce were only following the law of God as delivered in Malachi 2: "In quo hii pij principes cum secuti sint legem Dei Maleachi secundo." Milton reinforces this with another text: "Wherin those pious Princes follow'd the law of God in Deut. 24. 1, and his expresse charge by the Profet *Malachy*." [6] Perhaps Milton was thinking of the "law of God" in the Jewish sense as something distinct from the Prophets. In adding the reference to Deuteronomy, it is noteworthy, he dropped the chapter reference to Malachi. At the beginning of Chapter XXXV Bucer gives only a reference to Romans 7; Milton supplies the text.[7] However, in the next chapter it is Bucer who has the texts from Matthew and Corinthians, whereas Milton preserves only the references,[8] doubtless feeling that, since they had already been discussed, they would be in the reader's mind. In the whole work, Milton drops about as many quotations from Scripture as he adds.

Milton also adds numerous comments of his own, especially towards the end. Chapter XL contains three of these. The first, "and were still more and more straitn'd, as the Church and State of the Empire still more and more corrupted and degenerated," is hard to explain.[9] It upsets the flow of the argument, the next sentence of which goes back to the conditions prevailing under Theodosius and Valentinian. Milton apparently thought that Bucer was not making enough of the contrast between the early church, which permitted divorce, and the corrupt later church, which denied it. But the addition is scarcely happy.

The next addition is really a condensation. Bucer has a list of references to the Civil Law which Milton wants to drop: "I set them not down beeing easie to be found in the body of the civil law." [10] Technically an addition, this sentence is actually a bridge to get one across an omission.

The final addition in this chapter is more material. Bucer writes that Christian emperors permitted divorce by consent, then adds that Justinian revoked this concession. Milton drops the reference to Justinian's revocation but adds that the only impediment to divorce by consent was the necessity of providing for the children; if there were none, there was no difficulty in getting divorce by consent.[11] This

---

[6] *Scripta,* p. 121; above, p. 470.   [7] *Scripta,* p. 111; above, p. 458.
[8] *Scripta,* p. 114; above, p. 461.   [9] Above, p. 468.
[10] Above, p. 469. One suspects haste on Milton's part, for in abridging Bucer he has made a mistake. Bucer says that Justinian added four causes for divorce in all, one in Constitution 117 and three more in *de repudiis*. Milton misreads this to get a total of eleven!   [11] Above, p. 469.

represents a correction of Bucer by Milton, who had probably already made the intensive study of the Civil Law on matrimony which figures so prominently in *Tetrachordon*. Milton knew that Bucer's statement needed some qualification and proceeded to make it. The matter of Justinian's revocation was less important; he would take care of that impious and changeable emperor in *Tetrachordon*.

Milton has cut the quantity of Bucer's scriptural quotations considerably, often giving only the first few words of a text: "Deut. 21. 4. When a man hath taken a wife, &c," where Bucer has the whole passage.[12] Milton's scripture is most often from the Authorized Version, but often with the omissions and changes that Professor Fletcher has noticed so frequently in Milton's English works.[13] Thus, Romans 7:2 appears as "the woman is bound by the law of her husband so long as he liveth," [14] the wording of the AV, but with the omission of a clause: "The woman *which hath an husband* is bound," etc. Many passages could equally well be a translation of Bucer's Latin or the AV. Matthew 19:7, "They say unto him, why did Moses then command," though agreeing with the AV, is also a direct translation of Bucer's *"Dicunt illi: Cur ergo Moses jussit."* [15] One suspects that Milton's memory of familiar texts in the AV automatically supplied the wording.

In a few instances it can be shown that Milton is translating Bucer's Latin rather than relying on the AV. "I will that younger Widows marry," (I Timothy 5:14) obviously comes from Bucer's *"Volo juniores viduas nubere,"* [16] rather than the AV's "I will *therefore* that the younger *women* marry." Three times, all in one chapter, Milton translates paraphrases presented without italics in Bucer, as though they were scripture. Matthew 19:6, for instance, appears as "Those whom God hath joyn'd, let no man separate," which is closer to Bucer's "Quos Deus conjunxit, homo non separet," than to AV's "What *therefore* God hat joined *together*, let *not* man *put asunder.*" [17] But Milton has italicized the passage as though it were an exact quotation rather than a paraphrase.

On the other hand, immediately following this passage Milton has substituted for the AV text of Matthew 19:5 Bucer's paraphrase. Bucer has, "Propter hoc derelinquet homo patrem & matrem, & con-

---

[12] *Scripta*, p. 99; above, p. 454. A few instances in which Milton has the text, Bucer only the reference can be explained by the fact that Bucer has the full text in a previous passage omitted by Milton.

[13] Harris Fletcher, *The Use of the Bible in Milton's Prose*, University of Illinois Studies in Language and Literature, vol. XIV, no. 3 (1929), esp. pp. 23–29.

[14] Above, pp. 458–59.

[15] *Scripta*, p. 98; above, p. 453.

[16] *Scripta*, p. 96; above, p. 451.

[17] *Scripta*, p. 116; above, p. 464.

nexus erit uxori suae. Ex quo conclusit Dominus in Evangelio, oportere conjuges, quos Dominus matrimonio junxit, esse non duo, sed unam carnem." For this second sentence Milton has, "And they twain shall be one flesh." [18]

In a few instances Milton's text follows neither the AV nor Bucer. In Genesis 2:23 Milton is alone in using the singular, "bone of my *bone*" instead of the plural of the AV, "bone of my bones," and of Bucer, "*os de ossibus meis*." [19] Is it euphony that here governs Milton's practice? Or is it merely an oversight? Elsewhere Milton has "bone of my *bones*," just like Bucer and the AV.[20]

A special case is Milton's rendering of the textually corrupt Malachi 2:15–16. The AV reads, "For the Lord, the God of Israel, saith that he hateth putting away." But this was clean contrary to both Bucer's and Milton's understanding of the passage. Milton obviously spent some time in checking various translations and commentaries, and he sided with Calvin (and the Geneva Bible), Bucer, and the Vulgate against Tremellius, the standard Protestant translation into Latin, and the AV. The passage, says Milton in *Tetrachordon*,[21] definitely means that the Lord commands the man who hates his wife to put her away: "Take heed to your spirit, and let none deal injuriously against the wife of his youth. If he hate, let him put away, saith the Lord God of Israel. And he shall hide thy violence with his garment." [22]

This is not a literal translation of Bucer's "*Custodite spiritum vestrum, ne in uxorem iuuentutis tuae sis injurius. Si quis odio habeat, dimittat, dicit Dominus Deus Israel: & conteget violentiam tuam vestimento suo.*" [23] The first verse in Milton's rendering is close to the AV's "Therefore take heed to your spirit, and let none deal *treacherously* against the wife of his youth." Apparently Milton adopted the word *injuriously* from Bucer's *injurius*. The AV rendition of the next verse contributes nothing to Milton's, since it reads, "For the Lord, the God of Israel, saith that he hateth putting away." Nor does Milton follow Bucer's translation, except in the general sense of it. Clearly, Milton's main dependence is on his own probing of the Hebrew, though he has taken phrases from the AV in verse 15.

So much has been written about Milton's "Latinate" style that it is interesting to note that *Martin Bucer* affords scarcely any instances where Milton has used either a Latin derivative or a Latin construction where it is awkward or unusual in English. The rendering of *rité* by "rightly" (*i.e.*, ritely), where one would expect something like "with

---

[18] *Scripta*, p. 117; above, p. 465. [19] *Scripta*, p. 116; above, p. 463.
[20] Above, p. 586. [21] See *Tetrachordon*, above, pp. 615–16.
[22] Above, p. 454. [23] *Scripta*, p. 99.

due rites," would appear to be one such instance; [24] but the *Oxford English Dictionary* lists several examples of precisely this usage before Milton's time.[25] The case is similar with other apparently Latinate usages. "I will not praise her converted, unlesse I first absolve her guilty" mirrors the construction of "non laudabo conversam, nisi prius ream absolvero," [26] but such constructions appear to have been thoroughly naturalized in English by Milton's time, and anyway a completely slavish following of the Latin construction would produce something like, "I will not praise the converted one, unless first the guilty one I shall have absolved."

On the other hand, there are abundant examples of the avoidance of a Latin derivative which was perfectly acceptable in Milton's time. "Religiously considers" would be a natural translation of "religiose pensitet," but instead Milton gives us "seriously considers." [27] An extreme of this tendency appears in the translation of *repudiare* in the sense of divorce by "refuse." [28] *Repudiate* was well established in Milton's time, as numerous samples in the *Oxford English Dictionary* show. In fact, *refuse* in this sense was a bit archaic, most of the examples given in the *Oxford English Dictionary* coming from much earlier writers.

The same rejection of Latinism appears in Milton's frequent renditions of a passive by an active verb and of a subjunctive by an indicative or an infinitive. The passive, frequently economical and forceful in Latin, is often wordy and awkward in English. In translating "Dici autem non potest," Milton wraps up the impersonal verb, the negative, and the passive infinitive in one adjective: "For it is unspeakable." [29] In translating "Hoc facile perspiciet, quicunque ista Dei pronunciata, ex Spiritu Domini consideraverit & ponderaverit," Milton takes full advantage of the simplified tense and mood pattern of English. The future tense remains, but takes on the sense of inevitability often implicit in the use of *will*, and the future perfect (or perfect subjunctive) metamorphoses into the present indicative without any loss of meaning: "This he will easily perceave, who considers these things in the Spirit of the Lord." [30]

The compression of the original here illustrated is the chief quality of Milton's translation. Strictly speaking, this is not so much a matter of translation as of source adaptation. In *Martin Bucer* Milton has applied to a Latin original the techniques which Professor Cawley so

[24] *Scripta*, p. 86; above, p. 441.　　[25] *OED*, "ritely."
[26] *Scripta*, p. 94; above, p. 449.　　[27] *Scripta*, p. 100; above, p. 455.
[28] *Scripta*, p. 94; above, p. 448.　　[29] *Scripta*, p. 86; above, p. 441.
[30] *Scripta*, p. 114; above, p. 462.

neatly describes for the English sources of *A Brief History of Muscovia*.[31] But it is notably easier to compress English than to compress Latin, even the somewhat verbose Latin of sixteenth-century theology. Certainly the feat of rendering five words of Latin by three of English can have been achieved but rarely, yet Milton does it: Calvin's *"ab hominibus aliis occupationibus distractis"* becomes "by over-busied men."[32]

Milton's methods of compression are varied and sometimes marvelous. Paraphrases are deparaphrased. "Hunc virum Dei" becomes simply "Jerom," the particular man of God to whom Bucer was referring,[33] and "veteri suo populo" merely "to the Jews."[34] The single pronoun "they" takes the place of the circumlocution "illi matrimoniorum custodes," a change which improves the readability, since the reference is obvious.[35]

Throughout, Milton customarily omits words and phrases which in the context are unnecessary or redundant. In the discussion of Fabiola's second marriage in Chapter XXIII, for instance, Bucer wrote "etiamsi *his nuptijs* ab Euangelij vigore nonnihil deflexisset." Since the preceding page and more concerns Fabiola's second marriage, it is hardly necessary to say wherein she defected. So Milton drops the phrase: "Though she went somewhat aside from the vigor of the Gospel." Again, Jerome had written, and Bucer quoted, "quasi scopulus quidam & procella obtrectatorum eius opponitur, *quòd secundum sortita matrimonium, prius relinquerit,* non laudabo conversam, nisci prius ream absolvero." Jerome's explanatory clause is simply skipped: "There is a rock and storm of slanderers oppos'd against her, I will not praise her converted, unlesse I first absolve her guilty."[36]

All kinds of details and specifications fall under Milton's sharp pruning hook. Bucer writes with unnecessary fullness, "unum inter patrem & nos mediatorem, de cuius plenitudine Moses & Prophetae omnes, quaecunque tradiderunt, acceperunt." What Christian needs to be told that Christ is the mediator between the Father and us? Or that Moses and the prophets had their inspiration of Him? Hence Milton renders the whole passage by three words: "the only Mediator."[37]

Where Bucer has a doublet, Milton frequently makes one word do the work. "Considers" serves for "consideraverit & ponderaverit,"[38] and "civitatis optata constitutione atque sanctificatione," is "a right

---

[31] Robert R. Cawley, *Milton's Literary Craftsmanship*, Princeton University Studies in English, vol. XXIV (1941).   [32] *Scripta*, sig. β1; above, p. 422.
[33] *Scripta*, p. 94; above, p. 449.   [34] *Scripta*, p. 111; above, p. 459.
[35] *Scripta*, p. 92; above, p. 446.   [36] *Scripta*, p. 94; above, p. 449.
[37] *Scripta*, p. 99; above, p. 454.   [38] *Scripta*, p. 114; above, p. 462.

reformation of the Common-wealth," for "reformation" includes both ideas, of setting up and of making holy.[39] Likewise with Bucer's prescription to rulers to regulate the marriages of their subjects: "pios Principes & hoc maxime spectare convenit, atque procurare." Rulers will have to inspect (or look to) such matters if they are to procure the results Bucer counsels. Hence *spectare* is unnecessary. One also notices the dropping of the reinforcing "& hoc maxime" and of the adaptation of the advice to the England of Milton's time by rendering "Principes" by "magistrates." The result is "It will be the part of godly magistrates to procure." [40]

Milton prefers the straightforward to the round-about expression. The double negative of "non nisi, legitimè dissolvantur" becomes the simple affirmative of "be lawfully dissolv'd." [41] In one curious example a verb plus a passive infinitive yields a simple substantive verb: "nihil minus quam legitimi mariti, & uxores legitimae possunt numerari" becomes "such twain are nothing lesse then lawful man and wife." [42] Milton has been able also to lose one adjective because of the lack of gender agreement in English and he has substituted the generic singular for the plural, a frequent practice. Interestingly, however, the ambiguity remains. Bucer meant, and Milton meant, that such a couple are *not* lawful man and wife, for none are less lawfully joined than those between whom there is no love or harmony of soul.

Sometimes in the interest of straightforwardness Milton even substitutes plain statement for an image or figure, a practice one would scarcely expect in a poet. "Qui castrationem propter regnum coelorum non capiunt," though the image is based on Matthew 12:19, yields to the literal "who hath not the special gift from above." [43] Particulars likewise sometimes become generalities. Bucer's phrasing is often almost legalistic in its particularizing: "vel vir uxorem suam, vel uxor virum suum deseruisset, aut repudiasset" covers all cases. It reminds one of the wording of laws and ordinances: "Any applicant who registers his or her intention, or who has his or her intention," and so forth. Perhaps Bucer, who was at least suggesting a pattern of marriage law to the sovereign, found such specification necessary. It was not to Milton, who is arguing, not legislating. So the rather general "whatever cause ther had bin either of desertion or divorce." [44]

Lists of details are likely to suffer a similar fate. Bucer has to in-

---

[39] *Scripta*, p. 93; above, p. 447. Milton's usual rendition of *constitutio* by "reformation" is hardly a usage of a man overly concerned with the original Latin meaning of *reformatio*.   [40] *Scripta*, p. 91; above, p. 445.
[41] *Scripta*, p. 133; above, p. 476.   [42] *Scripta*, p. 112; above, p. 459.
[43] *Scripta*, p. 125; above, p. 472.   [44] *Scripta*, p. 93; above, p. 448.

clude all sorts of violations of the marriage compact, not just the more notorious ones: "non stupra tantum, & adulteria, sed etiam omnes vagas libidines, omnes illegitimas marium & foeminarum conjunctiones." For Milton the terser and more suggestive "whordom and adultery" suffices.[45] In another place Bucer gives complete details of what constituted marriage of persons of good fame with those of evil in Roman law. When a senator or his son, grandson, or great-grandson took a wife who had performed in the theater, been a prostitute or a pander, or been condemned in public judgment, the marriage was considered void, as was also the marriage of a female descendant of a senator with a man tainted with corresponding offenses. Milton apparently thought those details of little value to an English reader, and so he preserved only the general statement that Roman Emperors "counted those mariages of no force which were made between one of good repute, and the other of evil note." [46]

Perhaps the most frequent cause for the omission of extended passages, paragraphs or even whole chapters, is that they are not germane to Milton's purpose. Thus, in Chapter XXXVIII he omits a whole paragraph dealing with the love between parents and children, which comes naturally enough in Bucer's presentation, but does not pertain to the subject of divorce.[47] The whole of Chapter XLII, in which Bucer argues that incurable maladies ought to be a cause of divorce elsewhere, as they are in some German states, is omitted, because Milton does not treat this matter in *Doctrine and Discipline*.[48]

Occasionally the omitted material is not merely useless but positively prejudicial, or at least would require more explaining away than Bucer affords. In this category is a quotation from Ambrose to the effect that a man putting away his wife for adultery ought thereafter to remain unmarried, though he is not compelled to.[49] Why quote Ambrose at all when immediately afterwards you will have to dispute the matter with him? So Milton omits the passage, though keeping another quotation from Ambrose defending the Pauline privilege of separating from an unbeliever.[50] Elsewhere, Bucer after noting that according to Roman law "they who would divorce by mutuall consent, might without impediment" goes on to say that Justinian revoked this permission.[51] Milton drops the revocation. Doubtless some would accuse Milton of dishonesty in such omissions. The charge would be justified if Milton had promised a faithful translation. But he did not promise more than

---

[45] *Scripta*, p. 133; above, p. 476.   [46] *Scripta*, p. 119; above, 467.
[47] *Scripta*, p. 117.   [48] *Scripta*, pp. 123–25; above, p. 472.
[49] *Scripta*, pp. 112–13.   [50] *Scripta,* p. 112; above, p. 460.
[51] *Scripta*, p. 121.

to show wherein Bucer agreed with his own already expressed opinions. Hence it would be nearer the truth to say that Milton is here functioning as an advocate, not as a scholar.

Often simple omissions will not serve Milton's purpose of concentration. In such cases he combines several methods, picking out those words, phrases, and clauses which carry the essential meaning, shifting material about, recasting syntax, and adding whatever he finds necessary to accomplish his effect. Chapter XXXVIII has several samples of this operation. One sentence of Bucer's original will serve as a representative:

> Liquet ergo hinc, alterum esse conjugij proprium: *eos,* inter quos constat verum matrimonium, *oportere* sicut unà vivere, ita *rebus omnibus divinis ac humanis inter se communicare,* idque summa cum benevolentia & charitate, adeoque conjunctione sibi invicem cohaerere omnium arctissima, ut unam scilicet praestent carnem: id est, unum hominem, cui sit cor unum & anima una: ut *mulier* se viro ita subijciat, ut adjutorium ei se praestet, pro sua portione, & viribus, in rebus omnibus, *quae aliquod benè beatéque vivendum adferant momentum:* itaque *virum* suspiciat, *veneretur atque audiat, uti Ecclesia reveretur,* colit, *auditque Christum, caput suum.*[52]

Italics indicate the portions of the sentence which Milton saw as incorporating the essential meaning.

The sentence structure with its numerous clauses beginning *ita, idque, adeoque,* and *ut,* all indicating purpose or result, must have seemed diffuse and watery to Milton. It is too much like the house that Jack built. Hence he completely recast the syntax. By omitting the introductory *liquet ergo* ("wherefore it is clear") he transfers the substance from the accusative-infinitive construction of the Latin to the direct subject-verb-object one of the English. *Eos . . . . oportere* thus becomes "they must." To *communicare* he adds another verb, "communicate and consent," but *inter se* is redundant. *Rebus omnibus divinis ac humanis* he keeps unchanged, except for a reinforcing *both:* "in all things both divine and human." Then he skips down to the latter part of the sentence and picks up *quae aliquod ad benè beatéque vivendum adferant momentum,* which as Bucer wrote the passage belongs rather to the wifely duty than to the common duty, where Milton put it.

Then Milton starts a new sentence, with *mulier,* "the wife," as its subject. He makes it parallel with the preceding sentence by supplying

[52] *Scripta,* p. 117.

"must." The verbs *veneretur atque audiat* he renders "honour and obey," possibly relying on the marriage service for his phrasing, and the object *virum* he renders as "her husband," Milton supplying *her*. The clause beginning *uti* he preserves almost entire, only omitting one of the three verbs, *colit*, and rendering it so as to preserve the parallelisms between the wife and the Church. Both "honour and obey."

The finished result is thus, "They must communicate and consent in all things both divine and human, which have any moment to well and happy living. The wife must honour and obey her husband, as the Church honours and obeys Christ her head." [53] One is puzzled to know what to call this technique, which is found in many places in the work. Is it translation, paraphrase, or summary? Actually, it is all three. It has, in addition, the vigor and immediacy of original composition.

Beyond this technique, Milton has another, which does not involve any translation. It involves giving an epitome and perhaps a reason for skipping a large amount of material, usually a chapter. A series of chapters from XXIX to XXXIV exemplify this method, combined with others already described. Milton translates only the heading of Chapter XXIX, which in the original is only ten lines long, and does little more than restate the heading. The major part of Chapter XXX appears only in summary; the next to the last paragraph is translated with omissions, and the last paragraph omitted entirely. Milton then briefly summarizes the contents of Chapters XXXI–XXXIV and gives his reasons for not translating them: they deal with matters not taken up in *Doctrine and Discipline* or with points granted by all Protestants.[54]

ARNOLD WILLIAMS

Michigan State University

[53] Above, p. 465.
[54] Above, pp. 457–58.

INDEX

INDEX TO AUTHORS AND WORKS

Most works are indexed under the authors' names. Cross references are made from the names of editors and translators to authors. When a work has more than one editor or translator, reference is made only from the one whose name is listed first in the series. Compilations and works of multiple, anonymous, or uncertain authorship are indexed under the titles of these works. After the titles of such works will be found references to editors, translators, authors, and probable authors.

For many works short titles have been used. Starred page references indicate that the longer titles or additional bibliographical information will be found on the cited pages. As a further bibliographical aid, known dates of publication are included in the index for pamphlets and other works published during or close to Milton's lifetime, and for certain important titles for which dating aids identification.